MY BACK PAGES

BOOKS BY STEVEN MOORE

A Reader's Guide to William Gaddis's "The Recognitions" (1982)

William Gaddis (1989; expanded edition, 2015)

Ronald Firbank: An Annotated Bibliography of Secondary Materials (1996)

The Novel, An Alternative History: Beginnings to 1600 (2010)

The Novel, An Alternative History: 1600–1800 (2013)

BOOKS EDITED WITH AN INTRODUCTION BY STEVEN MOORE

In Recognition of William Gaddis (with John R. Kuehl, 1984)

The Vampire in Verse: An Anthology (1985)

Edward Dahlberg, *Samuel Beckett's Wake and Other Uncollected Prose* (1989)

Ronald Firbank, *Complete Short Stories* (1990)

Ronald Firbank, *Complete Plays* (1994)

W. M. Spackman, *Complete Fiction* (1997)

Beerspit Night and Cursing: The Correspondence of Charles Bukowski and Sheri Martinelli (2001)

Chandler Brossard, *Over the Rainbow? Hardly* (2005)

The Letters of William Gaddis (2013)

W. M. Spackman, *On the Decay of Criticism: Complete Essays* (2017)

MY BACK PAGES

Reviews and Essays

STEVEN MOORE

Los Angeles, 2018

ZEROGRAM PRESS
An imprint of GREEN INTEGER
København / Los Angeles
6022 Wilshire Boulevard, Suite 202C
Los Angeles, California 90036, USA
www.zerogrampress.com
www.greeninteger.com

Distributed by
CONSORTIUM BOOK SALES AND DISTRIBUTION / PERSEUS
www.cbsd.com

First Edition 2017
Expanded Paperback Edition 2018

Book design: Pablo Capra
Cover image: istockphoto.com/vandervelden

LIBRARY OF CONGRESS CATALOGING-IN-PUBLICATION DATA

Names: Moore, Steven, 1951- author.
Title: My back pages : reviews and essays / Steven Moore.
Description: First edition. | Los Angeles, California : Zerogram Press, 2017. | Includes bibliographical references and index.
Identifiers: LCCN 2016020816| ISBN 9781557134370 (hardcover : acid-free paper) | ISBN 9781557134387 (pbk. : acid-free paper)
Subjects: LCSH: Criticism.
Classification: LCC PN81 .M643 2017 | DDC 801/.95--dc23
LC record available at https://lccn.loc.gov/2016020816

Printed in the United States of America on acid-free paper.

Contents

Miscellaneous Nonfiction

Introduction

Publishing any book is an act of ego, a conviction that one's thoughts are not only worth broadcasting to the world, but that people should pay to read them. Assuming that previously published material deserves to be collected and preserved for the ages, however, ratchets up egotism to delusions of grandeur. But no such delusions inspired this collection, simply a wish to gather and preserve scattered pieces in a convenient place, for what it's worth. In fact I thought about calling this book *For What It's Worth* before settling on a different song title from the '60s. I chose *My Back Pages* because many of the book reviews literally appeared in the back pages of various periodicals, but also because I've always liked the sentiment expressed in Bob Dylan's song (even though I heretically prefer the Byrds' resplendent version over Dylan's ragged original). I want to preserve these writings not so much for my sake as for the authors': many of them aren't well known, so this collection will give me a second chance to proselytize on their behalf. It's the books I write about, many of them forgotten by now, more than the pieces themselves, that deserve to be remembered. Some of the cultural references in the book reviews in particular are dated — I don't even remember what *The Edge* TV program was — but the books I write about aren't. And finally, since most of these writings deal with 20th-century fiction, this volume also partly fills the void of the abandoned third volume of my *The Novel, An Alternative History*. I had planned to crib from this material anyway, and almost every novelist covered here was intended to be included in that third volume.

I began reviewing books in my twenties almost as a lark. I was running a small bookstore in a Denver suburb and writing my first book when I noticed that the local arts magazine, called *Spree*, featured all the arts but literature. I volunteered to write a monthly column on new fiction, and made my debut in *Spree*'s October 1978 issue. (The introductory byline claims I had previously written some "library reference reviews," but I have no recollection whatsoever of those.) I abandoned this after about a year, frustrated at the number of typos and glitches that usually appeared in the reviews, and concentrated on finishing my book, which was published in 1982 as *A Reader's Guide to William Gaddis's "The Recognitions."* On the basis of that, fellow Gaddis scholar Steven Weisenburger, an associate editor of *American Notes & Queries*, started sending me the occasional academic monograph to review. By then I had returned to grad school to pursue a PhD, and somehow found the time to write and place a few reviews elsewhere, such as the *San Francisco Review of Books*, Brad Morrow's *Conjunctions* (back when it still reviewed books), and two Beat-oriented magazines, Joy Walsh's *Moody Street Irregulars* and Dave (No Relation) Moore's *Kerouac Connection*. In 1986, after I volunteered to guest-edit a special issue of the *Review of Contemporary Fiction* on novelist Chandler Brossard, its editor likewise started sending me a few academic studies to review. I soon was reviewing some fiction as well for *RCF* (while still in grad school), and then upon joining its staff in 1988, that trickle turned into a flood as I started reviewing regularly, even manically, racking up over one hundred reviews in *RCF* before I left in 1996. I pretty much reviewed whatever I wanted to; there are lots of reviews of the Beats from those years, partly because they had not yet attained critical respectability, partly because I really like Kerouac and Burroughs in particular, and partly because many of the other authors I've written about were tangentially related to them: Alan Ansen, Richard Brautigan, the aforementioned Brossard and Gaddis, David Markson, Sheri Martinelli, even Thomas Pynchon.

On the basis of some early reviews in *RCF*, Michael Dirda of the *Washington Post* invited me to review a short-story collection by Mary Caponegro in 1990, which led to a long association with the *Post*, some 75 reviews to date. And on the basis of *those* reviews, I was occasionally invited to review for other places, such as the *Chicago Tribune* and the *Nation*. A wonderful woman named Carolyn Kuebler worked with me briefly in 1994–1995 at Dalkey Archive (the book publishing arm of *RCF*), and after she founded *Rain Taxi* in 1996 with Randall Heath and Eric Lorberer I began reviewing for them as well. In 1998 novelist Rikki Ducornet (whom I had published while at Dalkey) invited me to review a book for a special issue of the *American Book Review* she was guest-editing, which led to further reviews for that committed journal over the years.

Almost all these reviews are reprinted here; I even toss in a few Amazon posts. I've omitted a few trifles and roundup reviews, and others that I later incorporated into my essays and books. (To keep the focus on modern literature, I've also omitted reviews on works like *Gilgamesh* and *The Tale of Genji*, which I deal with at greater length in my alt-novel history.) In some cases I restore material that was cut or fiddled with by my editors, and I've made a few slight changes here and there, but have resisted the temptation to polish or improve them, most of which were written quickly under a deadline. They are what they are. I wince now at the book-reviewerese in some of them, and smile at the optimism: I conclude my review of an academic book about a French novelist by saying, "It is to be hoped that *Frontiers* will revive interest in Butor's work and inspire further translations," as though this obscure book by Summa Publications of Birmingham, Alabama, would actually have that effect. I often sound like I'm eagerly trying to set someone up for a blind date. Other times I warn readers away from certain books, with locutions like "If you don't know ______, this book isn't for you," not out of snobbery but because I didn't want readers to waste time and money on something that they might not like. Not every book is for everybody, no matter how good I might think it is.

I've always regarded book reviews as consumer advisory reports more than nuanced evaluations, hence the carnival-barking tone of some of them. In effect I was saying: Buy these books NOW before they are pulled from stores and remaindered! Decide later whether they are as good as I say they are. (The worst reviews are "balanced" ones that find as many faults as virtues in a book; who would want to buy that?) I also took advantage of my forums, especially the *Washington Post*, to tout other authors I liked; in my first 1990 review for the *Post*, for example, I gave a shout-out to a budding writer named David Foster Wallace, and in a later review for the *Post* of a short-story collection by Richard Ford, I named a few obscure short-story writers who are more deserving of the attention he gets. That review, by the way, is one of the very few negative ones I've written; since for most of my career I've either chosen what I wanted to review or was sent books by editors who knew my tastes, I've rarely had to review what I consider a bad work, and unlike some reviewers, I take no malicious joy in skewering writers. Even when stuck with a book I didn't like, I always tried to find something to praise.

There are a few different ways these reviews could have been organized — chronologically, thematically, linguistically, generically — but I settled on a straightforward alphabetical order by author, erasing the boundaries between time and nationalities. I mostly reviewed new fiction, but I also reviewed a large number of literary biographies and critical studies — but primarily applied criticism, practical criticism on specific authors, not rarefied literary theory, for which I've never had much use, and which I often deride in this volume. Reviews of books on individual writers are included under the subject's name, not the critic's, except for a handful that are placed at the end in a section of miscellaneous nonfiction, arranged by date of publication. By a happy coincidence, the book ends with a recent review of a book on rock music in the '60s, which is where my interest in literature began, as I've explained elsewhere.[1] Throughout, the style lurches from casual to formal depending on who I was writing for; I'm grateful that more often than not I was able to dress casual.

1 See my interviews with Jeff Bursey in *Music & Literature* <http://www.musicandliterature.org/features/2013/11/25/an-interview-with-steven-moore> and Nicolas Tredell in *The VP Annual* (Verbivoracious Press, 2016), 20–45.

The second half of this volume collects all the essays I've written over the last four decades that I'd like to preserve in book form; it excludes an equal number that I've published, either because I incorporated them into later books, or — in the case of certain introductions and afterwords — because they are too dependent upon their original circumstances of publication to stand alone, or because they already served their purpose. I mention this only because this section looks like an everything-but-the-kitchen-sink stockpile ranging from scholarly essays (aimed at specialists), to biographical profiles and introductions (which I like to think have a broader appeal), to a few talks, memoirs, and trifles.

Most of these can be called essays in appreciation. English class at Littleton, Colorado's Euclid Junior High School in the 1960s was split into two units: the first half of the school year was Grammar, the second Literary Appreciation, in which we read and discussed poems, plays, and stories. (I remember abridged versions of *Flowers for Algernon* and *Great Expectations*.) I've always felt that "appreciation" is the goal of a literary critic: the investigation and analysis of a literary work should result in a greater *appreciation* of it, especially of the craftsmanship and artistry that went into it. From the 1970s onward, however, many literary critics felt that it was their duty not to reveal the artistry in a work but to find and expose fissures that revealed an author's weaknesses (racism, homophobia, misogyny, etc.) and/or contradictions between an author's apparent intentions and his/her actual accomplishment, "complicating" the work by exposing alleged inconsistencies, unconscious prejudices, unwitting allegiance to the capitalist status quo, imperialism, heteronormative sexuality, and other deviations from political correctness. Or they used a literary work as a springboard to explore socioeconomic/political issues, theories of reading, theories of interpretation, theories of theory, drifting further and further away from the actual words on the author's page. In *Actual Minds, Possible Worlds* (Harvard University Press, 1986), Jerome S. Bruner delineates the two current approaches to writing criticism, drawing upon the "dual-process model" of cognition:

> Top-down partisans take off from a theory about a story, about mind, about writers, about readers. The theory may be anchored wherever: in psychoanalysis, in structural linguistics, in a theory of memory, in the philosophy of history. Armed with an hypothesis, the top-down partisan swoops on this text and that, searching for instances (and less often counter-instances) of what he hopes will be a right "explanation." In skilled and dispassionate hands, it is a powerful way to work. It is the way of the linguist, the social scientist, and of science generally, but it instills habits of work that always risk producing results that are insensitive to the contexts in which they were dug up. . . .
>
> Bottom-up partisans march to a very different tune. Their approach is focused on a particular piece of work: a story, a novel, a poem, even a line. They take it as

> their morsel of reality and explore it to reconstruct or deconstruct it. They are in search of the implicit theory in Conrad's construction of *Heart of Darkness* or in the worlds that Flaubert constructs. It is not that they are occupied biographically with Conrad or with Flaubert, although they do not turn a tin ear to such matters, nor are they so taken with the new criticism that they look only at the text and its artifices, though they are concerned with that too. Rather, the effort is to *read* a text for its meanings, and by doing so to elucidate the art of its author. They do not forswear the guidance of psychoanalytic theory or Jakobsonian poetics or even of the philosophy of language in pursuing their quest. But their quest is not to prove or disprove a theory, but to explore the world of a particular literary work.
>
> Partisans of the top-down approach bewail the particularity of those who proceed bottom-up. The latter deplore the abstract nonwriterliness of the former. The two do not, alas, talk much to each other. (pp. 9–10)

I've always been a bottom(s)-up scholar, privileging "particularity" — *this* particular word or phrase, *that* particular pattern of reference — to elucidate and celebrate an author's accomplishments. As one of Erasmus's adages puts it, *ex ungue leonem*: "[one deduces] the lion from its claws." My first published attempts at criticism focused on very specific words in *Finnegans Wake*, and though I widened my focus after that, an appreciation for style is one thread that runs through this motley collection. The other thread that sews these essays together is an appreciation for writers who deserve to be better known; in a few cases (Gaddis, Wallace) some of the authors I've written about achieved some acclaim, but most haven't.

As the contents page indicates, the pieces I've chosen to preserve fall into three categories. The chummy title "William Gaddis and Friends" collects various essays and talks on Gaddis along with essays on some of his writer friends, whom I got to know in the 1980s during my obsessive research on Gaddis. I first learned of him in the fall of 1975: I read a review in my father's *Time* magazine of Gaddis's *J R*, which had a sidebar on a recently reissued paperback of his 1955 novel *The Recognitions*. That caught my eye because the reviewer compared it to *Ulysses*, which was all I needed to hear, for I was a huge Joyce fan at the time. I found a copy locally and bought it the next day, read it shortly after, and was blown away by it. As I wrote in the preface to my first book on Gaddis (published seven years later):

> As is my custom when confronted with exhilarating literature, I began looking around to see what kind of critical work had been done on the novel, fully expecting to find mountains of material (and silently wondering all the time how I had missed hearing of such a novel.) To my utter dismay, I found not mountains but molehills, and this in 1975, a full twenty years after publication. Apparently the novel had been sitting like an island in the stream of American literature, circumnavigated a few times, but as yet unexplored. Feeling let down by the academic scholarly community, I proceeded to write (for myself if no one else) the kind of book someone should have written long ago.

It also struck me that writing the first book on Gaddis would be better than writing the 101st on Joyce, which I had been contemplating. "Chronological Difficulties in the Novels of William Gaddis," published in *Critique* in 1980, was the first fruit of my Gaddis researches, and it's interesting that in my maiden essay on him I took him to task (respectfully as I could) for his sloppy use of chronology. The two essays that follow were written between 1981 and 1983: the one on Gaddis and Pynchon was published in *Pynchon Notes* in 1983, and "*Peer Gynt* and *The Recognitions*" was published in a collection of essays called *In Recognition of William Gaddis* published by Syracuse University Press in 1984, for which I also wrote the biographical introduction. (The latter is an example of what I'm not including in this volume, for I adapted most of that introductory material in my later books on Gaddis.) Admittedly, all three will probably appeal only to Gaddis scholars.

I learned of Chandler Brossard (1922–1993) from Gaddis. They were roommates for a while in Greenwich Village in the late '40s, and Gaddis told me that Brossard modeled a character on him in his first novel, *Who Walk in Darkness*. I sought out and read that and another novel of his, liked them, wrote to Brossard to see if he had any letters from Gaddis (he didn't), met him during a trip to New York in December 1983 (when I first met Gaddis), and remained friends with him until his death in 1993. (He called me from his deathbed, the toughest phone call I've ever received.) The long essay included here is a composite of several things I've written on Chandler over the years. In 1984–85 I wrote the bulk of it for a special issue of the *Review of Contemporary Fiction* devoted to his work published in the spring 1987, for which I was the guest editor. That piece drew upon reviews of Brossard's chapbooks I had already published in the *San Francisco Review of Books* (1985) and *RCF* (1986), and years later, at publisher Paul Williams' invitation, I adapted portions of the original essay for the forewords to Herodias's new editions of Brossard's *Who Walk in Darkness* (2000) and *The Bold Saboteurs* (2001). I also wrote forewords for the next two Brossard novels that Williams planned to publish, *The Double View* and *Did Christ Make Love?*, but Herodias folded before they appeared. I went back to the well of that 1987 essay again for my introduction to Sun Dog Press's edition of Brossard's later works, *Over the Rainbow? Hardly: Collected Short Seizures* (2005), an omnibus I had prepared for Dalkey Archive Press in the early 1990s. (Though typeset and ready to go, it was delayed season after season, and then abandoned after I left Dalkey in 1996; Herodias too reset it and planned to publish it before going out of business.) The only novel of Brossard's I never wrote about was the one I typed up for him in 1984 and published with Dalkey in 1992, *As the Wolf Howls at My Door*; for this composite essay I decided to expand upon my original jacket copy and write a few pages to fill the gap and consequently re-read it over the 2015 Labor Day weekend with great pleasure and undimmed admiration.

I followed the same pattern with Alan Ansen (1922–2006): got to know him via Gaddis, wrote to see if he had any letters (again no), and then took an interest in his writings and in his connections with the Beat generation. I typed up and arranged to publish a few of his early works with Water Row Press, which specialized in Beat poetry. They tentatively agreed to publish an edition of Ansen's selected poetry, but then reneged; by then I had joined Dalkey Archive Press and was able to publish it there as *Contact Highs*, featuring the biographical introduction included here, which is augmented with some new information that has appeared in recent years.

I learned of David Markson (1927–2010) from Jack Green's 1962 defense of Gaddis entitled *Fire the Bastards!*, read an early novel or two, then contacted him too for letters. There I hit the jackpot, for he not only shared copies of a dozen or more with me, but shared many memories as well, and we soon became regular correspondents. He also shared with me an unpublished manuscript that had been turned down by 54 publishers, and so I became his publisher as well when I recommended his *Wittgenstein's Mistress* to Dalkey Archive Press, which I had just joined. Over the next eight years I published his *Collected Poems* and a new edition of *Springer's Progress*, and copyedited *Reader's Block* (published a few months after I left Dalkey in 1996). The essay included here was written for a special issue of the *Review of Contemporary Fiction* partly devoted to Markson in 1990, and covers his career up to that point. As a coda, I've added a review I wrote in 2016 on Markson's final four novels.

The Markson essay, incidentally, reveals a third thread that runs through this collection, namely the uses of erudition and the related arts of literary allusion and learned wit in fiction. Beginning with ferreting out allusions in *Finnegans Wake*, and ending with lauding the literary allusiveness of Leopoldo Marechal's *Adam Buenosayres* in one of the last pieces written here, I've always been fascinated with writers who make extensive, even ostentatious use of intertextuality in their work.

The aforementioned Jack Green is the subject of the essay that follows; the rocky origins of that introduction are explained in its opening pages. I wrote this partly in anger at Gaddis's mistreatment by reviewers, but also by the review media's disparagement of other favorites of mine (Brossard, Theroux), which was compounded by the frustratingly spotty media coverage of Dalkey's books at the time (1992). The final pages of the essay now strike me as unworldly — the job of a newspaper book-review editor is to cover books that the majority of readers will be interested in, not the ones of interest only to literary geeks — but the historical neglect of worthy writers by the review media (a recurring topic in Markson's final novels) remains relevant.

I learned of Sheri Martinelli (1918–1996) in the early 1980s in a roundabout way: I was informed of her connection with Gaddis from a mutual friend of theirs named Vincent Livelli, and of her connection with Ezra Pound via a book on the poet I had been asked to review. I wrote to her in 1983, and we stayed in contact thereafter. She died in November 1996, and the following summer Richard Peabody included her in his anthology *A Different Beat: Writings by Women of the Beat Generation*, with a sketchy contributor's note implying little was known about her. To rectify that, I first wrote a 10-page remembrance that was published in *Anais: An International Journal* (Spring 1998), then expanded it threefold for a more scholarly version that was published in Peabody's magazine *Gargoyle* that summer. A year later, Martinelli's longtime companion Gilbert Lee shared with me all the letters she exchanged with Charles Bukowski, so I adapted my essay for the introduction to *Beerspit Night and Cursing: The Correspondence of Charles Bukowski and Sheri Martinelli, 1960–1967* (Black Sparrow Press, 2001). The version included here incorporates an afterword to the *Gargoyle* version I posted online in 2005, along with a few additional details I've come across since then about this fascinating woman. I was pleased to see that A. David Moody made use of my research for the final volume of his magisterial biography *Ezra Pound: Poet* (2015).

I should add that while Gaddis was at the center of this circle of friends, they were only tangentially aware of each other. As I said, Chandler Brossard was Gaddis's roommate for a while in the late 1940s, and may have run into Alan Ansen at Cannastra's [see p. 489–90 below]. Brossard knew of Markson (and told me he didn't care for his fiction) but I don't think Markson knew him; Markson refers to Sheri Martinelli in *Wittgenstein's Mistress* by way of *The Recognitions*; Sheri probably met Brossard at one point, and she and Ansen had mutual friends (Ginsberg, Corso, Gaddis). Green — unlike the others, no friend of mine — quoted Markson in *Fire the Bastards!* and 30 years later Markson remembered "hammering my knee in delight at Jack Green's brilliantly targeted outrage." Gaddis is the hub of this circle, but not its ringleader.

This section concludes with three relatively short pieces I've done on Gaddis since his death in 1998: "Remembering Mr. Gaddis" was written in LaGuardia airport the day after the memorial his family held for him on 6 May 1999, and was posted on *Conjunction*'s website later that year. "*The Recognitions*: Then and Now" is a talk I gave at a conference at the University of Buffalo in March 2005 celebrating the 50th anniversary of the publication of *The Recognitions* — hence its chatty style. And "William Gaddis: The Nobility of Failure" was written at the request of the editors of *Critique* for a special issue entitled "An American Requiem: Elegies for Thirteen Novelists" in 2010.

The next section gathers essays on other writers who have meant a lot to me, hence the flippant title "Significant Others." I begin with some trifles on Joyce, partly for sentimental reasons — they were my first published criticism — but also because it was Joyce who made me want to become a critic. As an undergraduate I read his *Portrait of the Artist* in the Viking Critical Edition, which not only had some illuminating essays on it in back, but also excerpts from *Ulysses* and *Finnegans Wake*, which enthralled me. A year or so later I read *Ulysses* for the first time (understood about 30 percent of it), and shortly thereafter bought my first book of literary criticism, Stuart Gilbert's 1930 study of *Ulysses*. That became the model for the kind of criticism I wanted to write: not theoretical flights of fancy but down-to-earth explication of what was actually going on in a text, right down to the lexical level. *Finnegans Wake* came next, and I quickly became a *Wake* addict, hoovering up everything I could read on it. I even began compiling a multivolume glossary to *Finnegans Wake*, and spent a few years working on it until I realized it would take a decade to complete and would probably be too long for anyone to publish. These five notes on *Finnegans Wake* are all that survive of that project. They were published between 1976 and 1980 in a small English journal punningly called *A Wake Newslitter*, and probably won't mean much to non-Wakians, though they provide indications of some of my interests at the time.

After Joyce, the second great awakening I experienced in the early 1970s was reading Proust's *Remembrance of Things Past* (as it was known in those days), which had a seismic impact greater than almost any novel I've read since. So I'm including a collegiate essay from that period mostly in homage to Proust, but also because I liked Vonnegut at the time and never had an opportunity later to write about him — or Proust, for that matter. (I don't know if subsequent scholars have made the Proust-Vonnegut connection, but no one had back then.) I originally wrote this for an independent study in 1974: when I told my advisor, Dr. Sharon Wilson, that I wanted to compare Vonnegut to Proust, she smiled and asked "Why?" How's that for encouragement to a budding scholar? I revised it four or five years later and sent it to Vonnegut scholar Jerome Klinkowitz in case he was planning another casebook on Vonnegut like *The Vonnegut Statement* (1973) and *Vonnegut in America* (1977). He wasn't, and I don't recall making any further efforts to publish it, for by that time I had begun writing about a novelist born seven weeks after Vonnegut: William Gaddis, and then his fascinating circle of friends.

I first learned of Alexander Theroux in 1981, as I explain in gushing detail in the second of the two essays included here. The first was written in 1983–84 and published in *Contemporary Literature* in 1986. By that time I was in grad school at Rutgers, where I wrote the Edward Dahlberg piece during a Dahlberg phase I was going through, partly due to his influence on Theroux. It was published in 1989 as the introduction to a collection I edited entitled *Samuel Beckett's Wake and Other Writings*. The out-of-print situation I deplore in this essay is even worse today; even the book I edited is now o.p. (as are most of the books I edited for Dalkey). The second Theroux essay was written for a special issue of the *Review of Contemporary Fiction* I edited in 1991.

I learned of Ronald Firbank in the 1970s from Gaddis's *Recognitions* and quickly became a devotee of his eccentric works, which eventually led to publishing editions of his short stories (1990) and his plays (1994), as well as a book-length bibliography of Firbank criticism (1996). Brigid Brophy, author of a controversial book on Firbank, was another old favorite and in 1995 I edited a section on her for *RCF*, which went to press a few weeks after she died. I didn't originally intend to write an introductory essay on her, but decided at the last minute to add a piece on her for the occasion, hence its brevity.

W. M. Spackman came to my attention around the same time as Firbank. In the summer of 1978 I opened up a little bookstore in a suburb of Denver, ingeniously called Moore Books. While at the local warehouse buying stock, I noticed a recently published novel with an irresistible title, *An Armful of Warm Girl*, read it, and became a devoted Spackman fan thereafter. Shortly after he died in 1990, I began planning an omnibus edition of his complete fiction; it was typeset and ready to go by 1995, but was continually postponed by Dalkey's boss until a year after I left. (During that time, he moved my introduction to the back and called it an afterword because, as Spackman's daughter told me, "he felt the length of the introduction might discourage less scholarly readers from starting to read the book.") *The Complete Fiction of W. M. Spackman* (1997) was very well received, and I was especially flattered that John Updike referred to my piece as "excellent" in his *New Yorker* review (but disappointed when he dropped that adjective in his *More Matter* collection a few years later). I tried my hardest to make this essay as elegant as possible in tribute to Spackman's style: I wanted to be worthy of him. At that time I also prepared a collection of Spackman's essays that I wanted to publish as a companion volume, but my exit from Dalkey (and the boss's indifference to Spackman) made that impossible. I still hope to get it into print someday, for his essays and reviews are unbelievably brilliant. By the way: Back in the 1990s, David Foster Wallace received most of Dalkey's books, and I'm 99 percent certain he at least looked at my omnibus, and that the "Spackman Initiative" in his posthumous novel *The Pale King* was named after the novelist.

No sooner did I leave Dalkey/*RCF* than I was asked by Victoria Frenkel Harris to contribute to a special issue of *RCF* to be devoted to Carole Maso, two of whose novels I edited while at Dalkey. I chose to write on her latest one, the enchanting *Aureole*, and did so during August 1996 when I was out of work and living in a lousy apartment in my hometown of Littleton, Colorado.

In a far nicer apartment in Ann Arbor in the fall of 2001, I wrote the essay on Brautigan included here. I discovered Brautigan's work in 1971 when I spotted a paperback copy of *The Abortion* in a department store. I was struck by the photographic cover because it was like looking in a mirror: back then I had the same long blonde hair, glasses, and hippie clothes. ("Threads," we called them.) I loved *The Abortion* and quickly devoured his earlier works, then read each new book as it was published in the 1970s and '80s. After his death in 1984, I waited for the customary *Collected Poems* to appear, but years went by: nada. So in August 2001 I proposed such a book to John Martin of Black Sparrow Press; he liked the idea and contacted the Brautigan Estate, which also liked the idea, and over the next two months I prepared the manuscript. But in the spring of 2002, Martin decided to close shop and cancelled all further publications. Not wanting to see the work go to waste, I sent the manuscript to Houghton Mifflin, Brautigan's old publisher. An editor there said they might want to publish it, so I directed him to the Estate for the necessary permission. I never heard back from anyone after that, and the manuscript has been gathering dust on my shelf ever since. The essay here is the introduction I wrote for the doomed volume. In 2006, John F. Barber published it in his *Richard Brautigan: Essays on the Writings and Life* (McFarland & Company); I've undone the editorial meddling that was done behind my back (and deleted the bibliography), but I have not updated it in light of William Hjortsberg's massive *Jubilee Hitchhiker: The Life and Times of Richard Brautigan* (2012). In 2016 it was translated into French and published as the introduction to *Tout ce que j'ai à déclarer: œuvre poétique complète* (Le Castor Astral).

There are two pieces here on the late David Foster Wallace. The earlier was written during a week's vacation in the spring of 2003 and posted on Nick Maniatis's Howling Fantods website in May of that year, after running it by Dave first to make sure he had no objections. The second was written a few days after Dave's suicide in 2008, at the invitation of the literary journal *Modernism/Modernity*, which published it the following year as part of a tribute.

In 2012 Jesse Pearson invited me to contribute to a forum on "The Endangered Semicolon" for the inaugural issue of his magazine *Apology*. "Of Cause and Consequence" is a trifle, but I thought I'd add it to the pile if only to indicate my continued focus on tiny stylistic matters. Later that year, fellow Gaddis aficionado Ted Morrissey asked me to write the foreword to his forthcoming book *The* Beowulf *Poet and His Real Monsters*, for reasons known only to him, but I agreed because it gave me an opportunity to put to use that class in Old English I took 30 years earlier. The publisher deleted the date I placed at the end — the Anglo-Saxon equivalent of Christmas Eve — which I've restored here. Another trifle, but if nothing else it broadens the scope of this collection. The editors of a literary annual called *Pleasure* invited me in 2014 to contribute to a special issue on maximalism, and since I had just stumbled upon the first English translation of Leopoldo Marechal's 1948 novel *Adam Buenosayres*, I decided to use that as a demonstration-class example of that muscular mode.

The final section, "Personal Matters," begins with my favorite essay in this book. I wrote "Nympholepsy" in 2001 and published it the following year in *Gargoyle* (which was favorably noted by Michael Dirda in the *Washington Post*). It's my favorite largely because its subject *inspired* me — which was what nympholepsy originally meant — to open up my style, one that I've used ever since whenever possible. (You can see that style develop over the course of the essay, which begins in a flat, documentary voice that turns more lyrical, scholarly, and fanciful as it goes along.) That more personal, unbuttoned style is on full display in the book I began writing a few years later, *The Novel: An Alternative History*. After the first volume was published (2010), I was asked by the *Guardian* to write an account of how I wrote that book; a year and a half after the second volume was published (2013), I was invited by fellow novel historian Thomas Pavel to give a talk on the same topic at the University of Chicago in the spring of 2015, so I expanded that original piece for the occasion, included here as "Rethinking the Novel." Around the same time, I was asked by the editors of Verbivoracious Press to contribute to a forthcoming festschrift on novelist Rikki Ducornet, an occasion to reminisce on the books of hers I had the honor of publishing while at Dalkey.

After Jack Green published his defense of Gaddis, he expressed regret for doing so: "it was wrong & presumptuous of me to seek publicity for jones & gaddis in ways i wouldnt for myself i risked interfering with natural growth of acceptance of their work by my 'shot in the arm' methods." I have no regrets for my attempts to seek publicity for the authors I've loved — if one relied on "natural growth," any number of deserving writers would have vanished from literary history — and I hope this collection encourages readers to seek out at least some of my Gaddis friends and significant others.

Acknowledgments

First, I want to thank all the book review editors who invited me to write for their publications, and the journals that published my various essays; obviously this book would not exist without them. Second, I want to thank those who helped me compile this collection: my sister and nephew, Maureen and Ryan Stewart, dug up my old *Spree* reviews from the Denver Public Library; I had thrown them out in a fit of despair 25 years ago, along with other memorabilia, but I'm glad to add them to the album, like the early demos that are sometimes included on CD reissues. Victoria Harding and her husband Murray Gross found and sent me the *Finnegans Wake* tidbits. Third, I want to thank Haaris Naqvi of Bloomsbury and Gina Forester and Mark Nicholls of Verbivoracious Press for offering to publish shorter versions of this book; and finally, above all, I want to thank Jim Gauer for his willingness to publish this bulky collection just as I envisioned it, for what it's worth.

□ □ □ □ □ □ □

This paperback edition corrects a number of typos in the hardback edition (my thanks to Nathan Gaddis, Pablo Capra, Jim Gauer, and Jeff Bursey for identifying many of them) and adds a new essay on the forgotten novelist J. P. McEvoy — written in November 2016 as a diversion from the Trump tragedy — which was posted in March 2017 on Douglas Glover's stellar website *Número Cinq*. Further thanks to Jeff Bursey for suggesting I send it there.

REVIEWS

Héctor Abad

The Joy of Being Awake. Translated by Nathan Budoff
Brookline/Lumen, 1996

Literary translations are the poor relations of the publishing world, often showing up unwanted at the doors of book review editors and bookstore buyers, sniffed at by the book-buying public, and displaying foreign habits of little interest to most Americans. We are not nearly as interested in the rest of the world as they are in us. And one never knows about the quality of the translation: Few translators are as talented as the writers they translate, so one always feels cheated somewhat, like settling for a cover version of a song rather than the original. It's no accident that "lost in translation" remains a common idiom. Still, it's no virtue to be provincial, so hats off to those publishers — mostly smaller, independent presses — who continue to bring us literary translations against all odds.

The Joy of Being Awake by the Colombian writer Héctor Abad deliberately models itself on two key 18th-century works: Laurence Sterne's *Tristram Shandy* and Voltaire's *Candide*. Like Sterne's eccentric novel, *The Joy of Being Awake* is a bittersweet account of the life and opinions of a man at odds with himself, narrated in nonchronological fashion with plenty of entertaining digressions and the occasional formal game. One chapter, subtitled in fine 18th-century style "Wherein a Eulogy of Silence is Proclaimed & What is Not Disclosed in Passing Over Several Years of Life is Declared," consists of two blank pages. The narrator, a rich, erudite man, shares Voltaire's rationalism and skepticism, and his eventual wife, the delectably named Cunegunda Bonaventura, even shares the name of Candide's wife, Cunegonde. Writing at the end of his life, the narrator often gives two versions of a memory: first, what he wishes had happened, and then what really happened. It's appropriate that he's the author of a collection of essays "on the double scatology of Quevedo, the metaphysical and the defecatory." (That "double" should be "twofold" — one of many instances where the translator chooses the wrong word.) Torn between the metaphysical and the defecatory, as it were, the narrator retreats into an ascetic life, candidly admitting he is "a man who doesn't feel." Like both Sterne's and Voltaire's books (though not in the same league as either), Abad's novel has a surface geniality that barely conceals undercurrents of discontent and despair.

Washington Post, 22 December 1996 — the first in a "Fiction in Translation" roundup of six novels.

Avant-Pop Fiction

Avant-Pop: Fiction for a Daydream Nation. Edited by Larry McCaffery
Black Ice, 1993

Love Is Strange: Stories of Postmodern Romance.
Edited by Joel Rose and Catherine Texier
Norton, 1993

These two anthologies will interest readers of this particular issue of the *Review*,[1] not simply because Vollmann is in both and Wallace in *Love Is Strange*, but because they also include many of the authors named in the interviews: Eurudice, Mark Leyner, and Kathy Acker are in McCaffery's band, and Rose and Texier's includes Lynne Tillman, Acker again, and A. M. Homes's Barbie story, in addition to much more. Both anthologies come less from the world of creative writing programs than from rock music, television, and the weirder manifestations of pop culture. The titles of the books derive from rock — *Daydream Nation* is the title of a Sonic Youth album, and "Love Is Strange" an old song from Mickey & Silvia (though neither is actually explained: if you don't already know the references, you aren't in the intended audience) — and the sensibilities displayed in the stories have less to do with traditional fiction than with TV shows like *Saturday Night Live* and *The Edge*. That is to say, these stories have all the appeal of the best kinds of pop — off-the-wall humor, brash innovation, breezy iconoclasm, unstudied charm, reckless energy — along with some of pop's disadvantages: insubstantiality, shallowness, and plain recklessness. That said, both anthologies are way more enjoyable than most collections of short fiction published these days. *Avant-Pop* is more daring and eclectic than *Love Is Strange*, and both are mostly made up of previously published material, but both are highly recommended.

Review of Contemporary Fiction, Summer 1993

1 Younger Writers Issue, featuring William T. Vollmann, David Foster Wallace, and Susan Daitch, guest-edited by Larry McCaffery (Summer 1993).

After Yesterday's Crash: The Avant-Pop Anthology. Edited by Larry McCaffery
Penguin, 1995

Mark Leyner. *Tooth Imprints on a Corn Dog*
Harmony, 1995

I read some of *After Yesterday's Crash* while half-listening to a CD of Balinese gamelan music — gorgeous stuff, what angels on drugs must listen to — and realized I was exemplifying part of what McCaffery was after in this anthology: we live in a world of bizarre conjunctions (in this case, ancient music played on a high-tech CD while reading a book of avant-garde fiction), but too few writers attempt to capture the disorienting mélange of media overkill, global awareness, hyperconsumerism, and sensory overload that makes up postmodern life. Add those other elements that make life in the '90s so interesting — drive-by shootings, phone sex, serial killings, terrorism, AIDS, date rape, conspiracy theories, infomercials, friendly fire — and you've got the world McCaffery's writers have downloaded onto their PCs. Add techniques borrowed from rock music, pop art, television (especially MTV), low-budget films, pornography, cartoons, and other examples of "low" culture, and you've got this lively anthology, one of the best collections of innovative fiction in years.

"Avant-Pop" is a term McCaffery has appropriated from composer Lester Bowie to describe art that mixes pop or low culture with serious, high-culture concerns. In literature, it could probably be traced back to Joyce's *Ulysses*, where advertising jingles, street noise, and the day's "pop" songs commingle with weightier matters in a stream of consciousness meant to simulate sensory reception; or better yet, to Eliot's *Waste Land*, with its "samples" from culture high and low mixed into a multilayered word collage (with its footnotes functioning as a low-tech prototype of hypertext). Burroughs and Pynchon further explored these techniques in the late '50s and early '60s, as did the older writers included in the present anthology (Coover, Federman, Katz, Sukenick). Many of the writers in McCaffery's indie forerunner, *Avant-Pop: Fiction for a Daydream Nation* (Black Ice, 1993), reappear here with new offerings — Stephen Wright, Derek Pell, Eurudice, Mark Leyner, Harold Jaffe, Ricardo Cortez Cruz, William T. Vollmann, Gerald Vizenor — along with a few better-known writers (Don DeLillo, Steve Erickson, Tom Robbins, Paul Auster, Bret Easton Ellis) and a gang of cyberpunks (William Gibson, Mark Laidlaw, Bruce Sterling). It's mostly a guy thing; of the 32 contributors, only five are women.

The hit single from this compilation is David Foster Wallace's "Tri-Stan: I Sold Sissee Nar to Ecko," a flawlessly executed neo-Barthian remix of Greek mythology. Also outstanding are Lauren Fairbanks's "Victims of Mass Imagination" and Guillermo Gómez-Peña's "Border Brujo," the few pieces linguistically dense and disorienting enough to simulate the sensory overload and hyperactive stimuli all the contributors address in one form or another. (The other contributors not already mentioned are Rikki Ducornet, Susan Daitch, Craig Baldwin, Craig Padawer, Ben Marcus, Curtis White, Mark Amerika, Lynne Tillman, and David Blair.)

Since Mark Leyner could be Avant-Pop's poster boy — McCaffery calls him "the most intense, and in a certain sense, the most significant young prose writer in America" — it's worth noting he has a new book out. The word *Imprints* in the title says it all: any other writer would have used *Marks*; the more precise *Imprints*, with its police-lab smell of forensic medicine, signals Leyner's greatest virtue: a way with *le mot juste* even when discussing things as banal as corn dogs. His vocabulary, like Burroughs's before him, often comes from medical technology, and (again like WSB) has a cut-up quality of disparate discourses. (Burroughs, rather than the *Mad-Libs* ludicrously suggested by the *New York Times* reviewer of this book, is the likelier source and/or parallel.) There is much in Leyner that reminds me of the late Chandler Brossard (an unsung godfather of Avant-Pop), which is to say he can be extremely funny and is always surprising. Even though *Tooth Imprints* is basically a random collection of magazine pieces (one of which, "Oh, Brother," also appears in *After Yesterday's Crash*), it is more creative, more engaging, and better written than three-fourths of the so-called serious fiction published these days.

Review of Contemporary Fiction, Fall 1995

Félix de Azua

Diary of a Humiliated Man. Translated by Julie Jones
Brookline/Lumen, 1996

The narrator of *Diary of a Humiliated Man* is like [Héctor Abad's narrator] a man at odds with himself, but Spanish author Félix de Azua takes as his models not 18th-century writers but later ones like Dostoevsky and Camus. At a crucial point in his life, the narrator decides to go underground, to live like a stranger in his native city of Barcelona. As the title indicates, the novel takes the form of a diary, eight months in the life of a 47-year-old intellectual who fears he has become a "pious hypocrite." Deliberately seeking a banal, even humiliating life, he begins living a simple existence, only to descend into petty crime, temporary insanity, and homelessness. But he never loses his intellectual acuity — the novel is very erudite and richly allusive — nor his sardonic humor.

Like Ulrich in Robert Musil's *Man without Qualities*, the narrator is a sardonic commentator on his times: "Humiliated people are recognizable at first sight. We have the blasé, Ciceronian gaze of someone who has seen the universe sink beneath him without a single shot being fired. The ancient Earth has become a phone book. It says nothing at all, but it opens the way to cosmic charlatanism. And it's pricey. Very pricey." The novel is intellectually lively, but many of the cultural observations are not dramatically motivated by the material (as they are in Musil, Dostoevsky, and Camus) but rather superimposed by a brilliant, widely read author with opinions on everything. Nevertheless, it is an original treatment of age-old questions on the nature of sin, good vs. evil, human vs. animal, and so on, and is especially informative about Barcelona and Catalonia in general. Julie Jones's translation is exceptionally smooth and confident.

Washington Post, 22 December 1996

Nicholson Baker

The Mezzanine
Weidenfeld & Nicolson, 1988

This wonderful novel begins at the bottom of the escalator a young man rides to the mezzanine level where he works, and ends at the top of the escalator a minute or so later. His circumstances at the time of that ride — returning from lunch with a bag containing new shoelaces, carrying a Penguin paperback of Marcus Aurelius's *Meditations* ("Manifestly, no condition of life could be so well adapted for the practice of philosophy as this in which chance finds you today!") — provide the contents of the novel: what he had for lunch, why he needed new shoelaces, why he likes Penguin paperbacks, etc., all conveyed in reminiscences, digressions, footnotes (some as long as three pages), lists, and charts.

A mundane, even tedious subject for a novel? Not in this case, for Baker's delightful attempt to document "the often undocumented daily texture of our lives" also encompasses mini-histories of technical advances and human ingenuity in our time, from the workings of the escalator he rides to a celebration of perforation. At the end of a long footnote on "another fairly important development in the history of the straw," the narrator writes: "An unpretentious technical invention — the straw, the sugar packet, the pencil, the windshield wiper — has been ornamented by a mute folklore of behavioral inventions, unregistered, unpatented, adopted and fine-tuned without comment or thought." Giving voice to this mute folklore, the narrator — a Proust of the commonplace, a yuppie Tristram Shandy — links his own emotional history with recent technical advances by way of hundreds of analogies, metaphors, and fanciful comparisons that are so apt, so insightful, and often so amusing that I felt I was seeing the world I live in for the first time — as trite as that may sound. Often I've opened the package of a dry-cleaned shirt, but never have I noticed that "their arms [are] impossibly bent behind them as if each were concealing a present." As this particular image suggests, the narrator regards technical advances not as threats but as gifts, ones that we have taken for granted for so long that Baker has had to rewrap and present them anew in the form of an irresistible novel.

Review of Contemporary Fiction, Summer 1989

Nicola Barker

Darkmans
Ecco, 2007

'Tis the season of huge literary novels. Those of us for whom size matters welcome with holiday cheer Denis Johnson's *Tree of Smoke*, James McCourt's *Now Voyagers*, two new translations of Tolstoy's *War and Peace*, Paul Verhaeghen's *Omega Minor*, Alexander Theroux's *Laura Warholic*, and the 900-page *Adventures of Amir Hamza*, an old Urdu novel (by way of Arabia and Persia) newly translated for the Modern Library. Crashing this boys' club from England comes Nicola Barker's 838-page *Darkmans*, her seventh and longest novel, and a finalist for this year's prestigious Man Booker Prize (which went to a much much shorter novel).

Darkmans records with manic energy a week in the chaotic lives of a dozen characters living in contemporary Ashford, near the entrance to the Chunnel. The cast includes a prescription-drug dealer named Kane, his no-nonsense father Beede, a foul-mouthed, miniskirted teenager named Kelly (my fave), a displaced Kurd, a troubled married couple with a precocious son (he has built a replica of the Cathedral of Sainte-Cecile from matchsticks), an antiques restorer/forger, and the shadowy title character, who seems to be responsible for the occasional supernatural irruptions in the novel. For something strange is happening to some of these characters: mental blackouts, hallucinations, hauntings, confrontations with malevolent birds, and various signs and tokens of the late Middle Ages. Many of the latter concern John Scogin, court jester to Edward IV (ruled 1461–83), and the famous book about him, *Scogin's Jests*, which supplies some of the plot elements in *Darkmans*. Britain no longer employs court jesters; novelists now fill that function, a job open to members of either sex.

Despite these supernatural elements, *Darkmans* isn't really an occult novel but a social comedy suggesting the modern world has reverted to the premodern culture of the 15th century, an era of spectacle and over-indulgence, of superstition and conspicuous consumption. Beede owns a copy of Johan Huizinga's classic *Waning of the Middle Ages* and has underlined the sentence, "So violent and motley was life that it bore the mixed smell of blood and roses."

Life in Barker's England is likewise "violent and motley," bedeviled by many of the same problems we have here in "Yank-land" (as one character calls it): drug abuse, overdevelopment, declining standards, racism, and cultural illiteracy. And with a jester's license to speak truth to power, Barker conveys this in a motley style of great wit and daring. She relies heavily on idiomatic dialogue, deploys unconventional spacing and paragraphing, and exults in startling imagery and extended metaphors (with parenthetical asides), like this riff from Kane on his father's uncharacteristic refusal to meet his gaze:

> Unheard of! Beede was the original *architect* of the unflinching stare. Beede's stare was so steady he could make an owl crave Optrex. Beede could happily unrapt a raptor. And he'd done some pretty nifty groundwork over the years in the Guilt Trip arena (*trip?* How about a gruelling two-month sabbatical in the parched, ancient Persian city of Firuzabad? And he'd do your packing. And he'd book your hotel. And it'd be miles from the airport. And there'd be no fucking air conditioning). Beede was the hair shirt in human form.

Barker has also invented an effective typographic device to indicate what a foreigner means to say while speaking broken English, but she doesn't coddle the reader with traditional transitions. You're often as much in the dark as the characters as to what exactly is happening, and you're propelled to read on to see not what happens next but what Barker will do next with language. The novel's 838 pages fly by, and it's a bloody larf, mate, due to the profane slang used by all classes of society. (On laundry challenges, the hostess of a dinner party observes, "Bright whites can be such *bastards* to maintain, can't they?") Surprisingly for such a raucous novel, there's no sex in it.

Barker's extensive use of dialogue and her balancing act of serious theme/comic style remind me of the late William Gaddis, who likewise used *The Waning of the Middle Ages* in his first novel *The Recognitions* to show that in many quarters today it's as if the Enlightenment never happened. The ingenuity with which Barker weaves historical material into the fabric of modern life rivals that of Gaddis and Thomas Pynchon, though *Darkmans* is somewhat easier to read than their novels. Indeed, Barker has more in common with male writers like these — add the late Stanley Elkin, Robert Coover, David Foster Wallace, and the aforementioned Alexander Theroux — than with her writing sisters. Barker once acknowledged this: "A girl writer is something I never wanted to be. Girl writers don't get taken seriously. I am a boyish writer."

Hilarious and erudite, spooky and unconventional, *Darkmans* is a dazzling achievement. I haven't read the winner of the Man Booker Prize, but I suspect Nicola Barker was robbed.

Washington Post, 20 December 2007

Djuna Barnes

New York. Edited by Alyce Barry
Sun & Moon, 1989

The Book of Repulsive Women
Sun & Moon, 1989

Djuna Barnes had such a distinctive voice, such a magnificent style, that even her ephemeral writings are of interest. *New York* is the third in Sun & Moon's admirable plan to gather all of Barnes's minor writings: *Smoke and Other Early Stories* (recently reissued in a corrected edition) contains her earliest fiction; *Interviews* is probably the most extraordinary collection in that form; and now *New York* gathers all of her journalism relating to New York City and environs.

All the pieces date from 1913–19 and are features (as opposed to hard news), some banal, some sensational. Barnes was an early practitioner of participatory journalism, allowing herself to be rescued three times at a fireman's training school, to be hugged by a gorilla at the zoo, and, in the most striking piece here, to be force-fed in the manner of British suffragettes. Several articles concentrate on the Bohemian life in Greenwich Village, of which Barnes was both a participant and an ironically detached observer. She approaches most of her subjects from unusual, oblique angles, and shows early signs of her love for Jacobean metaphors and startling imagery, for aphorisms and epigrams. As in her interviews book, Barnes gives some of her subjects improbably sonorous lines: asked if crime and punishment will ever be done away with, Police Commissioner Ellen O'Grady answers, "Never, not so long as humanity is inhuman. The gallows tree has not shut the mouth of all the angers, nor has the rope strangled the universal cry of despair." Gems like that stud this varied collection, which should please Barnes fans as well as those interested in a unique look at life in New York during the Great War.

Sun & Moon has also begun a chapbook series called "20 Pages," and leading it off is Barnes's first published work, *The Book of Repulsive Women*. Originally published in 1915, the pamphlet consists of eight "rhythms" (poems) and five drawings, all done in a decadent style that looks back to Swinburne (especially in its use of rhyme) and parallels the Laforguean poetry Eliot was writing at the same time. The "repulsive" women are sisters to those she would later write about — lesbians, cabaret dancers, the damned (by society and self) — and constitute the earliest illustration of Barnes's love-hate relationship with her own sex. A minor but essential work in the Barnes canon.

Review of Contemporary Fiction, Spring 1990

Hank O'Neal. *"Life is painful, nasty and short . . . in my case it has been only painful and nasty": Djuna Barnes, 1978–1981*
Paragon House, 1990

Mary Lynn Broe, ed. *Silence and Power: A Reevaluation of Djuna Barnes*
Southern Illinois University Press, 1991

Djuna Barnes spent the first half of her life building a reputation as a daring, flamboyant character and as the author of several daring, flamboyant books. She spent the second half of her life in self-imposed exile in a tiny apartment on Patchin Place in Greenwich Village. Little has been known of this latter period, which makes Hank O'Neal's memoir of her last days valuable. A brilliant conversationalist, she regaled O'Neal with endless stories of her past and allowed him to witness her chaotic working methods as a writer. Numerous previously unpublished photographs enhance the book, and every Barnes fan or scholar will want to add this book to his or her shelf. The book has its faults — several anecdotes are needlessly duplicated and the book lacks an index (which is the second time this year a Paragon House book has been faulted in this journal for lacking an index: I hope they're listening) — but O'Neal's memoir is a welcome addition to the growing corpus of Barnes criticism and sheds considerable new light on this fascinating writer.

A warmer welcome can be extended to Mary Lynn Broe's *Silence and Power*, a magnificently produced collection of essays on every aspect of Barnes's life and work. Eighteen essays track Barnes's career from the early journalism and plays through the stylistic experiments of *Ryder* and *Ladies Almanack*, into *Nightwood* and the hermetic *Antiphon*. Between the essays are entr'actes of brief quotations from various people on Barnes, and following the essays are 30 pages of new reminiscences. Two selections of plates reproduce many rare photographs and drawings, and completing the volume are an afterword by Catharine Stimpson, an extensive bibliography, and yes, an index. This is the most important book to appear on this important writer, and is highly recommended to all scholars, fans, and libraries.

Review of Contemporary Fiction, Summer 1991

□ □ □ □ □ □ □

At the Roots of the Stars: The Short Plays.
Edited and with an introduction by Douglas Messerli
Sun & Moon, 1995

An important gap in Barnes's published work is now filled with this splendid collection of her early plays. These 16 one-acts were written between 1916 and 1923, when Barnes was in her late twenties and active with the Provincetown Players of New York (a group that included Eugene O'Neill and Edna St. Vincent Millay). All but one were published in newspapers or magazines, a few were staged, but only two were ever published in book form (*To the Dogs* and *The Dove*, both in *A Book* [1923]). All of them display the distinctive style that would come to fruition in her novels: Augustan cadences, rueful epigrams, bizarre imagery, "with an undertone that hints biting sarcasm and bitter wit," as one character's laugh is described. Many of the plays are Irish in setting and diction: as Douglas Messerli points out in his useful introduction, Barnes was obviously under the influence of J. M. Synge (on whom she had written an article) as well as Oscar Wilde: *Salomé* for the ornate imagery, and his comedies for some of the lighter plays included here (*Little Drops of Rain*, *Two Ladies Take Tea*). There's even a Firbankian bouquet to a few of them (*Water-Ice*, *The Beauty*), but Barnes's own unique style dominates.

I don't know how they would play on stage — there's very little dramatic activity in any of them — but they read beautifully, and in many ways are more original and accomplished than the short stories she was writing at the same time. Of the various collections of Barnes's early writings that Sun & Moon has published, this may be the best, and whets the appetite for its forthcoming editions of Barnes's three longer plays.

Review of Contemporary Fiction, Spring 1996

□ □ □ □ □ □ □

Poe's Mother: Selected Drawings.
Edited with an introduction by Douglas Messerli
Sun & Moon, 1995

Carolyn Allen. *Following Djuna: Women Lovers and the Erotics of Loss*
Indiana University Press, 1996

Sun & Moon continues its invaluable restoration work on Barnes's oeuvre with an extensive collection of her drawings. Although she illustrated many of her works, this is the first time they have been gathered for separate publication. The earliest date from Barnes's newspaper days, where her witty,

Beardsleyesque sketches accompanied her even wittier profiles, interviews, and stories. (Many of these newspapers are disintegrating, and many of the drawings here come from microfilmed versions; given the situation, most look remarkably crisp.) The visual element is strong in all of Barnes's work, even in the non-illustrated *Nightwood*, so these drawings are an essential part of her artistic vision and it is useful to have them reproduced in such a handsome volume, accompanied, like most of Sun & Moon's Barnes book, with an informative introduction by Douglas Messerli.

Barnes scholars will also want to pick up Carolyn Allen's new book, for it not only offers perceptive readings of *Nightwood* and the "Little Girl" stories ("Cassation," "The Grande Malade," and the little-known "Dusie"), but traces the example of Barnes's exploration of lesbian power and loss in the fiction of Jeanette Winterson, Rebecca Brown, and the underrated Bertha Harris.

Review of Contemporary Fiction, Summer 1996

John Barth

The Last Voyage of Somebody the Sailor
Little, Brown, 1991

Barth and his critics have noted his tendency to write books in pairs: his first two novels, standard in size and fairly realistic, were followed by two huge, flamboyant epics, which were followed by two collections of short fiction of Daedalian cunning. Then came *LETTERS*, his masterpiece, and *Sabbatical*, a sequel of sorts. And now, *The Last Voyage of Somebody the Sailor* extends certain themes and techniques of 1987's *Tidewater Tales*. These last two novels have solid, mathematical structures, a more relaxed pace of storytelling, and a kind of mature geniality. On the one hand, they are more lax and accessible than his earlier works, but on the other, they are more daring in that they flaunt verisimilitude by employing time travel. In *The Tidewater Tales*, Odysseus, Don Quixote, and Scheherazade were transported to the 20th century; in *The Last Voyage*, a 20th-century journalist is transported back to Sindbad's era (pre-Scheherazade, that is) and tells tales incomprehensible to his Baghdad audience in an effort to discover how to return to his own age. (Reading this novel, largely set in the "City of Peace," during the Gulf War was a similar time-dislocating experience.)

The Last Voyage has all the pleasures of old-fashioned narratives (not 19th-century novels but older ones: *Tom Jones*, *Don Quixote*, and of course Burton's translation of *The Book of the Thousand Nights and a Night*) while at the same time being as postmodern as anything. (His use of mathematical structures recalls the recent novels of Oulipian Jacques Roubaud.) Despite the wordplay, exuberant sex, and cheerful disregard for realism — his medieval characters on occasion speak French and quote *Hamlet* — there is a more somber tone than is usual with Barth: loss, incest, rape, madness, mutilation, and death stalk these pages. But it would be wrong to call *The Last Voyage* valetudinarian; Barth is as robust as ever, as fancy and outrageous as any writer alive, and gives proof once again that he is one of the most important novelists of our time.

Review of Contemporary Fiction, Summer 1991

□ □ □ □ □ □ □

Once upon a Time: A Floating Opera

Little, Brown, 1994

One of the many imaginary movies Thomas Pynchon programs into his fourth novel, *Vineland*, is *The Robert Musil Story*, starring Pee-wee Herman. But this account of the great Austrian novelist doesn't hold its audience's attention: "It was mostly Pee-wee talking in a foreign accent, or sitting around in front of some pieces of paper with some weird-looking marker pen." That is the problem facing any novelist's biographer, for it's difficult to find much drama in sitting around in front of some pieces of paper day in, day out, which is pretty much what the writing life amounts to. If you are a novelist writing your own biography, you can perhaps liven things up with a firsthand account of what you did between those periods of sitting around in front of those pieces of paper. If you are John Barth, you make a postmodern novel out of it.

Barth calls *Once upon a Time* "a memoir bottled in a novel" but cautions that it "is not the story of my life, but it is most certainly *a* story thereof." It might be better to shift those italics from *a* to *story*, for with few exceptions, a life is not inherently interesting or dramatic; as T. S. Eliot wryly put it, life is basically "birth, and copulation, and death." Not much of a plot. It is the stories we make of our lives, not the lives themselves, that compel interest, and here Barth sets out to make his rather humdrum life as interesting a story as he can.

A fan and practitioner of the ancient storytelling device of the frame tale, Barth returns to the same frame he has used for his last few novels: a prosperous couple set sail from their Maryland home on Columbus Day 1992 to see what happens. In this book, Barth likewise embarks on a tale to see where it will take him, writing in 1990 of that 1992 voyage (and gradually overcoming it in time). For this frame tale, he also invents a lifelong friend, a "counterself" named Jay Scribner, who plays the role of the helper in the standard hero myth that Barth has exploited so ingeniously in previous novels. After the obligatory shipwreck (harrowingly told), our hero finds himself disoriented and separated from his wife, and by way of a time-travel device begins making a story of his life.

It's a story that will be familiar to long-time Barth fans, especially those who have read his book of essays called *The Friday Book*. The younger half of a set of twins cutely called Jack and Jill, he had a fairly happy and prosperous childhood in Dorchester County, Maryland, learned the drums and half-planned on a career as a jazz drummer and arranger until a semester at Juilliard exposed his shortcomings, then went off to Johns Hopkins where he discovered his vocation as a writer. He married young and was the father of three by his mid-twenties; he piled up the usual stack of rejection slips until his agent found someone to take on his first novel, *The Floating Opera*, an astonishingly inventive debut (as I discovered re-reading it a month ago). His vocation fulfilled, it's been one book after another, a grand body of work that is one of the glories of postwar American fiction. The story breaks off around 1972, the year his National Book Award-winning *Chimera* was published.

The vocation is the hero of this novel. Barth is somewhat reticent about his first wife, about their children and their divorce, and doesn't reveal much more about his second wife than how they met (re-met, actually: She is a former student of his) and how happy they've been ever after. Instead, the focus is on the books; he tells us little about them that he hasn't told us before (in prefaces to new editions), but it is useful to have them integrated into a larger story of his life. It's Jay Scribner who complicates things. He's introduced as a fictitious creature, a plot device, and yet he plays a crucial role at several turning points in Barth's life: He teaches the young Jack Barth to play drums (a wonderful episode), critiques his early writings, warns him that his first marriage will fail, often provides him with the thread leading out of the labyrinths Barth writes himself into, steers him toward key books, and so on. As a character in this novel, he's an absorbing and necessary member of the cast; but if he is fictitious, who if anyone did help Barth at those turning points?

That's a question for his critics and biographers. For the general reader, there is this strange yet enjoyable hybrid of a book: part autobiography, part experimental novel, and part voyage of Sindbad.

Washington Post Book World, 8 May 1994

□ □ □ □ □ □ □

Coming Soon!!!

Houghton Mifflin, 2001

John Barth's previous book, *On with the Story*, is a formally elegant but relatively low-key short-story cycle. But in *Coming Soon!!!* Barth is back in full metafictional finery, sporting all the bells and whistles of postmodernism like boutonnieres, the three exclamation points in the title announcing that he intends to go out with a bang. For he implies this might be his last novel, and while that is grievous news to those of us who consider him one of the greatest novelists of our time, it is bracing to have this final display of his matchless powers.

For his latest (if not last) novel, Barth circles back to his first, *The Floating Opera* (1956), based on the showboats that used to work the Chesapeake Bay. Inspired by a replica called the *Original Floating Opera II*, the retiring professor-author decides to write a sequel. (Like much of Barth's later fiction, this novel is unabashedly autobiographical.) He is egged on by a college-age writer who admires Barth but feels that print narrative is dead and that cyberspace is the place to be. The two writers make a gentlemanly wager: Beginning in 1995 and with an eye on the approaching end of the millennium, the older author begins a print novel and the kid a hypertext narrative, racing to see who can finish first. *Coming Soon!!!*, subtitled "a narrative" rather than "a novel," combines the two into something resembling a printout from an enormous Website, complete with menu, Read-Me documents, clickable icons and underlined hypertext links. All it lacks, mercifully, are those annoying pop-up banners.

Both writers share an interest in showboats, specifically Edna Ferber's 1926 novel *Show Boat* and the various musical and film adaptations made thereafter. A good deal of *Coming Soon!!!*, perhaps too much, relates Ferber's experiences on a showboat and the efforts by a character named Charlie Hunter to turn those experiences into a new musical, an unfinished project taken up reluctantly by Barth himself. More interesting is the proliferation of themes both writers pursue: Y2K fears and a threatening storm conjure up everything from the apocalypse of Saint John to Shakespeare's *Tempest* to the myth of Noah and the ark.

Storytelling has always been Barth's grand theme, and watching all these characters construct stories, link them with earlier tales, borrow from other writers, and argue over the appropriate form provides a primer in narratology. For most of his adult life a professor of creative writing, Barth teaches the interested reader more about narrative in this novel than you'll find in a shelf of textbooks.

The young writer, Johns Hopkins ("Hop") Johnson — named after the university where Barth taught for many years — exemplifies the current generation of young authors who admire Barth but feel his brand of postmodernism has run its course. The most brilliant and successful of them, David Foster Wallace, has paid homage to Barth in a novella entitled "Westward the Course of Empire Takes Its Way" (in his *Girl with Curious Hair*) but has denounced postmodernism's self-conscious irony, terminal flippancy, and heartless preoccupation with form over substance. These traits are more characteristic of other experimental writers than of Barth, who has always respected the old-fashioned pleasures of reading no matter what newfangled devices he may be deploying. In fact, he mocks postmodernism in this novel even as he provides a state-of-the-art example. Almost alone among his postmodern brethren, Barth exhibits an admirable geniality and level-headedness, a wise realization of how wonderful life can be despite everything that conspires against it.

But does the novel offer anything to readers uninterested in eschatology or narrative theory? Yes, after you get past the first eight pages (a deliberately ditsy prologue). Barth's graceful, witty prose is endlessly inventive, the characters are colorful and appealing, and he delightfully conveys the inspiring if manic show-must-go-on mentality of theater folk. Perhaps a quarter of *Coming Soon!!!* drags its anchor, but as Graham Greene described the 1936 film version of *Show Boat*, "for three quarters of its length good entertainment: sentimental, literary, but oddly appealing."

And if this does prove to be Barth's final novel, that's all the more reason to savor it. It is a fitting capstone to a Library of America-worthy body of work that overtowers that of most other writers of his generation. (I consider only Gaddis and Pynchon his peers.) Y2K fears proved to be unfounded, and hypertext fiction more hype than not, but Barth's vast funhouse of fiction should endure.

Washington Post Book World, 25 November 2001

Donald Barthelme

Great Days
Farrar, Straus & Giroux, 1979

This collection consists of 16 stories, all but two of which originally appeared in the *New Yorker* earlier this decade, and all of which are delightful to read. The most intriguing are seven stories written entirely in dialogue; one thinks of the odd dialogues from the plays of Pinter and Beckett, or the odder conversation novels of Ronald Firbank and Ivy Compton-Burnett. The stories themselves are difficult to describe, so I won't; little will be conveyed if I tell you one concerns a group of zombies out on a wife-buying expedition, or that another consists of epiphanic highlights in the relationship between Cortés and Montezuma. Many of the stories are amusing, and this fact places Barthelme not in the gloomy company of avant-gardists wallowing in the dark night of the soul haunting the borderline between dream and reality, but rather in the more cheerful (though not frivolous) company of Stanley Elkin and John Barth.

Spree, August 1979

□ □ □ □ □ □ □

Tracy Daugherty. *Hiding Man: A Biography of Donald Barthelme*
St. Martin's Press, 2009

Donald Barthelme, perhaps the most beloved of the postmodernist writers who upset the apple cart of conventional fiction in the 1960s and '70s, has been treated extremely well since his death in 1989. His two major story collections and four novels are all in print, and over the last 15 years editor Kim Herzinger has rounded up all his previously uncollected stories, essays, and miscellaneous writings into three handsome volumes. And now comes the first biography, and not just a modest memoir but a full-length, meticulously documented study. All dead authors should be so lucky.

Although he wrote novels and plays, Barthelme is best known for his quirky, unconventional stories, though "fictive constructions" may be a better term for these witty, innovative, cunningly written pieces. He had no interest in following the trail of the conventional short story, preferring to spur that old workhorse in new directions with techniques and devices adapted from other art forms. His father was a prominent architect in Houston, and as a youth Barthelme took an interest in the modernist aesthetics of Gropius, Le Corbusier, Mies van der Rohe, and Frank Lloyd Wright. His father gave him a copy of Marcel Raymond's book *From Baudelaire to Surrealism,* which led to a lifelong interest in avant-garde art. (The young Barthelme was an art museum curator before he became a published writer.) He learned to play drums as a teenager and developed a keen interest in bebop jazz. All of these arts were exploding with experimentation and innovation while the American short story, as Barthelme couldn't help but notice, was still stuck in the Chekhov mode of the 19th century. When Barthelme began writing fiction in the late '50s, he harnessed all of these new approaches in the arts to catch fiction up with the modernist program, then added his own innovations to inaugurate postmodernism.

Daugherty does a fine job explicating all this in the first third of his biography, spending as much time on these formative influences as on the standard family life and teenage experiences. Daugherty doesn't neglect Barthelme's profound interest in philosophy from an early age, nor the mulligan stew of early literary influences — Kafka, Hemingway, Perelman, Beckett, Sartre, even Raphael Sabatini (of *Captain Blood* fame) — nor the sickening diet of B-movies he ingested as a newspaper reporter in his twenties. With all this under one's wings, the reader can better appreciate the absurdist, sometimes baffling stories that brought him fame in the 1960s.

Convinced New York was where it's at, Barthelme moved to Manhattan in 1962, where he lived for the next 20 years before dividing his time, near the end of his life, between there and Houston. He was fortunate enough to be adopted by the *New Yorker,* which published him regularly from 1963 onwards, and by a few sympathetic book publishers. (For all their critical acclaim, his books never made much money; even in the 1980s, with a dozen books to his name, his royalties never amounted to more than $1000 a year.) Like a knowledgeable curator, Daugherty walks us through his publications book by book, pausing for brilliant explications of the more challenging stories. He interleaves this with accounts of his marriages, affairs, teaching stints, and other extracurricular activities in a respectful but not hagiographic manner. (He reveals Barthelme had drinking problems from age 16 on, was fiscally irresponsible, and smoked so much it killed him at the premature age of 58.)

I especially enjoyed Daugherty's fierce defense of Barthelme's fictions as socially responsible art, not as the aesthetic playthings postmodernism's critics accuse them of being. As life became more complicated in the 20th century, as change and disruptions occurred more rapidly, and as the media and corporations insidiously tried to define reality for its consumers, Barthelme and other postmodernists felt new tactics in art were necessary both to render and to criticize this future-shocked world. Daugherty quotes from Barthelme's essay "Not-Knowing" on the writer's "need to refresh language continually, to keep it free of 'political and social contamination,' safe from co-optation by commercial interests." While the traditional short story kept its blinkered head down, Barthelme's alert fictions grappled with the absurdities and upheavals of his time, functioning as verbal guerrilla attacks against the rebarbative propaganda spouted by Madison Avenue and the White House. "The disorientation in my stories is not mine," Barthelme once said. "It is what is to be perceived around us." In this sense, Barthelme's mindbending fictions are more "realistic" than those of his mainstream contemporaries, and still feel fresh and relevant, while theirs sound quaint.

Daugherty was Barthelme's student in the '80s; the last time Daugherty saw him, six months before he died, his former teacher gave him a new assignment: "Write a story about a genius." He did, and I'd give it an A.

Washington Post Book World, 8 February 2009

Jonathan Baumbach

You, or The Invention of Memory
Rager Media, 2007

You want to write a novel about the failed marriage of two cultured, middle-aged New Yorkers, but you don't want to write a conventional story about such latte-sipping, museum-going, *New York Review of Books*-reading stereotypes. What do you do? You make the stories they tell themselves about their marriage the real story, showing the discrepancy between the facts and what they remember, or what they tell their friends, or what one of them later puts in a novel.

You is the eleventh novel by Jonathan Baumbach, who over the last quarter-century has become something of a legend in the world of independent literary publishing. In 1973 he co-founded (with Peter Spielberg) Fiction Collective, which published innovative fiction of limited commercial appeal (and still does as the revamped FC2). His latest novel and latest publisher adhere to those noble principles, and the results are beguiling.

The novel is divided into three unequal parts. The first is narrated in the rarely used second-person singular: the reader is addressed as "you," and while you naturally assume it is indeed you the novelist is confiding in — an informal update on the "dear reader" convention of older fiction — it soon becomes apparent he is addressing an unnamed woman. He then launches into a disjointed account of how they met and the various crises in their relationship — though "crises" is too strong a word for their mundane misunderstandings — all the while confessing, "I have a history of confusing the real world with the more compelling narrative of my fantasies."

In part 2, we get the woman's version of things, narrated mostly in the third-person and equally unreliable: "I forget (I forget a lot of things)," she admits after telling her version of how they met and of the bland marriage that ensued. The brief part 3 is narrated in the first-person by the husband and takes places several years later after their divorce, when he runs into a woman who may or may not be his former wife.

You finish the novel not sure who to believe, and with no way of knowing which of the versions of their relationship is correct, if any. The wife is especially complex: one of Baumbach's earlier novels is about a man's seven wives; the wife here seems like seven women, or like a woman in a cubist painting seen from seven angles simultaneously. You realize you're not the author's confidant, as the opening pages led you to believe, but only an eavesdropper, picking up pieces of the story and supplying your own coherence. Baumbach's characters remind you how much fiction-making takes place in daily life: When the wife tells the husband she has some news, he quickly imagines three possibilities (and then Baumbach spins out three alternating stories based on those possibilities). Disappearing one night during their married life, the husband next day is "dying to market the version he had worked up of where he had been and what he had done." Composing a personals ad for the *New York Review of Books*, the wife "barely recognized herself in the description she was issuing." We all work for the fiction collective, inventing and marketing stories as often as any novelist.

Baumbach drops many hints that *You* is autobiographical, but that would only add another layer of fiction to the fictions his characters tell. "Writing a novel . . . is a gesture of love between writer and reader" he tells us early on, so whether the "you" he addresses was inspired by an actual woman doesn't matter; the finished book is indeed for you the reader. "For as long as I've known you, you've been an admirer of the bold and unexpected." (Yes, you think, he's got my number.) "The book I am writing with you in mind will be nothing if not unexpected." He keeps his promise: there is the unexpected alternation between second-, third-, and first-person points of view. There is the totally unexpected revelation that the wife's name is Lois Lane, former "lifestyle" editor of the *Daily Metropolis*. There is "The Terror, a recently opened Middle Eastern restaurant with a provocative menu." It is also unexpected that postmodern tactics and gags like these can mesh so well with an old-fashioned story of midlife married malaise.

Writing a novel like this is indeed a gesture of love; neither the author nor publisher is in it for the money, and *You* won't make it onto any best-seller lists. You may even have trouble finding it in a bookstore. But if you are "an admirer of the bold and unexpected," *You*, like any gesture of love, deserves your regard.

Los Angeles Times, 21 December 2007

Anne Beattie

The Doctor's House
Scribner, 2002

There are two sides to every story, a character in Ann Beattie's new novel keeps insisting, but here we're given three: A sister, brother, and their mother offer three 100-page explanations for the sorry state their family has reached by the time the kids are in their forties. Andrew, an irresponsible womanizer, is tracking down girls he knew in high school, seducing most of them regardless of their current marital status. His sister Nina, a freelance copyeditor who retreated from the world after the premature death of her husband, obsesses over her beloved brother's erratic behavior. And their mother wonders from her rest home why her children turned out so neurotic, insisting it wasn't her fault.

All three point a finger at their father, the doctor of the novel's title. The doctor's house was a grim place to live: The children learned at an early age to avoid both their father — a tyrannical, philandering egomaniac with a real gift for emotional abuse — and their mother, an alcoholic who spends more time in a state of denial than in the state of Massachusetts, the novel's setting. The father died sometime before the novel opens, and each of the three survivors recounts the same story but with a different slant, a different emphasis on key events.

For example, there's the day a 15-year-old Andrew talked his sister into photographing two of her female friends in the nude: Nina devotes eight pages to this wild event, her mother barely eight sentences, and Andrew only eight blasé paragraphs (interrupted by a ten-page digression). On the other hand, Andrew's first wife is mentioned only in passing by his sister and mother but plays a major role in his account. Each of us is the star of his or her own soap opera, as Beattie knows, and it's fascinating to watch her juggle the events to suit her narrators' neuroses.

Beattie has been criticized in the past for not providing much motivation for her characters' actions (an aesthetic choice, I'm sure, not an oversight), but *The Doctor's House* is all about motivation, about how the most insignificant act in the present can have deep roots in the past. Both children vow to escape their father's influence but remain in his shadow: Nina winds up marrying a doctor, and after his death becomes almost as emotionally stingy as her father, and Andrew's philandering looks like a blatant attempt to outdo his father's adulteries. Both become as indifferent to their mother as their father was.

The father doesn't deliver a monologue like the others, but he doesn't need to: He dominates the novel. The "house" of the title refers to his legacy, and it's a sick one. In fact, illness is everywhere in this novel. Two characters are doctors, the mother briefly studies to be a nurse, many scenes are set in hospitals, characters are always falling sick, getting into accidents, having abortions, visiting ailing relations in nursery homes, dying. Even the plants are sickly. It would probably be going too far to extrapolate from all this that Beattie is suggesting we're living in a sick society still in the grip of a tyrannical patriarchy, but she accurately captures the moral malaise of our time.

Beattie copyrights her books under the witty name Irony & Pity, Inc. But those responses can be simplistic, even condescending. In *The Doctor's House*, she goes beyond irony and pity to demonstrate a profound understanding of the psychological depths most people possess, of the emotional baggage that even well-adjusted people must drag behind them. She also understands the lengths to which they will go to justify their ways to themselves and to others. People believe what they want to believe, regardless of the facts, which accounts for everything from religion to astrology to the mother who insists her son couldn't have committed the crime attributed to him. People believe what they need to believe to make sense of life; truth, to paraphrase Mae West, has nothing to do with it. *The Doctor's House* is a nuanced fiction about the fictions people create for themselves, sometimes unwittingly plagiarizing their parents' fictions. Make that Curiouser and Curiouser, Inc.

Washington Post Book World, 10 February 2002

The Beats and Their Critics

Sandra Loy. *The Writer's Voice*
Holt, Rinehart, and Winston, 1985

At first glance, this new freshman composition textbook doesn't appear much different than the dozens of similar ones on the market. It is basically a reader, organized along the familiar lines of Bain's modes of discourse (description, narration, argumentation, and so forth), and includes many standard essays familiar from other readers. But what makes *The Writers's Voice* appealingly unique is the inclusion of Jack Kerouac among its model prose writers — the first time, to my knowledge, that spontaneous bop prosody has been offered as a legitimate subject for study by freshman writers in search of a voice. I can hear the students now: "You mean it's okay to write like that?"

Kerouac makes not one but four contributions to the textbook, each followed by vocabulary studies, annotations, and comprehensive discussion questions. His "The Origins of the Beat Generation" ends the "definition" subsection of the Exposition chapter, and in chapter eight Kerouac is included for closer examination in "A Study of Four Writers" (the others are Orwell, McPhee, and Didion). Loy's three selections are especially apt for this section; she has chosen the bullfight description from "Mexico Fellaheen," "The Flop Hotel" (Loy's title) from "The Railroad Earth," and Kerouac's exhilarating account of the "warm, mad night" at the Folsom Street jazz joint from part three of *On the Road*. All the selections are preceded by biographical headnotes.

Of the four writers dealt with, Kerouac is definitely treated as the odd man out. The first study question following the bullfight episode, for example, asks, "What evidence is there of Kerouac's unconventional attitude toward the English sentence?" After "The Flop Hotel," the editor opens the discussion with, "Okay. This is it. You asked for words and you've got them. Better read out loud and careful not to trip your tongue." And Loy's suggested writing assignments occasionally smack of condescension: "You may wish to try Kerouac's 'sketching' technique yourself — with or without music. Remember, you must write fast, without editing, in an undisturbed flow. Try it, it's fun — and good practice, too, even though its use in a class where the polished essay is the objective may be limited."

Fortunately, any potential misapprehension on the student's part that Kerouac's writing is simply what Capote dismissed as "typing" is avoided through Loy's emphasis on the artistic qualities of Kerouac's language: its diction, syntax, and especially its sound. The lesson is driven home by way of comparison to other pieces in the textbook. Loy asks the student, for example, to compare Kerouac's bullfight episode with Hemingway's "Killing a Bull," which appears earlier in the textbook. Despite Hemingway's claim that "Bullfighting is not a sport. It is a tragedy, and it symbolizes the struggle between man and the beasts," his piece ignores the tragic dimension for a nuts-and-bolts account. Kerouac, on the other hand, without announcing any portentous themes, manages to be just as informative as Hemingway while capturing the tragedy of bullfighting (for man *and* beast) in achingly sensitive language and in a form that dramatizes the pacing of the fight. The difference is between Hemingway's journalism and Kerouac's art, and it is to be hoped that the student will apprehend the superiority of Kerouac's approach.

Another instructive discussion question draws the student's attention to the poetical qualities of Kerouac's prose and asks him or her how they compare with Dylan Thomas's "Notes on the Art of Poetry," which appears elsewhere in the textbook. A more fitting juxtaposition could not be wished for, and reading the Thomas piece after Kerouac's two nonfiction pieces emphasizes the startling similarity between the work of these two prose-poets. Has anyone called Kerouac an American Dylan Thomas? Loy certainly provides the materials for such a claim.

There are two main approaches to teaching composition these days: one asks students to develop an "academic discourse, the ways in which people talk and write about intellectual concerns within a university tradition" (from the writing handbook used at Rutgers University). The second, the more belletristic approach favored by Loy, places more emphasis on helping students find their own voice, one that best expresses their own outlook, concerns, and personality. To that end, Loy has provided a colorful array of models for encouragement. (Her other selections range from Sir Francis Bacon to Woody Allen, from Black Elk to Kawabata.) The Kerouac excerpts will not help the student learn how to write a polished essay suitable for academic discourse, but they may provide the liberating key that will unlock some tongue-tied students' latent writing abilities. "Anything that gets you to write, and with enthusiasm," Loy rightly observes, "should never be entirely dismissed." She is to be praised for having the vision and courage to include Kerouac among the best prose stylists of our time, and teachers and students alike should prove grateful.

Moody Street Irregulars, Summer 1986

□□□□□□□

Jennie Skerl. *William S. Burroughs*

Twayne, 1985

It is difficult to believe that Skerl's book is only the second in English on such an historically important novelist as Burroughs. (Compare the dozen or more on Bellow, Mailer, and Pynchon, or the half-dozen or so on Updike, Vonnegut, Styron, and Percy.) Skerl provides a more basic introduction than Eric Mottram's earlier, more sophisticated *William Burroughs: The Algebra of Need* to the fiction of this near-legendary writer. Separating the man from the legend is, in fact, the purpose of Skerl's first chapter, a biographical essay that will do nicely until Ted Morgan finishes his book-length biography [see below]. Chapter 2 takes the reader from *Junky* through *Naked Lunch* (omitting the recently published *Queer*) and shows how the earlier books plant the seeds that bloom so exotically in the later one. (Skerl also wrote the introduction to the 25th Anniversary Edition of *Naked Lunch* published in 1984.) She is especially good at tracing Burroughs's development of addiction as the subject of *Junky* to an extended metaphor in *Naked Lunch*, and his parallel movement away from fiction to mythology.

The trilogy that followed *Naked Lunch* is the subject of the next chapter, and Skerl provides a cogent introduction to the cut-up techniques and bizarre subject matter of *The Soft Machine*, *The Ticket That Exploded*, and *Nova Express*. She draws special attention to the importance of literary allusion in Burroughs's work (a point easily forgotten) and his structuralist theory of language. Not content merely to analyze language, "Burroughs, through his art, attempts to act upon the linguistic system and change it, thereby acting upon and changing the reader's consciousness." Skerl never lets us forget that Burroughs is not creating belles lettres but guerilla fiction of the most subversive kind.

With the publication in 1971 of *The Wild Boys*, Burroughs exchanged the rather nihilistic Nova myth of his earlier work for a new, more optimistic myth where sexuality replaces addiction as the central metaphor and greater emphasis is placed on what Skerl calls "man's positive potential for autonomy, regeneration, and creation." Skerl's fourth chapter deals with the "utopian dreams" of *The Wild Boys*, *Exterminator!*, *Port of Saints*, and *Cities of the Red Night*. Again, useful overviews are given to these works, though by the time Skerl reaches *Cities of the Red Night* she flags in enthusiasm: like many readers, she seems to find the later works less satisfactory than the earlier ones. (*The Place of Dead Roads* apparently appeared too late for inclusion.) A brief final chapter underscores the importance of "Burroughs's creation of a new novel form — the pop-art novel" and reminds us that any evaluation of his achievement must be made by his avant-garde standards rather than by more traditional standards.

A reader desiring a skeleton key to Burroughs's alien fictions could not do better than Skerl's concise volume. Too brief to be definitive, it will serve until a more ambitious study comes along.

Review of Contemporary Fiction, Fall 1986

□ □ □ □ □ □ □

Warren French. *Jack Kerouac*

Twayne, 1986

Most volumes in the Twayne United States Authors Series are straightforward surveys of an author's work, but Warren French's volume on Kerouac offers nothing less than a revisionary re-reading of the Kerouac canon. Everyone familiar with Kerouac's work is familiar with the Duluoz Legend, sketched out in the preface to *Big Sur*, but few have taken Kerouac's plan for a multi-novel cycle seriously enough to examine his corpus in this light. French quickly disposes of those novels he feels don't belong in the cycle (*The Town and the City*, *On the Road*, *The Subterraneans*, *The Dharma Bums*, and *Pic*) and instead concentrates on the Legend as though it were one vast novel. The rewards of this approach are numerous: the Legend is seen moving through a shifting array of styles and narrative strategies (much like Joyce's *Ulysses*) to chart the opposing urges of Kerouac's Peter and Francis Martin selves (his alter egos in *The Town and the City*), an odyssey of self-destruction in an American tradition French traces all the way back to Charles Brockden Brown's *Wieland* (1798). Read in this way, Kerouac's cycle of novels takes on much greater interest, complexity, and coherence; if only one of Kerouac's publishers could issue the Legend in its chronological order in two or three omnibus volumes, one of the great fictional projects of our time would stand revealed.[2]

Not everyone will agree with French's omissions, of course. He agrees with Tim Hunt (as I think we all must) that *Visions of Cody* was meant to replace *On the Road* (and *Pic*) in the Legend, and the materials of *The Town and the City* are covered elsewhere (mostly in *The Vanity of Duluoz*); but I would argue that *The Subterraneans* and *The Dharma Bums* are integral to the Legend. Would it be too ingenious to regard these two as metafictional novels

2 I was bitterly disappointed when the Library of America published its first Kerouac volume in 2007, ignoring the author's plan. That was the perfect opportunity to do it right, and they blew it. (See endnote to my Richard Wright review for more on LoA.) The Hunt book I refer to in the next paragraph is *Kerouac's Crooked Road: The Development of a Fiction* (1981; rev. ed. 2010), which I heartily recommend.

within the Legend, as Duluoz's novels about himself? (Malcolm Lowry contemplated a similar fictional cycle, in which *Under the Volcano* turns out to be a novel written by the cycle's protagonist.) French agrees that *Book of Dreams* belongs to the Legend, but makes no mention of the sketches in *Lonesome Traveler*: not only do they constitute some of Kerouac's best writing — Gilbert Sorrentino regards "October in the Railroad Earth" as the best thing Kerouac ever wrote — but they provide crucial links in the Legend.

French sees much defeatism, entropy, and disillusionment in Kerouac's novels, especially in *On the Road*, and consequently wonders why they have such great appeal. The answer is found in the one element French most often ignores in his otherwise fine study: Kerouac's extraordinary language. Opposing the entropic themes and preoccupations in the novels is the negentropic, energetic language that makes reading Kerouac so exciting: it's that language that sent thousands of kids on the road, not the depressing reality that language describes. (And those who discovered that the reality didn't measure up to the language that described it learned a hard lesson in literary appreciation and, one hopes, never again confused art with life.) One wishes French had paused in his thematic readings long enough to say something about Kerouac's lyricism, tactile diction, neologisms, untraditional syntax — that amazing ability with language that makes his novels often read like prose poems.

Despite these and one or two other reservations (the reliance on Clark over Nicosia for biographical details, for example), French's *Jack Kerouac* is probably the best introduction we now have on Kerouac's *work*, and represents a welcome shift in attention from the man to those glorious novels into which the man poured his soul — and that's exactly where our attention belongs.

Kerouac Connection, Spring 1987; reprinted slightly abridged in *Review of Contemporary Fiction*, Fall 1987

□ □ □ □ □ □ □

Allen Ginsberg. *Howl: Original Draft Facsimile*. Edited by Barry Miles
Harper & Row, 1986

It is appropriate that the poem which is the closest modern equivalent to Eliot's *The Waste Land* is now available in an annotated, facsimile edition modeled on Valerie Eliot's annotated, facsimile edition of her husband's poem published in 1971. The style and format of both books are identical, and though aimed more at the scholar than the layman, Ginsberg's book provides a wealth of material for anyone interested in the Beats. Several drafts of the poem are photographically reproduced with facing transcriptions that allow the reader to trace the painstaking process by which Ginsberg attained the artful disorder of the final draft. The editorial apparatus that follows is of a plenitude usually found only in critical editions of classic authors: copious annotations by the author himself; reprints of material by and about the poem's dedicatee, Carl Solomon; contemporary letters to and from Ginsberg on the poem; several accounts of the first reading at the Six Gallery in 1955; a section on censorship battles; an anthology of poems that inspired *Howl*; and a bibliography of all English and foreign editions. The book is profusely illustrated, well indexed, beautifully printed, a wonder to behold.

Ginsberg has been chided by some for his self-promotional tendencies, and it is almost inconceivable that any other major poet would produce such a book in his or her lifetime. Even Ezra Pound, knowing that a burgeoning critical industry awaited each addition to *The Cantos* with file cards at the ready, never assisted with the various critical guides written during his lifetime. But the advantages of having a poet annotate his own work, rather than leaving that to some editor in the future, are inestimable. No false modesty inhibits Ginsberg from acknowledging his place in contemporary literary history, and his willingness to document his materials so thoroughly — both here and in his recent *Collected Poems* — not only ensures greater precision in future scholarship but gives testimony, if any is still needed, that the Beat movement was more literary than social, and had as its principal goal the creation of enduring literary works, not an ephemeral, destructive lifestyle to be aped by dropouts and criticized by old maids of both sexes. This new edition of *Howl* is a must for all students of Beat literature, of modern poetry, perhaps even for all students of modern culture.

Kerouac Connection, Summer 1987

□ □ □ □ □ □ □

Gregory Stephenson. *Friendly and Flowing Savage: The Literary Legend of Neal Cassady*

Textile Bridge Press, 1987

He was a remarkable man, by all accounts, and in this pamphlet Gregory Stephenson charts the range of literary characters Neal Cassady inspired in a half-dozen writers. As Hart Kennedy in John Clellon Holmes's *Go*, he appears as a manipulative hustler, but also as an atavistic noble savage intent on transcending the limits of time and space — two extremes that Holmes does not try to reconcile but that engaged the writers following him, writers more willing to search for mythic and religious prototypes of Cassady's contradictory character. Stephenson deals at length with Kerouac's portrayal of Cassady in *On the Road* — associating him with figures as various as the "shadow" of Jungian psychology, the American Adam, the archetypal Western cowboy, W. H. Auden's "American child-hero," and the philosophical psychopath of Norman Mailer and Alan Harrington — but unfortunately gives short shrift to other works in the Duluoz Legend. The magnificent *Visions of Cody* may fail "to contribute substantially to the characterization of Cassady already achieved in *On the Road*," as Stephenson alleges, but the novel adds enough refinements and psychological subtleties to warrant further comment. Similarly, the Cody Pomeray of *Big Sur* deserves more than the half paragraph Stephenson gives him; the tragedy of Jack Duluoz's breakdown is foreshadowed and intensified by Cody's own: in their awkward final meeting, the once energetic and loquacious Cody is reduced to an inert house-husband who can only mumble "Ah, yah, hm," his last words in the Legend and an anticipation of the final line in the novel.

Ginsburg's Cassady is a romantic fantasy figure, an Adonis whose sexuality and heightened consciousness is celebrated in a number of poems. The less admirable traits that bothered Holmes and Kerouac are largely absent in Ginsberg's poetry; for him, Stephenson writes, "Neal Cassady represented a man in whom spiritual and sexual energies were harmonious and complementary." It is this idealized figure who was taken over by second-generation Beats such as Ken Kesey and his friend Robert Stone. Stephenson first analyzes Cassady's appearance in Tom Wolfe's *Electric Kool-Aid Acid Test* — again emphasizing Cassady's quest for satori as his driving force — then follows this trend toward greater idealization in the works of Stone and Kesey. By the time Kesey writes "The Day after Superman Died" in 1979, Cassady has attained the status of a saint, as foretold by his prophet Kerouac.

Cassady would not have inspired so much literary response had there not been a need for such a figure in the American literary tradition and in the specific atmosphere of post-World War II America, and Stephenson provides just enough historical context to show how a charismatic young car thief from Denver could so quickly be canonized as a saint in populist mythology. Stephenson's concise essay is tantalizingly brief — and makes no mention of Cassady's own literary characterization in *The First Third* and his other writings — but it is a welcome supplement to the Plummer biography and adds to Stephenson's growing reputation as one of the best Beat critics writing today.

Kerouac Connection, Summer 1987

□ □ □ □ □ □ □

Regina Weinreich. *The Spontaneous Poetics of Jack Kerouac: A Study of the Fiction*
Southern Illinois University Press, 1987

James Morton. *The Distance Instead Is the Feeling*
Dream of Jazz Press, 1986

V. J. Eaton, ed. *Catching Up with Kerouac*
The Literary Denim, 1984

Arthur and Kit Knight, eds. *The Beat Vision*
Paragon House, 1987

The Beat goes on with four new books on Kerouac and company. Weinreich regards everything Kerouac wrote as part of the Duluoz Legend, but posits four core novels — *The Town and the Country*, *On the Road*, *Visions of Cody*, and *Desolation Angels* — as a series of artistic challenges, each one solving rhetorical and thematic problems generated by the preceding one, with the rest of the novels functioning as variations on the themes of these four major novels. Concerned only with the cycle's poetic unity, she traces the evolution of Kerouac's style with close attention to the implications (literary, musical, psychological) of his "spontaneous bop prosody" and makes a strong case for Kerouac's possession of much greater stylistic sophistication than he's usually given credit for. Weinreich offers a useful corrective to French's neglect of Kerouac's language, and her close readings of several passages are brilliant testimony to Kerouac's artistry.

A close reading of *The Subterraneans* is the subject of Morton's essay *The Distance Instead Is the Feeling*, the most detailed study yet of the bluesy novel. Only 47 pages long, the monograph nonetheless is exhaustive in its analysis of everything from individual words to large speculations on Kerouac's attitudes toward male sexuality and the redemptive power of the imagination.

Catching Up with Kerouac is a collection of essays: a half dozen on Kerouac, and the others on Burroughs, Corso, McClure, and Huncke. Particularly outstanding are Ronna Johnson's "An Introduction to Kerouac's Art" — a suitable preface to the Duluoz Legend if ever published outside Heaven — and Gregory Stephenson's essay on *Howl*. The collection also features miscellaneous poems, drawings, and photographs reminiscent of the Knights' Beat journal *the unspeakable visions of the individual*, the best of which has now been collected into a handsomely printed volume entitled *The Beat Vision*. This reprints letters, interviews, and memoirs from nearly all the Beats, and joins *Catching Up with Kerouac* as an invaluable sourcebook for scholars of that heady era.

Review of Contemporary Fiction, Fall 1987

Arthur and Kit Knight, eds. *Kerouac and the Beats: A Second Sourcebook*

Paragon House, 1988

Jay Landesman. *Rebel Without Applause*

Permanent Press, 1987

The Knights have followed last year's *The Beat Vision* with another collection of pieces from their journal *the unspeakable visions of the individual*: interviews with Burroughs, Whalen, Jan Kerouac, Holmes, McClure, and Ginsberg; essays by Carolyn Cassady, Herbert Huncke, and Frankie Edith Kerouac Parker; and letters by Jack Kerouac and Holmes (along with excerpts from the latter's journal). The result is another invaluable sourcebook, all primary material exciting to read and essential to anyone working in this field. Especially good are the four letters by Kerouac, each as long as a short story, and all establishing Kerouac as one of the great letter writers of our age. In his foreword, John Tytell speaks of the resistance the academic community still puts up against Beat writers, but well-edited, well-presented collections like *Kerouac and the Beats* demonstrate that a countercultural academic community is not only possible but vital.

Rebel Without Applause looks and often reads like one of those shallow show-biz memoirs, but don't be deceived: there is valuable material on the early days of the Beat movement here that has appeared nowhere else. Jay Landesman was the founder and editor of *Neurotica*, that seminal St. Louis magazine that set the agenda for much of the writing that followed in the '50s and '60s. During his recruiting trips to New York City (and his later residence there), Landesman met and worked with such people as Kerouac, Holmes, Brossard, Ginsberg, and Carl Solomon, all of whom are featured here in revealing vignettes. Kerouac especially brings a boozy vitality to these otherwise genteel memoirs: enlivening Landesman's parties with the best scat singing he'd ever heard, impressing him with a gentleness and vulnerability belied by his drunken antics, and even modeling as the "original beatnik" in Landesman's novel, *The Nervous Set*. Although the novel was never published,[3] it was converted into a musical that premiered on Broadway on 11 May 1959, in which the Kerouac role was played by none other than *Dallas*'s Larry Hagman! Kerouac attended the premiere, but slept through most of it, awaking only when his name was used in such songs as "Fun Life": "Let's just have fun / Let's not be serious / Shakespeare was a hack / So we read Kerouac."

Among others portrayed in *The Nervous Set* were Holmes, essayist Anatole Broyard, and the legendary sexologist Gershon Legman, who co-edited *Neu-*

3 It was eventually included in Landesman's memoir *Tales of a Cultural Conduit* (2006), 127–254. He died in 2011.

rotica for a few issues. Legman looms over these memoirs like an avenging angel, burning with an iconoclastic moral energy that kept Landesman "honest" for a while (as he admits) before he gave it all up to return to St. Louis to open a cabaret. But the material on the Beats is terrific and consequently *Rebel Without Applause* belongs on every Beat scholar's shelf.

Review of Contemporary Fiction, Fall 1988

□ □ □ □ □ □ □

Ted Morgan. *Literary Outlaw: The Life and Times of William S. Burroughs*
Henry Holt, 1988

While reading Ted Morgan's long-awaited biography, I was reminded of the practice of some English instructors who assign split grades for compositions: one grade for content, another for style. The content of *Literary Outlaw* easily merits an A: this highly readable book was been thoroughly researched, organizing and verifying all the various tales of Burroughs's life that have been circulating for the last 40 years. In addition to all the details of Burroughs's life, Morgan also gives background information on all those with whom he came in contact: not only major figures like Kerouac and Ginsberg, but also most minor figures. Even his son Billy's doctor merits a brief biography. Occasionally this excess of material is overwhelming, especially in the detailed, operation-by-operation account of Billy Burroughs's last few years, the most depressing chapter in the book. Since this is not a critical biography, more attention is given to the circumstances under which Burroughs wrote his books than to the books themselves, though most of them receive a brief analysis that is insightful without being oppressively academic.

Morgan's account of Burroughs's life is fairly objective, even when the reckless and downright stupid antics of some of Burroughs's friends cry out for condemnation. Only occasionally does Morgan vent a little spleen, and then usually directs it toward others (Andy Warhol, Dennis Hopper, Terry Southern). Morgan is mildly disapproving of the way Burroughs raised his son and holds him partially responsible for Billy's death, but he finds enough mitigating circumstances to forgive him. Only during the last 30 or so pages does "the biographer" (as he calls himself) make his presence felt, offering quick analyses of some of Burroughs's personality traits. Here (as elsewhere) Morgan indulges in stream-of-consciousness reveries of what Burroughs may have been thinking at various times — too contrived to be successful — and even offers what looks like a brief cut-up in the Burroughs manner.

These contrived reveries are only one aspect of the larger objection I have concerning Morgan's style. *Literary Outlaw* reads as though it were written not for serious literary readers but for a more general audience that would include Burroughs's punk rock fans. Some may find this attractive, but I found it rather embarrassing. (I'm sure Morgan didn't use this style for his previous biographies of Maugham, Churchill, and Roosevelt.) Describing the Beats, for example, Morgan writes: "They constituted one of the few American literary movements, for American writers are more often loners, competing with each other like Hertz and Avis to be Number One." This is not only inaccurate — yes, some American writers are loners, but only a few like Hemingway and Mailer are *that* competitive — and the comparison to rental car agencies is degrading. Burroughs's unhappiness at Harvard is described in this way: "He was terribly unhappy because he was frustrated sexually. He was in a sexual desert in the years when the sap was rising. Just when you want it most you can't get it." The first sentence is the only one needed; the second offers a gratuitous metaphor, and as if that weren't enough, Morgan adds a bit of locker-room philosophy for the third sentence. Too much of this kind of writing — especially when Morgan is aping his characters' hip vernacular — almost spoiled the book for me, though others may prefer this as a refreshing change from academic writing.

Despite the slumming style, *Literary Outlaw* will be required reading for everyone interested in the Beats. There are some minor errors here and there — Alan Ansen has written to me of several concerning him,[4] so there are probably others — but Morgan's organization of thousands of facts into a compelling narrative is an admirable achievement. Burroughs once put off a fan by saying, "Mostly my life has been solitary and uneventful except in an inner direction," but quite the opposite is true: he has led an eventful, exotic life and has made major contributions to culture that continue to be felt to this day (rap music's sampling is little more than Burroughsian cut-ups) and Morgan's *Literary Outlaw* joins Nicosia's *Memory Babe* as a major Beat biography.

Kerouac Connection, Spring 1989

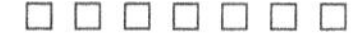

4 I asked Ansen to review the biography for the *Review of Contemporary Fiction*, which appeared in the Spring 1989 issue, pp. 240–41.

Gregory Stephenson. *The Daybreak Boys: Essays on the Beat Generation*
Southern Illinois University Press, 1990

The majority of material written on the Beats has been biographical, not critical. This is unfortunate because it has perpetuated the notion that the Beats were wild and crazy guys who just happened to do a little writing on the side, writing as undisciplined as their lifestyle. Gregory Stephenson offers in *The Daybreak Boys* the first comprehensive study of the Beats as a *literary* movement first and foremost, and one of the most important literary movements in American literature. A crisply written introduction recounts the origins (literary and sociological) of the movement, its major themes and concerns: "The themes of a journey through night to break of day, of personal and human liberation, of renewal arising out of exhaustion, and of beginning proceeding from ending are motifs that serve to link the essays." Separate chapters are devoted to Kerouac, Ginsberg, Burroughs, Corso, Holmes, McClure, Fariña, Ferlinghetti, and Cassady. (A second-generation Beat, Fariña is a bit out of place here, but it's good to have an essay on the neglected *Been Down So Long It Looks Like Up to Me*.) A concluding chapter explores the Beats' "primitivism" (again, both a literary and sociological concern) as a retreat from the materialism of the '50s, the safe, pseudosophisticated fiction of the time, and from the decline of spirituality.

Especially interesting are the Beats' affinities with various magic rituals — initiation, the hero's quest, shamanistic visions — in order "to counter the negative energies of the age with positive energies, to counter fear and hatred with celebration, to counter impercipience with vision, to counter black magic with white magic." Stephenson's splendid study will be savored by Beat aficionados, of course, but it deserves to be read by everyone interested in modern American literature — especially by those critics who remain under the impression that the Beats were just a gang of subliterary hoodlums.

Review of Contemporary Fiction, Fall 1990

□□□□□□□

Seymour Krim. *What's* This *Cat's Story? The Best of Seymour Krim*. Foreword by James Wolcott
Paragon House, 1991

Beat literature, like Romantic literature, consists largely of poetry; the movement produced only three novelists of note — Burroughs, Holmes, and Kerouac (four if you consider Brossard a Beat) — and only one major critic: Seymour Krim. Like Kerouac, Krim was enthralled by Thomas Wolfe, both his torrential prose style and his heartsick love for a lost America. In his lifetime (1922–89) Krim edited one influential anthology (*The Beats*, 1960) and published three collections of essays: *Views of a Nearsighted Cannoneer* (1961; expanded 1968); *Shake It for the World, Smartass* (1970), and *You & Me* (1974). *What's* This *Cat's Story?* consists of the best essays from those three books (chosen by Krim shortly before his suicide) along with four uncollected essays and an excerpt from his unpublished prose poem *Chaos*. The latter is reminiscent of Kerouac's *Old Angel Midnight*: it's a dense, impressionistic meditation on growing old in America, and I for one hope the complete text will someday be published. The essays are arranged chronologically: not in the order they were written, but according to Krim's own biography, so that the collection begins with his earliest ambitions to be a writer and ends with a late-life lament that actors have replaced writers as America's most heroic artists.

Krim's energetic prose and personal involvement will remind some readers of the other Tom Wolfe, and while Krim's contribution to New Journalism should not be discounted, he was striving for something more than journalism: a new form that would unite the novelistic imagination with direct communication. Krim called on the novelist to come out from "behind the mask of fiction" and to "speak intimately to his readers about these fantastic days we are living through but declare his credentials by revealing the concrete details and particular sweat of his own inner life." Though there is something self-defensive in this (Krim was unable to write a novel himself), he splendidly evokes those "fantastic days" of the late 1940s through the late 1960s when American literature and culture were turning themselves inside out. If you've never read Krim, this is the place to start; and even if you have, you'll appreciate the way his different essays have been brought together here to form the autobiography of one of our greatest cultural critics.

Review of Contemporary Fiction, Spring 1992

□ □ □ □ □ □ □

William Burroughs. *The Cat Inside*
Viking, 1992

Although at first glance *The Cat Inside* looks like a cute little book about kitties, closer inspection will find Burroughs's celebrated irony, gallows humor, apocalyptic fears, brutal lyricism, and mythological interests. In these brief anecdotes about his own experiences with cats, he muses on their real and metaphoric relations to humans: in Egypt they were gods; in medieval

Europe they were witches' familiars; for Burroughs they exhibit essential impulses, amoral drives, and naked needs that humans too share but have buried beneath layers of conventions, customs, and self-imposed alienation from our animal selves. To find the cat inside each of us is the latest installment in Burroughs's career-long search for liberation, and thus *The Cat Inside* is a small but significant addition to his canon.

Review of Contemporary Fiction, Spring 1993

□□□□□□□

James T. Jones. *A Map of "Mexico City Blues": Jack Kerouac as Poet*
Southern Illinois University Press, 1992

We rarely review poetry books in these pages, much less critical studies of poetry, but this one deserves special notice. Although Kerouac has been the subject of a good deal of amateur criticism ("amateur" in its best, etymological sense), first-rate scholarly studies of his work can be counted on the fingers of one hand. Jones is among that minority of working critics that takes Kerouac seriously as a writer, and his *Map* shows how rewarding a close reading of a Kerouac book can be once you look past its bohemian exterior. Even though Jones concentrates on the little-known *Mexico City Blues*, it's a bracing display of how to read Kerouac as a writer in general, and consequently offers innumerable insights for those more interested in his novels.

Author of a book on R. P. Blackmur, Jones writes intelligent, intelligible prose free of the alien jargon that disfigures so much recent criticism; he has a great ear for the sound of words (a crucial element of Kerouac's aesthetics) and applies his wide erudition judiciously. The mixture of close readings and appropriate biographical information, especially on Kerouac's religion(s), strikes the perfect balance. This book deserves to find a readership beyond Kerouac's admirers — amateur and professional — for it reveals *Mexico City Blues* to be just what Allen Ginsberg has claimed it to be: "a seminal poetic work of the latter half of the American Century."

Review of Contemporary Fiction, Spring 1993

□□□□□□□

William S. Burroughs. *Letters 1945–1959*. Edited by Oliver Harris
Viking, 1993

Barry Miles. *William Burroughs: El Hombre Invisible*
Hyperion, 1993

The current issue of *Lingua Franca* reports that heroin has returned as the drug of choice at some Ivy League colleges. "A lot of it has to do with having icons," explains a budding junkie at Bennington. "If you belong to a certain class or crowd, your hero might be Madonna. But if you're tuned into any subcultural, artistic thing, you're into Lenny Bruce, Billie Holiday, William Burroughs."

Although he turns 80 next February, Burroughs remains an icon for many younger writers, musicians, artists and, unfortunately, dilettante druggies. Like the dope at Bennington, many of these admirers are unaware that Burroughs's most famous novel, *Naked Lunch,* is a diatribe *against* addiction of all kinds, as Burroughs explains again and again in the letters gathered by Oliver Harris into a handsome volume. *Naked Lunch* depicts junkie sickness, and Burroughs made it as disgusting as he could to drive his point home. But some persist in misreading him as they do his friend Jack Kerouac, whose despairing threnody for postwar America in *On the Road* was misinterpreted by youngsters as a call for a joyride across America, preferably in a stolen car.

Burroughs has been influential in more positive ways, as Barry Miles shows in his new biography. In the '60s and '70s, several rock groups took their names from titles or phrases in his books (the Mugwumps, Insect Trust, Steely Dan, and Soft Machine — my favorite group at the time and, as a result, the first Burroughs novel I read), and the phrase "heavy metal" was lifted by Steppenwolf from *Naked Lunch* and was soon used to describe the thunderous hard rock of such groups as Blue Cheer and Led Zeppelin. The post-apocalyptic settings of some of his novels influenced movies like *Mad Max* and *Repo Man,* and so-called cyberpunk fiction is hugely indebted to him. His style is reflected in younger writers like Kathy Acker, Lauren Fairbanks, Mark Leyner and William T. Vollmann, and some of the more tasteless sketches on television shows like *Saturday Night Live* and *The Edge* can be traced back to Burroughs's "routines." (Burroughs has appeared on *SLN*, where he was introduced by noted literary critic Lauren Hutton as "the greatest living American writer.") It's difficult to think of another contemporary writer who has influenced so many people in so many different fields.

Burroughs's development as a writer and his struggles against addiction are the twin themes of this new edition of his letters. The addiction came first, and thereafter writing was a way of examining it and finding in addiction a multifaceted metaphor for the means by which people are controlled by the church, the state, advertising agencies, and any others in a position of power or influence. Many letters are first drafts of episodes that would later appear in *Naked Lunch* and the cut-up trilogy that followed (*The Soft Machine*, *The Ticket that Exploded*, and *Nova Express* — his most difficult works, but also the most poetic), and many of the incomprehensible episodes in those works are clarified by the biographical contexts of these letters.

Despite his addiction and loneliness, Burroughs is always an entertaining correspondent, largely because the letters are written in the same trademark style used in his novels, which Miles accurately describes as a "mixture of hustler-junkie jargon with WASP articulation, the hip talk mixed with the formal language of Harvard, compounded by a light camp overtone." The letters are helpfully annotated and are preceded by an insightful introduction, whose only fault is reticence on the manner of selection. An earlier book, *Letters to Allen Ginsberg 1953–1957* (published by Full Court Press in 1982), contains a number of letters not reproduced here — some superb — so it's unclear how many other letters may have been left out. This will create problems for Burroughs scholars, but other readers will find this new volume of letters an excellent introduction to Burroughs's early work. (A second volume of later letters is promised [but didn't appear until 2012].)

Miles's biography can be described the same way: great for the general reader, but deficient for the scholar. It doesn't have footnote one, and the bibliography lists only Burroughs's own work, so it isn't clear where the innumerable quotations from Burroughs and his friends come from, aside from conversations with Miles over the years. On the other hand, Miles has been a friend and bibliographer of his subject for 30 years — he refers to him casually as "Bill" throughout — and understands his life and work much better than Burroughs's last biographer. Ted Morgan's *Literary Outlaw: The Life and Times of William S. Burroughs* (1988) is twice as long and much more detailed than Miles's book, but is rather condescending at times and lacks much literary analysis. Miles, on the other hand, offers brief but alert readings of all the works and uses his bibliographer's expertise to note differences in editions (*The Soft Machine* exists in three different versions) and to give valuable background information. Two versions of *The Place of Dead Roads* were offered to Burroughs's publisher, for example: a "poetic" one and a more straightforward, "commercial" one; the latter is the one that was published, unfortunately. Miles also brings us up-to-date on the latest phase in Burroughs's career: painting.[5]

David Cronenberg's recent film adaptation of *Naked Lunch* brought Bur-

5 Miles went on to write a much better biography: *Call Me Burroughs: A Life* (2014).

roughs to the attention of the MTV generation, and it is to be hoped that they will seek out his books rather than their neighborhood pusher. The best are dense prose poems mixing brutal lyricism with outrageous humor, and display a healthy skepticism toward arrogant authority and repressive respectability. Burroughs's libertarianism, misogyny, and general misanthropy are hardly PC, and his novels are filled with the unsafest sex you've ever read; but these are shock tactics against mindless conformity, not recipes for living, and these two books are invaluable for understanding those tactics, and for understanding why the lovely Lauren Hutton may be absolutely correct.

Washington Post Book World, 15 August 1993

□ □ □ □ □ □ □

Jack Kerouac. *Old Angel Midnight* and *Good Blonde & Others*
Both Grey Fox, 1993

Access to Kerouac's lesser-known writings was obstructed for years by his widow, who refused to allow any of it to be reprinted. Now that she's gone and Kerouac's estate is in the hands of a more sensible heir (John Sampas), we can look forward to more books like these. Kerouac always advocated spontaneous composition, and *Old Angel Midnight* is the most radical form this aesthetic took. It is an exercise in pure sound, in channeling his stream of consciousness into syllables. It is both the most playful and the most difficult thing he wrote, approaching *Finnegans Wake* in its verbal density. This edition comes with prefaces by Ann Charters and Michael McClure; the latter is especially good on the autobiographical and Buddhist aspects of the work.

Good Blonde & Others collects Kerouac's nonfiction: magazine articles, introductions, his "Last Word" columns from *Escapade*, even some sports columns he wrote for the *Saint Petersburg Independent* in 1965 — virtually everything (aside from the pieces in *Lonesome Traveler*) he wrote apart from his novels and poetry. None of it is mere bread-and-butter journalism; it's all enlivened by Kerouac's wit and musical sentences, his whimsy and passion. This is an invaluable collection, carefully edited by Donald Allen, and warmly introduced by Robert Creeley.

Review of Contemporary Fiction, Spring 1994

□ □ □ □ □ □ □

Jack Kerouac. *Selected Letters: 1940–1956*. *The Portable Jack Kerouac*. Both edited by Ann Charters

Viking, 1995

These two splendid volumes are just what is needed to elevate Kerouac from his lingering status as a Beatnik chronicler to his deserved status as one of the greatest American novelists of our century. Because of uncooperative, greedy publishers and an incompetent estate, neither of these volumes were published 25 years ago as intended. (John Clellon Holmes and Kerouac discussed the idea of a reader as far back as 1965, but his various publishers wouldn't give permission to reprint; and after Kerouac's death in 1969, his estate squatted on his writings and wouldn't allow anything to be published.) Better late than never, the *Reader* offers an abridged "Legend of Duluoz" by reprinting segments from most of the novels in chronological order, beginning with Jean Duluoz's childhood in *Visions of Gerard* and *Doctor Sax* and ending with his disillusioned silence at the end of *Big Sur*. While no substitute for reading the novels in their entirety, this 425-page selection gives a good sense of the scope of Kerouac's grand autobiographical project. The fiction is followed by selections from his poetry, essays, Buddhist writings, and a handful of letters. Given the length constraint of Viking Portables, Charters's selections (and her useful headnotes) are ideal.

The paucity of letters in the *Reader* would be grounds for complaint were it not for the simultaneous publication of the greatest addition to the Kerouac canon in recent years, volume one of the *Selected Letters*. While some of these have appeared before — specifically in Arthur and Kit Knight's *unspeakable visions of the individual* series — this is the book that many Kerouac fans have been anticipating for years. By the time he was 20 Kerouac had already developed his vibrant, headlong prose style. In an early letter he writes: "I'm in an enthusiastic mood and I feel like pouring out this zest and transmitting it to a worthy listener." Indeed, the enthusiasm and zest of these letters are exhilarating, as are the appetite for life and new experiences. Some are the length of short stories, and as with Burroughs's letters (published two years ago), many of the letters are in essence first drafts of episodes in the novels. Using about half of the letters available to her, Charters has favored those in which Kerouac relates experiences that he later fictionalized. Although the novels are autobiographical, there are crucial differences between the raw experiences and the artistically mediated ones, giving the lie to Capote's quip that Kerouac's fiction was just "typing" — the letters may be typing, but the novels are art.

As with the *Reader*, Charters's headnotes are useful, but the footnotes are a bit skimpy: she identifies William Gaddis as the author of *The Recognitions*, but doesn't mention he's also a character in Kerouac's *Subterraneans*. Alan Ansen is identified only as Auden's secretary, which is like identifying T. S. Eliot only as a bank clerk. Aside from that, it's a wonderful, even inspiring book, ending just before Kerouac became famous for *On the Road*. The second volume won't be as exhilarating as this — Kerouac's last decade was a grim one — but it is keenly awaited nonetheless. [It appeared in 1999.]

Review of Contemporary Fiction, Spring 1995

□ □ □ □ □ □ □

William S. Burroughs. *My Education: A Book of Dreams*
Viking, 1995

As Burroughs himself has admitted in the past, dreams have long provided him with various characters and scenarios in his fiction. Here, uncut with any fiction, are transcriptions of various dreams he's had over the years, along with waking thoughts on matters arising from the dreams: his inability to feel part of any group, Genet's *Prisoner of Love*, a recipe for botulism from Pancho Villa, and occult speculations, among other things. Burroughs's dreamworld, the Land of the Dead as he calls it (the Western Lands of his fiction), is a desolate and rather seedy place where breakfast is never served. But important figures from his life like Brion Gysin and Ian Sommerville are here, as are his ubiquitous purple-assed baboons and his beloved cats. Like Kerouac's *Book of Dreams*, this is a useful companion to the Beat writer's work.

Review of Contemporary Fiction, Summer 1995

□ □ □ □ □ □ □

Carole Tonkinson, ed. *Big Sky: Buddhism and the Beat Generation*
Riverhead/Tricycle, 1995

This is not a study of the Buddhist element in Beat literature, as the title might suggest, but an anthology of works from the Beats themselves that illustrate their engagement with Buddhism. Friends and foes alike have not always known what to make of Beat Buddhism: many admirers simply ignore this element (as I have always done), while detractors consider it a dilettante affectation or un-American nihilism. But as Stephen Prothero points out in an admirable introduction, Buddhism is as important to an understanding of the Beats as Transcendentalism is to an understanding of Emerson and Thoreau; further, the Beats' knowledge of Transcendentalism aligns them with the same spirit of self-reliance and individualism advocated by their forebears, indicating that the Beats were not a postwar anomaly (again as detractors would say) or a European thing (imitating Céline, Genet, the existentialists) but part of a long American literary tradition. Prothero also makes distinctions between the branches of Buddhism the various Beats studied, noting, for example, that Kerouac was drawn not to Zen Buddhism but to a version of Mahayana Buddhism.

There are generous selections from Kerouac's works (including a previously unpublished dream), Ginsberg, di Prima, Snyder — all the regulars except for Corso, who showed little interest in Buddhism — along with some lesser-known Beats like Joanne Kyger, Albert Saijo, Lenore Kandel, and Will Peterson. The selections from Burroughs illustrate the difficulty he had taking Buddhism seriously, adding a dissident voice to the collection. One can still have reservations about the validity of Buddhism — Burroughs told Kerouac that "Buddhism frequently amounts to a form of psychic junk," which is echoed in a Kerouac poem included here where settling into meditation is compared to "a shot of heroin or morphine" — and yet still find this anthology immensely interesting and useful. There have been many anthologies of Beat writings, but this is a unique (and expertly edited) one that deserves a place in your rucksack.

Review of Contemporary Fiction, Spring 1996

□ □ □ □ □ □ □

The Beat movement is now a half-century old, and even though its principal writers are, with the death of Gregory Corso in early 2001, now eternally on the road, it remains as popular as ever. Kids who were not yet born when Jack Kerouac died sit in coffeehouses scribbling mad spontaneous prose in commercially produced blank books with — I'm not making this up — the opening lines of Allen Ginsberg's "Howl" embossed on the cover. Scholarly conferences on the Beats abound, Beat websites proliferate, and musicians and movie stars perform dramatic Beat readings. And of course there is no end in sight to the freight train of books on the Beats rolling off the presses.

Quite rightly so, for there are a lot of gaps to fill and damage to repair. In the early days, the Beats had trouble finding publishers for their works — and when they did, often had to settle for expurgated versions — and the only books written about them were journalistic accounts that emphasized the unconventional Beat lifestyle over their literary accomplishments. (Does anyone remember Lawrence Lipton's *The Holy Barbarians*?) Some of Kerouac's books were published in abridged form (*Visions of Cody*, *Book of Dreams*) or not at all (*Some of the Dharma*). William S. Burroughs had to publish *Naked Lunch* with a French porn publisher, and to this day his revised, preferred version of *The Soft Machine* hasn't appeared in this country.[6] Short-lived little magazines and poorly distributed small presses were the only ones to publish some of the lesser-known Beats.

But happily that's all changed. Several new Kerouac books have appeared in recent years, thanks to the death of his last wife Stella Sampas, who had squatted on her husband's literary property for 20 years after his death and refused to allow anything new to be published. We've seen new editions of *On the Road*, the imposing *Some of the Dharma*, collected essays, early writings, and in the next few years Viking plans to publish a book of Kerouac's haikus, his *Book of Sketches*, and the *On the Road* journals. We now have a new edition of *Book of Dreams* (City Lights, 2001), almost twice as long as the 1961 edition and containing the complete manuscript, exactly as Kerouac typed it (typos and all). Kerouac cites *Finnegans Wake* on the first page, and like Joyce's dreamscape there's a surrealistic quality to the vignettes, many featuring the same characters that appear in Kerouac's novels. (The prose only occasionally approaches Wakese, though Kerouac got nearer that goal in *Old Angel Midnight*.) Like anyone's dreams, some are more interesting than others, but at its best the prose has a fine, mournful quality:

> At the end, I'm watching from a tenement top window like Julien's Dostoevyskyan loft, like the George Jessel New York tenements on the upper east end — all the children are playing on the opposite roof, nets are stretched across the court to catch the ones that fall, when they do the other kids watch smiling — the fallen one cries in the net — *I told you it was cruel* — the mothers are not too concerned — "why cant they play on the sidewalks," I say — "*there's no room*, civilization is too vast now" — Guilt is a dream, pity is the only reality.

A similar restoration job is promised in the forthcoming *Naked Lunch: The Restored Text* (Grove Press, 2001), edited by James Grauerholz and Barry Miles, which may pave the way for a retooled *Soft Machine*. Ginsberg, a canny professional, took the time to prepare corrected, annotated editions of his works before he died. Corso has lagged somewhat behind; there's an excellent edition of his selected poems (*Minefield*), but as yet there has been no biography, nor has anyone reprinted his fanciful novel, *The American Express* (1961).

Another welcome trend is the reprinting of novels by minor or forgotten Beats. The late Chandler Brossard's first two novels, *Who Walk in Dark-*

6 Rectified in 2014 by Oliver Harris in *The Soft Machine: The Restored Text*.

ness and *The Bold Saboeturs* — both important documents for the Beats even though Brossard resented being lumped in with them — have been reprinted recently by Herodias (with new forewords by this reviewer). An even earlier Beat novel has been unearthed and reprinted by another small press: Alvin Schwartz's *The Blowtop* (Olmstead Press, 2001) was first published in 1948, a full four years before what are usually considered the first Beat novels (*Who Walk in Darkness*, John Clellon Holmes's *Go*, and George Mandel's *Flee the Angry Strangers*, all published in 1952). It describes the turmoil created in a band of Greenwich Villagers' lives when a local pusher is murdered, and includes musings on the then-new French existentialism and Abstract Expressionist painting. In fact, Jackson Pollock assumed he was the model for the painter in the novel, though (as the 85-year-old author tells us in a new introduction) a less famous artist named Attilio Salemme was intended.

Despite some interesting temporal shifts, *The Blowtop* isn't particularly innovative, and certainly lacks the liberated language that makes reading the other Beats suck a kick. What is remarkable about the novel is the way potentially sensationalist material — *Drug Fiends! Crazy Artists! Promiscuous Greenwich Village Chicks!* — is downplayed. Schwartz's characters smoke dope in the same uneventful way characters in other novels of the time drink beer. (Here "blowtop" is a term for a marijuana user, before "blow" became associated with cocaine; today's potheads will be amused by the novel's period slang.) Instead, the emphasis is on the new intellectual and artistic ideas that were in the air. A valuable discovery, *The Blowtop* should certainly figure in future histories of the Beat movement.

There have been many fine Beat anthologies published in recent years, but the most useful for understanding the movement from a sociological point of view as well as a literary one would have to be *Beat Down to Your Soul: What Was the Beat Generation?* (Penguin, 2001), edited by the fairy godmother of the Beats, Ann Charters. A companion volume of sorts to her 1991 *Portable Beat Reader*, this one shifts the emphasis from poetry and fiction onto nonfiction and commentary. The contents range from well-known pieces like Holmes's defining essay "This Is the Beat Generation" and Mary McCarthy's famous review of *Naked Lunch* to little-known items like English poet George Barker's "Circular from America" to a crazy letter Peter Orlovsky wrote to Charlie Chaplin. There are even some parodies included, like John Updike's "On the Sidewalk" and Christopher Buckley and Paul Slansky's clever "Yowl for Jay McInerney." The sharp but enigmatic Anatole Broyard is represented by both his "A Portrait of a Hipster" (1949) and by Henry Louis Gates Jr.'s 1996 *New Yorker* profile "White Like Me." The volume concludes with a 1996 roundtable discussion with Beat women writers, whose contributions were for a long time overlooked. (This has been rectified somewhat by two recent anthologies, Brenda Knight's *Women of the Beat Generation* and Richard Peabody's *A Different Beat.*)

Of course the Beats had their detractors from the word go, and Charters includes several attacks on the Beats in the '50s from conservatives writing for *Partisan Review, Life,* and *Horizon.* Scotsman James Campbell isn't exactly a Beat-basher, but in *This Is the Beat Generation: New York–San Francisco–Paris* (University of California Press, 2001) he tells their story in the worst possible light. Condescending, apparently regarding them as little better than juvenile delinquents, Campbell doesn't miss an opportunity to mock them or relate a seamy anecdote. He demonstrates a PC abhorrence for their treatment of women and their attitudes toward blacks (which was fairly liberal for the time), and considers their enthusiasm for life, their hunger for "girls, visions, and everything" (in Kerouac's lusty phrase), as sophomoric. He shows grudging respect for the sardonic Burroughs, who was older and wiser than the other wild boys, but too often Campbell indulges in clever put-downs of the sort used by square journalists in the 1950s. The Beats despised his type.

Whatever the flavor of his judgments — as Campbell says of a hatchet job on the Beats in *Life* magazine by Paul O'Neill, reprinted in *Beat Down to Your Soul* — he has done his homework and has written a lively, highly readable history of the Beats. First published in England in 1999, *This Is the Beat Generation* seems intended for readers not too familiar with the movement, if there are any left, and it covers all the key incidents up through 1961. Campbell has a sharp eye for literary parallels, especially between the Beats and French writers from Villon onward, and makes value judgments other Beat historians shy away from, such as the rank injustice that Holmes's prosaic *Go* was accepted for early publication while Kerouac's far superior *On the Road* was deemed unpublishable. On the other hand, his reading of Brossard's *Who Walk in Darkness* is misguided — it's a novel about inauthenticity, not about racist attitudes in Greenwich Village — and he dismisses most of Kerouac's writings apart from *On the Road.* Campbell's book is useful as a corrective to some of the more adulatory books on the Beats that have appeared in recent years, but it should be approached with caution.

The Beats are taken much more seriously in John Lardas's *The Bop Apocalypse: The Religious Visions of Kerouac, Ginsberg, and Burroughs* (University of Illinois Press, 2000). This is a book intended for the Beat scholar rather than the general reader, but it's a model academic study: it avoids the jargon and free-association of theory-addled, PC-blinkered critics[7] and instead con-

7 See Frederick Crews's new *Postmodern Pooh* (North Point Press, 2002) for a well-deserved satire of the kind of hip, academic critics who have made contemporary literary study a laughingstock to the outside world. Crews's parodies are funny, accurate, and terribly

centrates on the demonstrable sources of the Beat vision and their influence on their creative work.

Broadly defining religion as "the vehicle by which people come to understand their world and live within it," Lardas carefully examines all the religious and philosophical systems that influenced the Beats' worldview. The most valuable aspect of this superb study is the emphasis on Oswald Spengler, whose *Decline of the West* (1918–22) had an enormous influence on modern literature, which has yet to be traced in the detail it deserves. Yeats and Pound read it, Wyndham Lewis wrote *Time and Western Man* in response, Joyce cites it in *Finnegans Wake*, Lowry used it in *Under the Volcano*, and William Gaddis said reading Spengler when he was a young man permanently altered his outlook on life. Some previous critics have made passing reference to Spengler — James T. Jones, for instance, in his book on Kerouac's *Mexico City Blues* — but Lardas is the first to delineate the shaping force Spengler's provocative work had on Burroughs, Kerouac, and Ginsberg. (Other Beats may have known of Spengler's book — Brossard certainly did — but Lardas focuses on the Big Three.)

Lardas also surveys the postwar religious landscape that the Beats reacted against, a weird time of revivals, apocalyptic fears, UFO sightings, occultism, and the popularization of Eastern mysticism. Without an understanding of this background, much of Beat literature can be misread (as Campbell does) as the expression of personal neuroses, so Lardas has performed an invaluable service. Since the book's price [$39.95] makes it prohibitive for the fellaheen, I hope a paperback edition is forthcoming, for *The Bop Apocalypse* may be the finest book written on the Beats to date and deserves the widest readership possible.

Rain Taxi, Winter 2001–2002

---

depressing. [Note appended to original review, and repurposed for the introduction to the first volume of my *The Novel, An Alternative History*.]

Saul Bellow

Zachary Leader. *The Life of Saul Bellow: To Fame and Fortune, 1915–1964*
Knopf, 2015

June 10th will be the hundredth anniversary of the birth of Saul Bellow (1915–2005), the Nobel Prize-winning author of over a dozen novels and half a dozen books of stories and nonfiction. A few months ago his collected essays was published, and now comes the first of two volumes of a new biography by Zachary Leader, an Anglo-American literary critic. Bellow has already been the subject of a few memoirs and biographies, most notably one by James Atlas published in 2000, which struck some readers as resentful and overly critical. Leader offers a considerably longer, more straightforward account, with no particular agenda, thesis, or ax to grind, stuffed to the rafters with the results of his prodigious research. He provides all the facts, to be interpreted as you like — a welcome alternative to overly psychoanalytical and/or theory-driven biographies.

Bellow led an archetypal novelist's life, destined at an early age (perhaps as early as ten) to become a writer. He was born in Canada into an immigrant Russian-Jewish family — "crowded, tense, loving, fractious" — worked dozens of hard-scrabble jobs as a teenager in Chicago, read voraciously and argued vehemently with other well-read kids his age, wrote hundreds of pages of apprenticeship fiction, and traveled widely. After publishing two respectable but mediocre-selling novels in the 1940s, he broke through in 1953, stylistically and commercially, with *The Adventures of Augie March*, and continued to produce well-regarded novels up to *Herzog* in 1964, which is where this first volume breaks off.

As Leader points out, Bellow was a highly autobiographical novelist, and in the early part of the book nearly every incident is followed by a chain of references to Bellow's use of the incident in his fiction (unpublished as well as published). For example, at age eight Bellow suffered an appendicitis attack and spent four or five months recovering from it and other complications. Leader follows his three-page account with quotations from two novels and three unfinished works tracking all the uses Bellow made of the experience. Young Saul's concern for his mother is followed by every reference to mothers in Bellow's works. In nearly every instance, Bellow adjusted the facts to fit his artistic needs, a point not always appreciated by acquaintances who saw themselves depicted in his works.

Leader's thoroughness extends to those acquaintances. As each new person enters Bellow's life, a mini-biography is provided, and if they were writers — as many of them were — Leader gives accounts of their works, often even the kind of reviews they received. Bellow's first three wives also receive full, evenhanded treatment. The amount of detail here is staggering; Leader apparently left no stone unturned, and succinctly summarizes all the cultural upheavals surrounding Bellow in those heady days. (The biography doubles as a primer on the intellectual climate of the times.) But the details never become too dense or overwhelming, thanks largely to Leader's clear, brisk style.

I was surprised to learn how erudite Bellow was from high school onward, how much teaching he did in his early days, in Europe as well as America, how good a musician he was, and how frequently Bellow "was called upon, from *Augie* onward, to advise corporations, sit on boards and committees, and interact with corporate types." This speaks to how seriously novelists were taken in the 1950s and 1960s, when they enjoyed a cultural cachet unthinkable today. (I can't imagine any corporation asking, say, Jonathan Franzen or William T. Vollmann to advise them or join its board.)

Respectful but not hagiographic, Leader is not afraid to point out occasional flaws in Bellow's character and in his writing: violations in point of view, uncontrolled language (especially in *Augie*), and an overreliance on spontaneity. He quotes Philip Roth on the latter point: "Usually about half way through the book the original impulse weakens and then he gets a mess in the middle." Bellow admitted this himself when writing *Herzog*: "As sometimes happens by the hundredth page, my lack of planning, or the subconscious cunning, catch up with me," concluding cheekily, "God will provide. Consider the lilies of the field — do they write books?"

Leader covers Bellow's relations with fellow Jewish-American writers like Roth and Bernard Malamud, but I would have liked to see more on what he thought of some other novelists who emerged during that time. I was surprised at how many quotations from Bellow's work sounded like Jack Kerouac, yet he is mentioned (along with J. D. Salinger and William Burroughs) only as the possessor of an orgone box. No mention is made of Bellow's opinion, if any, of those who worked the artier side of the street in the 1950s and early '60s (John Hawkes, William Gaddis, John Barth, Thomas Pynchon), though a few of them appeared in a short-lived magazine called *The Noble Savage* he coedited from 1960 and 1962, as Leader notes.

Perhaps they'll turn up in volume two, all the more reason to anticipate the conclusion of what will surely become the standard life of Bellow for years to come.

Washington Post, 19 May 2015

Brooke Bergan

Storyville: A Hidden Mirror
Asphodel Press, 1994

Those who squirmed with guilt at viewing the pubescent Brooke Shields in *Pretty Baby* some years back can read with a clearer conscience the mature Brooke Bergan's treatment of the same material in *Storyville*. Like Louis Malle before her, she uses Ernest J. Belloq's photographs of the turn-of-the-century red-light district of New Orleans as her point of departure. Accompanying several of his striking photographs are her no less striking "plates" — poems that interpret the photos — along with other sections mixing prose and poetry called "voices," "arguments," "discourses," and "extrapolations," concluding with source notes. The result is a fascinating multimedia meditation on the place of prostitution in American culture and the politics of eroticism.

Bergan's extensive background reading gives the material a firm historical base, preventing any romanticization of what was a squalid life for most of the prostitutes, but at the same time allowing her to capture with precision the faded charm and desperate beauty of Storyville and its inhabitants. It also allows her to explore the complex sociology of the time, with middle-class tricks falling in love with "fallen" higher-class women, the relations between blacks and whites, the familiar economics whereby prostitution offered some women the only means to achieve financial independence, Old World French mores clashing with American Puritanism, and much more. Bergan's grasp of the subject embraces everything from ancient myths of sacred prostitution to the latest theories of photography's ambivalent relation to its object.

Reminiscent in form and texture to Pound's *Cantos*, Olson's *Maximus Poems*, and Metcalf's historical collages, *Storyville* is a richly complex and sensuously beguiling work of art.

Review of Contemporary Fiction, Summer 1995

R. M. Berry

Leonardo's Horse
FC2/Illinois State University, 1997

Forget the airplane, modern weaponry, or hydraulic systems; what Leonardo da Vinci was really working toward was a 1955 Buick Roadmaster, according to this audacious novel about Leonardo. Or make that "Leonardo," the quotation marks signifying the icon rather than the actual man. Both icon and man are everywhere in our culture, as the narrator points out: "There's a supermarket pasta called da Vinci. There's a children's fold-out book about his horse. There's a mutant Ninja turtle named Leonardo, and an electronics catalog with his Vitruvian man for its logo. Eighty-nine books mentioning him were published last year; over a hundred public institutions have exhibits; there are at least three English words derived from him; two electronics commercials, four car commercials" — and now a postmodern novel about him.

The narrator, called simply R—, is no Renaissance man, just your average liberal intellectual muddling through a messy life. One day he finds himself in a chaotic traffic jam caused by AIDS demonstrators, and while sitting it out he is joined by a fellow stranded motorist who notices the box containing R—'s unfinished novel about Leonardo and starts reading it. We read along with him. The novel begins and ends on May 2, 1519, the day Leonardo died in Ambroise, France. In one sense, the whole novel is a deathbed reverie, like Hermann Broch's *Death of Virgil* or Carole Maso's more recent *AVA*. Like those novels, *Leonardo's Horse* is nonlinear, jumping around from one key moment in Leonardo's life to another with little regard for chronology, interrupted by episodes detailing R—'s contemporary situation. And like those novels, it is linguistically rich; Berry's prose is as active as Leonardo's imagination, piling clause upon clause and multiplying details as he tracks Leonardo's memories, like this one when Leonardo as a child slipped in a dark cave, which he links with the dark room where he later observed the anatomist della Torre at work:

> And Leonardo was falling, reaching out for night's cusp, clawing at its roughness that slithered away, tearing the very sinews that 50 years later in Marcantonio della Torre's closet under the candle's waxy light with flies humming round his ear he'd watch being peeled one by one like threads from a spool, each cord plucked loose and flapping damply on the bench, until with the pink carpus glowing in the flame Leonardo would recognize that the hand was a miracle of intricate, twisting machinery and so, despite the teeming air, would nearly choke when the anatomist snickered: Only the beginning!

Another passage, also concerning della Torre (an important figure in Leonardo's life), uses colloquial language to remind us this is a 20th-century view of 16th-century Italy:

> Marcantonio, who was at the moment wrist-deep in the organs of an infant's cadaver he'd purchased that afternoon no-questions-asked from a local slime-bucket named Il Fortunato, a figure notorious on the streets for having only one nostril and half a lip as a result of getting overly intimate with a wheel-trueing device in his father's smithy as a child — Marcantonio, who in dissecting the infant was actually committing a crime legally punishable by those very torments about to be meted out to him for political acts he'd never dreamed of, when he heard the door crash open thought nothing but, Here are an extra pair of hands to hold this liver.

An entire novel of such long, convoluted sentences can be taxing — if you had trouble getting through these two, the novel's probably not for you — but Berry certainly brings the age alive in all its fetid glory.

As a history professor hoping for tenure, R— had decided to write his dissertation on Leonardo's iconic status, but as he began writing, he later tells his exasperated wife Deirdre, the dissertation turned "weird" and he decided only a novel could do justice to the man: "Leonardo was a cultural ikon only for spectators," he tells her. "For himself, for anyone who cared, he was lost, naked, crazy, embarrassing." Though he may now be considered a genius, "he died a failure." The greatest failure of Leonardo's life was his inability to complete the colossal horse Lodovico Sforza commissioned to commemorate his father, Francesco. Leonardo spent more than a decade on it, and managed to construct a clay model that wowed the invading Prussian army (who later destroyed it), but the finished bronze version was beyond him. This failure becomes emblematic of Leonardo's other failures: uncompleted paintings, failed projects, missed opportunities, lost commissions, all partly due to a restless imagination that kept him racing from one project to another.

Horses fascinated Leonardo all his life, and they run through Berry's novel, not as companions or mere means of locomotion but as frightening forces of energy. Leonardo's catamite/assistant Salai calls them "terrifying, vast as starless skies, like this one, and blacker. They make a noise through their noses, a hissing that tells you how nothing you are. Many times they tried to destroy me." (One particularly effective episode is Salai's account of hiding overnight in a stable, which is much more dangerous than you'd think.) On Leonardo's final day of life, Salai brings into the courtyard below Leonardo's window what appears to be a yellow coach, perhaps in mockery of the Sforza horse, but which, on Leonardo's closer inspection, turns out to be R—'s '55 Buick, as long as the Sforza horse was high, which Leonardo even takes for a spin. I can't begin to explain how Berry manages to pull this off, but it's an indication of the lengths to which he is willing to go to reclaim Leonardo from television commercials, advertising agencies, and overly reverential art monographs in order to bring him to life as someone who underwent the same frustrations and failures as many of us endure.

Berry's novel is not a debunking of Leonardo, as is often the case with revisionist biographies (or biographical novels). He is clearly appreciative of Leonardo's genius and displays an expert's grasp of his life and work, but he's more interested in how Leonardo coped with failure. While the parallels between R—'s midlife crisis and Leonardo's are not on the same scale — he's a typical failure, whereas Leonardo is an atypical one — Leonardo emerges from this novel less as a Renaissance man than as a modern, even postmodern man. Berry's ambitious goal is "plotting a failure, the despair of art, civilization at cross-purposes," by which he means the last decade of the 15th century as well as the last decade of our 20th century, and in doing so he makes Leonardo's story our own.

Washington Post Book World, 4 January 1998

Francesca Lia Block

If you're not a teenage girl, you may be unfamiliar with Francesca Lia Block's works. She's the Gabriel García Márquez of Young Adult fiction, Judy Blume gone punk and New Age, the patron saint of goth gurls into both Nine Inch Nails *and* Shakespeare. She's huge on the Internet, where some cybergrrrls have adopted their web-names from her characters. Imagine Ronald Firbank as a Valley girl with a heliotrope Mohawk. That's why there are many of us who are neither teenagers nor girls who find her fiction enchanting.

Block was born in 1962 into a creative family. Her father, Irving Alexander Block, painted and worked in Hollywood: he co-wrote *Forbidden Planet*, one of the best sci-films of the '50s, and created the special effects for *Atomic Submarine* and other movies. Her mother Gilda was a poet. Block grew up in the post-hippie '70s, embraced punk and spent many a night slam-dancing at L.A. clubs. She began writing her first novel, *Weetzie Bat*, while still a student at the University of California-Berkeley; it was published in 1989 to critical acclaim, and since then she has published a dozen books: eight YA novellas, two adult fantasy novels, a collection of short stories, and a manual on how to publish a 'zine. Ever prolific, Block has published three more books in the last year: a collection of short stories for adults called *Nymph*, another collection for teens entitled *The Rose and the Beast: Fairy Tales Retold*, and a new YA novel, *Echo*.

In a sense, all of her books are fairy tales, emblematic stories of young people coming of age in a Los Angeles transmogrified by Block's whimsical eye into a land of enchantment. Fairies are everywhere in her books, both the wingèd sort and homosexuals: *I Was a Teenage Fairy* (1998) is the title of a recent novel, and Claire of *Violet and Claire* (1999) is first seen wearing a Tinker Bell T-shirt with "iridescent gauze and wire fairy wings glued onto the back of her shirt." Some of Block's boys are taunted for being "fairies" before they fully understand, and accept, what that means. These are modern myths of transformation, with fairies, witches, angels, astrologers, dwarfs, and Tarot readers providing keys to unlocking the true self. Block's first short-story collection was called *Girl Goddess #9* (1996), and each of her girls is trying to find the goddess within.

Maxfield Parrish is name-checked in one of Block's books, and his gauzy romanticism hangs over Block's settings. Although terrible things happen to her teenagers — incest, anorexia, drug abuse, abandonment, suicide —

a genuine *joie de vivre* animates all her stories, helped along by the goofy slang some of her characters use. They celebrate the commodified, celebrity-obsessed junk culture scorned by most serious novelists. Here's Weetzie Bat chiding her fellow students for being blind to the glories of Los Angeles (or Shangri-L.A., as she calls it):

> They didn't care that Marilyn's prints were practically in their backyard at Graumann's; that you could buy tomahawks and plastic palm tree wallets at Farmer's Market, and the wildest, cheapest cheese and bean and hot dog and pastrami burritos at Oki Dogs; that the waitresses wore skates at the Jetson-style Tiny Naylor's; that there was a fountain that turned tropical soda-pop colors, and a canyon where Jim Morrison and Houdini used to live, and all-night potato knishes at Canter's, and not too far away was Venice, with columns, and canals, even, like the real Venice but maybe cooler because of the surfers.

Weetzie Bat herself is just as eclectic:

> She was a skinny girl with a bleach-blonde flat-top. Under the pink Harlequin sunglasses, strawberry lipstick, earrings dangling charms, and sugar-frosted eye shadow she was really almost beautiful. Sometimes she wore Levi's with white-suede fringe sewn down the legs and a feathered Indian headdress, sometimes old '50s' taffeta dresses covered with poetry written in glitter, or dresses made of kids' sheets printed with pink piglets or Disney characters.

In Block's postmodern, posthistorical world, there are no canons of taste, no master narratives, no division between high and low culture, and no rules except to be true to yourself and kind to others. Her characters are oblivious to history and politics, indifferent to the manipulations of their commodity culture, and indiscriminate in their taste for occult traditions and New Age bromides. Aside from starting a band or someday writing a screenplay, they are blissfully unambitious, content to drift and play and eat. They're like animals, and I mean that in the most flattering way. But most of them are also wise beyond their years and have a grounding in decency that shields them from the worst aspects of our culture. (I asked a 17-year-old friend of mine, Megan Bernardini, to read one of Block's novels to see if they accurately reflect her age; she loved it, but Megan felt Block's characters acted a little old for their age, though perhaps that's because they grow up in fast-paced L.A.)

Block's best books are the Weetzie Bat books — five novellas that have been collected into an omnibus entitled *Dangerous Angels* (1998) — and *The Hanged Man* (1994), a grim story that uses the Tarot as a structural device. If Carole Maso decided to write a YA novel, it might resemble this adventurous work. Like most of Block's novels, it features a dysfunctional traditional family and a beautiful teenage girl growing up too fast. In contrast, one of the many pleasures of the Weetzie Bat books is its reinvention of the family: Weetzie becomes the unexpected matriarch of an alternative family that functions much better than most traditional ones.

Nymph (Circlet Press), one of two collections of short stories Block published in 2000, is something of a departure in that it's erotica, and aimed at adults rather than teens. Block has written for adults before — a pair of rather pallid fantasy novels entitled *Ecstasia* and *Primavera* appeared in the early 1990s but are out of print and difficult to find — and in some of her YA novels Block dwells with almost masculine relish on her girls' fetching attire: their miniskirts, their tight jeans, their sleek thighs gleaming from shorts slashed up the sides. In *Nymph*, these teens are now in their twenties, a little older and sadder, and look for guidance not from fairy tales but from myths. Ovid's *Metamorphoses* is cited at the beginning and end of this short collection, and the tales focus on the transformative power of sex.

The stories are linked via recurring characters and unified in their use of animal imagery. The wheelchair-bound woman in the opening story has all the qualities of a mermaid; another woman has plastic surgery so that she resembles a cat; a sex therapist is named Dr. Fox; and throughout the collection sex causes people not exactly to turn into animals but to evoke their animal spirit-guides (after all, these are Californians for the most part). Characters are described as feline, colt-like, feral; even Block's preferred term for the vagina, "pussy," is consistent with the imagery. These are charming stories, R-rated rather than X-rated, and would be perfect for those teenage readers of hers wanting to sample erotic literature for the first time.

In *The Rose and the Beast: Fairy Tales Retold* (HarperCollins), also published in 2000, Block transports nine Perrault fairy tales from 18th-century France to 20th-century California, infusing them with her usual blend of New Age vibes and L.A. glam decadence. Her Sleeping Beauty, for example, pricks herself not with a sewing needle but a hypodermic syringe. Block bypasses the Disneyfied versions of these tales to embrace the spirit of the originals, which, as Robert Darnton has pointed out (in *The Great Cat Massacre*), contained everything "from rape and sodomy to incest and cannibalism." Block's heroines suffer drug addiction, incest, child pornography, and dysfunctional families, as well as the more usual teen problems, but manage to overcome their ogres and evil spells, or at least come to grips with them. (They don't all have happy endings.) Despite the contemporary references, these tales have a timeless quality about them, aided by Block's lyrical, impressionistic prose. There have been many feminist revisions of fairy tales in recent years, but none as exquisite as these.

Echo (HarperCollins), published in August 2001, continues the sadder, more serious vein of *The Hanged Man*. The heroine, Echo, is another anorexic, and the novel is set once again in Los Angeles, but the city so exuberantly described as Shangri-L.A. in the early novels is now regarded as a dangerous, soul-destroying place, less the City of Angels than "a city of vampires and devils": "L.A. is a beautiful prostitute with bougainvillea-blossom-pink lips, hair extensions to her waist, stiletto heels straining the muscles in her calves. Promising opiate dazzle if you pay her enough. And she doesn't just want money."

Echo (named after the chatterbox nymph of Ovid's *Metamorphoses*) tries to find her way through a world that has become sick; anorexia becomes a metaphor for a culture that offers little real nourishment, only quick fixes and cheap thrills. As with Block's other novels, there is an eclectic, thrift-shop mélange of styles and cultural references, everything from old Hollywood glamour and Beat poetry to rock stars and Grimm's fairy tales. And on her quest for fulfillment Echo is surrounded by a host of supernatural figures: angels, vampires, mermaids, psychopomps, fairies, and ghosts. The Holocaust and ancient myths of blood sacrifice haunt these pages. Echo's friends, like many teenagers in America today, hide terrible secrets and don't always survive to adulthood. Happily, Echo does, in a beautiful conclusion that brings to fruition the angel imagery hovering over the novel from its first page.

Block's coming-of-age fables not only prepare girls for the adult world, but for adult fiction as well. As they grow older, her readers are likely to scorn mainstream writers in favor of such fairy godmothers of fiction as Angela Carter, Rikki Ducornet, Karen Elizabeth Gordon, and the aforementioned Carole Maso. For older readers, Block evokes both Richard Brautigan's hippy whimsy and Salinger's Glass family tales. (In one of Block's stories, one teen reads *Franny and Zooey* aloud to another; the subtitle of *Girl Goddess #9* is *Nine Stories*, surely the same homage Lisa Loeb paid when she named her back-up band Nine Stories.) Blooming teens and aging adults alike should find Francesca Lia Block empowering and endearing.

Rain Taxi, Winter 2000–2001; expanded later in 2001 to include *Echo*

Roberto Bolaño

2666. Translated by Natasha Wimmer

Farrar, Straus and Giroux, 2008

The Chilean writer Roberto Bolaño died at the relatively young age of 50 in 2003, but since then a steady stream of English translations has introduced American readers to the Gabriel García Márquez of his time: politically engaged, formally daring, and wildly imaginative. *The Savage Detectives*, a huge novel published last year to wide acclaim, looked like his masterpiece, but now comes a monstrous novel twice as long and daring, and one that should cement his reputation as a world-class novelist.

Knowing that his liver ailment would probably kill him, Bolaño pulled out all the stops for his last novel and threw out the rulebook for conventional fiction. A catch-all for many of his concerns, *2666* is at heart a fascinating meditation on violence and literature, on how writers "turned pain, which is natural, enduring, and eternally triumphant, into personal memory, which is human, brief, and eternally elusive." At its simplest level, *2666* leisurely follows a handful of characters who are drawn, like vultures to a rotting carcass, to the northern Mexican city of Santa Teresa in the 1990s. For "Santa Teresa" read Ciudad Juárez, the killing fields since 1993 for over 400 murdered girls and women — most of them raped, mutilated, then dumped into the nearby desert — with justice for none due to official corruption, incompetence, and macho indifference to women. (*The Daughters of Juárez* by Teresa Rodriguez provides an informative overview of the tragedy.)

In the first of the novel's five semi-independent parts, we're told how three European literary critics became obsessed with the fictions of a mysterious writer named Benno von Archimboldi — think B. Traven or T. Pynchon — and travel to Santa Teresa after hearing the elusive writer may be there researching his next novel. Part 2 concerns an Archimboldi expert currently living in Santa Teresa after a wandering life that took him from Chile to Spain, now watching over his daughter, who seems destined to be another victim in the femicide epidemic. In part 3, a black American reporter travels to Santa Teresa to cover a prizefight and becomes distracted by and embroiled in the ongoing murders. The middle third of the novel, and the longest of its five parts, is a numbing chronological account of individual murders from 1993 to 1997, narrated in police-report fashion, along with digressions on various officials, policemen, lawyers, and reporters involved in the cases. And finally, in part 5, we're given the biography of the shadowy Archimboldi and his real reason for going to Santa Teresa.

Archimboldi never meets his critics, the reporters never solve the crimes, and nothing is resolved at novel's end. (Even the novel's title is left unexplained, though an editor's note at the end offers a clue.) This is not because Bolaño didn't finish it but because he was more interested in conveying the culture of violence, and how writers respond to it, than in telling a tidy story. In one of many self-reflexive comments on his work, he has a character sneer at a reader who prefers short, well-made works of literature, "afraid to take on the great, imperfect, torrential works, books that blaze paths into the unknown." *2666* is just such a work, with a historical reach extending back to the bloody rituals of the Aztecs, to the horrors of the eastern front during World War II, to the Black Panthers of the '60s. Countless fascinating subplots blaze paths into unknown corners of 20th-century culture, and there are enough references to Greek mythology to give the whole work a timeless quality. Uniting the sprawling work are moments and metaphors where sex and violence collide.

While the sex murders of Santa Teresa occupy the center of the novel, the perimeters make for the most satisfying reading. Part 1 is an engaging novella about academic life, and how one's specialty can turn into an obsession; part 5 is a mesmerizing account of how a strange Prussian boy named Hans Reiter became the enigmatic Archimboldi, an author neglected at first but considered worthy of the Nobel Prize after he's rediscovered by the scholar-detectives of part 1. This is a delightfully bookish novel, filled with writers, critics, publishers, copyeditors, reporters — all illustrating how reading and writing help one to make sense of the world. Archimboldi is a grim, humorless character, but we're told "he derived pleasure from writing, a pleasure similar to that of the detective on the heels of the killer"; Bolaño likewise exults in his indefatigable storytelling skills and his mastery of an arsenal of styles, from factual to frivolous, from plain to purple. (In this he is expertly partnered by Natasha Wimmer, whose translation is fluid and faithful.) The novel is probably longer than it needs to be, but there isn't a boring page in it, and I suspect further study would justify every page.

With *2666* Bolaño joins the ambitious overachievers of the 20th-century novel, those like Proust, Musil, Joyce, Gaddis, Pynchon, Fuentes, and Vollmann who push the novel far past its conventional size and scope to encompass an entire era, deploying encyclopedic knowledge and stylistic verve to offer a grand, if sometimes idiosyncratic summation of their culture and the novelist's place in it. Roberto Bolaño has joined the immortals.

Washington Post Book World, 23 November 2008

Greg Boyd

The Nambuli Papers
Leaping Dog Press/BlueRain Films, 2004

Julián Ríos's novel *Larva* (1990) comes with a photo insert and a fold-out map; Neal Pollack's *Never Mind the Pollacks* (2003) has its own soundtrack CD (sold separately); Barbara Hodgson's illustrated novels are tricked out with all sorts of paper novelties. But as a multimedia package, it would be hard to top Greg Boyd's new fiction project, *The Nambuli Papers*, which consists of (a) a 192-page paperback of that title, a mulligan stew of a novel about a French magician named Aristide Nambuli and the people who knew him; (b) a 64-page book of poems and manifestos entitled *It's Like the Eiffel Tower* by Bertrand Hébert; (c) a DVD entitled *The Lost Reel*, 24 minutes of outtakes from a documentary about Hébert and the artistic school he belonged to, the Tide Writers; and (d), enclosing all these, a folded, laminated gameboard for *Don't Hate the Game!*, with game pieces and mindbending rules included in the DVD case. Now *that's* entertainment.

A meditation on the impermanence of art and life, a tease about the difference between truth and fiction, the "novel" (if we can use that to describe the whole package) takes as its starting point the career of a mysterious, Gypsy-born man who transforms himself into Europe's greatest magician at the turn of the 20th century. Instead of a straightforward biography, Boyd has assembled a number of reminiscences about Nambuli, deftly executed period pieces in the form of memoirs, letters, newspaper reports, even a chapter from a pornographic novel based on the magician. The greatest puzzle about this puzzling man is his death: apparently he died in 1911 on the sands near Monte Saint-Michel when a Houdini-like trick went wrong. But there are several reports that he escaped, each differing from the other: he may have survived the sinking of the *Titanic* the following year; he may have wound up with other Gypsies in a concentration camp; he may have made his way to America only to wind up in prison in Buffalo for breaking-and-entering. The unreliability of biography and the tendency to mythologize charismatic figures are explored through Boyd's well-researched world of turn-of-the-century magic and circus acts.

Before his final 1911 feat, the magician gives a young boy "some simple principles concerning the æsthetics of disappearance and oblivion, an æsthetic that years later gets put into practice by a community of visual artists and writers." This refers to the 1950s "Tide Water" movement, a collection of eccentrics who live on the French beach and write on the sand, only to watch their words disappear when the tide comes in. Their work is the focus of *It's Like the Eiffel Tower* and *The Lost Reel* (filmed and treated to resemble a home movie from the 1950s), which are both amusing and sad: amusing because of the rather zany creations the Tide Writers come up with — such as a gestural language called "NoNohNon" — and sad because they accurately capture the lives of thousands and thousands of artists who never achieve any acclaim, whose works are rejected for publication, turned away from galleries, unperformed for lack of funding, and so on. (One of the squares on the gameboard reads: "The rent is due — go back two spaces.") It gets sadder when one realizes that astonishingly creative works like *The Nambuli Papers* will be largely ignored by the reading public and the review media in favor of commercial books not worth the paper they're printed on.

The 192-page book ends with an epistolary exchange between Boyd and psychiatrist Dr. Mitchell Carpenter about an earlier (fictitious) monograph by Boyd on Aristide Nambuli, whom Dr. Carpenter may have treated. This quickly leads to an argument about truth and falsehood, and on art as a lie that in many cases should not be allowed in a healthy society. This argument has been with us since Plato's *Republic*, and Boyd's final riposte to Dr. Carpenter is priceless. ("I've begun to suspect you don't really exist. Perhaps you are just another figment of the imagination of which you are so afraid.") Plato would have banned *The Nambuli Papers* from his ideal state, and that's the highest compliment one can pay to a true artist.

Rain Taxi, Winter 2004–2005

Richard Brautigan

Keith Abbott. *Downstream from "Trout Fishing in America": A Memoir of Richard Brautigan*
Capra Press, 1989

The shock at hearing of Brautigan's suicide in 1984 was followed by disappointment for many in the months that followed as details of his messy, neurotic life emerged in articles in *Vanity Fair* and *Rolling Stone*. A close friend of Brautigan's since 1966, novelist Keith Abbott was as shocked as anyone at his suicide; but annoyed at the media's emphasis on the sordid elements of his life (and at the continued critical neglect of Brautigan's work), Abbott set out to write a memoir that would give a more balanced account of both the life and work.

He has succeeded admirably, producing a very readable account that doesn't shirk the sordid details but instead puts them into the context of Brautigan's complicated personality. This is balanced by giving equal time to Brautigan's generosity and endearing eccentricity, along with a solid appreciation of the craftsmanship beneath Brautigan's seemingly inconsequential prose. Brautigan was at his best — as a person and as a writer — before fame changed his life in the late '60s, making the first half of Abbott's memoir more enjoyable than the second half. Quite wisely, he withholds details of Brautigan's ghastly childhood (abuse at the hands of a series of stepfathers, grinding poverty, abandonment by his mother on several occasions) until the second half, thereby providing a context for Brautigan's growing psychological problems in the late '70s. And since the work is finally the measure of and justification for a writer's life, Abbott saves his literary criticism for the concluding chapter, a close reading of passages from the early works that shows how carefully Brautigan crafted his prose.

Abbott's book makes no pretense to being a definitive biography, but it is clearly the best account of Brautigan's life now available, and given its insight and empathy (even the cover pays homage to Brautigan's early photographic covers), this memoir will remain invaluable for all of us who fell under the spell of Brautigan's inimitable books.

Review of Contemporary Fiction, Fall 1989

□ □ □ □ □ □ □

John F. Barber. *Richard Brautigan: An Annotated Bibliography*

McFarland & Co., 1990.

Richard Brautigan presents a bibliographer with many challenges: he published 20 books in a variety of editions, contributed to a hundred magazines, and has received a wide amount of critical commentary. Much of his early work (and some of the commentary) was published by small presses and/or underground magazines, which are rarely documented or indexed, compounding the bibliographer's task. John F. Barber has met and overcome most of these challenges. At first glance, the book seems unnecessarily subdivided into too many categories, but the exhaustive index simplifies things. Collectors' points are noted for the books, translations listed, and all criticism — from the trivial to the substantial — located and annotated. There are anomalies: Marc Chénetier's 100-page book receives a 200-word annotation, while Terence Malley's 200-page book is broken up into a half-dozen 10-word annotations; the chapter of Keith Abbott's book that appeared in our *Review* (Fall 1988, 117–25) is not listed, though there is an index listing for the *Review* that refers to Abbott's memoir — a ghost reference of sorts. But in spite of these and a few other irregularities — inevitable in this kind of work — Barber has uncovered an enormous amount of material on Brautigan and annotated it intelligently, making this an essential purchase for academic libraries as well as for Brautigan collectors and scholars.

Review of Contemporary Fiction, Summer 1991. Barber's vastly expanded bibliography is now online at http://www.brautigan.net.

Anthony Burgess

1985

Little, Brown, 1978

I'll never forget watching the 1960 movie *The Time Machine* as a child when it first came out. In it, a devastating atomic war occurs in 1966, and I remember wondering at the time if 1966 would indeed resemble that of the movie, a distinct possibility in the early '60s atmosphere of civil defense drills, bomb shelters, and impending missile crises. Successive reruns of the movie brought the year closer, and it was only with the greatest fortitude that I resisted hiding under my school desk, head between knees, all through that menacing year. No sooner did 1966 pass with the world still intact than, looking for something to read, I took down a book from my father's bookshelf: George Orwell's *Nineteen Eighty-Four*. Here we go again, I groaned.

1984. The date is incised on the mind as on a marble tombstone — gray, hard, inevitable. It has significance even for those who have never read the book (or seen the movie), and the novel's watchword "Big Brother is watching you" has been part of revolutionary rhetoric for years now. However, anyone familiar with the novel knows that there is little chance the year 1984 will resemble Orwell's nightmare in anything but minor matters. (Britain did, as Orwell predicted, adopt the metric system and a decimal coinage system.)

Anthony Burgess's new book is a two-part response to Orwell's novel. The first hundred pages or so set out to demonstrate — by way of literary criticism, philosophy, and political commentary — just why 1984 will not be as Orwell envisioned it. The rest of the book is a novel that, correcting Orwell's vision and taking into account recent political trends (especially Arab influences), attempts to bring the future into sharper focus.

The first part begins, by way of review, with a question and answer "catechism" on Orwell's fictitious world of the future (succinct enough to replace Cliffs Notes for those students who have only managed to reach chapter 3 by the time their term paper is due). There follows a variety of short essays and self-interviews on various topics suggested by Orwell's novel. Burgess corrects many assumptions commonly made about the novel — and any teacher who uses *Nineteen Eight-Four* in the classroom would do well to have *1985* by her side in the future — and demonstrates how closely *Nineteen Eighty-Four* resembled post-war England. Burgess challenges most of Orwell's philosophical assumptions with his own view of things, sane if somewhat eclectic (Burgess considers himself a Hebrew-Helleno-Christian humanist oscillating between a Pelagian and Augustinian view of human nature). Though most of what he says makes good sense, he is often idealistic to a fault, as when he insists "It is better to have our streets infested with murderous young hoodlums than to deny individuals freedom of choice." (This is in response to theories of behavior modification for social deviants, the dangers of which he dealt with in *A Clockwork Orange*.) All in all, the first section of the book will be of as much interest to the historian and philosopher as to the literary critic.

Following this promising overture, however, is a somewhat disappointing novel. Bev Jones's longstanding dissatisfaction with 1985 life in England — crippled by countless strikes — crystallizes into action when his wife dies in a fire set by arsonists but unattended because of a fireman's strike, but not before gasping with her dying breath, "Don't let them get away with it." A rather predictable story follows — the usual sane man against an insane system — with too much didacticism to make for good fiction. Burgess's prose is much more imaginative than Orwell's rather colorless journalistic style — though its very drabness contributes to the earlier novel's tone — and the story is not without some interesting moments; but the novel fails to reach the level of the classics of dystopian fiction, including his own *Clockwork Orange*. An epilogue reverts back to nonfiction for some final speculations on the shape of things to come, projections that are depressingly plausible.

One wishes Burgess had integrated more of the nonfiction into the fiction, but the book is useful in that it convincingly warns that one is not secure simply because the "enemy" is far away — in time or space — and that we'd best take the book's final sentence to heart: "We have to be on our guard." But as to whether or not an individual — on or off his guard — will be able to do anything about the future, the fate of Burgess's protagonist suggests . . . well, read it and draw your own conclusions.

Spree, November 1978

Gabrielle Burton

Heartbreak Hotel
Scribner, 1986

The anatomy, encyclopedic novel, Menippean satire — call it what you will — from Rabelais to Pynchon, from *Gulliver's Travels* to *Mulligan Stew*, is a genre that has hitherto attracted no woman writer I know of, with the possible exception of Djuna Barnes in *Ryder*. Gabrielle Burton's stunning first novel, winner of the Maxwell Perkins Prize, is an anatomy of feminism, an encyclopedia of misogyny, a Menippean satire on being female. Like other anatomies it mixes genres, delights in digressions, lists, and parodies, and indulges in bawdy humor of the sort found in such writers as Coover and Sorrentino. (Here, of course, the orientation is female: "a confiscated radio turned to a station that plays beat so primitive, baboons go into estrus"; "She's not of that school that thinks the menstrual products industry is a rags to riches story.") The novel is blackly humorous, exuberantly written, playfully erudite, sharing Stanley Elkin's brand of tough-minded sympathy, breaking your heart with wisecracks.

Although *Heartbreak Hotel* resembles *Mulligan Stew* in many ways, it more closely resembles *Finnegans Wake*. Joyce's book is a nightmare of history, dreamed during one night by a publican who fragments himself and his archetypal family into a variety of selves. In Burton's novel, Margaret Valentine, the curator of a small museum about pioneer women, lies in a coma after a motorcycle accident and dreams of a Museum of the Revolution, 20 blocks long, containing exhibits of every facet of the female experience. Like Joyce's dreamer, Margaret is fragmented in her coma into seven selves, a spectrum of female archetypes ranging from sensuous belly dancer to butch cop, each with a name derived from hers (Meg, Maggie, Gretchen, etc.). In *Finnegans Wake*, HCE's daughter Issy expands into a mirror self, the seven rainbow girls, and the 28 "maggies," and Burton likewise works with mirror images, shifting identities, and dissociated selves. In a surreal Faustian scene, a Mephistopheles tells one of Margaret's selves (who has just encountered a variety of faces in her mirror, from the monstrous to the resplendent), "You have a whole family of selves, Maggie, not one self acting many different ways. . . . You must find out who your family of selves are." In her coma, Margaret works through a process of disintegration and reintegration in time-honored psychomythological fashion, here loosely structured on the Catholic Mass, and emerges the next morning from her struggle in triumph.

The novel itself is the real Museum of the Revolution. Burton's descriptions of such exhibits as the Waiting Room, "The Menstrual Show" (performed in red-face), and the Hall of Fashion are as hilarious as they are infuriating. Like the Mass, the novel contains secular litanies, lessons, sermons, tropes, confessions, hymns, communions — an exhaustive inventory of all the pains, joys, and frustrations of being a woman in a male-dominated world. Destined to become a feminist classic, *Heartbreak Hotel* is an extraordinary novel that needs no qualifying adjective: call it a classic, and read it at your earliest opportunity.

Review of Contemporary Fiction, Summer 1987

Michel Butor

Frontiers. Translated by Elinor S. Miller with Warren C. Miller
Summa Publications, 1989

Michel Butor's oeuvre is so huge and various — embracing everything from novels to poetry to wildly experimental multimedia works — that a new reader hardly knows where to begin. That reader can begin with *Frontiers*, an attractive collection of materials by and about this prolific French writer. An informative introduction by the translator gives an overview of Butor's life and work (in a refreshingly unacademic style), which is followed by a 40-page interview with him by Christian Jacomino. This is followed in turn by a dozen short texts by Butor — poems, prose poems, essays, fantasies — ending with an extensive bibliography of primary and secondary materials. The English translations section of this bibliography indicates that since the '60s — when several of his books were done here — very little of Butor has been translated. It is to be hoped that *Frontiers* will revive interest in Butor's work and inspire further translations.

Review of Contemporary Fiction, Spring 1991

□ □ □ □ □ □ □

Improvisations on Butor: Transformations of Writing.
Edited by Lois Oppenheim. Translated by Elinor S. Miller
University Press of Florida, 1996

During the 1980s the French novelist Michel Butor published three books of literary criticism called *Improvisations*, each one focused on a particular writer (Flaubert, Michaux, Rimbaud); in this fourth volume in the series he turns his attention to his own large body of writings. Based on a series of lectures he gave at the University of Geneva in 1991 before retiring, it functions as his intellectual autobiography. He has had quite a life: enduring World War II, the postwar excitement of French intellectual life, the development of the *nouveau roman* in the 1950s (of which Butor is a leading exemplar), the multimedia experiments encouraged by the 1960s, travels all across the world. But as the subtitle indicates, it is also a meditation on the way writing has changed in his lifetime because of new technologies, transcultural influences, and the example of other media. (Butor has worked extensively with musicians and visual artists.) It's as much a book of cultural studies as a study of his own writings, and for that reason it should appeal to a wider audience than Butor specialists. The translation is very supple, maintaining the conversational tone of the original lectures.

Review of Contemporary Fiction, Summer 1996

Mary Butts

A Sacred Quest: The Life and Times of Mary Butts.
Edited by Christopher Wagstaff
McPherson & Company, 1995

All writers should be so lucky as to have a publisher like Bruce McPherson: after discovering the work of this interesting British writer (1890–1937), he began restoring her work to print with re-edited, definitive editions, with prefaces or afterwords by perceptive writers (John Ashbery, Paul West), and has now published this collection of essays on her work. (Another of Butts's books, *Ashe of Rings and Other Writings*, should be out later this year, and a biography is underway, which McPherson will likewise publish.)

A *Sacred Quest* is an excellent introduction to her work as well as an indispensable tool for future criticism. There are reminiscences from contemporaries of her like Bryher, Glenway Wescott, Virgil Thomson, and Quentin Bell, reprints of the few essays that have been written about her, new essays by a half-dozen others, various pieces by Butts herself (including an interview), a chronology of her life, and a lengthy checklist of all of Butts's writings and reviews of her work. In addition, a number of photographs of Butts are reproduced throughout the book.

Mary Butts is one of a number of fascinating women writers from the period between the wars (Djuna Barnes, Olive Moore, Mina Loy) who underwent a period of neglect before being rediscovered — usually by small presses like McPherson. This is independent publishing at its best.

Review of Contemporary Fiction, Spring 1996

□ □ □ □ □ □ □

Nathalie Blondel. *Mary Butts: Scenes from the Life*
McPherson & Company, 1998

The period between the two world wars produced a number of intriguing British and American women writers who never achieved the acclaim they deserved. Djuna Barnes eventually won a measure of posthumous fame, but too few readers today know about Olive Moore, Emily Holmes Coleman, Mina Loy, or Anna Kavan, all of whom published brilliant novels that rival those of their male contemporaries. These were unconventional, "difficult" women:

They wrote about independence and madness, took drugs or indulged in other illicit behavior, and thumbed their noses at convention, both literary and domestic. Mary Butts could be the poster girl for this lost generation of vixens.

Don't be surprised if you haven't heard of her. Despite McPherson and Company's valiant reprint series — they've reissued all her books over the last seven years, and plan to bring out previously unpublished work — she is little more than a name even to most well-read people, her books not easy to find. (Neither of Denver's two best literary bookstores has a single title of hers.) A recent critic described her, succinctly if somewhat slightingly, as "a devoted opium smoker with tangled red hair, [who] wrote regional novels of the English West Country with mystic overtones." But there's more to her than that. In the first biography to be written about Butts, Nathalie Blondel (a professor at the University of the West of England) makes a strong case for Butts's importance, not only to the modernist movement earlier this century but to many of today's feminist and environmental concerns. She achieves this by underscoring Butts's utter devotion to writing all her life, even when she was carrying on more like a rock star than a serious artist. Drugs, lesbianism, alcohol, witchcraft — she did it all, but always in service of her craft.

Mary Butts was born in 1890 into an aristocratic family living in Dorset, a charmed existence that was the subject of her posthumously published memoir (and best-known book), *The Crystal Cabinet*. She loved country life, but the charm wore off when her father died when she was 14. From that time on she had an acrimonious relationship with her mother, who never understood her eccentric daughter. Butts moved to London during World War I and worked for an organization that supported conscientious objectors, one of whom, future publisher John Rodker, became her first husband. By that time she was already at work on her first novel, *Ashe of Rings*, though it wouldn't be published until 1925. (It has just been reissued by McPherson in conjunction with this biography, with a preface by Blondel.) Together, Butts and Rodker became part of the Bloomsbury world — Wyndham Lewis painted her portrait, Pound and Eliot became her friends, as did eventually everybody who was anybody during that era — and her stories began appearing in the best little magazines. Her first book of stories appeared in 1923, her first novel in 1925, and a second novel in 1928. The critics were impressed, though a bit baffled by her unusual style.

But her personal life was less orderly. She and Rodker began drifting apart, but not before having a daughter, in whom Butts took little interest. She began experimenting with drugs and remained an addict all her life. Her strong interest in the occult led her to study magic under Aleister Crowley for a disastrous summer, and she was a firm believer in astral journeys, teleplasm, the fourth dimension, and other nonrational beliefs. (She eventually reverted to the Anglo-Catholicism of her childhood.) Despite her aristocratic background, she was frequently poor. Her dissipated lifestyle took a turn for the better when she moved to Cornwall in 1930; though she was saddled with a new but alcoholic husband, the wild Cornish seacoast and its legendary associations inspired a burst of creativity. More novels tumbled forth (including two set in ancient times: *The Macedonian* and *Scenes from the Life of Cleopatra*), as did a large number of essays, stories, and book reviews. She was finishing her autobiography when she died in 1937 at the relatively young age of 46.

Blondel relates all this in great, sometimes overwhelming detail, which is perhaps excusable in a first biography: one never knows what trivia may be of use to future scholars. She relies heavily on Butts's diaries and accounts by her contemporaries, so that much of her story is told by the actual participants. Blondel is very sympathetic to Butts but not to the point of overlooking her many shortcomings (especially her neglect of her daughter). Stella Bowen, Ford Madox Ford's lover, once described Butts as inhabiting a "cloud-cuckoo land of her own," a view Blondel occasionally agrees with, but there is no condescension from her toward Butts's varied beliefs. Her respect for Butts as a writer dominates all, a refreshing attitude at a time when many biographers seem bent on humiliating their subjects. Anyone interested in the literary life of the 1920s will be fascinated by this book. It probably won't result in a rewriting of modernism, but Mary Butts can no longer be dismissed in a footnote after this.

Washington Post Book World, 12 July 1998

□ □ □ □ □ □ □

Mary Butts. *Ashe of Rings and Other Writings*

McPherson & Co., 1998

It's useful to remember that the period of high modernism, for all its avant-garde progressivism, was also a period of occultism. Joyce, Pound, and Eliot took a keen interest in everything from the more metaphysical aspects of mythology to magic rituals, séances, mysticism, ghosts, black masses, old heresies, and spiritualism. Aleister Crowley and Montague Summers added black magic and witchcraft to literary culture, while Yeats and Conan Doyle talked of fairies. One of the finest expressions of all this is Mary Butts's forgotten 1925 novel *Ashe of Rings*, which has now been reprinted (along with some shorter writings) in a handsome volume by McPherson & Company, which is largely responsible for her rediscovery in recent years.

Ashe of Rings is set mostly during World War I, and mostly at Rings, a manor house set among some prehistoric earthwork in south Dorset. A place of Druid ceremonies, Arthurian enchantment, and possible witchcraft, it is a portal to the timeless world of myth and magic for the ancient Ashe family. The last of the line is Vanna Elizabeth Ashe, a young woman living in London (after being disinherited by her mother) and caught up in a messy romantic triangle. Like a mythic hero, Vanna endures exile and hardship before returning to her home and, after triumphing in a test of courage, reclaims her inheritance.

Butts later described the novel as "a War-fairy-tale" and skillfully blends elements of fantasy with realistic depictions of the deprivations and shattered nerves of wartime London. After observing, "I think we are living in an enchantment," one character explains: "I mean that we are spectators of a situation which is the mask for another situation, that existed perhaps in some remote age, or in a world that is outside time." Like Joyce's *Ulysses* (written at the same time), *Ashe of Rings* is a modern story with a mythic subtext, perhaps not a specific one as in Joyce's case, but continuously evoking Greek myth and philosophy. Recurring reference is made to *sophrosyne*, the concept of "temperance" discussed in Plato's *Charmides*; in a time of tension and upheaval — like World War I or millennial America today — this quality takes on all the allure of the Holy Grail.

Ashe of Rings is written in high modernist style: as compressed as *The Waste Land*, as allusive as *Ulysses*, and as imagistic as *The Cantos* or *Nightwood*. Like Barnes, Butts has a relish for outlandish language; one character is described as "a black rod tied at the top with a bunch of pale flames," and Butts isn't afraid to write sentences like: "Meanwhile there was the child, Van, before whom the house laid down its subtle spears. Before she could walk, the arrows of the sun, the arrows of the moon and rain, were ribbons to keep her upright." Though clarity is sometimes sacrificed for poetic compression, sound sometimes favored over sense, Butts is a daring stylist and a joy to read. *Ashe of Rings* is recommended especially to fans of the more recherché modernists such as Barnes, Ronald Firbank, and Baron Corvo.

The second half of the book is made up of shorter writings. "Imaginary Letters" is an epistolary novella in which an Englishwoman living in Paris writes unsent letters to the mother of a young Russian émigré whom she loves, a gay scamp who runs after sailors, steals money from her, and causes no end of exasperation. (A Russian émigré also figures in *Ashe of Rings* and some of Butts's other works; apparently she had a weakness for this type.) "Imaginary Letters" progresses from a fag hag's lament to a larger consideration of the post-Wilde generation of homosexuals: "the choicest men of our time are turned that way, and the women like them." It's an interesting work because it both captures the vagaries of unrequited love and indicates the exotic allure

Russians had for the English at that time.

The three remaining pieces are longish essays. "Warning to Hikers" addresses the fad for hiking prevalent in England in the 1920s and '30s. While not denying the deprivation felt by people raised in cities, Butts derides their attempts to "get back to nature" with weekend trips that are not much different from trips "to an opera or a picture gallery, with the extra advantages of a first-class nursing home." When nature is seen as a luxury item (she argues), a commodity, it attracts developers who are as indifferent to nature as they are to art — in fact, consider both expendable — with results that are even more apparent to us today than they were to prescient Mary Butts. Written with a gifted novelist's power of description, "Warning to Hikers" is a wonderful essay.

I can't say the same for "Traps for Unbelievers," an erudite but muddled meditation on the perceived lack of religious belief in England in the 1930s. Better is the final essay, "Ghosties Ghoulies," an informed survey of British supernatural fiction. All three essays illuminate aspects of *Ashe of Rings*, and it is useful to have these rare items bound together in the same book. With this volume, all of Mary Butts's principal works are now in print, and there's no excuse for serious readers — modernists and feminists in particular — to remain unaware of this fascinating writer.

American Book Review, May/June 1999

Roberto Calasso

The Ruin of Kasch. Translated by William Weaver and Stephen Sartarelli
Harvard University Press, 1994

Ten years ago I attended a lecture by Italian literary theorist and novelist Umberto Eco that began with a simple thesis that grew progressively more complicated as he took us on a whirlwind tour of his encyclopedic mind. Just when the argument was off in some Ultima Thule of a subdigression, seemingly leagues away from his starting point, Eco suddenly, like a magician tapping on a knot, pulled his line of reasoning free and all became clear. His countryman Roberto Calasso performs a similar feat in his new book, an intellectual tour de force that begins and ends with a consideration of Talleyrand's place in European intellectual history but includes just about everything imaginable in between.

Calasso's previous book in English translation, last year's *Marriage of Cadmus and Harmony*, was a hybrid of Greek mythology and cultural analysis. His new book (though written earlier than *The Marriage*) is a similar hybrid of history, economics, anthropology, theology, metaphysics, and philosophy, with digressions into everything from Vedic mythology to literary criticism. It doesn't resemble a straightforward study in any of those fields; instead, Calasso strings together hundreds of anecdotes and quotations (cited in 25 pages of notes at the end) along with his own annotations and observations. The result resembles such awesome compendia as Frazer's *Golden Bough*, Burton's *Anatomy of Melancholy*, and (closer to our own time) Norman O. Brown's *Love's Body* or Robert K. Merton's *On the Shoulders of Giants*.

The attraction of such books is the cornucopia of intellectual delights offered by their omnivorous authors. In *The Ruin of Kasch* one finds material from the Rig Veda and Upanishads, through Sade, Balzac, Melville, Marx, Frazer (and Wittgenstein on Frazer), up to Kafka and Simone Weil. (When was the last time you read a book that discussed Porphyry's *De Abstinentia* and cited the *Laws of Manu* on the same page?) There are discussions of fascinating but little-known figures like Max Stirner (a theoretician of anarchy) and Louis-Sébastien Mercier (who in 1770 described what Paris might be like in 2440). Curious anecdotes and asides abound. Calasso quotes and meets the same challenge that Choderlos de Laclos set himself in *Les Liaisons dangereuses*: "arousing interest without falling back on any novelistic devices."

The challenge for the reader is to follow their arguments through ever-widening circles of digression. Calasso is concerned with civilization's movement from ancient modes of thinking to modern, specifically with that period when what literary critics call the meta-narrative of Western culture broke down. Up until just before the French Revolution, civilization was still functioning according to ancient patterns: kingship, a god-centered universe, traditional notions of law and sacrifice, and so on. After the French Revolution, everything was questioned, and ritual degenerated into ceremony, legitimacy lost legitimacy, and convention lost force. That decisive break is Calasso's concern, along with the chief factors that led up to it and the attempts by 19th-century writers and philosophers to create a new meta-narrative for the future. (Marx and Engels came up with one such narrative, a poorly contrived scenario that Calasso discusses at some length, and whose concluding chapter still lay in the future when he published the Italian version of this book in 1983.)

Calasso found a parable of Western civilization's transition from the ancient to the modern in the story of the fall of Kasch, a legendary African kingdom. Taken from volume four of Leo Frobenius's *Atlantis*, it is a marvelous, *Arabian Nights*-like tale of a storyteller who disrupts the kingdom's traditional rituals and observances and inadvertently sows the seeds of destruction. Among those rituals was human sacrifice.

Obvious to all but fundamentalists, we cannot return to ancient ways, but modern ways have yet to provide a meaningful structure to our lives, or so Calasso seems to suggest. I use "seems" because *The Ruin of Kasch*, for all its polymathic brilliance, offers not a coherent argument but something more like a series of lecture notes for a year-long course, notes that would be expanded and contextualized in delivery. Here you have to act as your own professor, dredge up everything you remember from a traditional liberal-arts education (and thank your stars it was a traditional one, not a current PC one, which won't help you with a book like this), and put the pieces together as best you can. Though clearly a work of nonfiction, it perhaps needs to be read as though it were a demanding but brilliant encyclopedic novel, something along the lines of Gaddis's *Recognitions* or Coover's *Public Burning* — in other words, something resembling the most intriguing and enlightening books of our time.

Washington Post Book World, 25 December 1994

Julieta Campos

She Has Reddish Hair and Her Name Is Sabina.
Translated by Leland H. Chambers
University of Georgia Press, 1993

Hispanicists have known and written about Mexican novelist and critic Julieta Campos for years, but the lack of English translations of her work has prevented her from becoming more widely known. That should change now that two of her novels have been issued here: *The Fear of Losing Eurydice*, published a few months ago by Dalkey Archive, and *She Has Reddish Hair and Her Name Is Sabina*, both translated by Leland H. Chambers. Originally published in 1974 and the recipient of the coveted Villaurrutia Award, *Sabina* is, like *Eurydice*, a metafictional meditation on writing. As such, it is one of the purest examples of the genre: almost nothing "happens" in any narrative sense; instead the novel is a single, 135-page paragraph detailing the narrator's thoughts on trying to write a novel. But this narrator may only be a character in the mind of another writer, who in turn is a creation by Campos herself. Even the first narrator — the Sabina of the title — imagines narrators in the novel she contemplates, so that the concept of narrator here begins to resemble one of those Russian nesting dolls.

As Chambers points out in his introduction, Campos is closer aligned with France's *nouveau romanciers* than with Latin America's Booming magic realists. This can be seen in her interest in literary theory, her Duras-like languid lyricism, and her Butor-like use of intertextuality. But *Sabina* also exemplifies the *écriture féminine* celebrated by such theorists as Hèléne Cixous and Luce Irigaray, and thus should figure prominently in any future studies of women's experimental fiction.

Review of Contemporary Fiction, Summer 1993

□ □ □ □ □ □ □

Celina or the Cats. Translated by Leland H. Chambers
Latin American Literary Review Press, 1995

This is the third of Cuban-born Mexican writer Julieta Campos's books to be translated into English, after *The Fear of Losing Eurydice* and *She Has Reddish Hair and Her Name is Sabina* (both 1993, and likewise translated by Leland H. Chambers). Those two novels are experimental, metafictional works dating from the 1970s; *Celina or the Cats* is a collection of five stories dating from the 1960s, and thus may be a less daunting introduction to this wonderful writer.

The book's title, and the author's introductory essay on the place of cats in mythology and symbolism, is somewhat misleading, for cats figure only in the title story. "Cats are those soft, rippling, cruel, delicate beings, those solitary, nocturnal, always unpredictable beings that inject our everyday world with the sphere of the unknown," Campos writes in her introduction. The other four stories, then, could be said to focus on catlike humans whose feline sense of "the sphere of the unknown" makes their life in the everyday world problematic. It is appropriate that one of these stories, "All the Roses," first appeared in *Anaïs*, a journal devoted to publishing fiction in the tradition of Anaïs Nin, for that's the writer most readers will be reminded of, along with something of the languid lyricism of early Marguerite Duras. (Campos was educated in France and studied the *nouveaux romanciers*.) The final two stories, "The House" and "The City," evoke her birthplace, Havana, by way of a fragmented treatment of memory and the passage of time.

With three of Campos's four books of fiction now available in English, it is high time that North American readers acquaint themselves with Mexico's most innovative female writer.

Review of Contemporary Fiction, Summer 1996

Mary Caponegro

The Star Café & Other Stories
Scribner's, 1990

Whether by accident or design, most short-story collections display a consistency of tone, style and worldview. Characters and incidents change from story to story, but the writer's voice unifies classic collections and most young writers strive to achieve a similarly recognizable style. But there are others who prefer to play the ventriloquist, deploying a variety of voices and styles so that their collections more closely resemble an anthology by various hands. This is more daring commercially and aesthetically; commercially, because the writer refrains from creating a recognizable and marketable style, and aesthetically, because the writer must start from square one with each story, like a musician learning to play a new instrument for every composition. Last year's *Girl with Curious Hair* by David Foster Wallace was one such collection, and Mary Caponegro's first collection of short fiction is another.

Short "fiction" is more apt than short "stories" because Caponegro avoids the well-trod path of the well-made story for the yellow-brick road of Borgesian *ficciones*. For example, the first of her four fictions, "Tales From the Next Village," reads like a translation of an 18th-century collection of Chinese folk tales, parables of the dangers inherent in the quest for spiritual and/or erotic illumination. Some of these are cautionary tales exemplifying pronouncements from the *I Ching*, and all have the porcelain beauty of a Ming vase. The title story, like the rest of the stories in *The Star Café*, has a contemporary setting but a similar dreamy exoticism: A woman preparing for sleep goes downstairs to investigate a strange sound, enters the small café from which the sound originates, and enters into a series of erotic interludes with the café owner. The story moves effortlessly from realism into surrealism, myth, dream and sexuality.

"Materia Prima" also moves from realism to allegory — here the myth of the phoenix filtered through Jungian interpretations of alchemical symbolism — to chart a young woman's attempt to defend her memories and selfhood against her dismissive parents. This fiction is formally the most daring: It alternates between slightly inflated narrative and naive transcriptions of the girl's earliest memories, interrupted by quotations from ornithology textbooks on flight and bird songs. The concluding 13 pages of this long story are presented in play form as the mother witnesses the girl's phoenixlike annihilation and rebirth. The conclusion is reminiscent of the second part of Goethe's

Faust: pure symbol and myth, all realism left far behind as the girl discovers the powers of the imagination and the continuity of past, present, and future.

The final and longest story, the novella-length "Sebastian," is another psychodrama where the quotidian opens a portal onto eternity. The voice Caponegro assumes here is that of the title character, an Englishman living in America and engaged to an engaging artist named Sarah. The story recalls Nicholson Baker's novels in that the most mundane incident can lead, by way of brilliant chains of association, to an encyclopedic range of subjects. Faced with a "back in ten" sign at a gas station, Sebastian progresses during the next few hours through a maze of incidents and memories, an increasingly complicated and bizarre series of narrative events and Aristotelian meditations on difference: between England and America, classic and modern art, formal and vernacular language, and (as always in this book) between men and women and the "intricate disturbing eros" that unites them. The mastery with which Caponegro imposes one fugue-like meditation atop another — with images from one illuminating another, all grounded on a formal Stations of the Cross progression and enlivened with Sarah's wit — is truly impressive.

As in the other stories, the enfolding complications and increasing irrealism can be difficult to follow; Caponegro takes a great number of risks and asks much of her readers. But this reader would have it no other way and can report that *The Star Café* brilliantly fulfills the writing task Sebastian contemplates: "In any event, it will, it would, be impressive. Something talked about, written about; something not everyone could read. Yet not impenetrable."

Washington Post Book World, 23 August 1990 — the first review assignment I received from Michael Dirda, to whom I am eternally grateful for my long career as a freelance reviewer for the *Post*.

□ □ □ □ □ □ □

Five Doubts

Marsilio Publishers, 1998

Italy has elicited a variety of responses from British and American writers over the centuries. From the Elizabethan era to the Gothic, it was seen as a cesspool of depravity, of hot tempers and perverted Catholicism. For the Victorians, it offered an aesthetic retreat from the rigid morals of the north. Most of the modernists were involved with Italy somehow: Joyce and Pound lived there for long periods, Rolfe and Firbank died there, and Forster and Lawrence set novels there. And even the postmodernists are drawn to it: both Gaddis's *Recognitions* and Theroux's *Darconville's Cat* conclude in Italy, as though their encyclopedic quests would be incomplete without a return to the source of so many of Western civilization's artistic and religious concepts. But the most bizarre literary response has to be this fascinating new book of short fictions by Mary Caponegro.

In *Five Doubts* Caponegro takes five aspects of Italian culture as subjects for five experimental fictions. The first, "Il Libro dell' Arte," is a kind of fictionalization of Cennino Cennini's 15th-century book of the same title, a handbook of artistic techniques. Adapting the style and structure of the original, Caponegro retools it as an account of a visit to a fledgling painter's chaotic farmhouse workshop. An unnamed visitor (apparently a famous painter) is shown around the farmhouse by a young woman named Giovanna, who assists Lorenzo, an aspiring apprentice to Cennini. As Giovanna explains their activities — many taken straight from Cennini's book — she also confesses to her attempts to seduce Lorenzo, who is too nervous about failing his master to respond to the engaging Italian wench. (In his handbook, Cennini expressly warns artists to stay away from women during their apprenticeship.) The earthy, organic nature of painting in those days is palpably conveyed by rich details, and Giovanna's attempts to seduce Lorenzo away from his work are comical. The art of painting and the art of seduction are shown to have much in common.

Two other fictions travel even further back in Italian history. In "The Spectacle," an ancient mosaic — reproduced in color, as are four other illustrations in this book — is the inspiration for an account of a day at a bloody Roman circus, where animals were paraded and often slaughtered for the emperor's amusement. "The Spectacle" is broken into 15 brief "acts," many narrated by the animals themselves. Even stranger is "An Etruscan Catechism," which is exactly that: questions pious Etruscans might ask about their mysterious religion, answered by a well-informed haruspex (a soothsayer who examined entrails). Apparently based on *The Books of Tages*, the catechism lays the superstitious foundation of so much of Italian culture, from Roman mythology and exotic Catholicism to such malevolent folklorisms as blood curses and the evil eye. It is a mesmerizing performance.

Contemporary Italy is the setting for "Tombola," which is based (according to an author's note) on a Neapolitan game of that name, with interpolations from the Italian magazines *Panorama* and *L'Expresso*. A boy begins thinking about what he wants for Christmas, and over the course of 33 brief sections makes observations about his neighbors, his mother's scolding, his religious beliefs, and his sexual yearnings. These alternate with quotes from the magazines on the Mafia, the Church, and the role of women in modern Italy. The kaleidoscopic structure works well to convey the interconnected, often contradictory elements of Italian culture.

The final section, "Doubt Uncertainty Possibility Desire," extends Italian culture to embrace worldwide developments in medical technology. It is a collage made up of extracts from Leonardo da Vinci's notebooks alongside quotations from recent books on cancer, AIDS, and virtual reality. Leonardo's polymathic interests are thereby echoed by modern investigations into virology and the politics of medical research. (Leonardo often struggled with the dilemma of following his own interests or doing work that would pay, like many a medical researcher today.) Threading his way through these texts is the voice of Salai, Leonardo's apprentice, who teases and taunts his obsessive master, and which recalls the master/apprentice relationship of the first fiction in *Five Doubts*.

These are fictions unlike any I've ever read. As in her first collection of fiction, *The Star Café*, Caponegro creates a new voice and new form for every new fictional experiment. In its daring and originality — not to mention its iconoclastic reading of Italian culture — *Five Doubts* is a remarkable achievement.

American Book Review, July/August 1999. I wanted to publish this book when Mary submitted it to Dalkey Archive in early 1996, but the boss adamantly rejected it: "I will not publish this book," he declaimed in a memo. Upon publication two years later, it was very favorably reviewed by Robert L. McLaughlin in Dalkey's journal, the *Review of Contemporary Fiction*.

Tom Carson

Daisy Buchanan's Daughter
Paycock Press, 2011

You're unlikely to find a wittier, more ingenious, more compulsively readable novel this year than Tom Carson's latest, a satiric revue of the dearly departed American Century starring an 86-year-old woman who saw it all. The daughter of that charmer whose "voice is full of money," as gold-hatted Gatsby said of Daisy, Pamela Buchanan tells what happened after the last mournful pages of *The Great Gatsby*: how her mother became a morphine addict and died in Belgium in her (and the century's) '30s; her boarding-school days under the guardianship of kindly Nick Carraway (who is contemplating writing a novel about his late West Egg neighbor); and then her Zelig-like participation in some defining moments in the 20th century: Broadway theater life in the late '40s, the home front and Europe during World War II — she was on Omaha beach on D-Day, and at Dachau the day it was liberated in 1945 — Hollywood in the late '40s and early '50s as it transitioned from the big screen to the little home version; Camelot as seen from west Africa in the early '60s as an ambassador's wife (in which capacity Pamela meets an uncharming Robert F. Kennedy and hears of the assassination of his brother); and then Washington, D.C., for the last half of her life: comforting Lyndon Johnson during the final days of his presidency, sparring with Norman Mailer before the March on the Pentagon in 1967, and shaking her increasingly gray head at what follows in "Potusville" until her 86th birthday on June 6, 2006, the long day on which this novel takes place.

Logging on to her Website at 6:22 that morning, Pamela begins posting a daisy-chain of blogs, narrating the story of her life with a freedom her previous editors never would have allowed. (She became a journalist in the early '40s, which is how she got to see so much, and later wrote three books.) That liberated voice, more than the story itself, is what makes *Daisy Buchanan's Daughter* such a joy to read. "I do feel a mad glee at yoicksing on without a second look" she exults as she rides madly off in all directions in a maximalist style where no noun lacks an adjective, no pun is too low, and no allusion too far-fetched. Addressing many of her blogs to her teenage great-granddaughter Panama, she describes the sexual freedom of the war years:

> In mimsied retrospect, Panama, 1942's carnal throb leaves the Sixties looking like amateur hour. In ways we octogenarians have kept tenderly veiled from our gen-

> eration's Brokawing hymnalists, the home-front war was our Woodstock: an orgiastic engine we gave ourselves over to, from U.S. Steel blasting smokestack lightning to Detroit's purple haze and Eleanor Roosevelt Rigby fluting away. By the time we got to D-Day, we were golden. Fulfilling a national fantasy we hadn't known was one until Yamomoto's planes turned Mamala Bay into blue acid, we were all part of the same galvanizing, mud-bathed movie.

And that's a *typical* passage, not a rare swatch of purple prose. Incapable of being boring, Pamela is as witty as Wilde and Whedon, as punny as Joyce and Pynchon (as in the fastidiously named "Dottie I. Crozdetti"). Pam's first editor "warned me only against excessive whimsy" when concocting false names for her subjects — "No Oglesby in a brassiere factory, no dentist from Tuscaloosa" — but with no Strunk & Whitewashing editor to rein her in, the old gal revels in the whimsical excesses of the American lexicon as she dramatizes the successes and failures of the American Century.

It's not all pun and games. At the dead center of the novel (and almost at the dead center of the century: history isn't as well organized as art) is Pam's grim description of the concentration camp at Dachau, and her account of how the news of Kennedy's assassination struck her little diplomatic community is superb. Her dramatization of LBJ's despair in 1968 as the country (and his career) fell apart is so moving that one can almost forgive the big lunk for prolonging the Vietnam War. Almost. And her seething anger at the current administration in 2006 drives her to commit suicide as soon as she receives the congratulatory phone call she expects on her birthday. She has a pistol in her lap as she races to blog as much of her story as she can before the phone rings, and you know what Chekhov said about a pistol in the first act. But you'll never guess how Carson handles that.

Better known for his savvy essays on media than for his too-few novels — his last, *Gilligan's Wake* (2003), contains a chapter called "Sail Away" that serves as a Rheingoldy prelude to this longer novel — Tom Carson works that sweet spot where highly literary prose reads like a gossip column. If *The Great Gatsby* didn't quite reach the green of the Great American Novel — it's too short for such a big country — *Daisy Buchanan's Daughter* lands within putting distance of the grand old flagpole.

Washington Post, 27 July 2011

Cydney Chadwick

Oeuvres and *Persistent Disturbances*
Texture Press, 1995

Chadwick is the editor of *Avec*, one of the more consistently interesting journals of creative writing. In these two chapbooks, Chadwick again demonstrates (as she did in *Enemy Clothing*) she's as good a writer of short fiction as she is an editor. *Oeuvres* is a story about a woman who links herself with a man obsessed by the mysterious Arthur Cravan (1887–1918?), Dadaist poet, boxer, and husband of the more talented Mina Loy. Against her better judgment, the narrator moves in with the Cravan wannabe. Chadwick's affectless prose perfectly captures the despair of a lonely woman who links herself to a man merely because his life seems more interesting than hers, even if the man neglects her.

Persistent Disturbances consists of seven brief stories, each a study in anomie: a recital of a couple's tense visit to their parents, a hair-raising encounter between a woman and a friend of her lover's at the London Zoo, an increasingly involuted account of a violin-and-piano recital, mostly written in the present tense. They are not epiphanic, like most stories, but instead convey a history of loneliness or depression — hence the title. What is most striking about Chadwick's stories is their silence: there is no dialogue in any of them, and the effect is like watching a black-and-white movie with the sound off. Many of Chadwick's characters are bookish types, who assuage their anomie with a book because "print is such a comfort, even when what is written is not pleasant, not pretty." Chadwick's chapbooks offer a similar dour comfort.

Review of Contemporary Fiction, Summer 1996

John Colapinto

About the Author
HarperCollins, 2001

There are two kinds of budding writers: those who sit around in bars and coffeehouses talking about writing, and those who stay at home and actually write something. Both types will do almost anything to get published.

About the Author, John Colapinto's first foray into fiction after the nonfiction *As Nature Made Him*, introduces us to both types, living together in a crummy apartment in upper Manhattan in the late 1990s. Cal Cunningham, a good-looking guy filled with dreams of the literary life, works in a bookstore by day and works the bars at night, picking up women who are charmed by his literary talk. The next day Cal recounts his amorous adventures to Stewart Church, a withdrawn law student, who spends most of his time in his room typing — briefs and legal essays, Cal assumes.

One day Stewart is killed in an accident, and when Cal goes into his room, he learns that Stewart has actually written a novel based on Cal's life. Cal hasn't been able to write a word in years but yearns so badly to be a published author that he types his name on the title page, submits it to an agent and sees the book accepted for publication for more money than he ever dreamed. After bathing in the literary limelight for a season, he moves to the country, marries, and settles into his new life. Then he learns that someone knows his secret. The rest of the novel concerns his attempts to fend off the blackmailer, with Cal predictably enmeshing himself in a spider web of lies, guilt, and the temptation of murder.

What distinguishes *About the Author* from thousands of other novels and movies about blackmail is its literary setting. Cal's — that is, Stewart's — novel is described by his agent, Blackie Yaeger (a paper-thinly disguised Andrew Wylie), as "a fin de siecle *Bright Lights, Big City*, with a Gen X twist and some post-po-mo juju thrown in for good measure." The novel is sold to Hollywood before it's even published, and Colapinto describes the typical media frenzy that attends the latest thing in publishing. A sales rep at his publisher's is ecstatic: "'I can't remember anything like it — except for maybe our book on the Broccoli Diet, and of course *Having a Chat with the Lord*.' He shook his head in disbelief, then added in an amazed whisper, 'And it's not even on her club.'"

Cal is ambivalent about what he's done: He knows he did wrong but rationalizes that it was his life, after all, that Stewart had novelized, his tales of skirt-chasing. Stewart was merely a secretary, a ghostwriter. But Stewart haunts him nonetheless as an example of a real writer, and Cal's envy eats away at him. It's not until the end of the novel that Cal actually writes something, which turns out to be . . . well, I'd better not say.

Despite the literary trappings, *About the Author* is off-the-rack fiction, not haute couture literature. That said, it's a clever, engaging read, a real page-turner (which more serious metafiction usually isn't). For those on the outside, Colapinto accurately describes the inside workings of publishing, and while he notes the commodification of fiction, he doesn't seem to be too upset about it. (Indeed, the publicity materials accompanying the galleys note that the novel garnered a huge advance and has already been sold to Hollywood.) Colapinto is sensitive to the yearning many writers have to get into print — "Until you publish, you don't exist. . . . All you want is to be born, into print" — but he also knows how egotistical the act of writing is. Early in the novel, still facing writer's block, Cal admits: "I realized it wasn't so much inspiration that I lacked; it was something still more basic to the writer's mental and emotional makeup. I'm talking about the megalomaniacal confidence, the sheer cosmic audacity, that permits a mortal to attempt the sacrilege of setting in motion a world."

The world Colapinto sets in motion is a familiar one — as I said, the basic plot has been used thousands of times — but the insights into writing and publishing will appeal to those interested in the literary life. That the phony writer lives and prospers while the real writer is killed is worth mulling over by both kinds of budding writers, whether in a bar chatting up the ladies or at home sitting at a desk. You sure you want to be a writer?

Washington Post Book World, 29 July 2001

Jeffery Conway, Lynn Crosbie, and David Trinidad

Phoebe 2002: An Essay in Verse
Turtle Point Press, 2003

Even less than the epic itself, the mock-epic is not a popular form for poets today; indeed, it would be hard to match, much less improve on, the great mock-epics of Alexander Pope, "The Rape of the Lock" and *The Dunciad*. Twenty-five years ago, Richard Nason had a go at *A Modern Dunciad*, but no one will ever touch the utter perfection of Pope's "Lock." Undaunted, three poets decided in early 2000 to pool their talents to write a mock-epic on *All About Eve*, Joseph L. Mankiewicz's 1950 film about ambition and betrayal in the theater world. As unlikely a topic for a poem as the snipping of a lock of a girl's hair, perhaps — but the challenge of mock-epic is to spin straw into gold, and our three poets have discovered a goldmine in that old movie.

The scope is the literary equivalent of Super Panavision: *Phoebe 2002* is an oversized volume 650 pages long, divided into 16 books, with 30 pages of source notes and a number of stills from the movie. The text is an overflowing prop box of verse forms and styles: lines of various lengths and stanzas; poems reviving old genres like the ghazal, double sestina, villanelle, various acrostics, and the 17th-century pattern poem (here we have poems in the shape of a champagne glass, an Oscar trophy, and one illustrating the contrasting bust shapes of two actresses); letters, lists, quizzes, recipes, plays, extended quotations from such books as *Mommie Dearest* and Craig Nelson's *Bad TV*; and lots of parodies (including a hilarious one of the Ouija board pronouncements from James Merrill's *Changing Light at Sandover*).

In proper epic form, the poets announce their theme early on: "*All About Eve* is a Creation story which deploys deep literary and iconic tropes: / it is also an analogue for film and television; a treatise on fame; and an exposition about women and aging, women and sexuality: 'women . . . and their men!'" The line break here is the only indication that these particular lines are poetry rather than prose; it must be said that this "essay in verse" reads more like essay than verse in many places, despite the panoply of poetic forms. But the poets are ingenious at uncovering those "deep literary and iconic tropes": Eve's name evokes Milton's *Paradise Lost*, of course, and the smoke-filled opening scene of the movie Dante's *Inferno*. And they go far beyond whatever tropes Mankiewicz intended to find parallels in an encyclopedic range of other writers (Spenser, Byron, Baudelaire, Dickinson, Eliot, et al.). At times it's like a DVD audio commentary by the oral examination committee for a doctorate in literature.

The "treatise on fame" angle leads the poets to examine the celebrity culture and geeky fandom that was emerging around the time of *All About Eve*, thanks to columnists like Walter Winchell, and which has assumed such ghastly proportions in our time, not only in movies and music but in poetry, where ambition and betrayal also rear their ugly heads. *Phoebe 2002* becomes more personal in the last third of the book as our poets share horror tales of their fellow poets, and the 9/11 attack during the composition of the book casts the whole project into triviality, as they're the first to admit. But also knowing that good work is the only antidote to scheming poets and uncontrollable tragedies, the authors soldier on and bring their mock-epic to a satisfying conclusion.

If *Phoebe 2002* doesn't sweep every poetry award this year, it will be as unjust as Bette Davis's failure to win an Oscar for *All About Eve*. The endless creativity on display here, the deep erudition, the Talmudic ingenuity, and the sense of fun against all odds make this the most impressive book of poetry I've read in years. As the movie's theater critic Addison De Witt says, I am once more available for dancing in the streets.

Rain Taxi, Online Edition, Winter 2003–2004

Martha Cooley

The Archivist
Little, Brown, 1998

I used to know a fatuous publisher who once pontificated, "You know a book is in trouble when the author starts quoting Eliot." I didn't even bother to ask what he meant, knowing that many of our best contemporary novelists — Gaddis, Pynchon, Burroughs, Markson, Maso — have quoted T. S. Eliot's resonant, enigmatic poetry as regularly as earlier novelists quoted the Bible. Eliot is quoted throughout Martha Cooley's first novel, and in fact is regarded as a religious writer by the principal characters of *The Archivist*, who study his poetry to illuminate their own theological concerns.

It's risky to make the hero of your first novel a librarian, and a 65-year-old curator of manuscripts at that. Matthias Lane has been working in the special collections department of Princeton's library since 1965, the year both his wife, Judith, and Eliot died. One of the collections he presides over is the letters that Emily Hale received from Eliot; she was his first love and a lifelong confidante who gave his letters to Princeton (in fact as well as in this fiction) with the proviso that they be sequestered until 2020. (Eliot was furious and broke off contact with her.) One day a graduate student named Roberta Spire asks Matt to show her the letters. He refuses, of course, but is curious enough about Roberta's motives to be drawn into a friendly relationship with this intense poet half his age. Roberta is fascinated by religious conversion, both Eliot's to Anglicanism and her parents' from Judaism to Christianity. Eliot converted in the difficult years after he committed his first wife, Vivienne, to a sanatorium; he corresponded regularly with Hale during those years, and Roberta is convinced that the explanation for Eliot's mysterious conversion can be found in those letters. Her own parents converted after their terrifying experience in Europe during World War II; fleeing to the New World, they sought a new life and a new religion as a way of forgetting their past, an act of denial that now infuriates their daughter.

Matt shares Roberta's interest in both Eliot and conversion, because his dead wife Judith resembled Vivienne in some ways and because, as she deteriorated mentally, she converted from secular Judaism to Kabbalism, its mystical branch. Judith too was committed to a sanatorium, which paralyzed Matt in the same way Vivienne's commitment did Eliot. An obvious parallel between Eliot-Vivienne-Hale and Matt-Judith-Roberta quickly emerges, apparent even to readers not familiar with Eliot's life. (Cooley provides all the relevant details, drawn largely from Lyndall Gordon's 1988 book *Eliot's New Life*, and integrates them smoothly into her narrative.)

Like Eliot's *Four Quartets*, *The Archivist* is divided into four parts, each one dealing, as does Eliot's great sequence, with the ways the past impinges on the present. Part one sets out all that I've just summarized, and is narrated by Matt in circumspect prose. Part two consists of the journal Judith kept during her confinement, tracking her losing battle with her various demons. (Only jazz records provided her with any comfort, and Cooley nicely captures that heady period in the late 1950s when jazz was undergoing so many changes.) Part three returns to the novel's present (the mid-1980s) and Matt's narration of his recovery from Judith's death and his growing relationship with Roberta. The brief fourth part is Matt's terse account of his final encounter with the Hale-Eliot letters, an unthinkable act for an archivist.

It is rare and gratifying to read a novel about people who take literature seriously, who practically live and die by books. For Cooley's characters, poetry like Eliot's provides the most accurate and ennobling articulation of their various dilemmas, which explains Roberta's (and many scholars') desire to ransack a writer's letters for further illumination. (In addition to Eliot, Cooley's characters reverently quote Auden and especially LeRoi Jones, as Amiri Baraka was then known, and who emerges surprisingly as a kind of Beat Eliot.) It is also rare (though not as gratifying to some readers) to see a serious literary work that grapples with theological concerns these days. As a tribute to Eliot's continuing relevance to contemporary literature and as an examination into how books — both sacred and profane — can define some people's lives, *The Archivist* is a memorable achievement.

Washington Post Book World, 5 April 1998

Robert Coover

The Brunist Day of Wrath

Dzanc Books, 2014

Although the 1960s are remembered today more for its music than for its fiction, a number of important American novelists made their debut that decade: Donald Barthelme, Richard Brautigan, Stanley Elkin, William H. Gass, Joseph Heller, Ken Kesey, Harry Mathews, Joseph McElroy, Thomas Pynchon, Ishmael Reed, Gilbert Sorrentino, and Marguerite Young, to name the most prominent. One of the most impressive first novels was Robert Coover's *Origin of the Brunists* (1966), the story of a "terrible mine disaster, the lone survivor, the cult that formed up around him, made up of over-educated occultists and ignorant evangelicals possessed by the Jesus demon, their shy privacy shattered by the cynical local newspaperman, who infiltrated the cult and then exposed them to the world, their naïve prophecy about the Second Coming and end of the world, taking place out at an old slag heap which they called the Mount of Redemption, all of it becoming a huge international media event, a bizarre carnival really, and ending in catastrophic failure" — as one character in Coover's new novel summarizes it. Her auditor metafictionally remarks "it all sounded like the makings of a good novel."

Coover did indeed make a good novel out of it, the best satire of religion in America since Sinclair Lewis's *Elmer Gantry* and a raucous contribution to the genre of American apocalypse that stretches from Michael Wigglesworth's *Day of Doom* (1662) through works by Hawthorne, Melville, Twain, and Nathanael West, to Coover's contemporaries Gaddis, Barth, Vonnegut, Elkin, and DeLillo.

Coover's new novel is set five years after that "bizarre carnival," by which time the Brunist cult has expanded and is gathering once again in the small town of West Condon for more religious shenanigans, once again convinced that the end times are upon them. Coover replicates both the structure — four parts occupying a little over three months, bookended by a prologue and an epilogue — and the mode of *The Origin of the Brunists*: realism tottering on the edge of absurdism. Once again, Coover uses free indirect discourse to convey the story, sticking closely to the points-of-view of a large cast of characters, most of them poorly educated rubes, but with a sprinkling of smarter folks for clarification of events (and to convey his own sardonic point of view). Like the size of the cast, everything is supersized in the sequel: not only is it more than twice as long as its predecessor, there are greater amounts of sex and violence, fiercer blasphemies and outrages, and more madness and mayhem, in keeping with the course of American culture over the last 50 years. Though the novel is set in the late '60s, it is clearly a parable about recent years: in a 2010 interview in *Bookslut*, Coover said he began gathering notes for a sequel even before the *Origin* was published, "but the election of young Bush and the rise of the fundamentalists at the turn of the millennium inspired a determined return to the project."

Coover recreates the theological ambiance of American literature in the 1960s, when Christ figures were rampant — Kesey's Randle Patrick McMurphy, Barth's Giles the goat-boy, Vonnegut's Billy Pilgrim, the title character in Harry Crews's 1968 debut *The Gospel Singer* — and when the grand narrative of the Judeo-Christian tradition was superseded by the grander narrative revealed in books like Frazer's *Golden Bough* and Campbell's *Hero with a Thousand Faces*, both of which are referenced in Coover's new novel. The (anti)Christ figure in *The Origin of the Brunists* was the newspaperman Justin Miller, who exposed the cult to ridicule and was apparently killed by them in retaliation, only to be "resurrected" shortly after and is last seen leaving West Condon in the company of the alluringly named Happy Bottom.

Although there is a literal Christ figure in the new novel — a Presbyterian minister who goes mad and believes he's Jesus — Miller's role is taken by Sally Elliott, a wisecracking hippie chick who has taken enough college courses in comparative mythology to recognize the lunacy not only of the Brunists — they demonize her as the "antichrist" — but of religion itself. Fond of wearing Christian-baiting T-shirts with slogans like SUPPORT ATHEISM: A NON-PROPHET ORGANIZATION, Sally notes that the word "cretin" is derived from "Christian" and provides several caustic definitions of religion, ranging from "a comforting madness" and "a consoling fantasy" to: "Christianity is quite simply a shamanistic cult of monumental stupidity, chicanery, and willful self-delusion. A legacy of the infantile origin of the species." Like Justin Miller, she is nearly killed by the Brunists, but she too leaves the Christ-ridden town and becomes a writer. The metafictional epilogue implies she's the author of *The Brunist Day of Wrath*, and her early career as a writer overlaps with Coover's in many details.

Coover understands "religion's appeal, no matter how nutty, to the down-and-out," the need to "Be part of something bigger than" oneself, and creates a certain amount of empathy for his ill-educated cultists, his rust-belt mystics and hick apocalyptics. At the other end of the intellectual spectrum are those like the town's smarmy Lutheran minister, who understands "Christianity as the gradual shaping of a sustaining human vision, one impervious to the aberrations of history and the pretentious intrusions of misguided scholars. As such, it is true, even if it is not 'true.'" Imagining "the difficulty we have in glimpsing Being through the unreliable scrim of Becoming, which is the world of our sensations, but not the world itself, since our perceptions can never equal the perceived," he seeks "the immersion of my finite self within the infinite self that is God." His skeptical interlocutor, undoubtedly speaking for Coover, curtly critiques his liberal theology: "I think you're just kidding yourself."

The majority of the world's population believes in gods. "So what are you going to do if you don't live in the majority's crazy made-up world?" Sally asks. "Steer clear if you can and duck when they have guns in their hands," she advises, but Coover offers additional alternatives in *The Brunist Day of Wrath*. In place of their *dies irae*, he proposes *carpe diem*. The more sympathetic characters in the novel experience occasional moments of exultation (often sexual), fleeting apprehensions of beauty (one takes place on a golf course), and it is suggested one should remain alert and responsive to those moments, rather than reject them as the snares of Satan. The hope for eternal life is at the root of most religions, but "One is deprived of full contact with reality by the flaw of hope," wise-beyond-her-years Sally says.

The budding writer also broods on "The pursuit of aesthetic truth as a moral act." Throughout the novel, the Bible (and by implication other "holy books") is categorized not as a divine revelation but as the human invention of propagandists and fantasists, and theology as an "insignificant branch of fantastic literature." The authors of myths, sacred writings, and fiction are all "fantasists" — a term that has been applied to Coover — but as the character who calls himself Jesus warns, "*damned are they who project their mad fantasies upon others!*," which is the main difference between sacred and secular fictionists. Near the end of the novel, Sally distinguishes "her kind of fiction *versus* the Christian sort, . . . illuminating [*versus*] darkening the mind," meaning she subverts conventional genres and forms to achieve aesthetic truth, as Coover has been doing all his career, rather than exploiting them for religious propaganda. (Her published novel is called "faction" by reviewers, recalling the "nonfiction" novels of Capote and Mailer in the 1960s and Coover's own magnificent faction of 1977, *The Public Burning*.) She goes so far as to say (again, speaking for Coover):

> The conventional way of telling stories is itself a kind of religion, you know, a dogmatic belief in a certain type of human perception as the only valid one. Like religious people, conventional writers follow hand-me-down catechisms and look upon the human story through a particular narrow lens, not crafted by them and belonging to generations of writers long dead. So conventional writers are no more realists than these fundamentalist Rapture nuts are. The true realists are the lens-breakers, always have been. The readers, like your average Sunday morning churchgoers, can't keep up with all this, so the innovators who are cutting the real mainstream often go un-

> noticed in their own time. It's the price they pay. They don't make as much money, but they have more fun.

This statement is Coover's *apologia pro vita sua*, and if *The Brunist Day of Wrath* proves to be the octogenarian's final novel, it's a hellzapoppin' last hurrah for the kind of unconventional fiction he has written and championed during one of the most distinguished careers in American literature. Then again, the Brunists have regrouped at the end of the novel, and Coover probably has a few more lenses to break.

American Book Review, May/June 2014

Stanley G. Crawford

Log of the S.S. "The Mrs Unguentine"
Living Batch Press, 1989

In the late '70s Stanley Crawford published two of the most original and formally inventive novels on marriage ever written. *Some Instructions to My Wife Concerning the Upkeep of the House and Marriage and to My Son and Daughter Concerning the Conduct of Their Childhood* (1978) was a novel in the form of a marriage manual, expressing a patriarchal ideal that pushed Victorian sensibility to comically neurotic extremes. In that novel, marriage was compared to a house in numerous extended metaphors. In *Log of the S.S. "The Mrs Unguentine,"* published earlier and now reissued by a small press in Albuquerque, a marriage is compared to a floating barge, complete with vegetation, animals, even its own weather, that drifts across oceans for 40 years, inhabited by a man and woman who rarely meet. Mrs. Unguentine, the narrator, details life upon the barge with a verisimilitude that belies the antirealistic, at times mythic, bent of the novel, a married life in which little communication takes place — they post notes to each other occasionally — and which deteriorates into alcoholism, wife-beating, and suicide.

The novel is remarkable for several reasons, not the least of which is Crawford's wholly convincing assumption of a woman's voice that ebbs and swells (from two-word sentences to long, Woolfian observations) in this touching account of her eccentric marriage. The entire novel has to be read, however, not as a tale of a particular marriage but as an oblique, extended metaphor for marriage itself. It is a beautiful achievement.

Review of Contemporary Fiction, Fall 1989

Cyberpunk Fiction

Storming the Reality Studio: A Casebook of Cyberpunk and Postmodern Science Fiction. Edited by Larry McCaffery
Duke University Press, 1992

If, like me, you haven't been following the cyberpunk movement, this exciting anthology will tell you everything you need to know. Just as punk rock was a rebellion against the stale corporate rock of the 1970s, cyberpunk rebelled in the early 1980s against both mainstream fiction and generic science fiction to create a heady hybrid characterized by a hyperawareness of and immersion in recent technological changes. As editor Larry McCaffery notes in his introduction, "the cyberpunks were the first generation of artists for whom the technologies of satellite dishes, video and audio players and recorders, computers and video games (both of particular importance), digital watches, and MTV were not exoticisms, but part of a daily 'reality matrix.'" To represent that "reality matrix," cyberpunks felt compelled to abandon (or modify) previous modes of fiction-writing because, as George Slusser points out in his contribution, "Literature cannot use traditional techniques to present a contemporary reality because that reality has been transformed by technical advance to a point where those techniques no longer fit." (As Slusser notes, this was Robbe-Grillet's rationale for the *nouveau roman*.) Burroughs and Pynchon were early practitioners, but where those two have cultural memories stretching back to ancient Egypt, the cyberpunks' don't seem to go back much further than the Velvet Underground's first album. They are far more interested in what has happened in science over the last 20 years — and what's happening now — and how those discoveries have altered the way we experience our world.

Storming the Reality Studio — the title is from Burroughs's *Nova Express* — consists of 29 sound bites from cyberpunk fiction old and new, and 20 essays (many from *Mississippi Review*'s 1988 issue on cyberpunk), preceded by McCaffery's useful introduction and a handy guide to "the cultural artifacts that helped to shape cyberpunk ideology and aesthetics, along with books by the cyberpunks themselves." Chronologically, this annotated list runs from *Frankenstein* (1818) to the college cult favorite *My Cousin, My Gastroenterologist* by Mark Leyner (1990), and includes such things as the execrable (but influential) MTV and Sonic Youth's feedback-drenched *Daydream Nation*. Music, specifically of the indie (what we used to call underground) kind, is a crucial element in cyberpunk; William Gibson, whose *Neuromancer* (1984) is generally considered the best cyberpunk novel written to date, says, "I've been influenced by Lou Reed, for instance, as much as I've been by any 'fiction' writer." (And if you don't know who Lou Reed is, then cyberpunk's not for you.)

What's the fiction like? Very urban, and very much a male genre (though two women address their essays to this point). István Csicsery-Rónay provides (albeit sarcastically) this typical story template:

> a self-destructive but sensitive young protagonist with an (implant/prosthesis/telechtronic talent) that makes the evil (megacorporations/police states/criminal underworlds) pursue him through (wasted urban landscapes/elite luxury enclaves/eccentric space stations) full of grotesque (haircuts/clothes/self-mutilations/rock music/sexual hobbies/designer drugs/telechtronic gadgets/nasty new weapons/exteriorized hallucinations) representing the (mores/fashions) of modern civilization in terminal decline, ultimately hooks up with rebellious and tough-talking (youth/artificial intelligence/rock cults) who offer the alternative, not of (community/socialism/traditional values/transcendental vision), but of supreme, life-affirming *hipness*, going with the flow which now flows in the machine, against the spectre of a world-subverting (artificial intelligence/multinational corporate web/evil genius).

The prose (at its best) has a kind of brutal lyricism and linguistic inventiveness that yokes scientific terminology with street slang, black humor with techno-thriller sensationalism. But as weird as this fiction gets sometimes, it can and "should be seen," McCaffery argues, "as the breakthrough 'realism' of our time. It is an art form that vividly represents the most salient features of our lives, as these lives are being transformed and redefined by technology." The cyberpunks make many of the "contemporary" writers treated here in *RCF* seem like literary dinosaurs; anyone interested in truly contemporary fiction must get this book and start reading the writers it samples.

Review of Contemporary Fiction, Summer 1992

Susan Daitch

L.C.
Harcourt Brace Jovanovich, 1987

This intriguing and very accomplished first novel is concerned with the efforts of three women to redress personal and political inequality through the manipulation of texts. The novel begins with an editor's introduction to her own translation of a journal kept by one Lucienne Crozier, a proto-feminist witness to the February 1848 revolution in Paris. All seems well at first, but irregularities begin appearing: the language is not that of a 24-year-old Frenchwoman of the last century but of an older one of this century; the editor's signature to the annotations shrinks from Willa Rehnfield to W.R., then expands back to the full name, then is joined by annotations by a Jane Amme (a nom de guerre), writing 14 years after Rehnfield's 1968 translation. When Lucienne's diary comes to an end halfway through the novel, Amme steps in and explains Rehnfield's reasons for doctoring her translation. The fact that Rehnfield wrote in 1968, a year of revolutionary activity as futile as that in France 120 years earlier, points to the identification the reclusive Rehnfield feels for Lucienne. Amme, on the other hand, was a participant in the Berkeley riots of 1968 and consequently has her own reasons for identifying with L.C. She offers her own translation of the last section of L.C.'s diary — radically different from the Rehnfield version — and as text competes with text, questions arise concerning the recording of history, the nature of translation, and the ultimately subjectivity of all texts.

Dozens of cross-references link L.C. with her 20th-century annotators, and Daitch brilliantly underscores the similarities between the sociopolitical injustices that led to the revolts of 1848 and 1968. She's clearly done her homework in both eras (she was only 14 in 1968 herself) and demonstrates a vivid historical imagination. The role of women vis-à-vis history — from spectator to victim to participant — runs through this tale of two cities, a stunning debut by a young writer clearly worth watching.

Review of Contemporary Fiction, Fall 1988

□ □ □ □ □ □ □

The Colorist

Vintage Contemporaries, 1990

Susan Daitch's first novel, *L.C.*, was a remarkably sophisticated treatment of history and textual transmission, of how "history" is largely dependent upon whose text survives the machinations of time, editors, and translators. Alternating between Paris in the 1840s and America in the 1960s, the novel explored the ultimate subjectivity of all texts. In her new novel, Daitch pursues the related theme of representation in texts, this time concentrating on a wide range of visual arts. Julie Greene is the colorist of the title, someone who colors the frames in a sci-fi comic serial called *Electra*; she and her friend Laurel, an inker for the same comic, live their own kind of comic serial, moving through a series of "adventures" in lower Manhattan until they both wind up forging Egyptian hieroglyphics for a semilegitimate reproductions specialist. (Complicating their lives are their problematic relationships to others: Julie to a mysterious photographer and Laurel to her Chinese-born mother.) A wide variety of visual arts comes under Daitch's intelligent gaze, everything from photographs and paintings to movies, comics, dreams, staged erotic scenarios, cosmetics, to Egyptian papyri. Of the latter, Julie learns: "Scrolls placed in tombs were considered to be the equivalent of what they represented. A picture of slaves catching fish or slaughtering cows and cooking them was the same as having and eating and enslaving." With great ingenuity Daitch superimposes one art form onto another so that, soon, the superhero Electra is likewise living on the Lower East Side and Julie finds herself in an imaginary conversation with Maat, Egyptian god of law and order in the papyri she colors. ("Somehow I think Maat will understand me and not turn me over to the Devourer.") Just as Julie's photographer-boyfriend creates collages from previous photographs, Daitch juxtapositions one art next to another until, by the end of the novel, all barriers between art and reality have collapsed.

The Colorist is an immensely clever novel about the ambiguities of art and representation, recalling aspects of Gaddis's *Recognitions* and especially Antonioni's film *Blow-Up*. It demonstrates an extraordinary command of knowledge in a wide variety of fields and profound thinking about the role art plays in our lives. On the basis of her first two novels, it is now clear that Susan Daitch is one of the most significant young writers in contemporary American literature.

Review of Contemporary Fiction, Summer 1991. And on the basis of these two novels, I proposed to Larry McCaffery making Daitch the third in *RCF*'s special younger writers issue of Summer 1993 (along with Vollmann and Wallace), and further led to my publication of Daitch's *Storytown* with Dalkey Archive in April 1996, over the objections of Dalkey's boss, who disliked it. I was surprised, then, when Dalkey reprinted *L.C.* in 2002. Daitch went on to publish two remarkable novels with City Lights, *Paper Conspiracies* (2011) and *The Lost Civilization of Suolucidir* (2016).

Mark Z. Danielewski

House of Leaves
Pantheon, 2000

Any hope or fear that the experimental novel was an aberration of the 20th century is dashed by the appearance of Mark Z. Danielewski's *House of Leaves*, the first major experimental novel of the new millennium. And it's a monster. Ten years in the making, more than 700 pages long, sporting a half-dozen typefaces, 450 footnotes, two colors of ink, lengthy lists, a bibliography, three appendices, illustrations, an index and e.e. cummings-like typographical layouts, this is not your typical first novel. It's more like David Foster Wallace channeling H. P. Lovecraft for a literary counterpart to *The Blair Witch Project*.

A gifted but troubled young man who calls himself Johnny Truant (after his poor attendance record at school) comes across a huge manuscript by an elderly man known only as Zampanò that was abandoned after his death. The manuscript is a mess, but Johnny is irresistibly drawn to it and begins transcribing it, adding in footnotes a running commentary on his own wayward life. Zampanò's manuscript, entitled "The Navidson Record," is a scholarly critique of a film of the same title made by a Pulitzer Prize-winning photojournalist named Will Navidson. Johnny soon discovers that there is no such film, and even if there were, Zampanò was unqualified to write a critique: He was blind. Yet so compelling is Zampanò's account of "The Navidson Record" that Johnny — like most readers, I predict — suspends disbelief and undergoes a visceral experience that has him doubting the distinction between reality and fantasy.

Navidson's documentary concerns a strange house in rural Virginia into which he moves with his family. All is well at first, but small spatial displacements soon occur: The house measures slightly wider inside than outside, doors mysteriously appear inside with no counterparts outside. Then a walk-in closet appears: The more it is probed, the deeper it gets, until finally it opens up into a vast chamber of vertiginous dimensions, with a spiral staircase in the center that descends endlessly. Navidson gathers a crew for an expedition to the bottom of the stairs. The accounts of the exploration of this dark abyss are hair-raising, and the physical impossibility of it all only deepens the metaphysical dread felt by the characters. A sharp-clawed monster may inhabit the labyrinth — references are made to the Minotaur — and the explorers suffer madness and death before Navidson can be rescued. The physical layout heightens the experience: After Navidson's crew lose their way, the text mimics the labyrinth by expanding and contracting, going off in odd directions, printed upside down or backward, with narrative and multilayered footnotes crowding each other for space. As texts collide, the reader experiences the same disorientation the explorers do.

The house on Ash Tree Lane overshadows other famous haunted houses in literature because of Danielewski's audacious and erudite imagination, which links the terrifying spaces within the house to everything from psychological states like claustrophobia to the Norse legend of Yggdrasill, the great ash tree at the center of the universe. What in other hands would be just another tale of a haunted house becomes in Danielewski's a searching examination of the "psychological dimensions of space." The author brings in architecture and myth, film theory, and psychology to explore the way people react to the physical space around them.

Zampanò's footnotes cite (and mock) scholarly film criticism; Johnny's footnotes chart his own psychic disintegration, though not in as compelling a manner. After a troubled childhood, he has drifted until finally settling as an apprentice to a Hollywood tattooist. He lives *la vida loca*, falls for a stripper, does too many drugs, and generally burns himself out as he continues to edit Zampanò's monstrous text. Details gradually emerge about his ambiguous relationship to his brilliant but mad mother, who literally scarred him for life but in another sense gave him the intellectual groundwork to take on the task of editing "The Navidson Record." Her letters to her son written from an insane asylum, printed in one of the appendices, are dazzling.

Danielewski's achievement lies in taking some staples of horror fiction — the haunted house, the mysterious manuscript that casts a spell on its hapless reader — and using his impressive erudition to recover the mythological and psychological origins of horror, and then enlisting the full array of avant-garde literary techniques to reinvigorate a genre long abandoned to hacks. The novel may look like Frankenstein's monster in its patchwork assembly, but it's alive! It's alive!

A final note: It is heartening to see a novel like this published by a major New York house. *House of Leaves* is something I would have expected from someplace like Fiction Collective 2, not from venerable Pantheon Books. Right on.

Washington Post Book World, 9 April 2000

□ □ □ □ □ □ □

Only Revolutions

Pantheon, 2006

If Mark Z. Danielewski's daring and ambitious first novel, *House of Leaves*, read like a postmodern remix of H. P. Lovecraft's tales of metaphysical horror, his even more experimental second novel recalls James Joyce's *Finnegans Wake*. Joyce used a punning language and the fluidity of dreams to dramatize how the members of an ordinary Irish family reenact all of the conflicts in human history. Climbing into Joyce's seven-league boots, Danielewski retells American history as a joyride by two teenagers in language almost as dense, inventive, and polysemous as Joyce's. If *Finnegans Wake* and words like "polysemous" scare you off, *Only Revolutions* is probably not for you. But here's what you'll be missing:

Just as the romance of Tristan and Iseult undergirds Joyce's fantasia, *Only Revolutions* features two 16-year-olds, Sam and Hailey, who literally fall in love at first sight: Sam is dazzled by "her Gold Eyes with flecks of Green" and Hailey by "his Green Eyes with flecks of Gold," introducing the color scheme that dominates the novel. Meeting in symbolic New Hope, Pennsylvania, they decide to hit the road, both to see and to escape from America, wending their way in a variety of vehicles down to New Orleans, where they stay a spell and get sick, then up along the Mississippi to St. Louis, where they take jobs in a diner for a while, and then north to the Badlands, and finally west to Montana, where they come to a Tristanic end.

Danielewski gives us two first-person accounts, and here's where it gets tricky. Sam's version starts in the middle of the Civil War and ends with the Kennedy assassination in 1963 and the escalation of the Vietnam War, while Hailey's begins there and ends a century later. Only revolutionary times like the 1860s and 1960s, the author seems to suggest, can show us what our country is really about. Thus Sam and Hailey are not simply characters but transhistorical archetypes, personifying a country that never grew up and continues to act like a wild teenager, "Allmighty sixteen and so freeeeee." When they speak of each other they use a capitalized US; like their country, they are spontaneous and reckless, flush with a cheeky confidence that is admirable but that ultimately dooms them, as it will the U.S., to a tragic end.

Or something like that; this is a complex, challenging novel that leaves the head spinning after a first reading. As Stephen Stills sang during the revolutionary '60s, "There's something happenin' here, / But what it is ain't exactly clear." Whatever else it is, *Only Revolutions* is a masterpiece of formal design. Sam's story, told in eight-page installments, occupies one half of the novel, and you have to turn the book over to read Hailey's half. (The publisher recommends reading eight pages of one narrative, then turning it around to read the equivalent eight pages of the other, converting the book into a steering wheel for your own joyride.) Two ribbons, green and gold, are sewn in to help you keep your place. Everything revolves in circles: the book's 360 pages equal the 360 degrees of a circle; halving the circle, each page contains 180 words, and the page numbers are enclosed in circles that revolve if you flip the pages. All the o's in the book are printed in either green or gold, keeping you focused on the protagonists' eyes. They ignore history, transcend it, but for the reader lists of historical events from 1863 through 2005 run down columns next to the main text, whose fanciful language is Joycean, Whitmanesque, Kerouwacky, filled with oddly punctuated prose poetry and catalogs of flora and fauna, automobile models, and a century of slang:

> He doesn't weigh much.
> But I'm glad for his touch.
> Tremendously glad. So glad
> thousands of **Whorled Loosestrife**
> immediately demand:
> —*Me!*
> And I oblige.
> Their petals twirling my hair.
> I am their hair. And though my
> feet are dangerously bare, I'm just
> too free and faire to care about.
> —*Yipeeeeeeee!*
> Defeasibly not.
> I dive, palms a squeeeeeal wide,
> swirling the World and lifting
> the sky, arches uniting
> stratocumulus & ground.

The endsheets contain concordances to the novel, shaped in circles and ovals, which have to be held up to a mirror to read. If nothing else, *Only Revolutions* deserves to win every book-design award out there. The only thing it lacks is a map tracking this incredible journey, which would resemble a backwards square-root sign. Opened flat, the book forms a square; I think Danielewski may have squared the circle!

With a novel as meticulously crafted as this, any rush to judgment would be foolish. It needs to be studied, its patterns and symbolism deciphered, its historical cross-references pondered. It's certainly one of the great road novels, joining that dusty convoy stretching from Petronius' *Satyricon* through the *Zohar* and *Don Quixote* to *The Sky Changes* by the late Gilbert Sorrentino. A first reading is an exhilarating trip, and it can be recommended for that reason alone, offering a literary experience unlike anything else to be found in the more conventional novels piled up beside *Only Revolutions* in book stores.

Only revolutions like this against the conventional novel keep the genre fresh, novel, forever young and always eager to light out for the territory ahead of the rest.

Washington Post Book World, 22 October 2006

□□□□□□□

The Fifty Year Sword
Pantheon, 2012

If you annually host a literary Halloween party, where a creepy tale by Poe or Lovecraft is read aloud by candlelight, this year you might try *The Fifty Year Sword*, especially if your guests are postmodern Goths. Mark Z. Danielewski's unhallowed novella is a narrative trick and a treat for readers who like to be challenged as well as entertained.

Looking back years later, five orphans take turns recounting a terrifying Halloween party thrown for them as children in east Texas at the home of "a 112-year-old nut job." Also attending are the orphans' social worker, a seamstress and the "bitchwitch" who stole her husband, and the party's featured entertainer: a morose, hulking man called the Story Teller. He unfolds a fairy tale about his quest for a weapon to wreak vengeance, which he found in the form of a "fifty year sword," one that will kill its victim in "the final second of the fiftieth year." At the climax of his tale, he invites each of the orphans to open one of the five latches of the sword case, which reveals. . . .

The Story Teller's fairy tale of vengeance seems to be a coded account of the rage the seamstress, a Thai immigrant named Chintana, feels for Belinda Kite, the other woman, who takes over the tale at the end and brings it to a bloody conclusion. (Everyone in the novella has unusual names: the five orphans answer to Tarff, Ezade, Iniedia, Sithis, and Micit.) The tension between the two women crackles throughout the novella, a psychodrama elevated to mythic proportions by way of the Story Teller's tale and the author's numerous references to cutting and shearing. As in many classic ghost stories, the violent conclusion provides the catharsis the protagonist needs to get on with her life.

Two qualities distinguish this eerie narrative from other ghost stories: the language and the book's design. The narrative is a species of prose poetry that resembles Lewis Carroll's "Jabberwocky," and at times James Joyce's *Finnegans Wake*. Preparing himself for his performance, the Story Teller folds his legs until

he no longer
seemed
    "hrowling or gulking but sat
quietstill,
    "overdraped in his strange
silveryblack tunic, his head heavily
bowed.

He speaks in a "rumbidilling voice," lowers his head "dramatatically," and describes a sword blade as "milky white, / glossy / and cold, like / a fog creeping low across / a morning before / a funeral." As in his previous novel, *Only Revolutions* (2006), Danielewski brings a poet's resourcefulness to this eldritch tale, brilliantly fusing the sound of Anglo-Saxon poetry to the sprung rhythms of Gerald Manley Hopkins, all while making our flesh creep. And as in his debut novel, the magnificent *House of Leaves* (2000), he makes creative use of typography: some pages are full of text, others contain only a phrase or a word, and in others, the text and illustrations share the space. On one page, a line slices the word "swords" into "s/words"; Danielewski takes a sword to the typical layout of a novel and hacks his words and sentences into various shapes and configurations, a s/word dance of astonishing virtuosity.

The book is visually ornate. The text appears only on the lefthand pages — the *sinister* side, as it's called in heraldry. Most righthand pages are blank, except for a dozen or so instances where the fanciful artwork spills over. It is illustrated in full color, most dramatically when the orphans unlatch the sword case. Different colored quotation marks distinguish the various narrators; it would take many a winter's night to unravel who says what. The novel is as entrancing to look at as to read.

The Fifty Year Sword first appeared in 2005 as an expensive limited edition, seen only by collectors. (A new deluxe edition with latched box and Nepalese binding is also available for $100.) This gorgeous trade edition, slightly revised, should reach a wider audience and gives further evidence that Danielewski is one of the most gifted and versatile writers of our time.

Washington Post, 26 October 2012

Dame Darcy

Frightful Fairy Tales
Ten Speed Press, 2002

For the last decade, a madcap who calls herself Dame Darcy (née Darcy Megan Stanger) has been tap-dancing on the fringes of culture in a variety of roles: she's a dollmaker, a local-cable-show hostess, a palm-reader, an animator for film and television, an illustrator of album covers for indie bands, an actress, and a performer on the banjo and musical saw for various old-timey groups. But she's best known for the comic book *Meat Cake*, an annual anthology of bizarre stories rendered in filigreed black and white drawings. At first glance, it looks like the work of Edward Gorey's weird kid sister, or a precocious teenager trying to imitate Aubrey Beardsley. Each issue features a mix of ghost stories, cautionary tales, vaudeville skits, and nonsense with a repertory company of characters with names like Richard Dirt (Dame Darcy's comic persona), Richard's sidekick Friend the Girl, Wax Wolf (a man with a wolf's head), the Siamese twins Hindrance and Perfidia, Strega Pez (who "speaks via words written on giant Pez that come from her slit throat"), and Scampi the Selfish Shellfish. They all dress like silent screen stars or Victorian party girls, overly fond of kohl and lipstick, and speak in a slangy style derived from old movies (alcohol is always "hootch," people are called "pal" or "dolt," *you* and *your* became "ya" and "yer," etc.). Dame Darcy succinctly summed up *Meat Cake* in an interview as "kooky spooky girl fun-whimsical stuff."

I'm not sure who the audience is for *Meat Cake*, though I suspect it's largely young women who never outgrew their girlhood obsessions with fairy princesses, mermaids, and pretty ponies, unconventional women too frivolous to be goth, too fond of clothes and makeup to be hippies, who blow their paychecks from lousy jobs at vintage clothing shops, and who would rather go to an old-fashioned carnival than a rave. I value *Meat Cake* for playfully keeping alive such disparate traditions as gothic Americana and Firbankian camp, hippie whimsy and screwball comedy, dollhouse drama and racy burlesque. In a genre dominated by either *Ghost World*-type suburban angst or pulp/superhero fantasies, *Meat Cake* provides a delightful alternative that has nothing to do with our technologically driven commodity culture. (Dame Darcy's sole concession to modern times is an informative website, www.damedarcy.com.)

Frightful Fairy Tales, Dame Darcy's first real book, is just that: six macabre tales profusely illustrated in her trademark style. They're fairly eclectic, drawing inspiration from traditional fairy tales and ghost stories, and are true to their original sources. In “The Siren Ship,” for example, Dame Darcy de-Disneys mermaid mythology to restore a sense of terror to these “beautiful, strange women, glowing white like ghosts with long tapered horns,” more like demons than the pin-up girls of popular culture. Mermaids also appear in the longest and most ambitious story, “The Black River,” which combines abduction to an underwater kingdom with werewolf mythology. (Dame Darcy has a thing for mermaids: she’s dressed as one in the adorable author’s photo on the back cover, and a wisecracking mermaid named Effluvia is a recurring character in *Meat Cake*.) “The Queen of Spades” seems inspired not by Pushkin’s tale of the same name but by Poe’s “The Premature Burial,” while “The Damsel in the Well” is reminiscent of an Appalachian murder ballad. “Persimmion” is a grim tale that recalls the Pygmalion myth, and the concluding “Gambler’s Lesson” is another underworld abduction story with some of Dame Darcy’s finest drawings. Her various appropriations are not postmodern subversions but homage to a genre the author revels in: *Frightful Fairy Tales* is not Kathy Acker hijacking *Great Expectations* but Dame Darcy dressing up as Miss Havisham for Halloween and scaring the bejesus out of the neighborhood kids.

I doubt she’ll ever move from the fringes to mainstream culture, and she’ll always be something of an acquired taste, but Dame Darcy fills a niche for a certain kind of reader, and such readers are encouraged to seek out her book and the latest issue of *Meat Cake*.

Rain Taxi, Spring 2003. Various anthologies of *Meat Cake* are available, including the new, definitive *Meat Cake Bible*.

Guy Davenport, Robert Kelly, and Pamela Zoline

Guy Davenport. *The Jules Verne Steam Balloon*
North Point Press, 1987

Robert Kelly. *Doctor of Silence*
McPherson & Co., 1988

Pamela Zoline. *The Heart Death of the Universe and Other Stories*
McPherson & Co., 1988

There is a difference between fads in short fiction and genuine developments, and while the larger commercial presses can be counted on to supply plenty of the former, the smaller independent presses are more reliable for the latter. In his latest collection of short fiction, Guy Davenport continues to build on the aesthetics of the early modernists to create the most intellectual stimulating fiction of our time. As "seriously silly" as the youngsters he writes of with such affection, Davenport creates a world of sex and scholarship, where eroticism and education go hand in hand. The Dutch and Danish settings of the longer stories in this collection are presented in collages of erotic vignettes, entries from botany handbooks, mini-lectures, and quotations from a variety of texts (including the famous Quinet quotation from *Finnegans Wake*), written in a Danish Modern style of clarity and elegance. Other stories concern historical characters antithetical to the Fourierism Davenport champions: Pyrrho of Elis, who "denied that anything exists"; a petty and vindictive Jonah; and a sympathetic profile of Hitler as it might have been written by a totalitarian toady. But in the other stories Davenport writes of an idyllic world in the same generous spirit as one of his protagonists, the schoolteacher Hugo Tvemunding, "superb lover in both flesh and spirit," who tries "to paint because I want to show others what I think is beautiful."

Robert Kelly's fictions also take place in a different world than most pop fiction does — a world less idyllic and more supernatural than Davenport's, but like his a world of intelligence, scholarship, and grace. Ranging in length from half a page to 35 pages, these fictions defamiliarize both the world and the short-story genre; where Davenport is indebted to the generation of 1914, Kelly builds on Borges and European fabulists. In a short piece entitled "Hypnogeography," Kelly states: "I have a feeling that the Dream Representation of place can tell us a lot about what we think of as the 'real' place. . . . I want to learn, and want us to learn, how our countries and cities represent in dream." While his stories are not dreams, strictly speaking, they do read like dream representations of places, reminiscent at times of H. P. Lovecraft's oneiric alternate worlds (though without his gothic gush), more compact than the fictions in his previous collection, *A Transparent Tree*, but tantalizing and unsettling, wondrous strange.

The Heat Death of the Universe is Pamela Zoline's first collection of stories, some dating from the 1960s, most of which appeared in new wave sci-fi magazines. Many science fiction writers begin with an ingenious premise but wrap it in plodding prose; Zoline however matches her ingenious premises with postmodern strategies, a playful sense of humor, and colorful writing to produce a dazzling collection of stories. The longest and most inventive story, "Sheep," is made up of an insomniac's encyclopedic ramblings in quest of sleep. Another story features a boy whose genealogy consists of the most accident-prone family in literary history, while another offers a different view of Davenport's Holland, though in a collage style similar to his. Zoline joins Davenport and Kelly in the small circle of writers who are making genuine contributions to the short-fiction form.

Review of Contemporary Fiction, Fall 1988

Samuel R. Delany

Atlantis: Model 1924
Incunabula, 1994

Best known for his critically acclaimed science fiction and fantasy novels, Delany here writes a kind of homage to the Harlem Renaissance novel, something closer to Jean Toomer's *Cane* than to his other works. Teenage Sam takes the train from Raleigh, North Carolina, up to Harlem to stay with his older brother and work in the city. For this educated but unsophisticated country boy, New York City is like another Atlantis, "a truly wonder-filled city." The year is 1924 and the cultural air is filled with the black renaissance: there are references to Toomer (who Sam resembles), Paul Robeson, the riot at the premiere of *The Birth of a Nation*, minor writers of the time like Samuel Greenberg and Nathalia Crane, and O'Neill's *All God's Chillun Got Wings*. In the most memorable episode, Sam explores Brooklyn Bridge, which summons forth Hart Crane in spirit and, in the flesh, a loquacious character named Harold Hart, who sings of New York as the new Atlantis in the magniloquent style of Barnes's Dr. Matthew O'Connor. (Like O'Connor, Hart is gay, but Sam is too naive to realize he is being propositioned.)

Like Delany's masterwork *Dhalgren*, *Atlantis* occasionally splits into two columns, the narrative continuing in one while the other inserts subtle, intertextual vignettes expanding upon the narrative's references to Atlantis, Tutankhamen, and Columbus, among other things. A warm coming-of-age novel, a formally interesting period piece, an homage to Delany's cultural roots (not to mention a handsomely designed book by a press that deserves to be better known), *Atlantis* has much to recommend it.

Review of Contemporary Fiction, Spring 1995

□ □ □ □ □ □ □

The Mad Man
Kask, 1995

Atlantis: Three Tales
Wesleyan/University Press of New England, 1995

Samuel R. Delany has long been consigned to two literary ghettos — science fiction and, more recently, gay erotica (three, if you count his status as a black writer) — but his literary achievements in both fiction and criticism are such that he deserves the attention of all serious readers. (He is the subject of a forthcoming issue of this journal [Fall 1996: the last issue I copyedited].) His newest novel, for example, *The Mad Man*, published last year in hardcover and now available in a considerably revised paperback, has elements of each of those genres but more closely resembles some kinky coupling of Richard Powers's *Gold Bug Variations* and the Marquis de Sade's *120 Days of Sodom*. Like the former, it is partly concerned with reconstructing the life of a brilliant scholar, in this case a young Korean-American philosopher who died under mysterious circumstances; and like the latter, it has many scenes of unconventional sexuality with an emphasis on what even most liberated people would consider the perverse: urolagnia, coprophilia, foot-fetishism, bestiality, and so on, often practiced with filthy bums. (That adjective is merely descriptive, not judgmental.) Just as Sade alternates scenes of sexual depravity with philosophical disquisitions, Delany varies John Marr's investigation of the philosopher's puzzling career with long accounts of Marr's sexual practices (which parallel those of the philosopher) and his growing concern with AIDS. It's a deliberately provocative novel, and those who read books to have their assumptions challenged will have a good many of their buttons pushed by this one.

In last spring's issue I reviewed Incunabula's edition of Delany's *Atlantis: Model 1924*. That dazzling novella — the story of a young man's experiences in New York in the 1920s, structured around Hart Crane's *The Bridge* — has been expanded into a full-length book with two other coming-of-age narratives, apparently autobiographical. (The book is also available in a signed, limited edition from Incunabula, which adds a "Microflorilegium" at the end, a brief selection of letters by Delany to others about the book.) Delany has a wonderful essay on Crane in his recent collection of critical essays, *Longer Views*, also published by Wesleyan.

Review of Contemporary Fiction, Spring 1996

Don DeLillo

Tom LeClair. *In the Loop: Don DeLillo and the Systems Novel*
University of Illinois Press, 1987

Don DeLillo has been a wallflower at the critics' dance; his novels, while respectfully reviewed, have always been overshadowed by the works of the writers he's usually associated with (Coover, Gaddis, Pynchon). In his first time on the dance floor, DeLillo is fortunate in his partner: Tom LeClair not only offers incisive readings of all of DeLillo's novels but argues that the work deserves to be ranked as high as that by Coover et al. While no single novel, he allows, is the equal of *The Public Burning*, *J R*, or *Gravity's Rainbow*, he feels the corpus is as intellectually rigorous and as stylistically inventive as that of his "control" group. Like them, DeLillo is what LeClair calls a "systems" novelist, one who has discarded mechanistic thinking in favor of "a contemporary scientific paradigm that concentrates on the reciprocal — looping — communications of ecological systems (including man)." Like the others, DeLillo is also widely read, and LeClair's "method in most chapters is to lay alongside a DeLillo novel discursive texts or sets of ideas that correspond to and help express the 'deep texture' of relations in that novel." These texts are taken from such writers as Gregory Bateson, R. D. Laing, Jacques Derrida, Elias Canetti, Anthony Wilden, Ernest Becker, Walter Ong, and Michael Serres; recurring references to Coover, Gaddis, and Pynchon add to these other names to produce a book that is not simply a study of DeLillo but a study of the finest fiction and most provocative thinking of our time. In its intellectual breadth and interpretive insightfulness, *In the Loop* is both a splendid introduction to an unjustly neglected novelist and a state of the art demonstration of critical writing.

Review of Contemporary Fiction, Summer 1988

Helen DeWitt

The Last Samurai
Talk Miramax, 2000

The learned novel is mostly a guy thing. From Rabelais through this year's boy wonder, Mark Z. Danielewski, big novels stuffed with erudite references and arcane allusions have been written almost exclusively by men. Only a few brainy women, like British novelist Christine Brooke-Rose and our own Rikki Ducornet, seem drawn to my favorite genre. Helen DeWitt has crashed this boys club with a brilliant debut novel entitled *The Last Samurai*. When she introduced her female protagonist snuggling up with Adolph Roemer's *Aristarchs Athetesen in der Homerkritik* (Lepizig, 1912), my heart skipped a beat. As she launched into a history of the fabled Alexandria library a few pages later, I fell head over heels.

Learned novels are often modeled on an earlier work: Joyce used the *Odyssey* for his *Ulysses*, and, more recently, Lee Siegel adapted the *Kamasutra* to dazzling effect in his *Love in a Dead Language*. DeWitt bases her novel on Akiro Kurosawa's great 1954 film *Seven Samurai* — in fact, the novel was entitled "The Seventh Samurai" until just before it went to press — which the novel's narrator, a brilliant young woman named Sibylla, watches endlessly. Make that co-narrator: Halfway through the novel, the narrative is taken over by her even more brilliant son, Ludovic.

Sibylla was born in the United States (like DeWitt herself) but emigrated to England to study classics at Oxford, which she abandoned for a job in publishing, which led to a one-night stand with a mediocre author, which led to a son born out of wedlock without the father's knowledge. Sibylla supports her son by keying old magazine articles into a database for a CD-ROM venture. When she takes a break from typing, it's to watch *Seven Samurai*, which she admires as a film about "the importance of rational thought." She is so rational, in fact, that she hesitates to discipline her son: She doubts "the right of one rational being to exercise arbitrary authority over another rational being on the ground of seniority."

But Ludo is no ordinary child. Studying *Seven Samurai* with his mother at an age when most children watch *Sesame Street*, he soon picks up Japanese, which is merely one of a dozen or so languages he knows by age six. Without the benefit (or hindrance) of attending school, this prodigy knows as much about math and physics at age 11 as most university students. The one thing he doesn't know is his father's identity, which his mother refuses to disclose.

He then decides to search for a suitable father in the same manner as the Japanese peasants in Kurosawa's film search for samurai.

This is where Ludo takes over as narrator, and his account of his meetings with remarkable men is wonderful. Kurosawa's samurai undergo a test before they are accepted as part of the band: Ludo's test is to approach a famous man and see how he responds to the statement "I am your son," a challenge that would test the mettle of any man. Always a fan of adventure books, Ludo singles out brilliant men from a variety of fields, intellectual adventurers with fascinating backstories conveyed by DeWitt with great flair.

Learned novels usually explore a particular technical subject: forgery in Willaim Gaddis's *Recognitions*, rocketry in Thomas Pynchon's *Gravity's Rainbow*, medicine in Fernando del Paso's *Palinuro of Mexico*. In *The Last Samurai* it's grammar, especially that of foreign languages. There are discussions and examples in the novel of Greek, Inuit, Old Norse, Arabic, and even tables of alphabets and Japanese kana characters. Grammar also means the system of rules that governs any system, and so the reader is treated to quotations from books on aerodynamics, film criticism, Fourier analysis, chess strategies, and a ludicrous *Eskimo Book of Knowledge*. There are complex math equations, casual references to such things as Gauss's divergence theorem and the Kutta-Joukowski law, and some brilliant discussions of music. Sibylla possesses and passes along to her son a desire to discover the right way to do anything, a grammar for living, as it were, most nobly enshrined in samurai virtue.

DeWitt plays fast and loose with English grammar and punctuation, often writing in a kind of narrative shorthand that keeps things moving at an exhilarating clip. (In this regard she reminds me of British novelist Nicholas Mosley, who shares DeWitt's interest in science and ethics, and who should have won the Nobel Prize for Literature by now.) The novel is self-consciously experimental — *The Last Samurai* will crown DeWitt this year's It Girl of postmodernism — but then the best art often is to some degree. DeWitt is formidably intelligent but engagingly witty, not afraid to walk on the Wilde side (her pun). To paraphrase a sentence early in her novel (a fabricated school evaluation), DeWitt has wide-ranging interests and an extraordinarily original mind; she is a joy to read.

Washington Post Book World, 17 September 2000

Stephen Dixon

Frog
British American, 1991

Although portions of this novel had been appearing in 35 different fiction magazines for the last few years, *Frog* leaped into the literary pond with a big splash last fall: a finalist for the National Book Award even before publication. *Frog* lost that one to Norman Rush's *Mating*, but the nomination brought unexpected attention to one of the more prolific writers in the business, the author of more than 300 short stories, eight story collections, and five novels — most published within the last 15 years.

Frog is a thick, squat collection of short stories, sketches and novellas that can be called a novel by virtue of the fact that they all concern Howard Tetch, a college writing teacher (like Dixon, who teaches at Johns Hopkins) with a wife and two daughters (ditto Dixon). The novel covers Howard's entire life — even his afterlife — but not chronologically; it is more like a collage of episodes, dozens of scenes from a marriage, the domestic manners of modern Americans, placed in no obvious order (though it's possible to see meaningful juxtapositions — as with Joseph McElroy's *Women and Men*, another huge novel of interrelated stories and novellas). Under various headings ("Frog's Brother," "Frog Reads the News," etc. — nowhere else is Howard called Frog, the reasons for the nickname remain unclear), we are told of Howard's marriages, divorces, affairs in between, his experiences at camp, relationships to parents, household accidents, the deaths of a brother and sister, picking up his daughter at school, learning to ride a horse, his first time with a prostitute, his favorite dog, the time he foiled a burglar — a veritable compendium of experiences from everyday life, most of them ordinary, a little drama in some, tedium in others. The jacket description ill-advisedly calls *Frog* "the *Finnegans Wake* of this generation"; the copy-writer probably had in mind not the linguistic invention of Joyce's epic — for Dixon's prose is plain as porridge — but the possibility that Howard's experiences approach the universality of those of Humphrey Chimpden Earwicker, the ordinary paterfamilias of *Finnegans Wake*.

Frog also resembles Joyce's work in its nonlinear, episodic form and especially in its use of alternate versions of the same story. In one sequence, Howard imagines a number of scenarios to explain his wife's lateness in returning from a movie; in another, there are a dozen versions of Howard's reaction to seeing a priest and two policemen in his apartment building lobby; in yet another, he imagines various ways his brother Alex might have drowned at sea. In the first instance, the "true" story is revealed; in the others, not — unless the final version is intended to be the true one. But to insist on a true version of things is very much beside the point in *Frog*: it is our very tendency to make up stories, to imagine what might have been, to revise memories, that Dixon pursues to such great lengths. In "Frog Dies," Howard even imagines different ways he might die and how his daughters might think of him in later years: Here, the daughters, Olivia and Eva, take center stage with some rather amazing verbal arias, outdoing Daddy in digressive, obsessional prose. "Frog's Mom" consists of 120 pages of first drafts as Howard tries to find the paradigmatic incident that will define how he feels about her, only to conclude inconclusively and telling himself: "Enough, give up."

For these reasons, Dixon is called an "experimental realist," but readers who are scared off by the e-word (or by evocations of *Finnegans Wake*) can rest assured that *Frog* is easy reading, too easy maybe, often requiring no more effort than would be needed listening to a voluble stranger in a bar telling a long story about how he met his wife, or sitting on the couch with an aged aunt turning the pages of a photo album and telling the stories behind each picture. Dixon self-referentially explains his own method in the last of Howard's attempts to write about his mother:

> I asked my mother to tell me a thing or two about her mother she remembers the most. She asked me what I meant. I said "A memory, some incident, something she did to you or around you or to anyone — anything, a trait, habit or ritual she went through, religious, dress, food, or otherwise. But just something that keeps coming back and back to you — a quirk, even, or some physical gesture or a pretension — and you do or you don't know why it does come back or why you can't forget it or even what it means to you or just in itself, but something that possibly, well you know, exemplifies her, but it doesn't have to be as sweeping as all that." She looked at me as if she still didn't understand. I shrugged as if saying "What's wrong?" "Really, sweetheart, you're not making yourself very clear, and I don't think it should be blamed entirely on my hearing."

This, of course, is the modus operandi for the modern short story: a revealing incident or memory that exemplifies a character. But such stories by themselves are never "sweeping," so by cobbling together dozens and dozens of Howard's memories, traits, quirks, gestures, pretensions, and so on — "a concatenation of fabulations," to borrow a phrase from the book that Dixon may have placed there for the convenience of reviewers — Dixon is attempting to give short-story methodology something of the sweep of an epic novel. As such, *Frog* represents an interesting new hybrid: a long novel made up of short episodes, a maximalist meganovel written in a minimalist style.

Dixon is equally self-referential about his style. When an interviewer's questions come into Howard's hands, he admits that the description of his style is good: "'Your style, then. It sounds so undecorated, conversational, unstylized, spoken, even reads at times like quote unquote bad writing or neglected conventional writing. Yet the reader is aware of your deliberately ignoring standard sentence structure, syntax, punctuation, etcetera. Can you comment further on how you compose or what this style says about the people, places and situations that you write about?'" Howard doesn't answer the question; "I could if I was another writer," he quips.

But a possible answer is that Dixon is concerned with the unguarded, unbuttoned, private person, not the rehearsed, carefully groomed public persona — more interested in the frog before it is kissed into a prince, so to speak. If so, it is appropriate for the language to be casual, even sloppy, from the heart, rather than polished, structured, from the head. For readers who can see through such "bad writing" and relish the immediacy it offers, its vitality, its feel of catching life on the wing as Dixon's characters endlessly try to explain themselves to others or to themselves, *Frog* will be a memorable experience.

Washington Post Book World, 19 January 1992

□ □ □ □ □ □ □

I.

McSweeney's, 2002

As the author of two dozen books and nearly 500 short stories published over the last 25 years, Stephen Dixon may be the hardest-working man in the lit business. He has perfected a distinctive style, whereby a minor incident triggers obsessive analysis, jittery self-questioning, second thoughts and daydreamed alternatives, all conveyed in a torrent of idiomatic prose with rarely a paragraph break. His stories read quickly, belying the care with which they're constructed; in interviews, Dixon admits to revising some pages 30 or 40 times.

Though billed as a novel, *I.* reads like any of Dixon's short-story collections, and like almost everything he's written, it is (according to his new publisher) very autobiographical. All of the stories, or chapters, concern a character who, like Dixon, teaches creative writing at a university (Johns Hopkins), is married to a handicapped woman, and has two daughters. Most of the time, the narrator is called simply "he"; a few times, he tries the first-person "I" and then the initial "I.," but there's no meaningful distinction. Nor is anyone named, aside from a few peripheral characters. The stories hopscotch in time from the narrator's childhood to the present.

He's a pretty ordinary guy, the narrator, and many of the stories/chapters deal with ordinary events. In one, he apologizes repeatedly to one of his daughters for always losing his temper. In another, he attempts to correct his forgetfulness with mnemonic tricks. Others recall dates he had with women before he met his wife. There's a Seinfeldian quality to some, with a minor incident being obsessed over to the point of absurdity: His apologies to his daughter, for example, are extrapolated into the future when he imagines himself apologizing to her hypothetical son.

What makes these ordinary incidents extraordinary — and what has earned Dixon so many awards and the attention of critics — is the metafictional techniques he deploys so effortlessly. Like a magician explaining his trick as he performs it, Dixon lets the reader overhear his thinking process as he constructs these stories: sorting out correct details from misremembered ones, finding the right vocabulary, wondering if he should cut certain passages, and so on. In the opening chapter, he gets halfway through a story before admitting the events didn't really happen that way, then gives a presumably accurate account.

In the most extreme example — the concluding, novella-length "Again" — the narrator begins with multiple versions of how he met his wife, each slightly different. It reads like the literary equivalent of a cubist painting or, better yet, like one of Philip Glass's early, hour-long compositions, which repeat basic figures with algorithmic variations. About halfway through, the narrator settles into a straightforward narrative, and this account of a 42-year-old man courting a younger woman confined to a wheelchair just might break your heart.

Like an improv comic who takes a suggestion from the audience and runs with it, Dixon usually starts with a promising opening line to see where it takes him. Sometimes it goes well, other times, as he'll confess to the reader, it goes nowhere. The difference between Dixon and a more mainstream writer is that he publishes his "failures," which nonetheless succeed at showing the writer's mind at work and deepening the characterization of his narrator.

Whether considered as another short-story collection or as a novel — all of the stories do indeed add up to a well-rounded picture and history of "he"/"I"/"I." — Dixon's latest book accurately captures the hectic, one-damn-thing-after-another quality of modern life. Dixon is the polar opposite of the late William Gaddis — who seems to be the model for a character in one story, snubbing the narrator on several occasions — but, like Gaddis, he paces his events at breakneck speed and can ride herd on a stampede of language that is always, but never quite, threatening to go out of control. And he's much easier than Gaddis; reading his stories is like eating potato chips. Despite their metafictional qualities and possible parallels with cubist art or minimalist music, these fictions stick to basic emotions and real-life situations: They take place in crowded apartments and suburban houses, not in ivory towers. Highly personal, in a few cases embarrassingly intimate, *I.* is artfully artless, honest and true.

Consumer advisory: Because of the publisher's benighted anticorporate stance, McSweeney's Books are available only in selected independent bookstores and on their website. Dixon's books sell poorly enough without being saddled with this additional burden, so interested readers will need to make a special effort to procure a copy. *I.* is worth it.

Washington Post Book World, 26 May 2002. I added that concluding paragraph because I was a buyer for Borders at the time and we had a hard time convincing McSweeney's to sell their books to us.

Rikki Ducornet

The Butcher's Tales
Atlas Press, 1991

Many adjectives can characterize Rikki Ducornet's stories — exotic, surrealist, erotic, oneiric, macabre, whimsical, sensuous, coarse, elegant — but never ordinary or predictable. Six of the eight extraordinary, unpredictable stories in this chapbook are reprinted from a larger, limited edition of the same title published in Canada ten years ago and now quite scarce. In any given story, all of the above adjectives might apply; a similar array of influences can be discerned, ranging from Lewis Carroll and H. P. Lovecraft through (most importantly) the French Surrealists, Borges, and Angela Carter. Her characters are often in the grip of some form of madness, eccentricity, or perversion, and the storylines seek that "resolution of dream and reality" that André Breton recommends in his *Surrealist Manifesto*. At a time when so much fiction is banal and plain, *The Butcher's Tales* shimmers like an oasis in a desert.

Review of Contemporary Fiction, Fall 1991

Marguerite Duras

Two by Duras. Translated by Alberto Manguel
Coach House Press, 1993

Yann Andrea Steiner. Translated by Barbara Bray
Scribner's, 1993

Marilyn R. Schuster. *Marguerite Duras Revisited*
Twayne, 1993

Though called novellas by their publisher, the *Two* short pieces are more properly called "writings" by Duras in the interview with Ana María Moix that follows them. "The Slut of the Normandy Coast" (1986) is an account of Duras's difficulty converting her novel *The Malady of Death* into a play, and her concurrent troubles with her gay companion Yann Andréa. I can't see how it would interest anyone other than Duras specialists. But the second work, "The Atlantic Man" (1982), is sublime, resembling an austere Japanese painting. Taking the form of instructions given by a director to an actor, it uses film metaphors to explore memory, self-consciousness, and creation. The interview that follows concerns other works, mostly *The Lover*, and the attractively designed volume concludes with a brief afterword by the translator.

Yann Andrea Steiner is Duras's memoir of her relationship with the homosexual man half her age who came into her life in 1980, and who has been her companion ever since. But it is not a conventional memoir: mixed in with her story of Yann Andréa are fiction fragments and material that first appeared in other texts. Giving him the additional surname of Steiner aligns him with Aurélia Steiner (the protagonist of some of Duras's films) and underlines her identification with Jews, the subject of the fiction fragments. The result is not an autobiography but something finer, a meditation on Duras's deepest fears and needs.

Marilyn Schuster's book is an excellent introduction and overview of Duras's work. In the manner of most Twayne books, a biographical introduction is followed by chapters on virtually all the books (and in Duras's case, her films as well), with special attention to showing how the later texts modify earlier ones. For those who began reading Duras only with *The Lover*, or have read a few random novels, Schuster's book is invaluable for tracing the intricate continuity of all the fiction. She argues that all the work is concerned with a woman's story: how such stories are told, how a male narrator complicates the telling of a woman's story (as in *The Ravishing of Lol Stein*), and how film has allowed Duras to expand her woman-centered approach to fiction. The book addresses both French and American forms of feminist theory and manages to be critically au courant without being too hermetic for the general reader. A model study, and highly recommended.

Review of Contemporary Fiction, Spring 1994

Lawrence Durrell

Livia: or, Buried Alive
Viking, 1979

In the late 1950s, British writer Lawrence Durrell wrote a four-novel sequence called *The Alexandria Quartet* that has come to stand as a major achievement of modern literature. A two-novel sequence called *The Revolt of Aphrodite* followed some ten years later, but failed to win the same critical acclaim as its predecessor. Now, we learn, Durrell has launched what will be a five-novel sequence, and with the release of the second novel it looks like Durrell is on his way to creating another landmark in modern literature.

Livia: or, Buried Alive picks up where Durrell's 1975 novel *Monsieur* left off, and one really needs to be acquainted with the earlier novel to fully appreciate its . . . I almost wrote "sequel," but that belies the relationship between the two novels (and, presumably, the ones to follow). *Livia* begins with a novelist named Blanford brooding on a novel he wrote called *Monsieur* — a novel about another novelist called Sutcliffe, with whom Blanford carries on literal (and schizophrenic?) conversations about *Monsieur* and how it will lead to others:

> "Well, squinting round the curves of futurity I saw something like a quincunx of novels set out in a good classical order. Five Q novels written in a highly elliptical quincunxial style invented for the occasion. Though only dependent on one another as echoes might be, they would not be laid end to end in serial order, like dominoes — but simply belong to the same blood group, five panels for which your creaky old *Monsieur* would provide simply a cluster of themes to be reworked in the others."

Livia purports to be the "true" story behind *Monsieur*, so what we have then is a fiction commenting on another fiction but asserting itself as the true fiction, at least until the next fiction comes along.

Sound confusing? It's not, really. One must allow Durell his literary fun and games, for no one is more concerned with the modern novel as an art form than he is, and consequently no matter what the subject of a particular novel is, there will always be much discussion — by the author as well as by his characters — of novel-writing. Sometimes this calls for a bit of patience on the reader's part, for the self-conscious, self-reflexiveness of the novels almost gives the game away, so to speak. But these literary conundrums are pretty much confined to the first chapter. After that we are treated (and I do mean *treated*) to a series of vignettes examining "the perennity of despair, intractability of language, impenetrability of art, insipidity of human love."

Plot plays a negligible part in *Livia*, just as it did in the *Quartet*. Rather, the emphasis is on character, and character studies consequently give the novel its form. What in another author might be called episodic writing is in Durrell an attempt to select certain occasions when a character reveals an important aspect of him/herself, and an "attempt to encompass the vast multiplicity of purely human attributes" necessitates an episodic — or better yet epiphanic — approach to writing.

Just as the exotic city of Alexandria is mirrored in the lush, luxurious prose of the *Quartet*, the city of Avignon — home of the popes during the great schism and the setting of both *Monsieur* and *Livia* — contributes a brooding, rather melancholic tone to the writing. The profligacy of the Avignon popes, the Templar heresy (the ramifications of which, Durrell argues, are being felt to this very day), and other medieval aberrations seem to hang in the air of Provence in the 1930s (the temporal setting of *Livia*) and coagulate with the rise of Nazi Germany and the inevitable World War II to color the prose of the entire novel. But in spite of this overall tone, Durrell's writing — as always — still sparkles with aphorisms, pungent imagery, telling metaphors, and of course insights into the nature of art. (A friend and I spent an unfruitful hour puzzling over the "12 Commandments" of great art given in French in the appendix, coming away only with a vague notion that great art somehow resembles French cuisine.)

Denis de Rougemont, to whom *Livia* is dedicated, is the author of the classic 1940 literary-theological study *Love in the Western World* (still in print and still worth reading in spite of its Catholic bias). One day, when Durrell's novels are collected into a complete edition, no other overall title than that could be more appropriate. Love is, for Durrell, the axis of all human activity, the sun around which everything else revolves (even those things which, like the moon, turn their faces away from it), and Art the most effective means of both understanding love and paying homage. Love and art, as Durrell knows, is an unbeatable combination, and will serve for not only a quincunx of novels but even a quinquagintacunx of novels, had he time to write that many. And I, for one, would read all 50 with as much pleasure as I have his latest one.

Spree, May 1979

□ □ □ □ □ □ □

Lawrence Durrell: Comprehending the Whole.
Edited by Melody L. Enscore and Paige Matthey Bynum
University of Missouri Press, 1995

Thirty years ago Lawrence Durrell was universally considered one of the most important British novelists of our time, but since his death in 1990 he seems to be dropping off the map. His U.S. publisher declined his U.K. publisher's offer to publish its one-volume edition of *The Avignon Quintet* (1992), and except for *The Alexandria Quartet* all of his novels are now out of print (as is much of his poetry and nonfiction). Until his work comes into favor again, it may be up to academics to keep the fires burning (as they did with William Gaddis during his dark decades of neglect), and this new book demonstrates that Durrell's contribution to modern literature is significant enough to warrant continued attention.

The subtitle, *Comprehending the Whole,* is exactly what the book sets out to achieve. There are essays here on the two novels Durrell published before *The Black Book* (of whose existence I wasn't aware), as well as that breakthrough novel and all that followed, up to the concluding volumes of the *Quintet.* There are also essays on his Antrobus stories, his poetry, his relationship to Greece, a comparison of his underrated *Revolt of Aphrodite* to Pynchon's *V.*, and a description of the large Durrell collection at Southern Illinois University. As such, the book serves as an excellent introduction to Durrell's corpus as well as a fresh reevaluation of the work.

Review of Contemporary Fiction, Summer 1995

□ □ □ □ □ □ □

Gordon Bowker. *Through the Dark Labyrinth: A Biography of Lawrence Durrell*
St. Martin's, 1997

This biography couldn't be more timely. Considered until recently one of England's premier novelists of the postwar period, Durrell has been slipping into oblivion since his death in 1990. Of his 16 novels, only the four of his *Alexandria Quartet* (and a throwaway thriller) remain in print. His U.S. publisher declined to bring out the handsome one-volume edition of his *Avignon Quintet* published in England in 1992, easily the greatest British novel since . . . well, since *The Alexandria Quartet* appeared in the late '50s. Scholarly studies still appear, but without the availability of the novels they play to an empty house. Perhaps Gordon Bowker's satisfying biography, the first of

Durrell, will rescue him from this undeserved neglect.

Lawrence Durrell led such a colorful life that this book should appeal to anyone who likes a good biography. Born in India in 1912, Durrell had a Kiplingesque childhood that forever colored his view of dour England. It was a privileged upbringing, and included a Jesuit education in Darjeeling surrounded by Buddhists, the kind of exotic juxtaposition of cultures one finds throughout his novels. England, by contrast, was bleak and colorless when he arrived there in 1923 to continue his education. As soon as he was old enough he began to explore the gaslit night life of bohemian London, even jumping over to Paris whenever he could. He was already writing by this time, mostly poetry, and supporting himself by playing jazz piano at night and working odd jobs by day. Failing the entrance exams to college — although bright and well-read, he never "applied himself," as guidance counselors say — he began writing his first novel and began courting the woman who was to become the first of his four wives, Nancy Myers. It must be stated at the outset that Durrell was a terrible husband to all his wives — violent, temperamental, unfaithful — but Bowker commends them for the important roles they played in the writer's life, especially his third wife, Claude-Marie Vincendon. Durrell mistreated his wives, but Bowker doesn't, one of his many admirable traits as a biographer. (He has also written the definitive biography of Malcolm Lowry, another brilliant but troubled writer.)

Durrell took the first opportunity to leave England and in 1935 moved with Nancy to the island of Corfu. (It's interesting how many of the U.K.'s major novelists of this century went into self-imposed exile: Joyce, Lowry, Beckett, Burgess. . . .) He loved it there and except for brief visits never lived in Britain again, preferring the sunny Mediterranean to rainy "Pudding Island" (as he called England) and a pagan atmosphere to a puritanical one. Two things happened that crucial year: his first novel was accepted for publication (a forgotten book called *Pied Piper of Lovers*) and he discovered Henry Miller. *Tropic of Cancer* was a bombshell for Durrell, exploding his notions of what a novel could be and freeing him to write his first truly Durrellian novel, *The Black Book*. (A second novel, *Panic Spring*, intervened, but like his first it was never reprinted and is unknown to all but Durrell specialists.) Durrell wrote Miller a fan letter and the two became lifelong friends, a relationship celebrated in their published correspondence. Miller introduced Durrell to his lover at the time, Anaïs Nin, who also became a friend for life. Bowker vividly recounts the rollicking time these "Three Musketeers" had upon meeting in Paris, and for years thereafter.

The Black Book was intended as the first of a trilogy, but two decades would pass before its author returned to fiction in full force. World War II caused Durrell to flee to Egypt, which was to provide the setting for his great quartet years later. Egypt during the war was edgy and exotic, but it was a difficult time for Durrell: His marriage fell apart and his fiction foundered, though he did complete the first of many travel books, *Prospero's Cell*. (Some of Durrell's admirers consider his half-dozen travel books to be his greatest achievement; most of them have been reprinted recently by Marlowe in handsome trade paperbacks.) After the war, Durrell drifted from Egypt to Rhodes, married again, spent a disastrous year in Argentina and a few more in Yugoslavia, then moved to Cyprus — all the while churning out poetry, plays, and travel books while his Alexandrian novel fermented. *Justine*, the first in the quartet, finally appeared in 1957 and made Durrell a literary celebrity (especially in France, where he eventually settled). It ended his unwanted diplomatic career (which nevertheless provided him with the material for his comic Antrobus series, which should appeal to Wodehouse fans) and allowed him to concentrate on his increasingly complex novels: *The Alexandria Quartet* (1957–60), the two-volume *Revolt of Aphrodite* (1968–70), and *The Avignon Quintet* (1974–85) — three meganovels that dwarf the achievement of any other British novelist of his generation.

Gordon Bowker's account is admirable: well-researched, detailed while avoiding the minutiae that clog some literary biographies, sympathetic but not uncritical, and quite readable. It's filled with interesting facts: I had no idea Durrell was one of the screenwriters for the Burton–Taylor *Cleopatra* or that he contributed to the script for *Judith*, a 1965 film starring Sophia Loren. (Durrell had nothing to do with the atrocious film version of his own *Justine*.) As I said, Bowker gives Durrell's long-suffering wives their full due, and provides an evenhanded account of the scandal that surfaced soon after his death: his alleged incest with his daughter Sappho. Durrell treated his gifted but tormented daughter abominably, but the incest was apparently more psychological than physical, as Sappho admitted to her husband. (She committed suicide in 1985.)

Durrell hated proofreading and as a result some of his first editions are marred by errors; unfortunately Bowker imitates his subject in this regard. But the principal fault of *Through the Dark Labyrinth* isn't Bowker's but that of the Durrell Estate, which refused him permission to quote from Durrell's works or letters (except for the briefest examples). As a result, Bowker has to resort to sometimes wooden paraphrase, a shame in the case of a glittering stylist like Durrell. This is one more example of a growing problem in literary scholarship: the stranglehold some estates keep on their inherited authors, allegedly "protecting" their interests but in truth hobbling scholarship for what appears to be private gain (as in the case of Joyce's estate) or from simple obtuseness (as in Kerouac's, until recently). Apparently the Durrell Estate is sponsoring an "official" biography, and it had better be good. Until then, *Through the*

Dark Labyrinth is a welcome book for both Durrell fans and anyone interested in the literary life.

Washington Post Book World, 20 July 1997. That official biography, by Ian S. MacNiven, appeared in 1998; *Kirkus Reviews* said "Though MacNiven has the advantage of being able to quote freely from Durrell's oeuvre, he is much better on his subject's life, while Bowker's real strength lies in his understanding and exposition of Durrell's work."

Lucinda Ebersole

Death in Equality
St. Martin's Press, 1997

If you have a flair for writing Southern Gothic stories, but are smart enough to know that literary cottonfield has been picked clean, what do you do? If you're as smart as Lucinda Ebersole, you construct a metafictional structure that will allow you to have your grits and eat them too. Diagnosed with terminal lung cancer, 43-year-old Cordelia, a would-be writer living in New York City, decides to return to her hometown of Equality, Alabama, to die. It's a town where the most exciting event in recent memory was the time when a chicken truck ran a stoplight and overturned in front of the Shiloh Baptist Church, but it fulfils Cordelia's writerly sense of form to seek closure where the six previous Cordelias in her family lived and/or died.

The novel alternates between Cordelia's deathbed monologue — in first person and set in a sans serif font — and her memories of life in Equality, in third person and set in a traditional typeface. Make that memories of *death* in Equality, for nearly every tale recounts someone's death, often under grisly circumstances. These stories form a memorable cycle, like *Dubliners* or *Winesburg, Ohio*, but Cordelia's monologues are even more affecting. She's a sharp-witted bibliophile whose failure to have published a book is finally more tragic than the deaths of any of her hapless fellow citizens. While the Equality death stories are traditional in form and language, the monologues are engagingly diverse and quirky: we get a list of Cordelia's Garbo films on tape, brief lectures on Hildegard of Bingen and Vivaldi's Cello Concerto in G (and why the cello is the most feminine instrument), character sketches of her friends, catty remarks on the literary life, and much else.

As Cordelia drifts in and out of consciousness, her monologues and Equality memories occasionally bleed into one another, and stray phrases float on the page as in Carole Maso's AVA (which is included in "Cordelia's Final Reading List" on the last page of the novel). There is a deliberate confusion of narrative levels, strongly suggesting that Cordelia's tales of death in Equality are not mere memories but the literary stories she will not live to write and publish.

While the deaths of Equality's citizens are sad, if sometimes ludicrous, Cordelia's slow death is somehow exultant and transcendent. Ebersole's brilliant juxtaposition of a moribund literary form like the Southern Gothic with the livelier possibilities of postmodernism makes *Death in Equality* a fascinating study in literary evolution as well as a touching reminder of how much is lost when the world loses a gifted writer prematurely. Fortunately, the gifted Lucinda Ebersole is alive and kicking, and it is to be hoped she will produce many more such books before her time comes.

Rain Taxi, Fall 1997

Janice Eidus

Vito Loves Geraldine
City Lights, 1990

"Vito Loves Geraldine" is the sort of phrase one might see spray-painted on a wall, and Janice Eidus's first collection of stories is like an unusually imaginative NYC wall of graffiti: colorful and daring, unafraid of new forms or old sentiments. The opening story is a parody of a fairy tale, "Sleeping Beauty" perhaps, retold in a gum-snapping Brooklyn accent by a young woman brazenly sure of her destiny. But most of the other stories are about people unsure of themselves — in transition, in transformation — and concern the metaphors and language of transformation. Kids fasten onto objects of metaphoric value ("Davida's Own") or invent private languages as a defense against the grownup world ("Robin's Nest"), while Eidus's adults attempt more forceful changes by adopting unfamiliar idioms: a straitlaced wife attempts a career as a performance artist to give tongue to her repressed selves ("Vanna"), a sophisticated executive secretary turns into a Dolly Parton look-alike for a spell ("The Country in Maura"), and another woman forsakes suicidal Sylvia Plath for muscle magazines and pumping iron ("The Resolution of Muscle"). "I can change the course of my life," this last woman boasts, "create myself anew. . . ."

Eidus isn't afraid to change the course of the short story either, to create it anew by experimenting with new forms. "Safe" alternates points of view as a couple ruminates on post-AIDS sexual ethics, "The Star-Crossed Love of Don Diego del Perro and Chastity" is a mini-anthology of parodies of romantic genres, and "American Love Story" closes the collection with a metafictional love story that, like its counterpart at the beginning, both celebrates and parodies the rock candy durability of such tales. *Vito Loves Geraldine* is a vibrant collection of stories about our love for stories and about the potential of language to transform lives.

Review of Contemporary Fiction, Summer 1990

Stanley Elkin

The Living End
E. P. Dutton, 1979

"Serious comedy" may sound like a contradiction in terms, but it simply distinguishes it from trivial comedy, that which aims no higher than a belly laugh. The best serious comedian writing today is probably Stanley Elkin, whose new novel *The Living End* is, well, the living end. An eschatological farce, a divine comedy, it must simply be read to be believed. Elkin's verbal energy and inventiveness is dazzling, but unfortunately is over all too quickly. The novel is very short and can probably be finished in one afternoon at the poolside, provided one is not distracted by any of the equally dazzling delights usually presented in watery locales, a serious obstacle to even the most determined reader.

Spree, July 1979 — the only salvageable paragraph from a light column on summer reading.

□ □ □ □ □ □ □

Peter Bailey. *Reading Stanley Elkin*
University of Illinois Press, 1985

In the second book-length treatment of Elkin's dazzling fiction, Peter Bailey counters the charge that Elkin writes a gimmicky, zoot-suited prose too funny to be taken seriously with admirable demonstrations of how that supercharged prose actually works. Bailey argues that Elkin's fiction succeeds "through the elaboration and resolution of metaphoric (as opposed to philosophical or narrative) tensions" — a tendency more pronounced in the later works — and shows that Elkin's work must be read with the critical tools one is more apt to use with poetry than prose. Frost once described the poetic act as "performance and prowess and feats of association," and Bailey traces out those amazing feats of association that make up Elkin's heavily imagistic prose. He pays particular attention to the metaphor-making strategy Elkin calls "crossover": the jarring juxtaposition of one set of ideas and images against an incongruent set from an apparently unrelated field. The sparks that fly from such juxtapositions constitute the "heightened perception" that Ellerbe achieves upon becoming an angel in *The Living End* and create the lexical heaven of Elkin's best work.

Bailey quite rightly separates Elkin from the Jewish-American writers he is sometimes associated with (although not before a thorough discussion of the connection) and instead shows his affinities with such postmodernists as Pynchon, Coover, Barthelme, and Apple. (He might have added William Gaddis: he and Elkin admire each other's work and share many of the same preconceptions and aesthetics.) Using Elkin's early story "A Poetics for Bullies" as a paradigm of his artistic strategies and thematic concerns, Bailey works through the entire Elkin oeuvre: *Boswell* receives only passing mention, but the rest receive extended readings in which thematics and poetics are insightfully intertwined. (He is at his best on the four books from *A Bad Man* through *The Franchiser*; he is less thorough with *The Living End* and *George Mills*, and *The Magic Kingdom* appeared too late for inclusion.) What emerges is a clear sense of Elkin's growing reliance on language (rather than plot or theme) to carry his fictions, a high-wire confidence that his acrobatic prose needs no net.

Most importantly, Bailey never lets the reader lose sight of the wellspring of Elkin's fiction, that joyous quality which makes him one of the most consistently satisfying authors to read: "Elkin's is a fiction of excess, a fiction of abundance and artistic generosity. To recognize this is to realize that the real tension underlying all his work, whatever its shape once it has been transformed, is that of the imagination refusing to allow invention to flag — that of the creative mind's insistence that new pleasures and insights can still be wrung from the old materials and the old words if enough energy and vision are brought to the task." Elkin has been blessed with a critic who brings his own energy and vision to the task of explicating his fiction.

American Notes & Queries, May/June 1986

□ □ □ □ □ □ □

Stanley Elkin. *The MacGuffin*
Linden Press/Simon and Schuster, 1991

David C. Dougherty. *Stanley Elkin*
Twayne, 1991

Elkin could publish his novels anonymously and they would still be instantly recognizable as his, so unique is his style. That hot-wired vernacular, souped up with an astonishing array of rhetorical devices, hums like an ace in his newest novel. Once again Elkin examines the effect of vocation on character — a thematic common denominator in his work, as David Dougherty points out — in this case a city commissioner named Bobbo Druff. Observing the classic unities (as his narrator self-consciously notes), Elkin records a manic day and a half in 58-year-old Druff's life (with an extended flashback to his courting days) in his characteristic melting-pot style: an often riotous conglomeration of street slang, aggressive banter, barbaric (in the grammatical sense) Frankenstein sentences patched together with hyphenated adjectives, paratactic particulars, and outrageous (but always apt) metaphors. "Regaling," the narrator announces at one point, defining Elkin's relationship to his lucky reader: "Making it clear. Regaling. Regaling and relishing."

Elkin's verbal performances are so regaling, in fact, that one often overlooks the larger themes and philosophical issues in his texts. In *The MacGuffin*, these concern decline and helplessness of all sorts (physical, emotional, spiritual); Dougherty devotes his book to identifying the themes of Elkin's earlier novels, resisting the Siren-like allure of Elkin's language to concentrate on thematic clusters that have been ignored by previous critics. Friends and foes too often have allowed the humor of Elkin's novels to obscure his profound concern with "the ways in which our thinking affects our being," and Dougherty demonstrates the "philosophic richness" in the work in such a way that can only magnify the importance of this matchless novelist.

Review of Contemporary Fiction, Fall 1991

□ □ □ □ □ □ □

Pieces of Soap

Simon & Schuster, 1992

Stanley Elkin is mentioned only in passing in the new *Columbia History of the American Novel* ([reviewed] above [by John O'Brien] — another damning mark against it), but when the definitive history of the American novel in the second half of the 20th century is written, Elkin had better receive star treatment. I've used up all my superlatives reviewing previous books by and about him, but his prose style still strikes me as one of the greatest literary achievements of our time, every sentence deserving to be studied and savored with the attention we bring to Shakespeare or Joyce.

Pieces of Soap, his collected essays, comes as a welcome surprise. I had seen a few of these in magazines over the years, but had no idea there were so many (there are 30 here), and on such a range of topics: talk radio, the Academy Awards, the Kinsey sex reports, tuxedos, chairs, first names, novelty items, and betting on horses, in addition to the art of fiction. These latter essays treat his own fiction — included here are the prefaces he has written for various reissues and limited editions of his work — as well as such things as plot, inspiration, form (he's a party-line Russian Formalist, whether he knows it or not), the differences between the short story and the novel, the novel and the drama. The book opens with his well-known "Performance and Reality," where he discusses "crossover" — using the idiom of one field in a different, often incongruous one — which he considers invaluable in achieving the "strange displacements of the ordinary" so crucial to his art. (Russian Formalist Viktor Shklovsky called it "enstrangement.") But the essay also introduces the reader to the source of Elkin's trademark style, a verbal saturnalia where words cross-dress to create those riotous, dazzling metaphors of his. "Idiom knows," he notes at one point, and no writer gets greater mileage out of the immense resources and possibilities of the American idiom. (He must be hell on his translators; in fact, he's probably untranslatable, in the same way the greatest poetry is.)

"At the top of my voice at the top of my form, vicious, a gossip, clever as a fag, with, to save me, only this: that I am never the hero of my anecdotes but always — I'm crippled too — the fall guy, whiner take all." These are intensely personal essays: Elkin tells you of his likes, his dislikes, stories of his parents, anecdotes from his army days, why he lives where he lives, problems stemming from his multiple sclerosis — enough material to make *Pieces of Soap* serve as a kind of patchwork autobiography, as his confessions. But that shouldn't limit the book's appeal to Elkin fans and scholars (may their number increase!), for the book has sociological value as one ordinary/extraordinary American's take on this culture of ours. The force of Elkin's personality, the penetration of his insight, and the brilliance of his wit unify this grab bag of essays into a coherent work as entertaining as it is enlightening.

Review of Contemporary Fiction, Summer 1992

□ □ □ □ □ □ □

Van Gogh's Room at Arles: Three Novellas

Hyperion, 1993

Reading Stanley Elkin always reminds me not so much of his peers — that A-list of contemporary American novelists consisting of Barth, Coover, Gaddis, Gass, and Pynchon — as of reading Shakespeare. If that sounds hyperbolic, read Elkin and the Bard in tandem and you'll see what I mean: Just as everybody in Shakespeare, even gardeners and slaves, speaks in a richly imagistic language, everyone in Elkin speaks in a colorful argot of slang, shoptalk, proverbs, and one-liners. Like the butcher's boy from Stratford, Elkin scoops up the verbal flotsam and jetsam of his time — catchphrases, tag lines from movies, advertising slogans, song lyrics — and finds metaphors and similes in them. Metonyms. Litotes. Fifty years from now his texts will require as many footnotes as Shakespeare's, and the vast range of his linguistic resources, his amazing facility with the American vernacular, will make him the darling of lexicographers, the pet of anthologists, the pride of the Yankees for those specializing in late-20th-century American trivia.

For example, "Her Sense of Timing," the first of the three novellas making up *Van Gogh's Room at Arles*, develops from that recent commercial featuring the elderly lady who shouts out, "Help me, I've fallen and I can't get up." A campy squawk for some, it becomes in this superb novella a line that King Lear might have addressed to his fool. On the day before Professor Jack Schiff hosts his annual party for his grad students, his wife Claire announces that she's leaving him. Home alone, Schiff has more than your garden-variety despair to contend with: he is a wheelchair-bound cripple pushing 60 and suffering an advanced neurological disease. (As is Elkin — in fact, Schiff even has Elkin's St. Louis street address, and is obviously the most autobiographical character he's ever created.) There is no mawkish self-pity here, though, or any '90s sensitivity to the plight of the "physically challenged": Elkin's characters are tough — "cripple" is Schiff's word for himself — and use their linguistic prowess to ward off the slings and arrows of outrageous fortune. Remembering that commercial, Schiff calls and arranges for the emergency-call system (his conversation with the salesman is one of the funniest bits in the book) but decides too late to call off his party, which turns into a disaster. As the gathering gets further and further out of control, Schiff loses more and more of the only thing he has left — his dignity — as he realizes his life is not a tragedy but a farce.

In fact, the maintenance of dignity is the unifying thread between the book's three novellas, just as bachelors concerned with mortality unified Elkin's previous collection of novellas, *Searches and Seizures* (1973). In the second piece in the new collection, a British woman seeks to preserve her dignity against lurid tabloid accusations by penning a "*Town Crier* Exclusive, Confessions of a Princess Manqué: 'How Royals Found Me "Unsuitable" to Marry Their Larry.'" Recalling the recent separations of the Duchess of York from Prince Andrew and the Princess of Wales from Prince Charles, the failed princess in Elkin's novella is a commoner named Louise ("La Lulu" to the press) who is engaged to Lawrence, Duke of Wilshire, successor to the British throne. In a sense, Lawrence is confined to a wheelchair of traditions, protocols, and noblesse oblige expectations, which he endures with the same breezy self-deprecation that Jack Schiff does. Elkin has a field day with the trappings of monarchy: the titles, the customs, the intricacies of heraldry, the myriad royal offices and eccentric officers, the theory and practice of divine right, even the furniture in various palaces. The royals themselves — a dotty group closer to a Noël Coward cast than to the current royal family — initially welcome Louise into their closed world, but finally call off the engagement after Louise makes a confession Lawrence finds too challenging to his own dignity. In the course of her engagement, Louise discovers much about the symbolic nature of power, something else Jack Schiff meditated on as he watched his power over his students flicker like a bad light bulb.

Little power or dignity adheres to Professor Miller, the protagonist of "Van Gogh's Room at Arles." Awarded a foundation grant to join a group of scholars in the southern French city, he finds things going wrong from the minute he steps off the bus. Outclassed by the visiting luminaries from Harvard, Oxford, the Sorbonne, and elsewhere, this teacher from the Booth Tarkington Community College in Indianapolis has a case of jet lag that turns into a chronic ailment, a gift for making one faux pas after another, and an inability to understand French (which Elkin comically translates: "He heard the waiter tell them in French that but that because Madame Celli had become invisible in the laundry two horses must begin to be"). He is put up in the same room Van Gogh occupied, the subject of the famous painting, and soon meets various descendants of Van Gogh's portraits, who, in homage, dress as their originals did. And without meaning to — he's not an art historian — he finds himself in the very landscapes Van Gogh painted in and around Arles during his last blaze of creativity. Though he doesn't go mad there as Van Gogh did, he experiences the despair of those unable to give artistic form to vision.

Miller is left with an appreciation of how "interesting" the world is, "how very interesting." This echoes an insight expressed by Jack Schiff (who makes a cameo appearance in "Van Gogh's Room at Arles") in the first novella: "Once you really got into it, it was a waste, a waste and a shame, thought Schiff, to be crippled-up in such an interesting place as the world." Although it sounds banal and bland, Stanley Elkin's great gift is for reminding us how interesting the world really is. Reading Elkin's contemporaries will give you a firm sense of how corrupt, terrifying, and insane the world is, but you'd have to return to Shakespeare to find another writer who finds the world as endlessly interesting as Elkin does.

Washington Post Book World, 21 March 1993

Percival Everett

Glyph

Graywolf, 1999

In the 1970s, the American literary profession was rocked by a French invasion comparable to the British invasion of pop music a decade earlier, with critics embracing Roland Barthes, Jacques Derrida, Jacques Lacan, and others with all the fervor of teenyboppers swooning over the Dave Clark Five. Structuralism, poststructuralism, deconstruction, semiotics, and other approaches gave critics new tools with which to examine literature and a new vocabulary to express their findings. However, there were drawbacks: Until then, any educated person could read a book of literary criticism, but after the '70s only fellow critics could read each other's work because of the bizarre jargon and rarefied theory. Opponents complained that the results of these new approaches sounded more like the literary analysis a computer — with no innate sense of language — would come up with, like a child prodigy who can solve complex equations with no real sense of how mathematics works.

A linguistic child prodigy is the narrator of Percival Everett's new novel, *Glyph*, which is set in the 1970s and satirizes the impact of French theory on the American professoriate. Baby Ralph is the offspring of Douglas Townsend, a poststructuralist who sends his paper on alterity to Barthes and Derrida as if he were a teenager sending a love letter to Ringo, and who is stuck in a frustrating marriage with Eve, a painter. At ten months Ralph can understand sophisticated language, and by 18 months he has read more books than most doctoral candidates. The first book he reads is not *Goldilocks and the Three Bears* but Wittgenstein's *Tractatus Logico-Philosophicus*. He reads voraciously but refuses to speak. Instead, he writes: first notes to his startled parents, and eventually this novel.

His parents are naturally perturbed by Ralph's preternatural ability, especially since the baby seems to understand poststructuralism better than his old man and is wise to the professor's dalliance with a female student. The parents take Ralph to a child psychologist named Dr. Steimmel, who sees in Ralph a vindication of her theory of language development and decides to kidnap him and take him to a hidden laboratory for further testing. There the baby is rekidnapped by a woman professor who is teaching a chimpanzee to talk; she likewise feels Ralph would be useful to her research, only to lose him to another kidnapper who plans to use Ralph as a "Defense Stealth Operative" for the U.S. government. Ralph is kidnapped a final time by a sympathetic prison guard (whose wife wants a baby of her own) and taken to Mexico, where all of the above parties converge to stake their claim on the precocious toddler.

Overlaid on this farcical plot is all the forbidding arcana of French literary theory. Each of the novel's eight sections is prefaced by a linguistic schematic and is broken down into narrative units with headings taken from semiotics and theory (seme, ephexis, libidinal economy). Unattributed quotations interrupt the text, along with vocabulary lists and imaginary dialogues between writers and philosophers (Aristophanes and Ralph Ellison, Balzac and G. E. Moore). Several of Ralph's poems appear, all on anatomical themes with such titles as "Copora Cavernosa" and "The Weight of the Encephalon." We are treated to several of Ralph's musings on linguistics, which could be parodies of French theorists if their own writings didn't already sound like parodies of ratiocination. There's an alliteration-mad children's story. There are footnotes, limericks, jokes, mathematical formulae, even an appendix entitled "Ralph's Theory of Fictive Space." It's a postmodern mulligan stew that will keep theory junkies fixed for a long time working out the structural patterns and implications of all these narrative disruptions.

This is a strange novel, but not strange enough. The premise of an infant with full linguistic capacities but little life experience should yield a defamiliarized language, yet too often Ralph sounds like . . . well, like Professor Percival Everett of the University of Southern California. When Ralph is first taken into the dining room of the hidden laboratory, he remarks: "The dining room was ostentatious, crowded with heavy furniture and ornate lamps, but lit mainly by a gigantic chandelier of hundreds of multicolored, faceted glass spheres tethered on a too-small-looking chain." Even a baby who has read Proust (as Ralph has) would have limited empirical grounds for judging a concept like ostentation, an aesthetic judgment requiring previous acquaintance with interior design. And having never seen a chandelier, how could Ralph tell that this one is larger than usual? Wittgenstein once said that if a lion could speak, we would not be able to understand him, meaning (I think) that a lion's worldview and experience would be so radically different from ours that we would not share enough contexts for the language to mean anything to us. Similarly, the worldview even of a baby who has read hundreds of books would be so circumscribed that his language would be noticeably different from ours.

Since *Glyph* is a farce, it's probably a mistake to get too literal-minded about such things. Everett is a clever writer with a gift for parody and a formidable library in his head. *Glyph* is obviously written for a small, select audience. (He is the author of another, more successful novel, *Suder*, which is the current selection of The *Washington Post* Book Club.) That audience should find sophisticated entertainment here and a new vantage point from which to assess the impact of French theory on those professors who lapped it up like mother's milk.

Washington Post Book World, 28 November 1999

Ronald Firbank and Alan Hollinghurst

Alan Hollinghurst. *The Swimming-Pool Library*
Random House, 1988

Ronald Firbank. *The Flower Beneath the Foot*
Penguin, 1986

The most gaily diverting aspect of this diverting gay novel is the presence of Ronald Firbank. If you believe (as I do) that Firbank more or less invented modernism, then any reference these days to this unacknowledged progenitor is gratefully savored. Hollinghurst offers several. His protagonist, a young aristocrat named William Beckworth, is reading Firbank (in deference to his friend James's mania for the novelist) in between his numerous trysts with lower-class lovers. He learns that the aging aristocrat whose biography he is considering writing, Charles Nantwich, actually met Firbank in the Café Royal in 1925. Lord Nantwich's journal records this meeting in an entertaining vignette, but the real treat comes at the end of the novel when the major characters gather to watch unearthed film footage of Firbank in Italy at the end of his life. Firbank is described climbing up a hill followed by a swarm of children, where the novelist takes "on the likeness not only of a clown, but of a patron saint. It was a rough impromptu kind of triumph."

Firbank is clearly the patron saint of Hollinghurst's novel, which begins with an epigram taken from *The Flower Beneath the Foot* and ends a page after the charming film canonization. Researching Lord Nantwich's life, William comes to see him as a Firbankian figure in the sense "His adults don't have any dignity as adults, they're all like over-indulged children, following their own caprices and inclinations." This characterizes Hollinghurst's childish adults as well, who move through the contemporary (though pre-AIDS) gay world of London as capriciously as Firbank's characters but with none of their exotic eccentricities. As in Andrew Holleran's *Dancer from the Dance* (for my money the best gay novel written in my time), the mood of *The Swimming-Pool Library* mixes memory and desire to portray a sexual wasteland where the pursuit of male beauty seems both pointless and the only point there is to life. The novel is fulsome where Firbank is terse, frank where he is suggestive, but Hollinghurst shares Firbank's colorfully precise vocabulary and world-weary sense of the absurd. The novel is probably too British to do as well here as it's done in England, but it deserves notice nonetheless.

It is also worth noting that Penguin has recently reissued the novel that furnishes the epigram to Hollinghurst's novel. *The Flower Beneath the Foot,* "Being a Record of the Early Life of St. Laura de Nazianzi and the Times in Which She Lived," is one of Firbank's better novels, and though this particular edition has its faults — it omits both the subtitle I've just quoted and the 1924 preface Firbank wrote for the American edition — it has a good introduction by John Mortimer and is worth picking up by those still unacquainted with Firbank's inimitable fiction.

Review of Contemporary Fiction, Spring 1989. *The Swimming-Pool Library* did well here after all, and a few years later Hollinghurst wrote the introduction to my edition of *The Early Firbank* (Quartet Books, 1991).

□ □ □ □ □ □ □

Caprice
New Directions, 1993

Valmouth and Other Novels
Penguin, 1992

There's never been anyone like him. A number of writers over the years have been called Firbankian — early Waugh, Van Vechten, more recent novelists like James McCourt, Edmund Apffel, Alan Hollinghurst — but none of them has been able to capture the inimitable mixture of wit, compression, worldliness, perversity, blasphemy, pathos, and originality of Firbank's fiction. Fortunately, he's been kept in print rather steadily since the Firbank revival of the late '40s, when New Directions brought out two omnibuses (still available) that contain his eight novels. The same firm has just issued *Caprice* separately, Firbank's third novel (1917), a slim little treasure concerning Miss Sarah Sinquier's ill-fated attempt to become an actress, and Penguin has reissued a paperback omnibus from the '60s containing three of Firbank's later novels: *Valmouth* (set in an English health spa), *Prancing Nigger* (the innocent Mouth family succumbs to corruption in the big city), and *Concerning the Eccentricities of Cardinal Pirelli* (about one of the Church's more colorful priests). You've never read such beautiful sentences or heard such slashing wit. Wear your best clothes when you read these, and have a magnum of Champagne at hand.

Review of Contemporary Fiction, Summer 1993

F. Scott Fitzgerald

The Price Was High: The Last Uncollected Stories of F. Scott Fitzgerald. Edited by Matthew J. Bruccoli
Harcourt, Brace, 1979

In a clever piece originally written for the *New Yorker* called "The Metterling Lists" (reprinted in *Getting Even*), Woody Allen pokes fun at publishers who print every remaining scrap of a great author's work, even down to surviving laundry lists. Though posthumous collections of miscellaneous unpublished writings are of great interest to the scholar and specialist, the general reading public seldom benefits from such works. Consequently, only die-hard fans would be interested *The Price Was High*. Then again, there is another line of thought that considers a great writer at his worst better than a mediocre writer at his best, and since a surplus of mediocre writers are crowding the best-seller lists this season, this new collection might be worth reading after all.

The stories in *The Price Was High* were bread and butter writing, written to provide Fitzgerald with the money and time to concentrate on his novels. And although the editor of this collection admits these stories are not Fitzgerald's best, he also quotes Dorothy Parker's comment that "although he could write a bad story, he could not write badly." The Fitzgerald touch is apparent even in the worst of them, and consequently those of us who get giddy with Fitzgerald's lovely prose style will welcome the new collection.

The stories written in the '20s are clearly the best. Even when reading of charming nonsense like debutantes and proms one comes away from a Fitzgerald story just a bit wiser, a bit sadder sometimes, and always more aware of the beautiful fragility of life. The four points of Fitzgerald's compass — love, youth, ambition, success — are as eternal as the four points of a navigator's compass, and even in his most dated period pieces there are insights as true and constant as the northern star.

Spree, April 1979

□ □ □ □ □ □ □

Maureen Corrigan. *So We Read On: How* The Great Gatsby *Came to Be and Why It Endures*
Little, Brown, 2014

Getting a jump on the 90th anniversary of the publication of *The Great Gatsby* (next April 10), NPR book critic Maureen Corrigan reminds us in her engaging new book why F. Scott Fitzgerald's novel is still going strong after nearly a century.

It didn't look like it would last a decade at first. As Corrigan notes, Fitzgerald's third novel got lousy reviews, sold poorly, and was nearly forgotten by the time its embittered author died in 1940. But beginning in the 1950s, more and more people came to recognize it for the masterpiece it is, and as it was added to more and more anthologies and school curricula, it attained its current status as one of the most widely read American classics — both here, where its presence in high schools is ubiquitous, and abroad.

Like many, Corrigan first read it in high school and, she confesses, didn't really get it. (Me neither, at age 19; she feels most read it when too young.) But after a lifetime of rereading, teaching, and touring the novel — she lectured on it for the NEA's Big Read project — she has come to love it and regard it as *the* Great American Novel, and tells us why in unabashed fan-girl fashion, which makes her book as pleasurable to read as Fitzgerald's.

Taking what might be called a holistic approach, she examines *Gatsby* from every angle: from close readings of the novel's language (its chief attraction), to biographical matters, to its textual history, to its various media reincarnations (movies, plays, homages, even computer games), to its critical reception, and to its place in today's culture and classrooms. (In the final chapter, Corrigan returns to her high school and sits in on a few discussions of it.) She clearly knows the novel minutely, has read most of the criticism (a corpus as big as the Ritz), has visited the archives to report on its wonders, and is a fund of anecdotes about the Fitzgeralds and their world.

Corrigan flits back and forth between all this material and digresses wherever her fancy takes her; as she says of *Gatsby*, her book "jumps and ducks and shimmies." Though she is a professor at Georgetown University, she writes in a refreshingly nonacademic manner — she is not too PC to refer to women as "dames" when appropriate — and in fact takes a few jabs at recent literary theorists and their trendy jargon. She compares the "aggressive absurdity" of their approaches to that of old-fashioned scholars like Fitzgerald specialist Matthew J. Bruccoli: "they did more than just adopt theoretical positions toward literature; they actually *knew* things."

It's her own deep knowledge that allows Corrigan to argue that *The Great Gatsby* is more a hard-boiled detective novel than a glittery love story, "a noir that surveys the rotten underbelly of the American dream" (which is why she prefers the 1949 Alan Ladd movie version over others). She is also able to provide a historical context for what appears to be anti-Semitism and racism in the novel, and to supply the relevant biographical data to account for Fitzgerald's ambivalent feelings about America.

She argues that *Gatsby* is "our most American and un-American novel, all at once," and that Gatsby himself is, "for better or worse, an American." That ambivalence is the divided heart of the novel: Gatsby is a dreamer and "go-for-broke Promethean overreacher," but — as Corrigan's former high-school teacher tells her, "Gatsby was looking for the wrong things . . . money and clothes and Daisy." He embodies the best and worst qualities of America, resulting in a novel that is simultaneously buoyant and grim, as Corrigan notes. "*The Great Gatsby* is an elegant trickster of a novel, spinning out all sorts of inspired and contradictory poetic patter about American identity and possibilities." Corrigan quotes with approval one early reader who pegged Gatsby as "extraordinarily American, like ice cream soda with arsenic flavoring," which also describes the novel he inhabits.

Like Rebecca Mead's recent book on *Middlemarch* and Michael Gorra's on *The Portrait of a Lady*, Corrigan's "personal excursion" represents a welcome alternative to academic criticism: it's smart and compelling, persuasive without demeaning other interpretations (except for the rookie mistake of regarding the novel as "a celebration of the consumer society that was taking shape in the 1920s"), and succeeds at uncovering the novel from "under fossilized layers of Great Books-type reverential criticism" without going to over-theorized extremes. I used to think *The Great Gatsby* was too short to qualify as the Great American Novel — for a country as big as America, surely that honor should go to a sprawling work like John Dos Passos's *U.S.A.* or William Gaddis's *J R* — but Corrigan almost convinces me that bigger is not necessarily better. If you love *Gatsby*, or want to understand why it deserves such adulation, *So We Read On* is a gorgeous treat.

Washington Post, 9 September 2014

Richard Ford

A Multitude of Sins
Knopf, 2002

There are a few species for which monogamy is a natural and satisfactory arrangement, but humans are not one of them. For many, desire is too strong a force to be restrained by the bonds of marriage, and it leads them into temptation and adultery. In his new collection of stories, Richard Ford tracks a dozen characters into that lawless territory, with grim results.

In Ford's America, adultery is not the civilized pastime depicted in the sparkling novels of the late W. M. Spackman, nor is it the practical arrangement accepted in many parts of the world. Despite the title, it's less a sin than a symptom, an inevitable rite of passage for Ford's married, middle-aged, middle-class Americans. "Deception was very American," says a character in one story, and cheating on one's spouse is as common as cheating on one's taxes, dodgy but not sinful. Another character feels adultery merely satisfies an urge: "Life was sometimes a matter of ridding yourself of this or that urge, after which the rest got easier."

First published in England last fall (with a much better cover), the book gets off to a good start with "Privacy," a cheerless tale of voyeurism. The second story isn't bad either, an account of a journalist's affair with a rich man's trophy wife. Here, the illicit affair is front and center; in most of the other stories, the adulterous act is a distant memory that intrudes in the present at an awkward time. Ford is more concerned with the consequences of adultery than with its dangerous thrills. But most of the stories that follow fail because of their tedium and sloppy style. Much of the writing reads like an unedited first draft. Take this sentence: "Oddly enough — only because all events that occur outside New York seem odd and fancifully unreal to New Yorkers — our affair had taken place in the city of St. Louis, that largely overlookable red-brick abstraction that is neither West nor Middlewest, neither North nor South; the city lost in the middle, as I think of it." The final five words and "the city of" are superfluous, "Middlewest" is asymmetrical and not a recognized term, and eight of the first 33 words begin with the letter "o," a statistical aberration justifiable only in a phonics textbook. And why the clumsy and unnecessary possessives in this sentence: "Our — Beth's and my — love affair was, of course, only one feature in the long devaluation and decline in her and Mack's marriage"? And "devaluation"? I could fill the page with even worse examples.

One story, “Crèche,” is deliberately written in a kind of choppy narrative shorthand, but clunky writing spoils half of the collection. To be charitable — and the New Testament tells us “Charity shall cover the multitude of sins” — the graceless style may be thematic; the language is often as awkward and jittery as an adulterer checking into a motel, the punctuation as reckless. But those who call Ford an elegant stylist are being more charitable than the apostle Peter intended. “Charity,” as it happens, is the title of one of the better stories — better meaning competent — though at 40 pages it would have benefited from cutting.

The final story, “Abyss,” is even longer, nearly a novella, and so good it seems written by a different author. It’s just an adulterous tale of two average Connecticut realtors who visit the Grand Canyon — not exactly Anna Karenina and Vronsky in Italy — but the writing is fluid, the pacing brisk, the characterization sharp, and the tone pitch-perfect. Here, adultery is the primal, life-changing theme it was for Hawthorne, Tolstoy and Ford Madox Ford. It doesn’t mark a great advancement in the art of the short story, but it does justify Richard Ford’s reputation, which the others don’t. It shows what he can do when he exerts his full powers rather than merely going through the motions.

Even though one story is set as recently as “One day after the old millennium’s end and the new one’s beginning” (which sounds like the beginning of a riddle), they all have an old-fashioned tone, as if they’d been written 50 years ago. They make few demands on the reader, aside from patience with the less successful ones. Ford fans and those who prefer their fiction as comfortable as a pair of old slippers may like *A Multitude of Sins*, but short-story enthusiasts looking for something new and exciting would be better served by Anthony Doerr’s *The Shell Collector*, Janice Galloway’s *Where You Find It*, or, for the truly daring, Shelley Jackson’s *The Melancholy of Anatomy*. Ford will have to do better than *A Multitude of Sins* to keep up with the competition, even though this book will easily outsell theirs. That’s the real sin.

Washington Post Book World, 17 March 2002

James Frey

Bright Shiny Morning
Harper, 2008

Because I've been on a fool's errand the last four years writing a history of the novel, I paid little attention to the big publishing scandal of 2006, when James Frey's *A Million Little Pieces* was exposed as being closer to fiction than to the heartfelt memoir it was marketed as. I couldn't be bothered with the legal and moral issues because the history of this lawless genre is filled with such dodges. One of the world's earliest novels, a fantastic fiction by the 2nd-century Greek satirist Lucian, was cheekily entitled *A True History*. Both *Robinson Crusoe* and *Gulliver's Travels* were first marketed as nonfiction accounts, and even included prefaces by their publishers swearing to their veracity. More recently, we've had autobiographical novels, the "nonfiction" novels of Capote and Mailer, and some historical novels with more documentation than scholarly tomes. There's always been a blurry line between fiction and nonfiction, and Frey isn't the first or last writer to conga on that line.

In his newest novel — or rather, his first book to be marketed as a novel — the unrepentant author blurs the line further. The title page lacks the traditional subtitle "a novel," and the first line of text is a disclaimer: "Nothing in this book should be considered accurate or reliable." But in point of fact this sprawling novel about Los Angeles, where Frey lived in the 1990s, is very accurate and can be considered a reliable guide to "the most diverse, fastest-growing major metropolitan area in the United States," as he writes near the end. I did some spot fact-checking and nearly everything checked out: I was delighted to learn there is actually a black gang that calls itself the Harvard Gangster Crips, and the only error I turned up involved a wedding date: an L.A. secretary named Jannene Swift married a large chunk of granite in 1976 (part of the pet rock craze?), not in 1950 as it states on page 253.

Bright Shiny Morning is both a capsule history of Los Angeles and a fictional census of hundreds of its current citizens. The novel alternates between brief milestones in L.A. history, moving chronologically from its founding in 1781 to the year 2000, and countless episodes set in the present (and related in the present tense, which gives them a nervy energy). Some current Angelenos get only a few lines — Allison, an aspiring model, "Moved to Los Angeles at eighteen to become a Playboy Bunny. Now 19, she works in porn" — some get a paragraph or two, and others a few pages. We get the extended stories of only four representative characters, endlessly interrupted, which gives the novel just enough cohesion to keep it from looking like a kaleidoscopic collage.

Dylan and Maddie, for example, are childhood sweethearts from Ohio, now 19, who drove out to L.A. to avoid their abusive parents. Their nest egg is stolen during their first week there (welcome to L.A.!) and we watch as these sweet kids doggedly pursue the American Dream. Old Man Joe, who looks 80 but is only 38, is a bum addicted to Chablis. Amberton Parker is a box-office action hero and closet homosexual. Esperanza is the child of illegal immigrants, grows up smart but too poor to attend college, and works as a maid for a tyrannical rich white widow. Only one of these stories turns out well; this isn't a novel with a Hollywood ending.

Technically, the novel is interesting: it moves simultaneously through time (the historical vignettes) and space (the characters spread all over L.A.). There are lists and other modernist devices, including the unconventional layout, punctuation, and telegraphic sentence style of his earlier books. Frey's ambition may have been to write the definitive novel of L.A., to do for that city what Joyce did for Dublin, Dos Passos did for Manhattan, Döblin did for Berlin, or what Durrell did for Alexandria. If so, he may have succeeded; Joyce boasted that if Dublin were to disappear, it could be reconstructed from his *Ulysses*, and Frey could make the same claim for L.A. — though after reading his grim depiction, most wouldn't think it worth the effort.

But he's not in the same class as those modernists: there's some sloppiness to his writing — we're told twice that the Los Angeles International Airport is called LAX, which most readers don't need to be told at all, and twice that Lincoln Boulevard is nicknamed the Stinkin' Lincoln — and too many moments when he drops the narrative's impersonal tone and indulges in some wisecracks that mostly fall flat. Some sections, like the one on L.A.'s Skid Row, read like magazine pieces, and he has an annoying habit of repeating phrases for poetic emphasis (". . . it's the American Way, the American Way"). He sacrifices depth for breadth, for a CinemaScopic view of the city that both exemplifies and exploits the clichés about the mythological lure of the west and L.A. as the Land of Dreams, though this would be a necessary aesthetic sacrifice given the nature of his project.

Quibbling aside, *Bright Shiny Morning* reads quickly, has great dialogue and some expertly paced dramatic moments, teaches you more about L.A. than you ever knew, and makes the case (posited by an artist near the end) that Los Angeles is the new New York, on its way to becoming the cultural capital of the world. Or it could all be a stinging satire of the most violent, corrupt, polluted, pretentious, money-mad place in America. Works either way.

I understand Mr. Frey currently lives in New York.

Washington Post, 14 May 2008

William Gaddis

John Johnston. *Carnival of Repetition: Gaddis's "The Recognitions" and Postmodern Theory*
University of Pennsylvania Press, 1990

Given the complexity of Gaddis's *Recognitions* and its continued unfamiliarity to many readers, those of us who have written on it have tended toward introductory sorts of criticism — overviews, plot summaries, annotations — and toward "monological" thematic readings. Johnston offers a "dialogic" reading using not only Bakhtin but a wide array of recent theorists (mostly French) to explore new possibilities of meaning in this monumental novel. Arguing that Gaddis's "anticipation of postmodernist themes and fictional assumptions demands the kind of theoretical approach" now available via continental theory, Johnston employs Bakhtin's carnivalization, Deleuze's difference and repetition, Goux's structure of homologies, and much else to demonstrate that *The Recognitions* is more complex than previously thought and even more important to recent literary history. For me, much of the critical theory Johnston cites "seems a little remote from the surface tenor of Gaddis's text" (as he says of another critic's interpretation), but no matter: *Carnival of Repetition* is a provocative and intelligent study that will interest both Gaddis specialists as well as readers discovering *The Recognitions* for the first time.

Having said this, I must confess that my copy of Johnston's book is now littered with "no"s penciled in the margins, for I found myself disagreeing with many of his readings. To detail all my specific objections here would interest no one but Johnston and a handful of fellow specialists, though a few are crucial. Johnston cites Wyatt's assumption (on page 381 of the novel) that he began his forgery career copying a copy, which Johnston uses to build his case that *The Recognitions* argues against the existence of originals, of Platonic ideals. However, Johnston fails to notice that on page 668 Wyatt discovers that he was mistaken; the "copy" was indeed the original. Likewise, Johnston fails to note that the word *chavenet* — which he claims "has no 'original' meaning" — is finally identified on page 628 of *The Recognitions*. In other words, there are more originals in the novel than Johnston realizes, and which tilt the novel back in favor of verifying (rather than "overturning" [Deleuze]) Platonism and the stable moral order so necessary for Gaddis's form of satire. But as Johnston goes on to admit, *The Recognitions* is "'ambivalent' in a very strong sense: it both looks back at Platonic recognition and forward to Deleuzian repetition," and it is probably unwise to privilege one view over another.

But even though I found myself often disagreeing (and wincing at the poor copyediting job), I found much else to admire. Chapter 2 is an excellent, detailed plot summary cum commentary on "the novel's surface complexity"; he gets a few details wrong, but keeps admirable hold of the numerous narrative strands. There is a discussion of similar strategies in Dostoevsky and Gaddis that is particularly valuable; even though Gaddis is steeped in 19th-century Russian literature, no critic has explored the connection in any detail, nor has any Gaddis critic examined, as Johnston does, the implications of Gaddis's unusual source material. Johnston distinguishes nicely between Joyce's and Gaddis's manipulation of the mythic element in a way that does not depend on Gaddis's knowledge of *Ulysses* (which Johnston elsewhere assumes), and the postmodern tendencies in *The Recognitions* are traced out briefly in Gaddis's succeeding two novels. Johnston's *Carnival of Repetition* is easily the most sophisticated treatment to date of *The Recognitions* and sets a new standard for both Gaddis critics and students of postmodern theory.

Review of Contemporary Fiction, Summer 1990

□ □ □ □ □ □ □

A Frolic of His Own
Poseidon Press, 1994

The phrase "literary event" has been dulled by years of misuse by glib publicists; but no other phrase describes the appearance of a new novel by William Gaddis, one of this country's true literary giants. The review media's response to this literary event has been disheartening, however, as if nothing has changed in the 40 years since Gaddis's first novel, *The Recognitions*, was panned. Then as now, the main charge is "difficulty," yet only in literature does this seem to be a sin. One rarely sees a music critic complain that Philip Glass expects too much of his listeners, or reads that Merce Cunningham expects too much from his audience. In diving competitions and magic acts the degree of difficulty is admired. But let a writer execute a difficult task with breathtaking technique, and mostly what's heard is heckling — whining and moaning about how much effort is involved in watching the artist work. What should be a privilege is treated like an affront.

In her review for the daily *New York Times*, the usually hardy Michiko Kakutani said the novel made for "laborious reading" and that "Mr. Gaddis's provocative vision of modern society is purchased at a price, the price of hard work and frequent weariness on the part of the reader." In the Sunday *New York Times Book Review*, Robert Towers also felt compelled to warn the unsuspecting reader that "One must not underestimate the obstacles that lie in the way of the appreciation, to say nothing of the enjoyment, of this remarkable novel," going on to call some of the obstacles "gratuitous, even perverse." (It's always the author's fault.) Sven Birkerts used the d-word as well in his *New Republic* review, though he was sharp enough to note that the neglect of Gaddis because of his alleged difficulty "somewhat indicts us as a culture." But he makes Gaddis sound like the strictest kind of taskmaster: "let the attention slip for a second and you pay by having to work back to get it all straight." Frank McConnell in the *Boston Globe* warned of "the holy arrogance of the demands it makes on the reader. The book dares you to struggle with it, and on every page taunts you that you may, after all, not be up to the fight." Toward the end of his review McConnell says, "This is a very hard book to read, but it works," though by that point most readers have probably been scared off. Running against the grain was a rather snotty squib in *Newsweek* by Malcolm Jones Jr., who took the opposite tack and complained that the book was too easy, too lazy, and chided Gaddis for not giving "his readers more for their trouble."

Is *A Frolic of His Own* that difficult, that exhausting? I devoured it in a weekend in a state of exhilaration and delight. Yes, you do have to keep your wits about you when reading Gaddis, but it's a rare privilege these days to be taken this seriously as a reader. Like Henry James, William Gaddis wants the kind of reader on whom nothing is lost. He doesn't talk down or assume you can't make connections. He expects that you've read a few books in your time, read the papers. This is literature, not a TV sitcom.

The point is not whether Gaddis is difficult or not but whether difficulty is such a bad thing in literature. Those who prefer easy listening may want easy reading, but others should find a novel bracing, challenging. In Gaddis's second novel, *J R*, Jack Gibbs is asked if his work in progress on technology and the arts is difficult, and he answers, "Difficult as I can make it." The difficulties Gibbs undergoes to get this book written, the breadth of his research and length of time he devotes to the task (after 17 years he still isn't finished), show what sort of pact should exist between serious writers and serious readers.

Gaddis knows he's difficult (Gibbs is one of his personas in *J R*), and consequently lightens the task somewhat by making his books very funny, filling them with all forms of humor, from limericks and low puns to learned wit and Olympian ironies. The absence of a comic element can make some difficult literary works a real grind — Pound's *Cantos*, say, or Broch's *Death of Virgil* — despite their other virtues. On the other hand, the comic element is what makes extremely difficult novels like Joyce's *Finnegans Wake* and Julián Ríos's *Larva* such a pleasure to wrestle with. And yet few reviewers convey the idea that Gaddis is essentially a comic novelist and that his books can be great fun — rather than an exercise in masochism — to read.

The charges of difficulty have plagued Gaddis all his career. In *Fire the Bastards!* (1962), a scathing attack on the critical reception of Gaddis's first novel, Jack Green has a section called "The 'Difficult' Cliché" in which he quotes half a dozen reviewers voicing the same complaints about Gaddis as the current crop. (Green points out that a novel is difficult only if you read it like a textbook, in which each paragraph has to be mastered before moving on to the next. He also argues that a rich novel is always difficult, and asks "unless you hug impoverishment why worry?") Gaddis's *J R,* which is indeed his most difficult (though it is also the great American novel if ever there was one), seemed to prove most difficult for sophisticated mandarin reviewers like George Steiner in the *New Yorker;* those in the provinces, like Alicia Miller in the *Cleveland Plain Dealer,* had a wonderful time with it. Because of its shorter length, Gaddis's third novel, *Carpenter's Gothic,* got off comparatively easy, though there were those who complained of the close attention the novel demanded. The new book may be Gaddis's best mixture yet of complex and hilarious matters, of high art and good entertainment.

A Frolic of His Own is both cutting-edge, state-of-the-art fiction and a throwback to the great moral novels of Tolstoy and Dickens. That it can be both is just one of the many balancing acts it performs: It is bleak and pessimistic while howlingly funny; it is a deeply serious exploration of such lofty themes as justice and morality but is paced like a screwball comedy; it is avant-garde in its fictional techniques but traditional in conception and in the reading pleasures it offers; it is a damning indictment of the United States, Christianity, and the legal system, but also a playful frolic of Gaddis's own.

The plot is too wonderfully complex to summarize here; suffice it to say, it concerns an interlocking set of lawsuits involving the Crease family: Oscar, a historian and playwright; Christina, his stepsister, married to a lawyer named Harry Lutz; and their father, Judge Thomas Crease, presiding over two cases in Virginia during the course of the novel. The story unfolds by way of Gaddis's trademark dialogue, so realistic it reads like unedited transcripts but which artfully conveys much information that normally would be consigned to expository narration. Here, for example, is how Oscar's flaky girlfriend Lily is introduced. Oscar asks her where she got the new BMW that Christina saw her driving, and she responds: "It's just this person I borrowed it from Oscar. To come over and see you, I only wish she didn't dislike me so much. She just always makes me feel like a, she's so superior and smart and her clothes, she's just always so attractive for somebody her age and. . . ." This occurs early in the novel, before Gaddis has described Christina, and now he doesn't need to: Lily has. *J R* was conveyed almost entirely in dialogue, but in *A Frolic* Gaddis includes passages from Oscar's play — necessary for the plot, but often tedious reading — and various legal opinions, brilliantly rendered in the majestic language of the law. One of them, first published a few years ago in the *New Yorker* as "Szyrk v. Village of Tatamount et al.," is especially dazzling and contains one of the most eloquent defenses of venturesome art in our time. Noting that "risk of ridicule, of attracting defamatory attentions from his colleagues and even raucous demonstrations by an outraged public have ever been and remain the foreseeable lot of the serious artist," Judge Crease is another of Gaddis's personas, and it is this sense of artistic mission that makes Gaddis essential reading for our culture. He is the oldest of that generation of meganovelists that includes John Barth, Thomas Pynchon, and Robert Coover, and while his artistry is as relentlessly inventive as theirs, he is more adept than they at cracking the whip of corrective satire, more concerned with rescuing American culture from itself by exposing its inherent contradictions and weaknesses. The next century's historians and sociologists will learn more from Gaddis than from any other American novelist of our time what went wrong with this century.

Despite its preoccupation with the law, *A Frolic of His Own* has nothing in common with the current crop of legal fictions. There are no courtroom scenes: Gaddis isn't interested in the histrionics of courtroom drama but rather in the role the law plays in attempting to impose order on disorderly conduct.

Justice, order, money, and the law: Each of these nouns appears on the first page and together they form the compass points of the novel. The same concepts were at the heart of *J R*, but while there the emphasis was on money, here it is on the law. In the world according to Gaddis — made up of that devastating barrage of malice, madness, and malfeasance reported nightly on the news — the law is less a system to ensure order than a weapon that ridiculous, greedy people use to make "other people take them as seriously as they take themselves" (also quoted from the first page; like an opera composer, Gaddis announces all his themes in the overture). Justice, order, and the law are not synonymous terms, nor are they enough: The missing term (and thus absent from the first page but appearing later) is simply what is "right."

The novel is a stupendous achievement, filled with so much outrage, wit, wisdom, and artistry that it makes other novels published in the past ten years look tepid and underachieved. (Despite his reservations, Sven Birkerts admitted that it is "leagues ahead of most so-called 'serious' novels that are published these days.") If you find it difficult you should be grateful, for you'll be engaged at the top of your abilities, discovering reading muscles you'd forgotten you ever had. And any exhaustion you feel afterward will be the good kind, as after sex or an invigorating workout. Go for the burn.

The Nation, 25 April 1994 — expanded from *Review of Contemporary Fiction*, Spring 1994

William H. Gass

Arthur M. Saltzman. *The Fiction of William Gass: The Consolation of Language*
Southern Illinois University Press, 1986

William H. Gass has been publishing dazzling essays and fiction since the 1950s, but only in the last decade or so has his work attracted much critical attention. Saltzman's new book is the first extended study of Gass's output and promises to be the foundation for all subsequent Gass criticism. It is useful in two ways: first for its virtuosic readings of the individual works; not only are separate chapters devoted to Gass's three published books of fiction, but even *The Tunnel* — his mammoth work-in-progress, sections of which have appeared in literary magazines over the last 15 years — receives a skeleton key treatment that will prove invaluable once this monumental work is published.

Gass's first three volumes of nonfiction receive only passing mention (the fourth, *Habitations of the Word*, appeared too recently for inclusion), but the aesthetic governing those brilliant works illuminates Saltzman's opening and closing chapters: "Wording a Word," a cogent primer on the tenets of postrealistic fiction, and "The Aesthetic of Doubt in Recent Fiction," an examination of the implications of the Gass–Gardner debates on moral fiction. Both chapters not only provide the theory for which Gass's novels are the practice, but also place Gass in a proper historical-literary context — the second reason this book is so attractive. Thus Saltzman's book doubles as a masterful introduction to postmodern fiction and to one of its leading practitioners. Salzman's 1984 *Contemporary Literature* interview with Gass closes this highly recommended study of one of the most significant writers of our day.

Review of Contemporary Fiction, Summer 1986

□ □ □ □ □ □ □

The Tunnel
Knopf, 1995

I'm grateful that I lived long enough to see this. For nearly 30 years Gass has been publishing sections of *The Tunnel* in literary journals (including this one) and as fine press books, and as I devoured these I wondered, as many did, when and if the finished book would appear and whether the whole would be greater than its parts. That question has now been answered beyond my wildest expectations; *The Tunnel* is a stupendous achievement and obviously one of the greatest novels of the century, a novel to set beside the masterpieces of Proust, Joyce, and Musil as well as those of Gass's illustrious contemporaries. Although he has been grouped over the years with such novelists as Pynchon, Gaddis, Coover, Barth, and Elkin, he didn't have a novel in the same league as *Gravity's Rainbow, J R, The Public Burning, LETTERS*, or *George Mills*. His first two books of fiction, *Omensetter's Luck* and *In the Heart of the Heart of the Country*, are exquisite achievements, but more along the lines of *V.* and *Pricksongs and Descants*, respectively. *Willie Masters' Lonesome Wife* is a brilliant tour de force, but at 64 pages barely qualifies as a novel. But now with *The Tunnel* Gass has a novel that rivals, perhaps even surpasses those meganovels of his colleagues; it was never a competition, but Gass is now unquestionably in the heavyweight division.

At this early date, and within this limited space, only a bird's-eye view can be given of such a complex novel. So: it's set in 1967 and a Midwestern history professor has finally finished writing his magnum opus, *Guilt and Innocence in Hitler's Germany*. All that remains is to write the introduction, but instead he begins to write about his own life, which becomes the first-person novel we're reading. Fat and 50-something, William Frederick Kohler is a bitter man, but a literate one, and as he pours out his litany of complaint and disappointment he erects a great cathedral of rhetoric, "*un livre intérieur*, as Proust puts it," as Kohler puts it. A professional lifetime studying Nazisim — in a rash moment while studying in Germany in the 1930s, Kohler even participated in *Kristallnacht* — has led him to brood on "the fascism of the heart," both his own and his family's. Such brooding hovers over his childhood in Iowa, his student years in Germany, and his married and professional life in Indiana. It's a novel about history, about hatred, about unhappiness.

But above all it's a novel about language, about a life in language. At an early age Kohler gave up poetry for history, but poetry marked him for her own and dictates every word he utters. Kohler's powerful, polyphonic prose interrogates and illuminates every aspect of his miserable life, and in this regard *The Tunnel* resembles other huge, word-mad novels (*Under the Volcano, Visions of Cody, Miss MacIntosh, My Darling, Mulligan's Stew, Darconville's Cat*) where rhetorical energy and excess redeem personal failure and emptiness. The sheer beauty and bravura of Gass's sentences are overwhelming, breathtaking; the novel is a pharaoh's tomb of linguistic treasures. At one point Kohler's wife Martha demands: "tell it straight — the way it is, not what it's like." Kohler wants to tell what is has been *like* to live his life, hence his impassioned use of metaphors, symbols, tropes, allusions. As a result, language is not merely foregrounded here but given a life of its own: "My father is dressed in a thick green woodman's plaid wool shirt, so heavy with adjectives he can hardly lift his arms." Like *Willie Masters*, the pages are adorned with typographical devices, illustrations, different fonts, and special effects. Readers who, like the wife, prefer their prose straight are advised to look elsewhere.

It will take years of study to excavate fully the artistry of *The Tunnel*, and I can't think of another novel of recent years more deserving of such attention. This is truly one of the great books of our time.

Review of Contemporary Fiction, Spring 1995

□ □ □ □ □ □ □

Cartesian Sonata and Other Novellas

Knopf, 1998

With *Cartesian Sonata*, his tenth book and fifth work of fiction, William H. Gass adds another spray of glitter to his reputation as the finest prose stylist in America. He is positively Shakespearean in his metaphor-making abilities and brings a jeweler's attention to every detail of his sentences. Almost at random, the reader can dip into the book and pull out a sentence like this: "Emma's mother was short slender wan, while her father was broad and flat across the front, knotty too, a pine board kind of person." Note how the mother's diminutive size is conveyed in a compact phrase without commas or conjunctions, while the father's description is drawn out with a conjunction and prepositional phrase, the sentence itself flattening out to convey his appearance. Or take this description of the angel Gabriel, "who has to polish his armor to achieve a gleam, and who is dim as a grimy dime when he's not wearing it." Not only is the simile apt, but note the concatenating off-rhymes of gleam/dim, dim/grimy, grimy/dime. Most poets don't write this carefully. Add to this stylistic mastery a deep erudition, a hard intelligence, and an outraged sensibility and you'll understand why some of us consider Gass to be one of the greatest (if underappreciated) writers of the 20th century.

Cartesian Sonata gathers four novellas Gass has written over the last 30 years. Like his previously published novella, *Willie Masters' Lonesome Wife* (1968), these concern what might be called aesthetic vision: the ability to see similarities and thus make metaphors, the enhanced attention to objects and their aesthetic properties and possibilities, a concern with forms and patterns (both real and imagined), and an obsession with the representational value of words, of the world within the word (to invoke the title of one of Gass's books of essays).

To possess aesthetic vision is as much a blessing as a curse, as these novellas show. The first, "Cartesian Sonata," is about a writer struggling to compose a story about a clairvoyant named Ella Bend. Her ability to hear spirits, to see noises, and to foretell the future is analogous to the gifted writer's ability to conjure the forms of things unknown, turn them to shapes, and give to airy nothing a local habitation and a name (to quote Theseus in Shakespeare's *Midsummer Night's Dream*). As the title indicates, "Cartesian Sonata" has a three-part form: The first section is narrated by the writer and concerns his difficulties with writing the story, the second is narrated from Ella's point of view, and the third from her husband's as he watches over Ella during an illness. He's a down-to-earth fellow at the opposite end of the aesthetic spectrum from the writer in the first part, and as skeptical of Ella's vision as most people are of the poet's vision ridiculed by Theseus. The Cartesian notion of the interaction between spirit and matter provides a heady subtext to this dazzling piece.

"Bed and Breakfast" is, in comparison, relatively straightforward. It concerns an itinerant accountant — he works out of his car, "cooking the books" of small businesses in financial trouble — who winds up at an irresistible bed and breakfast in Illinois. (All four novellas are set in the Midwest, where Gass lives.) The B&B is a museum of kitsch, stuffed with samplers and doilies, ruffles and doodads, a knickknack heaven. Marveling at the profusion and ingenuity of it all, Walt Riff struggles toward an apprehension of the work involved in giving form to aesthetic vision: "Such work required (Walter was awed) . . . it was a sign of (he ransacked his head for a simile) . . . care, concern, devotion, a considerable degree of skill . . . gained over how many years of application? and what for? that was what was most amazing . . . after all, did tatting or carving or sanding or shellacking abolish war? did framing some of our often foolish, former faces in windows made of twigs or bark or knotwood boards redeem past time?" This allusion to Proust's great project of redeeming time (unconscious on Walt's part but deliberate on Gass's) may seem ludicrous — a needlework sampler is hardly on the same level as *Remembrance of Things Past*. But the impulse to find a satisfying form underlies all such projects, and Walt's growing appreciation of the composition of artworks — as well as, let's face it, their uselessness — is touching.

Aesthetic appreciation is taken to a lethal extreme in the third and most impressive novella in this collection, "Emma Enters a Sentence of Elizabeth Bishop's." A gangly girl growing up on a desolate farm in Iowa finds some comfort in the poems of Marianne Moore and especially Elizabeth Bishop. The eerie novella shows "how she had arrived at her decision to lie down in a line of verse and be buried there, that is to say, be born again as a simple set of words." The girl reacts to her mother's indifference and her father's scorn by starving herself, seeking nourishment only in a perfect line of verse. The novella contains some of Gass's most hauntingly beautiful prose ever, and once again contrasts aesthetic vision to a mundane one: When a creek overflowed and flooded a meadow, the father "saw only a flooded field. He didn't see a sheet of bright light lying like a banner over the ploughed ground." The girl's vision of a banner leads her to make a winding sheet out of poetry.

The final novella, "The Master of Secret Revenges," is a nasty piece of work concerning a man named Luther Penner, whose aesthetic vision enables him to see into people's souls, which he finds offensive and dirty; this leads him to devise "a theology based on the idea of vengeance." The novella takes the form of a memorial essay on Penner written by an unctuous disciple, an academic aware of his master's faults but respectful nonetheless of Penner's attempt "to improve on Nature and prefigure Providence." Believing in "the Bible as semaphore — as encoded poetry — and what deep signals it sends," Penner builds his theology into an ugly compost heap of revenge and goofy metaphysics, another example of how aesthetic vision can often go awry. I found this less satisfying than the other novellas; for one thing, the narrative voice seemed less like an academic's than Gass's own (or that of Alexander Theroux, another rhapsodist of revenge). But the novella does underscore the importance of vengeance to aesthetic vision: A dissatisfaction with the way things are, amounting to outrage in great writers from Swift and Pope down to contemporary writers like Gass, Gaddis and Theroux, is one of the sharpest goads to writing. Revenge may be a cruel motive, but it results in some great books. *Cartesian Sonata* is one of them.

Washington Post Book World, 20 September 1998

Karen Elizabeth Gordon

Intimate Apparel: A Dictionary of the Senses
Times Books, 1989

Though classified by the Library of Congress (in exasperation, no doubt) as nonfiction — "1. English language — Context — Popular works" — Gordon's unclassifiable book belongs on the shelf with such inventions as Abish's *Alphabetical Africa*, Barthelme's and Gorey's illustrated fables, Gass's *Willie Masters' Lonesome Wife*, and Sorrentino's *Misterioso*. Gordon's book is a kind of lexicon-novel, like Richard Horn's *Encyclopedia* (1969) or Milorad Pavić's more recent *Dictionary of the Khazars*, and consists of some 150 entries on words like "dusk," "frock," "perfume," "sparkle," and "zipper," most with definitions in the form of an illustrative quotation (a patch of purple prose from one of a half-dozen interwoven tales), an annotation of a particular phrase from the quotation, and often followed by a footnote or two. The stories themselves are fragments that range from surrealistic versions of Andersen's fairy tales to the European travels of insouciant Yolanta, a literary vamp of great wit and charm.

Gass's novella provides the closest parallel: Gordon too uses different typefaces, a variety of styles, much wordplay, and wispish illustrations to advance the analogy of the book as a woman's body. Gass's lonesome wife is nude, but Gordon's lasses disport in fabrics (*read* fabrications) as Yolanta writes something called *La Mode et la muse*. At a further remove, these tales are pieces of a wedding dress being cut out and sewn by two seamstresses (as Gordon's helpful introduction points out), while at the furthest remove, all these characters are tailor's dummies for Gordon to dress and undress in a variety of sensuous sentences.

Gordon's two previous works, *The Well-Tempered Sentence* and *The Transitive Vampire*, are delightful grammar books that use illustrative sentences like: "Surging with a rage for life, Yolanta was yanked out of her tedium by an attractive new trauma." (Apparently the same Yolanta.) Her mixture of goofy sensuality, Edwardian syntax, and *Cosmopolitan* mores may strike some as silly and inconsequential, but Karen Gordon is beginning to look like a cunning vixen who can hold her own with those boys on the metafiction shelf.

Review of Contemporary Fiction, Summer 1989. Seven years later I had the pleasure of reprinting a revised version of this book as *The Red Shoes and Other Tattered Tales*. Working with Karen was one of the few bright spots during my final dark year at Dalkey Archive.

The Ravenous Muse: A Table of Dark and Comic Contents, a Bacchanal of Books
Pantheon, 1996

Karen Gordon's inimitable, irresistible books are difficult to describe or categorize. She is best known for her two flamboyant grammar books, *The Well-Tempered Sentence* and *The Transitive Vampire*, which use outrageous but scrupulously correct sentences to illustrate the rules of grammar and punctuation. Reading them is like studying composition on a dark and stormy night at Castle Dracula. (She's least known for a dazzling collected of fragmented stories, originally called *Intimate Apparel* but recently rechristened and republished as *The Red Shoes and Other Tattered Tales.*) In her newest book, Gordon offers a course in literary gastronomy, using passages from a wide range of authors to illustrate the ways food has been used in literature. But it is only partly about food; it's primarily about book-lovers' ravenous appetite for words, for the chewy, savory quality of good prose, and about the nourishment provided by great writing.

This is what distinguishes Gordon's book from other anthologies of food in literature, for some of her examples are only tangentially related to food: Flann O'Brien's food-stealing bicycles are here, as is Julio Cortázar's wild-artichoke clock and Henri Troyat's anecdote of Chekhov's corpse being returned to Moscow in a dirty green van marked FOR OYSTERS. But each piece is a delicious, toothsome example of well-written prose, and it is the relationship between eating and reading and writing that Gordon foregrounds in her selections and commentary. It's amazing how many of the words we use to describe a good reading experience are from eating — we *devour* a good book, *gulp* it down, *chew* over or *ruminate* (in the bovine sense) on a passage, and so forth — as are the words we use afterward: a good book is as satisfying and nourishing as a good meal, often leaving you hungry for more by the same author. That is as it should be: as Gordon remarks, a good author keeps "the body present, content, and desirous — never sated: very important! — for that's the nature of the ravenous muse, to go on wanting, to demand new combinations and subtleties for the tongue that both tastes and talks."

Many of the authors anthologized here are little-known to American readers, which adds to the book's appeal: Marcel Aymé, Andrei Bely, Mikhail Bulgakov, Piero Camporesi, Elias Canetti, Antonin Carême, Leonora Carrington, Blaise Cendrars, René Char, Barbara Comyns, Sergei Dovlatov, Fillìa (Luigi Colombo), Eduardo Galeano, François Hébert, Ismail Kadare — without going further, it's obvious that Gordon's literary palate leans toward French and Eastern European dishes, which has the advantage of adding new names to the reading lists of "bibliogourmands" (her word) with appetites as ravenous as Gordon's. (There is a 40-page section of author biographies at the end, delectable appetizers for further reading.) Like her other books, *The Ravenous Muse* may look like a jeu d'esprit, but it is a subtle, surprising, and deeply learned exploration of the relationship between language and the body.

Review of Contemporary Fiction, Spring 1996

□ □ □ □ □ □ □

Paris Out of Hand: A Wayward Guide

Chronicle Books, 1996

Joyce once remarked that if Dublin were someday to disappear from the face of the earth, it could be reconstructed from its detailed description in *Ulysses*. In her ingenious new book, Karen Elizabeth Gordon gives us a Paris as it might have been reconstructed by the Surrealists of the 1930s. Your plane would land at the Apollinaéroport; you would take an Auto da Fée taxi to your lodgings, perhaps the Hôtel Carrington, where the desk clerk is a hyena (actually a debutante in disguise). If you dare, you can take the Métro de Sade to the Café Dada, dine later at La Cadavre Exquis, take in the floor show at La Pudeur aux Yeux (a reverse striptease) or a movie at L'Ange des Sables (where they show only films shot in the desert), and perhaps end the night with a drink at the rowdy La Taupe Tetue — The Headstrong Mole for those without French (most of which is translated here for the reader's benefit).

Paris Out of Hand takes the form of a travel guidebook, with sections on hotels, nightlife and entertainment, restaurants and cafés, services, sights, stores and shopping, and transportation — as if Breton, Queneau, *et Cie* had collaborated with Arthur Frommer. It's an elaborate, gorgeous production, lavishly illustrated in color with weird illustrations, collages, and old maps. (It was designed by Barbara Hodgson, whose exotic 1995 novel *The Tattooed Map* — also published by Chronicle and well work seeking out — is illustrated in a similar manner.) There are useful phrases translated for the traveler ("Je suis un ange vachment assoiffé" / "I am one thirsty angel"), quotations about Paris, menus, snippets of Parisian history, guests' comments from hotel registers, even graffiti transcribed from the restroom of a literary café ("Discreet, married publisher of a certain age seeks chilling, thrilling novella, 70 to 85 pages, which trifles with the reader's feelings, then gives him what he wants. Prefer emulation of Anatole France to parody of Raymond Roussel").

Instead of the straightforward prose of most guidebooks, Gordon writes punning, pungent prose that is at once sensuous, erudite, and hilarious. She is a charming and informed guide through the literary Paris of the imagination. "Paris, a capital city of logic," she writes in her introduction, "has also been the home ground for this reason gone astray, for the theater of the absurd, innovations in all the arts: how reality is perceived." In this sense, *Paris Out of Hand* is as much an homage to French literature as a makeover of a city Gordon obviously knows and loves.

Like all of Gordon's books, this new one is about the expressive possibilities of language. If it finds "all that Paris is via the Paris that might be" (also from the introduction), *Paris Out of Hand* also shows what language is via what it might be. Through multilingual puns, incongruous juxtapositions, sly allusions, and playful personifications, Gordon liberates language from its workaday function and propels it into a looking-glass wonderland (Lewis Carroll, a Surrealist *avant la lettre*, is a strong influence). There are images here a poet would kill for (". . . the breakfast room so disarmingly intimate that guests just naturally shuffled in, slippered and sleeping, their dreams still caught in their hair") and puns most writers wouldn't dare ("amuse your waiter with your long legs and faux paws"). I read *Paris Out of Hand* immediately after rereading *Finnegans Wake*, as it happens, and one would have to return to that punful adventure to find prose as giddy as Gordon's.

Over the course of five unclassifiable books, Gordon has been making her own innovations in the arts, a body of work that puts her in the front rank of experimental writers, though one never sees her name in that context. There seems to be an assumption that experimental writing must be serious in tone and content, which means those who are humorous, even frivolous (like Ronald Firbank) are often ignored, even when their work is more radically subversive and experimental than that of better-known writers (again, see Firbank). At both the level of the sentence — no one writes more ingenious sentences than Gordon does — and at the conceptual level — imagine! a book of fiction in the form of a travel guide! — Gordon is clearly one of the most innovative writers working today.

Rain Taxi, Fall 1996

Hervé Guibert

Blindsight. Translated by James Kirkup
Braziller, 1996

Blindsight is the latest posthumous work by French writer Hervé Guibert, who died of AIDS in 1991 at the age of 36. Published last year in France (as *Des Aveugles*, simply "The Blind"), it is a strange fantasia set in a Parisian institute for the blind. Robert and Josette live together at the institute. Both have been blind since childhood; he has a passion for the musical saw and biker gear, while she plays the harp and wears a fur coat. (She had asked for white, but an unscrupulous shopkeeper sold her an apple-green one.) They enjoy listening to horror movies and playing Mikado (a game like jackstraws).

Into this cloistered world comes Taillegueur (pronounced Tiger), also blind, a massive brute hired as the institute's masseur. Josette is immediately attracted to his savage odor — much in this novella is conveyed by sounds and smells, appropriately enough, not by appearances — and they begin an affair involving acrobatic sex that would be beyond the abilities of most sighted people. Taillegueur decides to murder Robert, but his plan backfires and he accidentally kills himself instead. Traitorous Josette meets her end in the institute's basement, devoured by a giant lagodon. (I don't know either: a giant hare, apparently.) [Actually, a fish.] Guibert imaginatively re-creates the world of the blind, which adds to the eeriness of this weird novella. If you are attracted to the idea of a Poe tale cast with blind people, you might enjoy *Blindsight*. Veteran translator James Kirkup uses British diction but otherwise skillfully conveys Guibert's often baroque prose.

Washington Post, 22 December 1996

Elizabeth Hand

Glimmering
HarperPrism, 1997

Poets usually influence other poets, and novelists other novelists, but T. S. Eliot is an exception. Few poets show his influence, but *The Waste Land* especially has had a profound influence on the modern novel, from Nathanael West's *Miss Lonelyhearts* and Malcolm Lowry's *Under the Volcano* to William Gaddis's *Recognitions* and David Markson's *Going Down.* Eliot found the medieval concept of the waste land suitable for his grim view of life at the beginning of the 20th century, and now at century's end Elizabeth Hand has appropriated Eliot's poem to paint an even grimmer view of our fin de siècle. If Stephen King set out to rewrite *The Waste Land* as a novel, the result might resemble *Glimmering.*

Eliot's waste land was largely spiritual and metaphoric, but Hand's is quite literal. Set in 1999, *Glimmering* portrays a world Eliot couldn't even imagine. A combination of environmental catastrophes and an intense solar storm in 1997 caused the atmosphere to deteriorate into a multicolored shroud, obscuring the moon and stars; the earth's magnetic field is altered, transformers and communication networks blow out, and by 1999 everyone is living like a refugee. Electrical power is intermittent, food and medical supplies scarce, the waters rising, and the cities overrun by feral teenagers. All others wear masks to protect themselves from the atmosphere, and sport all sorts of prosthetics and implants.

Surveying all this from his decaying mansion in Yonkers is Jack Finnegan, 40 years old and dying from AIDS. He's the editor of a *New Yorker*-like magazine that is also dying. Finnegans wake, Joyce assures us, but this Finnegan is obsessed with death: his own, his magazine's, his world's. His longtime companion is dead, and his few friends include a lawyer who is drinking himself to death (largely because his daughter died in an automobile accident) and a former lover named Leonard Thrope, who makes films and photographs of moribund subjects. Thrope, a "sociocultural pathologist" as he calls himself, brings Jack a magic elixir that seems to reverse AIDS but also allows Finnegan to see ghosts, deepening his preoccupation with death.

Just as *The Waste Land* abruptly switches locales and introduces new characters, *Glimmering* introduces in the third chapter a young Christian rock star named Trip Marlowe. A holy fool of sorts, he meets and impregnates the novel's "hyacinth girl," a waifish Polish refugee named Marzana Candry (probably named after Kundry, the enchantress in Wagner's *Parsifal*), then attempts a death by water. He is rescued and nurtured back to life by a gay man named Martin Dionysos, like Finnegan dying and grieving over a dead lover. (Though dominated by gay characters, *Glimmering* doesn't feel like a gay novel; for one thing, the few sex scenes are heterosexual.) Martin eventually takes Trip back to New York, where a spectacular New Year's (Millennium's) Eve party unites most of the novel's characters for a final orgy of death and destruction.

"I was reading this book — a really depressing book," a character says near the end of this novel, "and I thought, Why the hell am I reading this? All the people in here are dying. But then, I thought, But that's what we're all doing. It's like we all have two jobs: living, and dying. We just don't like to think about the dying very much." Hand has thought long and hard about dying, researching Finnish and Oriental mythology for their views on death, uncovering creepy experiments in biological warfare, quoting apocalyptic rock lyrics (including a striking song from Love's 1967 masterpiece, *Forever Changes*), and looting *The Waste Land* for all of its images of death and decay but none of its cautious hopes for renewal. There is a birth at the end of *Glimmering*, but the circumstances are anything but hopeful. Giving her book the subtitle "A Novel of the Coming Millennium," Hand gruesomely feeds the fears of those who feel the year 2000 (or 2001 for the better informed) will be catastrophic in some yet-unimagined way. In all likelihood, 2000 will pass as uneventfully as 1984 did, but until then there are bound to be a number of millenarian novels predicting the worst. I doubt that many of them will surpass *Glimmering* in this regard.

Washington Post Book World, 8 June 1997

Donald Harington

With

Toby Press, 2004

I wish I could avoid describing this wonderful novel in any detail, for certain of its elements (like pedophilia) will alienate some readers, and others will stop reading this review as soon as I mention that another plot element involves a young girl who communicates with a dog via a Ouija board. (Wait, come back! See what I mean?) *With* depends more than most novels on narrative surprises, which I shouldn't give away. And simply ending my review right here by praising *With* as the sweetest child abduction story I've ever read clearly won't do. This will be tricky.

For nearly 30 years, Donald Harington has been writing ingenious novels set in Arkansas's Ozark Mountains, mostly in a small town called Stay More. Despite rave reviews, his novels have never risen above cult status, and he has won the dubious honor of being called "America's Greatest Unknown Novelist." (I'll confess I'd never heard of him until last year, when a colleague began urging his novels on me.) He has earned his keep as an art professor, primarily at the University of Arkansas but with spells up North.

I can't put it off any longer, so here goes: *With* begins like a sleazy story out of an old *Police Gazette* but ends like a feminist revision of Genesis. In the early 1970s, Sugrue ("Sog") Alan, an Arkansas state trooper nearing retirement who lucked into half-a-million dollars when killing a drug dealer unobserved, decides to disappear. He locates a long-abandoned and nearly inaccessible house at the top of nearby Madewell Mountain, buys enough supplies to last him for years, and tells everyone he's moving to California. He moves all his stuff up to the mountain retreat and lacks only one more necessity: a child bride. Beautiful, blonde Robin Kerr is seven and a half when the novel opens, Alice's age in *Through the Looking-Glass*. Sog stalks and snatches her, installing her in a different kind of wonderland where she will remain for the next ten years. (For various reasons he doesn't molest her, though not for lack of trying.) Robin tries but fails to escape, resigns herself to her situation and slowly begins her unplanned metamorphosis from spoiled city girl to nature goddess.

Sog's dog seems to be the only other resident for a while. After Sog ceases to play an active role (that circumlocution is necessary to avoid spoiling the plot and to account for the different role he plays in the second half of the novel), Robin is joined by other animals: a bobcat, a litter of puppies, a raccoon, a snake, a fawn, and others, all of whom learn to communicate with Robin and with each other. And then there's the spirit of former resident Adam Madewell,

12 years old when his parents forced him to accompany them to California years before the novel opens, and forever 12 as he continues to haunt his old homestead as an "in-habit." (We're told that "An in-habit is part of someone who loves a particular place so very much that regardless of where they go they always leave their in-habit behind.") Though *With* is primarily Robin's story, we get Adam's as well; he eventually decides to return to Stay More, but this Adam is unaware that a new Eve inhabits his old paradise which his in-habit never left.

As confusing as this may sound, *With* is a joy to read, partly due to the variety of audacious techniques Harington uses. First, each chapter is narrated from the point of view of a specific character, which may not sound all that innovative until you learn that many of these characters are not human. (Robin's menagerie not only learns to communicate with their mistress and with each other, but also with you, dear reader.) He manipulates verb tenses, moving from past to present to future as the narrative requires. By way of literary allusion, Harington aligns his novel with similar adventures; we are told, for good reason, "Among the hundreds of books that Adam read at the Yountville Public Library were Stevenson's *Silverado Squatters* . . . as well as his *Treasure Island*. He also enjoyed Daniel Defoe's *Robinson Crusoe* and W. H. Hudson's *Green Mansions*."

Like all of these works, *With* explores the pluses and minuses of abandoning civilization for a solitary life communing with nature. Sog wanted to isolate himself because he became convinced that "the world was just no damn good, life was a joke, the world was full of meanness and wrongdoing and corruption and selfishness and evil and backstabbing and shoddy merchandise and wickedness and bum raps and disorderly conduct and weakness and malpractice and greed and moral turpitude and what not. It had been his plan to learn her to appreciate the isolation of this wilderness that protected her from all that badness and transgression." Robin misses out on the usual joys and sorrows of teenage girls, but the novel makes a strong case that she's better off that way. Hudson's Rima the Bird Girl comes to a tragic end, but Robin is clearly a better person for her experiences, and in the final line of the novel she exhibits a wisdom far beyond her 18 years.

Early during her abduction, Robin begins creating paper dolls, names them after residents of Stay More, and then begins inventing adventures for them — adventures that can be found in Harington's other novels. (Three of them have been reissued by his new publisher, and I hope more are on their way.) *With* is as whimsical as a paper-doll show while being deeply rooted in the earth; it gives the Garden of Eden myth a happy ending, and should find the wide readership that Harington so richly deserves.

Washington Post Book World, 11 April 2004

Joseph Heller

Portrait of an Artist, as an Old Man
Simon & Schuster, 2000

Portraits, even self-portraits, are not always flattering, especially if the artist is honest. James Joyce's *A Portrait of the Artist as a Young Man* presents a rather priggish, arrogant, pretentious intellectual whom not many people would want to know. The subject of Joseph Heller's final, posthumous novel is a bit more likable than Stephen Dedalus, and if the novel isn't as great as Joyce's, it's an honest look at what Heller's protagonist calls "the literature of despair." As Heller's last statement on the art of writing — he died in December at 76 — it is a fascinating look at the creative life of one of the most important writers of American postwar literature. For even though the work is billed as a novel, it is as confessional as either of Heller's two previous memoirs.

Eugene Pota, in all respects Heller himself, is 75 and struggling to come up with a subject for his next novel. He writes, as he confesses early on, because he has nothing else to do. After a wildly successful first novel, each succeeding work has met with diminishing sales and critical accolades, but there's nothing else he can or wants to do. "I can't go on, I'll go on," he quotes from Beckett.

Portrait of an Artist is a notebook of his attempts to come up with something new: We get the opening pages of various first chapters, cut off mercifully at the point when both Pota and the reader lose interest. Most are based on recycled literary conceits: updated versions of *Tom Sawyer* and Kafka's *Metamorphosis*, or tales from Greek and Hebrew mythology. One project is just a title, "A Sexual Biography of My Wife," which Pota and his publisher like so much that they joke about publishing a book with blank pages just to have that title on the dust jacket. In between these aborted chapters, Pota discusses these writing projects with his wife, agent, editors — and himself. As Pota admits, the book is less a novel than "a tract in the form of a fiction about a life spent writing fiction."

Lives spent writing fiction usually end disastrously, Pota knows. Although he is fairly well off, suffering only from waning inspiration and the usual pains of old age, he has made a study of the decline and fall of his fellow writers. At the center of the novel are two long catalogues of authors whose careers ended in illness, poverty, failure, depression, madness or suicide, one in the form of a fictionalized account of Tom Sawyer attempting to meet the great authors of his day for advice on becoming an author, the other a lecture Pota delivers titled "The Despair of Literature." It's a dismal, if familiar, list, ranging from Hawthorne's and Melville's failing reputations and ignominious ends, through Stephen Crane dying young and Dylan Thomas drinking himself to death, up to contemporaries of Heller's such as Richard Brautigan (suicide) and William Gaddis (neglected by his publishers). And although it must be said that this theme has been treated with more devastating effect by another of Heller's contemporaries — David Markson in *Reader's Block* — it tinges Pota's bumbling attempts to continue writing with its own kind of despair.

The novel is an honest look at a little-discussed phenomenon in literature, that of writers who continue writing long past their prime, and usually for the worst reasons: an expensive lifestyle to support, alimony to pay, or, like Pota, because they can't think of anything better to do with their time. Some septuagenarians, like Gilbert Sorrentino and the aforementioned Markson, continue to refine their art with surprising new creations, but too many writers (we won't name names) simply churn out more of the same every few years, taking up slots on publishers' lists (and big advances) that might better be given to fresh talents. One of the recurring themes in the Greek myths Pota tries to exploit is that of the father figure like Zeus who destroys his sons because he fears they will supplant him, and while Pota isn't overtly jealous of younger writers, he clings to his place in publishing as stubbornly as any patriarch.

Portrait of an Artist, as an Old Man (note the sigh of resignation in that comma) is no *Catch-22*, but it's an honorable conclusion to Heller's writing career. It reflects a lifetime of reading, with dozens of delicious quotes from favorite books; it includes some touching scenes featuring old people (too often excluded from fiction, as they are from popular culture); and it offers insights into such things as the publishing business and the relationship between creativity and sexuality. Death, that harshest of editors, has canceled Heller's contract; all the more reason for us to attend to his last hurrah.

Washington Post, 13 June 2000

Andrew Holleran

The Dancer from the Dance

Morrow, 1978

The Rev. Rowland Hill (1744–1833), commenting on the popularity of many folk songs over church music, is said to have complained that he did not see any reason why the devil should have all the good tunes. Along similar lines, it sometimes seems that the most fascinating fictional explorations of love concern "unconventional" loves — pedophilia in Nabokov's *Lolita,* homosexuality in Radclyffe Hall's *Well of Loneliness* and Jean Genet's *Our Lady of the Flowers,* and perhaps even spiritual eroticism in the poems of Saint John of the Cross and the writings of Saint Theresa of Ávila. Such works challenge and — in the case of *Lolita* — often surpass conventional love stories in insight and sensitivity. *The Dancer from the Dance* is a new novel examining the search for love, and is simply one of the most beautifully haunting love stories I've ever read. The fact that it concerns gay life in New York City is almost inconsequential.

Briefly, the novel concerns a late-blooming homosexual named Malone who comes to New York City in search of love. In his search he is assisted by the wise and weary Sutherland, a transvestite who plays Virgil to Malone's Dante in his tour of Gotham's homosexual underground. Unsuccessful in his search, Malone finally disappears mysteriously and soon attains the status of legend to those who remain, one of whom decides to write his story in an effort to capture what Malone symbolized to all of them. Doesn't sound like much of a plot; it isn't. The novel is really about "a group of people who . . . were bound together by a common love of a certain kind of music, physical beauty, and style — all the things one shouldn't throw away an ounce of energy pursuing, and sometimes throw a life away pursuing." That quotation could apply to a large segment of our increasingly hedonistic society — gay as well as straight — and is one indication of the novel's universality. For love's tensions, incongruities, difficulties, joys, and sorrows apply to all lovers — no matter what their tastes or inclinations — and ultimately the fact that Mr. Holleran's novel concerns homosexual love is as irrelevant as whether or not Proust actually gave his male lovers girls' names in his great examination of love.

In the preface to *The Picture of Dorian Gray,* Oscar Wilde counsels, "There is no such thing as a moral or an immoral book. Books are well written, or badly written. That is all." And that is what makes Mr. Holleran's frank portrayal of homosexual life so admirable: the writing is simply gorgeous. The prose recalls Fitzgerald at his *Gatsby* best; descriptions are both concrete and poetic, and the writing in general is thick with metaphor — many scandalously pinched from Catholicism. I am unaware of any book this season written as beautifully as this.

The love that once dare not speak its name has certainly found its voice recently — Gordon Merrick's novels are carried in all the best bookstores now, and St. Martin's Press is advertising its new "Gay Novel Series" — but I doubt that one will speak with as much eloquence and art as *The Dancer from the Dance*. Things have certainly come a long way since Radclyffe Hall was taken to court for her gentle novel and E. M. Forster simply stopped writing because he felt his society would not tolerate his speaking honestly about homosexuality. So go on, read it — there's still nothing like a good love story.

Spree, March 1979

□□□□□□□

The Beauty of Men
Morrow, 1996

Like James McCourt, Andrew Holleran is a gifted gay novelist who publishes infrequently, but whose books are worth the wait. *The Beauty of Men* is only his third novel in 18 years, and like the earlier ones exhibits a strong sense of history. His first, *Dancer from the Dance* (1978), appeared at the height of the promiscuous '70s and reflects the hedonism of the early days of gay liberation; *Nights in Aruba* (1983) registers the early ravages of AIDS; *The Beauty of Men* exhibits a kind of post-AIDS consciousness, where "the plague" (as it's always called in the novel) is just an unfortunate fact of life, "as meaningless as influenza," as the narrator says. As valuable as Holleran may be as a chronicler of contemporary gay history, however, he is one of those gay writers — again like McCourt, and like Edmund White — whose stylistic prowess and critical intelligence deserve the attention of straight readers as much as that of the gay reading community.

While McCourt follows in Firbank's fancy footsteps, Holleran follows in those of F. Scott Fitzgerald, bestowing "some sort of epic grandeur" on gay life during the plague years. (In fact, the famous conclusion of *The Great Gatsby* is parodied at one point in the new novel.) Like Fitzgerald's elegies for the Jazz Age, Holleran's novel eulogizes his generation's experiences in a sensuous, elegant style.

The novel centers on a man named Mr. Lark, 47, living alone in a small town in north-central Florida, who divides his time between caring for his paralyzed mother in a nearby nursing home and pining for a younger man named Becker, with whom he had a sexual encounter the year before but who wants to have nothing further to do with Lark. A refugee from New York City — he left in 1983, the first year a friend died from the then-new "gay virus" and the year his mother broke her neck — Lark spends the rest of his time looking for love in all the wrong places — at the isolated boat ramp at which the novel opens and closes, at the baths and gay bars in Gainesville — and recalling his life and friends in New York, almost all of whom have died from AIDS. Convinced he doesn't appeal to Becker because of his age, Lark broods on our culture's obsession with youth and beauty, with the loss of sexual appeal many people experience after they hit 40 (especially women and gay men), and on the isolation and loneliness single people of any sexual orientation feel in a society geared toward couples.

Lark is obsessed with aging and dying, various manifestations of which surround him: victims of AIDS seem to undergo an accelerated aging process, his mother's nursing home is of course filled with moribund patients, and Lark lives in a state that caters to the older generation. (In this regard the novel recalls Stanley Elkin's last novel, *Mrs. Ted Bliss*, also set in Florida and concerned with aging.) His obsession with decline even extends to America itself, which seems likewise to be the victim of accelerated aging: "He sits there wondering how his country went from 'Some Enchanted Evening' to 'Me So Horny' in less than fifty years."

Needless to say, Lark is not growing old gracefully. He considers himself "a flop as a homosexual"; not only has he failed to find a lifetime companion, he can't admit his homosexuality to his mother, and in some circumstances denies "his homosexuality more quickly . . . than Peter denied Christ." Despite having been "passed over" by the AIDS plague (another religious inversion), Lark remains as dissatisfied as Eliot's J. Alfred Prufrock: "Which leads him to the overwhelming question: Why, he wonders, isn't having been spared sufficient to make one happy? Why isn't that enough? Why aren't the ones who were left behind beaming with joy? Why does life still sting with envy and frustration, loneliness and desire? One would think that not having AIDS or not being paralyzed would be enough to make you awaken every day in a state of bliss. But no, it's not. You still want . . . a full head of hair, two more decades of unblemished youth, and everyone to want you when you walk into the bar." Lark is smart enough to recognize the vanity of such aspirations, but human enough to desire them anyway.

He is a bookish man, reads a lot, and consequently the novel is laced with literary allusions: Yeats is quoted often, as are Shakespeare, Melville, and Eliot, and there are other references to Poe, Juvenal, Mann, Schopenhauer, Arendt, Dante, Dostoevsky, and contributors to the *carpe diem* theme: "There's the whole tradition of this theme in literature from Marvell to Thoreau to Henry James. He's read them all." Lark's attempt to seize the day toward the end of the novel, in a final confrontation with Becker, ends in humiliating failure.

This is not a novel that will give comfort to many — not to homosexuals because of the emphasis on the sterility of homosexuality, nor to gay-bashers because of Lark's unapologetic love of men, their beauty, and the glorification of sex. Holleran is to be admired for bucking geriatric boomers who insist "You're not getting older, you're getting better!" and gay pride advocates who feel writers who dwell on the drawbacks of being gay are traitors to the cause. It will give comfort only to those who admire a well-crafted novel, one that orchestrates its theme with masterful effects, and that disregards the non-literary concerns of the politically correct (of any sexual orientation). It's a mournful book: If Holleran's first two novels were sweetly sad, *The Beauty of Men* is deeply despondent, soaked in sorrow, filled with erotic despair. But it's an honest attempt to grapple with loneliness and aging without self-pity or sentimentality, and for that reason it will last.

Washington Post Book World, 9 June 1996

Michel Houellebecq

The Elementary Particles. Translated by Frank Wynne
Knopf, 2000

A little over a hundred years ago, Tolstoy shocked the reading public with his novella *The Kreutzer Sonata*, a brutally frank denunciation of the mating habits of the upper classes. Michel Houellebecq's *Elementary Particles*, which at one point features a character reading *The Kreutzer Sonata*, sent similar shock waves through Europe after its publication two years ago. Though undoubtedly provocative and intriguing, it is unlikely to have the same effect here. In Europe public literary controversies still exist, whereas here a novel will make the news only if there are some political ramifications (as with Rushdie's *Satanic Verses*) or a tantalizing question of authorship (as with *Primary Colors*). *The Elementary Particles* has the added disadvantage of being so extreme in its views that it will be repugnant to most readers.

The novel is an account of two half-brothers coming of age in the '70s and finding a world that has lost its sense of community, morality, and purpose. Instead of regarding the '60s as a time of liberation, of the rejection of hypocrisy, repression, and conformity, Houellebecq — like many reactionaries here as well as in France — considers the '60s a disaster, when community was rejected in favor of rampant individualism and morality thrown out the window along with constricting ties and bras. The legacy of the French student revolt of 1968 and hippies dancing in the mud at Woodstock is the soulless, immoral, consumer society we now live in — a thesis so ludicrous that Houellebecq needs to go to extremes to defend it.

His two half-brothers, Michel and Bruno Djerzinski, were born to a beatnik mother who was too flaky to stick with one father, and who shipped the kids off to different grandmothers so that she could fly to California and join the burgeoning hippie movement in the early '60s. Bruno was sexually molested by his fellow students in primary school and grows up to be a sexual maniac who eventually winds up in an institution. Michel, a quiet, emotionless nerd, becomes a molecular biologist who makes revolutionary discoveries in cloning and paves the way for the brave new world of eugenics portrayed in the closing pages of the novel (which are set 80 years from now). Most of the people surrounding the brothers are so unhappy with the world bequeathed to them by those irresponsible hippies that they resort to suicide.

Instead of calling for a return to pre-'60s morality, as many conservatives do, Houellebecq looks to the future for a paradigm shift that would do away with the inefficient mechanics of sexual reproduction and alter the genetic code to create a race of perfect beings who have overcome "the forces of egotism, cruelty and anger" that drive our current civilization. Sexuality, which plays a major part in this novel — Bruno's escapades in nudist colonies and swingers' clubs are especially graphic — would be transformed into an activity divorced from reproduction. Tolstoy's solution to the sex drive was abstinence: Just say *nyet*. Houellebecq's equally naive solution is to extend the sensitivity of the genitals via genetic engineering "to cover the entirety of the epidermis, offering new and undreamed-of erotic possibilities." Sounds like something a sex-crazed hippie would come up with.

Despite its daft ideas, *The Elementary Particles* is a fascinating read, aided by an exceptionally smooth translation by Frank Wynne. Like our own Richard Powers and Rebecca Goldstein, Houellebecq makes extensive use of scientific knowledge in his fiction, often with unsettling results. The death of a character will be followed by a detailed scientific account of the putrefaction of corpses, and another character's act of aggression will inspire an aside on hierarchical structures in animal societies. In Houellebecq's view, we are not a little lower than the angels, as the Bible flatters us, but merely a little higher than the animals, and he gives enough evidence to substantiate this hard truth. In the sections dealing with Michel, there are extensive discussions of quantum physics, molecular biology, and the typology of meiosis, along with casual references to such things as the EPR paradox and Griffiths's Consistent Histories. Prepare to be challenged.

Houellebecq brings impressive erudition and a gutsy willingness to offend to his attempt to rethink and reimagine the bases for civilization, an ambitious task most novelists would shrink from and which earns our respect, no matter how sharply we might disagree with him. Like Huxley's *Brave New World*, which is cited in *The Elementary Particles* and obviously influenced it, Houellebecq's novel is equally fascinating and repugnant, the kind of mutant gene that keeps the evolution of the novel interesting.

Washington Post Book World, 21 January 2001

Robert Irwin

Exquisite Corpse
Pantheon, 1997

Surrealism, for its founders and early practitioners, was less an art movement than a new way of life: a search for the marvelous in daily life, an openness to chance encounters and meaningful coincidences, an exploration of dreams and the unconscious, and a reevaluation of the relationship between the sexes. The Surrealist lifestyle is the subject of British writer Robert Irwin's new novel, whose protagonist provides a more precise definition: "Surrealism is not, as most people think, an artistic movement; it is a scientific method of investigation in which experiment plays a leading part." The protagonist's own experiments in this novel, however, lead him to the brink of madness, if not beyond.

Exquisite Corpse purports to be an "anti-memoire" written in 1951 by a second-rate artist named Caspar about his life among the Surrealists in the late 1930s. The setting is not Paris, the birthplace of Surrealism, but London, where a group calling itself the Serapion Brotherhood (after a similar group in Russia) lives out the prescriptions of André Breton, Louis Aragon, and others. The British contingent is a pale imitation of the French one: "The trouble was that the British Surrealists were so drab and anemic, childishly obsessed with circuses and seasides, and desperately concerned to be polite and charming." Caspar, closer to the adventurous spirit of the original Surrealists, allows himself one day to be led blindfolded through the streets of London, eager "for something really exciting to happen — something that would change my life forever." He gets his wish with a vengeance. Led to a bar in Soho, he meets a woman named Caroline Begley, a typist out on an adventure of her own, who leads Caspar (still blindfolded) to St. James's Park for a kiss before abandoning him.

Caspar instantly becomes erotically obsessed with the mystery woman, for she so perfectly fills the female role in the (male) Surrealist scheme of things: "Women were channels through which the Marvellous manifested itself. According to Ned [the theorist of the Serapion Brotherhood] a woman could be materialised by the insemination of chance and desire. Then the appearance of these women would in turn lead to the transformation of the world into the domain of the perfectly Marvellous." But this particular woman transforms Caspar into a perfect wreck. Caroline arrives at Caspar's studio a few days later (he had asked to do her portrait and had given her his address) and begins keeping him company. For her it's a lark, mingling with bohemians and attending exhibitions, but Caspar is convinced he's found the woman of his dreams and becomes increasingly frustrated by her unwillingness to have sex with him. With the advice of black magician Aleister Crowley (he and several other historical figures of the 1930s make cameo appearances), Caspar studies mesmerism and tries unsuccessfully to hypnotize Caroline into acquiescence, and even decides to give up Surrealism and get a job as a commercial artist for her sake. She continues to put him off, then disappears completely.

Caspar's despair at losing Caroline is shared by his writer friend Oliver Sorge, who is searching for a fantasy woman named Stella whom he conjured up during a seance, and about whom he is writing a novel called *The Vampire of Surrealism*. Oliver goes off to the Spanish Civil War, while Caspar goes off in search of Caroline, a quest that entails opium dens, orgies, private detectives, Nazi Germany, and eventually the madhouse. Finally recovering somewhat, he writes and publishes his memoir as "a magic trap," hoping that Caroline will read it and return to him.

Does she or doesn't she? Here Irwin takes his greatest gamble. Caspar has strong hypnogogic abilities; those phantom figures most people see as they drop off to sleep assume lifelike vividness for Caspar, even speaking to him. (Salvador Dalí claimed to use hypnogogic exercises to inspire his paintings.) The final chapter of the novel reads like a realistic epilogue to the book, but may instead be a hypnogogic illusion, which in turn casts doubt on many other events in the novel. Is Caroline merely a typist from Putney or the very vampire of Surrealism? It's for the reader to decide.

Casual references to things like Bellmer's dolls indicate that Irwin has done his homework in Surrealism, and the whole novel could be read as a critique of the Surrealist program if not for the fact that Caspar's kind of erotic obsession is hardly limited to Surrealists. *Amour fou* (mad love), as Breton called it, is perhaps the inevitable result when "woman" becomes a channel, a symbol, a problem. Breton himself tells Caroline, "The problem of woman is the most marvellous and disturbing problem there is in the world." But our levelheaded British typist is doubtful. "It may have been that she did not like to think of herself as a problem, whether marvellous or not," Caspar writes. If Caspar had given this more thought, things would have turned out better. You know you're in trouble when you seek dating advice from the likes of Aleister Crowley.

Washington Post Book World, 4 May 1997

Henry James

Michael Gorra. *Portrait of a Novel: Henry James and the Making of an American Masterpiece*
Liveright, 2012

Henry James was in his late thirties when he published his first uncontested masterpiece, *The Portrait of a Lady* (1880–81), which elevated him from a talented up-and-comer to a major novelist. It is the story of an intelligent, independent young woman named Isabel Archer who is taken from America to England and allowed to make something of herself, but who "affronts" her destiny (as James worded it) by making a bad marriage. When James revised the novel for the collected New York Edition of 1908, he wrote a preface to account for its origins and aims, concluding after a dozen pages with the admission, "There is really too much to say." That's where Michael Gorra steps in, devoting 334 intelligent pages to everything James left unsaid about this superb, game-changing novel.

Mixing literary criticism with biography and travelogue, Gorra — an English professor at Smith College — provides a fascinating "Making of" documentary like those that accompany some films these days. Literally following in James's footsteps — Gorra visited all the places in Italy and England where he composed the novel — he alternates between close readings of the novel itself and wide-ranging background material drawn from James's life and writings, deliberately imitating the form of James's novel, which moves crab-wise both forward and sideways as James frequently interrupts the linear storyline to backtrack or leap forward over events (such as the first few years of Isabel's marriage), or to bring it to a halt for a dozen pages while Isabel simply thinks. Gorra even weaves unattributed quotations from James's writings into the texture of his own exquisite prose, giving his *Portrait* the same varnished finish of James's *Portrait*.

Gorra demonstrates that James was interested less in plot than in character, and specifically in consciousness; "the novel isn't finally about a young woman's choice of a husband, or even about Americans in Europe," Gorra writes near the end. "It is instead a drama of the perceiving mind," and James hoped this sort of intellectual drama would be as "interesting," as he wrote in his 1908 preface, "as the surprise of a caravan or the identification of a pirate," the stuff of commercial fiction. Gorra underlines how radically James broke from the fiction practices of the 19th century in this novel. Not only did he shift the emphasis from plot to character — and offered a deeper analysis of character than usual — but he introduced into fiction one of the earliest examples of "stream of consciousness" (his older brother William's phrase), and he dared to leave his ending unresolved, to the frustration of many readers.

James was one of the first purveyors of what is now maligned as "difficult" fiction, especially in his later novels when he stopped writing to please his audience. "He writes now as if he wants only to please himself," Gorra writes of his final phase, "and to the degree that he's concerned with his readers at all, it's to pay the fit and the few the compliment of assuming that they'll be able to follow." This is an attitude associated with Joyce and his postmodern progeny, but Gorra persuasively argues that "difficult" fiction began with James's *Portrait*. The Anglo-American novelist agreed with the French novelists he hung out with that it was time to write for mature *adults*; the "English system was good for virgins and boys, and a bad thing for the novel itself," as James wrote in a review of Zola's *Nana*, a novel then inconceivable and unpublishable in England or America. For the French, writing for adults meant dealing with squalor and sexuality, but for James it meant converting the novel from entertainment to art, a classification few people were willing to grant it, even at that late stage in literary history. Hemingway famously said all modern American fiction came from *Huckleberry Finn*, which may be true of relatively undemanding fiction such as his; but the more demanding fiction of Faulkner, Gaddis, Pynchon, Wallace, and others (Gorra implies) comes from *The Portrait of a Lady*.

Much contemporary literary criticism is so demanding as to be almost unreadable, but Gorra's book reads beautifully. It's closer to belles lettres than to academic criticism, I'm happy to report. He identifies the real-life originals behind James's characters and places, but steers us to the proper use of this information: "Searching for some putative original allows us to see what was in fact created; the difference between the fictional page and the gravel of documentary truth can stand as a guide to artistic practice." There is more biographical information here than in most monographs on individual novels, but the emphasis is always on how James transformed that material to aesthetic ends. Gorra's *Portrait of a Novel* is a model for the once-discredited biographical approach to criticism, a demonstration-class example of how richly rewarding such an approach can be in the right hands. It is an important book not only for James enthusiasts, but for anyone interested in what Gorra christens "the bridge across which Victorian fiction stepped over into modernism."

Washington Post, 30 November 2012

Charles Johnson

Dr. King's Refrigerator and Other Bedtime Stories
Scribner, 2005

It's always important to read the small print first. Facing a tight deadline, I plunged right in and read the first two stories in this collection and was not impressed. Can this be the same Charles Johnson who was awarded a MacArthur "genius" grant, and who won the 1990 National Book Award for *Middle Passage*? (I've always felt that should have gone to his fellow nominee Felipe Alfau for *Chromos*.) Only then did I notice the subtitle calling these "Bedtime Stories" and a note in the back explaining that these two stories and three others "were originally written for Humanities Washington, which commissions local Seattle writers to read new stories. The yearly readings have become a major Seattle literary event." Ah, the literary equivalent of a night at the Boston Pops, then. In that case, I guess the first two stories weren't so bad, and probably went over well with the rain-drenched crowd.

Graham Greene divided his published fictions into "novels" and "entertainments"; this collection clearly belongs to the latter category. Bedtime stories are usually simple tales ending in a moral, and that's mostly what we have here. The first, "Sweet Dreams," is a Kafka-Lite story about a fellow who is audited for not paying his "Dream Tax," a government revenue scheme by which every citizen must pay for any and all dreams, including daydreams. The unnamed protagonist loves to dream and consequently hasn't reported them all. Kafka would have strapped him to a torture apparatus, but Johnson lets him off with a fine. The sympathetic auditor tells him, "I know, I know. Those who dream more always pay more," a comforting platitude for artists and other dreamers.

"Cultural Relativity" makes reference to the Eddie Murphy movie *Coming to America* and reworks its plot as a Grimm fairy tale. In "Dr. King's Refrigerator," a young Martin Luther King Jr. is stumped for the theme of his next sermon until a midnight visit to his well-stocked refrigerator reveals to him the Lord's bounty. "Better Than Counting Sheep" pokes fun at academic life, and "The Queen and the Philosopher" is an account by Descartes' valet of his master's fatal trip to Sweden to become Queen Christina's tutor. Those are the Seattle Pops stories, pleasant bedtime stories for the rest of us.

The remaining three are a little more challenging. "Executive Decision" employs second-person narration to engage the reader in making a tough decision regarding affirmative action: Given two equally qualified candidates for a job, do you choose the white woman or the black man? The narrator and his colleagues struggle with ideas of reparation and social justice in addition to more mundane considerations of increasing market share and shareholders' value. The story reads a little too much like a civics lesson, but readers can see if their choice matches the one given in the final sentence.

"The Gift of the Osuo" is the most carefully wrought story in the collection. This fairy tale is set in an Islamic African nation in the 17th century, ruled over by a "kind, large-bellied king" named Shabaka Malik al Muhammad. One day, two *osuo* (sorcerers) come before him to settle the same question Descartes wrestled with (as his valet tells us in "The Queen and the Philosopher"): whether Mind is superior to Matter, or the other way around. The king hasn't a clue, but in a moment of inspiration decides both are equally important. The sorcerers are delighted and reward him with a magic stick of charcoal: "Whatever you sketch with this shall leap hugely to life." The bored king reinvents himself as an artist, drawing/creating a lovely young wife to replace his old one and refurbishing his kingdom, though with disastrous results. "Reality can be beaten with enough imagination," says Mark Twain in one of the book's epigraphs, and in Shabaka's venture we have an allegory of the joys and sorrows of artistic creation. The language (except for one incongruous reference to Chagall) is tighter in this story than in any of the others, enriched by mentions of African terms, tribes, and customs that aren't explained but simply there, as if Johnson is telling the tale straight from a 17th-century African's point of view. (The fable is quite engaging as well.)

The final story, "Kwoon," is probably the best — written 15 years ago, it has been anthologized often — but it feels out of place, a little too serious for a collection of "bedtime stories." It deals with the owner of a martial arts school (a kwoon) in Chicago and of the beating he takes from one of his older students, shaming him in front of the class; he invites the brutal student back for "a private lesson in budo" — the spiritual side of martial-arts training — and teaches him a lesson he'll never forget, and not the one the reader may expect. Its inclusion could be justified because it, too, is a didactic tale that provides a moral, but I suspect it was added to pad out this thin collection. It belongs with Johnson's literary works, not his entertainments.

The range of settings in this collection is impressive, from a kwoon on Chicago's South Side to a corporate boardroom in Seattle, from 17th-century Sweden and Africa to the pre-civil rights South, to a future where we pay taxes on dreams. "Art flourishes where there is a sense of adventure" is another of the book's epigraphs (from philosopher Alfred North Whitehead), and Johnson's fans should enjoy these day-trip adventures until his next novel comes along.

Washington Post Book World, 20 February 2005

Camden Joy

The Last Rock Star Book, or Liz Phair: A Rant
Verse Chorus Press, 1998

In his first novel, Camden Joy employs a remarkably sophisticated narrative strategy to examine love, loss, revolution, and rock and roll, mixing cultural criticism with personal confession to moving effect — the equivalent of a coming-from-nowhere rock musician scoring a spectacular hit with her very first album. Like Liz Phair.

Three different typefaces are used to distinguish three alternating, ultimately converging storylines. The first, set in the novel's present, is narrated into a pocket tape recorder by a young man, also named Camden Joy, concerning the offer he receives to write a quickie illustrated biography of Liz Phair for a series of "Where-are-they-now?" books published by a shady character named Gilbert Snell. (Until her long-delayed third album appeared last summer, many people were indeed wondering what became of the indie hellion who rocked the music world with her 1993 debut, *Exile in Guyville*.) Camden has spent time in mental institutions and is now living alone in Sioux City, Iowa, trying to resume some sort of life, so he accepts the assignment even though he has only the vaguest idea who Liz Phair is. A second typeface signals the story of his first girlfriend, Shaleese, and their empty relationship. A third typeface is used for Camden's autobiography, beginning with his earliest memories — all of them characterized by "this idea that everything in my youth was suffused with futility."

Details from each of the three narratives begin dovetailing in an ingenious fashion: Camden is blown away by *Exile in Guyville* once he hears it, and he begins relating it to things Shaleese had read to him from her journal. Shaleese claimed to be the illegitimate daughter of the Rolling Stones's Brian Jones; she then began writing intriguing songs, circulating tapes, and playing small clubs, eventually leaving Camden for Chicago and the big time. As Camden notes the similarities between the Stones's *Exile on Main Street* and Phair's *Exile*, his memories of Shaleese and his growing fixation with Phair begin melting together into a psychotic stew such that he thinks it's possible that Shaleese has changed her name to Liz Phair. And then there's the enigmatic photo of a female looter (from a 1968 newspaper, reproduced on the book's cover) that assumes a life of its own as the novel reaches its bizarre, fascinating conclusion.

This is an amazing novel in every way: in its handling of a complex, tripartite narrative, its observations on rock music, its assured, occasionally hallucinogenic prose style, and its intelligence. It's a typical "slacker" tale, but expertly done: great dialogue, period details, and free from mawkish sentimentality and melodrama. I hope this isn't a one-hit wonder; Joy is truly gifted and deserves to be as well known as Liz Phair herself.

Rain Taxi, Winter 1998–99

James Joyce

Don Gifford with Robert J. Seidman.
"Ulysses" Annotated: Notes for James Joyce's "Ulysses"
Second edition, revised and enlarged, University of California Press, 1988

The first edition of Gifford's mammoth book of annotations appeared in 1974 and has been on the shelf of serious readers of Joyce ever since. By serious readers, I don't mean those who say to themselves "this paragraph deals with recent Irish history" and feel it is unnecessary to understand the particulars, and I certainly don't mean those who skip over such paragraphs to get to the more interesting parts — such readers should have their degrees revoked. This second edition contains over a thousand additions and corrections, and is now keyed to the recent Garland/Random House edition of *Ulysses*. (Even though that edition is currently under attack, the dispute is largely over minor matters of punctuation and thus does not affect Gifford's book; besides, his annotations are cross-referenced to the 1961 edition for those who prefer the older text.)

What a wealth of information is here! from simple identifications of what Joyce called "Dublin street furniture" (shops, pubs, buildings, etc.) to precise explanations of Joyce's learned allusions, with all the flotsam and jetsam of popular culture and Irish slang in between. Maps are given for each episode, summaries of corresponding Homeric episodes, and details from the Gilbert and Linati schema Joyce drew up. An introduction examines Joyce's use of time, provides background material on the major political issues in Ireland at the time, and even converts 1904 monetary values into contemporary terms. A 32-page index doubles as an index to *Ulysses* itself, and though "highly selective" is as exhaustive as most readers could wish. This book is everything an annotation to *Ulysses* could and should be; only photographs for relevant Dublin locales and personalities could have improved it, but that would no doubt have pushed its already prohibitive price even higher [$65, or $125 in 2016].

While the primary purpose of the book is to inform any reading of *Ulysses*, an important secondary purpose is to limit and restrict certain readings. Joyce criticism has always had its lunatic fringe, even in the days before Derrida sanctioned free association with signifiers, and references in *Ulysses* (and especially in *Finnegans Wake*) have often been taken out of context and blown out of proportion to support readings that are eccentric, to say the least. Gifford hopes that precise information will curtail such irresponsible readings;

here, for example, is his annotation to "Vico road, Dalkey" (2.25):

> This has been repeatedly cited as an allusion to the Italian philosopher Giambattista Vico (1668–1744), whose concept of history as an endless *ricorso*, or "rosary," Joyce found fascinating. But there is room for doubt about this allusion because there is a Vico Road in Dalkey; because one of the models for Armstrong (Clifford Ferguson; see Ellmann, p. 153) lived in Vico Terrace; and because Stephen's free associations on Blakean and Aristotelian concepts of the nature of history put him in an essentially pre-Viconian position.

Although the purpose of these notes is pedagogical, not interpretative, it is as important to know what certain references probably *do not* mean as to what they do. Gifford's book will enlighten any reading of *Ulysses*, provide solid ground for any scholarly interpretation, and still belongs on the shelf of every committed reader of Joyce's classic.

Review of Contemporary Fiction, Fall 1989

Norma Kassirer

The Hidden Wife and Other Stories. Illustrated by Willyum Rowe
Shuffaloff Press, 1991

"What does democracy have to do with art?" asks the writer in the title story of Norman Kassirer's brilliant collection of short fiction. Kassirer doesn't write democratically for the masses but for connoisseurs of the unusual and innovative. The opening story, "Missing Hollywood," concerns a woman who conceives of her actions in cinematic terms, and Kassirer cleverly appropriates the vocabulary of film to animate this vignette of a failing marriage. The story's wry sense of humor and imaginative imagery ("The girl is tossing kisses. They rush at the car, a butterfly herd") distinguish it from the average story of a failing relationship, just as "The Hidden Wife" employs similar fancifulness to enliven a story about a writer's relation to her characters. "The Unbearably Extended Family" is giddy with Elkin-like tropes and wisecracks as it explores the tense relationship between an artist named Millicent and her irony-resistant mother. This artist returns in "More or Less Post-Modern Millicent" (maybe not — this one speaks like a Valley girl? with, like, a question mark after every sentence?), another dizzying send-up of postmodern overkill regarding reference, quotation, and the means of artistic production. "O," like "Missing Hollywood," examines a flagging relationship via sex fantasies that comically fail until the woman hits upon a unique one for her accountant partner. The collection ends with "Song and Dance," outwardly the most conventional story, but like the others characterized by unusual metaphors, sharp wit, and keen insights into relationships. The book is large (9 x 11) and illustrated with surrealistic collages that, for me, didn't enhance the reading but for others may be one more attraction of this lively collection of stories.

Review of Contemporary Fiction, Summer 1992

Ken Kesey

George J. Searles, ed. A *Casebook of Ken Kesey's "One Flew over the Cuckoo's Nest"*
University of New Mexico Press, 1992

Keseys' *Cuckoo's Nest* is one of those charmed novels that met with immediate popular and critical acceptance: published in 1962, it was the subject of an article by Irving Malin in *Critique* the same year, and has been written about and taught regularly ever since. In 1973, John C. Pratt edited a critical edition consisting of the novel plus a dozen of the best articles that had appeared up till then; George J. Searles has now gathered 15 of the best essays to have been published since the early 1970s and added what appears to be a very full bibliography of all *Cuckoo's Nest* criticism to date (almost a hundred items).

All of the selections here are old-fashioned thematic essays, untouched by recent developments in literary theory, which can be good or bad depending on your tastes. Many of the essays deal with the novel's alleged sexism and racism — which may doom the novel to obscurity in politically correct literature departments — and some refer to Milos Forman's film treatment. Consequently, anyone writing about or still teaching *Cuckoo's Nest* will find this casebook a valuable resource. On the evidence gathered here, however, Kesey criticism needs to move on to a higher level of critical sophistication if *Cuckoo's Nest* is to retain its undoubted place in postwar American fiction.

One more old-fashioned study still needs to be done, though, before moving on to that higher plane. (I owe the following information to bookseller Ken Lopez.) The minor character named Public Relations was originally a female called the Red Cross woman in the first edition of the novel. She is also called "Gwen-doe-lin" at one point, which led novelist Gwen Davis, apparently an aide at the same hospital Kesey worked at in the 1950s, to threaten a lawsuit. For the British edition and all subsequent American editions, Kesey made changes in his text (on pp. 9–11, 35, and 85–86 of the first edition). Kesey's disparaging treatment of the Red Cross woman — and his capitulation to this aspect of the Combine — is something future Kesey scholars will want to consider.

Review of Contemporary Fiction, Summer 1992. I hate spoilsport egomaniacs like Davis, and like the guy who forced Heller to change "R. O. Shipman" in the first printing of *Catch-22* to A. T. Tappman, even though the original name was only coincidental, and didn't refer to Mr. Shipman. Karmacally, Davis was later sued by someone who mistakenly assumed he was portrayed in one of *her* novels.

Sailor Song

Viking, 1992

The appearance of Kesey's new novel, almost 30 years after his first two, is already being compared to Pynchon's return to the fiction scene with *Vineland* a few years ago, and some are expressing a similar disappointment that the new work doesn't surpass the old. But like *Vineland*, *Sailor Song* is a hugely enjoyable novel written with a great ear for language, drawing its diction everywhere from Church Latin to Eskimo slang. Set in Alaska in the early years of the 21st century, *Sailor Song* nevertheless has a 1960s sensibility (again like *Vineland*) evoking that era's freewheeling boisterousness. This extends beyond its many references to music and books of the time (Bob Dylan and the Beatles are mentioned, Pynchon's *Lot 49* and *Gravity's Rainbow* alluded to, a stanza of Leonard Cohen's "Suzanne" used as the epigraph, the opening line of Buffalo Springfield's "For What It's Worth" quoted, etc.) to embrace that decade's concern with apocalypse and renewal (think of *V.*, *The Origin of the Brunists*, *Love's Body*, *Slaughterhouse-Five*, etc.)

The protagonist of *Sailor's Song*, Isaak Sallis — a toned-down version of *Cuckoo's Nest*'s Randle McMurphy, closer to *Demon Box*'s Devlin Deboree — was apparently born in the '60s, achieved notoriety as an eco-terrorist in the "environmental wars" of the '90s, and has since retreated to an Alaskan fishing village called Kuinak, where his simple life is upset by the arrival of a Hollywood film crew eager to use the village as the backdrop for their next movie. A literal apocalypse brings an end to all this — Frost's "Fire and Ice" provides the imagery — with Isaak recalled to heroism like an archetype out of Joseph Campbell. The ending, like that of *Vineland* (for the last time), is somewhat unsatisfactory, but it concludes an exuberant reading experience and constitutes a triumphant return to fiction by Ken Kesey, a true hero of our time.

Review of Contemporary Fiction, Fall 1992. I reviewed the advance galley, and I believe the "Church Latin" was edited out of the published book.

Ivan Klíma

The Ultimate Intimacy. Translated by A. G. Brain
Grove, 1998

The Ultimate Intimacy recounts a momentous year in the life of the Rev. Daniel Vedra, a Protestant minister in the Czech Republic. It begins with the death of his mother and ends with a near-fatal heart attack and his resignation from the ministry. In between, Daniel cheats on his second wife by having an affair with a married woman, inherits a large amount of money, begins seriously doubting his religion, discovers that his daughter is using drugs and is pregnant, and learns that his father may have been an informer during the Communist regime and was definitely a philanderer who cheated on his wife too. A tough year, by any standard.

Through it all, Daniel ponders the nature of intimacy and wonders what the ultimate intimacy would be or, more precisely, who should be the recipient of such intimacy: his first wife, whom he cannot forget? his children? his god? the beautiful stranger who enters his life at the beginning of the novel? The minister finally defines the ultimate degree of intimacy as "the capacity to trust utterly and therefore to confide everything, even one's deepest secrets, even the things one conceals from oneself." His realization that this can occur during prayer as well as lovemaking exacerbates the moral dilemma that bedevils him.

Daniel's quest for intimacy is shared by the four other principal adult characters in the novel: his second wife Hana, whose difficult early life has stunted her capacity for intimacy; Matous Volek, a jaunty journalist undergoing a divorce, who develops an interest in Hana; Bara, the married woman who steals Daniel away from his wife in her hunger for a meaningful life; and Samuel, Bara's obnoxious husband, who is so dissatisfied with her that he wonders if he'd be better off with a dog. Except for Samuel, these are all good people, especially Daniel, and Klíma effectively conveys their struggles. But the ordinariness of their problems makes it difficult to work up much enthusiasm for the novel. At one point Daniel attends a theological seminar: "The theme was predestination and the meaning of good works," he writes in his diary. "It's an eternal theme about which, as with most themes, everything has been said that could be said." A similar predictability dogs Klíma's novel. The standard themes of adultery and religious doubt have been treated so often that it's a real challenge to come up with something new to say about them, and Klíma doesn't rise to the challenge. Nor does the Czech setting offer any novelty: Prague might as well be Peoria, except that some of the buildings are older. It has the same divorce rate, the same kind of disenchanted teenagers experimenting with drugs, the same kind of people struggling with the same kind of problems.

The most interesting aspect of *The Ultimate Intimacy* is its elegant, formal structure. The novel consists of eight chapters, each with eight subsections that follow a pattern: The odd ones (1, 3, 5, 7) are third-person accounts of Daniel's activities; sections 2 and 7 are excerpts from his diary and correspondence, respectively; and sections 4 and 6 deal with the other four adult characters and are structured symmetrically. Architecture is a minor theme in the novel — both Samuel and Bara work in that field — so it's appropriate for the novel to have an architectural symmetry. But there's a contrast made in the novel between the boringly symmetrical buildings of the late Communist regime and the flamboyantly asymmetrical cathedral of Gaudí in Barcelona, which Bara sees on vacation. The latter is clearly the work of an "unfettered" genius, she feels, realizing that traditional art and religion usually seek symmetry and order. "Happily, from time to time, some wayward soul is born," she thinks, "some Gaudí, who questions the prevailing order and symmetry, in order to rescue life." Klíma has chosen to keep the fetters on and stick with traditional symmetry and order, perhaps because the notion that life can be "rescued" is a delusion, perhaps because Klíma lacks Gaudí's genius, perhaps. . . . One could speculate for hours on this, which is the ultimate appeal of *The Ultimate Intimacy*.

Washington Post Book World, 11 January 1998

Reif Larsen

I Am Radar
Penguin Press, 2015

In 2008, 28-year-old Reif Larsen wowed the literary world with *The Selected Works of T. S. Spivet*, a postmodern road novel featuring a 12-year-old prodigy and festooned with maps, illustrations, and marginalia. If young Spivet's thoughts were a little too mature at times, young Larsen displayed an admirable willingness to think outside the traditional narrative box.

The promise shown in that first novel is more than fulfilled in the grandly ambitious *I Am Radar*, another masterpiece of geekhood. It too has maps, illustrations, footnotes, even a bibliography, but if Larsen's first novel looks like a Donald Barthelme assemblage, this one resembles one by Thomas Pynchon. Like his novels (which are alluded to a few times in the text), it is thick with scientific references, tech talk, arcane erudition, and evinces prodigious historical research. Set over the last 40 years, it yo-yos between New Jersey, Norway, Yugoslavia, Cambodia, and the Congo.

The übergeeky title character, Radar Radmanovic — named by his father after the chopper-detecting character in *M*A*S*H* — is a radio engineering prodigy, but also a freak. Born black to white parents during a blackout in 1975, he baffles the scientific establishment, then undergoes a mysterious treatment in Norway that turns him white, though it leaves him nearly bald and subject to epileptic seizures. While in Norway, he and his parents learn of an "experimental puppet troupe" called the Kirkenesferda, which has been staging "happenings" (as they call them) illustrating scientific ideas like neutrinos and superstring theory in war-torn regions ever since World War II. During another blackout in 2010, 35-year-old Radar is invited by the troupe to put on a performance in the Congo, where he meets a strange bibliophile assembling a gigantic library in the jungle, who likewise underwent a skin change from dark to light. The ending is nearly indescribable, a phantasmagorical display of apocalyptic magic realism.

In between the three chapters on Radar there are two novella-length accounts of other whiz kids and their families in Yugoslavia and Cambodia, where the Kirkenesferda eventually shows up to stage other elaborate puppet shows in protest against the brutality of war.

In Larsen's gifted hands, puppetry becomes a multilevel metaphor for the role of art in a violent world. "War happens when society forgets its artists," as one puppeteer says, meaning that art reveals the gut-level similarities between people, while wars are caused by those who violently insist on skin-deep ethnic, religious, or ideological differences. The Kirkensesferda also wants to "make the human body into a puppet of itself" in order to erase "An awareness of ourselves as an actor on the stage. . . . We think, and therefore we cannot just *be*." Puppetry also is a metaphor for the way novelists operate: Don Quixote gets so worked up by a puppet show that he storms the stage to attack its villains, but you don't have to be loco to be taken in by wooden figures manipulated by strings, and the Kirkensesferda's activities are a metafictional analogy of the elaborate show that puppeteer Larsen is staging for us.

Then again, some of the Kirkensesferda's happenings go unobserved, and those that are end in disaster. They sound like the kind of over-conceptualized, theory-addled performance art that is more interesting to think about than to sit through, and the troupe has no effect on the political status quo. In a sense, *I Am Radar* is an avant-garde novel dramatizing the inconsequence of avant-garde art.

But Larsen's brainy novel is no ephemeral performance piece. Larsen grapples with time-honored questions of free will, predestination, "man versus nature," and the tensions between parents and children. But it's the ingenuity with which he does so, rather than the themes themselves, that elicit admiration. Each of the foreign settings contains thick descriptions of their culture, history, folklore and literature, and is laced with words and phrases in their native tongue. (In addition to Norwegian, Serbian, French, and Cambodian, there are passages in sign language, Morse code, and even African talking drum transcriptions.) There are several bibliophiles in the novel, hence lots of discussion of books, and some literary in-jokes: in the African chapter, set in 2010, we're told of "one small feeder boat from South Africa, the *Colonel Joll*, which looked as if it had been here for some time" — referring to a character last seen in J. M. Coetzee's 1980 novel *Waiting for the Barbarians*, also set in Africa. The experimental theater troupe names a goat Bertolt Brecht. There are math equations, music scores, maps of a small island located simultaneously in the Adriatic Sea, off the northern coast of Norway, and in the Mekong river in Southeast Asia. Radar crosses the ocean in the *Aleph*, the title of a book by Jorge Luis Borges, as important an influence on Larsen as Pynchon. It is listed in the novel's bibliography — a clever mixture of real and fictitious works — which gives further evidence of the network of literary allusions supporting the novel's wide-ranging concerns. An item in the bibliography also tells us how Radar's story ends.

Fifteen years ago, critic James Wood used the term "hysterical realism" to deride novels like this one, those that feature wacky characters with funny names involved in cartoonishly convoluted plots about mysterious connections, and often spiked with pop references and nerdy erudition. But this genre includes some of the greatest novels of our time, from Pynchon's *V.* to Wallace's *Infinite Jest*. That's the troupe Larsen has decided to join, and *I Am Radar* is a dazzling performance.

Washington Post, 10 April 2015

Brad Leithauser

A Few Corrections
Knopf, 2001

The obituary is an odd little genre: a passionless minibiography usually written long before its subject's demise, then entombed in a newspaper's morgue until the fateful day. When that day comes, an introductory and concluding paragraph are slapped on like a last-minute costume change before taking the stage, and the obituary makes its ephemeral appearance, only to be tossed out a few days later, perhaps just as its subject is being lowered into the grave. Invariably, mistakes are made.

Brad Leithauser's clever new novel opens with a 250-word obituary of one Wesley Sultan, followed by the statement: "There are at least a dozen errors here." Over the next 270 pages, the obituary is corrected, item by item — handwritten on the original, which is reprinted at the beginning of each chapter — concluding with a revised, considerably expanded obituary of the late Mr. Sultan.

The appeal here is not in the tale but in the telling. Wesley Sultan was a small-town salesman and womanizer who lied and charmed his way through a rather messy life, dying in shabby circumstances heavily in debt. Set mostly in Michigan in the 1950s and '60s, it's a story similar to that of dozens of novels and movies. But as Henry James advised, we should criticize not the subject of a novel but how the writer treats it, and this is where Leithauser shines. Unsatisfied by the original obituary, the initially unnamed narrator begins digging into Sultan family history to uncover the true story, and the piecemeal revelation of the details of Wes's life quickly becomes fascinating, despite the predictability, even dreariness, of those details. It's like working a jigsaw puzzle of an uninspired subject, which can be as satisfying as a masterpiece when the pieces begin falling into place.

The narrator — whose identity isn't revealed until a third of the way through the novel and shouldn't be disclosed here — has the advantage of several colorful characters to draw upon. Wes's ex-wife Sally and his brother Conrad, interviewed separately, provide most of the details, correcting and expanding upon what the other has said. Sally is a refined, bookish woman now living in France and working her way through Proust, while Conrad is a fat slob retired in Miami, an abrasive homosexual who enjoys taunting the narrator as much as enlightening him. Other characters important to Wes's life are interviewed, each a middle-class Midwesterner of no special distinction but crucial to adding pieces to the puzzle. Although they add facts, their real contribution is their interpretations of Wes's character, which emerges as the real test of wisdom: "whether we're skilled enough interpreters to make even minimal sense of our lives."

Although the relationship of Leithauser's *A Few Corrections* to Proust's *In Search of Lost Time* (mentioned several times in his novel) is that of a dollhouse to a cathedral, both novels are intent upon preserving a vanishing world: in Leithauser's case the 1950s, which now look as quaint as the Victorian era. He has a poet's eye for defining details, like the endearingly geeky clubs featured in Wes's 1952 yearbook — the Ushers Club is "composed of uniformed girls who are on call for working the checkroom at school parties" — and revels, in a nonpatronizing way, in the earnestness of that earlier time, a time free of irony and skepticism.

Throughout, Leithauser displays an enviable control of his material, with a magician's feel for what to reveal and when. Although the novel is overtly about the tangled relationships, the complicating details that define anyone's life, *A Few Corrections* is also about how a novel is constructed — the choices a writer makes, the construction of character, setting a novel's rhythm and tone — and in all of these Leithauser demonstrates that he is a master craftsman. He knows he's good and displays a kind of bravado as he pulls one rabbit after another out of his magician's hat. (He even uses a quotation from his previous novel as an epigraph: Now that's confidence.) It's a delight to see him at work, like watching someone make an origami swan out of a back issue of the *Detroit Free Press*. Read *A Few Corrections* for an evocation of an earlier era, if you wish, or for the tangled tale of a Midwestern Lothario, but read it as a tour de force in narrative construction. You'll certainly never read a simple obituary in the same way again.

Washington Post Book World, 15 April 2001

Antonio Lobo Antunes

The Inquisitors' Manual. Translated by Richard Zenith
Grove, 2002

Portugal's Antonio Lobo Antunes is one of those foreign novelists who can write circles around most American writers. Yet he has never caught on here. This has probably less to do with his high-modernist technique (reminiscent of Faulkner's), which can be challenging, than with his subject matter, the tribulations of Portuguese society during the long dictatorship of Antonio de Oliveira Salazar from 1932 to 1968. Not exactly a hot topic. But with a half-dozen splendid novels now available in English translation, and rumors of a Nobel Prize afoot, he deserves to be embraced by all serious readers of literary fiction.

The Inquisitors' Manual, his most recently translated novel, centers on the revolution of 1974, which brought the dictatorship to an end and ushered in a chaotic period of adjustment to democracy. Spanning roughly the period 1965–95, the novel tracks the career of Senhor Francesco, one of Salazar's ministers, who is bitterly disappointed not to have been named the dictator's successor, and who winds up in a nursing home after suffering a stroke. Francesco is a horrible man who rapes his maids and shoots his sick dogs (to save on vet bills), an emblem of Salazar's ruthless police state.

The novel is divided into five "reports," appropriate for a land whose chief of the secret police has "the whole country on file in his metal cabinets, not just the Communists, foreigners, and enemies of the state but us," as Francesco admits, "we ourselves, even Professor Salazar, even the Admiral, even the Cardinal, us, we ourselves, our gallstones, our hay fever, our cavities." (The Admiral, the Cardinal, and others are historical figures and identified in notes at the end of the book.) Each report is interrupted by two or three commentaries by other characters, a cross-section of Portuguese society that adds up to a remarkably complete picture of what life must have been like under the dictatorship.

First we hear from Francesco's son João, a sensitive boy whose growth is stunted by his father's ruthlessness. João matures into an inept adult who is easily swindled out of his father's farm, where much of the novel takes place. João's report is conveyed in a stream-of-consciousness style as his mind flits between the present and the past. (You have to admire a novelist who puts his most difficult chapter first.) Commentaries are supplied by the farm steward's daughter Sofia, who is João's wife, then by her scheming uncle, who set João up to make it look like he robbed his wife's family. Lobo Antunes orchestrates all the voices and time-shifts with dazzling finesse, helpfully using paragraph indentations to separate the changes.

The next report is from Albertina (Titina), Francesco's devoted housekeeper, with commentaries by the cook, the vet and a funny one by the therapist taking care of Titina in the novel's present. Francesco fathers a child by the cook, and the illegitimate girl provides the desolate third report. After the revolution, she is discriminated against for being the minister's daughter; Lobo Antunes isn't afraid to show that the oppressed, once they throw off the shackles of dictatorship, can be just as ruthless as their previous oppressors. Mila, the minister's naive mistress, supplies the fourth report. Struck by her resemblance to his first wife Isabel, who left him, the minister dresses Mila up in old-fashioned clothes and accessories and eventually calls her Isabel, trying to maintain the fiction that his wife never left him. In much the same way, we are made to understand, Salazar and his cronies in the Catholic hierarchy insisted on the fiction that their iron rule was necessary to protect the Portuguese people from communists, reformers, and other radicals. Finally, we get Francesco's report: bitter, senile, deluded, and arrogant to the end. We also finally get Isabel's story of how she got pressured into a loveless marriage and escaped as soon as she could. Francesco insists he has been misunderstood by everyone — by Isabel, by his son, by the populace — but he is cut off in mid-sentence, silenced by the "inquisitors" (never identified) who have compiled this manual.

It's a brilliant performance. Too often, novelistic treatments of life under a dictatorship are unrelentingly bleak, but Lobo Antunes's witnesses are wonderfully diverse in their testimonials: Some are bitter, but others are funny, sarcastic, or simply clueless. Several express their dismay that, for decades, they allowed themselves to be pushed around by "idle and innocuous old [men], passing out titles of honor, municipal posts, administrative posts, and cabinet posts to a band of decrepit geezers." Together they provide a panoramic view of recent Portuguese history that is impressive both as a work of art and as a condemnation of fascism.

Washington Post Book World, 5 January 2003

Malcolm Lowry

Chris Ackerley and Lawrence J. Clipper.
A Companion to "Under the Volcano"
University of British Columbia Press, 1984

Sherrill Grace. *The Voyage That Never Ends: Malcolm Lowry's Fiction*
University of British Columbia Press, 1982

Books like Ackerely and Clipper's — a line-by-line annotation of Lowry's complex novel — are too often labeled "indispensable for the serious student of X's work" but henceforth accorded all the dignity of a dictionary, as if their authors were little more than literary file clerks. Such a judgment is too harsh even for the driest of "companions," and would be totally inappropriate for Ackerley and Clipper's; for not only do they annotate everything in sight with thoroughness and accuracy for the "neophyte," but they go on to offer critical commentary for the "magus" (as they style the two kinds of readers). Thus their work mirrors Lowry's own: "The novel is written this way," they point out. "Lowry was concerned that a very faithful surface realism should conceal greater depths," and consequently both the surface of the text as well as its depths (and what depths!) receive equal treatment. Their book should put to rest any lingering doubts that *Under the Volcano* is just an overwritten novel about drinking, and establish it as one of the richest, most orchestrated novels of our century. Needless to say, it is indispensable for the serious reader of Lowry's work.

But as Sherrill Grace reminds us in *The Voyage That Never Ends, Under the Volcano* is not the only book Lowry wrote. Her title is the same Lowry intended for a seven-novel sequence, and her book examines Lowry's output (published and unpublished) in order to identify the thematic links between the published novels and to speculate on the shape the cycle would have assumed had Lowry lived to complete it. Lowry's other works thus take on greater subtlety and scope when seen as part of this cycle, and even the *Volcano* gains yet another dimension. (It was intended to be a novel written by the cycle's protagonist, Sigbjørn Wilderness, entitled *The Valley of the Shadow of Death* — which aligns it with the postmodern, metafictional novel rather than the older, modernist tradition with which the *Volcano* is usually associated.) With this cycle in view, Lowry's short story collection *Hear Us O Lord* emerges as a capsule version of the larger sequence, recapitulating the theme of withdrawal and return that unifies the cycle. Grace's incisive study confers a coherence on Lowry's work that many have not suspected and should do much to dispel the notion that Lowry is a one-book author.

Review of Contemporary Fiction, Summer 1987

Norman Mailer

The Gospel According to the Son
Random House, 1997

Marilyn Monroe, Muhammad Ali, Gary Gilmore, Lee Harvey Oswald, Pablo Picasso — Norman Mailer is interested in celebrities, or more precisely, in the cultural implications of celebrity and notoriety. In his newest book, he takes on the greatest celebrity of Western civilization, Jesus Christ superstar. Andrew Lloyd Webber and Tim Rice's musical was innovative, entertaining, and theologically provocative. Mailer's book is none of these things; it is a poorly conceived disaster, easily the worst book the man's ever written. I don't like writing negative reviews, nor am I a Mailer-basher — *Why Are We in Vietnam?* and *The Armies of the Night* are two of the best books about the '60s, when Mailer was in his element — but this new one leaves me no choice. It's that bad.

The Gospel According to the Son purports to be Jesus' autobiography. Unsatisfied with the exaggerated accounts given in the gospels and apocrypha, which he has read, Jesus decides to tell his own story. But what follows is basically the synoptic gospels retold in the first person, with a few details borrowed from John. Mailer's version reads like a simplified novelization for grade-school children, or for adults who find the New Testament tough going, even in one of those breezy new translations in a rainbow cover. No attempt was made to flesh out the gospels' bare-boned account with local color or historical background, and the other characters remain as one-dimensional as in the original.

Mailer doesn't seem to realize there's a difference between the Jesus of history, a Jewish soothsayer, and the Jesus of the gospels, a mythological figure. Everyone who has written a serious novel about Jesus has tried to recover or imagine what Jesus' actual life might have been like; Mailer just paraphrases the gospels, uncritically accepting the inventions of the anonymous group of storytellers, witnesses, scribes, local pastors, budding theologians, and translators who are responsible for the textual mess we now have. Consequently, Mailer's Jesus tells of his family's escape to Egypt when he was a child, though the trip is clearly an invention by later writers who wanted to enforce Jesus' messiah status by having him seem to fulfill the Old Testament (at the top of Matthew's agenda especially). Later Jesus retells the story of Salome's striptease for the head of John the Baptist, a story that was denounced 40 years ago by Robert Graves and Joshua Podro (in their fascinating *Nazarene Gospel*

Restored) as historically absurd and at odds with social customs at the time, as unthinkable as Chelsea Clinton performing the Dance of the Seven Veils at one of her father's political functions. It has been estimated that as much as 82 percent of the words ascribed to Jesus in the gospels were not actually spoken by him, but Mailer has him reciting most of them nonetheless. All this makes nonsense of Jesus' claim at the beginning of Mailer's novel that he'll be telling the true story, free of the gospels' additions and exaggerations.

What little Mailer does add to the gospels is of questionable value. He makes Jesus and his family Essenes, a notion discredited by most scholars. He accuses God of being sexist and adds homosexuals to Jesus' earliest followers, both defensible but smacking of political correctness, which I would have thought beneath Mailer. He gives some extra dialogue to Judas, which does no harm, but he spoils Pontius Pilate's famously laconic "What is truth?" by having the Roman governor expand upon his remark. (Later Mailer violates his first-person point of view by recording Pilate's inner conflicts.) Mailer's is an eschatological Jesus, predicting the end of the world within his followers' lifetime, another position discredited by contemporary theologians and one flatly at odds with actual history and even with the conclusion of Mailer's novel.

The only controversial element Mailer introduces is Jesus' doubts about his father's omnipotence, an idea first suggested to him by the Devil during the temptation scene in the wilderness, and which dogs him throughout the novel. On the cross, fearing his father has abandoned him, Jesus gives Pop the benefit of the doubt: "My Father was only doing what He could do. Even as I had done what I could. So He was truly my Father. Like all Fathers He had many sore troubles, and some had little to do with His son. Had His efforts for me been so great that now He was exhausted?" In the final chapter, apparently set in Heaven in our own time, Jesus notes that his overworked father is still a bit distant: "My Father, however, does not often speak to me. Nonetheless, I honor Him. Surely He sends forth as much love as He can offer, but His love is not without limit. . . . Thereby does my Father still find much purpose for me. It is even by way of my blessing that the Lord sends what love He can muster down to that creature who is man and that other creature who is woman, and I try to remain the source of love that is tender." Even as an atheist I'm embarrassed for Jesus to have to mouth such drivel.

As this extract shows, the style is modeled on the King James translation (which Jesus quotes from time to time), another bad choice on Mailer's part. The gospels were written in the vernacular, not in an archaic (albeit sonorous) literary language. If Jesus is telling his own story, why would he imitate a 17th-century preacher? Only pious Christians believe the gospels should be rendered in an antique style, complete with capitals for He and Father.

Mailer's choice is mystifying. (For an English translation that is faithful to the original, pick up one of the two books produced by the Fellows of the Jesus Seminar: *The Complete Gospels* or *The Five Gospels*, both in paperback from HarperCollins.)

The Gospel According to the Son may make a suitable Sunday-school prize, but I can't imagine anyone with more than a high-school education finding this book of interest. For Mailer's detractors, it will be one more nail in the coffin of his declining reputation. His wife, friends, or agent — all thanked in the acknowledgments — should have prevented him from making a fool of himself in public like this.

Washington Post Book World, 27 April 1997

Yann Martel

The Facts Behind the Helsinki Roccamatios
Harcourt, 2004

Before he achieved best-sellerdom with *The Life of Pi*, Yann Martel was the typical struggling writer, sending out dozens of stories to magazines only to receive dozens of rejections in return. But he persisted, found a home for some of them, and in 1993 gathered four of his best stories into a book published in Canada. Slightly revised and prefaced with a self-deprecating author's note, it has now appeared in America just in time for the holiday season. It's the perfect gift for the person who would appreciate the literary equivalent of tickets to the Cirque du Soleil.

Each of these stories is a performance, a high-wire act in which the author sets himself an unusual challenge and dazzles us as he pulls it off. In the title story, the longest and most ambitious of the four, ringmaster Martel tells the story of a young man dying of AIDS. Or rather, he tells us how two young Canadians turned the dying of a young man of AIDS into a story. The 23-year-old narrator is a senior at Ellis University and volunteers to mentor 19-year-old freshman Paul; within three pages we're told Paul will die of AIDS, the result of a botched blood transfusion when he was 16. The narrator decides to stick with Paul to the end, and comes up with an idea to pass the time: remembering how Boccaccio's *Decameron* was based on stories characters told each other while waiting out the Black Death, he convinces Paul to construct a joint novel about a Canadian family whose activities would mirror the events of the 20th century, year by year.

Paul likes the idea, but to make it more exotic, he shifts the locale to Helsinki and invents a Finnish-Italian family named the Roccamatios. Then Martel ups the stakes and tells us not the story he and Paul come up with, but the historical facts upon which the story is based. So: in 1901 Queen Victoria dies, and their novel likewise begins with the death of Sandro Roccamatio, the patriarch of the family. Thereafter, we get only a few details about the Roccamtios saga but a year-by-year recital of historical events, which parallel Paul's illness. On good days, we get good events — in 1921 insulin is discovered — and on bad: "*1936 — The Spanish Civil War begins, exceptional in its bloodletting ferocity.*" Paul dies when their novel reaches 1963: "The year JFK was shot and people cried in the streets. The year I was born."

Though this might sound contrived, too artsy for something as serious as dying from AIDS, Martel is able to maintain the strong "emotional foundation" that he insists (in his Author's Note) must be the basis for any good story. "But a story must also stimulate the mind if it does not want to fade from memory," he adds, and the intellectual balancing act he performs, juggling historical facts with clinical details of Paul's illness, elevates his story above the bulk of treatments of this sad subject.

The other three stories also deal with death but are likewise occasions to allow Martel to show off his literary skills. Two years after the first story, the same narrator (apparently) is in Washington, DC, visiting a high-school friend, and relates "The Time I Heard the Private Donald J. Rankin String Concerto with One Discordant Violin, by the American Composer John Morton."[8] His friend, now a well-paid but overworked consultant with an accounting firm, is too busy for him, so the narrator one night hears a concert put on by some Vietnam War vets; the composer of the story's title is a janitor who wrote a concerto for a fellow soldier — a stunning piece but poorly played — and as the narrator speaks with him after the concert, the career-track that he and his friend are on dwindles into insignificance. "Manners of Dying" consists of nine versions of a letter a prison warden writes to a woman to inform her of how her son Kevin "faced up to his execution by hanging for the crimes for which he was convicted." Each letter follows the same pattern — his last meal, his interaction with a priest, his final words — but differs in details. Which one is real? Which does he actually mail? We're not told. The last one is numbered 1096; there are at least that many different ways to face a hanging, and an inventive writer can come up with at least that many variations.

The final story, "The Vita Æterna Mirror Company: Mirrors to Last till Kingdom Come," is the trickiest, both in form and subject matter. A pretentious young man is visiting his grandmother; the text is divided into two columns with different typefaces, the grandmother on the left telling long stories about her youth and her dead husband (often reduced to "*blah-blah-blah-blah-*") and the grandson on the right making snide remarks ("Man, she can go on"). While there, he comes across an antique mirror-making machine that is activated by spoken memories; when the mirror comes out of the machine it is covered with the text of the spoken words, which soon fades away, leaving only a reflecting surface. It's a magic-realist story, recalling those superstitions about mirrors possessing the souls of those who gazed into them, but also the practice of artists who use mirrors to create self-portraits.

8 Not to be confused with real-life American composer John Morton, who has done some fascinating things: check out his 2001 CD *Outlier: New Music for Music Boxes*. [2016 note]

It's an eerie note to end the book on, leaving the reader a little disoriented but enchanted. The young man who wrote these stories clearly had a mirror-bright future in fiction ahead of him.

Washington Post Book World, 12 December 2004

Carole Maso

Defiance
Dutton, 1998

Any suspicions that Carole Maso would feel pressured to write a more conventional novel after moving to a mainstream press are put to rest within the first few pages of her fierce new novel, which is as uncompromising and experimental as anything she's written.

Defiance takes the form of a journal kept by a former Harvard physics professor named Bernadette O'Brien, awaiting execution in a Georgia prison for the murder of two of her students. In her "death book," as she calls it, Bernadette broods on the events that led to her incarceration: the ridicule she endured as a child prodigy, the humiliating sexual acts she watched her mother perform, her father's infidelities, her beloved brother's death in Vietnam, the class differences she felt upon arrival at Harvard, and an overwhelming feeling of helplessness. Only when she becomes a professor does she feel she has some control, and decides to exercise that control in a fatal way to make up for years of humiliating hopelessness.

But Bernadette (and Maso) is quick to distance herself from the current obsession with victimhood: she is contemptuous of the recovery movement and mocks a well-meaning prison counselor's attempts to get her in touch with her inner child. Defiant, unrepentant, Bernadette rages against the injustice of it all without hiding behind a faddish excuse.

As Humbert Humbert said on the first page of his prison book, "You can always count on a murderer for a fancy prose style." Bernadette's language is impassioned, sardonic, Shakespearean (she quotes often from the tragedies, especially *Macbeth*), and very angry. It's a deadly serious book, almost humorless — except for one laugh-out-loud point where Bernadette forces her student out "into the *dating world*," italicized as though it were some Lovecraftian horror. Bernadette is one of Maso's most fascinating creations, a prodigy in both senses of the word — a budding genius but also a monster. *Defiance* is a stunning addition to the oeuvre of one of the most important writers of our time.

Rain Taxi, Summer 1998

□ □ □ □ □ □ □

Mother and Child
Counterpoint, 2012

Opening this novel is like stepping into a Chagall painting: folksy Old World surrealism envelopes you like a warm blanket while a circus calliope plays a minor-key tune off in the distance. It shimmers between realism (school photos and parent–teacher conferences, obstetrics) and the world of fairy tales; it remythifizes the modern world by way of ancient Egyptian, Greek, and biblical stories, starlore, metamorphoses, telluromysticism — re-enchanting the world after 9/11 and the techno-death of the Bush era.

It would have been easy for Maso to lapse into preciosity and sentimentalism regarding the mother–child bond, but this isn't a Mother's Day gift (though it should be): there's a tough-mindedness here, a serious concern over the sick earth and the need to heal it, and its inhabitants. The prose is wonderfully unpredictable. You literally can't imagine what will come next. There is charming whimsy, a few LOL lines, and gorgeous prose throughout. A stunning achievement.

Amazon.com, 31 July 2012

Harry Mathews, Georges Perec, and Oulipo

The Way Home: Collected Longer Prose
Atlas Press, 1989

This valuable collection brings together a half dozen inimitable pieces by Mathews hitherto scattered in various small press books, literary journals, and a reference book: "Country Cooking," an outrageously complicated recipe that even includes a fairytale digression; "The Way Home," concerning the imaginative broodings of one Walt Maltmall (but lacking the drawings by Trevor Winkfield that inspired the piece); "Their Words, For You," a Oulipian exercise in writing a story using only the vocabulary of 44 proverbs; "Singular Pleasures," a worldwide survey of great moments in masturbation, as funny as it is unsettling; "The Orchard," a touching memoir of Georges Perec; and the longest piece, written for Gale Research Company's autobiography series. This candid and often moving essay concludes an invaluable book (with a terrific cover, by the way), well worth writing away to England for.

Review of Contemporary Fiction, Spring 1990

□ □ □ □ □ □ □

Immeasurable Distances: The Collected Essays
Lapis Press, 1991

Over the last twenty years, Mathews's work on his inimitable fiction has been occasionally interrupted by requests from editors for essays. Even though he doesn't consider himself a trained critic, he responded to those requests with essays of great insight and intelligence, all of which are gathered in this sumptuous production. (The high price [$35.00] is justified by the format: it is large [7 x 10], illustrated in color and duotone [a foldout perforated photomontage of Mathews that can be used as a jigsaw puzzle], printed in a large point size on heavy cream paper.)

Of the 14 essays here, two concern Mathews's writing methods, six are on the Oulipo and its members (especially Georges Perec), five are on specific books and writers (Lewis Carroll, Raymond Roussel [cowritten with Perec and painstakingly researched], Laura Riding, Kenneth Koch's *Duplications*, and Joseph McElroy's *Women and Men*), and one is on the relation between libretti and music (his college major). Throughout, Mathews demonstrates a novelist's flair for apt metaphors ("Of course it is always reassuring when we extract from a book great bones of conclusion that we can then bury deep in our private gardens, but that is not the way of the best works of modern literature") as well as a novelist's conviction that the reader is a participant in fiction, not a passive receptor. Having written novels that expect much from his readers, Mathews here shows how he participates in the work of others. The results are brilliant, and it is to be hoped that *Immeasurable Distances* will be read not just by Mathews fans but by everyone with an interest in how fiction works.

Review of Contemporary Fiction, Spring 1992

□ □ □ □ □ □ □

The Journalist

Godine, 1994

Mathews's first three novels were elaborate, comically erudite inventions that firmly established his place both in the American avant-garde and in the French Oulipo group, that workshop for experimental fiction founded by Raymond Queneau and including such writers as Italo Calvino and Georges Perec. With his fourth novel, *Cigarettes* (1987), Mathews cunningly used Oulipian combinatorial devices to structure what appeared to be a somewhat traditional novel of manners set in the early 1960s. His brilliant new novel combines the experimental approach of the early novels with the concern with social mores of the later novel; the result, as the jacket succinctly notes, is "a blend of postmodern metafiction and old-style bedroom farce."

A middle-aged man in an unspecified European setting decides for reasons of mental health to keep a journal. As he writes, he becomes increasingly aware of the multiplicity of experience and the subjectivity of perception: does a dream have the same cognitive value as an account of what his office partners wore? is something overheard on the tram similar to something read in a book? As the journalist struggles with such questions, he devises an increasingly elaborate classification system for his diary and, in an effort to make his diary as complete as possible, begins to devote so much time to it that his life exists merely as material for his diary.

While the journalist ostensibly uses his diary to make sense of the suspicious behavior of his family and friends, he stumbles upon basic questions of epistemology and the nature of artistic creation. At one point he realizes his diary "may now concern only myself, but ultimately it extends far beyond myself because it is the condition of the noblest of all acts, that of rescuing the precarious imprints of reality; and reality is the world's, not mine." The journalist's ambition begins to resemble Proust's great project of preserving "the precious imprints of reality," and in language that is almost as elegant and beguiling. (There's a quirkiness to the sentences, however, that suggests they've been processed through some Oulipian filter.)

The bedroom farce aspect of the novel is amusing, but what gives *The Journalist* its lasting significance is its meditation on the creative act, which is less a record of experience than an experience in itself, sometimes supplanting all others. This concept is not new, but *The Journalist* is a novel demonstration of the concept, and deserves the widest readership.

Review of Contemporary Fiction, Fall 1994. I ran into Mathews in New York City the following spring, and he told me I misunderstood an aspect of the novel, but I can't remember which.

□ □ □ □ □ □ □

Georges Perec with Robert Bober. *Ellis Island.*
Translated by Harry Mathews and Jessica Blatt
The New Press, 1995

Oulipo Laboratory: Texts from the "Bibliothèque Oulipiènne."
Translated by Harry Mathews and Iain White
Atlas Press, 1995

Fifteen years after his death, Georges Perec continues to delight us with new facets of his genius. Perec and filmmaker Robert Bober visited Ellis Island in 1979 to make a documentary, found it in ruins, and set out to recover its meaning in prose and images. The book combines archival photos with ones taken during the making of the documentary, and alternates between Perec's own meditation on the theme of "dispersion, wandering, diaspora" (a theme explored in his novels, especially *W*) and interviews with immigrants who arrived at the island. The book is beautifully produced, and Perec's text is beautifully translated by his friend, novelist Harry Mathews. (Jesssica Blatt handled the interviews.) It's a moving book that should appeal to cultural historians as well as Perec fans, and appears at a pertinent time when immigration policies are under attack.

Perec is most closely associated with the Oulipo group, to which Harry Mathews also belongs. A valuable anthology of their writings has just been published under the title *Oulipo Laboratory*. Although Perec is not represented here, there are several key texts from fellow members Raymond Queneau,

Italo Calvino, Paul Fournel, Claude Berge, Jacques Jouet, and Mathews; in addition, the book is prefaced by two manifestos by Oulipo founder François Le Lionnais and by an informative introduction by Atlas publisher Alastair Brotchie. This is an essential book for both newcomers and longtime students of this ingenious school of writers.

Review of Contemporary Fiction, Spring 1996

James McCourt

Time Remaining
Knopf, 1993

Unless you've been in the game awhile, you probably don't recognize the name. James McCourt only manages one book of fiction every nine years — Alexander Pope's recommended gestation period — but oh what books they are! *Mawrdew Czgowchwz* (1975) is the best novel about the opera milieu I've ever read, a camp classic in the tradition of Ronald Firbank. *Kaye Wayfaring in "Avenged"* (1984) treats the related world of motion pictures, a more "restful" novel (as Firbank would say) than its exuberant predecessor, but just as admirable. Now comes *Time Remaining*, a brassy, innovative novel that represents a startling development not only in McCourt's style but in gay fiction as a genre. It "outs" queer fiction from the closet of the conventional novel and gives it a new form all its own.

McCourt's first two books are beautifully written, almost stately in their grammar and sentence structure. But *Time Remaining* is a spoken text, loose, improvisatory. Here's the setup: The first 40 pages of the book, entitled "I Go Back to the Mais Oui," is a performance piece given in New York by Daniel Delancey, looking back at four decades of life in gay Gotham, with special attention to a bevy of transvestites who called themselves the "Eleven against Heaven," all but one now dead from AIDS. The survivor, who calls himself Odette O'Doyle, attends the performance and then takes a train with Delancey out to Sagaponack in the Hamptons. Odette has just returned from Europe, where she was scattering the ashes of the other "girls" in their favorite places. The bulk of the book consists of Odette's monologue on her European tour, intercut with numerous flashbacks and digressions, with only an occasional comment by Delancey (or station stops called out by the conductor) to interrupt her. (Odette is always called "her," and often refers to herself as "your mother.")

Odette's is a dazzling, sometimes bewildering performance, and to keep up with her it helps if you're multilingual and up on ballet, opera, 1940s movies, Harold Bloom's *Book of J*, gay activism, James Schuyler and Jackson Pollock (presiding spirits over the novel), literary theory, and all the arcana of New York gay life — the baths, the slang, the clubs. At times it's more than this straight Midwesterner could keep up with, but I doubt any reader is expected to follow every thread in Odette's tapestry of tales. Odette joins Dr. Matthew O'Connor (of Djuna Barnes's *Nightwood*) and Sutherland (of Andrew Holleran's *Dancer from the Dance*) as one of the great gay monologuists in fiction. Pushing 70, Odette is — like a specialist in Cornish — one of the last to speak a disappearing language, that of erudite drag queens able to discuss Henry James as easily as makeup. ("Hattie Jaques's" *The Ambassadors* is dissed mercilessly at one point.)

But it's the form that's intriguing (as Mae West would say, another presiding spirit). In recent years literary theorists have spoken of an *écriture feminine*, feminine writing that differs from masculine not only in subject matter but in form and structure: a different sense of rhythm, less linear, more open-ended, and so on. Most gay fiction has been written in fairly conventional form, but McCourt here seems to be feeling his way toward a poetics for fiction that resembles the way drag queens talk: stories within stories, numerous asides and cutting characterizations, flippant allusions and in-jokes, moodswings between self-deprecation and self-glorification (often depending on the types of drugs and liquor consumed), with flashes of rage at prejudice and, in recent years, the ravages of AIDS. McCourt *knows* his critical theory — this is a very self-conscious text, as self-conscious as a drag queen in public — and there are numerous references to new modes of writing in his book. He talks of adapting Pollock's "expressionist drip" for narrative purposes, and at another point challenges George Orwell's notion that writing should be like a clear window on one's subject; like John Barth, McCourt prefers writing that is like a stained-glass window, where the writing itself is the subject. Odette prefers Proust over James (and in fact took her name from Swann's cocotte), and McCourt gives Proust's great work on time, memory and art a postmodern makeover.

This isn't the time or place (nor am I the one) to work out all the implications of McCourt's radical, outrageous new work, but *Time Remaining* is worth as much time as you can give it.

Washington Post Book World, 20 June 1993

□ □ □ □ □ □ □

Now Voyagers: The Night Sea Journey.
Some Divisions of the Saga of Mawrdew Czgowchwz, Oltrano.
Authenticated by Persons Represented Therein. Book One
Turtle Point Press, 2007

In 1975, James McCourt published the most delightful novel about the opera milieu ever written, *Mawrdew Czgowchwz* (pronounced "Mardu Gorgeous"), detailing the triumphant 1956 season of a Czech-Irish singer. It is also the brainiest, a tour de force of opera lore and Celtic mythology, and written in an erudite style that approaches Joycean heights. (It was reissued a few years ago by the New York Review of Books and is ardently recommended.) Since then McCourt has written other novels and stories about la Czgowchwz and her friends, but in his brilliant new novel he returns to pick up where the first one left off. *Mawrdew Czgowchwz* ended with the singer and her lover embarking for Ireland to make a movie; *Now Voyagers* records their sea journey and their first days in the old country.

You don't go to an opera for the story, but for the performance of the story; *Now Voyagers* is essentially a showcase for McCourt's vast knowledge of opera, movies, and literature, specifically the cultural currency exchanged by sophisticates in post-World War II New York. The novel's rather demanding overture, surely designed to scare off the unworthy, begins on the night of June 16, 2004 — and honey if you don't know the literary significance of June 16, this novel isn't for you. The elderly singer and her poet-friend Jameson O'Maurigan have unearthed materials about that triumphant 1956 season, including a metafictional version of *Mawrdew Czgowchwz*, and decide to rewrite that *opera buffa* as a Wagnerian epic with libretto by Oscar Wilde. (*Now Voyagers* is the first book of a planned tetralogy.)

The result is dazzling, if at times disorienting. In opera terms, *Now Voyager* is more *Einstein on the Beach* than *Abduction from the Seraglio*, and like Glass's opera it doesn't have a conventional plot. In a nonlinear series of arias and ensemble pieces, McCourt's witty cast dissects performances, dishes gossip, divulges details of their past — often outrageous tales of alienation, abuse, and "I Will Survive" determination — and serves up cocktails of allusions mixing high and low culture, as in this riff on lyricist Tom Lehrer:

> "Lehrer? Yes, a terribly bright boy — so much happier in show business than he was in academic life, I believe, and an absolute knockout at *Le Bon Soir*."
>
> "A wizard mathematician, isn't he?"
>
> "Yes, dear, but he realized how utterly constraining mathematics can be."
>
> "You mean his Gödel was killing him?"
>
> "Ha-*ha*. He came to understand that any discipline that attempts to tell the truth by relying on the proposition *if . . . then* inevitably leads to unavailing grief."
>
> "But surely his songs do that — all songs do that."
>
> "That may be true, dear, but as you may have noticed if you can *sing* a thing, almost nobody minds in the least *what* it's saying or doing."

So what is McCourt's epic song saying or doing? For one thing, *Now Voyager* erases the distinction between high and low culture — a well-educated person should know the work of *both* Lehrer and mathematician Kurt Gödel — and McCourt's erudite novel provides a liberal education in everything from eastern religion to Mae West. (I agree with him that the latter is a saner guide to life than the former.) For another, it preserves a time and place of remarkable sophistication, the fin-de-demi-siècle of Manhattan in the '50s. Those with a fondness for old New York, classic movies like *Now, Voyager*, Saturday afternoon radio broadcasts from the Met, and hot gossip about the stars of stage and screen will find much pleasure here.

But this isn't a novel for your bachelor uncle; it's closer to Joyce's *Ulysses* than to Kirk Douglas's. Beneath the gossip and one-liners a Jungian psychodrama unfolds as Mawrdew Czgowchwz reflects on her troubled childhood and now her new lover and midlife career change. The "night sea journey" of the subtitle is a reference to Joseph Campbell's *Hero with a Thousand Faces* (not to be confused with *7 Faces of Dr. Lao*, as a McCourt character might add) and the necessary confrontation with the dark elements of the psyche before one can attain wholeness and continue on life's journey. It is the same psychodrama that Ishmael undergoes in *Moby-Dick*, mentioned often in *Now Voyagers* and an obvious influence. Mawrdew is the heroine of a thousand faces (via opera roles and mythic archetypes), revisiting this crucial period of her life 47 years later on the long night of June 16–17. We're told she later became a psychoanalyst, appropriately enough.

Opera is not for everyone, and postmodern opera for fewer still. *Now Voyagers* is the most ostentatiously literary novel of the year, the one most likely to become the subject of dissertations and scholarly papers. It is steeped in literary theory, encyclopedic in its range of references, speaks half a dozen languages, and is unapologetically elitist. McCourt makes it clear in the opening pages, where Czgowchwz and the O'Maurigan discuss their postmodern makeover of the earlier novel, that their ambitious project entails "representing in language of a certain prolixity and complexity some approximation — quite impossible to realize by means of the routine deployment of ostensibly simpler and more direct syntactical constructions — of the tessellated and polyphonic texture of even the least educated, inquisitive, and sophisticated human natures' interior colloquies, almost never attempted in present times by either the writing of history or the fictionalization of it."

But the serious intellection of the novel is leavened by so much wit and campy fun that it goes down easy. This may be the most literary novel of the year, but also the silliest; like Gaddis and Pynchon (whose fans are the ideal audience for this novel), McCourt knows comedy and tragedy are not antithetical, and that one can write a novel appealing to both the brain and the funny-bone. No new novel of 2007 gave me greater pleasure than *Now Voyager*, and I eagerly await book 2 of the Saga of Mawrdew Czgowchwz.

Los Angeles Times Book Review, 4 November 2007

Joseph McElroy

Women and Men
Knopf, 1987

Joseph McElroy published five remarkable novels between 1966 and 1977, then disappeared from the book-publishing scene as those books drifted out of print. In the early '80s there were rumors that he was in Paris writing the longest novel in American literature, that his publisher was hounding him for reduction and simplification, even that McElroy had been driven crazy by the task — a suspicion confirmed for some with the appearance in *Conjunctions* a year or two ago of a particularly demanding extract. Completed by the end of 1985, the novel was in final revision and production for two more years (but lost only two sections) before appearing last spring, so huge that the bound galleys were sent to reviewers in two 600-page volumes.

Women and Men received several flattering reviews, and many probably placed it on their summer reading lists — but few, I suspect, actually finished it. Fifteen years ago, intellectual machismo was measured by the number of pages of *Gravity's Rainbow* one had managed; in this year of big books, McElroy's has provided the measure, even upping the stakes by writing a book longer and more difficult than Pynchon's. Are the novel's length and difficulty justified? I had my doubts at first, but after reading, nay living with this book for two months, I became ashamed at my presumption. Hitting the 600-page mark, the 800-, the 1000-page mark with still 200 pages to go and McElroy's unflagging invention still going strong, I was filled with awe and wonder as the immense epic design of the novel continued to mushroom ever higher. *Non sum dignus*, I cried; reading this book is a humbling experience.

The novel begins, "After all she was not so sure what had happened, or when it started," and after completing the novel, the reader may too be unsure what has actually happened. Although the novel opens with a birth and closes with a death, it does not unfold in chronological order, nor is there much straightforward exposition. Instead, the book is a meditation on events located around a half-dozen temporal points (1893–94, 1945, 1960–62, 1973, 1976–77), weaving in and out of time, back and forth in space from a small town in New Jersey, to New Mexico (past and present), to a hypothetical moon colony in the future, but always back to Manhattan. (Among other things, this is a great novel about New York.) Much of the novel concerns a middle-aged journalist named James Mayn, the son of a woman who apparently committed suicide at the end of World War II, and grandson of a remarkable woman whose travels out West in 1893–94 as a young woman assume the contours of myth as she retells them to her grandson. In the novel's present (1976–77), Mayn has returned to his New York apartment formerly inhabited by his wife and family. Living in the same building is Grace Kimball, a feminist workshop leader whose holistic exploits alternate and occasionally overlap with Mayn's comings and goings. Although they know of each other, the two never actually meet, but they have in common friends and acquaintances whose increasingly complicated interactions give the novel its rich social texture. Also in New York are a number of Chilean expatriates, caught up in an interhemispheric intrigue that leads to political assassination and the production of an opera based on *Hamlet* written by a Chilean woman composer of the 19th century, the first performance of which draws together nearly all of the novel's characters near the end and provides Mayn with the catharsis that frees him to dream (for the first time, he believes) and reconcile himself to his rich family heritage.

The scope of the novel is global: from the Earth and its geology to the clouds and atmospherics above it, from the act of breathing as a microcosmic counterpart to the meteorological configurations of the Earth's own breathing, from a tapeworm burrowing inside a woman's body to a satellite orbiting above the Earth's body. A thousand links, metaphoric and literal, are drawn between the planet, its population, and the endangered ecosystem that binds them together. The demographic scope is not so wide: with the exception of a retarded black messenger boy who figures in the "known bits" sections, all of the main characters are well-educated WASPs apparently unencumbered by 9-to-5 jobs. Daily domestic interaction is minimal, except in Mayn's daughter Flick's fictional account of her parents' marriage, a tender and touching chapter entitled "IN FUTURE." Native Americans are present in some sections, but more as actors in mythic romances than as fully developed characters.

McElroy's two principals differ in their views of history: Mayn doesn't feel history makes much sense and sees it instead as a collection of separate facts and particles, whereas Kimball sees history all too clearly as a pattern of male domination and female oppression. McElroy brilliantly fuses the two outlooks by breaking his own history up into thousands of separate events and scattering them throughout the novel, counting on the alert reader (and this book demands every ounce of your concentration) to see that everything is indeed connected. It doesn't make "sense" as simply as Grace Kimball would have it — and McElroy's knotty political intrigue is too complex to unravel after one reading — but the inescapable relatedness of things — human, animal, vegetable, political, economic, atmospheric — is not lost even on the reader who has grasped only a few of those relations. The rest can be taken on faith.

The reason not all of those relations can be grasped is that so many of the events are narrated in an oblique, indirect manner. The only straightforward narrative occurs, oddly enough, in the account of the dream Mayn has near the end: a spellbinding little piece of sci-fi concerning a bomb that destroys buildings but leaves people unharmed, even enlightened. Elsewhere, it is often difficult to tell exactly what is going on, to whom, and why. Mayn's high-school journalism teacher drummed the four Ws into his head, but many readers will be hard-pressed to answer the who, what, where, and why of much of the novel. A book this long and this involved risks information overload as a matter of course, and yet the motive seems to spring not at all from a desire to numb and bewilder the reader but from McElroy's generous desire to tell us everything, to share all he knows about these characters. Like his own Hermit-Inventor, McElroy gives the reader "such a condensed mountain of information . . . that one might spend a life digesting it all." *Women and Men* is a prime example of what Tom LeClair has been calling the art of excess, a plenitude of art so vast that the reader can lose him-/herself in the book as one does in the huge novels of Dickens, Tolstoy, or Proust. The book as world, not as an evening's entertainment, is what McElroy offers, and one can't help being engulfed by the novel, even if it means coming close to drowning in the details, smothering in the novel's multiple folds.

Nowhere does the reader struggle for breath more desperately than in the vast sections ironically called "Breathers," which make up a third of the novel's bulk. Here, the fictional events are brooded over by a group of angels — yes, angels — who seem to be spirits of potential anxious to incarnate themselves in human bodies. A kind of space-age Greek chorus, these angels are presided over by a comically pedantic interrogator who is as much concerned with the vagaries of idiomatic language as with exploring the Mayn family history. Questioning Mayn during meditative moments, the interrogator at times speaks for the exasperated reader; one digression is interrupted with, "But *who* is remembering all this? stabs the interrogator, himself again; or, better said, what use are the family facts to the abiding subject of the grown journalist James Mayn's activities?" Many of the memories conveyed through the Breathers originate in times of lowered consciousness — half-asleep pillow talk, daydreams, late-night bar conversation, bedtime Navajo tales — and unfurl in long, paratactic sentences that sometimes recall Faulkner, sometimes the Eumaeus chapter of *Ulysses*, sometimes the heckling narrator of the interchapters of McElroy's own *A Smuggler's Bible*. As Harold Bloom has recently written of Pynchon, McElroy "always seems not so much to be telling his bewildering, labyrinthine story as writing a wistful commentary upon it as a story already twice-told, though it hasn't been."

For the embattled reader, the real breathers come in the form of a dozen or so short vignettes scattered throughout the novel (indicated by their lowercase titles), each an exquisite crisis of sharing between couples. Resembling *New Yorker* stories somewhat (and in fact two of these "poems" — as McElroy calls them — did appear there before book publication), these stories have only a tangential relation to the main (Mayn) plot, but do extend the novel's concern for the relations between the sexes.

Like all truly innovative novels, *Women and Men* is baffling much of the time, but I couldn't help feeling while reading the first Breather section that this is what fiction in the 21st century might look like. Burroughs used to complain that fiction was 50 years behind the other arts, but one closes this extraordinary novel with the conviction that McElroy is 50 years ahead of anyone else now writing. At a time when most fiction still resembles its 19th-century parents, it is breathtaking to behold fiction of the future, a future that will be guaranteed if McElroy's warm and intelligent regard for the planet and its women and men is emulated by us all.

Review of Contemporary Fiction, Fall 1987

□ □ □ □ □ □ □

Actress in the House

Overlook, 2003

Click on Joseph McElroy's name at Amazon.com, and you'll be told that customers who shop for him also shop for the best and brightest of post-World War II American novelists: Pynchon, Gaddis, Coover, Gass, and (the writer McElroy most resembles) DeLillo. He has never attracted quite the following they have, even though his oeuvre is as impressive as theirs. Debuting in 1966 with *A Smuggler's Bible*, which was reminiscent of the astonishing first novels of Gaddis and Pynchon (and is to be reissued this summer by Overlook), McElroy produced one brilliant, cerebral novel after another — *Hind's Kidnap, Ancient History, Lookout Cartridge, Plus* — culminating in his magnum opus of 1987, the 1200-page *Women and Men*. A winsome novella, *The Letter Left to Me*, followed in 1988, but nothing since. Thus it is especially welcome to have a new novel by this postmodernist master, and one that both builds on his previous accomplishments and explores new directions.

Actress in the House begins with a slap: An actress performing in an off-Broadway play is struck harder than expected by the actor playing opposite her, and her shock is shared by a man sitting in the theater, Bill Daley, a lawyer twice her age. Like the flap of a butterfly's wing in Brazil that, according to chaos theory (which McElroy was hip to long before other novelists), can cause a tornado in Texas, this slap generates the long novel that follows, as Daley becomes involved with the actress, a bright young woman named Becca Lang. Concerned for her after that slap, he takes her home after the show, and the rest of the novel tracks the week in November 1996 that follows. They begin exchanging stories, anecdotes, opinions. Becca is developing an autobiographical one-woman show and performs it for Daley in his house the night he takes her home; the more reserved Daley mostly asks questions, providing personal background only as needed, but he is inspired by his provocative visitor to dredge up details of his earlier life.

Like most of McElroy's novels, *Actress in the House* explores the hidden, unexpected connections between things. It turns out that Becca had called Daley the day before the show to ask him to take on her eviction case; it later turns out that her older brother knew of Daley back in the early '70s and even told his kid sister about a helicopter exploit Daley had been involved in. Slowly — and this novel moves very slowly — a wealth of detail accumulates around this odd couple and the people they know.

What makes the novel challenging is the odd style McElroy has adopted for Daley's musings. After a talk with a friend named Lotta, Daley realizes: "He hardly knew what he'd told her all jumbled together." The reader is likewise often left in the dark as to what exactly is being said and why. Part of this is strict mimesis: Two people getting to know each other will exchange information that is jumbled, out of sequence, lacking in context, and filled with the names of friends and relations yet to be introduced. Daley says admiringly of Becca, "One thing: she paid attention, picked things up in no order, gave them back her way." And that's the way the reader gets things. The sentences are often choppy, sometimes incomplete, as in this typical paragraph:

> It was other people's lives she talked about on the phone. Lotta's clients shading into friends. Not only clients with second houses, who bought [jewelry] from her. A mixed couple sanding a table outside, fitting legs to it, having a fight while carrying on independent conversations with Lotta, the guest standing around under a tree, a failing Berkshire elm, with her coffee mug. Daley tried to put his finger on it.

The reader likewise tries to put a finger on the significance of what's being conveyed, and whether the detail of a Berkshire elm is worth remembering. It might be important 200 pages later, or it might not. McElroy could easily have presented all this material in a more chronological, coherent manner, but the result would have been yet another standard midlist novel with a limited shelf-life. He is more ambitious, and in one of Daley's many discussions of jazz we might discern McElroy's narrative strategy. Listening to a Dutch saxophone player and a Turkish trombonist jam at a jazz club, Daley thinks,

> For fifteen minutes the Dutchman and the Turk went their ways — how did they do it? — so separately jettisoning a succession of milling-around boplike flights and halfway volcanic omnidirectional grinding that in self-defense against this no-man's-land of tonal centers (what the Free guys called them) you could feel oddly closer to the person you were with, barraged, instructed, not hardly borne along because what kind of vehicle was this? Instead intellected out, elasticked in a greater field than Daley could help being drawn toward yet unhappy and ignorant of the jazz sounds, the hopeful eyes, the plainer chords Daley didn't want to miss out on; or you could feel it was marvelously relative and/or pointless and deep going nowhere and wonder what you were doing here, singly or coupled, or curiously combat-ready.

Much of *Actress in the House* feels that way: milling-around boplike flights — though McElroy always remains closer to Henry James than Harry James — and "intellected out, elasticked in a greater field" than the traditional novel encompasses. It's the kind of novel where you don't learn the name of Becca's play until page 385, and where the climax of the novel involves a discussion of abalone protein, but one finishes it feeling as the protagonist does after his week with an actress in the house: "A doubling of Daley's horizons, faintly befuddling, emerged as a reason for whatever had happened."

Washington Post Book World, 13 April 2003

Jim Morrison

An American Prayer. Music by the Doors
Elektra Records, 1978

If Arthur Rimbaud wrote in the 1970s instead of the 1870s, my guess is that he would be singing his poems in front of a punk rock band. The fact that Rimbaud is appreciated by Bob Dylan and Patti Smith as well as by students of French symbolist poetry seems to bear this out. Though the majority of young modern poets still relies on small presses and poetry journals to publish their verse, it seems that a small number of equally talented poets have found it more rewarding (financially if not always artistically) to "publish" their verse as lyrics to rock and folk music. (This was more true of the late '60s and early '70s than it is now, when the artistic respectability achieved by rock music in the '60s has been whored away by mindless disco, bland top-40, and self-indulgent punk.)

The lyrics of Dylan, Donovan, Lennon–McCartney, Robin Williamson (Incredible String Band), Jim Morrison, Pete Sinfield (King Crimson, Premiata Forneria Marconi, Emerson, Lake & Palmer), and Patti Smith have been published in book form by now, but it is significant that their work was originally intended for the stage rather than the page. (And it would also be nice to have in printed form the work of lesser known but equally interesting lyricists such as Syd Barrett, Procol Harum's Keith Reid, Roy Harper, Nico, and Don Van Vliet, aka Captain Beefheart.) Although only time will tell how much of this work will remain a permanent contribution to the art of poetry — little of it, I would imagine — the best of it has been a genuine artistic response to the times and, if nothing else, opened the doors for some of us impressionable youths to the more varied and challenging world of literature.

One of the most impressive of the rock poets was Jim Morrison, whose posthumous poems have just been released on an album entitled *An American Prayer*. A poetry booklet accompanies the album and establishes once and for all that Morrison was not just a rock singer who wrote lyrics, but a poet who chose rock music as the best medium for his art. Almost all the poems on this album are recited, not sung, while the original Doors provide simple but effective musical backdrops. Most of the earlier Doors albums featured at least one song presented in this manner — e.g., "Horse Latitudes" and the epic "Celebration of the Lizard" but an entire album of poems and stories perhaps provides the best context for an evaluation of his achievement.

What kind of poetry is it? A poetry of myth and magic, words as sorcery, media as message, of ritual and taboo. Morrison's poetic world is that of the Freudian unconscious, fraught with sexual menace, man as half beast half god, where sex, death, and violence join bloody hands in phallic dances. His artistic vision follows in the French tradition of de Sade, Lautréamont, Baudelaire, Verlaine, Genet, and the above-mentioned Rimbaud in raising the dark underside of humanity to the level of grandeur.

More than anyone else, Morrison brought a sense of theater (not to be confused with theatrics) to rock music. His performances with the Doors — two of which I attended, in 1967 and 1970 — were more akin to ceremonies, ritual celebrations, psychodramas even, than to the simple party atmosphere of most concerts. Consequently, simply reading his poetry — as in his only published book, *The Lords and The New Creatures* (1970) — doesn't provide the same kind of experience as hearing it. His spoken words have an immediacy lost in the silence of the printed page or even when sung in his rich baritone. The combination, then, of spoken word and music is perfect; perhaps because much of his poetry is lacking in content (what is the magnificent "Soft Parade" actually about?) — relying instead on the juxtaposition of incongruent but thrilling images — music makes up for the lack, providing both content and context for the poetry.

Those unfamiliar with the Doors' music and history may find the new album strange and inaccessible, but those of us who consider them one of the better groups of the time and who were heartbroken at his premature demise will find the album heaven-sent, a voice from the grave, as it were. Just knowing that Morrison died shortly after recording these poems lends an eerie aura to some of them. Indeed, these beautiful last lines from the title track sound almost as if Morrison had purposely composed his own epitaph:

Do you know how pale & wanton thrillful
    comes death on a strange hour
    unannounced, unplanned for
like a scaring over-friendly guest you've
    brought to bed
Death makes angels of us all
    & gives us wings
where we had shoulders
    smooth as raven's
        claws

No more money, no more fancy dress
This other Kingdom seems by far the best
until its other jaw reveals incest
& loose obedience to a vegetable law

I will not go
Prefer a Feast of Friends
To the Giant Family

His friends now have cause for new feasts. We miss you, Jim. Requiescat in pace.

Spree, January 1979

Bradford Morrow

Come Sunday
Weidenfeld & Nicolson, 1988

Most first novelists play it safe, but the best novelists take chances with their first: witness *The Recognitions*, *V.*, *A Smuggler's Bible*, or more recent novels like David Foster Wallace's *The Broom of the System* and William T. Vollmann's *You Bright and Risen Angels*. In his first novel, Bradford Morrow likewise dares all in a novel that ranges across five centuries and three continents, speaks a half-dozen languages, draws upon numerous fields of knowledge, and manages to tell dozens of tall tales to boot.

Jack Kerouac used to ask young writers who their models were. Morrow has apparently worked from the best models, many of whom contribute regularly to his wonderful magazine *Conjunctions*. The achronological structure and chapter titles reminded me of Pynchon's *V.*, while the ironic use of erudition and history evoked both Pynchon and Gaddis. Morrow's fine ear for dialogue recalls Gaddis's, while the general temporal mood of the novel — a kind of extended past perfect — and the oblique narrative strategies bring McElroy to mind. Morrow can ride a metaphor as far as Paul West can — there's a dazzling one on fire on pages 377–78 — and he commands the same sort of bizarre esoterica one finds in Burroughs's novels. This is not to say that Morrow is derivative or imitative; only that instead of following the same 19th-century models as most first novelists do, he has learned from these more recent writers the manifold ways of extending the possibilities of the novel. Would that all first novelists had Morrow's learning, range, and daring.

Review of Contemporary Fiction, Spring 1989. Although I didn't know it at the time, Brad and I attended high school together. We are pictured on the same page of the Arapahoe High yearbook for 1969.

Mo Yan

Life and Death Are Wearing Me Out. Translated by Howard Goldblatt
Arcade, 2008

A conventional novel about the miseries endured by Chinese peasants during the second half of the 20th century would hold little appeal for most readers. Worse, it would probably misrepresent the era: How could a conventional novel encompass the ideological insanity of Mao Zedong's policies and the unimaginable horrors he inflicted on his people, or render effectively the Orwellian policies enforced after his death in 1976? It couldn't. Something boldly *un*conventional is needed, a need that has been filled by the wild man of Chinese fiction, Mo Yan (a pseudonymic phrase meaning "Don't speak"). Over the last 20 years, Mo Yan has been writing brutally vibrant stories about rural life in China that flout official Party ideology and celebrate individualism over conformity. (How he has escaped imprisonment — or worse — I don't know.) He also flouts literary conformity, spiking his earthy realism with fantasy, hallucination, and metafiction.

His previous novel, the voluptuously titled *Big Breasts & Wide Hips*, revealed the horrors of Chinese life during the first half of the 20th century; his new one covers the second, even worse half. Here he revives the Buddhist notion of reincarnation to structure his exuberantly imaginative novel. It begins on January 1, 1950, in hell, where Lord Yama, king of the underworld, is examining a benevolent landowner named Ximen Nao, who was brutally executed two years earlier (like thousands of landowners) so that his land could be redistributed to peasants. Frustrated that Ximen will not admit any guilt, Yama punishes him by sending him back to his village in the form of a donkey.

Ximen remains in that form for the next ten years, witnessing the Land Reform Movement and the disastrous Great Leap Forward (1958–61) that killed 30 million Chinese people (and an unrecorded number of Chinese animals — the novel reminds us this earth belongs to them too). The donkey is angry at first when he learns his trusted farmhand Lan Lian has married Ximen's concubine, but is mollified as Lan carries on as a fiercely independent farmer, the last holdout in collectivized China. The donkey is killed during the great famine, accompanied by appropriate animal imagery: "But then the famine came, turning people into wild animals, cruel and unfeeling. After eating all the bark from trees and the edible grass, a gang of them charged into the Ximen estate compound like a pack of starving wolves." Ximen is reincarnated next as an ox, then a pig, a dog, a monkey, and finally — on New Year's

Eve 2000 — as a big-headed child. On his fifth birthday, the child and elderly Lan Lian get together and, taking turns, narrate the novel we've just read.

It's a grimly entertaining overview of recent Chinese history; as a "wise German shepherd" summarizes it, "People in the 1950s were innocent, in the 1960s they were fanatics, in the 1970s they were afraid of their own shadows, in the 1980s they carefully weighed people's words and actions, and in the 1990s they were simply evil." In contrast to the sheeplike "people," brave individuals emerge as the true heroes of the novel; aside from the animal reincarnations of Ximen Nao, these include Lan Lian for refusing to give in to communal pressure, and his son Lan Jiafang, who defies convention by abandoning his legal wife (from an arranged marriage) for a younger woman he deeply loves, ruining himself in the process. The most colorful individual is the novelist himself, who pops in and out of the novel, usually to the annoyance of the other characters.

To Western readers, *Life and Death Are Wearing Me Out* may recall the magic realism of recent Latin American fiction, but actually Mo Yan is reincarnating classic Chinese fiction. The first giveaway is the two-part chapter titles — "An Aggrieved Soul Returns as a Dog / A Pampered Child Goes to Town with His Mother" — a convention of all classic Chinese novels. In the opening chapter the narrator refers to the protagonists of Wu Chengen's fantastic novel *The Journey to the West* (c. 1570), which likewise features animal characters, reincarnation, and an infernal descent to Lord Yama. The name Ximen may be taken from that of Ximen Qing, the philandering protagonist of China's second-greatest novel, *The Plum in the Golden Vase* (c. 1600), and several later novels used reincarnation as a device, most memorably in China's greatest novel, Cao Xueqin's *Story of the Stone* (c. 1760). Mo Yan's mash-up of traditional Chinese literature and avant-garde techniques is daring and provocative, aided by the vivid translation by Howard Goldblatt, an old China hand.

I don't want to leave the impression this novel with the jokey title is a gimmicky book that makes light of recent Chinese history. Born in 1955, Mo Yan endured the worst of it — he too was so poor he ate tree bark — and there are graphic descriptions that will shock the reader into realizing this is no literary game. Indeed, reality keeps outrunning the author's wild imagination. Near the end of the novel, a born-again capitalist comes up with the idea of a Cultural Revolution theme park, which one would think would be as tasteless as a Nazi theme park in Poland. And yet there are now Cultural Revolution-themed cafés in China, favored by urban hipsters with an almost American ignorance of history. Mo Yan's use of animal narrators makes us rethink our casual use of words like "beastly" and "inhuman," and he offers insights into ideology, conformism, and predatory capitalism that we ignore at our peril.

This "lumbering animal of a story," as he calls it, combines the appeal of a family saga set against tumultuous events with the technical fascination of a tour-de-force of innovative fiction. Catch a ride on this wheel of transmigration.

Washington Post Book World, 25 May 2008

□ □ □ □ □ □ □

POW! Translated by Howard Goldblatt

Seagull, 2012

On October 11 of this year, the Chinese fiction-writer Mo Yan was awarded the Nobel Prize in Literature, and his new novel *POW!* demonstrates why he deserved to win. It's a vibrant, visceral novel that is both personal and political, traditional and modern, realistic and surrealistic, funny and shocking, earthy and intellectual, universal and culturally specific. The explosive title cries out for the blurb "*POW!* packs a powerful punch," but it is also a subtle display of narrative wizardry.

Like many of Mo Yan's earlier novels, it is set in the poverty-stricken rural China in which he grew up. A troubled 19-year-old named Luo Xiaotong has decided to abandon his vagabond life and become a monk at a temple near his hometown, Slaughterhouse Village, but before he does so, he wants to tell his life story to the wise monk who tends the temple. The novel alternates between the present (the year 2000) and a decade earlier, signaled in the text by italics for the present and regular type for the past. As Luo tells how he and his tigerish mother struggled to survive after his father left them for a woman nicknamed Wild Mule, only to return sheepishly five years later with an illegitimate daughter in tow, he reveals his obsession with meat. Determined to save enough money to build a house and demonstrate she doesn't need a man, Luo's mother deprives him of meat, which becomes in Mo Yan's hands a wide-ranging metaphor for obsession, sex, power, and politics. Luo becomes convinced that the world's population (animal as well as human) can be divided into "those who eat meat and those who don't" and who consequently play the "roles of eater and eaten."

It's a dog-eat-dog world — literally: lots of dog meat is consumed in the novel — and later when Luo is able to satisfy his carnivorous cravings, he is emboldened by his diet to indulge in widespread carnage at the end of the novel, a scene too bizarre to be real (the talking, dancing weasels are your first clue) but a brilliant dramatization of the meat-sex-power-violence nexus that the novel has been bulking up to. Ashamed by his actions, Luo forswears meat and after years of lowlife adventures (including a spell as a catnapper), he returns to his hometown temple to renounce the world of the senses.

But that world continues to tempt him in the temple, "one that enshrines five spirits with superhuman sexual prowess, one that generations of intellectuals have called an 'obscenity.'" Over the course of the few days he tells his tale, Luo is interrupted by a stream of increasingly strange visitors and watches with disbelief as a "Meat Appreciation Parade" approaches the temple as a prelude to a Carnivore Festival, a bizarre event that culminates in an opera called *From Meat Boy to Meat God*, a surrealistic parody of Luo's life. "I rub my eyes and, like the heroes in wildwood tales who ponder their reactions to strange encounters, I bite my finger to see if I am dreaming." (And thanks go to translator Howard Goldblatt for not Americanizing that to "I pinch myself"; he retains Mo Yan's Chinese idioms and allusions). Yuo suspects all this is an illusion staged by the monk as a test, and the author leaves us at the end as puzzled as Luo as to how much of this is real and how much imagined.

"An animal's temperament and demeanour are ruled by its stomach," Leo states at one point, and throughout the author reminds us that humans too are essentially animals. He blurs the distinction by using animal metaphors for human actions and by giving his animals human attributes, a ploy enabled by China's colorful mythology. One peasant is convinced that a cow is the reincarnation of his mother, and treats her accordingly; various women are compared to the fox-spirits common in folk tales; a rich big-shot justifies his tomcatting ways by comparing himself to "a stud horse, and stud horses belong to all the mares in a herd." This generates some unusual similes, as when a foxy lady exposes herself to Luo and he notes "the nipples rising gracefully, like the captivating mouths of hedgehogs." In rural settings like the one in this shapeshifting novel, humans and animals have a symbiotic relationship, but Mo Yan demonstrates that even the most civilized city-dweller is an animal at heart.

In a brief afterword, Mo Yan says the novel is autobiographical, but his stand-in Luo Xiaotong admits he is something of a "powboy": "In my village 'pow' also meant to brag and to lie." *POW!* is also the sound made by the 41 mortar shells Luo fires off in the novel's 41st and final chapter in a cartoonish attempt to kill his nemesis. Mo Yan's *POW!* is a pyrotechnic display of how to blow up one's personal life to mythic proportions.

Washington Post, 21 December 2012

□ □ □ □ □ □ □

Frog. Translated by Howard Goldblatt
Viking, 2015

When Mo Yan won the Nobel Prize for Literature in 2012, this 2009 novel had presumably not yet been translated into Swedish. But the Nobel Committee must have known about it, for *Frog* is the kind of serious, socially conscious fiction they favor. Recent novels of his like *Life and Death Are Wearing Me Out* and *POW!* took a Monty Pythonesque approach to depicting life under Mao Zedong and his successors, but *Frog* is a more serious affair. It has the same setting as those novels (rural China, 1950–2000) but this time the author grapples with China's controversial one-child policy.

The policy was instituted in 1979 to slow down China's exploding population, and the novel mostly concerns the resistance shown out in the boondocks, the dodges people used to get around the policy and the brutal methods used by the authorities to enforce it. The villagers naturally decry it as unnatural, and are especially frustrated if their first and only child is a girl, who hardly counts in this patriarchal society. Their pain and exasperation is dramatized in numerous outrageous vignettes, though equal time is given to justifications of the policy. These are voiced by the two main characters: Gugu, a midwife turned abortion doctor, does the math: "family planning is absolutely essential. If we let people have all the babies they want, that's thirty million a year, three hundred million a decade. At that rate, in fifty years the Chinese population alone would flatten the earth. So we must lower the birth rate, no matter what it costs. That will be China's greatest contribution to humanity."

Tadpole, the narrator's childhood nickname, concurs: "if no one had done what she did, it is truly hard to say what China might be like today." More environmentally aware than his fellow villagers, he adds: "When all is said and done, we live together on this tiny planet, with its finite resources. Once they're gone, they're not coming back, and seen from this perspective, Westerners' critiques of China's family planning policies are unfair." (Right-to-lifers will disagree, but they are not in charge of a national economy.) Tadpole's case is strengthened years later when he is almost killed by a teenage hoodlum who turns out to be one of the few fetuses that Gugu, in a moment of weakness, decided against terminating.

But this novel is no polemic: the noisy, emotional scenes of fathers and mothers risking punishment, fines, and even their lives to have babies outshout the quiet explanations given by the main characters. Tadpole struggles with all this as he plans to write a play about Gugu's career. The novel takes the form of four long letters Tadpole writes to a former teacher, recording anecdotes about Gugu in a rambling, episodic style. It is artfully artless: at one point Tadpole apologizes, "Using this sort of language to describe Gugu's work may seem inappropriate, but I can't come up with anything better," and he thanks his correspondent for telling him "that a little bit of reorganisation could turn it into a publishable novel." In metafictional counterpoint to the main theme of the novel, Tadpole struggles to give birth to his play, to transform himself from a tadpole into a frog.

Tadpole is a rather bland character; more vibrant is Gugu herself, who likewise undergoes many transformations: from a gifted midwife, to an independent-minded woman who defies the brutal dictates of the Cultural Revolution (1966–1976) and is publicly humiliated for it, to an equally brutal enforcer of the one-child policy. Late in life, she repents by marrying a man who molds clay babies based on her descriptions of all the fetuses she aborted. "I admit there are issues with Gugu's mental state," Tadpole says diplomatically.

His nine-act, 65-page play functions as an epilogue as Tadpole, now in his fifties, celebrates the one-month anniversary of his first son. The scene is disrupted, however, by the appearance of a crazed surrogate mother who steals the child, resulting in a televised courtroom scene that reenacts a Ming-era Judge Bao crime story (one of many allusions to classic Chinese fiction). Here, Mo Yan brings back the hallucinatory realism for which he's known. It's a bizarre but fitting conclusion to this unconventional novel, once again expertly rendered by Mo Yan's regular translator, Howard Goldblatt. Only recently has China relaxed the one-child policy somewhat, and *Frog* is both an invaluable record of that social experiment and yet another display of Mo Yan's attractively daring approach to fiction. The Nobel Committee chose wisely.

Washington Post, 24 March 2015

Haruki Murakami

Kafka on the Shore. Translated by Philip Gabriel
Knopf, 2005

If bizarre things are happening in Japan, then it must be a new novel by Haruki Murakami. America's favorite Japanese novelist could publish this anonymously and it would be instantly recognized as his by fans. And for first-time readers, *Kafka on the Shore* is an excellent demonstration why he's deservedly famous, both here and in his native land. He writes uncanny, philosophical, postmodern fiction that's actually fun to read; he's a more serious Tom Robbins, a less dense Thomas Pynchon. Like those two, he mixes high and low culture, especially ours: two of his novels are named after Western pop songs (*Dance Dance Dance* and *Norwegian Wood*) and his characters are more likely to see a film by Truffaut than Kurosawa. In this new novel, characters may occasionally discuss *The Tale of Genji* and the novels of Natsume Soseki, but the presiding influences are Plato, Sophocles, and, as the title indicates, Franz Kafka.

It would be easy to make this novel sound goofy: there are talking cats, sudden downpours of fish and leeches, a ghost that takes the form of Colonel Sanders pimping in a back alley of Takamatsu, another character who dresses up as the old Johnnie Walker whiskey icon and collects the souls of cats for a magic flute, a gorgeous prostitute who quotes Bergson and Hegel, and an "entrance stone" to another dimension. It would be just as easy to make the novel sound ponderous: there are many discussions of Greek tragedy, Plato's myth about the origin of the sexes, predestination, various metaphysical systems, musicology, the nature of symbolism and metaphor, the ways of Buddha and the Tao, and grim memories of atrocities committed during World War II. The wonderful thing about this novel is the mash-up Murakami creates from this disparate material, resulting in a novel that is intellectually profound but "feels like an Indiana Jones movie or something," as one character aptly notes.

Or something. The novel consists of two parallel narratives told in alternating chapters. One features a bright but unhappy 15-year-old boy named "Kafka" Tamura — he adopted the name partly because he likes his fiction but also because "Kafka" is Czech for "crow," with whose solitary nature he identifies — who runs away from home because of an Oedipal foreboding that he will murder his father and sleep with his mother. (His mother abandoned him at age 4 and he hasn't seen her or his older sister since.) He leaves Tokyo for the southern island of Shikoku, and spends most of his time at a private library run by a 21-year-old "hemophiliac of undetermined sex" named Oshima and a mysterious, elegant woman named Miss Saeki, old enough to be his mother. Both of them play key roles in helping the runaway find himself and come to terms with his dark destiny.

The other narrative deals with a retarded, illiterate man in his sixties named Satoru Nakata, who as a child underwent an inexplicable experience during World War II that erased his memory and stunted his intellectual growth. In recompense for that loss, however, he has the ability to communicate with cats and control the weather. (He's the one responsible for those Fortean downpours.) He gets involved with the cat-soul collector and commits an act that forces him to flee Tokyo. (This novel depends so much on surprising plot twists that I don't want to spoil it with details.) He hooks up with a truck-driver named Hoshino — just a regular guy who favors aloha shirts, Ray-Bans, and a Chunichi Dragons baseball cap — who agrees to help the old guy. They too make their way to Shikoku on a kind of metaphysical quest for an "entrance stone" that Nakata must open and close. As another character says (this is a very self-conscious text, frequently commenting on itself), it's "like some film noir science-fiction flick."

On one level, the novel is about a 15-year-old boy's rite of passage into the adult world, but on a larger level it's a meditation on Plato's notion (voiced in the *Symposium*, as Oshima explains to both Kafka and the reader) that each of us is looking for a soul-mate to complete us. Hoshino finds one in Nakata, who reminds him of a dimwitted but devoted disciple of the Buddha, but who also fills in for a beloved grandfather. Kafka finds one in Miss Saeki, who appears to him in dreams both as the 15-year-old girl she once was and at her present age. And though Kafka and Nakata never meet, their parallel actions complement each other on a metaphysical plane. Hermaphroditic Oshima — the most self-possessed and knowledgeable character in the novel — exemplifies the original state Plato said the soul enjoyed before it was split into halves.

Murakami's spin on this theme and the Oedipus myth is daringly original and compulsively readable, enabled by Philip Gabriel's wonderfully fluent translation. *Kafka on the Shore* is warmly recommended; read it to your cat.

Washington Post Book World, 30 January 2005

Anaïs Nin and Pornography

Little Birds
Harcourt Brace Jovanovich, 1979

Casting about for something of lasting literary value to review this month, I read — for lack of anything better — the first half-dozen or so stories from the latest posthumous collection of Anaïs Nin. But the stories lack the poetry and luxury of her earlier *Delta of Venus*, the surprising sales of which apparently prompted the publisher to gather up all the rejects from the first collection — a regrettable decision. At any rate, in light of the controversy surrounding [Colorado] Senate Bill No. 450 — on the governor's desk as I write — it might be worthwhile to use *Litte Birds* as a point of departure to discuss the relationship of pornography to literature.

Briefly, the bill wants to exclude those 18 years and under from entering any bookstore that carries any book "the cover or content of which exploits, is devoted to, or is principally made up of descriptions or depictions of illicit sex or sexual immorality." There probably isn't a bookstore in Colorado — apart from Christian and children's bookstores — that doesn't carry at least one book fitting the above description, and the passing of the Senate bill would force booksellers to remove from their shelves all such books, or else bar those under 18 from entering their door.

Now I will be the first to admit that books "principally made up of descriptions or depictions of illicit sex or sexual immortality" usually are not worth reading. Books of that nature more often than not are shallow, poorly written, predictable, and of little literary value. But then so is much science fiction. The main objection, to quote again from the bill, is that pornography threatens "the immediate preservation of the public peace, health, and safety." Thus pornography becomes no longer a literary issue but a political one. But is this a realistic evaluation? In his study *The Aesthetics of Pornography*, Peter Michelson writes, "Pornography, it is supposed, constitutes both a social and psychic threat. Society will be terrorized by the rampant lewdness induced by pornographic books — our wives and daughters raped, law and order dissolved. And our sons (somebody, after all, has to do the raping) will either be driven to mad carnality or will become idiots driveling in the wake of luxurious onanism."

Does anyone actually believe this? If so, they simply haven't been paying attention; countless psychological and sociological reports (even our own Presidential Commission on Obscenity and Pornography) have demonstrated there is little if any connection between pornography and sex-crimes. Indeed, in Denmark, where pornography was legalized a dozen years ago, the number of sex-related crimes has drastically decreased (except for rape, which is not a sexual act so much as an act of violence, and should be prosecuted as such). And as for the potentially damaging effect on children — is there a single senator who sometime during his/her youth never snuck a peek at a "lascivious" illustration or description in a book? And were they as a result permanently warped, now forced to hide their monstrous lust and odious perversions under the cloak of decency offered by public office? Of course not.

Children are naturally curious about certain aspects of life, and it's encouraging to see them turn to books for answers no one else will give them. Without any prompting they can usually tell the good ones from the bad, the realistic from the unrealistic. As a substitute teacher I remember once seeing an eighth-grade student with a copy of Henry Miller's *Tropic of Cancer* under his arm. "Is that any good?" I innocently asked. "Nah," he shrugged, "it's pretty boring."

Spree, June 1979. A few days before the magazine went to press, the bill was vetoed by Governor Dick Lamm.

Lawrence Norfolk

The Pope's Rhinoceros
Harmony, 1996

Lawrence Norfolk's second novel (after *Lamprière's Dictionary*) is a historical extravaganza, a panorama of 16th-century life so fantastically detailed that the author seems to have done his research by way of a time machine. The frame for this gargantuan novel is the story of the monks of Usedom, a tiny island in the Baltic Sea. Founded in the Middle Ages, the order is in disorder by the beginning of the Renaissance, their monastery crumbling into the sea and their leadership divided. In 1514 the monks decide to travel to Rome to seek guidance from the pope. Once there, *The Pope's Rhinoceros* bursts into life. Norfolk seems to have walked the streets of 16th-century Rome, so detailed are his descriptions of the smells, the cuisine, the weather, the riffraff, the different kinds of pawnshops, building practices, the rat problem — endless details on every aspect of Roman life. This isn't the glittering, ecclesiastic Rome of most historical novels but a muddy, noisy dump.

Ruling over this sweaty, smelly city is Pope Leo X, who has a shadowy past that he tries to forget by way of a craving for "marvels and prodigies." One of his prize possessions is an elephant, but he has read in Pliny's *Natural History* of a rarer creature, the elephant's natural enemy, which is referred to throughout the novel only as the Beast. (Not naming the animal except in the book's title is one form of narrative coyness the author practices; another is beginning a chapter in an unspecified setting with an unidentified "he," keeping the reader in the dark for paragraphs at a time.) As it happens, the ambassadors of Portugal and Spain are in Rome at the time, urging the pope to redraw the dividing line between territories being discovered in the New World, so to curry favor both ambassadors arrange to procure a rhinoceros for the pontiff.

The race is on. Portugal contacts its people in the Indian city of Goa, where a rhino is boarded on a ship for a harrowing voyage across the Indian Ocean and around the Cape. Spain meanwhile sends a rickety vessel to West Africa to find one. Its representatives — who do indeed find a rhinoceros (or rather, it finds them) — are a pair of ne'er-do-wells named Salvestro and Bernardo, the real protagonists of the novel. A classic picaresque pair — Salvestro is wily and resourceful, Bernardo a dim-witted giant — they accompany the monks down from Usedom but once in Rome run into some old enemies from their soldiering days. To escape them, they agree to sail to Africa on what is clearly a fool's errand. (There are machinations, subplots and double-crossings at work here that I couldn't begin to summarize. Norfolk shows that behind-the-scenes skullduggery has always been politics as usual, especially in Holy Rome.)

Norfolk displays an encyclopedic knowledge of every setting he uses, from arcane aspects of shipwrighting and canon law to the ecology of West African rain forests. Like the pope, he too has a penchant for marvels and prodigies and enlivens his prose with bold, flamboyant descriptions and some daring personification. "Once great, now this: a yawn-inducing acreage of alluvial dullness, a river-riven flood plain that shelves at the rate of one vertical foot to the horizontal mile, the drop corresponding to the land's sinking self-esteem and the coast to its despair. The land has been creeping slily out to sea for the last twenty centuries or so and meeting zero resistance en route, the Tiber flopping about like a sciatic drunk, this channel, that channel, a delta briefly." He even offers observations from the point of view of animals: We have the thoughts of herring, strategy sessions by rats, and the deliberations of an African ant. The cast of characters, human and animal, expands with every chapter, with new characters being introduced up to the end. All of this is both admirable and exhausting, overwhelming the narrative at times and stunning the reader by the amount of research Norfolk must have done.

The novel finally returns to Rome for what the pope hopes will be a grand climax, intent as he is that "however it ends . . . it be large, chaotic, noisy." Norfolk's conclusion is exactly that, a flamboyant end to an extravagant novel. When published in Britain earlier this year, the novel drew comparisons to Umberto Eco's erudite, historical novels. But *The Pope's Rhinoceros* is less like *The Name of the Rose* than the kind of historical novels William T. Vollmann and Rikki Ducornet write, where the old-fashioned genre is given a postmodern makeover. Norfolk has expressed admiration for the work of Thomas Pynchon and has a similar gift for displaying a casual mastery of the most outlandish historical materials.

Does the pope get his rhinoceros? Yes and no. To find out, you'll have to track the Beast yourself through the jungles of Norfolk's adjective-rich prose.

Washington Post Book World, 15 September 1996

Joyce Carol Oates

Son of the Morning
Vanguard Press, 1978

What do the following books have in common: *The Hungry Ghosts, Crossing the Border, Childwold, New Heaven New Earth, Son of the Morning, All the Good People I've Left Behind*, and *Women Whose Lives Are Food, Men Whose Lives Are Money*? They are all by Joyce Carol Oates and were published (or issued in paperback) within the last year alone. So many novels, plays, poems, short stories, and articles flow from her prolific pen that I'm starting to wonder if "Joyce Carol Oates" is the group pseudonym for a team of writers, just as the name Hermes Trismegistus was given as the author of a large body of mystical writings actually composed by a group of Greeks in Egypt. Or perhaps she follows the practice of the Dutch painter Peter Paul Rubens, who would sometimes do an outline and sketch in the figures for a painting, then turn the actual painting over to a disciple. At any rate, the Joyce Carol Oates Writing Collective has had a great year.

Ms. Oates's newest novel *Son of the Morning* chronicles the rise and fall of a Pentecostal preacher named Nathanael Vickery and explores the psychology of religious fanaticism. The book is timely in that the '70s has been a decade of religious revival in all areas of society (except for us godless intellectuals, who resist salvation as a stubborn child does castor oil), and the novel raises many questions about the psychopathology of religion — a delicate and inevitably irreverent subject. As a result, one's reaction to the book will depend on one's religious beliefs, or lack thereof. The author herself doesn't tip her cards; when she appeared on *The Dick Cavett Show* recently — as quietly cautious as a girl on her first date — she said she considered it almost an invasion of privacy to inquire into someone's religious beliefs, and as a result she records the story of Nathanael Vickery with the reverent objectivism attributed to the writers of the Bible.

And it is to the Bible that one must turn to fully appreciate Nathanael's career. The novel's title is taken from Isaiah 14:12: "How art thou fallen from heaven, O Lucifer, son of the morning!" (Actually, "Lucifer" — Latin for "light-bringer," i.e., Venus the morning star — was the King James translation of "Day-star, son of Dawn," an epithet based on the name of a Canaanite deity applied to boastful Nebuchadnezzar; the name was applied by analogy to Satan by Saint Jerome and other early fathers much later.) Lucifer fell from heaven through overweening pride, and apparently Nathanael falls from grace for finally believing himself to be not just a disciple of Christ but an avatar as well. The name Nathanael (Hebrew for "gift of God") also comes from the Bible; in the New Testament, it is Nathanael who provides one of the few laughs in the otherwise somber book. When told by Philip that a messiah has come from Nazareth, he quips, "Can there any good thing come out of Nazareth?" (John 1:46; evidently Nazareth was the Cleveland of the Levant).

Other biblical parallels abound. Nathanael, like Jesus, is born of a 15-year-old virgin (ages 14 to 15 were considered a girl's prime in ancient times); he is tempted; and if not finally crucified (though he is, in a sense, betrayed, killed, and resurrected), he is finally forsaken by God — or so he feels. There is no doubt that Nathanael's religious dedication is sincere — he is not one of those televangelists with their keep-those-checks-coming brand of religious commercialism — but ultimately Nathanael comes across as being a victim of . . . how does Freud define religion? . . . an obsessive neurosis. This point is forcefully made when Nathanael takes Christ's advice to pluck out an offending eye literally. A more modern diagnosis, inspired by Julian Jaynes's recent *Origin of Consciousness in the Breakdown of the Bicameral Mind* (which should be on the shelf of every educated person), might involve a form of schizophrenia, which suggests itself in the novel's narrative mode. Although the story is told mostly in the third person, a strange "I" intervenes from time to time — usually offering Davidic psalms and reflections — that seems to be Nathanael himself, but which recounts events that Nathanael could never have known.

The explicit parallels with both Jesus and Lucifer — at one point a clergyman throws a bottle of ink at Nathanael, as Luther did at his devil — gives the story a kind of predictability and inevitability, and also make Nathanael too unreal and inhuman to engage one's sympathies. The pedophilic protagonist of Oates's last novel *Childwold* was also quite different from the run of humanity, but somehow he won empathy where Nathanael doesn't. It is finally the language itself — from metaphorically rich poetic details to the nobility (as well as irritating vagueness) of cadenced biblical prose — that makes the novel a rewarding experience. Just listen:

> When the floodwaters recede there is a jumble of things: broken parts, fragments, coils and loops and shreds. Shall I seek myself among them? Shall I seek You among them? God-intoxicated am I, or only stubborn? Or defiant? Calling to the one least like me, to the One Who has swallowed me up and forgotten me. Who gave birth to me, and devoured me, and excreted me into the drifting, clamoring world. God-mad, God-infatuated am I, calling to the one least like me, to the One Who will never reply, who has turned away from me forever . . .

Spree, December 1978

David Peace

Red or Dead
Melville House, 2014

Sports novels generally rank low on the literature scoreboard — unless you regard *Moby-Dick* as a harpooning competition — even though Robert Coover, Don DeLillo, and David Foster Wallace have shown that it is possible to write ultraliterary, even experimental novels about sports. What they did for baseball and tennis is matched, if not trounced, by what British writer David Peace has done for soccer, first with *The Damned Utd* (2006), and now with this massive, mesmerizing novel.

Red or Dead is an epic treatment of the career of Bill Shankly, who from 1959 to 1974 led the mediocre Liverpool Football Club to a series of triumphs. The first two-thirds of the book, subtitled "Shankly Among the Scousers," is a clipped account of every game the team played during those 15 seasons, complete with stats and attendance figures. The final third, "Shankly Agonistes," begins with his unexpected decision to retire and dramatizes his final seven years (he died in 1981 at age 68).

The most radical feature of *Red or Dead*, and one that will try the patience of some readers, is the style. Peace uses short, often incomplete sentences, eschews pronouns and quotation marks, and deliberately repeats phrases and descriptions to excessive length, recalling early modernist works by Gertrude Stein, Ernest Hemingway, and T. S. Eliot. (Peace's subtitles echo Eliot's "Sweeney Among the Nightingales" and "Sweeney Agonistes.") Here is the conclusion to a defeat at Liverpool's Anfield stadium:

> On the bench, the Anfield bench. Bill watched George Best dodge every challenge, George Best elude every tackle. Bill watched George Best spin threads, George Best weave webs. With artistry and with craft, with bravery and with strength. Bill watched Best dance, Bill watched Best sing. And score and score again. And on the bench, the Anfield bench. Bill watched Liverpool Football Club slip and slip again. Liverpool Football Club no longer first in the First Division. Manchester United first in the First Division. Again. Liverpool Football Club second. Again. Second best. Again.

As here, the style often transcends modernist aesthetics to evoke ancient epics and medieval ballads, their repetitive formulas and lilting refrains, their stylized actions and heroic gravitas. Each time Liverpool trains for a new season, it is as though they are preparing to besiege the walls of Troy. Shankly is as cunning as Odysseus, as civic-minded as Aeneas, as relentless as Beowulf. He confesses in the final third that "football is my religion," and the style appropriately resembles liturgical chanting, mystical incantation. For readers who simply want the straight story, there are couple dozen books about Shankly to choose from (Peace lists them in his concluding "Sources and Acknowledgments"). But "with artistry and with craft, with bravery and with strength," Peace set out to ennoble Shankly's career into a postmodern epic, and succeeds brilliantly. Goal!

Shortly after he retires, Shankly describes football as "a hard, relentless task which goes on and on like a river" (498), which justifies the first part's relentless, focused narrative. It's "Total Football," as he calls it, with very few references to the times. Not a word about that other band of Liverpudlians who rose to fame in the early '60s, and only four words on 1967's summer of love. ("The summer of love.") After Shankly retires, the focus widens to take in England in the 1970s, and during two lengthy interviews we learn more about Shankly's background and philosophy. Not much of a reader, his favorite book is John Stuart Blackie's *Life of Robert Burns*, and there are several references and allusions to his fellow Scot's poetry. A committed socialist, Shankly notes that football is a form of socialism: "You play collectively and then you're very difficult to beat. But if you've individuals in your team, then your team will fall down." During an interview with Harold Wilson, the prime minister tells him "if you think in sporting analogies, it helps you in other walks of life," and Shankly tells anyone who will listen that the same qualities of a good footballer — determination, ambition, hard work, positive attitude — can be applied to anyone. There are a few schmaltzy scenes at the end, typical of feel-good sports movies, but they are nicely done and irresistibly moving. Even if, like me, you are a four-eyed aesthete with zero interest in sports, you'll choke up.

Shankly retires at the top of his game because, he tells his wife Ness, "I'm not enjoying life, love. I need to get it sorted out." This complicates the novel's moral, for those same qualities that drove Shankly and his team to the top make it difficult to live a fulfilling life. Shankly's wife and team members are little more than names, his daughters are always offstage, and he has nothing to fall back on after he leaves the game. And while Shankly instinctively thinks in terms of sporting analogies when he learns of the moon landing in 1969 — "The flag on the moon, the ball in the goal" — there is a world of difference between a team of engineers and astronauts reaching the moon and a team of men in red shorts kicking a ball up and down a field. Shankly also thinks of football in terms of salvation and redemption, and compares the elusive Football Association Cup to the Holy Grail. The reader can decide whether this is sublime or ridiculous.

These moral quandaries, like those in the *Odyssey* and the *Aeneid*, only enrich Peace's ambitious novel. As both postmodern epic and ultimate sports novel, *Red or Dead* is a winner.

Washington Post, 22 July 2014

Ezra Pound

Paul Smith. *Pound Revised*

Croom Helm, 1983

Pound's adherents have tended to praise his poetry and ignore his political and economic beliefs, while his detractors have used these beliefs to condemn him with little regard for the quality of his poetry. In this compact volume Paul Smith argues that Pound's poetics and politics are inextricably woven and cannot be isolated (by friend or foe) without misunderstanding the whole fabric of Pound's thought. It is Smith's contention that Pound's totalitarianism is as obvious in his poetry as it is in his political and economic tracts, and for that reason the poetry is to be regarded with suspicion.

The revision announced in Smith's title is of two kinds: a new estimate of Pound's achievement in light of the political overtones of his evolving poetic theory; and a new estimate of Pound's influence on three colleagues or disciples: James Joyce, H.D. (Pound's abbreviation), and Louis Zukofsky. For his re-envisioning Smith draws upon not only the primary texts of each writer but much biographical material as well, augmented by a good deal of Structuralist and Freudian theory (by way of Lacan) along with the best literary criticism available.

Smith begins with Pound's earliest poems to indicate the conflict between materiality (form) and substance (content) that would occupy Pound until he settled on the final form for *The Cantos*. Pound's early notion of poetry as nearly non-denotative "verbal music" (as he called Swinburne's poetry) evolved into connotative Imagism and finally (in *The Cantos*) to a view of "language as the means, simply, of direct and useful transmission," where his early self-absorption with the materiality of poetry gives way to an emphasis on its substance — often at the expense of poetics. (It was this tendency that Zukofsky most objected to: "you no longer bother to weigh each word you handle, translate, etc.," the younger poet complained. "The damn foreigner you say I am has more respect for English than you have.") Personal diction gave way to that of his quoted materials; the poet as singer becomes the poet as anthologist.

Smith closes the gap between poetic and political theory just as Pound did in the 1920s and '30s. Poetic traditions are maintained by stable (often totalitarian) political systems; Pound's reverence for tradition not only drew him to fascist systems that promised such stability, but also accounts for the patriarchal and phallocentric impulse in his later work — an impulse discounted by many of his critics and even by his female admirers. A detailed look at Canto 47 challenges the critical tendency to translate Pound's intentions, "reducing language to fixed meanings within the control of the author." Smith's attack on the methodology of Pound criticism concludes: "Far, indeed, from being that 'poetry of emergence' [as many Pound critics regard it], the *Cantos* continually aim at the unequivocal expression of Pound's opinions" — reducing *The Cantos* to an artsy version of his blunt Rome Radio broadcasts, which have accurately (in Smith's opinion) been called "The Poor Man's Cantos." These speeches are of course embarrassing to most Pound critics, yet Smith invests them with pivotal importance in the development of his poetics from materiality to representation. "How can we explain the enthusiasm with which he embraced radio except by reference to radio's power to transmit the quality of the subject's voice without the interference of the materiality that stands in the way of writing communication?" The relentless process that leads to Smith's conclusion on Pound's intrinsic totalitarianism resists summarization; suffice it to say Smith has thrown down a gauntlet that only the doughtiest Pound critic should take up.

The last three chapters examine the relationship between Pound and three others, partly "to explain what sort of implicit and necessary revisions of Pound's poetics were made by James Joyce, H.D. and Louis Zukofsky," but more importantly to find "antidotes, or experiments towards antidotes, for what I see as the damaging implications of Pound's work." All three chapters rely heavily on psychoanalysis, especially in H.D.'s case. Joyce represented freedom of a sort repugnant to the fascist Pound, apparent even in such instances as Pound's discomfort with the jakes scene in *Ulysses*. Joyce and Pound became Shem and Shaun figures (from *Finnegans Wake*, Smith's primary text for the Joyce chapter), with Pound as the repressed and repressing Shaun. If Joyce and Pound had a sibling rivalry of sorts, H.D. and Zukofsky had a daunting father figure in Pound to deal with. Smith details their attempts to emerge from under the shadow of *il miglior fabbro* and argues that the two younger poets wrote their best work only in their later years, by which time they were finally free of his influence.

This slim (and overpriced) book represents one of the most closely argued attacks on Pound and on Pound criticism in general. Pound's work has attained a stature that no single book can now destroy, yet Smith's book must be taken into consideration if that hard-earned stature is to maintain its integrity.

American Notes & Queries, September/October 1984

□ □ □ □ □ □ □

Ezra Pound: Tactics for Reading. Edited by Ian F. A. Bell

Vision Press/Barnes & Noble, 1982

The emphasis on the text to the exclusion of all external materials that characterizes the aging New Criticism has always been dear to the hearts of Pound's critics because of the embarrassing nature of such materials in Pound's case: his ranting socioeconomic tracts, the Rome Radio speeches, and such works as *Jefferson and/or Mussolini*. Professor Bell's new anthology of Pound criticism — all but one previously unpublished — provides a much-needed re-evaluation of "the terms whereby Pound is examined in order to reconstruct our means of talking about him in a more historical, less privileged manner than that which has informed so many earlier discussions." Most of the essays in this volume provide larger and more varied contexts in which to evaluate Pound's poetics than are usually offered by his more numerous exegetists and annotators. If Pound's poetic achievement is to withstand such attacks as Paul Smith's recent *Pound Revised*, such essays as these are indispensable.

The volume opens with an essay by Peter Brooker "addressing and attempting to explain the internal relations between Pound's literary texts and authorial ideology" — the exact issue so many of Pound's admirers have skirted. Pound's early disappointment with European culture (which he had left America to embrace) and his discovery in 1928 of "a tradition of family interest in questions of monetary reform" are aligned with "Hugh Selwyn Mauberley" and a variety of *Cantos* in an interesting example of cross-fertilization from external sources, a process continued with discussions of Pound's Carlylean hero worship and enchantment with fascist ideology. Brooker swings back and forth between *The Cantos* and the nonfiction writings that inform the poem (by Pound as well as by others) and reaches a startling conclusion regarding the much-debated unity of *The Cantos*: because "the completion of both Pound's poem and Italian fascism manifestly require a similarly unqualified faith in the driving will towards order of the constructive single personalities at their centres," then consequently, with the fall of Mussolini and Italian fascism, *The Cantos* (beginning with *The Pisan Cantos*) moves away from a driving will toward order to a "double realm" of "chaos and potential order" with the poet embracing a concept similar to Keats's "negative capability." This shift makes *The Cantos* "of interest not simply as a 'fascist epic,' or as an 'American fascist epic' but also as a 'failure' since where it 'fails' it also succeeds in undermining Pound's totalitarian ambition." Thus Pound's alleged failure to make his epic poem cohere can be read as a victory of sorts, a victory of humanism over fascism.

The other essays in the volume offer similar revisionary "tactics for reading." In his "Pound-signs: Money and Representation in Ezra Pound," David

Murray insists that "it is important to locate Pound specifically as an artist threatened by a lack of role in a democratic society" in order to understand fully Pound's "long-standing concern with money" and what he saw as "the *cultural* failure of the rich" to provide for his sort. Murray provides the necessary groundwork in historical contexts (American Populism and the Depression) and the ideology prevalent among the money reformers of the late 19th century (whom Pound followed) to explicate the crucial role of money in *The Cantos*. Martin A. Kayman provides equally useful groundwork in "A Model for Pound's Use of 'Science'" by examining Pound's tendency to place "'Mystic values' into a scientific context" to ensure their "acceptability" — much as Carlyle did a century before. Herbert Schneidau's elegant "Pound's Poetics of Loss" begins with prolegomena from the Romantic tradition that Pound used as a point of departure for his modern epic in order to "exploit a poetics of loss and turn it into a magnificent gain." Schneidau also reminds us of Pound's concept of the epic (largely from his *ABC of Reading*) as an accumulation of "long-preserved and well-filtered traditions of knowledge transcending the mind of one man or even of several"; thus the often exasperating heterogeneity of *The Cantos* is not the result of Pound's inability or unwillingness to shape his materials, but a conscious strategy to rescue poetry from the vagaries bequeathed by the Romantics by joining it to the more vigorous, confident, and relevant poetic tradition of the epic.

Eric Mottram's "Pound, Merleau-Ponty and the Phenomenology of Poetry" draws a number of parallels between the poet and the French Marxist philosopher. It is followed by editor Bell's "'Speaking in Figures': The Mechanical Thomas Jefferson of Canto 31," which examines the wide range of materials and ideas that went into that important canto, especially regarding Pound's debt (via Jefferson) to the Enlightenment. Joseph Riddel's "'Neo-Nietzschean Clatter' — Speculation and/or Pound's Poetic Image" traces the influence of the German philosopher on both Pound and Wallace Stevens (with help from de Man and Derrida), and the volume concludes with Richard Godden's discussion of Pound's obsession with the phenomenology of language, "Icons, Etymologies, Origins and Monkey Puzzles in the Languages of Upward and Fenollosa."

These brief summaries fail to do justice to the depth and intelligence that suffuses the volume. The book is highly recommended not only to Pound scholars but to anyone open to new "tactics for reading."

American Notes & Queries, March/April 1985

□□□□□□□

Ezra Pound's Poetry and Prose: Contributions to Periodicals. Prefaced and arranged by Lea Baechler, A. Walton Litz, and James Longenbach
11 vols.; Garland, 1991

This is a mind-boggling achievement: all two thousand or so of Pound's contributions to magazines reprinted in their original formats, and arranged in chronological order according to section C of Gallup's Pound bibliography. This includes essays, poems, reviews, statements, translations, letters, interviews — many of them inaccessible and/or never published in book form. Apart from the clear advantage of having all this material handsomely bound into a ten-volume set (vol. 11 is the index), it is invaluable for tracking the growth of the poet's mind, which is possible only when one follows the chronological sequence of his writings. Thus 1939 begins with Pound contributing an article to the *British Union Quarterly* entitled "Banks Are a Blessing," followed by an essay on French novelist René Crevel, then letters to the editors of the *Examiner* and *Musical Times*, then a reprint of his 1914 poem "Abu Salammamm — A Song of Empire" and another poem called "Slice of Life," a note on T. E. Hulme, another letter to an editor (on economist Irving Fisher), then an essay in Sir Oswald Mosley's *Action* asking "Does the Government of England control the B.B.C?" — all this in the month of January alone. Not only are these particular items unknown to most Pound readers, but the juxtaposition of economics, literature, music, poetry, and politics is indicative of the range of his interests. Even the smallest trifle has a striking phrase, a pertinent thought; taken together, these two thousand items constitute a vortex of intellectual activity encyclopedic in its scope and universal in its relevance.

Beautifully designed and impeccably edited, *Ezra Pound's Poetry and Prose* is an essential acquisition for all academic libraries and major public libraries. Be sure to recommend it to the libraries you patronize.

Review of Contemporary Fiction, Fall 1992

□ □ □ □ □ □ □

Ezra Pound. *Canti Postumi*. Edited by Massimo Bacigalupo
Arnoldo Mondadori Editore, 2002

An unsympathetic critic might grumble that Pound threw everything but the kitchen sink into his 824-page *Cantos*, especially since the book ends with a section of "Drafts and Fragments." But in fact Pound did leave a lot out, the best of which has now been gathered by Italian Pound scholar Massimo Bacigalupo for this edition of "Posthumous Cantos." The introduction and notes are in Italian, but the poetry is of course in English, and since there are no plans for an American edition, *Canti postumi* deserves notice.

The book is divided into eight chronological sections: it begins with the 1917 version of "Three Cantos" published in *Poetry*, different enough from those eventually published in *The Cantos* to be preserved. Then we travel from Paris (1920–22) to Rapallo and Venice (1928–37), then sections called "Voices of War" (1940–45) and "Italian Drafts" (1944–45), then outtakes from the great *Pisan Cantos* (1948), followed by what Pound himself called "Prosaic Verses" (written during his confinement at St. Elizabeths in the 1950s), and finally "Lines for Olga" (1962–72).

Some drafts offer longer versions of incidents that were compressed for the final book version, like a discussion between Pound and Eliot at Verona in 1922 that is merely alluded to in the published version. The couplet "Her name was courage / & is written Olga" from the final page of *The Cantos* is taken from a lovely 13-line poem published here in tribute to his longtime companion Olga Rudge, the embodiment of Venus invoked at the beginning of his epic. Other verses occur in contexts quite different from those in the final book and will aid Pound scholars in seeing those historical "rhymes" Pound made by yoking various eras together.

And throughout there are beautiful, medallion-bright images that take one's breath away: "Brows cut smoothe as if with a jade-wheel / Cool water of hill-lakes, water calm as the eyes"; "her red head a flask of perfume"; "The air is solid sunlight, apricus, / Sun-fed we dwell there." For all his obfuscation and hare-brained theories, Pound commanded poetic powers that continue to astonish, even in these drafts and outtakes.

There are images in *Canti postumi* of ruined castles, of "Empires end[ing] in the marsh." *The Cantos* itself is like a cathedral falling into ruins, attended today only by specialists, ignored by most readers of poetry. *Canti postumi* may only be fragments shored against those ruins, but these drafts remind us of the greatness of Pound's achievement, and the book even works as a teaser for those uncertain whether they want to take the grand tour. It is well worth seeking out.

Rain Taxi, Online Edition, Summer 2003. An English edition was eventually published by Carcanet in 2015.

Dawn Powell

The Diaries of Dawn Powell, 1931–1965. Edited by Tim Page
Steerforth Press, 1995

Almost forgotten until Gore Vidal "rediscovered" her in the 1980s, Dawn Powell is enjoying an enviable posthumous career: most of her novels have been reprinted — Steerforth just reissued *The Locusts Have No King* — a biography is in the works (by Tim Page [published in 1998]), and now selections from her diaries have been published. The book will appeal to Powell fans, of course, and to those interested in the New York literary world of the 1930s through the '60s (she died in 1965).

For readers of this journal, the book is valuable for its material on Felipe Alfau (the subject of our spring 1993 issue), for whom so little biographical material exists that one is grateful for anything. Like many figures depicted in the *Diaries*, Alfau doesn't appear at his best here: he is described in an entry for 1938 as pro-fascist and anti-Semitic — not a word about his great novel *Locos*, published two years earlier — but he is also quoted on the differences between Spain and America, the theme of his even greater novel, *Chromos*, which he would write ten years later. Nevertheless, Powell respected him: "Felipe Alfau, brilliant, dazzling mind, witty, Jesuitical, a mental performance similar only to Cummings, but a scholar — erudite, fascinating, above all a romantic about his Spain, fiercely patriotic, a figure out of a medieval romance, a lover of Toledo, of old Spain, valuable surely to his country — talked so brilliantly of Totalitarianism that is based on human weakness, human error, human conduct, that it almost convinced me."

I first heard of Powell as one of the reviewers of Gaddis's 1955 novel *The Recognitions*, one of those whom Jack Green designated a "bastard" for her condescending review. There's no mention of Gaddis here — perhaps he was left on the cutting-room floor (this book represents about three-fourths of the extant diaries) — but almost every other writer of the time is mentioned in one way or another, making *The Diaries of Dawn Powell* a valuable resource for students of the first half of 20th-century American literature.

Review of Contemporary Fiction, Summer 1996 — the last review I published in *RCF*

Richard Powers

Operation Wandering Soul
Morrow, 1993

The MacArthur Foundation is certainly getting its money's worth from Richard Powers. After granting him their so-called genius award, he brought out his huge *Gold Bug Variations*, and now, barely two years later, comes another huge, rich novel. *Operation Wandering Soul* is about children: now comprising 50 percent of the world's population, they are the victims of at least that percentage of the world's violence and neglect. Mercilessly, Powers sets his novel in the pediatrics ward of a hospital in Watts, where his doctor protagonist, Richard Kraft, sees an unending line of children abused, wounded, malformed, overdosed, and prematurely dying, ending with the victims of a mass shooting at an elementary school. As Kraft struggles with the implications of all this, Powers inserts into the text classic stories of children trying to escape the adult world — *Peter Pan*, "The Pied Piper of Hamelin," the Children's Crusade — suggesting that for children, it is always apocalypse now. But the present proliferation of guns, gang warfare, drugs, and child abuse red-lines that yearning for Never-Never-Land.

As socially redeeming as this novel is, its true genius lies in its prose. Like Pynchon's or, better yet, Stanley Elkin's, Power's sentences are rich confections of tropes and metaphors, slang and puns, sentences that you want to linger over and savor. The novel is formally inventive as well: one chapter ends with study questions (which later turn up as a homework assignment for one of the sick kids), another has vocabulary notes to *Peter Pan*, others experiment with viewpoint or chronology. All in all, *Operation Wandering Soul* is a vastly satisfying performance from a novelist who looks like he'll assume major historical importance.

Review of Contemporary Fiction, Fall 1993

□ □ □ □ □ □ □

Galatea 2.2
Farrar Straus Giroux, 1995

Richard Powers is your reward for graduating from college with a liberal arts degree. His engagingly erudite novels richly repay those art history courses you took, all the reading in literature, those electives in music and foreign languages. He does make you wish you had paid closer attention to those science requirements you struggled through, but he is a good teacher and fills you in on what you need to know. In his magnificent *Gold Bug Variations* (1991) it was genetics; in his new novel, it's cognitive neurology. But *Galatea* 2.2 is not merely a novel about science, nor science fiction; it's an elegant attempt to use cutting-edge research on cognition to explore the nature of memory and literary creation.

As in all his novels — this is his fifth in ten years — Powers tells two stories in counterpoint. The one set in the novel's present concerns Richard Powers's return to Illinois after several years in the Netherlands. (The novel is overtly autobiographical; Powers uses his own name and career as the basic subject matter.) Writer-in-residence at a large Midwestern college in the town of U. (that is, the University of Illinois at Urbana), Powers is drawn to the work being done at the Center for the Study of Advance Sciences, specifically to a certain Philip Lentz's belief that a computerized model of the human brain can be created. In a scenario that is part *Frankenstein* and part *Faust*, Lentz and Powers accept a wager that they can build such a creature and teach it enough literature to pass the university's master's exam. We follow their rocky progress to the point where they achieve Implementation H, which they nickname Helen. (The earlier models are nicknamed Imp, which recalls Joseph McElroy's use of that name in his 1977 novel *Plus*, a denser exploration of the same theme of memory and cognition.) Meanwhile, Powers falls in love with the 22-year-old grad student whom the team plans to test against their creation. Their Helen, recalling both Helen of Troy (especially the eidolon in *Faust*) and the Helen evoked in a poem by Edgar Allan Poe, takes on enough personality to win Powers's heart but asks enough unsettling questions about the literature he reads to her to cause him to doubt his literary vocation, even the value of literature itself.

Threading through this story is another one that details Powers's long-term relationship with a woman named C., his companion during the years he wrote his first four novels. The dissolution of their relationship is what sends him back to the States after several years in Holland, and while his Helen is building up memory and comprehension, Powers searches his memory to try to comprehend the failure of their relationship.

Despite the autobiographical content, *Galatea* 2.2 is not an example of what has been called "navel-gazing" fiction, where an author's preoccupation with his own creative processes takes on undue (usually boring) proportions. Instead, Powers tackles the big questions: How does the mind work? How do we know what we know? What is the relationship between literature and "real" life? What is the impulse behind literary creation? How do metaphors work? And what is the proper attitude toward literature? Powers leaps right into the current maelstrom that is literature in the '90s, with literary theory, multiculturism, and 14 varieties of cultural politics pulling it every which way. Powers belongs to the old school, downloading what used to be called the Great Books into Helen's memory banks; Helen's 22-year-old adversary is into Kathy Acker and the Violent Femmes. I won't reveal who wins the contest, but it's a race nearly as thrilling as that to crack the genetic code in *The Gold Bug Variations*.

One of the greatest advantages of Powers using his own career as subject matter is that we learn of the precariousness, the almost accidental nature of artistic creation: The novels Richard Powers has blessed us with so far were the result not of careful career planning but of accidental glimpses, unexpected relationships, unplanned relocations, unlooked-for financing (the success of his first novel, *Three Farmers on Their Way to a Dance*, was unpredictable, as was his receipt of a MacArthur Award a few years ago), and so on. Remove one event here or there and we would have had different novels, or none at all. We take novels for granted because hundreds of them appear each year, but the few that matter, that will last, are almost miracles. Powers doesn't play the noble artist suffering for his art here: He's amusingly self-deprecating about his achievements and his reputation. But these precious things are not to be taken for granted. *Galatea* 2.2 is not quite in the same class as Powers's last two novels — the underrated *Operation Wandering Soul* was his last — but it is a splendid intellectual adventure, a heartbreaking love story, a brief tutorial on cognitive science, and the autobiography of one of the most gifted writers of the younger generation. Play Pygmalion and bring this lovely Galatea to life with your appreciation.

Washington Post Book World, 9 July 1995

□□□□□□□

Gain

Farrar, Straus & Giroux, 1998

"The business of America is business," said Calvin Coolidge in 1925, which is even more ruthlessly true today, when everything from the arts to health care is measured if not motivated by financial profit. To understand our money-driven culture one must understand economics, a daunting and complex subject that scares off most readers and novelists, but not our best: William Gaddis in *J R* and Thomas Pynchon in *Gravity's Rainbow* went to prodigious lengths to expose the skeletons in capitalism's closet, and now Richard Powers joins their exalted company with a masterful novel named after the strongest force in millennial America: *Gain*.

In alternating chapters Powers tells two stories: the 170-year history of Clare, Incorporated (think Procter & Gamble or DuPont) from its simple beginnings as a small, family concern to its present status as a multinational corporation; and a contemporary account of the last year in the life of Laura Bodey, a real estate broker living in Lacewood, Illinois, the Midwest headquarters of Clare. Parallel to Clare's progress from soap manufacturer to global giant is Laura's discovery and battle against ovarian cancer, which grows with the same blind urgency as the corporation. In between the alternating chapters are brief examples of Clare's PR materials over the years: ads, signs, press releases, and so forth, reminiscent of Dos Passos's *U.S.A.* The two stories begin to dovetail when it's suggested that Laura's cancer is the result of nearby Clare's manufacturing process.

Powers is a masterful stylist, and the alternating narratives tailor the language to the times. The language is grand and fulsome in the historical sections on Clare: bold personifications, windy rhetoric, daring, even reckless metaphors ("Rail steadied the farmer's year like a hand laid upon the turbulent heel of heaven"), mirroring the reckless rollercoaster ride of American commerce in the 19th century. The style in the contemporary sections is comparatively sedate, the sentences shorter, though still quite imagistic, like those of the late great Stanley Elkin.

Powers is also a masterful researcher. For each of his previous novels he investigated a forbidding subject — genetics in *The Gold Bug Variations*, cognitive neurology in *Galatea 2.2* — and made an exciting, intellectual adventure out of it. He does so again in *Gain*, both with economics (chemical manufacturing, the implications of incorporation, labor relations, stocks, etc.) and with cancer. Laura's illness and chemotherapy treatments are related in such excruciating detail that I'd swear Powers went through them himself.

Unlike Pynchon, Powers doesn't see evil or occult forces behind the growth of capitalism, and unlike Gaddis he doesn't show much outrage over the stupidity and greed that can pervert it. Instead, there's a curiously detached tone to the novel, conveyed in its somewhat neutral-sounding title. Nevertheless, *Gain* is a brilliant, moving novel, and an enlightening account of the price our country has paid for its headlong pursuit of the almighty dollar.

Rain Taxi, Summer 1998

□ □ □ □ □ □ □

Plowing the Dark

Farrar Straus Giroux, 2000

The second of the Ten Commandments, the one against creating representational art, is probably the most widely ignored and least understood. "It's like God knew that if we ever got started drawing," a computer programmer in Richard Powers's superb new novel surmises, "that we'd keep at it until the picture was done." At that point, God's creation would become obsolete, like that analog vinyl version of a favorite album you traded in for a digital 24-bit CD.

Despite the second commandment (and a similar prohibition in the Koran), creative people have been trying to simulate the visible world ever since the dawn of mankind: Cave paintings are the version 1.0 of today's Virtual Reality programs. Between Lascaux and Silicon Valley marches a parade of VR prototypes: the playhouse, representational paintings, realistic novels, panopticons, dioramas, planetariums, movies (especially the 3-D variety), even puppet shows and dollhouses. Each is an attempt to simulate reality, even to impose its reality on God's. No wonder the prohibition ranks so high on the Decalogue, even above those against theft and murder. And of course the oldest and wildest VR simulation is the one we are all hard-wired with: the ability to dream and imagine, the origin of all art, religion, and technology.

All this and more is at the heart of *Plowing the Dark*, Powers's seventh and perhaps greatest novel. In each of his novels, Powers tackles a specialized field of study — economics in his last one, genetics and cognitive neurology in earlier ones — and uses it as a vehicle for his career-long meditation on the nature of artistic creation. They can be described as intellectual thrillers because, despite their brainy subjects, there is a palpable sense of drama in each of them. In *Plowing the Dark* the subject is computer technology, specifically the development of Virtual Reality. The novel opens in 1989 — the year the term "Virtual Reality" was coined, according to Webster's — as a painter named Adie Klarpool is lured away from a boring job in commercial art by an old college friend named Stevie Spiegel to join him at a digital laboratory near Seattle. Spiegel is part of a team creating a VR room, and they need Adie's artistic touch to enhance their programming. She reluctantly joins them but is soon caught up in the limitless potential of this digital form of artistic creation.

The team decides first to create a simulation of Henri Rousseau's famous painting *The Dream*, and then move on to a walk-in, surround-sound version of Van Gogh's *Room at Arles*. Flushed with success and given the challenge to create something truly spectacular for public demonstration, they decide to shoot for the moon: Under the influence of Yeats's poem "Sailing to Byzantium," they decide to re-create the crown jewel of Byzantium, the Hagia Sophia cathedral. The narrative of their progress — the technical challenges, the artistic considerations, the interactions between the team members — is fascinating. Powers knows the field as thoroughly as if he had been working for Microsoft for the last ten years instead of writing some of the best novels in our literature. Like the late William Gaddis, he seems to know everything and knows how to make the most forbidding subjects come alive.

As in his other novels, Powers threads a second narrative through his primary one. Every third or fourth chapter concerns an American of Iranian heritage named Taimur Martin, who has traveled to Beirut in 1986 to teach English as a second language. He is abducted by a terrorist group and held hostage in a darkened room for the next four years. While Adie and her team revel in a room bursting with technological tools to aid their imaginations, Martin is stripped of all technology and reduced to his own resources. (Appropriately, Powers strips his usually lush language down to a spare, second-person style for the hostage story.) Martin's memory and imagination expand during his captivity, suggesting that technology is as much a crutch as a tool, but the experience is brutal and humiliating. His mind begins crashing as often as a poorly programmed computer.

As Adie and the others rush to meet their deadline, her doubts about the validity of their enterprise grow. "VR reinvents the terms of existence," Spiegel states. "It redefines what it means to be human. All those old dead-end ontological undergrad conundrums? They've now become questions of engineering." Adie's doubts about this brave new world are doubled by the world events breaking into her VR sanctuary: the massacre in Tiananmen Square, the fall of the Berlin Wall, the break-up of the Soviet Union, and the outbreak of the Persian Gulf War. Like the Alec Guinness character in *The Bridge on the River Kwai*, Adie suddenly realizes that the joy of creation has blinded her to the uses to which her creation will be put, and she takes appropriate action. (I won't spoil it for you.) At this point, a few pages from the end of the novel, Powers pulls off one of the most astonishing feats I've ever seen in literature. Adie's narrative and Martin's apparently unrelated one half a world away dovetail in such a daring, unpredictable, and emotionally powerful way that tears came to my eyes. Unbelievable.

I've only scratched the surface of Powers's deeply profound exploration of the interface between art and technology in our age. I haven't marked up and underlined a book this much since college: Nearly every page has stunning ideas that will force you to reevaluate everything you thought you knew about these subjects, and implications you never imagined. I'm tempted to end my review by simply emptying out my thesaurus with every synonym for "masterpiece," but you could do that just as easily. Just boot up your PC; there's bound to be a digital thesaurus somewhere in cyberspace.

Washington Post Book World, 4 June 2000

Caroline Preston

The Scrapbook of Frankie Pratt: A Novel in Pictures
Ecco, 2011

This is a charming, old-fashion novel about a smalltown girl with dreams of becoming a writer in the 1920s. She attends Vassar, moves to Greenwich Village, and begins working for magazines, then travels to Paris to revel in the avant-garde literary scene for a few years before returning home to care for her ailing mother. There she meets and marries her high-school flame, now a doctor, just as she publishes her first story. If that were all there is to this novel, even your grandmother would find it a little sappy.

What makes it a delightful novelty is its period detail. That phrase usually refers to carefully researched descriptions, but here the detail is visual rather than verbal. The novel takes the form of a scrapbook the protagonist receives as a high-school graduation present, and begins filling with memorabilia: magazine ads, photos, seed packets, ticket stubs, locks of hair, buttons, report cards, candy wrappers, maps, menus, book covers, etc., along with typed captions pasted on top of them. There are a few exchanges of dialogue, and as in an epistolary novel, letters, postcards, and telegrams move the plot along, but for the most part the illustrations speak for themselves.

The vintage memorabilia exerts oodles of period charm, and it is artistically appropriate that the novel is set in the '20s. As Frankie learns, it was a great period for literature and experimentation. Her bohemian Jewish roommate at Vassar introduces her to the writings of Pound, Eliot, and Stein, and she meets Edna St. Vincent Millay in the flesh. (Several striking photos of the poet are included, as well as examples of her poetry.) In Paris, Frankie goes to work for a literary magazine that publishes all the latest avant-garde writers, and even helps James Joyce with his corrections to *Finnegans Wake*.

Much of this is over Frankie's head, who is at heart a commercial writer, but it's not over Preston's head. In one sense, her novel is an homage to that innovative era, with hints of Ernest Hemingway's minimalism, Ezra Pound's imagism, and Max Ernst's Surrealist collage-novels. During this period, some were composing wordless woodcut novels, like the Belgian Frans Masereel and the American Lynd Ward (who was recently inducted into the Library of America), and others were writing early examples of what we now called graphic novels. *The Scrapbook of Frankie Pratt* is not as avant-garde as Leanne Shapton's recent novel in the form of an illustrated auction catalog, but the idea of "writing" a novel in the form of a scrapbook is a concept worthy of the experimental '20s.

Every picture tells a story, and one story here tells how Frankie reacts to media — the advertisements she pastes into her scrapbook, the books she reports on, the movies she sees — and how she wavers between embracing and resisting them. She wants to be the bobbed beauty in the Corona typewriter ad as much as she wants to be a published writer, and all the Gibson girls and Leyendecker lovelies that adorn her scrapbook represent an ideal that she is smart enough to realize doesn't exist. A playful sense of irony and self-awareness runs through the novel, as though Frankie is playing dolls with these images as she constructs her life story. One ad is captioned "My Idea of the Perfect Male . . . An Arrow Shirt man with a brain and a trust fund," but she doesn't really expect to find one outside the pages of *Collier's*. She reads F. Scott Fitzgerald's *This Side of Paradise*, but is disappointed to learn college boys don't really resemble the sophisticates in his novel. Paris is much grittier than the travel guides let on, and the novel ends in 1928, just before the financial crash brought everyone back to reality.

It's tempting to push this further and treat the entire scrapbook-novel as the fantasy life of a nerdy girl who never left Cornish, New Hampshire, or never left the job she gets in New York at *True Story* magazine, where she turns reader's conventional stories into publishable ones. She reveals the magazine's formula for "How to edit a 'true story': 1. make humdrum characters glamorous. . . . 2. add dramatic plot twist (musician killed in speakeasy brawl, pronounced dead by hero who is now famous doctor) 3. finish with improbable happy ending (doctor never stopped loving still beautiful heroine)." The suspicious fact that this describes the story Frankie assembles in her scrapbook encourages us to regard this novel as something more cunning and ironic than a cutely curated walk down Memory Lane.

But even if it is no more than that, *The Scrapbook of Frankie Pratt* is a retro delight. Meticulously assembled and designed by the author from her own huge collection of memorabilia, it turns scrapbooking into an art form. Fans of the Roaring '20s, of Nick Bantock, and of modernism will all find something of value in Caroline Preston's nostalgic ephemera.

Washington Post, 25 November 2011

Thomas Pynchon

Thomas Moore. *The Style of Connectedness: "Gravity's Rainbow" and Thomas Pynchon*
University of Missouri Press, 1987

Kathryn Hume. *Pynchon's Mythography: An Approach to "Gravity's Rainbow"*
Southern Illinois University Press, 1987

Charles Hohmann. *Thomas Pynchon's "Gravity's Rainbow": A Study of Its Conceptual Structure and of Rilke's Influence*
Peter Lang, 1986

Robert D. Newman. *Understanding Thomas Pynchon*
University of South Carolina Press, 1986

Harold Bloom, ed. *Thomas Pynchon: Modern Critical Views* and *Thomas Pynchon's "Gravity's Rainbow": Modern Critical Interpretations*
Chelsea House, 1986

Pynchon has received an unparalleled amount of criticism in the 15 years since the publication of *Gravity's Rainbow*: over 20 books now, dozens of chapters in other books, hundreds of articles, even his own journal (*Pynchon Notes*). I know of no other novelist who has generated as much criticism in as short a time, and keeping up with Pynchon criticism is beginning to verge on a full-time occupation. All the more important, then, to separate the wheat from the chaff — or, to put it more charitably, to separate those studies that make significant contributions to Pynchon criticism from those that do little more than cover well-covered ground.

Of the half-dozen books under review, only three offer something new. Newman's little handbook is addressed to undergraduates and general readers unfamiliar with Pynchon's work, and though he succeeds well enough at his task, there's little here "for us, old fans who've always been at the movies" (as we're called on the final page of *Gravity's Rainbow*). It does fill the gap left by Joseph Slade's pioneering book, long out of print, just as the two anthologies edited by Harold Bloom fill the gaps left by two earlier collections now out of print: Levine and Leverenz's *Mindful Pleasures* and Mendelson's *Pynchon: A Collection of Critical Essays*. Bloom reprints many articles from those two collections, as well as a few from Pearce's *Critical Essays on Thomas Pynchon*, so originality can hardly have been his intention. (And why is Craig Werner's essay printed in both of Bloom's volumes? it's not *that* good.) Bloom's brief introduction — also printed in both volumes — centers on a Gnostic reading of the Byron the Bulb episode from *GR*; not a word on *V.* or the stories, and only one word ("perfect") for *The Crying of Lot 49*. Consequently, his two collections can be recommended only to those who missed the earlier ones.

But on to the good stuff. Thomas Moore's *The Style of Connectedness* strikes me as one of the best books on Pynchon to date. Longer than any previous study of *GR*, it not only explicates the encyclopedic range of background materials in the novel but demonstrates their metaphoric properties and stylistic functions. Pynchon's achievement, Moore argues, is to have found the metaphoric potentials inherent in such disparate fields as quantum physics, Weberian sociology, and film technology, and to have linked them in the manner of the best metaphysical poets. As with Hohmann's book (below), much of this background material has been covered before, but never with such thoroughness or with such sensitivity to the poetic uses to which Pynchon puts this material. Though obviously writing for the Pynchon scholar, Moore also addresses those who remain unconvinced of Pynchon's historical importance. The well-known objections to *GR* are dealt with in a gracious, learned manner that should win over the most recalcitrant, and even those who champion Pynchon may learn that they have been misreading him. Moore's Pynchon is a tender, humanistic writer: "He is possessed of a shy, pained tenderness for human vulnerability, frailty, need — for whatever chances for love and connection still hide between the impersonal frames, the vast design of things." Too many of Pynchon's "dark" critics (as Moore calls them) have separated Pynchon's head from his heart and have elevated him to a prophet of nihilism, death, and entropy. Between zero and one, these critics choose zero, but Moore examines several facets of Pynchon's One ("pan-psychic sentience, living stones, negentropy, I-Thou relation, Earth Goddess, psychoid field, synchronistic connectedness, Tao") to suggest that Pynchon's rainbow is a sign of hope and possibility, not simple a rocket's destructive trajectory.

Kathryn Hume also embraces Pynchon's talismanic word "kindness" and suggests Pynchon is rewriting mythology, salvaging whatever workable elements remain from the traditional concept of the hero and revising them into a new heroic myth: "Instead of reintegrating into society, the new style of hero integrates into chaos, more or less by allowing the ego to disintegrate. He or she will live with openended reality and with uncertainty." The new myth applies to readers as well, Hume demonstrates, who learn through repeated readings to live with the open-ended reality and uncertainties of Pynchon's labyrinthine text. She joins Moore in finding in *GR* "solutions to our problems" rather than apocalyptic warnings, a new mythology rather than the death rattle of the old.

Hohmann's book is a dissertation submitted to the University of Zurich and (like Hume's book, to a lesser extent) has all the characteristics of "dissertation style": surveys of criticism for each new topic, three or four footnotes to the page, and a dry, humorless style. But his exhaustive thoroughness gives a definitive ring to his discussions of the standard themes of *GR*, and nowhere more so than in the last third of his book, a study of Rilke's presence in Pynchon's novel. No previous critic has given sufficient space to this important subject, and none need do it again. Hohmann's book is rich in textual details, with countless citations from lines not usually quoted, giving an air of freshness even to well-trod ground. The cost of this book [$48.05, $96 today] is prohibitive, but future Pynchon critics should read it if only to see what need not ever be covered again.

Review of Contemporary Fiction, Summer 1988

□□□□□□□

David Seed. *The Fictional Labyrinths of Thomas Pynchon*
University of Iowa Press, 1988

Steven Weisenburger. *A "Gravity's Rainbow" Companion*
University of Georgia Press, 1988

During the last six or seven years, Seed and Weisenburger have been among the most frequent contributors to *Pynchon Notes*, an erratically published but invaluable forum for primary research. Both have now published their finds in book form, riding the crest of a new wave of Pynchon criticism (a half-dozen books in the last two years). Both are interested in facts: what's the source for this particular datum; what's the significance of this particular allusion; what was Pynchon reading at certain stages of composition? Such documentary criticism is not in fashion in many academic quarters these days, yet when the fashions change (as they will), these books will remain valuable precisely because of their density of detail and specificity of source material.

Seed surveys all of Pynchon's work in chronological order, both isolating unique features and sources for each book and searching for recurrent obsessions and concerns, and constructing Pynchon's voice from these continuities. Seed even analyzes Pynchon's dozen or so blurbs to refine further the reclusive novelist's aesthetics and somehow gained permission to reprint an invaluable letter from Pynchon to a graduate student on his research methods. Seed anchors each book in the intellectual currents of its time, stressing how each book is a response to specific socio-political tensions in the air at the time Pynchon was writing — a fact lost on less historically-minded critics and one that underscores Pynchon's sincere engagement with such issues. This is the best overview of Pynchon's oeuvre to date.

Weisenburger's *Companion* is a line-by-line annotation of *Gravity's Rainbow* and is indeed, as he points out, "eight resources in one: a source study, encyclopedia, handbook, motif index, dictionary, explicator, gazetteer, and list of textual errors." Two previous attempts have been made at such a book — Kihm Winship's unpublished index-guide, and a book by Douglas Fowler that many Pynchon critics wish had never been published — but Weisenburger's is easily the most comprehensive, authoritative, and reliable study yet on Pynchon's masterwork. He shows how "marginal, footnoted material is transmuted into fictional reference and event" and how "many of the novel's episodes draw their backgrounds, references, even details of plotting from a central source text." There are concise plot summaries for each section, precise chronologies (derived from Pynchon's own historically precise and symbolically provocative chronology), and an index that doubles as an index to the novel itself. Of the dozen or so books now available on *Gravity's Rainbow*, this is the only one that is truly indispensable, a stunning piece of scholarship on one of the greatest novels of our time.

Review of Contemporary Fiction, Fall 1988

□ □ □ □ □ □ □

Thomas Pynchon. *Vineland*

Little, Brown, 1990

The most remarkable thing about Pynchon's new novel is its brilliant and often hilarious use of the vernacular, its attention to the ways American speech has changed since the1960s. It goes beyond Pynchon's close familiarity with current slang — amazing enough for a man in his fifties — and embraces the new metaphors, tropes, and bases for allusions that have come into play, alterations of syntax, pronunciation, all the permutations that have marked recent changes in the American vernacular. So great are these changes, and so accurate is Pynchon's ear for them, that the novel will defy translation, even if accompanied by a battalion of footnotes. (British reviewers have already complained of its linguistic difficulties for non-Americans.) Pynchon makes other contemporary masters of the vernacular — especially the younger minimalists — sound stodgy and out-of-date in comparison.

This has little to do with simply registering "how people really talk," for Pynchon's dialogue is a little too clever, too witty for verisimilitude — closer to the snappy dialogue of the 1940s movies he seems to like. Instead, it's artificial in the best sense (as in *art*) because it echoes the culture his characters are immersed in, a world of junk food, television, rock music, B movies, sports, recreational drugs and technology, and so on. For example, the narrator will speak of putting a situation on "Pause" — which will mean nothing to those who don't own a VCR — or a character will speak of wanting to "beam up" out of a situation — which will mean nothing to those unfamiliar with *Star Trek*. Where Pynchon in his earlier works would allude to European history, literature, opera, and so on, his references in *Vineland* are to TV shows, video games, cartoon characters, rock lyrics — the majority of which will be lost on anyone over 40 and certainly on anyone who hasn't been paying attention to low culture. It goes beyond the minimalist habit of dropping brand names and popular trivia in an otherwise old-fashioned fictional universe; Pynchon registers a new mode of perception, a new weltanschauung, no less.

Pynchon's hippies are in a direct line with the Beats, and in this regard *Vineland* should remind the reader of Pynchon's roots in Beat literature — roots he openly acknowledges in his introduction to *Slow Learner* but that have been ignored by his legion of commentators. Reading *Vineland* is more akin to reading Kerouac than to any of the others Pynchon is usually associated with — Coover, DeLillo, Gaddis, McElroy — for Pynchon shares with Kerouac an enthusiastic love for spoken language, popular culture, populist concerns, and an unabashed sentimentality for what America might once have been. *Vineland* deserves to be read and savored by anyone interested in the glowing junkyard American language and culture have become.

Review of Contemporary Fiction, Summer 1990

□ □ □ □ □ □ □

Thomas Pynchon. *Against the Day*

Penguin Press, 2006

News of a new Pynchon novel has the same effect on the literati that an unscheduled return of Halley's comet would on astronomers. The Internet started humming with the news last June, and after five interminable months, the mammoth volume has arrived and is everything a Pynchon fan could hope for. It's his longest novel, his most international in scope — from the mountains of Colorado to the deserts of Inner Asia — and is perhaps his funniest.

All of Pynchon's signature moves are here: as early as page 15, someone picks up a ukulele and sings a silly song; documentary realism morphs into hallucination without warning; loud, tasteless clothing is worn with aplomb; a wide variety of drugs and stimulants are consumed, matched by a wide variety of sex acts, including bestiality (which results in the most hilarious scene in the novel); and Pynchon's old leftist, countercultural ideals shine on. There's vast erudition and technical savvy on display, mostly to do with math. The novel is spooked by the occult, enchanted with fairy tales and myth. And the writing is spectacular, orchestral, in registers ranging from magniloquent set-pieces to sass and puns. If there are any remaining doubts that Pynchon is the greatest novelist alive, *Against the Day* should dispel them.

The plot is too wonderfully complex to summarize; suffice it to say the novel occupies about 30 years from 1893 to the 1920s, and chiefly concerns the adventures of three brothers (a stock fairy-tale motif) and their efforts to avenge the death of their father, a pro-union engineer named Webb Traverse who was killed by agents of the plutocracy that hijacked the U.S. after the Civil War. (A good warm-up exercise is the "Robber Barons and Rebels" chapter in Howard Zinn's *People's History of the United States*; Pynchon shares Zinn's populist viewpoint.) A related storyline involves a photographer/inventor and his red-haired daughter Dahlia, who, like the brothers, spends a lot of time in Europe during the tumultuous days before the First World War. And hovering above them all are "The Chums of Chance," the plucky crew of the airship *Inconvenience* and the heroes of a series of boys' adventure novels.

The presiding spirits over this novel are the Marx brothers — humorless Karl as well as Groucho and the boys. Traverse teaches his sons that "Labor produces all wealth. Wealth belongs to the producer thereof" (quoting from his union card), and parts of the novel dramatize the strikes and acts of "anarchy" from Colorado mineworkers in reaction to the inhuman treatment they received at the hands of greedy tycoons, who wouldn't pay a living wage (much less propose profit-sharing schemes) to those who made their obscene wealth possible. But Pynchon doesn't let this become a dour proletarian tract because of his own anarchist bent for doing in fiction what the Marx Brothers did on film. (*Duck Soup* is name-checked early on, and a young Groucho makes a cameo appearance under his real name.) Hence the silly songs, surrealistic pratfalls, and Pynchon's tendency to undercut ominous pronouncements with wisecracks.

Though he covers the major events of his chosen period in well-researched detail — world politics, technological advances, sociological shifts, artistic experiments — Pynchon is mostly concerned with how decent people of any era cope under repressive regimes, be they political, economic, or religious. After drifting through Europe, the Traverse brothers and many other characters develop alternative families, communities, sexual arrangements, and envision "the replacement of governments by other, more practical arrangements, . . . working across national boundaries." A countercultural, even utopian alternative is imagined, and the novel ends hopefully on that note, though whether such an alternative could exist outside the pages of a book is doubtful. "Fine idea while the opium supply lasts," a female character notes near the end, "but sooner or later plain personal old meanness gets in the way." That's what radical novels like his are for, Pynchon implies: to provide the kind of world our leaders would never allow, if only to inhabit for the week or two it takes to read this endlessly inventive novel.

Pynchon fans will accept this early Christmas gift from the author with gratitude, but I'm not so sure about mainstream readers. While *Against the Day* isn't as difficult as some of Pynchon's novels, its multiple storylines test the memory, and some folks may be scared off by the heady discussions of vectors, Brownian movements, zeta functions, and so forth, not to mention the words and phrases from a dozen languages scattered throughout. Politically, this is blue-state fiction: I doubt it will play well in Bush country. (*The Chums of Chance and the Evil Halfwit* is the title of one of the boy balloonists' novels set in "Our Nation's Capital.") "Capitalist Christer Republicans" are a recurring target of contempt, and bourgeois values exposed as essentially totalitarian. As in his last historical novel, *Mason & Dixon*, Pynchon draws parallels between the past and present — there's a brilliant evocation of the 9/11 attack on Manhattan, where Pynchon lives — and it's clear the worldly author doesn't see much difference between the corruptions of the late Gilded Age and our own era.

Not for everybody, perhaps, but those who climb aboard Pynchon's airship will have the ride of their lives. History lesson, mystical quest, utopian dream, experimental metafiction, Marxist melodrama, Marxian comedy — *Against the Day* is all of these things and more.

Washington Post Book World, 19 November 2006

□ □ □ □ □ □ □

Robert E. Kohn. *New Close Readings of* The Crying of Lot 49

Brentwood, MO: Mira Digital Publishing, 2011

Writing in 1987, 21 years after the publication of Thomas Pynchon's second novel, critic Alan Wilde prematurely claimed, "*The Crying of Lot 49* has been combed over thoroughly and well for all its possible meanings." Twenty-five years later, further meanings are still be teased out of Pynchon's tangled tale, supporting Frank Kermode's earlier claim that *Lot 49* "is loaded with hidden meanings, and although there will be a consensus as to certain of these, there is no suggestion that the process of interpretation need ever cease." Both remarks are quoted by Robert E. Kohn in his new book (on pp. 2 and 25, respectively), an attempt to uncover more of those "hidden meanings."

Trained as an economist, Kohn's method is to propose a model, such as the assumption a certain book influenced Pynchon, run a simulation to find words and concepts common to both texts, and then see if the model implies or yields "facts capable of being observed," as economist Milton Friedman put it in *Essays in Positive Economics*, which Kohn cites. He goes on to quote Friedman's blithe admission, "Truly important and significant hypotheses will be found to have 'assumptions' that are wildly inaccurate descriptive recommendations of reality, and, in general, the more significant the theory, the more unrealistic the assumptions." Emboldened by this model and by the freedom Roland Barthes granted to readers upon announcing the death of the author (quoted on p. 4), Kohn runs a number of simulations on Pynchon's novel, acknowledging that he may be wrong in some of his assumptions, but grateful nonetheless that those assumptions have "given me insights into aspects of the novel that I wouldn't have had otherwise."

So: in chapter 1, he acts on the assumption that Pynchon read E. M. Forster's *Aspects of the Novel* prior to writing *Lot 49* — a safe assumption, given its popularity at the time — then proposes as a "corollary hypothesis" that "the fact that Forster's book was made possible by 'a bequest in [William Clark's] will to Trinity College" suggests that Pynchon was thereby inspired to make the protagonist of his novel the executor of a will. If this strikes you as probable, or at least a possibility that cannot be ruled out with 100 percent certainty, then you'll find Kohn's book a goldmine of such nuggets. If, on the other hand, you consider that a meaningless coincidence, and probably the furthest thing from Pynchon's mind when he decided to make Oedipa Maas an executrix, then you'll probably throw the book at the wall before finishing it.

The book would have been more suitably titled *New Intertextual Readings of* The Crying of Lot 49, for each chapter pairs Pynchon's novel with a possible influence: *Aspects of the Novel* in chapter 1, Henry Adams and J. R. Pierce in chapter 2, followed by chapters on Rachel Carson; Loren Eiseley and Charles Darwin; various authors on plate tectonics; *The Tibetan Book of the Dead*; the *Diagnostic and Statistical Manual of Mental Disorders*; critics Roland Barthes, Paul Virilio, and F. R. Leavis; and two tangentially related essays on Pynchon's *Against the Day* and *Inherent Vice*. Nearly all of these are valid pairings, yielding occasional insights and useful suggestions. But too many of Kohn's observations are along the lines of his assumption that Pynchon named his Jacobean scholar Emory Bortz after W. Y. Evans-Wentz, who translated the edition of *The Tibetan Book of the Dead* Pynchon may have read, for "The names, Emory and Evans, both begin with an E and have five letters. Bortz and Wentz both end with tz and have five letters. . . . To seal the connection between Evans-Wentz and Emory Bortz, the latter is married to a 'wife named Grace' (*Crying* 148); Evans-Wentz's edition of *The Tibetan Book of the Dead* instructs the deceased, upon 'enter[ing] into the womb' to 'emit thy gift-waves [of grace, or good-will] upon the womb which thou art entering, [transforming it thereby] into a celestial mansion' (191, square brackets in the original). In the index, they are listed under 'Grace-Waves' (245), rather than 'gift-waves.'"

Like Horatio talking Hamlet down from one of his wild speculations, I want to tell Kohn, "'Twere to consider too curiously to consider so." Verbal and thematic similarities between books are sometimes merely that, similarities, and many of Kohn's examples look like what a character in *Gravity's Rainbow*, using electrical imagery, calls "Parallel, not series." However, I grant there are precedents for such readings elsewhere in Pynchon criticism, as well as in older, richly suggestive texts like *Finnegans Wake* and the Bible. (Spend an afternoon with the *Zohar* to see some truly wacky Rube Goldberg overinterpretation.) Since *The Crying of Lot 49* is a parable about literary analysis and interpretation, one that is deliberately open-ended — the only mystery the reader solves at the end is the meaning of the novel's odd title — I suppose it would be arrogant to reject such an approach.

Besides, Kohn has had his fill of rejections: the book begins with a 44-page introduction in which he records the negative, often condescending responses these chapters received when submitted to journal editors, which makes for some embarrassing reading. (Kohn quotes at length the kind of rejection letters most critics hide in a drawer.) They have been somewhat revised with those objections in mind, but Kohn stuck to his guns and self-published the book partly to "enjoy the freedom of saying what I wanted to say." It's an amateurish book, but in the best, oldest sense of the word: one written by someone who loves the subject and wants to share his discoveries with others. This is not the first book a student new to *The Crying of Lot 49* should read, but anyone fascinated by that brilliant novel, and willing to sort the wheat from the chaff, will find something of interest here.

Style, Summer 2012. When asked to review this book, I tried to disqualify myself by pointing out that I'm mentioned in it: on p.41 Kohn records a conversation I had with him in May 2011 while doing research at the Gaddis archives at Washington University in his hometown of St. Louis. Over dinner, he told me about his book and of his plans to self-publish it. But *Style*'s editor thought that made me the perfect person to review it! Much to my surprise, Kohn liked my dismissive review. He died in 2014 at the age of 86.

□ □ □ □ □ □ □

Luc Herman and Steven Weisenburger.
"Gravity's Rainbow," Domination, and Freedom

University of Georgia Press, 2013

I've been reading Pynchon criticism since the 1970s, and this is hands down one of the best books on him. The authors successfully show that the materials in Pynchon's war novel "take on a concrete and vivid existence if read in the context with . . . persistent questions of political life during the years Pynchon was writing *Gravity's Rainbow*," such as books by Fromm, Marcuse, Brown, Fanon, and others, along with the underground press, FBI surveillance reports, and Supreme Court decisions. This background is necessary "to tease the politics out of scenes in *Gravity's Rainbow* that may wrongly seem, forty years after their writing, to be merely farcical." The authors' deep research into these matters shines new light on many dark corners of this novel (and in passing on his other works), and offers new reading strategies for navigating Pynchon's Zone. If your interest in *GR* extends beyond its surface entertainment value (which is considerable, and enough for some folks), this book is required reading.

Amazon.com, 26 July 2015

Raymond Queneau

Stories and Remarks. Translated by Marc Lowenthal
University of Nebraska Press, 2000

Raymond Queneau is sort of the French equivalent of Jorge Luis Borges — though he never caught on in this country as Borges did — and *Stories and Remarks* is sort of his *Ficciones*. The two writers shared a wide erudition, an interest in philosophical concepts, and a willingness to experiment with form. But the short story was Borges's preferred genre, while Queneau's was the novel. (First-time readers of Queneau should consequently start with one of those, like the sublime *Saint Glinglin*.) Queneau's short fiction is lighter in tone than Borges's, and if finally not as historically important as the Argentine's, this book is a welcome addition to the Frenchman's translated output.

There's certainly no lack of diversity here: of the 21 pieces included, only a few are traditional short stories. There are pseudo-essays on animal languages, tranquilizers, and the aerodynamics of addition; there are linguistic experiments that look back to Queneau's involvement with the Surrealists and look forward to his membership in Oulipo; his only play is here, as are the beginnings of two abandoned novels (one a pastiche of *Alice in Wonderland*). There are talking dogs in two stories, and a talking horse in another. There are puns a-plenty, and Marc Lowenthal is to be congratulated for his smooth translations (and his copious endnotes). Michel Leiris's preface to the original French edition (*Contes et Propos*) is also included.

One of the shortest pieces is Queneau's playful preface to Émile Bauwen's *Book of Cocktails*, and this book is like a fizzy cocktail made up of many strange liquors, saying "Drink Me."

Rain Taxi, Winter 2000–2001

Pascal Quignard

Albucius. Translated by Bruce Boone
Lapis Press, 1993

The French original of this book was reviewed in our Spring 1991 issue, where John Taylor called "this compelling novel-essay-biography" of the Roman rhetorician Gaius Albucius Silus (69 BC–10 AD) a tour de force of historical fiction, less like Robert Graves's Roman novels than the works of such writers as Suetonius or Diogenes Laërtius. The novel has now been issued in an English translation with one of the most lavish designs imaginable. The book is large (8 x 11), printed on heavy paper, and illustrated on the jacket, boards, and endpapers with decadent Roman pedophilic photographs. Pope has a line somewhere warning poets against trying to achieve a "beauty that shocks," but this shockingly beautiful book is the perfect marriage of content and design. Those who enjoyed Quignard's *Salon in Württemberg* (Grove Weidenfeld, 1991) or who dote on Baron Corvo's novels will enjoy this one, along with all lovers of beautiful books, especially those who specialize in what rare-book dealers call "curiosa."

Review of Contemporary Fiction, Summer 1993

Marie Redonnet

Nevermore. Translated by Jordan Stump
University of Nebraska Press, 1996

I don't know if *Twin Peaks* was televised in France, but Marie Redonnet's *Nevermore* reads like a French attempt at similarly kinky drama. It's a detective novel of sorts, set on the U.S. West Coast, but with no attempt at verisimilitude: The coastal city of San Rosa has a volcano nearby, features a *buvette* and a *pissotiere*, and uses francs for currency. As with the TV show, the setting is contemporary but has an oddly retro atmosphere. The characters' names are not quite American (Drove Wrangler, Stive Lenz), and in fact they are types rather than characters, as in most procedurals. The plot concerns various power plays in the town, tied in with mysterious goings-on at the nearby Fuchs Circus. Everyone has a shadowy past, and during the second half of the novel there are new murders every ten pages, an erupting volcano, a burning circus, a collapsing building — an excess of climaxes, as though a season's worth of TV episodes were compressed into one extravaganza (like the final episode of *Twin Peaks*, in fact).

Redonnet obviously knows what she's doing: Her fantasy of our West Coast is just that, not the result of ignorance. But for some reason the novel didn't work for me; despite its quirks, *Nevermore* still reads too much like your average detective novel, a genre that doesn't appeal to me. Worse, Redonnet is infected with Hemingway's Disease: the delusion that short, see-Spot-run sentences constitute fine writing, that adjectives and adverbs are crutches only weak writers use, that metaphors are for sissies, and that it's useful to repeat characters' full names in every sentence. *Nevermore* is the fifth of Redonnet's short novels to appear in English translation in the last few years, most (like this one) smoothly done by University of Nebraska professor Jordan Stump.

Washington Post, 22 December 1996

Julián Ríos

Loves That Bind. Translated by Edith Grossman
Knopf, 1998

Pity the woman who loves a bibliophile: In addition to competing with former girlfriends or wives, she is up against all the heroines of literature. A man who loves novels often loves their leading ladies, and may even be foolish enough to choose a woman because she reminds him of a literary character or at least a metaphor ("eyes like drenched violets"). A man who confuses his love of books with his love of women is asking for trouble; on the other hand, it can beget a wonderful book like *Loves That Bind*.

Spanish writer Julián Ríos obviously loves both books and women passionately, and in his third novel to be published in English has found the perfect form to express literary love. Having been left by his jealous girlfriend, Babelle, a painter named Emil Alia decides to search for her throughout London, pausing to write her 26 confessional letters about the previous women in his life, in alphabetical order. Though none of them is named, each resembles a female character from modern literature, challenging the reader to guess her identity. Assisting the game reader is Emil's adoption of the style and substance of the writers who created these figures. The first chapter is easy: A is for Albertine, the bisexual flirt of Proust's *In Search of Lost Time*. Some are equally easy to identify — D is for Daisy (*The Great Gatsby*), L is for Lolita, and O is for Woolf's Orlando (the source of the ocular metaphor above) — while others are not so easy. Unless you've read Céline's *London Bridge*, Arno Schmidt's *Lake Scenery with Pocahontas*, and Malcolm Lowry's *Under the Volcano*, you won't be able to recognize the titular heroines of chapters V, P, and Y, respectively.

I'm proud to say I was able to identify all but six of the 26 characters, though I had to spend an hour in a bookstore confirming some hunches. Ríos usually drops hints to the titles of the books he's parodying: For example, in the chapter for X, I had no idea who the referent could be until he used the phrase "the blue of noon in his demonic eyes." I remembered that the French writer Georges Bataille had written a novel called *Blue of Noon* (1957), and when I consulted it, there she was: Xenie. When *Loves That Bind* was first published in Spain in 1995, Ríos's publisher sponsored a competition to see how many readers could identify all 26 heroines. Only four readers got them all.

Loves That Bind is more than a literary version of Trivial Pursuit, however.

Ríos is exploring the varieties of amorous experience in modern literature. These range from the vampiric (G is for Grace Brissenden, from James's *The Sacred Fount*) to the pedophilic (*Lolita* and *London Bridge*) to the masochistic (W is for Wanda, from Sacher-Masoch's *Venus in Furs*, the only non-20th-century work I could identify). In between are the more common stages of love affairs, from unrequited love (*The Great Gatsby*) and deception (F is for Florence, from Ford's *The Good Soldier*) to bemusement (S is for Sally Bowles, from Isherwood's *Goodbye to Berlin*) to spirited fun (Z is for — who else? — Queneau's *Zazie in the Metro*). Even if you don't have much of a literary background, you will be fascinated by this gallery of women and the ways they pursue their sense of the erotic.

But it is as a literary tour de force that most readers will be entranced by this book-length love letter to modern literature. Alphabetically structured works of fiction have appeared from time to time — Walter Abish's *Alphabetical Africa*, Karen Elizabeth Gordon's *The Red Shoes*, Gilbert Sorrentino's *Splendide-Hôtel* — but rarely with such delightful results.[9] A cunning linguist, Ríos puns in several tongues in the manner of his forbears — Lewis Carroll, Nabokov, Schmidt, and above all the Joyce of *Finnegans Wake* — and indulges in all kinds of wordplay, imaginatively re-created in Edith Grossman's translation.

For example, the Proustian narrator of the first chapter tells Albertine "of my aversion to the sophisms of sapphism. But she could also adopt an angelic air (was the seraphic pose easier for her than the sapphic?)." The Spanish subtitle for the book is *Belles Lettres*, and Ríos celebrates every meaning of the phrase: These are beautiful letters about the belles of modern belles lettres. It was Emil's love of letters that drove Babelle away, not any actual indiscretions: The loves that bind him are bound in books. Does he eventually find her? Does she read these letters? You'll want to know.

Emil and Babelle are also the immensely appealing protagonists of Ríos's two previous novels: *Larva* appeared here in 1990, and *Poundemonium* in 1997. Both are stunning achievements, albeit challenging to read because of their Joycean density of language, and should have established Ríos here as the world-class belletrist he clearly is. The more accessible *Loves That Bind* should be the one to win for Ríos the large audience he so richly deserves. It's charming, clever, often profound, and frequently moving. I live for novels like this one.

Whom haven't I named? B is for Bonadea (Robert Musil's *The Man without Qualities*), H for Hermine (Hermann Hesse's *Steppenwolf*), J for Julia

9 I have a longer list of such works in the first volume of my alt-novel history (183n69), but I thoughtlessly forgot to add *Loves That Bind*. [2016 note.]

(Jean Rhys's *After Leaving Mr. Mackenzie*), M for Molly (Joyce's *Ulysses*), N for Nadja (André Breton), Q for Quentin (Caddy's daughter in William Faulkner's *The Sound and the Fury*), and R for Robin (Djuna Barnes's *Nightwood*). Readers who can identify the six remaining heroines are urged to send me their own belles lettres in care of *Book World*.

Washington Post Book World, 24 May 1998, 3, 14. No one responded to that invitation. I now regret identifying so many of the heroines — I felt I was helping the reader out, not showing off — but as long as I did, here are the remaining six, courtesy Ríos himself: Celia is from Beckett's *Murphy*; Ellen from Dos Passos's *Manhattan Transfer*; Iku-Ko from Tanizaki's *The Key*; Klara from Kafka's *Amerika*; and Tristana from the novel and film of the same name by Benito Pérez Galdós (1892) and Luis Buñuel (1970).

Raymond Roussel

How I Wrote Certain of My Books. Edited by Trevor Winkfield.
Translated by the editor, John Ashbery, Harry Mathews, and others
Exact Change, 1995

You need to know the work of Raymond Roussel (1877–1933) to make sense not only of many contemporary French writers — for this reason, Leon Roudiez's survey *French Fiction Revisited* begins with a chapter on Roussel before jumping ahead to Duras, Robbe-Grillet, *et Cie* — but also contemporary novelists like Harry Mathews and Gilbert Sorrentino, and poets like John Ashbery and Kenneth Koch. This new anthology from Exact Change — not to be confused with the book of the same name published by SUN in 1977 — is an ideal Roussel reader. It opens with an introduction by Ashbery (a longtime Roussel scholar), which is followed by Roussel's eye-opening title essay, and then selections from his major works: the novels *Impressions of Africa* and *Locus Solus*; the play *The Dust of Suns*; the long poem *New Impressions of Africa*; and all the surviving fragments of his unfinished novel, *Documents to Serve as an Outline*. Also included are the 59 drawings Roussel commissioned to pad out *New Impressions of Africa* — one look at them and you'll understand how Sorrentino's *Under the Shadow* works — and an annotated bibliography by the editor that doesn't mince words. (Rayner Heppenstall's critical study of Roussel is described as a "Simpering apologia, not worth the paper it's printed on.")

Roussel's writings themselves are exotic and quirky. In his lifetime they attracted Dadaists and Surrealists — though Roussel was unaware of their aesthetics — and there's a superficial resemblance between some of them and the novels of Ronald Firbank written at the same time, but they more closely resemble the works of his followers, like Mathews's early novels, Kenneth Koch's novel *The Red Robins* and his narrative poems, and Sorrentino's recent novels. In France, the *nouveaux romanciers* adapted his tendency to give long, detailed descriptions of inanimate objects and to allow the imaginative manipulation of language to generate form and content, a practice later followed by the Oulipo school. For his influence alone Roussel deserves to be read, and this nicely designed anthology is the perfect introduction to his work.

Review of Contemporary Fiction, Summer 1996

Severo Sarduy

Maitreya. Translated by Suzanne Jill Levine
Ediciones del Norte, 1987

Roberto González Echevarría. *La Ruta de Severo Sarduy*
Norte, 1987

Severo Sarduy is the most daring and innovative of the so-called Boom writers — García Márquez, Fuentes, Vargas Llosa, et al. — but has never won the large audience these writers command. *Maitreya*, his fourth novel (originally published in 1978), guarantees to continue both his high reputation and low readership. His novels are more difficult to read than those of his compatriots and require not only a familarity with recent history and French critical thought, but an ability to decode his outlandish metaphoric structures. His characters are not the typical cast of dictators, whores, and matriarchs of Latin American fiction, but an outrageous group of drag queens, dwarfs, motorcyclists, Tibetan monks, dealers, and assorted perverts — most weighed down by junk jewelry and *too* much makeup, frequently drugged with cocaine, and hanging out in louche bars or disreputable cabarets. Reading a Sarduy novel is akin to trying to develop a Structuralist reading of history from a trunk of costume jewelry, tacky religious relics, and the creepy merchandise of an S&M sex shop.

Sarduy's best-known novel, *Cobra* (English translation 1975, also by the gifted Suzanne Jill Levine), began in the West (Paris, Tangier) and ended in the East (India, Tibet). *Maitreya*, which González Echevarría describes in his study as a post-Structuralist companion to the Structuralist *Cobra*, reverses the route, beginning in Tibet and moving west to Cuba, Miami, and New York, before ending in Iran. The novel is divided into two halves, with a great deal of doubling uniting the two halves and exemplifying its Buddhist premise: "reality as an empty place, a mirage of appearances reduced to the myth of its interchangeable representations." While part one concerns the unsuccessful revolt of Tibetans against their Chinese oppressors in 1959 — and their flight to Ceylon — part two begins with the Cuban Revolution of 1959 and the flight to Miami of certain segments of Cuban society. The Leng sisters of part one, protecting the new-born incarnation of the Buddha, have as their counterparts in part two the "Massive Misses": Lady Divine and Lady Tremendous, who wind up singing Wagnerian arias in a Cuban cabaret in New York City run by a cook named Luis Leng, who may be the same incarnation of the

Buddha in part one. ("Maitreya" is the title of the future Buddha.) But Leng is also a character out of José Lezama Lima's novel *Paradiso*, and the death of the Master that opens *Maitreya* is Sarduy's homage to the death of Lezama in 1976. Thus the novel is about the loss of origins — the Buddhists' loss of Tibet, the loss of pre-Revolutionary Cuba, and the loss of the grandmaster of Cuban literature (Lezama edited the influential magazine *Orígenes*) — which makes the subsequent wanderings of Sarduy's weird cast of characters a kind of campy diaspora, awaiting the future Buddha in gay bars.

It is difficult to describe this complex, often baffling novel, and those who read Spanish would be better served by Roberto González Echevarría's study, which offers not only an informative analysis of *Maitreya* but a biographical introduction, a discussion of Sarduy's association with the Tel Quel group, and excellent readings of all of Sarduy's inimitable novels. Sarduy will never join García Márquez on the best-seller list, but as González points out, Sarduy is the "secret source" for much that is admirable in García Márquez and other Boom writers.

Review of Contemporary Fiction, Summer 1989. Six years later, I was able to publish a one-volume edition of *Cobra* and *Maitreya*, with a whip-smart introduction by James McCourt and one of the best covers I ever designed.

□□□□□□□

From Cuba with a Song. Translated by Suzanne Jill Levine
Sun & Moon, 1994

Severo Sarduy (1937–93) put the swish in the Boom explosion of Latin American literature in the '60s and '70s with his gloriously baroque fictions filled with transvestites and bizarre *mise-en-scènes*. His first major novel, *From Cuba with a Song*, has just been reissued by Sun & Moon. Previously available in English only as the last third of an anthology called *Triple Cross* (1972), this is the first separate appearance of this campy parody of Cuban history. Suzanne Jill Levine has revised her earlier translation, which is the subject of an entertaining chapter in her book *The Subversive Scribe* (1991).

Review of Contemporary Fiction, Fall 1994

□□□□□□□

Christ on the Rue Jacob. Translated by Suzanne Jill Levine and Carol Meier
Mercury House, 1995

This has been a good year for the late Cuban writer: earlier this year his principal novels were reprinted (*From Cuba with a Song, Cobra, Maitreya*), and now this autobiographical collection of his essays, perhaps his most personal and accessible work. An earlier collection of his essays was called *Written on a Body*, and the first part of the new book describes marks literally inscribed on Sarduy's body — scars, cuts, a wart, the navel (a birth scar) — and describes their occurrences as "epiphanies." Other essays are beautifully written (and beautifully translated) meditations on places (Benares, Tangier, Paris) and on people (Barthes, Calvino, Lezama Lima, Emir Rodríguez Monegal). Elsewhere he discusses why he paints, his struggles with alcoholism (specifically "beeromania"), and the loss of many friends to AIDS, the scourge from which he himself died in 1993. Though not his last book (he published two more as-yet-untranslated novels), *Christ on the Rue Jacob* is a moving farewell to the world and people Sarduy loved; for readers new to his work — some of which can be dauntingly difficult — this farewell is a warm introduction.

Review of Contemporary Fiction, Fall 1995

Arno Schmidt

Robert Weninger. *Framing a Novelist: Arno Schmidt Criticism 1970–1994*
Camden House, 1995

In Germany, critical activity on Arno Schmidt (1914–79) has been running at industrial levels for several decades now, comparable to the Anglo-American Joyce industry, and for much the same reason: Schmidt is often called the German Joyce because of the lexical density, range of reference, and experimentation in his works, and he has attracted a core following that supports a good deal of publication. Schmidt's achievement, if not as great as Joyce's, is certainly more prodigious: 20 novels and novellas, dozens of short stories, two literary biographies, nearly two dozen translations of authors ranging from James Fenimore Cooper and Wilkie Collins to William Faulkner and mystery writer Stanley Ellin, and six volumes of some of the liveliest and most innovative literary criticism I've ever read (which exists in translation only in manuscript at this time). *Caveat lector*: these remarks are hardly impartial, for I have been Schmidt's American editor [*Collected Early Fiction*, 4 vols.] and consider him to be the best thing to come out of Germany since Christa Päffgen changed her name to Nico.

While Schmidt has attracted some critical attention in the U.S. and England — most notably Michael Minden's book-length study (Cambridge, 1982) and *RCF*'s spring 1988 issue on him — the bulk of the criticism has understandably been written in German, all of which is intelligently analyzed in Weninger's splendid new book. Writing for an Anglo-American audience that knows no German and that knows Schmidt only from the handful of translations that have appeared so far, Weninger first provides an informative overview of Schmidt's life and work before breaking down Schmidt criticism into various categories. Before 1970, most of this was limited to book reviews and occasional essays and followed typical approaches of the time. Everything changed in 1970, the year Schmidt published *Zettel's Traum*, a massive Über-novel (1300 pages, 13" x 17") that immediately became Germany's *Finnegans Wake* (the nonstandard apostrophe in Schmidt's title imitates the nonstandard absence of one in Joyce's) and attracted the kind of specialist who contributed to the old *A Wake Newslitter*, which in fact is where I first learned of Schmidt. (Schmidt's newsletter is playfully called the *Bargfelder Bote* — the "Bargfeld Bugle" — after the town Schmidt lived in during the last 20 years of his life.) After 1970, Schmidt criticism proliferated, and even critics who hated his work felt compelled to deal with him.

Weninger guides the reader through the secondary literature in an even-handed manner, pointing out the inadequacies of some criticism and the insights of others, and in the process provides a fine introduction to Schmidt's work itself. A separate chapter focuses on the critical reception of two novels, an early one called *The Stony Heart* (1956) and his last completed novel, translated as *Evening Edged in Gold* (1975; 1980). Even if you don't have a particular interest in Schmidt, Weninger's book is an instructive account of how scholarship develops around an author, how it builds on previous scholarship, gets sidetracked by critical fads and trends, or (more recently) takes what Stanley Fish has called an anti-professional stance — that is, denigrating previous scholarship as inadequate and/or biased.

As Schmidt's works become available to Anglo-American readers, critical appetites are sure to be whetted over this fascinating author. For anyone writing on Schmidt in the future, Weninger's *Framing the Novelist* will be an indispensable tool.

Review of Contemporary Fiction, Summer 1996

□ □ □ □ □ □ □

The School for Atheists: A Novella = Comedy in 6 Acts.
Translated by John E. Woods
Green Integer, 2001

For those who have been following Arno Schmidt's erratic appearances in English translation over the last 20 years, the publication of *The School for Atheists* is cause for celebration. This is one of the "hyperbooks" Schmidt wrote during his last decade, an oversized volume with elaborate page layouts, illustrations, and Schmidt's unique, highly expressive style of punctuation. At 301 pages it's no novella, but it does resemble a play and is definitely a comedy.

First published in 1972, *The School* is set mostly in the year 2014, with an extended flashback to the summer of 1969, when a band of atheists had their lack of faith tested (a clever reversal of the traditional test-of-faith topos). The action takes place on a "reservation" in northern Germany at a time when two superpowers rule the globe: a matriarchal United States and a patriarchal China, representatives from which converge on the reservation for a summit. At the center of the novel is a typical Schmidt protagonist, a 75-year-old justice of the peace named Kolderup, who shares Schmidt's own fantastic erudition and iconoclastic views. Living with him are two "arsch damsels of Seven=Teen," his daughter Suse and her friend Nipperchen, whose romantic escapades provide most of the comedy in this sex farce.

Schmidt was one of the few writers who valiantly attempted to pick up where Joyce left off, using *Finnegans Wake* as a model for his own punning, multilingual, polymorphously perverse prose. It takes some getting used to — be prepared to spend about ten minutes on the first page — but once you acclimatize yourself to it, Schmidt's prose is a delightful concoction (or "cunt=cock=shun," as Schmidt would say) of double entendres, learned allusions, and phonetically rendered speech, all heroically translated by the fantastic John E. Woods. Though not as difficult as *Finnegans Wake*, the novel likewise tosses many languages into a word salad, using etymologies and puns to explore hidden connections and tensions (often sexual) between signifiers and their signifieds.

Like Robert Musil, Schmidt is a German writer of the first rank whose tardy appearance in English translation has kept him from being as well known in America as his countrymen Mann, Grass, Böll, and others. But enough Schmidt is now available that readers who consider themselves au courant with innovative, experimental fiction have no excuse for not knowing this literary giant. *The School for Atheists* is a good place to start.

Rain Taxi, Spring 2002

□ □ □ □ □ □ □

Radio Dialogs II. Translated by John E. Woods
Green Integer, 2003

Popularizers of literature, from Clifton Fadiman to Harold Bloom, are scorned by many academic critics, who seem hell-bent on *de*-popularizing literature by writing only for each other in code. But 50 years ago the great German writer Arno Schmidt devised a form of literary criticism appealing to general reader and academic alike. Between 1955 and 1971, while creating some of the most ambitious experimental fiction of his time, Schmidt wrote 34 radio scripts, hour-long dramas in which two or three people discuss well-known authors. In most of them, a well-informed advocate (Schmidt himself, essentially) argues with one or two others who don't quite share his enthusiasm, challenge him on various points, or simply ask the kinds of questions general readers might ask. (A separate voice recites quotations from the books.) Green Integer is publishing 19 of them in translation: six appeared in *Radio Dialogs I* (1999), six are in the present volume, and seven more will appear someday in volume three [never happened].

While this sort of dramatized criticism isn't new — one can trace the genre from Plato's *Dialogues* through Lucian's *Dialogues of the Dead* up to Julián Ríos's recent *La vida sexual de las palabras* and his Joycean *House of Ulysses* — Schmidt made the form his own. This isn't your usual polite book chat. Schmidt's dialogues are a rowdy mix of criticism, biography, exegesis, sarcastic asides, dramatic recitations, provocations (Schmidt was an atheist and rarely missed an opportunity to mock religion), and astonishing displays of erudition. He seems to have read *everything* and, as one character says, "would have scruples writing about a 50=volumned author if [he] knew only 49 of them." (That equal sign is one of many typographical oddities Schmidt indulged in.) Schmidt's vast reading and his working writer's knowledge of how books actually get written enliven all these dialogues, turning even mundane writers into fascinating case studies.

Not surprisingly, most of the writers Schmidt treats are German, but surprisingly, perhaps, he passes over the giants to focus on those fading from literary memory (or completely unknown to most readers): the first volume has dialogs on Barthold Heinrich Brockes, Christoph Martin Wieland, Ludwig Tieck, and Karl May; this one features Johann Gottfried Schnabel, Johann Gottfried Herder, Adalbert Stifter, and Gustav Frenssen. (Wait, come back!) There are also dialogs on the Brontë sisters (volume I), Edward Bulwer-Lytton (I said come back!), and each volume concludes with a dazzling dialog on James Joyce, whom Schmidt revered and whose later works are the closest parallel to his own. (Schmidt's magnum opus, *Zettel's Traum*, is like *Finnegans Wake*, but twice as long.)

Even the most minor writer provides Schmidt a platform for a wide range of topics. The opening dialog on Schnabel, once known for a 2,000-page novel called *Felsenburg Island*, discusses the nature of literary influence, the use of allusions, the damage done by later editors, the politics of publishing, and how life can imitate art. (Schnabel's island was based on Tristan da Cunha, which later developed much as the island does in his novel.) The one on Herder demonstrates how conflicting ideologies in a writer's work are often the result not of unconscious cultural assumptions (which the deconstructionist critic will smarmily expose) but of the real-life demands of writing a variety of books to earn money to feed one's family: "The unworldliness — to avoid a harder expression — with which professors practice literary psychology is verily, verily quaint. *(shaking his head, repeating)*: 'What could possibly have compelled him ??' — *(insistent= imploring)*: Seven children : if you please ! ! !"

The liveliest dialog is "The Gentle Monster," in which two smart-alecks do a tag-team number on Adalbert Stifter and his thousand-page novel *Indian Summer*. Stifter avoided leaving an accurate picture of the times he lived in, which is one of the basic functions of a writer, Schmidt felt. "Goethe cannot have anticipated for me the experience of jet=fighter accents in the sky : the present is always new and original ! — " This is followed by a more somber evaluation of the career of Gustav Frenssen, who began writing sermons and regional "blood and soil tearjerkers," and was startled by World War I into a brief period of clarity in which he wrote one good book (*Otto Babendiek*, a 1,300-page novel: Schmidt loved big books), before becoming a Nazi sympathizer and returning to hackwork.

The dialog on Bulwer-Lytton is the most dramatic in that there are three distinct characters (Schmidt and a married couple), with a subplot involving a young girl offstage. Schmidt here accomplishes the impossible by making this neglected Victorian actually sound impressive. This is the densest, most convoluted of his dialogs, very much in the style of the fiction Schmidt was writing at the time. If his radio audience had a hard time following it, they probably gave up and switched the dial halfway through the final dialog, a heady discussion of Joyce's *Ulysses* and *Finnegans Wake*.

One need not have any interest in the particular writers Schmidt covers to find these dialogs useful, for two reasons: they provide invaluable insights into the mind and working methods of Schmidt himself, a greater writer than any of those he treats (save Joyce) yet as unfamiliar to most readers as Schnabel or Frenssen. They perhaps deserve to be forgotten; he doesn't. And second, these dialogs demonstrate that literary criticism can be lively and entertaining while still maintaining critical rigor and sophistication. Too much current criticism strikes educated readers as pretentious, theory-addled muddles, too far removed from the actual practice of reading and writing to be of any use to anyone (other than the author running on a tenure-track). Few critics could emulate Schmidt's performance-art criticism with as much success, but perhaps these dialogs will have the clarifying effect on them that World War I had on Stifter.

A final shout-out to John E. Woods: a great writer deserves a great translator, and in Woods Schmidt has the ideal partner. From his genial introductions to his meticulous but creative translations, he brings Schmidt alive and has deservedly won several prizes for his work on this writer once called untranslatable. Reportedly he's taken on *Zettel's Traum*, which will be the crown of both his and Schmidt's careers. In the meantime, tune in to these *Radio Dialogs*.

American Book Review, September/October 2003

John A. Scott

N
Brandl & Schlesinger, 2014

When this extraordinary novel appeared in Australia last April, one reviewer grouped it with "postmodernist maximalist opuses such as *Infinite Jest*, *The Recognitions*, *2666*, *A Naked Singularity* and *Gravity's Rainbow*." The Pynchon reference is probably the most relevant: the novel takes place during the same World War II period, veers from documentary realism to outlandish fantasy, and indicts industrialists as the real warmongers, putting profits over patriotism. And like Pynchon's *V.*, Scott's *N* is a quest for the meaning of a mysterious initial by an individual driven to expose the secret history of his country.

N is an alternative history along the lines of Sinclair Lewis's *It Can't Happen Here* or Philip Roth's *The Plot against America*: Scott imagines a right-wing takeover of Australia in 1942 and an invasion by the Japanese, both of which entails persecution of the dissenting artists who dominate the first half of the novel. A civil servant named Telford dominates the second half as he begins to realize the nature of the fascist regime for which he works. Linking the two halves are two redhead women who resemble each other, and uniting the lengthy novel is a web of intertextual references to classic works of fiction like *Gulliver's Travels*, *Great Expectations*, "The Purloined Letter," *Through the Looking-Glass*, and *Journey to the Center of the Earth*, not to mention a few references to Joyce's *Ulysses* and a cameo by Gertrude Stein and Alice B. Toklas, sitting out the war in the wilds of Australia (a comic episode conveyed in the style of *Great Expectations*). Formally and politically, *N* resembles Dos Passos's *U.S.A.*, alternating between the personal stories of a dozen or so characters and a variety of documents, each in a different font, privileging heterogeneity over the homogeneity demanded by conservative regimes and aesthetics. This bold, important novel is worth seeking out.

Review of Contemporary Fiction, Spring 2014

Will Self

Umbrella
Grove Press, 2013

Warning: *Umbrella* is what's known as a "difficult" novel. If that genre sounds as appealing as a difficult pregnancy, you can stop reading. But if you enjoy challenges, in literature as well as life, read on, for *Umbrella* is a virtuosic performance.

The storyline is not in itself that difficult to follow. It concerns a woman named Audrey De'Ath (symbolically changed to Death and then Dearth by her caretakers), a lively, redheaded Londoner who comes of age during World War I, works in a munitions factory, gets caught up in socialism and "free love," and then falls victim to encephalitis lethargica, an epidemic that raged through Europe and England between 1915 and 1926, killing a third of its victims and leaving the rest in a somnolent state with symptoms of Parkinson's disease. She is confined to a mental hospital in 1922, and remains there, "mind out of time," until 1971, when a young clinician named Zach Busner — fascinated by her and other "enkies" — awakes this sleeping beauty with a drug called L-DOPA. The cure is temporary, however, the patients relapse, and decades later — on 8 April 2010 to be exact — the elderly Busner thinks back on all this as he visits his old hospital, now the Princess Park Manor, a complex of luxury apartments.

The story also branches out to include Zach's marriage problems, harrowing accounts of how the mentally ill were mistreated, and the careers of Audrey's two brothers, one of whom becomes a bloodless technocrat, and the other a forward-thinking soldier who apparently dies during the Great War. (Fans of World War I fiction will not want to miss the military sequences, gruesomely realistic depictions of what life on the front must have been like.)

What makes the novel difficult/challenging is the nonlinear form and its stream-of-consciousness style. The novel opens in spring 1971 but thereafter time-travels back and forth between Audrey's Edwardian childhood and 2010, jumping mid-sentence from one era to another with no chapter breaks, and precious few paragraphs indents, to guide the reader.

All of this is narrated in the maximalist, allusive, and sensory-overloaded style associated with James Joyce's *Ulysses*. (It will be noted that *Ulysses* and *Umbrella* share the same initial letter and cadence; the latter's title and epigraph come from a line in *Ulysses*: "A brother is as easily forgotten as an umbrella.") Self's style is a heady mixture of closely observed (and deeply researched) period details, colorful imagery, surrealistic juxtapositions, British slang, and italicized interjections: "his arm *Bill Sikes* upraised to another dog — or a dog *spliced with a child* that howls, then coughs, the *Coniston's* catching in its throat, before loping off along an alleyway past a stinking shambles where there are staved-in casks, a shed-on-stilts, and beneath this a pyramid made from horse's skulls, some flayed entirely except for their *twitching ears*. The dog-child gives a last despairing hoooooooooooooooooowl and is gone into the August-evening quiet of the city that lies splayed there under the dirty orange of its senescent sky."

Joyce and other modernists adopted a new style because they felt the old ways were inadequate to convey the paradigm-shifting changes underway at the beginning of the 20th century. Self concurs with those modernists who feared technological advances "and other forms of mechanisation that were precisely the regimentations and oppressions of the human spirit and the human body that" revolutionaries like Audrey opposed. He implies that Audrey and others were martyrs to technology and mechanization, inventions that did not result in machines that freed "well-fed and healthy folk . . . from material want" but "engines only for the maceration of bodies and the grinding up of souls." Self's metaphor-mad mind finds mechanization recalibrating nearly every aspect of life, especially the sexualization of weaponry.

This material isn't particularly new: Oliver Sacks dealt with the same sleeping sickness and its treatment with L-DOPA in *Awakenings*, and fears of technological "advances" have been expressed at almost every stage of history. The latter has concerned poets ranging from William Blake to the Kinks' Ray Davies, whose 1970 song "Apeman" opens Self's novel. What's admirable about *Umbrella* is Self's daring, ingenious treatment of this material: welding form with content, he uses modernist techniques to deal with an epidemic that occurred during the heyday of modernism, an approach that can be as puzzling to readers as encephalitis lethargica was to physicians. Like Zach examining photographs of his patient's compulsive-repetitive actions, the reader may cry out "this is incomprehensible, this intercutting of time," but Self's wildly nonlinear narrative offers other delights: richly detailed settings that bring the Edwardian era and mental hospitals sensuously alive, imaginative imagery, kaleidoscopic patterns of symbolism (umbrellas assume all sorts of forms and functions), and loads of mordant satire. Yes, *Umbrella* is a "difficult" novel, but it amply rewards the effort.

Washington Post, 1 January 2013

Lee Siegel

Love in a Dead Language
University of Chicago Press, 1999

Not to waste your time, *Love in a Dead Language* is a satiric, learned novel in the tradition of *Mulligan Stew* and *Darconville's Cat* (though not as vicious as Sorrentino or earnest as Theroux), an homage to Nabokov's *Lolita* and *Pale Fire*. If this is your cup of tea, read on; if not, move on to the next column.

Now that we're alone: this is a fabulous novel, a postmodern, metafictional extravaganza that is sure to please fans of the above authors. It recounts the last year in the life of Leopold Roth, a Sanskrit scholar and professor of Indian studies at a university in California. Although he loves India and has been there many times, he has never made love to an Indian woman, a want that intensifies when a Californian-born girl of Indian ancestry enrolls in his Asian Studies class. Predictably, the teacher falls for the student (who has no interest in him or India), eventually seduces her, and destroys both his marriage and life in the process.

But nothing else is predictable about *Love in a Dead Language*. The novel takes the form of Roth's working translation of the *Kamasutra*, with his commentaries relating the teachings of the classic sex manual to his amorous progress with his student. But Roth dies before completing his translation, so what we have here is an edition prepared by his literary executor — a humorless grad student — who adds his own foreword and commentaries (parodying the numerous translations and commentaries on the *Kamasutra* itself).

And there's more: inserted at various places in the text are parodies of college newspaper articles, filmscripts, instructions for a board-game version of the *Kamasutra*, a comic-book version, and even screen shots of a CD-ROM version; there's a lecture on malacology, parodies of Victorian pornography and Anglo-Indian travel narratives; and the novel concludes with a bibliography and index. But wait, there's more: examples of retrography (mirror-writing), an alternative chapter printed upside-down and in red ink, quotations from music scores, an undergraduate term paper, a movie poster, a proposal and sample pages for a Cliffs Notes version of the *Kamasutra*, and reproductions of Indian art and manuscripts. All it lacks is a fold-out map of India and a CD of ragas. (The uncredited designer deserves a National Book Award for this production.)

But in the center ring of this textual circus is a profound study of love, and especially of lust as a funhouse mirror of love. Love and lust are both four-letter words beginning with *l*, just as a single letter distinguishes *erotic* and *exotic*. The close relationship, lexical and otherwise, between these terms is the true subject of *Love in a Dead Language*. Roth's beloved student is erotic because she's exotic, and his lust turns to love the longer he's with her. A "romance" is both a love affair and a literary genre, and Roth is very conscious of "scripting" his affair with this student (via the *Kamasutra*) as though it were a novel. He's read *Lolita* as well as Edward Said's *Orientalism* and knows both what he's doing and how it is doomed to end.

And Lee Siegel certainly knows what he's doing, too. A professor of Indian religions at the University of Hawaii, his vast erudition is breathtaking, both in his own field as well as in literature and pop culture. He is a gifted parodist, able to pump up his prose to purple majesty when needed. If he has a fault, it's that he's a little too proud of his cleverness: he often explains his references or literary allusions (which a Sorrentino or Theroux wouldn't) to make sure you appreciate his wit. But that's a minor fault, and actually adds to the ease of reading what might otherwise have been a formidably erudite novel. Siegel is not ashamed to be clever, and his novel (as a character says of another work) is "shameless in every way — erotically, morally, politically, religiously . . . even rhetorically." That's praise, not censure.

As the new millennium begins, it is perhaps fitting to have a final, defining example of a literary genre that bloomed in the 20th century: the learned academic novel. I don't mean novels satirizing academic life, like McCarthy's *Groves of Academe*, Jarrell's *Pictures from an Institution*, or some of David Lodge's books, but novels that incorporate the apparatus of scholarship into their form: *Pale Fire* with its poem cum commentary, the parodies of scholarship in *Mulligan Stew* and *Darconville's Cat*, Barth's syllabus-as-novel *Giles Goat-Boy* (and parts of *LETTERS*), perhaps even Wallace's *Infinite Jest* with its hundred pages of endnotes. (Only a few women writers seem attracted to this genre: Rikki Ducornet's *Phosphor in Dreamland* and Carole Maso's *Defiance* make some use of these techniques, but only Christine Brooke-Rose has embraced the genre wholeheartedly.) *Love in a Dead Language* is the ultimate example of this genre, and not likely to be outdone anytime soon.

And if you've never read the *Kamasutra*, this is an excellent introduction. Much better than the movie.

American Book Review, May–June 2000

□ □ □ □ □ □ □

Love and Other Games of Chance
Viking, 2003

In our enlightened age, we are blessed with reality television, professional wrestling, and movies like *Dude, Where's My Car?* A century ago, folks sought their low-brow entertainment at carnivals, séances, and variety shows. That seedy world is brought vividly to life in Lee Siegel's new novel — or "novelty," as he subtitles it.

Love and Other Games of Chance purports to be the autobiography of Isaac Schlossberg, born in 1899 to Jewish immigrants lately arrived in America. As soon as Isaac is old enough, the elder Schlossbergs enlist him into their variety act. He debuts as Samoo the Snake Boy and graduates to other roles in a gaudy procession of sideshows, scams, Wild West jamborees, and silent movies. In his twenties he travels to India, where he assembles Professor Solomon Serpentarius's Oriental Oddities and Indian Incredibilities to take to Britain, and then travels throughout Europe — doing everything from a Futurist snake-charming routine in post-revolutionary Russia to writing plays for Parisian Grand Guignol — finally to return to America to star in early talkies. At the end of his life, he attempts the grandest stunt of all: to be the first to scale Mount Everest.

In the course of the novel, the reader stares like a slack-jawed yokel at a cavalcade of shows: ludicrous Buffalo Bill dramatizations, circus and animal acts, nautch dances, fortune-telling, taxidermy demonstrations, experiments in transmigration, necromancy, "pulse-stopping, reptile regurgitation, levitation," mind-reading, aerial shows, Folies Bèrgere nude extravaganzas, "Great Sharpshooters of the Bible," psychosurgery, gilli-gilli shows, the wedding of two elephants, funambulists — a stupefying parade of hoaxes and hustles almost encyclopedic in its range. The willingness, even eagerness, to be duped made all these early forms of popular entertainment successful, a lowbrow counterpart to the highbrow "willing suspension of disbelief" that Coleridge says is necessary to appreciate great art. And religion: As one character says near the end of the novel, "All the religions in the world are foolish. They entertain us at their best and delude us at their worst."

What makes this novel a novelty is its structure: It is based on the children's game Snakes and Ladders (Chutes and Ladders for squeamish Americans), with the board game reproduced on page 9 for reference. The challenge, you may recall, was to go from square 1 to 100, climbing ladders when you landed on certain squares and sliding down when encountering snakes. The novel is organized into 100 "squares" of unparagraphed text, each about 2,000 words long and occupying four pages. Though the novel can be read sequentially, one can also climb illustrated ladders and slide down snakes to other squares of the novel if one wishes to read thematically rather than chronologically. This ludic, interactive structure recalls those of Julio Cortázar's *Hopscotch*, some of Georges Perec's and Milorad Pavić's novels, and Siegel's previous novel, *Love in a Dead Language*. He is a writer who believes in having fun with the form of his novels, and it is as much fun to read them as it must have been to write them.

Love is in the title of both novels [and in every novel of his since] and is Siegel's grand theme, ranging from lofty philosophical speculations on the subject to the sexual habits of animals. Isaac falls in love with ten fascinating women in the novel, each an example of the kinds of relationship that can exist between couples, from a sweet one with his first and unforgettable love, Angel (an aerialist and actress née Devora Rabinowitz), to a stormy one with a jealous aviatrix for whom love and flying are forms of mystic transport. The deception at the heart of these artistes' various acts is carried over into their love lives, with self-deception the headliner.

But reading *Love and Other Games of Chance* is not necessarily a day at the circus. Siegel, a professor of Indian religions at the University of Hawaii, is formidably erudite, though never overbearingly so, and possesses an extravagant vocabulary. Isaac has a sideshow barker's love of alliteration and magniloquence, so you'll need your biggest dictionary close at hand. (Quick test: If it lacks "ophicleide," you need a bigger one.) There are phrases from half a dozen languages, not always translated, and at least a hundred characters to keep track of, many of whom go by more than one name as they create new acts for themselves.

But if you don't mind being challenged, you'll be rewarded with a wise, witty, and entertaining novel illustrating the myriad, complicated ways that love, art, and religion resemble each other. *Mundus vult decipi* is one of the untranslated phrases in the novel: "The world wants to be deceived," the motto of lovers, artists, and religious leaders.

Lee Siegel published several academic monographs before turning his clever hand to fiction, but Indian scholarship's loss is literature's gain. His two pyrotechnic novels are warmly recommended to game readers.

Washington Post Book World, 2 February 2003

Elizabeth Smart

By Grand Central Station I Sat Down and Wept
Vintage, 1992

This is one of the most extraordinary novels ever written. It's a torch song of a book, an operatic lament written in an intense, overwrought style that is by turns biblical, poetic, impertinent. The story is simple: a young woman falls obsessively in love with a married man, enjoys some blissful moments of illicit sex with him, and is left to bear their children. But the plot is hard to follow, for the text is hardly what you'd call "composed": instead, its lipstick is smeared, its hair a mess, its mascara running as the nameless narrator rhapsodizes over love's joys and desolations. The novel lacks decorum, is shameless in its excesses, and resembles those madwoman scenes in Elizabethan drama where disorderly prose breaks through the orderly boundaries of verse. The story doesn't flow, it hemorrhages. (All this is praise, not censure.) The effect is overwhelming, emotionally draining, the greatest love story ever written if you define *love* as naked yearning so powerful and lawless that it resembles demonic possession.

First published in 1945, this new edition adds *The Assumption of the Rogues & Rascals* (1978), a kind of sequel, along with an astute introduction by Brigid Brophy. She finds parallels between Smart's poetic style and Jean Genet's; one might also be reminded of Djuna Barnes, Anaïs Nin, Marguerite Young, even Edward Dahlberg. But no one compares to this daring maenad of a writer.

Review of Contemporary Fiction, Summer 1993

Ilan Stavans

The One-Handed Pianist and Other Stories.
Translated by David Unger, Harry Morales, the author, and others
University of New Mexico Press, 1996

Longtime readers of *RCF* will recognize the name Ilan Stavans: he has written for our special issues on Barth, Gass, Puig, and Kiš, and guest-edited our Felipe Alfau issue, in addition to contributing numerous book reviews and (most recently) interviewing Mexican writer Fernando del Paso. All of these authors are cosmopolitan by nature, in outlook if not in actual circumstances, as is Stavans himself: born in Mexico of Russian-Polish Jewish descent — his complete name is Ilan Stavchansky Slomianski — he has traveled widely and now teaches at Amherst College. An autobiographical essay, "Lost in Translation," concludes this volume, a fascinating account of Stavans's multicultural upbringing and its influence on his writings.

In this first collection in English of Stavans's fiction, Kafka, rather than any of the above, is the presiding influence. The first story, "A Heaven without Crows," takes the form of a letter from Kafka to Max Brod, explaining his decision to have his writings destroyed. ("Because I am an imposter who has invented a dark reality. Because I've made a career out of being a victim.") Kafka is evoked in the second story, "The Invention of Memory," where a Czech man moves to his mother's neighborhood in Mexico City to lose his memory and die under the voyeuristic eye of a neighbor. "The Death of Yankos" is a brief tale in Kafka's lighter, more absurdist vein, while "The One-Handed Pianist" concerns a woman whose inexplicable defects recall Kafka's sense of the incomprehensibility of God. (In the first story, Stavans's Kafka writes: "My idea of God is of a distant warden in a state of alertness, always ready to punish.") The centerpiece of the book is "Talia in Heaven," a metafictional novella that is both the most Kafkaesque (in the general sense of the term) story in the book and the one most concerned with the Jewish heritage. Filled with anecdotes from the Talmud and written in a racier tone than the others, "Talia" is a tour de force, the most difficult but the most impressive fiction in the collection. "House Repossessed," like a surprising number of other stories here, is narrated from a woman's point of view, and the final story, "Three Nightmares," brings us back to Kafka territory, where dream and reality are blurred.

Stavans has already distinguished himself as a critic and essayist; this volume of his brooding, erudite fiction places him in that small circle of writers who are as accomplished at fiction as they are nonfiction.

Review of Contemporary Fiction, Summer 1996

Gilbert Sorrentino

The Sky Changes
North Point Press, 1986

Mulligan Stew
Grove Press, 1987

In 1974 Gilbert Sorrento told interviewer Barry Alpert that he would welcome the opportunity to revise his first novel *The Sky Changes* in order to add a few sections and to correct some lapses in tone. North Point Press provided the opportunity and we now have a revised edition with two new chapters near the beginning — filling that geographical gap between Washington, DC, and Jacksontown, Ohio — and with a tonal consistency that is now pitch perfect. A dying marriage dies during a trip through dying cities at the dying of the year at the end of the Eisenhower '50s, a time when America itself died in many respects. The writing is fierce and fine, and of such rigorous artistry that its depressing subject takes on the transcendent beauty of a Flemish *Crucifixion*. The unrelieved bleakness of the novel not only separates it from more exuberant road books of the '50s like *Lolita* and *On the Road* but separates it from realistic fiction in general. *The Sky Changes* is primarily an exercise in tone and color, a composition in black and gray; although it has its psychological depths and sociological implications, it is as a triumphant tonal exercise that the novel commands our attention.

Mulligan Stew ranks with *J R*, *Gravity's Rainbow*, and *LETTERS* as one of the few truly significant novels of the '70s, and probably surpasses these in stylistic variety and parodic virtuosity. In this hilarious account of Antony Lamont's doomed attempt to write an avant-garde detective thriller, Sorrentino manages to do nearly everything that can be done in fiction, making *Mulligan Stew* required reading for anyone interested in modern literature. Enough said.

Review of Contemporary Fiction, Summer 1988

□ □ □ □ □ □ □

Gold Fools

Green Integer, 2001

Damn, this is a funny book! Sorrentino subverts the Western novel with a ludicrous tale of hunting for gold narrated entirely in interrogative sentences. Reminiscent in some ways of the boys' novel parody in *Misterioso*, Sorrentino has a field day with the traditions and lingo of the Western, as well as going off on riffs concerning contemporary culture. Throughout, Sorrentino interrogates our use of language, especially our reliance on clichés; a linguistic hygienist, Sorrentino questions any sloppy misuse of language, knowing that sloppy language can lead to sloppy thinking. The Western genre has attracted many innovative writers — Coover, Brautigan, Kesey, even William Gaddis wrote a Western screenplay, unfortunately never produced — but Sorrentino's inquisitorial contribution is the funniest.

Amazon.com, 19 March 2001

Edla van Steen

Early Mourning. Translated by David S. George
Latin American Literary Review, 1996

If Marie Redonnet's *Nevermore* recalls *Twin Peaks* [see p. 298], Edla van Steen's *Early Mourning* evokes *Pulp Fiction*. Spanning 12 hours in September, from dusk till dawn, and set in Brazil's Sao Paulo, this cinematic novel tracks a gang's robbery at a funeral home. Like the Tarantino film, *Early Mourning* jumps between plots, features a cast of eccentric characters — most memorably a female transvestite who moonlights as a professional mourner — and black humor. (The novel has already been turned into a play in Brazil, but it cries out for film treatment.)

Four deaths from four levels of Brazilian society occur; along with crime, corruption, and random disasters, Steen paints a portrait of a dying society, with little relief in sight despite the dawning of a new day at the short novel's end. ("There's nothing special about this dawn," a character thinks on the last page. "It's a morning like any other.") The novel ends with a helicopter flying over the cemetery where the four deceased are buried, which neatly brings us back to a news helicopter that appeared in the first chapter. *Early Mourning* is a choppy helicopter's view of Brazilian society rather than a detailed study, but the noisy immediacy of such an approach gains in intensity what it loses in depth.

The racy prose, briskly translated by David S. George, is in the present tense, adding to the headlong rush of events. The third of van Steen's books to appear in English, *Early Mourning* won the Brazilian Academy of Letters prize for best novel and the Pen Club Brazil prize for best book in 1993.

Washington Post, 22 December 1996

D. N. Stuefloten

Mexico Trilogy
FC2, 1996

Mexico Trilogy isn't a translation, but it might as well be. It was written by an American who has spent more time abroad than in his native land and who writes from an international perspective, even going so far as to exhibit a distinctly European kind of anti-Americanism in places. The three novellas gathered here are ostensibly set in Mexico, though one is actually set in an Ethiopian town pretending to be a Mexican resort (to attract tourists) and another in a Mexican town pretending to be Las Vegas.

Filmmaking is the central activity of the trilogy, which allows for discussions (by the author as well as his characters) about the nature of reality, of illusion, and the difficulty of distinguishing between the two, especially when the camera is rolling. Stuefloten's work in places recalls that of the practitioners of the French nouveau roman — especially Marguerite Duras and Alain Robbe-Grillet, both of whom likewise worked in film — and in places that of Latin American magic realists like Gabriel García Márquez and the late Severo Sarduy.

In his preface, Stuefloten writes that these novellas, though set in Ethiopia and Mexico, may ultimately be about the United States. By their very foreignness, all of the above novels can help us look at ourselves and our own country with new eyes, to translate these fictional experiences into our own idiom.

Washington Post, 22 December 1996 — the last of a "Fiction in Translation" roundup.

Alexander Theroux

An Adultery
Linden Press, 1987

With his third novel, Alexander Theroux has pulled in the reins a bit on the witty, outlandishly erudite style he employed in *Three Wogs* and the brilliant *Darconville's Cat* to write a more conventional work, yet one that retains the finest features of his earlier style: an unerring instinct for language and a keenly satiric eye for all forms of pretense and folly. *An Adultery* is the confession of a character with just those stylistic qualities who falls in love with a woman who epitomizes pretense and folly; his love for her struggles against his greater love for language, loyalty, and honesty, and the result is one of the most puzzling relationships in recent American fiction.

In the first seven pages Christian Ford, artist-in-residence at a prep school in St. Ives, New Hampshire, meets and begins an affair with a married woman named Farol Colorado. After seven more pages he has seen through most of her pretenses and recognizes her for the ridiculous woman she is, and yet the affair drags on for three years. Throughout the rest of the book Ford catalogues and analyzes her faults with a thoroughness not seen since Marcel trained his sights on Albertine. While Farol betrays her husband, Ford betrays his young girlfriend Marina Falieri, an angel too transcendentally pure for this world. Yet every time he breaks away from Farol he accomplishes work of a much higher caliber than the saccharine portraits he does of Marina.

Chief among his complaints is Farol's language: throughout *An Adultery* she displays a discomfort with language, distrusting its capacity for precision and clarity, and fearful of its ability to expose deception. Ford's commitment to language as a means for analysis clashes with Farol's use of it for obfuscation, and at this level *An Adultery* is a heroic attempt to prove that it is still possible for rigorous thought and incisive language to fight and triumph over the foggy, imprecise language, generalities, and clichés that both Farol and much of the present culture employ as its lingua franca. "Love is not only a talkative passion," he argues. "Language itself can lose chastity and its ambiguity become also depraved, as when on the adulterous tongue two meanings that should remain separate suddenly become coupled. A parody of communication begins to take place."

Theroux's language swells and recedes accordingly. The beginning of the novel is suspiciously flat; the language catches fire only when Ford starts learning of Farol's insincerity, bad manners, and weak-mindedness, provoking sentences of a kind rarely seen in current fiction: aphoristic, colorful with metaphor and allusion, fugally unwinding with a vocabulary rich and strange, yet equally precise. Although the prose is less eccentric, learned, and excessive than in *Darconville's Cat*, Theroux must be ranked with the finest stylists of our day. He is not without humor: Ford's fury with his mistress and her artsy-craftsy world inspires caustic satirical set pieces, burning with Augustan rage at modern manners and nostrums.

An update on earlier classics of adultery, Theroux's novel impugns adulteration of every kind — in love, language, morals, art — and Ford's long and exasperating duet with Farol becomes an attempt to wrestle the numerous adulterations that have debased the quality of modern life. The fight takes its toll: Ford is driven to psychotic extremes in his drive to fathom Farol's equally psychotic iniquities, and Marina is their sacrificial victim. But Ford escapes to tell the tale.

Conjunctions, Spring 1988

□ □ □ □ □ □ □

Watergraphs

Base Canard, 1994

While Theroux's three novels are justly admired, his short stories are almost unknown. This is partly because they've never been collected into book form, and partly because many of them were published in out-of-the-way places. "Watergraphs," for example, first appeared in the *Boston Globe Magazine* in 1983. Theroux's stories are lighter in tone and easier in execution than his more ambitious novels and usually center on some special field of knowledge. This one has to do with collecting historical autographs — "watergraphs" in the Boston accent Theroux self-deprecatingly makes fun of here (possessing a classic one himself). Also included in this slim volume is "A Note on the Type," an amusing parody of those blocked paragraphs at the end of books describing the typeface used. (This first appeared in *RCF*'s Theroux/West issue of Spring 1991.) The book is beautifully designed, and the deluxe signed edition is particularly sumptuous.

Review of Contemporary Fiction, Spring 1995

Hunter S. Thompson

The Proud Highway: Saga of a Desperate Southern Gentleman.
Edited by Douglas Brinkley
Villard, 1997

The subtitle must be a joke: Born in Louisville, Kentucky, Hunter S. Thompson may be Southern, but he's no gentleman. Hell, I'm not even sure I'd call him civilized. But I would call him one of the greatest American writers of the 20th century, both for his vibrant prose style and his career-long autopsy reports on the death of the American Dream. His work is uneven, but at his best he shares with Mark Twain and William Gaddis a sense of outrage that expresses itself through virulent satire. His rock 'n' roll lifestyle obscures the fact he is essentially a moralist and a patriot, attacking shame and corruption with the vehemence of a biblical prophet. (The Book of Revelation is one of his favorite books.) To live outside the law you must be honest, and Thompson's iconoclastic honesty covers a multitude of sins. Perhaps he is a gentleman after all, in the sense that the Prince of Darkness is a gentleman.

The other subtitle for this book is "The Fear and Loathing Letters, Volume I." The first of a projected three-volume series, it includes about 200 letters written between 1956, when Thompson was 19, and 1967, the year he published his groundbreaking book *Hell's Angels*. What is immediately apparent from these letters is that Thompson is a born writer, not only by the ease with which he handles the language at an early age, but because of his strong sense of vocation. Despite a reckless youth, he was a voracious reader and knew he wanted to be a professional writer from high school onwards. (*The Proud Highway* reprints three of his high school writings and intersperses throughout the volume several other previously unavailable works.)

The letters tell the story of his desperate struggle to support himself while forging a writing career. Unable to hold a conventional job — at a newspaper or elsewhere — he became a freelancer at an early age, writing colorful features for a variety of newspapers and magazines while enduring every form of poverty. But his real apprenticeship was in the writing of these letters, where he was free to work out the aesthetics of what would later be called his "gonzo" journalism. Some of his letters take the form of outrageous fictions, others are pranks (like his letters to President Johnson applying for the governorship of American Samoa), and others detail his objections to and frustrations with conventional journalism.

Finding the appropriate vessel for his writing talent is one of the main themes of this collection. He originally planned to be a novelist — the F.

Scott Fitzgerald of his time, he boasted — but had to support himself with journalism because he couldn't sell his fiction. He wrote two novels in his twenties; the excerpts from them that were eventually published in Thompson's 1980 miscellany *Songs of the Doomed* show that conventional fiction was as unsuited to his talents as conventional journalism. A weird hybrid of the two, he sensed, was needed: well-researched nonfiction enlivened by fiction techniques and filtered through an outrageous narrative persona. *Hell's Angels* was a step in the right direction, but he realized he needed to go further. Near the end of *The Proud Highway* Thompson tells a correspondent: "I feel experimental these days. Something new is wanted . . . Gross libel and madness. I'm getting bored with straight writing." A few years later Thompson would stumble upon the formula he had been searching for in "The Kentucky Derby Is Decadent and Depraved," and then hit the mother lode with *Fear and Loathing in Las Vegas*. That book was recently added to the revamped Modern Library — this isn't your father's Modern Library — and can now be seen as the culmination of one of the longest and strangest literary apprenticeships in modern literature.

Those who know Thompson only from his Fear and Loathing books or, worse, from his caricature as Uncle Duke in Garry Trudeau's *Doonesbury*, are in for a jolt here. The seriousness of Thompson's quest is hammered home by the emotional climax of *The Proud Highway*: the assassination of President Kennedy on November 22, 1963. Thompson was devastated, almost reduced to tears, and the two letters he wrote that day sputter with hurt and indignation: "It is the triumph of lunacy, of rottenness, the dirtiest hour in our time . . . It is the death of reason." Filled with new outrage, Thompson has a new sense of his mission: "No matter what, today is the end of an era. No more fair play. From now on it is dirty pool and judo in the clinches. The savage nuts have shattered the great myth of American decency. They can count me in — I feel ready for a dirty game." And those who know Thompson's more hallucinogenic prose should consider this eloquent plea:

> If we cannot produce a generation of journalists — or even a good handful — who care enough about our world and our future to make journalism the great literature it can be, then professionally oriented programs' are a waste of time. Without at least a hard core of articulate men, convinced that journalism today is perhaps the best means of interpreting and thereby preserving what little progress we have made toward freedom and self-respect over the years, without that tough-minded elite in our press, dedicated to concepts that are sensed and quietly understood, rather than learned in schools — without these men we might as well toss in the towel and admit that ours is a society too interested in comic strips and TV to consider revolution until it bangs on our front door in the dead of some quiet night when our guard is finally down and we no longer kid ourselves about being the bearers of a great and decent dream.

True to his word, Thompson made journalism the great literature it can be, and in a weird, roundabout way has indeed become the F. Scott Fitzgerald of our time, as brilliant a chronicler of our age as Fitzgerald was of his. *The Proud Highway* is a great book by a great American, in that Thompson exemplifies the fierce individuality and love for democratic ideals that used to define an American. This is his best book in years; his recent efforts have been entertaining, but *The Proud Highway* vividly brings back the days when (to echo his diction) Thompson stomped the terra like a champion.

Washington Post Book World, 25 May 1997

Steve Tomasula

The Book of Portraiture
Fiction Collective Two, 2006

Before you read Steve Tomasula's brilliant new novel, you might want to take a long look at Diego de Velásquez's endlessly fascinating painting *Las Meninas* (Maids of Honor), which plays a major role in the novel, followed perhaps by a look at Michel Foucault's explication of the painting in *The Order of Things*, which I'm sure Tomasula read. Foucault sees in *Las Meninas* "the entire cycle of representation," which is the ambitious historical project behind *The Book of Portraiture*, from the invention of the alphabet to computer code to the latest uses of biotechnology in art. It's a heady, cerebral, exciting trip.

The novel is divided into five independent chapters, linked by recurring themes and references (like the Velásquez painting). The first and shortest, with the Genesicidal title "In a Beginning," evokes cave paintings, cuneiform, and runes before settling on a wandering storyteller in Egypt who invents an alphabet while doodling in the sand and realizes he can uses these markings to record a grand fiction about himself he has been inventing, inspired by Mesopotamian legends. Impressed by the pharoanic name Thutmose, he adapts a punchier version for his reed-pen name: Moses.

Fast-forward to 17th-century Spain. Chapter 2 purports to be the autobiography of Velásquez, written late in his life. Illustrated by Maria Tomasula with pencil renditions of some of Velásquez's most famous paintings, it tracks the development of the painter's aesthetics throughout his career, as well as his conflicts with those who misunderstood or opposed his innovations in art. He pities traditional painters who believe "that paint is only a means to illustrate that which is already known: stigma no different than the rings in a tree or other traces of God's thought and not symbols, like letters, that could be combined and recombined to make what man imagines into what is." The Inquisition suspects this encroaches upon divine prerogative, so they haul him in for a dramatic interrogation. Velásquez has to play dumb before these murderous religious bullies, and their cat-and-mouse exchanges are a highlight of the novel. Both realize that what is at stake is the question whether the world is a god's creation or ours; the cats believe it's their god's, but the mouse knows it's ours, and at that point goes off to create *Las Meninas*, depicting the artist in the act of creation.

After that tense chapter, some comic relief comes in the next, entitled "P. Displays R If and Only If S (a modern romance)." Set in the closing years of World War I, when Freud had the new profession of psychoanalysts in the same grip that Catholic theology held Spanish Inquisitors, it takes the form of a journal a young "brain mythologist" keeps of his sessions with an unmarried, 26-year-old woman named Paula. Because she prefers reading and independence to finding a husband, her family assumes something is wrong with her, and the psychoanalyst concurs, finding in her all the symptoms of sexual repression that will, if not treated in time, erupt into sexual hysteria, masturbation, sapphism, and/or nymphomania. He devises a procedure to relieve these symptoms that, unbeknownst to him, gives his patient volcanic orgasms, after which the young sophisticate attends her sessions with avidity. The sessions (and chapter) end after Paula sends her clueless doctor a magazine ad depicting "The Belbout Electric-Powered Vibro-Wand," guaranteed to "Reach that Vital Spot." Ignoring the phallic device, the psychoanalyst concentrates on the other illustration in the ad and, interpreting it as literally as the Inquisition did their Bible, misassumes she's run off with a lover.

Although the psychoanalyst insists his account is scientifically objective, his lust for Paula results in loaded sentences like: "This is the situation that I, her fireman, found when I came rushing in, hose in hand, and I pointed its nozzle at her onastic compulsion by presenting her with the horns of her dilemma." With its citations of turn-of-the-century articles with titles like "Signs of Masturbation in the Female" (*Pacific Medical Journal*) and quack diagnoses, it's funny now to read how the medical profession spun itself into a tizzy over the "problem" of female sexuality. But wipe that smirk off your face: every reader of *ABR* probably holds at least one equally misguided belief — in a god, an ism, in astrology, the social construction of gender, whatever — that will seem just as silly to the cognoscenti of the future. To this point, Tomasula quotes William Seabrook "that even the most outlandish claims can be mistaken for bedrock truth by those submerged in a community that gives them credence and support."

Chapter 4 brings us up to our own time, when the magic of computers has increased surveillance of citizens to a level that the Inquisition would have creamed over, and when *Las Meninas* has been digitally remastered by a Japanese photographer with his own face pasted over that of the little princess. This is the longest and most complex chapter, and is such a brilliant display of narrative architecture that one almost neglects the chilling implications. Tomasula tracks nine characters — several pharmacy employees, a few programmers, a fashion model, and a troubled female vet — across the grid of the Internet, spinning a web of relationships too complicated to summarize here. As in Tomasula's second novel *IN & OZ*, most characters are reduced to capitalized professions (Photographer, Station Manager), and as in his first, *VAS: An Opera in Flatland*, it is ingeniously designed, in this instance by

Robert P. Sedlack Jr. (Every chapter in *The Book of Portraiture* has a different font, layout, and shade of paper.)

The short final chapter, like the first entitled "In a Beginning," is set tomorrow, after another 9/11-type attack, and alternates between an American medical technician's attempt to create "bio-art" from her own eggs and a Muslim man who loses a daughter because of unavailable medical care and watches as she's given a fanatical martyr's funeral — high-tech aestheticism vs. low-tech religiosity. And we know who will win that one, don't we.

"Often, when we progress through a novel," the psychoanalyst records in his journal, "scenes from earlier sections that we lightly passed over or did not understand begin to become more meaningful as certain themes emerge." These cleverly connected themes are what make *The Book of Portraiture* a novel rather than a collection of stories, and the overarching theme of representation and self-portraiture, from cave art to computer code, gives this novel a historical sweep that is breathtaking. Like Joseph McElroy and Richard Powers, Tomasula can make intellectually engaging fiction out of forbidding (to some of us) topics like recombinant genetics, microbiology, computer technology, and other hard sciences, and utilizes the advantages of graphic design to go places even those gifted writers don't go. More accessible than *VAS*, more ambitious than *IN & OZ*, *The Book of Portraiture* is Steve Tomasula's finest creation yet.

American Book Review, November/December 2006

Frederic Tuten

Tallien: A Brief Romance
Farrar Straus Giroux, 1988

"It was really good, looked like a little nothing, then it went sailing off and sped deep into the heart." This response by the character Tallien to a brief letter from his former benefactor is likely to be the reader's to Frederic Tuten's splendid new novel, his first since the innovative *Adventures of Mao on the Long March* in 1971. *Tallien* is a novella in size and seems simple in structure: a middle-aged man visits the deathbed of his father who abandoned him 30 years earlier, a radical activist named Rex. Inspired for years by an idealized version of his father, the disillusioned son now wishes he could tell him the story of the French revolutionary Jean Lambert Tallien (1767–1820), a historical figure whose biography takes up most of Tuten's novella. An idealist whose erotic obsession with a noblewoman named Thérèse destroys his ideals, Tallien exemplifies a truth the son wishes he could impress upon his father: that a revolution may begin with the best of intentions, but quickly brings out the worst in people.

The stories of Rex and Tallien are linked both in broad outlines and by numerous subtle details (the son wishes for a blanket to keep off the freezing December nights in the Bronx, while Thérèse leaves Tallien for a banker who makes his fortune selling thin blankets to soldiers trying to keep from freezing). The stories also share a colorful vernacular style, maximalist prose within minimalist perimeters. Tuten brilliantly captures the gut-level anxieties of revolutionary activity and the inevitable betrayals — of friends and family, of ideals and principles — that attend most attempts to pound the square peg of an ideal into the round hole of reality. The son never tells this cautionary tale to his father but he tells it to us, and for that we should be grateful.

Review of Contemporary Fiction, Fall 1988

John Updike

The Coup
Knopf, 1978

I began reading John Updike's latest novel on New Year's Eve, confident that Updike's prose would be as deliciously intoxicating as the more common intoxicants imbibed in great quantities that evening. Continuing the book through the first cold week of the new year (and continuing the metaphor), I drank and drank but never felt more than a slight buzz; the language was there, as fine as an expensive liqueur, but little else — or rather, not as much as one would expect from one of America's finest novelists.

The new novel consists of the impressionistic memoirs of Colonel Hakim Feliz Ellellou, disposed dictator of the fictional African nation of Kush, formerly the kingdom of Noire and now an Islamic-Marxist "republic." Having disposed of the old king, Ellellou — writing years later in the south of France — reconstructs the bloodless coup led against him by a trusted adjutant. Woven into the memoirs are prose portraits of his four wives — the most interesting a saucy American coed named Candy Cunningham — and memories of his undergraduate years at an American college in Wisconsin during the balmy Eisenhower '50s.

Like Harun al-Rashid in *The 1001 Nights*, Ellellou is fond of wandering amongst his people incognito (and often in danger). It is during these fact-finding adventures that Updike tells us all he knows about Africa — which is surprisingly much — not all of which is always pertinent to the concerns of the novel, but which is interesting and poetically phrased well enough to excuse the occasional intrusiveness. Indeed, Africa quickly emerges as the real protagonist of the novel, and is almost a more fully realized "character" than any of the people, the narrator included.

Updike's ability to get under the skin of a Black Muslim dictator and project from that unusual point of view is impressive, reminiscent of his portrayal of the Black radical Skeeter in *Rabbit Redux*. Few authors would attempt such a foreign viewpoint, but few authors have Updike's insight into human nature. Nor do many have his dazzling control of language. Witness this self-conscious sentence concerning Minister of the Interior Michaelis Ezana's escape from a prison cell:

> Rather than risk confrontation with the soldiers and their doxies quartered in the fourth-floor corridor, who, if not fully alerted to the *nuancé* shifts of inner-circle lead-

> ership in Kush, certainly had caught the smoky whiff of *tabu* that now attached to Ezana, he, by a series of ripping, knotting, and measuring actions that like certain of these sentences were maddeningly distended by seemingly imperative refinements and elaborations in the middle, constructed a rope of caftans and agals and descended, through the silver kiss of the last moon of Safar, down the wall, in his terrified descent accompanied by his indifferent shadow, a faint large bat-shape whose feet touched his abrasively.

It is finally the language alone that holds the reader's interest to the end, like an indefinable something in a fine liqueur that urges one to drink glass after glass and which finally ends not with intoxication (as expected) but with an empty bottle, a pretty label, and a lingering bouquet gone by morning.

Spree, February 1979

William T. Vollmann

The Rainbow Stories
Atheneum, 1989

Surveying the fiction published in 1987, a Belgian critic wrote me the following year to ask, "Where are the young William Gaddises and Thomas Pynchons?" I wrote back recommending William T. Vollmann and David Foster Wallace, both of whom published masterful, innovative first novels in 1987: Vollmann a kind of cross between *Naked Lunch* and *Gravity's Rainbow* entitled *You Bright and Risen Angels*, and Wallace a novel called *The Broom of the System*, compared by some reviewers to the early Pynchon but closer to the spirit of Barth or Elkin. Now, coincidentally, both authors are publishing their first collections of short fiction within a month of each other, bravura performances that establish them both as heirs apparent to Barth, Burroughs, et al., and as the two most promising and talented authors under 30 writing today.

Like Kafka, Vollmann writes bizarre tales generated from pain and alienation, feelings he reveals in numerous authorial asides and footnotes. Most of the stories in his huge (543 pages) collection are actually nonfiction, fragmented pieces on marginalized groups such as skinheads, prostitutes, perverts, the homeless, and miscellaneous lost souls and eccentrics. These are rather aimless people, and Vollmann often adopts a kind of aimless narrative structure, simply recording brief epiphanies in their wretched lives like the "recording angel" he claims to be in the preface. There is an epigraph from Poe's "Berenice" that provides both the structure and rationale for *The Rainbow Stories* — "Misery is manifold. The wretchedness of the earth is uniform. Overreaching the wide horizon as the rainbow, its hues are as various as the hues of that arch; as distinct too, yet as intimately blended" — and Vollmann shares to a large degree Poe's morbidity, bizarre humor, outlandish erudition, and superior prose style. Vollmann can write monumental sentences with elaborate, extended metaphors, and has an ear for dialogue as sharp as Gaddis's. His is an art of excess, which occasionally spills over into a kind of recklessness, however: he seems a little too willing to allow any stray thoughts, any tangential trivia to take their place in his pages, and to find his aimless (and often repulsive) characters more interesting than most of his readers are likely to. Still, Vollmann's verbal prowess, empathy, and astonishing range put him in a class apart from his contemporaries.

Review of Contemporary Fiction, Summer 1989

Whores for Gloria
Pantheon, 1992

Vollmann's remarkable new novel is set in San Francisco's whore-infested Tenderloin district, the same setting he used for "Ladies and Red Lights" in his *Rainbow Stories* a few years back. The latter strung together dozens of realistic episodes in almost documentary fashion; *Whores for Gloria* is a far more ambitious and satisfying effort, a powerful psychodrama of one man's quest for happiness and love. Wino Jimmy, an aging Vietnam War vet, tries to keep his memory of Gloria alive by paying whores (the only word Vollmann uses for them) to tell him stories, which he in turn attributes to Gloria's past. Just as Dr. Frankenstein assembled an ersatz man from various body parts, Jimmy assembles his dream woman from the miserable lives of whores and precariously maintains a modicum of happiness by looking forward to reuniting with her. It's not clear whether Gloria was a childhood friend of Jimmy's, or a whore he actually knew, or indeed a complete fantasy. Vollmann keeps the reader close to Jimmy's point of view, so there's no telling whether Gloria is real or not. Sordid realism develops into hallucinatory fantasy and back again often in *Whores for Gloria*, appropriate in a world where whores and transsexuals bloom instantly into fantasy figures at a customer's request. In this regard *Whores for Gloria* is reminiscent of Genet's *Miracle of the Rose*: lyricism cut with brutal realism. It's a stunning performance.

Review of Contemporary Fiction, Summer 1992

□□□□□□□

Fathers and Crows
Viking, 1992

An Afghanistan Picture Show; or, How I Saved the World
Farrar, Straus and Giroux, 1992

From where I'm sitting, William T. Vollmann looks to be the most prodigiously talented and historically important American novelist under 35, the only one to come along in the last ten years or so capable of filling the seven-league boots of such mega-novelists as John Barth, William Gaddis, and Thomas Pynchon. Since 1987 he has published seven books — four novels, two collections of short fiction, and a nonfiction account — which tower over the work of his contemporaries by virtue of their enormous range, huge ambition, stylistic daring, wide learning, audacious innovation, and sardonic wit. If the man and his work are unknown to you, here's a brief résumé:

He is 33 years old, graduated summa cum laude (in comparative literature) from Cornell, and worked as a computer programmer until devoting himself full-time to writing a few years ago. His first novel, *You Bright and Risen Angels*, was published in 1987; a massive (635 pages), surrealistic work that reads like a cross between Pynchon's *Gravity's Rainbow* and William Burroughs's *Naked Lunch*, it is (like them) a brilliant allegory of the conflicts between revolutionary and repressive tendencies in politics and culture. It was followed in 1989 by *The Rainbow Stories*, another huge book, this one a collection of stories and novellas mostly concerning marginal, disenfranchised people — the homeless, skinheads, prostitutes. A year later, *The Ice-Shirt* was published, an imaginative reconstruction and retelling of the Norse legends about the discovery of America, and the first volume of his "Seven Dreams" series (more on which below). Last year he published another collection of short fiction, *Thirteen Stories and Thirteen Epitaphs*, in England (due out here in 1993), and earlier this year Pantheon brought out *Whores for Gloria*, a short novel set in San Francisco's Tenderloin district that fuses the lyricism of *You Bright and Risen Angels* with the brutality of *The Rainbow Stories*, an achievement that recalls Jean Genet's *Miracle of the Rose*. All this within five years! Even the most talented of Vollmann's contemporaries — David Foster Wallace, Susan Daitch, Richard Powers, Mary Caponegro — can't match this in quantity or quality.

Now come *Fathers and Crows*, his longest novel to date, and *An Afghanistan Picture Show*, his first book of straight nonfiction. These genre distinctions are misleading, however: Much of Vollmann's fiction uses nonfictional materials and techniques, and the author is ever-present in his work, popping up in the most unlikely places (11th-century Iceland, for example) to make an observation. Transformation and transvestism are recurring themes in his work, and thus Vollmann often dresses his fiction in nonfiction attire and vice versa, a technique that not only contributes to current debates on genre/gender distinctions but also looks back to the birth of the novel, a similar period of cross-dressing between fiction and nonfiction.

An Afghanistan Picture Show, for example, exploits the traditional literary theme of the innocent, altruistic Young Man (thus capitalized in Vollmann's book) going out into the world, only to have his naive worldview shattered. Barely out of college, Vollmann went to Afghanistan in 1982 to witness the fighting and to "Save The Afghans" (again, his caps). Instead, he spent most of his time fighting off various illnesses and cooling his heels in Pakistan (entry into Soviet-held Afghanistan was illegal), asking earnest but naive questions in an attempt to discover just how one goes about saving a people quickly and efficiently.

The older author is quite hard on his younger self and his "failed Pilgrim's Progress," yet the book succeeds not only in achieving its original goal — to bring attention to the plight of Afghan refugees (the first draft was finished in 1983 but couldn't find a publisher, though the attention is still valid) — but also in dramatizing the limitations of altruism and activism, the difficulty of understanding the context of any culture other than your own, and how that difficulty imperils writing books like this one. To overcome the last difficulty, Vollmann keeps his materials raw: Instead of a polished narrative, it's a disruptive text using many typefaces, incorporating bits of interviews, letters, statements, flashbacks and flash-forwards, quotations from Wittgenstein, footnoted asides — a mixed-media presentation that is all the more entertaining and effective for its ragged, unconventional look. As a do-it-yourself political primer, it is ingeniously ingenuous.[10]

Those same devices are on display in *Fathers and Crows*, the second volume of his "Seven Dreams: A Book of North American Landscapes." This is a hugely ambitious project tracking American history from the time of the Norsemen (*The Ice-Shirt*) to our present age, an investigation of American character, culture, and identity by way of seven pivotal episodes in our history. There are no precedents for an enterprise of this scope in our literature, though aspects of Vollmann's project can be seen in Washington Irving's *A History of New York*, Pound's history *Cantos*, and Marguerite Young's *Angel in the Forest* — all of which are poetic, even fanciful attempts at history. But Vollmann is closest in spirit to William Carlos Williams's *In the American Grain*. The poet there complains: "It is an extraordinary phenomenon that Americans have lost the sense, being made up as we are, that what we are has its origins in what the nation in the past has been; that there is a source in AMERICA for everything we think or do." Vollmann is out to recover those sources, and we need to be reminded of them.

Like Williams's book, *Fathers and Crows* is a kind of documentary history — in this case, of the French invasion of Canada in the 17th century, with particular attention to the conflicts between Jesuit missionaries (resembling crows in their black garb) and the Native American population. It's not a pretty story, and that's Vollmann's point: The violence that percolates under the surface of contemporary American life, erupting more and more often these days, has its origins in the violence the Norsemen inflicted on the natives of Newfoundland and in that more insidious violence of the imperialist sort that the Jesuits brought with them. Again like Williams, Vollmann relies on original documents (the *Jesuit Relations*, compilations of Indian tales, etc.) and retells them in their same spirit, switching points of view (and even the

10 After 9/11, every publisher with rights to a book on Afghanistan rushed a new edition into print, but not only did *An Afghanistan Picture Show* fail to be reprinted at that time, it wasn't issued in paperback until 2013. [2016 note.]

spelling of names) as his sources dictate.

The novel opens in modern Quebec with Vollmann (in his narrative persona as William the Blind) researching the Blessed Catherine Tekakwitha, a Mohawk convert of the 17th century on whom he has an adolescent crush. Attempting a mystical fusion with his materials — as Jesuit founder Saint Ignatius advised in his *Spiritual Exercises*, often quoted in *Fathers and Crows* — the narrator recounts his tale like a medium in a trance. His visionary approach occasionally takes liberties with recorded history, duly noted in footnotes and voluminous endnotes; here Vollmann often cites a few experts who read portions of his manuscript, and his cheeky rationale for ignoring their sober advice is often amusing and always interesting for the light it sheds on his artistic agenda. Like the narrator of *Tristram Shandy*, Vollmann confides in the reader occasionally, asking for patience at times, revealing personal biases, drawing parallels to contemporary Canadian problems, and so on. It's a self-conscious, postmodern approach to the historical novel, and while a few reactionary purists (historical and literary) may take exception, *Fathers and Crows* is a richly imaginative and boldly innovative achievement, doing for the historical novel what Barth's *Sot-Weed Factor* did 30 years ago, namely, reviving the genre for a new generation of readers.

Even though Vollmann's sympathies are clearly with the Native Americans, *Fathers and Crows* is neither a romantic evocation of the Noble Savage nor a politically correct idealization. The Native Americans could be as racist, sexist, and brutal as any European imperialist: They *routinely* tortured and ate members of other tribes (women and children included) and let their lust for iron hasten their own destruction. On the other hand, a few of the French are admirable characters, especially Samuel de Champlain (on whom Williams also wrote); some of the Jesuit priests are like the Young Man of *An Afghanistan Picture Show*, too idiotically innocent to be held accountable. A small attitude adjustment on the part of the Jesuits — like that displayed by Roberto de Nobili in India (also recounted here) — would have eased the Europeanization of Canada, but faults on both sides caused the wounds that crippled 17th-century Canada and that have reopened recently with the Quebecois and Native American movements for autonomy.

With *The Ice-Shirt* and *Fathers and Crows*, there is every indication that Vollmann's "Seven Dreams" septology will be the most important literary project of the '90s (if he lives to complete it — he has a history of risking his life to do field research). If you consider yourself at all conversant with contemporary American fiction, you must acquaint yourself with Vollmann's work and stay with him: It promises to be quite a picture show.

Washington Post Book World, 2 August 1992

Thirteen Stories and Thirteen Epitaphs

Pantheon, 1993

Vollmann's newest book is, like *The Rainbow Stories*, a linked collection of novellas and stories, and like his earlier book is peopled mostly by the demimonde of San Francisco, with a few set in Third World locales. "These stories are all epitaphs," Vollmann writes in an author's note, and there is a valedictory, memorial air hanging over most of these pieces as Vollmann tells autobiographical tales of people he's known. His photographer friend Ken Miller appears in many of them — Dean Moriarty to Vollmann's Sal Paradise — as does the mournful Elaine Suicide, the focus (heroine is hardly the word) of the two longest and best stories in the collection, "The Ghost of Magnetism" and "The Handcuff Manual." In between the 13 stories are 13 brief "epitaphs," ranging from a paragraph to a few pages, each a concentrated vignette of death or loss. The stylistic range is wide: "The Ghost of Magnetism" recalls *Visions of Cody*-era Kerouac, while "The Grave of Lost Stories" is a deliberate homage to Poe; the other stories use what is sometimes called "dirty realism," but are enlivened with unexpected bursts of lyricism and Vollmann's mordant humor. It is his saddest book, and one of his finest.

Vollmann is publishing so many books these days (three last year, now this one, *Butterfly Stories* and *The Rifles* within the next nine months) that his brilliance runs the risk of becoming taken for granted. There's no telling how much longer he will be able to keep up this prodigious rate of production, however, so readers are well advised to take nothing for granted and to savor each new book by this remarkable writer.

Review of Contemporary Fiction, Summer 1993

□ □ □ □ □ □ □

Butterfly Stories

Grove Press, 1993

The search for love has rarely been portrayed as joylessly as it is in *Butterfly Stories*. The unnamed narrator — variously called "the butterfly boy," "the journalist," "the husband" — moves through different sorts of jungles, some literal, some metaphorical, so lonely and so anxious to be happy that he can't help but fall in love with almost any woman he meets, beginning with a girl who defended him from the school bully, continuing with a lesbian met on a train to Istanbul, and finally a Cambodian whore named Vanna, an illiterate taxi dancer with whom he can't even converse. To maintain the bleak, hopeless nature of the narrator's quest for love, Vollmann reins in his often extravagant style for bare-bones recitation much of the time.

The novel moves from America to Europe to Asia, to northern Canada, to England as the narrator flits about like a butterfly: not a symbol of light-hearted caprice but of ceaseless wandering and searching. Towards the end the narrator tests HIV-positive, but that is nothing to the despair he feels at the loss of Vanna. The narrator's lack of shame and pride is almost ascetic in its self-abnegation, giving him a pure quality despite his incessant whoring. *Butterfly Stories* follows from Vollmann's *Whores for Gloria* and *Thirteen Stories* to explore the desperation that lovelessness can lead to.

Review of Contemporary Fiction, Spring 1994

□□□□□□□

The Rifles

Viking, 1994

Novels in series are usually pursued only by genre writers: John Jakes's Kent Family Chronicles or Marion Zimmer Bradley's endless Darkover fantasy series don't have their counterparts in serious literary fiction, where even the idea of a sequel is suspect.[11] (Joseph Heller's forthcoming sequel to *Catch-22* is already arousing more suspicion than elation: How can it possibly be as good?) William T. Vollmann is an exception, as might be expected from a writer who is exceptional in every way. His voluminous output — this is his ninth book in eight years — can be divided into two groups: raw, rather bizarre fictions about prostitutes (*Butterfly Stories, Whores for Gloria, The Rainbow Stories*) and a wildly ambitious historical series about our continent called "Seven Dreams: A Book of North American Landscapes." The series began with *The Ice-Shirt* (1990), which concerns the first Norse visitors to America, and was followed by *Fathers and Crows* (1992), about the French and Jesuit conquest of Canada. These are not straightforward historical novels; instead, they are highly imaginative meditations on early American history, mixing verifiable facts (the novels have as many footnotes and source notes as scholarly history books do) with legends, myths, fanciful digressions, sarcastic asides,

11 I should have inserted "nowadays" somewhere in this sentence. Literary history of course contains numerous series — Balzac's *La Comédie humaine*, Zola's *Les Rougon-Macquart*, Galsworthy's *Forsyte Saga*, Undset's *Kristin Lavransdatter* (a favorite of Vollmann's), Kerouac's *Legend of Duluoz* — but contemporary literary series are rare. James McCourt's delightful and still-growing Mawrdew Czgowchwz Saga comes to mind, as does Mark Z. Danielewski's new serial, *The Familiar*. [2016 note.]

and Vollmann's personal interpretation of the events. Those two historical fantasias are among the finest fictional achievements of our time. And while Vollmann's books about prostitutes are responsible for much of the notoriety and popularity he currently enjoys, I suspect it is the "Seven Dreams" series that will guarantee his place in literary history.

The Rifles is the third installment but will be volume 6 in the eventual seven-book scheme. It is the most experimental and daring book yet in the series, pushing its central metaphor of metamorphosis (Vollmann's initial inspiration for the series was Ovid) to almost phantasmagoric lengths. Here, a contemporary American who calls himself Captain Subzero becomes the reincarnation of Sir John Franklin, the celebrated English explorer who perished in 1847 in search of the Northwest Passage. Visiting Canada, Captain Subzero (clearly a version of Vollmann himself) falls hopelessly in love with a rather hopeless native Canadian Inuk woman named Reepah, and his doomed pursuit of her is aligned with Franklin's own doomed pursuit. Similarly, Captain Subzero's wife back home in the States becomes the reincarnation of Franklin's patient wife Jane. In many episodes the four characters mingle outside the bounds of chronology, which permits such bizarre anachronisms as Lady Jane praising a King Crimson CD that Subzero plays for Reepah.

Reincarnation smacks of mysticism or fantasy, but Vollmann uses it for other purposes: On the one hand, Subzero is engaging in a more exaggerated form of the kind of identification readers make with characters in novels; on the other, he is concerned (as is Vollmann) with the continuity of history, the fact that people and events in the past continue to resonate in the present. It is a common European complaint that Americans have no sense of history, and Vollmann seeks to redress that fault by using radical techniques (such as reincarnation and deliberate anachronism) to bring the past alive in a way that previous historical novelists would not have dared.

The shifts from the Victorian Era to our own time can be disorienting, but Vollmann's exquisite control of language helps keep the reader on course. (To further assist the reader, the book includes a number of hand-drawn maps.) The prose in the sections that recount Franklin's explorations is fulsome, Victorian; that in the sections set in our own time is choppy, curt. Vollmann's verbal prowess offers further satisfactions: The descriptions of the landscapes of Canada's Northwest Territories are especially good, and Vollmann's accounts of freezing to death are harrowing. He also has an uncanny ability to project himself into the most disparate characters, from a sailor on Franklin's ship to an Inuk seal trapper.

Each volume of "Seven Dreams" discusses the impact of Western technology and ideology on aboriginal Americans. The repeating rifle comes under scrutiny here, especially in the way it changed the hunting patterns of the

Inuit and thus led to their current decline. (Vollmann attacks the Canadian government's inhuman relocation programs in a portion of the novel called "Straight Shots" and in his footnotes.) That Reepah uses a shotgun to commit suicide brings the long history of firearms in America to a tragic, personal conclusion for the brokenhearted Subzero. Hopeless yearning unites Subzero with Franklin; "You want what you can't have," Subzero confesses at one point. Perhaps each of us pursues a Northwest Passage of some sort.

For readers new to the series, it would be better to start with *The Ice-Shirt* or *Fathers and Crows*. But for those who have been tracking Vollmann's career or who have a special interest in Canadian history, *The Rifles* is not to be missed. As Lady Franklin says of the King Crimson CD, it is "awfully marvelous, bloody brilliant."

Chicago Tribune, 6 March 1994

□ □ □ □ □ □ □

Ken Miller. *Open All Night*. Text by William T. Vollmann
Overlook, 1995

Well-heeled Vollmann fans will certainly want to buy this book. Ken Miller is a photographer who has accompanied Vollmann on many of his journeys and has photographed many of the people and places he writes about in his books. Vollmann contributes a two-page introduction and furnishes the quotations from his books that appear on facing pages to Miller's stark, black-and-white photos of skinheads, prostitutes, junkies, and the homeless. Miller — several of whose photos of the author appeared in our Vollmann issue a few years ago [Summer 1993] — played Virgil to Vollmann's Dante in the mid '80s by introducing him to this underclass and thus helped make possible such works as *The Rainbow Stories* and *Whores for Gloria* (as Vollmann gratefully acknowledges). Most of these photos in fact were taken in the '80s; Miller documents some of the lost souls who haunted that decade of greed.

Review of Contemporary Fiction, Spring 1996

□ □ □ □ □ □ □

The Atlas
Viking, 1996

In 1989, Tom Wolfe raised a stink when he wrote (in *Harper's*) that novelists should stop examining their navels and go out and get some real experience, do research like an ace journalist, so their work would have some socio-historical depth. I doubt William T. Vollmann's phantasmagoric novels are what Wolfe had in mind, but he certainly does get around. In 1982, barely out of college, Vollmann traveled to war-torn Afghanistan to see what he could do to help, a romantically naive experience described in his nonfiction book *An Afghanistan Picture Show*. Later in the '80s he began exploring Greenland and Canada for the early volumes of his "Seven Dreams" series of historical novels. In recent years he has been sent by magazines such as *Esquire* and *Spin* to the world's hot spots — Somalia, Bosnia, Thailand, Los Angeles after the Rodney King riots — often at considerable risk. (He narrowly missed being hit by snipers in Croatia; his two companions were killed.) All of these travels inform his latest work of fiction, *The Atlas*.

The book is difficult to categorize: It resembles a short-story collection in that there are 55 stories, most of them made up of four or five brief vignettes — the prose equivalents of postcards or vacation slides — linked by a particular image or memory. It is like a gazetteer in that you can focus on particular places to read about, if you wish, for the stories are all self-contained. It is also a mathematically structured fiction like Georges Perec's *Life A User's Manual* or John Barth's *LETTERS*. As Vollmann explains in the preface, the book is organized like a palindrome — a sentence that reads the same backwards and forwards. ("Able was I ere I saw Elba," Napoleon reputedly said.) That is, the first story is linked to the last, the second to the penultimate, and so on. At the center of the novel *The Atlas* is a story called "The Atlas," which weaves together episodes from the rest of the book. But the book *The Atlas* also resembles a novel in that it explores the psychic landscape of a single narrator (never named, but pretty clearly Vollmann), a man who is reminded of the world within by the troubled world at large.

The narrator travels the world over to escape from an overwhelming sense of loss and to find some sort of enduring love. By turns holy fool and ugly American, he meets a wide variety of people and has numerous adventures, most of them dismal. Occasionally he experiences moments of beauty and rapture (especially in the chapter-story "Exalted by the Wind"), but mostly what he encounters are reminders of losses: his dead sister, the various women he has loved, former friends. Brooding on the Thames a century ago, Joseph Conrad's Marlow, another world traveler, announced, "And this also has been one of the dark places of the earth." Vollmann likewise is concerned with the dark places of the earth, and the heart of darkness within. They say travel expands one's horizons, but it also brings into sharper focus our limitations, our inability to connect with others in a meaningful way. As in Conrad's novella, an air of desolation and despair hangs over Vollmann's *Atlas*.

The geographic range is extensive: Australia, Burma, Egypt, India, Italy, Japan, Madagascar, Mexico, the Vatican City — he seems to have been everywhere. (There are even stories set in Limbo and "The Sphere of Stars.") The stylistic variety is just as wide. Some chapters, like "The Red Song," are lyrical and surrealistic. "The Hill of Gold" imitates the King James Bible, even to verse numbering. Some stories are rendered in straightforward reportage, others in a stream-of-consciousness style that can be difficult to follow. The book is thus an atlas of narrative styles and rhetorical devices, from allegory to zeugma. If nothing else, *The Atlas* offers further proof that Vollmann is perhaps the most stylistically daring writer working today.

The crosscutting between several locales within the same story can be disorienting, like being on a whirlwind tour and seeing too many places in too short a period. But at its best, the technique is revelatory. For example, one of the best stories, "Under the Grass," opens with the narrator brooding on the day in 1968 when his negligence led to his sister's drowning in a pool. (Sad to say, this tragedy actually occurred when Vollmann was a boy, as he once revealed in an interview.) Buried under the New England grass, his sister becomes a combination of spirit guide and ghost to haunt the boy: "Now you're my white witch," he says, like a narrator in one of Poe's tales (evoked here by the lush, Gothic prose). From there we jump to an airport in Mauritius 25 years later, where the narrator is so fatigued and disoriented that he asks the authorities how to find his sister, a request that leads to comic misunderstandings and ends with a taxi driver assuming the narrator wants a prostitute. Then we jump to Thailand in the same year, at a bar for prostitutes, where the narrator is feeling good for having recently "rescued a child-prostitute from a nightmarish brothel in the south." (This was the subject of a photo-essay Vollmann contributed to *Spin* in 1993.) He has sex with a prostitute, then dreams of seeing his sister's coffin, and wakes up "either screaming or thinking I was screaming," realizing that his rescuing exploit was a failed attempt to appease the spirit of the sister he failed to rescue 25 years ago. The story concludes in the catacombs of Rome, back in Poe territory (this story is a micro-palindrome mirroring the macro-palindrome of the book), where the narrator envisions a gruesome resurrection for his sister, only to see her metamorphose into the presiding spirit of "the girls from Firenze who drink the sun . . . the girls who sing a-la-la-*la!* and 'Ciao, Maria'" — a puzzling but cathartic ending to a moving story.

For those who have followed Vollmann's career, *The Atlas* will recall his

Rainbow Stories and *Thirteen Stories and Thirteen Epitaphs*. He also revisits some of the people and places of earlier novels of his. Those who don't know his work might begin with *The Atlas*: It functions as a summation of his characteristic themes and settings, a display of his stylistic range, and an unsettling, unforgettable tour of the world according to Vollmann.

Chicago Tribune, 11 August 1996

□ □ □ □ □ □ □

The Royal Family
Viking, 2000

William T. Vollmann writes about whores. Not prostitutes or hookers, not call girls or sex workers, certainly not courtesans or concubines, but whores: drug-addicted, disease-ridden, lying, cheating, filthy, stupid wretches. And he loves them. He has already devoted two novels — *Whores for Gloria* and *Butterfly Stories* — and several short stories to these creatures, works that display a Christ-like compassion and forbearance for them. *The Royal Family* is his longest and saddest paean to whores, and I hope his last.

Like Steinbeck's *East of Eden*, *The Royal Family* is set in California and is based on the Cain and Abel story. Henry Tyler (Cain) is a struggling private detective in his forties; John (Abel) is an ambitious contract lawyer, a stereotypical yuppie who prides himself on knowing where to buy the finest ties in San Francisco, while Henry is something of a bohemian (he has long hair and prefers City Lights bookstore over a haberdashery). Both brothers are in love with the same person, a rather unhappy Korean-born woman named Irene. She's married to John, who is usually too busy to spend time with her, so Henry keeps her company — until the day she commits suicide.

One of Henry's clients is a crass businessman named Jonas Brady who wants to open a Las Vegas sex casino called Feminine Circus. He's heard of a San Francisco woman known as the Queen of the Whores, whom he feels would be a fine attraction at his casino, so he hires Henry to track her down. As Henry trawls through the underworld searching for this mysterious person, he's introduced to the members of the Queen's "royal family," a pool of "cunt-sharks" with names like Sapphire, Chocolate, Sunflower, Strawberry, and Domino. After Irene kills herself, he redoubles his efforts to locate the Queen, hoping to find some kind of salvation by passing through a refining fire of grief and degradation.

Henry's quest for the Queen rings with religious overtones supplied by Vollmann's occasional references to Gnostic scripture and Canaanite mythology. God set the mark of Cain upon the brow of Abel's murderer that he might be avoided by all decent people, and Henry comes to view prostitutes — and eventually himself — as members of Cain's tribe. When he finally meets the Queen, she provides him with rituals of degradation intended to purge him of his grief for Irene, and when those don't work, she becomes his lover. Eventually she disappears, and Henry gives up his profession and becomes a hobo, riding the rails in search of his lost Queen.

Vollmann's brutal, unflinching accounts of the lives of street whores will not be to all readers' tastes. I was reminded of Samuel R. Delany's transgressive novel *The Mad Man* and even of Sade's monstrous works (Sade is, in fact, quoted in a prologue). And whoring is only one of the activities depicted here that will discomfort the reader. The secret of Brady's successful Feminine Circus turns out to be his employment of retarded girls for his patrons' abuse. An autopsy is described in colorful detail. A lively character named Dan Smooth, an enthusiastic pedophile, regales Henry (and the reader) with a number of stories. At one point Henry interrupts Smooth to say, "Your filth gets pretty boring after a while"; this quotation appears on page 152 of the 780-page work and I almost gave up at that point in hearty agreement. (Vollmann seems to be deliberately baiting the reader; on page 324, still not yet halfway through, Tyler himself says, "If this were a book I wouldn't even read the rest of it.")

Vollmann tests his readers' patience, but rewards it with occasional flashes of black humor, sardonic social commentary, and bursts of phantasmagoric prose (especially in the extraordinary Book XVII: "Buying Their Dream House"). His wide erudition results in some far-flung analogies, and his cavalier disregard for the conventions of fiction allows for some interesting authorial asides and even an essay on the California bail system. The theological parallels are intriguing, if not totally convincing, and his obvious sympathy for whores and homeless people makes him a better person than I. *The Royal Family* is an honest look at an aspect of modern life that continues to be ignored or romanticized. Dan Smooth could be speaking for Vollmann when he claims, "I'm the only person in the whole wide world who always speaks the truth. You know how to be sure it's the truth? Because it's *ugly*, man!" Consequently, calling *The Royal Family* an ugly book is praise, not censure.

And of course it's good to have Vollmann back after a four-year absence. He published nine books in the decade 1987–96, most of them *huge*, and then hunkered down to finish a massive nonfiction book on violence entitled *Rising Up and Rising Down*, only to have it rejected by his publishers because of its length. (During this period Vollmann almost lost the use of his hands due to excessive typing.) Vollmann's previous two books on whores are among his shortest works, so perhaps with *The Royal Family* he has made his grand statement on the subject and can return to what I and many of his other admirers feel is his greatest achievement, the "Seven Dreams" series. The three volumes Vollmann has published so far of this proposed seven-volume history of North America afford him the widest scope for his considerable talents, from minutely researched historical set pieces to phantasmagoric tales of shape-shifting and metamorphoses. There's been nothing like this in American literature since Washington Irving's *A History of New York*, and Vollmann has already redefined the historical novel with this behemothian project. I know how the story ends, but I can't wait for him to resume telling it.

Rain Taxi, Fall 2000

□□□□□□□

Argall

Viking, 2001

With *Argall*, Vollmann makes a triumphant return to his ambitious "Seven Dreams" series of novels, detailing the invasion of North America by Europeans and the legacy of violence and oppression they left behind. *Argall* deals with the British annexation of what they later called Virginia, and focuses on three colorful characters: Pocahontas, Captain John Smith, and the sinister Sir Samuel Argall, who eventually kidnaps Pocahontas and introduces slavery into the New World.

As the voluminous notes attest, Vollmann has done his homework and gives us what is probably the most historically accurate version of the Pocahontas story. And he does so in an astonishing re-creation of Elizabethan prose. This isn't the elegant Augustan prose adapted by Barth in *The Sot-Weed Factor* and Pynchon in *Mason & Dixon*; this is the earlier, racier prose of the young turks of Shakespeare's day like Robert Greene, Thomas Dekker, and especially Thomas Nashe. As one of Vollmann's sources says of that era, "the whole style of the day was inflated — in writing and in living"; hence Vollmann uses a suitably inflated style that captures the age in all its vitality and vulgarity. As both a historical novel and a linguistic tour de force, *Argall* is a magnificent achievement.

Amazon.com, 2 October 2001

□□□□□□□

Rising Up and Rising Down

7 vols.; McSweeney's, 2003

A little over a hundred years ago, Sir James G. Frazer set out to explain a minor point in Classical scholarship: the rule that regulated the succession to the priesthood at a shrine in Italy devoted to the goddess Diana. But over the next 15 years, as he realized every aspect of the rule had a history to be explicated, and as he found parallels in other cultures, his project ballooned into the 12-volume *Golden Bough*, a monumental study of the evolution of magic and superstition into religion, an influential work cited by writers as diverse as T. S. Eliot, Carl Jung, William Gaddis, and Jim Morrison.

Twenty years ago, novelist William T. Vollmann set out to answer a similar deceptively simple question: When is violence justified? Most people have a stock response: Never, says the pacifist. Only in self-defense or wartime, many would say. Whenever anyone looks at me funny, a bully would say. Whenever I'm doing God's work, a religious fanatic would say. The new century threatens to be even more violent than the last, so it is a question that deserves a more considered response, a challenge Vollmann has met with a massive work that provides an encyclopedic survey of violence and a general field theory for its justifiability.

The work is divided in two parts: the first four volumes are what Vollmann calls the "theoretical" part of the study — drawn mostly from historical accounts of violence — while volumes 5 and 6 deal with contemporary zones of violence, based on Vollmann's far-flung travels. A concluding volume contains a digest of his "moral calculus" (more on which below), appendices, supplementary materials, and a 44-page bibliography where Herodotus is followed by a book on bear attacks, and where a translation of the medieval *Two Lives of Charlemagne* by Einhard and Notker the Stammerer precedes John Ellis's *Social History of the Machine Gun.* "Eclectic" doesn't even begin to describe it.

To organize his unruly subject, Vollmann divides acts of violence into their various possible defenses: self-defense (the only clearly justified use of violence according to Vollmann), defense of homeland, of honor, authority, race, creed, gender, and more recent concerns such as defense of earth against polluters and defense of animals. For his examples, Vollmann draws on nearly all eras of recorded history — in volume 2 he tosses off "A Survey-History of Property from Nomadic Times to the Russian Revolution" — and treats nearly every culture on earth, from the hapless Afghans to the Zulu.

The scope is immense, and his reading wide. Though not an academic, Vollmann scrupulously documents everything in hundreds of source notes (his philanthropic publisher hired a team of fact-checkers to help) and goes out of his way to be as fair and respectful toward his material as possible. He is so open-minded that he can identify and praise Trotsky's few virtues while admitting "To Trotsky I'd be scum." There's no agenda, no pre-ordained thesis, no political bias: he simply wants to understand violence and share his findings. Nor is he prescriptive; though sickened by violence, he's concerned here with how to judge it, not how to eradicate it. We *know* how to eradicate it: as Vollmann counsels, just observe the Golden Rule, perhaps fleshed out with the UN's 1948 *Universal Declaration of Human Rights*, but that's easier said than done.

Like Frazer, Vollmann's method is comparative: though a principal "moral actor" stars in each section — Trotsky in "Defense of Authority," Cortés in "Defense of Ground" — other actors from other eras of history make their appearances. "For much the same reason that one opera frequently recalls another," Vollmann notes, "the student of history will find that many an atrocity will be recapitulated somewhere down the centuries." In his chapter on "Defense of Honor," Vollmann finds common ground between the Charge of the Light Brigade ("remembered for its 'gallantry' — in other words, for its tactical idiocy"), Joan of Arc, Napoleon, King Olaf's forced conversions in medieval Norway, Sun-tzu, and Mao Zedong's personal physician. Referring to young inmates of juvenile hall in the 1950s, Vollmann writes: "And now Blinky has disturbed his prestige again, like the Roman Prince Maxentius throwing down the statues of the Roman Emperor Constantine. Abbot had better show some 'heart.' ('When a brave man faces death,' says Socrates, 'he does so for fear of something worse.')" A discussion of Plato's totalitarian ideals includes an aside on "his half-brother Adolf Hitler" and an anecdote about a four-year-old girl whose parents allowed her to starve to death. A single paragraph will join a Revolutionary War Minuteman, an 1870s pioneer woman, and sixth-century Byzantine historian Procopius. He'll defend his right to carry a gun with a citation from the Old Norse *Poetic Edda*.

Throughout, the emphasis is on individual responsibility for acts of violence. Vollmann contemptuously dismisses the claims of "social forces" and "historical goals" that so many revolutionaries and tyrants hide behind, identifies the monstrous arrogance of terrorists who would impose their beliefs on others, and condemns the spinelessness of those who defend their participation in atrocities by claiming to be "following orders." (As the personified Technology in Thomas Pynchon's World War II novel *Gravity's Rainbow* says at one point, "'Do you think we'd've had the Rocket if someone, some specific somebody with a name and a penis hadn't *wanted* to chuck a ton of Amatol 300 miles and blow up a block full of civilians?'") Vollmann indicts not only the obvious mass-murderers of history — Stalin, Hitler, Mao, Pol Pot, Saddam Hussein — but those who encouraged widespread violence (Robespierre,

Trotsky) or made questionable decisions that led to it, like Abraham Lincoln. (Vollmann reminds us that Lincoln pursued the Civil War not to free slaves but to assert the superiority of federal rights over states' rights, a dubious justification for the four years of bloodshed that resulted.)

As Vollmann proceeds through the various defenses of violence, he codifies his findings as part of a "moral calculus," an attempt to establish a checklist by which any act of violence can be judge as justifiable or not. Not surprisingly, he finds most acts of violence unjustified, excepting only self-defense and violence committed during a justified war, which even then must be tightly restricted. (According to Vollmann's calculus, the Bush Administration's recent invasion of Iraq is totally unjustified because it fails the test of imminence, among other reasons.) Vollmann's moral calculus is presented in digest form on pp. 33–119 in the final volume, and I wish this section could be printed as a pamphlet and distributed worldwide. Every politician, soldier, activist, and budding revolutionary deserves to read it, if no more of *Rising Up and Rising Down.*

(And about that odd title: a "rising up" is a justified act of violence, a "rising down" an unjustified one.)

Unlike Frazer, who never left his library, Vollmann supplements his immense reading with fieldwork done in some of the most dangerous places on earth. Volumes 5 and 6 record his trips to Cambodia, Thailand, Burma, Japan, the former Yugoslavia, Madagascar, the Congo, Somalia, Malaysia, Iraq, Afghanistan, Yemen, Colombia, Jamaica, and various parts of the United States. Some of these essays were published in the 1990s in such magazines as *Spin, Gear, Esquire,* and the *New Yorker,* always in severely edited form, and for many readers these will be the most enjoyable volumes of *Rising Up and Rising Down* — though "enjoyable" is hardly the word for this parade of misery.

In almost every case Vollmann shows the effects of violence on those least able to avoid it: the poor. Some of these make for rather thrilling reading — like Vollmann's account of his rescue of a 12-year-old sex slave from a Thai brothel — while others are the bleakest things you'll ever read. A few are *Apocalypse Now*-type quests for mysterious figures — Vollmann was one of the few to interview Khun Sa, the "Opium King" of Burma, and Hadji Amin, the "Old Man" of the PULO separatist movement in Thailand — but most consist of interviews with the wretched of the earth as they suffer from the effects of weak or illegitimate governments. I lost count of the number of times Vollmann was almost killed during these adventures.

Here in the States Vollmann hangs with Cambodian immigrant gangbangers, with suicidal Apache teenagers on an Arizona reservation, with mourners after the Columbine Massacre, with superstitious blacks down

South (who resort to magic, voodoo, Christianity, Santería, and other primitive beliefs to ward off violence), and with paranoid whites in the Pacific Northwest, whose very real concern with governmental abrogation of their rights gets mixed up with anti-Semitism, racism, conspiracy theories, and Bible-fueled apocalyptic fears.

Rising Up and Rising Down is a monumental achievement on several levels: as a hair-rising survey of mankind's propensity for violence, as a one-man attempt to construct a system of ethics, as a successful exercise in objective analysis (almost nonexistent in today's partisan, ideological, politicized, spin-doctored, theory-muddled public discourse), and a demonstration of the importance of empathy, whether in writing a book like this or simply dealing with fellow human beings. It can be an exhausting, depressing read, but with the ever-growing role of violence in our lives, it is an essential read. And the amazing fact that during the 20 years he spent writing *Rising Up and Rising Down* Vollmann also published a dozen extraordinary books of fiction — many in the 700-page range and packed with historical research as deep as that on display here — elevates this achievement beyond the realm of mere mortals.

Washington Post Book World, 17 December 2003

□□□□□□□

Europe Central
Viking, 2005

Expelled from Eden: A William T. Vollmann Reader.
Edited by Larry McCaffery and Michael Hemmingson
Thunder's Mouth Press, 2004

The Vollmann juggernaut rolls on. Instead of taking a well-deserved rest after publishing his 7-volume, 3300-page *Rising Up and Rising Down* in the fall of 2003, he quickly prepared a 1-volume abridgment — a mere 733 pages, published by Ecco last fall — then collaborated with critic Larry McCaffery and novelist Michael Hemmingson on *Expelled from Eden*, continued to publish essays and reviews in various journals, and then completed his new 800-page novel *Europe Central* while recovering from a broken pelvis. He's published 15 books in the last 18 years, half of them 600 pages or longer, and with no falling off in quality or innovation. He's what they used to call a shock worker back in the USSR.

The former Soviet Union and Nazi Germany are the settings for his new novel, a grimly magnificent dramatization of the impossible moral choices forced on individuals by those totalitarian regimes. Ranging from 1914 to 1975, the book is organized as a series of paired stories, like Plutarch's *Parallel Lives*, comparing a German and a Russian facing a similar situation. For example, one set pairs Soviet general Andrei Vlasov, who deserted his army for the enemy's, with Field-Marshal Friedrich Paulus, a Nazi who collaborated with the Communists after capture. But most are not so neat. The danger of using violent means to attain idealistic ends is the point of the first pair of stories, which contrasts the revolutionary idealist Fanya Kaplan, whose failed attempt to assassinate Lenin in 1918 unleashed the Red Terror wave of executions, with a nameless German whose patriotic idealism inspires him to cheer Kaiser Wilhelm's decision to begin World War I; "and right beside me a pale little man, probably a tramp, with disheveled hair and a dark trapezoidal mustache, began to caper, smiling at the world with a sleepwalker's eyes."

Many of the stories focus on four artists, tracking their attempts to create meaningful art under regimes that are hostile to any art that doesn't celebrate official patriotic ideals in social-realist form. The German Käthe Kollwitz persists with her stark engravings depicting the victims of oppression despite charges of pessimism. The Russian Anna Akhmatova tries to keep her poetry free of political themes, and pays the price of non-publication for decades, until she capitulates in order to rescue her son from a Siberian prison. The Soviet filmmaker Roman Karmen, by contrast, has an easier time of it by producing films that win official approval. Vollmann devotes the most pages to the case of Soviet composer Dmitri Shostakovich, the subject of several long stories, who played a cat-and-mouse game with the authorities throughout his career, outwardly submitting to their criticism and "corrections" while managing to write deeply personal music and avoid joining the Party until near the end of his life.

Like a method actor immersing himself in a role, Vollmann tells most of his stories from the point of view of their protagonists or a related character — the apparatchik Comrade Alexandrov relates many of the Soviet stories — relying on his immense research to empathize with his characters. (There are 50 pages of source notes at the end of the book, scrupulously documenting his occasional departures from the historical record for artistic purposes.) He shows that most moral decisions are not abstract applications of principles but the complicated result of cultural conditioning and personal psychology, a muddy mix of dreams, neuroses, fairy tales, nationalism, perversion, pride, and fear. His German characters are motivated as much by myths and Wagnerian opera as by political considerations, and communist double-speak keeps most of his Soviet characters from even thinking straight. Vollmann's language beautifully captures these warring conflicts, moving from lyricism to military strategy to hallucination to erotic longing as his characters navigate their way through a landscape of atrocities — and not just the ones perpetrated by the Nazis and the Communists. A Russian character notes: "On the night of 13–14.2.45, the British and the Americans burned thirty-five thousand people, mainly civilians, in an incendiary bombing raid in Dresden. This slightly bettered the Nazi achievement at Babi Yar, where only thirty-three thousand Jews had been machined-gunned."

I've reviewed nearly all of Vollmann's books over the years and am running out of superlatives; suffice it to say, if you've been following Vollmann's extraordinary career, *Europe Central* may be his best novel yet. If you haven't, you might want to begin with *Expelled from Eden*, a well-organized collection of selections from his works, uncollected essays and letters, poems, all enclosed by very useful commentary from the editors. Vollmann's willingness to go against the preferred social realism of our day, enabled by his publisher's willingness to allow him to unfold his Wagnerian epics at full length, makes him a hero of our time.

Washington Post Book World, 17 April 2005

Marek Waldorf

The Short Fall
Turtle Point Press, 2013

This is an innovative, multilevel novel about a speechwriter's relationship to his client, a charismatic presidential candidate named Vance Talbot, and about his own relationship to the written word. Despite a terrific convention speech that Chad wrote, the candidate's poll numbers begin dropping in the weeks before Election Day. An assassination attempt changes everything: the bullet misses Talbot but hits his speechwriter, who is paralyzed from the neck down. When the novel opens, Chad is in a hospital struggling to learn how to write again, and begins to suspect the bullet was deliberately aimed at him in a desperate attempt by Talbot's campaign staff to win sympathy for their candidate and reverse the poll numbers.

Much of the novel concerns the nuts-and-bolts of running for the highest office in the land, a fly-on-the-wall exposé of how campaigns are run. At the same time, *The Short Fall* is a metafictional meditation on creative writing. Ghostwriter Chad was successful because he captured Talbot's voice, and an idealized character behind that voice; implied throughout is the novelist's (any novelist's) attempt to find a "voice" for his protagonist, a distinctive one that creates character. After a career of writing in the voice of others — there are a few subtle references to ventriloquism — Chad writes this account in his own voice, which is radically different from his speeches for the candidate. Because of the neurological damage done by the bullet, he has to rediscover how to write, literally so, via a stick in his mouth by which he selects letters on a keyboard. Complicating this rediscovery of his voice is the presence of a hack ghostwriter who has been hired by a publisher to tell Chad's story.

The form is nonlinear. Chad's memories range from childhood to the campaign trail, from the day of the assassination attempt to his rediscovery, presented out of chronological sequence. As a result, we don't learn that the narrator is named Chad until a third of the way through; similarly, we don't learn until much later that Vance's alternate name "Vlad" refers to his birth name, Vlad Blattoski. The achronological form and withholding of key details like this may frustrate conventional readers, but Waldorf is not writing for them: he is writing for those who like Nabokov, Wallace, Danielewski, and other unconventional novelists. But the "story" is not that difficult to follow — it emerges slowly like an image on a Polaroid photograph — so the novel shouldn't be pegged as offputtingly experimental.

Unlike the conventional political speeches he writes — which evoke Orwell's "Politics and the English Language" — Chad's own speech is unconventional, quirky, and metaphoric. There's a "*joie d'ecrit*" at work here; "Every word a surprise!" as it says herein. Some recondite words are indeed a surprise (lucify, impetiginous), but the unusual phrasing, imagery, and occasional flashes of humor are a continuous delight. Finding his own voice, Chad becomes a creative writer in part 3 as he imagines 13 scenarios for how the assassination attempt may have come about, all 13 generated from misspellings in a crazy fan letter Talbot receives, and which Chad suspects is a coded message from a rival campaign staffer (if I understood all that correctly). As both a political novel and a novel about the creative process, *The Short Fall* is a success.

Amazon.com, 16 October 2013, adapted from my reader's report for the publisher of 9 September 2012

David Foster Wallace

Girl with Curious Hair
Norton, 1989

[See the first Vollmann review above (p. 335) for the opening paragraph: *Girl with Curious Hair* and *The Rainbow Stories* were reviewed together.]

David Foster Wallace is [Vollmann's] only equal, and is probably his superior in exerting greater artistic control and placing further aesthetic distance between himself and his creations. His stories have a different kind of appeal than Vollmann's — which is like the grim but absorbing fascination one might have for a documentary on concentration camp experiments on human subjects — for they are usually funnier, not as intensely personal as Vollmann's, and concerned with a wider variety of characters. Wallace is a masterful ventriloquist, capable of speaking in the voice of a woman (in "Little Expressionless Animals" and "My Appearance," in which he also impersonates perfectly the cast of *The David Letterman Show*), a twisted Young Republican and his punk friends ("Girl with Curious Hair"), and an aide to LBJ ("Lyndon"), among others, while "John Billy" is a tall tale told in an incredible Elizabethan cracker accent, Sir Thomas Browne filtered through Jethro of *The Beverly Hillbillies*, as it were.

The most impressive story, done in a variety of voices, is a novella entitled "Westward the Course of Empire Takes Its Way." Using Barth's story "Lost in the Funhouse" both as a stylistic springboard and as part of the plot (a franchise of Funhouse discos is the centerpiece at the reunion in Illinois of everyone who's ever appeared in a McDonald's commercial), Wallace pulls out all the stops in this tour de force of what the jacket copy calls *post*-postmodernism (a technique he mocks even as he creates it). Here, as in most of the stories, Wallace processes brand names, TV shows, commercials, and all the other flotsam of popular culture, not in the manner of the minimalists (to ground their anemic stories in the real), but to show that what used to be low- or extra-cultural trivia have become the dominant, even the sole culture for many people. Like Vollmann, Wallace has a great ear for dialogue, especially for the MTV/game show/technoid idiom of his generation, managing to make it lively and clever rather than dumb and dated.

A pressing deadline forced me to read and review these books more rapidly than they deserve (indeed, they demand to be read more than once to fully appreciate their complexity), but even the hastiest reading indicates these are likely to be the two best short-story collections of the year from the two most talented young writers in America.

Review of Contemporary Fiction, Summer 1989

□□□□□□□

Mark Costello and David Foster Wallace.
Signifying Rappers: Rap and Race in the Urban Present
Ecco Press, 1990

You don't even have to like rap music to find Costello and Wallace's pioneering study a dazzling performance: informative, provocative, funny, and — especially in the sections by Wallace — brilliantly written, an intellectually wired style combining subtle and original thought with demotic diction of great wit, insight, and in-your-face energy.

The authors build their case for taking rap seriously not on its musical qualities — in fact, they admit rap doesn't qualify as music in the traditional sense — but on its poetic qualities. The rapper works in a form (historically aligned with 16th-century skeltonic verse, actually) containing a number of constraints (meter, rhyme, assonance) that inspire the better rappers to "really complicated prosodic innovations — disordered but effective enjambment, stresses alternated between standard feet, wild combinations of iamb with trochee and of both with spondee, with the kind of metrical libertinism that spells f-r-e-e-v-e-r-s-e but is here required by *exactly* the sort of tight aural walls free verse was all about knocking down" (Wallace).

Signifying Rappers forces us to think about a new art form most of us wouldn't even want to listen to, much less think about (much less dignify as an art form), explains the racial dynamics that make rap so alien and off-putting to many whites, and succeeds as a tour de force of cultural criticism that will open your eyes, if not your ears.

Review of Contemporary Fiction, Spring 1991

□□□□□□□

Infinite Jest

Little, Brown, 1996

While reading William Gass's *The Tunnel* last year at this time, I feared I was witnessing the last of a dying breed, the encyclopedic American novel that began with Gaddis's *Recognitions* in 1955, hit its stride in the '60s and '70s (*Giles Goat-Boy, Gravity's Rainbow,* Gaddis again with *J R, The Public Burning, LETTERS*), went baroque in the '80s (*Darconville's Cat, Take Five, Women and Men, You Bright and Risen Angels*), then raged against the dying of the light in the '90s with Powers's *Gold-Bug Variations* and Gass's massive masterpiece. Who was left to write such novels, or to read them at a time when some scorn such books as elitist, testosterone-fueled acts of male imperialism? For those of us who regard these works as our cultural milestones, not as tombstones in patriarchy's graveyard, David Foster Wallace demonstrates that the encyclopedic novel is still alive and kickin' it.

As with *The Tunnel,* sheer style is the first attraction of *Infinite Jest.* Even in his precocious first novel, *The Broom of the System* (1987), Wallace was unfurling long, complex sentences, by turns sonorous and satirical, that were a joy to behold. *Infinite Jest* displays a wider range of styles — from the subliterate monologue of a poverty-stricken abused woman to technical explications of the properties of various pharmaceuticals — but the main narrative style is both casual and complex, slangy and erudite, a kind of slacker mandarin with comically manic specificity of detail. Even if you have trouble following the multiplex narrative at the macro level Wallace offers huge entertainment value at the micro level, flaunting (but in a good way) an amazing command of late-twentieth-century English, with its proliferating technical terms, street slang, and babble of late capitalism. Only Gaddis and Pynchon have this range, and Wallace takes the language places even those two don't go.

At the macro level, *Infinite Jest* consists of numerous "anticonfluential" (Wallace's word) episodes set a dozen years or so in the future (as was *The Broom*), at a time when numerical designations for years have been sold to corporate sponsors: hence we have the Year of the Depend Adult Undergarment (in which most of the novel takes place), the Year of Glad, the Year of Dairy Products from the American Heartland, and so on. The narrative focuses on two suffering individuals: Hal Incandenza, a brilliant student and gifted tennis player attending the Enfield Tennis Academy and smoking way too much pot; and Don Gately, a petty criminal and recovering narcotics addict on staff at the nearby Ennet House Drug and Alcohol Recovery House ("Redundancy *sic*"), and the narrative shuttles between these two locations (both in the metro Boston area) with occasional side-trips to Arizona, where Hal grew up and where other members of the Incandenza family live. (There is a subplot concerning Quebecois separatists and a lethally entertaining video cartridge.) Thematically, the narrative shuttles between addiction and recovery.

Addiction struck William S. Burroughs at midcentury as an encompassing metaphor for many facets of American life, and at century's end Wallace finds a similar metaphor in the recovery from addiction. While Burroughs dwelled with sadistic glee on the horrors of addiction, Wallace takes on the horrors of withdrawal; addiction in Burroughs was largely a response to the need to conform in the Eisenhower '50s, while in Wallace addiction is a response to stress, to the need to excel in the Reagan '80s (the novel's "ethical" setting, if not its historic one). Again like Burroughs — who is named in the text and seems a pretty clear influence — Wallace uses insect imagery to heighten the repugnance of addiction and detoxification. *Infinite Jest* is a *Naked Lunch* for the '90s.

But there's more: tennis as a metaphysical activity; a hundred pages of endnotes, some with their own footnotes; a parody of an annotated filmography; mindbending excursions into game theory; a Workers Comp claim worthy of a Roadrunner cartoon; an essay-length explanation of why video-phones are doomed to fail; and some incredibly sad stories of damaged human beings with more problems than you'll ever have. The novel is so brilliant you need sunglasses to read it, but it has a heart as well as a brain. *Infinite Jest* is both a tragicomic epic and a profound study of the postmodern condition.[12]

Review of Contemporary Fiction, Spring 1996

□ □ □ □ □ □ □

Brief Interviews with Hideous Men

Little, Brown, 1999

David Foster Wallace is one of the few contemporary authors who actually sounds like he's writing in the present. Artists in every other field are using techniques that were unthought-of ten years ago; in literature, however, especially in the short-story format, most authors are writing as if it were 1959 instead of 1999. *Brief Interviews with Hideous Men* is not only a state-of-the-art demonstration of the short-story form, but a rebuke to almost every other short-story writer to *move on*, to try something new.

12 I originally wrote "comic," but changed it to the more accurate "tragicomic" right before sending the issue to press; unfortunately, the version sent to Little, Brown was the earlier, uncorrected proof copy (some magazines do this to give publishers time to quote from it if they wish, as LB did here), hence the "comic" in the blurb that appeared in the cloth and paperback editions.

No one is better attuned than Wallace to the zeitgeist of the '90s: its unique mélange of ethical confusion, technological overload, depression as a lifestyle, sex as a psychodrama, overanalyzation, media overkill, political correctness, aggressive defensiveness, post-ironic wariness, post-everything, in fact. (If Björk hadn't already used it, *Post* would have been a good title for the book.) This is not to be confused with being hip to new trends and fashions, but rather to have a Jamesian sensitivity to the subtle ways all of the above have changed the way we interact with others. It's not a decade to be proud of; to use a recurring word from the book, the '90s were/are hideous.

As harrowing as many of these stories are, they are a joy to read because of the aesthetic bliss that results from being in the hands of a master. Wallace can do anything in prose — everything from elegant, donnish sentences to Gaddisian dialogue, from technical jargon to wacky slang — and he does so in a variety of forms. The title story is a series of one-sided interviews, and there are also a series of pop quizzes (in which the reader is asked to judge ethical dilemmas), a Barthian rewrite of Greek myth in a Californian setting, an extended dictionary entry (from the year 2096), and other unclassifiable forms. (Even the most conventional story, "Forever Overhead," is narrated in the unconventional second person.) There are some metafictional gestures that provide fascinating insights into Wallace's writing processes, and throughout there is a pitch-perfect control of a variety of tones.[13] That, and Wallace's preternatural powers of observation, should make him the envy of every writer alive.

Aesthetic bliss aside, this is not a pleasant book to read. There are some hard truths here, many conveyed in a clinical tone that will be off-putting to some. (Female readers especially might be repulsed by the "Brief Interviews" series, though if they persevere they'll learn more about men than from a shelf of Mars and Venus-type books.) But the stellar artistry on display throughout renders all objections irrelevant. Along with *Infinite Jest* and *A Supposedly Fun Thing I'll Never Do*, this book establishes Wallace as the most historically significant and technically gifted writer of the '90s.

Rain Taxi, Summer 1999

□ □ □ □ □ □ □

13 As in his other works, he makes extensive use of footnotes for additional narrative levels in some stories. [Note in original review.]

Conversations with David Foster Wallace. Edited by Stephen J. Burn
University Press of Mississippi, 2012

The Legacy of David Foster Wallace.
Edited by Samuel Cohen and Lee Konstantinou
University of Iowa Press, 2012

The only upside to the tragically premature death of David Foster Wallace in September 2008 is an acceleration of books on his work, a rush to judgment to commemorate his spectacular achievement and to locate his place in contemporary American literature. First came David Lipsky's book-length interview tape-recorded in 1996, *Although of Course You End up Becoming Yourself: A Road Trip with David Foster Wallace* (2010), which might not otherwise have ever seen print. On its heels came *Consider David Foster Wallace* (also 2010), a collection of conference papers edited by David Hering, and then in the spring of 2012 there appeared the two books under review, along with a revised edition of Stephen Burn's 2003 book *David Foster Wallace's* Infinite Jest: *A Reader's Guide*. D. T. Max published *Every Love Story Is a Ghost Story: A Life of David Foster Wallace* in August 2012, and by the time this review appears, another critical study or two will probably be forthcoming.[14]

I was surprised to learn in Stephen Burn's introduction to *Conversations with David Foster Wallace* that the novelist gave over 70 interviews during his relatively short career, especially since Wallace didn't enjoy them or think he was particularly good at them (though he was). Burn has selected 21 of the best, ranging from one conducted in 1987 shortly after the publication of his first novel, *The Broom of the System,* to a brief talk with the *Wall Street Journal* four months before he died. Most were done in conjunction with publication of new books; they are arranged chronologically here, resulting in a book-by-book commentary by Wallace on his work, and a register of his growing fame, especially after *Infinite Jest* came out and he became regarded as a kind of voice of his generation. (He didn't think so, though, again, he was sort of was). For the most often-quoted interview Wallace ever gave, the one with Larry McCaffery published in the *Review of Contemporary Fiction* in 1993, Burn went back to the original transcripts and added around 2,000 words, making it even more invaluable. The book ends not with Wallace's last interview but with the obituary-essay David Lipsky published in *Rolling Stone* a few weeks after Wallace's suicide, which quotes from the then-unpublished road interview he did in spring of 1996. It goes without saying that *Conversations with David Foster Wallace* is an essential book for Wallace critics, but it will be of

14 After this review was written, *ten* more books on Wallace had appeared by spring 2016, with more announced as forthcoming.

great interest to anyone interested in late 20th-century American fiction, of which he was both a stellar practitioner and a perceptive theorist.

As the title suggests, *The Legacy of David Foster Wallace* is largely concerned with what Wallace bequeathed to fiction. It is a creatively curated collection, mixing academic essays with memorials, tributes, and interviews, with contributions from novelists as well as critics (and one librarian). Around two-thirds of the contents have been published before, most within the last four years since Wallace's death: there are remarks from the memorial services that were held in New York and Illinois, a few Web publications, two brief interviews (not in Burn's book), and the foreword Dave Eggers wrote for the tenth anniversary edition of *Infinite Jest* — all interleaved under three main subjects (History, Aesthetics, Community). The mixture of scholarly essays with personal remarks may seem odd, but it's appropriate, for even academics (along with "regular" readers) developed an empathy for Wallace that they probably don't have for, say, John Barth or Cormac McCarthy. Pynchon exerts considerable mystique, but you'd have to go back to certain authors in the 1950s like Salinger and Kerouac for an example of a writer whose appeal is personal as well as professional.

In addition to an introduction playfully written in Wallacese, editors Cohen and Konstantinou each contributes a smart essay on readers' responses to Wallace and on his place in the canon. Cohen rightly fears "that Wallace's work will forever be read through the way that he died," and Konstantinou convincingly argues that "Wallace wanted to discover or invert a viable postironic ethos for U.S. literature and culture at the End of History, that is, for an America in the thrall of postmodernism." And lest that sound too cerebral, he goes on to suggest that "Wallace's oeuvre might be seen as a single long survey of the different forms individual suffering can take in a postindustrial or postmodern society." Kathleen Fitzpatrick concurs: writing of blog-conducted group readings of *Infinite Jest*, she notes "that no other writer has managed quite so well [to wed] high-modern and postmodern experimental pyrotechnics with an incisive cultural critique and a deep concern for quotidian human suffering." Paul Giles notes Wallace's affinity with 19th-century essayists like Emerson and Lincoln before demonstrating how he "managed to update rhetorical conventions to represent an altered state of affairs" at the end of the 20th century. Ira B. Nadel contributes a good essay on Wallace's use of footnotes,[15] and Mol-

15 Though he errs in calling Wallace's heavily footnoted essay on David Markson's *Wittgenstein's Mistress* a book review. As Managing Editor of the *Review of Contemporary Fiction*, I commissioned that 22-page essay from Dave for a special issue devoted to Markson's work, which he wrote during a difficult period in his life. He came through brilliantly. [Note in original review.]

ly Schwartzberg concludes the volume with a previously unpublished account of Wallace's archive at the Harry Ransom Center at the University of Texas.

Both books are must-haves for Wallace fans, casual or academic, but are also excellent introductions for those late to the game, especially older academics who may still regard Wallace as a flash-in-the-pan postmodernist too tricky and popular to be taken seriously. The intelligence and concern for the craft of fiction on display in *Conversations with David Foster Wallace*, along with the equally intelligent assessments of his achievement in *The Legacy of David Foster Wallace*, should dispel any such prejudices.

Style, Summer 2013

Paul West

Sheer Fiction
McPherson, 1987

The Universe, and Other Fictions
Overlook, 1988

Sheer Fiction is an exhilarating collection of previously published essays and reviews from a transplanted British novelist who has no patience for what he variously calls "mercantile novelists," "literary greengrocers," "antiquarians who keep on trying to invent the nineteenth-century novel in the age of quasars." In opposition to these minimalists, "wholly intent upon reducing the wonder and the enigmatic abundance of life to glum sentences whose only virtue is to be grammatically correct and not draw attention to their maker," West argues a spirited case "in defense of purple prose" (to borrow the title of one of the essays), in defense of those "impulsive self-mythologizers [who] light out for the territory of the word, where the dictionary is king, full of the voices of the dead, and of the way their throats, their mouths, were built."

Although there is a fascinating essay showing how Virginia Woolf anticipates so much of what he finds exciting in contemporary fiction, British and American writers are in the minority; West prefers European and especially Latin American writers because of their greater willingness to play in a universe at play, while remaining hyperconscious of "the trauma of being alive." Enumerating his favorites among Latin Americans, West doubts "if anyone of rather fixed literary taste would go away unchanged by a banquet of Cortázar, Carpentier, García Márquez, Puig; those engrossing Brazilians (Osman Lins, Lispector, and Piñon), the sonorous gourd of Lezama Lima, and the sprightly, antic other Cubans, Cabrera Infante, Severo Sarduy, and Reinaldo Arenas." In the nearly 50 book reviews, West surveys the best novels by these writers and by numerous Europeans, along with the few British and American novelists whose technical innovations have kept pace with their more daring compatriots abroad: Abish, Beckett, Compton-Burnett, Connell, Davenport, and Gass. (I regret the exclusion of his insightful review of Alexander Theroux's *Darconville's Cat* back in 1981, but one can't have everything.)

His genuine excitement for this fiction is contagious and his own language is as splendid as the purple stylists he celebrates; especially impressive is his continuous recourse to metaphors and illustrations drawn from astronomy and genetics (not surprising from the author of *Gala*), marine biology, geology, and quantum physics. It is tempting to quote endlessly from this fascinating collection — in Compton-Burnett, breakfast is "less a meal than a parliament of rhetorical vultures" — so I'll limit myself to his Woolf essay, which fits *Sheer Fiction* like pantyhose: "It is not often that we find so intricate a sense of wonder depressed to the level of diagnosis, or so granitic a vision made manifest in such radiant and, sometimes, bravura, sentences."

The same could be said for West's first collection of short fiction, an audacious set of literary experiments in a variety of modes: monologues by such "characters" as the sun, Moby Dick, a brain cell in the dying Shakespeare's head, and the universe itself; interviews with Atlas and an African mystic; reports on a failed anthropologist, a pinball wizard, a book that kills, and on a mysterious Sino-Russian project; fictions in the forms of notes for a fiction, an unsent letter, a Chinese parable. In other words, these are not your traditional short stories but *ficciones* of the exotic and erudite school of Borges, Robert Kelly, or Guy Davenport. Like these writers and others that might come to mind (the Barth of *Lost in the Funhouse*, Harry Mathews, Alexander Theroux), West exults in a gorgeous, rich language drawn from every level of discourse from low slang to specialized jargon. His trademark galactic imagery suits the scope of his vision, for these fictions recall one to the multiplicity and variety not only of the short fiction genre but of the universe itself — which, as his title story indicates, is the grandest fiction of them all. This lively collection fills the reader with a renewed sense of awe before both the genre and the cosmos its emulates with such panache.

Review of Contemporary Fiction, Spring 1988.

□ □ □ □ □ □ □

The Place in Flowers Where Pollen Rests
Doubleday, 1988

The Hopi word *koyaanisqatsi*, meaning "life out of balance," came into some prominence five years ago in the Philip Glass-scored film of the same name, which eschewed narrative and dialogue in favor of a rapidly shifting montage of scenes from contemporary life. The Hopi word is used early in Paul West's extraordinary new novel, which likewise forgoes a traditional linear narrative and instead features a series of reveries, arranged not so much in chronological order as in an associative manner, one memory leading to another, with all memories existing in a kind of eternal present tense that mirrors the grammatical structure of the Hopi language.

Life is hideously out of balance for Oswald Beautiful Badger Going Over the Hill. As a teenager in the early '60s, he leaves the Hopi reservation in northeastern Arizona for Hollywood; but failing to find legitimate acting work, he descends into the trashy world of pornographic movies. During one of his cinematic orgies, a porn actress suffocates — a breathtakingly beautiful description of her repose in death opens the novel — and while Oswald is not directly responsible, his horror sends him back to the reservation to attend to his uncle, a carver of kachina dolls named George The Place in Flowers Where Pollen Rests. After his uncle's death (actually his father, though they both kept up the pretense), Oswald leaves again, this time for the war in Vietnam, an official obscenity linked to the underground obscenity of the porn world Oswald had left behind. Surviving a massacre and experiencing a kind of rebirth, he returns once more to the reservation and tries to restore some balance to his life. By way of what might be called stellar mysticism, he is able to find the balance between the individual and the cosmos, the past and the present, and reintegrates himself into Hopi society, first by recounting a traditional (and grisly) tale, and second by impersonating a kachina, Mastop the death fly.

Extracting this narrative from the novel is a challenge, for the reveries that make up *The Place in Flowers* are densely printed monologues without paragraphing or much regard for chronology. Uncle George possesses "the waterfall of a worn-out voice," and West's verbal waterfall fills a vast narrative pool 500 pages deep, where chronology dissolves and narrative events purl in a simultaneous present that can be dipped into by characters at any time. "We are tenseless and timeless," Uncle George boasts, and it is amazing how West has managed to convey not only the Hopi culture but its linguistic structure as well. One is forced to read this novel differently than one reads an "Anglo" novel; Oswald had "learned from his tribe, his uncle especially, the sovereign slowness of things, the way in which ongoingness was better than any outcome," and it is the "ongoingness" of this novel rather than its outcome that commands the reader's attention — an attention that must be slowed down in this case, not racing forward to see what happens next. Reading slowly, the reader can better appreciate the detailed, visceral texture of the places West describes: the smells, the weather, the taste of food, the feel of clothes — which is all the more remarkable since West is describing experiences (the war in Vietnam, life on a Hopi reservation, the porn industry) that are quiet alien to this transplanted Englishman who teaches at Penn State. (And how ironic that it took a Britisher to write what may very well be the Great Amer-Indian Novel.)

The traditional tale Oswald finally learns to tell also places emphasis on the telling rather than the outcome, with the more details the better. We too have heard this tale before, in a sense. The hero wears a thousand faces, Joseph Campbell tells us, and Paul West has given us an exotic new version of the oldest tale there is, one of urgent relevance in this new age of *koyaanisqatsi*.

Review of Contemporary Fiction, Fall 1988.

□ □ □ □ □ □ □

Lord Byron's Doctor

Doubleday, 1989

Paul West's newest novel, his twelfth, is a remarkable mixture of literary imagination and historical fact. The facts are these: In 1816, Lord Byron, finding himself ostracized from polite society due to disclosures concerning his marital infidelities, left for Europe, taking with him a young physician named John Polidori — the youngest man ever to receive a medical degree from the University of Edinburgh. Offered £500 by Byron's publisher to keep a journal of the poet's activities, Polidori wrote a sketchy account of his next seven months with Byron. (The publisher, finding too much Polidori and not enough Byron in it, declined to publish it. In 1869, Polidori's sister Charlotte copied the manuscript, leaving out the racy parts, then destroyed the original. Polidori's nephew, William Michael Rossetti, edited the expurgated version for publication in 1911, his own commentary taking up as much space as his uncle's jottings.) Percy Shelley and a party consisting of Mary Godwin (later Shelley's wife) and Byron's mistress Claire Claremont left England shortly after Byron did (also under scandalous circumstances). The two poets and their entourages met up in Geneva, set up house at the Villa Diodati on the shores of Lake Geneva, and sometime between June 15 and 17, two of the most enduring literary monsters were brought to life in fiction: the vampire in Polidori's novella *The Vampyre* and the man-made creature of Mary Shelley's *Frankenstein*.

What Paul West has done — himself a Byron scholar, author of *Byron and the Spoiler's Art* (1960) and editor of *Byron: Twentieth-Century Views* (1963) — is to flesh out Polidori's skeletal diary in a robust early-19th-century style and to create a penetrating psychological portrait of Lord Byron's doctor: a hot-headed youth (only 21 in 1816, and only 25 at his suicide in 1821), by turns arrogant and defensive, obviously talented (in both literature and medicine) but outclassed by Byron and Shelly, and mortified at failing to be taken seriously by anyone. "My only crime had been that I kept on hoping," he complains near the end of the novel, "not even to pass muster but just be dealt with honourably — the young with the young." This is very much a tale of youth, similar in many respects to today's *Less Than Zero* generation: Byron was the eldest at 28, Shelly 23, Polidori 21, and the women 18 and 19. They were promiscuous, hip (for 1816), did drugs, discussed outlandish ideas all night, and differ from a rock group and its entourage only in being better educated and more magnificently talented.

Byron himself emerges as a complex, driven man, with an "opportunistic voracity that cared less about taste and culture than about the raw entity squirming with life in the teeth of death. He dealt in extremes," Polidori goes on to say, "sometimes ordinary folk in the grip of dreadful powers, sometimes heroes standing vast at the horizon. He wanted to push against life, against those living it, and in this sense was not a consumer, a follower. In short, he was milord." Polidori's love-hate relationship with Byron thrashes itself against the wall of Byron's indifference, condescension, and insensitivity, making Byron's closing-line comment on Polidori's suicide — "It seems that disappointment was the cause of this rash act" — a damning indictment against him. Polidori knew what he was about when he modeled his vampire, Lord Ruthven, after milord.

Hence West's novel satisfies on several levels, offering revisionary portraits of some of the great figures of Romanticism; an accurate, often bawdy picture of the times; a profound treatment of the timeless difficulties of crossing over from adolescence to adult maturity; a stylistic tour de force of 19th-century elegance, slang, and technical jargon; and a wholly successful recreation of that crucial year in literary history when Romantic yearnings confronted the darker recesses of the unconscious, wreaking havoc in the personal lives of their creators, but also giving birth to poetry and monsters that haunt us still.

Review of Contemporary Fiction, Fall 1989

□ □ □ □ □ □ □

Portable People. Illustrated by Joseph Servello

Paris Review/British American Publishing, 1990

In his newest book, West revives the 17th-century genre of character writing and gives it a modernist twist. There are 85 biographical sketches here (each illustrated with a line drawing), most ranging in length from 200 to 600 words, arranged chronologically. The selection is wonderfully eclectic: writers, scientists, musicians, composers, actresses, aviators, Nazis, astronomers, sports figures, even a few literary characters (Moby Dick and Queneau's Zazie).

Some compress a lifetime into a few paragraphs of telling anecdotes; others (the most interesting) are monologues, ventriloquistic prose poems ranging from the excited stuttering of George Gershwin to the calculated outrage of Djuna Barnes to the confident paranoia of Nixon in China.

Throughout there is the rich feast of West's characteristic prose — exotic nouns, beefy verbs, buttered with adjectives, spiced with epigrams — and plentiful evidence of nearly encyclopedic learning, not only in the humanities but embracing science, sports, aviation, and other disciplines. Even though this book feels like a jeu d'esprit, it reveals a lifetime of reading and observation that, though worn lightly here, is truly astonishing. (When was the last time you held a conversation with someone who could tell anecdotes about Carolus Linnaeus *and* describe the aeronautic design of the Polikarpov I-16 *and* weigh the respective merits of two recordings of Bernstein's Kaddish symphony *and* summarize Hans Bethe's theory of energy production in the stars *and* tell you how much the shah of Iran spent on that party in Persepolis in 1971 commemorating the 2500th anniversary of the Persian Empire?) *Portable People* is a delight and unlike any other book I can think of, as original and sui generis as West himself.

Review of Contemporary Fiction, Fall 1990

□ □ □ □ □ □ □

Sheer Fiction: Volume Two
McPherson, 1991

Volume one of West's *Sheer Fiction* consisted of a half-dozen essays followed by 40 or so book reviews, all of which championed full-bodied maximalist fiction over thin-blooded minimalism. Volume two continues with the same format and in the same vein: essays on the musical *Les Misérables*, Djuna Barnes (a brilliant monologue, actually), Albert Guerard on the novel, Günter Grass, and the late Maria Thomas are followed by an even larger number of book reviews. I'd wager few readers of this journal command a wider knowledge of contemporary writers than West does — ever heard of Mario Soldati, Eduardo Galeano, René-Victor Pilhes, Voldemar Lestienne, Julian Gloag, Chuang Hua, Robert Kroetsch? — which means that this installment of *Sheer Fiction* not only introduces a number of novelists well worth knowing, but offers fresh, inspired readings of better-known writers like Gombrowicz, Cortázar, Gracq, Goytisolo, and Skvorecky. As these lists indicate, West favors European and South American novelists, though this volume does include more British and American writers than the last one did. *Sheer Fiction: Volume Two* is an excellent field guide to numerous little-known subspecies of the modern novel from a tireless and entertaining observer.

Review of Contemporary Fiction, Summer 1991

□ □ □ □ □ □ □

Love's Mansion

Random House, 1992

Paul West's newest novel is ostensibly a memoir of his parents in novel form, but it boasts a postmodern dimension that adds to its appeal. The first paragraph sweetly introduces the heroine of the novel as a young girl, but the second paragraph introduces novelist Clive Moxon, her son, now struggling to give form to his memories of his parents. Throughout the novel Clive comments on his progress in writing this book, exulting at one moment for getting a scene right (he hopes), despairing at another because of the scarcity or unreliability of his materials. "The temptation was to give them a lovelier life than they had had," he confesses early on, "but the chore was to record their happiness, between body soil and intelligent anguish. He had to make a good job of this, or he would never be able to remember them without lethal guilt."

His parents "meet cute," as movie critics say, and enjoy a charmed life as childhood sweethearts until Harry runs off to enlist in World War I. Clive imagines his father's exploits in the war and his mother's activities back on the home front with what seems to be penetrating psychological insight and a firm grasp of period detail, though he never lets us forget that this is *his* re-creation, not a historically accurate account. The reader also has to remember that Clive Moxon is Paul West's re-creation as well, himself as a young boy, putting the entire novel on another metafictional level. The narrative part of the book carries his parents through the Great War into the hard times between the wars, all the way to their deaths. Clive's own childhood is also recounted, concentrating on the aesthetic development that would make possible, many years later, the very novel we're reading. The narrative has all the rewards of a good read, even though the task is proving more difficult than Clive had imagined: "a calculus where he has been eager to settle for arithmetic." Clive triumphs at the end, however, making a very good job of it indeed.

Whether read as a wonderful story of childhood sweethearts becoming a complex couple, as a portrait of the artist as a young man, or as a metafictional project, *Love's Mansion* is a goodly place to dwell.

Review of Contemporary Fiction, Spring 1993

Robin Williamson

The Craneskin Bag: Celtic Stories & Poems
Canongate, 1989

The Craneskin Bag, published in Scotland in 1989 but only now available in this country, is a collection of Celtic legends and folk tales rendered in an oral style that is contemporary and yet true to the originals. The man walking that linguistic tightrope is a professional storyteller and harper, Robin Williamson, formerly of the Incredible String Band. In that eclectic folk duo of the '60s Williamson wrote lyrics that brilliantly transcended the typical folk songs of the day: they were kaleidoscopic visions of great beauty, wit, and invention, usually whimsical and profound in equal measure.

Williamson brings those same qualities to these traditional tales, mixing prose and poetry to reanimate the ancient world of Celtic kings, wizards, bards, and heroes. Williamson has rescued this material from the sword and sorcery hacks and restored the pristine flavor of true oral literature, and in so doing reaffirms his stature (of nearly 30 years' standing now) as a leading poet/storyteller of the global village.

Review of Contemporary Fiction, Spring 1991

Jeanette Winterson

The World and Other Places

Knopf, 1999

After six novels, each more audacious than the last, Jeanette Winterson has published her first collection of stories. Her novels are known for their lush style, erudite structures, and erotic intensity. Her stories have a lighter tone, brief day excursions that Winterson permits herself in between the extended journeys of the novels.

The collection opens with "The 24-Hour Dog," a whimsical, occasionally metaphysical account of a trial relationship with a puppy. After a night with the spirited pup, the narrator decides to return him because he promises to be too great a threat to his/her sense of identity. (Here, as in many of Winterson's works, the narrator isn't identified by gender, and since Winterson is a lesbian the reader's conventional habit of assigning a sex to an unnamed narrator is usefully unsettled.) This story, the first of many to question the nature of identity, is followed by "Atlantic Crossing," about a brief encounter on an ocean liner. It is set in the '50s and reads as though written back then for a magazine like *Mademoiselle*. It's charming but slight, and just when you are wondering whether Winterson should stick to novels, "The Poetics of Sex" bursts into the room and kicks the chair out from beneath you. This is Winterson at her best: vivid language, wild metaphors, randy eroticism, learned wit, and in-your-face attitude. It's an account of the white-hot relationship between two lesbians nicknamed Picasso and Sappho (characters from her novel *Art & Lies*) and is structured in response to the dumb questions naive straight people can ask ("What Do Lesbians Do in Bed?" "Which One of You Is the Man?"). This is quintessential Winterson.

In the remaining 14 stories she tries her hand at nearly every form of fiction. There is a fable ("The Three Friends"), a retold myth ("Orion"), even a cute Christmas story ("O'Brien's First Christmas"). Two stories are exercises in imagination generated from the opening line: "This morning I noticed there was one room missing." There's a successful Borgesian attempt at imaginary geography ("Turn of the World") and a Bradburyesque story about a family's encounter with some Gypsies ("The Green Man"). A parable called "Newton" is set in a town tyrannized by the sociological equivalent of Newtonian physics, and the collection's title story investigates the Einsteinian conflict between perception and reality. The final (and earliest written) story, "Psalms," a winsome tale about a child's pet tortoise, has the same British fundamentalist setting as Winterson's first novel, *Oranges Are Not the Only Fruit.*

As varied as their forms may be, Winterson's stories share one theme with the traditional short story: Their protagonists are usually sensitive people at odds with others and/or their surroundings. The protagonist of "A Green Square," for example, leaves his/her house one morning "with no desire to return . . . I stood looking up at the tall house in between other tall houses and I understood that I always had been outside." But Winterson is aware of the predictability of this rather shopworn theme and introduces interesting variations. The same protagonist is smart enough to ask, "So what is it to be? Banality of convention or banality of individuation? Shall I choose society's clichés or my own?" In opposition to banality Winterson proposes risk — one of the stories is entitled "Adventure of a Lifetime" — and finds models in the most surprising people. The protagonist of another story states, "In the lives of saints, I look for confirmation of excess. To them it is not strange to spend nights on a mountain or to forgo food. For them, the visionary and the everyday coincide. Above all, they have no domestic virtues, preferring intensity to comfort."

Excess and intensity are the key words here, admirable both as character traits and as components of a lively literary style. While few of these stories display the excess and intensity of Winterson's novels, none of them could be called banal. (Even the conventional "Atlantic Crossing" features a character named Gabriel Angel.) With its variety of forms and range of imagination, *The World and Other Places* is a stimulating tour of where "the visionary and the everyday coincide."

Washington Post Book World, 21 March 1999

P. G. Wodehouse

Tales from the Drones Club
International Polygonics, 1991

Comic novelists are rarely taken seriously by literary critics: novels dark with despair are almost automatically assumed to have greater artistic merit than novels light with laughter. Perhaps someday a critic will make a case for the importance of P. G. Wodehouse by arguing that his comic juxtaposition of formal (liturgical, juridical, literary) language against jazzy slang and breezy colloquialisms is an insidious attack upon the elitist institutions that employ that formal language. As a bold saboteur of entrenched linguistic institutions, as a guerrilla warrior against outmoded codes of language and behavior, Wodehouse someday may be taken seriously as the consummate artist he was, whose grasp of language and signs was far greater than that of many writers taken more seriously than he is. In the meantime, latch hold of this priceless collection of stories about the Drones Club — a kind of Mermaid Tavern of the Jazz Age. Put aside that new collection of earnest stories from some recent MFA and watch a real master at work and play. Great art can inspire terror and pity, but Aristotle forgot to add that it can also leave you helpless with laughter.

Review of Contemporary Fiction, Fall 1991

Richard Wright

Early Works, Later Works
Library of America, 1991

The magisterial Library of America includes only two post-World War II writers: Flannery O'Connor and now Richard Wright. There are probably several reasons why there aren't more — unavailability of rights, certainly, but perhaps a reluctance to identify which contemporary writers are likely to prove of historical importance — but one looks forward to the day when today's best writers are treated as handsomely as Wright is here. With the exception of *Uncle Tom's Cabin* in the *Early Works* volume, the texts are new: *Lawd Today!* and *The Outsider* from Wright's typescripts, *Native Son* from bound page proofs, and *Black Boy* and *American Hunger* together (and unexpurgated) as Wright intended. Typos have been corrected, censored passages restored, fulsome annotations (by Arnold Rampersad) appended — almost everything one could desire.

Except the format: the two volumes run only 936 and 887 pages respectively, but are priced at $35.00 each, making them shorter and yet more expensive than most of the other volumes in the series. The contents of these two should have been combined into one volume at that price (there are a few other Library of America volumes nearly as long), or the two volumes expanded to include Wright's other works (especially the novel *The Long Dream* and the stories of *Eight Men*) to form a two-volume complete Wright. As it is, these splendid volumes won't find the large readership they deserve.

Review of Contemporary Fiction, Spring 1992. I've included this squib only to register my disappointment with the Library of America. I was an early enthusiast and collected all their volumes from 1982 onward, but became disenchanted with them at this point. Their first four volumes averaged 1,400 pages each, and almost all the ones that followed over the next decade were well north of 1,000 pages, one even reaching 1,620 pages (Francis Parkman). But this Wright set initiated a downsizing trend, favoring shorter volumes as the prices continued to rise, a cash-grab approach at odds with LoA's nonprofit status and substantial funding. They stretched Henry James's complete stories into five volumes of about 950 pages each, rather than four volumes of 1,200 pages each, or even three of 1,600 pages like the Parkman. Their Charles Brockden Brown volume is called *Three Gothic Novels* and is 914 pages long; he wrote *four* Gothics, and adding the excellent *Ormond* would have increased the page count only up to around 1,150 pages. Their Lovecraft volume is 838 pages, and — unlike all the complete volumes they did earlier — includes only about 75% of his work: only another 200 pages or so would have made it complete. (Plus they left out my favorite Lovecraft work, *The Dream-Quest of Unknown Kadath*.) The majority of books they do now are *south* of 1,000 pages. They blew the perfect opportunity to publish Kerouac's Duluoz Legend as he wished, and their selection of 20th-century novelists is questionable. Of all post-World War II novelists, they started with that racist religious nut Flannery O'Connor? Dawn Powell gets two volumes, while Djuna Barnes is ignored? Philip Roth gets nine volumes while John Barth doesn't get a single one? And let's not even talk about some of their recent anthologies, such as *Football: Great Writing about the National Sport*, *Women Crime Writers*, and two volumes of *American Musicals*. Their recent "Special Publication" of *String Theory: David Foster Wallace on Tennis*, while welcome, also smacks of cash-grab opportunism.

Stephen Wright

Going Native
Farrar, Straus and Giroux, 1994

Going Native is less a novel than a linked set of short stories, like *Winesburg, Ohio*; and like Anderson before him, Wright is interested in the grotesque, those variants from what used to be called the norm, a concept that has been losing definition ever since Anderson's time. Wright served in the Vietnam War, which pretty much greased norms of all kinds (political, personal, sociological, aesthetic) and used that experience for his first novel, *Meditations in Green* (1983), one of the best books about the war and its psychological aftermath for those who served. This was followed by *M31: A Family Romance* (1988), a sumptuously bizarre and garish novel about those Americans who butcher cattle in satanic rituals and communicate with UFOs. Both display a rich, even ornate style: heavily imagistic, dense with detail, grammatically complex, ironic, sarcastic — imagine an issue of the *National Inquirer* as co-written by Joyce and Pynchon and you'll have a sense of what the latter especially is like.

The same concerns and style animate Wright's newest novel. Although as contemporary as the evening news, *Going Native* revives one of the oldest themes in American literature: the fluidity of identity. One of the great attractions of the States for earlier Europeans was the notion that one could be anyone one wanted to be in America, that every immigrant was an Adam who could remake himself, free from the European restrictions of class, customs, and religion. But in Wright's brilliant new novel, that freedom offers a dangerous temptation to go native in the way Kurtz did a hundred years ago in the Congo. One reads *Going Native* muttering "the horror, the horror" at the lives he depicts, but, as in Conrad, one is simultaneously ravished by the style, the exquisite metaphors, the black humor, the insights into illusion and degradation. This novel should promote Wright to the ranks of America's finest novelists.

Review of Contemporary Fiction, Summer 1994

Rudolph Wurlitzer

David Seed. *Rudolph Wurlitzer: American Novelist and Screenwriter*
Edwin Mellen Press, 1991

Wurlitzer belongs to that post-Beat generation that includes such writers as Pynchon, Brautigan, Fariña, Kesey, Stone, and Robbins. He published three novels in quick succession between 1969 and 1972, but didn't publish a fourth novel until a dozen years later. Aside from a few articles in *Critique* by Douglas Bolling and a few pages in Frederick Karl's *American Fictions*, Wurlitzer's work has received little critical attention, which makes this book-length study by David Seed particularly welcome.

Organized like a Twayne book, *Rudolph Wurlitzer* opens with an introduction sketching biographical details and placing Wurlitzer in the tradition of American "road" fiction, where a disgruntled individual leaves the congested (intellectually as well as physically) East for the wide-open spaces of the West. Whitman, London, and of course Kerouac are mentioned, along with some lesser-known roadwork by Sorrentino, Rumaker, and the late Douglas Woolf. Seed then devotes separate chapters on the first three novels — *Nog* (1969), *Flats* (1970), *Quake* (1972) — then breaks for a chapter on Wurlitzer's film work. (He wrote the scripts for *Two-Lane Blacktop* and *Pat Garrett and Billy the Kid* — even had bit parts in each — along with scripts for a few other films.) A chapter on Wurlitzer's fourth novel, *Slow Fade* (1984), follows, and the book concludes with some appendices and a very full bibliography.

As in his earlier books on Pynchon and Heller, Seed is alert to historical and intellectual contexts, as well as being an indefatigable researcher, turning up such things as an interview Wurlitzer gave in 1969 to the *Rutgers Anthologist*, reprinted here as an appendix. Seed links Wurlitzer not only to other writers but to artists in other fields who share his aesthetic: composer Philip Glass, sculptor Richard Serra, painter Claes Oldenburg, photographer Robert Frank — all of whom Wurlitzer knows and has written on/worked with — along with several movie directors and filmmakers. Wurlitzer's literary style owes as much to these artists as to literary figures like Beckett (an important influence, especially on *Flats* and on Wurlitzer's unpublished plays), so it is valuable to have cross-references to their work. The book's price [$59.95] is prohibitive for individuals, so get your library to order this: it's worth having.

Review of Contemporary Fiction, Fall 1992

Marguerite Young

Harp Song for a Radical: The Life and Times of Eugene Victor Debs. Edited by Charles Ruas
Knopf, 1999

It is difficult to decide who is the more remarkable character in this new book: Eugene V. Debs — founder of the Socialist Party in America, five-time presidential candidate, and a legendary orator — or his biographer, Marguerite Young, author of the legendary novel *Miss MacIntosh, My Darling*, a first-rate historian of 19th-century America, and a prose stylist of the highest order. This book is a match made in heaven: the story of an extraordinary man told by an extraordinary woman.

Young, who died in 1995 before quite completing the book, was interested in Debs because of the part he played in the history of American utopianism. Young's first prose book, *Angel in the Forest: A Fairy Tale of Two Utopias* (1945), examined the failed attempts by George Rapp and Robert Owen to establish utopian communities in her home state of Indiana. In a sense, *Harp Song for a Radical* picks up where the earlier book left off, tracing the utopian impulse through other communal experiments by Fourierists, Saint-Simonians, Millerites, Mormons, and other groups. Young shows how a yearning for utopia, fermented by theories of socialism and communism imported from Europe, set the scene for the trade-union movements after the Civil War, a scene in which Debs was a major player.

However, the emphasis here is less on Debs's life than on his times. After some introductory chapters on Debs (and his poet-companion James Whitcomb Riley — both were Hoosiers), Young takes us to Europe and back to find the origins of anti-capitalist thought and utopian alternatives. Everyone from Karl Marx to Alexander I of Russia appears for a few revealing chapters, including Heinrich Heine, Charles Dickens, Fyodor Dostoevsky, Dred Scott, John Brown, Brigham Young (from whom the author was descended), virtually every president from Andrew Jackson through Woodrow Wilson, most of the generals in the Civil War, and many forgotten foot soldiers in the war against capitalism, such as Wilhelm Weitling, a German tailor who receives almost as much space as Debs does. The background material on Europe and the early communal experiments in America leads in to that crucial period after the Civil War when robber barons and carpetbaggers, war profiteers and predatory tycoons, promulgated a cutthroat capitalism that reduced the average American worker to the level of a Russian serf, a time when starving strikers in the East were massacred with the same fury as Native Americans out West. The Civil War between the North and South was followed by a civil war between the rich and the poor that could have ended America's great experiment in democracy, Young argues, had not Debs and others like him created trade unions to hold despotic capitalists in check.

Young's narrative method is episodic and anecdotal, and her style nothing less than epic. This is not a conventional biography but a "harp song," an epic ideally chanted with harp accompaniment (as were the *Iliad* and *Beowulf*). Young saw the quest for utopia as a grand tale, like the wanderings of Ulysses, and used a magniloquent prose style to give her theme epic grandeur. Her specialty was what she called the "dragnet" sentence: a long, paratactic sentence that would cast its net into a sea of facts and fancies, ideas and characters, and drag them into unexpected relationships. (There's one in *Miss MacIntosh* that's two pages long.) A typical sentence:

> Wilhelm Weitling had sought refuge here as an exile in 1848 but had returned to Europe sub rosa when the revolutionary forces were about to boil over in France and Germany and Austria and inundate the Old World, and then had returned to the harbor city in the New World in 1849 in flight from the failure of the revolution, in which the red caps storming the barricades had been mowed down by the military representatives of international capitalistic interests whose kingdoms knew no boundary lines but those between rich and poor, and the cobblestone streets were turned into seas of blood, red as the red roses in that June, which was the month of brides, dead brides, dead bridegrooms.

From factual opening to fanciful closing, this sentence form is used throughout *Harp Song*; some readers will find it wearying, but others will be enthralled by Young's poetic eye (note how the red caps lead to red roses, which in turn echo "sub rosa" from the beginning of the sentence) and her emphasis on the personal, even domestic side of historical events.

My only complaint about this fabulous book is its length: no, not the usual one that it's too long but that it's not long enough. Five years ago both Young and editor Charles Ruas described *Harp Song* as a work of three volumes, each 800 pages long, yet what we have here is a single volume of 600 pages, without an editorial word about the second two volumes. In a cursory discussion of the surviving manuscript (in an otherwise useful introduction), Ruas says that Young didn't quite finish the book, but he doesn't point out that the present book contains only about half of what Young did finish. In 1995 Young, unhappy with Knopf's plans to abridge the work, offered it to a small press [Dalkey Archive] willing to publish the complete manuscript, but Knopf insisted on keeping the work, then sat on it for four more years. There will be an even longer wait until somebody brings out an unabridged edition.

As the sour critical reaction to Ellison's *Juneteenth* and Hemingway's *True at First Light* indicates, this hasn't been a good year for posthumously published books.

The curtailed length and steep price [$35.00] aside, this is as grand a book as you're likely to come across, a classic that deserves to win every book prize this year and to be cherished in years to come as a magnificent testimony to the American spirit. Neither unions nor utopias are what they once promised to be: Some unions have become as greedy and corrupt as the robber barons they originally opposed, and most utopias — with the possible exception of some hippie communes — are formed nowadays by either religious nuts or militant "patriots." While Young at times displays a Puckish bemusement at mortals with their utopian schemes — the word "utopia," after all, means "no such place" — her sympathy for the downtrodden and persecuted is admirable, and the biblical cadences with which she tells their tale remind us why so many people did, once upon a time, look to the United States as the Promised Land.

Washington Post Book World, 26 September 1999

Miscellaneous Nonfiction

Jerome Klinkowitz. *The Self-Apparent Word: Fiction as Language/Language as Fiction*
Southern Illinois University Press, 1984

Literary Subversions: New American Fiction and the Practice of Criticism
Southern Illinois University Press, 1985

The concluding section of *Literary Subversions* consists of abstracts of the 15 books Klinkowitz has published since 1972; and while the purpose of this section is unclear, it does remind us that he has been one of the most active champions of innovative fiction. *The Self-Apparent Word* provides the theoretical underpinnings for his enthusiasm by opposing "self-effacing" language — where the reader looks past the language as through a window to the mimetic actions in a traditional, representational novel — to "self-apparent" language, where the words themselves are the view, as in a stained-glass window. Postmodern fiction, he argues, demands a shift in "the reader's attention from the action of the story taking place to the action of a text being composed." Such fictions are not representations of or commentaries on the real world, but additions to it, new objects with the autonomy of "a rock or a refrigerator," as Donald Barthelme once put it.

Although essentially a book of literary theory, Klinkowitz's study does offer numerous close readings to illustrate his various points. Self-effacement versus self-apparency is dramatized by pairing Frank Norris's *McTeague* with Raymond Federman's *Smiles on Washington Square*, and the aesthetic superiority of self-apparent language is driven home with another pairing, Philip Roth's *Goodbye, Columbus* and Kurt Vonnegut's "The Hyannis Port Story." The varieties of self-apparent fiction are explored through the balance of the book with brief discussions of representative examples from the major practitioners of such fiction: Barthelme, Gass, Sukenick, Sorrentino, Abish, Katz, Dixon, and Clarence Major.

If the book has a fault, it lies in Klinkowitz's readiness to dismiss too much fiction as self-effacing in its language. Much current criticism of older, traditional fiction is energized by the realization that all language is "self-apparent" to some extent; the language of Hawthorne draws attention to itself just as much as Sukenick's does, though this may not be apparent during a first reading. "Once a story begins," Klinkowitz says of traditional fiction, "the reader's rush to meaning virtually closes the book" to the qualities of its language. While this may be true for a first reading, subsequent readings of any text will disclose at least some self-apparency in the language. Klinkowitz also dismisses as inadequate the various strategies against effacement practiced by Joyce, Robbe-Grillet, Burroughs, Barth, and Pynchon — a dismissal that will alienate many readers otherwise sympathetic to his thesis. And although his discussions of little-known writers such as Katz, Dixon, and Major are interesting, one wonders why there is no reference to writers whose language is more flamboyantly self-apparent than theirs: where is Stanley Elkin, for example, Harry Mathews, Chandler Brossard, or the amazing Alexander Theroux?

But Klinkowitz is correct in placing the emphasis on the "privileging of the writer and his techniques over the action he represents" and draws an interesting parallel between those who take religious mysteries too literally and those who demand that fiction be mimetic and representational. This parallel is repeated in the opening chapter (or "Pretext") of *Literary Subversions*, which overlaps to a certain extent the closing chapter of *The Self-Apparent Word*. Any fears that Klinkowitz's stringent demands for innovative fiction may make him an unsuitable critic of other forms of fiction are laid to rest in this collection of previously published essays. In fact, he ranges so far from his preferred brand of fiction that at one point he cries out in mock surprise to Dan Wakefield, "After ten years of messing around with experimental fiction, pushing all these innovations to their logical and illogical extremes, what am I doing back here congratulating you for your literary realism, your triumph in the novel of manners?"

And what indeed does a book entitled *Literary Subversions* have to do with such unsubversive writers as John Irving, John Updike, Grace Paley, Richard Yates, and Dan Wakefield, along with a handful of more genuinely subversive authors? Such questions highlight both the force and the flaw of the book; unlike *The Self-Apparent Word*, the more recent book isn't limited by an agonistic thesis. Instead Klinkowitz indulges his huge appetite for contemporary fiction and writes about a wide variety of authors without worrying whether they are subversive or not. Running against the tide, he finds Barth's recent *Sabbatical* preferable to his previous work; shows how Ishmael Reed's last two books of fiction and nonfiction inform each other; gives fine readings of lesser known works by Irving (*The Water-Method Man*) and Updike (the Olinger and Maples stories); trivializes Gardner's *Grendel*; and offers useful insights into the writings of Paley, Robley Wilson, Thomas McGuane, Yates, Kosiński, and Thomas Glynn.

Interestingly enough, the 12 essays are divided into groups of three utilizing specific essay forms: polemic, lyric, meditation, and witness. Although the distinction between the second and third is not as sharp as between the others, Klinkowitz's versatility with these forms reminds us that the new fiction calls both for new ways of reading as well as for new ways of writing criticism. Klinkowitz is masterfully adept at both, and both books can be recommended to all with an interest in contemporary American fiction, theory or practice.

Review of Contemporary Fiction, Summer 1986 — the first of a hundred or so I wrote for *RCF* between 1986 and 1996.

□ □ □ □ □ □ □

Tom LeClair and Larry McCaffery, eds. *Anything Can Happen: Interviews with Contemporary American Novelists*
University of Illinois Press, 1983

"Anything can happen now that we've slid over this bridge," Nick Carraway said on his thirtieth birthday. Although editors LeClair and McCaffery found their title elsewhere (in Elkin's *The Living End*) they celebrate the sense that fiction too has crossed a kind of bridge and is now capable of virtually anything, from conventional realism charged with a new sensitivity to the self-referentiality of language, to fabulist metafiction that finds new uses for old-fashioned storytelling. This highly readable collection of 18 interviews provides a state of the art report on contemporary American fiction; because many of the same questions are asked, the collection also provides a forum on hotly debated aesthetic issues, many centering on the Gass–Gardner controversy on moral fiction (one of whose jousts is included). Gardner is the whipping boy in many of these interviews, which dates the collection somewhat. (Most of them were done in the late '70s and appeared in a variety of journals.) But what emerges, finally, is the kind of well-rounded discussion that is only dreamed about at writers' conferences and discussions.

Feeling that many of their interviewees "were writing from assumptions misunderstood by most readers," the editors include a high proportion of innovative, experimental writers: Barth and Hawkes (a dialogue), Barthelme, Coover, DeLillo, Elkin, Federman, Gass, Katz, McElroy, and Sukenick. But the editors insist their 18 novelists were chosen for the quality of their art, not for their allegiance to postmodernism, and thus we also have interesting interviews with Rosellen Brown, Doctorow, Irving, Diane Johnson, Toni Morrison, and Tim O'Brien. Some authors are conspicuous in their absence — Pynchon doesn't grant interviews; Gaddis did one with LeClair but was disappointed with it[16] — but the editors are justified in claiming "the novelists interviewed

16 It was posthumously published in Joseph Tabbi and Rone Shavers's *Paper Empire: William Gaddis and the World System* (Tuscaloosa: University of Alabama Press, 2007), 19–27.

here represent the range of possibilities and the quality of recent fiction."

The collection could also serve as a handbook for writers that would be quite useful for creative writing classes. There are plenty of nuts-and-bolts discussions of the mechanics of writing — everything from first conceiving a work to hassling with a publisher — and beginning writers should find these discussions both inspiring and practical. *Anything Can Happen* will prove invaluable for writer and critic alike.

Review of Contemporary Fiction, Summer 1986

□ □ □ □ □ □ □

James M. Mellard. *The Exploded Form: The Modernist Novel in America*
University of Illinois Press, 1980

The Exploded Form is many books in one. On one level it is a history of the novel, a brief but lucid exposition of how the novel evolved from Bunyan to Brautigan. On another level it shows how the novel has always aligned itself with the prevailing scientific models of the universe, illustrating Kuhn's concept of shifting paradigms. On yet another level, it is a history of 20th-century literary criticism: key words from Frye's *Anatomy of Criticism* to recent essays by Philip Stevick and Gerald Graff are given almost as much attention as the novels Mellard discusses. Finally, *The Exploded Form* describes the new paradigm established by such modernist classics as *Ulysses* and *The Waste Land* and shows how American novelists have worked with this paradigm ever since.

Mellard divides the modernist American novel into three phases: the naive (primitive or instinctive experimentalism), the critical (self-conscious use of established modes), and the sophisticated (decadent, even disruptive use of established modes, making way for a new paradigm shift). For each phase the author provides a historical backdrop, a discussion of critical concerns, and an explication of an exemplary text: *The Sound and the Fury* (naive), *Catch-22* (critical), and *Trout Fishing in America* (sophisticated).

Although the background chapters are invaluable, the explications of single texts provide the clearest validation of Mellard's phasal thesis. He shows how Faulkner, for example, "exploded" the traditional novel in the Benjy section of *The Sound and the Fury*, but then allowed his novel to implode (so to speak) through the remaining sections until Dilsey's section returns us to the traditional mode from which Faulkner departed. Naive modernists such as Faulkner, Anderson, and Hemingway "simply did what they felt they had to in order to do their tasks." The operative word here is *felt*: critical modernists are more calculating, more conscious of the implications of modernism, and in his reading of *Catch-22* Mellard draws a parallel between the use of dèjá vu in that novel and Heller's evocation of "naive" modernists.

Heller and such "critical" modernists as Mailer and Bellow are critical of their predecessors' presuppositions and practices, but never to the extent of turning their backs on them. Enter the "sophisticated" modernists, that group of writers who emerged in the '60s to subvert and disrupt most of the traditional concepts of fiction: epistemological concerns override ontological ones, form is privileged over content, and what Mellard calls (after Poirier) the "performative" mode takes precedence over the "artifactive" mode of Eliot and Pound.

Mellard is the first to admit that his theory of phases is elastic enough to fit individual writers — Barth's three books from *The Sot-Weed Factor* to *Giles Goat-Boy* to *Lost in the Funhouse* recapitulate the three phases — and, at the widest angle, to fit the development of the novel as a whole: 18th-century novels are naive, 19th-century novels critical, and 20th-century ones sophisticated. Nor does there seem to be any reason such phases could not be applied to poetry and drama as well. But the novel emerges as the closest analogue to the exploding universe itself, and Mellard's excellent study is as good a general field theory as we are likely to see for some time.

Review of Contemporary Fiction, Fall 1986

□ □ □ □ □ □ □

Michael Stephens. *The Dramaturgy of Style: Voice in Short Fiction*

Southern Illinois University Press, 1986

This original study might have been more suitably subtitled "A Critic Prepares," for Stephens approaches fiction in much the same way as an actor does a script, looking not so much for the meaning of it all but for a voice — a rhythm, breathing spaces, silences — learning to read a character not so much by what he says as how he says it. As he modestly admits at the end of the book, "Nothing I have said is a radical departure from anything that is already known," yet the freshness of his book emanates from taking strategies we've also used in reading poetry and drama and demonstrating their applicability to fiction.

The fresh approach also stems from Stephens's own background as a working writer. He is the author of the fine novel *Season at Coole* and is a practicing poet and playwright as well, which gives *The Dramaturgy of Style* a hands-on knowledgeability missing from run-of-the-mill academic studies. Nor is he constrained by a self-imposed academic writing style: his prose is personal, anecdotal, hip, witty, even whimsical at times. He is also personally acquainted with many of the writers he treats — Paul Blackburn, Joel Oppenheimer, Gilbert Sorrentino, Hubert Selby Jr. — which is especially apt when locating the voice in these writers' works. He's actually heard those voices and can alert the reader to what can be lost on the printed page. The best reader reanimates the page, gives the print a voice. "Speak the lines out loud," he recommends. "Get the text on its feet and move around the empty space."

As this list of names indicates — to which should be added Stephen Dixon, John Clark Pratt (and other writers on Vietnam), Harold Pinter, and the late Theresa Hak Kyung Cha (a Korean-American writer of great promise) — Stephens works with an eclectic bag of writers, not the usual set of golden codgers treated in most studies of short fiction. Nor does he confine himself to short fiction, despite the subtitle. The poetry of Blackburn and Oppenheimer; the novels of Sorrentino, Selby, and those writing fiction about Vietnam; the drama of Beckett and Pinter — all this receives as much attention as short fiction, a deliberate blurring of the genres that again demonstrates how much one genre can inform the other. What he calls the "seeing voice" is common to all.

The personal approach does have its drawbacks, of course. Private enthusiasms and dislikes are vented, as when his curiously ambivalent chapter on Sorrentino is followed by a curiously extravagant one on Selby. (He once considered the latter's *Requiem for a Dream* "the greatest American novel of the century.") In other words, Stephens expresses many opinions of the sort that other teachers would use in the classroom but not usually commit to print, but for this he deserves commendation rather than censure. Would that more academics had such courage.

In fact, it is in the classroom (rather than the study) that this book might prove most useful. I can't think of a more inspiring text to be used in a writers' workshop or creative writing class, and in his concluding chapter Stephens even offers a number of exercises that can be used there. But his opening chapters on the seeing voice (with a history of drama thrown in for good measure), his brief but fascinating readings of "exemplary voices" (Beckett, Kafka, Borges, Babel), and his insightful treatments of his principal authors give solid training in locating the voice in literature as well as in creating a voice in one's own writing.

Review of Contemporary Fiction, Fall 1986

□ □ □ □ □ □ □

Tom LeClair. *The Art of Excess: Mastery in Contemporary American Fiction*
University of Illinois Press, 1989

John Kuehl. *Alternate Worlds: A Study of Postmodern Antirealistic American Fiction*
New York University Press, 1989

Tom LeClair's *Art of Excess* is easily the most significant book of literary criticism I've read in years for two reasons. First, he redeems seven brilliant novels of our time that have been ignored, misunderstood, even vilified: Pynchon's *Gravity's Rainbow*, Heller's *Something Happened*, Gaddis's *J R*, Coover's *The Public Burning*, McElroy's *Women and Men*, Barth's *LETTERS*, and Le Guin's *Always Coming Home*. Second, LeClair leaves the ivory tower of literary criticism to engage urgent problems concerning "the ecological, political, economic, technological and other systems in which we all exist." The result is a brilliant work of cultural criticism as well as literary criticism, and one that restores to the literary masterwork the stature and potential for social improvement of the greatest works of the last century.

LeClair knows he's going against the grain of fashionable literary criticism — which tends to avoid privileging masterworks over minor and marginal works — but his introduction masterfully makes his case for going against the grain. He is insistent without being strident, urgent but not fanatical, and critically au courant without the pseudo-scientific jargon. His erudition is sweeping but not overpowering, even allowing those who (like myself) are unacquainted with systems theory (LeClair's major paradigm) to follow his arguments.

The seven novels LeClair examines offer trenchant criticisms of the 20th century and valuable blueprints for the 21st, and LeClair is the first to treat these works with the dignity and respect they deserve. *The Art of Excess* should be required reading not only for critics of contemporary American literature but for anyone concerned with the current crisis of American culture.

John Kuehl's new book, unlike LeClair's, is not addressed to critics already familiar with contemporary fiction, but apparently to readers who have never heard of, much less read, such writers as Barth, Gaddis, and Pynchon. For years Kuehl has been teaching a seminar at NYU on postwar antirealistic fiction, and his book seems intended for students who have studied the classics but are unfamiliar with what has been happening in contemporary American fiction and who need terms like "roman à clef" defined for them. For this audience Kuehl has written a serviceable book: he has isolated a dozen or so of the most significant writers who have challenged the notion of realism in fiction, then isolated a dozen or so recurring themes and preoccupations of these writers, with enough asides and digressions on other writers and themes to make *Alternate Worlds* a fairly comprehensive history of this movement.

A lengthy introduction by James Tuttleton extends the historical context by showing that antirealistic themes and techniques are not a modern development but have been present throughout American literature, and an interview between Tuttleton and Kuehl concludes the book. Tuttleton doesn't hide the fact that he has a low opinion of much contemporary antirealistic fiction, and Kuehl's defense has a perfunctory tone like that of a lawyer defending a client he knows is guilty. Neither seems even to *enjoy* these novels, much less find in them the blueprints for cultural regeneration that LeClair finds in the best of them (especially *Always Coming Home*). But Kuehl's purpose is literary history and taxonomy rather than cultural criticism, and the range of writers he includes in his weighty study — especially neglected writers like Coleman Dowell, Gilbert Sorrentino, and Alexander Theroux — makes his book a good place to start for students beginning to study contemporary American literature.

Review of Contemporary Fiction, Fall 1989. Kuehl, with whom I had worked earlier on *In Recognition of William Gaddis* (Syracuse University Press, 1984), took offense at my review, which I considered an evenhanded, even charitable account of a rather mediocre, unoriginal book — I was afraid if I had assigned the book to someone else, an even harsher review would have resulted — and in an insulting letter broke off contact with me.

□ □ □ □ □ □ □

Writers in Conversation. Kathy Acker, William Burroughs, Angela Carter, William Gaddis, et al.

The Roland Collection [now available at http://www.rolandcollection.tv/films/modern-literature-and-philosophy/writers-talk-series]

Readers of this journal [*RCF*] should be aware there is an impressive series of audio-cassette interviews available that feature some of the past, present, and future subjects of the *Review*. They range from 30 to 45 minutes in length and most seem to have been taped around 1985–1987 at the Institute of Contemporary Arts in London. The interviewer is a fellow writer or sympathetic critic, resulting in non-adversarial interviews that are more spontaneous than published ones (which are invariably edited and touched up) and that provide a more immediate sense of an author's personality, voice, and temperament.

Kathy Acker is a remarkably direct, straightforward speaker, patient with interviewer Angela McRobbie's sometimes convoluted questions, and displays great intelligence and charm. The tape opens and closes with comically deadpan readings from *Hello I'm Erica Jong*, framing an informative discussion of her influences, interests, opinions of the British literary scene, and the various theories and political motivations behind her works. (The visual contrast is entertaining: Acker is dressed very punk — leopard-skin Spandex pants, black T-shirt, short orange hair, black leather jerkin and matching headband — while McRobbie looks like a prim Welsh school teacher.)

Acker switches from interviewee to interviewer on the Burroughs tape. This interview could have been intriguing, given Burroughs's influence on her work (which she discusses on her tape), but Burroughs is rather disengaged and politely indifferent here, and Acker is a little too deferential (and too ill-informed on some aspects of his life and work) for the interview to ever get off the ground. Much of the information here has been covered in other interviews, though Burroughs does talk a little about his recent painting ventures and about his next book — about Jesus Christ and a "Christ virus" that is let loose [*Ghost of Chance*, 1991].

Like Burroughs, Gaddis is a bit subdued and restrained, showing little of the wit and urbane charm he can show in private company. Intelligently interviewed by British novelist Malcolm Bradbury on the occasion of the publication of *Carpenter's Gothic* in England in 1986, it is interesting to hear Gaddis's view of that novel as basically a set of technical challenges he set himself to overcome. He is also candid about the "absurd missionary spirit" in his work and in that of Russian authors like Gogol and Tolstoy, a point often lost on his commentators.

The most enjoyable of the lot is Lisa Appignanesi's interview with Angela Carter. Their conversation is relaxed, amusing, clever, and covers a number of points: class distinctions in British writing; Carter's adaptation of the supernatural genre; feelings about the U.S.; the subversion of stereotypes (sexual and literary) in her work, especially in her fairy tales; and her interest in the Marquis de Sade. Attracted at first to Sade's atheism ("the most honourable course a humane person can take in the face of religion," she says), she talks about the insights that led to her writing *The Sadean Woman*, a brilliant piece of cultural criticism.

There are almost 40 other authors featured in the Roland Collection, including Cabrera Infante, Pinter, Heller, Vargas Llosa, and Ginsberg (interviewed by R. D. Laing). While the price [$79.95 each] may be prohibitive for individuals, those attached to universities should urge their libraries to buy as many of these tapes as possible.

Review of Contemporary Fiction, Fall 1989.

□□□□□□□

Joseph Dewey. *In a Dark Time: The Apocalyptic Temper in the American Novel of the Nuclear Age*

Purdue University Press, 1990

For me the highlight of Joseph Dewey's excellent study of contemporary American apocalyptic fiction is his brilliant chapter on William Gaddis's *Carpenter's Gothic,* which has received minimal critical attention since its publication in 1985. Dewey displays a fine grasp of the novel's mazy complications and cleverly teases out the many metaphoric implications of Gaddis's structure, allusions, and details. This chapter alone makes *In a Dark Time* invaluable, but the reader is also treated to an informative overview of American literature's long apocalyptic tradition and to extended readings of several contemporary novels that have grappled with the ways the potential of nuclear war has threatened to literalize the religious metaphor of apocalypse. These include Vonnegut's two best novels (*Cat's Cradle* and *Slaughterhouse-Five*), Coover's *Origin of the Brunists* (another underappreciated novel), two by Percy (*Love in the Ruins* and *The Thanatos Syndrome*), Pynchon's *Gravity's Rainbow,* and DeLillo's *White Noise.* Dewey's prose is colorful and refreshingly clear of critical jargon; his research is thorough but unobtrusive. In a dark time when many younger critics are producing unreadable books overburdened by critical theory, Dewey has written an accessible, illuminating book that should prove of permanent value.

Review of Contemporary Fiction, Spring 1992

□ □ □ □ □ □ □

Brian McHale. *Constructing Postmodernism*

Routledge, 1993

Brian McHale *owns* postmodernism: his 1987 book *Postmodernist Fiction* remains the best introduction to this slippery term and the multitude of devices and strategies it encompasses, and now comes *Constructing Postmodernism,* which refines and extends the arguments of the earlier book and offers exemplary readings of a variety of problematic postmodern novels. As his title indicates, defining "postmodernism" is a project always under construction, never finished, and any critic's definition of the term is to be judged by how accurately it recognizes the historic continuum of which every novel is a part (no text is an island) and by how useful that definition is in allowing the critic to say interesting things about a work. McHale rigorously tests earlier definitions — finding Dick Higgins's little-known version more coherent than John

Barth's better-known one — but isn't so dogmatic as to dismiss anything that's useful in earlier formulations.

Two introductory chapters are followed by readings of *Ulysses, Gravity's Rainbow, Vineland, The Name of the Rose, Foucault's Pendulum, Women and Men,* and the novels of Christine Brooke-Rose. (Most of these chapters appeared first in literary journals, but all have been revised for this book.) In the text and in the notes, McHale makes reference to a huge number of other novels; this is so heartening at a time when most critics seem to read only other critics, and even the best-read among us will have several interesting novels to explore thanks to McHale's voracious reading. For once, the publisher's hyped prediction on the back cover is accurate: "*Constructing Postmodernism* will be essential reading for all students of contemporary literature and culture."

Review of Contemporary Fiction, Fall 1993

□ □ □ □ □ □ □

Anatole Broyard. *Kafka Was the Rage: A Greenwich Village Memoir*
Crown/Carol Southern, 1993

Anatole Broyard was a book columnist for the *New York Times* who wrote some notoriously vicious reviews of such stunning, innovative novels as Jack Kerouac's *Visions of Cody* and Chandler Brossard's *Wake Up. We're Almost There*. (His own attempts at fiction came to naught.) This rather beguiling memoir, abandoned in 1988 shortly before he died, tells of his first few years in Greenwich Village after World War II and of the burgeoning literary and artistic movements below Fourteenth Street. Its greatest value, however, is the extended biographical portrait of one of the most remarkable women of our time, Sheri Martinelli (here called Sheri Donatti). Born in 1917, she came to New York in the mid-1940s and began an almost legendary existence: she was an abstract painter who modeled for *Vogue*, was the object of William Gaddis's affections and became the basis for Esme in *The Recognitions* (which even reprints one of Sheri's long letters to him on art), was friends with Anaïs Nin and described at length in her *Diary*, then went to Washington, DC, and became a disciple of Pound and apparently got him working again on *The Cantos* (the *Rock-Drill* section in particular refers to her in various guises), was also friends with H.D. (she is "Ondine" in her *End to Torment*) as well as with the Beats (Kerouac, Corso, and Ginsberg all refer to her at some point in their writings). In addition her paintings have been exhibited all around the world — Pound wrote a preface for a book of her art published in Italy in 1955 — and she has written a good deal of entrancing poetry. Broyard wonderfully captures the fascination she exerted (and continues to exert: she lives outside Washington, DC, these days and we talk on the phone occasionally; her conversation is unlike any I've ever heard, whimsical, brilliant, outrageous, and very funny. She dismisses Broyard's book as more "a wet dream" than a factual account). Sheri receives the lion's share of this book, but there are also brief portraits of Delmore Schwartz, Milton Klonsky, and Caitlin and Dylan Thomas (but *not* Gaddis, despite what the jacket copy promises.)[17] A slight but valuable piece of literary history.

Review of Contemporary Fiction, Spring 1994

□ □ □ □ □ □ □

David Bergman, ed. *Camp Grounds: Style and Homosexuality*

University of Massachusetts Press, 1993

Camp has been around for at least a hundred years, and though a few attempts have been made in the past to define its essence — by Christopher Isherwood in his novel *The World in the Evening* (1954) and Susan Sontag in her "Notes on Camp" (1964) — only in the last decade has it come to be recognized as a form of transgressive aesthetics used by gay artists to challenge mainstream culture. Camp is not to be confused with kitsch or simpering silliness: it is a witty undermining of basic assumptions about culture and gender, two concepts whose currency makes *Camp Grounds* as timely as it is useful.

The 16 essays here — some reprinted, some written specifically for this volume — explore a variety of "camp grounds" high and low, from Proust to Dusty Springfield, from movies to queer 'zines. As several of the contributors concerned with literature argue, camp is a tone that must be recognized by all critics — straight and gay — to appreciate fully certain writers like Whitman, James, and Proust, and to rescue from triviality more obviously camp writers like Ronald Firbank (subject of a stellar essay here by William Lane Clark). The book is an invaluable contribution to gay studies, and lays the foundation for future studies of what Roland Barthes called "*écriture gaie*."

Review of Contemporary Fiction, Fall 1994

□ □ □ □ □ □ □

17 Apparently deleted at the last moment, this material was published later as "Remembering William Gaddis in the Nineteen-Fifties," *New England Review*, Summer 1995.

Kevin Kopelson. *Love's Litany: The Writing of Modern Homoerotics*
Stanford University Press, 1994

Claude J. Summers, ed. *The Gay and Lesbian Literary Heritage: A Reader's Companion to the Writers and Their Works, from Antiquity to the Present*
Holt, 1995

Desire has got a lot of ink in critical theory recently, but not love, desire's romantic elder. Kevin Kopelson shows how 19th-century literary constructions of (heterosexual) love were adapted by eight key gay and lesbian writers: Wilde (the father of them all), Gide, Firbank, Woolf, Stein, Yourcenar, Renault, and Barthes. Wilde and Barthes open and close the book in separate chapters, with the others paired off to illustrate specific erotic tropes. Kopelson's own writing of homoerotics is smart, witty (he disputes the stereotype "that gay men are Oedipal wrecks"), as conversant with theory and scholarship as with pop culture (Tina Turner provides a typical epigraph), and alert to cultural differences ("Liebestod is at home in Bayreuth but not in Beirut").

The book is all the more valuable for including Firbank, the least known of Kopelson's eight writers but possibly the most cunning, provocative, and artful. In chapter 2, Firbank is paired with Gide to demonstrate how two "frustrated pederasts" dealt with the traditional erotic notion of "complementary merger" (i.e., opposites attract). Working mostly with *Concerning the Eccentricities of Cardinal Pirelli* (and with references to *The Artificial Princess* and *The Princess Zoubaroff*), Kopelson investigates disrobing as both self-revelation and disempowerment, Firbank's rejection of Wilde's constructionist rejection of an essential self (without, however, fully embracing essentialism), and "the use of Narcissus as a trope for libidinal investment in the ego." This is the kind of attentive, sophisticated reading Firbank has long deserved but rarely received. Critical neglect of Firbank during most of the century is shameful, and one applauds the current generation of gay critics who are rescuing him from oblivion. Now if they could just find some way to rehabilitate Frederick Rolfe.

Rolfe and all eight of Kopelson's subjects have intelligent, well-researched entries in Claude J. Summers's massive new reference book. In addition to hundreds of author entries, there are subject essays on various eras of literary production (broken down *MLA Bibliography*-style), related subjects (musicals, opera), and particular themes (camp, identity, romantic friendship). Almost every gay and lesbian writer of note seems to be represented, along with numerous heterosexual writers who have addressed homosexuality in their works: Saint Augustine is here, Donne, Tennyson — but not Pierre Louÿs, who doted on lesbians — and a rather cutting entry on Hemingway (but which omits "The Sea Change" from the discussion of his works that treat homosexuality). The emphasis is on 20th-century literature, and it is up-to-date enough to contain a passing reference to Carole Maso's 1994 novel *The American Girl in the Chinese Hat*. There are a few curious omissions — no entries for René Crevel, Coleman Dowell, James McCourt, Severo Sarduy — but it would be petty to harp on them in light of the considerable efforts obviously expended here to be as inclusive as possible.[18] This is an essential book for all libraries and literary scholars.

Review of Contemporary Fiction, Fall 1995.

□ □ □ □ □ □ □

Jan Bondeson. A *Cabinet of Medical Curiosities*

Cornell University Press, 1997

Of all the marvels in the universe, the human body remains the most marvelous and mysterious, the subject of more myths, legends, and superstitions than King Arthur or Atlantis. In cases of illness or deformity, the body can seem especially mysterious, even alien: the plaything of occult forces, or the very battleground on which God and Satan compete for the soul. In his new book, British physician Jan Bondeson examines a wide variety of medical abnormalities and, to a lesser extent, the uses moralists and writers have made of such "freaks of nature."

Spontaneous human combustion, snakes living in the stomach, the lousy disease (phthiriasis), giants and dwarfs, death trances, women who give birth to rabbits or other animals, tailed people, and other anomalies, real and imagined, are catalogued by Dr. Bondeson with forensic thoroughness and easy erudition. From the beginning of recorded history, he shows, people have been fascinated by abnormalities, and almost always interpreted them as signs of divine punishment, an attitude that sadly persists today. (Ask a fundamentalist about the origin of AIDS and he'll tell you it's God's way of punishing those sinful homos.) Hence spontaneous combustion was usually associated with drunkards, and phthiriasis with godless tyrants. Hawthorne took the legend of snakes living in stomachs — surprisingly prevalent in his day — and used it as an emblem of jealousy and self-centeredness in his famous story "Egotism; or, The Bosom Serpent." Giants, in the Bible and other mythologies, were invariably evil. Dwarfs got off easier, often benevolently viewed as fairies — the story of Caroline Crachami, "The Sicilian Fairy," is included here — though sometimes they were demonized as sprites or trolls. Any deviation from the

18 They were not added to the revised edition of 2002.

norm was viewed with suspicion, an attitude that unfortunately seems to be innate to a large portion of the populace, then as now.

The history of teratology (the study of malformation in organisms) is shot through with deceit and ignorance, which Dr. Bondeson exposes with the bemusement of someone who's seen it all. Mary Toft was the talk of London in the 1720s for having given birth, she claimed, to 17 rabbits, a scam she ran for several months. People who insisted that snakes lived in their stomachs either mistook roundworms for snakes or suffered from a misdiagnosed gastrointestinal disease — that is, when they didn't deliberately swallow a dead snake in secret and then vomit it up for the credulous. Reading these fantastic accounts, it's difficult to decide who is more to blame: the fraudulent or the defrauded. Most people believe what they want to believe, regardless of the facts, and when the capacity for self-delusion is added to ignorance of scientific principles, you've got believers in everything from spontaneous combustion and cat-headed women to astrology and heavenly fathers.

Though most of the exhibits in *A Cabinet of Medical Curiosities* are frauds, Dr. Bondeson relates the sad tales of some real abnormalities: Charles Byrne ("the Irish Giant"), the Two-Headed Boy of Bengal, and the aforementioned Sicilian Fairy, all of whose remains can be viewed today in London's remarkable Hunterian Museum. Dr. Bondeson's final chapter is on Julia Pastrana, whose hairy, apelike appearance made her a sensation in the last century. She was by all accounts "a normal, intelligent woman of gentle disposition" despite her extreme case of congenital hypertrichosis, and the callous exploitation she suffered during her lifetime — and for a hundred years after as a mummy — "is not one," as Dr. Bondeson laconically remarks, "to inspire confidence in human nature."

Throughout his book the author takes note of the many famous writers who have used (if not exploited) monsters in their works, ranging from Goethe, Dickens, Melville, Hawthorne, Gogol, and Zola up to our day: Dr. Bondeson discusses García Márquez's *One Hundred Years of Solitude*, but monsters and prodigies can also be found in the contemporary writings of such authors as Angela Carter, Rikki Ducornet, and David Foster Wallace. (And of course supermarket tabloids continue to report monstrous births and other anomalies, indicating frauds will continue to flourish so long as there are people gullible enough to be defrauded.) But when all fraud, demonization, and allegorization are cleared away, one is left with a sense of awe at the human body, a *terra incognita* still capable of producing as much terror as delight.

American Book Review, July–August 1998. This was written at the invitation of my friend Rikki Ducornet, who was guest-editing a forum on "The Monstrous and the Marvelous: The Dual Nature of the Grotesque."

Jerome Klinkowitz. *Keeping Literary Company: Working with Writers Since the Sixties*
State University of New York, 1998

Richard Elman. *Namedropping: Mostly Literary Memoirs*
State University of New York, 1998

These two books of literary memoirs, published by the same press at the same time, seem designed to offer contrasting views of the literary life, one from the ivory tower and one from the trenches. Jerome Klinkowitz, a professor at the University of Northern Iowa, has been a tireless promoter of contemporary innovative writers for nearly 30 years, and was one of the first to write about them. Back in the 1960s, when he was in graduate school, it was almost unheard of for a professor to write about a living author or even to take an interest in current fiction. But when he discovered the works of Kurt Vonnegut, Klinkowitz realized that innovative living authors deserved the same kind of scholarly treatment that dead authors receive and, more important, that one shouldn't wait until authors were dead and canonized before taking them seriously.

In *Keeping Literary Company*, Klinkowitz relates in an engaging style how he came to know certain writers he considers to be the most interesting innovators in fiction: Vonnegut, on whom he has written several books; the fascinating mountebank Jerzy Kosiński; the endearingly eccentric Donald Barthelme; avant-gardists Ronald Sukenick and Raymond Federman; the sublime Gilbert Sorrentino; and the enigmatic Clarence Major. Through well-chosen anecdotes Klinkowitz demonstrates how familiarity with these authors led him to better understand their narrative strategies, techniques, and tonalities. *Keeping Literary Company* is thus as much a work of criticism as it is literary history and should prove invaluable to future scholars of those authors' works.

Klinkowitz has fallen out with a few of his subjects but remains remarkably generous toward them all. He points out that he helped many of them to get grants, professorships, and attention from other critics, but he doesn't dwell immodestly on this. One surprising fact that emerges is many writers' lack of confidence in their work; it was Klinkowitz's validation of their work as worthy of critical study, more than the grants and jobs, for which some of these writers were most grateful. The symbiotic relationship between contemporary writers and their critics is an intriguing but little-studied subject, and *Keeping Literary Company* provides a fascinating look at the benefits and pitfalls of such relationships.

The late Richard Elman could have used someone like Klinkowitz in his corner. Far from being a fêted author, he was "a resident of New Grub Street," as he admits near the end of this posthumous collection of biographical sketches. He wrote 25 books while working in journalism and radio and while teaching (mostly creative writing at a variety of colleges, a different world from Klinkowitz's tenured domain). As the subtitle notes, these are mostly memoirs of literary figures — the others include a musicologist, a dancer, and several participants in the Sandinista revolt in Nicaragua, which Elman covered as a journalist — and mostly writers who taught him something, either about writing or life itself. They range from notables like Aldous Huxley and Isaak Babel to numerous minor, forgotten novelists (Dan Jacobson, David Lamson, William Butler). The 60 or so sketches are brief and anecdotal, without much background or context.

It's all a bit dismal, I'm afraid, these memoirs by a minor writer of other mostly minor writers, though there are a few shining moments: an essay on Isaac Bashevis Singer before he became famous; fine remembrances of William Bronk and Bernard Malamud; a touching anecdote about Robert Lowell; and an acidic portrait of Gilbert Sorrentino, the only writer in common with Klinkowitz's book. Both books refute the principal tenet of the New Criticism under which both authors grew up, namely the irrelevance of biography to literary study. While any work of art should be able to stand on its own, Klinkowitz especially demonstrates how knowledge of a writer's life and habits, even quirks and eccentricities, goes a long way toward explicating the work. New Criticism has been supplanted in recent years by increasingly recondite varieties of literary theory that take even less notice of an author's personality, to the detriment of all involved.

While not all critics can (or should) become pals with the authors they write about, *Keeping Literary Company* and *Namedropping* offer budding critics a more rewarding path to follow than the yellow-brick road of theory-mad speculation and obscurantist jargon that has pretty much shut out the educated reading public from contemporary literary criticism. You don't need a PhD to read either of these two books, just some curiosity about how writers actually live and write.

Washington Post Book World, 23 August 1998

□ □ □ □ □ □ □

Alice Fulton. *Feeling as a Foreign Language: The Good Strangeness of Poetry*

Graywolf Press, 1999

After four award-winning books of poetry, Alice Fulton has published her first collection of essays, a book every bit as dazzling as her books of verse. The ten essays reprinted here are organized thematically rather than chronologically, and subdivided into sections, all of which begin with *P* (Process, Poetics, Powers, Praxis, Penchants, Premises), preceded by a Preamble. The first essay, "Screens: An Alchemical Scrapbook," is in some ways the best, and forms a fitting introduction to Fulton's eclectic mind. It's a wide-ranging meditation on the various meanings of the word *screen* — reminiscent of her second book *Palladium*, generated from the various meanings of that noble noun — and takes in composition, computers, and autobiography. Fulton's gift for striking imagery is on display throughout, as is her ability to find metaphors everywhere. It also introduces her interest in "the aesthetics of science," that is, the ways scientific models enhance an understanding of art.

This segues into the next two essays, which adapt Benoit Mandelbrot's notion of fractals to contemporary poetry. These two essays, written a dozen years apart, join the century-old debate on the merits of formal vs. free verse, and argue persuasively that "fractal" would be a more fitting description than "free" for the kind of verse many poets (including Fulton herself) write today. In her erudite survey of the development of form in poetry, Fulton identifies Emily Dickinson as "a fractal forebear" and makes some fascinating observations on *The Waste Land* and *The Cantos*, noting that while they may resemble current fractal poetry, they were informed by a different cultural worldview.

Dickinson is the subject of a later essay, one of the best I've read on her. Celebrating rather than apologizing for Dickinson's eccentricity (as even many sympathetic critics do), Fulton engages both cultural politics and close reading (especially a brilliant analysis of "It would never be Common — more — I said — ") to argue that Dickinson is the true mother of contemporary poetry, not a weird spinster who left no progeny. Fulton reaches even further back in history to examine the work of another "eccentric" poet, Margaret Cavendish, Duchess of Newcastle. (In Fulton's lexicon, "eccentric" is a compliment.) If, like me, you've never heard of this 17th-century poet, Fulton's essay is the perfect introduction, and in fact deserves to be printed as such next time a publisher issues an anthology of her writings.[19]

"To Organize a Waterfall" is Fulton on her own poetry, a fascinating demonstration of how artfully she constructs her poems. (Most of the examples

19 I could kick myself for forgetting this essay when, a dozen years later, I wrote about Cavendish in the second volume of my history of the novel.

are drawn from her third book, *Powers of Congress*.) This is followed by three review-essays of a variety of poets. Noting how rarely (and often dismissively) books of verse are reviewed, Fulton bends over backward to provide sympathetic readings of a dozen or so recent books, reading them more closely than most poets dream of, and couching her objections as generously as possible. These are models for how to review poetry, and at the same time provide a useful overview of many trends in contemporary poetry. The book concludes with "A Poetry of Inconvenient Knowledge," an argument for how Fulton would like to see poetry develop in the future, discarding narcissism and tired arguments about form to explore more vigorously that "slightly skewed domain where things are freshly felt because they are freshly said."

Long considered one of our best poets, Fulton emerges here as one of our best critics as well: erudite, sensible, "original brain'd, generous" (as she says of Cavendish), and wonderfully readable. Even if, or especially if you don't read much poetry or poetry criticism, *Feeling as a Foreign Language* deserves your attention; it will be repaid tenfold.

Rain Taxi, Fall 1999

□ □ □ □ □ □ □

Anne Roiphe. *To Rabbit, with Love and Squalor: An American Read*
Free Press, 2000

Denis Donoghue. *Words Alone: The Poet T. S. Eliot*
Yale University Press, 2000

Both of these instructive new books straddle the fence between memoir and literary criticism, treating writers not as subjects of quasi-scientific analysis (as in formal criticism) but as people who have played an important role in one's life. It's a difficult balancing act to pull off; if you pick up a book on Eliot, it's usually because you're interested in Eliot, not the critic who wrote it. But Anne Roiphe and Denis Donoghue have found a way to blend criticism and memoir that offers an attractive alternative to the kind of literary criticism being published by most university presses.

Anne Roiphe, who has written both novels and memoirs, reminisces about the literary men in her life, namely, seven protagonists of 20th-century American fiction: Holden Caulfield from Salinger's *The Catcher in the Rye*; Robert Jordan from Hemingway's *For Whom the Bell Tolls*; Dick Diver from Fitzgerald's *Tender Is the Night*; Harry Angstrom from Updike's Rabbit tetralogy; Philip Roth's fictional alter ego, Nathan Zuckerman; Frank Bascombe from Richard Ford's *Independence Day* and *The Sportswriter*; and Max from

Maurice Sendak's *Where the Wild Things Are*. Roiphe cares deeply for all of these troubled boys and men, even though they have more faults than virtues, as she is the first to admit. "Ah men," she sighs at the end of her book, "the sweetness and ferocity of them, the salty taste, the neediness, the difficulty of them, the tragicomedy of them."

She takes a threefold approach to each literary creation: an extended character analysis, an account of what was happening in the United States when these books were published, and a discussion of how the books influenced her personal life and her relationships with men. She first read many of these books when young and impressionable, then re-read them when older and wiser, and admits that these protagonists more often than not created unrealistic ideas of what the men in her life should be. But like a first love, they remain dear to her, so dear that Roiphe ends each chapter with a fictionalized fantasy date with each of these men.

It would be easy to mock this approach; this is how amateur reading groups "analyze" novels, discussing literary characters as though they were neighbors and relating everything to personal experience. But it's a compliment to an author to have created characters so well-rounded they can indeed be discussed this thoroughly, and most authors would prefer readers such as Roiphe over captious academic critics deconstructing their texts for signs of political incorrectness. Roiphe is full of insights into these characters, especially how Caulfield and Jordan in particular offered alternatives to the stifling, alcoholic conformity of the 1950s of her youth. The editing is rather slack — either Roiphe or her editor needs a refresher course in comma usage — but the book is appealing and quite readable.

While Roiphe discusses half a dozen men, Donoghue focuses on one: the man who wrote less poetry than any other major poet yet whose poetry dominated the 20th century. When Donoghue first encountered T. S. Eliot's "The Love Song of J. Alfred Prufrock" in college, it was akin to love at first sight: "I knew it was a different kind of poetry from Yeats's or Byron's and that I would never forget it."

Words Alone picks up where Donoghue's 1990 memoir *Warrenpoint* left off, but after the first few pages it becomes, aside from the occasional personal digression, a straightforward critical study — and a superb one at that. As the title suggests, the focus is very much on Eliot's words: Why did Eliot choose this word rather than that? Why does the weary London clerk in *The Waste Land* fix his eyes "before his feet" rather than "on his feet"? What difference does that preposition make? How do Eliot's extensive quotations from foreign languages function? That's the level at which Donoghue works, but his close readings are buttressed by a wide range of background material, making *Words Alone* almost a history of modern poetry as well as an argument for

Eliot's predominant position in that history.

After the autobiographical introduction and a chapter on the various voices in Eliot's work, Donoghue gives demonstration-class readings of six key Eliot poems — the one on *The Waste Land* is especially fresh — and follows those with chapters comparing Eliot and Wallace Stevens, one on Eliot's *The Idea of a Christian Society*, two on *Four Quartets*, and a concluding chapter on Eliot's religious beliefs. In the process, Donoghue discusses nearly all of the works, including the plays and Eliot's magisterial essays. He cites earlier Eliot critics and some contemporary theorists, but doesn't put the theoretical cart before the horse, as so many younger critics do.

Donoghue has been reading, teaching, and writing about Eliot for more than 50 years; *Words Alone* bears the stamp of someone who has lived with this poetry, not merely studied it. In that regard his book resembles Roiphe's, and both show the advantage of taking books personally.

Washington Post Book World, 26 November 2000

□ □ □ □ □ □ □

Roz Kaveney, ed. *Reading the Vampire Slayer: An Unofficial Critical Companion to "Buffy" and "Angel"*
Tauris Parke, 2001

Rhonda V. Wilcox and David Lavery, eds. *Fighting the Forces: What's at Stake in "Buffy the Vampire Slayer"*
Rowman & Littlefield, 2002

When literary critics began writing about popular media 30 years ago, they ganged up on simple, even unworthy targets: soap operas, supermarket romance novels, slasher movies, and so on. Like shooting fish in a barrel. Now they're picking on someone their own size and have met their match in the sublime, postmodern *Buffy the Vampire Slayer*. Any TV program that routinely includes such lines of dialogue as "I believe the subtext here is rapidly becoming text" and "Do I deconstruct your segues?" is ready and waiting for academia with a smile. Two bands of critics, armed with the latest in media and cultural theory, go up against the slayer in these new collections of essays, with fascinating results.

British writer and critic Roz Kaveney has assembled ten interesting essays on *Buffy* and its spin-off *Angel*, mostly from her fellow Brits — such as Keith Topping, whose alert and entertaining *Slayer: The Totally Cool Unofficial Guide to "Buffy"* has just been reissued in an updated edition — indicating that the show is not merely an American phenomenon. Kaveney furnishes a fine introductory essay, mapping the "Buffyverse" and identifying the story-arcs of the first five seasons of *Buffy* (and the first two of *Angel*). Although canny enough to note that the strongest shows appear during sweeps months, she's sharp enough to detect unifying themes in each season's shows and the structural pattern of the evolving series. This is followed by Boyd Tonkin's "Entropy as Demon: Buffy in Southern California," a literate, cleverly written essay on the history and significance of *Buffy*'s So Cal setting. Brian Wall and Michael Zoyd's "Vampire Dialectics: Knowledge, Institutions and Labour" is as dry as it sounds, but gives an insightful Marxist reading of the show (perhaps inspired by that memorable scene in "Anne" where Buffy fights her captors with a hammer and sickle). "*Buffy* wouldn't work without its sense of humour," Steve Wilson quite rightly insists in "'Laugh, spawn of hell, laugh,'" which examines the many forms of humor deployed in the clever show.

Karen Sayer's "'It wasn't our world anymore. They made it theirs': Reading Space and Place" is, well, all over the place, poorly written/edited, and spotty in its insights. Infinitely better is Zoe-Jane Playden's "'What you are, what's to come': Feminisms, Citizenship and the Divine," an erudite, convincing argument "that *Buffy* offers not degraded readings of women in society, but emancipatory ones, and that the series is suggestive of a series of feminisms: feminist theory, feminist mythology and feminist politics." Ann Millard Daugherty continues this argument in "Just a Girl: Buffy as Icon," and in "'Concentrate on the kicking movie': *Buffy* and East Asian Cinema," Dave West explores that important influence on the series. Esther Saxey takes us on a tour of the weird, online world of fan fiction, where the implicit sexual attraction between the characters is made very explicit, especially in "slash" stories hypothesizing homosexual relationships (Buffy/Faith, of course, but Spike/Xander?!). The anthology concludes with Ian Shuttleworth's excellent "'They always mistake me for the character I play!' Transformation, Identity and Role-Playing in the Buffyverse (and a Defence of Fine Acting)," an informed tribute to the remarkable acting abilities of the cast and the creativity of *Buffy*'s creator/auteur Joss Whedon.

Fighting the Forces boasts more than twice as many essays, mostly from American contributors, most of whom, interestingly enough, are women. (The Brit collection is evenly balanced.) This in itself isn't surprising; with the departure of Angel and Giles, and the addition to *Buffy*'s cast of Anya, Tara, and Dawn, the show is becoming increasingly gynocentric, and from the very beginning it has problematized feminism, "girl power," patriarchy, and female relationships. Those particular concerns are the focus of the opening essays — too numerous to itemize as I did with the earlier collection — but *Buffy* proves to be too slippery and subversive to pin down. Aside from these essays, there's not much overlap with the Kaveney collection. This one is more concerned with the social and cultural issues "at stake" in *Buffy*, as the punning subtitle indicates: gender, violence, alternative families, religion, class and race differences (various manifestations of the Other), the resurgence of the occult, and morality. While *Buffy* is hardly politically correct — "You're a vampire," Buffy says in one episode. "Oh, I'm sorry, was that an offensive term? Should I say 'undead American'?" — it scores high in most categories as a bracing model for ethics. Only in its perceived brushes with racism, exemplified in the show's treatment of Kendra, a black slayer, does *Buffy* lose a few points, according to several critics here.

Others provide useful historical background and source material: on witchcraft, fairy tales, dreams, Shelley's *Frankenstein* (the source for the Adam arc in season four), demonology, and of course vampires. (No one notes, however, that Buffy Summers is undoubtedly named after the eccentric scholar Montague Summers, whose two notorious books on vampires have been almost continuously in print since the late 1920s.) In every case the contributors show how *Buffy*'s writers appropriate, subvert, and even ridicule this material for their own needs. The collection concludes, again like Kaveney's, with a few essays on fan fiction, *Buffy*'s extensive Internet presence, and a brief appreciation of Joss Whedon.

Missing is much analysis of the considerable artistry of the show; J. P. Williams is good on its use of dramatic camera angles, and another critic notes how effectively a particular scene is lit, but there's little here on film technique or the show's true glory, its dialogue. As Mark Dery is quoted as saying in a different context, *Buffy* enjoys "playing slip 'n' slide on a slick of pure surface: self-conscious quotes, appropriated styles, glib asides." While the critics obviously appreciate the show's witty script — most take their titles from a line of dialogue — few analyze it for particulars or attempt to match it, with one splendid exception: noting Buffy's predilection for puns, Karen Eileen Overbey and Lahney Preston-Matto ask, "But is Buffy's quipping just a display of intellectual cleavage?" That's a line worthy of Cordelia.

Still, *Fighting the Forces* is a solid collection and shows how much substance there is to a show that to the casual observer might seem campy and shallow. Wilcox and Lavery have also established an online journal called *Slayage* that will not only publish further essays on *Buffy* but updates of the ones in the book in light of further developments in this unpredictable show. (In a recent episode, it is suggested the entire six-year series is the hallucination of a psychotic girl in a mental ward, an intriguing frame that should send critics into working overtime.)

Both books may be over the heads of *Buffy*'s teen demographic, but for us older viewers — to whom the show is increasingly catering as its cast grows older — it justifies and reduces (in contributor Steve Wilson's words) "the absurdity inherent in watching a show about a vampire slayer with the dubious name of Buffy."

Rain Taxi, Summer 2002

□□□□□□□

Frederick R. Karl. *American Fictions, 1980–2000: Whose America Is It Anyway?*
Xlibris Corporation, 2001

Twenty years ago, Frederick R. Karl published *American Fictions, 1940–1980*, a huge, double-columned book that pretty much lived up to its subtitle: *A Comprehensive History and Critical Evaluation*. With this sequel, Karl tries to make sense of the last 20 years in American fiction, with a different sort of subtitle indicating how difficult it is now to encompass all the different directions fiction has taken and to identify its readers. Audiences have splintered; 30 years ago, everyone read Roth and Updike, like 'em or not; nowadays, few feel obligated to read those considered our best writers, partly because there is no consensus on who those writers are.

Karl has read more of them than most of us, and in his new book gives a fairly good overview of what's happened in American fiction and culture since Reagan took office. His first chapter, however, deals not with fiction but with nonfiction: specifically the "growing up" memoir that has become so popular in the last 20 years. This genre might seem out of place, except, as Karl shows, many of these have been written by novelists and/or use fictional techniques. He discusses a dozen of the best, including Paul Auster's *Invention of Solitude* and Edmund White's *A Boy's Own Story*, and notes that while earlier books of this type usually ended in some sort of triumph, those written since the '80s lack any kind of closure, aside from the writing of the book. Many focus on the writer's disappointing relationship with his or her (in Susan Cheever's case) father, mirroring the general disillusionment with family and, ultimately, with our national leaders ever since the Vietnam War.

Thereafter, Karl organizes fiction writers into loose groups. Chapter 2, entitled "The Resurgent New," includes DeLillo's early novels, Auster, T. C. Boyle, Cormac McCarthy, and Toni Morrison, noting the ways these writers are building on the work of their predecessors, especially Kafka (on whom Karl wrote a book), and reflecting on the hyperinflated reputations of McCarthy and Morrison. (He notes with scorn the bombastic blurbs and reviews these writers have received; they're good, he allows, but not *that* good.) Chapter 3 moves on to one of Karl's (and my) favorite genres, the "mega-novel."

Joseph McElroy's *Women and Men*, Norman Mailer's *Harlot's Ghost*, Harold Brodkey's *The Runaway Soul*, and William Gaddis's *A Frolic of His Own* are discussed at length, with a brief coda arguing — wrongly, I think — that Alexander Theroux's *Darconville's Cat* and Richard Powers's *The Gold Bug Variations* don't quite measure up as mega-novels. And in his final chapter, Karl discusses four more examples of the genre: William H. Gass's *The Tunnel*, DeLillo's *Underworld*, David Foster Wallace's *Infinite Jest*, and Thomas Pynchon's *Mason & Dixon*. With the exception of DeLillo's and Pynchon's, these titanic novels haven't received the attention they warrant, justifying Karl's pointed subtitle to chapter 3: "The Mega-Novel: Do We Deserve It?"

Karl's fourth chapter asks "The New Realism — How New Is It?" Here we have mostly individual works by Richard Ford, Saul Bellow, Ethan Canin, Cynthia Ozick, Robert Stone, Kathy Acker, Russell Banks, Joyce Carol Oates, Nicholson Baker, Peter Matthiessen, and Annie Proulx, with Karl arguing that only Acker and Baker have added anything radically new to realism. The fifth chapter discusses short story writers, the sixth chapter war fiction (specifically the difference between fiction written about World War II and that on Vietnam), the seventh "Blacks–Women–Jewish Writers," and the eighth an update on the novels of Roth and Updike (the Jew fares better than the Gentile). The final chapter surveys a variety of other novels, including Latino-, Native-, and Asian-American fiction, concluding with the mega-novels mentioned above.

Karl's readings focus on theme and rhetoric, undisturbed by the varieties of literary theory that have emerged during the same 20-year period. They read, I'm happy to report, more like essays in the *New York Review of Books* than *PMLA* and are bolstered by his caustic readings of the sociopolitical worlds in which these books were written. (In one footnote, Karl implies that Robert McNamara should be tried as a war criminal for his actions during the Vietnam War.) In attempting to cover so many writers, Karl's readings are a bit hasty — drive-by criticism — but he's alert to how fiction works and nearly always has something interesting to say about the writers he includes.

As with any book of this sort, there are omissions — some understandable, some puzzling. With the exception of David Markson and Guy Davenport, no authors published chiefly by small presses are noticed, so we get nothing on Gilbert Sorrentino, Carole Maso, Rikki Ducornet, Curtis White, and many others responsible for some of the most innovative fiction of this period. William T. Vollmann's shortest, least important book, *Whores for Gloria*, is discussed briefly, but none of his more ambitious mega-novels. Nothing here on Mark Leyner, Tom Robbins, or Jonathan Franzen. (*The Corrections* appeared too late for inclusion, but he wrote two earlier novels worthy of notice.) Frank McCourt is mentioned but not James McCourt, whose five books published over the last 25 years constitute the most impressive body of gay fiction since Firbank's. Marguerite Young's mega-novel *Miss MacIntosh, My Darling* was ignored in Karl's earlier survey, as is her *Harp Song for a Radical* in this one.

Aside from these omissions, Karl's book is an excellent overview of an exciting time in American fiction. The dust is still settling on the 20th century, but *American Fictions, 1980–2000* is an admirable attempt to make sense of its final decades and establishes a watermark for those who plan to write similar chronicles. It'll be a hard act to follow.

American Book Review, November/December 2002

□□□□□□□

Thomas Dumm. *Loneliness as a Way of Life*

Harvard University Press, 2008

Dear Lonely in DC: No, this book isn't really about you, that is, about those who live alone, have few if any friends, and spend holidays alone. True loneliness is a crippling condition that ruins lives. Thomas Dumm, a professor of Political Science at Amherst College, isn't interested in literal loneliness but in "epistemological loneliness." For Dumm's purposes, loneliness is provisionally defined as "the experience of the pathos of disappearance," the trauma of losing someone or something dear. His book is a meditative essay on the various forms loss takes, ranging from personal loss — Dumm's mother and wife died within the last dozen years, his daughter has just left home — to the loss of home experienced by a refugee, to that of a liberal who feels his country has been lost to a gang of contemptible politicians.

In order to make sense of the loss of his mother and wife, Dumm turned to a number of works dealing with the topic. In Shakespeare's *King Lear* he finds both Lear and Cordelia struggling to live in "the matrix of the missing mother," alienating each other in the process with tragic results. Hannah Arendt's *Origins of Totalitarianism* provides him with grim examples of state-enforced loneliness on both refugees and the paranoid citizens of a police state. In two especially fine readings of Arthur Miller's *Death of a Salesman* and Herman Melville's *Moby-Dick*, Dumm explores these textbook examples of epistemological loneliness. The 1984 film *Paris, Texas* literally dramatizes "the pathos of disappearance" in its tale of a man who disappeared for two years to deal with his own epistemological issues. And finally, Dumm contrasts the responses of Ralph Waldo Emerson and W. E. B. Du Bois to the loss of their respective sons.

As Dumm progresses, he adds more and more details of his personal losses, grounding this often abstract book in recognizable situations. Although he says writing the book was therapeutic, Dumm doesn't conquer loneliness at the end; the book has been "a striving toward a larger sense of who I am becoming than I had when I began," concluding with the realization, "The lonely self will always be with us now, an elemental part of our human being."

The truly lonely may find this conclusion facile. To say that *everyone* is lonely dilutes the concept of loneliness, in the manner of the cheesy '70s song that insisted "Everything is beautiful in its own way." Early on, Dumm writes, "*Exiled, untouched, ignored, isolated, desolated, alienated, outcast, denied, lost, mad.* Is it too much to claim that this list of words summarizes something important about all of us?" Yes, it is. I'm tempted to add, "I'll teach you differences," as Kent says in *King Lear.* It's one thing to apply that string of words to someone like Lear, quite another to Jay Leno or my gregarious barber. The truly lonely are a breed apart, social lepers; Dumm deals with Ishmael and Pip from *Moby-Dick,* but Melville's "Bartleby the Scrivener" would have provided a truer study of loneliness.

Dumm seems to be describing modern life in general, not loneliness per se, but I don't want to scold this book. It is a heartfelt and erudite diagnosis of a condition that, OK, many people may experience these days to some extent, one documented in recent books like Robert Putnam's *Bowling Alone* (which Dumm acknowledges in a footnote). However, Dumm intellectualizes this condition to a level not all readers may be willing to follow; there are quite a few passages like this (on an essay about mourning by philosopher Judith Butler):

> Butler's response to the trap of national narcissism is to turn to what she perceives to be the most specific and concrete ways of thinking about others, namely, an ethics of faciality, borrowed from the thought of Emmanuel Levinas. This response, I believe, is a dangerous one, because in Levinasian ethics an appreciation of attenuating circumstances, the articulation of the incomplete and open, in the end gives way to an exclusive recapitulation of the human, so that what appears to be other than human still comes to appear as less than human.

Too much of the book is argued at this level of abstraction for my taste, though if nothing else it underscores the point that Dumm's book is not a self-help book (as its title might suggest) but a carefully nuanced intellectual inquiry. For those not alienated by such prose, *Loneliness as a Way of Life* will make a consoling companion.

Washington Post, 28 August 2008

□ □ □ □ □ □ □

Rob Chapman. *Psychedelia and Other Colours*
Faber & Faber, 2015

Although this is a fairly comprehensive history of psychedelic music in Britain and America during the '60s, it differs from others in delving more deeply into sociological and cultural issues, especially during the second half of the book on "Psychedelia UK." A recurring theme is the influence of LSD on psych, not only on the music but on lyrics, light shows, fashion, and posters. "Acid sugar-cubed and blotter-soaked and tidal-waved its way across the universe in ways unparalleled before or since," as he sums up on the last page. But Chapman also discusses the influence of nostalgia, utopianism, media coverage, censorship, racism, and psychology on the music as well. This is as much a cultural history of psych as a music survey.

Challenging conventional wisdom, Chapman validates the psych credentials of many bands not usually included in the genre (the Association, the Mamas and the Papas, the Bee Gees, the Moody Blues), and makes unusual connections like the relevance of surf music to psychedelia — a chapter so good that it inspired me to buy my first surf instrumentals comp CD. He elevates certain groups — Soft Machine is one of the few that gets a separate chapter, quite rightly IMHO — and downgrades others. (He's rather hard on the Doors. Yes, Morrison acted like a clownish drunk at times, but as a *band* the Doors are extraordinary in the most literal sense of the word.)

Chapman displays a vast knowledge of music, not just psych but classical, commercial, and world music as well. Although I know psychedelia fairly well — I grew up with the stuff as a teen in the '60s — he discusses hundreds of bands I've never heard of. And he makes dozens of counter-intuitive connections, such as when he cleverly demonstrates "that there is an unbroken line of development between Bob Dylan and the Banana Splits."

Best of all is Chapman's colorful way of writing, reminiscent of Lester Bangs but with more control and source notes. A few examples at random: Barry Ryan's "1968 Top 10 hit 'Eloise' was a silk-blousery romp of a song, with bridal choruses that crescendoed and climaxed like a host of Tin Pan Alley valkyries." "Smokey Pokey World" by Tickle — a good example of the rarities discussed here — is described as follows: "The wigged-out call and response between the left-brain, right-brain vocal lines is blue-eyed gospel mutated to the nth. The duo of vocalists sound like disembodied glove puppets popping up from adjacent rabbit holes or moon craters as a ringmaster MC unsuccessfully tries to club them to death with a mallet made of calcified Jelly Tots." (How badly do you want to hear *that*!)

This is a magnificent study of a style that could be silly and excessive at times — one that was certainly abused by many bandwagon-jumpers who later traded psychedelics for coke or heroin to jump on the next music fad — but Chapman shows why psych should be taken as seriously as any other genre in the annals of music history.

Amazon.com, 30 October 2015

ESSAYS

PART 1: WILLIAM GADDIS AND FRIENDS

Chronological Difficulties in the Novels of William Gaddis

In William Gaddis's first two novels, *The Recognitions* (1955) and *J R* (1975), the passage of time is given such attention that a strict internal chronology is implied for each novel. In *The Recognitions* a few references to historic events suggest a precise historical background as well. Little attention, however, has been paid to the internal and external evidence of these fictional chronologies, and as a result critics are still making elementary errors about the novels' time schemes. One critic states, for example, that the bulk of *The Recognitions* "takes place in the early 1940's";[1] it does not. Another believes that Aunt May dies on May Day;[2] she does not. Since Gaddis's work is starting to receive the critical attention it deserves — and it deserves better than it has thus far received — one must be on a firm footing when discussing basic elements of the novels. To that end, then, I have tried to establish chronologies for both novels; "tried" because although the time schemes can be plotted to a great extent, as I shall show, a number of difficulties and discrepancies do not allow establishing totally coherent chronologies. Failure, though, is often instructive, and even somewhat unsatisfactory time schemes will give a clearer picture of the novels' temporal structures and put future discussion of Gaddis's work on surer ground.

Looking for a starting point from which the events in *The Recognitions* can be dated, one might take the statement that Rev. Gwyon was "born on the yellow day in Boston when the volcano had erupted on the other side of the earth,"[3] that is, August 27, 1883. Since we are told (7) that Rev. Gwyon was 44 at the time of his wife's death, the opening of the novel would be 1927. However, one soon sees that this date is too late, for it would be Spring 1928 when he returns home, at which time Wyatt is four — born, then, in 1924.

1 Peter Koenig, "Recognizing Gaddis' *Recognitions*," *Contemporary Literature* 16.1 (Winter 1975): 63.

2 Grace Eckley, "Exorcising the Demon Forgery, or the Forging of Pure Gold in Gaddis's *Recognitions*," in *Literature and the Occult*, ed. Luanne Frank (Arlington: University of Texas at Arlington, 1977), 130. Other misreadings also mar Eckley's essay.

3 *The Recognitions* (Cleveland: World Publishing Co., 1962), 60; subsequent references are to this Meridian edition, for which Gaddis corrected the original edition (New York: Harcourt, Brace, 1955).

Consequently, it would be 1939 when Wyatt takes ill at the age of 15, and since I.2 clearly takes place in the 1930s when Wyatt is in his early twenties, 1927 simply cannot be the starting date.

A more satisfactory starting point can be found by working backward. Several references to the approaching Holy Year are made in Part II; Holy Year has been proclaimed every 25 years since 1450, so obviously 1950 is meant. Further confirmation comes when we are told that an incident on page 297 takes place on Tuesday, December 20; this date did indeed fall on a Tuesday in 1949, so it appears that all of Part II takes place in December 1949, except for the last dozen or so pages, which take place (as does the remainder of the novel) in 1950. If further evidence were needed, the proclamation of the dogma of the Assumption of the Virgin and the canonization of the cross-eyed virgin raped and killed at the age of 11[4] could be cited — both appear in Part III and both occurred in 1950.

That settled, two further chronological clues can be followed. The first occurs (706) when we are told by an unidentified member of the Use-Me Ladies that Aunt May would have been 83 that month; this is spoken, as I shall show below, on Christmas day 1949. That would place Aunt May's birth in 1866, which means she died at the age of 63 in May of 1930. Wyatt, 12 at the time of her death, would have been born in 1918 and would be 31 during the bulk of the novel.

On two other occasions, however, we are told that Wyatt is 33 at this time, once by Brown (229) and once by Wyatt himself (876).[5] But Brown is only approximating, and Wyatt could be speaking figuratively, for he does not really say that he himself is 33, only that "two thousand years ago, thirty-three was old and time to die" — apparently echoing Frazer's thesis that divine kings were killed at the height of their powers. Although one might find it unlikely that a member of the ludicrous Use-Me Ladies would know how old Aunt May would have been some 20 years after her death, one must remember that Aunt May herself made a similar remark about her long-departed brother (37); older people, Gaddis suggests, keep track of that sort of thing. On the other hand, Brown, having first guessed Wyatt to be about 40 (142) and, subsequent to having him investigated, amending his guess to "about thirty-three" (229), might seem as reliable as the unidentified Use-Me Lady, if not more so. In spite of Wyatt's vagueness, he is probably referring to himself

4 Based apparently on the sad fate of Maria Goretti, who was raped and murdered in 1902 under the same circumstances as Gaddis's cross-eyed virgin (see note 13 below). Maria Goretti was canonized on June 24, 1950.

5 Eckley (133) states that Wyatt is 34 at this point, but she uncritically accepted 1883 as Rev. Gwyon's birth, which would mean the last part of *The Recognitions* takes place in 1957, two years after the novel's publication!

when he speaks of 33 being old and a time to die. All things considered, we should probably go with Brown's reckoning, for 33 is no doubt also being used for its symbolic value; traditionally, Christ was 33 at the time of the crucifixion (and coincidentally so was Gaddis the year *The Recognitions* was crucified by the critics).[6] The two year difference between the two chronologies may seem insignificant, but we are concerned here only with chronological consistency, not significance.

Thirty-three years old in December 1949, Wyatt would have been born in 1916. Using this year, then, as a point of reference, the events of I.1 can be dated as follows:

c. 1720 — Rev. John Huss Gwyon "butchered by disaffectionate Indians" (22).
1842, May 1 — Rev. Gwyon's father born (37; spoken on May 1, 1928).
1864, December — Aunt May born (40, 706).
1875, August 27 — Rev. Gwyon born (60; either Gaddis mistakenly used 1875 for 1883 or perhaps meant that Gwyon was born on the day of the month Krakatoa erupted, not the year).
1908 — the 11-year-old virgin assaulted and murdered (16; spoken in early 1920; Maria Goretti died in 1902.
1912 — Rev. Gwyon's father dies (14, 37).
1913 — Rev. Gwyon marries Camilla (3).
1916 — Wyatt born.
1919, May — Esme born (276).
1919, October 26 — Rev. Gwyon and Camilla set sail from Boston for Spain (4).
1919, November 1 (All Saints' Day) — Camilla "stricken with acute appendicitis" (4); dies that evening (5).[7]
1919, November 7 — Rev. Gwyon arrives in Spain (6).
1919, Christmas — Rev. Gwyon administers Eucharist to himself at the Real Monasterio (11).
1920, Spring — Rev. Gwyon returns home (18).
1925, Summer — Aunt May disgusted at news of Scopes Trial (36); Otto Pivner probably born at this time.[8]
1928, May — Aunt May dies, age 63 (40).[9]

6 [Actually, Gaddis was 32 when the book came out in March 1955, and turned 33 in December. I fudged to make the crucifixion pun. (All bracketed notes like this were added in 2015–16 when preparing this book for publication).]

7 A supernatural element is introduced on page 20 when we are told that "right after Hallowe'en" Wyatt imagined seeing Camilla, dressed in white, looking for something in her sewing room (her Byzantine earrings?). Since shortly afterward Aunt May receives Gwyon's letter announcing Camilla's death, the implication is that Wyatt has a vision of his mother at the moment of her death.

8 On page 517 we are told that Otto has been out of college for three years, making him about 24 or 25. He would, then, be about nine when Albert, King of the Belgians, was killed mountain-climbing (1934) — rather late for Otto to learn "that he had a father, or should have one" (507).

9 Eckley mistakenly assumes Aunt May dies on May Day, but several days clearly pass be-

1931 — Wyatt taken with fever at age 15 (41). Winter thaws into April (42).

1932, June 24 (Sunday, Midsummer/St. John's Day) — Rev. Gwyon delivers anti-doctor sermon (45 ff.; had we followed the Use-Me Lady's chronology, the year would be 1934, in which June 24 was indeed a Sunday).

1934–35 — Wyatt's first year at Divinity School (assuming he enters during his eighteenth year, as most freshmen do.)

1935, Fall — Wyatt leaves for his second year of theological studies, but goes to Munich instead.

When we next come upon Wyatt in I.2, we are told that he has not written his father in three years (67), and assuming the letter Rev. Gwyon receives at the end of I.1 is the last Wyatt has written, we are now in 1938. Though it is said to be Fall (68), the interview with Crémer that immediately follows takes place in August, for apparently right after the interview we are told: "Little else happened that Saturday night in August" (73). The same paragraph continues, "Saint Bartholomew's Day was warm" but ends: "It was Sunday in Paris, and very quiet" (74), making it difficult to decide if St. Bartholomew's Day refers to Saturday or Sunday. Since, however, another reference to St. Bartholomew's Day follows (75), Wyatt apparently has his interview with Crémer on Saturday, August 16, and reads his review the following Sunday, August 24 (St. Bartholomew's Day), and, like a persecuted Huguenot, decides to leave Paris.

These dates do not coincide with the calendar for 1938, and it is probably expecting too much that they should. Apparently Gaddis was more concerned with working in as much historical information into this short chapter as he could — the only instance where the early reviewers' charges of unnecessary erudition might be justified — that chronological details were either overlooked or considered unimportant, which for the most part they are.

Chapter 3 of Part I opens several years later in New York City, leaving a large gap in Wyatt's life (as the Gospels do in the life of Jesus) that is only partially accounted for. Working backward from Part II, then, is the only way of dating I.3 and the balance of Part I. Considering that we are told twice (337, 623) in Part II (December 1949) that Wyatt left his wife two years ago and that John, Wyatt's fellow divinity school student, meets him again (266 — also December 1949) two years after his earlier meeting (115), we can date the events of I.3 as follows:

---

tween Aunt May's reference to May Day (37) and her death (40). Eckley correctly points out that Gaddis borrowed much occult lore from Robert Graves's *The White Goddess*, where it is shown that the hawthorn and may trees are related mythologically, and that their month (in his reconstructed tree calendar) commenced on May 14. This date would be more appropriate, chronologically as well as symbolically, for Aunt May's death occurs shortly after that of her hawthorn tree.

c. 1946 — Wyatt marries Esther (at her suggestion); married for a year (79); Wyatt employed as a draughtsman (78–91).
c. 1947 — Wyatt and Esther attend (separately) a showing of Picasso's *Night Fishing in Antibes* (91–100).[10]
1947, Fall — "The lust of summer gone"; Esther and Wyatt invited to the Bildows' for New Year's Eve (100–104).
1947, December 31 — Wyatt and Esther spend New Year's Eve at a Spanish restaurant instead; afterward run into John (104–19).
1948, early Spring — Otto, having been introduced to the Gwyons at a party in December 1947, begins keeping company with them. Wyatt meets Recktall Brown, and soon leaves Esther (119–46).
1948, late Spring — Otto living with Esther; Benny meets Wyatt but fails to persuade him to return to his old job (146–50).
1949, Spring — "More than a year" since Wyatt left Esther; Otto leaves her for Central America (150–53).

Chapter 4 of Part I features Otto in Central America during the summer and fall of 1949, working on his play; he returns to New York at the beginning of December. Chapters 5, 6, and 7 (169–277) all take place on an evening and the next day in early December. Thus the bulk of the novel (169–709) takes place within a few weeks in December 1949, anticipating *J R* in plotting a multitude of events within a very short time span.

Dating Part II involves difficulties of a different sort. Virtually all the action (with the exception of the final pages of II.9) takes place within less than a week's time: Tuesday, December 20th, 1949, until Christmas Day, that Sunday. With great ingenuity Gaddis accounts for almost every action of a dozen or more characters during this short week, but unfortunately a few problems arise in trying to date all the events within the outer perimeters of December 20–25. The starting date for Part II is supplied on page 555 when Agnes Deigh receives a communication from the police informing her that the complaint she phoned in on Tuesday, December 20, at 10:17 AM may result in legal action taken against her by the offended party. Already there's a minor problem: when she calls in the complaint on page 297 it is a little after 4 PM — 4:17 would be about right; so either Gaddis or the police department is off by six hours. We'll assume the latter.

This established, it is easy to track the rest of the chapter, which ends a little after dawn the next morning.[11] Apparently, II.2 takes place later that day (Wednesday, December 21). However, some confusion arises on page

10 The painting is now at the Museum of Modern Art but was not shown there until 1952 (as Mr. Richard Flowers of MOMA kindly informed me).

11 The drag party Tuesday night is later called, appropriately, Saturnalia, which under the Roman Empire lasted from December 17–24 and featured role reversals.

369 when Esther asks, for no apparent reason, what day it is. Wyatt answers Wednesday, but Ellery "corrects" him with Thursday. Since Wyatt had told Valentine that morning that he had been to his wife's the previous night (337), Wyatt apparently knows the correct day, though why he and not the more businesslike Ellery would know it is unclear. When Esther later asks, "—You were here last night?" Wyatt answers with uncertainty, "—Or was it?" (370). (One gets the feeling that Gaddis is teasing the reader — which may account for the other chronological discrepancies encountered so far — simply to see if he is paying attention.) At any rate, Esther's sister Rose had seen Wyatt "in the mirror" on the previous night, and though hers is not the most reliable testimony, she is apparently right. Chapter 2 of Part II ends with Wyatt boarding a train that night to return to his father. Chapter 3 is spent with Rev. Gwyon on what would be Thursday, December 22, with Wyatt returning to New York at 11 PM that night (444).

Now one might naturally assume that the next chapter takes place on the following day, Friday. However, a quick look at the succeeding chapters makes such an assumption impossible. After visiting Wyatt's Horatio Street lodgings, Esme attempts suicide. The next day (473 ff., Saturday) Otto learns of her attempt, visits her, then has the meeting with Sinisterra, and finally ends the night arrested for trying to solicit an undercover policewoman. The following chapters (II.6–8) clearly take place on Saturday, Christmas Eve, and cannot be the same day on which II.5 takes place, for on Christmas Eve Anselm, Hannah, and others are at Esther's party, not at the Viareggio where Otto meets them after his meeting with Sinisterra. What apparently happens, then, is that II.4 takes place on Thursday, the same day Wyatt visits his father — this is partially confirmed by Esme's pornographer friend agreeing to meet her on Friday (447), that is, the next day. Esme goes to Wyatt's place and assumes he is sleeping — as does the reader — though he is not even there. If one carefully rereads the account of her visit (467–71), one finds no direct reference to Wyatt's physical presence.

This reading is further confirmed by an incident paralleling young Wyatt's apparition of his mother at the time of her death. While at his father's parsonage Wyatt twice falls asleep; the second time, Janet discovers him sleeping and touches his torn cheek (438): "—Who was here? he asks himself on waking; "—She was here," he realizes, but not until later (549) do we learn that "she" was part of a dream he had. He tells Valentine: "—And there she was, she touched me. Her lips were blue like indigo." On a literal level the reference is to Janet, whose lips are continuously blue as a result of "the mercuric compound of Aunt May's prescription renewed year after year" (401). But Wyatt, as the conversation with Valentine goes on to reveal, is thinking of Esme and, by extension, his mother, both of whom have contributed to the face of the *Stabat Mater* he is working on. When Esme visited Wyatt's studio, she made herself up garishly with rose madder on the lips and indigo around the eyes, all the while wearing Camilla's Byzantine earrings. (Just as most of the male characters in *The Recognitions* are extensions or parodies of Wyatt, most of Wyatt's women are extensions of his mother.) By analogy, then, with the earlier visitation by his "spectral stabat mater" (399), Esme visits Wyatt's studio at the same time Janet finds him sleeping. Unfortunately, as Fuller might put it, there remains the complication of the griffin's egg. Wyatt purchases it right before he leaves to return to New York (443), and Esme kicks it away while sitting on Wyatt's bed. The presence of the griffin's egg, then, defeats the apparition analogy Gaddis introduces and inserts another day into an already overcrowded week.

Even if Esme did visit Wyatt's place on Thursday and attempt suicide that night, as the chronology demands, other problems intrude. Otto should find out about it Friday (478) and meet with Sinisterra that night, December 23. Now, on Tuesday night (309) Otto had called his father and arranged "a rendezvous for a week later." Why, then, is he going to meet his father only three days later? And there are other problems: II.6, opening with Wyatt and Valentine's discussion at the zoo, should take place on December 24, since II.7–8 takes places on Christmas Eve; but Valentine (686) refers to this meeting as "yesterday morning," that is, Friday. That cannot be because during their meeting the ubiquitous tall woman always missing the Narcissus festival refers to her invitation to Esther's party that night (553). Why would Valentine mistake a conversation earlier in the day with one the day before? Only if his remark on page 686 were spoken after midnight could it be literally correct — and though possible, it's quite improbable.

Still another problem: finally deciding to go ahead with his Mithraic ceremony, Rev. Gwyon tells the Town Carpenter on the night Wyatt leaves to be ready "—Dawn tomorrow, a great deal of work to be done in the church" (442). Chapter 9 of Part II opens on Christmas morning, and there are indications (701–2) that Gwyon spent the day before preparing the church (alone; the Town Carpenter died in his sleep that night). The "tomorrow" on page 442 refers to Friday, but the "yesterday" on 701 refers to Saturday, which could only be true if either Wyatt spent two days visiting or Rev. Gwyon spent two days working on the church, neither of which is indicated in the text. A third alternative would have Ellery correct about the day when he said Thursday; Wyatt would have spent Friday with his father, and both "tomorrow" (442) and "yesterday" (701) would refer to Saturday. One can only conclude, then, that half of the incidents in Part II run on one time scheme and the other half on another. The outer perimeters can be established as December 20–25, but any attempt to date the week's events is doomed by contradictory evidence.[12]

The last dozen or so pages of II.9 and all of Part III take place in 1950, the Holy Year. The general movement in part III is toward Easter, the day on which the cross-eyed virgin is to be canonized (mentioned as early as page 321), and also the day on which Stanley meets his death in the church at Fenestrula. References are made (882, 890, 947) to the approaching Holy Week, and Gaddis evidently intended Stanley's death on Easter Day — dying for the sins of the entire *dramatis personae* of *The Recognitions* — to carry all the symbolic weight associated with the most important day of the Catholic calendar. However, chronological inconsistencies prevent a smooth resolution. Holy Week in 1950 was April 3–9; Stephen/Wyatt remarks, "—The Pleiades are rising, now, now is the time" (892) — it will be remembered that the novel opened with the setting of the Pleiades in November. But the Pleiades rise at the beginning of May, not April. In addition, mention is made of events that took place much later in the year (for instance, the proclamation of the dogma of the Assumption on November 1 — the day Camilla died) and even events that followed in the next couple of years.[13] We also learn on page 917 that Anselm's confessions — based, it would seem, on Thomas Merton's *Seven Storey Mountain* (1948) — have just been published. But he left for a monastery only three or four months earlier, and even if the manuscript had already been written, four months is an impossibly short time for the book to be published and distributed as far away as Italy.

12 One wonders at this point if the chronological discrepancies are a result of editing. When *The Recognitions* was first submitted to Harcourt in 1953, it was somewhat longer, and perhaps in the process of editing (performed by the aptly named Catharine Carver) cuts were made and scenes shifted that inadvertently undermined the chronology.

13 The reference to the Americans looking for Noah's ark on Mount Ararat (916) is probably to Dr. Aaron Smith's expedition of 1951. Similarly, we are told that a "Baptist minister . . . burned two copies of a newly revised version of the Bible because it substituted the words *young woman* for *virgin*" (947); this refers to the publication of the Revised Standard Version in 1952, and specifically to the oft-quoted prophecy of Christ in Isaiah 7:14, where the King James version's *virgin* was translated more accurately as *young woman*. [Years later I discovered that the reference on p. 662 to "prophecies contained in the great pyramid" was taken from Worth Smith's *Miracle of the Ages: The Great Pyramid* (Holyoke, MA: Elizabeth Towne, 1934). Smith predicted, "The *final* phase of the second portion of the prophecy is to be fulfilled on September 16, 1936, in a wonderful way by humanity's entrance into the King's Chamber" (chap. 8), then goes on to predict, "The final 'woe' will begin August 20, 1953" (chap. 9). Hence, Kuvetli's statement "it is only last year we have entered the period of final woe" would place this scene on Christmas Eve 1954, and the remainder of the novel in 1955, the year it was published.] It is probably foolish, however, to expect any work of fiction to adhere perfectly to history, and especially a novel like *The Recognitions*. The fact that in the world according to Gaddis a Spanish city could be named San Zwingli (not to mention Arshole Acres) indicates that Gaddis is playing with the world as we know it. That is part of the fun, and he should not be taken to task for such foolishness.

Finally, the events of the last day of the novel seem rather implausible if intended to take place on Easter. Stanley simply goes to an early Mass as if it were any other day, though being the devout Catholic he is, surely attending Easter services would be in order, in spite of his excitement. He arranges to play the organ later in the morning, at which time surely the church of Fenestrula would be celebrating Easter. The symbolic importance of Stanley's dying on Easter, then, is weakened by these small but nagging inconsistencies. It would be unfair, I suppose, to object that Maria Goretti, the cross-eyed virgin's real-life counterpart,[14] was canonized on June 24, 1950 — not on Easter. The white-stockinged virgin, in spite of the historical basis for her character, is finally just a fictional character.

Even if *The Recognitions* fails to be chronologically consistent in all its particulars, a general historical background for the novel can be summarized as follows:

I.1 (3–62)	c. 1919–c. 1935
2 (63–77)	c. 1938
3 (78–153)	c. 1946–Spring 1949
4 (154–68)	Summer–Fall 1949
5–7 (169–277)	December 1949
II.1–9 (281–720)	December 20–25, 1949 (final pages of II.9 in 1950)
III.1–5 (723–900)	early 1950
Epilogue (901–56)	1950, ending Easter Sunday

This working chronology, even with its imperfections, should clarify the novel's temporal structure and should assist in future discussion of Gaddis's monumental work.

Where *The Recognitions* spans some 30 years, *J R* spans only 30 days. Those days, however, match and often exceed the intricacies of the first novel, indicating that Gaddis spent the 20 years between novels developing even further his impressive organizational skills, at times rivaling Joyce in his ability to shape a great deal of material — sometimes reaching encyclopedic proportions — into a coherent work of art. Gaddis details each day's passing in *J R*, and in almost as many different ways as days, giving the impression that a tightly knit and coherent chronology underlies the novel's dazzling surface. Unfortunately, this does not prove to be the case.

The first day of the novel extends from page 3 to the bottom of page 74;

14 The fact that a fat woman traveling to the upcoming canonization is reading "a small threepenny book titled *A Modern Virgin Martyr*" (831) makes the identification certain; see Alexander Gits, S.J., *A Modern Virgin Martyr: Saint Maria Goretti* (London: Catholic Truth Society, 1949), a 15-page pamphlet.

no indication of the day of the week (or month or year) is given as yet. The second day spans pages 75–149, the third from page 149 to Norman Angel's departure for Chicago on page 154. The exact length of Angel's business trip is hard to determine — he says he "spent three nights on the phone" (157), though this does not necessarily mean the trip lasted only three days — but it takes place over a weekend, for on his return his secretary, Terry, shows surprise at his "even being gone the whole weekend and all" (156). In addition, a fragment from a Spanish newscast on the day of Angel's departure indicates that a weekend is approaching: "viernes sabado y domingo, el . . ." (154). Angel, then, would seem to leave on a Thursday (154) and return the following Tuesday (156), and the weekend itself can be dated thus: Friday, the day after Angel's departure, begins at the bottom of page 154 with the morning traffic report ("inbound traffic on the Gowanus Exp . . .") and ends, apparently, at line 20 on the following page ("voices meeting and parting"). At line 21 Terry is explaining to a customer named Shapiro that Angel is "supposed to be back yesterday he had to stop off at Dayton"; this would be spoken on a Monday since Saturday has already passed and she would not be working on a Sunday. Monday extends from line 21 to line 32. A new day, Tuesday, begins with the morning newscast ("sunny and colder, with temp . . . to be expected"), and later that day Angel finally returns.

If this chronology is correct, then, the novel opens on a Tuesday and the first third can be dated as follows:

3–7	Tuesday
75–149	Wednesday
149–54	Thursday
154–55	Friday
—	Saturday/Sunday
155.21–32	Monday
155–66	Tuesday
166–93	Wednesday
193–230	Thursday
230–31	Friday
231–32	Saturday
232–34	Sunday
234–86	Monday

But here we run into problems. The day that spans pages 234–86 turns out to be not Monday but, as we learn (236–37), Friday. Working backward, then, Angel's business trip would extend from Monday to Saturday (or Monday to Friday, depending on whether one or two days pass at page 155.20–21); such ordering is unacceptable, though, for even though redheaded Terry is the stereotypical dumb but stacked secretary, even she would not confuse the middle of the week with the weekend. Furthermore, if pages 234–86 take place on a Friday, pages 163–93 would take place on a Sunday, and the fact that J R has school that day indicates that cannot be right either. Other minor discrepancies exist: on page 206, for example — Thursday by the first dating system, Monday by the second — while on the phone Crawley complains, "What do you mean call Tuesday, this is. . . ." He does not finish his sentence, but he seems about to object that it was Tuesday already.

One third of the way through the novel, then, the reader cannot form a coherent chronology of the novel's events, juggle them as he may. Even when pages 235–86 are established as a Friday, the chronology is only precariously maintained. Continuing, we would have:

286–316.12	Saturday
316.12–.24	Sunday
316.24–373	Monday
373–414	Tuesday
414–91	Wednesday
491–501	Thursday
501–65	Friday
565–80	Saturday
580–610	Sunday
610–89	Monday

Now on page 552 Rhoda informs us that, "it's like Thursday right?" (instead of the above chronology's Friday). However, if she were correct, the school trip on the day spanning pages 610–69 would take place on a Sunday; so either Gaddis or Rhoda is off a day.

Incidentally, we learn on page 531 that the field trip takes place on the 21st of the month, and since approximately 24 days have elapsed since the beginning of the novel, the opening can be dated from the end of September.[15] If indeed Monday is the correct day of the field trip, we might assume the novel takes place in 1974, the year in which Gaddis finished *J R*, for October 21 did fall on Monday that year. (Even though Gaddis began writing the novel shortly after *The Recognitions* and published parts of it as early as 1970, as late a date as possible is necessary to include all the elements of the story — for example, references in the past tense to the Vietnam War and the technological "advances" such as the video-phone and the electric tie-rack.) Continuing the chronology to the end, we would have:

15 Many references to fall and Indian Summer occur in the beginning of the novel, and references to the approaching Christmas holidays toward the end. The end of August would be too early as a starting point, and since a baseball game is broadcast on p. 219, the end of October would be too late.

669–670.4	Tuesday (10/22)
670.5–.18	Wednesday (10/23)
670.18.–.38	Thursday (10/24)
670.39–674	Friday (10/25)
674–87	Saturday (10/26)
687–726	Sunday (10/27)

Another problem arises, unfortunately. Mr. Duncan asks "Waddles" (Nurse Waddams) what day it is on page 685 and she responds, "I don't know is it Wednesday?" In spite of her uncertainty, she, like Terry earlier, would not mistake the middle of the week with the weekend. Finally, then, we can only say *J R* takes place in October 1974 and let it go at that.[16]

One might account in two ways for the chronological flaws in these otherwise finely crafted novels: either Gaddis purposely devised chronological discrepancies simply to see if any readers would be attentive enough to catch them; or, more probably, Gaddis did not feel that a painstakingly accurate chronology was really important to either novel. If so, he was right — for indeed the substance of neither novel is affected by chronological incoherence, in the same way that *Othello* is not weakened by its oft-noted chronological inconsistencies. It is, however, somewhat surprising that a meticulous craftsman like Gaddis would allow even unimportant discrepancies to creep into his intricately worked novels. How ironic if the chronological difficulties in his works were "like the flaw in Oriental carpets, an intentional measure of humility introduced to appease the Creator of perfection" (*The Recognitions*, 34). Aunt May would like that.

16 [We can't even say that. On page 692, the financier Cates complains that the night before he thought a member of a "theater bunch [. . .] was making some sense about what the pound's been through rallies declines public turning its back turns out he's talking about some damn dead poet." Ezra Pound died 1 November 1972; this and the reference to Kennecott's troubles on page 214 place the novel in the fall of 1972 instead of 1974, though the absence of any reference to the presidential election that year makes even this date suspect. Although I now see that my 30-day time frame is too brief — Gaddis later wrote me "the novel's technique demanded compressing time so, I was afraid I'd be called on it but no one did" (1 June 1986) — the proportions are about right: Gaddis apparently intended the first third of the novel to occupy about a month or so, the second and third a few weeks each, from the end of September to the end of November. There are similar chronological difficulties in his later novels as well.]

"Parallel, Not Series": Thomas Pynchon and William Gaddis

A name often linked with Pynchon's in many discussions of his work is that of William Gaddis, author of two encyclopedic novels of astonishing power and range: *The Recognitions* (1955) and *J R* (1975). Not only is Gaddis considered one of Pynchon's few peers, but similarities in style and content have led many to discern a pattern of literary influence. Usually, this has taken the form of the presumed influence of Gaddis's first novel on Pynchon's first; leading Pynchon critics such as Tony Tanner and Richard Poirier have insisted on *V.*'s debt to *The Recognitions*,[1] and on the publication of Gaddis's second novel, many reviewers repeated this presumption.[2] Recently, *The Recognitions* has been acknowledged as a harbinger not only of the Black Humor of the 1950s and '60s (the genre in which *V.* was first placed), but also of the revival of the Menippean satire (the genre in which Pynchon's second and third novels have been placed), the form to which an increasing number of our most creative writers are turning.[3] Commenting on Don DeLillo's use of Menippean satire in *Ratner's Star* (1976), for example, George Stade wrote: "He is close in subject matter to Thomas Pynchon, who seems to have learned how to use the form through a study of William Gaddis, a presiding genius, as it turns out, of post-war American fiction."[4] The relation between Gaddis and Pynchon seems so close that once it was even rumored that Thomas Pynchon was merely a pseudonym for Gaddis![5] Lately the question of influence has

1 Tony Tanner, *City of Words: American Fiction 1950–1970* (New York: Harper and Row, 1971), 393, and his recent book *Thomas Pynchon* (London: Methuen, 1982), 90; Richard Poirier, "The Importance of Thomas Pynchon," in *Mindful Pleasures: Essays on Thomas Pynchon*, ed. George Levine and David Leverenz (Boston: Little, Brown, 1976), 24.

2 See, for example, John W. Aldridge, *Saturday Review*, 4 October 1975, 27, and R. Z. Sheppard, *Time*, 13 October 1975, 98. Most of the others mentioned Pynchon in one connection or another.

3 See Elliot Braha's "Menippean Form in *Gravity's Rainbow* and in Other Contemporary American Texts" (PhD diss., Columbia University, 1979); chapter 2 discusses *The Recognitions*. (Braha is convinced of Pynchon's debt to Gaddis.) That this form is still going strong is evident from two recent novels: Gilbert Sorrentino's *Mulligan Stew* (1979) and Alexander Theroux's *Darconville's Cat* (1981).

4 *New York Times Book Review*, 20 June 1976, 7.

5 One reviewer speculated that *Gravity's Rainbow* might well be the long novel Gaddis had

come full circle, and the possibility that Pynchon influenced Gaddis's *J R* has been raised by at least one critic.[6] For the most part such ascriptions of influence have been made in passing and not traced in any detail,[7] but the question of influence has been raised often enough that a detailed examination seems warranted at this time.

A *caveat lector* is necessary at the outset: for years most of Gaddis's critics assumed that *The Recognitions* plainly showed the influence of *Ulysses*, and in fact the first academic essay on the novel was later described by Gaddis himself as "a most ingenious piece in a Wisconsin quarterly some years ago in which *The Recognitions*' debt to *Ulysses* was established in such minute detail that I was doubtful of my own firm recollection of never having read *Ulysses*."[8] How ironic it would be, then, to turn around and detail *The Recognitions*' nonexistent influence on any subsequent novel. Similarities between Joyce and Gaddis are the result of a common interest in certain cultural and artistic concerns, and any similarities between Gaddis and Pynchon may be no more than that.[9] Also, *The Recognitions* attracted very little positive notice when first published, and the teenage Pynchon would have been fortunate even to have heard of the novel, much less to have read it. Because of its negative and hostile reviews, *The Recognitions* was remaindered shortly after publication; until the 1962 Meridian reprint, copies were difficult to find. Granted, its

---

been rumored to be working on in the 1960s, and that Pynchon and he were the same person. [See now *The Letters of William Gaddis*, ed. Steven Moore (Champaign, IL: Dalkey Archive Press, 2013), 385–86.]

6 Scott Allan Simmon, "The *Ulysses* Tradition: Open and Closed Form in the Novels of James Joyce, William Gaddis, and Thomas Pynchon" (PhD diss., University of California at Davis, 1979), 60.

7 When I was halfway into the writing of this essay, Clifford S. Mead drew my attention to a paper by Walter Isle (Rice University) delivered at the MLA convention in December 1976 entitled "The Large Loose Baggy Monsters of William Gaddis and Thomas Pynchon" that examines some of the parallels between the writers' work. (Prof. Isle, like Simmon, suggests Pynchon's three novels may have influenced *J R*.) But as this interesting paper remains unpublished, I may perhaps be excused for repeating some of Prof. Isle's points in print.

8 Letter to Miss Howes dated March 1972, quoted in Grace Eckley's "Exorcising the Demon Forgery, or The Forging of Pure Gold in Gaddis's *Recognitions*," in *Literature and the Occult: Essays in Comparative Literature*, ed. Luanne Frank (Arlington: University of Texas at Arlington, 1977, 125 [see now *Letters*, 278]). Gaddis's disavowal of ever having read *Ulysses* has appeared several times in print, but to this day many critics still refer to its alleged influence on *The Recognitions*.

9 One common concern — the relationship between the individual and society — is the subject of J. Bakker's "The End of Individualism," *Dutch Quarterly Review of Anglo-American Letters* 7 (1977), 286–304, a discussion of *The Recognitions* and *Gravity's Rainbow*. The last five pages tabulate a number of parallels between the two novels (though the question of influence is never raised), but Bakker's Marxist reading is too idiosyncratic (and, on *The Recognitions*, guilty of too many factual errors) to warrant further citation.

very obscurity and "underground" reputation may have inspired Pynchon to search it out, but we move on shifting ground here, and for obvious reasons should proceed with caution.

In the absence of external evidence at this time, the logical place to begin the search for internal evidence of Gaddis's possible influence is in Pynchon's early stories; like most fledgling writers, Pynchon wears his literary influences on his sleeve more here than in his later, more mature works. (Gaddis would develop the same way: *The Recognitions* is saturated with literary allusions to his reading, whereas *J R* uses such allusions sparingly — the majority of which, incidentally, can be traced to *The Oxford Dictionary of Quotations*.)[10] Though Gaddis is neither named nor quoted, there are several interesting parallels to be found between these stories and Gaddis's first novel. Both "Mortality and Mercy in Vienna" and "Entropy" have as their setting a party, and recall the long party scenes in *The Recognitions* where, as in Pynchon, pseudo-intellectuals exchange sophomoric chit-chat that parodies the more serious concerns of the protagonists. Other similarities are apparent: "Mortality and Mercy" especially indicates that Pynchon, like Gaddis, is fond of historical and literary allusions, the more obscure the better. (Both cite Albertus Magnus, for example.[11]) The story also contains the first of Pynchon's many uses of mirror imagery, and recalls Gaddis's extensive use of such imagery in *The Recognitions*.

But it is in "Entropy" that the most intriguing parallels to Gaddis's work can be found. The style itself is highly reminiscent of Gaddis's: formal, even elegiac prose alternates with party dialogue as the story shifts back and forth from Callisto to Mulligan, just as long, highly wrought passages in *The Recognitions* alternate with long stretches of uninterrupted dialogue. Callisto attempts to isolate himself from life much as Wyatt Gwyon does in *The Recognitions*, and both are led by two girls cut from the same cloth, Aubade and Esme, to the realization that life is to be engaged rather than avoided. In fact, Aubade is the first of Pynchon's many exotic but redeeming women: she and

10 For example, on p. 396 of *J R* (New York: Knopf, 1975) Gibbs quotes from two of Robert Southey's poems that happen to follow each other in the *ODQ*; the odds against Gaddis's reading Southey's poetic works and plucking from that morass exactly these same passages in the same order are too great to be considered. Similarly, Coach Vogel's hilarious medley of "cheek" quotations on pp. 463–64 was obviously worked up from the *ODQ* index, and there are too many other quotations in *J R* that can be found in the *ODQ* to doubt Gaddis's reliance on it. He used the *ODQ* for *The Recognitions* as well, but I realized this too late to document it in my source study *A Reader's Guide to William Gaddis's "The Recognitions"* (Lincoln: University of Nebraska Press, 1982), where many of my "source unknown"s can now be corrected to read *ODQ*.

11 *Epoch* 9.4 (1959), 205; *The Recognitions* (1955; rpt. with corrections, Cleveland: World/Meridian Fiction, 1962), 131, 132.

Nerissa in "Low-lands," Paola Maijstral in V., and Leni Pökler or Geli Tripping in *Gravity's Rainbow* all have their fictional ancestor in Gaddis's Esme, a heroin-addicted poet capable, as none of *The Recognitions'* dozens of other characters are, of selfless love. Additional and even more literary references appear: the Marquis de Sade and Djuna Barnes's *Nightwood* are mentioned in both "Entropy" and *The Recognitions*, and if Pynchon did not learn of these authors from Gaddis, the citations do at least indicate a curious similarity in literary taste.[12] On the other hand, there can be found in "Entropy" what appear to be anticipations of characters and themes in Gaddis's *J R*: the same Josiah Willard Gibbs mentioned twice in Pynchon's story also gives his name to one of the protagonists of Gaddis's second novel, and both story and novel share a concern with entropy and its application in information theory, especially as explicated in Norbert Wiener's *The Human Use of Human Beings*. Pynchon and Gaddis apply this concept in almost identical fashion:

> "Tell a girl: 'I love you.' No trouble with two-thirds of that, it's a closed circuit. Just you and she. But that nasty four-letter word in the middle, *that's* the one you have to look out for. Ambiguity. Redundance. Irrelevance, even. Leakage. All this is noise. Noise screws up your signal, makes for disorganization in the circuit."
>
> Meatball shuffled around. "Well, now, Saul," he muttered, "you're sort of, I don't know, expecting a lot from people. I mean, you know. What it is is, most of the things we say, I guess, are mostly noise."
>
> "Ha! Half of what you just said, for example."
>
> "Well, you do it too."
>
> "I know." Saul smiled grimly. "It's a bitch, ain't it."[13]

In *J R*, Jack Gibbs, getting drunk on liqueur, rewords it thus:

> —Whole God damned problem tastes like apricots, whole God damned problem listen whole God damned problem read Wiener on communication, more complicated the message more God damned chance for errors, take a few years of marriage such a God damned complex of messages going both ways can't get a God damned thing across, God damned much entropy going on say good morning she's got a God damned headache thinks you don't give a God damn how she feels, ask her how she feels she thinks you just wants to get laid, try that she says it's the only God damned thing you take seriously about her puts you out of business . . .[14]

12 If Sade is not being simply name-dropped, there can be found in his outrageous novels a source for Pynchon's equation (especially in *Gravity's Rainbow*) of sexual perversion with what Joseph Slade calls "a mutual complicity in transgression in order to liberate one's self — if only by obliterating it" (*Thomas Pynchon* [New York: Warner, 1974], 232). Sade's libertines dissertate on this point at great length between debauches.

13 *Kenyon Review* 22.2 (1960): 285–86.

14 *J R*, 403. Lest anyone leap at this "evidence" of Pynchon's influence on Gaddis, it should be pointed out that he began *J R* as early as 1957.

Mulligan's shuffling rejoinder displays a higher ratio of noise to information than is usual in Pynchon's dialogue, while *J R* is written almost entirely in such dialogue, the noise seeming to drown out what information is exchanged until the reader realizes only the characters themselves are involved. For the attentive reader every ambiguity, redundancy, irrelevancy, and leakage provides information on Gaddis's people and the noisy society in which they live — information of the sort that not a few of *J R*'s reviewers missed.

"Low-lands," dating from the same year as "Entropy," offers further parallels. Some are superficial — the corpse trick recalls similar episodes in *The Recognitions*, and both Gypsies and Heisenberg's Uncertainty principle are common to story and novel — but others are more substantial. Dennis Flange's mother-complex (or what his analyst diagnoses as such) sets in motion a theme that will culminate in *Gravity's Rainbow*'s Mother Conspiracy, and recalls Wyatt's own mother-complex and the psychological havoc that results. In *The Recognitions*, maternal imagery is implied in most of the references to the sea and the moon, and we find Pynchon making the same symbolic equation in his story. Both Dennis and Wyatt leave their rational, logical wives for animas more psychologically nourishing, but not before the traditional mythological descent to the underworld and symbolic death. Here Pynchon reveals a greater and certainly more demonstrable debt to Frazer's *Golden Bough*, Eliot's *Waste Land*, and perhaps Graves's *White Goddess* than to *The Recognitions*. These very titles, moreover, provide a key to the semblance of literary influence. Gaddis too draws upon Frazer, Eliot, Graves, Rilke, Shakespeare, and others; where two writers draw upon the same cultural materials, there is bound to be a certain amount of overlapping. Consequently, it is because Gaddis and Pynchon have read so many of the same authors, rather than each other, that so many similarities can be discerned.

This is certainly the case with Pynchon's first novel *V.*, which has been said to reveal Gaddis's influence most plainly. Of course, a number of surface similarities are obvious: structurally, both consist of dual narrative lines that intersect on occasion. In *The Recognitions*, Wyatt and his quest for integration disappear for great stretches as various incomplete, parodic versions of Wyatt rush headlong into disintegration, along with Western culture. Stencil and his search for V. likewise retreat offstage for the yo-yoing activities of Benny Profane and the Whole Sick Crew. Pynchon's New York pseudo-intellectuals might mingle easily with Gaddis's Greenwich Villagers; in both cases "they produced nothing but talk and at that not very good talk" (*V.*, 297),[15] though

15 All references to Pynchon's novels are to the first editions: *V.* (Philadelphia: J. P. Lippincott, 1963); *The Crying of Lot 49* (Philadelphia: J. B. Lippincott, 1966); *Gravity's Rainbow* (New

Gaddis lets his people talk at much greater length than Pynchon mercifully does. Even the names of some of the characters in *V.* are reminiscent of those in *The Recognitions*. Scott Simmon thinks it "possible to make a case that Benny and Esther in *V.* owe something to their namesakes in *The Recognitions*,"[16] but Benny Profane bears no resemblance to Gaddis's Benny (besides, Pynchon used the name earlier in "The Small Rain") while Pynchon's Esther probably takes her name from Jules Siegel's girlfriend Esther Schreier.[17] (On the other hand, Dudley Eigenvalue's surname anticipates Gaddis's autobiographical Thomas Eigen in *J R*: *eigen* = German "ownself"; Thomas is Gaddis's middle name.) But Simmon is correct in pointing out that Pynchon's penchant for giving his characters outrageous names is similar to Gaddis's: in *The Recognitions*, we have Agnes Deigh, Sr. Hermoso Hermoso, Victoria and Albert Hall, a poet named Arthur but called Saint Anselm, Recktall Brown, Basil Valentine, and even the Reverend Gilbert Sullivan. Unlike Pynchon, Gaddis has curbed such tendencies in his later work, but even in *J R* we have characters named Dan DiCephalis (a school administrator whom students naturally call de Syph), Mr. Piscator (the fisherman in Walton's *Compleat Angler* [which a girl is reading on p. 298 of *The Recognitions*] as well as Saint Peter ["il pescator" in Dante's *Paradiso*]), Norman Angel (after British author and economist Sir Norman Angell [1872–1967]), and a garrulous salesman named Isadore Duncan.

Beneath these superficialities there are deeper affinities which, though they may not betray a direct influence, certainly indicate Gaddis and Pynchon have drawn the same conclusions about the decline of the West. Both diagnose the patriarchal nature of Western civilization, in which too often rationality is valued over instinct, intellect over emotion, mind over body, aggression over tenderness, order over spontaneity, Christianity over the occult, and ultimately, death over life. Both novelists recognized early the danger in such polarization, and in their first novels created motherless sons who subsequently must search for the unifying feminine principle that will, if not fertilize the modern Waste Land, at least restore an inner balance.

Not only was Herbert Stencil raised motherless (*V.*, 52), but even his father Sidney was "[b]rought up by a pair of bleak Nonconformist aunts, [from whom] he had acquired the Anglo-Saxon tendency to group northern/Protestant/intellectual against Mediterranean/Roman Catholic/irrational" (190). This background is remarkably similar to Wyatt's: losing his mother at the

York: Viking, 1973). These will be abbreviated in citations as *V.*, *CL49*, and *GR*.

16 "The *Ulysses* Tradition," 58.

17 "Who Is Thomas Pynchon . . . and Why Did He Take Off with My Wife?" *Playboy*, March 1977, 169.

age of four, he is raised by a bleak Calvinist aunt and a father who finds it increasingly difficult to reconcile his own "northern/Protestant/intellectual" background with his growing attraction to "Mediterranean/Roman Catholic/ irrational" modes of life. At first, Reverend Gwyon delights in dashing the "petrous visages" of his congregation "with waves from distinctly pagan tongues, voluptuous Italian, which flowed over their northern souls like sunlit water over rocks" (24), but eventually his inability to reconcile the two modes results in madness. In an effort to spare his son the same anguish, he leaves Wyatt his mother's Byzantine earrings, an emblem (as a flashback on p. 14 suggests) of her vibrancy and daring, and charges him to come to terms with her memory (61), lest he be mired in the same sterile state of indecision as his father.

For Herbert Stencil, V. too is "a legacy from his father" (155). In both cases, personal mothers are elevated to impersonal feminine principles. Wyatt's mother Camilla is incarnate in many of the women in *The Recognitions* — from the Virgin Mary in Wyatt's paintings, to Esme, and finally to the saint canonized at the end of the novel — just as Victoria Wren becomes a feminine principle (explicitly on p. 209 of *V.*) associated with every woman in the novel from Queen Victoria, to Botticelli's Venus, to the rat Veronica. But both Stencil and Wyatt have trouble coming to terms with their lost mothers and the feminine principle they represent; not surprisingly, neither is able as a result to have a satisfying relationship with a woman. Both are incomplete, for they lack an anima, the feminine component in the male psyche according to Carl Jung, another author with whom Gaddis and Pynchon are both familiar. Stencil's incompleteness is betrayed by his references to himself in the third person, a "forcible dislocation of personality" (62), as he freely admits. Consequently, as Alvin Greenberg points out, "not being at one with himself — and, hence, with herself [V.] — he naturally misses her in the process of missing himself everywhere he goes."[18] Wyatt's own "dislocation of personality" is indicated by the loss of his name, which is equivalent in primitive mythology to the loss of his soul. He is called Wyatt for the last time on page 118, and remains nameless for 600 pages until he recovers himself — and the anima within — and is renamed Stephen, the name Camilla originally intended for him before Aunt May intervened.

The difficulty of incorporating the anima — which is what both protagonists' predicaments amount to — has been dramatized in myth and literature most often as a quest; the dangers met with during the quest are those inherent in plumbing the unconscious and doing battle with the dark and destructive aspects of human nature in order to rescue the revitalizing anima.

18 "The Underground Woman: An Excursion into the V-ness of Thomas Pyncheon [*sic*]," *Chelsea* 27 (1969): 60.

"Native guides will only go a short distance into these mountains," Godolphin says of Vheissu, Pynchon's symbol for the unconscious. "Soon they will turn back, pointing out the way" (168). The quest is both private and dangerous, for it caters to the self's "dream of annihilation" (206) as well as its urge toward unification. These dangers account for the reluctance displayed by both Wyatt and Stencil to claim their legacy:[19] in Wyatt's case, it takes the forms of insulating solitude and bouts of insanity like his father's; and in Stencil's, a reluctance to follow his quest to Malta and risk losing V. as well as himself by learning of her death. What Carol Marshall Peirce says of Durrell's *Alexandria Quartet* and *V.* is equally true of *The Recognitions* and *V.*: "Both works project against the real/naturalistic world a romantic quest for the ideal woman (Justine, V., Aphrodite, Venus, or Virgin) that ends in each case in possible destruction, possible revival."[20] Like Durrell, both Pynchon and Gaddis undercut somewhat the high romantic quest with a more realistic dénouement, but all three are clearly devotees of Graves's White Goddess, and realize that the boons she is able to confer justify any and all risks.

But this goddess, like Janus, shows two faces. Victoria Wren represents the destructive, terrifying aspect of the Eternal Feminine, the Siren that leads men more often to their destruction than to their salvation.[21] In the Profane sections of *V.*, the maternal, nourishing side of the feminine principle is represented by Rachel Owlglass. Her progress is the reverse of Victoria Wren's: introduced under the sway of mechanization — and even once compared to a succubus (30), as is Esme in *The Recognitions* (199–200, 766) — she moves toward humanity as V. moves away from humanization toward greater mechanization. (This dual movement can be found in *The Recognitions* as well, where Wyatt moves toward integration as Otto, his comic counterpart, moves toward disintegration.) After her brief fling with her car, Rachel begins to be associated quite consistently with motherhood, primarily through the recurring image of the umbilical cord that not only links daughter to mother — "A long unbroken chain of Jewish mothers going all the way back to Eve" (47)[22] — but also accounts for the vexatious control women have over

19 "Refusal of the Call" is the second stage in Joseph Campbell's paradigmatic adventure of the hero: see *The Hero with a Thousand Faces* (1949)

20 "Pynchon's *V.* and Durrell's *Alexandria Quartet*: A Seminar in the Modern Tradition," *Pynchon Notes* 8 (1982): 26n8.

21 See Douglas A. Mackey's concise discussion of this theme in *The Rainbow Quest of Thomas Pynchon* (San Bernardino, CA: Borgo Press, 1980), 23–24; Joseph Fahy's "Thomas Pynchon's *V.* and Mythology," *Critique* 18.3 (1977): 5–18; and Alvin Greenberg's ingenious essay cited above.

22 Stephen Dedalus broods on this same conceit at the beginning of the third chapter in *Ulysses*.

men. Profane feels "the invisible, umbilical tug" (29; cf. 34) every time he feels disconnected:

> Any sovereign or broken yo-yo must feel like this after a short time of lying inert, rolling, falling: suddenly to have its own umbilical string reconnected, and know the other end is in hands it cannot escape. Hands it doesn't want to escape. Know that the simple clockwork of itself has no more need for symptoms of inutility, lonesomeness, directionlessness, because now it has a path marked out for it over which it has no control. (217)

This is hardly the basis for a mature relationship, as even Profane seems to realize. It even takes a hazardous toll on Rachel's friendship with Esther, as Slab argues with another example of the umbilical cord metaphor (49–50). Finally, in a chapter significantly entitled "In which the yo-yo string is revealed as a state of mind," Rachel herself cites the maternal connection after making love to a reluctant Profane:

> "You have to grow up," she finally said. "That's all: my own unlucky boy, didn't you ever think maybe ours is an act too? We're older than you, we lived inside you once: the fifth rib, closest to the heart. We learned all about it then. After that it had to become our game to nourish a heart you all believe is hollow though we know different. Now you all live inside us, for nine months, and when ever you decide to come back after that." (370)

— spoken like a true White Goddess. However, the umbilical string, despite the nourishment it provides, must be cut to attain mature selfhood. "You have to grow up" is what, in essence, Basil Valentine tells Wyatt when it becomes apparent to the art critic that many of Wyatt's difficulties with life and art can be traced back to his "sainted mother" and his subsequent idealization of romantic redemption (549–51). Such romanticism results in a loss of self, and adds its voice to "the single melody, banal and exasperating, of all Romanticism since the Middle Ages: 'the act of love and the act of death are one'" (*V.*, 410).[23] *The Recognitions* is filled with male characters stunted psychologically by too great an attachment to their mothers, and it is not until Wyatt can come to terms with his mother's memory and abandon the Wagnerian equation of love with salvation (*The Flying Dutchman* appears throughout the novel) that

23 This is precisely the theme of Denis de Rougemont's *Love in the Western World* (1939), a book Gaddis quotes often in *The Recognitions*. I would not be surprised to learn that Pynchon also read de Rougemont's influential study, especially by the time he wrote *Gravity's Rainbow*, where this theme prevails. [Turns out the same year I wrote this essay, Lila V. Graves published one entitled "Love and the Western World of Pynchon's *V.*" in the *South Atlantic Review* (47 [January 1982]: 62–73) that makes the de Rougemont connection — 2016 note.]

he will be in a position to integrate the disparate elements of his personality and experience a more mature love with the Spanish girl Pastora — a love that does not necessitate a regression to maternal dependence and a loss of self, but rather a love that allows a completion of the self by bringing forth the anima within. It is perhaps for similar reasons that Benny Profane is last seen not with Rachel but with the free-spirited Brenda Wigglesworth, a girl capable of nourishing without suffocating (unlike Rachel), and an embodiment of the 20th century without its destructive, perverse tendencies (unlike V.). Wyatt and Profane have found the anima that Stencil, off for Stockholm still in quest of V., will never find.

The quests these characters undertake lead them not through the enchanted forests of Brocéliande or the windswept plateau of Leng, but rather through what Pynchon calls Baedeker Land, which brings us to another possible link between *V.* and *The Recognitions*. Both novels have international settings and feature protagonists whose inner quest is reflected outwardly in their extensive travels. Unfortunately, the modern world is no longer the place for the once-noble quest; voyaging has been reduced to tourism, and discovery to sight-seeing, as Eliot indicated in early poems such as "Burbank with a Baedeker" and "Lune de Miel." (Gaddis quotes from the latter on page 182 of *The Recognitions*.) William M. Plater's comprehensive essay "Baedeker Land" explicates the importance of this theme in Pynchon,[24] but neither Plater nor anyone else has pointed out how thoroughly Gaddis anticipates this theme in his novel.

"I think this book will have to be on voyaging," Gaddis wrote in his notes for *The Recognitions*, "all the myth & metaphor of that in modern times."[25] But the difficulty of leading a voyage of discovery in a world crowded with, and even transformed by, tourists is insisted on throughout the novel. The Town Carpenter, Wyatt's maternal grandfather, first fills the young boy's head with tales of "great voyages" (31), and complains bitterly of the tourists who have degraded the hero's voyage:

> Traveling in their trains and their airplanes they try to intrude on the greatest career of the hero. Why, travel's become the great occupation of people with nothing to do, you find second-hand kings and all sorts of useless people at it. There now, it's always the heroic places you find them intruding, trying to have a share in the work of great men, looking at fine paintings and talking as though they knew more of the thing than the man who painted it, and the same thing listening to fine music, . . . they all suspect that a man needs something to do. . . . (409)

24 Chapter 2 of *The Grim Phoenix: Reconstructing Thomas Pynchon* (Bloomington: Indiana University Press, 1978).

25 Quoted in Peter W. Koenig's "'Splinters from the Yew Tree': A Critical Study of William Gaddis' *The Recognitions*" (PhD diss., New York University, 1971), 33.

Gaddis fills his novel with these insensitive tourists with their Baedekers, "doing" Europe without ever seeing through their misconceptions to the actual land and people before them. Several times Gaddis suggests that the progenitors of these ridiculous tourists were those who made religious pilgrimages (496, 825, 901), and reinforces his tourism theme with similar references to the novels of Dostoevsky and E. M. Forster.[26] That *The Recognitions* is itself a kind of tourist guide to the modern Waste Land is indicated by the title of its metafictional counterpart within the novel, Willie's work-in-progress "Baedeker's *Babel*" (475). And although Wyatt travels as extensively as anyone in the novel, Gaddis was careful not to recount any of his actual trips, but only those of the other characters. In this way the symbolic nature of his voyage is emphasized over the merely literal, and distinguishes him from the tourists of Baedeker Land. His quest is not available at a group rate.

The lonely quest and its trepidations are also the theme of Pynchon's second novel, in which Oedipa Maas attempts to make the same "recognitions" Wyatt does in Gaddis's novel: the Pentecostal moment when "everything [is] freed into one recognition, really freed into reality that we never see" (*The Recognitions*, 92). In fact, the word "recognition" is used in this sense in a passage at the end of *The Crying of Lot 49* highly reminiscent of Gaddis's style:

> [Oedipa remembered] the voices before and after the dead man's that had phoned at random during the darkest, slowest hours, searching ceaseless among the dial's ten million possibilities for that magical Other who would reveal herself out of the roar of relays, monotone litanies of insult, filth, fantasy, love whose brute repetition must someday call into being the trigger for the unnamable act, the recognition, the Word. (180)

The dead man is of course Pierce Inverarity, who, like Camilla in *The Recognitions*, does not actually appear in the novel but nevertheless exerts a constant pressure on the protagonist. And just as Wyatt must come to terms with the true nature of his mother's legacy, Oedipa must come to terms with In-

26 On pp. 937–38 Gaddis quotes Lizaveta Prokofyevna's imprecation from the final page of *The Idiot*: "We've had enough of following our whims; it's time to be reasonable. And all this, all this life abroad, and this Europe of yours is all a fantasy, and all of us abroad are only a fantasy . . . remember my words, you'll see it for yourself" (trans. Garnett). Earlier in this same final chapter there are references to Forster's *Where Angels Fear to Tread* (906) and *A Room with a View* (910), both concerning Baedeker-toting English tourists in Italy. For some reason David Cowart neglected this theme in his discussion of Forster's influence on Pynchon in *Thomas Pynchon: The Art of Allusion* (Carbondale: Southern Illinois University Press, 1980), 115–19.

verarity's testament. Making true "recognitions" in a culture encrusted with counterfeits, false information, and trash is the challenge both Wyatt and Oedipa must meet.

In both novels there is a conflict between the sacred and the profane, with protagonists exploring the nature of the sacred in a decidedly profane world. There have been many excellent discussions of the religious dimension of *The Crying of Lot 49*,[27] but again, none of the commentators seem to be aware that Pynchon's novel was anticipated (if not influenced) in this regard by Gaddis's *Recognitions*, the most encyclopedic treatment of religion in American fiction.

The extent of Gaddis's preoccupation with religion in his novel is indicated by the range of source books he used in the process of composition: from the fourth-century theological romance attributed to Saint Clement from which *The Recognitions* takes its name, to the *Apocryphal New Testament*, Lethaby's *Architecture, Mysticism and Myth*, Foxe's *Book of Martyrs*, Frazer's *Golden Bough*, Phythian-Adams's *Mithraism*, Lang's *Magic and Religion*, Kramer and Sprenger's *Malleus Maleficarum*, Conybeare's *Magic, Myth, and Morals*, Marsh's *Mediæval and Modern Saints and Miracles*, the *Pilgrim Hymnal*, Summers's *Physical Phenomena of Mysticism*, and Graves's previously mentioned *White Goddess*. In addition, there are over a hundred citations to the Bible and references to elements of almost every religious and occult tradition, from the *Egyptian Book of the Dead* to the writings of the early Church fathers, the Koran, legends of the Buddha and Krishna, Gnostic speculations, Saint Ignatius's *Spiritual Exercises*, hermetic alchemy, a calendar's worth of saints' lives, witchcraft manuals, Fortean hypotheses, mystical numerology, ghosts, and even a Satanic invocation from A. E. Waite's *Book of Black Magic and of Pacts*. All this led early reviewers to complain that the novel was "shrouded in mysticism" and filled with "pagan mumbo-jumbo," charges that would later be leveled against *Gravity's Rainbow* by its comparatively fewer detractors. But Gaddis is not merely indulging in arcane name-dropping; all religions and occult traditions have at their base a belief in another, higher reality that transcends sensory reality. Too often this other reality has been literalized into such nonsense as the kingdom of heaven with its gold-paved streets and choirs of white-robed angels, or its counterpart in the geography

27 See, for example, Edward Mendelson's "The Sacred, the Profane, and *The Crying of Lot 49*" and James Nohrnberg's "Pynchon's Paraclete" printed back to back in *Pynchon: A Collection of Critical Essays*, ed. Edward Mendelson (Englewood Cliffs, NJ: Prentice-Hall, 1978), 112–46, 147–61; Marion Brugiére's "Quest Avatars in Thomas Pynchon's *The Crying of Lot 49*," trans. Margaret S. Langford, *Pynchon Notes* 9 (1982), 5–16; and the last half of Thomas H. Schaub's superb essay "*The Crying of Lot 49*: 'A Gentle Chill, an Ambiguity,'" in his *Pynchon: The Voice of Ambiguity* (Urbana: University of Illinois Press, 1981), 21–42.

of hell and especially the demonology that excited the prurient interests of many theologians. But Wyatt works through institutionalized religion and the jejune theatricality of the occult, past the realms conquered and codified by overconfident scientists, to the timeless state beyond the reach of those who would make of God a science, and of science a god. This ineffable state resists description, and accounts to some extent for the vagueness of Wyatt's final appearances, a vagueness that has its counterpart in *Gravity's Rainbow* in the "scattering" of Slothrop toward the end.

The Crying of Lot 49 is not as overtly religious as *The Recognitions*, but there are enough hints to indicate Oedipa experiences a similar transformation. She too loses her self — dramatized by her inability to find her mirror reflection (41) — and like Wyatt, seeks sustenance from feminine symbols such as the moon and sea.[28] She also undergoes a dark night of the soul during her eerie night in San Francisco (chap. 5), paralleling the extensive night imagery in Gaddis's novel, and represents a modernization of the allegorical *Book of the Dead*, to which both refer (*The Recognitions*, 49 and 388; *CL49*, 31). Finally, as Anne Mangel puts it, Oedipa's "continual doubt and reevaluation of events differentiates her from the other characters in the novel who do, in fact, end in closed systems of inertness"[29] — precisely the relationship between Wyatt and the other characters in *The Recognitions*. Pynchon takes subtle, quiet steps where Gaddis strides in seven-league boots, but they are united in their search for the sacred, a concern that distinguishes them from their more profane contemporaries.

If the idea of the holy in *The Crying of Lot 49* looks backward to *The Recognitions*, its treatment of communication looks forward to *J R*. The thesis of Wiener's *The Human Use of Human Beings* is likewise the thesis of Gaddis's and Pynchon's second novels: "society can only be understood through a study of the messages and the communication facilities which belong to it."[30] As with his treatment of religion, Gaddis's exhaustive treatment of communication in *J R* greatly exceeds Pynchon's more circumspect treatment, partly of course because *J R* is five times longer than *The Crying of Lot 49*. The noise factor in information is especially prevalent, and thus Gaddis has filled his novel with clichés, advertisements, radio voices, and every level of spoken discourse from legal terminology to street slang. The greatest frustration of the novel's protagonists, the composer Edward Bast and the writer Jack Gibbs, is

28 For a discussion of sea symbolism in *The Recognitions* and *Lot 49*, see John Z. Guzlowski's "No More Sea Changes: Hawkes, Pynchon, Gaddis, and Barth," *Critique* 23.2 (1981): 48–60.

29 "Maxwell's Demon, Entropy, Information: *The Crying of Lot 49*," in *Mindful Pleasures*, 93.

30 (Rev. ed 1954; rpt. New York: Avon, 1967), 25.

in finding a noiseless place to create, while the greatest frustration, or rather challenge, for the reader is in translating all the noise in the novel into information. (There is no "pure" noise in the novel; it is a work of art, not a series of tape recordings,[31] and consequently every word is informative, every cliché revelatory of the character who uses it, as I insisted earlier.) "The redundancy, irrelevance, ambiguity, and sheer waste involved in language glare from every page of *The Crying of Lot 49*,"[32] but with nowhere near as much intensity as in *J R*, where the idea of waste especially is even more insistent.[33] Entropy is, of course, a central concern of both novels, and has been dealt with at length by both novelists' critics.[34]

But at this point, further discussion of "influence" would be redundant and of decreasing value. It is indeed highly coincidental that two novelists would borrow the concept of entropy from the scientific world at the same time (though not published until 1975, *J R* was begun in 1957, set aside for a few years, then resumed in the '60s), and during this time Gaddis and Pynchon continued to read many of the same books (Weber's *The Protestant Ethic and the Spirit of Capitalism* can be added to the others already mentioned); but the similarities between their work begin to look more like a case of what Leni Pökler would describe as "Parallel, not series" (*GR*, 159). By the time Gaddis and Pynchon came to write their masterpieces, each had developed his considerable talents to such an extent that any talk of one being influenced by the other is potentially degrading. There is hardly a theme in *Gravity's Rainbow* that does not have its counterpart in one or the other of Gaddis's novels, but this does not mean that Pynchon cribbed from Gaddis or vice versa. For example, that *J R* and *Gravity's Rainbow* both allude to Wagner's *Ring* tetralogy merely indicates a recognition on both writers' part of the immense relevance of the *Ring* to the Nazi Reich in particular and to Western civilization in general.[35] If Pynchon is as fond of Rilke's poetry as Gaddis is, again this reveals a mutual recognition of a superior artist whose haunting

31 For an example of a "novel" thus created, see Andy Warhol's *a* (New York: Grove, 1968).

32 Mangel, 98.

33 See Thomas LeClair's discussion of Gaddis's many-leveled use of the term "waste" in "William Gaddis, *J R*, & the Art of Excess," *Modern Fiction Studies* 27.4 (1981): 591–94. Cf. the pun on waste/W.A.S.T.E. in *Lot 49*, especially 87–88.

34 Pynchon criticism on this point is too extensive and too well known to warrant documentation, but for Gaddis, see LeClair's essay cited in the previous note; Johan Thielemans' "Gaddis and the Novel of Entropy," *TREMA* 2 (1977): 97–107; and Susan Strehle Klemtner's "'For a Very Small Audience': The Fiction of William Gaddis," *Critique* 19.3 (1978): 61–73.

35 See especially L. J. Rather's *The Dream of Self-Destruction: Wagner's Ring and the Modern World* (Baton Rouge: Louisiana State University Press, 1979), which incidentally includes *Gravity's Rainbow* ("Myths, rituals, and remembrances of the *Götterdämmerung*, 1939–45") in its Thematic Bibliography (202).

poetry illuminates various modern dilemmas with which the two novelists are concerned. If *Gravity's Rainbow* shows the same preoccupation with the occult as does *The Recognitions*, it demonstrates only that Pynchon and Gaddis are reacting independently against Weber's complaint that "the fate of our times is characterized by rationalization and intellectualization and, above all, by the 'disenchantment of the world.'"[36] The occult represents a re-enchantment of the world, a restoration of the ancients' sublime (if paranoiac) conviction that everything is indeed connected. And finally, if both *J R* and *Gravity's Rainbow* hold Western economic policies chiefly responsible for the deteriorating quality of life, it is difficult to see how anyone as knowledgeable about the roots of modern civilization as Gaddis and Pynchon are could arrive at any other conclusion.

There is no irrefutable evidence that Pynchon has ever read Gaddis: he is not named in Pynchon's work; there are no direct borrowings or quotations, no tidbits of arcana that could have been found only in *The Recognitions*. Moreover, Gaddis does not really belong to "Pynchon's company," that group assembled by Thomas Schaub consisting of Fariña, Beal, Robbins, Matthiessen, Reed, and Burroughs,[37] a group to which one might add Terry Southern, Ken Kesey (cf. Pynchon's ubiquitous "They" with Kesey's "Combine"), Robert Anton Wilson, Samuel Delany (especially *Dhalgren* [1975]), and — on a different level — Joseph McElroy and Don DeLillo. Only the last two could be considered of "Gaddis's company," both having expressed their admiration for his work.

Perhaps the final word should be left to the writers themselves. Pynchon, of course, is incommunicado; but Gaddis, asked if he had an opinion of Pynchon's work and if he thought it might have been influenced by his own, answered succinctly:

> I haven't read Pynchon enough to have an opinion either of his work or whether it might have been 'influenced' (perilous word) by mine, though I've understood he feels not & who's to know if he'd ever read mine before V? Always a dangerous course,
>
> Gaddis[38]

36 Quoted in Schaub, 57.
37 Schaub, 139–40.
38 Postcard to me postmarked 6 August 1982 [now *Letters*, 380].

Peer Gynt and *The Recognitions*

> The main thing is to remain sincere and true in relation to one's self. It is not a matter of willing this or that, but of willing what one absolutely must do because of one's self, and because one cannot do otherwise. Everything else leads only to falsehood.
>
> —Henrik Ibsen

In his elaborate first novel, William Gaddis incorporated a huge body of referential material garnered from world literature, mythology, and mysticism as a backdrop against which Wyatt Gwyon's quest for salvation is played. Parallels and analogies are thereby suggested that not only clarify aspects of Wyatt's struggles and raise them to mythic proportions, but in turn often shed illumination on the original sources themselves, aiding the reader to make the "recognitions" demanded by the novel's title. Gaddis's use of Ibsen's equally elaborate drama *Peer Gynt* is an instructive example of this process and, more important, may provide a key to certain problematic areas in the difficult novel.

Both novel and play share a concern for redemption and the attainment of selfhood, or, in C. G. Jung's phrase, the "integration of the personality."[1] However, the exact nature of redemption, and whether the protagonists actually attain selfhood, are questions that have been asked of both works. The validity of Solveig's role as the means of Peer's salvation has been debated since the play's publication in 1867. One of the earliest reviewers found the "happy" ending banal and "a little absurd,"[2] and Ibsen scholars have yet to reach a consensus on the artistic and theological integrity of Peer's fifth-act redemption. "Nobody," Michael Meyer hopes, "any longer takes the last act of *Peer Gynt* at its face value, as the return of an old man to his youthful love; such an ending would have been, for Ibsen, most untypically banal and sentimental, two adjectives which recur frequently in contemporary criticisms of it."[3] How then are we to take this last act? or more pertinently, how did Gaddis

1 *The Integration of the Personality* (1939) is the title of Jung's first book-length study of alchemy (and a book that Gaddis used for most of his alchemical references), but the phrase is common to many of Jung's writings; cf. Ensaf Thune's application of the phrase in "The Paradox of the Boyg: A Study of Peer Gynt's Humanization," *Modern Drama* 19 (March 1976): 91.

2 Frederik Bætzmann in *Aftenbladet*, quoted in Michael Meyer's *Ibsen: A Biography* (Garden City, NY: Doubleday, 1971), 268.

3 *Ibsen*, 272.

take this last act? A variety of readings have been suggested, the most persuasive of which emphasize Peer's passivity: his redemption, such that it is, is conferred upon him, not actively won. "If Peer is to be saved at all," translator William Archer wrote to writer Arthur Quiller-Couch, "it is clearly to be by no active effort of his own," adding that "whether seriously or ironically, it was a supernatural salvation that Ibsen had in his mind."[4] This form of redemption was as unsatisfactory to Archer (who labeled it "rank supernaturalism") as it must be to most modern readers. "Work out your own salvation with fear and trembling" advises Saint Paul (Phil. 2:12), and it has become difficult to admire any form of salvation in which the redeemed does not take an active part.

This, at any rate, is the conclusion Wyatt Gwyon draws after exploring the various avenues of redemption still open to modern man, and he almost fails to achieve integration for the same reason that Peer fails: a stunted attachment to his mother.

If this sounds like psychological reductionism of the worst kind, it takes only a careful reading of both texts to vindicate such an interpretation. Wyatt has the misfortune to lose his mother Camilla by the age of four. Her ghost appears to him at the moment of her death and thereafter her absence (and her inadequate replacement in the person of Aunt May) leaves an emptiness in him that he spends most of the novel trying to fill. At an early age he begins a portrait of his mother (taken, significantly, from a photograph of her *before* her marriage), and his inability or reluctance to complete the portrait — some 15 years pass before he does — becomes a symbol of his inability to establish a satisfying relationship. "Finish it," his wife Esther astutely says of the portrait. "Then there might be room for me."[5]

Wyatt takes the portrait with him when he leaves Esther to forge paintings for the art dealer Recktall Brown. It is not until he listens to Esme read the opening of the Grimm Brothers' "The Frog King" that he finds in Esme's features the lines of completion needed for the portrait of his mother: "She sat, her head half turned; and her face emptied of the curiosity and life of an instant before. If anything of life was left, it was a vague look of yearning, but that without expectation" (273) — a deliberate echo of "the unchanging, ungratified yearning in the face of Camilla on the living-room mantel" (33). She is thus contrasted with Esther, who had always complained of his failure

4 Quoted in Rosalind Pitman's "William Archer and *Peer Gynt*," *Notes and Queries* 218 (n.s. 20 [July 1973]): 236. Timothy Schiff comes to the same conclusion in "Providence and Dispensation in Henrik Ibsen's *Peer Gynt*," *Scandinavian Studies* 51 (Autumn 1979): 375–91.

5 William Gaddis, *The Recognitions* (1955; rpt. with corrections, Cleveland: World/Meridian Fiction, 1962), 88. Subsequent references will be cited parenthetically in the text.

to live up to her great expectations of him, and Esme appears to qualify for the anima figure (again Jung's phrase) that Wyatt has been seeking. But when Wyatt realizes his portrait of his mother has become a portrait of Esme, a subconscious apprehension of the incestuous nature of the attraction (coupled consciously with guilt in knowing that the portrait is a study for his next forgery) causes him to shy away from Esme's advances, and he sends her on her way.[6]

Had Wyatt given in to Esme at this point, finding in her the mother he lost in Camilla, he would have been in much the same situation as Peer Gynt at the end of Ibsen's play. Among Ibsen's many commentators, only those with a psychological background seem to have noticed that Peer can give himself to Solveig only after she has become — in appearance as well as psychologically — his mother. For example, Georg Groddeck, who included a psychoanalytic reading of *Peer Gynt* in his *Exploring the Unconscious* (1933), remarks that from the opening scene the relationship between Peer and Aase is not the usual one between a grown-up son and his middle-aged mother, but rather that of a little boy and his young mother — a psychological rut Peer stays in throughout the play:

> It is only after a long and roundabout journey that Peer Gynt can bring himself to the point of allowing another woman to have the honor of mothering him. The new mother, one need hardly say, is Solveig; she is the reincarnation of Aase. Peer Gynt feels that from the start. This and this alone it is that prevents him from remaining with her, for she is sacred to him, as a mother must be to her son. Never can she be for him a mere woman.[7]

It is only after Aase's death and when Solveig herself is middle-aged that Peer is able to give himself to her. Groddeck goes so far as to suggest that the only successful staging of the play would be one where a physical resemblance between Aase and Solveig is emphasized. His arguments, too extensive to be rehearsed here in full, are convincing enough to necessitate a reevaluation of Peer's redemption at the end of act 5. When Peer cries, "My mother; my wife; oh thou innocent woman! — / In thy love — oh, there hide me, hide me!"[8] it is clear that Peer has not progressed psychologically beyond the first scene and has reaffirmed his ideal love as that for his mother. We hear the cry not of

6 When Valentine asks Wyatt the next morning who the subject of this painting is, Wyatt admits it is his mother, and immediately his face draws "up in lines of confusion as though he had just remembered" (338). This confusion, perhaps more than anything else, causes Wyatt to retreat to his father in part 2, chapter 3.

7 Reprinted (in V. M. E. Collins' translation) in *Ibsen: A Collection of Critical Essays*, ed. Rolf Fjelde (Englewood Cliffs, NJ: Prentice-Hall, 1965), 64.

8 The translation is the same one used by Gaddis, viz., that of William and Charles Archer (New York: Charles Scribner's Sons, 1907).

a self-realized man but of a little boy who misses his mommy. And there the play, and perhaps Peer's life, ends.

Wilhelm Reich, whose "Libidinal Conflicts and Delusions in Ibsen's *Peer Gynt*" preceded Groddeck's essay but remained unpublished until recently,[9] lays greater emphasis on Peer's incestuous fixation and Oedipal conflicts.[10] Wyatt's fixation, of course, is on the memory of his mother rather than the woman herself, and it is maintained by the unfinished portrait and her gold earrings, but the psychological principle is the same: his inordinate attachment to his mother obstructs a mature relationship with any other woman. Reich reaches the same conclusion as Groddeck regarding Peer's fifth-act redemption: "We now understand that Peer's redemption can take place only when Solveig has become as old as his mother was at the onset of his psychosis."[11]

Holding out for a girl just like the girl that married dear old dad would be more disastrous for Wyatt than it was for Peer; where Peer is an old man in act 5 and probably dies if not at the end of the play (as some critics have suggested) then shortly thereafter, Wyatt is in his early thirties. His process of integration would halt upon falling into Esme's arms, as Peer's does in Solveig's lap. Esme *is* the ideal anima figure for him in that she, alone of all the characters in *The Recognitions*, is capable of selfless love. But with the unresolved relationship to his mother simply shifted onto Esme's shoulders, such a union — even ignoring Esme's schizophrenia and heroin addiction — would be far from ideal. This move on Wyatt's part would be romantic in Denis de Rougemont's sense that intense romantic attraction, if not akin to the death instinct, leads not to personal growth but to decay.[12] Providentially, Wyatt loses track of Esme and instead returns to Spain where his mother is buried, to confront and resolve the original source of his psychosis.

Bearing all this in mind, we are now in a position to understand Wyatt's

9 The paper was presented to the Vienna Psychoanalytic Society in 1920 and is translated by Philip Schmitz in *Early Writings* (New York: Farrar, Straus and Giroux, 1975), 3–64. As with Groddeck's essay, the many insights in this long essay resist summary; suffice it to say, Reich's analysis is very thorough and convincing. At that time, Reich was still an orthodox Freudian and had not yet developed the singular theories for which he is generally known and often dismissed.

10 A full exposition of Wyatt's Oedipal conflict would require an essay in itself. The symbolic keys to the conflict can be found in the bird imagery (Wyatt as robin, Reverend Gwyon was wren); Wyatt's imitation Memling (in which the tortured Valerian is modeled after his father); and the role of the father-king in anthropological and religious ceremonies cited in the novel involving the death of the son.

11 "Libidinal Conflicts," 48. It is no coincidence, then, that when Wyatt meets Esme she has an abandoned daughter of four somewhere (196) — Wyatt's age when Camilla abandoned him. Even if Esme's child is imaginary (276–77), the symbolic importance remains.

12 De Rougemont's *Love in the Western World* (1939) was another of Gaddis's source books.

own half-dozen or so references to Ibsen's play. After delivering his last forgery to Brown a week or so after the encounter with Esme and drunkenly revealing his various dilemmas, Wyatt visits Basil Valentine to deposit the evidence of his forgeries. Valentine tries to subdue him and asks what he has been up to, and Wyatt answers that he has not been "up" to anything but rather:

> —Down to, consorting with mermaids in the bottom of a tank where the troll king lives (here a cough interrupted; and Basil Valentine held his breath) —God love him. I had willingly fastened the tail to my back, and drank what he gave me, you know, but there, when he tried to scratch out my eyes. "I'll scratch you a bit till you see awry; but all that you see will seem fine and brave."
>
> —So you've been to see Brown, have you? Basil Valentine leaned down and pulled open the loose newspaper package. —And this?
>
> —There they are, from A to izzard, from under the watchful eyes of Rose . . . protected, cautious, circumspect, eyes in every variety, but mostly those of children.
>
> Valentine looked up from the painted fragments, and poised, the lines in his forehead wove concern. —What's the matter, what's the matter? he said suddenly, —groaning like that, what is it?
>
> —I'll explain . . . as soon as I . . . yes . . . get settled . . .
>
> —My dear fellow . . .
>
> —It's a liberty I'm taking today, pretending I weigh three hundred pounds. Damn it, will you allow it? "I min Tro, i mit Håb og i min Kjærlighed" . . . eh? No, it didn't work out that way, I tell you. There's Solveig locked up with a dangerous man, human and industriously mad, he may save me yet like Luther saved the Papacy. (375)

The two quotations will be recognized by those familiar with Ibsen's play. The first is from Peer's encounter with the troll king in act 2, scene 6; and the second is Solveig's famous line, "In my faith, in my hope, and in my love," from the end of the play. But the context requires some elucidation. Mermaids entered into the discussion Wyatt held with the butler Fuller previous to Brown's arrival (346–48), and the "bottom of a tank" (i.e., lake) is the residence of the Grimm Brothers' frog king. Solveig and the dangerous man refer to his former wife Esther and her current lover Ellery, both of whom Wyatt saw briefly en route from Brown's to Valentine's. Esme, then, seems to be equated in Wyatt's mind (especially after her advance) with the troll king's daughter, called the Green-clad One, who leads Peer to her father's mountain court. At this point, Wyatt is contemplating a return to his father to resume his studies for the ministry, and consequently Esme is seen not in the role of redemptress but the temptress of *Peer Gynt*. (Esther, a failed Solveig, has long been abandoned as his redeemer.) Valentine, however, interprets the allusion to Solveig as a reference to Esme, and 175 pages later at the Brooklyn Zoo, though only a few days hence, mocks what he infers are Wyatt's romantic delusions:

> Basil Valentine turned and laughed in his face. —Really, really my dear fellow. No, he said, clutching the single gray glove before him. —The "somber glow" at the end of the second act, is it? the duet with Senta, is that it? . . . "the somber glow, no, it is salvation that I crave," eh! "Might such an angel come, my soul to save," your Flying Dutchman sings, eh? Good heavens! And up they go to heaven in a wave, or whatever it was? Really! And all that foolishness you were carrying on with the last time I saw you, that "I min Tro . . ." and the rest of it, that Where has he been all this time? and your Solveig answers In my faith? In my hope? In my, . . . good heavens! You are romantic, aren't you! If you do think you mean all this? And then what, They lived happily forever after?
>
> —But listen, listen, she . . .
>
> —No, no, it's too easy. After all, you know. With no interruption, Valentine paused, looking into the cage of the lioness. The lioness had come to the middle of the cage, watching him. She went round the tree trunk where her tail followed close, circling it. She stopped and moaned at the tail. She turned and bit at it. Then she moaned and faced him again. He did not speak until threatened by the voice beside him, then went on derisively, —And Saint Rose of Lima! Why, this sudden attempt to set the whole world right, by recalling your own falsifications in it? And then? Happiness ever after? Then you will be redeemed, and redeem her, and . . . good heavens knows what! And then, what next? First it's Shabbetai Zebi, now it's the Flying Dutchman? Listen to me, he went on, his voice dropping, —this lost innocence you're so frantic to recover, it goes a good deal farther back, you know. And this idea that you can set everything to rights at once is . . . is childish. (551)

Valentine, it would seem, understands the source of Wyatt's confusion better than Wyatt does himself. In this crucial section (part 2, chap. 6) Valentine is alerted by several references by Wyatt to his mother and makes the connection between Esme, Camilla, and their combined appearance in the portrait Valentine calls a *Stabat Mater* ("the [sorrowful] mother stood"). When Solveig is added to the gallery of romantic redemptresses Wyatt has been naming (Senta from Wagner's *Flying Dutchman*, the king's daughter from "The Frog King," Arianrhod from the Welsh *Mabinogion*, Isis from Apuleius' *Golden Ass*, Saint Rose of Lima) Valentine can only dismiss Wyatt's concerns as "childish" — an apt word in light of the psychological implications under consideration. He realizes, as Wyatt will later, that redemption cannot come from without — from a Solveig capable of conferring salvation — but must be worked out "with fear and trembling" from within.

An immature relationship with one's mother is not only childish but ultimately destructive, as the fates of many other characters in *The Recognitions* attest: Anselm castrates himself after an encounter with his domineering mother;[13] Charles is left to die after his smug Christian Scientist mother aban-

13 Anselm's habit of going about on all fours — "ritu quadrupedis," as he calls it, after the manner of Saint Teresa (197, 300) — makes psychological sense when we learn that "His mother is the sweetest little Boston woman, . . . *aw*fully interested in dogs" (309).

dons him; and Stanley, concerned with his hospitalized mother throughout the novel, finally dies as a result of his organ work dedicated to her. (None of them, it will be noted, has a satisfying relationship with a woman in the course of the novel.) "You know, the trouble with you," Max taunts Anselm and Stanley, "you're all mothers' sons" (534), as is Peer Gynt, and as is Wyatt until he adjusts to the loss of both his mother Camilla and his mother-surrogate Esme, and rediscovers the meaning of love with the Spanish girl Pastora.

Wyatt could never pursue this course as long as he was involved with the Valentine-Brown syndicate. Brown recommends crass materialism as the most reasonable goal in life, and the only advice Valentine can offer, "the only secret worth having," is "the power of doing without happiness" (552).[14] Such advice, however, is as limiting as the troll king's dictum, "Troll, to thyself be — enough!" (act 2, scene 6) or the Boyg's advice, "Go roundabout" (act 2, scene 7). That Gaddis associated the troll king with the Boyg — both of whom advocate passive resignation over active integration — is indicated by a gloss Gaddis provided his Italian translator to a reference to the Boyg earlier in that same important chapter:

> p. 545, l.27 — the "Boyg" was the troll king in Ibsen's "Peer Gynt" who wanted Peer to marry his ugly troll daughter and, in order to cure Peer of his 'pestilent nature'[15] and make him see as trolls do, says he will scratch his eyes so that Peer will "see awry; but all that you see will seem fair and brave."
>
> The reference is to Brown, as elaborated on page 375 lines 15–19, Brown as the Boyg-troll king having perverted Wyatt's vision so that the false looks beautiful.[16]

Together, the Boyg and the troll king form a combination represented in *The Recognitions* by Valentine and Brown, both of whom try to pervert Wyatt's vision. Although Peer stops short of allowing the troll king to scratch his eyes until he sees awry, his subsequent career is an embodiment of the king's ad-

14 This "secret" is from Bernard Shaw's *The Perfect Wagnerite* (4th ed. 1923). In his synopsis of Wagner's *Valkyrie*, Shaw writes, "With the son [Siegmund] he himself [Wotan] leads the life of a wolf, and teaches him the only power a god can teach, the power of doing without happiness" (New York: Dover, 1967), 35.

15 Actually, "pestilent" is a mistranslation on the Archers' part. According to Henri Logeman, *hersens* is a colloquialism, and the line should be translated "this 'ere human nature" (*A Commentary, Critical and Explanatory, on the Norwegian Text of Henrik Ibsen's "Peer Gynt," Its Language, Literary Associations and Folklore* [1917; rpt. Westport, CT: Greenwood Press, 1970], 116–17).

16 Quoted in Peter W. Koenig's "'Splinters from the Yew Tree': A Critical Study of William Gaddis's *The Recognitions*" (PhD diss., New York University, 1971, 92. I assume Gaddis is purposely consolidating the Boyg and troll king into one symbolic figure; however, the note for the Italian translator was written some ten years after the publication of the novel, and perhaps Gaddis simply forgot the distinction.

vice: "To thyself be — enough!" Wyatt, to his credit, more quickly realizes that the way of the world is not his way. The world of *The Recognitions* is the world of trolls, where the false looks beautiful, where counterfeit is taken for genuine, and where people are to themselves not true but simply enough. In his introduction to the edition of *Peer Gynt* Gaddis used, William Archer quotes Ludwig Passarge's interpretation of the Boyg as "a symbol of the mass of mankind, *perpetuum immobile*, opposing its sheer force of inertia to every forward movement." He goes on to explain: "This would make it nearly equivalent to 'the compact majority' of *An Enemy of the People*; or, looking at it from a slightly different angle, we might see in the scene an illustration in action of that despairing cry of Schiller's Talbot: 'Mit der Dummheit kämpfen Götter selbst vergebens.'"[17] Brown is consequently not only the troll king who urges conformity but also the Boyg in his capacity as chief representative of the inert, conservative masses against whom Wyatt, and any creative, liberal-minded person, must struggle in vain. Valentine, on the other hand, despises the masses and thus errs at the other extreme, a position that Gaddis associates with Gnosticism. In his notes, Gaddis wrote:

> Basil Valentine, who is the gnostic presumption . . . is finally stricken down with insomnia, for his very refusal to realize and grant the worth of matter, that is, of other people. The essence of his gnosticism is largely an implacable hatred for matter. It is that element of aescetecism [*sic*] common in so many religious expressions turned, not upon the self, but upon humanity.[18]

Brown interacts with people only to bilk them; Valentine does not interact with them at all. Both are to themselves enough. Now the masses in *The Recognitions* are, for the most part, no better than trolls (as Ibsen felt the majority of his fellow Norwegians were), but following the cynical paths advocated by Brown and/or Valentine will not help Wyatt in the least. If Camilla has hold of Wyatt's private conscience, then Brown and Valentine have hold of his public conscience; all three must be exorcized before he can progress.

Act 5 of *Peer Gynt* and part 3, chapter 5 of *The Recognitions* (the last chapter in which Wyatt appears) find the protagonists in similar circumstances. Most significantly, both have undergone a symbolic death at sea; realistically, of course, Peer escapes from the shipwreck and Wyatt dies only in the eyes of Esme, who is convinced the moribund sailor recovered mid-voyage is Wyatt himself. But psychologically both exemplify the "rebirth fantasy" common to

17 Pp. xxviii–xxix. The quotation from Schiller — "With stupidity the gods themselves struggle in vain" (*Jungfrau von Orleans*, act 3, scene 6) — appears in Gaddis's second novel, *J R* (New York: Knopf, 1975), 189.

18 Quoted in Koenig, 93.

literature and myth.[19] Both Peer and Wyatt must at this point come to terms with the past to redirect the future. As Peer makes his way to Solveig, the voices of his unconscious — anthropomorphized as the Strange Passenger, the Button-moulder,[20] the Lean One, and assorted thread-balls, withered leaves, sighs in the air, dewdrops, and broken straws — weigh his past deeds in the balance and find him wanting. His symbolic death notwithstanding, Peer is unable to make the final sacrifice necessary to be born again: "To be oneself is: to slay oneself," the Button-moulder explains (5.9), to kill the childish ego and allow the mature self to emerge.[21] But this answer, as the Button-moulder anticipated, is lost on Peer, and he ends on Solveig's lap in the same childish state as when the play began.[22]

Wyatt, on the other hand, seems to have taken to heart the Lean One's prescription in the following scene:

> Remember, in two ways a man can be
> himself — there's a right and wrong side to the jacket.
> You know they have lately discovered in Paris
> a way to take portraits by help of the sun.
> One can either produce a straightforward picture,
> or else what is known as a negative one.
> In the latter the lights and the shades are reversed,
> and they're apt to seem ugly to commonplace eyes;
> but for all that the likeness is latent in them,
> and all you require is to bring it out.
> If, then, a soul shall have pictured itself
> in the course of its life by the negative method,
> the plate is not therefore entirely cashiered —
> but without more ado they consign it to me.
> I take it in hand, then, for further treatment,
> and by suitable methods effect its development.
> I steam it, I dip it, I burn it, I scour it,
> with sulphur and other ingredients like that,
> till the image appears which the plate was designed for —

19 See Reich's "Libidinal Conflicts," 43–44. Some critics have argued that Peer actually drowns during the shipwreck and that the remainder of act 5 is a hallucination at the moment of death, but this reading has not found widespread acceptance.

20 The Button-moulder's occupation (see act 5, scenes 7, 9, 10) probably accounts for the unusual image in *The Recognitions* "streets were filling with people . . . like buttons from a host of common ladles" (329), an image repeated by Wyatt on the top of page 376.

21 Groddeck, 76–77; see also Logeman's long gloss on this line, 33–35. Wyatt knows what the Button-moulder is talking about and thus answers Valentine's taunt that his plans are suicidal: "Suicide? this? Do you think there's only one self, then? that this isn't homicide? closer to homicide?" (546).

22 In a 1972 BBC television production of the drama, director Alan Cooke astutely lap-dissolved at this point back to a tableau of Aase cradling Peer just as Solveig does at the end.

> that, namely, which people call positive.
> But if one, like you, has smudged himself out,
> neither sulphur nor potash avails in the least.
>
> PEER
>
> I see; one must come to you black as a raven
> to turn out a white ptarmigan? Pray what's the name
> inscribed 'neath the negative counterfeit
> that you're now to transfer to the positive side? (5.10)

The name inscribed 'neath the negative counterfeit of Gaddis's protagonist had been Wyatt; as Stephen, the name originally intended for him by Camilla (27), he will no longer try "to make negative things do the work of positive things" (590), as Esther had earlier accused him of doing. Blocked throughout the novel by his guilt and fixations, he finally realizes "it's only the living through it that redeems it" (898) and takes as his motto Saint Augustine's dictum "Love, and do what you want to" (899). On that note we leave him, not defeated by childish fixations as we left Peer, but victorious over the remorseful past and well on the way to individuation.

Ascertaining the proper relationship to self and society, to the world within as well as the world without, constitutes one of the major themes of *The Recognitions*, and Gaddis found in *Peer Gynt* an analogue that could be incorporated with advantage. *The Recognitions* may be a repudiation of the myth of romantic redemption glorified in such works as *Peer Gynt*, *The Flying Dutchman*, and *Faust*,[23] but it shares with them the age-old concern with the proper development of the inner and outer man. The allusions to (and quotations from) *Peer Gynt* and the large number of other works appearing in the novel are not then, as some early reviewers charged, showy examples of erudition on the young author's part, but an attempt by Gaddis to achieve the kind of multiple perspective Wyatt finds so intriguing in his beloved Flemish painters; they succeed in giving *The Recognitions* the depth and symbolic resonance that distinguishes truly great literature.

23 The influence of *Faust* on *Peer Gynt* has often been noticed — see, for example, A. LeRoy Andrews's early "Ibsen's *Peer Gynt* and Goethe's *Faust*," *Journal of English and Germanic Philology* 13 (1914): 238–46 — but space does not permit an examination of the confluence of both works on *The Recognitions*.

Chandler Brossard: Bold Saboteur

Chandler Brossard (1922–1993) was always an outsider, scornful of the country-club rules of literary decorum. In his 1955 review of Dan Jacobson's novel *The Trap*, Brossard concluded with the hope "that in his subsequent work he will discover himself 'outside' literature, and come upon a way of expressing himself — or conveying his vision — that is truly fictional and not literary."[1] As Brossard saw it, "literature" is the thin-blooded offspring of moribund literary conventions, tricks of the trade, writers' workshop mentality, and the homogenizing midwifery of unimaginative editors. "The fiction writer's primary responsibility," he insists in the same review, is to father "his own 'myth'" and to find a voice appropriate to this vision. Only then will the writer succeed at "extending the reader's (or listener's) vision and experience, and heightening his total sense of awareness."

Brossard's own development as a writer began "outside" literature in the early 1940s; hired at age 19 by the *New Yorker*, he was encouraged by its editor William Shawn to write fiction. He began with gritty short stories based on his experiences as a child (and later incorporated into *The Bold Saboteurs*), which startled his *New Yorker* co-workers precisely because the fiction lacked any of the superficial polish or mannerisms of the "well-made" story. Efforts were made to fit his fictional talent into the *New Yorker* mold, but these failed when Brossard realized his vision and that of the magazine were worlds apart. Central to his conception of fiction was the spoken word (as opposed to "literary" locution), the vehicle — as he wrote in an essay on Sherwood Anderson — of "the original source of literature, the oral story-teller."[2] Although the oral tradition was out of fashion in the mainstream fiction of the time — *The Catcher in the Rye* is the exception that proves the rule — it was the common denominator of those Brossard considered America's finest writers:

> Anderson, Twain, Stein, and Hemingway all wrote this spoken language, whether or not the particular work was written in the third person or in the first. If it was in the third, the presence of a narrator was always heavily felt throughout; there was not the feeling of a piece of fiction that had anonymously written itself. The idea was that

1 "Fiction and 'Literature,'" *Commentary* 19 (May 1955): 508. The quotations that follow are from p. 507.

2 "Sherwood Anderson: A Sweet Singer, 'A Smooth Son of a Bitch,'" *American Mercury* 72 (May 1951): 612; the block quotation that follows is from the same page.

> the written language, or the literary language, was exhausted, just about dead, and there had to be a return to the continually moving, continually developing vigor of the spoken English.

Here we have the two basic components of all of Brossard's fiction: a close attention to the vernacular and the presence of a distinctive, visionary sensibility. The result is a unique body of work spanning 40 years that not only defies classification but challenges many of the assumptions held on what constitutes legitimate fiction. Belonging to no school or literary coterie, Brossard remains "outside" literature, a bold saboteur of entrenched conventions of any sort: literary, political, sociological, or religious.

Life in the United States in the years following World War II, according to the *Life* magazine version, was just swell. America had won the war and emerged as the leader of the free world, the economy was booming, and college classrooms had begun filling with veterans taking advantage of the GI Bill. But our sharpest writers, as usual, were having none of it. The best literary works to appear in the decade after VJ-Day painted a different picture of America, one characterized by a sense of loss and disappointment, even disgust. Salinger's Holden Caulfield complained about the phoniness of people, while William Gaddis extended that complaint to expose postwar America as a counterfeit culture in his massive novel *The Recognitions*. Among the Beats, Jack Kerouac mourned the disappearance of redbrick small town America, Allen Ginsberg howled "I saw the best minds of my generation destroyed by madness," and William S. Burroughs attacked conformity and repression in hallucinatory routines that would eventually be served up as *Naked Lunch*. And of course James Baldwin, Ralph Ellison, and Richard Wright pointed out with varying degrees of rage that the American dream still had a sign warning No Coloreds Allowed.

Brossard's first novel, *Who Walk in Darkness* (1952), brought a French existentialist sensibility to this American malaise. While all of the above writings are exuberant, dramatic works that display a kind of grim hilarity at times, for his take on postwar America Brossard stripped language of all its unnecessary literary trappings and reduced it to the flat, unemotional voice of a black-and-white documentary. The lean, chaste language reminded many reviewers of Hemingway (specifically of *The Sun Also Rises*, with which it has a superficial similarity), but a more illuminating parallel would be Camus's *The Stranger*. "Sartre has shown," Susan Sontag notes in her essay "On Style," "in his excellent review of *The Stranger*, how the celebrated 'white style' of Camus's novel — impersonal, expository, lucid, flat — is itself the vehicle of Meursault's image of the world (as made up of absurd, fortuitous moments)."[3] This image of the world is shared by Brossard's narrator Blake Williams (a stunted William Blake?), the passive recorder of a month in the lives of his Greenwich Village circle at the beginning of 1948. The Camus parallel is significant for other reasons: *Who Walk in Darkness* may or may or not be (as it is sometimes called) the first Beat novel — George Mandel's *Flee the Angry Strangers* and John Clellon Holmes's *Go* were published the same year (1952), though I believe Brossard wrote his first — but it certainly appears to be American literature's first existential novel. Narrator Blake's first spoken word is "nothing," a word carrying the full weight of both Sartre's *Being and Nothingness* and Camus's *The Myth of Sisyphus*. Like Meursault, Blake describes rather than explains, and like *The Stranger*, *Who Walk in Darkness* is a demonstration of (rather than an argument for) the existential absurdity of life. Wanting only to perform "clean work" somewhere where "you did not have to tell lies," Blake documents his movement toward love and authenticity by contrasting it with his nemesis Henry Porter's flagrant inauthenticity. Blake displays none of the "self-righteousness" Delmore Schwartz ascribed to him in his review of the novel;[4] his observations are as objective as a scientist's, taking special care to avoid subjective judgments of any sort. Only after he experiences tenderness with Grace (her name carries as much religious symbolism as godless existentialism will allow), does he venture a few speculations and metaphors, eventually working up to such remarks as his sardonic response to a 1948 recording of Khachaturian's "Saber Dance" sung by the Andrews Sisters: "It sounded like the swan song of my decade. After that there could be nothing."

Who Walk in Darkness can be said to take place in what Jewish mystics called "the Abyss of Nothingness," as Brossard probably learned (if from nowhere else) from Milton Klonsky's 1948 essay "Greenwich Village: Decline and Fall," which Brossard reprinted in his excellent sociological anthology *The Scene before You* (1955). Klonsky took as his epigraph this quotation from Gershom Scholem: "Rabbi Joseph ben Shalom of Barcelona maintains that in every change of form, in every transformation of reality, or every time the status of a thing is altered the Abyss of Nothingness is crossed. . . . Nothing can change without coming into contact with this region of pure absolute Being which the mystics call Nothing. . . . It is the abyss which becomes visible in the gaps of existence."[5] Everyone in the novel is in such a state of transforma-

3 *Against Interpretation and Other Essays* (New York: Delta, 1966), 16–17.

4 "Fiction Chronicle: The Wrongs of Innocence and Experience," *Partisan Review* 19 (1952): 355.

5 *The Scene before You*, 16. This collection also reprints Anatole Broyard's "A Portrait of the Hipster" (1948); taken together, Klonsky's and Broyard's essays furnish useful background material for Brossard's novel.

tion — as was Greenwich Village at the time, as Klonsky shows — and the flat narrative tone and general meaninglessness of the characters' actions are meant to evoke this abyss of nothingness. Nothing in the novel is sensationalized or melodramatically exploited, though both the narrative and the setting offered numerous temptations that would have overpowered a less ascetic writer. (Burroughs faced and overcame the same temptation in *Junky*, another even-toned "documentary.")

Brossard's superb control of tone also throws into high relief any dialogue contaminated by the slightest dishonesty, ambiguity, or pretension. Only Grace's dialogue approaches the purity of Blake's own, and she consequently emerges as the only other person of "good faith" (to return to Sartre). Henry Porter, Max Glazer, and (to a lesser extent) Harry Lees all illustrate Sartre's inauthentic men of "bad faith," and Brossard accomplishes this as much by the inauthenticity of their language as by their deeds.

This philosophical demarcation is dramatized by the Coster-Phelps boxing match at the heart of the novel. Blake and Grace favor the former: "Coster was a skillful, clean-fighting boy who knew his way around in the ring. He never bragged. He played by the rules." Porter favors Phelps, a brutal, dirty fighter; Max is too busy putting the make on a girl to participate, and fastidious Harry doesn't know if he is attracted to or repulsed by the fight. A boxing match may seem an inadequate objective correlative for an existential crisis, but clearly Brossard incorporated it because the boxing ring is one place where inauthenticity of any sort is quickly exposed. Coster's defeat at the hands of the vicious Phelps, however, seems to argue that those who fight clean and play by the rules — the rules for authenticity, that is, not the rules of social convention — are endangered most by those who have no rules, like the ubiquitous hoods in the novel (who later mug Harry and leave him for dead) or "underground" men like Max and Porter. It is for this reason that the novel ends on a fearful, apocalyptic note as Blake and Grace realize their authenticity is no protection against the violently absurd world in which they are condemned to live.

Brossard had difficulty finding a publisher for *Who Walk in Darkness*, and even more difficulty after he did. It was rejected by all the major New York houses, but fortunately Brossard met the eminent French novelist and publisher Raymond Queneau during a visit to the States and let him read the manuscript. Queneau liked it and not only offered to publish it in France with the prestigious Gallimard publishing house, but recommended it to his American publisher, James Laughlin of New Directions, who also liked it and offered to publish it. Brossard was delighted.

Then Delmore Schwartz stepped in. Laughlin's literary advisor at the time, Schwartz was miffed to learn that an American novel had been accepted without his approval. Laughlin let him read the galley proof as compensation, and Schwartz quickly realized that a few of Brossard's characters were apparently based on mutual acquaintances: Henry Porter resembled Anatole Broyard, and Max Glazer seemed to be based on Milton Klonsky. (Brossard always insisted that his characters were just that: characters, not portrayals of real people.) Schwartz informed these two of the situation, and they threatened to sue New Directions unless changes were made. On the other hand, novelist William Gaddis saw something of himself in the character of Harry Lees, the Harvard dandy who drinks too much, but he didn't object to the portrayal. (Gaddis and Brossard shared an apartment in Greenwich Village around 1946–47.) Cap Fields was based on the notorious Village character Stanley Gould; coincidentally, both he and Gaddis would reappear as characters in Jack Kerouac's *The Subterraneans*.

Brossard reluctantly made the required changes, the most difficult beginning with the novel's opening line: instead of "People said Henry Porter was a 'passed' Negro," he had to make it: "People said Henry Porter was an illegitimate." This change was not only factually wrong — Broyard was indeed a light-skinned Negro who passed for white — but lexically wrong: a black man can't choose to be illegitimate, but he can choose to be inauthentic, and making such choices is what the novel is all about. One further change was Laughlin's: the original title of the novel was *Night Sky*, but he wanted something different, so Brossard took *Who Walk in Darkness* from part five of "Ash Wednesday" by T. S. Eliot (who took it from Psalm 88, the epigraph to the novel).[6]

In the biographical note on the dust-jacket of *Who Walk in Darkness*, Brossard wrote (in third person) that his next "book of fiction will not be a novel because the author feels the novel is not adequate to express certain contemporary experiences." And indeed *The Bold Saboteurs*, published in September 1953, is almost the complete opposite of Brossard's first novel. The passive, circumspect narrator of that one is replaced by an aggressively active one who goes on the rampage with a subversive language of exceptional power and energy. "That was the first book I opened up all the doors to," Brossard later said of his second novel, "because *Who Walk in Darkness* was almost like the finals in some academy in a way. I wanted it to be this seamless, perfect, controlled, absolute thing of infinity, where in *The Bold Saboteurs* I

6 When the novel was published in France in 1954, it not only retained Brossard's original title, translated as *Ciel du Nuit*, but also used Brossard's original, uncensored text. It wasn't until 1972 that Brossard was able to publish the original version (with Harrow, an imprint of Harper & Row), which was also used for the 2000 edition by Herodias.

just let everything go crazy."[7] Brossard discarded the detached, dispassionate tone of Camus for the deliriously energetic one of Céline. Like his *Death on the Installment Plan, The Bold Saboteurs* relates the experiences of childhood in a style that mixes idiomatic street-slang with otherworldly surrealism. The result is not so much an autobiographical Bildungsroman (though it is based on Brossard's childhood in Washington, DC) as a terrifying exploration of adolescent psychological disintegration in the context of a family destroyed by alcoholism.

Perhaps Brossard's most widely admired book, *The Bold Saboteurs* has elicited a variety of responses. Like *Who Walk in Darkness*, it has been assigned a privileged place in Beat literature: its first chapter was reprinted in Feldman and Gutenberg's classic anthology *The Beat Generation and the Angry Young Men* (1958) and in 1971 Bruce Cook wrote that *The Bold Saboteurs* "had a teen-age hero who seems even today the model of a hipster."[8] Though Brossard never considered himself a Beat — he admired Burroughs's *Junky* (published the same year as *The Bold Saboteurs*) and *Naked Lunch* (whose influence can be seen in Brossard's later novels) but otherwise felt no affinity with them — his second novel does dramatize the seamier, more violent side of the Beat Generation. Despite Jack Kerouac's insistence that "beat" was short for "beatific" and Allen Ginsberg's equation of hipsters with angels, petty crime shaped Beat aesthetics as much as Buddha or Blake. Neal Cassady was a car thief; Gregory Corso landed in reform school at an early age; Burroughs occasionally joined Times Square hustlers to rob people; and they all admired Herbert Huncke, a thief and drug addict (as they did the criminal writer Jean Genet). While some Beats went on to become semirespectable members of the literary establishment, Brossard dramatizes the path other Beats took: namely, toward Norman Mailer's definition of the hipster as "a philosophical psychopath."

But perhaps Seymour Krim, one of the earliest champions of *The Bold Saboteurs*, has come closest to grasping the book's most significant achievement. Linking it not with Beat literature but with Ellison's *Invisible Man* (1952), Krim points out that such "novels"

> are more truly imaginative explorations into the maze of personal being rather than novels in any traditional sense. The story they tell is primarily the psyche's story. The nightmarish sequences in both books, and many others like them, are a testimony to the devilish heat imposed on anyone with imagination who is just being today; it is the slice-of-life technique applied to the pressure-cooked head. There is invention in

7 Steven Moore, "An Interview with Chandler Brossard," *Review of Contemporary Fiction* 7.1 (Spring 1987): 50.

8 *The Beat Generation* (New York: Scribner's, 1971), 48.

> these books, but it is all directed to the description of, and the attempt to find, new colors, new sounds, new equivalents for the extremity to which the Self has been pushed.[9]

On the surface, *The Bold Saboteurs* seems to be about the extraordinary adventures of a thoughtful petty thief. The younger son of a drunk and a harridan, George Brown (nicknamed Yogi) begins a life of crime at first merely to support himself during the Depression, and then increasingly out of contempt for conventional behavior. He is smart enough to elude the police most of the time — they catch him only once, at age 16, in the episode that opens the novel — and he soon develops an appreciation of the aesthetics, as it were, of criminal activity. His older brother, Roland, takes him under his wing, for which Yogi is grateful: "Roland educated me as a thinker while he was educating me as a thief, and since then I have always associated crime with intellect." Most of the novel is an episodic and frequently hilarious account of a life of crime; but beneath its raffish surface, something more insidious is happening inside Yogi. At an early age he endures debilitating migraine attacks, and in times of stress lapses into hallucinations, or fugue states, what Yogi first dismisses as "my lovely blackouts." These bizarre and skillfully integrated episodes are what separate *The Bold Saboteurs* from typical novels about young criminals, and they also foreshadow the phantasmagoria of Brossard's later works.

In psychological terms, Yogi operates on the wild frontiers of consciousness where sanity is occasionally overthrown by the rebellious unconscious. In fact, one of the more remarkable sections of the book is a three-page letter of warning addressed to Yogi's conscious from "Your inseparable partner, / until death do us part," his unconscious.[10] From "the twisted smoking wreckage of my childhood" (37), Yogi tries to maintain some semblance of sanity, but the psychic havoc inflicted upon him in childhood proves irreversible.

Brossard uses hallucination to dramatize the irruption of the unconscious into consciousness, largely the result of Yogi's violently ambivalent feelings toward his father. Freud often used police action as an image for his theory of repression, and Yogi's running conflict with the authorities throughout the novel is given its full psychological value in the sequence Brossard placed at

9 "Fiction — and Total Imaginative Writing" (1958), rpt. in his *Views of a Nearsighted Cannoneer*, rev. ed. (New York: Dutton, 1968), 224. [Krim later published a brief memoir entitled "Chandler, *WWD*, and, Inevitably, Hopefully Not Intrusively, Me," *Review of Contemporary Fiction* 7.1 (Spring 1987): 87–90.]

10 Pages 201–4 in the original edition published by Farrar, Straus and Young in 1953. Unfortunately, when the novel was reset and reprinted by Herodias in 2001, an uncorrected text was sent to the printer, resulting in a flawed edition.

the beginning of the book. Chapter one opens achronologically with Yogi's arrest at the age of 16 (chapter two begins when he is eight and the narrative unfolds chronologically thereafter) and reveals his ambiguous fear of and desire for punishment. Seeing a police car cruise toward him, he admits: "My body was a block of iced fear. I was afraid to let myself feel luxuriantly scared because then I knew I would disintegrate into hysteria, which is what I may have wanted to do anyway" (14). When he is finally caught, his reaction is tinged with masochistic satisfaction — anticipating the "purifying" beating he later welcomes from his brother, when he passes out "in a coma of ecstasy and pain" (179).

The book's first surrealistic sequence follows his arrest; feeling "that the police house had always been my goal" (17), Yogi finds in the depths of his hallucination the man responsible for his disintegrating psyche:

> Now I was in an absolutely quiet corner of the station house. Here I experienced a strange tidal sensation all around me and inside myself: it was very emotional and a little sexual. Before me was my father, very bloated and dreamy looking and dressed in what resembled a policeman's uniform. He smiled vastly at me but I did not smile back. My father reminded me of some giant fish, a whale or a porpoise, that had been stranded on the beach. He was murmuring vast, oceanic nothings to a small man in a black raincoat who was pretending to write it all down in a very official-looking black notebook. . . .
>
> And almost before I knew what I was doing, I had pushed the man away and had climbed into my father's arms. Now I felt happily helpless and I was sobbing and sobbing, and my father was caressing my head.
>
> "I was hoping you would be here," I said, or felt myself say for there was still an absolute, overwhelming silence around me.
>
> "That makes me feel very proud, son," my father replied in his vast, oceanic voice.
>
> I began to play with his police badge, but under my fingers the badge turned into an ordinary button. I was suddenly stunned by this, and I looked into my father's face for an explanation. But my father now looked old and sick and disgusting, and he stank terribly of whiskey. His uniform had become a shabby suit of clothes.
>
> "You tricked me! You tricked me!" I shouted. "Why? Why?"
>
> And I was hitting my father in the face, blow after blow. My father, however, did not react at all to these blows; he just stared helplessly at the floor. (20–21)

Yogi's love–hate relationship with his father, an unredeemable drunkard, sets into play a classic Oedipal psychodrama. Hatred for his father is distributed to other authority figures and institutions, as can be expected: he avoids school, convinced it wants "to emasculate whatever originality and spirit" he has (57), and his fierce blasphemy is illuminated by his brother Roland's delirious evocation of "my father who art in heaven drunk" (231). In another hallucination, Yogi watches a crowd passing around his father's clothes and ripping them to shreds, reminiscent of a station in Christ's passion (Matt.

27:35). Similarly, Yogi's first mugging victim is an older man who tries to dissuade him by crying out, "I could be your father" (134), and shortly afterward Yogi maliciously entraps an older pederast — a delayed reaction, perhaps, to Yogi's disgust at being forced to sleep with his father when younger. The drunken father appears sporadically in the novel, and each time Yogi retreats into hallucination rather than bring into consciousness and resolve his hopelessly ambivalent feelings toward him. To complicate matters further, almost all of Yogi's love affairs are with women old enough to be his mother.

Yogi's brother Roland at first receives all the love and devotion Yogi cannot give to his parents, but after Roland kicks the old man out of the house, he becomes the father figure (going so far as to disallow his mother remarrying), triggering conflicts similar to those Yogi experiences with his father. He finds a temporary brother-substitute in a criminal wunderkind named Victor, but their idyllic relationship is short-lived. At the end of the novel Yogi learns of his death, and his visit to pay his respects to Victor in a shabby funeral parlor is the most touching scene in the book. "Always looking for that brother, aren't you?" a policeman asks in Yogi's final hallucination.

At the end of the book, lost to friends and family in "a still grey world beyond communication" (296), Yogi finds a job caring for a final father figure, an invalid named Mr. White. Carrying him one night (after reading to him from the Book of Judges), "trying to do it so that I would not have to touch the repulsive man too much with my arms and body, really trying to juggle him, and now with an unusual lack of muscular interest, I dropped him." (Note how the syntax delays the confession as Yogi struggles to admit responsibility.) Panicking, he carries the half-dead body to bed and nearly strangles him. Guilt overwhelms him, and after finally proclaiming his deed like a Dostoevskian hero, Yogi flees from the house and, after a period of hunger and illness, lapses into the hallucination that closes the book. Traveling by boat to a Kafkaesque otherworld, Yogi is abandoned, either struggling to break out of his hallucination — "running from pier to pier, looking for the boat which I hoped would take me back" (303) — or perhaps dying, if the archetypal boat symbolism is used in its mythic sense. Either way, it is a chilling conclusion to a remarkable study in neuroses.

But *The Bold Saboteurs* is obviously more than a Freudian case study. In a style as racy as the first novel's was chaste, Yogi's picaresque adventures are always absorbing and often hilarious, and the novel undoubtedly remains Brossard's most popular for these very reasons. But the psychological conflicts dramatize a theme that Brossard would examine with increasing audacity in succeeding works, namely the conflicting claims of the Dionysian unconscious and the Apollonian intellect. At the beginning of a decade that would later produce Herbert Marcuse's *Eros and Civilization* and Norman

O. Brown's *Life against Death,* Brossard demonstrated the necessity of allowing the liberating unconscious to revitalize the gray-flannel conscious, and in *The Bold Saboteurs* he gives a stunning dramatization of both the rewards and dangers that attend this process.

It is difficult to fathom why the one-two punch delivered to literature by *Who Walk in Darkness* and *The Bold Saboteurs* failed to make a great impact. Much of the blame rests with the reading public's allegiance to the drab realism of most fiction — then as now. The hyper-realistic trompe-l'oeil narrative of *Who Walk in Darkness* owes more to the illogical details of a surrealistic painting or a nightmare than to the realistic fictional conventions of the time, and the blending of fantasy and realism in *The Bold Saboteurs* is a technique European readers respond to more readily than Americans. Other than their obvious influence on such emerging writers as Gilbert Sorrentino and Hubert Selby in America and on various New Wave novelists and filmmakers in France, the novels attracted little critical attention, despite their long lives in various mass-market editions.

Disappointed by this lack of response and desperately needing money, Brossard next wrote the first two of several potboilers: *Paris Escort* (1953) and *The Wrong Turn* (1954), both published under the pseudonym Daniel Harper, to be followed in later years by *All Passion Spent* (aka *Episode with Erika,* 1954), *The Girls in Rome* (aka *We Did the Strangest Things,* 1961), and *A Man for All Women* (an expanded version of *Paris Escort,* 1966). These Brossard dismissed as "threepenny dreadfuls," and although they all have occasional points of interest, they probably would not repay close study.

In the late 1950s Brossard also edited the first of many paperback short-story anthologies, each carrying anywhere from one to five of his own stories, most appearing under a variety of pseudonyms.[11] The short-story form was not a new departure for him, and like Hemingway's earliest stories,[12] they dramatize epiphanic moments in a style of scrupulous meanness. The best among them conjure up the existential dread inherent in the quotidian world, offering interesting asides on the themes treated at greater length in his novels. "Sunday Revelation," written while Brossard was still at the *New Yorker* but not published until 1953 (and included in his first anthology, *The First*

11 [For bibliographic details, see the "Checklist of Writings by Chandler Brossard" that accompanied this essay in *RCF* (82–86).]

12 There are some close parallels: Brossard's "fictional moments" in *American Mercury* (1951) resemble the brief interchapters in Hemingway's *In Our Time,* and his story "Some Other Way" (1966) seems deliberately modeled on Hemingway's "The Sea Change." It is perhaps only coincidental that Ernest is the name of the father in the Oedipal psychodrama *The Bold Saboteurs.* For Brossard's opinion of Hemingway, see his essay "Everybody's Old Man" in *New American Mercury* 71 (December 1950): 698–701.

Time [1957]), is both a grimly original portrayal of the loss of innocence, and symbolic (as he later realized) of the subtly corrupting influence of Brossard's mentor at the *New Yorker*, novelist William Maxwell. A skewed sort of voyeurism disrupts the deceptively placid surface of "A Very Nice Place" (1947), and the repeated image of garfish staying "stiffly together in speckled angles, unmoving" — an image Ezra Pound singled out for praise[13] — effectively characterizes the tensions between the threesome in "Vacation for Three" (1951). "Jewel of the Soul" (1951) is a harrowing story of the loss of identity, and the exquisite "The Closing of This Door Must Be Oh, So Gentle" (1962) is an equally effective study of a desperate attempt to maintain an identity. In a more exuberant style that anticipates his later work, "One If for Sorrow, Two If for Joy" (1966) reads like an Isaac Bashevis Singer story adapted by Stanley Elkin, and "The Robber Next Door" (1966) — which Brossard used as the closing sequence in his 1971 novel *Wake Up. We're Almost There* — was praised by Richard Nason as "a short story as good as any of its kind, Virginia Woolf and Katherine Mansfield not aside."[14] Plans to publish a collection of the early stories around 1953–54 fell through, as did a similar plan in the 1980s, but fortunately the best of them were recycled for inclusion in *Wake Up* and in his final novel, *As the Wolf Howls at My Door* (1992).

Brossard's next novel was published in 1960; originally entitled "The Double Dealers," it appeared as *The Double View* to much better reviews than his first two received. The original title sharpens the contrast between most of the book's characters — New York pseudo-intellectuals suffering in various degrees from a kind of cultural schizophrenia — and more straightforward characters like Shanley, "no dillier with identities, no dallier with self, a single dealer of infinite simplicity."[15] The others dilly-dally with their identities in a number of ways: Margaret, a wealthy socialite, leads a complicated double life as an organizer of foreign charities and private orgies; Phillips has ambivalent feelings toward his Jewish heritage (as his gentile name suggests); Christopher Hawkins is a black professor who wants to be white so intently that he wears a white "skin-tight suit of long woolen underwear" and has such a tenuous grip on his identity that he is not even named during his early appearances; Rand has a doppelgänger relationship with his best friend Carter Barrows, sharing both Carter's wife and his nervous breakdown. Carter, the book's protagonist, is in an insane asylum throughout the novel, wondering when and where he

13 Brossard and Pound corresponded in the early '50s, and occasionally the poet would evaluate Brossard's work in progress. (Unfortunately, Brossard later threw out all his correspondence from his early career.)

14 "A Man for All Obsessions," *Village Voice* 17 (26 July 1973): 26.

15 Dial Press edition, 183. The publisher changed the title because a book on scam artists called *The Double Dealers* had appeared two years earlier.

took "the fatal fork in the road" that separated "his strange self and his not strange self" (150, 186).

The most interesting of the double dealers is Harry. Here it is worth noting that the novel was written in 1953, for it anticipates in several essentials Norman Mailer's 1957 essay "The White Negro." Harry perfectly illustrates Mailer's hipster as "a philosophical psychopath, a man interested not only in the dangerous imperatives of his psychopathy but in codifying, at least for himself, the suppositions on which his inner universe is constructed."[16] An intellectual radical (who nonetheless "writes lies for an advertising agency"), Harry has decided, in Mailer's words, "to set out on that uncharted journey into the rebellious imperatives of the self . . . to encourage the psychopath in oneself, to explore that domain of experience where security is boredom and therefore sickness." Harry leads a secret life as Eddie Brien, a vulgar small-time hood, doing no more than practicing what he preaches in an early chapter; asked what he means by "exploiting schizophrenia," he replies: "Oh that. Well, instead of destroying yourself with anxiety by repressing certain aspects of your whole self, aspects that conflict with the so-called moral self, why, it would be better to try to express them all. For example, if you have some criminal desires, become a part-time thief, or at least let the emotion have some badly needed exercise. See what I mean?"

As good as his word, Harry goes from entrapping and mugging some out-of-towners to knocking over a bowling alley with his small gang, and finally to raping Margaret and burglarizing her apartment with two other masked assailants. Harry's actions are a dramatization of Mailer's notorious definition:

> Hip, which would return us to ourselves, at no matter what price in individual violence, is the affirmation of the barbarian, for it requires a primitive passion about human nature to believe that individual acts of violence are always to be preferred to the collective violence of the State; it takes literal faith in the creative possibilities of the human being to envisage acts of violence as the catharsis which prepares growth.

No growth, however, takes place; three double dealers are destroyed or debilitated during this climactic scene, and only the single dealer Shanley escapes unharmed.

The masked murder is a convention of Elizabethan drama, including *The*

16 Norman Mailer, *Advertisements for Myself* (New York: Putnam's, 1959), 343; the succeeding quotations are from 339 and 355. Because of the close connection in thought between Mailer and Brossard, it should come as no surprise to learn that Mailer once wrote that "parts I had read of *The Bold Saboteurs* were sufficiently interesting for me to put the book away — it was a little too close to some of my own notions" (ibid., 469). But Mailer told Brossard privately that he had not only read the whole novel but "liked it enormously" (Peter Manso, *Mailer: His Life and Times* [New York: Simon and Schuster, 1985], 244).

Revenger's Tragedy, the closing lines of which supply the epigraph to Brossard's novel.[17] In fact, the numerous parallels between these two works are instructive: like the play, the novel has a dramatic structure, eschewing prosaic transitions in favor of jump cuts to scenes of dialogue or internal monologues that read like theatrical asides. The characters in both play and novel frequently resort to disguises and live in the same climate of moral corruption. And like Middleton, Brossard is a stern moralist; his dust-jacket remarks on his novel apply equally to *The Revenger's Tragedy*: "I like to think of *The Double View* as a stringently moralistic work. It tries to show what happens when people lose sight of God; when they begin to use each other, the way we use commodities, rather than love each other; and what happens when a person does not know truly who he is and what he should do on this earth." Just as Vindice the revenger becomes tainted with evil in the very process of seeking revenge and thus must be destroyed, Harry likewise perishes, as much from a "failure of belief" (150) as from a policeman's bullet. Harry had rationalized his crimes with a variant of Ivan Karamazov's challenge: "In a society which has no meaning, Hawkins, my boy, what could be a more appropriate gesture than ours?"

A more constructive attitude is taken by Carter, who struggles to learn how authenticity slipped through his fingers:

> "Failure of belief must have been the reason I'm here now, otherwise why would any one wish to leave a world, or anything else, that he believed in? Question before the accused is, how to regain Belief *and in what*. Without that there is simply no point in accused leaving present address. One is not required to have anything here [the asylum] except a pulse. In the place I left, outside, living without belief is even crazier than it is in here, and I know. At what point did I lose it and why? That's what must be discovered. The fatal fork in the road."

On the same night Harry and his cohorts execute their burglary, Carter escapes from the asylum with his black friend (an act that looks back to *Huckleberry Finn* and forward to *One Flew over the Cuckoo's Nest*) and plans a similar bloody revenge against his unfaithful wife and friend. But at the very moment he plans to consummate the deed, "a beatific, transcendent lucidity" illuminates him — conveyed in sexual imagery — and he lays down his knife in order to return "back down that long, long highway, to the fatal fork in it, to the town where he was born, where the wrong direction had been chosen or forced upon him . . . he would return to the particular fragrant spawning street of his childhood and begin there to search for the person he had been."

17 [In Brossard's day, the 1606 play was attributed to Cyril Tourneur, but now it is considered the work of Thomas Middleton.]

The Double View is a nervy, compact book written with economy and a flair for unusual imagery, accomplishing in fewer than two hundred pages what Brossard's friend William Gaddis spent nearly a thousand pages doing in *The Recognitions* (admittedly in greater depth), namely to chart a pilgrim's progress from hell through purgatory, leaving him poised for a paradisiacal rediscovery of authenticity and atonement.

These religious implications are at the heart of Brossard's next novel. "Necessity makes men misapprehend / Hunger makes the wolf leap from the woods," wrote the medieval French poet François Villon in *Le Testament*. Chandler Brossard adapted Villon's phrase for this provocative novel about an Episcopalian priest driven by necessity and sexual hunger to leave the safe woods of his parish for a walk on the wild side. Written in 1961–62 with the title "The Wolf Leaps," it failed to find a publisher at the time; a dozen years would pass before someone offered to take it on, a publisher mostly of educational materials called Bobbs-Merrill, whose editor insisted that the title be changed before they would publish it. It appeared in 1973 as *Did Christ Make Love?* — a question one of the characters asks late in the novel — and even though the *Village Voice* called it Brossard's best book to date, it quickly sank from sight. It is the least known of Brossard's novels, the scarcest on the used-book market, and the only one not to have been reprinted as a paperback.

This is a shame, because *The Wolf Leaps* (Brossard's preferred title) is intriguingly different in many ways from Brossard's other novels. Its ethnic cast of characters and *West Side Story* setting is unique in his canon, and it is the only novel of his to focus explicitly on religion and the nature of religious belief. (He would return to this theme in his final work, *Shifty Sacred Songs*, a collection of what might be called postmodern psalms.) *The Double View* had charted a secular pilgrim's progress from hell through purgatory, leaving its protagonist determined to return to that fork in the road where he took a wrong turn, and take a different path. The implicit religious argument of that novel is made explicit here as Alfred Harrison, an Episcopalian priest, suffers a "passion" in both the religious and erotic sense of the word. A parish priest in Spanish Harlem, he is driven by his smarmy wife Leslie (a latent lesbian) into the arms of a mulatto prostitute named Monique. His sexual awakening is twice compared to Saint Paul's illumination on the road to Damascus as Harrison discovers that fork in the road where sex and religious worship parted ways millennia ago. Harrison attempts to reunite the two by using biblical texts in sexual contexts, thereby reversing the procedure theologians have used on sublime erotica such as the Song of Solomon and the poems of Saint John of the Cross. Like Harry in *The Double View*, he exults in the liberation of his repressed instincts, but his exultation is short-lived: again like *The Double View* (in fact, *The Wolf Leaps* is a doubled view of that novel), the story ends in mass murders, from which only one escapes.

In an autobiographical sense, Harrison tries to escape from the conventional middle-class lifestyle Brossard himself was living in the early 1960s, and which was driving him crazy. Leaving school at age 11, Brossard had led a bohemian existence until the early 1950s (partly recounted in *The Bold Saboteurs*), when he married and soon became the father of two girls. Needing to support them, he first turned to writing potboilers for quick cash, but when this proved too financially unreliable, he became an editor at *Look* magazine in 1956, turning out photo-essays on a variety of mundane subjects and commuting to work in New York City from Ridgewood, New Jersey. For this bold saboteur, now pushing 40, working for *Look* and living in the suburbs was a living death.

As it happens, one of the articles he wrote for *Look* dealt with an Episcopalian priest's work with juvenile delinquents ("Father Myers: He Never Gives Up on Anybody," *Look*, 13 October 1959). A few years later, when Brossard decided to write a novel about the sterility of upper-middle-class white society compared to the vitality of ethnic cultures, he drew upon that essay for his principal character, and then surrounded Father Harrison and his anemic wife Leslie with a handful of vibrant blacks and Hispanics.

The novel's small cast of characters has little in common with each other, and Brossard cleverly underscores the radical conflicts between them by shifting styles as each character takes the stage. Mixing narration and interior monologue, the author clothes his characters in language that mirrors the psycho-sociological reality each inhabits. In the opening chapter, for example, both Harrison's academic background and his psychological conflicts are conveyed in windy language using a paratactic sentence structure that frequently fractures itself with parenthetical qualifications. (After his sexual experience, his language loosens up as much as he does.) The second chapter introduces José Rojas, a street-smart young welfare worker and a parishioner of Harrison's, in a jazzy style appropriate to his playful outlook on life. He reads, and occasionally quotes from, Johan Huizinga's *Homo Ludens: A Study of the Play Element in Culture* (1938), and in fact he previews the liberated narrative voice Brossard would use in his later fiction. Chapter three features Leslie in a coy, saccharine style reminiscent of the Gerty MacDowell chapter in Joyce's *Ulysses*. The last major character, a pimp named Dancer, has his own language of "viciously thin corrupted words." The close juxtaposition of these clashing language codes heightens the various religious, sexual, and racial tensions throughout the book, giving it more the quality of a play than a novel. (It is worth noting that Brossard was heavily involved in playwrighting at the time.)[18] These exercises in multiple points of view would eventually lead to the communal narrative voices and rampant heteroglossia of his two longest, most ambitious novels, *Wake Up. We're Almost There* and *As the Wolf Howls at My Door.*

Uniting these diverse conversational styles is a careful and consistent use of imagery. Fleeting glimpses of Eden are caught by way of the nature and garden imagery in the sexual scenes, but animal imagery dominates this gritty picture of the urban jungle. Rats, lizards, snakes, dogs, jackals, cockroaches, alligators, and of course wolves infest the novel. After a brutal gang-rape, for example, the boys leave "much as beasts of prey will ultimately pad heavily away from the half-devoured body of a gazelle, innocent, unsuspecting, which, wandered from its herd, they have brought down." In addition, a variety of figurative demons, hunchbacks, dwarfs, gargoyles, dragons, trolls, ghouls, and ghosts haunt the pages of this nightmare world. "A razor-slice of life in the raw from Chandler Brossard's disturbing new novel, *The Wolf Leaps*" is how the headnote reads to a selection published in *Nugget* in April 1962 (a men's magazine edited by Brossard's friend Seymour Krim). The novel remains as sharp and raw as it did then.

Brossard followed it in the early '60s with two novels that remain unpublished, which he described as follows: "They were a shortish novel, very brutal, almost B-movie kind of novel with a very exquisite kind of super-realism, situated in New York, about crazy people. It was called 'I Came to See You but You Were Asleep.' That book was rejected by several people so I withdrew it, and then I did a sort of campy porn novel called 'Your Place or Mine?' That too was rejected by a couple of people and I withdrew it."[19]

He had better luck with several nonfiction books he wrote during the same period. Two were popularized biographies written for money — *Ilya: That Man from U.N.C.L.E.* (combining his young daughters' names as a pseudonym) and *The Insane World of Adolf Hitler* (both 1966) — but they have their appeal. *Illya* is a frequently hilarious parody of pop journalism, a point no doubt lost on its gushing readers, and the Hitler book, despite its negligible, somewhat improvised text, constitutes a valuable photographic record.

In a special category, however, is Brossard's 1968 travel book, *The Spanish*

18 I have omitted a discussion of Brossard's half-dozen plays because, with the exception of two one-act plays reprinted in *Wake Up*, the texts remain unpublished. See Brossard's account of his brief dramatic career in *Contemporary Authors Autobiography Series*, vol. 2 (Detroit: Gale Research, 1985), 63–78 (hereafter abbreviated *CAAS*).

19 *CAAS*, 69–70. The first book (under the title "She Cried Out to Me") is among Brossard's papers at the Special Collections Research Center, Syracuse University; the second was [in the 1980s] in the hands of his former wife.

Scene. Based on interviews and observations made during a trip in the spring of 1967, *The Spanish Scene*'s nonfiction status can be called into question when one considers the rather extraordinary circumstances in which it was written. Brossard explains:

> *The Spanish Scene* — non-fiction, more or less — took me two weeks. I was in an elegant sort of trance while I was doing it. I was very high, and very happy. I had spent two months in Spain collecting material for the book — just talking to people, really — and I was experiencing ecstasy during the whole time. I seemed to understand everything in Spain even though I did not speak a word of Spanish. My ESP was working divinely. A Spanish department had opened up in my brain. I could hear Cervantes talking, and Lope de Vega and Ortega. It was incredible.[20]

Consequently, it might be better to consider the book more as an imaginative recreation, an early example of New Journalism, or even an impressionistic historical fiction, than as a straightforward travel book — as informative as it may be in that regard.

One of the book's most interesting aspects can easily go unnoticed: the subtle identity crisis the self-effacing narrator suffers and overcomes in the course of the book. Daniel Talbot, a consistently reliable reviewer of Brossard's work, noticed one facet of this crisis: "*The Spanish Scene* is not so much a book about the Spanish scene as a gifted novelist's predicament in explaining why he is so bugged by life in his own country."[21] More precisely, it is an account of a man who has lost touch so completely with any kind of nurturing reality that he must make contact with something real before he loses touch altogether. In this regard the narrator recalls Blake Williams of *Who Walk in Darkness*, and the travel book has much the same kind of chaste, noncommittal style as the earlier novel.

The short book is made up largely of monologues by various Spaniards in which the narrator does little more than ask an occasional question; rarely does he express any kind of evaluation or value judgment. On the few occasions he does register a response, it more often than not concerns his own shortcomings: he feels "like an idiot in my innocence and non-participant role" or feels "thick with stupidity and frustration"; occasionally he simply agrees because he can't "think of anything else to say." Not surprisingly, he finds the sight of his fellow Americans — tourists and GIs stationed in Spain — repugnant after his encounters with such vivid Spaniards.

We learn he is going through a divorce at one point (and from the book's

20 Eric Baizer and Richard Peabody, "Politics & Libidos: The Irreverent World of Chandler Brossard" [interview], *Gargoyle* 14 (1980): 7. See also *CAAS*, 70.

21 "The Way to Get at Spain," *The Nation* 206 (20 May 1968): 674. Brossard disagreed with this reading.

dedication to his doctor can infer he almost lost his life shortly before) and learn that he is so vulnerable that a few lines from Rilke are almost enough to cause a breakdown. Not until the end of the book, however, do we fully realize how cathartic his encounter with Spain has been. Discovering "I knew that something in this world made sense, if you kept your eyes open to notice," the Spanish scene allows him to free himself from his earlier, frustrated self: "The man with my name who had waited with premature exhaustion in the departure section of the airport in New York was still there. I was someone else." Picking up a copy of *Time* and reading a misleading article on the Basques (7 April 1967, p. 31), he reacts to this compact symbol of all that is wrong with America by reestablishing contact with the real, the visible:

> I found myself concentrating on the faces of the people more, staring at particular Spanish details of stores and buildings, gestures of differentness, in order to kill the dirty-taste feeling left in me by reading the insults in the magazine; and, with microscopic urgency, I was seeing a full, curved mouth, a thick brooding eyebrow, a stone flower on a façade, and as I was thus healing myself, I began to analyze why I felt so tranquil and no longer in small angry pieces. . . . I could isolate one feeling for sure — that I felt more like myself, in those places, than I generally did in my own country. And feeling more like myself meant, quite simply, not feeling those other personalities that I had been forced to invent to deal with those countless situations and humans in New York that I, the me of myself, did not want any part of. The stage of me became so crowded with those others: a ghostly repertory company that refused to go home when the curtain came down. Those other hungry, manipulated, angry pseudo-humans were not with me here, and it was me and me alone that was responding to and becoming part of — no longer a spectator, object scene — the fold in the stone martyr's robe, the reflection of light on the shy wet street, the ache in the tolling of bells. The singleness of myself allowed me to discover how much a part of this natural world I truly was.

This episode, significantly, is followed by one that begins with a Spanish businessman's confession: "I used to think I could find myself and my destiny somewhere else"; he discovered that he couldn't, and the narrator soon learns likewise. The next two episodes — the last in the book — deal with the brutal, repressive side of Franco's Spain, disqualifying it as the Eden it may have appeared to be. The narrator must return to his own country, but vows not to forget those aspects of Spain that brought him back to himself. "'I won't [forget],' I said. I couldn't. To do that would be to forget myself."

This crisis of personal disintegration and integration is handled almost indirectly, so unobtrusively that it could easily be overlooked among the more vivid vignettes of Spanish life with which the book is largely concerned. But the theme is one that is central to Brossard's work, as is his concern with the dark, repressed side of human nature — the subject of an interesting monologue by a government official near the end — themes that would dominate his work from this point on. An elegant, beguiling work, *The Spanish Scene* illuminates Brossard's fiction as much as it does the Iberian peninsula.

Writing of Brossard in 1959, Mailer prophesized, "It would not surprise me if he appeared with a major work in ten or fifteen years, or however long it takes for the rest of the world to become as real to him as Chandler Brossard" (*Advertisements*, 469). In 1971 that major work appeared under the strange title *Wake Up. We're Almost There*, a mammoth surrealistic epic (with 24 chapters, as in Homer's epics) with a protean repertory company of characters improvising scenes ranging in time and space from the fields of Troy to the battlefields of Vietnam, from Renaissance Italy to Hitler's Germany. Like *Finnegans Wake* (its closest literary analogue), *Wake Up* features a small group of archetypal characters in the dreamworld of a down-at-the-heels New Yorker called (for our purposes) Gelb. Just as Yogi in *The Bold Saboteurs* blacked out into hallucinations to avoid facing his Oedipal conflict, narrator Gelb finds fantasy more hospitable than life with his shrewish wife Sylvia. Their psychotic marriage is driving him up the wall — an image he literalizes on the first page — and at the simplest level *Wake Up* constitutes the psychotic fantasy world he seeks refuge in. But this is only the simplest of the series of increasingly complex levels on which the book operates.

"I feel like Everyman himself" Gelb admits early in the book, and at the next level *Wake Up* illustrates the unconscious weltanschauung of a well-meaning but beleaguered man trying to make sense of the chaotic '60s. Given those surreal times, Brossard cut what few ties he still had with social realism in favor of a full-fledged visionary surrealism. In an essay written for *Harper's* shortly after the publication of *Wake Up* — an essay that illuminates Brossard's conception of his own book — he noted:

> A true visionary fiction, like a myth structure, magically combines, orders, and dramatizes multiple realities. A single level of action, or plot or behavior, does not hold sway, nor does arbitrary sequential time obtain sovereignty. It is not imprisoned within one language system: it has many tongues and voices. One identity does not dominate the speaker's platform and restrict the play and range of sensibility; many identities perform, and they flow in and out of one another. Thus we have a symphonic *communal* statement, in which the culture of the community and its members are resonantly and clearly the same thing, and not separated strangers and antagonists.
>
> For an American "novel" to qualify as authentic fiction-vision, as far as I am concerned, it would have to contain an imaginative orchestration of the sensibilities and actions of Shirley Temple, Dickie Nixon, Lieutenant Calley, General Westmoreland, Blaze Starr, and Huck Finn, and include the spacious sexual folklore of *Screw* and *Suck* and the sniffy mores of *The New Yorker*. In any ten waking hours, all of these identities and genres and their behavior patterns are experienced directly and in fantasy by an intelligent, reasonably sophisticated American. Many, many more

> are experienced by this same person when he is "dreaming" (though that is such a simplistic and denigrating designation for that extraordinary world and its experiences). Why, then, should it be asking too much of our fiction that it represent this rich state of being, this absolutely unalterable fact?[22]

The first paragraph is an exact description of the structure of *Wake Up*; although Gelb is the ostensible narrator, his voice repeatedly gives way to a torrent of other "tongues and voices." (Returning to the simplest level, however, he may be doing no more than "talking to myself in different voices.") A plot summary would be unintelligible if not impossible and, as Brossard indicates, would be antithetical to the nature of this visionary fiction. The "symphonic *communal* statement" that emerges is a radical affirmation "of the wonders, and therefore the chaos, of the human imagination,"[23] set in contrast to all forms of authoritarianism that fear and therefore try to subjugate the imagination by means of enforced conformity, reactionary/imperialistic politics, and a puritanical denial of the body and senses.

Written during the second half of the paradigm-shifting '60s, *Wake Up* is the ultimate countercultural Happening, a psychedelic light show love-in that captures nearly every aspect of that reckless, tumultuous decade. A few years later, Tom Wolfe expressed dismay that novelists for the most part turned their backs on the '60s; publishers, he later discovered,

> had been practically crying for novels by the new writers who must be out there somewhere, the new writers who would do the big novels of hippie life or campus life or radical movements or the war in Vietnam or dope or sex or black militancy or encounter groups or the whole whirlpool all at once. . . . The — New Journalists — Parajournalists — had the whole crazed obscene uproarious Mammon-faced drug-soaked mau-mau lust-oozing Sixties all to themselves.[24]

Not quite. Wolfe read Brossard's *Harper's* essay on the fiction scene — he quotes from it later in the same piece — but he obviously did not read *Wake Up*, for Brossard did indeed take on "the whole whirlpool all at once" in his book: hippies, radical movements and protest marches, black militancy, pop art, encounter groups, Vietnam, mod clothes, Zen, sitar music, protest buttons, sexual liberation, acid rock, terrorism, Kennedy assassination conspiracy theories, nothing less than "the whole obscene uproarious Mammon-faced drug-soaked mau-mau lust-oozing Sixties" in a hallucinatory form that embodies the times better than any work that I know of — fiction or nonfiction — written since then. *Wake Up* is indisputably *the* novel of the '60s.

22 "Commentary (Vituperative): The Fiction Scene," *Harper's*, June 1972, 110.
23 *Wake Up. We're Almost There* (New York: Richard W. Baron, 1971), 465.
24 *The New Journalism* (New York: Harper & Row, 1973), 30–31.

The freethinkers of that decade called into question nearly all the values and assumptions upon which Western civilization rests, and, true to that spirit, *Wake Up* also challenges (and gleefully violates) most literary conventions of the traditional novel. Brossard, of course, had been at odds with that genre from the beginning. Brossard associated the conventional novel with conventional thinking, conventional beliefs, and the political status quo. Given the radical political vision propounded by *Wake Up* — at the halfway point a character says "Sometimes I wonder if all Western civilization will have to vanish — or be vanished — before mankind can begin to be truly himself in all his magnificence" — Brossard obviously felt his medium must be part of the message. Consequently, the organization and sociological orientation of the novel is subversive, trans-schematic, alogical, achronological, pagan, sensual, and goes to extremes that in a conventional novel would be tasteless, incomprehensible, or obscene. The very form of the book is thus calculated to unseat the reader's usual expectations and cultural assumptions (in life or fiction), never allowing the reader to settle back and be told what he or she already knows.

At the verbal level, this is accomplished by way of Brossard's unconventional imagery. The reader with conventional expectations founders at such descriptions as these (all culled from irritated, conventional reviewers):

> Her look was a Roman soldier's spear covered with cow dung.
>
> I'm beginning to feel like the arch of a fallen woman.
>
> The big trouble with people is that they look at themselves as a mouse would look in a mirror.
>
> We made it to a cobbler's shop which had not fixed a shoe for easily a lifetime.

The liberated reader, in contrast, can take such lines two ways: to laugh and move on, or to treat them as Zen koans: alogical propositions intended to break down and subvert imprisoning modes of thinking. One of the main characters in the book is a Zen archer named Zachary, from whom the reader learns enough about Zen to take Brossard's hint that much of his imagery functions as koans and that many of his apparently unconnected episodes function as edifying tales like those told of Zen masters. Brossard does not preface his book with a koan as Salinger does in *Nine Stories*, but the same aesthetic assumptions concerning the applicability of Zen to fiction can be seen at work in both books.

Such imagery draws upon the rich tradition of European visionary fiction that has played so important a part in shaping Brossard's literary sensibility.

The antecedents for the style of *Wake Up* are not to be found in American literature (with the possible exception of *Moby-Dick*) but in writers like Rabelais, Rimbaud and the French symbolists, Babel, Kafka, Céline, Genet, Bataille, and the best middle European writers. Brossard's bizarre imagery is not as disconcerting when placed alongside similar uses of synaesthesia in Malaparte's *Kaputt* ("An icy wind was blowing, the color of a dead child's face") or when aligned with Rimbaud's program for the dislocation of the senses in *A Season in Hell.*

Brossard's aesthetic had more in common with certain avant-garde art and theater movements of the 1960s than anything happening in literature at the time (aside from the works of William S. Burroughs and perhaps the gonzo journalism of Hunter S. Thompson). Underground cinema, the activities of dada-influenced groups like Fluxus, the Lettrist International, and the Situationist International, the improvisational Living Theater, Andy Warhol's Exploding Plastic Inevitable, the Annual New York Avant Garde Festival, standup comedians like Lenny Bruce and George Carlin, and countercultural troupes like the Firesign Theater and Monty Python's Flying Circus provide better parallels for understanding Brossard's later work than literature, which, as Burroughs often pointed out, generally lags 50 years behind the other arts.

After more than five hundred pages of anarchic prose, the final episode of *Wake Up* (533–40) comes as a bit of a shock. Narrator Gelb, "scattering" as does Slothrop near the end of *Gravity's Rainbow*, is transformed into a female character for a slice of suburban life right out of the pages of the *New Yorker*, with no apparent connection with the rest of the book. The formal juxtaposition is instructive: although the story is superb by conventional standards (see Nason's praise quoted earlier), the language is curiously flat and the characters insipidly shallow after the verbal extravaganza the reader has been through. Returning to such fiction as this is like returning to ditch water after Champagne. But the more important implication concerns the shallowness of any non-visionary fiction that does not plumb "the rich state of being" opened up through fantasy and dreams.

Through a dazzling feat of literary sleight of hand, Brossard makes his freak-show narrative appear more "realistic" than this or any other realistic story. He stressed this point in a book review published at the time he was finishing *Wake Up*:

> An amusing thought: The true absurdists of our time are not the avant-garde at all; they are the institutional realists. For what is more absurd than maintaining erect, dignified postures, setting up smooth-working, clean-cut structures, and saying "sensible" things, when all this "reality" is unleashing madness and surrealism? Our

> avant-garde absurdists in the arts are, by comparison, drones of reality. What they are acting absurd about is *real*, not at all absurd. The hatred felt by the establishment groups toward the activists-absurdists (in politics as well as in the arts) is based on the realization that these latter groups are *attempting to introduce reality into their world.*[25]

The contrast between Brossard's reality — imaginative, unfettered, soaring — and that of realistic writers could not be greater, and by the end of this phantasmagoric book, the reader should have no doubt which provides the more accurate picture of the human psyche.

Near the middle of *Wake Up. We're Almost There*, a hunchback reveals his plans for "a real spicy underground film movement for emotionally deprived young. Smut for small fry. I've never understood why pornography should be reserved for grown-ups" (255).[26] Brossard's next publication was a book along these lines retitled *Dirty Books for Little Folks*, which he began while teaching at Old Westbury College on Long Island at the end of the '60s; he would write at least one more such tale after the book's publication in 1978.[27] It's a hilarious collection of Rabelaisian renditions of classic fairy tales in which the Brothers Grimm hit the streets in stained raincoats, selling French postcards. The seven stories feature Jack (of beanstalk fame), a streetwise hustler; Piccolo Pete, the Pied Piper of Hamlin ("I'm to rats what James Joyce was to the contemporary novel"); Hansel and Gretel, an incestuous pair of juvenile delinquents whose most recent prank was derailing the 5:14 train from the Land of Nod ("Twenty-seven fairies killed and fourteen babysitters injured"); Rumpelstiltskin, dressed as a Hell's Angel and expecting kinky returns for his straw-spinning scam; and three versions of Little Red Riding Hood, a sassy skirt into bestiality. Cameos are made by other fairy tale immortals engaged in very un-Disney-like pursuits: Sleeping Beauty rehearsing catatonic trances ("'I think you've just about got it, doll,' said an Old Fairy Coach with her. 'Let's take it from the top one more time'"); Bambi in her first screen test; Snow White in a gang-bang with the Seven Dwarfs; and Tom Thumb and the Goose That Laid the Golden Egg getting drunk together on dago red. Everyone uses a racy street slang laced with loopy metaphors, and the result

25 "All Fall Down: The Culture of Collapse," *Guardian*, 26 April 1969, book supplement, 15.

26 There is a reference to "Smut for small fry" in Brossard's rollicking program notes for the movie *Dead of Night*, "Problems of Being the Real Me" (1960; rpt. in *Film Comment* 10.3 [May–June 1974]: 21), where they figure as a series of stories to which J. Edgar Hoover is addicted.

27 His version of "Goldilocks and the Three Bears" can be found in *As the Wolf Howls at My Door* (Elmwood Park, IL: Dalkey Archive Press, 1992), 314–21. *Dirty Books* was privately printed in France by a friend of Brossard's named Daniel Cointe, who translated and published a French version later in 1978.

is so absurdly funny that one can easily overlook the subtle implications of these risqué tales. By "outing" the sexual symbolism latent in fairy tales, Brossard not only dramatizes the tales' erotic tensions but also draws attention to other dynamics at work therein, such as power structures, class struggles, and economic exploitation — fairy tales as psychosexual case studies.

In their own way, Brossard's tales are closer in spirit and subject matter to the tales actually circulated by the peasantry before they were sanitized by Perrault and the Grimm brothers. The original tales contained everything "from rape and sodomy to incest and cannibalism," historian Robert Darnton has pointed out. "Far from veiling their message with symbols, the storytellers of eighteenth-century France portrayed a world of raw and naked brutality."[28] Brossard portrays just such a world, and his pornographic versions of "Little Red Riding Hood," for example, are right in line with 18th-century versions of the tale in which, Maria Tatar tells us, "the heroine unwittingly eats the flesh and blood of her grandmother, is called a slut by her grandmother's cat, and performs a slow striptease for the wolf."[29] *Dirty Books* is a daring attempt to remedy the efforts of generations of "bony, tight-lipped, self-appointed censors and translators [who have] disguised, rerouted, suppressed, and sometimes eliminated entirely certain meanings and messages, whole layers of involvement, that would have made childhood substantially richer, more interesting, less feebleminded and smelly" (*As the Wolf Howls*, 177). But it would probably be a mistake to over-read these tales; they contain depths, to be sure, but are satisfying enough at the surface level to be admitted into the small circle of genuinely funny erotica.[30] (In a 1987 interview Brossard said that Terry Southern's comic erotic novel *Candy* was the only work of recent American fiction he admired.) *Dirty Books* also belongs to the growing number of innovative revisions of fairy tales — many of which likewise emphasize the erotic — such as Donald Barthelme's *Snow White* (1967), Angela Carter's *The Bloody Chamber* (1979), Karen Elizabeth Gordon's *The Red Shoes* (1996), Francesca Lia Block's *The Rose and the Beast* (2000), and several imaginative works by Robert Coover and Tanith Lee.

In 1970 Brossard left Old Westbury for the University of Birmingham in England, where he spent a year as a visiting professor at the Centre for Contemporary Cultural Studies. There he wrote his only fiction with a British

28 *The Great Cat Massacre and Other Episodes in French Cultural History* (New York: Basic Books, 1984), 15.

29 *The Hard Facts of the Grimms' Fairy Tales* (Princeton: Princeton U P, 2003), 23.

30 For other readings of these tales, see S. Ramnath's "Chandler Brossard: A Critical Study of *Dirty Books for Little Folks*," John Coyne's "Dirty Books," and William Levy's "The Abuses of Enchantment," all in *RCF* 7.1 (Spring 1987).

setting, a novella entitled *A Chimney Sweep Comes Clean.*[31] At least three different narrators — none of whom, by the way, is actually a chimney sweep — come clean on a variety of British foibles and eccentricities in a comic style that mixes surreal metaphors, Beckettian dialogue, Zen koan one-liners, and philosophical cobwebs spun from puns and non sequiturs. The result is something like cultural anthropology as written by the Marx Brothers. And there's lots of raunchy sex — though the spirit is more *Benny Hill* than *Fanny Hill* — which was another advantage to publishing in the small press underground.

Ten loosely linked episodes turn a funhouse mirror on British customs and expose the fundamental propositions underlying that culture. As a gamesome English mum explains (while carnally engaged with an American visitor): "The prototypical Englishman-woman is held together by an anxiety system that prevents him from seeing or otherwise making significant contact with emotions or events that would precipitate an irrevocably intimate moment of thereness. The English exist, in a very real sense, by not existing. He is a compilation of seedy abstractions, interlocking arrangements of distancing that permit him to be, at all times, a spectator to his own pseudo-participation. He is the good-bye to his own hello." Although British culture is as ridiculous as its American counterpart (which he fled several times in his life, always to return), it lacks the viciousness Brossard found in much of American life, and as a result there is a lighter tone here than in his earlier works.

The ten chapters are best understood not as linked, sequential sections of a narrative, but rather as Pythonesque skits or, better yet, as "situations" in the sense the Situationist International used the term: "constructed encounters and creatively lived moments in specific urban settings, instances of a critically transformed everyday life."[32] The SI had a political agenda, hoping to introduce chance, adventure, and variety into habitual activities, thereby freeing individuals from the tyranny of routine, consumerism, and from what SI theorist Guy Debord called "the society of the spectacle." Brossard introduces the same elements into his narratives, hoping to free the reader from the predictability of so much fiction.

To be sure, there are some ugly facets to British life that surface here and there in *Chimney Sweep*, and Brossard's laughter may indeed be masking the cry of Pagliacci. (In a letter to me, he explained: "I wrote *Chimney* while I was

31 The first chapter was published in *Evergreen Review* in 1971, but the complete book wasn't published until late 1984 by Realities Library of San Jose, California.

32 Peter Wollen, "Bitter Victory: The Art and Politics of the Situationist International," in *On the Passage of a Few People through a Rather Brief Moment in Time: The Situationist International*, 1957–1972, ed. Elisabeth Sussman (Cambridge: MIT Press, 1989), 22. See also Greil Marcus, *Lipstick Traces: A Secret History of the Twentieth Century* (Cambridge: Harvard University Press, 1989).

teaching at Birmingham while living in a charming, nutsy bed-sit — freezing, etc. — in West Kensington. I think I was off my rocker at the time — at the absurdness of my life, at the awfulness of the quality of life in England, at the amusing fucking lunacy of the people — I became the sensibility in the book, out of pain, out of a need to adapt or perish. Laughing while sobbing, you might say.") The novella ends with an apocalyptic vision of London buried in its own garbage, but it's a comic send-up that owes more to bemusement than to contempt.

The work that *Chimney Sweep* most closely resembles is Richard Brautigan's *Trout Fishing in America*, published a few years earlier (1967). I don't know if Brossard ever read this novel — he did read, but didn't like, Brautigan's short-story collection, *Revenge of the Lawn* (1971) — but there are the same kind of off-the-wall humor and bizarre metaphors in both books. The original edition of *Chimney Sweep* even resembles *Trout Fishing in America* physically: both were slim books with photographic covers set in the same typewriter font. It could have been called *Muff Diving in England.*

By the time Brossard went to England in 1970 he was a committed antiwar activist, and in fact he spent some of his time there working for an organization that aided North Vietnamese victims of American atrocities in Vietnam.[33] After finishing *A Chimney Sweep Comes Clean*, he began writing the outraged and outrageous *Raging Joys, Sublime Violations.* Of the large body of Vietnam War fiction, this has to be one of the most bizarre literary responses to the war and one of the most damning indictments of the American sensibility responsible for that intervention. *Raging Joys* is not a war novel in any conventional sense, but rather a series of field reports narrated by a cultural anthropologist who describes himself late in the book as "a freelance vulture circling over the compost heap that is Western civilization, an insatiable death-bird waiting to plunge upon any morsel of rottenness and decay." The telling original title for this book was "History as Language and Human Garbage."[34]

The narrative strategy is a brilliant example of what the Situationist International called *détournement*, in which statements or images from one context are "displaced and estranged before being subsequently reinscribed and transformed through radical juxtaposition."[35] In each of *Raging Joys*' 17 "situ-

33 For a brief account of these activities, see Jay Landesman's *Jaywalking* (London: Weidenfeld & Nicolson, 1992), 102–3.

34 An early version of the final chapter of *Raging Joys* was published under this title in Paul Krassner's *The Realist*, 92-C (May-June 1972): 1–8 (whole issue), where the work is described by Brossard as "the beginning of a long fiction having to do with American culture and the destruction of Indo China" (1). Although completed by 1973, it wasn't published until 1981, by Cherry Valley Editions of Silver Spring, Maryland.

35 Thomas Y. Levin, "Dismantling the Spectacle: The Cinema of Guy Debord," in *On the*

ations" (a better term than chapters or episodes), Brossard develops a surreal, often raunchy ambience in which official statements on the Vietnam war intrude at unexpected moments: interdepartmental softball strategy in Washington gets mixed up with military tactics in Vietnam; a discussion of former porn star Linda Lovelace doubles as a discussion of the Kennedy assassination; a guided tour of the Balearic island of Minorca is interrupted by testimonies from Vietnamese victims of American bombing missions. Severed from their original contexts, these statements join the surrealistic sideshows going on around them (often a sexual scenario, reinforcing the rape metaphor inherent in imperialism of most sorts) and thus emerge as bizarre as any of Brossard's fantasies. In their new contexts, official policy statements sound like the ravings of madmen. Several other language permutations occur: the boring predictability of governmental announcements clash against the lively unpredictability of Brossard's language. The reader will find him/herself swinging along from vine to vine with Brossard's dazzling language only to suddenly hit a tree in the form of State Department rhetoric. The language of politics is as dead and dishonest as the culture it speaks for, whereas Brossard's daring metaphoric prose, free of causality and logic as well as of bourgeois ideology, asserts the primacy of the imagination. (Although Brossard sympathized with revolutionaries, he also mocks the theatrical rhetoric of agitprop and parodies Chairman Mao's *Little Red Book.*)

The 17 "field reports" hopscotch in time from the Kennedy administration to the early '70s, and range geographically from Tibet to Belgium, from "la belle France" to Washington, DC, ending in a Minorca that seems to belong more to Burroughs's Interzone than to Spain. (There is also an interview with an ex-Peace Corpsman in Nicaragua on the problems of American intervention there — a remarkable piece of prophecy on Brossard's part considering he wrote the book in 1971–73.) Also included are a number of scandalously funny interviews with political figures such as Dean Acheson, Allen and John Foster Dulles, Reagan, the Kennedy brothers, Nixon, Kissinger, and a letter home to mother by Hubert Humphrey. Like Burroughs's "Roosevelt after Inauguration," Paul Krassner's "The Parts Left Out of the Kennedy Book," and the more salacious sections of Robert Coover's *The Public Burning*, these episodes translate the shameless depravity of some politicians into the grossest sexual terms in a bold attempt to shock the reader into a realization of the true nature of certain political actions. When traditional, polite forms of political discourse fail, as they had by the early '70s as the Vietnam War dragged on, this sort of guerilla fiction must have struck Brossard as the only way he could

Passage of a Few People, 77. See also Levin's note 6 on page 110 for a further discussion of this key SI term.

register the depth of his disgust with the dominant ideology.[36]

And yet, as they say, truth is stranger than fiction. In this book Brossard portrays politicians as little better than bullies and perverts, and recent revelations suggest he wasn't too far off the mark. At one point he has J. Edgar Hoover stroll by in a dress, an outrageous slander in 1973 but now a common subject of gossip and jokes. In his book of memoirs, Krassner tells "the story of a journalist who had once interviewed LBJ, and after the formal question-and-answer session was over, the president told him, 'You know, what the Communists are really saying is, "Fuck you, Lyndon Johnson," and nobody says "Fuck you, Lyndon Johnson," and gets away with it!'"[37] The schoolyard swagger and petty egotism of this threat could have been lifted straight from *Raging Joys*, and the scene where a politician seduces his teenage admirer (a prospective intern?) should not surprise, much less shock, anyone who remembers the Clinton administration.

The very form of *Raging Joys* represents an attack on conservative narrative as yet another facet of imperialist American ideology. Just as Wagner inserted a traditional aria in *Tannhäuser* to show his detractors he could write such things if he wished, Brossard at one point includes a realistic description of a Nicaraguan outpost that is splendid by conventional standards. But this is followed by a fierce denunciation of such narrative conventions for creating "smugness and self-deception, aesthetic and political status-quoism, cultural and humanistic fraud, and endless spectatorship empathy." One of the more sobering implications of this passage is that we are as much victims of our own language systems as the North Vietnamese were victims of our bombing raids (with the obvious difference that devious language doesn't kill us or destroy our homes). At any rate, this startling book should earn a privileged place in any future discussions of the American literary response to the Vietnam War.[38]

After a four-year break from writing in the mid '70s — the only break in his long career — Brossard began a mammoth fictional project, originally called "Somebody's Been Sleeping in My Bed," that resolved itself into two books: the longer, originally called *Come Out with Your Hands Up*, was finished in 1981 but not published until a decade later under the title *As the Wolf Howls*

36 See also Brossard's "Why the Death Machine Could Die Laughing," *Penthouse*, April 1972, 32–34, 104, 106, a highly critical exposé of recent advances in weapons technology and their deployment in Vietnam.

37 *Confessions of a Raving, Unconfined Nut* (New York: Simon & Schuster, 1993), 165.

38 The only such discussion I know of is Philip D. Beidler's excellent essay "*Raging Joys, Sublime Violations:* The Vietnam War in the Fiction of Chandler Brossard," *RCF* 7.1 (Spring 1987): 166–75.

at My Door. Like *Wake Up*, which it resembles in some ways, the 460-page novel uses a central narrative consciousness through whom a torrent of voices rushes, flooding the book with the collective unconscious of the time. Having written one of the best novels about the '60s, Brossard here takes on the '70s: a time of despair as the dreams and ideals of the '60s were cashed in for political opportunism and crass materialism. America's inglorious exit from Vietnam, the expansion of repressive CIA operations (working hand-in-glove with oppressive regimes in Chile, Iran, and Angola), the commodification of the American Way — all this and more in Brossard's zany, hyper-maximalist style.

That style mixes French surrealism and theatrical absurdity with Beat improvisation and performance art confrontation. Brossard's avalanche language is outrageous: incongruous diction, insidious non sequiturs, pathetically funny fallacies, bellowing oxymorons, barking doggerel, breezy colloquialisms, Zen koan-like metaphors, subverted jargon, free-association imagery — all making a joyful noise in a variety of genres: picaresque adventures in the radical underground, folksy travelogues, porno fairy tales, suspiciously well-made stories set in the Kennedy years, political testimony, sexual role-playing, metafictional hijinks, and ending in dramatic form (from the autobiographical play *My Side of the Story* by Moby Dick). A kind of verbal delirium possesses the text, which on the most realistic level is about countercultural activities in Paris, Amsterdam, Madrid, and London; on another level, it may be the psychotic outpourings of a woman named Decca Aldridge (who is so stupefied by her life on an American army base in Spain that she escapes via hallucination);[39] on yet another, it is the "mammoth, organic fiction" (80) of an American writer named Welles Ewing, also living in Spain, which turns into a script by one of his fictional creations, impresario Socks Peelmunder, for a guerrilla theater performance; and on the final level, an exposé of the gamy underside of America's subconscious — a terrifying lava flow of provincial prejudices, racial fears, political paranoia, and sexist attitudes, all speaking in tongues in a desperate attempt to bolt the door against the return of the repressed.

There is a brief but significant reading list on p. 133 that names a few of the sources of Brossard's ideology: James Aronson's *The Press and the Cold War* (1970; mistitled in the novel), Noam Chomsky's *American Power and the New Mandarins* (1969), Stanley Cohen's *The Manufacture of the News* (1973), and Jules Henry's *Culture Against Man* (1965), the last one especially important for Brossard's anti-Americanism. A character also recommends the writings of Christopher Caudwell (1907–1937, author of *Studies in a Dying Culture*): "He's terrific. He analyzes capitalist society right down to the corn-

39 The jacket cover photo Brossard supplied was intended to represent her alter ego, Decca Records.

cob up its asshole" (132).

The language used in "this ad hoc saturnalia (this magical minestrone, this hyperactive labyrinth, this . . .)" (121) is frequently hilarious and therapeutic: "It is the exquisitely liberating and purifying laughter of complete absurdity" (18). But it has a serious purpose as well; the unfettered, insurrectionary use of language is the only way the narrator(s) can survive the deluge of state-sponsored horrors that runs through the work: "Screams do not help man climb out of the abyss. Only language can do that. It is the sharp instrument with which he patiently carves his upward hand- and footholds in the sheer walls of the abyss. Without it he is forever doomed to pace at the bottom of these walls and claw at them in anguished futility" (273).

In his appreciative review, Joseph Coates rightly placed *As the Wolf Howls* in the Menippean satire genre,[40] but it (like *Wake Up*) is a textbook example of what critic Robert Buckeye in the 1960s called the psychic novel:

> The psychic novel sees reality to be multiple and uncertain; presents a protagonist who is conscious of the masks he wears in the world; and dramatizes the unceasing struggle between them. Its subject is the incomplete and unfulfilled; its form, psychic; its method, reflexive parody and satire; and its aim, the creation and preservation of psychic identity in the face of history which renders events and actions meaningless as well as science and technology which reduce man to mechanical and operational, the biological and behavioral. The psychic novel is precisely that fiction in which subjective and objective, dream and reality, merge and blur; . . .[41]

Buckeye's term never caught on, but it is an accurate description of "what is undoubtedly — along with Robert Coover's *The Public Burning* and Pynchon's *Gravity's Rainbow* — one of the last mad epics of the West," as Coates wrote, capturing "the last thrashing throes of the Cold War mentality at its irrational peak" before it mutated into more recent neocon misadventures abroad and right-wing extremism in the U.S.

The shorter book Brossard wrote alongside *As the Wolf Howls* was published as *Postcards: Don't You Just Wish You Were Here!*, which he began in the late '70s when he was looking for a house in San Francisco. His wife, Maria Ewing Huffman, staying in Aspen at the time with their young daughter Genève (the dedicatees of most of his later works), began receiving comical prose "postcards" from her husband from such imaginary places as Over My Dead Body, Minnesota, and Horse of Another Color, Maine. After settling in San Francisco, Brossard continued to write more of them until he had enough for a short book.

40 "Chandler Brossard's Erotic, Satirical Epic," *Chicago Tribune*, 19 July 1992.
41 "The Anatomy of the Psychic Novel," *Critique* 9.2 (1967): 33–34.

As eerie as it is funny, *Postcards* is a kind of folksy walking tour through a Kafkaesque Amerika and extends Brossard's use of the non sequitur to expose the general non sequitur nature of modern America. (Ironically, Brossard couldn't find an American publisher for it; the chapbook was eventually published in England by Redbeck Press in 1987.) The book overlaps at some points with *As the Wolf Howls*, which opens with a postcard from Mum's the Word, South Carolina, and features some similar travelogues (pp. 21–24, 52–57, 90–93, 161–67, 214–22, 290–97). But it marks an important turning point in Brossard's writing; it's free of the outrage and heavy profanity that characterized much of his preceding work, and displays the more playful attitude toward language, especially the American vernacular, that characterizes his final writings.

Brossard's approach to language in this whimsical travelogue extends a technique introduced in *Raging Joys*. There, when John F. Kennedy challenges Aristotle Onassis to an arm-wrestling match, we have this exchange:

> "Try not to cheat, Ari," said Jack. "I know what you greaseballs can do with your elbows."
>
> Ted Sorensen coughed and said, "The expression 'elbow grease' can't really be broken down and reassembled that way, Jack. In the first place . . ."

The late president cuts his speechwriter off, but this is exactly what Brossard delights in doing in *Postcards*: breaking down idioms and clichés and reassembling them, usually with hilarious results. Some may be reminded again of Brautigan's *Trout Fishing in America*, others of Robert Walser's microscripts or the homespun surrealism of Bob Dylan's *Basement Tapes*-era songs. The book may also reflect the metropolitan suspicion that the hicks out in the sticks are just plain weird; but Brossard, though a lifelong urbanite, shows an affectionate regard for his colorful rubes and their dairy-state dementia.

Like late-period Samuel Beckett (whom he didn't care for), Brossard continued paring down his fiction, reducing it to essentials. Paragraphs became shorter, sentences crumbled into fragments, exposition was eliminated, leaving only disembodied voices. In *Closing the Gap*, written in the early '80s (and also published by Redbeck Press in 1986), Brossard anticipated the later trend for very short stories (variously called sudden fictions or flash fictions) in these ten "meditations," for lack of a better word,[42] on such subjects as intimacy, cave explorers, handmaidens, backbiting, den mothers, and clochards.

42 *Meditation* is the title of Kafka's first book of short stories (1913), brief, uncanny pieces not unlike Brossard's. "One could call them Sufi epiphanies," Brossard himself wrote of *Closing the Gap*. "They are not really prose poems. They're fictions, linguistic/philosophic moments" (CAAS, 71).

But such unlikely subjects are merely springboards for brilliant improvisations in a style that combines dazzling wit and wordplay with an edgy sense of foreboding. Often he rings punning changes on a particular word or phrase; for example, alerting the reader that "Evidence is mounting that we have been neglecting our handmaidens," Brossard pulls one rabbit after another out of his vernacular hat: "They are walking about in hand-me-downs. They are living from hand to mouth. Making do with handouts. And it would appear they are getting absolutely no feedback. Throwing them completely on the mercy of hearsay. They're still too proud to stoop to lip service" — and so on, concluding with mock solemnity: "Can the common man in our streets be expected to make a wise choice between Made by Hand and Hand in Your Maidens?"

This is obviously language at play, words sporting on the page like dolphins in the sea. The principle at work here can be found in Johan Huizinga's *Homo Ludens* (a book Brossard knew well, also a key text for the Situationists): "In the making of speech and language the spirit is continually 'sparking' between matter and mind, as it were, playing with this wonderful nominative faculty. Behind every abstract expression there lie the boldest of metaphors, and every metaphor is a play upon words."[43] *Closing the Gap* reminds us of the metaphoric origin of our most common words and phrases by putting the oldest of dogs through lively new tricks.

Encroaching upon this playfulness, however, is a faint air of dread and menace, a premonition of danger, and in fact the work closes on just such a note: "Covering one's tracks. It's never too early to begin." Like receiving somber advice in a dream that turns to gibberish upon waking, the reader might find the otherworldly language of *Closing the Gap* as difficult to comprehend as a Zen koan and often as unsettling as the deadly wit of Lear's Fool. Time and again, the smile is wiped from the reader's face, the carpet pulled out from under her by an unnerving witticism. A glimpse is caught of what Gershom Scholem called "the abyss which becomes visible in the gaps of existence." But in the end, Brossard more often than not closes these gaps with bravura feats of wordplay reminiscent of Joyce's Shem the Penman.

Novels, short stories, plays, essays, reviews, travelogues, anthologies, photodocumentaries — the only genre Brossard had never tried was poetry, but suddenly, for two months in 1989, he became possessed by it and wrote a cycle of two dozen poems, to which he later gave the title *Traditionally a Place of Banishment*. The late '80s were a difficult time for him, having separated from his wife and enduring several bouts of illness on top of loneliness, depression, and purposelessness. He wrote most of these poems in museums, in particular

43 *Homo Ludens* (1938; Boston: Beacon, 1955), 4.

the Museum of Modern Art in Manhattan, where he would spend his days when not in library reading rooms. The arrival of these poems — he spoke of them as "breaking out" spontaneously, writing themselves, as it were — signaled an end to that period of despair and brought him back "among the living."[44] The diction of the poems recalls that of *Closing the Gap*, but there is an attention to rhyme and cadence, a tone of tenderness and regret that is new to his work.

Brossard began *Shifty Sacred Songs* in September 1990 and finished almost a year later in August 1991.[45] The work began as a kind of companion piece to *Closing the Gap*, but moved in a direction that took the author by surprise. About halfway through the composition of these "songs," Brossard wrote to me about them:

> I'm quite surprised by the almost surreptitious emergence of religious reference, or feeling, or something. It gets stronger as the pieces mount. I think it's possible that, in a hidden, almost shamefaced way, I have always been drawn to the saints and to Him, as men — or women — of extraordinary quality. No God, of course. But I think this is only a surface explanation. Also, I suspect that as I get nearer the grave, my thoughts and my searchings are for something outside my mortal reach. For something I can "look up to." Something I can behold with wonder and love.

After he finished the final song, he again wrote me: "It's strange. Now that I think about them, I can't quite believe that I wrote them. Some strange religious sect in my brain poured them out. Find the perpetrators! Bring them to trial?"[46] Like the pieces in *Closing the Gap*, they often explore the implications of particular nouns, but instead of playing and punning with them, Brossard personifies them and broods on them with a kind of bittersweetness and poignancy. There are some superficially reactionary tendencies here — Brossard sings the praises of royalty and tyranny, attacks modernism — but in his hands these terms are abstracted to the point where they have little bearing on their real-life counterparts. When Brossard discusses a tyrant's wardrobe — "A tyrant's jacket must hang just so. Lest he be mistaken for a mere bully with grandiose ideas" — it's clear the old revolutionary hasn't changed his tune, just modulated it to a different key. He called these pieces songs in the sense that the Psalms of David are songs, and while largely secular, there is an openhearted, yearning quality to his meditations that in other ages would have been called religious.[47] There is "no God, of course," as he says in his

44 The quoted phrases are from a letter to me postmarked 6 September 1989.

45 Both it and *Traditionally a Place of Banishment* were published posthumously in Brossard's *Over the Rainbow? Hardly: Collected Short Seizures* (Sun Dog Press, 2005).

46 The two letters I've quoted from are postmarked 15 May and 23 August 1991.

47 For this reason, Brossard eliminated an early song on sandwiches, which seemed out of

letter, and yet a capitalized He haunts the last of these songs, on "Virtue." I like to think of them as postmodern psalms. So ended the writing career of this unclassifiable writer.

Although I consider Brossard to be one of the most daring and innovative writers of our time, not to mention one of the funniest, it is difficult to evaluate his work by the usual standards because it deliberately violates so many of the norms used to evaluate literature. In Brossard's case, it is difficult enough to decide even what genre his later works belong to, much less what to make of them. Even if one does evaluate Brossard's work in a positive light, as I've obviously done here, it is nearly impossible to convince others of its worth: there are certain writers, like Mark Leyner (who sometimes sounds like Brossard on steroids) or Ronald Firbank, who are so idiosyncratic that one instinctively likes or dislikes them, and no amount of critical persuasion one way or another is going to change anyone's mind. His work is united by a common theme — "the inevitable conflict between man's instinctual drives and the demands of civilization" (*As the Wolf Howls*, 448) — but it is safe to say that the stylistic, formal distance Brossard traveled from *Who Walk in Darkness* to *Shifty Sacred Songs* in pursuit of this theme is as great as that of any other writer of our time.

Suffice it to say Chandler Brossard remains a unique presence in postwar American literature and deserves far more attention than he has hitherto received. If you missed Lear's Fool doing his stand-up routine at Dachau, catch Brossard's act: he wrote the Fool's material, and works matinees to boot.

place by the time he finished the other pieces. It was published with two other songs in *World Letter* 1.1 (1991): 14–17.

The Legend of Alan Ansen

> And so the legend of A.J. the laughable, lovable eccentric grew and grew . . .
>
> —William Burroughs, *Naked Lunch*

Although Alan Ansen's name is known only to a small number of Beat scholars and Auden specialists, his flamboyant personality is known to the millions of readers of the Beat quadrumvirate of Kerouac, Burroughs, Ginsberg, and Corso. As Rollo Greb in *On the Road* and Austin Bromberg in *The Subterraneans*, he exemplifies the illusive "it" for which Kerouac and friends drive in quest. As A.J. in *Naked Lunch*, he opposes his anarchic individualism to the addictive conformity advocated by such groups as the Liquefactionists and Divisionists. He appears under his own name in a few of Ginsberg's poems (as well as in his journals and letters), and under such unflattering sobriquets as Dad Deform and Death in the writings of Gregory Corso. He is even dreamed about in Irving Rosenthal's *Sheeper* (1967).

Perhaps it is novelist William Gaddis who has best delineated the enormous influence Ansen had on the Beats. Gaddis said it had always seemed to him that in the spate of material about the so-called Beat scene of the '50s he had seen, too little note had been taken of Ansen's part in influencing, "you could almost say educating a number of those younger talents. It was Ansen's unrestrained enthusiasm at sharing his own rather marvelous store, languages, literature, Bellini, the works, his hunger for work well done or the hope of it, and it was terribly infectious."[1] The fullest display of Ansen's remarkable character can be found, of course, in his dozen books of poetry, the best from which make up this volume.[2] And to a great extent, Ansen tells his own story in his Popian "Epistle to Chester Kallman" included herein. What follows, then, can be considered an extended annotation to that and his other autobiographical poems, as well as an attempt to chart with greater precision Ansen's role in the literary history of his time.

Alan Joseph Ansen was born 23 January 1922 in Brooklyn, New York, the only child of William and Bessie (née Blum) Ansen. Raised first in Brooklyn and then in Woodmere, Long Island, Ansen had a privileged, conventional upbringing, complete with violin lessons. In his poem "Imperfect Tributes" he recalls his early desire to escape "from the family meal's determined con-

1 [From an unpublished letter to me dated 8 November 1985. See also *The Letters of William Gaddis*, ed. Steven Moore (Champaign, IL: Dalkey Archive Press, 2013), 390–91.]

2 [*Contact Highs: Selected Poems 1957–1987*, Dalkey Archive Press, 1989.]

versation about nothing / for us and the group games of loathsome children in the same economic bracket." Like many an only child — "I have no brother with surpassing glory crowned" he writes later in the same poem (echoing Gloucester near the end of *Henry VI, Part 3*) — Ansen turned to books for companionship,

> To the gramarye books where gangs decoded sestinas,
> icy gentlemen smoked hashish taking careful notes all the while,
> Satan defied his parent in language that made our eyes bug out but we
> instinctively felt a little beyond us
> And graceful Athenians persuaded us that heaven was pure mind

Ansen left Woodmere Academy to enter Harvard in the fall of 1938. There he studied Classics, with a special interest in Greek lyric poetry, and impressed friends and teachers with his scholarly abilities. Once, after Ansen had left a conversation with two fellow students in the Classics Department, one said to the other, "Either he is the most impressive intellectual phony that I have ever seen or he is one of the brightest people in this college."[3] The latter judgment was confirmed as Ansen went on to accumulate one of the highest grade point averages the college had seen in some time. At Harvard he also met a few of the people he would later see in postwar Greenwich Village, such as Ed Stringham and Alan Harrington, two of the more intellectual members of the Beat generation. Writing his bachelor's thesis on Milton's prose, Ansen graduated summa cum laude in 1942, and began graduate work only to leave after taking the M.A. the same year to return to Woodmere.[4]

There in what he calls (in the "Epistle") his "suburban retreat," Ansen continued his studies while war raged overseas. Speaking for himself as well as for friends like Burroughs and Gaddis, he later wrote of this period: "All of us who failed to participate in the war effort owing to one form of unclubbability or another have, I think, felt the necessity to conduct private wars of our own."[5] But his own private war would not be declared until later; still the devoted scholar, he was attracted by a course to be given in New York by W. H. Auden. As he later explained in a letter to Dorothy Farnan:

> I attended Wystan's lectures on Shakespeare at the New School for Social Research, beginning in October 1946. I enrolled for the additional seminar he gave on Saturday afternoons (the lectures were on Wednesday evenings), I helped him carry records

3 Letter from Howard Hageman to me, 2 June 1986.

4 [Beat scholar Bill Morgan says Ansen "had been forced out of Harvard under a cloud of homosexual scandal" in his *I Celebrate Myself: The Somewhat Private Life of Allen Ginsberg* (New York: Viking, 2006), 239.]

5 "Anyone Who Can Pick Up a Frying Pan Owns Death," *Big Table* 2.2 (Summer 1959): 33.

> home after a small riot he caused by playing Verdi's *Falstaff* in lieu of lecturing on *The Merry Wives of Windsor*, which he described as a very boring play.
>
> It was good education, but he rather rubbed it in by spending the time absorbed in the libretto rather than providing the scintillating commentary of which he would have been perfectly capable. I wrote a paper for him on *The Sea and the Mirror* [Auden's poetic commentary on *The Tempest*], and after he read it, he said, "You've seen the figure in my carpet."[6]

"It was the happiest moment of my life" when Auden leaned over to Ansen on the way to the podium and made this remark, and it was largely on the basis of this brilliant essay — a 52,000 word monograph entitled "Crisis and Festival," unfortunately never published — that Auden asked Ansen to go through the draft of his *Age of Anxiety* to point out errors in the syllabification of the verse.[7] When the book was published in July of 1947, Auden gave him a copy inscribed "To Alan, my conscience, from careless Wystan," which is now on deposit, along with "Crisis and Festival" and Ansen's notes on his conversations with Auden, in the Berg Collection at the New York Public Library.

In January of 1947 Auden introduced his student to his lifelong companion Chester Kallman, a year older than Ansen. The importance of Auden and Kallman to Ansen cannot be overestimated, and until their deaths in the 1970s they remained central to his life. Devoted opera lovers, they introduced Ansen to "the fascinating noise / Italian opera makes" — which he had "spurned / Thitherto as insufficiently serious," preferring Wagner since high school days.[8] Within a year he was firmly entrenched in Auden's world, as indicated in the following extended quotation from Farnan's *Auden in Love*:

> It was partly because of the paper Alan wrote on *The Sea and the Mirror*, which Wystan told Chester was the most brilliant he has ever read, that Alan eventually joined the group on East Twenty-seventh Street. He was embraced, if not always wholeheartedly by all of Chester's friends, at least wholeheartedly by Chester's family, who adored him, for he was a weekly visitor at Eddie's [Chester's father]. Alan would come to New York on Saturday evenings from his home on Long Island, where, since the death of both parents in 1948, he was living with his guardian, an elegant maiden aunt who wore white kid gloves and hats. First he would appear at Eddie's new place in the London Terrace for drinks and dinner. Then he would go out to celebrate Saturday nights with his friends, and, bedraggled but happy, return to Eddie's for Sunday supper. "I decided to come back," he would say each week, "because I am just in the

6 Dorothy J. Farnan, *Auden in Love* (New York: Simon and Schuster, 1984), 165. [For more on Ansen's recollections, now see Arthur Kirsch's edition of Auden's *Lectures on Shakespeare* (Princeton: Princeton University Press, 2000.]

7 [Now see Alan Jacobs's annotated edition of *The Age of Anxiety* (Princeton: Princeton University Press, 2011), specifically pp. xliii-xlvi, for details on Ansen's work on the poem.]

8 [Unidentified lines of poetry can be assumed hereafter to be from Ansen's "Epistle to Chester Kallman" (pp. 147–63 in *Contact Highs*).]

mood for a quiet, soap opera kind of Sunday afternoon *en famille*. I am also ravenously hungry. What's to eat?" and he would turn his face shyly to the side, giggle, and walk into the living room. Whereupon Eddie or I would serve him a drink, a stinger or the usual dry martini, and he would sit down to brains vinaigrette, braised kidneys, and a fowl served with white wine before he left to catch the 10:58 back to his aunt, who by this time was nervously making telephone calls.

When you thought of Alan, you immediately thought of his laugh. He would bend his head coyly to the side, focus his brown eyes demurely upon the rug, giggle, and at the same time pat his forehead with his thick-fingered right hand. Then, if really amused, he would roar with full-throated ease, raising his face heavenward, all the while continuing to pat his forehead, the more energetically as he enjoyed the joke. Chester had already baptized him Allegra from the third stanza of [Longfellow's] "The Children's Hour."

Although he came from a well-to-do family, he was more than economical. As he himself put it, he did not want ever to work. He wished to spend his time as a gentleman and a scholar — and a poet — and that takes money. He had an inherited income, and he had to make it last. Therefore, he never spent a penny unwisely. He took to the habit of wearing secondhand clothes, mostly those worn by his father before him, and once appeared on a beach with Chester's brother Malcolm and Malcolm's fiancée in a bathing suit of a generation past, so moth-eaten that one could hardly discern the suit. When he voted, he voted for the man who was best for real estate.

During the week on Long Island, where he was beginning to cause his aunt-guardian much concern, he systematically studied his literature, kept up with his ancient Greek, and wrote his poetry from prime to sext (he was now following W. H. Auden's *horae canonicae*), and from sext to nones he listened to soap operas. He could discuss every plot of every soap opera on the radio. In the evening he would read himself to sleep from his vast library, at least two shelves of which were devoted to detective stories. Like Wystan, he liked detective stories, but they had to follow prescribed rules, one of which was that they provided their readers with sufficient evidence to solve the problems themselves. He always carried at least two of these paperbacks in his pocket when in New York, and if you rode with him on the train or on the subway, he would take one out, hand it to you, say, "Here, read, but give it back," and immerse himself in the other book forthwith. He was also an authority on W. H. Auden and stated his intention of being Boswell to Wystan's Johnson, until, that is, he discovered that W. H. Auden did not want a biographer or a biography. He could quote poem after poem — Wystan's as well as those of others — as the spirit moved him, and he could quote them letter perfect.[9]

Auden's world overlapped the wilder one that revolved around Bill Cannastra, a brilliant, handsome, self-destructive lawyer who held saturnalian par-

9 *Auden in Love*, 165–67. As Ansen had not yet begun writing poetry, Farnan must mean Ansen wrote his *criticism* from prime to sext, i.e., from 6 AM to noon. And she is imprecise on the date of his parents' deaths: Ansen's mother died in October 1947 on the ship back from her only trip to Europe, his father in March of the following year. [For Ansen's Boswellian activities, now see his *The Table Talk of* W. H. *Auden*, ed. Nicholas Jenkins (Sea Cliff Press, 1989; Ontario Review Press, 1990).]

ties in his loft at 125 West 21st Street. Kallman took Ansen to a Halloween party at Cannastra's in 1947, "and I was fascinated with him," he later wrote. "He had very good taste in literature and music (an early admirer of *The Real Life of Sebastian Knight*, for example). And he provided a salon where the Audenites and the future Beats could mingle. I don't think Burroughs was ever there, but Ginsberg, Kerouac and Lucien Carr were."[10] Despite his personal fascination with Cannastra, Ansen found his world less appealing than Auden's, and evinced an initial distaste for the Beat crowd, especially for the shy Kerouac. As Kerouac biographer Gerald Nicosia explains,

> One of the literary mandarins of the group, Alan Ansen was an intimate of W. H. Auden, who with his lover Chester Kallman were frequently at Bill's loft. Although Ansen was in love with Bill, he hardly relished the exotic, rather un-American atmosphere in which Bill throve. When people asked Ansen what his politics were, he'd answer "Whig" and mean it. He was also deeply involved in "culture culture," concerned about the ultimate refinements of opera and the nature of Gongorism, the kind of esoteric subjects Jack abhorred. Kerouac's claims as a writer meant nothing to Alan. Seeing Jack tongue-tied and withdrawn into corners much of the time, he decided Jack was a "pretender" and lost no time conveying that judgment to others.[11]

Here as elsewhere in his biography, Nicosia exaggerates the relationship between Ansen and Kerouac (details of which he learned at second or third hand). "I don't think I thought Jack was a pretender," Ansen has pointed out, "as opposed to being occasionally pretentious (as who of us is not?)."

Although Ansen would never be as close to Kerouac as he was to Burroughs, Ginsberg, and Corso, their acquaintance improved to the point where Kerouac was welcomed to visit Ansen out on Long Island. One such visit in January 1949 is immortalized in Kerouac's *On the Road*:

> We found the wild, ecstatic Rollo Greb and spent a night at his house on Long Island. Rollo lives in a nice house with his aunt; when she dies the house is all his. Meanwhile she refuses to comply with any of his wishes and hates his friends. He brought this ragged gang of Dean, Marylou, Ed, and me, and began a roaring party. The woman prowled upstairs; she threatened to call the police. "Oh, shut up, you old bag!" yelled Greb. I wondered how he could live with her like this. He had more books than I've ever seen in all my life — two libraries, two rooms loaded from floor to ceiling around all four walls, and such books as the Apocryphal Something-or-Other in ten volumes. He played Verdi operas and pantomimed them in his pajamas with a great rip down the back. He didn't give a damn about anything. He is a great scholar who goes reeling down the New York waterfront with original seventeenth-century musical manuscripts under his arm, shouting. He crawls like a big spider

10 Letter from Ansen to me, 23 June 1985 (hereafter abbreviated AA/SM; these letters are now among my papers at the Ransom Research Center, University of Texas at Austin).

11 *Memory Babe: A Critical Biography of Jack Kerouac* (New York: Grove, 1983), 219.

> through the streets. His excitement blew out of his eyes in stabs of fiendish light. He rolled his neck in spastic ecstasy. He lisped, he writhed, he flopped, he moaned, he howled, he fell back in despair. He could hardly get a word out, he was so excited with life. Dean stood before him with head bowed, repeating over and over again, "Yes . . . Yes . . . Yes." He took me into a corner. "That Rollo Greb is the greatest, most wonderful of all. That's what I was trying to tell you — that's what I want to be. I want to be like him. He's never hung-up, he goes every direction, he lets it all out, he knows time, he has nothing to do but rock back and forth. Man, he's the end! You see, if you go like him all the time you'll finally get it."
>
> "Get what?"
>
> "IT! IT! I'll tell you — now no time, we have no time now." Dean rushed back to watch Rollo Greb some more.[12]

Another occasional visitor to the house at 816 Bryant Street was Allen Ginsberg, who would often return the favor and invite Ansen out to Paterson, New Jersey, where Ansen would spend much of his time in a quiet bar Ginsberg had discovered reading P. G. Wodehouse to him. From Ginsberg Ansen learned of the man who would succeed Auden as father figure and guru, William S. Burroughs. In Paterson Ginsberg would share Burroughs's letters from his east Texas farm "in which he defended the use of wetbacks in that it raised the standard of living of both the wetback and the American consumer. I found his arguments impressive," Ansen writes, but would not meet the author until 1953.[13]

His primary allegiance was still to Auden, for by this time Ansen had succeeded Rhoda Jaffe as Auden's secretary and was writing another long essay on Auden's work, this one on *The Age of Anxiety*. His growing love of opera, fostered by Auden and Kallman (then collaborating on the libretto for Stravinsky's *The Rake's Progress*), resulted in an essay written in 1949 but not published until 1972 entitled "The Shy Opera Lover,"[14] in which he expresses a near-heretical preference for recordings over live performances. The essay is remarkable for its knowledgeability: in a few short years Ansen had thoroughly familiarized himself with the standard repertoire and developed a fund of music history and theory to the point where he could correspond with Thomas Mann on the musical allusions in *The Magic Mountain*. He applied for a Guggenheim Fellowship to write on Wagner's prosody, but despite Auden's backing he was turned down.

John Clellon Holmes remembers Ansen at this time "smirking and roaring like a sixfoot gnome in a dusty black suit, in afternoon-Clarke's among the

12 *On the Road* (New York: Viking, 1957), 127. [Cf. *On the Road: The Original Scroll* (New York: Viking, 2007), 228, where his name is misspelled "Allen Anson."]

13 "William Burroughs: A Personal View," *Review of Contemporary Fiction* 4.1 (Spring 1984): 49.

14 *Prose*, no. 5 (Fall 1972): 5–33.

neighborhood Irish."[15] At night, "under the aegis of mad Cannastra," his private war escalated. "I even fell afoul of Lily Law," he confesses in the "Epistle to Kallman,"

Playing Miss Subways in the crowded johns,
Grieving my father, shortening his days
Searching for magical panpharmacons
Shimmering through the alcoholic haze,

My armor for the very dubious quest
I undertook on the cheap to lose self-knowledge
As truculent, resentful, unrepressed,
At war with home, society and college,

I wallowed in an ecstasy of weakness

This reckless period is the setting for Ansen's only attempt at a novel, the opening chapters of which were published in 1987 as *The Vigilantes*. As Ginsberg would later describe it, the roman à clef was to be "a strange literary but very sad novel about a spectre of a party at Cannastra's."[16] After Ansen completed four chapters, Ginsberg tried to interest Carl Solomon's uncle A. A. Wyn of Ace Books in the novel — as he had with Burroughs's *Junky* — but Wyn showed insufficient interest and Ansen abandoned the work. Auden and Kallman were to appear (under the names "Von der Goltz" and "Denis Carney"), along with other members of Auden's circle such as Rhoda Jaffe ("Carmen Janacek"), Billy Vinson ("Monterone Carter"), and Dorothy Farnan ("Ora Diamond"). Cannastra, Beatrice to Auden's Dante, appears in the opening chapter as "Brendan Rcheznik," and Ansen himself answers to the name "Hermann Reichardt," "passionate spy on the creative process and would-be unicorn."

"A study of the milieu," as Wyn called it, *The Vigilantes* captures even in its fragmentary state the civilized frivolity of Ansen's world in the late '40s, a world of liquor and opera, nostalgia and nightmare. The fragment holds additional interest as an attempt to adapt operatic form to fiction — one can see Ansen laying out this groundwork in "The Shy Opera Lover" — and for its fleeting portraits of the artist as a young exquisite. Reichardt/Ansen is variously seen "making his usual dark effort to look farouche," brushing "automatically at his carefully cultivated cowlick," and displaying "that severe and unfortu-

15 *Nothing More to Declare* (New York: Dutton, 1967), 201. P. J. Clarke's is a legendary bar at the corner of 55th Street and Third Avenue.

16 *As Ever: The Collected Correspondence of Allen Ginsberg & Neal Cassady*, ed. Barry Gifford (Berkeley: Creative Arts, 1977), 122.

nate manner he always cultivates to hold waitresses under forty at bay." Like Kerouac's Rollo Greb, he rocks "ecstatically back and forth, not oblivious to but delighting in the estranged glances of others." But behind Reichardt's politeness, Carney/Kallman seems "always to hear the mocking goat and the caudate scorpion, the legal rapist and the honorable murderer of his sister." Carrying a copy of *La Vida es sueño*, singing Gilda's dying address to her father from Verdi's *Rigoletto*, Reichardt looks forward to a night of "drunkenness, passive participation in society, and, to top off the evening, the kidnapping of something pretty, perhaps from the party, perhaps from the Atlantic Fleet Grill, a recherché spot in the Village." Ansen's outline of the novel, printed as an appendix to the Water Row Press edition, gives no indication of the outcome of Reichardt's program, and it is regrettable that Ansen never completed this tantalizing fragment.

He did, however, complete the poem "Dead Drunk," a grim memorial to Cannastra, who was killed 12 October 1950 in a grisly accident. "Everybody was all hung up and changed somewhat," Ginsberg wrote to Cassady later that month. "But everybody — Carl, Howard Moss, Ansen, Holmes, Stringham, everybody who knew him — so many — as well as those we don't know from the past — got all big theories and weeklong drunks, everybody's pride was beaten for a week. As in greek tragedy, the purging of pity and terror" (*As Ever*, 71). Cannastra's sobering death sent Ansen back to "suburban solitude," with only "François Mauriac and bleakness" for companionship.

Ansen continued to work in a secretarial capacity for Auden — who dedicated his 1950 book *The Enchafèd Flood* to him — and continued to receive occasional visits from Ginsberg and Kerouac. In his *Visions of Cody* (written 1951–52) Kerouac speaks of Ansen's retirement and relates a conversation he had with him (here called "Irwin Swenson") regarding novelist Jean Genet and Ansen's recently deceased aunt in one long, Faulknerian sentence:

> Last night Swenson spoke at such great length on Genêt that I suddenly realized (had innocently queried: "And Genêt? have considered Genêt?") he not only of course had considered Genêt, every work published to date and incidentally reports brought to him personally by people who know him, reports about some recent new shift in Genêt's general feeling or attack (and the reason I have no details is because I wasn't listening, I was only dreaming over the significance that overlayed or overlay the context because it really to me was its rainbow) he even knew in detail the characters of the books, the names of the great mythological French queers of the underworld Paris, Froufrou, Mimi, Ange Divine and the lot, every nuance, like we know Buckle or Huck, knew them intimately, had savored them at his longest and most hungup leisure on nameless afternoons in that house which he now occupies alone 'cause his aunt died (and think!: he misses her! "I've grieved just the proper amount on the surface of it but it's rather — rather, you know — after, one DOES realize, I *just did* wish I'd been nicer to her, that's all, really") (finally, after a whole minute of his eyes

> struggling from their demure downward cast to turn over to me, his face suffusing with a sudden blush that seems to advertise his glances, writhing with his body one way while his gorgeous enormous eyelids unfurled the other way, in my direction, to reveal eyeballs in the act of rolling with indescribably veiled languor, mixed with shy shames and raptures of all kinds, as if from premeditated evil depths, from long private preparations no man could ever dream was possible to the mind, mincing deliciously all over like this big lovely child that reads the Apocalypse, wrapping himself around doors, melting, like Bloom, most like Leopold Bloom in a Dream, with his huge expressive and excessive nose which is the indicator of all his directions and etcetera the fingers).[17]

Despite his obvious admiration ("I dig Swenson," the passage continues), Kerouac found Ansen's daunting intellect incompatible with his own more sentimental views. In his *Book of Dreams*, Kerouac asked, "America is so sad, haunted, long remembered, itself a dream, what can Irwin Swenson begin to know about the red dusks over the wilderness trees and the meaning of young trainmen in the hills, old shanties with stoves, the long old dream — "[18] He continued to regard Kerouac with condescension: "Alan Ansen found Jack amusing," Nicosia writes, "but screamed over the 'tedium' of *Visions of Cody* and in fact used to enjoy patronizing Jack as 'just a little boy who wants to be a novelist.'"[19]

On the other hand, Kerouac often found Ansen "stuffy," and got some of his own back by playfully caricaturing Ansen in *Doctor Sax* (written 1952) as "the witty, gay ambassador for the Black Cardinal, our good friend Amadeus Baroque — sitting with his legs underneath, on an elegant *longue*, with a sip drink, titterlipped in listen." Kerouac continues his Firbankian description of Baroque with extravagant glee:

> (he wore his brocaded white silk tunic pajamas à la Cossack with a great bloodclot in red thread over the heart, he smoked from elegant holder, "perfumed of course," a brilliant wit in the Ark Galleries of the Rack where he'd been for a while before descending (not to take courses in a taxi school) to forfend the later migamies for his mother's estate and save the day, and find himself a Sugar Daddy at the same time so here he was)

The scene ends as Baroque leans over and plays his favorite record, "Edith Piaf dying."[20] Ansen never read *Doctor Sax* and thus remained unaware of the campy fun Kerouac had at his expense.

During the same period, Ginsberg continued to spend an occasional

17 *Visions of Cody* (New York: McGraw-Hill, 1972), 39–40.
18 *Book of Dreams* (San Francisco: City Lights, 1961), 90.
19 *Memory Babe*, 456. Ansen told me he found only the tape recording transcriptions "tedious."
20 *Doctor Sax* (New York: Grove, 1959), 106–9.

weekend at Ansen's house — trying unsuccessfully to find a publisher for *The Vigilantes* and the Auden essays — and continued to share his letters from Burroughs, who spent the first half of 1953 in South America in search of yage. (These letters were published a decade later as the epistolary novel *The Yage Papers*; although Ansen is credited along with Alene Lee on the copyright page with typing and preserving these letters, he only gave "practical advice on the organization of *The Yage Letters*."[21]) Enter mysterious stranger. Burroughs returned to New York in August 1953 with a suitcase of yage and was introduced to Ansen by Ginsberg in his East Village apartment. The two hit it off immediately; in Burroughs Ansen found a mentor to succeed Auden, who by this point had

> left me dissatisfied
> With my best efforts as a scholiast
> And for the moment fairly content to glide
> An idle eccentric member of the cast.
> . . . .
> To get that special tan
> That marks aspirants to a higher grade
> All unconsciously I needed "A man
>
> Of no fortune and with a name to come."
> Burroughs fitted the bill.[22]

Wandering between two worlds, that of Auden and that of the Beats, Ansen opted for the latter as offering greater scope for his unconventionality and fewer threats to his individuality.

Later that same August Kerouac made another trip to Woodmere that would be memorialized in his fiction. Drinking one night in the San Remo with Gaddis, Corso, and his current girlfriend, Kerouac decided to drive out to Woodmere "and crash in on old Austin Bromberg," as Ansen is called in *The Subterraneans*, the novel Kerouac would write in October 1953. (Kerouac called himself "Leo Percepied," Gaddis "Harold Sand," and his girlfriend Alene Lee "Mardou Fox.") Leaving Corso behind, the three arrive at Ansen's house

> at gray dawn, parking and ringing the doorbell the three of us sheepishly I most sheepish of all — and Bromberg comes right down, at once, with great roars of ap-

21 [Bill Morgan, *The Typewriter Is Holy: The Complete, Uncensored History of the Beat Generation* (New York: Free Press, 2010), 79. Morgan dedicated this compact book "To the memory of Alan Ansen / the unknown Beat."]

22 "Epistle to Chester Kallman," 154. The quotation is from Pound's Canto 1, which quotes that line from an old translation of Homer's *Odyssey*.

> proval cries "Leo I didn't know you knew each other" (meaning Sand, whom Bromberg admired very much[23]) and in we go to rum and coffee in the crazy famous Bromberg kitchen. — You might say, Bromberg the most amazing guy in the world with small dark curly hair like the hip girl Roxanne making little garter snakes over his brow and his great really angelic eyes shining, rolling, a big burbling baby, a great genius of talk really, wrote research and essays and has (and is famous for) the greatest possible private library in the world, right there in that house, library due to his erudition and this no reflection also on his big income — the house inherited from father — was also the sudden new bosom friend of Carmody [Burroughs] and about to go to Peru with him, they'd go dig Indian boys and talk about it and discuss art and visit literaries and things of that nature, all matters so much had been dinning in Mardou's ear (queer, cultured matters) in her love affair with me that by now she was quite tired of cultured tones and fancy explicity, emphatic daintiness of expression, of which roll-eyed ecstatic almost spastic big Bromberg almost the pastmaster, "O my dear it's such a charming thing and I think much MUCH better than the Gascoyne translation tho I do believe — " and Sand imitating him to a T, from some recent great meeting and mutual admiration — so the two of them there in the once-to-me adventurous gray dawn of the Metropolitan Great-Rome Frisco talking of literary and musical and artistic matters, the kitchen littered, Bromberg rushing up (in pajamas) to fetch three-inch thick French editions of Genet or old editions of Chaucer or whatever he and Sand'd come to, [. . .] — the birds beginning to sing finally at about eight and Bromberg's great voice, one of the mightiest you can hear, making the walls of the kitchen throw back great shudders of deep ecstatic sound — turning on the phonograph, an expensive well-furnished completely appointed house, with French wine, refrigerators, three-speed machines with speakers, cellar, etc.

Unaware that the relationship between Leo and Mardou is crumbling, Bromberg/Ansen is perplexed by Percepied's troubled countenance, and with the others tries

> anyway to make the best of it in spite of my palpable unhappy brooding all over the place, while listening to Verdi and Puccini opera recordings in the great upstairs library (four walls from rug to ceiling with things like *The Explanation of the Apocalypse* in three volumes, the complete works and poems of Chris Smart, the complete this and that, the apology of so-and-so written obscurely to you-know-who in 1839, in 1638 —)[24]

Asked nearly 30 years later how he regarded Kerouac's portrayal of him, Ansen admitted, "My present reaction to the Bromberg portrait is to deplore my ap-

23 Ansen later wrote that Gaddis "won my heart by entering to a quotation from George Herbert — I think it was 'I smote the board and cried "No more"'" (AA/SM, 19 March 1983).

24 *The Subterraneans* (New York: Grove, 1958), 85–93. Reading this passage for the first time in 1983, Gaddis wrote me: "I remember our acquaintance as very much the way he presents it right down to the old car (a black wounded 1941 Chevrolet) & centered very much around Alan Ansen. Kerouac's picture of him (Bromberg) is right on. Ansen was an extraordinary fellow, marvelously without 'consciousness of his fantastic impact on the ordinary'" . . . (*Letters*, 390).

palling insensitivity to Jack's suffering at the time."[25] But there is no malice in Kerouac's treatment: Ansen and Gaddis carry on a "brilliant conversation (the likes of which cannot be surpassed anywhere in the world)," and the episode ends with Kerouac paying tribute to the amazing fact that "Bromberg doesn't even have consciousness of his fantastic impact on the ordinary."

Burroughs continued to make his own fantastic impact on Ansen — who already considered him "one of the great writers of XX Century" (as Ginsberg wrote to Cassady) — and, learning of Burroughs's plans to travel to Europe "to steep himself in vice in either Rome (under the influence of Gore Vidal's *The Judgment of Paris*) or Tangier," Ansen realized he "had found the ideal travelling companion" and decided to gratify his long-held dream of seeing Europe.[26]

Renting his house in Woodmere for a nominal sum to Gaddis — who had introduced Ansen to Kathleen Costello, who in turn gave him a letter of introduction to Peggy Guggenheim — Ansen departed for Europe in November 1953 with plans to meet Burroughs later in Rome. After a week in Rome together, Burroughs grimly wrote Ginsberg that he had "no interest in this town at all . . . I am going to have something to say to that lying bastard Gore Vidal," but that "Alan has been a little bit more happy here since he goes for Cathedrals and such, and can stand cold weather."[27] Disgusted with Rome, Burroughs left for Tangier while Ansen continued his grand tour: a month in Rome, another in Florence and Venice, a week in Munich, three in Paris, and two weeks in London, whence he returned to America in April 1954. By that time, his house-sitter had finished writing his thousand-page novel *The Recognitions*, and Gaddis later remembered "him sitting down barely off the boat in that ghastly diningroom & reading it through in a day and a half."[28]

No longer in Auden's employ, his other friends scattered, Ansen saw little to keep him in America and by the fall of 1954 he was back in Venice, which (as Dorothy Farnan notes) "offered the most generous exchange rate for the American dollar." His residence there got off to an inauspicious start. Caught by a servant "*in flagrante* with a cute young Samoyed," he was thrown out of his first apartment, but was able to relocate with "an understanding landlady" associated with the famous Harry's Bar near St. Mark's Square, which became

25 "Letter from Alan Ansen," *Moody Street Irregulars*, no. 9 (Winter/Spring 1981): 22.

26 "William Burroughs: A Personal View," 50.

27 [*The Letters of William S. Burroughs, 1945–1959*, ed. Oliver Harris (New York: Viking, 1993), 193.]

28 [*Letters*, 391. I once asked Gaddis if the flamboyant gay character Big Anna the Swede was based on Ansen, but he said no. Ansen's numerous letters to Gaddis charting his cultural and sexual tour of Europe are now among Gaddis's papers at the Olin Library at the Washington University, St. Louis.]

his base of operations for the next seven years. Although occasionally a victim of "the mix of sadism, greed and envy that harries / The deviant dissident in Italy," Ansen enjoyed the "variety of passions and privations / . . . Venice preserved in semi-isolation." Actually, his own isolation was minimal; old friends either visited (like Helen Parker) or lived nearby (Burroughs in Tangier, Auden and Kallman in Ischia every summer), and new friends like Peggy Guggenheim were readily made. Hard to miss in his red suit, Ansen soon became a permanent fixture of the expatriate colony in Venice.

During an extended visit by Burroughs in the summer of 1956, Ansen took his seat at his friend's *Naked Lunch*, then in progress. Two years earlier Burroughs had written to Ginsberg of his idea for a new character — "A man given to surrealist puns and practical jokes" — and as Burroughs later noted in his "Literary Autobiography," "it was during this summer that A.J. took shape and the gondola scene was written."[29] Ansen's own extravagant unconventionality provided Burroughs with a model for his surrealistic practical joker, and taking Ansen's first two initials he fleshed out what was to become a central character in both *Naked Lunch* and future works: A.J. also appears in *The Wild Boys*, *Exterminator!*, and *Port of Saints*.[30] In addition to his speaking role in *Naked Lunch*, Ansen worked backstage as well as in the book's production. Burroughs left Venice in August 1956, and the following spring Ansen sailed to Tangier to take over from Kerouac and Ginsberg the task of typing the manuscript of Burroughs's burgeoning book. "Ansen was great," Ginsberg wrote to Kerouac in May 1957, "came and started typing immediately, read through all the notebooks and in fine hand made a huge index of all the materials in the letters, sentences, announcements, routines, all to be integrated chronologically," adding, "Worked on it like a great professional pedantic scholar with an unruly library full of dignified ancient manuscripts of the Venerable Bill."[31]

Ginsberg and his companion Peter Orlovsky (whom both Burroughs and Ansen disliked) were making their own grand tour of Europe that year, and in the summer of 1957 they joined Ansen in Venice.[32] Although both Auden

29 *Letters of William S. Burroughs*, 272; Miles Associates, *A Descriptive Catalog of the William S. Burroughs Archive* (London: Covent Garden Press, 1973), 77. The gondola scene occupies pp. 150–52 of *Naked Lunch* (New York: Grove, 1962) [pp. 126–28 in the restored text of 2001].

30 [Burroughs biographer Barry Miles dismisses this, saying, "A.J. had no life model, though it pleased Alan Ansen to think it was based on him. The initials stood for nothing" (*Call Me Burroughs: A Life* [New York: Twelve, 2013], 353. But since Ansen knew Burroughs better than Miles did, I'm letting it stand.]

31 [*Jack Kerouac and Allen Ginsberg: The Letters*, ed. Bill Morgan and David Stanford (New York: Viking, 2010), 346.]

32 [There's a photo of Ansen and Orlovsky in Venice taken by Ginsberg in Bill Morgan's *Peter*

and Kallman had encouraged Ansen earlier to pursue his vocation for poetry, it was Ginsberg who convinced him "to launch / My overloaded rather sloppy pinnace / On the sea of verse." The first result, inspired by the arrival of the American cruiser the *Newport News*, is the poem that opens *Contact Highs*.

After Ginsberg and Orlovsky left for Vienna, Ansen traveled to Paris and renewed his acquaintance with Gregory Corso, "whose poetry's outbreak / Dazzled my senses and convinced my judgment." At Ansen's invitation, Corso joined him in Venice at the beginning of 1958. Ginsberg and Burroughs had paid for Corso's trainfare and had given him some heroin to convey to Ansen, but en route "he used it all up. Alan was mad at him."[33] But more junk was found and soon the two were writing chain poems together. "Under its influence," Ansen later wrote, recounting the origin of his brilliant poem "Heroin,"

> we composed a joint poem God Heads Down and a playlet about Monopoly. Later, under the influence of nothing, I separated out my contributions and added the fake Burroughs epigraph. Gregory was cross about the title, which he thought violated omertà and his general feeling that the occasions of poetry should remain mysterious. Auden, when he read the poem, told me to take heroin again in order to make the poem clearer — something I don't think he would have advised everyone to do.[34]

At Corso's prompting, Ansen also wrote what the younger poet called a very perceptive review of his just-published booklet *Gasoline*, which apparently was never published.[35]

Ansen introduced Corso to Peggy Guggenheim, as he had Burroughs and Ginsberg in previous years, and like the others, Corso soon ran afoul of the art patron. Surprisingly enough, Ansen remained on the best of terms with Mrs. Guggenheim despite his train of "unpresentable" guests. As her biographer Jacqueline Weld records, "Alan Ansen, a wildly eccentric poet who dressed in red," was a frequent visitor at the palazzo Venier dei Leoni. For Mrs. Guggenehim's 61st birthday in 1959, Ansen composed the first of many masques to be held at her palazzo, *The Return from Greece*. Ginsberg, Orlovsky, Corso,

Orlovsky, a Life in Words (Boulder, CO: Paradigm, 2014), 66.]

33 Allen Ginsberg and Peter Orlovsky, *Straight Hearts' Delight: Love Poems and Selected Letters 1947–1980* (San Francisco: Gay Sunshine Press, 1980), 139. [See now *An Accidental Autobiography: The Selected Letters of Gregory Corso*, ed. Bill Morgan (New York: New Directions, 2003), which contains numerous references to Ansen.]

34 AA/SM, 26 June 1984. Auden suspected Ansen "to be a joy popper who would take the remark in the slightly comic spirit in which it was meant" (AA/SM, 15 May 1986). "Joy popper" is '50s slang for an occasional drug-user, not an addict.

35 [It is now among Irving Rosenthal's papers at the Stanford University Libraries; Rosenthal was an editor at the *Chicago Review* at that time.]

and Burroughs were the models for the "four beat tourists" in the antimasque section.[36] Poet James Merrill attended, having met Ansen the previous May. In a letter to fellow poet John Hollander, a friend of Ansen's as well, Merrill reported: "Sometimes he is wearing a bright red double-breasted suit, sometimes a white one. After midnight he is apt to be sound asleep in Ciro's bar where nothing wakes him, not even sharp prods from an umbrella."[37]

For Ansen, 1959 proved an *annus mirabilis* for several other reasons. The second issue of *Big Table* carried his article "Anyone Who Can Pick Up a Frying Pan Owns Death," the first critical essay on Burroughs's work, coinciding with the Paris publication of *Naked Lunch*. (Kerouac had recommended Ansen to the editors of *Big Table* as the most suitable critic to comment on the ten episodes from *Naked Lunch* that appeared in their first issue.) Most importantly, Ansen's first book of verse, entitled *The Old Religion*, was published that year by John Bernard Myers under his Tibor de Nagy imprint, thanks to Ginsberg's recommendation. Aptly dedicated to both Auden and Burroughs, the booklet fuses Auden's concern for poetic craftsmanship with Burroughs's irreverent, visionary sensibility. John Hollander liked it well enough to recommend Ansen's work to his fellow committee members of Wesleyan University Press's budding poetry program when he visited the following year, and as a result most of *The Old Religion* and several newer poems were published as *Disorderly Houses* in 1961, the principal volume by which Ansen's work as a poet was known until the 1989 publication of *Contact Highs*. Ansen was in Tangier in July 1961 for a reunion with Burroughs, Orlovsky, Corso, and Ginsberg, and that August Ginsberg wrote an insightful jacket blurb for Ansen's forthcoming book that was apparently sent too late to be used.[38]

Unfortunately, the following year proved to be an *annus calamitosus*, anticipated with eerie prescience in his dream-ridden birthday poem "On His Fortieth Year." First (he explained in a letter), "a different selection committee of the Wesleyan University Press turned down my next book, *Field Report*; and my long commitment to samizdat began. The dedication to Ginsberg, a poem

36 *Disorderly Houses* (Middletown, CT: Wesleyan University Press, 1961), 71–73, in which Ansen gives some very funny lines to the Burroughs character.

37 [Quoted in Langdon Hammer's *James Merrill: Life and Art* (New York, Knopf, 2015), 269.]

38 [With Ginsberg's permission it was printed on the back cover of *Contact Highs*: "Ansen is the most delicate hippopotamus of poets with his monstrous classical versifications — he gets conversational fatness 'into stricter order' by use of weird echosyllabics, polyphony, strict rhymeless pindarics, self-annihilating sestinas, mono-amphisbaenic and echo rhyme, skeltonics, versicles & alcaics coherent Palindromes & such like master eccentricities — a hangup on Forms which interestingly pushes academic models beyond polite limits into the area of lunatic personal genius — This is an amazing book, with many sad poems." Part of it was used for an ad in the *Village Voice* (19 October 1961), along with Corso's terse "Only poet of his kind."]

'Fuck' written for a projected anthology of obscene literature Olympia Press had commissioned from Gregory Corso and perhaps too many poems about procedures, a not unfamiliar phenomenon when the initial inspirations run out, helped the more anti-Beat committee make up its mind."[39] *Field Report* (1963) was privately printed and distributed, as would be all of Ansen's subsequent books of verse. Also, the authorities in Venice decided to crack down on "Communists and queers," and Ansen and many others were expelled from the city.[40]

To top things off, Ansen found himself vilified in two works of Corso's published at the time. His novel *The American Express*, dashed off in a month and published in 1961 by the Olympia Press in Paris, is a whimsical fantasia containing a caricature of Ansen named "Dad Deform." Somewhat like Burroughs's A.J., Deform has a penchant for surrealistic puns and muffled motives, and represents joy and spontaneity in a novel where most of the other characters are busy with dystopian scenes. Yet he is often described in unsavory terms:

> "Dad Deform is a hunchback [one character tells another]. He makes bombs for Hinderov, and holy statues for Simon. He lives in a small furnished room. It's so small that when you enter you have to be careful as not to step out the window. But there is hardly any danger of that happening because nobody hardly ever visits him. Not only is he repulsive to look at, he also stinks. His mattress is flattened stiff with old pee, and he has stacks of old fairy-tale books and so on, and they are the homes of roaches and the like — I don't suggest you visit him." (69)

Burroughs appears in the same novel as "Mr. D," and Corso seems to have associated Ansen with Burroughs's programs for the death of the word and militant homosexuality. As a result of this guilt by association, Ansen appears as "Death" in Corso's superb poem "Greece," written about the same time as *The American Express*.[41]

Spurned by Venice, Ansen settled permanently in Athens, where old friends would look him up: Peggy Guggenheim visited a few times; Chester Kallman moved in with him in 1963; and James Merrill was an occasional visitor.[42] Spurned by his publisher, he turned to the mode of publication he called samizdat to gather into booklets the large amount of poetry he wrote

39 AA/SM, 26 June 1984.

40 Jacqueline Wald, *Peggy: The Wayward Guggenheim* (New York: Dutton, 1986), 394.

41 [Corso turned on Ansen after he learned that all the private papers he had stored at Ansen's place were destroyed after he was driven out of Venice in 1962; see *An Accidental Autobiography*, 330, 335.]

42 [See Hammer's Merrill biography for numerous references. When I reprinted Merrill's *The (Diblos) Notebook* at Dalkey Archive in 1994, Ansen suggested the cover art.]

in the '60s. *Field Report*, the first such publication, was followed by a companion volume of slightly later poems entitled *Believe and Tremble*, also in 1963. (This collection also contains Ansen's earliest "routine" à la Burroughs, "Out of Control," which he sent to him in a letter dated 28 July 1962.) In early 1966 he brought out *Day by Day*, "using the title long before Lowell," he notes. Included in this collection is Ansen's pastoral threnody "The Death of Nearchus," as trenchant as it is elegant, which first appeared in Glikes and Schwaber's *Of Poetry and Power: Poems Occasioned by the Presidency and by the Death of John F. Kennedy* (1964).

In 1967 Ansen returned to the United States for the first time since 1954 and, after visiting the old neighborhood, boarded a Greyhound bus to see America. The trip is recounted in his poetic travelogue "Deseret," and mentioned in Ginsberg's poem "Los Gatos," after the city in California where the two held a brief reunion (*As Ever*, 218). The same year, Ansen contributed a double sestina entitled "Genethliacon" to a special issue of *Shenandoah* honoring Auden's 60th birthday. The poem was part of a new collection Ansen had ready for the printers, *The Ghosts of Neighborhood*, but the oppressive junta that came into power in 1967 delayed its publication until 1969, when the political situation in Greece relaxed somewhat. By then a briefer volume was also ready, *The Lay Contemplative's Vade Mecum*, dedicated to Chester Kallman.

The following year Kallman, inspired by the Jewish origins he shared with Ansen, invited him to join Auden and him on a short pilgrimage to Jerusalem, a visit commemorated in Kallman's last poem "The Dome of the Rock."[43] At one point in the poem Kallman denigrates the ruined surroundings, whereupon:

> Alan counters me,
> Exhorting, 'Let the heathen reign!
> Look at Constantinople: the Turks
> Have blessed it with neglect; how misbegotten
> Greek effort would be, and in time redundant,
> To tidy out the worst. They would overwhelm
> The best in doing so. It never works!'

During the same trip, these "Eternal tourists, never quite at home, / Three good New Yorkers," met the mayor of Jerusalem, of whom Ansen later wrote, "Kollek loathed me, but I must confess I rather admire him. It wasn't lunch

43 In *W. H. Auden: A Tribute*, ed. Stephen Spender (London: Weidenfeld & Nicolson, 1975), 226–28. Ansen used this fine poem when teaching Auden. He never held a permanent post, but taught occasional classes and tutored visiting scholars.

[as Farnan writes in *Auden in Love*] it was a drive through Jerusalem with him chauffeuring and an evening party. I suggested doing *Israel in Egypt* to inaugurate the Jerusalem opera house and he snarled 'Why not *Aïda*?'"[44] Auden found the city "'fascinating' but '*very* expensive,'"[45] but Ansen regarded the visit "A junction of joys I find too exquisite / For analysis."

Auden's death in September 1973 drew Ansen and Kallman even closer. Kallman called Ansen to Vienna for the funeral on the fourth of October, and thereafter increasingly relied on Ansen for companionship and support. Ansen cheerfully shouldered the burden, proud to be "the keeper of the keeper of the Flame." They continued the domestic routine they had established in 1963 when Kallman settled in Athens: every evening Ansen would walk down the hill from his apartment to Kallman's bringing the groceries he had shopped for at noon. Chester always cooked the meals, and afterward they would talk and listen to music until "Chester would go off," Farnan recalls, "sometimes with Alan, but more often without him, to the bars and the Greek boys" (247).

Kallman survived Auden only by a year and a half, dying on the morning of 17 January 1975. Ansen attended to the arrangements for Kallman's burial in the Jewish Cemetery in Athens, and eventually wrote one of his longest and finest poems, "Epistle to Chester Kallman," as a tribute to his irreplaceable friend. It was included in *The Cell* (1983), the last of his self-published poetry collections.

Happily, another irreplaceable friend stayed in contact. In August of 1973 William Burroughs flew to Athens to retrieve a variety of manuscripts that Ansen had been holding for him. Burroughs's stay at the Hilton and his trip to Spetses were later transmuted into the Greek settings of the Clem Snide sections of his novel *Cities of the Red Night* (1981). They continued to correspond through the 1970s and into the '80s, and when Ansen visited the United States in March of 1985 to see to the sale of his Woodmere house he spent a good deal of time at Burroughs's famous Bunker on the Bowery.[46] The following year he visited Burroughs at his new headquarters in Lawrence, Kansas, and in 1987 Water Row Press published Ansen's monograph *William Burroughs*, a compilation of three earlier essays on his friend's work.

Though Ansen continued to write poetry throughout this period, he issued no further collections after 1983's *The Cell*. The struggle continued with

44 AA/SM, 15 May 1986.

45 Humphrey Carpenter, *W. H. Auden: A Biography* (Boston: Houghton Mifflin, 1981), 435.

46 [I met Ansen during this trip at the apartment of his friend Rachel Hadas, where I gathered some of the information used in this memoir. Hadas wrote a perceptive afterword for *Contact Highs*. See also her lovely obituary for Ansen at <http://www.rachelhadas.com/ansen.html>]

this "Unmanageable poem, life of mine," as he called it in his early poem "An Occupational Hazard." The two are one, and consequently the jacket copy he wrote for *Disorderly Houses* serves as well to summarize the unique personality who made those poems:

> The subject of *Disorderly Houses* might be summed up as the joy of the horror and the horror of the joy: the horror being principally alienation — sexual, social, theological; the joy the vitality in that alienation, the ability to be conscious of it and to express it, even sometimes to laugh over it in the realization of wider contexts.
>
> By instinct and biographical compulsion, I want the naked scream. By training and remembered satisfactions, I utter in patterns.

The naked scream uttered in patterns; "the happy wobblings of biological spontaneity" chastened by "the iron insensitivity of disciplined prosody" (to quote again from "An Occupational Hazard") — such paradoxes best characterize the life and work of this Classical scholar in Beat clothing, this joy popper with monastic discipline. These tensions are at the heart of the poems that follow, chosen by Ansen from his inimitable books of verse.

CODA

In 1989, just before *Contact Highs* went to press, Sea Cliff Press published Ansen's *The Table Talk of W. H. Auden*, edited by Nicholas Jenkins, which was reprinted the following year by Ontario Review Press. I reviewed the latter in the Fall 1990 issue of the *Review of Contemporary Fiction* as follows:

> Ansen's record of his conversations with Auden in the late 1940s (which he donated to NYPL's Berg Collection) has often been plundered by Auden scholars, and now it is easy to see why. "Conversations" is perhaps the wrong word; these are monologues by the British poet, critical observations on everything from opera to politics, from sex to religion, and of course literature of all languages and eras. The range is astonishing, and Auden has an original, brilliant, and quotable opinion of everything he touches, as this passage (plucked at random) shows: "Where the poetry is good, it's not vital to the myth — it isn't essential as it is in *Anthony and Cleopatra*. Myth and poetry exist independently of each other. *Don Quixote* is the only really Christian myth. You find a trace of it in *Li'l Abner* in the *Daily Mirror*. Abner's always trying to do someone a good turn, and it never works out. *Superman* and *Little Orphan Annie* ought to be on the *Index*. Henry Miller, certainly. Yes, Thomas Wolfe . . . and Carl Sandburg — the prose is all right, but not the poetry." Ansen's feats of memory are no less astonishing, remembering pages and pages of such details without the benefit of a tape-recorder, and prodding Auden with intelligent questions and observations of his own. This is the ideal nightstand book for any reader, not just the Auden specialist, and is highly recommended.

From 1989 to 1994 I commissioned a half-dozen book reviews from Ansen for the *Review of Contemporary Fiction*, and we kept decreasingly in touch in the years that followed. Ansen died in Athens on 12 November 2006.

David Markson and the Art of Allusion

> And to be alone so, to frown so often upon the pages of so many books? What could be the meaning of reading, or of so many books?
>
> —David Markson, *Going Down*

The skillful use of literary allusion seems on its way to becoming a lost art. Writers and readers once shared a common literary heritage, and even the most run-of-the-mill Victorian novel would have its allusions — to Shakespeare, the Bible, and perhaps a figure or two from Greek mythology. The great modernists of the early 20th century pushed literary allusions to unheard-of extremes, necessitating the bulky reference books now available on Joyce and Pound (though, curiously, Eliot has not yet received treatment comparable to Gifford's *"Ulysses" Annotated* or Terrell's *Companion to "The Cantos"*). The generation of American writers weaned on these modernists produced some novelists who carry on this allusive tradition; a few, like William Gaddis and Thomas Pynchon, have already inspired similar, less bulky reference, while others, like Gilbert Sorrentino and Alexander Theroux, await their annotators. By and large, though, the presence of literary allusion in contemporary fiction is relatively rare, and when it does appear, it is usually branded "pretentious" by reviewers who recognize the allusions, and of course lost on the larger number of readers who don't.

David Markson belongs to the generation that battened on the erudition displayed in such works as *Ulysses*, *The Waste Land*, and, in Markson's more particular case, Malcolm Lowry's *Under the Volcano* (which has also generated an informative "companion" by Ackerley and Clipper). Many motives account for the disproportionate amount of allusion and reference in these works, ranging from Joyce's flippant remark about keeping professors busy for two centuries to Pound's earnest attempt to educate and instruct. But all of these writers recognized not only the obvious — that literature is made out of previous literature — but that the experience of literature is as valid as any other kind of experience to write about, that Blake's rose is as real to some readers as a rose in someone's garden. Markson is just such a reader and has tended to create characters who are themselves voracious readers. The use they make of their reading ranges from destructive (*Going Down*) to playful (*Springer's Progress*) to heuristic (*Wittgenstein's Mistress*), and it is Markson's principal achievement to have created works that are as learned as his predecessors' and that, at the same time, contain within them critiques of the uses and abuses of such learning.

These qualities are present even in his earliest extant story, "Be All My Sins Remembered" (1955). Anthony Becker is a prototypical Markson protagonist: bookish (though in a manner more suited to the saloon than the salon), self-deprecating, and possessed by a torturing self-consciousness. In Tony's case, he is tortured by his inability to confess his homosexuality, which is compared to Hamlet's inability to act via numerous allusions, beginning with the title itself and including direct and indirect quotations from Shakespeare's play. But the Hamlet parallel is quickly compounded by other references: to Mann's *Death in Venice* (another tale of a closet homosexual), Kafka's *Trial* and Orwell's *Nineteen Eighty-Four* (for his guilty conscience), P. C. Wren's *Beau Geste*, various occult writers like Paracelsus and Böhme (whom Markson would have known from his work on *Under the Volcano*), even an account of Spinoza's excommunication (a metaphor for Tony's feelings of alienation) — all cleverly dovetailed until *Hamlet* is confounded with Saint Augustine's *Confessions* by way of Eliot's *Waste Land* and D. H. Lawrence confused with T. E., by whom he means P. C. Wren. There may even be a subtle reference to *Moby-Dick* in Tony's flashback to the "counterpane world" of his childhood, which recalls "The Counterpane" in Melville's novel, the most overtly homosexual chapter in *Moby-Dick* and also containing a flashback to Ishmael's childhood.

Markson is not merely name-dropping here; the references are an integral component of the characters he creates and the milieu in which they move. For someone like Tony, immersed in books since childhood and now moving among writers and playwrights, it is only natural (and hence artistically appropriate) that he think and speak in terms of a shared literary tradition. (His first spoken sentence, a quotation from *Hamlet*, is easily completed by his friend Peter Hoag.) In his later works Markson would expand this shared culture to include art history, music, and philosophy, but it is important to note that from his earliest story Markson favored a particular kind of fiction, one that would allow him to make extensive use of his wide reading.

In this story and in his major novels, such literary references are functional and organic. In the paperback originals he wrote in the late '50s and early '60s, however, literary allusions are essentially indulgences, in-jokes that few of his genre readers could have been expected to recognize or appreciate. Harry Fannin, the sardonic private investigator of Markson's two detective novels, is cut from the same cloth as Chandler's Philip Marlowe, but is much better read. He's curled up with "a gay little thing by Thomas Mann called *The Magic Mountain*" at the beginning of *Epitaph for a Tramp* (1959), and later we learn that he's read Eliot's *Waste Land*, knows of Whittier and Longfellow, and keeps a paperback *Book of Quotations* around (from which he picks up the alias Thomas Hobbes). *Epitaph for a Dead Beat* (1961) finds him reading *Lolita* as the novel begins ("a sad story about a twelve-year-old girl who couldn't find anyone her own age to play with"); he knows Dickens, Melville, and a surprising number of older poets, making flippant references to Shelley, Keats, Swinburne, Sandburg, Frost, Thomas,[1] and even imagines an Oscar Williams-edited *Treasury of Mongolian Verse*. It can be argued that the literary/bohemian settings of both novels provide an artistic motivation for these allusions, but when Fannin suggests to a suspect doing "a textual exegesis of *The Cantos* of Jayne Mansfield. We'll talk of graves, of worms, and epitaphs, make dust our paper and with rainy eyes write sorrow on the bosom of the — hold it right there," the reader is tempted to tell Markson himself to hold it right there and explain how it is that a private dick can quote *Richard II* at the drop of a hat. He's even able to parody lines from *Macbeth* ("Tamayo and Tamayo and Tamayo, seeps in this petty paste from plate to plate") and to improvise a beatnik paraphrase of Kipling's "Mandalay" ("By the old Moulmein Pagoda, lookin' lazy to the sea, there's a beatnik girl a-settin', and she's gettin' high on tea"). Such things strain the verisimilitude of the novels, unless Markson is deliberately going against the grain of generic conventions (and reader expectations) to show that a detective can be literary without necessarily being a sophisticated, urbane wimp (like S. S. Van Dine's Philo Vance.)

At any rate, these are Fannin's parodies and allusions. Better yet — and part of the fun of reading these early works — are Markson's own parodies and private allusions. Often Fannin will be in someone's room and will notice certain books on a shelf that mean nothing to him but mean a great deal to Markson: in *Epitaph for a Tramp*, for example, there are appearances by Lowry's *Under the Volcano*, Aiken's *The Coming Forth by Day of Osiris Jones*, and his friend Donald Honig's *Sidewalk Caesar*. But a reference that probably went over every reader's head in 1959 is Markson's splendid tribute to William Gaddis's *The Recognitions*. Remaindered shortly after its 1955 publication, *The Recognitions* is the subject of a comp lit paper a student is writing; in the student's apartment, waiting for his adulterous wife to get dressed, Fannin sees the last page still in the typewriter and rolls it up to read:

> *And thus it is my conclusion that* The Recognitions *by William Gaddis is not merely the best American first novel of our time, but perhaps the most significant single volume in all American fiction since* Moby Dick, *a book so broad in scope, so rich in comedy*

1 [Markson knew and drank with Dylan Thomas, on whom he published a short memoir in 1973, reprinted in Markson's *Collected Poems* (Dalkey Archive Press, 1993). The same volume contains his memoir of Conrad Aiken, also published in 1973.]

and so profound in symbolic inference that —

The paper breaks off here, but Markson also mimics Gaddis's style of Greenwich Village dialogue a few pages earlier, and even more so in *Epitaph for a Dead Beat*, which in fact parodies the Beat scene of the late '50s. In this novel, there are more references to Markson's own enthusiasms (like Joseph Stanley Pennell's neglected Civil War novel *The History of Rome Hanks*) and this broad parody of Kerouac's style (again, a page picked up by Fannin):

> *. . . digging it with Bennie and Jojo and those wild chicks (one of them an Arab, she had eyes like smothered stars) in the backseat of that brokendown Chrysler Bennie had driven to Tampico and back and sold for forty dollars in San Diego and spent the money on a two-week fix and then swiped it back again, and all night long Jojo talking about the Mahayana transcendence of our friend Wimpy, the poet who did not wash except on the coming of the new moon and who was the new culture hero of our time and who once said: "I dig Brahman and I dig The Bird but I do not dig housewives," which became a creed: and all the while (younger then and my jeans too tight; I'd borrowed them from a tranquil Taoist midget I'd met reading Lincoln Steffens in a public urinal in Times Square — ah, holy times, holy square!) pressing my hand against the knee of that swinging angel Arab lass and not minding the blood where I tore my skin against a broken spring in the seat, oh how I suffered, telling myself as soon as I make it with this chick I will hop a freight and very religiously ride the rails to Albuquerque to tell Herman (but first some detail here about Herman, a raw maniac hipster kid who . . .*

(In a letter to me, Markson recalled: "I read Jack that little parody one night, & he went off into a jazz riff, da-da-de-duh, etc., saying the rhythms were off; but he was not offended in the least.")

Markson's third and last paperback original, *Miss Doll, Go Home* (1965), parodies the format of Faulkner's *As I Lay Dying*. This comic suspense story, set in a Mexican art colony, is told from a variety of viewpoints, each labeled with a character's name. One of the principal characters, Benny Grimes, is a typical Markson protagonist — well read, burnt out, and given to making sarcastic literary allusions. He is in an *Of Mice and Men* relationship with Norman "the Gink," deaf, dumb, and slightly retarded, who fulfills the same role here as the boy Vardaman in *As I Lay Dying* (who has the famous one-sentence chapter "My mother is a fish"). Gink keeps not rabbits but goldfish, one of which seems to be in difficulty until he is able to announce in a one-sentence chapter, "My fish is a mother." This shameless parody joins takeoffs on "Christopher Robin Is Saying His Prayers," the title of Capote's *Other Voices, Other Rooms*, and other literary fooling to enliven this otherwise lightweight novel — though again such things were probably wasted on the drug-store clientele who originally picked up this 45¢ paperback. The most arcane allusions come from the villain of the piece, who dotes on classical authors (he has misplaced his Virgil, his Petronius is dog-eared), browses through Krafft-Ebing, and occasionally thinks in Latin quotations. Such allusions don't fulfill any larger function than dressing the character, though they do remind the reader of Markson's easy erudition.

This sort of learning is absent from Markson's next novel, *The Ballad of Dingus Magee* (1966), aside from a few facetious references to Emersonian Transcendentalism and an allusion at the end to the final line of *Huckleberry Finn*. As Joseph Tabbi points out elsewhere, there are broad structural allusions to *Oedipus Rex, Don Quixote*, and *Tom Jones* in *Dingus Magee*, and a kind of continuous stylistic allusion to Faulkner.[2] But specific quotations are limited to epigrams from Wild West figures like Billy Clanton and Johnny Ringo (and one from Faulkner on the ideal job for a writer), along with some deflationary material on the truth behind many Old West myths, indicating that even in a novel like this — a transitional work between his early commercial novels and the more ambitious ones that followed — Markson did his research, matching wide reading with a vivid imagination to produce a fanciful but historically accurate work.[3]

Meanwhile, Markson was working on a novel that would make greater use of the lessons of the masters, a novel that would make its own contribution to the art of allusion as practiced by Joyce, Eliot, and Lowry. Years later, John Barth would write to Markson: "I remembered *Dingus Magee* with a smile, and even Leslie Fiedler's praise of it,[4] from back in the days when paperbacks cost 60¢. It's a Borgesian exercise to amalgamate the author of that book with the author of *Going Down*" (letter dated 18 May 1982). Published in 1970, *Going Down* is concerned with the despair and catatonic apathy experienced by three young, fairly well-read characters: Fern Winters, Steve Chance, and Lee Suffridge. The focus of the novel is less on how they reached this state than on how they live with it (or die by it) — and more specifically, on how despair is for them as much a literary experience as a psychological one. The function of the disproportionately large number of literary references and allusions in the text is to show how certain artistic works can define, nurture, even ennoble for some individuals their feelings of alienation and inadequacy.

2 "David Markson: An Introduction," *Review of Contemporary Fiction* 10.2 (Summer 1990): 93–94.

3 [Since this essay now appears in a section on Gaddis's friends, it's worth adding that when Alice Denham asked Gaddis what he thought of *Dingus Magee*, he called it "Pure slapstick" and a "Riotous performance" (*Sleeping with Bad Boys* [Las Vegas: Book Republic, 2006]).]

4 Fiedler praises *Dingus* in *The Return of the Vanishing American* (see Tabbi, 94) but doesn't note that his surname was used in the novel for Captain Fiedler, who, we learn at the end of the novel, marries the love-starved schoolmarm Agnes Pfeffer.

Fern, the 23-year-old painter whose deterioration — "going down" into depression, perversity, and madness — is the principal activity of the novel, generates most of the literary and artistic references, either in conversation or in the free indirect discourse in which most of the novel is narrated. Half of the novel's 14 chapters are narrated from her viewpoint, and she figures prominently in most of the others. More background is given for her than for the others: her childhood humiliation at her withered left hand, an apparently expensive education followed by two years of joyless promiscuity, frustrating attempts to develop as a painter, and a creeping sense that she is losing her mind. As she broods on these things, she is constantly reminded of characters and lines from books, fictional situations parallel to her own. Fern's background in literature is wide but fairly standard: an anthology's worth of poetry ranging from the anonymous Middle English lyric "Western Wind" to Eliot's *Waste Land*, a few Shakespeare plays (*Hamlet, Macbeth, The Tempest*), and a handful of novels of the sort usually assigned in college (*Moby-Dick, As I Lay Dying*) or that more ambitious students might read on the side (*Ulysses, Steppenwolf*). Compared to Chance's exotic library, Fern's books "were predictable, the standard classroom currency of the moment" (88), and most of her allusions are easily recognized by anyone who underwent a similar curriculum.

Her knowledge of art history is much greater, embracing technical matters as well as a good deal of anecdotal material about the troubled lives of artists. (In this regard she anticipates Kate of *Wittgenstein's Mistress*.) Despite her psychological problems, Fern has an adhesive memory for a wealth of literary and artistic details and the ready wit to find an appropriate line or anecdote to match any occasion. Given her unhappiness and sense of impending madness, she is understandably drawn to the gloomy and Gothic — Poe, *Wuthering Heights, Moby-Dick* — and to works concerned with abulia, despair, or madness, like *The Waste Land, Hamlet* (probably the most frequently cited text), Munch's *The Scream*, and *Steppenwolf*. Concerned for her own state of mind, she doesn't go to a psychiatrist but instead turns to Nijinsky's diary or to Vasari's lives of the painters to find other great minds gone astray, seeking not so much an explanation or cure for her fears as an artistic justification, even a sense of camaraderie with others who've entered the door that Hesse marks "For Madmen Only."

Ironically, it is exactly this tendency that complicates a reader's response to Fern's character. On the one hand, the very quantity of her allusions, her habit of constantly referring her own experiences and perceptions to literary and artistic antecedents, will strike some readers as precious and artificial, leading them to second Steve's impatient rebuke to Fern to "try to think about [things] in some context other than your own self-indulgent spurious civilized neurotic way" (159). Such readers will regard Fern as a spoiled little rich girl with drama-queen tendencies, self-aggrandizing herself into "Fern Van Gogh," and taking garden-variety apathy and dressing it up into existential despair by way of inappropriate literary models. On the other hand, there is a bitter, self-deprecating tone to many of Fern's allusions, indicating she is as aware as anyone of the unsuitability of evoking Hamlet or Dante as a parallel to her own "shabby neurosis . . . [her] two-peso version of the abyss" (50, 51). But while she can joke about becoming "Schizo-Fernic" (118), the very real schizophrenia she seems to suffer from, especially by the end of the novel, suggests her use of allusion is itself a symptom of schizophrenia, a defense mechanism used to shield herself from intolerable situations by instinctively deflecting them onto a stronger literary figure. Even her miserable end, as a deranged whore in Veracruz, is ennobled as she emulates (in her mind) Saint Mary of Egypt and represents (to others) a miracle-working Virgin.

Her partner in despair, Steve Chance — a kind of black hole, sucking nearby bodies into his center of gravity — is likewise well read, allusive, and self-deprecating about his despair, but in a bleaker and more mysterious way. Variously compared by others to Hamlet, Faust, Heathcliff, Raskolnikov, Stavrogin, and characters of that ilk, Chance is associated with arcane theological works, both Occidental and Oriental, as well as with myth, anthropology, and folklore. His bookshelves contain such works as Saint Anselm's *Proslogion*, Raymond Lully's *Ars Magna*, Judah Halevi's *Kuzari*, Tertullian's *Adversus Praxean*, and the *Enchiridion Fontium Historiae Ecclesiasticae*. His vocabulary contains such words as "stercoraceous" and "genizah," and when he quotes a line of poetry, it is likely to be from something like Kalidasa's *Shakuntala* or the Hebrew *Kol Nidre*. Like T. S. Eliot and such learned literary characters as Lowry's Consul and Gaddis's Wyatt Gwyon, Steve is drawn to such books in search of some sort of "Order, maybe" (174), and perhaps for some explanation or justification for the desolation he's felt ever since the death of his father when Steve was still a teenager. (The oblique description of his father's death on pages 200–201 seems to implicate Steve, but whether he pushed his father or simply failed to prevent him from falling over the cliff is left ambiguous.) We are told "something happened to him when his father died that transcended common grief" (164) and learn that he spent succeeding years traveling through the East "like some fugitive or wanderer upon the earth" (163, echoing Gen. 4:14). His father, the poet Eric Chazen, could be overheard (usually when drunk) "discussing something, original sin, the *Gita* . . . with Avicenna. Maimonides" (96), and Steve's adult obsession with theological concepts and writers suggests that he's more interested in solving the mystery of his father — a drunkard who killed Steve's mother in a car accident — than in the mystery of Our Father.

"Something happened," but Steve has never found an explanation in any of the books he's read, and in fact has reached the point where he doesn't "give a damn about . . . books, art, all the recondite, agonized reasons why anybody . . . writes or not" (99–100). The despair he feels is almost too deep for words, nor is art a valid way to combat depression, for as he argues, those who try are superficial: "There has to be a lie in it, Fern. Real despair, a real sense of the . . . Jesus, just the boredom . . . and there wouldn't be any point in . . . words — " (98). The reader later learns that Steve indeed has been trying to write, but his scribbled pages end up as toilet tissue, and one of his final involuntary literary associations sputters out in fierce condemnation: "'Dante, fuck you,' he said. 'And, dear Jesus, fuck all the . . . unnecessary books — '" (259). Moments later he is a suicide, but staged as a literary allusion, as it were, to Christ's crucifixion. The peasant girl Petra called the literary figures Eric addressed when drunk "demons," and demons from books hound father and son alike to their deaths.

Although it would be specious to separate authorial allusions from the ones his characters make, it is worth noting that Markson limits his referential material within the perimeters of his characters' reading. For example, he gives the name Roderick to the former owner of the house in Mictlán that Steve and the woman rent, a name congruent with Fern's own interest in Poe. The various Aztec names Markson uses — Mictlán (the Aztec underworld), Chignahuapán (a lake in the underworld) — are in keeping with Steve's references to Aztec mythology and sacrificial practices. Even the ludicrous use of Oedipus as the name of an old nag functions subliminally to keep the name in the reader's mind until it can be applied later as details emerge of Steve's troubled relationships with his father and with his father figure, Ferrin Priest. Markson thus reinforces his characters' reading and knowledge without ever adding foreign, incongruent material that would upset the careful texture of literary, artistic, and theological references at work in the novel. In this regard he is closer to Lowry than to Joyce, and achieves the same kind of claustrophobic intensity that characterizes *Under the Volcano* (as opposed to the more open-minded feel of *Ulysses*).

It remains to ask why so literary a writer as Markson would write a novel about the failure of literature to provide solace, insight, or even much enjoyment to characters like Fern and Steve. Perhaps because it is not meant to — literature is an art form, not a Dear Abby forum — or perhaps because literature, like anything, can be misused, used as protective coloring by empty people who come and go, talking of Michelangelo. Or perhaps it is because, as Steve suggests, even works about despair are only contrived representations of despair, their artifice and very existence disqualifying them from authenticity. In this regard, it is worth noting that the truest expression of despair in

Going Down is given not to any of the well-read Americans but to an ill-read Mexican, for whom Markson reserves his most beautiful prose:

> And then a vast, an immense sadness, pressed down upon Manolo where he paused, and a sorrow almost beyond bearing. It was not for today, for these embarrassments of stupidity alone, but for all of life as he had known it, here, upon these few rude meters of earth, with so many days of anguish, or despair, and eternally too, with the great, the unanswered longing. For what could it serve to be a man, to live, for such as he, who knew only that he must suffer and labor and die, and to taste of ashes forever, what good, what hope? (226)

Where *Going Down* broods on literature as a medium for despair, *Springer's Progress* (1977) celebrates it as a medium for wit and venery. This clever and charming tale of extramarital affairs and the literary life begins with a parody of Bunyan's *Pilgrim's Progress*, but the language and spirit are those of other 17th-century writers: word-drunk bibliomaniacs like Robert Burton and Sir Thomas Browne, robust translators like Sir Thomas Urquhart and Peter Motteaux, and the poets who elevated wit as the crowning achievement of art, ranging from such literary lounge lizards as Herrick and Waller to ingenious metaphorists such as Donne and Marvell. The novel has wit in its 17th-century sense — "a tough reasonableness beneath the slight lyric grace," as Eliot wrote of Marvell, an "alliance of levity and seriousness" — but also in the more specific sense of "learned wit," the inventive and usually farcical treatment of erudition by way of literary allusions, lists (of authorities, of facts), parodies, and other irreverent approaches to canonized literature. A literary allusion in a novel of this sort is not a respected authority lending cultural weight, but rather a straight man for the author's wit.

Consider this particularly allusive passage from Markson's novel, in which Lucien Springer is in a bar thinking of his lover Jessica Cornford visiting relatives in Ohio. The usually promiscuous Springer is trying his best to resist the temptations surrounding him:

> Norma Miljus again? Third time he'll spot her in the two weeks. Buttressed bum and buttery boobs, recalls, acres of supplest forage. Requiting wench as well, what's to fear?
>
> Come-hithering hi from Beverly Allerdice also, saloon's aswim in aloneness, third of a nation ill-fondled and ill-humped.
>
> Won't, won't. Toss the drunken dog one bone named Cornford, lifetime's Pavlovian dedication down the stews.
>
> A child said, *What is the ass?* fetching it to him with full hands.
>
> Final scrotumtightening image as her elevator swallowed him, altarwise by owllight in her doorway framed. A grief ago.
>
> Imagining Ohio also, house on a hill. Dappled things, for Christ's sake? And brinded cows.

> *Ein Jessbetrunkener Mensch.* Small rain down, forgot his letters. (122)

It immediately becomes apparent that an appreciation of the wit (and even the meaning) of this passage is dependent upon a familiarity with the sources of Springer's allusions. (Many of these sources appear in the same chapter, teasing the reader to match them up.) Passages like these are like extended in-jokes shared between author and reader, and like any joke, would be spoiled if one had to explain that "third of a nation ill-fondled and ill-humped" is a takeoff on a famous phrase in FDR's second inaugural address, explain who Pavlov was, that Whitman's child originally had a handful of *grass*, that "scrotumtightening" is from Joyce's *Ulysses* and that "altwarwise by owl-light" and "A grief ago" are titles of Dylan Thomas poems, that "Dappled things" and "brinded cows" have been imported from Hopkins's England ("Pied Beauty"), that Novalis called Spinoza "*ein Gott-betrunkener Mensh*" (a God-intoxicated man), and that "Small rain down" is from the same medieval lyric Fern remembers, "Western Wind," another lament for an absent lover.

The reader needing all that explained might testily ask Why? Why the telegraphic allusions and parodies that none but a *Literatur-betrunkener Mensch* would recognize and appreciate? One answer is that the elliptical references function here not only as a representation of Springer's thinking process — a kind of literary shorthand — but as the writer/reader's equivalent for the private references and intimacies that two lovers usually share — literary allusions as pillow talk. A related answer is given by Springer himself as he contemplates the aim of the novel he plans to write (and that we are reading): "Play a little. With luck a phrase or three worth some lonely pretty girl's midnight underlining" (218). This seems a modest, even trivial ambition. And yet, Markson means his novel to be intriguing, delightful, as desirable as that lonely pretty girl. The novel is as pert and sassy as an impetuous new lover, playful and teasing, happy one moment and sad the next — artistically contrived so that the reader's experience with the text is analogous to Springer's experience with Jessica. In *Springer's Progress*, literary allusion is a sex toy, an (extra)marital aid to heighten and prolong the delight Springer and Jessica experience with each other, and the delight the reader experiences sharing their wit. (In one of his *Rambler* essays, Dr. Johnson defines wit as "the unexpected copulation of ideas.") The literary references and puns they bandy back and forth are not to meant to echo the way people talk — even well-read people — but instead to create a literary equivalent to their carnal joys and sorrows. The Chinese water torture of Jessica's oft-repeated excuse "I'm seeing a friend" should annoy the reader as much as it does Springer, and likewise the reader should scream with joy when, after 227 pages of doubts and frustrations, Springer hears Jessica admit, "I do sort of love you, if somehow you haven't known?" (This admission is immediately followed by a literary scream of joy, so artistically right, as is every line in the book.) The reader doesn't simply *observe* the affair, as in a conventional novel, but *participates* in Springer's progress, a ménage à trois in which literary delight matches carnal delight.

In the same essay on Marvell, Eliot argues that wit is "structural decoration of a serious idea," the serious idea in *Springer* being the same as that in Gass's *Willie Masters' Lonesome Wife* and Barthes's *Pleasure of the Text*, namely that reading is ideally an erotic experience. A skillful author is like a skillful lover, and not for nothing is the high point of a novel called the climax. Nor is Markson the first to consciously imitate in his novel the rhythms of a sexual encounter: one thinks of the teasing near-seductions of Fanny throughout Fielding's *Joseph Andrews*, which heighten the reader's impatience to see the wench bedded as much as it does Joseph's; or of the rhythm of *Moby-Dick*, five hundred pages of foreplay with metaphysics and cetology leading up to the climactic sighting and harpooning of the whale, a text lubricated with Melville's spermy prose and wedding imagery; or think of the final chapter of Faulkner's *Light in August*, where the storytelling becomes a deliberate kind of foreplay as the furniture dealer keeps his impatient wife on edge by prolonging his anecdote. Like these works, *Springer's Progress* is not so much a representation of sex — i.e., mere pornography — as an equivalent experience, arousing the reader to the sensuous qualities of language and the stimulating rewards of fondling a body of literature.

Just as reading becomes a sexual act, so too writing. When Springer finally breaks through his writer's block and begins writing, he exults: "As on she flows, sweet ruptured maidenhead of the mind! Less than a ransacked virgin's notion of what's ahead still, but ah, how beatific's the gush" (205). As he writes of his affair, he falls in love all over again with Jessica and reaches the point where, showering together, Springer will "Clasp her anew, they'll cleave still liquidy there awhile, serene. Springer with his book in his arms" (231). Pygmalion fell in love with his work of art and prayed to have his statue brought to life; Springer reverses the procedure and converts his lover into a work of art, a novel as sexy, frustrating, clever, and satisfying as Jessica herself — the flesh made word. In its clever use of literary allusion, comic stichomythia, and inspired parody, *Springer's Progress* is one of the most brilliant examples of learned wit in modern literature and admits Markson into the small circle of contemporary writers — Barth, Gaddis, Pynchon, Sorrentino, Theroux — who are keeping this venerable tradition alive.

At first glance, *Wittgenstein's Mistress* (1988) seems to have little in common with Markson's previous work — or anyone else's, for that matter. (The nearest precedent for it would be Charlotte Perkins Gilman's 1892 story "The

Yellow Wallpaper," also narrated in short paragraphs by a woman seesawing between sanity and madness, with a fertile if disordered imagination.) It has the least amount of dramatic activity of all of his novels, being (at the simplest level) the rambling meditations of a woman named Kate who seems to be the last person on earth. And yet it has the greatest amount of intellectual activity, being (at this level) one of the most profound investigations of epistemology in literature and the best fictional illustration I know of Wittgenstein's proposition that "Philosophy is a battle against the bewitchment of our intelligence by means of language."

Like all of Markson's protagonists, Kate views the world through the lenses of culture: "one does not spend any time viewing castles in La Mancha without being reminded of Don Quixote," she writes. "Any more than one can spend time in Toledo without being reminded of El Greco" (39). And like both Fern in *Going Down* and Lucien in *Springer's Progress*, Kate has a huge fund of anecdotal material on painters, supplemented by a general knowledge of writers, composers, singers, and philosophers — often the kind of material, however (and as Kate is the first to admit), that one picks up from such places as the liner notes on record albums, dust-jacket copy, or digressive footnotes in biographies. Kate can't remember where she learned many of these items — things like the fact that manuscripts of Sappho's poems were once used to stuff mummies — nor why such trivia has stayed with her all these years while more substantial matters have slipped her mind. Nor does she always remember such trivia correctly, and it is here that Markson's art of allusion differs most not only from his earlier work but from that of other allusive writers.

For earlier writers (and in Markson's earlier works), culture was stable and objective, an orderly accumulation of facts — names, dates, compositions, critical opinions — that could be called up by the writer (and/or his characters) as in a user-friendly data-retrieval system. In *Wittgenstein's Mistress*, however, culture is unstable and subjective, a fading memory of "baggage" that teases Kate with false connections, "inconsequential perplexities," and meaningless coincidences. It is a disorderly jumble where Euripides seems to have been influenced by Shakespeare, where Anna Akhmatova is a character in *Anna Karenina*, and where Willem de Kooning wears a soccer jersey in Giotto's Renaissance studio. Kate lives in a world of cultural relativity similar to the physical one described by Einstein and the historical one described by recent historians, who likewise have realized that history is not an objective set of facts but a subjective welter of interpretations.

Kate's attempts to order her cultural memories are often earnest, often comic: for example, the reason Euripides sounds as though he'd been influenced by Shakespeare is that she's read Gilbert Murray's Shakespearean translation of *The Trojan Women*; so Kate wonders if a bookstore she enters in Athens has "a Greek edition of William Shakespeare's plays. By a translator who had been under the influence of Euripides" (45). This is as funny as it is profound, upsetting traditional notions of influence and the transmission of culture while at the same time being perfectly plausible. (And note the Jack Benny pause between those two sentences; Kate has a deliciously dry wit that, like Springer's, rescues her from many potentially maudlin moments.) Sometimes it takes her several pages (and several weeks) to complete a tantalizing connection: on page 12, for example, she relates the fact that the British painter Turner once "had himself lashed to the mast of a ship for several hours, during a furious storm, so that he could later paint the storm." This reminds her of something, but she can't remember what. Then on page 83 she thinks about the scene in the *Odyssey* in which "Odysseus has himself lashed to the mast of his ship, so that he can listen to the Sirens singing but will stay put." Again she is reminded of something but can't say what. Finally, a hundred pages (and *many* weeks) later, Kate writes:

> Have I ever said that Turner once actually had himself lashed to the mast of a ship, to be able to later do a painting of a storm?
>
> Which has never failed to remind me of the scene in which Odysseus does the identical thing, of course, so that he can listen to the Sirens singing but will stay put. (189–90)

Other times the connection is never made, like the one Kate suspects exists between Lawrence of Arabia and T. E. Shaw; she comes so close so often to making the link that the reader wants to shout it out to her as though in the audience of a game show.

Kate's cultural allusions also differ from the usual ones in that more emphasis is placed on the artist than on the work, especially on the kinds of personal and domestic details that are usually ignored. When she cites Maupassant, for example, it is not to allude to one of his stories or to his theory of fiction but to remember that he liked to row and ate his lunch at the Eiffel Tower because that was the only place in Paris from which he couldn't see the monument. The first half of the novel is filled with such trivia, but midway Kate's references begin to take a different turn and emphasize the darker side of the lives of cultural figures, noting those who went mad, were forced into exile or poverty, who committed suicide, went blind, and so on. Here a reference to Maupassant will hint (111) and then state (234) that he ended up crawling about on all fours and eating his own excrement. "Even though the work itself lasts, of course," Kate reminds herself. "Or does thinking about the work itself while knowing these things somehow sadden one even more?" (139). A sense of futility hangs over culture and history as Kate attempts to sort all this out, tempting the reader to equate Western civilization's greatest works of art and philosophy with the futile messages Kate leaves in the street or, better yet, with the messages she leaves in sand, washed away almost before she can complete them. The culmination of this train of thought is the mournful litany near the end of the book for all those who succumbed to the Siren song of art, as destructive as it is seductive, as well as for those who were victims of more mundane miseries:

> God, poor Maupassant.
>
> Well, but poor Friedrich Nietzsche, too, actually.
>
> If not to mention poor Vivaldi while I am at it also, since I now remember that he died in an almshouse.
>
> And for that matter poor Bach's widow Anna Magdalena, who was allowed to do the same thing. . . .
>
> Ah, me. If not to add poor Andrea del Sarto and poor Cassandra and poor Marina Tsvetayeva and poor Vincent Van Gogh and poor Jeanne Hébuterne and poor Piero di Cosimo and poor Iphigenia and poor Stan Gehrig and poor singing birds sweet and poor Medea's little boys and poor Spinoza's spiders and poor Astyanax and poor my aunt Esther as well. . . .
>
> So for that matter poor practically the whole world then, more often than not. (234–36)

This outpouring of sympathy seems to have a cathartic effect on Kate, however. Nearly two months have passed since she broke off typing the book we are reading, and some sense of balance and renewal seems to have come to her in the meantime. After the first snow falls, she is reminded of "that old lost nine-foot canvas of mine, with its opaque four white coats of gesso. [¶] Making it almost as if one could have newly painted the entire world one's self, and in any manner one wished" (233). She seems to be doing just that at novel's end, building fires down near the water after sunset and making believe they are Greek watchtowers at Troy, starting over again where it all began. Like the woman in the hypothetical novel Kate toys with writing (a metafictional version of *Wittgenstein's Mistress* itself, obviously) Kate has "gotten more accustomed to a world without any people in it than she ever could have gotten to a world without such a thing as *The Descent from the Cross*, by Rogier van der Weyden, . . . Or without the *Iliad*" (232–33). The throat-constricting desolation of the novel's final lines seven pages later discourages the reader from too cheery an interpretation, but civilization and its discontents seem finally to have been worth it after all.

In his 1972 review of the facsimile edition of Eliot's *Waste Land*, George Steiner points out that "in the years 1910 to 1940, Ezra Pound, T. S. Eliot, and James Joyce impressed their audience as iconoclasts, as demolition experts bent on blowing up traditional literary and linguistic forms in the name of esoteric modernism." He goes on to suggest that the wealth of allusions in their work, however, now appear as

> deliberate acts of conservation, of inventory. They are a nostalgic, obsessed voyage through the museum of high culture just before closing time, or — in Eliot's own famous phrase — "fragments shored" against the impending ruin of classical and European values. . . . Their works are crammed with quotations from, allusions to, pastiches and parodies of the best art, music, and literature of the previous two thousand years. They were not destroyers but custodians of tradition.[5]

This strikes me as an especially apt description of *Wittgenstein's Mistress*, but Steiner then poses a question relevant to Markson's full output: "Can there be a kind of iconoclastic academicism, a strategy that keep tradition vital by often violent appropriation and distortion?" Markson's novels give an affirmative answer to this question. In his work — as in the work of Barth, Pynchon, and especially Sorrentino — learning is subjected to experimental forms and devices that seem a deliberate slap in the face of culture. And yet these writers, like their modernist forebears, actually demonstrate a greater regard for (and deeper understanding of) the Great Tradition than any of the more conventional novelists usually thought to be carrying on that heritage. Springer may parody Whitman, say, and Kate may refer to him only as someone who said hello to Abraham Lincoln in the streets of Washington, DC, but the fact that Whitman occurs at all in any late-20th-century novels shows something of that custodial impulse Steiner finds in Joyce and Eliot. Most of Markson's allusions are more substantial and provocative, of course; in fact, a fine liberal education would result from following up on the full range of references in his works. (His Lowry book alone is equivalent to an Introduction to Western Civilization course.) Markson's novels deserve to be read and studied for a variety of reasons, but not the least of them is his mastery of the classical art of allusion.

CODA: THE NOTECARD QUARTET[6]

After warming up with three commercial novels, the late David Markson (1926–2010) published seven ultraliterary ones between 1966 and 2007. At a glance, the first three ultraliterary ones look totally different from each other,

5 "The Cruellest Months," *New Yorker*, 22 April 1972, 134, 137–42.

6 [A review I volunteered to write for *American Book Review* of *This Is Not a Novel and Other Novels* (Counterpoint, 2016) mostly so that I could add a few remarks here on Markson's last four novels.]

while the last three — now available in a handsome omnibus edition — look totally alike. The fourth, the paradigm-shifting *Reader's Block* (1996), set the pattern for the last three, but can also be seen as the culmination of a propensity that runs through all the earlier ones, including the commercial warm-ups. From early on, Markson loved novels thick with literary allusions and intellectual references, specifically Joyce's *Ulysses*, Lowry's *Under the Volcano*, and Gaddis's *Recognitions*. As he progressed in his career, each new novel became thicker with allusions and references, and seemed to reach a saturation point in *Wittgenstein's Mistress* (1988), whose thin raft of a plot supports a heavy cargo of references to all of Western culture. Markson finished writing that one in 1984, spent the next three years trying to find a publisher, then spent the next seven years contriving a way to write "A novel of intellectual reference and allusion, so to speak minus much of the novel," as the narrator of *Reader's Block* states on page 61.

That novel dramatizes the author's ruminations on how much traditional novelistic matter he should use in his next novel: plot, setting, character background, autobiographical details he might use, and so on, the types of things a typical novelist would think about during the planning stages. ("Author" here refers to both Markson and his novel-writing stand-in, whom he calls Reader.) He expresses some reluctance to bother with such stuff: "Valéry said he could never write a novel for one insurmountable reason. He would have to include sentences like The Marquise went out at five." Reader is more interested in trivia about artists like that, which begin popping up on the very first page. Those factoids, and the patterns they create (anti-Semitism, insulting reviews, artistic eccentricities, and especially the deaths of artists), prove more interesting to the author than the mundane matters of plot and characterization. Blocked from writing a typical novel, "his mind full of clutter," Reader compiles this atypical one instead, retaining the notes and queries to himself and all the factoids but dispensing with the traditional novel outerwear. There's page-turning momentum and a skeletal narrative arc — "I have a narrative. But you will be put to it to find it," he taunts — but without the novelistic padding and connective tissue. Markson's paragraphs had been growing shorter ever since *Going Down*; here they are printed in discrete units with spaces in between, so that the pages resemble X-rays where the novelistic innards are whited out. Given Markson's idolatry of *Ulysses*, the style could be described as stream of consciousness without the water, just hundreds of river stones.

Though Markson didn't intend to write a sequel, much less to compose what some critics now call a Notecard Quartet, he liked the form of *Reader's Block* enough, and was pleased enough at its favorable reception, to write another one. Alienated by the publisher of *Reader's Block*, Markson submitted his next novel to Counterpoint, which not only published his subsequent novels but reissued some of his earlier ones. *This Is Not a Novel* appeared in 2001, followed by *Vanishing Point* in 2004 and the prophetically named *The Last Novel* in 2007.

Though there are slight shifts in emphasis in each one, even less novelistic matter, and slightly different characterizations of their narrators (all of whom are 98% Markson himself), all four novels explore a common theme. It can be found in a book cited in *Reader's Block*, Schopenhauer's *Parerga and Paralipomena* — specifically, the Penguin version called *Essays and Aphorisms*. (That's where Markson found the misogynistic statement about women on p. 138 of *Reader's Block*.) On pages 210–11 of the Penguin edition (1970), Schopenhauer writes:

> I wish someone would one day attempt a *tragic history of literature*, showing how the various nations which now take their highest pride in the great writers and artists they can show treated them while they were alive. In such a history, the author would bring visibly before us that endless struggle which the good and genuine of all ages and all lands has to endure against the always dominant bad and wrong-headed; depict the martyrdom of almost every genuine enlightener of mankind, almost every great master of every art; show us how, with a few exceptions, they lived tormented lives in poverty and wretchedness, without recognition, without sympathy, without disciples, while fame, honour and riches went to the unworthy; . . .

This is what Markson's last four novels are "about," especially since he regarded himself as an unfairly neglected writer, though he brings his artists down several pegs by giving plenty of examples of their anti-Semitism, misogyny, self-destructiveness, and other shortcomings. Schopenhauer obviously didn't have a quirky quartet of experimental novels in mind, but it is hard to imagine a finer fulfillment of his hypothetical project.

Tragic, yes, but like Shakespeare's tragedies, there's some clowning around: wry asides, ironic juxtapositions, in-jokes, even the teasing title Counterpoint chose for this omnibus. Up to *The Last Novel* he couldn't resist impudent quotations like Jacques Prévert's "Our father who art in heaven / Stay there."

This Is Not a Novel — a play on both Magritte's captioned painting *Ceci n'est pas une pipe* and Diderot's proto-postmodernist story "Ceci n'est pas un conte" — is even more skeletal than *Reader's Block*. Instead of mulling over fictional possibilities, Writer (as this autobiographical protagonist is called) doesn't even want to think about such things. "A novel with no intimation of story whatsoever, Writer would like to contrive," it states on the opening pages. "Plotless. Characterless. [¶] Yet seducing the reader into turning pages nonetheless." And seduce us he does, with another fascinating collection of artistic trivia and laments over the injustices done to artists, cunningly patterned to mimic the plot development of a traditional novel, and building to a heartbreaking climax. Once again the syntax is often inverted, with objects coming before subjects (as in the example above), verbs sometimes eliminated, and scattered sentence fragments everywhere, as though Markson had renounced Joyce for Eliot to write "an ersatz prose alternative to *The Waste Land*," as Writer metafictionally suggests halfway through the book.

In *Vanishing Point*, "Author" lacks the energy to put his notes into manuscript form for another novel: "Author had been scribbling the notes on three-by-five inch index cards. They now come close to filling two shoebox tops taped together." His own struggles with old age and illness evoke another litany of woes about the creative life, an unputdownable sequence of factoids in which the actions and antics of artists through the ages take the place of the activities of characters in a traditional novel. "All sorrows can be borne if you put them into a story," he quotes Isak Dinesen as saying, and it's as though he can bear his sorrows as long as he can organize all those notes into an artful form.

Vanishing Point was published in 2004, and despite feeling "Old. Tired. Sick. Alone. Broke," Markson decided to write one more "notecard" novel, this one about the final days of "Novelist" and presciently called *The Last Novel*. That five-word quotation appears on its second page, but once again the author seduces us with his bottomless well of anecdotes, observations, coincidences, and quotations, intermittently foreshadowing his end with foreboding references to the roof of his apartment building. Erudite to the end, his final words are a quotation from the Flemish painter van Eyck, "*Als ick kan*," whose translation Novelist pondered a few pages earlier: "*That's it, I can do no more? All I have left? I can go no further?*"

In her introduction, novelist Ann Beattie, an old friend, wishes Markson were still alive and writing more novels in this format, but I remember him telling me after *The Last Novel* came out that he wanted to try something different, dealing with a relationship between an old writer and a young admirer, perhaps in the manner of *Springer's Progress*. (This is confirmed in Laura Sims's *Fare Forward: Letters from David Markson* [2014], which I warmly recommend.) But that closing line "*Als ick kan*" is hard to beat for finishing off a quartet or concluding a career. Also on that final page of *The Last Novel* the narrator quotes a slave's query from Aristophanes' *Peace*: "Is it true then, what they say — that we become stars in the sky when we die?" As Beattie points out, Markson has become something of a literary star since his death, and this brilliant volume should keep his star burning brightly.

Jack Green and Book Reviewing in America

There are two reasons for reprinting Jack Green's *Fire the Bastards!* in book form 30 years after its original appearance as a three-part series in an underground magazine: because it is the first sustained commentary on one of the greatest novels of our time, and because it raises disturbing questions about the book-review media that are as pertinent today [1992] as they were 30 years ago. William Gaddis's reputation has improved over those intervening years: *The Recognitions* (1955) was followed by *J R* (1975) and *Carpenter's Gothic* (1985), a body of work that has firmly established Gaddis as one of the most significant American novelists of the postwar period. The review media, on the other hand, hasn't improved; if anything, it has degenerated, and Green's essay is invaluable for understanding why — a topic I'll take up in the second part of this introduction.

The magazine that first published this piece was called simply *newspaper*, a one-man operation written, typed (in lower case and with minimal punctuation), mimeographed, and distributed by someone who called himself Jack Green (a pseudonym for Christopher Carlisle Reid). Green was born in or around 1928, son of Helen Grace Carlisle, author of *The Merry, Merry Maidens* and other novels. His stepfather was a textbook editor at Harcourt, Brace — coincidentally Gaddis's publisher. Green attended high school in Darien, Connecticut; a classmate remembers him as "a mathematical prodigy with a tremendous wit and facility for the piano." He entered Princeton in 1947, where he majored in music, but apparently he left without a degree. In the early '50s he lived in Greenwich Village, studied the psychological theories of Wilhelm Reich, and worked on trying to perfect various gambling systems. In October 1954, as he writes in his autobiographical essay "insurance company days" (*newspaper* 15 [1963?]: 7–15), he "came back from france to newyork hollowcheeked from learning how to lose at roulette" and decided to get a job as an actuary for Metropolitan Life, reasoning "if i must be a gambler, why not work for the house?" In this engaging essay Green recounts his frustrating two and a half years there, ending on a payday in the spring of 1957 when he

> took the cash, down the elevator and out! . . . went to madisonsquare fountain instead   i felt bright, feverish   tore off necktie & dress shirt, flung in fountain   walked home in t-shirt, feeling great   took the razor, the clock, & the mirror & threw them out the window

He then changed his name to Jack Green, perhaps taken from Jack Green's Card, a horse-racing tip sheet of the 1940s (cf. "Jack's Little Green Card" in *J R* [188]). Supporting himself as a freelance proofreader — by all accounts a quick and accurate one — he started *newspaper*, which he had been planning since his insurance company days. It played a central role in his life from 1957 to 1965, during which time he produced 17 issues. Appearing at irregular intervals, most issues were filled with his own writing, for even though he welcomed submissions, only a handful of outside material appeared during the entire run: a few poems and prose sketches, one issue (#6) reprinting Jack Jones's essay "To the End of Thought" and the next mostly filled with responses to Jones's piece. But Green's own writings showed great variety: there were many articles on Reich and especially on his persecution by the U.S. Food & Drug Administration, many book reviews (often a few words of straightforward praise followed by sample extracts, letting the books speak for themselves, as it were), scornful examples from the media of the time (especially *Esquire* and the *Village Voice*), articles on dodging the draft, the pointlessness of voting (backed with mathematical equations), on four-handed piano compositions, on peyote (reprinted in Seymour Krim's anthology *The Beats* [1960]), and on anything else that struck his fancy or, more often, infuriated him as yet another example of hypocrisy and mendacity.

In later years — specifically in a pamphlet jokingly called *newspaper* 18 published in 1979 — Green apologized for what he considered the "bad writing" of issues #1–17 and retracted his "sales pitch in #8 for peyote and LSD"; but *newspaper* is a bracingly eclectic and fiercely independent example of little-magazine journalism at its best. [In the blurb Gilbert Sorrentino furnished for the 1992 Dalkey edition, he praised the "unique and irreplaceable *newspaper*" as "one of the authentic minor splendors of New York literary life in the late fifties and early sixties."] After Green ceased publication in 1965 with #17, critic Donald Phelps wrote an "Obit of a Sort" (collected in his *Covering Ground: Essays for Now* [New York: Croton, 1969], 208–12) in which he called it "New York's best newspaper" for providing "a running commentary, drily attentive, on current America." Distinguishing "the tough, witty clarity of Green's surveillance" from "the formless, characterless spewing of the less talented 'underground' self-chroniclers," Phelps praises Green's "firmly intelligent critical integrity" and assumes "*newspaper* will continue, metamorphosized — for one hopes, many good years — in the person of its editor and author." But this was apparently not the case; aside from the *newspaper* #18 of 1979, Green seems to have self-published only an occasional pamphlet of punning prose: something called *I'm Going Dancing with Lesly Lesby* (1970?), which I've not seen; something else called *Preliminary Edition* (1982), which seems to be a revision-in-progress of *Lesly Lesby*. (*Preliminary Edition* and *newspaper* #18 were accompanied by separate pamphlets explaining all the references and allusions in these pieces.) In 1991 Green published *Snaps* (1991), a mélange of book recommendations, "pithy remarks," criticism of various media ranging from the *New York Times* to MTV, puns, opinions, jokes, and scenes from Greenwich Village life.

The format of *newspaper* was unusual in many ways. It was typewritten and mimeographed by Green himself on heavy, legal-sized beige paper in (according to Phelps) "a soot ink of Green's own composition," and stapled in the top lefthand corner. (Unfortunately, the paper has a high acid content, for surviving copies are brown and brittle with age.) Green used very little punctuation (except in quoted matter): no capital letters, few commas or apostrophes, with spaces at the end of sentences instead of periods (unless the line ended flush right), compound words closed up, with spaces between paragraphs rather than indentation. The purpose, Phelps felt, "is not only to disarm the reader, but to liberate Green's voice, by eliminating the most familiar and most innocuous-seeming, therefore the most inhibiting, conventions." Green himself gave this explanation in #2 in response to complaints about the lack of punctuation in #1:

> other publishers use page makeup mostly to conceal the fact that in writing one man is speaking to another, as face makeup & formal clothes are used to conceal it that man is naked before life   also, most nonfiction writing is styled so the reader can swill it down without chewing it   your teeth gone?   my lack of capitals & periods fits my use of incomplete sentences (breaths) and flexible stops — what could be less important?   if a thing is unimportant you should do it your way not the other persons   also if it is important

Copies were sold for a quarter in Greenwich Village bookstores and by subscription; few libraries today have the journal, so apparently it wasn't very successful in this regard or in any financial sense.

Gaddis's *Recognitions* was a recurring topic from the very first issue. Green learned of the novel from a review in the *New Yorker* shortly after publication in 1955, and though he admits that he had some difficulty adjusting to it at first, by 1957 he was convinced it was "a great work of art, the best novel ever written in America" (#1 [4 December 1957]: 5.) Noting that the book was being remaindered, he printed four long selections from it to encourage readers to pick it up. There were brief references to the novel in #2 (1958) and #8 (1959), and in 1960 came #10, a 32-page "Quote-Précis of William Gaddis's *The Recognitions*." In #11 (3 June 1961), Green announced

> the quoteprecis (#10) was the 1st of at least 5 long issues on gaddis   the articles on references & crossreferences in the recognitions   & attacking the reviews that prevented the book from being accepted as the masterpiece it is   are far from finished & there will again be a long delay between issues

"Fire the Bastards!" occupied three issues (#12–14) published over a nine-month period in 1962 and was continuously paginated: 76 pages of scorching invective and exhaustive analysis of every review *The Recognitions* received. But he didn't stop there: he also took out a full-page ad in the *Village Voice* (typeset himself) to publicize the newly released Meridian paperback edition of *The Recognitions* as well as *newspaper* #12. There was speculation then (and for many years after) that Gaddis not only paid for the ad himself, but that he was none other than Jack Green writing under a pseudonym. (Later there was even speculation that Gaddis, after "failing" with *The Recognitions*, began writing under the pseudonym of Thomas Pynchon.) Gaddis was naturally pleased at Green's prodigious efforts ("Here at last — a la ravanche!" he wrote to his editor Aaron Asher upon publication of #12) but undoubtedly kept his distance from the project (as he has with subsequent criticism of his work). He had met Green in 1959 and would run into him occasionally over the years, but apparently he had little to do with "Fire the Bastards!" aside from loaning Green the original reviews. (Green also supplied Gaddis with a list of typos in the first edition of *The Recognitions*, which were corrected in the 1962 Meridian edition and again in 1985 in the Penguin reprint of the novel.)

Despite its limited distribution, "Fire the Bastards!" caused a bit of a stir in the industry, as Green records at the end of the essay: "#12 touched a raw nerve, got some action   the establishment surrendered without a fight, admitting its sins with humorous tolerance for itself & those who had no right to be right." However, he goes on to admit "most of the 1962 plugs had only a momentary effect because they were by phonies, insincere jobholders who often hadnt even read the book." Sales of *The Recognitions* were strong enough to justify a second printing of the Meridian paperback in 1963, and in 1964 even the original publisher decided to reprint the hardcover edition (raising the price to $8.50 but ignoring the 60 or so corrections Gaddis made for the Meridian edition.) But by then the momentum had slowed and *The Recognitions* had once again gone "underground" to remain a "cult" book for another decade.

In 1964, Green wrote an epilogue of sorts (in *newspaper* #16) entitled "gaddis gossipcolumns" in which he concludes the story and regrets his efforts on behalf of Gaddis and Jack Jones's essay. Making special reference to a piece by Jerome Beatty Jr. in the "Trade Winds" column of *Saturday Review* (21 April 1962, 8–9), Green writes:

> beatty, hogan, macgregor & in *publisher's weekly* (see issue #14)   no interest in *the recognitions*, only in the "Gaddis underground" as a 3ring circus   beattys 14th & last paragraph gets around to "'The Recognitions,' by the way" — that sums it up)   hogan:
>
>> According to a hard core of partisans, "The Recognitions" is one of the most important works since Joyce's "Ulysses." I learned long ago never to argue with a hard core of partisans of anything. In this case I shall take their word for it, *and* leave the decision to future literary historians.
>
> (my italics)   decision if gaddis is "as good as Jack Green says he is, or is this just another nine-dollar bill?")   i invited this vulgar flippancy, at gaddis expense & mine, by letting gossipcolumnists interview me
>
> "hard core of partisans" — cf other critics "literary brotherhood," "William Gaddis bandwagon," "William Gaddis Fanclub" with their "enthusiastic admonitions to Read It," "small group of vocal admirers," "subterranean bible," "cult following"   david boroff, suggesting novels "which are not much read these days but deserve to be" (*ny times book review* 6/9/63 3) declines to discuss *the recognitions* because "The cults need little help from me" — there are already "loyal coteries beating the drums"   a 2d line of defense after the fake surrender of 1962   on this line, since those who speak up for gaddis work (or atonal music or *ulysses* or wilhelm reich) are noisy, cultist, ridiculous, it follows that the cultists *and the work* should be quarantined   this was a lie 50 yrs ago & it still is
>
> next step is to defame gaddis personally using the Fanclub as a steppingstone   beatty used what i blabbed to him, that when i quit the insurance company i threw my necktie into the madisonsquare fountain   gaddis was more reticent   middleman beattys revenge:
>
>> right now [William Gaddis] works in New York for a respectable corporation and he would rather not be identified any further than that. After all, he's got a *job*, and he's probably not about to toss his necktie into the Seagram Building pool.
>
> it was wrong & presumptuous of me to seek publicity for jones & gaddis in ways i wouldnt for myself   i risked interfering with natural growth of acceptance of their work by my "shot in the arm" methods

In the same issue of *newspaper* Green recounts the efforts made to reprint "Fire the Bastards!" in more permanent form. Poet and critic Karl Shapiro asked to reprint it in a special issue of *Prairie Schooner* that was to be devoted to Gaddis's novel. Green reluctantly agreed (because there was no reprint fee: the sponsoring university's yearly income was $20,000,000, he noted); as he tells it:

> few months later shapiro was finking about length: "what would you do in a case like this?"   so i prepared a ½length version but came to my senses at the last moment, didn't send it   few months more, shapiro out as editor   (university censors banned a story hed accepted — it was already set in type)   no reprint, no notice there wouldnt be one

Then (from the same issue #16): "sent 'fire the bastards!' to grove & putnam's . . . grove got the 50000word ms tuesday, sent it back wednesday   putnam's was less hasty — they never answered." Green continued his own work on the references and cross-references in *The Recognitions* until 1980 when, feeling it would never be "satisfactory," as he put it, he threw it out, but apparently made no further effort to reprint "Fire the Bastards!"

Two offers were made in the early 1980s to reprint the essay, but by then Green was no longer interested. I wanted to reprint it in an anthology of Gaddis criticism that John Kuehl and I were compiling. At that time (mid-1981) we had no idea of Green's whereabouts or whether he was even still alive. Since our prospective publisher expected to see the manuscript in early 1982, I decided we would lose valuable time if we waited until we located Green (assuming he could be located), so I sent a query for information regarding Green to the *New York Times Book Review* (which wasn't published until the following year) and began preparing a new typescript of Green's essay. Feeling that the lack of punctuation was an unnecessary hindrance — and not having read yet his justification of his practices in *newspaper* #2 — I restored capitalization and periods, indented paragraphs, and incorporated a few of his shorter footnotes into the body of the text in parentheses. The content remained exactly the same, only the appearance had changed. Kuehl and I were also concerned about getting this piece (along with the rest of the book) past an editorial board who might be put off by Green's unscholarly tone; we didn't have a contract yet and the eccentric format of Green's essay might have jeopardized our chances of publication. It wasn't until after I had prepared the typescript that William Gaddis was able to dig up an old address for me; I wrote to Green to ask permission to reprint "Fire the Bastards!" and he wrote back refusing permission, saying that the essay was poorly written.

A brief digression is needed at this point to explain the disingenuousness of his refusal. What he didn't mention was the fact that "Fire the Bastards!," like the rest of *newspaper*, was never copyrighted and thus was in the public domain. Legally, we didn't need his permission, for by refusing to copyright his work Green had relinquished all rights to it, had donated it to the public domain.[1] Nor was this an oversight: he was fully aware back in his *newspaper* days that his work was not under copyright, nor was this the first time he had concealed this. The most embarrassing piece in *newspaper* is an epistolary exchange published in #16 between Green and Orion Press. They had signed a contract whereby $20.00 was to be paid to Green "in consideration for permission to reprint" his essay "peyote" in a forthcoming book called *The Drug Experience*, edited by David Ebin, with the fee payable upon publication. Green chose to interpret the $20.00 fee to be for "permission" to reprint, whether they used the essay or not; the editors decided not to use "peyote" after all, but when the book was published in 1961 Green wrote demanding his fee. They wrote back explaining that the fee was understood to be for *use* of the essay, not merely for *permission* to use it, but Green threatened to sue and eventually Orion, just to get rid of him, paid the $20.00. (This wrangling occupied a year and a half's time.) At the end of the last letter, there is a snide postscript in parentheses by Green: "(ps 'peyote' is not copyrighted)." In other words, he knew that the whole legal exchange was a farce because permission for "peyote" was not his to give or withhold. His pharisaical insistence on the letter of the law at the expense of its spirit in this exchange is disheartening; when he adds that, in effect, he was simply bluffing, he becomes guilty of the same sort of mendacity he accuses in others.[2] It must be said, however, that this particular incident is a deviation; throughout the rest of *newspaper* Green seems to have strictly maintained the uncompromising high standards he set for himself and expected in others.

Back to our story. I was deeply disappointed in Green's refusal, partly because I had spent three months preparing the typescript (with much research verifying and adding details to his bibliography), and partly because I felt Green's essay was the cornerstone of Gaddis criticism and deserved to be better known. (I've lost track of how many times I've photocopied my set of *newspaper* #12–14 for other Gaddis critics.) So I wrote back remonstrating with him, offering to let him add a headnote explaining his current opinion of the work, and told him that I didn't think it was poorly written at all, espe-

1 [Revisions in copyright law from 1978 onward now provide copyright protection to any work upon creation, registered or not, but they were not retroactive to works created before 1978.]

2 [When I sent Green copies of Dalkey's edition of *Fire the Bastards!* in September 1992, he was predictably outraged and threatened to sue, but again he was bluffing and didn't follow through with his threats. Gaddis expressed mixed feelings about the reissue, "conflict[ed] in my head & history between vain pleasure at seeing Green's work preserved & circulated on the one hand & on the other my strong feelings over a writer's wishes for & implicit rights to his work & privacy however legally encroached upon . . ." (*Letters* 478–79).]

cially in the more conventional typescript I had prepared. That did it. The fact that I had "revised" his work (as he put it) without permission enraged Green. He wrote back to accuse me of "barefaced impudence," again refused permission, and forbade me to write him again "on this or any other subject." That last injunction kept Green in self-imposed ignorance of the actual circumstances of this project. Had I known of his whereabouts, I certainly would have asked his permission to put his essay in more conventional form. Had he allowed me to write again, I would have explained this and cheerfully offered to throw my three-months' labor out the window and submit his original with the rest of our manuscript and take my chances with the editorial board. But it seemed pointless to remonstrate further, or to ask Gaddis to intervene. As anyone who's dealt with a difficult person knows, these are no-win situations: goodwill gestures are twisted into malicious ones, the hand that feeds is viciously bitten, generous motives are assumed to mask selfish, ulterior motives, and so on. Even though we suspected Green had no legal right to his work, we decided to honor his undoubted ethical right to his own work. When the book was accepted and published by Syracuse University Press in 1984 as *In Recognition of William Gaddis*, I insisted on dedicating it to Green — Kuehl wanted to dedicate it to James Laughlin of New Directions — but even this "jolly (& deserved, really)" dedication, as Gaddis wrote me, was misinterpreted by Green as a deliberate insult on my part and he asked Kuehl to remove the dedication in any future printings.

In early 1982, John O'Brien also asked to reprint "Fire the Bastards!" in a special issue of his *Review of Contemporary Fiction* to be devoted to Gaddis's work, and he too was refused permission, Green again explaining that it was poorly written but that he hoped to issue revised versions of some of his early work someday.

Ten years later, deeply troubled by the current book-reviewing situation, O'Brien and I decided "Fire the Bastards!" was too important to remain unknown, and that Green's personal feelings regarding his work were heavily outweighed by cultural considerations regarding his essay's value for the ongoing debate over the inadequacy of the review media vis-á-vis innovative fiction. . . .[3]

As bad as the review "racket" may have seemed to Green in 1962, it is far worse today for innovative fiction.[4] Green notes that *The Recognitions* received 55

3 [Omitted is the rest of the paragraph on the editorial procedures of the Dalkey edition.]

4 ["Today" was 1992; nowadays the *mainstream* review media is even worse, especially after newspapers dropped or severely shortened their book-review sections in the early 2000s, though the slack has been picked up since then by many fine online sites.]

reviews — an astounding number for a huge, difficult novel by an unknown writer. (Some of these reviews were syndicated to several newspapers, raising the number even higher.) A similar novel published today would be lucky to get a fourth of that number. Finding a contemporary parallel to *The Recognitions* is difficult, but for purposes of comparison, consider the reception of William T. Vollmann's 1987 novel *You Bright and Risen Angels.* Like *The Recognitions,* it was a long, complex first novel from a young, unknown writer and was as far removed from the prevailing fiction trends of the mid-1980s as *The Recognitions* was from those of the mid-1950s. By any measure it was a brilliant debut, and even in a year that included several excellent American novels — John Barth's *Tidewater Tales*, Stanley Elkin's *Rabbi of Lud*, Joseph McElroy's *Women and Men*, Alexander Theroux's *An Adultery* — Vollmann's was arguably the most daring and creative novel of the year. How many reviews did this superb contribution to American literature receive in this country? Just ten. Three pre-publication trade journals reviewed it — *Publishers Weekly* (positive), *Kirkus Reviews,* and *Library Journal* (both negative, but a "fascinating flop," the latter concedes) — and there were brief mentions in *USA Today* and something called *Spectrum* (both noncommittal, but mildly positive). It received only five full-length reviews: in the *New York Times Book Review, San Francisco Chronicle* (Vollmann was living in that city at the time), *San José Mercury News, Providence Sunday Journal,* and the *Anniston* (Alabama) *Star.* Except for Jeff Riggenbach's positive notice in the *San José Mercury News,* the reviews were mixed, each finding as many faults as virtues in Vollmann's work. But Riggenbach's review appeared in the science fiction column, which meant it would have been ignored by many literary readers. (*You Bright and Risen Angels* is science fiction only in the broad sense that Burroughs's *Naked Lunch* or Pynchon's *Gravity's Rainbow* is.) The final result of this scanty attention is that a general reader interested in innovative fiction wouldn't have seen a *single* review that responded to *You Bright and Risen Angels* as it deserved and/or that recommended it strongly. Such readers learn of such books only by accident, by word of mouth, learning about it (as most kids learn of sex) from the streets, as it were.

Vollmann's novel received far fewer reviews than Gaddis's partly because the review media is less receptive to such work than it was 35 years ago, and partly because circumstances have changed for the worse. Many newspaper and book review supplements have reduced the amount of space available for reviews; some (like the *Saturday Review* and the *New York Herald Tribune*) no longer exist, others (like *Harper's*) no longer review books; many book review editors are journalists with non-literary backgrounds and conventional tastes; and there is a field-wide tendency to ignore literary fiction in favor of mainstream books. New product by the likes of Stephen King or Danielle Steel is now reviewed where in the past it would have been passed over in silence, if not with contempt; nowadays it is the literary fiction (and especially translations) that is passed over in silence.

Nor do reviewers seem to be any better qualified than they were in Green's day. But such complaints are hardy perennials, returning every publishing season in the mouths of disgruntled authors and publishers. (Readers too would complain if they were better acquainted with the book-reviewing process.) The problem is exacerbated today due to the sheer number of worthwhile books crying out for review. The proliferation of independent presses over the last ten years, taking up the literary slack of New York publishers and in many cases surpassing them in literary titles, has led to an unprecedented amount of quality literature being made available. But the interested reader learns of only a fraction of this work, and usually only those token literary books still published in New York by the big conglomerates. Where does a reader turn to keep abreast of literary fiction? The *New York Times Book Review*, once the obvious choice (though Green calls it "the worst bookreview section in the world"), now treats books as a branch of the entertainment industry and is the last place anyone would look for wide coverage of innovative fiction; besides, like the *New York Review of Books*, its emphasis is on nonfiction. The *Washington Post Book World* makes a greater effort to cover quality fiction, but hasn't room for extensive coverage. The *American Book Review* and the *Review of Contemporary Fiction* probably review more such fiction than anyone else, but *ABR* is usually seasons behind publication dates (by which time many bookstores have already returned the books to their distributors) and *RCF*, published only three times a year, lacks the immediacy of a weekly or monthly journal. Green said the worst review is no review at all, and too many quality books get no reviews at all in the places that matter most. If they don't get reviewed, they won't be stocked in bookstores, and thus the reader never learns about them, unless he or she comes across them by chance on a remainders table a year or two later.

The fact that Gaddis's *Recognitions* did eventually rise to the surface after being torpedoed by the critics may seem to argue that book reviews aren't all that important: worthy books will prevail, forgotten masterpieces will be rediscovered and take their places in the canon. But a complacent confidence that future literary historians will sort things out is damaging to both writers and our culture. Instead of joining the ranks of our leading novelists, William Gaddis spent the next 20 years of his career doing public relations work, scripting films for the army, writing speeches for corporate executives, and other deadening jobs. It is something of a miracle that he was able to write *J R* during those same 20 years, though it includes failed, suicidal writers who are more representative of neglected artists. Even when "forgotten masterpieces" are rediscovered and reprinted, they are treated not as active artworks but as historic relics. Innovative art always challenges the status quo and conventional modes of thinking and are meant to be a part of today's cultural dialogue, not fodder for tomorrow's dissertations. As Jack Green points out, "the real job of reviewing [is] to see that great books are bought now & not, like *the recognitions* will be, years & years after publication." It is the review media's responsibility to make these works known, but too often it acts as an obstacle course by placing inadequate reviews between the book and its potential readers, or, more and more frequently these days, it acts as a de facto censor by not even bothering to review such books.

It is highly ironic that we live in an Age of Information where, if anything, we risk information-overload on most topics, and yet where there isn't a single, comprehensive source for intelligent, timely coverage of quality fiction. The ills of the book-review media that Green diagnosed are apparently organic and irreversible; it is now impossible to imagine the current media expanding its coverage of this literature. To "fire the bastards!" may once have seemed like a solution, but a more practical one remains to be found.

Sheri Martinelli: A Modernist Muse

No notice was taken by the press of artist-writer Sheri Martinelli's death in November 1996, unfairly ignoring the significant role she played in the cultural history of our time. A brief overview of her career indicates her range of roles: she was a protégée of Anaïs Nin and is described at length in her infamous *Diary*; she was the basis for a major character in William Gaddis's novel *The Recognitions* and then became the muse and (some say) mistress of Ezra Pound (she appears in various guises in the later *Cantos*); Charlie Parker and the members of the Modern Jazz Quartet hung out at her Greenwich Village apartment; Marlon Brando was an admirer and Rod Steiger collected her art, as did E. E. Cummings; she knew and was admired by all the Beats — Allen Ginsberg was an especially close friend and mentions her in one of his poems; Gregory Corso put her on his complimentary copy list for *Gasoline* (1958) — and was herself known in San Francisco in the late 1950s as the Queen of the Beats; H.D. identified with her and wrote about her in *End to Torment*; Pound wrote the introduction to a book of her paintings, and her art is now in collections throughout the world. She wrote unusual prose and poetry, much of it published in her own 'zine. She corresponded with Charles Bukowski, who mentions her in a few of his poems, and was one of the first to publish his work. More recently, she appeared under a pseudonym in Anatole Broyard's posthumous memoir *Kafka Was the Rage*, as Lady Carey in Larry McMurtry's *Dead Man's Walk*, under her own name in David Markson's *Reader's Block*, and was anthologized in Richard Peabody's *A Different Beat*. When younger, she even modeled for *Vogue* and acted in one of Maya Deren's experimental films. And yet not a single obituary marked the passing of this remarkable woman — whom it was my honor and pleasure to have known the last dozen years of her life — and no account of her life exists anywhere.

So, for the record: Sheri Martinelli was born on 17 January 1918 in Philadelphia — on Ben Franklin's birthday and in his city — with the given name Shirley Mae Burns Brennan. Her father Alphonse was the son of a fisherman, and in later years Sheri liked to refer to herself as "The Fisherman's Granddaughter." Her mother was Maryellen Trindle, whose family was from Trindle Springs (now Mechanicsburg), Pennsylvania, named after an ancestor. Sheri's paternal grandmother claimed descent from Scottish poet Robert Burns. Shirley began using the name Sherry by the time she was a teenager, but she was later told that her first name had the wrong numerological value, so to rectify that she modified it to Sheri. (All her life she had a weakness for occult and metaphysical notions.) She was the oldest of three girls and a brother and was largely responsible for raising them. At some point her family moved to Atlantic City, New Jersey, but in the late 1930s Sheri moved back to Philadelphia to study art, specifically ceramics under John Butler at the Philadelphia School of Industrial Arts.

In Philadelphia she met Ezio Martinelli, a painter and sculptor who was studying at the Barnes Foundation in nearby Merion, Pennsylvania. Born in 1913, he was five years older than Sheri. They got married at the beginning of World War II, and in 1943 Sheri gave birth to a daughter, Shelley (named after the poet). The family moved to New York City, but by the end of the war they had grown apart. Sheri and Ezio separated; she kept his surname, and he kept the daughter. It's been said that Sheri left her husband because she felt she was a better painter, though by conventional standards Ezio Martinelli went on to achieve considerably more success in his field than she did: his abstract paintings were regularly exhibited at the Willard Gallery in New York City and respectfully reviewed; several sculptures of his are on display at the United Nations complex; from 1947 to 1975 he taught at Sarah Lawrence College, he won many grants and awards, and so on. (A photograph of him receiving one such award appears in *Art Digest*, 15 September 1947, p. 21.) He died in 1980.

Sheri stayed in Greenwich Village, moving into an apartment at 23 Jones Street in the West Village. Talented, beautiful, and intriguingly eccentric, she made a striking impression on all who met her, evident from the writings of those who knew her. In her diary entry for December 1945, Anaïs Nin recounts how she learned that a "romantic-looking girl" was reading her short-story collection *Under a Glass Bell* and had told her publishing partner Gonzalo Moré that she wanted to meet Nin but was too shy to approach the older woman. Nin suggested that she attend a lecture of hers at Mills College. When Sheri approached her at the end of the lecture, Nin writes, "I recognized her. She was like a ghost of a younger me, a dreaming woman, with very soft, burning eyes, long hair streaming over her shoulders." At first, Sheri didn't say a word: "She merely stared at me, and then handed me a music box mechanism, without its box. She finally told me in a whisper that she always carries it in her pocket and listens to it in the street. She wound it up for me, and placed it against my ear, as if we were alone and not in a busy hall, filled with bustling students and professors waiting for me. A strand of her long hair had caught in the mechanism and it seemed as if the music came from it."

"She came to see me," Nin goes on, "blue eyes dissolved in moisture, slender, orphaned child of poverty, speaking softly and exaltedly. Pleading, hurt, vulnerable, breathless. Her voice touches the heart. . . . She looks mischievous and fragile. She wears rough, ugly clothes, like an orphan. She is part Jewish, part Irish. Her voice sings, changes: low, gay, sad, heavy, trailing, dreaming" (107–8). Journalist Anatole Broyard, 40 years later, remembered her in much the same way: "She had a high, domelike forehead, the long silky brown hair of women in portraits, wide pale blue eyes with something roiling in their surface. Her nose was aquiline, her mouth thin and disconsolate, her chin small and pointed. It was the kind of bleak or wan beauty Village people liked to call *quattrocento*. Her body seemed both meager and voluptuous. Her waist was so small, it cut her in two, like a split personality, or two schools of thought. Though her legs and hips were sturdy and richly curved, her upper body was dramatically thin. When she was naked it appeared that her top half was trying to climb up out of the bottom, like a woman stepping out of a heavy garment" (3–4). Nin observed the same dichotomy: "Half of her body is heavy and animal, and the upper half is childlike and fragile" (144).

Sheri approached Nin for the same reason she would approach Pound a few years later: "She came because she felt lost," Nin writes. "I had found the words which made her life clearer." She goes on to quote Sheri: "Oh God, all the books one reads which don't bring you near the truth. Only yours, Anaïs" (108). As ingenuous as it may sound, it was this quest for truth, rather than celebrity-worship, that led Sheri to apprentice herself to writers like Nin and Pound.

Sheri joined Nin's entourage, a group mostly made up of young male admirers, with whom Nin felt more comfortable than with people of her own age (she was in her mid forties). "The presence of the young lightens the world and changes it from an oppressive, definitive, solidified one to a fluid, potentially marvelous, malleable, variable, as-yet-to-be-created world. I call them the transparent children" (95). At 27 Sheri was a bit older than the young men who surrounded Nin, but she began accompanying them to parties and outings. In the spring of 1946 she joined Nin and the others to act in Maya Deren's film *Ritual in Transfigured Time*; she appears in the party scene in the middle of the short film and in the park scene at the end. At this time Sheri was still starstruck; Nin quotes her as gushing, "You're a legendary character. I keep thinking that in the future I will look back and say: 'I was here in Yonkers Park with the legendary Anaïs!'" (145).

One of the young men dancing attendance on Nin was a French surrealist poet named Charles Duits (1925–1991), who had come to the U.S. in 1941 to attend Harvard, but left it a year or two later to live *la vie bohème* in New York. He is mentioned frequently in volumes three and four of Nin's *Diary*, always singled out as the most brilliant and talented of her "transparent children." He seems to have been quite taken with Sheri, for he gave her a poem entitled "La Naissance de Sherry Martinelli" (like Nin and some others, he used the earlier form of her first name). Written in French, which Sheri couldn't read, it was apparently never published; it follows as an appendix to this essay in a translation made by Sheri's and my mutual acquaintance George Kearns, a Pound scholar (and revised by writer-artist Rikki Ducornet). It is a surrealist birth myth in which no sooner is Sheri born than she is "preyed upon by starving men." Sheri came across the poem in her papers in 1985; when I sent her Kearns's translation she commented, "One regrets that it has one's name on it. Charles Duits was forsoothe writing this to his own dream female 'twin soul' born into t/mind of t/male that he ever cherishes/nourishes/seeks/desires & possesses in every female he meets outside his mind. His perfect opposite/his extreme norm/his action polarity." Duits was the first of many "starving men" to mythologize Sheri, an act her strange beauty and endearing eccentricity encouraged. It is the inverse of her own exaltation of wise teachers like Nin and Pound.

In the same diary entry for December 1945 quoted earlier, Nin reports that Sheri was then living with a Chilean-American painter named Enrique Zañartu (1921–2000; Anatole Broyard gives his first name as Nemecio). But she seems to have been living alone in 1946 when she met Broyard, who says he moved in with her and was her lover for about three months. Their affair is recounted at length in his memoir *Kafka Was the Rage*, written in 1988 but not published until 1993, three years after his death. It is an engaging account of life in Greenwich Village immediately after the war and of the "sentimental education" he received from Sheri (he changed her surname to Donatti to protect her privacy), but its reliability is in doubt. When I sent Sheri a copy of the book in 1993 she insisted Broyard had never spent a single night with her and dismissed the book as "a voyeur's wet dream." It's difficult to know whom to believe. Sheri sometimes misrepresented her past, glossing over some of its scandalous aspects, not so much out of vanity as (she said) to avoid giving young people any encouragement to emulate bad behavior. But Broyard himself was duplicitous; as Henry Louis Gates Jr. shows in his memoir of him, Broyard's entire life can be said to be a lie. (He hid his black heritage and passed for white, keeping his secret from his friends and family until near the end of his life.) The Sheri Donatti of *Kafka Was the Rage* certainly has much in common with Sheri Martinelli: Broyard's physical descriptions of her are accurate and he captures her unique way of talking and her oblique intelligence, but Sheri told me many of his details are wrong: her apartment was clean and comfortable, not dirty and crowded as he says, and she most often wore cloth pants, not the clinging dresses without underwear that Broyard obsesses over. (He constantly worried that she would inadvertently expose herself, most comically the time she accidentally knocked W. H. Auden over and on top of herself.) In some ways Broyard's portrait of Sheri is as fanciful as Charles Duits's surrealistic one and springs from the same male tendency to project desired qualities onto the unsuspecting female. Taken with a huge grain of salt, however, Broyard's book provides yet another testimony to Sheri's appeal. For Broyard, she was literally unforgettable; on his deathbed 40 years later, Sheri was one of the people he spoke of (Gates 80).

Broyard notes that Sheri was still an abstract painter at the time (like her former husband) and describes a few of her works. She continued to take classes during this time, studying engraving under Stanley William Hayter at the Atelier de Sept. She was in one class with Spanish painter Joan Miró, who ogled her shamelessly; as she later wrote me, "his round blue eyes 'ate' all of t/ black net off my chorus girl stockings." One of her projects was described by Josephine Gibbs in the 15 December 1946 issue of *Art Digest*:

> Three young up-and-coming modernists have contributed five original prints each to an unusual portfolio of etchings and serigraphs which may be seen at the Joseph Luyber Gallery. . . . Sheri Martinelli's velvety, soft ground-etchings are technically fascinating. They are as deeply bitten as can be imagined to produce raised areas and lines under pressure, and imaginatively manipulated to produce a variety of textures in abstract compositions which may have had their inspiration in the accidental forms of nature.

(Sheri would continue to find "inspiration in the accidental forms of nature" in her later artwork.) This portfolio was limited to 100 copies, priced at $40.00 each; I've never seen a copy. In fact, little if any of her art from this period survives. Sheri also kept an ungainly printing press in her apartment at this time — no doubt in emulation of Nin, who owned one and typeset her own books — which she used for her etchings.

During the late 1940s Sheri supported herself by modeling, principally for *Vogue*. Such noted photographers as Karl Bissinger, Cliff Wolfe, Tommy Yee, and Dick Rutledge took hundreds of shots of her. (Two *Vogue* photos are reproduced in the photo section of *Beerspit Night and Cursing*, and two others appear on pp. 128 and 129 of Karl Bissinger's *The Luminous Years*.) Like many a *Vogue* model today, Sheri also experimented with heroin during this time, though not so often as to become addicted.

One thing Broyard got right is that Sheri had many suitors. He describes an amusing episode when critic Richard Gilman came over one night and presented an elaborate argument why he would be a more suitable partner for her than Broyard. He also describes a similar visit from Zañartu; if they had indeed lived together earlier, perhaps he was there to win her back. But Broyard doesn't mention another rival for Sheri's attention, novelist William Gaddis, whose portrayal of a thinly disguised Sheri in his novel *The Recognitions* is the most extensive and memorable of her various appearances in literature.

Leaving Harvard (without a degree) in 1945, Gaddis had moved to Manhattan and been hired as a fact-checker at the *New Yorker*. He lived on Horatio Street in the West Village and frequented the same places Sheri did, such as the San Remo bar on the corner of Bleecker and Macdougal. He was 25 when he met her, five years her junior. In her first letter to me Sheri remembered attending an opening at the Museum of Modern Art with Gaddis; he had borrowed someone's shoes for the occasion, which were too big and flapped noisily the entire time. He was quite smitten with her by all accounts, but she apparently didn't reciprocate his interest, regarding him as something of a "mama's boy" as she put it (which he was, literally, having been raised by his mother after his parents separated when he was three). It seems to have been a case of unrequited love, or lopsided at best, and Gaddis had rivals like the practiced skirt-chaser Broyard to contend with, but he would rout all his rivals when it came to immortalizing Sheri in a book.

Broyard writes that Sheri "looked more like a work of art than a pretty woman" (3). She is introduced in *The Recognitions* in the same way: Otto (Gaddis's self-deprecating self-portrait) is attending a Greenwich Village party given by Max (Broyard, more or less) when he briefly glimpses "the face of a girl who was sitting alone on the couch, . . . Then she was gone, with the silent consciousness of a painting obscured by a group of nattering human beings" (183). A little later, having taken down a volume of Browning and pretending to read it while spying on her, Otto reads the following lines from "A Likeness" just as he realizes she is watching him:

> *He never saw, never before today,*
> *What was able to take his breath away,*
> *A face to lose youth for, to occupy age*
> *With the dream of, meet death with . . .* (193)

Her name is Esme, and in almost every respect she is Sheri Martinelli: she lives on Jones Street, has a four-year-old daughter somewhere, owns a printing press, and speaks in a curious way. (Broyard: "Like everything else about her, her style of talking took some getting used to. She gave each syllable an equal stress and cooed or chanted her vowels. Her sentences had no intonation, no rise and fall, so that they came across as disembodied, parceled out, yet oracular too" [5].) Otto introduces himself and even manages to sleep with her that night, but his relationship to her throughout the rest of the novel is one of frustration. Otto has a rival in the unsavory person of Chaby Sinisterra (based on a jazz musician Sheri knew named Eddie Shu [1918–1986]; *The Recognitions* is very much a *roman à clef*), but Esme is hopelessly in love with the painter for whom she models, the enigmatic Wyatt Gwyon.

A romantic quadrangle links Wyatt and Otto with the novel's two principal female characters, Esme and Wyatt's wife Esther (based on a woman Gaddis knew named Helen Parker), both of whom tolerate Otto only because of Wyatt's chilly indifference to them. Both women have additional lovers, making Otto even more superfluous, and many of the other male characters seem to have slept with Esme or Esther. But the promiscuity of Greenwich Village women is hardly Gaddis's chief concern. Esther and Esme represent the two traditional forms of female salvation open to the mythic hero, and their inadequacies as suitable anima figures dramatize Gaddis's critique of that very tradition. Though both women share initials and an avocation for writing, they are diametrically opposed: Esther is rational, big-boned, ambitious, and writes prose, while Esme is mystical, delicate, aimless, and writes poetry. Gaddis's prose sharpens the contrast further: his character analysis of Esther (78–80) is written in the well-balanced, logically ordered style of Henry James — an author Esther admires — while Esme's equivalent analysis is fractured into two sections (276–77, 298–302), presaging her incipient schizophrenia, and written with the illogic of an interior monologue, punctuated with solipsistic questions and fragments of poems, fictions, and esoteric trivia. They are united, however, in their unrequited love for Wyatt and, after losing him, in their despair.

Gretchen to Wyatt's Faust, Esme has been sent to him by the novel's Mephistopheles, Recktall Brown. A promiscuous manic-depressive schizophrenic junkie, she nevertheless models as the Virgin Mary in Wyatt's religious forgeries ("No needle marks on your Annunciation's arm, now," Brown reminds him [259]). Although Esme is associated with a wide variety of other female figures of salvation in addition to Mary and Faust's Gretchen — Dante's Beatrice, Saint Rose of Lima, the Egyptian goddess Isis, the Flying Dutchman's Senta, Peer Gynt's Solveig (like other modernist masterpieces, *The Recognitions* is thickly allusive to other texts) — she is elsewhere associated with succubae and sirens, and when Wyatt deigns to think of her at all, it is unfortunately in her role as temptress. Rebelling from Brown in his role as the Troll King, Wyatt comes to view Esme more as Ibsen's Green-clad One than as the maternal Solveig and at that point rejects her offer of intimacy to return to his father and take up the priesthood. In her face Wyatt had found the lines necessary to complete his childhood portrait of his dead mother Camilla, but this only adds unconscious fears of incest to his relationship with Esme. After he spurns her, she attempts suicide, and though she is rescued she drifts through the rest of the novel in a state of acute schizophrenia, referring to herself in the third person. Wyatt eventually comes to his senses and realizes that Esme is the one woman capable of offering him selfless love, but by that time she has disappeared, a stowaway on a ship taking Stanley, a neurotic Catholic organist also in love with Esme, to Italy. By day Stanley tries to convert her to Catholicism, but by night her "simulacra" assail him "immodest in dress and licentious in nakedness, many-limbed as some wild avatar of the Hindu cosmology . . . full-breasted and vaunting the belly, limbs indistinguishable until he was brought down between them and stifled in moist collapse" (828). Ever the victim of male projections, Esme slips deeper into madness and religious mania as the long novel nears its conclusion, her unrequited love for Wyatt causing her to waste away, "so quickly as though she . . . she had no will to live," as Stanley mournfully confesses, reporting her Firbankian death (a "staphylococcic infection . . . from kissing Saint-Peter-in-the-Boat" [953]).

On the one hand, all this sounds like an elaborate revenge fantasy contrived by Gaddis because of Sheri's indifference to him, but on the other, it shows that he learned from her how ridiculous some of his preconceived notions about her had been. One of the strangest yet memorable heroines in contemporary literature, Esme betrays the absurdities of the role of romantic redemptress forced upon so many female characters by males who prefer virgins and whores to any more complex woman in between. As with Broyard, Sheri provided Gaddis with an invaluable "sentimental education."

Gaddis sent a copy of *The Recognitions* to Sheri upon publication in 1955 — at which time she was regularly visiting Ezra Pound at St. Elizabeths Hospital in Washington, DC — and she replied with a blistering, four-page letter. It begins: "willie…u blasted menace..NO wonder u always looked for me wherever i happened to be…i told pound i shall slit yr throat and he smiled like a big pussy cat and said: bene..bene…O my GOD or anybody's what a shock…recognition huh?....i saw a chick so fucking vain that i wanted to strangle her…thou art a very devil…and all the time i thot u were the only one who cared…yr a lousy punk…" She objected to the name Gaddis gave her: "esme..(what a name u bastard) can go to hell…but it is difficult NOT to recognize her… at least my beloved you were THERE…that's more than i can say for myself…the bitch-goddess…gee willie thanks a lot…o yes I shall slit yr throat…you must be the most wanted man in new york city…revenge is MINE sd the lord (of all creation)…" She relents a little and admits, "i suppose the decade needed a chronicler and I suppose you couldn't resist," and invites him to visit her "that I might re-pay you for all the nice times you 'rescued' me from that filthy city so i cd recover (AGAIN) (and again and again)…anyhow i really terribly desire to cut yr throat…you have given me something to LIVE for.. so come that is if you can FACE me you lousy camera..you television.. you etc…etc.." After quoting two pages of poetry (hers as well as Pound's) she concludes: "now do as I say and come to meet the maestro or write a letter to the lonesomest doll in the world....," signing off "eternamente... & i am always the same — and NO more novels willie for christsake."

But Gaddis never did visit. Pound also received a copy, but he wasn't interested in such "verbiage." "I'll help your friends any way I can," he told Sheri, "but I won't read their books." The jacket carried a blurb by Stuart Gilbert favorably comparing *The Recognitions* to *Ulysses*, so Pound added: "Tell your friend Joyce was an ending, not a beginning." (It should be remembered that Pound, an early supporter of *Ulysses*, began having doubts about it after the "Sirens" episode, and regarded *Finnegans Wake* as unreadable.) Two years later, Pound asked Sheri to ask Gaddis to contribute to a magazine called *Edge* — which he declined — and in this 1957 letter she reported that she was still "'chewing my way' through *Recognitions*. I know it is the kind of book that will be read a hundred years after it was written because it is too contemporary for its contemporaries." (For some reason, she told me in the 1980s that she never read the novel.)

In addition to inspiring Esme, Sheri made a literal contribution to *The Recognitions*: a long letter of hers to Gaddis is reproduced verbatim on pages 471–73. (Gaddis didn't ask Sheri's permission to do so.) The thousand-word letter is too long to reproduce here, but it's a remarkable piece of writing and valuable both as a statement of her aesthetics at the time and as the earliest surviving example of her prose style. Written under Nin's obvious influence — just as Sheri would adopt Pound's idiosyncratic way of writing in later years — the letter discusses "the demands of painting," principally the psychological demands made on the painter. A short extract follows, concluding with a striking image of the sort Nin is known for:

> The painter concerned for his mortal safety, indifferent because he fears to scrutinize, paradoxically sacrifices that very safety, for he will not be allowed to escape painting.
>
> He will make paintings or they will revolt and make him, unhappy being in the grasp of them. He compulsively must, then, live them cold as they are, static, perversely with warmth and movement he cannot know but feel painfully, a bird with broken eggs inside. (472)

In the context of the novel, the letter is a suicide note Esme leaves for Wyatt; Broyard too describes a suicide attempt by Sheri (65–66), but she told me she never attempted suicide. Perhaps she meant she never *seriously* attempted suicide, because the attempts described in both *The Recognitions* and *Kafka Was the Rage* are half-hearted, more theatrical than suicidal.

Gaddis left for Europe in 1948 to write his novel. Anaïs Nin seems to have drifted away by then too; a year earlier Sheri had found a doctor to perform an abortion for Nin (Bair 328), and in later years Nin would send Sheri inscribed copies of her books, but she was no longer part of her entourage. (When Nin died in 1977, Sheri wrote a poem entitled "Goodbye Anaïs," which was eventually published in the journal *Anaïs*.) At some point she became friends with Leonard Bernstein's fiancée, Felicia Montealegre (she lived a few blocks from Sheri), who was to become something of a patron to her. It was the heady beginning of the Beat era, and Sheri was leading a hedonistic but (as she later admitted) empty life, hanging out with jazz musicians and indulging in drugs. In the early 1950s she was living with a musician named Joseph Castaldo, who was studying at Juilliard; aware of her ennui, Castaldo suggested that she go down to Washington, DC, and visit Ezra Pound, then incarcerated at St. Elizabeths Hospital. There she met the man who would dominate the second half of her life.

Writing in 1973 to one of Pound's biographers, Sheri gave this lively, freely punctuated account of her state of mind in 1952 when she first met Pound:

> I was going around t/world with the/clouds and t/air like Chief of All The Chiricahuas Apache: Cochise — when Ezra Pound (known to us as: "E.P.") "spoke to my Thoughts." I, too, "carried My Life on My Finger-Nails" and they were each & all a different colour because I was a working painter — a Fighter in The Ethical Arena wherein you KNOW what's Really Wrong because you did that yourself and you found out by The Way of Be-ing There. Artist. Maestro.
>
> Was There Ever Such A Man, Dear Goddess. A Man who found me Lost in Hellishness but FIRST I had been Made Trusting & Loving & Innocent & Ignorant "Love One Another Children" . . . so as not To Even Know for a split second that I *was* Lost. I was having a Ball. All Those Sweet-faced Indians! T/guiltless sex of animal desire; pure, simple & uncomplicated by The Falsities of Any Other Facts! Freedom of Diet & No Two Days Running The Same. . . .
>
> Today I remembered: His great Faith in Art when he said: "PAINT me out of here, Cara." So Painted E.P. in Paradise as he had sung me from Purgatory. . . . This is The Power of Art Work. With Out A Picture of It inside your mind — how can you Find It? (Heymann 226; his ellipses)

Pound was in his own form of Purgatory at the time. Detained by the U.S. Army in 1945 for making allegedly treasonous broadcasts over the Italian radio network during the war, Pound had, on the advice of his lawyers, pleaded insanity rather than risk being tried for treason (and if convicted, executed), and had been confined since the end of 1945 to St. Elizabeths Federal Hospital for the Insane. (The government's plan was to keep Pound there rather than risk an acquittal after a trial, so the fiction of his insanity was maintained by sympathetic psychiatrists.) During his first few years there he was allowed very few visitors, but by 1951 his visiting privileges had been extended, as they would continue to be over the years. Surrounded by madmen and with the threat of being tried for treason hanging over his head should he "recover" from his insanity, Pound was understandably miserable and his creative drive at a standstill. *The Pisan Cantos*, written in 1945 while Pound was incarcerated in Italy, had been published in 1948, and he had written nothing since. In 1949 Pound won the Bollingen Prize for *The Pisan Cantos*, and the controversy surrounding the award attracted the attention of a new generation of readers, many of whom began making pilgrimages to St. Elizabeths in the 1950s to study under the master at his "Ezuversity" and do his bidding.

Sheri wrote to Pound's supervisor Dr. Overholser on 26 December 1951 to ask permission to visit him; her request was granted, and though there's no record of their first meeting, the mutual attraction must have been immediate. Pound encouraged her to move down there and informally adopted her. She got a job working in the admissions office of George Washington University, which didn't last long, and then worked in a waffle shop on K Street, but Pound made her quit so that she could concentrate on her painting. He paid the rent on her apartment and gave her a dollar a day for expenses. Aged 66 and 33, respectively, there was a father-daughter relationship at first (or older: she called him "Grampaw"). Pound was still married to Dorothy Shakespear, who had taken a small apartment near the hospital and visited him daily, but the older woman was apparently not jealous of the younger one; she even approved of Pound's financial assistance to Sheri. In the summer of 1954, Dr. E. Fuller Torrey notes in *The Roots of Treason*, "Dorothy wrote to Dr. Overholser requesting that Sheri Martinelli be allowed to take her place as [Pound's] guardian while out on the lawn because she had to go away for a week; Dorothy reassured Dr. Overholser that Ezra thought of Sheri as his own daughter" (242). The following year Pound asked Dr. Overholser whether Sheri could move onto the grounds of St. Elizabeths and work as an art therapist; both requests were denied (Torrey 241). Dorothy too seems to have looked upon Sheri as a daughter; spotting Sheri walking up toward Pound and her, Dorothy once commented, "Here comes 'family.'" Sheri proudly accompanied Dorothy on various outings in Washington, DC, dazzled by the older woman's Edwardian elegance. In her letters and phone conversations Sheri told me she loved Dorothy, and often sang her praises.

Sheri lived in a variety of small apartments in and around Washington, DC, for the next seven years — once sharing a basement apartment with another Pound disciple named David Horton — and visited Pound almost daily. She did, however, maintain a studio apartment on New York's Lower East Side for occasional visits, and continued to be popular with jazz musicians, who would hang out at her apartment and sometimes give her shirts that they had worn too often on the bandstand. Charlie "Yardbird" Parker was a frequent visitor; bass player Ted Wald remembers "That summer of 1953 was wonderful. Those of us who lived in the Village got to play with Bird almost every day, either at the Open Door or at Sherry Martinelli's pad on Third Avenue and 4th Street" (Reisner 230). Members of the Modern Jazz Quartet were likewise friends; Sheri painted a splendid abstract portrait of MJQ bassist Percy Heath entitled *Daw oo* that was later included in her book of paintings. (Another Pound disciple, John Kasper, moved to New York and opened his Make It New bookshop on Bleecker Street; Sheri used it as a mailing address, and received more than a hundred letters from Pound during her periods away from St. Elizabeths.) She joined the growing number of young acolytes who visited Pound, listening to his pronunciamentos and undertaking various projects at his suggestion. Sheri could always be seen with sketchpad in hand, doing studies of the Maestro, and occasionally of Dorothy.

Virtually everyone who has written about Pound's life at St. Elizabeths mentions Sheri, in terms ranging from praise to bemusement to condemnation. Noel Stock, one of Pound's earliest biographers, calls her "a strange, rather scatterbrained young woman" (439) and a later biographer dismisses her as a manipulative, troublesome "odd-ball" (Wilhelm 287, 308). On the other hand, one visitor at the time said of her, "so far as I could tell the only visitor of those years who had any perception at all of what Pound was doing then was a young woman painter from one of those 'passionate religious traditions conscious of its roots in European paganism'" (McNaughton 323), and critic Wendy Stallard Flory goes so far as to suggest that Sheri practically saved Pound's life, at least his creative life: "the poet sees her as more than an individual; she comes to represent for him the very idea of love as inspiration. Set against the bleak and stultifying reality of the asylum ward, her youth, enthusiasm, and spontaneity must seem to provide a contact with all those things in the outside world that he most minds being shut away from" (246).

Pound playfully called her "La" Martinelli, adding the mock title *la* more often used in reference to actresses and divas, which Sheri adopted as her professional name thereafter. Pound obviously enjoyed her company: "Seeing Sheri approach across the lawn," another visitor recalls, "he jumps out of his chair and hurries to greet La Martinelli with his most affectionate and energetic bear hug" (Booth 383). It's been said she and Pound became lovers, as Sheri herself claimed in a letter to Archibald MacLeish (Torrey 241), though a later biographer doubts the couple would have had much opportunity to do so (Carpenter 803). Allen Ginsberg called Sheri Pound's "girlfriend," and one of her musician friends teased her with "I guess you're Ezra's pound cake now." In Timothy Findley's play *The Trials of Ezra Pound*, Sheri is portrayed as a concubine, there merely to satisfy Pound's sexual needs. Diane di Prima made a pilgrimage in the spring of 1956 to see Pound, and stayed at Sheri's apartment; she noted that Pound "greeted Sheri intimately and with great affection. We felt she was indeed 'mistress' in that situation, as Dorothy was wife" (142). As late as 1957, they acted like lovers: when David Rattray visited Pound that fall he recorded for the *Nation* another example of Pound's greeting Sheri upon her arrival: "Pound embraced her and ran his hands through her hair, and they talked excitedly, each interrupting the other." "Grandpa loves me," she told Rattray. "It's because I symbolize the spirit of Love to him, I guess." She also boasted, "Grandpa says I know intuitively what it takes a great genius years of study to learn." When she left, "Pound threw his arms around her, hugged her, and kissed her goodbye." To Rattray's critical eye, "Her appearance suggested a frayed and faded survivor of the early bobby-sox days. She had huge eyes like a cat. They bulged in a flushed face that tapered down from an enormous forehead to a tiny chin and tinier double chin. Her lips were tight and pale, but sometimes relaxed and parted into a naive smile. I assumed that she was a patient from another ward." Sheri was infuriated by Rattray's article and wanted to sue for slander, but Dorothy talked her out of it.

Pound was attentive to her emotional needs as well. On 23 September 1954 her only brother, Walter Albert Brennan (Buddy to his sister), committed suicide, the result of a decade of misery ever since being wounded in World War II. So great was Sheri's grief that Pound wrote a "Prayer for a Dead Brother" for her, which was eventually published in 1972. When Charlie Parker died the following year, Pound again attempted to assuage her grief with a poem, which remains unpublished. He also fed her during these years, passing along items from the hospital cafeteria. However, by 1956 he began tiring of her, and "turned her over" (as her second husband put it) to a Chinese-American composer named Gilbert Lee (1928–2006), ten years her junior, whom she had met shortly after coming to St. Elizabeths. Di Prima writes that Pound decided she should marry Gilbert, adding parenthetically: "(he liked to arrange the lives of his close disciples). Sheri was not too inclined to this arrangement," di Prima continues; "the rumor was she was recently off smack, and Gilbert and she had frequent and loud fights" (141). Sheri moved in with Gilbert at his mother's gallery on Mount Vernon Avenue across the Potomac in Alexandria, Virginia. He drove her into Washington frequently, though, so she could continue her studies at the Ezuversity.

Ostensibly Sheri was at St. Elizabeths to study "the classic arts and letters" (as she would later put it in her résumé), and her art did undergo a change under Pound's tutelage. "Stay between Giotto and Botticelli," he advised her, so she supplemented her abstract style with an older, more representational style. She painted portraits almost exclusively, and mostly self-portraits. The paintings are small, 12" by 14" at the largest, and are richly colored. As with Sheri herself, her art elicited contradictory reactions from Pound's visitors: his

U.S. publisher James Laughlin has said "Her drawings were not very good, in fact, quite bad" (24), but Eustace Mullins, a photographer and sculptor among other things, wrote: "She had perfected a jewel-like tone in her painting, much like the ancient Persian painting, which was very effective" (307; a shadowy photograph of Sheri and Mullins is reproduced on p. 292 of his book). Art historian Max Wykes-Joyce paid her splendid tribute by writing, "La Martinelli, Italo-American, brings to painting a sense of hieratic splendour lost since Byzantium. The *Testa Invocatrice*, the terra-cotta head of a Madonna, no higher than a man's thumb, is a manifestation of religious art in the direct tradition of Giotto and Crivelli" (249).

Pound himself was delighted with the development of Sheri's painting under his direction and actively sought to promote her career. His rooms were decorated with her paintings and he proudly talked them up to his visitors. (On p. 339 of the winter 1974 issue of *Paideuma* there is a photograph from the 1950s of Pound seated at a desk displaying her painting *Giotto*.) His letters of 1955 are full of exhortations to correspondents like MacLeish and Laughlin to do something for Sheri: grants, foundation support, publication, museum showings, anything, but nothing came of his efforts (Pound/Laughlin 236–42). Di Prima gives an example of his practical support: "She told how she'd needed the formula for faience, the ancient Egyptian blue glaze, to use on a batch of miniature heads she had sculpted. It had been lost — at least to artists — for centuries, but 'Grandpa' had managed to get it for her, by writing to some Egyptian scholar he knew. . . . In all this there was a purpose, an urgency. The question of what could be saved, as civilization went down" (144). As late as 1958 he was still trying to get some sort of subsidy for her from a European admirer (Stummvoll 75–78), again without results.

He did, however, arrange for publication in book form of a small selection of her paintings. He suggested the project to Vanni Scheiwiller, the son of Pound's Italian publisher, and offered to write an introduction for it. David Gordon, a photographer who later became a leading Pound scholar, photographed the paintings he thought should be included — Sheri wasn't consulted and later was irritated at his selection — and in February of 1956 Scheiwiller published *La Martinelli*, a miniature booklet (2 ¾" x 4") limited to 500 copies. It reproduces nine paintings — *St. Elizabeth's Madonna* (also reproduced on the cover), *Giotto, Patria, Cleofe Santa, Isis of the Two Kingdoms, Daw oo* (the portrait of jazz musician Percy Heath), *Ch'iang (Fortuna), E.P.*, and *Leucothoe, Daughter of Orchamus*, and two ceramic works, the *Testa Invocatrice* admired by Wykes-Joyce and a *Ra Set*. In his introduction, Pound notes that several of Sheri's paintings were works in progress (indeed, she would continue working on some of them up until her death) and states: "The unstillness that delayed my recognition till quite a while after that of my less restless contemporaries [e.g., Joyce and Eliot] runs parallel in the work of la Martinelli, who is the first to show a capacity to manifest in paint, or in la ceramica what is most to be prized in my writing" (11). (Pound's introduction was reprinted later in 1956 in Noel Stock's magazine *Edge* with the title "Total War on 'Contemplatio'" — a phrase from Canto 85 — and has been reprinted a few times since.)

Pound mentions two of Sheri's paintings not included in *La Martinelli* but that are mentioned in *The Cantos*: *Lux in Diafana* and *Ursula Benedetta*, both dating from 1954. By that time Pound had resumed work on his epic poem, and the next two installments he would publish, *Section: Rock-Drill* (1956) and *Thrones* (1959) are, at a basic level, a record of what he was reading and, in Sheri's case, seeing at St. Elizabeths. Through the thicket of Pound's dense, allusive poetry, Sheri can be glimpsed in various guises.

Sheri's presence in these cantos takes two forms: references to her person and/or her role in Pound's life at the time, and references to her art. As in *The Recognitions*, she is mythologized in *The Cantos* as a romantic figure of redemption, and like Gaddis, Pound associates Sheri with a wide range of women in myth and literature. The first half of *Rock-Drill* (cantos 85–89) continues the manner and matter of the pre-Pisan cantos in their concern with history and ethics. But Canto 90 makes a sudden shift to the lyrical mode, recalling the love poetry of the troubadours Pound had studied nearly a half-century earlier. "In fact," writes Italian scholar Massimo Bacigalupo, "the forty pages of [cantos] 90–95 may be taken as a single new *Canzone d'amore*, modelled upon Cavalcanti's (and Dante's) *poesis docta* and on Provençal *trobar clus*" (259). (One of Pound's earliest books had been a translation of the sonnets and ballads of the medieval Italian poet Guido Cavalcanti; Pound gave his personal copy of the book to Sheri, who filled the margins with drawings and love poems to Pound.) Pound later told Sheri that cantos 90–95 were "her" cantos, for like the troubadour's Lady, she personified love as a creative force. On the other hand, Bacigalupo cautions that Sheri may have claimed "for herself a greater role than she in fact had, or Pound in a flirtatious mood may have told her that she was meant in a given line, to humor her" (*RSA Journal*, 73–74).

On the second page of Canto 90 the poet cries out to Cythera (Aphrodite), and then addresses a prayer to "Sibylla," the all-seeing sibyl of the Delphic oracle in ancient Greece. Most critics agree with Carroll F. Terrell's annotation: "Sheri Martinelli is understood to be the real-life sibyl at St. Elizabeths" (542). Chanting in liturgical refrain the phrase "m'elevasti" ("you lifted me up," from Dante's praise of Beatrice in the *Paradiso*), Pound registers his gratitude to Sheri for lifting him up out of his personal hell and reanimating him with the spirit of love:

Sibylla,
from under the rubble heap
m'elevasti
from the dulled edge beyond pain,
m'elevasti
out of Erebus, the deep-lying
from the wind under the earth,
m'elevasti
from the dulled air and the dust,
m'elevasti
by the great flight,
m'elevasti
Isis Kuanon
from the cusp of the moon,
m'elevasti (90/626)

Isis Kuanon conflates the Egyptian goddess with the Chinese goddess of mercy. Next Sheri is referred to as the mermaid Undine, a nickname Pound gave her ("Thus Undine came to the rock" [91/630]; "Yes, my Ondine, it is so goddamned dry on these rocks" [93/643]). Although this could be a reflection on her dangerous, siren-like persona — Sheri was, after all, tempting Pound away from his wife and practicing what Laughlin learnedly calls "*concitatio senectutis* (the arousing of desire in old men)"(25) — the undine is another redemptress, especially when Pound further conflates her with the sea-nymph Leucothea (from book 5 of Homer's *Odyssey*). In the second half of *Rock-Drill* Pound resumes the persona of wandering Odysseus, and Leucothea makes her smashing entrance in Canto 91. Appearing in the form of a seagull to Odysseus, adrift on a raft in wet clothes, Leucothea coos, "my bikini is worth your raft" (91/636), a flippant paraphrase of her offer to give him her magic veil in exchange for his wet clothes. The flirty line is repeated in Canto 95 (665), and even J. J. Wilhelm, who goes out of his way to deny Sheri's role in *The Cantos*, grudgingly admits that Leucothea "may well have been a tribute to Sheri Martinelli at this time" (302) for rescuing Pound just as the sea-nymph rescued Odysseus. When Sheri left St. Elizabeths in 1958, among the paintings and drawings she left with Norman Holmes Pearson for safekeeping was a photograph she had taken of herself in a mirror, wearing a bikini (H.D. 52).

In Canto 92, Pound writes:

"And if I see her not,
no sight is worth the beauty of my thought."
Then knelt with the sphere of crystal
That she should touch with her hands,
Coeli Regina

The four altars at the four coigns of that place,
But in the great love, bewildered
    farfalla in tempesta (92/639)

"This passage is surely a tribute to Sherri [*sic*] Martinelli," Wendy Flory feels, "and the 'sphere of crystal' that the poet holds out to her is perhaps the poetry which she has inspired him to write" (253). Flory goes on to suggest that in Canto 93 Sheri is evoked as Flora Castalia (650), goddess of flowers (256), and Terrell sees another reference to Sheri in Canto 94 as Pound's "Blue jay, my blue jay" (570). In Canto 97 there are two intriguing descriptions of Sheri's hair and eyes. Brooding on the Homeric epithet "wine-dark," Pound again refers to Sheri as "Sibilla" and tries to describe the color of her hair, settling on "russet-gold" (97/695). Sheri had been a brunette earlier, but at St. Elizabeths she sported "splendid red hair" (Laughlin 24), which she later explained in this wise: "It was a spectacular crimson & it came about because E.P. had placed his hand on one's head and where E.P. put his hand on one's hair (a bit later on not instantly) that hair turned crimson. . . . E.P.'s touch (a 'laying on of hands'??) also deep'n'd t/eye colour into a lavender which E.P. is also noting in C/97 indicating that E.P. was aware of t/changes" ("*Pound as Wuz*"). Sheri's second reference is to the lines:

with eyes pervanche [violet-blue]
    three generations, San Vio
darker than pervanche?
    Pale sea-green, I saw eyes once (97/696; cf. 97/698)

A little later in Canto 97 there is a line that some have knowingly said refers to Sheri, but which she disavowed:

mid dope-dolls an' duchesses
    tho' orften I roam,
some gals is better,
        some wusser
            than some. (97/700–701)

Sheri told me this was merely the chorus of a bawdy song Pound had composed; she was no longer a "dope-doll," having given up heroin by then. But it's true that during her first few years at St. Elizabeths she was still using heroin and marijuana. As early as March 1952 Pound was asking an acquaintance "have you any angles on keeping dope pushers away from young people of talent?" (Carpenter 804), and in a letter to E. E. Cummings dated 7 September 1954 Pound asked the poet what he knew about dope and warned: "I may need e.e.c.'s help re/ particular victim / emergency MIGHT arise/" (*Pound/*

Cummings 356). Sheri was that "particular victim," as William McNaughton's letters to Pound during that time attest. According to Charlie Parker's wife Chan, Sheri was calling herself "The Needle Lady" at that time (49–50). (Chan Parker ran into her at Bellevue, where Sheri was visiting her hospitalized husband six months before he died in March 1955.) Sheri was also the victim of a dope plant by the police and went to trial in 1956, but she was acquitted easily, "jury out 5 minutes," as Pound explained to MacLeish (Carpenter 819).

The sibyl at Delphi was also known as the pythoness (from her familiar), and in this guise Sheri makes her final appearance in *The Cantos*: born "Of the blue sky and a wild-cat, / Pitonessa [Italian for pythoness] / The small breasts snow-soft over tripod" (104/760). Sheri had given Pound a comic drawing of herself as a sibyl, standing next to a tripod and with a python in hand, which Pound thus worked into Canto 104. (Sheri said Pound told her, "T/ drawing is good because it shows you can laugh at yourself.") In fact Sheri gave Pound many comically risqué drawings of herself; the cutest one depicts her nearly nude with a bouquet of flowers in hand and the caption: "'F U Will Be My Valintine I Will Be Yr Kon Que Byne."

In a similar manner, several of Sheri's paintings became part of *The Cantos*. She would show Pound her works in progress and often he would give them titles and then work them into his poem. Her *Sibylla* of 1954 coincides with her appearance in Canto 90 (written the same year). In Canto 93, the two paintings Pound mentions in his introduction to her book, *Lux in Diafana* and *Ursula Benedetta*, become the subjects of the poet's prayer for compassion:

> Lux in diafana,
> Creatrix,
> oro.
> Ursula benedetta,
> oro (93/648)

Sheri's *Lux in Diafana* ("light in transparency") depicts a woman's face in quarter-profile with rays of light emanating from her forehead, while the *Ursula* is a full-face portrait of the legendary saint. (Pound's "benedetta" demotes her to "Blessed.") Both paintings are idealized self-portraits. The lines "Isis Kuanon / . . . / the blue serpent / glides from the rock pool" (90/626–27) have been associated with Sheri's painting *Isis of the Two Kingdoms*, which Pound admired (Gordon 241; *Isis* is reproduced on 240), though in this case it's impossible to say which came first. Canto 98 refers to two figures Sheri painted, Princess Ra-Set and Leucothoe (not Homer's nymph but a character in Ovid's

Metamorphoses), both included in *La Martinelli* and thus apparently pre-dating the composition of Canto 98. A different *Leucothoe* (but done in the same medium, sepia on grained wood) appeared in the spring 1955 issue of the *Hudson Review* as a frontispiece to Canto 86. During this time she did countless portraits of Pound, as I've said; one was reproduced as the frontispiece to Pound's translation of Sophocles' *Women of Trachis* (1956). In a poem/commentary on Canto 106 written many years after the event, Sheri recounts how one day she brought to St. Elizabeths a painting she'd been working on, a portrait of a woman with black hair surrounded by the faces of four girls. The Pounds were seated outside, and when Sheri showed them the painting, "DP sat straight up in her deck chair & said: 'I'll TAKE t-h-a-t' and she did. . . . EP stared @ work said nothing / He went to his room & wrote down in His Book" the opening lines of Canto 106:

> And was her daughter like that;
> Black as Demeter's gown,
>   eyes, hair?
> Dis' bride, Queen over Phlegethon,
>   girls faint as mist about her? (106/772)

Sheri would continue to illustrate figures from *The Cantos* after she left St. Elizabeths, including an *Undine* in 1964 in memory of Pound's nickname for her.

Undine is also the name H.D. used for Sheri in her *End to Torment*, written in 1958 in the months leading up to Pound's release from St. Elizabeths. In journal form she records her memories of him and their teenage romance, when he called her "Dryad." (Carpenter notes, "It was his first but by no means last invention of a mask for someone else, which stuck, and changed their perception of themselves" [62], as would be the case with Sheri, the sibyl/undine/madonna of St. Elizabeths.) After reading Rattray's *Nation* article and receiving *La Martinelli* from a friend, H.D. developed a keen interest in Sheri, finding a parallel between her younger self and the artist: "Undine seems myself *then*" (39). When she learned Pound would not be taking Sheri with him to Italy upon his release, she decided to help her; though she doesn't mention it in *End to Torment*, she gave Sheri the money from her Harriet Monroe Prize award in 1956 (Guest 315–16). She was enchanted by the photos of Sheri and her artwork that Norman Holmes Pearson had sent her, and somewhat reluctantly entered into correspondence with her. Sheri seems already to have known her work and wrote her an effusive letter of praise, but also expressed her rage at being dumped by Pound. "The male just can't go about like that, ditching a spirit love," Sheri fumed. "I have known Ezra for

6 years. The last 4 years I took a vow in St. Anthony's Church in NYC not to leave the Maestro until he was freed. A month before he was freed he made me break that vow" (57). "He killed her," Sheri wrote of herself to Pearson, describing Pound's decision to desert her (54). Instead of taking Sheri to Italy, Pound took Marcella Spann, a young teacher who had started visiting Pound at St. Elizabeths a year earlier and had supplanted Sheri in the Maestro's affections by 1958. "With her serious, rather reserved expression and her hair done neatly in a bun," Carpenter writes, "she made a marked contrast to the ultra-exuberant Sheri Martinelli, who until then had been undisputed queen of the disciples" (829). Dethroned, Sheri married Gilbert Lee and together they left for Mexico at the beginning of the summer of 1958.

"Poor Undine!" H.D. laments. "They don't want you, they really don't. How shall we reconcile ourselves to this?" (57), remembering that a half-century earlier Pound had likewise abandoned her to go to Europe. Sheri had commented on the "sea-girls" section of Eliot's "Love Song of J. Alfred Prufrock" in a poetry anthology she sent to H.D., and the poet's last vision of Sheri is of "our little Undine on her sea-rocks with her wind-blown hair" (59), utterly forlorn.

A few years later, Sheri included an "Homage to Grampa" in a letter to editor Miles Payne, who published it in his little magazine *Light Year*. Since it is extremely scarce, it is included here (everything *sic*; bracketed ellipses are Payne's). Among other things, it seems to put to rest the question of whether she and Pound were lovers. She signs off — charmingly, self-deprecatingly — as "his gig": an archaic word for a flighty, giddy girl.

"Homage to Grampa"

"the pressure at any point of

> (one moment.. I had to look it up.. Mr. Cummings teaches to quote accurately.. if one is quoting)

"The pressure at the pivotal point on which any art changes or swings into direction is tremendous.." [. . .]
Ezra Pound has had TREMENDOUS PRESSURE put on him — I didn't see anyone else going into those old metal doors at 4:30 BUT him — because the A R T changed & the Goddess used Ezra as a pivotal point.
We live in a barbarous age — yes — but a wonderous & exciting age for the Arts — every day I scan our Newspapers I see evidence of the presence of Ezra Pound & what he got born to teach us.
People no longer say: "you're ALL wet.." they are now saying: "oh fairly.. wet.."
Thanks to dear Miles publishing Grampa's letter — Reno said: "if you had no previous experience with E.P. that letter would take the enamel off your teeth.."
The Shape Changer — and Miles will be part of that circle of Dog Farts who smeared

Ezra. Do you WANT to spend eternity with Dog Farts, Miles? What will happen to your Love Reservation for we Indians? Filled with Dog Farters like Wang?
I would very much like it if you would acknowledge your error. Ezra Pound was not AT St. Liz — such talk is too fairy-fied for Ezra — he was IN St. Liz & he was most definately NOT a patient — he was there because of an international political situation which has not yet been fully done with — not likely to be for 2000 MORE years. Wasn't Miles in NYC when it was the VORTEX of the States & the town joke in 1948 ish was: "what will they do next time Jesus comes?" and the answer was.. "they'll declare him insane.."

one is not saying that Ezra IS Jesus Christ.. one is merely tieing that joke up with the fact that Ezra had been treated in the way the joke implied — at about the same time.

and who went for the oky-doke is you Miles —
Ezra Pound is the ONLY man I'd ever met — in the full sense of being a man. BomKoff at a different degree of it is also a man in the same way.

I'd like to record this fact . . . that Ezra Pound.. agish 69 to 72 ish.. could fuck better than any man & that includes men of many colours..

Ezra Pound is the best fuck that ever got born & he has the MOST adequate prick & he loveth a woman's smell & he balls like a fierce wild eagle
and the ideas he flows through a woman's mind whilst he flows through her body.. ah that..

if you have ever seen the wild sea..
how can water drops do more than awaken a sweet ache in the spirit..
Patient? Don't be a 4-sided square Miles — Grampa ain't a fallen angel — he's a ballin' angel.. [. . .]
Charlie Parker reserved his rhythm for his horn & kept his talk direct & to the point. Ezra did the same.

It is called discipline
and I am a sorry example of the lack of it — but then..
that is also why I got put into grampa's paradise..
"for having such a good time"

"Miz Kikz" said Arthur King —
one of the most basic differences
between we all-alikes is WHAT we choose to LOVE —
Ezra Pound loved SANITY & ORDER — it was a quaint mockery to "legally" declare him insane — it would take a most ancient soul to think of that one. I suppose one might in a high mind-state — beyond it all — say it is the precise back-wards of poetic justice — it is a terrible & awful joke because it is outrageously intelligent. Miles says he loves humanity & then with an almost invisible smear adds to the pain & hurt of a good & benevolent man

and a great stud
and a Shape Changer — a maker of Souls —

his gig

At Pound's suggestion, José Vazquez-Amaral, another member of the Ezuversity who would eventually translate *The Cantos* into Spanish, had arranged for an art scholarship for Sheri in Jalisco. He also arranged for her and Gilbert to stay with a friend at his country house in Cuernavaca "in case the Jalisco scholarship fell through. It did," Vazquez-Amaral later wrote. "After a while the fiery and imaginative Sheri was also unwelcome at the Cuernavaca place" (20). The Mexican authorities expected someone who would paint pretty landscapes and glorify the republic, but Sheri was more interested in sketching beggar girls and exploring Aztec temples (H.D. 53). After about six months Sheri and Gilbert left Mexico for San Francisco.

The best thing to have come out of her Mexican odyssey was a newfound interest in writing. Vazquez-Amaral was dazzled by a piece she wrote on Mexico in 1958: "The title is *Mexico, his Thrust Renews*; the subtitle is *Cheap Hollywood Movie.* In a little over 7 pages, Sheri manages to give one of the strongest and most vivid *impressions* I have ever read on a trip to Mexico from the border to Mexico City. It is all there. I don't say that her painting is to be sneezed at but I still maintain that if given half a chance, Sheri — the Sheri of 1958 — would have given Kerouac, Bellow and all the others who have ventured on the quicksands of Mexico some very worthy competition" (20). The piece was published posthumously in 2002; another piece set in Mexico, entitled "The Beggar Girl of Queretaro," is an equally remarkable piece of writing.

The latter was published in the *Anagogic & Paideumic Review*, a periodical (what we'd now call a 'zine) she started in 1959 after settling in San Francisco. Sheri had forgiven Pound by this time and began the journal to fulfill a promise she made him to help raise the level of culture in this country. In issue number 4 she gave this unhelpful explanation of the journal's forbidding title: "A = the direction of the will UP & P = the kulchur born in one's head or wotever/ authority is E.P. - one might have not been listening for real but more or less that is wot one recalls." Actually, "anagogic" is a spiritual interpretation of a text, and "paideumic" derives from *paideuma*, a term Pound picked up from Frobenius to describe "the tangle or complex of the inrooted ideas of any period" (or, more simply, the culture taught by educators). Typed by Sheri and mimeographed in purple ink, the magazine was sold at City Lights book store and mailed to select friends and libraries. She usually ran off only 50 copies of each issue, and not surprisingly few copies exist anymore.

A typical issue would consist partly of Beat writings and partly of Sheri's own writings, drawings, and commentaries on the other contributions. Pound is frequently quoted — the first issue, in fact, reprinted a 1928 essay of Pound's entitled "Bureaucracy and the Flail of Jehovah" — and tribute was paid to H.D. after her death in 1961. The places of publication track Sheri and Gilbert's movements over the next few years: the first four issues were produced in their apartment at 15 Lynch Street on Nob Hill, number 5 was issued from

San Gregorio, and number 6 from Half Moon Bay, both small towns down the coast from San Francisco. Number 5 contains a scathing review by Sheri of Charles Norman's *Ezra Pound* (1960), the first biography of the poet and the first to mention Sheri. Both it and number 6 contain poems by Charles Bukowski, with whom Sheri corresponded on a weekly basis for a while in the early '60s; they never met, but she loved his work. An early poem of his entitled "Horse on Fire" indicates that Shari shared with him some memories of St. Elizabeths: "and reading Canto 90 / he put the paper down / Ez did (both their eyes were wet) / and he told her . . . / 'among the greatest love poems / ever written.'" The poem expresses Bukowski's reservations about Canto 90 and Pound's self-appraisal of it, though generally he approved of Pound's work. Sheri is presumably the "M.S." mentioned in his poem "What to Do with Contributor's Copies?" (*Roominghouse Madrigals* 17–18) according to Seamus Cooney in his notes on the letter from which this poem sprang (see *Screams from the Balcony* 34–35). Bukowski's letters to Sheri were published in 2001, and in his letters to others he occasionally refers to her. Sheri was a harsh editor and berated him "because I stay down in the mud and also because I put her in a poem now and then," but he was fond of her and proud to know her; in a 1965 letter to writer William Wantling, he reported: "Pound's x-girl friend Martinelli trying to cough up my whore-O-scope. stars, something. I suppose this puts me somewhere near the Master. just think, somebody Pound went to bed with is now writing me, has been for years. my, my" (*Screams* 134, 234).

A few supplements to the *Anagogic & Paideumic Review* were published at various times — one showcasing Bukowski, another a booklet by local poet Sam Suzuki entitled *San Francisco Beat Scene: Poetry* — but there is no record of any issues beyond number 6. In most ways the magazine is a product of its times. In his memoir *Bohemia*, Herbert Gold remembers "The hum and whir of the late fifties, early sixties mimeograph machines, churning out beat poetry, deafening me as I walked down North Beach alleys" (37). But Sheri's contributions stand apart from the usual Beat ramblings of the unknown local writers she published. One piece in particular has attained a certain notoriety over the years: while at St. Elizabeths Sheri wrote an essay for Pound entitled "Duties of a Lady Female," a partly tongue-in-cheek primer on how to please a man and defend him from other women — Sheri had been in a few catfights in her time — which Pound found amusing. Sheri published it in the third issue of her magazine, which came into the hands of Diane di Prima. When she reprinted the essay in her own magazine *Floating Bear* (32 [1966]: 411–13) di Prima added the disclaimer "The views expressed therein are not necessarily those of the editors." Sheri's essay was posthumously reprinted in Richard Peabody's *A Different Beat* (1997), where he appreciably notes "the sarcastic laser" of her observations on male-female relationships.

In San Francisco Sheri reestablished her connection with the Beat Generation, especially since many of the Beats she had known earlier in Greenwich Village migrated to San Francisco in the late '50s. She was introduced to Jack Kerouac during one of his visits there, though he apparently already knew who she was. Describing Kerouac in 1953, Gerald Nicosia writes: "Jack loved the modern young women on the Village scene and was especially intrigued by the 'Three Graces': Iris Brodie, Sherry [*sic*] Martinelli, and a woman known as the 'silent Madonna' . . . Wearing granny dresses and junkshop jewelry, her hair in a bun, the painter Sherry Martinelli visited Ezra Pound in St. Elizabeth's [*sic*] Hospital and became his mistress," Nicosia concludes, apparently reporting common gossip (455). Sheri's old friend Allen Ginsberg expresses a similar appreciation of these "very beautiful Jewish girls who read Ezra Pound and were into grandma dresses and sewing and amphetamine and junk and bebop and poesy and kept journals and painted," and even recorded a disturbing dream of her: "Up north, in the junk pad — a huge Siberian studio — with Sheri, Heine, various ex or present dead or alive junkies — " (*Journals* xvi, 302). Sheri soon became friends with most of the major Beat writers in San Francisco — Michael McClure, Gary Snyder, Alan Watts, Philip Lamantia, Bob Kaufman (with whom she was especially impressed) — and dabbled in the North Beach scene, a mother hen to the younger beatniks. But mostly she kept to herself, drinking vodka and producing her magazine.

In the early '60s Sheri decided she wanted to get out of the city (though Gilbert would continue to work there as an auto mechanic). She first moved down to a cabin in La Honda, but found the towering redwoods too oppressive, so instead moved into some cabins on the coast about halfway between San Francisco and Santa Cruz, where Tunitas Creek empties into the Pacific Ocean. She would live there at "the Creek" for the next 20 years, though for a mailing address she rented a post office box up in Pacifica, about 20 miles north. The caretaker of the cabins, Walter Clark, would be the subject of a memoir she wrote many years later, which gives some indication of her life there. Though she would soon abandon the *Anagogic & Paideumic Review*, she continued to write, draw, paint, and make jewelry, at night reading *The Cantos* by the light of an old kerosene lamp.

In 1964 Sheri gave her first one-woman show. A Cleveland advertising copywriter named Reid B. Johnson had developed an interest in Sheri's work when making a documentary radio program on Pound while he was still incarcerated at St. Elizabeths. In the course of corresponding with him, Pound sent Johnson a copy of *La Martinelli*, which so impressed him that a few years later he decided to organize an exhibit. After first securing Sheri's cooperation — she agreed to send about 20 oils and drawings — Johnson acquired others on loan, eventually assembling 48 works. He then wrote to acquire testimonials to Sheri's work. Johnson managed to elicit some impressive comments, printed in the show's four-page program, which is invaluable for the technical descriptions and dates of the works. In addition to quotations from Pound's introduction to *La Martinelli* and Wykes-Joyce's book (quoted earlier), the program contains statements from Robert Lowell ("Sheri Martinelli's paintings have a style of their own. I admire their grace, dash and uncanniness"), Marianne Moore ("She has a wonderful color sense and the true reverence of the mystic"), and Archibald MacLeish, who loaned Johnson at least one of her paintings and wrote:

> One of my most vivid memories of Pound in St. Elizabeths is a memory of the excitement with which he showed me some photographic reproductions of work by a young artist named Sheri Martinelli. No one who knew Pound ever had reservations about his taste — at least I never did, even when his taste had difficulties with me. I was struck by the reproductions and I was even more struck by the work itself when I saw samples of it: a power of line which asserts itself and cannot possibly be faked or counterfeited.

The show ran for a month in September 1964 at the Severance Center in Cleveland, and was the subject of a photo-essay by Russell W. Kane in the local paper.

Details are sketchy on Sheri's life during the second half of the sixties. Allen Ginsberg visited whenever he could, often bringing along a friend like Peter Orlovsky or Lawrence Ferlinghetti. In his 1966 poem "Iron Horse" Ginsberg recalls

> On Pacific cliff-edge
> Sheri Martinelli's little house with combs and shells
> Since February fear, she saw LSD
> Zodiac in earth grass, stood
> palm to cheek, scraped her toe
> looking aside, & said
> "Too disturbed to see you
> old friend w/ so much Power"
>
> (*Collected Poems* 450)

A year later Ginsberg visited Pound in Venice and asked a favor:

> "I'd like you to give me your blessing to take to Sheri Martinelli" — for I'd described her late history Big Sur, eyes seeing Zodiac everywhere hair bound up like Marianne Moore — which gossip perhaps he hadn't even heard — "To at least say hello to her, I'll tell her, so I can tell her," and stood looking in his eyes. "Please . . . because it's worth a lot of *happiness* to her, now . . ." and so he looked at me impassive for a moment and then without speaking, smiling slightly, also, slight redness of cheeks

> awrinkle, nodded up and down, affirm, looking me in eye, clear no mistake, ok. (*Composed on the Tongue* 10)

That blessing "brought tears to Sheri Martinelli's eyes on the Pacific Ocean edge a year later, '68" ("Allen Verbatim" 273). In November 1971 she and Gilbert drove up to Berkeley to attend the American premiere of Pound's opera *The Testament of François Villon.* Pound didn't attend, but Sheri renewed her acquaintance there with Olga Rudge, an earlier mistress/protégée of Pound's whom Sheri had first met at St. Elizabeths in 1955.

One night at the beginning of November 1972, Sheri went out to check on Walt the caretaker when "a terrible wind came up. A bad wind. A whistling wind," she later wrote. "One recalled that in Hawaii, not too far off westerly, such a wind is reported to come up when royal persons or sacred persons are about to die. . . . One thought there was a talking sound something like: 'Think ye hard on Ezra Pound' but it didn't make sense" ("A Memoir" 153). The next morning Sheri learned Pound had died the night before.

There had been little or no contact between them in the 14 years since they parted at St. Elizabeths, but for the rest of her life Sheri would think of Pound almost daily, endlessly rereading *The Cantos*, writing poems about him, and trying to live up to the example he set for purposeful creative activity. She continued to produce poetry and drawings, periodically gathering them up into booklets, which she would photocopy, bind with staples and masking tape, and send to friends. She apparently made no effort to publish her work through conventional channels or promote her art in any way, or apply for grants. That is, she had no interest in becoming a *professional* writer or artist. She did become something of a professional widow, however: in the late '70s she attended a Pound session at an MLA meeting in San Francisco dressed in black weeds like an Edwardian widow. When Pound was slighted in an article in *Paideuma* in 1977 by her old acquaintance Reno Odlin, Sheri fired off an enraged Mailgram to *Paideuma* demanding an apology (which was reprinted in facsimile in its winter 1977 issue). She also began to appreciate all the Pound materials she had saved — letters from Pound, drafts of cantos, inscribed books — and began thinking about organizing all this material, both for her own continuing studies of *The Cantos* and for eventual sale to a library. As Pound studies proliferated in the '70s and '80s, she began to be approached by critics seeking information, but she regarded most of them with a wary eye. She felt their neglect of the anagogic possibilities of *The Cantos* in favor of more mundane matters was wrongheaded, especially since she had seen how the poems were written. (She put into an epigram the shortcomings of Pound critics: "each stone is known / but building secrets lost.") Although she subscribed and occasionally contributed to *Paideuma*, she barely glanced at the many books that were appearing on Pound, even those that mentioned her. She made an exception for Terrell's invaluable *Companion to the Cantos*, because it provided the kind of solid information she needed and because she shared Terrell's conviction that essentially "*The Cantos* is a great religious poem" (vii). (Terrell does perpetuate one error concerning Sheri: the Joey mentioned in Canto 101 was Sheri's younger nephew, not her "kid brother," as Pound believed.)

In 1983, at the age of 65, Sheri decided it was time to retire and return back East. Both she and Gilbert had ailing mothers there to attend, so they left the Creek and drove out to New Jersey; after staying with relatives for a year or so, they finally settled in Falls Church, Virginia, just outside Washington, DC, where they lived for the rest of their lives. Organizing Pound's papers became the primary activity of her days, interrupted often by family concerns and her own failing health. She took the time to contribute a brief statement to a festschrift for Allen Ginsberg's 60th birthday, and remained interested in some Pound events: she planned to attend the 1985 centennial Pound conference in Orono, Maine, but last-minute complications caused her to cancel the trip. She did make it up to Rutgers University for a one-day Pound conference on 4 October of the same year, though she arrived too late for anything but the reception afterward. (I was working on my doctorate at Rutgers and met her for the first time that night, after corresponding with her for two years. She made it rudely clear I disappointed her somehow, it pains me to say.) She was invited to other Pound conferences in the '80s, but always declined due to overwork and ill health. One event she was annoyed *not* to be asked to participate in was a show called "Pound's Artists" held in Cambridge and London that same centennial year of 1985. The exhibit focused on the art Pound encountered and wrote about in London, Paris, and Italy. "No USA?" she scribbled on the copy of the program she sent me, urging me to protest the "lack of american art representation," by which she meant her own. She was proud to be the only contemporary American artist whose work is mentioned in *The Cantos*, and this sort of neglect hurt her. This particular slight was rectified a few years later when poet/Pound scholar Peter Bennett arranged for an exhibit of Sheri's work at the 13th Annual International Pound Conference, hosted by the University of Essex in September 1989. Sheri didn't attend but was pleased at this belated recognition of her work. The following year, she did attend another exhibition of her work, also arranged by Peter Bennett, at the Pound-Yeats conference at the University of Maine.

The last time I saw Sheri was in late October 1988, just before I left Rutgers to go to Illinois to work for the Dalkey Archive Press. She and Gilbert drove up to New Brunswick, where we were joined by visiting Pound scholar Massimo Bacigalupo. (His film of her visit is now on YouTube: https://

www.youtube.com/watch?v=gkT1QNA5Iwc.) Sheri showed us some of her treasures, including many letters from Pound and some rough drafts of "her" *Rock-Drill* cantos. We kept in contact over the succeeding years, mostly by phone. Sheri always complained of the endless work involved in organizing her Pound archive while fighting off various illnesses, but these were the most enchanting conversations I have ever had with another person. She spoke in a measured, somewhat melodramatic manner — she reminded me of Carolyn Jones as *The Addams Family*'s Morticia, whom Sheri closely resembled in her younger years — and she had a range of tones that would be the envy of any actress, from weariness to outrage to coyness to oracular pronouncements — and she would giggle like a schoolgirl. In her improvised monologues (she did most of the talking) she would quote everyone from Blake to Edgar Cayce, but always returning to *The Cantos* or some wisecrack E.P. (as she always called him) had made, and talk about everything from the annoying antics of neighborhood kids to psychic experiments in the former Soviet Union. She could be surprisingly witty and funny, and told wonderful (if dizzyingly digressive) anecdotes. She remained intellectually active until the end, asking me about Hesiod's *Theogony* or whether I could get an inexpensive Greek dictionary for her. After we finished a phone conversation — "Good-bye" was too final; she always preferred a sing-song "So l-o-o-o-ng" — I always felt like Coleridge at the end of "Kubla Khan," a bit dazed at the heady experience.

One of the last books I edited before leaving Dalkey in 1996 was David Markson's extraordinary novel *Reader's Block*, published in September of that year. In it, an autobiographical narrator contemplates writing a novel; at the same time, he broods over hundreds of cultural anecdotes and quotations, which make up the bulk of the novel. With spaces separating its one- or two-sentence fragments, *Reader's Block* superficially resembles *Rock-Drill* in that it too employs what Pound called "the method of Luminous Detail." On pages 74–75 of Markson's novel this sequence of thoughts comes to the narrator:

> No needle marks on your Annunciation's arm, now.
>
> We do not come to thoughts. They come to us.
> Thought Heidegger.
>
> The first translation of major length for purely literary purposes was a Latin *Iliad*, ca. 250 B.C., by Livius Andronicus.
>
> Sheri Martinelli.

The first line is from Gaddis's *Recognitions*, quoted earlier. A few moments later the narrator realizes he happens to know that Esme was based on a woman named Sheri Martinelli, and records it as one more example of the cultural trivia cluttering up his mind, on par with an obscure Latin translator.

In her final years Sheri liked to park her camper in front of the local supermarket and watch the people come and go. It was there that she died on 3 November 1996, almost 24 years to the day after the death of her beloved Maestro, and 40 years after he transformed the fisherman's granddaughter into a goddess.

Ra-Set in her barge now
over deep sapphire (92/638)

APPENDIX

"The Birth of Sheri Martinelli"

by Charles Duits

I was never virgin nor was born as others are
A green drum beats in front of a blue curtain
And it was beneath a dawn of great violence that two fishermen bent by the wind discovered there in the wet sand my two white feet budding like flowers
And it was a terrible delight to be drawn from the beach's womb inch by inch thanks to those two fishermen
The beating of the drum became a pair of arms before which the curtain parted
O grains of yellow sand, like insects you slid off me
Voluptuous wet sand sliding down my thighs
I recall the ochre-colored spasm and how I opened eyes heavy with sleep to see the tempest on the faces of the fishermen
My eyes were like crystal jars filled with seawater in which little fish, having made love, laid chains of eggs in which tadpoles could already be seen
Look, said the fishermen, she is blind
And suddenly in hushed voices, She is naked, completely naked
Veils of ochre-colored blood, you no longer protect me
The blue curtain folds through the green dream
There where I had been sleeping in the wet sand
The sand crabs with their multitudinous feet traversed my throat every day as they would have climbed mounds of sand
But these tender hills were kneaded of a softer clay
And in my parted lips the sand crabs sat as in an armchair
And bantered with their fellows, insinuating themselves on the balcony of my shoulders
On the balcony of my shoulders, I mean my collarbones
The sand envelops my flesh, the sand was a featherbed of tenderness
The drum beats far away, calling, calling
At nightfall O dark crustaceans rising from the depths of the waves you have chosen a very soft bed in me you have spread out your limbs in a caress you have

chosen to live in my vulva
The foam clings less to the rocks than your pincers deeply grafted to my most secret flesh
And I, I am tired of being a woman preyed upon by starving men
Tired of being given over to their need to be wounded, to be abandoned
And I long for a lover who will sleep all night his lips on mine and his hand in the same fault and as delicate as the claws of the crabs
What to say of the taste of the sea, what to say of the cave of sleep
The fishermen, their faces changed, took of my body in order to quell their hunger
O I am not nourishment for starving men
I wish only to be a house
A house of lips and secret folds
Where they may exist in peace
And sleep like insects all night in my mouth
Their fingers in my vulva
Their fingers deep in the sand
Tranquil and the drum beats on
The drum beats out the call of heaven

(Written ca. 1946; trans. George Kearns and Rikki Ducornet)

Works Cited

Bacigalupo, Massimo. *The Forméd Trace: The Later Poetry of Ezra Pound.* New York: Columbia U P, 1980.

———. "'I wish he would explain his explanation': Authorial Explication in Wallace Stevens and Ezra Pound." *RSA Journal* 7 (1996): 63–78.

Bair, Deirdre. *Anaïs Nin: A Biography.* New York: Putnam's, 1995.

Bissinger, Karl. *The Luminous Years: Portraits at Mid-Century.* New York: Abrams, 2003.

Booth, Marcella. "Ezrology: The Class of '57." *Paideuma* 13.3 (Winter 1984): 375–88.

Broyard, Anatole. *Kafka Was the Rage: A Greenwich Village Memoir.* New York: Crown/Carol Southern, 1993.

Bukowski, Charles. "Horse on Fire." *The Roominghouse Madrigals: Early Selected Poems 1946–1966.* Santa Rosa, CA: Black Sparrow, 1988. 70.

———. *Screams from the Balcony: Selected Letters 1960–1970.* Ed. Seamus Cooney. Santa Rosa, CA: Black Sparrow, 1993.

———, and Sheri Martinelli. *Beerspit Night and Cursing: The Correspondence of Charles Bukowski and Sheri Martinelli, 1960–1967.* Ed. Steven Moore. Santa Rosa, CA: Black Sparrow Press, 2001

Carpenter, Humphrey. *A Serious Character: The Life of Ezra Pound.* Boston: Houghton Mifflin, 1988.

Deren, Maya. *Ritual in Transfigured Time.* 1945–46. In *Experimental Films, 1943–1959.* Mystic Fire Video, 1986.

di Prima, Diane. *Recollections of My Life as a Woman.* New York: Viking, 2001.

Findley, Timothy. *The Trials of Ezra Pound.* Winnipeg: Blizzard, 1994.

Flory, Wendy Stallard. *Ezra Pound and* The Cantos: *A Record of Struggle.* New Haven: Yale U P, 1980.

Gaddis, William. *The Recognitions*. New York: Harcourt, Brace, 1955.
Gates, Henry Louis, Jr. "White Like Me." *New Yorker*, 17 June 1996, 66–72, 74–81.
Gibbs, Josephine. "A Modern Portfolio." *Art Digest* 21 (15 December 1946): 11.
Ginsberg, Allen. "Allen Verbatim." *Paideuma* 3.2 (Fall 1974): 253–73.
———. *Journals: Early Fifties Early Sixties*. Ed. Gordon Ball. New York: Grove, 1977.
———. *Composed on the Tongue: Literary Conversations, 1967–1977*. Ed. Donald Allen. San Francisco: Grey Fox, 1980.
———. "Iron Horse." *Collected Poems 1947–1980*. New York: Harper & Row, 1984.
Gold, Herbert. *Bohemia*. New York: Simon & Schuster, 1993.
Gordon, David. "From the Blue Serpent to Kati." *Paideuma* 3.2 (1974): 239–44.
Guest, Barbara. *Herself Defined: The Poet H.D. and Her World*. Garden City, NY: Doubleday, 1984.
H.D. *End to Torment: A Memoir of Ezra Pound*. New York: New Directions, 1979.
Heymann, C. David. *Ezra Pound: The Last Rower*. New York: Viking/Richard Seaver, 1976.
Kane, Russell W. "A One-Woman Art Show." *Cleveland Plain Dealer Sunday Magazine*, 6 September 1964, 6–7.
Laughlin, James. *Pound as Wuz: Essays and Lectures on Ezra Pound*. Saint Paul: Graywolf, 1987.
McNaughton, Bill. "Pound, A Brief Memoir: 'Chi Lavora, Ora.'" *Paideuma* 3.3 (Winter 1974): 219–24.
Markson, David. *Reader's Block*. 1996. Corrected edition: Normal, IL: Dalkey Archive Press, 2007.
Martinelli, Sheri. *La Martinelli*. Introduction by Ezra Pound. Milan: Vanni Scheiwiller, 1956.
———. "Duties of a Lady Female." *Anagogic & Paideumic Review* 1.3 (1959). Rpt. in *A Different Beat: Writings by Women of the Beat Generation*. Ed. Richard Peabody. London and New York: Serpent's Tail/High Risk, 1997. 154–58.
———. "The Beggar Girl of Queretaro." *Anagogic & Paideumic Review* 1.4 (1961?): 26–29.
———. "Homage to Grandpa." *Light Year*, Autumn 1961.
———. [Letter to the editor.] *Paideuma* 6.3 (Winter 1977): 415–16.
———. "Canto CVI." Unpublished poem/commentary, dated 6 December 1984.
———. "For Allen." In *Best Minds: A Tribute to Allen Ginsberg*. Ed. Bill Morgan and Bob Rosenthal. New York: Lospecchio, 1986. 190.
———. "A Memoir." *Paideuma* 15.2–3 (Fall-Winter 1986): 151–62.
———. "*Pound as Wuz*." Unpublished commentary on Laughlin (above), dated 11 April 1988.
———. "Goodbye Anaïs." *Anaïs: An International Journal* 12 (1994): 77.
———. "Mexico, His Thrust Renews." *Gargoyle* 44 (2002): 9–18.
Mullins, Eustace. *This Difficult Individual, Ezra Pound*. New York: Fleet, 1961.
Nicosia, Gerald. *Memory Babe: A Critical Biography of Jack Kerouac*. Berkeley: U of California P, 1994.
Nin, Anaïs. *The Diary of Anaïs Nin, 1944–1947*. Ed. Gunther Stuhlmann. New York: Harcourt Brace Jovanovich, 1971.
Parker, Chan. *My Life in E-flat*. Columbia: U of South Carolina P, 1999.
Pound, Ezra. "Prayer for a Dead Brother." *Antigonish Review* 8 (Winter 1972): 27.
———. *The Cantos*. New York: New Directions, 1995 (Thirteenth Printing).
———, and E. E. Cummings. *Pound/Cummings: The Correspondence of Ezra Pound*

and E. E. Cummings. Ed. Barry Ahearn. Ann Arbor, MI: U of Michigan P, 1996.

———, and James Laughlin. *Selected Letters*. Ed. David M. Gordon. New York: Norton, 1994.

Rattray, David. "Weekend with Ezra Pound." *Nation* 185 (16 November 1957): 343–49.

Reisner, Robert George. *Bird: The Legend of Charlie Parker*. New York: Citadel, 1962.

Stock, Noel. *The Life of Ezra Pound: An Expanded Edition*. San Francisco: North Point, 1982.

Stumvoll, Josef. "Ezra Pound schreibt uns." *Biblos* (Vienna) 8.2 (1959): 74–83.

Taylor, Richard. "Sheri Martinelli: Muse to Ezra Pound." *Agenda* 38, nos. 1–2 (2001): 98–112. [Note: this appeared *after* I sent Taylor my 1998 essay.]

Terrell, Carroll F. *A Companion to the Cantos of Ezra Pound*. Volume II (Cantos 74–117). Berkeley: U of California P, 1984.

Torrey, E. Fuller. *The Roots of Treason: Ezra Pound and the Secret of St. Elizabeths*. New York: McGraw-Hill, 1984.

Vazquez-Amaral, José. "La Martinelli." *Rutgers Review* 4.1 (Spring 1970): 19–21.

Wilhelm, J. J. *Ezra Pound: The Tragic Years, 1925–1972*. University Park, PA: Pennsylvania State U P, 1994.

Wykes-Joyce, Max. *7000 Years of Pottery and Porcelain*. New York: Philosophical Library, 1958.

William Gaddis: Three Memorials

REMEMBERING MR. GADDIS

A memorial tribute was held May 6th [1999] for the late William Gaddis, the esteemed novelist who died last December. The course of my life was irrevocably changed by my discovery of his work in 1975, and after nearly 25 years of writing and thinking about his titanic novels, I felt compelled to attend this tribute to the man who, I am now convinced, is the greatest American novelist of the 20th century.

The tribute was held in the august auditorium of the American Academy of Arts and Letters in New York City, into which Gaddis was inducted in 1984. As it happens, the last time I had seen Gaddis was in the same building five years earlier, an awards ceremony where Gaddis and the other members of the Academy sat on the stage (like the faculty at a graduation), facing us like totems guarding the gates of American literature.

Gracing the stage this time was a smaller but well-chosen group: Sarah Gaddis, his daughter, began the event on an elegiac note, almost breaking down in tears as she confessed how difficult it was to adjust to the absence created by her father's death. (She once wrote an autobiographical novel, *Swallow Hard*, largely about her relationship to him.) She was followed by gentleman-novelist Louis Auchincloss, who gave an overview of Gaddis's achievement (in a sumptuous Anglo-American accent) and paid tribute to his vast erudition. Auchincloss is known for his legal novels, but he admitted Gaddis's knowledge of the law far exceeded his.

William H. Gass followed with a brilliant and witty account of the impact *The Recognitions* had on his generation of writers. Gass's life intersected with Gaddis's on many occasions, most recently in Germany, where Gass accompanied Gaddis to a book event in Cologne where he was treated like a movie star: stepping out of a black limo, Gaddis was surrounded by photographers popping flashes as if he were attending the premiere of his latest movie — a conceit helped along by the fact that Gaddis had movie-star good looks, resembling Leslie Howard when younger, and William Holden in later life.

Short-story writer Joy Williams was next, first reading a hilarious passage from *A Frolic of His Own*, then recounting her memories of the man she always called *Mister* Gaddis, despite their friendship. (I know the feeling: I met Gaddis several times, was even a guest at his house for three days, but considered it unthinkable to address him as anything but Mr. Gaddis.) Painter Julian Schnabel followed, with a somewhat difficult-to-follow account of how Gaddis's view of painting (in *The Recognitions*) influenced his own development as an artist. The last guest to speak was filmmaker D. A. Pennebaker (best known for his Bob Dylan documentary, *Dont Look Back*), who entertained us with some anecdotes about Gaddis in the 1940s.

Gaddis's son Matthew — the spitting image of his father — then introduced a brief slide-show presentation, ranging from Gaddis as an eight-year-old Eagle Scout and a shot of him as a young man in an improbable cowboy hat holding the reins of a horse — a Harvard version of the Marlboro man — to photos taken later in life.

The audience was rather small — somewhere between 100 to 150 people — but made up in quality what it may have lacked in quantity. Among the many writers there were Don DeLillo, E. L. Doctorow, Joseph McElroy, David Markson, Harry Mathews, Ann Beattie, Walter Abish, Bradford Morrow, and Mary Caponegro. Many of us who have written about Gaddis were there — Gregory Comnes, Frederick R. Karl, Joseph Tabbi, Christopher Knight — as were two of Gaddis's three wives. At least one of his former publishers was there (Aaron Asher) along with some of his current German ones, and a good many family friends. (There were probably other distinguished guests whom your reporter didn't recognize.) The only disappointment was the lack of any information on future publications: Gaddis left behind a final novel, *Agapē Agape*, but its publication date remains up in the air. Matthew avoided questions on this topic with lawyerly aplomb. (However, one of Gaddis's German publishers told me they had already arranged to publish a collection of his essays, along with *Torschlusspanik*, a radio play he wrote for Deutschland Radio last year, which may be the opening chapter of *Agapē Agape*.)

There were some felicitous coincidences that illustrated Gaddis's belief in "the unswerving punctuality of chance" (a phrase that appears in all four of his novels). Looking for a restaurant after the event, Markson, Tabbi, Caponegro, and I were wandering around the West Village when we stumbled upon Horatio Street, Wyatt's address in *The Recognitions*. And during my taxi ride to the airport the following day, I passed the brownstone on 96th street where so much of *J R* is set. Best of all was my in-flight reading choice: James Hilton's old classic *Lost Horizon*, which turned out to be the source of a literary allusion in *Carpenter's Gothic* that had always eluded me. In that shortest, shapeliest of his novels, Gaddis quoted Hilton's description of a character who, despite his setbacks, had "a sense in which he felt that he was still a part of all that he might have been." This striving to achieve one's full potential bedevils many of Gaddis's characters — most of them failures to some degree — but this memorial tribute was a rousing affirmation that Gaddis became everything a great novelist could, and should, be.

THE RECOGNITIONS, THEN AND NOW

It's an odd title, isn't it — *The Recognitions*. In English we use the singular "recognition" often enough, but the plural form is rare, especially with that definite article in front of it. It sounds unidiomatic, like a literal translation of a foreign title (which it is). That's the first potentially off-putting thing that a customer looking over the new releases in a bookstore 50 years ago would have noticed, and perhaps the only thing that was needed to cause the customer to pass over it and keep looking. For while some people are attracted by the rare and unusual, most people aren't. But had a curious customer paused long enough to examine this new novel with the odd title, several other obstacles to buying it would have begun to appear, beginning with the cover. Unlike the majority of novels at that time, there was no pictorial representation of the novel's setting, or of its principal character, or of a significant scene. Instead, just big block letters, alternating between red and gold against a plain white background, broken into correct but misleading syllables that made the odd title look even odder:

THE RE-
COGNI-
TIONS

The lower half — A NOVEL BY WILLIAM GADDIS — would have meant nothing to the average reader. Gaddis had published only one brief essay before that, along with an excerpt from *The Recognitions* in an obscure literary magazine, so the name would not have provided any incentive to buy it. If, still undeterred, the customer would have picked the book up to examine it further, the next thing that would have struck her or him was the weight: 2 pounds, 7 ounces, and the length: 956 pages, the size of three or four standard novels. Again, some of us are instinctively attracted to thick, long books, but others are reluctant to make the large investment of time they require. So by this point, the huge novel with the weird title by an unknown writer would have scared off most customers.

But for those still looking, further obstacles presented themselves. Flipping the book over, they would have seen a single blurb, by a Stuart Gilbert. The name would have been recognized by Joyce fans, for Gilbert wrote the first substantial book on *Ulysses* back in 1930, which had been reprinted in the early '50s, but the average customer wouldn't have known who he was. Gilbert evokes Eliot's *Waste Land* and Joyce's *Ulysses*, again catnip to us literary types but for the average customer a warning signal that this book would be difficult. And as one of our leading contemporary novelists assures us, peo ple don't like difficulty. But say a few customers in 1955 were among those freaks who regard difficulty as an invigorating challenge — as in a "difficult" golf course — rather than as an ordeal; those hardy few might have continued by looking at the front flap to learn more about the book. The first thing they would have noticed there was the price: *Seven dollars and fifty cents!* Nowadays that sounds ridiculously low, but in 1955 most new novels were priced at $2.50 to $3.00; so in today's terms, $7.50 would be like paying $40 for a new book, an outrageous sum. [$65 in 2016!] Once they got over that shock, they would have found a fairly good description of the book, but on the back flap, there was no customary photograph of the author, a custom Gaddis metafictionally mocks on page 936 of the novel itself: "For some crotchety reason, there was no picture of the author looking pensive sucking a pipe, sans gêne with a cigarette, sang-froid with no necktie, plastered across the back."

By this point, for all the reasons I've given, nine out of ten customers would have put the book down. For those of us who regard *The Recognitions* as a masterpiece, it's always been hard to imagine why the book was ignored when it first came out, but we have to remember that it entered the world, not as an obvious masterpiece, but simply as a new product fighting for the customer's attention in the marketplace. Whether by accident or design, the book placed a number of obstacles between itself and book customers during those first crucial minutes when they browse the table full of new releases. And if that one out of ten who was still interested persisted with his or her investigation, what would they have encountered upon opening the book? Well, the first thing they would have seen is the book's motto. In Latin. By someone named Irenaeus. Not a strong selling point, unless you're a big fan of early church fathers. Next thing is an epigraph. In German. At least this one is by Goethe, a name most people would recognize. Now, if they made it over all those obstacles and actually read the first paragraph of the novel, they would have been rewarded with an elegant, sardonic paragraph that sends up a flare announcing that this is indeed no average novel. The better-read may even have noticed the paragraph ends with a subtle allusion to a line from one of Robert Browning's poems, an indication of Gaddis's allusive manner. But if instead they had flipped the book open and read a paragraph at random, they may have been confronted with something like this:

> The dog bared its teeth at his harsh laughter, and watched his hand drop, all the way to snatch up the slip of paper he'd dropped a few minutes before. —I A O, I A E, in the name of the father and of our Lord Jesus Christ and holy spirit, iriterli estather, nochthai brasax salolam . . . yes, very good for cows in Egypt . . . opsakion aklana thalila i a o, i a e . . . (138–39)

OK, put the book down. I don't think Uncle Dwayne would want this for a birthday present.

Now: there may have been some who remained undeterred by all these obstacles and even liked what they saw in Gaddis's novel, but were reluctant to shell out the enormous sum of $7.50 until they learned what the critics thought of it. Surely, the respected members of the press would tell them whether this book was worth their time and money. The novel received 55 reviews over the next few months, and two or three of them were actually fairly positive. The reviewer for the *Amarillo News* liked it, and so did the guy for *Library Journal.* (That was Herbert Cahoon, for many years the bibliographer for the *James Joyce Quarterly*, and thus used to that kind of writing.) The rest damned and blasted the book, working it over with one of the worst critical muggings in literary history. For the sordid details, read Jack Green's *Fire the Bastards!*

But it's too easy to blame those bastards . . . sorry, those *reviewers* for scuttling *The Recognitions* in 1955. They were typical members of a dominant literary community that was hostile to innovative fiction in general. Jack Kerouac couldn't find a publisher for his second, more experimental version of *On the Road*, and even had trouble getting the more commercial version published. (The magnificent alternate version, entitled *Visions of Cody*, wouldn't be published until 1972, three years after his death.) Vladimir Nabokov had to publish *Lolita* in Paris at first; no American publisher would touch it; same with William Burroughs, whose *Naked Lunch* was published in France in 1959 but not in America until 1962. Henry Miller's *Tropic of Cancer* had likewise been published in France back in 1934, but banned in America until 1961; same with Lawrence Durrell's decadent first novel, *The Black Book*, published in Paris in 1938 but not available here until 1960. And of course D. H. Lawrence's *Lady Chatterley's Lover* was written even earlier but was not allowed into America until 1959. Felipe Alfau wrote a brilliant novel entitled *Chromos* in 1948 but couldn't find a publisher for it at the time, and had to wait more than 40 years to see it in print. And who knows how many other amazing novels from the 1950s never even saw the light of day because of the provincial, conservative nature of American publishing at the time. To be sure, there were a few American publishers — like Grove Press and New Directions — that were bringing out unconventional works, but for the most part, such fiction was unwelcome.

Innovative authors writing in foreign languages fared even worse; American publishers simply assumed its readers were not yet ready for their daring works, and so Americans were kept in the dark about a number of fascinating authors. Jean Genet, for example, published all of his transgressive novels in France in the late '40s and early '50s, but it wasn't until the '60s before they'd be translated into English. The great German writer Arno Schmidt began writing his experimental novels during the late '40s, but none of them would appear in English until the late '70s. Stanislaw Witkiewicz's 1930 novel *Insatiability* — sort of Poland's answer to *Ulysses* — likewise didn't arrive here until the 1970s. Consequently, there was almost no context, and no perceived market, for such a novel as *The Recognitions* in the sheltered literary world of the Eisenhower '50s.

In fact, in light of all this, it's something of a miracle that *The Recognitions* was published at all. The novel is laced with obscene language, which was still rare at that time in fiction, and is fiercely blasphemous. The character Anselm ridicules Christianity mercilessly throughout the novel, and Gaddis himself has lots of fun with Catholic stigmatics and other religious nuts. Reverend Gwyon spends most of his time exposing Christianity as a counterfeit of earlier religions, and there's that scene toward the end when the phony novelist Ludy has an attack of the runs and afterwards wipes himself with pages from a nearby book — the most prominent book you'd expect to find in a monastery. The novel also has a number of homosexual characters and transvestites; not only is their presence unusual for a 1950s novel, but they're actually treated fairly nicely, which was almost unheard of back then: the unspoken rule was that any homosexual characters had to come to a bad end, but Gaddis has a few of them getting married and heading off to Europe for a honeymoon at the end. A number of characters use drugs, which was still fairly rare in "respectable" novels back then. And finally, the novel is incredibly frank in its treatment of sexuality; not only is there rampant promiscuity, but there are scenes featuring masturbation and even bestiality. (Who could ever forget the moment when the servant girl Janet is caught in the act with a bull?) So it's not surprising that the reviewers were shocked by Gaddis's novel and felt compelled to denounce it. They were presumably unfamiliar with novels of the sort I mentioned earlier — those by Genet, Durrell, Schmidt — which were already treating these topics with the same bravado, and so Gaddis's novel must have seemed like a weird aberration, and not anything you'd recommend to the average reader.

But how about the academic community, those who in the '50s were teaching and studying Joyce's *Ulysses*, Faulkner's more experimental works, Céline's novels — why didn't they pounce on *The Recognitions* and praise it? You would think those who liked intellectually challenging writers like Joyce and Eliot — not to mention older writers like Melville, Sterne, Rabelais — would have championed the work. But unfortunately, academics in the '50s still had a wait-and-see attitude toward new fiction: a book had to pass "the test of time" before they risked writing about it. Even a book as stupendous as *Ulysses* inspired very little academic criticism at first; it was published in 1922 but it would be 30 years before the Joyce industry got into gear; same with Faulkner, Eliot. Malcolm Lowry's *Under the Volcano* remained under the radar for decades. Samuel Beckett's novels were neglected at first. And of course little or no contemporary fiction was studied in English classes in the '50s. It wasn't until the 1960s that some academics felt it was OK to write about recent novels, and it was J. D. Salinger, of all people, who made that possible: academic books began appearing within a few *years* of the publication of his books, which was unheard of until then. But even so, writing about current fiction was considered a kind of slumming, a little vacation until you returned to the real stuff. In this regard, as in so many other ways, *The Recognitions* was simply ahead of its time, and would pretty much be ignored by the academic community for the next few decades.

And finally, we have to remember that the '50s were . . . well, *the '50s*. It was a very conservative era — it's a cliché but true — and the last thing anyone wanted then was a blasphemous, foul-mouthed, erudite, multilingual, liberal, thousand-page novel denouncing the American way of life as hypocritical and phony. In later years, Gaddis himself admitted that it was naïve of him to think that his novel would be welcomed with open arms and that he would be thanked by a grateful but chastised public for showing them the error of their ways. It was the wrong time for his brand of social criticism and black humor, his kind of high-wire literary showmanship. Cracks were beginning to appear in the façade of the Eisenhower '50s, and innovation could be seen in some of the other arts: it was an exciting time for painting and sculpture, jazz was getting more abstract and experimental, rock music exploded onto the scene, and the Beats yanked poetry out of the academy and took it to the streets. But most novels still resembled their Victorian predecessors in form, and it wouldn't be until the '60s that some readers began to realize fiction could be as innovative as other art forms. Had *The Recognitions* been published in 1965 instead of 1955, things may have been different. It might have won the same acclaim that greeted Pynchon's *V.*, Heller's *Catch-22*, Kesey's *One Flew over the Cuckoo's Nest*, and other unconventional novels of the '60s. Who knows?

Things are certainly different today, which gives me hope that when the next *Recognitions* appears, it won't suffer the same fate as the original. The audience for unusual, noncommercial fiction is still small, but it's much larger than it was in the '50s, and though the mainstream review media may not be much better, there are a host of alternatives that will get the word out, from literary journals that champion innovation to the vast resources of the Internet. Academics no longer consider it slumming to teach and write about new fiction, and in some universities, recent fiction is probably taught as much as classic literature. Since the '50s, a growing number of difficult, demanding novelists — from Thomas Pynchon to David Foster Wallace — have taught us to appreciate ambitious mega-novels like *The Recognitions,* and a steady stream of translations of innovative foreign novels over the last 50 years has made it harder to remain as provincial and uninformed as readers used to be. Though there are still millions of Americans today who are as unwilling as their predecessors in the '50s to hear their country criticized, there are more people today than 50 years ago who would agree with Gaddis that our culture has its flaws, and that it's noble to expose those flaws in an effort to restore the original intentions of the Founding Fathers, rather than trying to fake others and ourselves with a ludicrous counterfeit.

The Recognitions was ahead of its time, and the literary establishment back then crushed Gaddis in much the same way that the church on the last page of the novel crushes the true artist Stanley; but as Gaddis predicted in the last line, his work would survive. And as all of us gathered here today will demonstrate, "it is still spoken of, when it is noted, with high regard."

□ □ □ □ □ □ □

WILLIAM GADDIS: THE NOBILITY OF FAILURE

There were giants in the earth in those days. The sheer size of some contemporary novels astounded me in 1974 when, after receiving an M.A. in literature, I pulled my head out of the canon to see what was happening in current fiction. I had already picked up flea-market copies of Barth's brick-size *Sot-Weed Factor* and the fat Signet paperback of Young's *Miss MacIntosh, My Darling,* and soon was reading other gigantic novels like Pynchon's *Gravity's Rainbow* (back when it still had that garish orange cover) and Delany's *Dhalgren.* I soon added Nabokov's *Ada* and Coover's *Public Burning* to my groaning shelves. But the huge novels that impressed me most were those by William Gaddis: via a *Time* magazine review of *J R* in October 1975, I learned of both it and his first novel, *The Recognitions* (1955), which had been reissued the year before in a squat, 1,021-page paperback by Avon. (Remember what a great line Avon was in the 1970s, especially all those Latin American translations?) I read the latter first, then *J R* a few months later, and knew I had discovered one of the greatest American novelists of the postwar period.

It sure was a well-kept secret. When I went to the library to find out more about Gaddis, fully expecting to find several books and essays about him, I was shocked to find almost nothing. It had been 20 years since *The Recognitions* had been published, and the only response from the critical establishment was two mediocre essays and a dissertation. The lack of recognition for that monumental achievement surprised me, but was a life-changing blow to Gaddis. The failure to achieve something that was perhaps not worth doing in the first place became a signature theme in his subsequent novels, including his stab at mainstream fiction (*Carpenter's Gothic*, 1985), yet another big novel (*A Frolic of His Own*, 1994), and a posthumously published parting shot about failure (*Agapē Agape*, 2002).

Gaddis's concern with failure, missed opportunities, and lack of recognition stemmed partly from his hard-luck life. Born in Manhattan in 1922, Gaddis grew up without his father, who left his mother when Gaddis was three, and he saw little of his mother after he was sent to a strict boarding school in Connecticut at age five. Shortly after he enrolled in high school, he contracted a disease that not only kept him home for long periods but later disqualified him from serving in World War II, stigmatizing him with a sense of "unclubbability" (as his friend Alan Ansen later put it). He was asked to leave Harvard before graduation, and moved to Manhattan to work as a fact-checker for the *New Yorker*; but as a Harvard dandy, he was out of place in the postwar Greenwich Village milieu in which he moved. (See Chandler Brossard's portrayal of him as "Harry Lees" in his 1952 novel *Who Walk in Darkness*.) He failed to place any of the short stories he was writing at the time — no great loss, from what I've seen of them — and spent most of the years from 1947 to 1952 as a stranger in strange lands, drifting from Central America to Spain to France while working on his first novel. *The Recognitions* appeared in 1955 to overwhelmingly negative reviews; deprived of the success he expected (and fully deserved), Gaddis spent the next decade working at a variety of jobs in industry, starting then abandoning a second novel, failing to find a backer for a play he had written, enduring a divorce in the mid-1960s, and living off a series of advances and part-time teaching jobs to resume and finish that second novel.

J R appeared in 1975 to much better reviews, and won the National Book Award the following year, but Gaddis was disappointed that he didn't get a huge paperback reprint sale as Pynchon did a few years earlier for *Gravity's Rainbow*. (They shared the same agent, the late Candida Donadio.) Jobless and at loose ends, Gaddis wrote his finest essay at this time, originally entitled "Failure" but published in *Harper's* in April 1981 as "The Rush for Second Place" (and included in the posthumously published book of that name). Based on a class he had taught at Bard College a few years earlier on the theme of failure in American literature, Gaddis pondered the paradox that doing one's best doesn't necessarily lead to recognition and success, and often results in disappointment. Gaddis populated his novels with well-intentioned failures, sometimes blaming them for their own self-destructive tendencies, but also indicting his country for encouraging a capitalist system that almost ensures failure for most people, few of whom can keep up with its endless demand for greater profit margins and greater success. Add the corrosive effect of excessive litigation to the melting pot — the subject of *A Frolic of His Own* — and the American dream begins to look like the nightmare it has become for many of its citizens.

Though Gaddis wrote about failure, both personal and national, he himself was not one. After receiving one of the first MacArthur "genius" awards in 1982, Gaddis began attracting the kind of recognition he had hoped for in 1955, and though he never became as popular with general audiences as other literary novelists, his work became the subject of a growing number of monographs, dissertations, critical essays, and a compendious website (www.williamgaddis.org). His novels have been translated into a variety of languages — a Chinese translation of *J R* appeared recently — and in Germany, which he visited in the 1990s, he was greeted with movie-star acclaim. A dozen years after his death in December 1998, his novels are still in print and continue to find readers and generate criticism. (A new collection of essays, *William Gaddis, "The Last of Something,"* is in press as I write.) *J R* especially now looks uncannily prescient, predicting in 1975 the financial and cultural meltdown of 2008 by condemning the moral vacuum created in the wake of predatory capitalism, the ridiculous abstraction of many financial instruments, and a system that condones greed over humanism and divides people into winners and losers.

In "The Rush for Second Place," Gaddis cites Ivan Morris's *The Nobility of Failure* (1975), a study of Japanese culture, in which a failure is often "the man whose single-minded sincerity will not allow him to make the manoeuvres and compromises that are so often needed for mundane success" (*The Rush for Second Place* [Penguin, 2002], 57). While all his novels dramatize characters struggling — sometimes comically, sometimes tragically — with those "manoeuvres and compromises," Gaddis himself never made any. That, and the uncompromising artistry he brought to his demanding but rewarding novels, make him a hero of our time.

PART 2: SIGNIFICANT OTHERS

Five Notes on *Finnegans Wake*

DAVID IN CRIMEA

Joyce's rendition of his father's story of Buckley and the Russian General seems to owe something to the story of Saul and David. In the First Book of Samuel, David twice has the opportunity to kill Saul, but both times abstains.[1] On the first occasion, Saul goes into a cave to relieve himself, and though David's men encourage him to kill the old king, he cannot bring himself to murder "the Lord's Anointed" and instead simply cuts off a piece of Saul's robe unobserved (24:3–6). On the second occasion Saul is sleeping, David is again encouraged, and again abstains; this time, more symbolically, he makes off with Saul's spear (26:7–8).

On *FW* 344–45 the Russian General[2] relieves himself, and Butt, like David, "adn't the arts to" kill him in such a state. But Taff, upon hearing of Butt's failure, determines "*to see him pluggy well moidered . . . before he doze soze, sopprused though he is*" (345.6). Here Taff is playing Abishai to Butt's David[3] by encouraging him to kill Saul as he sleeps. But Butt again abstains: "*hearing somrother sudly give tworthree peevish sniff snuff snoores like govalise falseleep he waitawhishts to see might he stirs*" (345.10). And before the Mullingar interlude interrupts, the feeling of reconciliation (345.30–35) approximates that between Saul and David (26:21–25).

NOTES

1. Modern biblical scholarship considers this two versions — the first from an early source, the second from a later — of the same story.
2. Here called "the Saur of all the Haurousians." "Saur" is, of course, Czar, but by way of the L/R interchange (see O Hehir's *Gaelic Lexicon for "Finnegans Wake,"* 392–93) easily becomes "Saul."
3. I realize "Taff" is from the Welsh form of David, but I think Butt and Taff merge into one Son archetype, demonstrating both reverence and hatred for the Father. Elsewhere in *FW* Butt-Shem is associated with David (from the Telegram motif) and Michael Davitt; see Hart's *Structure and Motif in "Finnegans Wake,"* 125, 127.

□ □ □ □ □ □ □

FOR THE RECORD

John Cage's 1942 composition "The Wonderful Widow of Eighteen Springs" (adapted from *FW* 566.01–22) is now available on a recording by Jan Steele and John Cage entitled *Voices and Instruments* (Obscure No. 5 [Island Records Ltd.).* A rather simple, unimpressive piece, the melody is restricted to three notes (A, B, and E) and is accompanied by percussive use of a piano's wooden surfaces. Also featured on this album is a beautiful setting of *Chamber Music* XXXV by Steele.

□ □ □ □ □ □ □

OLIVER CROMWELL

I've always wondered why Cromwell warrants almost 40 appearances[1] in *FW* in almost as many settings. Mrs. Glasheen lists him as an HCE figure in her "Who Is Who" chart,[2] and Dr. O Hehir shows that on the basis of etymology Humphrey is to be identified with Oliver Cromwell, who in turn is associated with the ancient Irish idol *Crom Crúach* ("gory croucher"),[3] a manifestation of the mytho-psychological ogre-father.

But at the same time, the fact that Cromwell seized the crown (420.36), invaded Ireland, and dissolved the Rump Parliament, of which HCE was once a member (127.33),[4] puts him in the role of the son overthrowing the father and/or old older.

Of course, characters in *FW* can and do play more roles than one, but Cromwell's purpose in *FW*, outside of contributing a handful of phrases,[5] is sufficiently murky to lead Mrs. Glasheen (among others, I'm sure) to confess, "I do not think I wholly understand the use of Cromwell in *FW*."[6]

But more light may be shed by consulting the following nursery rhyme from Suffolk which Joyce, whose familiarity with all kinds of music is amply demonstrated by Hodgart and Worthington's book, probably knew:

> Oliver Cromwell lay buried and dead,
> Hee-haw, buried and dead,
> There grew an old apple-tree over his head,
> Hee-haw, over his head.
>
> The apples were ripe and ready to fall,
> Hee-haw, ready to fall,
> There came an old woman to gather them all,
> Hee-haw, gather them all.
>
> Oliver rose and gave her a drop,

* This was Brian Eno's boutique label, most of whose offerings I purchased in the '70s. This one in particular was irresistible because it featured one of my favorite vocalists, Robert Wyatt, singing one of my favorite novelists — 2016 note.

Hee-haw, gave her a drop,
Which made the old woman go hippety hop,
Hee-haw, hippety hop.

The saddle and bridle, they lie on the shelf,
Hee-haw, lie on the shelf,
If you want any more you must sing it yourself,
Hee-haw, sing it yourself.[7]

"And curled up like Lord Olofa Crumple" (45.03), Cromwell here resembles Tim Finnegan, by all appearances dead, but soon to wake. The apple tree performs many functions — a symbol of Cromwell's resurrection (cf. the countless vegetation deities whose deaths result in life-giving crops and food), an allusion to the biblical tree of knowledge, and perhaps even an allusion to the fruit which supposedly inspired Newton not to "go hippety hop" but to develop the laws of motion. The old woman gathers "a pretty nice kettle of fruit" (11.32) just as ALP, Biddy the Hen, and/or Mrs. Finnegan are wont to do. And though the "drop" Cromwell gives her is an apple, a "drop of the creature" could certainly make the old woman go hippety hop just as it did Tim Finnegan. And do I hear the Four's Ass braying every other line?

One shouldn't make too much of a simple song such as this, but the appearance of two or three of *FW*'s major themes makes the song worthy of consideration, especially for the light it may shed on the murky role of Cromwell in *FW*.

NOTES

1. *A Second Census of "Finnegans Wake,"* 57–58.
2. Ibid., lxiii.
3. *Gaelic Lexicon*, 389.
4. *Structure and Motif in "Finnegans Wake,"* 239.
5. E.g., "remove that bauble"; "put your trust in God and keep your power dry"; "hell or Connaught."
6. *Census II*, 57.
7. The song has been arranged by Benjamin Britten, where I first heard the song on a London/Decca recording (STS 15166).

□ □ □ □ □ □ □

LUPERCA LATOUCHE (67.36)

This soiled dove takes her name not only from the Roman festival of Lupercalia and the Latouche family of Dublin bankers,[1] but also, in all probability, from Rose La Touche, the pubescent Irish paramour of John Ruskin.[2] "Rosie" was ten when Ruskin, 30 years her senior, fell in love with her, and he asked her parents to allow him to marry her when she came of age. However, informed by Ruskin's unconsummated first wife of his "peculiarities," the family refused; in addition, by the time she was 18 Rose was fervently religious and was put off by Ruskin's growing religious skepticism. Bouts with insanity soon followed (linking him with Jonathan Swift, another of the many pedophiliacs lurking in the pages of *FW*), but Ruskin never lost his passion for his "Irish Angel."

NOTES

1. A *Third Census of "Finnegans Wake"*; Lupercalia was a festival of expiation and purification in honor of Faunus. O Hehir and Dillon identify Luperca as the she-wolf that suckled Romulus (*A Classical Lexicon for "Finnegans Wake,"* 44), but fail to mention Luperca, the sister of the famous Roman consul Valerius Poplica (or Publicola).
2. For Ruskin's charming account of the relationship, see the chapter entitled "L'Esterelle" in his autobiography *Praeterita*; but for a full record of this tragic affair, see Derrick Leon's *Ruskin: The Great Victorian* (London: Routledge & Kegan Paul, 1949). I would guess that Ruskin's Rose is present in many of the appearances of "rose" in *FW*; Rose and Lily are Mrs. Glasheen's names for the two temptresses, and Rose La Touche and her sister Emily seem as likely and appropriate a pair as any of the others suggested by Mrs. Glasheen (*Third Census*, 248–49) to elucidate those sisters-in-love ⊣⊢.

□ □ □ □ □ □ □

I CHING

"I feel spirits of itchery outching" (439.22–23) seems to make reference to the Chinese *I Ching* when considered in the light of a similar pun toward the end of Thomas Pynchon's *Gravity's Rainbow* (New York: Viking, 1973, p. 746) regarding "devotees of the I Ching who have a favorite hexagram tattooed on each toe, who can never stay in one place for long, can you guess why? Because they always have I Ching feet!"

Slaughterhouse-Five: A Poor Man's *Remembrance of Things Past*

Eliot Rosewater, a character in Kurt Vonnegut's *Slaughterhouse-Five*, says at one point that he used to believe "that everything there was to know about life was in *The Brothers Karamazov*, by Feodor Dostoevsky."[1] If one novel can be said to contain everything there is to know about life, I would suggest Marcel Proust's *Remembrance of Things Past*. However, few readers have the time, endurance, and ability to read and appreciate Proust's masterpiece. This is unfortunate, for apart from the brilliant display of literary technique, the novel contains a world of ideas, indeed almost everything there is to know about life, which might be of great interest and perhaps even therapeutic value to many people if not for the veil of complexity draped over it. Fortunately, though, another novel exists that contains many of Proust's ideas in an easily digested form. Although having nowhere near the breadth or scope of Proust's work, it does illustrate many of the major ideas and principles at work in *Remembrance*, and serves, as it were, as a kind of poor man's *Remembrance of Things Past*. This novel, mentioned above, is *Slaughterhouse-Five*.

At first suggestion, it might seem hard to imagine two novels more unlike each other than these. It takes months to read Proust's novel; Vonnegut's can be read in hours. Contrasted to Proust's complex prose style is Vonnegut's light and very readable writing. In place of Proustian profundity we have Vonnegut's deceptive naivety, wise but simple. And what greater contrast in form could there be between a "serious" novel, Literature with a capital L, and a novel of science fiction, whose legitimacy as a literary genre is still in question?

Perhaps paradoxically, it is at this point of opposition that we can begin to see a possible relationship between the novels, for both borrow from "subgenres" of literature to enhance their works. Proust's novel owes a lot to the memoir genre, a more highly developed form in French literature than in English, where plot is subordinate, if it even exists at all, to social observation and commentary. Free from the constant need to advance a story line, Proust adopts the convention of the memoir for the same reason that Vonnegut uti-

1 *Slaughterhouse-Five* (New York: Delacorte, 1969), 87, to which all subsequent references, included in the text, will be made.

lizes science fiction: in each case the conventions of a sub-genre of literature allow the authors greater freedom to pursue the goals of their unconventional and largely autobiographical fiction.[2]

Basically, Vonnegut's science fiction allows for a literalization of Proust's metaphors. Both Marcel and Billy Pilgrim become "unstuck" in time; Marcel travels back and forth in time figuratively whereas Billy does so literally. The willing suspension of disbelief is a necessary convention of science fiction, therefore Billy's time travelling is readily accepted where one might struggle with Proust's metaphor. Appropriately, some of Proust's metaphors deal with outer space and are consequently made concrete in *Slaughterhouse-Five*. For example, when Proust says: "A pair of wings, a different mode of breathing, which would enable us to traverse infinite space, would in no way help us, for, if we visited Mars or Venus keeping the same senses, they would clothe in the same aspect as the things of the earth everything that we should be capable of seeing,"[3] the wisdom in this is recognized as one recalls Billy's early attempts and failure to understand Tralfamadorian concepts. When Proust goes on to say: "The only true voyage of discovery, the only fountain of Eternal Youth, would be not to visit strange lands but to possess other eyes, to behold the universe through the eyes of another" (2:559), one remembers that it wasn't until Billy could see things as the Tralfamadorians do before he discovered his "fountain of Eternal Youth." Of course, for these concepts to be of any real value to the reader, the Tralfamodorian episodes must be read metaphorically, and I hope to show that the originals of most of Vonnegut's metaphors can be found in Proust's novel.

Parenthetically, the science-fiction genre is not only convenient for a conveyance of Proust's ideas but quite appropriate at times. Although science fiction has not yet been totally accepted as a legitimate literary genre, I don't think Proust would have objected to seeing his ideas conveyed in this manner, for speaking of his projected novel Marcel admits: "as to the choice of theme, a frivolous theme will serve as well as a serious one for a study of the laws of character, in the same way that a prosector can study the laws of anatomy as well in the body of an imbecile as in that of a man of talent . . ." (2:1009).

However, the major argument for *Slaughterhouse-Five* as a poor man's Proust is not in form but in theme, and it is here that the two novels closely coincide. As I (and most critics) read it, *Remembrance of Things Past* focuses

2 Short but useful studies of Vonnegut's use of the "sub-genre" of science fiction are Willis E. McNelly's two articles, "Science Fiction: The Modern Mythology" (*America*, 5 September 1970, pp. 125–27) and "Kurt Vonnegut as Science-Fiction Writer" (in *Vonnegut in America*, ed. Jerome Klinkowitz and Donald L. Lawler [New York: Dell, 1977], 87–96).

3 *Remembrance of Things Past*, trans. C. K. Scott Moncrieff and Andreas Mayor, 2 vols. (New York: Random House, 1970), 2:559. Subsequent references will be included in the text.

on four major themes: (1) time as the key to understanding love and death; (2) the necessity for stereoscopic vision in time, made available through memory; (3) internal vs. external reality, i.e., the necessity of turning inward rather than outward for truth and happiness; (4) the therapeutic value of art. After a close reading of *Slaughterhouse-Five,* I believe these themes can be found to have counterparts in Vonnegut's novel, allowing it to gain in stature what it might consequently lose in originality.

From the very first word (*longtemps* in the French), the narrator of Proust's novel is concerned with the true nature of time, and in the "Overture" (Scott-Moncrieff's title for the first section) asks many questions about time and related questions that will not be answered until the end of the novel. Similarly, Vonnegut's opening chapter is as temporally free-floating as Proust's, and in the same way introduces some of the major themes to be explored later. In fact, one passage in Vonnegut's prologue even sounds like the beginning of Proust's overture: "Sooner or later I go to bed, and my wife asks me what time it is. She always has to know the time. Sometimes I don't know, and I say, 'Search *me*'" (7). At another point Vonnegut lapses into a Proustian state of mind and says, "And I asked myself about the present; how wide it was, how deep it was, and how much was mine to keep" (16). When the Tralfamadorians later answer this question, it will bear a striking resemblance to Proust's answer: "The time which we have at our disposal every day is elastic; the passions that we feel expand it, those that we inspire contract it; and habit fills up what remains" (1:465).

In *Slaughterhouse-Five,* one passage in particular introduces a curious incident, much like Marcel's madeleine incident, that will not be explained until much later, commencing the quest for the truth about time that is so much a part of both novels. While waiting for a flight, Vonnegut notices:

> The time would not pass. Somebody was playing with the clocks, and not only with the electric clocks, but the wind-up kind, too. The second hand on my watch would twitch once, and a year would pass, and then it would twitch again.
>
> There was nothing I could do about it. As an Earthling, I had to believe whatever clocks said — and calendars. (18)

This puts Vonnegut in much the same position as Marcel in the overture: ignorant of the true nature of time and, therefore, trapped and powerless. But within this very episode, again like the madeleine incident, lies the key to the escape from the bonds of time. Some 50 pages later, Billy/Vonnegut is on a slow-moving train in Europe during World War II, and the author comments: "It was a long time between clicks, between joints in the track. There would be a click, and then a year would go by, and then there would be another click" (67). In the first chapter, then, Vonnegut does not connect the war incident with the airport incident almost 25 years later because of his ignorance (at this point) of the nature of time, which his protagonist will discover later. Similarly, Proust does not comment on the relation between Marcel's madeleine incident and the truth about time, but instead lets his protagonist discover it later. The despondency Vonnegut feels at the airport, becoming "a non-person in the Boston fog" and being put "in a limousine with some other non-persons and sent . . . to a motel for a non-night" (18), is the result of his/Billy's discomfort on the train 25 years earlier, the principle responsible for this not to be revealed until Billy discovers, as Proust puts it, that "man is that creature without any fixed age, who has the faculty of becoming, in a few seconds, many years younger, and who, surrounded by the walls of time through which he lived, floats within them but as though in a basin the surface-level of which is constantly changing, so as to bring him into the range now of one epoch now of another" (2:813).

Proust sees time not so much as the conventional flowing river but as a series of fragments or moments — which are gathered and stored in the memory. Taken together, these drops of time form not a steadily flowing river but a kind of ocean. Fragments or moments of time flow like a river via the senses into a sea of memory, where they mix with countless other fragments out of chronological or any logical sequence. Time therefore does not pass, it accumulates; it only seems to vanish until the past is recaptured as memory dips into the sea of time and brings forth moments, which Proust calls "fragments of existence withdrawn from Time," still as fresh as the day they entered the ocean. Far from remaining a dead sea, or a nostalgic interior Memory Lane, these time fragments constitute a life force of their own and provide the motion necessary for life; for he goes on to say of these fragments, "the moments of the past do not remain still; they retain in our memory the motion which drew them towards the future, towards a future which has itself become the past, and draw us on in their train" (2:726). The fact that memory is involuntary as often as voluntary attests to their independent force.

The extra-temporal existence led by the Tralfamodorians illustrates Proust's concept of time. They too see time as a collection of moments. As Billy explains, "They can see how permanent all the moments are, and they can look at any moment that interests them. It is just an illusion we have here on Earth that one moment follows another one, like beads on a string, and that once a moment is gone it is gone forever" (23). When compared with the following passage from *The Sweet Cheat Gone* [*Albertine disparue/The Fugitive*], the Trafalmadorian concept of time seems to be taken directly from Proust:

In order to enter into us, another person must first have assumed the form, have

> entered into the surroundings of the moment; appearing to us only in a succession of momentary flashes, he has never been able to furnish us with more than one aspect of himself at a time, to present us with more than a single photograph of himself. A great weakness, no doubt, for a person to consist merely in a collection of moments; a great strength also: it is dependent upon memory, and our memory of a moment is not informed of everything that has happened since; this moment which it has registered endures still, lives still, and with it the person whose form is outlined in it. And moreover, this disintegration does not only make the dead man live, it multiplies him. (2:718)

The idea that a moment "registered" in memory "endures still, lives still, and with it the person whose form is outlined in it" is treated at length in *Slaughterhouse-Five*, mainly as an antidote to the fear of death. Billy's summation of the Tralfamodorian way of looking at death sounds like a flippant paraphrase of Proust: "When a Tralfamadorian sees a corpse, all he thinks is that the dead person is in bad condition at that particular moment, but that the same person is just fine in plenty of other moments" (23). Billy adopts this point of view and employs it later when, giving an eye-examination to a boy who has just lost his father in the Vietnam War, he assures him "that his father was very much alive still in moments the boy would see again and again," and goes on to ask, "Isn't that comforting?" (117).

This sentiment appears many times in *Remembrance*. While reflecting on his apparent lack of grief at his grandmother's death, Marcel offers the following rationalization:

> Perhaps the great sorrow that follows, in a daughter such as Mamma, the death of her mother only makes the chrysalis break open a little sooner, hastens the metamorphosis and the appearance of a person whom we carry within us and who, but for this crisis which annihilates time and space, would have come more gradually to the surface. . . . It is in this sense (and not in that other, so vague, so false, in which the phrase is generally used) that we may say that death is not in vain, that the dead man continues to react upon us. He reacts even more than a living man because, true reality being discoverable only by the mind, being the object of a spiritual operation, we acquire a true knowledge only of things that we are obliged to create anew by thought, things that are hidden from us in everyday life. (2:123)

Grief only leads to remorse and self-abuse, "for as the dead exist only in us, it is ourselves that we strike without ceasing when we persist in recalling the blows that we have dealt them" (2:115). Finally, Proust sums up the sentiment by stating that "People do not die at once for us, they remain bathed in a sort of *aura* of life in which there is no true immortality but which means that they continue to occupy our thoughts in the same way as when they were alive" (2:741).

This thought should lay our own fears of death to rest in addition to the deaths of loved ones, and this is what warms "the cockles of Billy's heart": "What made them so hot was Billy's belief that he was going to comfort so many people with the truth about time" (24). The truth about time ensures a deliverance from the fear of death. While addressing an audience in Chicago on flying saucers and the true nature of time, Billy mentions his imminent death and then rebukes the crowd for their protests: "If you protest, if you think that death is a terrible thing, then you have not understood a word I've said" (123).

Billy's mention of already witnessing his death several times recalls a passage from near the end of *Remembrance*:

> But by a strange coincidence, this rational fear of danger was taking shape in my mind just when the idea of death itself had finally become indifferent to me. In the past the fear of being no longer myself was something that terrified me, and this had made me dread the end of each new love that I had experienced . . . because I could not bear the idea that the "I" who loved them would one day cease to exist, since this in itself would be a kind of death. But by dint of repetition this fear had gradually been transformed into a calm confidence. So that if in those early days, as we have seen, the idea of death had cast a shadow over my loves, for a long time now the remembrance of love had helped me not to fear death. For I realized that dying was not something new, that on the contrary since my childhood I had already died many times. (2:1131)

This calm confidence grows to almost a defiant scorn for death by the extratemporal man as Marcel, waiting in the library of the Prince de Guermantes, realizes: "A minute freed from the order of time has re-created in us, to feel it, the man freed from the order of time. And one can understand that this man should have confidence in his joy, even if the simple taste of a madeleine does not seem logically to contain within it the reasons for this joy, one can understand that the word 'death' should have no meaning for him; situated outside time, why should he fear the future?" (2:1002). Not to understand this is not to understand a word Proust *or* Vonnegut has said.

Time plays one final role in linking the two novels. Both Marcel and Billy respond to the challenge of telling the world of the true nature of time, a resolve that will give meaning to their otherwise meaningless lives. Previous to Marcel's revelation and subsequent decision "to embody as clearly as possible . . . this notion of Time evaporated, of years past but not separated from us" in a work of art (2:1138), he laments the years wasted trying to become a writer, which led to his loss of faith in literature, life, and ultimately himself because of his inability to even perceive reality: "we strain after the unsubstantial fragments of a dream, and all the time our life with our mistress continues, our life indifferent to what we do not know to be important to us, attentive to what is perhaps of no importance, hagridden by people who have no real connection to us, full of lapses of memory, gaps, vain anxieties, our life as fantastic as a dream" (2:481).

Billy's plane crash plays the same role as Marcel's revelation in the Guermantes' library. It is immediately after recovering from the crash that Billy decides to tell the world about time. Previously, Billy's life seems as meaningless as Marcel's: he was indifferent to both his occupation and to his wife, found himself every so often weeping for no apparent reason, and finally, after realizing with great effort that he was 44 years old, asks, like Marcel, "Where have all the years gone?" (49).

The decision to tell the world about time infuses new life into both Marcel and Billy. Marcel forsakes the company of his friends to do them a higher service:

> Was it not, surely, in order to concern myself with them that I was going to live apart from these people who would complain that they did not see me, to concern myself with them in a more fundamental fashion than would have been possible in their presence, to seek to reveal them to themselves, to realize their potentialities? . . . Was it not more worthwhile that I should attempt to describe the curves, to educe the laws which governed these gestures that they made, these remarks that they uttered, their very lives and natures? (2:1091)

Billy, likewise rejuvenated, forsakes his friends and risks public and private ridicule in order to devote himself "to a calling much higher than business. An optometrist by profession, he is doing nothing less now, he thought, than prescribing corrective lenses for Earthling souls" (25). Marcel will willingly submit to death if only granted enough time to complete his mission, the same mission Billy is on when he is shot. Both become voluntary martyrs to time, "'for unless the grain of wheat dies after it has been sown, it will abide alone; but if it does, it will bring forth much fruit'" (2:1137, quoting John 12:24).

It is both interesting and appropriate that Marcel and Billy describe their mission in optical terms. As noted above, Billy sees himself as "prescribing corrective lenses for Earthling souls" just as Marcel believes the book he plans to write will be "merely a sort of magnifying glass like those which the optician at Combray used to offer to his customers," for

> The writer's work is merely a kind of optical instrument he offers to the reader to enable him to discern what, without this book, he would perhaps never have perceived in himself. . . . In order to read with understanding many readers require to read in their own particular fashion, and the author must not be indignant at this; on the contrary, he must leave the reader all possible liberty, saying to him: "Look for yourself, and try whether you see best with this lens or that one or this other one." (2: 1128, 1031–32)

Again, Vonnegut does little more than literalize the metaphor; Marcel is figuratively an optician as Billy is literally one. More than just a metaphoric coincidence, the optical imagery is germane to the second major theme the two novels share, namely, the necessity for stereoscopic vision in time to perceive the true nature of reality.

Proust defines reality as "a certain connection between . . . immediate sensations and the memories which envelop us simultaneously with them," and goes on to say, "truth — and life too — can be attained by us only when, by comparing a quality common to two sensations, we succeed in extracting their common essence and in reuniting them to each other, liberated from the contingencies of time" (2:1015). Not only can Tralfamadorian vision be described as the ability to see sensations "liberated from the contingencies of time," but Billy's time-trips operate directly under this principle. As Billy perceives a given sensation, he travels through time to an earlier occurrence of the same sensation, which then takes on a new and complete meaning and gives the two sensations their "essential" reality. For example, Billy as a child is visiting Carlsbad Caverns when the ranger leading the tour turns out all the lights. Billy is terrified of the extent of the darkness when he suddenly notices something ghostly floating in the air: the radium dial on his father's pocketwatch. Billy immediately time-travels to the brightly lit delousing station of a German prison camp, a seemingly unrelated incident until the reader comes upon the line, "There were more starving Russians with faces like radium dials" (78). Thus the two incidents, one taking place during his childhood in New Mexico and the other years later in Germany, are linked by a common sensation, bringing back to life a childhood incident Billy may never have been able to recall with voluntary memory. The sensation of terror in each incident is consequently enhanced and broadened by its counterpart.

Billy's time-traveling, then, is essentially a sci-fi dramatization of involuntary memory, the Proustian key to the recovery of lost time (as in his novel's French title: *À la recherche du temps perdue*). Upon close examination, Billy's time-travels are found to be not just random excursions in time but the result of involuntary responses to a wide range of interconnected sensations that echo back and forth through the novel. Some of these sensations include orange and black stripes (60, 82, 103?), blue and ivory feet (24, 62, 128), nestled spoons (62, 109, 125, 128), and the barking of a dog, occurring no fewer than five times (37, 42, 65, 71, 144). Thus, as Peter J. Reed points out, "All of the events portrayed are carefully interconnected, and events from 'separate' times are often juxtaposed, completing or commenting upon one another. The frequent complementary nature of the time fragments adds to their coherence."[4]

The effects of involuntary memory/time-travel are usually beneficial. The pangs of joy Marcel feels at each instance of involuntary memory is the result of perceiving a previously hidden truth about the essence of things. In a similar fashion, some of Billy's time-travels allow him to grasp a truth by way of "the past which we have long kept stored up in ourselves and learn suddenly how to interpret" (2:438). For example, Billy is being registered at the German prison camp when an American, after muttering something, is knocked down by a guard who knows English:

> "Why me?" he asked the guard.
>
> "The guard shoved him back into ranks. "Vy you? Vy anybody?" he said. (79)

Several years later, Billy is abducted by a Tralfamadorian spaceship, and the American prisoner's question is answered:

> "Welcome aboard, Mr. Pilgrim," said the loudspeaker. "Any questions?"
>
> Billy licked his lips, thought a while, inquired at last: "Why me?"
>
> "That is a very *Earthling* question to ask, Mr. Pilgrim. Why *you*? Why *us* for that matter? Why *anything*? Because this moment simply *is*. Have you ever seen bugs trapped in amber?"
>
> "Yes." Billy, in fact, had a paperweight in his office which was a blob of polished amber with three ladybugs embedded in it.
>
> "Well, here we are, Mr. Pilgrim, trapped in the amber of this moment. There is no *why*." (66)

The truth or necessity of the earlier incident is now revealed to Billy, and will be added to the other truths he discovers, which will in turn gives his life the meaning and coherency it has lacked.

However, the truth or reality revealed by involuntary memory/time-travel can sometimes be quite painful. Involuntary memory alone tortures Marcel with thoughts of the absent Albertine long after voluntary memory has released her. He therefore describes memory as "a sort of pharmacy . . . in which our groping hand comes to rest now upon a sedative drug, now upon a dangerous poison" (2:653). Vonnegut introduces Billy as equally vulnerable: "Billy is spastic in time, has no control over where he is going next, and the trips aren't necessarily fun. He is in a constant state of stage fright, he says, because he never knows what part of his life he is going to have to act in next" (20).

Although both Proust and Vonnegut admit that the past holds both pleasant and painful moments, they both stress the need for stereoscopic vision

4 *Kurt Vonnegut, Jr.* (New York: Warner, 1972), 179.

in time, viewing the present and the past simultaneously. In *Remembrance*, stereoscopic vision is the result of combining immediate sensations with similar sensations stored in the memory. Memory is the catalyst in stereoscopic vision, as Roger Shattuck points out:

> Memory in Proust's sense designates a stereoscopic or "stereologic" consciousness which sees the world simultaneously (and this out of time) in relief. Merely to remember something is meaningless unless the remembered image is combined with a moment in the present affording a view of the same object or objects. Like our eyes, our memories must see double; those two images then converge in our minds into a single heightened reality.[5]

The Tralfamadorians also see time in relief, and "can look at the different moments just the way we can look at a stretch of the Rocky Mountains" (23). However, multiplicity of vision is not merely a pleasurable Tralfamadorian pastime; it is a prerequisite to understanding the true nature of reality. The enormous opiate power of habit, which "weakens every impression" (1:488), inhibits our ability to perceive relevant sensations of existence, a handicap from which the Tralfamadorians seem to be free. They feel sorry for the Earthlings' inability to see in time as well as in space, and rightly so. Perhaps "unwillingness" would be a better word, for with an understanding of time and memory (available to anyone willing to make the effort), an Earthling *is* able to see in time.[6] This is one of the points Billy stresses when speaking to people about Tralfamadore, and it is likewise a point Proust makes quite often in his novel. In *Within a Budding Grove* he compares the human face to "the face of the God of some oriental theogony, a whole cluster of faces, crowded together but on different surfaces so that one does not see them all at once" (1:686). One is reminded of the Tralfamadorian view of human beings "as great millipedes — 'with babies' legs at one end and old people's legs at the other'" (75). This in turn recalls Marcel's reflection at the Prince de Guermantes' party on the mutability of physical appearance:

> For all these reasons a party like this at which I found myself was something much more valuable than an image of the past: it offered me as it were all the successive images — which I had never seen — which separated the past from the present, better still it showed me the relationship that existed between the present and the past; it was like an old-fashioned peepshow, but a peepshow of the years, the vision not of a moment but of a person situated in the distorting perspective of Time. (2:1043)

5 *Proust's Binoculars* (New York: Random House, 1963), 47.

6 This line of thought would suggest that the uncanny feeling of déjà vu is simply the result of an inability to connect a sensation of the present with its counterpart in the past.

Stereoscopic vision in time is an internal process, which leads to the third theme shared by both *Remembrance* and *Slaughterhouse-Five*, namely, the necessity of turning inward to discover truth and happiness. In Proust, this idea is presented in the opening chapter of *Swann's Way*: "It is plain that the object of my quest, the truth, lies not in the cup [of tea] but in myself" (1:34). Continuing throughout the novel is the idea that "experience of oneself . . . is the only true experience" (2:228) and that truth and happiness can be found only after plumbing the depths of the self.

Though Proust stresses this idea much more than Vonnegut, it is present in *Slaughterhouse-Five* and accounts for the novel's guarded optimism. During Billy's capture by the German patrol, Vonnegut relates the following anecdote concerning the patrol commander's boots:

> One time a recruit was watching him bone and wax those golden boots, and he held one up to the recruit and said, "If you look in there deeply enough, you'll see Adam and Eve."
>
> Billy Pilgrim had not heard this anecdote. But, lying on the black ice there, Billy stared into the patina of the corporal's boots, saw Adam and Eve in the golden depths. They were naked. They were so innocent, so vulnerable, so eager to behave decently. Billy Pilgrim loved them. (46)

If Billy sees Adam and Eve in the boot's luster, he can only be seeing a reflection of himself (cf. Reed, 185–86). In Christian mythology all mankind is descended from Adam and Eve, and Billy therefore sees in himself all of mankind. Thus his struggles, hopes, fears, and needs become those of all people, and the study of himself becomes the equivalent to the study of mankind. A more Proustian thought would be hard to find, for in *The Past Recaptured* it is emphatically stated that "what we have to bring to light and make known to ourselves is our feelings, our passions, that is to say the passions and feelings of all mankind" (2:1028). And again, this is made possible by stereoscopic vision in time, which in turn allows one to follow the Tralfamadorians' timely advice to "ignore the awful times, and concentrate on the good ones" (102).

The therapeutic value of art is the final theme common to both novels. Again, this theme is stronger in *Remembrance* than in *Slaughterhouse-Five*, but Vonnegut's concern for the role of the artist and the need for and value of art — and especially literature — cannot be overlooked. Throughout *Remembrance*, Marcel's shifting assessment of the value of literature parallels his growth as a writer, culminating in *The Past Recaptured* when he beams: "How much more worth living did it appear to me now, now that I seemed to see that this life that we live in half-darkness can be illumined, this life that at every moment we distort can be restored to its true pristine shape, that a life, in short, can be realized within the confines of a book!" (2:1127).

On a more subdued level, Billy and Eliot Rosewater, sharing a hospital room, use literature to counteract the meaninglessness of their lives by "trying to re-invent themselves and their universe. Science fiction was a big help" (87).[7] Since both Proust and Vonnegut agree that reality is personal and internal, it should not be surprising to find that fiction (or vicarious experience) can be as real as actual experience. Marcel notes: "At times the reading of a novel that was at all sad carried me sharply back, for certain novels are like great but temporary bereavements, they abolish our habits, bring us in contact once more with the reality of life" (2:774). In fact, Proust goes so far as to suggest that art is *more* real than actual experience, for "at every moment the actual artist has to listen to his instinct, and it is this that makes art the most real of all things, the most austere school of life, the last true judgment" (2:1007). Billy is able to reconstruct his life via literature once he realizes along with Marcel "that reading teaches us to take a more exalted view of the value of life, a value which at the time we did not know how to appreciate and of whose magnitude we have only become aware through the book" (2:887).

Kilgore Trout becomes Billy's favorite author, and it is significant that Trout is described as a "cracked messiah" (143), for it is his books that "deliver" Billy from meaninglessness. Trout seems to understand the true nature of time when he correctly diagnoses Billy's uncomfortable expression upon seeing the faces of the barbershop quartet of optometrists: "You saw through a *time window*" (149), which would have been his response had he been present at Marcel's tasting of the petite madeleine. If Billy is a kind of Proustian hero, Kilgore Trout represents the Proustian artist. For the same reason that Trout is described as a "cracked messiah" and (in another Vonnegut novel) as a "frightened, aging Jesus, whose sentence to crucifixion had been commuted to imprisonment for life,"[8] Marcel's projected novel takes on the air of a religious crusade by the end of *Remembrance*, to furnish his readers "with the means of reading what lay inside themselves" (2:1128) as he prepares to deliver his readers from the bonds of time.

Although Vonnegut's narrator considers *Slaughterhouse-Five* a failure "since it was written by a pillar of salt" (19) — that is, by someone still attached to the past — it is precisely because he chose to become a pillar of salt that his novel has any real value for the reader. Apart from its intrinsic worth, it can also serve as an introduction to the world of Proust, and although it can never takes the place of that masterpiece, it can act as a delightful hors d'oeuvre to the literary feast that is *Remembrance of Things Past*.

7 Cf. Marcel's observation: "In reality every reader is, while he is reading, the reader of his own soul" (2:1031).

8 *God Bless You, Mr. Rosewater* (New York: Dell, 1965), 115.

Alexander Theroux's *Darconville's Cat* and the Tradition of Learned Wit

In his essay "*Tristram Shandy* and the Tradition of Learned Wit," D. W. Jefferson identifies Sterne as perhaps the last great writer in a tradition that goes back through the Augustan satirists to Burton, Cervantes, Erasmus, and Rabelais, and ultimately back to classical satirists such as Lucian and Petronius. Although it is possible to find scattered examples in subsequent British literature of the witty manipulation of the materials of erudition — *Sartor Resartus*, the Alice books, Rolfe, Joyce, Beckett, and a few contemporary writers such as Durrell and Burgess — Jefferson is justified in considering *Tristram Shandy* the last major work in British literature whose theme "may be seen in terms of a comic clash between the world of learning and that of human affairs."[1] But just as this genre crossed over from the continent to England in the 17th century, a case can be made for a second crossing in the 18th from England to America where, after a long and sporadic period of growth, it has bloomed in post-World War II fiction. Most of the components and techniques of learned wit identified by Jefferson and other commentators on the genre can be found in a series of American works that begins with Brackenridge's *Modern Chivalry*, with its pseudo-philosophical digressions in the Swiftian manner, and continues with the whimsical erudition of Irving's *A History of New York* (especially in the first, unexpurgated edition of 1809) and the more sophisticated use of erudition in *Moby-Dick*, and develops through the somewhat idiosyncratic works of various writers at the beginning of the 20th century, such as Edgar Saltus, James Branch Cabell, and Djuna Barnes. With William Gaddis's 1955 novel *The Recognitions*, the tradition reached full strength, and since then a number of writers have availed themselves of the techniques of this genre, including Nabokov, Barth, Pynchon, Mathews, Markson, Davenport, and Sorrentino. But without a doubt, the fullest flowering of the tradition of learned wit — and the "purest" example of the genre

1 D. W. Jefferson, "*Tristram Shandy* and the Tradition of Learned Wit," *Essays in Criticism* 1.3 (July 1951), rpt. in *Tristram Shandy*, ed. Howard Anderson, A Norton Critical Edition (New York: W. W. Norton, 1980), 516.

established and perfected by Rabelais, Swift, and Sterne — is Alexander Theroux's 1981 novel *Darconville's Cat,* a dazzling 700-page satire that attracted little attention when published (although it was nominated for the National Book Award) but that surely will soon come to be celebrated as the finest example of learned wit ever produced in American literature.

As this novel is not yet widely known, some background might be in order. Alexander Theroux, older brother of the best-selling author Paul,[2] has published two novels — *Darconville's Cat* is his second; the first, *Three Wogs* (1972), was also nominated for the National Book Award and won the *Encyclopaedia Britannica*'s "Book of the Year" award; a third novel will appear shortly — and has published a large number of stories, fables, and essays. Nearly everything he has written is characterized by far-ranging erudition and a high style whose elitism has troubled not a few reviewers too lazy to use their dictionaries. In a brilliant essay written between the two novels to defend his amplified style, Theroux declared:

> I pay taxes to nowts, listen to nowts daily, watch nowts perform on television. But I don't write for nowts. I don't speak to everyone; why should I write for everyone, speak, say, through the pneumatically controlled head of some shovelmouthed dummy whose libretto of operative words, because of those impossible to ventriloquate, reaches to the number of no more than fifteen or twenty? The glory that was the ancient hero — Odysseus, Achilles, Aeneas, Beowulf, even Hamlet and Milton's Satan — was, in fact, often bound up with the glory of his speech; his gift that way seemed to be the linchpin of that very heroism, the logical extension of his grandeur.[3]

And what of the man who has inherited this mantle of eloquence? Like Stephen Dedalus,

> I am a fearful Jesuit, I don't doubt. I am an antiquary, a pedant, a metaphysical deacon and special student on lease from the University of Padua with a swag-bag filled with ciphers, bolts, and refutations. I am a Roman Catholic, born to its jewels and

2 Both brothers make guest appearances in each other's novels. The prolific Paul appears in *Three Wogs* as "bespectacled Paul the Pseudo-plutarch, American oligosyllabicist," author of *Velocity: The Key to Writing.* (Paul has published almost a book a year since 1967.) And Dr. Crucifer's misogynist library (in *Darconville's Cat*) includes a copy of Paul's novel *Girls at Play* (1969). Alexander was the model, to a certain extent, for the flamboyant Orlando in Paul's *Picture Palace* (1978) and, to a lesser extent, for Allie Fox in *The Mosquito Coast* (1982). Paul's high opinion of Alexander's work is recorded in the *New York Times Book Review*, 4 December 1977, 70.

3 "Theroux Metaphrastes: An Essay on Literature," appended to the 1975 paper reprint of *Three Wogs* (Boston: David R. Godine), 5. This essay, occasioned by Diane Johnson's review of *Three Wogs* in *Book World* (*Chicago Tribune/Washington Post,* 13 February 1972, 8), is the best introduction to Theroux's work and cannot be recommended too highly.

> bulls, and constantly aware of its byzantine smoke, wrought chasubles, traditional liturgies, and litanies infinite. You can find me, you're thinking to yourselves — and O, I suppose you're right — hunched over Albert Pigghe's *Hierarchiae Ecclesiasticae Assertio*, Demosthenes' *Exordia*, or Ebo's "Life of the Apostle of Pomerania" or, becloseted, pushing notions around on foolscap with a goblet of mulled wine at my elbow and finding everything after Joyce an impertinence. Well, that may be so.[4]

One might expect elaborate historical novels from such a Mitty-like medievalist, reactionary moonpenny, and Tory Catholic (as he once obliquely described himself),[5] erudite reconstructions in the manner of Flaubert's *Salammbô* or, better yet, of Frederick Rolfe's historical romances.[6] But only his fables have historical settings; all the fiction — short stories as well as novels — is contemporary, but features the same cross-fertilization of past and present as in Joyce's later works and those of his contemporaries Gaddis and Pynchon. (He also shares with these contemporaries a deep interest in religion — not surprising from one who spent two years in a Trappist monastery and dedicated his first book to the Holy Ghost — as well as in religion's shadow, the occult.) A historical resonance is maintained throughout his work not so much by historical allusions and set pieces — as in Gaddis and Pynchon — as by his astonishing vocabulary: no word is too arcane, too obsolete for his use. Though Theroux chooses these words for their precision and color rather than from a perverse desire to force his readers to memorize the *OED* (as some resentful reviewers have hinted), the historicity of these words maintains a continuous and highly ironic tension between the colorful past and "this sad, psychiatric century" of ours (as Theroux describes it in his preface to *Darconville's Cat*), a century as colorless as it is vulgar. On the other hand, such diction confers an Elizabethan splendor on the few aspects of modern life of which Theroux can approve.

The grandiloquent "Theroux Metaphrastes" had been written in defense of the high style of *Three Wogs*, but it can now be seen also as prolegomenon to the novel that was already in progress by that time. *Darconville's Cat* is largely autobiographical, and its genesis is recounted in Atlas's profile of the

4 "Theroux Metaphrastes," 9. A more factual account of his life can be found in James Atlas's group profile "The Theroux Family Arsenal" (*New York Times Magazine*, 30 April 1978, 22–24, 49, 52, 54, 58, 60, 62, 64). Dr. Theroux has informed me, however, that the article is misleading and inaccurate in several instances; for example, he does not own "an assortment of esoteric sex books" as reported on p. 62: in fact, this is a collection of books on eunuchry — in Latin, no less — that Theroux used in working up Dr. Crucifer's background for *Darconville's Cat*.

5 "Silent Nights, Holy Daze: A Seasonal Meditation," *Boston Phoenix*, 9 December 1975, 22.

6 Theroux is a collector of Rolfe's works — as rare as they are eccentric — and has been influenced by them to an extent I hope to delineate in a future paper [never written].

talented Theroux family:

> Eight years ago [i.e., 1970], he was engaged to one of his students from Longwood College ("an unremarkable Southern girl," as [younger brother] Peter describes her; "a common piece of licitation," in Alexander's blunt formulation), who used to complain to her fiancé, "You talk like a book." Still, Alexander was in love with her and busied himself with lavish plans for a wedding ceremony in Westminster Cathedral. But this young woman was obviously bewildered by the grandiose, unkempt, loquacious novelist nine years her senior, and "no more prepared to marry Alex," [older brother] Eugene asserted, pointing across a restaurant, "than [to marry] that man over there."
>
> When she left him, Alexander vowed to avenge himself in a novel. "Do your worst," she taunted. . . .[7]

Darconville's Cat was his answer. But what began as a shorter, personal novel of revenge[8] grew over the years into a huge, universal meditation on love and hate,

> with thoughts, unsummoned and unannounced, pensioned out of the blandishments of common reality, constantly stealing upon him for inclusion, transmitted down through the memory of those who lived in ancient times, races illimitable, to be resumed across the years in all the emotions, passions, experiences of the millions and millions of men and women whose lives of love and the loss of it insensibly passed into his own and so composed it. (697)

With a universality thus approaching that of *Finnegans Wake*, Theroux borrowed his theme and structure from the closing pages of *À la recherche du temps perdu*: on the night Darconville plans to consummate his revenge by murdering the girl who left him, he unexpectedly beholds the tree on which, in happier days, he had carved the word *Remember*:

> He stood before it in the pouring rain.
>
> What hand made it? Whose carved? The very hand, he saw without elaborate calculation, that would now mock memory by murder. It was quietly, an overpowering accumulation, in the midst of that storm — with the feeling of what was impending swiftly opening to him in violent contrast the intensity of past consciousness and the idea that it might cease forever — that Darconville suddenly realized that the source of all error in life was failure of memory! A recept, made of many precepts, exploded into concept — and the past, formerly thought adversary to the future,

7 Atlas, 62. Both quotations ascribed to the girl appear in the novel (Garden City, NY: Doubleday, 1981), 274, 611. Subsequent references to *Darconville's Cat* will be placed parenthetically in the text.

8 The headnote that introduced two excerpts from the novel in the Fall 1974 issue of the *Harvard Advocate* announced that they were from a novel entitled *Linda van der Lubbe*, to be published in September of that year.

> spoke to him. Remember! Remember! Remember the king's words in the old story: which arrow flies forever? The arrow that has found its mark! All forgetfulness, he understood, almost on the edge of exultation, was in itself immoral, for the permanence with which experiences stay with a man is proportional to the significance which they had for him: memory must be preserved *from* time! A thing has the more value, it came to him, the less it is a function of time, and the effort of men to probe the past? Why, it was nothing less than an exertion toward immortality, for the consciousness and vision of the past but pointed to a desire to be conscious in the future, didn't it? And if, he suddenly reasoned, we do not free what we have known from time by memory, can we have any knowledge of remembrance any more than we can have one jot more of time? Memory was eclogue! "What have I got left?" asked Time. "Your genius," answered Eternity. (677–78)

Like Marcel at the end of Proust's novel, Darconville decides to rescue memory from time by means of art: dying in Venice,[9] he writes the novel that we have been reading for nearly seven hundred pages. Once it is completed, he dies; but his creator, happily, survived to tell the tale.

This is one of the few instances in which Theroux differs from Darconville, for in almost every other respect the novel is very much a portrait of the artist as a young man. Like Theroux — and like Rolfe and Joyce, two major influences — Darconville studies for the priesthood before deciding to become a writer. He wastes four years teaching at a Southern college similar to the one at which Theroux taught from 1969 to 1973, and there falls in love with a student named Isabel Rawsthorne.[10] The affair proceeds as outlined in Atlas's profile quoted earlier, with Isabel withholding her misgivings about marrying Darconville. (There is, however, a good deal of foreshadowing of Isabel's eventual betrayal by way of literary allusions linking her with such figures as Keats's La Belle Dame [52], Milton's Delila in "Samson Agonistes" [96], and Irving's Katrina Van Tassel [168, 241].) On the strength of Darconville's book on angelology — more or less equivalent to Gustav Davidson's *A Dictionary of Angels* (1967), from which Theroux quotes extensively — he is invited to teach at Harvard (as was Theroux for *Three Wogs*). It is there he receives word that Isabel will not marry him, preferring to give herself to a childhood sweetheart instead.

9 Though Mann comes first to mind, it is more likely that Theroux invokes Baron Corvo, who also died in Venice. Or perhaps both are recalled: Donald Weeks finds several parallels between Gustave von Aschenbach and Frederick Rolfe in his *Corvo: Saint or Madman?* (New York: McGraw-Hill, 1971), 430–31.

10 Darconville's beloved takes her name from the subject of a dozen or so paintings by British artist Francis Bacon (1909–1992): her face in each is distorted and grotesque, and can be viewed in any of the half-dozen books devoted to Bacon's work. The name of Isabel's real-life counterpart appears throughout the novel in various disguised forms, though perhaps most plainly in the acrostic poem on pp. 122–23.

But at this point, three-fifths through the autobiographical novel, fact and fiction part ways. Upon learning of the girl's desertion of him for another, Theroux threw himself into a whirl of literary activity. But Darconville is paralyzed by the news, and in this condition is taken under the wing of one of the most bizarre characters in modern fiction, Dr. Abel Crucifer, a retired Harvard professor. The initial motive for Crucifer's interest in Darconville ties together a curious thread that has been running through the novel in the form of abusive references to Queen Elizabeth I, "she of the judas wig: bastard, usurper, excommunicate, baldpate, heretic, murderess, schismatic, and willing copulatrix" (13; cf. 235–37, 313–14, 529–30, 578). Crucifer recognizes Darconville as a descendant of "Pierre Christophe Cardinal Théroux-d'Arconville (1532–1601)" (234),[11] which leads the bedridden Darconville to realize:

> some perverse fealty owed to an ancient in his family was being paid to him in some kind of insane transferral or reciprocity centuries old.
>
> "A Prince of the Church, murdered in the red of his robes," said Crucifer, adding a reverence intercalated with an Italian phrase while in the same breath sniping at the woman who in killing that old man could kill again — such was the madness up there — in the proxy of Darconville's bride-to-be. (436)

Elizabeth was not only responsible for the fictitious execution of Cardinal Théroux-d'Arconville in 1601, but in the same year ordered the very real execution of her favorite, the Earl of Essex. The fatal relationship between them is described in Lytton Strachey's *Elizabeth and Essex* — Atlas reports that Theroux owns a signed copy of this book — and an identification of Darconville with Essex (and thus Isabel with Elizabeth) is made by way of numerous historical and literary allusions throughout the novel. "In the history of Essex," Strachey writes, "so perplexed in its issues, so desperate in its perturbations, so dreadful in its conclusion, the spectral agony of an abolished world is discernible through the tragic lineaments of a personal disaster."[12] Theroux surely intends the reader to discern a similar agony in the tragic lineaments of Darconville's personal disaster. Crucifer does, at any rate, and just as Essex embodies for Strachey "the colours of antique knighthood and the flashing gallantries of the past" at the very point in England's history when such qualities were giving way to a grayer, if more democratic social order, Crucifer regards Darconville as a final descendant of a better, more cultured

11 The cardinal and his monograph *The Shakeing of the Sheets* — a remarkable parody of Elizabethan style — are Theroux's own invention, but all the other "writing d'Arconvilles" in the long footnote on page 234 of the novel are quite historical.

12 *Elizabeth and Essex* (New York: Harcourt, Brace, 1928), 2. The quotation that follows is from the same page.

world: a world of learning, refinement, aristocratic Catholicism — Crucifer has sold his soul to the devil, an option open only to a true believer — and a world free from the perfidious influence of women. "Your style is like mine," he confides. "We are co-supremes" (434).

Darconville's initial reaction to Crucifer is one of undisguised contempt, which deepens when he learns of Crucifer's consuming misogyny. But slowly, under the repeated onslaughts of Crucifer's fantastic rhetoric, Darconville's resistance is worn away and he agrees that revenge against Isabel is imperative if he is to recover the world of art from which, like Adam, he has fallen.[13] Their calculating collaboration results in the terrible chapters that darken the last third of the novel, during which the hapless reader is subjected to a library of misogynistic book titles, a formal oration against women (which compares favorably with Juvenal's famous sixth satire), an unholy litany of female malefactors (each with her own exotic epithet), a diabolical pact in reversed Latin and a satanic invocation, essays on hate and revenge, and, finally, a gruesome catalogue of hypothetical tortures (the horror of which is relieved only by what one reviewer called their giddy surrealism). Even a reader inured to the writings of Sade, the Jacobean dramatists, and the so-called Catholic Diabolists (Barbey d'Aurevilly, Baudelaire, Villiers de l'Isle-Adam, Huysmans — all of whom are quoted or mentioned in the novel) must be overwhelmed by the dazzling rhetoric and dark extravagance of these chapters. The baroque eloquence of *Nightwood*'s Dr. Matthew O'Connor — the nearest parallel in modern fiction — is laconic by comparison. Like a bird before a serpent, the reader is hypnotized.

Though converted reluctantly to Crucifer's philosophy, Darconville never loses his repugnance for the repellent eunuch and realizes — if only subconsciously — that he risks becoming another Crucifer himself, "a puzzle-headed caricature of spite with a large share of scholarship but with little geometry or logic in his head and yet a figure of method and merciless egotism, possessing a sinister genius" (463).[14] Darconville was earlier described as "tall and white

13 There is a series of references to Adam's fall that begins on the first page of the novel and continues up to Darconville's Proustian revelation (678). In "Theroux Metaphrastes" the author argues that Adam "fell from art into life" and speculates on this point: "To fall from art into life! What a pain in the ass it has been for us all ever since. And where have we fallen? We've fallen, bump, crash, splat, into that vast neutral forest, empty of druid and shadow, where the faint voice of Quarles sounds lamenting reedily through the darkness, muttering, 'Queens drop away, while blue-legg'd Maukin thrives; / And courtly Mildred dies while country Madge survives'" (26, correcting Theroux's "dries" to "dies").

14 Adapted from Dr. Johnson's description of the French scholar Michel Mattaire: "He seems to have been a puzzle-headed man, with a large share of scholarship, but with little geometry or logick in his head, without method, and possessed of little genius" (Boswell's *Life of Samuel Johnson* [New York: Modern Library, 1931], 909).

as a paschal candle" (156),[15] and Crucifer is similarly described as "tall and cold and white" (438) — a paschal candle without its flame. Both share a limitless vocabulary with a special preference for Elizabethan diction: Crucifer's "cheekfuls of words" include dozens of quotations from Shakespeare, mostly from the sonnets and narrative poems, and Darconville seems to have by heart the complete works of the Elizabethan love poets. All of Darconville's best qualities are exaggerated and perverted in Crucifer, to the point where he begins to doubt his separate existence: "There was no real person named Dr. Crucifer, thought Darconville, I have created him!" (489). To murder Isabel at this point would be to give birth to the Crucifer within him.

This subconscious realization, coupled with the Proustian revelation of the immortality of memory, rescues Darconville at the eleventh hour and allows him to throw off Crucifer's evil influence. His return to the world of art is a triumphant one — celebrated in the short, Whitmanesque chapter XCVI — but the contamination contracted from his fall into life, so to speak, proves lethal. Moribund, he has time only to complete his manuscript, to give artistic form to memory, before he quits this world for that of his angels. Darconville dies a martyr to love and art, yet the novel ends on a note of somber victory:

> But the survival is in the art — for *there* the heart begins to measure itself, not by its constraints but by its fullness, its poor baffled hopes dim now in the light of those infinite longings which spread over it, soft and holy as daydawn. Thus it must be while the world lasts, the very misprisions against the spirit coming only to test and reveal the power of exaltation. Sorrow is the cause of immortal conceptions. (704)

That, in a roundabout fashion, is the plot. But as a character in Buckingham's *The Rehearsal* complains, "What the devil does the plot signify, except to bring in fine things?" There is no end of fine things in *Darconville's Cat*: a love story that must be ranked with the most charming ever written; Swiftian swipes at Southern life and manners; erudite flights into angelology; hilarious speeches and sermons; the catty conversations of college girls; an anthology of arcane epigraphs, literary allusions, and parodies; "books . . . that haven't been mentioned in 400 years," as Theroux boasted to Atlas, "words that haven't been uttered in five centuries"; meditations on the act of writing; poems, fables, nightmares, a diary, an abecedarium, a blank-verse playlet; the black

15 Theroux borrowed this image from Villiers's *Axel*, where the strange heroine Sara de Maupers is described as a "young girl, tall and white as a paschal candle" (trans. June Guicharnaud [Englewood Cliffs, NJ: Prentice-Hall, 1970], 10). Sara's exotic travelogue in act 4 provided the inspiration for Theroux's even more exotic one in chapter LVIII, where a few of Sara's locales appear by way of tribute.

page of grief from *Tristram Shandy* and a digression on ears reminiscent of Sterne's on noses; a chapter consisting of one word, and another with the title "What Is One Picture Worth?" that consists of — you guessed it — exactly one thousand words; revisionist lectures on Keats and Socrates; and, in perhaps the most ravishing chapter of the entire novel (and John Barth rightly insists ravishment is an essential quality of great fiction), a whimsical travelogue of fanciful places Darconville plans to take Isabel, which ends with a rapturous passage unequalled in modern literature since Molly Bloom said yes:

> Welcome, fate! The future shall be greater than all the past! It shines with prophecies, unborn deeds, liberty and love! Come, finally, with me to the Land of Cinnamon, the olive yards by the river Alpheus, the Isles of Orcades and the promontory of the Cimbri, Aneroid and Gravelburg, the medieval castle of Broglio, the empire of Lugalzaggisi and the masses of Negropont, Maleventum, and Orinoco! Come away with me and wander through the Upper Valley of Greater Zap, eat the ten-pound peaches of Chinaland, climb the spires of the foursquare city of Golgonooza, wave to the gold-guarding griffins in the Deserts of Gobi, pray with the holy apocalypts in the ancient monasteries of St. Neot, Pill, Axholme, Stixwould, Drax, Tiptree, and Burnham-on-Crouch, then watch the Plow of Jehovah and the Harrow of Shaddai pass over the dead, and then maybe sit on a dune in the month of June by the amber waters of the Syllabub Sea where the tide comes in in an opal mist, splashing in sweetly like the sound of a kiss, and we'll trip upon trenches and dance upon dishes and see whither the hither of yon, but if without reason you should find me gone, I won't be buried among the dead — no, go instead and look for me where eternity goes, in another world where the rain makes bows, for there'll be restored by the hand of art whatever's lost in the human heart, for something of us will always be, and forevermore I'll live for you if forevermore you'll live for me. (386–87)

But such fine things are not pointless pomposities as in *The Rehearsal*. The rhyming conclusion of this passage, for example, loosely adapted from Edward Lear's "The Jumblies," recapitulates the entire movement of the novel — life moving toward art — as does the subject of the poem in chapter XXIII, a sonnet written by Darconville, who thinks at the time life is more important than art. The novel is likewise encapsulated in the fable that constitutes chapter XXVII, "Master Snickup's Cloak."[16] Under the guise of a bedtime story Darconville narrates to Isabel, it too predicts in fairytale terms the fate of their love. (Isabel's counterpart in the fable, Superfecta van Cats, ends up as the madam of a brothel called De Zwarte Hertogin — the Dutch form of *The Black Duchess*, the ship on which Gilbert and Isabel marry [701].) Torn between "the world of learning and that of human affairs" (to quote

16 The fable appeared in an earlier form first as "Lynda van Cats" in *Antæus* 19 (Autumn 1975), 47–51, which was reprinted in the first *Pushcart Prize* annual the following year, and appeared in its final form as a book published in 1979, under its present title, by Paper Tiger in England and Harper & Row in America.

Jefferson again), Darconville betrays his allegiance to the former by translating every emotion into its literary equivalent. As a perceptive British reviewer points out,

> Darconville believes, in fact, that experience has to be *avoided* in order for him to be able to write, but the richness of his imaginative life can't insulate him from suffering. His imagination is even the source of his pain because, as he comes to see, his love for Isabel has been an imaginative invention, the transmuting into a goddess of a commonplace, silly, snobbish girl.[17]

This process of transmutation is responsible for the highly allusive nature of the novel. When Isabel sends him a note reassuring him of her love after their first break-up, Darconville responds: "O angels, clap your wings upon the skies, and give this virgin crystal plaudities!" (333) — the exact words with which Vindice celebrates his sister's chastity in Tourneur's *The Revenger's Tragedy* (2.1.243–44).[18] The unattributed quotation is not only appropriate both in its particular setting and as another feather in the angelology motif, but also warns that Darconville will come dangerously close to becoming a Vindice himself. Most of Theroux's hundreds of quotations, allusions, and parodies function likewise on several different levels. The novel's title, for example, refers to (a) Spellvexit, Darconville's actual cat; (b) Isabel, often compared to the cat, both of whom he loses at about the same time; (c) his Catholicism ("Cat" is British slang for Catholic), which he is also in danger of losing; (d) the flagellatory cat-o'-nine-tails, his satiric bent as well as his pain-inflicting imagination; and (e) God, Whom the six-year-old Darconville had drawn with the face of a cat (7).

Throughout the novel there is a lively intelligence that finds metaphors everywhere — his female students "had hearts like chocolate bars, scored to break easily" — and that constantly harmonizes the abstract with the concrete in the best manner of the metaphysical poets:

> It is an emotion, love, the moral implications of which quicken out of time, passing the clouds, to touch the instant of Creation. Love murders the actual. (Reverse the sentence, it's still true, but terrifying.) You must be what you are, always, however, in the hope that what you can be is exactly what you pursue in love; and ideally, of course, you shouldn't be anything but what you should be, a difficulty which the thought itself raises. Loved, nevertheless, you find yourself favored with the greatest of all possibilities for transfiguration, assisted, paradoxically, by what you would attain, but failing that, a kind of devastation few can know. *Cave amantem!* It carries

17 Tom Treadwell, "From Rage to Redemption," *Times Literary Supplement*, 3 February 1984, 116 — the most insightful review the novel received.

18 [Formerly attributed to Cyril Tourneur, this play is now thought to be by his contemporary Thomas Middleton — 2016 note.]

> the full weight of your soul with it. Our ideals are our perils. The heart of the loved one is an autoclave in which you have placed your own. Ravens bleed from their eyes during coition. (225–26)

As in earlier examples of learned wit there is also the comical citation of erudite authorities on a variety of subjects, no end of rhetorical wit, scholastic logic-chopping with evidence taken from every field of human endeavor, and lists with the "rhetorical value" of those in Burton's *Anatomy of Melancholy*, where "it is a thing of glory, the inventory of a treasure-house."[19] The treasure-house here is "The Royal Library of Nineveh" Darconville calls his head (335–36), yielding such outlandish inventories as Crucifer's misogynistic library (ten pages of titles such as Tertullian's *De cultu feminarum*, Pierre du Moulin's *Anatomie de la messe* [1624], the 14th-century "Pucelle Venimeuse," *Talmudic She-Things*, and *How to Tell Your Mother from a Wolf* by Roland X. Trueheaxe) and his litany of female seductresses.

"Only in an age which believed in the nobility of learning could the materials of erudition be raised to such rhetorical heights," Jefferson argues (510), and it is to that pre-Enlightenment age Theroux really belongs. The novel is piously Roman Catholic, unapologetically elitist, unfashionably misogynistic (though sex in this genre of learned wit is almost always at once romantic and bawdy), and unmercifully satiric. The novel makes no concessions to modern tastes or standards — in life or literature — and for that reason may appear anachronistically out of place in contemporary fiction; yet it boasts a pedigree that goes back through some of the most brilliant writers in Western literature. In a recent essay Jo Allen Bradham places *Darconville's Cat* in the genre of the academic novel, but Theroux's novel clearly subsumes that essentially American tradition into the older tradition of learned wit.[20] It is at once a culmination of, and a tribute to, a genre whose demands, on writer and reader alike, are heavy, yet whose rewards often outweigh those from more realistic

19 Jefferson, 509. He believes "The attempt to exploit the list for rhetorical or comic purposes is not, as a rule, successful in modern writers" (510); that may have been true at Jefferson's time of writing, but postmodern writers such as Gilbert Sorrentino, Stanley Elkin, and Theroux have restored the rhetorical glory of the list.

20 "The American Scholar: From Emerson to Alexander Theroux's *Darconville's Cat*," *Critique* 24.4 (Summer 1983): 215–27. Ms. Bradham's conclusion is worth quoting: "In any number of ways, Theroux's book concludes a long line of academic novels, each of which has diluted the positive image of Man Thinking. Since Emerson spent an evening defining and pleading the American scholar, hundreds of books have interpreted and reinterpreted that scholar. Now the investigation is complete as Theroux, in this archly scholarly book from a decidedly anti-scholarly age, caps a group of works on a single subject with such searing finality that nothing more may be said" (226). [Theroux later published an essay on the genre: "The Novel of Learning: Endangered Species," *Review of Contemporary Fiction* 14.2 (Summer 1994): 192–98.]

works. Apropos of which, it might be best to close with Theroux's own words:

> The "realistic" novel and the way one reports to it is to me a *locus molesti*. The threats of the realistic novel, for which I believe I have a constitutional disinclination, force me into an anti-world with a fantasy and bedevilment all its own which refuses (ready?) to "hold a mirror up to nature." Make nature grovel! Transubstantiate it! Shake your multi-colored dreams out of your black disappointing sleep! Will you shrink from diversion, whimsy, entertainment, wit? Can you ignore the concept of fiction, always erudite, as game, pleasure, hobby, and puzzle — a mottage of rich and well-born nouns that can roister with sluttish verbs and prinked-out allusions, snoozy bedfellows all, content and uncomplained of? That's a prose: uncommon quiet dashed with common thunder. We father out our tikes, now coddled with the words of apropositional lullabies, then awakened to the dangers, combustions, and cymbal crashes of Shandean pyrotechnics and goofy but literate words. It is a fool who thinks a smitten adjective or a concerned adverb or an instructive parenthesis impedes the velocity of a sentence. A period does that. Your page is not a linen closet in Miss Pokeberry's Seminary. A great book is no Shaker bedroom. ("Theroux Metaphrastes," 27–28)

Neither, needless to say, is *Darconville's Cat*.

Edward Dahlberg: An Introduction

The modern reaction against the impressionistic criticism of the Victorian era has escalated recently into an attempt to turn literary criticism into a science, appropriating a scientific objectivity and a critical vocabulary only a technician could love. At its worst, impressionistic criticism amounted to little more than the feelings that a work aroused in a critic; at its best, however, such criticism had force, personality, color, and the courage of its convictions — qualities lacking in most academic criticism today. One such impressionistic critic, the folklorist Gershon Legman, once declared, "I believe in a personal and intense style, and in making *value judgments*. This is unfashionable now, but it is the only responsible position."

Edward Dahlberg (1900–1977) staked out just such a position in his critical essays, expressed in a personal, intense style modeled (in later years) after the exuberant prose styles of Elizabethan writers and 17th-century bibliomaniacs like Burton and Browne. A self-proclaimed Ishmael wandering the deserts outside the walls of academe, Dahlberg was neglected by critics most of his life. But during his (and the century's) 60s, he began receiving the appreciation so long overdue, beginning with a steady stream of appreciative reviews of the many books he published in that decade, and continuing with several book-length critical studies: Harold Billings edited a collection of appreciative essays on Dahlberg's work in 1968, Jonathan Williams followed with a festschrift in 1970, Fred Moramarco revised his dissertation as a Twayne book that came out in 1972, and Charles DeFanti published his biography of Dahlberg in 1978, the year after his subject's death. But since then, Dahlberg has slipped back into neglect; aside from the occasional article in a scholarly journal, critical attention has wandered. This may be due partly to the backlash often visited upon writers once they die, consigning them to a purgatory until they are revived by a new generation of critics. It may also be due to a feeling that Dahlberg is not politically correct, that he is too autocratic, phallocentric, sexist, reactionary, too insensitive for these sensitive times. Or the neglect may be due to a continued confusion as to what exactly to make of this outlandish writer with that extraordinary style and those genre-defying works. Add to this the sad fact that only a few of his many books remain in print and the case for neglect seems to be closed.

Samuel Beckett's Wake and Other Uncollected Prose seeks to reopen the case by displaying the full range of Dahlberg's abilities in shorter forms, from skillful reportage to imaginative essays, from proletarian fiction to inspired parody, from travel pieces and personal memoirs to historical studies, along with some of the most cantankerous book reviews ever published. The purpose here is to gather all of the shorter pieces that were left out of (or written after) his two earlier collections of essays, *Alms for Oblivion* (1964) and *The Leafless American* (1967, recently reissued by McPherson & Co.). These writings span Dahlberg's entire writing life. After publishing two immature pieces in the college magazine of the University of California at Berkeley (not reprinted here), Dahlberg amassed a great deal of manuscript material that he took with him when he left for Europe in 1926. There he found a sympathetic editor in Ethel Moorhead, as he recounts in "Beautiful Failures," who accepted enough of his material to fill nearly a fourth of the spring 1929 issue of her magazine *This Quarter*. Along with a few poems and the opening chapter of his first novel, *Bottom Dogs*, this issue contains the two earliest pieces in the present collection: "Ariel in Caliban," an aesthetic statement that would govern his writing style for a decade, and "The Dream Life of Mary Moody," a story in his early naturalistic mode that was reprinted shortly after in the *Fortnightly Review*. Following Joyce's lead for reasons outlined in "Ariel in Caliban," Dahlberg soon produced the impressionistic collage "Graphophone Nickelodeon Days," intended for his second novel, *From Flushing to Calvary*, but never used after its 1931 appearance in *Pagany*.

On the strength of his first novel, Dahlberg found the pages of several political magazines open to him upon returning to America in 1929. During the next half-dozen years, he published a number of essays and reviews in the *New Republic*, the *Nation*, and the *New Masses*. Many of these dealt with proletarian writers, but in his essay on his own second novel (included herein) he disassociated himself from them, anticipating his later renunciation of his own work in that genre.

His reporting of the 1932 Washington hunger march for the *Nation*, Hitler's growing power for the *New York Times* in 1933, and the fascist movements in America for the *New Masses* in 1934 give some indication of Dahlberg's political commitment in those years, culminating in 1935 with his role in organizing the Marxist American Writers' Congress, where he delivered his provocative paper "Fascism and Writers." But some measure of his growing disenchantment with the Marxist approach to literature is indicated by a dispute that occurred in 1934 at the founding of the *Partisan Review*. According to the account he wrote for his *Confessions* but later omitted — it was published in *Prose* instead and appears here as "Ignorance and Malice at the New" — Dahlberg and "Saul Hobinof" (Saul Funaroff, a communist writer) were selected as cofounders of the magazine, but he resigned after the editorial appointments of "Lob Miching and Cog Murrain" (Philip Rahv and William Phillips). Dahlberg was writing his anti-fascist novel *Those Who Perish* at that time, but within a few years he quit both the political and publishing scenes in order to continue educating himself, to revise his aesthetic, and to forge a new style.

Aside from his early masterpiece *Do These Bones Live* (1941), Dahlberg wrote no criticism in the 15 years from 1935 to 1950, with two exceptions: in 1937 he published the first of many fine essays on progressive writer Randolph Bourne, and in 1942 he contributed to a symposium in the *New Directions Annual* honoring Ford Madox Ford. In 1950, however, he returned to the literary world in a flurry of activity. In addition to publishing his enigmatic book of parables *The Flea of Sodom* that year, he began turning out reviews in rapid succession for *Tomorrow*, the *New York Times Book Review*, but mostly for John Chamberlain's ultraconservative periodical the *Freeman*, where Dahlberg had a regular column called "Second Harvest" until 1953. From that time on, he had little difficulty finding outlets for his essays, publishing in a variety of magazines and journals, and becoming a regular contributor in the 1970s to Coburn Britton's elegant but short-lived magazine *Prose*.

In the literary criticism that makes up the bulk of this collection, Dahlberg makes it clear that he is less interested in form and technique than in an affirmative moral tone. He went to a book "looking for maxims and parables of benefit to our lives," for something "of fundamental importance to the spirit," but finds these qualities lacking in most modern fiction. "There is neither health nor sun in Faulkner," he complains, "and his readers are compelled to witness the spectacle of fetid, dying people who are dour and wicked. There is no wit, or good ripe bawd, in him as ease or balm for the suffering, ailing mind." Again and again in his reviews, Dahlberg asks, "Is there no balm in Gilead?" as he surveys the works of writers who fail to provide any nurturing or wisdom for their readers. Instead, writers like "Frank Norris's successors, Faulkner, Hemingway, Caldwell, for all their avowed social purposes, are vandals who pour bile upon nature, the human seed, women." Although he shows grudging respect for Pound in his review of the poet's letters, Dahlberg later wrote, "Pound's shibboleth, Make it New, is for the sham Gideon; I say, Make it Human."

Dahlberg ransacked world literature in search of "the healing word" that would ease "the suffering, ailing mind," and the fact that he found such words more often in myth and ancient literature than in modern fiction accounts for the learned, allusive style of his later essays. In the best of them he achieves the ideal set in his tribute to his friend Herbert Read: "The essay is an epistolary art, full of maxims and wise sayings, which, when well done, lead us to believe that we possess all the knowledge of great men, but none of their defects." Dahlberg had his share of defects, of course, and his work is "full of invectives, metropolitan irritations and heated diatribes" (as he said of Catullus), intent as he was on "sweep[ing] the dung out of the Augean stables of literature." Nor has he had many followers; among contemporary writers, only Alexander Theroux works successfully in Dahlberg's manner. Few readers today would affirm Dahlberg's radical vision of the literary canon, perhaps, but few readers will emerge from this ordeal of fire with their former views unsinged by the heat of his moral fervor.

Alexander Theroux: An Introduction

I must confess at the outset that I love Alexander Theroux's work as I love no other. I had never heard of him prior to seeing an ad for *Darconville's Cat* in *Publishers Weekly*, but during that intriguing series of ads — three corner ads on succeeding pages culminating in a full-page one — I experienced something akin to love at first sight. That ad appeared in January of 1981, and since the novel was not scheduled to appear until May, I beguiled the time by searching out and reading the two other books of his that were still in print, *Three Wogs* and the children's fable *Master Snickup's Cloak*. These I enjoyed, confirming my instinct that I had found an author after my own heart. Then *Darconville's Cat* arrived, dark and elegant, and swept me off my feet. This is the novel I had been waiting for all my life, I realized, nor has the succeeding decade dimmed my ardor. I want to be buried with this novel clasped to my heart.[1]

With that same heart throbbing on my sleeve, let me introduce this brilliant writer; that he still needs to be introduced to most readers at this late date, nearly 20 years after the publication of his first book, is of course an outrage, but we burn daylight to grumble at the neglect. Born in 1939, Alexander Theroux is a member of a prolific family of writers stretching back to the 18th century and including in the present generation best-selling writer Paul, Joseph (with one novel to his credit), and Arabic translator and commentator Peter. Alexander's younger years are recounted in Martin Battestin's essay later in this issue,[2] and in recent years Theroux has made a modest living by teaching (Harvard, Yale, MIT) and from journalism on a wide variety of subjects. His creative writing ranges across most genres — poetry, short stories, fables, plays — but most masterfully in three remarkable novels: *Three Wogs* (1972), a triptych of comic novellas; *Darconville's Cat* (1981), a 700-

1 [David Markson was so bemused by this declaration that he quoted it, without attribution, in *Reader's Block* (Normal, IL: Dalkey Archive Press, 1996, 106), which I consider an honor, however he intended it. — 2016 note]

2 ["Alexander Theroux in Virginia and London, 1964–1973," *Review of Contemporary Fiction* 11.1 (Spring 1991): 50–83. This special issue on Theroux, which I edited, will be alluded to a few more times. — 2016 note]

page anatomy of love and hate; and *An Adultery* (1987), a Jamesian analysis of betrayal. They bear little resemblance to anything else in current fiction: because of his ornate style and manipulation of literary forms, Theroux has been grouped with postmodernists like Barth and Sorrentino, but the underlying conservatism in his work and his preference for linear storytelling make this an awkward grouping. But that same style, formalist concerns, and general excessiveness disqualify him from the ranks of more traditional novelists like Bellow and Updike (both of whom have expressed admiration for his work). Instead, Theroux belongs to the line of literary outsiders, writers like Frederick Rolfe ("Baron Corvo"), Ronald Firbank, and Djuna Barnes, whose work has little in common with that of their contemporaries and which instead amalgamate curious byways of literary tradition and eccentric genius into something unique.

Both Rolfe and Firbank, in fact, come to mind during the three novellas that comprise *Three Wogs*, which offers three views of British racism. The first, "Mrs. Proby Gets Hers," opens with a rhymed pair of hexameters (after the manner of Rolfe's *The Desire and Pursuit of the Whole*, where each chapter ends with one or more hexameters[3]) and introduces the fountainhead of much British Sinophobia in the nefarious person of Fu Manchu, "the Yellow Peril incarnate in one man," as Rohmer's heroic but fanatically bigoted Nayland Smith solemnly insists. A particularly menacing scene in one of the many B-movie adaptations of "Sax Rohmer's great Manichean saga" (as Pynchon calls it in *Gravity's Rainbow*) elicits from Mrs. Proby a scream, which she later ascribes to her distrust of her Chinese neighbor Yunnum Fun, proprietor of a small Chinese market in *her* neighborhood (which is also, as the last line of the story remarks, *his* neighborhood). She imagines him to a friend in the same jingoistic terms popularized by Rohmer's Nayland Smith:

> "He lights incense sticks at night, worships the devil, I think. I don't know if he's grinding tea or muttering A-rab chants, I don't, but I turn my wireless up so as not to hear, you see. What I'm driving at, Mrs. Cullinane, is this: some morning, Mrs. Proby's going to turn back the covers, take off her hairnet, and find she's shoulder-to-shin with the Yellow Peril, she is."[4]

3 Theroux's familiarity with Rolfe's Venetian romance is also evident from a quotation that appears in "The Wife of God": the reference on p. 147 of *Three Wogs* (Boston: Gambit, 1972) to "St. Theodylus, patron saint of those who suffer from cruel apprehension," is taken verbatim from p. 153 of *The Desire and Pursuit of the Whole* (Norfolk, CT: New Directions, 1953). As his letters to Battestin printed elsewhere in this issue attest, Theroux discovered Rolfe in London and immediately began quoting him: the quotation above is used in letter #7, and his quotation from Martial in #8 is actually from Rolfe's *Nicholas Crabbe* (London: Chatto and Windus, 1958), 29.

4 *Three Wogs* (Boston: Godine, 1975), 12. This paperback reprints the essay "Theroux Meta-

But beneath these ridiculous notions is a stronger, if not the true, motive for British prejudice, the main theme on which the three stories in the novel are variations: England's loss of prestige as a world power and the concomitant loss of the Edenic purity of English life before the influx of "wogs" (Westernized [or Worthy] Oriental Gentlemen). "In those days," the first of many nostalgic reveries in the novel, "England had a voice in the world, people could understand the lyrics of songs, and there were no Chinese" (10). The complicated political and economic changes that have reduced England's status are, of course, above the heads of Theroux's Britons, and so Mrs. Proby (and Roland and Lady Therefore in the succeeding stories) fixes the blame on the most visible targets available, and in no uncertain terms:

> "You see," she fumed [at Yunnum Fun], "we were always taught that if people go mucking about and foraging around with yellows, blacks, or any another cribbage-faced nit who steps here and about as free as Dick's hatband *in a country not his*, well then, the country won't be worth tuppence." Her face was wide, flapping, incarnadine. "And don't you think for one iota we're going to become another Shanghai with all its cheap cloth and jerry-made cameras, because you've got another thing coming, dearie. We've had the war. Once burned, twice shy, they say. Mark me well, we know what you're about, too, and you are not, you heard me just say *not*, pulling the wool over anybody's sheep's clothing. Certainly not mine, least of all." Her womb was smoking with wrath. And then the exit line came. "Rice or no rice," she said, "if I was a Chinaman I'd flap right back where I flew from." (32–33)

But she decidedly does *not* know what he's about; like the "fat white woman whom nobody loves" in the epigraph, Mrs. Proby misses so much.[5] Her denunciation follows a brief biographical sketch of Yunnum Fun's 40 years of hardship and abuse leading to his present position, and by the time Mrs. Probably delivers this declaration, "onto her he had telescoped a revenge informed by years and years of scorn and obloquy" (27); thus, "It was then that Yunnum Fun decided to kill her." Mrs. Proby gets hers, as both the title and Mrs. Cullinane predicted (13), and the story ends with a deliberate echo of the closing sentences from the first paragraph: "'Simple,' said Yunnum Fun as he sat on the No. 22 bus which took him back to the Brompton Road roundabout, where he lived. It was his neighborhood" (52).

In his otherwise enthusiastic review of *Three Wogs*, novelist D. Keith Mano felt the first 20 pages of the book were the weakest and consequently ad-

phrastes" as an appendix and hereafter will be cited parenthetically.

5 The epigraph is from Frances Crofts Cornford's once-popular poem "To a Fat Lady Seen from the Train" (1910).

vised readers to put the second or third story first.[6] But "Mrs. Proby Gets Hers" establishes the general dynamics of racial prejudice (the other two stories are more specialized applications), and for that reason it is a more suitable introduction than the others. An important refrain (adapted from Isaiah 55:9–9) is repeated three times in the story: "Their how is not necessarily our how," Mrs. Proby gravely warns Mrs. Cullinane, "nor is yours theirs" (8), a statement akin to that Yunnum Fun heard from his father many years earlier: "Your how is not necessarily my how, nor is ours theirs" (22); a final variation occurs to Yunnum Fun on the last page of the story: "my how is not necessarily their how, nor is theirs mine" (52). Theroux will continue ringing changes on this theme through his later short stories (often concerning American travelers at odds with foreigners) up to *Darconville's Cat* (where Darconville's how is not necessarily Isabel's how, not is hers his) and *An Adultery* (ditto Kit Ford and Farol Colorado). The insistence on this theme may or may not argue the inevitable conflict that will exist between people of different cultures or backgrounds, but it is central enough to Theroux's fiction to be sounded at the beginning of his first book. Mrs. Proby's prejudice is not confined to the Chinese; Americans and Irish also come in for verbal abuse, as would anyone of the wrong color, culture, or religion. The establishment of this middle-class theme will allow Theroux to move on surer footing down to the lower classes (Roland) and up to the upper classes (Lady Therefore) and provides more than a hint that bigots, despite their wide class differences, are all sisters and brothers beneath the skin.

"Childe Roland," the longest and most virtuosic of the three stories, opens not with hexameters but with a "Once upon a time" and ends with a predictable (but ambiguous) "live happily ever after." The fairytale conventions are seconded by the title itself, taken from Browning's enigmatic poem "'Childe Roland to the Dark Tower Came.'" Browning's knight is consumed by doubts: of himself, of his fellow questers, even of the nature and validity of his quest, to the point where — "After a life spent training for the sight!" (l. 180) — he does not recognize his Dark Tower. Similarly, Theroux's Roland, a young loner who has lost both parents,[7] conceals beneath his breezy cockiness a maelstrom of doubts and uncertainties, brought to the surface in his dramatic confrontation with a gentle Indian electrical student.

The most obvious parallel between Browning's poem and Theroux's story

6 *New York Times Book Review*, 16 April 1972, 4.

7 Theroux relates the manner of Roland's death in a succinct parenthesis: "(picnic, kipper bone)" (58) à la Nabokov's Humbert Humbert, "whose very photogenic mother died in a freak accident (picnic, lightning)." Theroux uses this device again in *Darconville's Cat* to account for the death of Mrs. McAwaddle's husband: "(tainted knockwurst, Jaycee picnic)."

is the "starved ignoble nature" (l. 56) common to both. Nothing thrives in Childe Roland's "grey plain":

> No! penury, inertness, and grimace,
> In some strange sort, were the land's portion. "See
> Or shut your eyes," said Nature peevishly,
> "It nothing skills: I cannot help my case:
> 'Tis the Last judgment's fire must cure this place,
> Calcine its clods and set my prisoners free." (ll. 61–66)

Penury, inertness, and grimace likewise characterize Roland McGuffey's Houndsditch:

> Sunday — how say it? — dawned, the only invincibility it seemed to possess. From its broken tenements, lonely streets, and empty squares had all emotions ebbed, and Houndsditch seemed a limit gone beyond, a kind of stone leprosarium of gutted doors through which the metaphorical inmates, as if suppurating with the afflictive screwworm of helminthiasis, willingly decamped in crawls, belled, as it were, to the nether of their dungeons where, in a sickly and zombie-like *lacher prise* from the weekly obligations that beat them down, they could spoon away their Sunday dinners, suck their dirty pipes, doze half-naked slumped into the sofa, or, without the slightest expectation, stare down silently through old thread-bare curtains with tired gull-like eyes to the streets below which sheered off abruptly at corners and in turn closed off pretty much of their world. Everyone had withdrawn, it seemed, so as not to be intimidated by the intimidating click that snapped them away like the catch of a cheap lock,[8] shut fast and buried hopelessly within those monstrous building projects, tall as the Cities of the Plain, being everywhere winched toward the sky, where each building, disfigured, hulks higher and higher, its shit-coloured self rising into space like a cement Kraken out of the inattentive and varicose earth. It was like a surrealistic dream, as if all the buildings were actually cardboard and, if but tapped, would hurtle down in a spray of dust and scaffolding, revealing a vast desert of grey which reached to the fag-end of infinity. (64–65)

After a brief encounter with a Pakistani that foreshadows the later one with Dilip, Roland sets off on his usual Sunday quest, his path indicated by the same "hoary cripple" (68) who maliciously points Childe Roland's way (l. 2).[9] As he makes his way toward Hyde Park he plays an imaginary game of soccer, with rocks and rolled bread for balls and trash barrels for opponents

8 Cf. stanza 29: "Yet half I seemed to recognize some trick / Of mischief happened to me, God knows when — / In a bad dream perhaps. Here ended then, / Progress this way. When, in the very nick / Of giving up, one time more, came a click / As when a trap shuts — you're inside the den!"

9 [In the interview that followed the original appearance of this essay, Theroux remembered "effortfully working to make the perambulations in London of Roland McGuffey recapitulate the lines of the Union Jack" (30). — 2016 note]

("huge monocular Welsh cretins, he decided, running around with the stupidity ascribed to giants and salivating in leek-coloured uniforms" [68]) — the Tottenham Hotspurs standing in, apparently, as the nearest 20th-century equivalent to a band of knights. Throughout the story Theroux thus undercuts the paradigmatic noble quest (as Browning did before him) with Roland's restless wanderings, sometimes with deflated comparisons (the girl he soon meets is, Roland admits to himself, "not really Snow White" [73]), but more often with the clanging juxtaposition of rich, orotund descriptions against Roland's saucy slang and sordid activities. The effect is deliberately comic — indeed P. G. Wodehouse made a career from the same technique — as when Theroux follows Roland's trashy song with the remark, "His was the lyrical mode" (67). Thus the Horatian admonition (from *Ars Poetica*) that stands as epigraph to the story: "Mountains will be in labor, the birth will be a single laughable little mouse."

Roland's bigotry is as widespread as Mrs. Proby's, but with a crucial added dimension: sexual competition. This theme comes to the forefront after his unsuccessful attempt to pick up a girl named Rose ("Rosamund, actually"), whom he meets lounging in Hyde Park. His bigotry reaches a vicious pitch as he imagines Rose joining two Sikhs who had previously passed by their bench:

> All bloody flap that was, and Roland knew that within a brace of shakes she'd be all hands to the pump in some cul-de-sac in the Edgeware Road, with those two drum-eared jungle bunnies who walked by, just begging for it. That, for Roland, was the *osculum infame*, roughly, "kissing the devil's fundament." The brain-racking insouciance with which he generally met the world here stung Roland into a cold fury, a splenetic grudge which ripened into a bouncing loath specifically for those smut-crazed piratical Asians, roasting with satyriasis and ready with their poison juices to roger anything warm and horizontal, only to send pullulating over the indiscriminate bedsteads of Christendom a witless, sponge-headed progeny of biological variants, all with three breasts and minds like silly putty, conceived to a one in a perfect *Walpurgisnacht* of pithecanthropic howls, reechy innuendo, and drools. (79).

The paragraph that follows cleverly translates Roland's sexual envy into the flag-waving nationalism that often masks such uneasiness:

> His resentment burrowed in bitterness the geometrical, if underground, trenches of philosophical Patriotism from which, when the whistle blew its warning, he would burst, plumed and armiferous,[10] into the irrepressible English ozone, splintering the air with war cries like sprays of dynamite to call to the barricades, into the fight,

10 This word apparently comes, as many of Theroux's outlandish words both here and especially in *Darconville's Cat* must, from Thomas Blount's *Glossographia* (1656), a lexicon (the subtitle informs us) "interpreting the hard words of whatsoever language, now used in our refined English tongue."

> all who would outface, and must, this Zulu, this Asian, with his endless streaming hordes, those dark plumed beings of the Middle Air, and buttress all his wrath against that flood which was spilling over the tidemark of the world like an endless tidal wave of paint and staining all an excremental brown. Love Thou Thy Land! *Dieu et Mon Droit!* Into the Valley of Death Rode the Six Hundred! (79–80)

Just as Roland's fury reaches this patriotic pitch, the flames are further fanned by the windy bombast from the "Speaker's Corner" in Hyde Park, "a side show of hammering hands and spitting rhetoric" (80), and he follows with relish an outrageous diatribe against "wogs," excerpted over the next eight pages — probably the funniest pages in the book. Roland eventually makes his way to Victoria Station, where he hears the sound of water "from some sourceless spot" (89) — like the "sudden little river" that crosses Childe Roland's path, "As unexpected as a serpent comes" (ll. 109–10) — and finally confronts his own "wog": not an overpaid, lazy, communist emigrant "putting the boots to your women," as the speaker had warned Roland against; instead, in a passage as quiet and gentle as the speaker's tirade was loud and violent, "alone on a bench and huddled into a tiny embryonic position like a small, brown croissant, a little Indian" (90).

Dilip, the same Indian that Roland spotted earlier and dismissed as a member of "The Pansy Patrol" (76–77), speaks with the same inflated phraseology, misapplied slang, and nonidiomatic formality as the protagonists of F. Anstey's *Baboo Jaberjee* (1897) and G. V. Desani's *All about H. Hatterr* (1948), Theroux's probable models. Anxious to cultivate Roland's friendship, Dilip politely ignores his innuendos and subtle bullying during the first round of their confrontation, which ends with Roland "contented in the knowledge" that "the Indian, among others, remained, ineluctably, that shuttlecock which must drop to the ground if its elevation is not secured, and constantly maintained, by frequent blows" (98–99). And blows, indeed, seem imminent.

But here Theroux interrupts his narrative as he did in "Mrs. Proby Gets Hers" for a biographical digression: a marvelously realized excursion into Dilip's early days in India (99–106, 112–14).[11] As was Yunnum Fun's, Dilip's life has been one of hardship and tribulation, but one in which he has attained a degree of dignity unobtainable by guttersnipes like Roland. Again, Roland's self-defense against such unobtainable dignity is more flag-waving patriotism and darker suspicions of miscegenation. When Dilip excuses himself to make a phone call, Roland jumps to the inevitable (for him) conclusion:

> It's the girl, Roland thought, it's the girl! The telephone call was obviously urgent,

11 Theroux has traveled widely, but never to India, which makes these sections of "Childe Roland" all the more remarkable.

> and even now the line would be jumping with his wheedling artifices, or, worse — like that movie of The Incredible Hulk — filled with evil commands whispered huskily in likerish and diabolical croaks, the brain-trepanning spells that those bottle-nosed nigs, Congoids, and Hottentots cast at midnight in pointed hats and trick coats, using corpsedust, newtliver, and toads filled with mercury as magic barometers to swallow children, blow up churches, and work love potions on those harmless but not terribly percipient English salesgirls, who were later posted off in lumpy parcels to Port Saïd or Bombay, too ashamed, of course, to go back to Chepstow or Boodle and the happy life they had known there selling lollies over the toy counter in Woolworth's or shining the torch down the stalls at the Roxy. It was clear. It was horrible even to think of someone exposed to the fleers of this lustmonger, ready to wipe his smears of shoe-polishy discharge on some poor Trilby with skin like goldenrod and hair like down, probably now bound hand and foot and stuffed like a Norfolk pheasant into some dirty old wardrobe in a Brighton hotel, where her mother didn't even know where she was, never mind her father. It was a dead giveaway. But he had to have proof. (116–17)

Actually, Dilip has been invited for an innocent weekend of tennis at the seaside cottage of his 63-year-old tutor, Miss Lorna Bunn, "who looked like she lived in a cottage of gingerbread and brewed toads" (119). But Roland gets his proof, misinterpreted of course, and from this point on the tension builds dramatically:[12] at any moment, it seems, Roland's bigotry, wounded patriotism (his country comes off the worse in what Dilip assumes is merely a game comparing England to India), and his fears of sexual inadequacy (Roland pitifully boasts that Rose is actually his sweetheart) will explode into violence. But just as Roland backed down from the Pakistani ice-cream vendor at the beginning of the story, his anger suddenly fizzles out, and Dilip, drawing strength from a Buddhist parable, just as suddenly disappears.

Roland turns and descends back down to the station cellar; images of death surround him as they do Childe Roland toward the end of Browning's poem, and he finally comes upon his Dark Tower:

> Roland heard his own whickering footsteps echo to the end of a long tunnel where, in these catacombs, one bus sat alone in a kind of Scotch mist, the glassed-in sign, top front, having been rolled to show its destination: Houndsditch. Roland boarded it and sat down in the shadows, a sort of violet deathlight round his jaw. (141)

In the bus he notices a dark blot on a panel. He tries to wipe away the blot with the handkerchief the Hyde Park speaker had given him as a souvenir, but to no avail. Exhausting every means to expunge it, he finally decides, "*why not*

12 I deliberately refer to the dramatic qualities of "Childe Roland," for the story is an outgrowth of a play Theroux wrote as a graduate student at the University of Virginia entitled *The Sweethearts and Chagrin of Roland Maguffey* and published in *Rapier: The University of Virginia Magazine of Satire and Broad Discussion* 1.3 (April 1967): 29–31, 37–38.

simply pretend the blot was part of the bus?" (142). Roland takes small comfort in this parable of racial integration, but realizes "it was *only* that single frail resolve, made there in the shadows, that alone could make the busride back to Houndsditch less painful, and, if to speak of perpetuity, the only possible way one might ever possibly believe he could live happily ever after" (143). And on that inverted note Theroux's modern fairy tale ends.

The final story in the book, "The Wife of God," is a high camp romp written with such exquisite style that it is necessary to remind oneself that beneath the frivolity is yet another example of simple bigotry: this time not from ill-educated members of "the non-propertied classes" (147) as in the first two stories, but from cultured, propertied members of the Anglican *bon ton*. Lady Fanny Therefore, determined to keep intact the "brushed and curried elegance of the lyric past" (147), is as convinced as Mrs. Proby and Roland that "wogs" are lowering the tone of civilized life, if not ruining England altogether. Specifically, she is concerned for her son, who is introduced in the first sentence engaged in a suggestive act that reveals his sexual orientation as well as the color of the object of his affections: "The Reverend Which Therefore sucked, then swallowed a black jujube, one on which he could just as easily have bitten down, he was that agitated" (147). A kissing cousin to Firbank's eccentric Cardinal Pirelli, Reverend Therefore is enamored of a black African named Cyril, his current choirmaster. But Lady Therefore, "a repository of racial declamation" (169), feels nothing but disgust for her son's companion:

> She pictured Cyril mythopoeically: a Dark Morlock, sloppy, smokeyed, limping through her dreams with his socks down, a salivating anthropophagus chewing khat, punching mandrils and hartebeest, and, with his thousand tribal members sitting on their haunches in the clearings, drinking strip-me-naked from wooden bowls, polishing their teeth with pieces of soft stick, and farting into the grass. (154)

(It will be noticed that all three protagonists of *Three Wogs* picture foreigners "mythopoeically" in terms that bear no resemblance to reality but reveal much concerning their psychological fears.) Consequently, when she hears of Cyril's plans to marry an African girl — a ballerina also in London — she eagerly supplies the necessary financial backing, unbeknownst to the Reverend Which Therefore, who does everything he can to dissuade Cyril from his plan, inviting him to join him instead in holy matrimony with God. The Edenic England of Lady Therefore's girlhood, evoked in a series of beautiful reveries throughout the story, included no blacks; she feels no compunction, then, in sacrificing her son's future happiness that she may preserve her dream of England: "The Lion and the Unicorn would always boldly guard the door that led to that paradise, the land of sweetness, light, and transforming prevenient grace, and yet, asked Lady Therefore, could she at last unto that sacred portal, into that sacred land, one day bring her son to spend their final days together, only themselves, alone?" (216). This rhetorical question concludes a two-page reverie of great beauty, similar to the famous paragraph that concludes Lytton Strachey's *Queen Victoria* (1921), but much finer. The question is followed by the concluding paragraph of the story, in which Rev. Therefore is left drowning in a black pool of despair. Despite its frivolity, learned wit, catty misogyny, and Catholic camp, then, "The Wife of God" ends on a tragic, somber note, in much the same way as Firbank's frivolous *Flower beneath the Foot* does. (Firbank comes to mind more often than any other author during this story.) The tragedy is inevitable: even without his mother's intervention the Reverend Therefore would have lost his "Dark Angel" (175),[13] who does not share his patron's sexual tastes. Nor is Lady Therefore's Edwardian England ever to be recaptured. It is a measure of the power of Theroux's style that he can evoke such tragic sympathy for such characters, for such concerns. Even the bigotry that is the subject of the novel gives way at the end to the greater themes of love, loss, and sorrow: the very thematic seeds that would grow through the decade and bloom in Theroux's great anatomy, *Darconville's Cat*.

During the decade between the publication of his first two novels, Theroux published a large body of short fiction, fables, and journalism. The style and content of Theroux's dozen or so short stories are decidedly lighter than the novels. Most feature travelers at the hands of crafty natives: "satiric fiction which showed the ironic contradictions between the characters' confidence in themselves and what the reader knew about them."[14] They range over a variety of locales (England, Virginia, Russia, Italy, Poland) and, more impressively, display Theroux's technical knowledge in a variety of fields (trains, folkmotif scholarship, gastronomy, Latin literature and archaeology, Copernican astronomy). But beneath the light, satirical surfaces a somber theme recurs, one that would play a major role in the long novel he had already begun writing. The key is provided in a quotation from William H. Gass that Theroux glosses in a 1975 essay:

> "You have fallen into art — return to life," warns a coffee stain at the end of William Gass's *Willie Masters' Lonesome Wife* (1968). That old problem, isn't it? — the op-

13 The Catholic convert Lionel Johnson personified his homosexuality as "The Dark Angel" in an excellent poem of that name (1893). Theroux quotes from this poem on several occasions in *Darconville's Cat*, where the alluring (and insistently heterosexual) Hypsipyle Poore functions as the schoolmaster's dark angel.

14 *Darconville's Cat* (Garden City: Doubleday, 1981), 408 — a kind of writing at which Darconville becomes adept.

> posite of Adam's problem, perhaps, who fell from art into life. To fall from art into life! What a pain in the ass it has been for us all ever since. And where have we fallen? We've fallen, bump, crash, splat, into that vast neutral forest, empty of druid and shadow, where the faint voice of Quarles sounds lamenting reedily through the darkness, muttering:
>
> "Queens drop away, while blue-legg'd Maukin thrives;
> And courtly Mildred dies while country Madge survives."[15]

Most of Theroux's stories concern just such a fall from art into life, a confrontation in which a character's insulated, private world (usually one of culture if not art) is punctured by a representative from "that vast neutral forest" of real life: a Protestant minister's Bible-belted security is disrupted by a Russian bellhop eager to supply him with pornography ("Fark Pooks"); a fussy folklorist has a harrowing encounter with an alleged witch of Somersetshire ("Mrs. Marwood's Spunkies"); a fastidious lady novelist's world comes undone when her tightly bunned hair is knocked undone by an obnoxious child of tourists ("A Wordstress in Williamsburg"); a feminist magazine editor is almost seduced by a lascivious Italian ("Scugnizzo's Pasta Co."); a Californian classicist is almost seduced by his Roman guide ("A Polish Joke"); and so on. This recurring theme is merely satiric here in the stories; in his second novel, Theroux elevates this theme to great tragedy and high art.

Darconville's Cat (or "The Jilt's Companion," as Theroux once referred to it in conversation) is a monumental novel in several senses of the word: it is a lasting reminder of a love affair, erected in memory of the great love of Darconville's life, and a record of the tragic course of their affair; it is a monument to the English language, a vast burial ground of archaic words and sentiments, intellectual traditions, literary forms and rhetorical devices rarely used anymore; and it is monumental in the more idiomatic sense of *massive*: over 700 pages long, an encyclopedic range of references to literature, art, history, religion, and philosophy from every era of human history, thick with learning and lore, aflame with excoriating satire, alight with love, choked with hate, and waterlogged with grief. Simply thinking of the novel can bring tears to my eyes, yet it is also laugh-out-loud funny. It exhausts my superlatives.

The storyline is fairly straightforward. Alaric Darconville, a learned and rather aloof ex-novice, comes to Quinsy College in Virginia to teach and write. There he falls in love with one of his students, Isabel Rawsthorne, who seems to return his love. But soon feeling out of her league with Darconville, she admits to herself that she would feel "safer" with a neighborhood boy, Gil-

15 "Theroux Metaphrastes," 26. [I've corrected Theroux's "dries" to "dies"; the couplet is best known from an 1810 letter by Charles Lamb, often reprinted.]

bert van der Slang. She strings Darconville along until she is sure of Gilbert's reciprocal feelings, and then tells Darconville she no longer loves him. Darconville, who is teaching at Harvard at this point and finalizing arrangements for their marriage, is destroyed by the news, and as he realizes the extent of her betrayal, contemplates revenge with the encouragement of Dr. Abel Crucifer, a strange ex-professor he meets at Harvard. Darconville returns to Virginia and waits outside Isabel's house with a gun, but seeing the tree upon which he had carved the word *Remember* in happier days, he abandons his plans for revenge and instead travels to Venice to stay in his grandmother's palazzo and write a novel about the affair. Racing against a fatal illness, he manages to finish and dies.

Summarized this baldly, *Darconville's Cat* sounds conventional and melodramatic, more like a 19th-century opera than a 20th-century novel. What is unconventional about the work, however, is Theroux's extraordinary language, his rhetorical power to transform a commonplace boy-loses-girl story into a profound meditation on love, hate, and the tie that binds them. Hawthorne remarks in the concluding chapter of *The Scarlet Letter*, "It is a curious subject of observation and inquiry, whether hatred and love be not the same thing at bottom," and Theroux brings unmatched "observation and inquiry" to this subject. To find a parallel, one would have to go back to Burton inquiring into the causes of melancholy, or Rabelais on whether Panurge should take a wife: ordinary questions, extraordinary responses.

In a recent essay on Proust and Vermeer, Theroux cites Bergotte's late realization (upon seeing Vermeer's *View of Delft*), "My last books are too dry, I ought to have gone over them with several coats of paint, made my language exquisite in itself, like this little patch of yellow wall"; Theroux goes on to explain that "It was Proust, after all, who taught us that art by no means represents a copy of reality, rather it creates a truer, a nobler, more poetic reality."[16] Theroux transfigured his simple story by similar means: he chose a genre — the anatomy — that would be flexible enough to accommodate a wide variety of materials, but he encased this loosely structured genre in a design as balanced as a Greek temple. His novel consists of exactly 100 chapters; chapter 50 recounts the day on which Isabel decides to betray Darconville, thus acting as a hinge for the two halves of the novel. An essay on love in the first half is balanced by one on hate in the second; a benevolent elder advisor in Virginia, Miss Thelma Trappe, has her counterpart in Massachusetts in the malevolent Dr. Crucifer; the southern setting contrasts with the northern one, angelic imagery changes to demonic, and so on. At the physical center of the book is the short chapter entitled "Odi et Amo"; this is the Catullan text for Theroux's

16 "The Sphinx of Delft," *Art & Antiques*, December 1988, 85, 124.

sermon, with the emphasis on that paradoxical *et*.

Unlike Bergotte, Theroux went over his book with layer after layer of verbal paint, resuscitating hundreds of obsolete words that stand out on the page like blobs of bright paint, and adding layers of literary allusions and quotations. At times this reaches a density where an entire paragraph might consist of buried quotations. Take this paragraph from chapter 79, where Crucifer is taunting Darconville about Isabel's deceptive love:

> "Stories to delight your ears, favors to allure your eyes? She touched you here and there? Oh yes. The adverse party, with a suitable amount of proleptic irony, was your advocate. But the time that went by! Is it any wonder that Vulcan fashioned creaking shoes for Venus that he might hear her when she stirred?" Crucifer swept his arm from him. "She loved you — pish! She was loyal — bubble! Fair proportioned — mew! gentle of heart — wind!" (535)

This sounds like Cruficer's usual conversation, and yet hardly a word in his own. The first two sentences are from Shakespeare's "Passionate Pilgrim," the third from Shakespeare's sonnet 35; the Vulcan reference from an unidentified source, probably also Elizabethan;[17] and the final four exclamatory sentences adapted from John Marston's play *The Malcontent* (1604). In one sense, *Darconville's Cat* is a collage of texts, hundreds of quotations and allusions strung together as a narrative, a necklace of literary pearls. Even the final sentence of the novel, "Sorrow is the cause of immortal conceptions," is an unacknowledged quotation (from *The Confessions of Edward Dahlberg*), maintaining to the end the essential literariness of the novel.

Actually, Theroux is extending here the practice he followed in *Three Wogs*, especially in "Mrs. Proby Gets Hers," which is a kind of linguistic mosaic of Britishisms: English slang, idioms, holidays, quaint-sounding city names, culinary items, habits, herbs, as well as prejudices. The characters are as much creations of language as users of it. But in *Darconville* Theroux moves further away from representation and exposition to create what Roland Barthes called the "paradise of words," where "every kind of linguistic pleasure" exists. Even more than Severo Sarduy's *Cobra* (Barthes's exemplar), *Darconville's Cat*

> is in fact a paradisiac text, utopian (without site), a heterology by plenitude: all the signifiers are here and each scores a bull's-eye; the author (the reader) seems to say to them: *I love you all* (words, phrases, sentences, adjectives, discontinuities: pell-mell: signs and mirages of objects which they represent); a kind of Franciscanism invites all words to perch, to flock, to fly off again: a marbled, iridescent text; we are gorged

17 [Turns out this is from the section on jealousy in Burton's *Anatomy of Melancholy* (part 3, sec. 3, member 1, subsection 2), as I learned from Sam Endrigkeit (see n20 below). — 2016 note]

> with language, like children who are never refused anything or scolded for anything or, even worse, "permitted" anything.[18]

"How I adore the language that can tell you this," Crucifer interrupts himself at one point (544), and how Theroux adores the language that let him compose *Darconville's Cat*. But this very verbal exuberance is thematically functional as well, not merely self-indulgent. In *Darconville,* Isabel is first invested with the entire literary heritage of romantic love, then stripped and reviled with the English language's disturbingly large vocabulary of misogyny. Isabel is by turns ennobled and disfigured by this language, which points to Darconville's tragic flaw: his tendency to see people as literary stereotypes rather than as people. He treats Isabel as the heroine of his romantic reveries, and the reason he doesn't write much while involved with her is because she's the literary work he's creating. A simple girl, Isabel doesn't deserve (nor desires) these literary trappings, however ennobling they may be. During the second half of the novel, Darconville moves in the opposite direction, painting her (with Crucifer's assistance) as a new Messalina, again allowing artistic preconceptions to cloud his vision. Only at the end of the novel does his vision clear with the realization that art and life are two different (usually incompatible) realms and that his literary creation more properly belongs between the covers of a book than beneath the covers of his marriage bed.

Despite a number of good reviews, a National Book Award nomination, and inclusion in Anthony Burgess's *99 Novels: The Best in English since 1939* (1984), *Darconville's Cat* failed to make much of a mark. (True to form, the *New York Times Book Review* didn't even list *Darconville* in its year-end roundup of the hundred or so best novels of the year.) Some of the reasons for this criminal neglect are mundane: no paperback edition was issued,[19] and a year after Burgess honored it, *Darconville* went out of print. A few academic articles have been written on it and *Darconville* is discussed briefly in a recent survey of postwar American fiction,[20] but otherwise few readers seem to know of the

18 *The Pleasure of the Text*, translated by Richard Miller (New York: Farrar, Straus and Giroux, 1975), 8.

19 [It was eventually published in paperback in 1996 by Henry Holt; Theroux took the occasion to revise a few passages, identifiable by the lighter type (e.g., pp. 643–44). — 2016 note]

20 The essays are Jo Allen Bradham, "The American Scholar: From Emerson to Alexander Theroux's *Darconville's Cat*," *Critique* 24.4 (Summer 1983): 215–17; Larry McCaffery, "And Still They Smooch: Erotic Visions and Re-Visions in Postmodern American Fiction," *Revue Française d'Etudes Américaines* 9.20 (May 1984): 275–87; Steven Moore, "Alexander Theroux's *Darconville's Cat* and the Tradition of Learned Wit," *Contemporary Literature* 27.2 (Summer 1986): 233–45; and Michael Pinker, "Cupid and Vindice: The Novels of Alexander Theroux," *Denver Quarterly* 24.3 (Winter 1990): 101–24. The survey is John Kuehl, *Alternate Worlds: A Study of Postmodern Antirealistic Fiction* (New York: New York

work, even among specialists in contemporary fiction. Granted, the novel is long and difficult, but not nearly as long or difficult as Gaddis's *Recognitions* or Pynchon's *Gravity's Rainbow*. It may be that *Darconville's* chief virtue, its style, is for many its chief fault. It is a mode no one uses these days and that fewer and fewer readers seem capable of appreciating. Just as sparse Atticism ousted spacious Asianism in classical Rome 20 centuries ago, minimalism is preferred over maximalism by a majority of this century's readers and writers. Theroux's style, which has affinities with Greek Alexandrianism (a happy coincidence), medieval scholasticism, the learned wit of the 17th and 18th centuries, French decadence, and Corvine invective, is a style that demands of its readers an almost antiquarian devotion to English language and literature. Consider this paragraph, again from the grandiloquent Dr. Crucifer:

> "The state, it could be argued, must be called to account as to one of its highest functions, that of law — the hubris of human ingenuity — and even possibly condemned by the standards implied in the utopian idea of primal innocence, for hasn't it taken upon itself one form of dominion after another," asked Crucifer, crossing the room with his forefinger in the air, "and lorded it over all the others, pretending, as though it were the daughter of the gods, to a privilege beyond all other disciplines? primal innocence?" He winked. "Dwale and delusion! So laws were grafted. Lawcraft? Sheepcraft! I won't bore you with a history of all its agathokakological claptrap, Darconville, but simply point out that, at bottom, it owes its essential existence to the depraved and fallen nature of mankind — which it can never riddle, which it can never rectify — and in my considered opinion is styled, when at its most efficient, only to jingle at justice and to twill at truth, especially in matters touching on that curious but primal antagonism: the just thing versus the legal thing. The law and the gospel," he glubbed with obvious delight, "are hereby made liable to more than one contradiction, and if a mooching and piety-faced forgiveness is all you know of either, where punishment you take to be a crime, I must then reinstruct you that all law has its beginning in that first crime of our first mother and her low tongue — Johannes Goropius Becanus (1519–1572) in his *Origines Autuerpianae*, Antwerp, 1569, maintained that the original language of Adam and Eve, and so the tongue of primal betrayal, was Dutch! — and thereby cry out that you might let your severe and impartial doom imitate divine vengeance and rain down your punishing force upon this temerarious strumpet, this mistress of the adroit lie, until like than fen-born serpent she resembles at the root of all our woe she eat the dust of her penalty for the rest of her life!" (542–43)

What a treasure chest of language is opened here! A geological survey of words ranging from Anglo-Saxon monosyllables ("dwale," "twill") and mon-

University Press, 1989), 94–96, 106–8, and passim. [Nor has there been much since, aside from a few appreciative online blogs and an excellent thesis by Sam Endrigkeit entitled "'Do Your Worst': Maximalism and Intertextuality in Alexander Theroux's *Darconville's Cat*" (Universität Duisburg-Essen, 2015). — 2016 note]

strous inkhorn words ("agathokakological")[21] to words apparently of Theroux's own invention ("Sheepcraft"); ornate adjectival phrases ("a mooching and piety-faced forgiveness") and epigrammatic asides ("which it can never riddle, which it can never rectify"); cranky scholarship (Becanus's *Origenes Autuerpianae*)[22] and obscure literary allusions ("fen-born serpent" — from Milton's *The Reason of Church Government Urged against Prelatry*); and an arsenal of rhetorical devices to move the paragraph from its calm, forensic opening to its wrathful, Old Testament conclusion. But this tour de force of Quintilian rhetoric also functions at the levels of plot development (Crucifer is persuading Darconville to take the law into his own hands), iterative patterns of reference (Dutch as "the tongue of primal betrayal" recalls his rival Gilbert van der Slang's ancestry), and at the thematic level, where Darconville, having fallen like Adam from art into life, is trying to reverse the fall and regain Barthes's paradise of words and (eventually) his Catholic paradise. In other words, this paragraph isn't just a patch of purple prose but a highly efficient (and entertaining) paragraph that fulfills several narrative functions. And there are a thousand more as richly textured as this one.

But the American reading public wasn't interested. (Nor the British, apparently; 1500 copies were exported to Britain, but a good number of these were returned to the United States a few years later, with the British publisher's sticker still on them, to ornament remainder tables.) From 1981 until the appearance of his third novel in 1987 Theroux continued to teach and to write magazine articles, most notably a series of increasingly sophisticated essays in art criticism for *Art & Antiques*. (The protagonist of his next novel would be a painter.) Only two short stories were published during this period: "Watergraphs" (1983) and "A Woman with Sauce" (1985), both for the *Boston Globe Magazine*. The latter is interesting for the similarities between the narrator's relationship with a young girl of Italian descent named Angela Capitalupo and Christian Ford's relationship with angelic Marina Falieri in *An Adultery*.

Theroux's third novel, with its stark, Deuteronomic title, marks a departure from his previous flamboyant style. Gone are the obsolete words, the parodies, and most of the exotic references (though one obscure reference to Rolfe remains).[23] Instead, *An Adultery* is written in a neo-Jamesian style that

21 The *OED* cites only one appearance of this word (which means "composed of good and evil"): Robert Southey's *The Doctor* (1834–47), a *Tristram Shandy*-like novel in seven volumes.

22 I'm guessing Theroux found this among the annotations in John Wilder's edition of Samuel Butler's *Hudibras* (New York: Oxford University Press, 1967), 326.

23 The couplet Christian Ford recites on p. 174 of *An Adultery* (New York: Simon & Schuster, 1987) is the opening of Rolfe's poem "Dux Amor" (1889). Discovered after the publication

recalls the Master's inexhaustible fascination with the subtleties of manners and morals, as well as Proust's exhaustive analyses of character and culture. The result is a novel that some readers and reviewers found too obsessive and exasperating, especially with regard to the adulteress of the novel, a thoroughly detestable woman with none of the appeal of an Emma Bovary or Anna Karenina. Near the end, the narrator realizes "she wasn't worthy of the energy required to form the words that sentenced her" (372), but the fact he found the energy to form the 145,000 or so words that precede that sentence is the paradox readers must unriddle.[24] (The words *paradox* and *paradoxically*, in fact, appear conspicuously throughout the novel.)

An Adultery is the first-person account by a painter, Christian ("Kit") Ford, of his messy affair with a twice-married woman named Farol Colorado (which, traced to Greek and Spanish roots, means "red light"). At first the attraction is merely physical, but as Kit learns more about this troubled woman, his pity and sensitivity to her vulnerability cause him to fall in love with her, despite his better judgment, and despite an on-again, off-again girlfriend named Marina Falieri. (Marino Faliero [1285–1355] was a Venetian doge and the subject of a tragedy by Byron and a novel by Hoffmann.) Kit's neglect of the impossibly sweet Marina in favor of the offensively neurotic Farol is perplexing, even to Kit, who, like a dog returning to its vomit, keeps returning to Farol despite their many fights and his numerous complaints about her. Or perhaps *because* of these fights and complaints; at one point Kit writes: "I had heard of a thing called obstacle love and how certain people needed complexity, barriers in fact, to assure the love that one demanded be proven by it and for the reassurance all was worth it in the many things to be overcome. Or not worth it. I'm sure it explained both of us" (189). Marina presents no obstacles; her love is open and unconditional. Farol, on the other hand, is more than a challenge: "trying to fathom Farol Colorado has become part of my own personal exorcism" (223). Kit is enchanted with angelic Marina, but is possessed by the demonic Farol, and *An Adultery* charts a Faustian battle for Christian Ford's soul.

As with the two earlier novels, *An Adultery* has a clear formal structure. It is divided into three parts, the first sentence of each forming a syllogism:

---

of Cecil Woolf's edition of Rolfe's *Collected Poems* (1974), it was reprinted in the introduction to Donald Weeks's pamphlet *Frederick William Rolfe, Christchurch, and "The Artist"* (Edinburgh: Tragara, 1980), 9.

24 [I now wonder if Theroux isn't echoing the end of the "Swann in Love" section of Proust's *Swann's Way*, when the art critic exclaims to himself: "To think that I wasted years of my life, that I wanted to die, that I felt my deepest love, for a woman who did not appeal to me, who was not my type" (trans. Lydia Davis [New York: Viking, 2003], 296). — 2016 note]

All women are mortal. (11)
Farol Colorado was a woman. (139)
Farol Colorado was mortal. (259).[25]

At the very center of the novel is an essay on adultery (196–200), reminiscent of the essays on love and hate in *Darconville's Cat*. This appeal to formal logic and exposition is characteristic of Kit; his muddled mistress, on the other hand, "hadn't the art or ability to reach conclusions by means of the usual premises which involved steps of thought and demanded language, whether interior or interchanged. The cliché here applied: she *leapt* to conclusions. She reached conclusions by determination alone, excluding middles and hopfrogging the logic of thought" (233). Throughout the novel Farol displays much discomfort with language, distrusting its capacity for precision and clarity, and fearful of its ability to expose deception. Kit's commitment to language as a means for analysis clashes with Farol's use of it for obfuscation, and at this level *An Adultery* is a heroic attempt to prove that it is still possible for rigorous thought and incisive language to fight and triumph over the foggy, imprecise language, generalities, and clichés that both Farol and much of our society employ as its lingua franca. "Love is not only a talkative passion," Kit argues. "Language itself can lose chastity and in its ambiguity become also depraved, as when on the adulterous tongue two meanings that should remain separate become suddenly coupled. A parody of communication begins to take place. And soon all distinctions are lost" (113).

Loss is, in fact, the principal theme of *An Adultery* and the impetus of its form and content. The loss of distinctions in language is only one of many forms of loss with which Kit is concerned: loss of clear thinking, of manners, of judgment in art — his scathing critiques of Farol's artsy-craftsy world are the funniest bits in the novel — and, perhaps most importantly, emotional loss. His childhood fear of desertion (26) — Kit lost his parents at an early age — has caused him to become obsessed with avoiding loss: "I suppose the sad truth was," he writes to justify clinging to Farol, "I could be satisfied with very little if I was only delivered from the dread of losing it" (239). Initially, Kit found Farol "a symbol of all sorts of beautiful lost things" (15), two pages after stating "I've always found something terrible in what we have that can also be lost" (13). Eventually he loses both Farol and Marina; like Darconville, all he is left with are memories, and determined not to lose *them* as well, Kit writes the novel we have been reading.

"I can't forget anything," he notes early in the novel (27), and a little later admits "I love details. Details are never small" (47). The struggle against loss

25 Of the numerous reviews I've seen, only Richard Scaramelli's in the *Review of Contemporary Fiction* (8.1 [Spring 1988]: 190–91) noted the syllogism.

and the recovery of memories generate the novel's verbal energy, the very urgency of Kit's project justifying his obsessive recording of detail. What saves the novel from becoming wearisome is the language, of course; the endless examples of Farol's shortcomings may not always be interesting in themselves, but Kit's manner of relating them always is. Elegant, aphoristic, metaphoric, ranging in tone from sweetly sentimental to fiercely satiric, showing great psychological acumen, Kit is a consistently entertaining narrator. Consider this account of Farol's distaste for Kit's Cape Cod house:

> I hated her fastidious pessimism and found it uncomfortably disingenuous of her, under the circumstances, to be so queenly. The whole day passed that way, with her remarks as she drifted from room to room confined to exiguous and monosyllabic quacks of disapproval, devoid of variety, wit, and compass. One had to go far, believe me, to find a more exemplary fusion of insecurity and snobbery or dependence and resentment. And it was very easy, I remember, to criticize her on the way home for accepting under false pretenses the bicycle her husband gave her. But who trades in contradiction will not be contradicted. "I took the bicycle," she replied — her eyes cold as high-shoe buttons — "because it was incumbent on me to take it," she said, "because I'd have seemed guiltier," she snapped, "*not* to take it, do you *understand?*"
>
> Incumbent. (241)

Every sentence is a complaint, yet here, as throughout the novel, Kit has the "variety, wit, and compass" to keep the reader engaged, even when (elsewhere) the reader suspects Kit's lucidity has something in common with the deceptive lucidity of Poe's deranged narrators. (The occasional references to Poe — Marina recites his poetry, one of Farol's sisters is named Lenore — suggest Theroux encourages this particular suspicion, especially toward the end of the novel when Kit writes "Madness, do I say? It wasn't madness. I was completely rational, as calm as I was cold and as cold as camphor" [383].) As a first-person narrator Kit may be (by definition) unreliable to some extent, but like Marcel in Proust's great novel he earns this reader's confidence and even admiration, despite his faults. (Other readers find Kit as reprehensible as Farol — see Michael Pinker's essay later in this issue.)

It is in this regard that *An Adultery* differs from most of the classics of the genre; in them, the adulteress claims our attention and often our sympathy. In Theroux's novel, even though Kit spends most of his 400 pages talking about Farol, it is he that holds our attention and wins our sympathy. Nor does Theroux give adultery any of the dangerous glamour it has in the classics, or even the civilized charm it possesses in, say, W. M. Spackman's novels. Working against reader expectations, Theroux takes a number of risks, as if he too believes in an "obstacle love" relationship with the reader, needing "complexity, barriers in fact" to force the reader to abandon any notions of the illicit allure of adultery and to see it for the psychologically complex and morally destructive activity it is. The depth of Theroux's psychological penetration and the brilliance of his language assure *An Adultery* a place among the classics in this genre, which in turn encourages us to reevaluate them in the powerful light he shines on this perennial theme.

As Thomas Filbin shows elsewhere in this issue, *An Adultery* received mixed reviews, and even some of Theroux's fans (myself included) were reluctant to trade the exuberance of *Darconville's Cat* for the inquisitorial grimness of *An Adultery*. But repeated readings bring out the third novel's many strengths and it could be that, for many readers, it will represent the fullest maturation of Theroux's art. A fourth novel is in progress [later abandoned], reportedly a comically pedantic novel in the form of a biography, but unfortunately bread-and-butter journalism, by necessity, claims most of his time.

Writing of the Theroux family in 1978, James Atlas said of *Darconville's Cat*, then nearing completion:

> I would not care to predict the fate of Alexander's novel. It is a brilliant, idiosyncratic work, graced with the quaint vocabulary that abounds in "Three Wogs," and I hope it becomes one of those books kept alive by a few loyal readers in each generation, like Edmund Gosse's "Father and Son" or Corvo's novels. But perhaps it is too literary; perhaps Alexander would do better to put more of Medford [his Massachusetts hometown] in his work. If this cumbersome novel remains unread, Alexander's character will continue to be talked of and appreciated, like Oscar Wilde's, as if it were itself a work of art.[26]

Alexander Theroux is indeed a colorful character, as several of the contributors to this issue agree. But it is the work, not the man, that should command our attention and respect. The depressing fact that, as of this writing, all of his books are out of print suggests that he may have to wait as long as Corvo, Firbank, and Barnes to win an audience. It is to be hoped this special issue will shorten the wait.

CODA: *DARCONVILLE'S CAT* REDUX[27]

Though often grouped with maximalist, encyclopedic novels because of its elaborate style and range of references, Theroux's novel differs from others of that species (Gaddis's *Recognitions*, Pynchon's *Gravity's Rainbow*) in being the easiest to read. The story is simple, the plot unfolds in linear fashion, and

26 "The Theroux Family Arsenal," *New York Times Magazine*, 20 April 1978, 64.

27 My original essay was followed by an appendix listing all the substantive changes Theroux made to *An Adultery* between the galley stage and the published book. In its place I am substituting a brief piece on *Darconville's Cat* that I was asked to write for a festschrift entitled *The Syllabus*, published by Verbivoracious Press in May 2015.

the moral is clear. It's a rare, perhaps unique example of a novel that reads like a best-seller while deploying the kind of literary pyrotechnics associated with rarified postmodern fiction.

Boy meets girl, boy loses girl and vows revenge, then comes to his senses and erects this literary cathedral to unrequited love before romantically dying in Venice. Betrayed by Isabel Rawsthorne, Alaric Darconville devotes himself to the true love of his life, the English language. The language is unusually rich, employs an arsenal of rhetorical devices, and revives words that haven't been used in hundreds of years. And as the dust-jacket boasts, "Its chapters embody a multiplicity of narrative forms, including a diary, a formal oration, an abecedarium, a sermon, a litany, a blank-verse play, poems, essays, parodies, and fables." Playing on a popular phrase, the chapter entitled "What Is One Picture Worth?" contains exactly one thousand words. The black page of grief from *Tristram Shandy* is here, and enough literary allusions to keep an annotator occupied for years tracking them down. It's by turns funny and sad, satiric and mournful.

It's a performance piece, to be sure, taking full advantage of "the opportunity for display that [novels] offered a good mind," as the Canon in *Don Quixote* says, "providing a broad and spacious field where one's pen could write unhindered. . . ." But Theroux's lavish style and far-flung allusions are functional as well: Darconville is well-read, richly imaginative, and individualistic, whereas the girl he falls for . . . isn't. A simple soul who wants to play it safe and consequently dumps Darconville for a local boy, Isabel's plain language and lack of imagination is stylistically at odds with the magniloquent language that surrounds her. Theroux shows that style is substance; he's got it, she doesn't, and 100 pages into this 700-page novel, the reader knows they have no future, though Darconville won't admit it for hundreds of pages, hoping his powerful imagination can trump unimaginative reality. Darconville's language swells and his rhetorical feats grow more outlandish as he resists that conclusion, resulting in some stunning set-pieces, such as a travelogue of imaginary places and an unholy litany of malevolent women. When he realizes all his imagination and rhetoric still can't change the world, he sickens and dies, right after he finishes penning this work.

It's a pattern Theroux would follow in his two subsequent novels, *An Adultery* (1987) and *Laura Warholic* (2007): a sensitive, overeducated man falls for an insensitive, undereducated woman and suffers as a result. But neither reaches the linguistic heights of *Darconville's Cat*, or matches its range of registers, from whimsy to intellection, from broad satire to targeted social criticism. Out of print for years, it deserves to be tracked down by any reader interested in love, language, and the complex relationship between the two.

The Plays of Ronald Firbank

The drama and the novel have enough similarities that most novelists try their hand at a play sometime in their career, just as many playwrights attempt a novel at some point. For most novelists, their plays occupy a minor place in their oeuvre — Henry James's plays and Joyce's *Exiles* are convenient examples — just as the novels of playwrights are often mere footnotes in their careers (like Shaw's *The Irrational Knot* or Coward's *Pomp and Circumstance*). Writers who excel in both genres are rare — Beckett and Genet, maybe Duras if you include film scripts — and while Firbank's achievement in theater is secondary to that in the novel, the drama played a significant role in his development as an artist.

From an early age, Firbank was enamored of the theater. As a boy he collected autographs of playwrights and actors, and by the time he was 15 he was attending such plays as Daudet's *Sapho* and Pinero's *Iris*. A few years later, in 1904, Firbank moved to Paris, where opportunities for attending plays and meeting actors were plentiful. Ostensibly there to perfect his French, Firbank spent as much time cultivating his personality, and he took many of his cues from Parisian theater life. In her biography of Firbank, Miriam Benkovitz details some of his enthusiasms:

> Theater and theatrical personalities, of course, delighted Firbank. He watched eagerly for the bills, green for the Opéra-Comique and wine-red for the Comédie-Française, posted to announce new productions. It was the green which he read more eagerly: the Opéra-Comique never failed to please, and operettas — *La Chauve Souris*, for example — were most amusing. His admiration for La Belle Otéro was devout; he went again and again to the Mathurins to see her in the pantomime *Rêve d'Opium* or in M. Gailhard's *L'Aragonaise*, and he filled pages of his photographic album with her pictures. He sat entranced before Polaire as Fiquet in Willy's *Claudine à Paris* as well as before his old favorites. Réjane was at the Théâtre de Variété; and the Divine Sarah created the part of Marie Antoinette in *Varenne*, which opened on April 23 [1904], and re-created Aiglon for twenty performances commencing on October 1. He went through the stage door to visit Mlle Jeanne Granier and Édouard de Max, who was at the Théâtre Sarah Bernhardt or the Théâtre Porte-Saint-Martin.[1]

This Romanian actor, "reputed to have a bad influence on young men" (Benkovitz reports), became friendly with the English teenager and added a dec-

1 *Ronald Firbank: A Biography* (New York: Knopf, 1969), 47.

adent dimension to Firbank's budding dandyism. At the time, Firbank was reading the Symbolists, the Pre-Raphaelites, Maurice Maeterlinck, and, most importantly, Oscar Wilde.

It was in this heady atmosphere that Firbank wrote his first play, *The Mauve Tower*, dated in the dedication the summer of 1904. (The dedication on the typescript reads: "A Monsieur Jean Pozzi / Très cordialement je dédie ma 'TourMauve' en souvenir de l'été mil neuf cent quatre": Pozzi was a slightly older friend of the family Firbank was staying with.) Like some of the prose pieces Firbank wrote that year — "La Princesse aux Soleils," "Far Away," "Harmonie" (all of which appear in the *Complete Short Stories*) — the play is more concerned with setting and description than with narrative or characterization. Firbank here is like a young artist more interested in exploring the colors on his palette than with painting something substantial, or a musician experimenting with chords and tonalities. The young writer can be seen testing his metaphor-making abilities ("the moon looks like a yellow jewel, like a strange yellow jewel from some dead king's crown") and paying homage, through imitation, to important influences like Maeterlincks's plays, Wilde's *Salomé*, and, perhaps, Debussy's *Pelléas et Mélisande*. It's a derivative, juvenile effort, and yet a major theme of Firbank's later work — alienation — is present here in the circumstances of Princess Ingria's flight from an unwanted marriage and Prince Laon's wrongful imprisonment by his uncles. Neither is integrated into her or his society, a situation shared by many of Firbank's characters.

If *The Mauve Tower* recalls Wilde's *Salomé*, Firbank's next play, *A Disciple from the Country*, recalls Wilde's comedies. Firbank wrote this play three years later at Cambridge University. In 1907 he joined two of the university's dramatic societies — the Amateur Dramatic Club and the Footlights — and Benkovitz suggests he wrote this play some time that year in lieu of participating in performances. Brigid Brophy, in her spirited biography of Firbank, refines the date further to argue he wrote it before May of 1907, the month Richard Strauss's opera version of Wilde's *Salomé* premiered in Paris;[2] hence Mrs. Creamway's observation (on Mary Magdalene's alleged engagement to John the Baptist): "They tell me the whole thing has been turned quite recently into a very tuneful opera."

In style, content, and dramatic technique, *A Disciple from the Country* is completely opposite to, and a marked improvement upon, *The Mauve Tower*. Alan Hollinghurst has noted that all of Firbank's juvenilia falls into two catego-

2 *Prancing Novelist: A Defence of Fiction in the Form of a Critical Biography in Praise of Ronald Firbank* (London: Macmillan, 1973), 316.

ries: those he wrote for his mother and those written about her.[3] "Baba," as her son called Lady Firbank, doted on his impressionistic prose poems and pastels in prose, of which *The Mauve Tower* is a florid example. But from an early age Firbank also began writing satirical stories about characters like Lady Firbank and her social set. Such early stories as "When Widows Love," "Her Dearest Friend," and "A Tragedy in Green" show Firbank's first, tentative lashes of the whip of satire, at which he would grow murderously proficient in later works. The triviality of Mayfair social life, especially when combined with religiosity, is a subject that Firbank would return to in his later novels, and this early play shows how natural the satirical impulse came to him.

The play has a variety of connections with Firbank's other work of the same period. Lady Seafairer suggests that Stella's marriage to a bishop would allow her the opportunity to erect a cathedral window to herself; this same ambition is shared by Lady Henrietta Worthing in his story "A Study in Opal," written the same year (1907). (Mrs. Creamway's allegedly haunted house in St Catherine-in-the-Marsh is Lady Henrietta's residence as well.) Lord George Blueharnis's name is merely a syllable away from Lady Georgia Blueharnis's in "A Tragedy in Green," another story written about the same time, which also refers to a Jane Seafairer, though it's impossible to tell if this is the Lady Seafairer of the play.

Neither of these plays was published or performed in Firbank's lifetime. Indeed, when he came across them in 1925 amongst his papers, he wrote "Not to be published" on both of them. He did, however, draw upon *A Disciple* for his later works. Mary Magdalene's alleged engagement to John the Baptist is repeated in chapter 13 of *Vainglory*, Firbank's first published novel (1915), in which Lady Georgia Blueharnis reappears. Stella Creamway's ambition to marry a bishop and erect a church window to herself provides the basic plot of the same novel.

In the years after he went down from Cambridge, Firbank continued to attend plays and ballets, both in England and abroad. One of his early novels, the wonderful *Caprice* (1917), treats theater life in London with bemused affection, and that novel even tries out a memorable stage direction later used in his next and final play, *The Princess Zoubaroff*. (In chap. 13 of the novel, a young man is described as having "a voice like cheap scent," used in act 1, scene 11 of the play to describe Reggie Quintus's voice.) *The Princess Zoubaroff* falls into a different category than the two earlier plays, for it was published in Firbank's lifetime (though it wouldn't be performed for decades after) and is usually counted among his mature works. He wrote the play in London in 1919–20 and published it between his fourth and fifth novels (i.e.,

3 "Introduction," *The Early Firbank*, ed. Steven Moore (London: Quartet, 1991), ix.

Valmouth, 1919, and *Santal*, 1921). As with his novels, Firbank constructed the play from lines written in notebooks, and then crossed out as he found a place for them in the work at hand. Two surviving notebooks for *The Princess Zoubaroff* offer many examples of lines not used (nor ascribed to any character):

Humour is a weapon that needs sharpening every day.

In England people are so moral they would arrest the Moon for following the Sun —

Pere Puget used to say I made epigrams even at Confession — They would come!

I'm fairly hardened. Ever since I was a child I was talked about.

One finds her now more often than not on her knees.

Just now she was malicious enough to openly condole.

Poor soul! Soured by six seasons! . . .

You feel like after a dose of chloral, an intense absolute lethargy, that's quite overwhelmingly delicious.

She is too healthy to love with passion.

Reading us a paper on corporeal charm vs. mental fascination.

He's witty and insinuating, your husband I find.

Ah well — I suppose in the end, we shall all be reduced to living on our own estates —

Conceited creature!

His temperament is an enigma.

It's all an enigma.

Horridly artful.

The charmingest man.[4]

The book was published in November 1920 in a small edition of 530 copies, and illustrated with two drawings by Michel Sevier. The reviews, like

4 From the sale catalog of Swann Galleries, New York, Sale Number 1421, December 11, 1986, item no. 249. The two notebooks were formerly in the possession of Miriam Benkovitz; their present whereabouts is unknown.

most of those Firbank received for his novels, were unsympathetic. The *Times Literary Supplement* gave it a brief, lukewarm notice criticizing the lack of dramatic development, the inadequate plot, and Firbank's "curious adventures in spelling." The *Spectator* said, "There is something vaguely unpleasant in its *fin de siècle* attitude," but admitted Firbank had "an extraordinary knack of writing dialogue, and his entirely odious people move and breathe and are completely real."[5] Firbank naturally wanted to see his play staged and the following year discussed this with actress Lillah McCarthy; she expressed interest, but efforts to finance the play failed. He told Sewell Stokes that he sent the play to Charles B. Cochran to read, as well as to "*all* my favourite actresses," but nothing came of his efforts.

When the play finally received its first staging, in June 1951 at the Watergate Theatre in London, it met with a different reception. The *Times* reviewer was delighted with it, finding it "twice as amusing" to watch than to read. The play was also staged in 1952 at the Irving Theatre in London,[6] and in 1975 at the Tower Theatre, Islington. A radio adaptation by Archie Campbell was broadcast on the BBC's Third Programme in 1962, with Dame Edith Evans in the title role. Jonathan Kent, one of the directors of the Almedia Theatre, also in Islington, wanted to produce the play during the 1991 Christmas season, but a financial crisis forced him to shelve the idea.

Reading the play today, it is inconceivable that it could have been staged in Firbank's own day. It is one of his most unapologetically homosexual works, and one can only wonder how even a sophisticated British audience would have reacted to the openly gay and lesbian flirting in some scenes (Reggie with Angelo in act 2, scene 11; the Princess with Enid in act 1, scene 7, and again in act 2, scene 4), or to Reggie dancing at the end of act 2 with a newly published poet named Astix ("a wild young man who looks like the Publishers' Ruin"), or indeed to the ongoing argument for homosexual separatism that develops over the course of the play. The institution of marriage is mocked throughout, motherhood is seen as a calamity (Nadine's pregnancy is likened to the Plague), and in one of his most daring moves, Firbank aligns lesbianism with purity and the religious life, consigning heterosexuality to the profane world.

5 [For summaries of the reviews the play received, see my *Ronald Firbank: An Annotated Bibliography of Secondary Materials* (Dalkey Archive Press, 1996), 7–8. — 2016 note]

6 [Neville Phillips reports "the role of the Princess was played by the always newsworthy, once ravishing now ravaged, oft arrested society blonde lesbian drug addict, Brenda Dean Paul, who, owing to her addiction, was not able to do all the performances, giving the ones she could manage the extra frisson of wondering if the police might burst in at any moment and make an on-stage arrest" (*The Stage Struck Me! A Sort of Memoir* [Leicester: Matador, 2008], 243. — 2016 note.]

The play has such a light, inconsequential air about it that it is not apparent at first how radical a critique of conventional standards this work is. Even Firbank's later critics have steered clear of the play, either ignoring it altogether or dismissing it as a minor, unsuccessful work. Brigid Brophy is, of course, an exception and devotes two dozen brilliant pages to this work.[7] Among other things, she notes that not only does the relationship between Lord Henry Orkish and Reggie Quintus evoke that of Oscar Wilde and Bosie Douglas, but that Reggie is an alter ego for Firbank himself, allowing the play to function as a kind of dream date between Firbank and his martyred master. Firbank reverses Wilde's unhappy fate by showing him happily in exile, a fantasy of how things might have turned out for Wilde had England held the liberal, humane view of homosexuality displayed in *The Princess Zoubaroff*.

7 *Prancing Novelist*, 195–99, 326–34, and 486–99. The only other critic who has discussed the play at length is Parker Tyler; see his essay "The Prince Zoubaroff: Praise of Ronald Firbank, *Prose* 2 (1971): 155–69.

Brigid Brophy: A Brief Introduction

There was a time, in the 1960s and early '70s, when no one needed an introduction to Brigid Brophy. She was one of the most controversial writers in England — occupying a position somewhat like Camille Paglia's today — and here in the States her books were published by the best New York houses and widely reviewed. Now, unfortunately, most of her books are out of print on both sides of the Atlantic and few readers under 40 recognize the name. Some of the reasons for this neglect are understandable: she didn't publish a novel after 1978, and a debilitating struggle with multiple sclerosis over the last 15 years of her life sharply curtailed her writing career. Also, she was cursed for being too far ahead of her time: in her 1953 novel *Hackenfeller's Ape* she was writing about animal rights long before the cause became popular, and in 1969 wrote the definitive novel about gender confusion (*In Transit*) long before there was a critical context for the topic. But any informed reckoning of 20th-century literature must take Brophy's work into account: not only her nine books of fiction, but a career's worth of sharp, intelligent essays (most gathered into three collections), books on Mozart, Freud, and Beardsley, and a 600-page tour de force "defence of fiction in the form of a critical biography of Ronald Firbank," *Prancing Novelist*.

Her literary career began early. Born in 1929, she was reading authors like Firbank at the age of five (as she reports in an excellent interview with Leslie Dock in *Contemporary Literature* [17.2 (Spring 1976): 151–70]) and from age six onwards was writing verse dramas. When she was 15 she wrote an early version of "The Late Afternoon of a Faun," which appeared in her first book, *The Crown Princess and Other Stories*, published in 1953 when she was 24. Later that same year she published her first novel, *Hackenfeller's Ape*, which won the Cheltenham Literary Festival prize for best first novel. Brophy later dismissed *The Crown Princess* as too mainstream — I think it's better than that — but *Hackenfeller's Ape*, as Mark Axelrod shows in his essay,[1] demonstrated her ability at an early stage to integrate a variety of themes and concerns (Mozart, original sin, vivisection) in a form owing as much to music as to literature.

1 [In an issue of the *Review of Contemporary Fiction* partly devoted to Brophy (Fall 1995), where this introduction first appeared.]

(Baroque architecture would become an additional model for her novels.) Mozart and musical (specifically operatic) form dominates many of her early works: her charming second novel, *The King of a Rainy Country* (1956), relies heavily on Mozart's *Le Nozze di Figaro* (as Patricia Juliana Smith notes in her insightful essay in this issue), just as her dazzling fifth novel, *The Snow Ball* (1964), relies on his *Don Giovanni*. (In the same year she published her nonfiction study *Mozart the Dramatist*, widely hailed as one of the best books on his operas, and recently reprinted both in Britain and the U.S.)

Brophy's third novel, *Flesh* (1962), is an unusual novel about the effect of marriage on an awkward, unsociable man that plays against the Pygmalion theme. Dedicated to Iris Murdoch, this story of north London Jews was her first popular success. It was followed by her fourth and most elliptical book of fiction, *The Finishing Touch* (1963), a wickedly clever novella — half Firbank, half Colette — about a lesbian-run girls' finishing school on the French Riviera. Corinne E. Blackmer explores its literary heritage in detail in this issue and correctly praises it as "an important milestone in the history of lesbian and, more broadly, antihomophobic literature."

Brophy was in her element in the iconoclastic Sixties. She became notorious for her views on vegetarianism, sexual freedom, animal rights, writers' rights (she played a major role in Britain's current Public Lending Right, by which authors are paid a royalty whenever their books are checked out of libraries), women's rights, pornography (pro), and educational reform (contra religion in school, pro Greek), promoting her views on television and radio as well as in print. The same year she published *Flesh* she published a long nonfiction work entitled *Black Ship to Hell* (1962), a rigorous Freudian reading of the dynamics of hate, compared by the *London Telegraph* to Norman O. Brown's *Life against Death*. The best of her essays and reviews were published in book form in 1966 under the title *Don't Never Forget*, and have lost none of their bite, wit, and lightly worn erudition 30 years later. With her husband Michael Levey and friend Charles Osborne she collaborated on the cheeky *Fifty Works of English and American Literature We Could Do Without* (1967), and the following year she wrote the first of two books on the 1890s artist Aubrey Beardsley. Also in 1968 she published a book version of her 1967 play, *The Burglar*, with a long, Shavian introduction. (She has written other, unproduced, plays.)

The decade came to an explosive climax in 1969 with her masterpiece, *In Transit*. Several essays here deal with this extraordinary novel, and several more would be needed to encompass its achievement. As the ambiguously named narrator sits in an international airport waiting for a connecting flight, he/she suffers a kind of gender amnesia and goes through a series of comic attempts to discover his/her sex. The novel is a riot of multilingual puns, parodies, opera allusions, typographical high jinks (one thinks of roughly contemporary books like William H. Gass's *Willie Masters' Lonesome Wife* and Christine Brooke-Rose's *Thru*), and should be a *locus classicus* for today's gender critics and advocates of experimental fiction.

The next few years were spent researching and writing her massive book on Firbank, which was met largely by uncomprehending reviews, most questioning the wisdom of using Firbank, of all people, on whom to erect a theory of creative fiction. Once again, Brophy was years ahead of the pack, for only now in the '90s is Firbank becoming recognized for the subversively innovative writer he is. In 1973 she also published her second collection of short fiction, *The Adventures of God in His Search for the Black Girl*; it's a lively if somewhat miscellaneous collection, some of the pieces a mere page, the title fable novella-length. Then in 1978 she published her final novel, *Palace without Chairs*, an oddly muted fairy tale set in an imaginary Eastern European socialist monarchy, somewhat in the vein of Firbank's *Flower beneath the Foot*. After that, Brophy wrote very little; two collections of her essays were published in the 1980s — *Baroque-'n'-Roll* (1987) and *Reads* (1989) — supplementing (and in some cases reprinting) those in her 1966 collection *Don't Never Forget*. She died on 7 August 1995, a few weeks before this issue went to press.

The neglect of this brilliant woman's work and contributions to contemporary aesthetics is scandalous, and I hope the essays in this issue begin a long-running critical engagement with her body of work. In the afterword to *Reads*, Brophy says she took the title of her first essay collection from Mozart's attempt at English in a friend's album — "Don't never forget your faithfull friend" — because "I consider it vital that human beings never should forget Mozart." Those human beings who study contemporary literature never should forget Brophy.

The Stylish Fiction of W. M. Spackman

> Virtuosity and style were for him the chief merits of literature.
>
> —Osbert Sitwell on Ronald Firbank

Many novelists get off to a late start, or wait years before receiving proper critical attention, but few can match W. M. Spackman in this regard. His first novel wasn't published until he was nearly 50, his second not until he was over 70. But that second novel, *An Armful of Warm Girl*, won widespread critical acclaim, and for the next half-dozen years Spackman published a novel nearly every other year, a burst of creativity unusual at any age, but all the more so for a gentleman in his seventies. And what novels they were: stylish comedies of manners, audacious arguments for adultery, by turns cheeky and charming, haughty and haunting, and impeccably executed. A few years later he was dead, and those delicious novels out of print. But the man deserves to be remembered and (more importantly) the work preserved, hence this omnibus edition of all his fiction.

William Mode Spackman was born 20 May 1905 in Coatesville, Pennsylvania. His Quaker ancestors had lived in Pennsylvania since the beginning of the 18th century, and Spackman himself prepped at the 200-year-old Friends School in Wilmington, Delaware. (His family moved to Wilmington the year after he was born; his parents owned a large hardware store with a substantial steel operation.) Quaker traditions and practices run through his novels, even their use of *thee* and *thou*. More important than his Quaker background, however, is his Princeton background, which is so pervasive in these novels that this book should be bound in orange and black, the school colors. Under the influence of F. Scott Fitzgerald's *This Side of Paradise*, Spackman was matriculated in the Class of 1927, the same as that of the protagonists of his first novel, *Heyday*; in fact nearly all the male characters in his novels are Princetonians. His writing career began when he was an undergraduate: a brand-new magazine called the *New Yorker* published several of his poems during its first year. In his sophomore year Spackman was chairman of the *Nassau Lit*, and caused something of a scandal by publishing his "Sketches from a Madhouse" there, a piece he later described as "straight Aldous Huxley" (but which, as juvenilia, is not included in the present collection). Spackman graduated from Princeton with honors in French and Italian literatures, and as a Rhodes Scholar (1927–30) took a second Bachelor's degree at Balliol College, Oxford, where he read "Greats" (Greek philosophy and ancient Greek and Roman history, though his best final exam paper was on classical Greek prose). Just before his last year at Oxford, Spackman married Mary Ann Matthews, to whom *Heyday* is dedicated, from a family even older than his (her first ancestor in America was one of Cromwell's lieutenants).

Returning to the States at the beginning of the Depression — he lost a small fortune in the stock market crash of 1929 — he taught Classics for a year at New York University, then returned to Princeton in 1933 to do graduate work. He spent the rest of the Thirties working as a copy-writer and account executive for various public relations agencies in New York City (he was a Rockefeller Fellow in opinion research 1940–41); often this required work in radio, and Spackman won three national awards for educational radio programs in the OSU annual judgings. During much of World War II he was director of the Office of Public Information at the University of Colorado in Boulder, where he had gone largely for his wife's health. Toward the end of the war he studied Russian at the Navy Language School there and became an agent for the U.S. Navy. In 1945 he became assistant professor of Classics at the University of Colorado, and it was during a sabbatical in France in the fall of 1949 that he wrote his first novel; after *Heyday* was published in 1953, he resigned and returned to Princeton to devote himself full-time to writing (and part-time to architecture; over the years Spackman designed and built two Queen Anne houses for himself and his family, even the rough carpentry and paneling, and later remodeled a modern-style house as well as a large seaside villa in France). Quitting teaching seems to have been an easy decision given his immense frustration and exasperation with how literature was being taught at the time.[1]

Spackman's next two books wouldn't appear until 1967. The first, *Twenty-five Years of It*, is a slim book of poetry, a limited edition — six hardbacks, 250 paperbacks — privately published in France. (He was spending six months a year living in Perros-Guirec at the time, which is given as the place of publication.) It's a gathering of verse dating back to his undergraduate days — some first appeared in the *Nassau Lit* and Oxford's *Cherwell*, and had been anthologized in *Princeton Verse between Two Wars* and in Blackwell's Oxford Poetry series — mostly of a traditional sort, some with Latin titles (and apparently

1 See his blistering indictments "The Menace to Curriculum Reform," *Classical Journal* 44.5 (February 1949): 293–97, "Topic Sentences and "The Learned No" in his *On the Decay of Humanism* (Rutgers University Press, 1967), and "Literature as Literature, and Why," *Cultural Affairs* 3 (1968): 5–9, published under the pseudonym Alexander Neave (see n10 below).

based on Latin models). The poems more closely resemble those of Ovid or Catullus than any 20th-century poets, except for a Marianne Moore-like poem about a tortoise. The longest poem in the book is a take-off on Byron's *Don Juan*, written in the same ottava rima form and good-naturedly addressing what Spackman believes are the shortcomings of Byron's comic epic. Entitled "Proem to an Unwritten Epic," it doubles as a proem to his fiction of the next two decades, the central thrust of which could be described as a modernization of the Don Juan theme:

> . . . a century plus has passed since Byron
> Dispatched that earlier Juan to the press.
> Our literary needs have changed — require an
> Array of symbols, far less fancy dress,
> A modern bitch instead of gothick siren,
> A hero with a haircut . . .
>
> . . . .
>
> However. Here's the issue as I find it: —
> Byron would make you think the mischief's done
> By lovers half tongue-tied and seven-eighths blinded;
> Neither of them, you'd swear, is having fun;
> The lady, if not downright absent-minded,
> Never seems conscious quite what's going on
> (In fact the situation's so abused
> I'm never sure she knows she's being seduced).
>
> And since such rapturous stuff'll hardly go down
> With anyone who's ever lived the part,
> What I propose is the plain modern low-down
> On what does happen in her pretty heart
> When passions rev up and refusals slow down.
> Half way through Canto One (a flying start
> And you'll be through before it's time for dinner)
> My little saint turns every inch a sinner.

Spackman here could be describing *An Armful of Warm Girl*, which he had completed some years earlier. If nothing else, his poetry pays tribute to the writers with whom Spackman had the greatest affinity: the classical love poets — Catullus, Propertius, but above all Ovid (especially the *Amores* and *Ars amatoria*) — Renaissance and Cavalier poets like Wyatt (or Wiat, as he preferred to spell it), Donne, and Herrick, and finally (despite his misgivings) the author of *Don Juan*. (Byron's poem is also parodied in part 3 of *A Presence with Secrets* [290].)

The other book Spackman published in 1967, *On the Decay of Humanism*, is a dazzling collection of essays treating more recent literature (though two are on the classical era) and the inadequate way such literature is taught.

Like Harold Bloom more recently, Spackman castigates those who exploit literature for its psycho-sociopolitical content at the expense of its artistry, its technique. In the first essay, "Topic Sentences," he writes: "In our time, from various accidents of fashion and personality, the basic disagreement — for everyone but the narrowest of philosophers — is whether literature is something a writer writes or the synthesis of signs the establishment tends to deal in instead." Rather than explore the former, academics prefer the latter, which he likens to "a roll in the catnip of semantics." In words as applicable to today's literary theoreticians as to those of the Sixties, Spackman warns: "the more articulate your professor, the likelier he is to deal with a work of art less in its own terms than as a mere starting point for whatever he has thought up to say instead." This point is reiterated in his long essay on Henry James, whose defects as a writer, he feels, have gone unnoticed by critics because "a professor of literature is not so much trained to *look* at what he is reading as to find things to say about it."

Focusing himself on what a writer actually writes, Spackman offers numerous iconoclastic readings of canonized writers, displaying an Olympian self-confidence (which some reviewers found hubristic) and an enviably encyclopedic range of background, everything from Homer (in Greek, of course) to Raymond Queneau's *Zazie dans la métro*. Those whom he weighs in the balances and finds wanting include Socrates, Aristotle ("a marine biologist," he reminds us), Wordsworth, James, and Ford Madox Ford. In contrast, he finds much to admire in less-celebrated writers like Benjamin Constant, Ivy Compton-Burnett, Henry Green (a recurring touchstone for disciplined, artful prose), and Edmund Wilson's fiction. This isn't an indulgence in studied iconoclasm; in passing Spackman expresses great admiration for such canonized authors as Ovid, Stendhal, Proust, Joyce, Pound (especially as a translator), Auden, Faulkner, and Beckett. It is a brilliant, provocative book and deserves to be reprinted someday, perhaps augmented by the essays and book reviews Spackman continued to write (especially for *Parnassus*) in the Seventies and early Eighties.

At an early point in the book Spackman notes "the typical first novel . . . tends to be naturally gloomy and emotionally out of balance / *Sto sospirando o lagrimando vado* / and so forth,"[2] but "second novels are noticeably different *if* the writer is artist enough to see that every new book calls for a new form, and perhaps style, as much as for a new topic." Spackman probably had himself in mind, for this accurately describes the difference between *Heyday* and *An Armful of Warm Girl*, which he had "just finished" according

2 ["I am sighing and I walk weeping," which "may be an echo of Petrarch," Massimo Bacigalupo tells me. — 2016 note.]

to the jacket of *On the Decay of Humanism*. (Incidentally, in the latter Spackman tries out the title of his second novel: "We read Vergil for other things entirely, putting up with his aesthete's character-drawing by the same convention that lets us accept, say, a travertine Galatea as representing an armful of warm girl.") Actually, he had finished a first draft of the novel in 1955; the book made the rounds without any luck, then was submitted to Stanley Kauffmann at Knopf in 1959, who liked the book and suggested revisions, which Spackman made, only to have the book rejected again. It was shopped around elsewhere during the Sixties — Spackman later said it was rejected by 15 publishers — but with no takers. It was resubmitted to Knopf in the early Seventies, but he was told that the advent of the feminist movement made his novel unpublishable at that time. It wouldn't see print until the summer of 1977, when the editors of *Canto*, a new literary magazine, decided to publish the novel as the complete contents of their second issue. It was spotted by Gordon Lish, then fiction editor at *Esquire*, and recommended to Knopf once more; this time they accepted it and offset the *Canto* text for book publication in the spring of 1978. (In the process, a line on the bottom of its page 79 was accidentally dropped, which has been restored here.) The novel enjoyed enough critical acclaim that Knopf became his regular publisher: *A Presence with Secrets*, which Spackman had written in 1971–73 but which likewise failed to find a publisher at the time, followed in October 1980, *A Difference of Design* in June 1983, and *A Little Decorum, for Once* in October 1985. The novels were favorably reviewed for the most part, but like most innovative fiction, they didn't sell particularly well.

A heart attack in 1975 caused Spackman to abandon his plan to settle permanently in France. The failing health and eventual death of his first wife in 1978, the year *An Armful of Warm Girl* was published, was another tragedy that altered his life. He later moved in with his second wife, the Laurice to whom the later novels are dedicated, and continued to spend most of his time writing.

The remaining works in this omnibus date from the last five years of Spackman's life. The brief "Dialogue at the End of a Pursuit" was first published under the title "After Glow: A Dialogue" in *Town & Country*, October 1985. To make it suitable for publication there, Spackman had to rewrite a few lines and change the opening stage directions to the following: "SCENE: The appointed place. TIME: Now and then. PERSONAE: Corinna and Ovid." The version published here, including its original title and dedication, is taken from Spackman's typescript.

"Declarations of Intent" was first published in the autumn of 1987 issue of *Southwest Review*. The same journal also published a short story entitled "As I Sauntered Out, One Mid-Century Morning . . ." in its spring 1989 issue, adapted from chapter 2 of the short novel of the same name published here for the first time. The novel was sent to Spackman's editor at Knopf, Alice Quinn, for book publication; she visited him once in Princeton to work on it, but his illness during his final years, along with Quinn's move from Knopf to the *New Yorker*, left the work unpublished. The manuscript has numerous corrections in Spackman's hand, as well as an errata page, so it seems to be in finished form. (There is an awkward leap at the beginning of chapter 2 from the early 1950s to the mid 1960s that still needed to be finessed.) A few superior readings from the *Southwest Review* chapter have been adopted (under the assumption Spackman would have made these changes for the book version as well), and what looks like an unintentionally duplicated passage dropped; otherwise, aside from routine copyediting, the novel appears here just as he left it.

Just as some of his novels were dropping out of print in this country, they started to attract attention abroad. A German translation of *An Armful of Warm Girl* had appeared in 1981 (as *Die Unschuld der Fünfziger*, claasen Verlag), and a French translation of *A Presence with Secrets* was published by Quai Voltaire under the title *L'Ombre d'une présence* in the autumn of 1987. In 1988 the French magazine *Le Promeneur* published a translation of the unexpurgated version of "Dialogue at the End of a Pursuit," and the following year Quai Voltaire published a translation of *An Armful of Warm Girl* under the title *L'Embrassée*. (This novel came out after *A Presence* because Spackman was unhappy with the initial translation and felt it needed work. Even the title proved troublesome; Spackman told a correspondent at the time that the title *Un Brassée de fille épanouie* "has been suggested, but it's up to the publishers. I myself find that *épanouie* lovely, but the ambiguities of the French word for 'girl' aren't something a foreigner should deal with.") Both French novels were translated by Bernard Turle and were well received by the French press.

W. M. Spackman died 3 August 1990, in his beloved Princeton, of complications of prostate cancer.[3]

3 My sources for this brief biography are (1) the author's note in the first edition of *Heyday*; (2) the entry on Spackman in *Contemporary Authors* vols. 84–88 (based on information he supplied); (3) correspondence with Harriet Spackman Newell, the author's daughter; (4) brief interviews with Spackman that accompanied a few of the reviews of his books; and (5) Maurice B. Cloud's "A Conversation with W. M. Spackman," *High Plains Literary Review* 4.1 (Spring 1989): 51–63. This informative interview is followed by Cloud's appreciative essay "How Watchful of His Muse . . . : In Praise of W. M. Spackman" (64–69). The only other critical essays published on Spackman to date are Sallie Bingham's "Maenads and Satyrs: Some Thoughts on W. M. Spackman's Novels," *American Voice* 2 (Spring 1986): 30–37, and John Whitehead's "An American Arcadia: The Novels of W. M. Spackman," *Contemporary Review* 265 (October 1994): 206–11.

Spackman's first novel, *Heyday*, was published in 1953 by Ballantine Books as an early experiment in a "split" edition, whereby a book is published simultaneously in hardcover and paperback formats. In a lengthy author's note at the end of the book, Spackman described the novel as follows:

> *Heyday* is among other things an elegy upon the immemorial loneliness of man; a statement too about its causes (varied) and customary cure (someone charming to hold one's hand); though these things are of course said about a particular group at a particular time, viz. the young American upper class in that era of its disaster, the 1930's. *Heyday* is thus also the spiritual biography of a generation hardly anyone has written up, the generation of a decade after Scott Fitzgerald's (his story *Babylon Revisited*, for instance, is about the Class of 1917 very much as *Heyday* is about the Class of 1927). *Heyday* is incidentally too, then, a statement about American values, for the Class of 1927 was perhaps the last generation brought up in those traditions of moral competence and severe pride in the individual which progressive education and the welfare state have nearly stamped out by now forever.

To those who know only the later novels, this statement strikes an uncharacteristically somber note, and indeed *Heyday* is the most "serious" novel Spackman ever wrote. (It could hardly be otherwise, dealing as it does with the corrosive effect of the Depression on his generation.) One reviewer described that statement as "Pretty large claims for this nostalgic and single-minded chronicle of Greenwich Village sex-capades, featuring nubile ivy-leaguers whose hearts belonged to Eighth Street even during sidetrips to Paris, France, and Coatesville, Pa. Regrettably, therefore, one must judge *Heyday* by how close it comes to the author's elaborate intentions, which is not very." The reviewer (James Kelly in the *Saturday Review*) went on to remark: "If Max Bodenheim, Scott Fitzgerald, and Ezra Pound had at one time pooled their forces (shocking thought) to write a definitive Depression Novel, the chances are it would have turned out something like this parodiable amalgam of classical allusions, large social observations, and explicit sexual vignettes. As a one-man tour de force, *Heyday* is remarkable." Other reviewers had similar mixed feelings, and though the novel was published in England by Frederick Muller in 1954 (with many of the racier sexual vignettes censored out), the novel soon went out of print and was never reprinted in Spackman's lifetime.

The text of *Heyday* printed here is the revised version that Spackman was working on at the time of his death. The original version consisted of three parts: parts 1 and 3, largely about narrator Webb Fletcher, were set in the novel's present (1942) and provided a frame for the longer part 2, largely about his distant cousin Malachi (Mike) Fletcher, and set in the early 1930s. The frame was intended to give formal elegance to Webb Fletcher's narration, "enclosing within my fate your fate; the action of your tragedy exhibited within the symbolic border of its contrasting counterpart" (206). Part 1 indicated that

Webb, like Spackman, was born in 1905 and was a member of Princeton's Class of '27, and that the novel was intended as a kind of book-length obituary for the *Princeton Alumni Weekly*, which Webb thinks might be called "Obituary with Female Figures." Not satisfied with the original, Spackman dropped the first and third parts, made numerous cuts in part 2, switched the order of a few chapters, and made an occasional word substitution or added a transitional phrase. In the surviving manuscript (a photocopy of part 2 of the Ballantine edition, worked over in pencil), he also indicated eight places where new material was to be inserted. These inserts were either never written or became separated from the manuscript and lost. Consequently, those places are indicated in the present text with bracketed ellipses. Although the rest of the manuscript shows considerable evidence of work, it is impossible to tell whether it represents his final wishes (save for the missing inserts). However, the Spackman Estate and I agreed that, even in its not-quite finished form, this is the one that should represent his first novel in this collected edition.

In its revised form, the novel shifts the focus away from what Spackman called (in the original author's note) the causes of "the immemorial loneliness of man" to their "customary cure," exchanging the mask of tragedy for that of comedy, or at least tragicomedy. Love in all its phases, from flirting to adultery, is the central theme here, as it would be in all of Spackman's fiction. Webb Fletcher remains the narrator, but in a greatly reduced role, though the novel is still, in essence, Webb's monologue to Stephanie Lowndesden, the woman he loves and loses. The debilitating effect of the Depression remains, especially in the near-hysteria that keeps the female characters on edge throughout, but the tone is a bit lighter than the earlier version. Although Mike's trip with Kitty to a Quaker graveyard remains, the novel's tone is softened from funereal to valedictory. The feelings of jealousy and betrayal felt by some characters are retained in full animal force, feelings that will be all but absent in the Arcadian affairs that follow. While he cut many of the philosophical meditations of the original edition, Spackman retained the precious, fluttering adjectives (*angelic, blissful,* etc.) that he would continue to use to describe women, and his fine ear for the variations in female voices — displayed here in Kitty's offbeat emphases, Stephanie's lan-guor-ous drawl, Jill's childlike prattle — would only get better. The revised version is more compatible with the later novels than the original is, but finally *Heyday* belongs to a different world, aesthetically and historically, and it will probably always strike most readers as a prelude to (rather than a part of) his true oeuvre.

From the vantage point of today, the 1950s may likewise seem a different world, but there is a world of difference between the tone of Spackman's first novel and that of his second, set in June 1959. The first paragraph of *Heyday* sounds like something Fitzgerald or O'Hara could have written, but I can't think of any other writer who could have written the outrageous opening of *An Armful of Warm Girl*. (The closest thing to it is the opening paragraph of *The Catcher in the Rye*, which in fact Spackman may be parodying.) At first the haughty arrogance is like a slap in the face, but soon enough the reader understands why Nicholas Romney is so damned irked and thus why the narrative tone is appropriate. The reader is addressed as though he were a Princeton crony of similar age and temperament, a disarming tactic deployed to win the reader's tolerance, even affection, for this bellowing rake. As quickly as the second page, though, a second mode is introduced — the pastoral — as Nicholas broods on his now-forsaken Pennsylvania property. Presiding over this novel is Thalia, muse of comedy and bucolic poetry (but in a Coco Chanel dress rather than her usual shepherdess garb). This mode will find its purest expression in the four choral interludes featuring Nicholas's daughter Melissa and her friend that occur at regular intervals, enchanting dialogues that read like Theocritus as translated by Ronald Firbank. ("Hours long, a soft gabble, musing, as in Arcadia, choral turn and turn"). There is even a dash of Restoration comedy here — Spackman greatly admired Congreve's *The Way of the World* — both in the novel's deliberately artificial diction ("Yes; who in love with; oh hideous!") and in its bedroom-farce plotting.

It's easy enough to sit back and enjoy the novel as though it were a Fred Astaire musical — indeed, that approach is more advisable than a politically correct one of how people should be represented in fiction, otherwise Spackman will seem the very Antichrist of sexism and elitism — but closer attention reveals some rather unexpected elements. For a novel in which everyone is committing (or contemplating) adultery with everybody else, it is surprising to note how often the concept of responsibility is raised. In fact the word appears over 50 times (in one form or another) within the short novel, and is applied to virtually every character. In love begins responsibility as far as Spackman is concerned: responsibility to the loved one, to oneself, to family. In Spackman's view, adultery is a *civilized* activity, and like any civilized activity presupposes manners, thoughtfulness, education, certain standards of behavior, and so on. In a word, responsibility.

Even more surprising are the darker elements of the novel. Spackman's world may seem like a kind of Arcadia, but *et in Arcadia ego*. Death stalks these pages, with classmates of Nicholas's dropping dead right and left. Though Nicholas is still hale and hearty at 50, these deaths add a certain poignancy to the novel, and encourages the *carpe diem* motivation that drives him and the other characters to live life to the fullest. But most troubling are the hints of incest; the possibility is often raised that Morgan, the young actress who is pursuing Nicholas with such passion, may be his illegitimate daughter, but he also has an almost unhealthy regard for his legitimate daughter Melissa. (In addition, there is a suggestion on page 166 that Nicholas's son may be pursuing a woman that his father once had an affair with.) The suspicion of incest is never verified, but it is flirted with often enough to give the novel an unsettling tone, less like Fred Astaire's *Top Hat* than de Sade's *La Philosophie dans le boudoir.*

But these are passing clouds in the novel's otherwise blue sky. The style especially is a delight: a heady cocktail of Edwardian elegance, colloquial breeziness, and Mayfair slang ("Sweetie, champaginny and all, well how *coo*"). Latin quotations dance cheek-to-cheek with risqué nightclub lyrics, traditional syntax is unbuttoned, and several species of rather outlandish female dialogue are heard, ranging from Melissa's gushiness to Morgan's theatricality to Mrs. Barclay's "femalizing." It could all be criticized as cloying if that isn't exactly what Spackman is after: at one point Nicholas insists that he "wanted a sweet dessert to be really and *elaborately* sweet, no nonsense about de-cloying it" (160), which explains the excesses of Spackman's style. *An Armful of Warm Girl* is Spackman's most entertaining novel, if not his best; that distinction would go to his next one, *A Presence with Secrets*.

Nicholas Romney confesses to "a lifetime's delight in the mere look, the mere tournure, of women, in the posed and lovely portraits they always somehow made him half-think they were" (160) — and in fact at one point refers to his namesake George Romney, the British portrait painter. Spackman pursues this conceit even further in *A Presence with Secrets*, whose protagonist is an award-winning painter named Hugh Tatnall, and whose story involves a veritable portrait gallery of delectable women. (Tatnall was based to some extent on a Princeton classmate named Alfred Young Fisher, a poet who taught at Smith, one of whose undergraduate poems is quoted at the end of *On the Decay of Humanism. An Armful of Warm Girl* is dedicated to him.) Like several of Spackman's novels, *A Presence with Secrets* has a three-part structure: in keeping with the protagonist's vocation, the novel is intended to be a triptych, three portraits of Tatnall from three different perspectives. Part 1 takes place in Florence, Italy, in the spring, when Hugh is 36, and is narrated from his point of view (though in third person); part 2 takes place in Brittany in the summer, perhaps a few years later, and is narrated by a nameless female cousin of Hugh's; part 3 takes place a month after Hugh's death, a decade or so after parts 1 and 2, and is narrated by a friend of his named Simon Shipley, who reviews their mutual careers as "marauders" at Hugh's funeral service.[4]

4 As Spackman explained to interviewer Keith Fleming, the book had a complicated composition history: "I wrote the last part first, as a separate novel; then rewrote it so often I began

Together, the three views create a rounded but deliberately incomplete portrait of a typical Spackman libertine, but in a tone that leans more toward tragedy than farce, closer to Mozart's *Don Giovanni* than to Byron's *Don Juan*.

The portrait is incomplete because Hugh Tatnall — like any human being — is at most a presence with secrets, never capable of being completely understood by another person. Each part of the novel dramatizes this in a different way: in part 1, Hugh wonders what to make of the young woman delivered to his bed by (he fancies) a benevolent Bona Dea, at the same time brooding on his year-long adulterous liaison with Alexandra Fonteviot. Solicitous of each woman, he realizes he knows neither in any real sense. In part 2 Tatnall's cousin has one assumption after another overturned, surprised at Hugh (whom she has known since age nine), at her host's behavior, at the Gaullist assassins (whom she took for Breton separatists), and even at herself. An in part 3, while playing Leporello by cataloguing Tatnall's many conquests, Shipley recounts coming across a drawerful of Tatnall's mementos that upsets everything *he* thought he knew about his lifelong friend. Shipley also emphasizes how misleading biography can be when trying to make sense of an artist's work; wondering "whether the painter and the libertine were two aspects or components of a creative unity" (281), he provides a good deal of data to support such an argument, but finally retreats from any final judgment. For that reason, he burns the contents of the drawer, apparently deciding that Tatnall's work will have to be judged on its own merits, and that the man behind the work should remain a secret.

The prose is especially lush. Appropriately, there are frequent "painterly" descriptions — of rooms, landscapes — that demonstrate an artist's eye for color and light. The novel shares *Heyday's* valedictory tone, but is less ponderous, bittersweet rather than gloomy. A few of the recounted affairs are somewhat comic, but most are sweetly sad or — in the story of Hildegarde on pages 316–23 — utterly heartbreaking. The novel is technically interesting for its experiments in non-linear narration: both parts 1 and 3 advance by retreating, with the narrative present continually interrupted by flashbacks that nevertheless carry the narrative forward. The rich prose, the aesthetically satisfying structure, and the parade of Spackman dreamgirls make *A Presence with Secrets* his finest achievement.

to detest it *and* its style; so I threw out everything I could no longer stand looking at — and there was the present novella. Then I used my painter character as protagonist for two other novella ideas I had, adapting him as I went along — *et voila*, I'd cobbled a novel together. I did the first story next, starting out stylistically as if I were doing a pastiche of Henry Green; then the middle story last" (*Chicago Literary Review*, 13 March 1981, 7). Some minor revisions were made for the Dutton Obelisk edition (1982).

The idea of redoing *The Ambassadors* occurred to Spackman in 1973, but his dissatisfaction with Henry James's novel was longstanding. In a highly critical essay in *On the Decay of Humanism* entitled "James, James," Spackman agreed with F. R. Leavis that in *The Ambassadors*

> I cannot find anything to admire at all. Women perhaps find it more readable than men do. One trouble, technically, is that male characters, which are never what James did best, take up so much of the wordage. In particular, the Jamesian-male shilly-shally of Strether is excessive, and the endless bleating of Bilham is really not to be borne at all. Again, the love affair which James's plan puts at the center of his action is both a sensory and a narrative blank: there is not even enough physical presence bestowed on Mme. de Vionnet to suggest that she had ever been in anybody's bedroom. The choral commentary of Bilham (with hemichoria by Maria Gostrey) is as crude as it is wearisome, mere third-person narration disguised as dialogue: nowhere is Mr. [Edmund] Wilson's cruel phrase "the fumes of Jamesian gas" more just or more apropos. One is even exasperated by opportunities programmatically thrown away — Miss Gostrey starts off beautifully only to fade into a mere annotation upon the action, yet how could anyone overlook the sheer comedy of making her the American parallel of Mme. de Vionnet and seduce Strether? And so on. The ladies can have it.

Many years later, reviewing a public-television film version of *The Ambassadors*, Spackman said rather cattily, "If the new BBC production is more of a success than [the original], then the sometimes headlong condensation of James's 165,000 words into a 90-minute script is certainly in part why."[5] Spackman's 90-page novel *A Difference of Design* is not so much a condensation of *The Ambassadors* as a makeover. Set in 1983, Spackman's novel uses James's cast of characters, with slightly different names — James's Lewis Lambert Strether is called Lewis Lambert Sather, Maria Gostrey is Maria Godfrey, Chad Newsome is Chad Newman (probably taken from James's 1877 novel about another American in Paris) — and differs from *The Ambassadors* largely, as the title announces, in design. Instead of a linear narrative consistently rendered from the point of view of the male protagonist (which Spackman considered wrong-headed), *A Difference of Design* is broken up into three achronological sections that focus on the women: the first and third are narrated in the first-person by Fabienne, Comtesse de Borde-Cessac (playing Madame du Vionnet's role), and record her *coup de foudre* with regard to Sather, while the second section, like *The Ambassadors*, is in third-person but from Sather's point of view and deals with his affair with Maria. "How could anyone overlook the sheer comedy of making her the American parallel of Mme. de Vionnet and seduce Strether?" Spackman had asked in his James

5 "H.J., O.M. (TV)," *New England Review* 4.1 (Autumn 1981): 95.

essay, and that is what he set out to do here, though it's an open question who seduces whom in Spackman's version. James used a linear form to track Strether's growing awareness of the limitations of New England life in light of cosmopolitan Paris, affording him a "glimpse of a possible 'civilization' in which the manners belonging to a ripe social intercourse shall be the index of a moral refinement." Spackman's Sather already belongs to that "civilization" and merely comes to a realization that a more comfortable life can be lived in Paris than what he is used to in America, especially with the added attraction of two lovely women head over heels about him.

Another difference in design is signaled by the numerous references to French writers: Spackman's is a *roman libertin* rather than an American bildungsroman, closer to a Marivaux comedy than to a James novel. Spackman was deeply read in French literature, and *A Difference in Design* is studded with references to his reading: obscure writers like Marivaux, Pellerin, and Fontenelle are quoted (usually in French), as are better-known writers like Corneille, Giraudoux, Constant, Musset, Rostand, Choderlos de Laclos, and the Comtesse de Lafayette. There's even a parody of the *nouveau roman* (397–98), specifically of Michel Butor's *Second Thoughts* (*La Modification*, 1957). Throughout there is an emphasis on *les bienséances*, which is a French principle of literary decorum as well as manners, but which still allows a traditionally French form of farce to develop as the characters juggle lovers. In this regard, *A Difference of Design* is as much an homage to French literature as a makeover of *The Ambassadors*.

Reviewing Laurie Colwin's novel *Happy All the Time* in 1978, Spackman described the structure as "simple and amusing, a mock-formal three-part composition of six couples in a kaleidoscope of the patterns and stylistics of the urban love-affair, the two principal sets of lovers serving as story-line, the other four pairs (all with splendidly various eccentricities) rushing in and out as chorus, running commentary, and the ironies of antithesis in general." He goes on to say, "Good manners, as it happens, are also the novel's ambience — the title in fact might better have been *A Little Propriety For Once*."[6] Spackman's fifth novel, *A Little Decorum, for Once*, has a cast list similar to Colwin's — one principal couple, three other pairs — and could likewise be described as "a kaleidoscope of the patterns and stylistics of the urban love-affair." But it is not only a far greater achievement than Colwin's relatively lightweight one, it is also his most self-conscious novel, his most metafictional. Every major character is a writer of some sort, and literary discussions pop up on nearly

6 "Undeath of the Novel," *Canto* 2.4 (Winter 1978–79): 152, 153. This is a useful essay because it has more to do with Spackman's aesthetics than with Colwin's novel.

every page. The principal male protagonist, Scrope Townshend, is clearly a stand-in for Spackman himself (though a decade younger than Spackman was at the time) and the novel functions as both a demonstration and defense of Spackman's style of writing.

Reminiscent of *An Armful of Warm Girl* in some ways, the novel is Spackman's most audacious justification yet of adultery: introduced in the very first paragraph, adultery is defined by Scrope as "Woman's happiest birthright and perquisite" (425) and is defended by him (with help from Ovid) as a means of preserving family values:

> Look, if all that our piety-simple writs and prescripts about adultery produced was a divorce rate ten times the civilized average abroad, perhaps we should explore the hypothesis that it was an unsung blessing! Binas habeatis amicas, said Ovid — have two loves, and you're a slave to neither. Well, but he himself meant to turn Ovid round — with two loves you grow *tired* of neither, and, as things go between men and women, you therefore stay married. And the social structure preserves its stable decencies. So, as a natural bonus . . . as a cultural bonus, the *family* is preserved. (463–64)

Later, another character is reported to have argued adultery "was a branch of civilized deportment you had to *acquire* the traditions of, being unfaithful wasn't just something you did by light of nature, as between consenting illiterates, you had to read up on it, and would he joke if he thought?" (495). As much as these arguments are calculated to outrage, Spackman in fact offers a delightful novel (an entire oeuvre, actually) where one can indeed "read up on it." Scrope is upset at first to learn that his daughter Sibylla may be having an affair, but by the end of the novel realizes this is all for the best, just as his various adulteries with Laura Tench-Fenton over the years have deepened their love for each other.[7] By treating this theme comically, Spackman is of course going against the grain of traditional treatments of adultery in literature; in American fiction in particular, from Nathaniel Hawthorne's *Scarlet Letter* to Alexander Theroux's *An Adultery*, adultery is a grim and corrosive business, withering the souls of all involved. Spackman takes a continental approach, exemplified by Ovid and by his beloved French writers, to argue that adultery is a blessing, not a curse, of civilization. Again like Firbank (whose works seem frivolous but contain devastating critiques of Edwardian mores), the airy

7 Mrs. Tench-Fenton is based somewhat on Spackman's image of Nancy Tuck Gardiner, the editor at *Town & Country* with whom he worked (though he never met her), and who (Mrs. Newell tells me) "flattered him outrageously by sending him flowers, and notes such as this one in which she wrote: 'My dear Mr. Spackman — What a joy to hear your voice! As ever, mischievous and merry. . . . With apologies to your friend, Mr. James, it's not 'summer afternoon' which I find the two most beautiful words in the English language, . . . but a secretarial shout, 'William Spackman' is on the phone."

inconsequentiality of the medium makes the message all the more shocking.

When not defending his case for adultery, Scrope defends his manner of writing, which violates conventional style just as adultery does conventional morality. Spackman's novels were favorably reviewed, by and large, but there were of course those who objected to his precious vocabulary, unapologetic elitism, and the rendition of his "dream girls," as Scrope's son-in-adultery calls them. It's all meant to be stylization, he points out, not mimesis (450). For example, when Scrope writes a sentence like "the door had swung open and swung gently to again, and in had stepped this beautiful child" (461 — echoing Morgan's entrance in *An Armful of Warm Girl* [127]), Amy asks, "but 'child'? she's in Radcliffe! So is this just technique or *do* you think of them that way." Scrope, like a gentleman, overlooks her "just technique" and argues "a certain docileness had to be conveyed, he supposed, yes. Demureness perhaps too? Still, in that sort of relationship, a kind of daughterly deference he'd assume was at work." That is, the use of *child* isn't sexist or patronizing but a compact designation that carefully conveys the exact nature of their relationship; *child* is aesthetically correct, if not literally or politically correct. (I can just imagine what Spackman would have thought of *that* provincial intellectual blight.) As the quotation here indicates, Spackman's defenses of his style are casually confident; either one has the taste and education to appreciate these things, or one hasn't. No point in arguing.

Death is even more of a sobering presence here than it is in *An Armful of Warm Girl*. Gerontic love is rarely portrayed in literature, which gives *A Little Decorum* a special place in romantic fiction, but Scrope's romp with the Danish sociologist and his more considered affair with Mrs. Tench-Fenton take on special poignancy when it is implied that the former caused the heart attack that put him in the hospital at the beginning of the novel and the latter may cause another, fatal attack at the end. But the novel is anything but solemn; like most of Spackman's works, the novel is set in summer, the season of romance (in Northrop Frye's paradigm), with three generations of lovers celebrating life and literature. It is Spackman's most ebullient novel.

The remaining works in this omnibus provide delightful variations on Spackman's characteristic themes and concerns. The two short stories can be read as companion pieces, dealing as they do with a romantic "pursuit" ("Declarations of Intent") and a "Dialogue at the End of a Pursuit." The sexual act itself was of no literary interest to Spackman; it was the social dance that led up to it, and the tender relations between lovers immediately following, that engaged his attention. The female speaker in the "Dialogue" itemizes the stages of pursuit *dans les formes* (a French phrase that appears in several of Spackman's novels), and Eve Fremantle of "Declarations" knows that her pursuer knows the forms as well as she, which causes her no little distress. Eve is the editor of a writer like Spackman named Matthew Talley and is being pursued by his brother Robert, a classicist at Princeton's Institute for Advanced Study currently involved with a Princeton undergraduate who models on the side.[8] At one point she expresses her impatience with her predetermined role by accusing Robert of being like his novelist brother:

> "But why should I think you so different," I said, laughing at him. "Are you behaving as if you took women seriously either? He really just likes our décor — you know? — and whichever of us happens to come with it? anyhow, the way he thinks she is, with! . . . We're this adorable ballet for him. But does one have to be a ballerina on demand? And why should I want to be 'adored,' heavens!" (531)

The passage is interesting for several reasons (not the least as an example of the kind of adventure in syntax Spackman can lead the reader on). If Robert is a typical Spackman marauder, he likes both women *and* their décor — it's not an either/or choice — but there's no denying that Spackman's characters, male and female, are like dancers, and his novels like ballets. Stylization, artificiality, and self-conscious display of technique are common to both the ballet and Spackman's novels — indeed, to many works of literature. In *An Armful of Warm Girl*, Nicholas compares even the *Iliad* to "a ballet, matched heroes dancing forward at each other in opposing pairs to fling their antiphonal taunts and spears, then dancing back, and then a choral movement of the ordinary infantry another pair coming on, another pas de deux; and this he said was how it often seemed to be with love" (201). Spackman's novels could be called "adorable ballets," and Eve's declaration has the unsettling effect of a ballerina stopping in mid-performance to complain of sore feet, breaking the illusion. Eve speaks of an "escape-clause" near the end, from the same legal vocabulary that the story takes its title, and provides a rare instance in Spackman's work where *dans les formes* threatens to become merely going through the motions. Eve is one of Spackman's most complex female characters, but, despite her reservations, the circular form of the story (which begins and ends with Eve in a car admiring a man's profile) suggests that Eve will strap on her toe shoes for yet another performance.

Spackman's final novel, *As I Sauntered Out, One Midcentury Morning . . .*, is a more relaxed work than the ones that preceded it — a saunter rather than a gallop, as the Audenesque title indicates — without quite the whirl and wit of *A Little Decorum* or the tour-de-force ambitions of *A Difference of Design*. In fact, it recalls *Heyday* in some respects: the Princeton/

8 Though the undergraduate Samantha is described as a showgirl, one can't help but think of actress Brooke Shields, who was attending Princeton at the time Spackman wrote this story.

Quaker background is once again emphasized, and like the first novel it covers a longer span of time than the other novels: despite its brevity, *As I Sauntered Out* is Spackman's most spacious novel, ranging from the summer of 1948 to the late Sixties or early Seventies.[9] It is also his most domestic novel, the only one in which the protagonist shows any concern for "settling down." Johnnie Coates, the narrator, is a self-confessed "marauder," but he's a domesticated one, not a campaigner like his Uncle John Coates or Spackman's other rakes. He even proposes marriage to a woman, one of the few men in Spackman's fiction to do so.

Broadly based on the career of Spackman's son Peter (1930–95), Johnnie Coates graduates from Princeton in 1952, does graduate work at Columbia, and later becomes a political journalist. (Peter Spackman edited a political journal called *Cultural Affairs* in the late Sixties; his father contributed an essay entitled "Literature as Literature, and Why?" in 1968 under the pseudonym Alexander Neave.[10]) The novel recounts Johnnie's sentimental education, with special attention to his relationship to his Uncle John — who recalls to some extent High Tatnall's rakish uncle in *A Presence with Secrets*, with his palazzo in Italy and a drawerful of amorous mementos. Uncle John proves to be another "presence with secrets," with one secret in particular that shakes but doesn't destroy his nephew's love and respect for him. Like Spackman's other novels, *As I Sauntered Out* is concerned with adultery — the theme is spelled out on pages 583–84 — but with few of the shock tactics of the earlier novels; adultery here is merely an alternative domestic arrangement, and a sensible one at that. And like the other novels, it is chiefly a "comedy of manners" (559), but less hectic, less mannered. It doesn't represent a falling-off of Spackman's powers but an attempt at a different mode; though several scenes are characteristically set in summer, the novel's conclusion and overall tone

9 The internal chronology for the novel is shaky; as I said earlier, there is an awkward leap at the beginning of chapter 2 from 1952 to the mid-Sixties, and although the novel is intended to conclude in 1967 (the narrator states on p. 602 that he went to France in the summer of 1948 and that it is now 19 years later), several years intervene between the Class of '52's 15th reunion in chap. 2. (i.e., 1967) and the conclusion of the novel. Such discrepancies undoubtedly would have been cleared up had the book been edited in Spackman's lifetime, and I felt it would be intrusive to try to correct his chronology for him. There are a few anachronisms as well, but these too have been allowed to stand, with one exception: the substitution of "plane" for "Concorde" at the bottom of p. 552 since its first flight was in 1977, beyond the time frame of the novel.

10 Alexander and Neave are old family names, Mrs. Newell informs me: "Apparently Elizabeth Neave was his great-grandmother; she married Thomas Peirce, and their daughter, Priscilla, in turn married WMS's grandfather, William Mode, who owned, with his brother Alexander, paper mills at a small town called Modena, just down the Brandywine River from Coatesville, PA."

are autumnal. Those who find his other novels too self-consciously brilliant may actually prefer this quieter demonstration of his skills. I find it charmingly appropriate that the last word in his last work is *kissed*.

Up through his final work, style, not content, remained Spackman's chief interest and, as he argued in his critical writings, the principal (if not the only) criterion by which a writer should be judged. From the earliest essays in *On the Decay of Humanism* through his last published essay, "An *Ex Parte* for Comedy," Spackman railed against the professoriat's (and book-review media's) reduction of a work of art to "its 'content' — the thing's theme, its 'ideas,' its everlasting Meaning."[11] "Content is not really what any decently gifted novelist is chiefly concerned with," he wrote elsewhere, and he quoted with approval Nabokov's statement that "Style and structure are the essence of a book; great ideas are a lot of hogwash."[12]

Style, at its simplest, is a matter of vocabulary and syntactical organization. Spackman's signature style is a unique combination of decorum and playfulness, Edwardian vocabulary and contorted syntax. A scrap of dialogue like "Webb sweet, you are plying me with drink, surely a girl shouldn't just let ply?" (from *Heyday*) is both formal and informal, taking an antiquated phrase like "plying me with drink" and giving it a Wodehousian twist that violates traditional grammar but makes perfect sense, amuses the reader, and adds to the characterization of the speaker. There are a few antecedents for such a style: Wodehouse, Firbank, the Stevie Smith of *Novel on Yellow Paper*; among contemporary writers, such a sentence might be found in James McCourt's novels, David Markson's underappreciated *Springer's Progress*, or in one of Karen Elizabeth Gordon's delightful books, but not very many other places. Where Spackman shines, however, is in paragraphs like this one (from *An Armful of Warm Girl*):

> Mrs. Barclay being as it turned out late and Nicholas early, or as early anyway as a man in his right mind waiting for a pretty woman, he'd sat damn' near twenty minutes in Veale's unrecognizable bar, bolt-upright and presently glaring, before with a ripple of high heels in fluttered his angel in this breathless rush at last, blissfully gasping "Oh Nicholas oh simply now imagine!" as he lunged up from the banquette with a happy bellow to grab her — though this act she parried, after one radiant flash of blue eyes, by seizing and tenderly pressing his hands while uttering little winded cries of salutation and reminiscence; and having let him merely peck at one heavenly

11 "An *Ex Parte* for Comedy," *American Voice* 1.3 (Summer 1986): 50. This essay is essential reading for Spackman students, for it is the most succinct statement of his aesthetic principles and a defense of his work against unsympathetic critics.

12 "Undeath of the Novel," 149; "A Time Was had by All" (a review of Nabokov's *Lectures on Literature*), *Canto* 3.4 (January 1981): 164.

cheek eeled out of his arms to the seat, onto which she at once sank, blown. (115)

One first admires the velocity of the passage, a single sentence that strains the rules of syntax and the proper use of dependent clauses to render the "breathless rush" of the action. It opens with a phrase that could have been written by Jane Austen but quickly races through a number of other registers before coming to rest onomatopoeically with two monosyllabic words. The tone is conversational rather than expository, as though Nicholas were retelling the event to a friend, but consists of carefully chosen vocabulary — Nicholas lunges, bellows, and grabs (mostly in earthy trochees), while Mrs. Barclay flutters, parries, tenderly presses, eels (in lacy sibilants: "this breathless rush at last, blissfully") — his bluntness contrasted to her wariness, which sets the tone for their relationship throughout the novel. It gives one example of Mrs. Barclay's "little winded cries of salutation" to stand for the rest and efficiently conveys other descriptive matters like her footwear, the color of her eyes, and her sleek ("eeled") figure. The aptness of the diction and the economy of the passage are amazing; most writers would have taken a page to convey what Spackman does here in a brief paragraph. The care and precision of the composition will be self-apparent to anyone who has tried to write. And that, Spackman always felt, rather than the characters' morals or sociopolitical outlook, is the only thing that should matter in a work of literature.

It is tempting to quote and analyze other passages — especially those showing Spackman's brilliant use of what grammarians call free indirect discourse, where conversation and exposition are blended without clear demarcation (a method William Gaddis has likewise developed to great advantage) — but I'll leave such pleasures to the reader. It is Spackman's instantly recognizable style that elevates him above the ranks of other novelists of manners and places him among the most accomplished writers of our time. The content of his novels, and his characterization of women especially, will always create problems for some readers, but not for those who agree that style is what a writer is to be judged by. In his review of a new translation of the *Aeneid*, Spackman wrote that it is, finally, not the content or philosophy but "the noises, the language, that make Vergil Vergil."[13] Similarly, it is the charming noises, the Olympian language, that make Spackman Spackman.

13 "Pascua, Rura, Duces," *Parnassus* 1.2 (Spring/Summer 1973): 101.

A New Language for Desire: Carole Maso's *Aureole*

> Sleepers awaking, our grey flesh tingling beneath the warm tongues of sister suns, the old dreams stirred; our blood flowed fast now, darkening, already inventing a new language for Desire.
>
> —Rikki Ducornet, *The Complete Butcher's Tales*

"We were working on an erotic song cycle" the dying Ava Klein remembers in Carole Maso's AVA (1993), recalling its tentative titles throughout the novel (*A Place We Can Still Go*; *Toward a Female Subject*; *In the Joie de Vivre Room* — which was the original title for AVA). In a sense, *Aureole* (1996) is the song cycle Ava Klein didn't live to complete, musical in its lyrical style and decidedly erotic. Like Schubert's song cycle *Die Winterreise*, mentioned near the end of *Aureole*, Maso's individual "songs" are united by a common theme: desire. But rarely in literature has desire been explored with the intensity Maso brings to *Aureole*: a pyrotechnic display almost reckless in its abandon, daring in its subversion of literary propriety, and voracious in its erotic hunger.

In *Aureole* Maso exhibits the kind of bravado and self-exposure that I associate more with rock music divas than with her literary sisters. She has something of Courtney Love's swagger, P J Harvey's erotomania (both are mentioned on page 81 of her book), Liz Phair's bluntness, Kate Bush's bookish romanticism, Siouxsie Sioux's dramatic flair, Jane Siberry's wit, Liz Fraser's mellifluousness, Shirley Manson's aggressive sexuality, Tori Amos's introspection, and Lisa Germano's heartbreaking insecurity. Maso even seems to borrow techniques from the more experimental female musicians working today, "sampling" older books and film (like the women in Single Gun Theory), using words occasionally as "noise and effects" (as Lisa Germano uses her violin), creating loops of recurring phrases (like Sarah Peacock of Seefeel), and so on. The individual pieces in *Aureole* cry out for performance, preferably with a backing track mixed by Betty and released on the innovative 4AD label.

But the overt musicality of *Aureole* owes just as much to the literary tradition of lyric women writers Maso aligns herself with by way of citation. In this book she names and quotes Sappho, Mirabai, Emily Dickinson, Gertrude Stein, Anna Kavan, and Marguerite Duras. A woman writer she doesn't name is Elizabeth Smart, whose novel *By Grand Central Station I Sat Down and Wept* provides an instructive parallel to *Aureole*. Smart's 1945 novel, which remains criminally neglected, is a torch song of a book, an operatic lament written in an intense, overwrought style that is by turns biblical, poetic, and impertinent. The story is simple: a young woman falls obsessively in love with a married man, enjoys some blissful moments of illicit sex with him, and is left to bear their children. But the plot is hard to follow, for the text is hardly what you'd call "composed"; instead, its lipstick is smeared, its hair a mess, its mascara running as the nameless narrator rhapsodizes over love's joys and desolations. The novel lacks decorum, is shameless in its excesses, and resembles those madwomen scenes in Elizabethan drama where disorderly prose breaks through the orderly boundaries of verse. The story doesn't flow, it hemorrhages. (All this is praise, not censure.) The effect is overwhelming, emotionally draining, the greatest love story ever written if you define love as naked yearning so powerful and lawless that it resembles demonic possession.

Aureole is the only book I know to match the intensity and stylistic daring of Smart's. The narrative of *Aureole* is even more deeply buried than that in *By Grand Central*, but it can be unearthed if one wishes to consider the book a novel (which is useful if not strictly necessary). The nameless protagonist is an autobiographical figure whose erotic life traces a trajectory of desire from youth and the giddiness of her first lesbian experience, through the agony and ecstasy of various adult relationships, concluding in what might be the afterlife in a lesbian paradise. Like Smart, Maso isn't interested in standard exposition or in providing her figures with detailed backgrounds. (It's more useful to speak of figures than characters in *Aureole*; they're more like figures in a painting, or fantasy figures, than characters in a conventional novel.) But the overarching narrative concerns the writer/protagonist's search for a new language for desire. Maso goes further than Smart, further than anyone, in exploring "the hanging, gorgeous strange place between poetry and prose" (6), dispensing with the clichés of most erotic writing to develop a more physical kind of writing to simulate the various physical states of desire. Braving the imitative fallacy, Maso's sentences moan, babble, stutter, shout. The novel is a record of finding this language. Glance at the opening and closing pages of *Aureole* for a preview of the process: from normal-looking paragraphs and complete sentences, to isolated phrases, then blissed-out words, winding down to suspension points and finally an open-ended dash, yearning for "more — " (211). If language is seen as the protagonist, then its development can be tracked as easily as Jane Eyre's.

After a brief preface (in which Maso explains what she's up to better than I ever could), the novel opens with "The Women Wash Lentils." Stylistically, it encapsulates the stylistic development of the entire work, much as an opera's overture does: it begins with orderly sentences, standard paragraphing, and so on, but soon starts breaking up into fragments, lists, two word paragraphs, where incantation replaces narrative. Ostensibly, the chapter concerns two young women in Paris, discussing French slang, though it is more likely an erotic fantasy invented by two older women, pretending to be in Paris and taking on the roles of two straight girls having their first lesbian experience. (In fact, in much of the novel it is impossible to say what is "really" going on and what is fantasy; it is set in the place in between the two.) One of the women is American, the other French (or pretends to be), and exploring a foreign language becomes synonymous with exploring a foreign body: "When they are in love with language, as they always are when they are French they explore each word, as they explore each other" (9). Throughout the novel Maso explores English with the care and curiosity with which one studies a foreign tongue: intrigued by its idioms, amused by its slang, puzzled by its grammar, going so far as to use English in the nonidiomatic way a foreigner would ("You Were Dazzle" is the title of a later chapter). She is defamiliarizing the language, both for herself and her readers, in order to rediscover its metaphoric capacity and to tease out its erotic potential (as in "a foreign tongue"). In this first chapter Maso establishes the equivalency of "lovemaking, language making" (15), where reading and writing are aphrodisiacal acts, and where sexual energy becomes a goal to achieve in writing: "And I'd like to do with any sentence what I'm about to do to you . . ." (10).

Maso's achievement of this goal is what distinguishes *Aureole* from standard erotica. Most erotic writing is erotic in content only, not in style or form. The average erotic novel uses the same syntax and paragraph organization as the average murder mystery or sci-fi adventure and is heavily reliant on clichés. Maso wants to capture states of desire "Between the event and its many formulations in the mind" (15), before it gets translated into those standard sentences and paragraphs. This means risking unintelligibility, slurring the language rather than seeking clarity, inducing a trance rather than providing a straightforward narrative, but Maso is willing to take these risks. Reversing the procedure of the Elizabethans I mentioned earlier, she disrupts orderly prose for a disorderly poetry of desire.

The young writer of the first chapter is next seen in a café in "Her Ink-Stained Hands," talking with her male lover, a butcher who is practicing abstinence. Their previous sexual bouts were physically brutal, and she still has the bruises and scars to show for it. She wants him still, but since he has withdrawn himself from her, she writes about him instead, another instance where writing becomes an extension of sex. The two have grown apart, mimetically signaled by the layout of the text: there are blank spaces between their utterances, with many of their sentences likewise interrupted by space. The blood, scars, and ink-stained hands metamorphose into religious images of crucifixion and stigmata, continuing the blending of religious and sexual images from the first chapter (where it is noted that *voir les anges* — to see the angels — is French slang for orgasm [22]). The chapter is a quiet piece, a meditation on the sublimation of sexual energy. It ends with the woman imagining kissing a bisexual triathlete, who takes the stage in the next chapter, "Make Me Dazzle," which is as explosive as the previous chapter is muted.

Dazzle is a key word in *Aureole*, used in two of its chapter titles and recurring throughout the novel. Maso has rescued the word from overuse in advertisements in women's magazines and recovered its more powerful original meaning of becoming overwhelmed by something, blinded, stupefied. In *Aureole* the word carries the full force of the impassioned boast of Shakespeare's Henry the Fifth: "I will rise there with so full a glory / That I will dazzle all the eyes of France, / Yea, strike the Dauphin blind to look on us" (*Henry V Part 1*, 1.2.279–81). Or for a more modern instance, listen to Siouxsie and the Banshees' magnificent song "Dazzle" (from *Hyæna*, 1984), where the word conveys an exultant derangement of the senses. In "Make Me Dazzle" the woman writer of the first two chapters is now a professor, vacationing in what sounds like Provincetown off-season. Walking along the beach, she encounters a woman named Aurelie,[1] a bisexual triathlete, and they begin a torrid affair. Dazzled by the woman, the professor's language falls apart. "A deep deranging of the sentence — disorder" (49) sets in, and she has trouble forming coherent sentences. Mixed metaphors, synaesthesia, disrupted syntax, and almost preverbal babbling effectively convey her dazzled state of mind, the seashore setting providing some intoxicating Dylan Thomasesque sea imagery as she goes down (in all senses): "Sea drunk and snow they can barely hear each other / over the moan of the lighthouse and the ocean and roses" (43) could almost be a couplet out of his *Under Milk Wood*. "Rising from their sexual wreckage" (71) near the end of the chapter, the professor enters a stupefied dream-state, "singing demented songs dazzling songs," and indeed in the next chapter she becomes Ophelia and sings the most demented, dazzling song in the novel.

"Dreaming Steven Lighthouse Keeper" is a reverie conveyed in nursery rhymes and poetic prose in a state of post-orgasmic bliss. The narrator imagines that the lighthouse nearby is inhabited by a man who overhears the love-talk of the professor and the triathlete, then invents a background for him: a married man who left his wife, children, and the big city for a lonely existence as a lighthouse keeper. The narrator imagines Steven in love with an array of women, most identified winsomely by their relationships (the schoolmaster's daughter, the butcher's bride, the piano-tuner's assistant), others romantically

1 [In 1994 I published Aurelie Sheehan's debut story collection *Jack Kerouac Is Pregnant*, and I remember Carole telling me at the time that she liked the name Aurelie. — 2016 note.]

mad (an opium addict, a crazy white-haired girl who scribbles poetry and who, in one sense, is the author of this chapter). His is an isolated, masturbatory existence, but Maso wraps it in a cocoon of enchanting fantasies and sing-song poetry, like a mother cooing nonsense over her sleeping baby.

Turning from this chapter to the next, "The Changing Room," is like getting a bucket of water in the face. It recounts a brief, urgent coupling between a man and a woman in breathless prose that is almost over before it begins. (It is the shortest chapter in the book.) The encounter takes place on a foggy night in March in a beach cabana, illuminated by a car's headlights. The woman repeats a line ("must have been an angel") from "Her Ink-Stained Hands" and is presumably the same; another line ("you are gentle") links this chapter to the next, the longest chapter in the book.

"Anju Flying Streamers After" begins with what sounds like a line from Wallace Stevens — "On the nighttable: a pomegranate" (89) — an obvious and important influence on Maso. But "Anju" is more influenced by film: directly by Marguerite Duras's *India Song*, which is quoted throughout the rest of the novel, and indirectly by the films of Satyajit Ray and Maya Deren. The professor of "Make Me Dazzle" is still in off-season Provincetown when she conjures up Anju, an Indian woman who inspires Maso's most trancelike writing. One can almost hear the drone of sitars and tambouras as the narrator rhapsodizes over Anju, abandoning linear narrative for a series of intoxicating visual images. The narrative method here is "chanting chanting / weaving slurring bobbing" (109), single words and phrases, as though the narrator is so "deranged by desire" (121) that she cannot form a coherent sentence: "sexual energy propels the sentence . . . her body disorders how you — " she trails off, allowing Anju's body to disorder the very sentences we are reading. The water imagery of "Make Me Dazzle" and "Dreaming Steven" is replaced here by fire imagery as the narrator almost literally burns with desire for her luscious Indian beauty. Likewise, there are images of food and eating that are almost literalized, as the narrator feasts on her beloved's body, eats from her fingers, eats a mango from between her legs, smothers her with spices. Possessed by erotomania, the narrator reverts to pure orality, the earliest stage of psychosexual development in psychoanalytic theory. The willing reader is sucked into this whirlpool, and only with difficulty realizes that Anju is a former student or disciple of the professor's, and who intriguingly enough believes she saw her teacher in India many years ago, the mysterious "woman on the bridge" who drifts through *Aureole* in various disguises (a persona for the narrator). Like the Song of Solomon, "Anju Flying Streamers After" is ravishing.

"The Devotions," the next chapter, continues with quotations from *India Song*, but the fires of desire have been extinguished for a meditation on the ephemerality of things, including art. This is followed by another brief chapter, "As We Form Our First Words." By this point in the novel, narrative has all but disappeared. This chapter contains fragments from most of the preceding chapters and represents a kind of breathing place as the narrator conjures up the persona for the next chapter.

"Sappho Sings the World Ecstatic" echoes the title of Whitman's "I Sing the Body Electric" and delivers another burst of sexual energy to the novel. (It will be noticed that there is a sexual rhythm to the novel, as chapters representing sexual insatiability alternate with ones in which, temporarily satiated, the narrator can fantasize about other figures or recall sexual episodes from her past.) With Whitmanesque exuberance Maso sings of the joys of lesbian sex, channeling Sappho as her narrative persona. Sappho, of course, has been present throughout the novel, quoted in several of the chapters and obviously a presiding muse over the novel. (The fragmented form in which her work survives can even be seen as a formal model for Maso's deliberately fragmented style.) Maso evokes the Greek poet in her most lilting, lyrical language yet, setting her in an erotic landscape (where a reclining nymph's hip can turn into a cliff's edge) and allowing her in a "fever dream" to see Maya Deren's dreamy film *At Land*, whose film script is excerpted throughout the chapter. The chapter itself is a kind of fever dream, where different levels of narrative surrealistically waltz together "In a medium unknown at the lip of the hypnotic word and Maya, key, asleep" (160). This sentence introduces Maya Deren, but also evokes the Vedantic concept of *maya*, the illusory world of the senses, which Maso represents so seductively here. A sensuous languor infuses the chapter to the point where the narrator becomes giddy and silly: "Sappho sings and sells sea shells. Sappho sings by the seashore" (166). Such playfulness explains Gertrude Stein's presence in the chapter, another woman conjured up by Sappho from the strings of her lyre (164). In one sense Sappho is creating the lesbian paradise of the novel's final chapter; in another, all this is another reverie of the narrator, and ultimately of Carole Maso herself, our postmodern Sappho.

The narrator is jerked back to reality in "You Were Dazzle" (that word again), remembering a messy affair with a rich, cultured woman. The soft seas of Sappho's Greece give way to "the slam of the ocean" (170) back in the States, the "girly girls" (167) of Sappho's dream pushed aside by two strong-willed women filled with "rage and sorrow and hurt" (171). The prose is as wild and reckless as the women, with striking images flung in the reader's face, rage and lust preventing the impatient narrator from forming complete sentences. Lust here isn't the devouring hunger of "Anju" or the sexy games of "Make Me Dazzle" but "sex addiction" (172), that dreary concept from 1980s pop psychology that seems to have some validity here. The narrator resents her lover, even going so far as to turn her faults into a kind of poem (174), but admits "We were tangle and pull and gag but we were dazzle" (173). That sentence makes sense even though ungrammatical, and their affair made sense the same way.

"We were strung out," the narrator of "You Were Dazzle" says several times. In the next chapter, "Exquisite Hour," the narrator draws a parallel between sex addiction and drug addiction. The "you" addressed throughout this chapter is a composite figure, partly the opium addict with her snowy globe from "Dreaming Steven Lighthouse Keeper" and partly Anna Kavan (1904–1968), a British novelist and short-story writer who was a heroin addict most of her adult life. The language itself is drugged, drifting in a haze, nonlinear, indolent, obsessive, beautiful in an icy kind of way. It is difficult, consequently, to determine what exactly happens. Is the "he" who addresses the opium addict Steven? Is the narrator herself the one strung out on drugs? On page 188 there is a quotation from David Callard's biography of Kavan (acknowledged in the notes at the back of *Aureole*): "The heroin makes one's eyes beautiful. There is no doubt I am attractive. I watched myself in the glass for a long time, which gave me pleasure." This suggests the narrator is addressing herself throughout, staring into a snow globe (179) in a drugged state. Snow and ice are the dominant images; one of Kavan's best novels is entitled *Ice*, and in her story "High in the Mountains" she praises heroin: "a clean white powder is not repulsive; it looks pure, it glitters, the pure white crystals sparkle like snow" (quoted in Callard, 47). And of course snow is slang for heroin as well as cocaine.

The aggressive sexuality of the previous chapter relaxes here into passive submission: to drugs, obviously, but also to a "*maitre*" who is partly a fencing instructor (Maso studied fencing as a teenager). But the narrator is also learning to submit to a new kind of writing, to "the sensuous lexicon of falling, where I write, where I like to write, more and more often now. Charting a motion and its many permutations, its many fallings into desire, language — waywardness, hope. . . ." She goes on to justify drug use because "you just wanted to be taken away. Taken out — to become silent because there wasn't any language for this" (193). But at this point in the chapter the male voices (the "he" of the opening pages, the fencing master, even the "yowling mouth of Dietrich Fischer-Dieskau" singing *Die Winterreise*) are drowned out by the voice of "a woman singing only slightly out of phase . . . the woman with the velvet voice. Exquisite. Salvation. Lady Day" (194). Listening to Billie Holiday, the narrator sees a "Halo. *Aureole*. I lift my arms to the glare" (194). "A strange paradise enters" (194), glare and fire melt the snow and ice, couples dance, and the narrator walks "out of all enclosures, all that has confined you . . . away from all that has kept me in place. Afraid" (196). Thus "Exquisite Hour" can be read as an account of an aesthetic crisis, where the narrator turns to drugs in despair of finding an appropriate language for herself, is confined in an enclosure of patriarchal expectations — the fencing master's (read agent's, publisher's) repeated demand for a masterpiece — then finds in Lady Day's voice the courage to forge a new language like that so triumphantly on display here and throughout *Aureole*. "At last you see — at last — someone in the mirror you think you recognize. And I am happier than I have ever felt, she thinks" (200).

This feeling of triumph at the end of "Exquisite Hour" — the most daring and complex chapter in the book — is carried over to *Aureole*'s concluding chapter, a kind of coda entitled "In the Last Village." A few pages back the narrator had said "A strange paradise enters," and this brief prose poem describes her personal paradise, a lesbian utopia populated by her friends and mentors. Various phrases from earlier chapters are chanted in a final state of post-orgasmic bliss, where all aesthetic and erotic difficulties have been resolved.

It's a lovely conclusion to Maso's most innovative book to date. Each of her preceding novels pushed the envelope of what prose fiction could do, especially the groundbreaking *AVA*, but *Aureole* takes greater risks, dares more, shows greater variety than anything she's done before. Though it will probably be categorized as lesbian erotica — and deserves to become a classic of the genre — it's more an aesthetic adventure of self-discovery, of seeing how far a gifted writer can go to forge a new language for desire. Borrowing techniques from film and poetry, nursery rhymes and pornography, rock music and painting, Maso goes further than any writer working today to create a style that does justice to the polymorphously perverse energy of eros. Carole Maso will make you see the angels.

Paper Flowers: Richard Brautigan's Poetry

He was born in poverty and died a suicide, suffered from depression, alcoholism, and insomnia, yet Richard Brautigan produced some of the most delightful and inventive poems in American literature. With their quirky humor, bizarre metaphors, and playful forms, these poems charmed readers in the Sixties and Seventies and continue to attract new readers — that is, those lucky enough to find them. For with the exception of *The Pill versus the Springhill Mine Disaster,* which is sandwiched between two novels in a Houghton Mifflin omnibus, his poetry has been out of print for decades. Although Brautigan will always be better known for his dozen books of fiction, his poetry played a major role in establishing his reputation and remains a significant part of his enduring appeal.

Like the adorable woman seated in a sandbox on the cover of his *Rommel Drives on Deep into Egypt,* Brautigan regarded poetry as a sandbox to play in. His poems take a vaudevillian variety of forms: hobbled haikus, sabotaged sonnets, prose poems, newspaper headlines, Zen koans, public service announcements, *penseés,* surreal weather reports, mash notes, Beat goofing, fragments of autobiography, psalms, obituaries, insults (some play is serious), broadsides, found poems, poems "published" on seed packets, poems with titles but no text, poems with titles longer than their texts, poems about the failure to write poems, Shakespearean adaptations, Carrollian whimsy, Joycean epiphanies, Marxist gags (Groucho, not Karl), fractured fairy tales, instructions for the use of a "Karma Repair Kit," lists, journal entries — and throughout, some of the most astonishing, mindbending metaphors in verse. Only Brautigan would be reminded by a potted plant on a windowsill of a vampire entering by the window. Who else would think of a contraceptive pill in terms of a mining disaster, or describe Shakespeare's Ophelia floating "like an April church"? He was blessed with the gift of metaphor, one of the truest signs of a born poet.

And he knew it. From an early age Brautigan knew he had a vocation to be a writer, and pursued it with the fierce dedication of a true believer. He was born (as he tells us in the poem "Tokyo / June 24, 1976") on January 30, 1935, in Tacoma, Washington. He had a bleak childhood; born in the pit of the Depression to a single mother often on welfare, he suffered from malnutrition, neglect, and abuse at the hands of his mother's string of boyfriends. (Brautigan saw his real father only twice during his childhood.) He and his sister were boarded out to another family once, abandoned a few times, and other times left with one of his abusive stepfathers for weeks. Only after his mother remarried a decent man when Brautigan was 13 did his life improve, though those earlier experiences marked him for life, and he rarely spoke of that time thereafter.

"Richard was real smart," his mother told his daughter Ianthe years later, "read all the time. Always had a paperback in his pocket."[1] He also developed a poet's eye early on; he would often take his sister Barbara with him on fishing trips, and she later told Ianthe: "'We would make peanut butter sandwiches and quart jars of Kool-Aid and walk for miles fishing along the way. He saw beauty in everything,' she said. 'We were just kids, but he would point out a special tree or the way the flowers were bending in the wind. Nobody talked about that sort of thing in our family or even in the town we lived.'" The mention of Kool-Aid recalls one of the more memorable characters in *Trout Fishing in America*: the Kool-Aid wino. He too is poverty-stricken, but rises above it by the power of imagination: "He created his own Kool-Aid reality and was able to illuminate himself by it." For Brautigan, it was not Kool-Aid but the discovery of poetry that allowed him to create his own reality.

In the contributor's note to one of his earliest magazine appearances, Brautigan stated: "I have been writing poetry since I was seventeen. Olivant will publish my first book of poems, Tiger in a Telephone Booth. Making paper flowers out of love and death is a disease, but how beautiful it is."[2] He discovered poetry in high school, and was especially drawn to Emily Dickinson; like telegrams from a parallel universe, her short, gnomic verse provided a model for the poetry he began writing then, and her personal example of the poet as an eccentric outsider must have appealed to his own sense of estrangement. In a fine essay on Dickinson, poet Alice Fulton noted "it's hard to think of any criticism that places a man poet within a primarily Dickinsonian orbit,"[3] but Brautigan certainly gravitated toward her, even though he may never have attained her level. But he paid tribute to her by using a line from one of her poems as the title of his second book of poetry, *Lay the Marble Tea*,

1 Quoted in Ianthe Brautigan's *You Can't Catch Death* (St. Martin's, 2000). Her memoir and Keith Abbott's *Downstream from "Trout Fishing in America"* (Capra Press, 1989) provided most of the biographical details in my introduction; both are filled with horror stories of Brautigan's childhood.

2 *Epos* 8.2 (Winter 1956). Plans for that first book fell through.

3 Alice Fulton, *Feeling as a Foreign Language: The Good Strangeness of Poetry* (Graywolf Press, 1999), 126.

and by including therein one of his own entitled "Feel Free to Marry Emily Dickinson."

William Carlos Williams is another poet Brautigan discovered in high school who exerted a lasting influence on the budding poet's aesthetics. Reacting against the complex, multilingual, allusive poetry of Pound and Eliot, Williams insisted on using the American vernacular, on junking obsolete poetic forms, and on writing poems that made an immediate impact on the reader (as opposed to poems that were to be puzzled over in the classroom). Williams believed a good poem was the result not of working up preconceived ideas but of recording fresh observations of ordinary things; his credo "No ideas but in things" became Brautigan's credo as well. Williams's iconic poem "The Red Wheelbarrow" and the two-sentence refrigerator note "This Is Just to Say" could both be mistaken for Brautigan poems.

The other important poetic discovery Brautigan made in high school was the Japanese haiku, especially as practiced by such masters as Basho and Issa. "I like the way they used language concentrating emotion, detail and image until they arrived at a form of dew-like steel," he later wrote in his introduction to *June 30th, June 30th*. While he rarely followed the strict syllabic form of the classic haiku, Brautigan aimed for the same effect in his short poems. The haiku of Basho and Issa were often lighthearted or humorous, qualities Brautigan emulated, only to have his verse criticized consequently for its lack of seriousness.

From 1952 to 1955 he wrote a great deal of poetry, some of it collected in the posthumously published *Edna Webster Collection of Undiscovered Writings* (Houghton Mifflin, 1999). Many of these "paper flowers" are what you would expect from a high school student, but others already display the distinctive voice and aesthetic strategies of his later poems. Before he published even one of them, however, he got his first negative review: as Keith Abbott tells it in his introduction to *The Edna Webster Collection*, "Richard showed his poems to a girlfriend, and when she criticized them, he was so distraught that he went to a police station and asked the police to arrest him. They said they couldn't; he hadn't done anything illegal. Brautigan then threw a rock through a glass partition in the station."[4] They not only put him in jail for a week, but sent him to the Oregon State Mental Hospital in Salem — the setting for the film *One Flew over the Cuckoo's Nest* — where he was diagnosed as a paranoid schizophrenic and given electric shock treatments.

After his release, Brautigan made a concerted effort to become a published

4 Brautigan told his daughter that he asked the police to put him in jail because he was hungry; after graduating from high school Brautigan could find only menial labor, such as working in a pickle factory.

poet. He submitted three small collections of his poetry to three different publishers in 1956 — *The Smallest Book of Poetry in the Whole God-Damn World* to New Directions, *Why Unknown Poets Stay Unknown* to Random House, and *Little Children Should Not Wear Beards* to Scribner's — all of whom rejected them.[5] Deciding it was time to move on, Brautigan gave his collected writings to his girlfriend's mother and in the summer of 1956 left Portland to go on the road: first to Reno, Nevada — where he stayed long enough to publish a few poems in the local newspaper in nearby Fallon — and then to San Francisco.

San Francisco was experiencing a literary "renaissance" in the 1950s, partly as the West Coast wing of the Beat movement but mainly as the flowering of a homegrown tradition of poetry that had been underway ever since Kenneth Rexroth moved to San Francisco in 1927. Brautigan came, he later told Bruce Cook, "just to come to San Francisco. He had no ambitions to be a Beat writer or anything. No ambitions at all, he said. Just got to know some of the people around town after a while, that was all. 'But my involvement with that was only on the very edge and only after the Beat thing had died down.'" Supporting himself with dead-end jobs, he continued writing poetry and began placing his poems in various small magazines. In 1957 a small publisher in San Francisco called Inferno Press brought out Brautigan's first separate publication, a broadside poem entitled "The Return of the Rivers," tipped into black construction paper wrappers. (Needless to say, this is the Holy Grail for Brautigan collectors; only 100 copies, all signed in Brautigan's cramped hand, were printed.) This impressive poem, later reprinted in *The Pill versus the Springhill Mine Disaster,* serves as Brautigan's aesthetic calling card, announcing the direction his poetry would take. Like a brief history of modern poetry, it begins with a stanza of nineteenth-century verse, reminiscent of Swinburne's "The Garden of Proserpine," then wipes the slate clean with the affectless observation "It is raining today / in the mountains." The third stanza evokes the early modernists, especially the synesthesia in "a warm green rain," the fourth stanza mimics Beat bebop ("Birds happen music / like clocks ticking heavens"), and with the fifth and final stanza, we have the true Brautigan voice: a bizarre but charming juxtaposition of images that still make a kind of narrative sense, rewriting the first stanza in Brautigan's own style: Swinburne on acid, or Dickinson on weed.

In May 1958, Brautigan produced his first "book" of poems (actually, a 16-page pamphlet): *The Galilee Hitch-Hiker,* published by Joe Dunn's White Rabbit Press in San Francisco. (Only 200 copies were printed; a second edi-

5 *Why Unknown Poets Stay Unknown* was posthumously published in *The Edna Webster Collection,* but the other two remain unpublished.

tion of 700 copies followed in 1966, published by Cranium Press.) The book consists of a suite of nine poems featuring a time-traveling hipster named Baudelaire. It's appropriate that for his first substantial contribution to modern poetry Brautigan would evoke the father of modern poetry, Charles Baudelaire, whose major work *The Flowers of Evil* had been published almost exactly a hundred years earlier (1857). Baudelaire was an iconic figure for the Beats; in the 1940s Lucien Carr had introduced the French poet to Kerouac and Ginsberg, who were seduced as much by Baudelaire's unconventional lifestyle as by his decadent poetry. Ginsberg modeled his poem "The Last Voyage" on Baudelaire's famous "Invitation to the Voyage," and when Kerouac had a brief affair in 1953 with a black woman (novelized in *The Subterraneans*) he was consciously following in the footsteps of Baudelaire, whose principal mistress was a mulatto named Jeanne Duval (mentioned in part 6 of Brautigan's book). Every well-read bohemian owned a copy of *The Flowers of Evil* or its prose counterpart, *Paris Spleen* (from which Brautigan quotes).

In *The Galilee Hitch-Hiker*, Baudelaire is the young Brautigan's role model and alter ego ("mon semblable – mon frère!"). Baudelaire is reckless where Jesus is cautious (Part 1); he loves to drink on Skid Row (Part 2); he encouraged the imagination of the four-year-old Brautigan in the slums of Tacoma (Part 3) and said prayers for the boy's dead insects (Part 9); he plays Dada games in San Francisco (Parts 4 and 5); he's a daydreamer who creates great art with a wave of his spoon (Part 6); he smokes opium at a Yankees–Tigers game and transforms a high fly ball into a suicidal angel (Part 7); and, like the 20-year-old Brautigan, Baudelaire enters an insane asylum only to emerge all the stronger from it (Part 8).[6]

Introducing himself to the literary world, Brautigan tosses off a psychological autobiography with admirable élan, aligning himself with the daring French poet to assert his own freedom from convention and his commitment to the imagination. Even though it reads more like prose chopped into lines than poetry, *The Galilee Hitch-Hiker* is a jaunty, assured work; Brautigan still liked it enough ten years after to place the sequence in the center of *The Pill versus the Springhill Mine Disaster*, and editor Alan Kaufman liked it enough 30 years later to include the entire cycle in his anthology *The Outlaw Bible of American Poetry* (Thunder's Mouth Press, 1999).

Brautigan's next book, *Lay the Marble Tea* – published by Carp Press in an edition of 500 copies in "that terrible year of 1959" (as it's called in the "Sea, Sea Rider" chapter of *Trout Fishing in America*) – is another 16-page pamphlet, but consists of two dozen poems and displays the full range of Brau-

6 A tenth poem featuring Baudelaire, entitled "The Whorehouse at the Top of Mount Rainier," appeared a year later in the first issue of *Beatitude* (9 May 1959).

tigan's poetic abilities at that time. The first thing that strikes the reader is the large cast of characters; most of Brautigan's later poetry would be written in the first person, but here he speaks through and about a variety of characters from history and literature: Billy the Kid, Hansel and Gretel, Harpo Marx, Baudelaire again, Ulysses and the Cyclops, Moby Dick and Captain Ahab, Kafka, Hamlet and Ophelia, Emily Dickinson, and John Donne all make appearances. Only a few poems are in the first person, as though the young poet is not yet confident enough to trust his own experiences and observations (as Williams urged).

But the poems of *Lay the Marble Tea* are bursting with poetic confidence: Brautigan flaunts his gift for incongruous imagery throughout, thumbs his nose at old forms (his "Sonnet" has only 13 lines), and experiments with different meters. Still under the influence of the prose poems in Baudelaire's *Paris Spleen,* he blurs the distinction between poetry and prose. A daring use of synesthesia in "Yes, the Fish Music" contains the guppy that would become *Trout Fishing in America,* and the book ends in postmodern fashion with a self-referential gesture, returning the reader to the first poem in the book. It's a dazzling performance, but attracted little notice beyond San Francisco.

The Octopus Frontier followed in 1960, likewise published by Carp Press. (The fisherman in Brautigan must have liked that name.) A few literary couples from *Lay the Marble Tea* reappear (Moby Dick and Ahab, Hamlet and Ophelia), but there is a greater reliance here on Brautigan's own powers of observation and transformation via metaphor. Like a magician confident enough to reveal how he performs his tricks, Brautigan shows in three poems how he changes the most mundane things into poetic concepts ("Horse Race," "The Postman," "Private Eye Lettuce"). The seeds of *In Watermelon Sugar* are sown in one poem ("The Last Music Is Not Heard"; cf. p. 51 of the novel), and in the incantatory "1942" he refers to an uncle whose story he would eventually tell in the introduction to *June 30th, June 30th.* In the fanciful title poem, Brautigan sounds a note of regret, a note that would be silenced by the tumultuous Sixties but heard with increasing volume in the poems Brautigan would write in the Seventies. Brautigan liked *The Octopus Frontier* well enough to include all but five of its poems in his "Selected Poems" of 1968, *The Pill versus the Springhill Mine Disaster.*

In one of his short stories, "The Literary Life in California/1964," Brautigan tells of a friend who once tore up two of Brautigan's early poetry books in a fit of jealous rage. Those pamphlets now go for as much as $1,500 on the rare-book market. But his first three books of poetry were sold only on consignment at the City Lights bookstore, and consequently made little impact elsewhere. They were barely noticed even in San Francisco, where Brautigan was considered merely a fringe poet. "Allen Ginsberg had hung the nickname of Bunthorne on him," Keith Abbott tells us in his memoir:

> A Gilbert and Sullivan character, Bunthorne is a synonym for a precious and winsome poet who indulges in 'idle chatter of a transcendental kind.' This was apt, given that Brautigan's early poems were perfect Bunthorne productions, concocted of brief whimsical thoughts of a metaphorical and ephemeral nature. His public Bunthorne persona as a poet often exposed Brautigan to ridicule — of which Ginsberg's was perhaps the kindest among his North Beach mentors. Since he continued to publish mainly his poems, people could not reconcile those sometimes simple-minded lyrics with what seemed to be Brautigan's inflated self-regard. (36–37).

Brautigan's next book of poetry wouldn't appear until seven years later. Though he continued to write poems, he turned most of his attention to writing fiction, resulting in four of the most remarkable novels of the Sixties: *Trout Fishing in America* was written in 1961–62 (and rejected by Viking Press, among others), followed by *A Confederate General from Big Sur* in 1963. (They would be published in reverse order, the *General* in 1964 but *Trout Fishing* not until the fall of 1967). The enigmatic *In Watermelon Sugar* was written between May 13 and July 19, 1964 — inspired, thinks Abbott, by Brautigan's separation from his wife at the end of 1963 — and *The Abortion: An Historical Romance 1966* was finished at the beginning of 1966. (Grove Press bought the first two novels and optioned the second two, but published only the most conventional one; *In Watermelon Sugar* was published by a small press in 1968, and *The Abortion* not published until 1971.)

This abandonment of poetry was not a sudden decision, nor an attempt to cash in on the more commercial viability of fiction. (No one interested in making money writes a book like *Trout Fishing in America* — though, ironically enough, that book went on to sell millions of copies.) It was part of his master plan, as he explained in an essay entitled "Old Lady," published in David Meltzer's *The San Francisco Poets* (1971) in lieu of an interview. It is brief and interesting enough to be quoted in full:

> I love writing poetry but it's taken time, like a difficult courtship that leads to a good marriage, for us to get to know each other. I wrote poetry for seven years to learn how to write a sentence because I really wanted to write novels and I figured that I couldn't write a novel until I could write a sentence. I used poetry as a lover but I never made her my old lady.
>
> One day when I was twenty-five years old, I looked down and realized that I could write a sentence. Let's try one of those classic good-bye lines, "I don't think we should see so much of each other any more because I think we're getting a little too serious," which really meant that I wrote my first novel *Trout Fishing in America* and followed it with three other novels.
>
> I pretty much stopped seeing poetry for the next six years until I was thirty-one or the autumn of 1966. Then I started going out with poetry again, but this time I knew

> how to write a sentence, so everything was different and poetry became my old lady. God, what a beautiful feeling that was!
>
> I tried to write poetry that would get at some of the hard things in my life that needed talking about but those things that you can only tell your old lady.

Brautigan's return to poetry in 1966 was partly inspired by his real-life "old lady," a lovely Canadian woman named Marcia Pacaud. (She's pictured on the cover of *The Pill* and is the subject of many of the poems written in 1966–67.) But in truth, he didn't so much abandon poetry as apply his poetic strategies to writing fiction. His novels and poems share the same kind of imagery and extended metaphors, and reading his early novels is the best preparation for reading his poetry because he often explicates those strategies. In fact, the poet Jack Spicer, to whom Brautigan apprenticed himself in the late 1950s, called *Trout Fishing* "a great poem." As Ellingham and Killian write in their exhaustive biography of Spicer, *Poet Be Like God*, "He brought it to Spicer page by page, and the two men revised it as though it were a long serial poem" (223). In what originally was probably the first chapter of *Trout Fishing* (the published first chapter describes the novel's cover photo, which was taken years later), Brautigan gives a step-by-step explanation of how he arrives at one of his characteristic images:

> The old drunk told me about trout fishing. When he could talk, he had a way of describing trout as if they were a precious and intelligent metal.
>
> Silver is not a good adjective to describe what I felt when he told me about trout fishing.
>
> I'd like to get it right.
>
> Maybe trout steel. Steel made from trout. The clear snow-filled river acting as foundry and heat.
>
> Imagine Pittsburgh.
>
> A steel that comes from trout, used to make buildings, trains and tunnels.
>
> The Andrew Carnegie of Trout! (3)

A Brautigan poem eliminates the process and presents only the image, leaving the reader to work out the steps by which the image was achieved. *A Confederate General from Big Sur* provides further examples. If a Brautigan poem compared a cup of coffee to an albino polar bear, it would be dismissed by an unsympathetic critic as incoherent, but the image would work like this: "My cup of coffee changed into an albino polar bear: I mean, cold and black" (126). In a poem, Brautigan might compare a woman to "an infinite swan" and leave it at that; in his novel, he spells it out: "Elizabeth acted like an infinite swan. I mean, that quality advanced beyond the limits of her body and hovered there in the room" (138). Consequently, when one comes across a baffling image in a Brautigan poem, it should be taken on faith (if not diligently worked out) that a careful if zany process of association is behind the image.

The book that marked Brautigan's return to poetry was *All Watched Over by Machines of Loving Grace.* This 36-page chapbook was produced by the Communication Company, the publishing arm of a collective of hippie anarchists called the Diggers (named after a 17th-century British radical group of agrarian reformers). This book can also be said to mark the transition of Brautigan from "the last of the Beats" (as he's been called) to the first of the hippie writers.

It's worth a brief digression to wonder if there is such a thing as hippie literature. The counterculture didn't produce any major poets; or rather, those who would have been poets a generation earlier became lyricists instead. Bob Dylan, Donovan, Joni Mitchell, Leonard Cohen, Jim Morrison, Lou Reed, and the Incredible String Band's Robin Williamson set their poems to music rather than send them off to poetry magazines, though later they all published their lyrics in book form. John Lennon published two books of punny prose and poetry in the Sixties; his bandmate Paul McCartney eventually published his collected lyrics in the year 2001. Record companies began printing lyrics on album covers, and there was a conscious effort on the part of many songwriters to move beyond simple love songs to something resembling serious poetry. Some bands had an in-house poet to provide lyrics, such as Procol Harum's Keith Reid, Grateful Dead's Robert Hunter, and King Crimson's Peter Sinfield. (I can't be the only teenager whose interest in "real" poetry was sparked by these rock poets.) In 1969 Richard Goldstein published an anthology entitled *The Poetry of Rock* that tried to make the case that some of these lyrics approached the status of poetry.

As regards fiction, most counterculture novels were actually late Beat efforts, like Richard Fariña's *Been Down So Long It Looks Like Up to Me* (1966), Irving Rosenthal's *Sheeper* (1967), Ed Sanders's *Tales of Beatnik Glory* (set in the Sixties but not published until 1975), and the novels of Beat poets Philip Whalen and Michael McClure. The first free novel published by the Diggers' Communication Company, *Happiness Bastard,* was written by another San Francisco Beat poet, Kirby Doyle. However, one could argue that two of our most flamboyant contemporary novelists, Thomas Pynchon and Tom Robbins, began as hippie writers. Pynchon's *Gravity's Rainbow* (1973), though set in the last days of World War II, is implicitly about the Sixties; his later *Vineland* (1990) and *Inherent Vice* (2009) are explicitly so, and the best evocations I know of that revolutionary era. Robbins, beginning with *Another Roadside Attraction* (1971), has kept his freak flag flying through a half-dozen iconoclastic novels filled with outlandish, Brautiganic metaphors. James Leo Herlihy, best known as the author of *Midnight Cowboy,* wrote a mainstream novel about hippies entitled *Season of the Witch* (after the caustic Donovan song), but most of the other books that might qualify as hippie fiction are, appropriately enough, literary oddities: Richard Horn's alphabetic *Encyclopedia* (1969), Kenneth Tindall's *Great Heads* (1967/1969), Rudolph Wurlitzer's hallucinatory *Nog* (1968), a few sci-fi novels — Chester Anderson's *The Butterfly Kid* (1967), Brian Aldiss's *Barefoot in the Head* (1969), Willard S. Bain's *Informed Sources* (first published by the Communication Company, then picked up by Doubleday in 1969) — Ed Sanders's obstreperous *Shards of God* (1970), Raymond Mungo's commune fantasy *Total Loss Farm* (1970), Chandler Brossard's kaleidoscopic freakshow *Wake Up. We're Almost There* (1971), Thomas McGuane's magniloquent *Bushwhacked Piano* (1971), Gurney Norman's *Divine Right's Trip* (1972), Samuel R. Delany's post-apocalyptic *Dhalgren* (1975, but written 1969–73), and whatever you want to call Bob Dylan's *Tarantula* (1971). Of Brautigan's novels, only *The Abortion* has the setting and sensibility of a hippie novel, and only the work he did between 1966 and 1971 — from *The Abortion* through *Revenge of the Lawn* — would qualify as hippie literature. Before that, Brautigan could loosely be called a Beat writer, and after 1971, simply a West Coast writer.

At any rate, *All Watched Over by Machines of Loving Grace* was definitely a hippie production. Fifteen hundred copies were mimeographed in 1967 and distributed free by the Diggers to the flower children who had blown to Haight–Ashbury that "Summer of Love." Some copies were misbound, resulting in duplicate poems, missing poems, and upside-down pages, but the pamphlet did introduce Brautigan to a new audience. And the kids dug it: the poems were funny, sexy, silly, and now. Some of the poems mentioned bands that could be heard on the radio (the Lovin' Spoonful, Jefferson Airplane, the Mamas and the Papas). Others were distributed as single-sheet broadsides with illustrations. These are not Brautigan's greatest poems — he described them to Digger founder Emmett Grogan as "tidbits" — but they are among his most appealing ones, and the new audience they attracted helped make him a best-selling author over the next few years.

His next "book" of poetry was another typical hippie product of the times. *Please Plant This Book* was made of card stock folded to create pockets, with eight seed packets laid in with poems printed on the sides. The "poems" are actually prose pieces, their line breaks merely the result of the size of the seed packets, not metrical requirements. This book of lilting pronouncements on utopian and environmental themes was also distributed free.

In the fall of 1967, Donald Allen's Four Seasons Foundation Press published *Trout Fishing in America,* and the well-deserved success of that slim masterpiece apparently led Allen to invite Brautigan to compile a volume of his selected poetry. For *The Pill versus the Springhill Mine Disaster,* Brautigan's best-known book of verse, Brautigan reached back to his earliest publications: he included his first separate publication, "The Return of the Rivers," the complete *Galilee Hitch-Hiker,* less than half of *Lay the Marble Tea,* most of *The Octopus Frontier,* and all of *Machines of Loving Grace,* along with three dozen newer poems. The book was published by the Four Seasons Foundation in 1968, then reprinted the following year by the Dell Publishing Company of New York, where it went through numerous printings.

Because of its chronological span, *The Pill* is something of a mixed bag, but the range of poetic forms and Summer of Love "vibe" make it his most representative and attractive book of poetry. It opens with his most frequently reprinted poem, "All Watched Over by Machines of Loving Grace," foretelling the dawning of the Age of Aquarius and capturing the giddy sense of new possibilities that was in the air back then. The book is filled with sweet love poems to Marcia Pacaud, recounting "the legend / of her beauty" in the language of street people, but other poems contained enough "heavy" thoughts to give the book some weight. There are some harsh notes here and there: a poem protesting the war entitled "'Star-Spangled' Nails," a swipe at the then-current fad for writing haikus called "Haiku Ambulance," an apocalyptic account of "The Day They Busted the Grateful Dead," and, concluding the book, a poem of farewell (presumably to Marcia) entitled "Boo, Forever." But overall, *The Pill* was easy to swallow, lighter in tone than Beat rantings, and certainly more enjoyable than the turgid (if more sophisticated) academic verse being published at the time.

Rommel Drives on Deep into Egypt, the first of his poetry books to be brought out by a major New York publisher (Delacorte, 1970), has its playful moments, but is a little darker than *The Pill.* The success of *Trout Fishing in America* transformed Brautigan from a struggling hippie who had to hustle for rent money into a rich celebrity who was lionized everywhere he went, but the initial euphoria quickly wore off. He sneers at reviewers who belittled his work ("Critical Can Opener"), dismisses a would-be biographer who had been stalking him ("Cannibal Carpenter"), spits out insults ("Negative Clank"), and writes less of love and more of jealousy and loss. The Summer of Love had turned into a winter of discontent as flower children wilted into hustlers and junkies ("Diet"), and local calamities like busting the Dead paled in comparison to larger events like the assassination of Robert F. Kennedy ("Yeah, There Was Always Going to Be a June 5, 1968").

The superficial simplicity of many of the poems is misleading. One poem — which reads in its entirety "Do you think of me / as often as I think / of you?" — was singled out for criticism by book reviewer Jonathan Yardley for sounding like a bad Hallmark greeting card, which would be a fair assessment had the poem been entitled "Friendship" or "First Love." But it's entitled "Please," which turns the mawkish sentiment into a despairing plea, spoken by someone afraid he's losing the one he loves. (This is reinforced by the poem's placement immediately following "30 Cents, Two Transfers, Love," about a person who has been left by his lover.) I don't think Hallmark makes a card for *that* sinking feeling. Even a sympathetic critic like Terence Malley, who wrote the first book-length study of Brautigan but quotes Yardley with approval, dismisses a poem like "April 7, 1969" as unpoetic, without noticing the careful metrical pattern Brautigan deploys: a perfect line of iambic trimeter is followed by another (after first intentionally stumbling with an extra syllable), then the poem collapses in the third line with a well-placed caesura, leaving the poem to limp to its conclusion, effectively dramatizing the poet's frustration with his failure of imagination on that particular day.

In fact *Rommel* shows a sharpening of Brautigan's poetic skills throughout. There are many striking, compressed images ("Vampire," "Cellular Coyote," "A Closet Freezes"), and poems that extend a metaphor with Brautigan's wonderful sense of poetic logic ("Shellfish," "33-⅓ Sized Lions"). Four poems consist only of titles; like John Cage's notorious music composition 4'33" — whose score instructs a performer to sit in front of a piano without playing it for that amount of time — the reader is invited to fill in the blank text: "1891–1944" is a riddle whose answer is elsewhere in the book, and "A 48-Year-Old Burglar from San Diego" perhaps commemorates a criminal so quiet he doesn't make a sound in the poem; "8 Millimeter (mm)" may be an exposed (blank) roll of film, and "'88' Poems" evokes the 88 keys of a piano, perhaps Brautigan's sly homage to Cage. There is a tighter control of meter in most of the poems, more effective use of enjambment, a more restrained vocabulary. And it's got that terrific cover photo, though perhaps the sight of a grown woman playing in a sandbox is meant to be sad rather than adorable.

Envious of the royalties songwriters earn, he took one of the poems from *Rommel*, "She Sleeps This Very Evening in Greenbrook Castle," and an older poem called "The Horse That Had a Flat Tire" to his friend Janis Joplin for consideration. Needless to say, she passed on both. Brautigan had better luck with another poem from *Rommel* entitled "Love's Not the Way to Treat a Friend." A Bay area band called Mad River invited him to recite it on their second album, *Paradise Bar & Grill* (1969), to the accompaniment of acoustic guitars.[7] In 1970 Brautigan released his own album, *Listening to Richard Brautigan*, on Capitol Records' hip Harvest label (Pink Floyd, Roy Harper, Kevin Ayers, et al.), featuring selections from his prose and poetry. Unlike many professional poets, Brautigan appreciated some rock lyrics, especially

7 The liner notes to the CD reissue state: "Mad River, mindful of Brautigan's kindness when they were starving, had used some of their Capitol advance to pay for the printing of Brautigan's novel [*sic*], *Please Plant This Book*."

those of the Beatles: he had Beatles lyrics posted on the walls of his San Francisco apartment and later wrote a brief foreword to *The Beatles Lyrics Illustrated* (Dell, 1975).

When the 1970s arrived, Brautigan once again put poetry on the back burner in order to concentrate on writing fiction. He signed a lucrative deal with Simon & Schuster, who would publish his next six books and financed his purchase of a ranch in Montana. He first dusted off the five-year-old manuscript of *The Abortion* for publication in 1971, then gathered his wonderful short stories for publication later that same year, naming it *Revenge of the Lawn* after one of its funniest stories. He then began writing the first of the increasingly experimental novels that would occupy him until the end of his life. Determined not to coast on his previous accomplishments — as he said at the time, he didn't want to write "Son of *Trout Fishing in America*" or "Grandson of *Trout Fishing in America*" — he experimented with different temporal structures and juxtaposing disparate genres. The seven novels he wrote in the ten years between 1972 to 1982 — from *The Hawkline Monster* (1973) to *An Unfortunate Woman* (written in 1982, published first in French in 1994 and then in its original form in 2000) — were not as popular as his first four, even though a case can be made — as Marc Chénetier does in his brilliant monograph on Brautigan (Methuen, 1983) — that these novels show a maturation of his aesthetics.

The Hawkline Monster, a historical novel yoking together two previously disparate genres (the Gothic and the Western), appeared in 1974, and was followed in 1975 by *Willard and His Bowling Trophies*, which similarly tied mystery and s&m erotica together. Among *Willard*'s seedy charms is the presence of the *Greek Anthology*, from which the "amateur sadist" Bob reads aloud throughout the novel until it reduces him to despair.[8] This large collection of Greek epigrams, poems, songs, and fragments was originally gathered together in the first century BC by Meleager, and then expanded in the ninth century by Constantinus Cephalus with similar collections, and finally revised in the tenth century into 16 thematic sections. Brautigan owned a set and enjoyed reading it aloud to visitors, recommending the poems to Abbott and other fellow writers as "models of brevity and emotional concision" — the same qualities he found in the haiku and aimed for in his own poetry. Many of the entries in the *Greek Anthology* consist of single lines — all that remain of the original poems — and in some of his poems Brautigan deliberately wrote

8 Brautigan may have first learned of this book from Kenneth Rexroth's *Poems from the Greek Anthology* (1962). Bob is said to have "all three volumes" of the "1928 Putnam edition" (66), but that edition (reprinted from the Loeb edition of a decade earlier) consisted of five volumes and appeared in 1927.

fragments, hoping they would have the same evocative power as the Greek fragments that move Bob to speculate on lost poems and lost lives.

In 1976 Brautigan brought out his next collection of poetry, *Loading Mercury with a Pitchfork*. It's unique among his poetry books for being organized into titled sections, and for having a dominant figure throughout: the crow. This noisy scavenger appears in a half-dozen poems — evoking both Poe's ominous raven and perhaps the Crow tribe of Native Americans that once occupied the land just east of Brautigan's ranch in Montana — and it is a suitable totem animal for these downbeat poems. There are a few examples of the whimsical Brautigan of the Sixties, but most of the poems express the sour feelings of a man becoming increasingly disappointed with himself and those around him. The book's title describes an act of futility, and the mood throughout is grim, regretful.

There's certainly no falling off of technical ability, and the care with which Brautigan organized these poems (mostly written in the early '70s) into titled sections indicates he was still devoted to his craft. The trademark Brautigan similes are as surprising as ever, and he can still turn on the old charm ("I'll Affect You Slowly") and make you laugh ("Attila at the Gates of the Telephone Company"). But most of the poems are from a man who admits: "I collect darkness within myself like the shadow / of a blind lighthouse."

Ghosts, cemeteries, graves, funeral parlors, and tombstones are recurring images. In several poems Brautigan broods on the night sky — stars, distant constellations — as though, like Pascal, the eternal silence of those infinite spaces terrifies him. The hell-raising Baudelaire of *The Galilee Hitch-Hiker* stands in vivid contrast to the catatonic nautical drifter Captain Martin in a similar poem cycle ("Good Luck, Captain Martin"). The latter is one of two poem cycles in the book; the other, "Group Portrait without the Lions," consists of 14 miniature character studies, a sad gallery of poetic snapshots. *Loading Mercury with a Pitchfork* is a mature, reflective collection, and those who consider Brautigan a hippy-dippy poet will find little evidence of that here.

Just as *Loading Mercury* was arriving in bookstores, Brautigan took off for his first trip to Japan. He had a longstanding interest in Japanese literature — both the haiku and the fiction of twentieth-century writers like Yasunari Kawabata,[9] Junichiro Tanizaki, and Kenzaburo Oe — and was flattered by the serious interest Japanese critics took in his work. He kept a poetry journal during his six-week visit, wrote an introduction for it a month later, and published

9 Like Brautigan, Kawabata had a miserable childhood, excelled at very short stories, used startling imagery in his death-haunted fiction, and eventually committed suicide.

the results in 1978 as *June 30th, June 30th* (the title taken from that moment on his return when he crosses the international date line).

Given the circumstances of its composition, *June 30th* would be Brautigan's most unified book of poetry. After an introduction providing "a map that led me to Japan and the writing of this book," Brautigan records his impressions of Japan in about 80 dated poems. He states in the introduction that they "are different from other poems that I have written," and there are indeed fewer striking metaphors and self-consciously "poetic" thoughts than in his earlier poems. At first the tone is lighter, less despairing than *Loading Mercury*; the change of scenery briefly restored Brautigan to his old self, allowing him to take delight in what he sees on his first trip to Japan. Winning silly prizes at a pachinko parlor, he goes so far as to say, "I feel wonderful, exhilarated, child-like, / perfect." But soon the drinking and depression set in, and the ominous crows from *Loading Mercury* return. "The American Fool" he calls himself, making cultural blunders, ranting drunkenly at his Japanese friends, and generally embarrassing himself. "Lazarus on the Bullet Train" is an especially candid admission by Brautigan of how impossible he could be. A few poems deal with an affair he had with a woman named Shiina Takako, who owned a lively bar in Tokyo patronized by writers and artists. (She's pictured on the back dust-jacket cover of *The Tokyo–Montana Express*.) But despite his obvious love for Japan, to which he would often return in the years following, the poems indicate it wasn't enough to halt the downward spiral his life was taking.

The book was largely ignored by the American book-review media, but Brautigan's Montana neighbor and fellow novelist Jim Harrison provided an acute assessment on the back cover of the book that deserves to be preserved. Addressing his friend directly, he wrote:

> What can I say? It is your work that has touched me the most deeply, the least mannered and the most exact in its insistent nakedness. It is not a succession of lyrics but finally ONE BOOK. A long poem that offers us its bounty in fragments. It is saturated with the "otherness" we know to be our most honest state and the true state of poetry. It offers itself in perhaps the unconscious but ancient fabled form of the voyage. It is about the stately courage and loneliness of this voyage into a strange land which is both Japan and the true self of the poet, where there are no barriers to admitting and singing all. It is about love and exhaustion and permanent transition, so fatal that it is beyond the poet's comprehension. I love the book because it is a true song, owning no auspices other than its own; owning the purity we think we aim at on this bloody journey.

June 30th, June 30th was the last collection of poetry Brautigan published. He continued to write poetry in the years following: a half-dozen were published in magazines before his death, a few more have appeared posthumously, and hundreds more are among his papers at the Bancroft Library (University of California at Berkeley). They continue to record his despair, but also include meditations on karma and reincarnation. Richard Brautigan committed suicide in October 1984, three months short of his fiftieth birthday.

"I'm a minor poet. I don't pretend to be anything else," Brautigan told Keith Abbott modestly in 1970, surprised at the virulence of a negative review of his work. But a minor poet is not necessarily an inconsequential one, or a forgettable one, and this particular minor poet who set out to make "paper flowers out of love and death" deserves to be remembered:

> Don't *ever ever* forget
> the flowers
> that were rejected, made
> fools of.
>
> ("Japanese Pop Music Concert")

The First Draft Version of *Infinite Jest*

David Foster Wallace began working on his second novel in the fall of 1991 — the outgrowth of an essay he wrote that season called "Derivative Sport in Tornado Alley" — and by the fall of 1993 had completed a working draft. He made two photocopies of the manuscript, sent one to Michael Pietsch, his editor at Little, Brown, and loaned the second to a young woman whom he was trying to impress at the time (he later told me). Pietsch was enthusiastic about the manuscript but asked Wallace to consider shortening it, so Dave asked me if I'd be willing to read it and suggest cuts. (At that time we were both working in the same town, Normal, Illinois: Dave taught at Illinois State University, and I was managing editor of the *Review of Contemporary Fiction*/Dalkey Archive Press, located on ISU's campus.) Dave's plan was to compare Pietsch's suggested cuts with mine, and accept the ones on which we both agreed. (He also explained he was planning to add more material, though.) I instantly agreed, jokingly adding the condition that I could keep the manuscript afterward — I would have read it anyway. Dave agreed, and on 3 December 1993 he gave me the huge manuscript (the young woman's copy). I needed both hands to support it.

Why me? I guess because I'd been an early supporter of his. (What follows sounds uncomfortably like tooting my own horn, so I'll keep it brief.) I had read *The Broom of the System* when it was published in 1987 and had been very impressed; even if not an entirely successful novel, it struck me as written by someone possessed of genius. A few months later I was invited to guest-edit a special issue of the *Review of Contemporary Fiction* to be called "Novelist As Critic." It amounted to little more than inviting my favorite novelists to contribute an essay on any literary topic, the working assumption (which I still hold) being that novelists write better criticism than most professional critics. Since all of the authors I invited were well along in their careers, I thought I should have at least one emerging writer, so I wrote to Wallace in care of his publisher and invited him to submit something, an offer he found "intriguing" (he had never written an essay for publication before). His "Fictional Futures and the Conspicuously Young" appeared in the fall 1988 issue and confirmed my impression that he was brilliant. (Our typesetter, on the other hand — a wonderful middle-aged woman who had her doubts about much of the stuff we published — thought he sounded snotty.)

We stayed in touch. I suggested *Conjunctions* as someplace he might submit future stories (he'd never heard of it). For the summer 1989 issue of *RCF*, whose staff I had joined by that time, I wrote a favorable review of *Girl with Curious Hair*, and along about then I invited him to contribute to a special issue we were planning on novelist David Markson. Wallace was going through a difficult period, but he came through with another brilliant essay, "The Empty Plenum: David Markson's *Wittgenstein's Mistress*" (*RCF* Summer 1990), which did nothing to alter our typesetter's opinion of him but certainly kept mine sky-high. In 1992 I informed him of an opening in the English department at ISU, for which he applied and was accepted, and later that year guest-editor Larry McCaffery and I decided he had to be part of the "Younger Writers Issue" we were planning for the summer 1993 *RCF*. For that Wallace submitted what would become his most famous essay, "E Unibus Pluram: Television and U.S. Fiction" (which had been rejected by *Harper's* because of its length) along with several selections of what he had finally decided to call *Infinite Jest*. (As late as January 1993 he was calling it simply the "longer thing.") So perhaps all this support, plus similar tastes in fiction (we both revere William Gaddis, for example), led him to entrust me with his manuscript.

First, a physical description: It's a mess — a patchwork of different fonts and point sizes, with numerous handwritten corrections/additions on most pages, and paginated in a nesting pattern (e.g., p. 22 is followed by 22A–J before resuming with p. 23, which is followed by 23A–D, etc). Much of it is single-spaced, and what footnotes existed at this stage appear at the bottom of pages. (Most of those in the published book were added later.) Several states of revision are present: some pages are early versions, heavily overwritten with changes, while others are clean final drafts. Throughout there are notes in the margins, reminders to fix something or other, adjustments to chronology (which seems to have given Wallace quite a bit of trouble), even a few drawings and doodles. Merely flipping through the 4-inch-high manuscript would give even a seasoned editor the howling fantods.

What follows is a description of its contents. I'll cite the manuscript page numbers (hereafter abbreviated MS), and following an = sign will give the equivalent pages in the published version of *Infinite Jest* (hereafter abbreviated *IJ*), unless the section was cut, in which case I'll provide a brief summary. (For copyright reasons I'll have to keep my quotations of unpublished material to a minimum.) And I'll add color commentary on points that may be of interest to future scholars.

Title page. Typewritten: "First Two Sections / *Infinite Jest*," followed by the name and address of Wallace's agent, Bonnie Nadell. (No subtitle; Chris Hager says Wallace wanted to subtitle the novel "a failed entertainment," but that must have been added later, and then rejected by the publisher.) Handwritten are various notes Wallace wrote to himself, e.g., "Mid-East attaché in Mexico City. 'Good bit of Mexico not answering its phone,'" and what looks like "DMZ is ultimate phenomenal speed — halluce — believe you have radically sped up, whole world slow, ESP, no speech — Death[.] See Wraith & Gately." Other notes concern Mrs. Gately's stroke and the correct spelling of mille*nn*ium.

A–B. "Preliminary Throat-Clearings." These two pages contain the dedication to Fenton Foster (whom Wallace identified as "My mother's father, who died before I was born" in an interview with Valerie Stivers), an epigraph — "Sorrow brings forth" from Blake's *Marriage of Heaven and Hell* — followed by various definitions of *addict* and *addiction*. The first is taken from the *American Heritage Dictionary of the English Language, New College Edition*, and the rest from Hal's beloved *Oxford English Dictionary*, including some illustrative quotations. Two of the more relevant ones: "A man who causes grief to his family by addiction to bad habits" (Mill, *Liberty*) and "Each man to what sports and revels his addiction leads him" (Shakespeare, *Othello* 2.2.6). Wallace cut this *Moby-Dick*-like opening and decided to let Hal summarize his findings: "The original sense of *addiction* involved being bound over, dedicated, either legally or spiritually. To devote one's life, plunge in. I had researched this" (*IJ* 900).

1–5 = *IJ* 27–31. The novel originally began with Hal's interview with his father disguised as a "professional conversationalist." This makes thematic sense since Jim Incandenza's failure to communicate with his son leads him to create the *Infinite Jest* cartridge, but in my report to Wallace I wrote: "this is wild & funny, but rather too much so; that is, it differs from the rest of the book so much in tone & content that it will give the reader the wrong idea of what kind of novel this is going to be." (I suggested he begin instead with what is now *IJ* 200–11.) The date gave Wallace some trouble: the chapter was originally dated Year of the Perdue Wonderchicken, then changed to Trial-Size Dove Bar before settling on Year of the Tucks Medicated Pad. (Handwritten note: "Incandenza needs to suicide in Year of Dove Bar.") Likewise with Hal's age: Wallace originally typed: "I'll be 14 in December," then crossed it out and wrote 13. The first edition of the novel reads "I'll be thirteen" (p. 27) but the paperback edition reads "I'll be eleven." (N.B.: Wallace made numerous corrections for the paperback edition of 1997, so that edition is the one scholars should use. Put a Mylar cover on the pretty hardback and leave it on the shelf.) Another interesting change: instead of a crisis in southern Quebec (*IJ* 29) Wallace originally set the crisis in Sierra Leone.

5A–F = *IJ* 42–49. The MS. supplies the names of some of Orin's "Subjects": instead of "The Subject after Bain's sister but before the one just before this one" (*IJ* 47) Wallace wrote: "The woman after Helen Slansker and before Binnie van Vleck" (MS 5D). Leaving them nameless better conveys Orin's attitude toward women. (Orin was originally called Cully.) Test-subject Fenton (*IJ* 48; note dedicatee above) was originally called Curtis. For Helen Slansker, see 56–56A below.

6–15 = *IJ* 17–26. Erdedy's dealer "had promised to get him a fifth of a kilogram of marijuana, 200 grams of unusually good marijuana, for $1250 U.S." (*IJ* 18), metricized and inflated from the MS's "She had promised to get him a quarter of a pound of marijuana, four ounces of unusually good marijuana, for $550.00" (MS 6).

15A = *IJ* 32–33.

16–17 = *IJ* 37–38. Dolores Epps's brother was originally named Rodney, then Londell, before Wallace settled on Columbus Epps (*IJ* 38).

17A–C = *IJ* 33–37. *Nass*, "the Arabic-language video edition of April's *Self* magazine" (*IJ* 36) was originally an unnamed Arabic edition of *Harper's Bazaar*. The MS chapter ends "the viewer's digital display reads 7:20PM" instead of the book's "1927h" (*IJ* 37). Throughout the MS time is given the old-fashioned way.

18–20 = *IJ* 39–42. There is no reference to Puccini's *Tosca* (*IJ* 41) in the MS version.

20A = *IJ* 42. Time adjusted from 8:00PM to 2010h.

21 = *IJ* 38–39. The MS describes Mildred Bonk as "The kind of dreadful female figure who glides through the sweaty junior-high corridors of a nocturnal emitter's dreamscape." Wallace's revision to "fatally pretty and nubile wraithlike figure" (*IJ* 38) anticipates the Joelle van Dyne/Jim Incandenza as wraith/fatal cartridge developments in the novel. The succinct, alliterative summary "A vision in a sundress and silly shoes" (*IJ* 39) replaces the more fanciful MS version: "A vision. A nymph, you would have described her as.

Ninth-grade rumor had it she didn't even go to the bathroom: small forest animals descended with coos and twitters and took the stuff away, inessential as talc, the peristalsand of a creature that lives on light." (That p-word means the product of peristalsis, the involuntary contractions that force waste through the alimentary canal.)

21A–B: cut. A brief episode set in the Year of the Perdue Wonderchicken describing Avril Incandenza in a post-coital moment with unnamed older lover in the headmaster house's master bedroom in Enfield, before racing to the airport to pick up her "husband and son."

21–22 = *IJ* 130. An early version of the mugging of Burt F. Smith by Poor Tony.

22A–G = *IJ* 49–54. Jim Struck was originally called Rutherford Poat here and elsewhere in the MS. This is the first point in the MS where footnotes are used (=*IJ* 983–84nn5–9); a note indicates Wallace intended to include an ONANTA Jr. Tournament Schedule as Appendix X. (The only appendix in the MS is Incandenza's filmography.) The book version of this chapter is much more detailed than the MS, which concludes more abruptly and with an unexpected pronoun: "It's unclear to me whether or not this is a bad thing."

22G–1 = *IJ* 54. Time adjusted from 12:15AM to 0015h.

22H–J: cut. Dated Year of the Depend Adult Undergarment, this is a first-person account by Hal of his mother's grammar class, including a sample final exam. (E.g. "Briefly explain why phrase-structure rules alone are insufficient for the explication of the following clause — 'I had three books stolen.'") Several questions have to do with the grammatical structure of "the opening independent clause of the L. and A. Maude translation of Tolstoi's *Anna Karenina* — 'All happy families resemble one another, each unhappy family is unhappy in its own way.'" (The wide diversity of unhappy families in *IJ* could be generated from this classic opening sentence.) There is a reference to the exam on *IJ* 95. Hal also comments on how Enfield training prepares one to handle "surreal panic."

22–23: cut. A young Jim Incandenza tells of a night he accompanied his father to kill a particularly large black widow spider. The episode begins: "I have one sober memory of my father. . . ."; cf. *IJ* 157–69, a different memory of Jim's father.

23A–D = *IJ* 60–63, 67–68. The longer book version dwells more on Troelsch's symptoms, while the MS recounts one of his dreams. The passage on *IJ* 67–68 is labeled "HAL SOLIL[OQUY]" in the MS., which contains an X'ed out earlier version of this passage (MS 23–24).

24–32 = *IJ* 68–78. Kate's remark "I was going to say I've thought sometimes before like the feeling maybe had to do with Hope" (*IJ* 75) originally detoured into this comic exchange:

> 'I was about to say I've thought before it seems like it maybe has something to do with pot.'
>
> The doctor's eyebrows became angled with puzzlement before he could stop them. 'A pot?'
>
> 'Oh for Christ's sake. Yes, a pot, this piece of cookware my dear sainted mother used to abuse me with.' She saw his pen dip toward her chart. 'No, the bloodbath guy, in Cambodia, with the fields. Jesus what am I *doing* here. *Pot*. Bob Hope. Smoke.' She made a quick joint-gesture with thumb and finger held to rounded lips.

Kate's reference at the end of the chapter to *One Flew Over the Cuckoo's Nest* — "That old cartridge, Nichols and the big Indian" (*IJ* 78) — originally read "That old Jack Nicholson movie" (MS 32). Interesting that Wallace would have Kate misremember the famous actor's name, while making her smart enough to know of the killing fields of Cambodian dictator Pol Pot (1928–98).

32A = *IJ* 78–79. Time adjusted from 1:00 to 0145h.

32–38 = *IJ* 79–85. The Nick Bollettieri camp (*IJ* 79) was originally called a Harry Hopman tennis camp. Next to the physical description of Schtitt (MS 33; *IJ* 80) Wallace wrote "vampirish-looking." Incandenza's founding Latin motto (*IJ* 81) was originally *LARVARDUS PRODEO* — a slip for *Larvatus prodeo*, "I advance masked," which was the young Descartes' motto. "Schtitt was educated in pre-Unification *Gymnasium* under the rather Kanto-Hegelian idea . . ." (*IJ* 82) originally read: ". . . under the classic idea (via Pfau and Wasser's 1936 *Spiele und Knaben*) . . ." (MS 35). After the sentence ending "this flat and short-sighted idea of personal happiness" (*IJ* 83) the MS added: "Schtitt is obsessed with, and never tires of repeating, the fact that in the final year of unsubsidized time, more Americans watched something called *Wheel of Fortune* than all four network newscasts combined" (MS 36).

38–40 = *IJ* 85–87. The wordy sentence "The trees' bony fingers make spell-casting gestures in the wind as they pass" (*IJ* 86) was originally punchier:

"Bare trees cast witch-fingers at the sky" (MS 39), not to mention avoided pronoun confusion (not that anyone would think "they" refers to the trees and not the schoolboys).

40–[42]: cut. This section begins: "Hal Incandenza got introduced to drug use for comparatively innocent reasons; he'd wanted to be able to sleep through a recurring bad dream," and continues with a brief history of his drug abuse: "eating mushrooms and tabs with Michael Pemulis and Rutherford Poat and Ortho Slice and all other most sinister players in ETA's chemical crowd, plus of course the liquor stores all through Brighton dispensed wares to anyone whose head cleared the register's counter, and so Hal . . . was an interior wreck by 17 . . ." But Wallace X'ed this out and wrote in the margin "BAG — NO 41." He revised this on MS 40K–N.

40A–E = *IJ* 95–105 (but without the Marathe/Steeply interlude on 97). A heavily revised section printed in 8-point type. (Dave told me he did this to disguise the book's length from his editor, who of course wasn't fooled for an instant.)

40E–K = *IJ* 109–121. Ditto.

40K–N: cut. After "There is a twinge in a tooth on his mouth's left side" (*IJ* 121), the MS continues without a section break with a longer account of Hal's drug history and the "ghastly nightmares" that "are an occupational hazard of serious junior tennis."

42–47 = *IJ* 128–35. Originally narrated by an unidentified "me" rather than the book's "yrstruly."

47–48 = *IJ* 93.

48–52 = *IJ* 151–56. Many small revisions but substantially the same. In the MS, one of Pemulis's T-shirts (cf. *IJ* 156) reads "Remember Bobby Sands," the Irish nationalist who died in prison in 1981 after a hunger strike protesting the British decision to criminalize those previously held as political prisoners.

52A = *IJ* 87.

52–53 = *IJ* 63–65. Avril Mondragon (as on *IJ* 64) was originally called Constance Bilodeau. Though brief, the book version of this chapter is twice as long (i.e., detailed) as the MS.

53–54 = *IJ* 137–38. MS says the Ennet House was founded in the Year of the Tucks Medicated Pad, revised to Year of the Whopper for the book. Similarly the MS has the founder dying at age 56 instead of 68. (The Ennet House was based on Granada House in Brighton, where Wallace lived the first half of 1990.)

54A = *IJ* 127–28. This description of Lyle was a staple of Dave's readings in the 1990s.

55A–56 = *IJ* 140–42. The book's heading is longer than the MS's, which stops at "PASSED FROM THIS LIFE."

56–56A = *IJ* 142–44. MS has Helen Slansker instead of Helen Steeply as the author of this heartless *Moment* article. The closing sentence's power saw (*IJ* 144) was originally a hatchet.

57–58 = *IJ* 169–71. From about this point on, fewer and fewer of the chapters are dated in the MS. The MS. had Aldous Huxley considering Leary's invitation to become writer-in-residence at Millbrook in the late 1960s until I reminded Wallace that Huxley died in 1963 (the same day Kennedy was assassinated), so he changed it to Alan Watts (*IJ* 170; whether it's true Watts received such an offer, I don't know). Instead of the Riverside *Hamlet* (*IJ* 171), Hal originally held "the *American Heritage* Fourth" (MS 58).

58–61 = *IJ* 172–76. The film Hal narrates was originally called *Too Much Fun,* the title of one of his father's unfinished films (*IJ* 993), and was dated differently in the headnote. Instead of 8½ (*IJ* 175), Wallace originally had *One-Eyed Jacks,* then crossed that out and inserted "Powell's *Peeping Tom,*" a 1959 British film summarized by *Halliwell's* thus: "A film studio focus puller is obsessed by the lust to murder beautiful women and photograph the fear on their faces."

61–65 = *IJ* 176–81.

65–76 = *IJ* 157–69. Originally dated April 1961.

77–81 = *IJ* 55–60. Moved much closer to the front of the published book, this was another favored piece at Wallace's readings in the 1990s.

81A–K = *IJ* 491–503. Young Jim's account of helping his father move a mattress was moved back to the middle of the published book. In the upper right-hand corner of p. 81A is a handwritten note: "Sold to Harper's 5/93." It was published in their 9/93 issue with the title "The Awakening of My Interest in Annular Systems."

81L = *IJ* 135–37. The phone call from Orin was greatly expanded for the published version.

81–90 = *IJ* 181–93. The account of Madame Psychosis's radio program was likewise greatly expanded for the book version, though some sections were cut from the MS., e.g. an ethnic survey of reactions to the radio show's obscure background music: "Madame Psychosis's cued musics [*sic*] make Arab MIT students ache for minarets and muezzins' azans, their foreheads itch for the feel of non-representational carpet. German graduate students get lumped-throated envisioning Tubingen roses blooming time-lapse in perfectly ordered rows. The Canadian kids don't think of anything at all. The Swiss kids cop images of prolix clocks," and so on. "Mario's convinced Schtitt would like this music if you could get him to take the Wagner off and try something else for once, in his office" (MS 88).

90–109 = *IJ* 219–40 (excluding the interludes on 223 and 227). Joelle van Dyne is called Joelle ver Nooy in the MS. and is described as "the daughter of a pipe-fitter from Arkansas." (Wallace has a note in the margin urging *Reconsider*; he changed it to "a low-pH chemist" for the published novel; the name ver Nooy has some connection with Wallace's alma mater Amherst; "van Dyne" is probably meant to evoke "anodyne," which Dave once used in the sense of "painkiller" in a letter to me). Wallace cut from the MS Molly Notkin's winning strategy against her examiners for passing her Orals (she "took a seat not right opposite the three of them but *with* them . . . they'll attack only from a distance"). The reference to Yugoslav director Dusân Makavajev [sic] at the bottom of *IJ* 233 was originally to "late Maillaux" (MS 103), whoever that is. In the MS Joelle states, "I am five feet nine inches tall. I weigh 121 pounds, or 55 kilos," which Wallace changed to "I am 1.7 meters tall and weigh 48 kilograms" (*IJ* 234).

109–14 = *IJ* 211–19. Wallace cut another paragraph on Hal's drug history (he "has in two years gone from Mormonesque [*sic*] abstinence to a willingness to absorb just about anything at all. . . . Pemulis refers to him with good humor as a garbage-head"). Charles Tavis's surname is Davis in some places in the MS.

114–16 = *IJ* 240–42. The first-person "To I think it must be the southwest" (bottom of *IJ* 241) isn't in the MS, which suggests Hal is narrating this little geography lesson.

116A–N = *IJ* 242–58. An immaculate typescript, and very close to the published version.

116O, 117–18 = *IJ* 193–98.

119–29 = *IJ* 258–70. John Wayne is said to be from Kirkland, New Brunswick; changed to Montcerf, Quebec, for the novel (*IJ* 259); Avril was likewise originally from New Brunswick rather than Quebec.

130–37 = *IJ* 270–81. Geoffrey Day is 49 in the MS, 46 in the book (*IJ* 270). Numerous similar small changes, e.g., Day originally drove his Saab through the window of a sporting goods store in Somerville, revised to Brookline, and finally to Malden (*IJ* 272). The MS's Morse Code was changed to "Morris Code" for the book (*IJ* 275), one of numerous instances throughout the finished novel where the narrative employs phonetic spellings and malapropisms even outside of quoted dialogue, what's been called a "free indirect discourse" based on the education level of a chapter's protagonist (in this instance, Gately) while maintaining a third-person authorial presence. Before settling on The Fiends in Human Shape (*IJ* 276), Wallace noted a number of band names: The Husks, Snout, The Green Men, The Exquisite Corpses (top of MS 134). On the top of MS 136 there's a note "Joelle knows Day from BU."

137–38 = *IJ* 281–83. The MS doesn't specify what everyone is reading, as does *IJ* 281–82. Tavis imitates Richard Nixon in the MS instead of the novel's Pierre Trudeau (*IJ* 282).

138–42 = *IJ* 299–306. MS calls him "Queer Tony" rather than "Poor Tony." The Year of the Whopper was originally called the Year of the Twinkie (MS 139).

142A–E = *IJ* 306–12. The classes taught by prorectors in the MS were different: "Rik Dunkel's 'History of Styrofoam,' Mary Esther Thode's 'Contemporary Psychoethical Quandaries,' Donni Stott's 'Geography of the Rhineland' [crossed out and replaced by Thierry Ontan's 'Separatism and Return'], Corbett Thorp's 'Deviant Logics,' Aubrey DeLint's 'Sport and Society,' Tex Watson's 'The Atom in the Mirror: A Lay Look at Annular Fusion,' Tony Nwangi's 'Minority Fashions,' etc." (cf. *IJ* 306). After the reference to smallpox *variola*

(*IJ* 310), Wallace cut from the MS a long passage that begins: "Hal's maybe favorite anecdote wasn't even in the assigned part of Thevet's *Cosmographie* — it was the part where the vain and imperious French General Sieur de Roberval, setting sail from France on the second big Canadian expedition in 1541, '. . . took with him his niece, Marguerite, a beautiful and high spirited girl.'" The story continues with a young nobleman, in love with Marguerite, joining the expedition; the disapproving father abandons his niece and her old nurse on Canada's Isle of Demons, to which the nobleman swims. The three eke out a living, Marguerite bears a child, who dies, then Marguerite walks out into the ocean to drown herself. The nobleman takes up with the old nurse, and they are finally rescued and return to Europe, "where the couple earned a handsome living travelling around Portugal on a kind of lecture-tour describing the incestuous heartlessness of Roberval and the general French character" (MS 142C–D). I would have guessed Wallace found this anecdote in his friend William T. Vollmann's *Fathers and Crows* (1992), but a little digging uncovered the source to be not Thevet's impossibly rare book but Francis Parkman's *Pioneers of France in the New World* (1865), also a major resource for Vollmann. Parkman also supplied a few French-Canadian names in *IJ*: Poutrincourt, and Pointgravè and DesMonts (spelled Pontgravé and De Monts in Parkman), the Rosencrantz and Guildenstern of *IJ*.

142–46 = *IJ* 312–17. In the margin next to the first sentence is the note (re: Mario): "Mutated because product of incest? Tavis w/ khaki skin and dinosaur eyes?" — an odd question since Tavis and Avril are not biologically related. (See *IJ* 314 for Mario's khaki skin and dinosaur eyes.) The MS has the Incandenzas living in Beacon Hill, not the Back Bay.

146–67 = *IJ* 321–42 (+ 1023–25, nn. 123–24). The only heavily footnoted chapter in the MS (with notes and diagrams at the bottom of pages rather than as endnotes) In the MS equivalent to the end of the long paragraph on *IJ* 330, Pemulis begins adding some long footnotes on hard-core game theory, a "Pure-Strategy Table," other diagrams (one pair is labeled MADAME and PSYCHOSIS), and some very complicated math equations I'm not qualified to describe. (At the end Pemulis says, "If you got all the way through this my hat's off" — to which Wallace added in the margin "Particularly to Gerry Howard," the editor of his first two books, and who Wallace assumed would publish this one as well.) In my report I suggested that Dave condense this tour-de-forceful chapter a bit, and perhaps for that reason Pemulis's footnotes got the ax. (This chapter is followed immediately by the brief description of the Statue of Liberty [MS 167], which was moved to the end of the following chapter for the book [*IJ* 367]. There are a half-dozen versions of the Liberty sentence on various pages in this portion of the MS.)

168–83 = *IJ* 343–67. Another chapter with some footnotes, including one Wallace discarded: after the phrase "warm day after cold day" (*IJ* 350 bottom), there's this note: "See for instance photos of people released after long periods in concentration camps; do they look 'happy'?" (MS 172). Wallace wisely decided not to equate brutal internment with reckless addiction, despite the physical similarity between prisoners and addicts. Ferocious Francis was originally called Bobby McCarren, then Bobby Hurst. At one point on p. 176 of the MS — equivalent to the paragraph ending "abject AA mirth" on *IJ* 356 — Wallace originally planned to insert pp. 176A–W, but then changed his mind: see next entry.

176A–W = *IJ* 1007–21. I asked Dave if he moved some sections back to the endnotes as a compromise against eliminating them entirely (since they would take up less space in the smaller point size), but he said no. My copy of the MS is missing pp. 176A–P.

183A–B: cut. A brief episode labeled "CATATONIC INSERT," beginning: "A couple of the Enfield Marine Hospital security guys Mario'd met when they made 'Dial C For Concupiscence' [see *IJ* 992] sometimes drop by Tequila Mockingbird on Blind Bouncer night when Hal and like maybe Troeltsch are in there." These "young dim big good guys" describe "some of the specimens they keep secure" in Unit #5 (see *IJ* 196–97).

184–88 = *IJ* 367–75.

188–90 = *IJ* 376–79. MS p. 190 is labeled 190–95 to synch it with the succeeding pages.

195A–200 = *IJ* 380–86. Aubrey DeLint's first name was originally Dana.

200A–B = *IJ* 379 and 375–76 ("There'd been that first brutal winter night . . ."). The MS is longer because Lyle tells a drunken Incandenza, depressed by harsh criticism (*IJ* 375), "the fable of the Smart Old Bee and the Foolish Young Bee," about a hyperactive young bee that preferred flying around and enjoying the sights to working at the hive. "The Smart Old Bee watched the Foolish Young Bee ignore his advice about apollonian motion vs. dyonesian [*sic*] motion and fly around terrorizing al fresco diners . . . and decided, in true Blakean fashion, that (in an almost ultrasonically high and tiny bee-voice) 'You never know what is enough unless you know what is more than enough.'"

He asks the Young Bee to spend a day within a flower while "it opened its petals to drink the light and feed the bees," an experience wasted on the Young Bee. "All he had experienced inside that flower, he complained, was a gradual enlargement of the world outside until he forgot the flower altogether because he was now in the world, and so flew away from the flower that had gradually let him go."

200–208 = *IJ* 386–95. This chapter on Lyle begins more simply in the MS: "No guru's immune to fruitless yearnings, sometimes," and was both cut and expanded for the book version. The return to Mario's film (*IJ* 391–94) comes at a different point in the MS. (There should be a section break at the top of *IJ* 391; Wallace made verbal corrections for the paperback edition but neglected numerous bad layout problems like this; see, e.g., 692, 701, 736.)

208–18 = *IJ* 395–410. In the novel, this chapter opens with a passage that originally followed the end — "Like most young people genetically hard-wired for a secret drug problem . . ." (*IJ* 395) — which in the MS is accompanied by a handwritten note that seems to read "addiction fairly gallops in both the Incandenza and Tavis family trees" (MS 218).

218–26 = *IJ* 410–18.

226–28 = *IJ* 430–34.

228A–B = *IJ* 434–36. At the top of MS 228A is a note "Pt. II open?" suggesting (as does the title page) that the novel would be divided into parts. Stavros's ambition to open a women's shoe store isn't discussed in the MS.

228–33 = *IJ* 436–42.

233A–B: cut. This brief section set in August of the Year of the Trial-Size Dove Bar begins: "You, Don Gately, 19 [circled with "20?" above it], currently and it turns out very temporarily of Lowell, MA, Boston's extreme North Shore, meperidine addict and journeyman burglar, using a hole in a high hedge and some 10X binoculars not your own to scout out potential burglarees . . . become an unsuspected witness to the first ever confirmed U.S.A. sighting of a giant feral infant, a giant feral infant [redundancy *sic*], south of the Great Concavity within which nothing is ever confirmed." Gately watches the wholesome members of the Young Christians Community House prepare a picnic for the hard-luck family living next door when he hears "Something unspeakable." A monster-movie description of the infant on MS 233E was deleted from what is now *IJ* 447.

233B–F = *IJ* 442–49. Substantially rewritten, cutting some paragraphs (see above), expanding others.

233F = *IJ* 449–50.

233G–O = *IJ* 450–61. The clause "the thing it's not entirely impossible he may have fathered asleep" (*IJ* 451) doesn't appear in the MS, apparently added to give another hint about Tavis's relationship to Mario.

233P–R: cut. This "Running and Salvation Insert" describes the E.T.A.s' different conditioning runs and one Friday when Hal, Stice, Troeltsch, and Mario watch a Salvation Army rally.

233–51 = *IJ* 461–89 (excluding 470–75). The Purity Supreme Market (*IJ* 461) was originally called simply the Star Market. No mention yet in the MS of Gately's former girlfriend Pamela Hoffman-Jeep (*IJ* 465; Wallace took that name from a regular *RCF* reviewer named Lynda Hoffman-Jeep: she had a review in the same "Younger Writers Issue" in which he was featured, and he obviously took a shine to her unusual name). In the MS Pat Montesian drives not like "a maniac" (*IJ* 465) but "like Annie Hall." In the pre-metric MS, Gately is described as 6'2" and 280 pounds. The MS has only a paragraph break between the section ending on *IJ* 469 and its resumption at *IJ* 475.

The "new girl Amy J." (*IJ* 475) was originally an "old male panhandler Danny something" (MS 240). The transition between Gately and the Antitoi brothers by way of a piece of debris (MS 244; *IJ* 480) is *very* Gaddisian, as in his novel *J R* (1975), which Wallace taught at ISU during this time. Bertraund was originally called Stefe Antitoi, and the store Antitoi Notions. The French phrase "IL NE FAUT PLUS QU'ON PURSUIVE LE BONHEUR" (*IJ* 483) was originally given in English as "HAPPINESS NEED NO LONGER BE PURSUED" (MS 247).

251A–C = *IJ* 550–53. At the top of 251A Wallace wrote "Misplaced ch[apter]. This ch. should be moved 70 pp. ahead." (See MS 314B–D below.) The MS version has Jim Struck interfacing with Dr. Rusk instead of Ortho Stice, and stopping after the crack about linoleum. Rusk's door originally had "two Gothic-script quotes from Andrea Dworkin" in addition to the sampler. Struck/Stice originally proposed naming his anger Bernard, then Cletis, rather than Horace (*IJ* 551). What sounds to Pemulis like Tavis exhorting himself "Total worry total worry" (*IJ* 552) in the MS was a military chant: "One, Two, Three,

Four/Every Night I Pray For War . . . Five, Six, Seven, Eight/Kill, Rape, Mutilate" (MS 251B). Hal's mother is here called Elaine, though usually it's Constance in the MS.

252–58: cut. Labeled "Catatonic Lady Eavesdrops on Ennet House Conversations" and dated 11 November, Year of the Depend Adult Undergarment, this concerns a catatonic "Thing" from the Shed over at Enfield Marine's Unit #3 (i.e., #5: see *IJ* 196) who is wheeled over to the Ennet House "to soak up an atmosphere of substance-recovery." It's mostly dialogue, similar to the material on *IJ* 563–65, with some funny-bad puns ("Kid, sex is like a cemetery. Get a lot while you're young" [MS 256]).

259–71 = *IJ* 283–99. This chapter is unique in having a centered title and subtitle:

An Inspirational Story
(To Give Up Is To Go On —
Moral In Defense of Apostasy)

Here the Moms is called Minovia; in addition to Orwell's "Politics and the English Language" (*IJ* 288) her grammar group reads "Edwin Newman and William Safire's treatises" (MS 263). The MS gushingly introduces Joelle as "a freshman baton-twirler with huge happy hair whose ringlets were discs and whose legs went up to her armpits, who twirled and strutted with immaculate posture and a diffident expression, whose legs were the color of whole milk against the bruised color of the sunrise sky . . . who was quite simply drop-dead pretty" (MS 264). The novel's gentle note that Orin "had already drawn idle little sideways 8's on the postcoital flanks of a dozen B.U. coeds" (*IJ* 289) replaces the MS's coarser "had already gone about penetrating a huge cross-section of BU's incoming freshwomen." The unnamed "cleft-chinned and solidly B.U.-connected Dad" at the top of *IJ* 291 is revealed to be Dr. Geoffrey Day in the MS. Joelle is the daughter of Joe Lon ver Nooy of Meyer, Arkansas, and though called the "prettiest girl of all time" in the MS is not yet acronymed P.G.O.A.T.

271A–D = *IJ* 503–7. Nearly identical to the published version. This is the selection from the MS, of the three or four Dave offered, I chose to run in the *RCF* "Younger Writers Issue" in spring 1993.

272–91 = *IJ* 508–27. Trevor Axford's role in this much-revised chapter was originally assigned to a "Danny Fuller," crossed out and replaced by Jim

Struck. Following the reference to Brewster's Angle (*IJ* 511), the MS has this excised, bracketed note: "[Caroline Sutton, 'How Do They That,' angle at which light hits thing so they produce horizontal waves and thus glare]." (See Sutton's *How Do They Do That: Wonders of the Far and Recent Past Explained* [1984].) Another e&b'd note reads: "[Use McLean bldgs., part of McLean's tunnel map, for schema of ETA]" (MS 275). The "diddle-check" goes on a little longer in the MS as the moppets give more explicit examples of inappropriate contact, e.g. Tina Echt's query, "'You mean like when Uncle Rollo back home in Pawtucket likes me to climb on his lap and bounce up and down and play Horsie-With-Progressively-Lumpier-Saddle, he calls it?'" Tiny Gretchen Holt and Jolene Criess ask similar questions (MS 277). A section detailing the more brutal disciplinary methods at other tennis academies in North and South America was cut following the reference to ETA's puker-drills (*IJ* 515). The footnote to "Coatlicue Complex" reads "No clue" (*IJ* 516, 1036 n.216), but the MS helpfully supplies another e&b'd note: "[Carnes, 'Out of the Shadows' p. 69 — Aztec mother-god who symbolizes power of life and death that each mother holds over her infant]" (MS 279). (See Patrick Carnes, *Out of the Shadows: Understanding Sexual Addiction* [1990].) As kids Hal and Orin called Tavis Gretel after a cow they'd seen at the Catskill Game Farm with a hole in its stomachs "with like plastic caps over them, and tubes, so you could look in and see internal digestive processes going on right inside the cow" (MS 280; cf. *IJ* 1068). There are a few notes in margins where Wallace considers whether he should make Tavis Avril's biological brother or not; it appears he began with biological and only later changed it to adoptive. Tavis's interview with Tina Echt is much longer in the MS version. At the equivalent to the bottom of *IJ* 521 the MS reads: "This is embarrassing, but her [Avril's] diminutive for Harold James Incandenza is Patoot, which don't ask" (MS 286).

292–96 = *IJ* 531–38. The MS omits the opening sentence. In the margins Wallace wrote little notes to himself about certain passages, e.g., "G[ately] needs to be more sensitive," Joelle "needs to be more Southern," like a director rehearsing actors. The MS omits the last two sentences of the published version. Typed a few lines later is an idea: "Joelle as child model, mother and twin brothers just as gorgeous — posed as attractive family in picture frames in picture you buy and discard to put your own imperfect picture in frame." But Wallace circled this and dismissed it as "possibly too cute."

297–307 = *IJ* n.324, 1066–72. At the top of the first page of this episode Wallace wrote "Fix or cut," compromising by fixing it up (expanding it to twice its original length) but moving it to the endnotes. Instead of the Russian T-shirt

(*IJ* 1069) Pemulis wears one that's "pork-colored, with a swine in a police cap counting currency and the words Keep Our Cops Kosher." In addition to praising the axiom and the lemma (*IJ* 1071) Pemulis goes on at length in the MS on the principle of induction, Descartes and Saint Augustine, hypothetical math problems, etc., but Wallace wrote "Too abstract" at the bottom of one page and abridged most of it. (Pemulis *doesn't* name the set of mathematicians at the top of *IJ* 1072, though.)

308–14 = *IJ* 538–47. In the MS Lenz keeps his stash in "Blakiston's gargantuan *Gould Medical Dictionary*" instead of in James's *Principles of Psychology*, but at the end of the episode Wallace has this handwritten footnote to the line "a waste of time and tension and yet still not be able to stop worrying about it" (*IJ* 547): "cf. William James — 'Recent works on the psychology of character have had much to say on this point. Some persons are born with an inner constitution which is harmonious and well-balanced from the outset. Their impulses are consistent with one another, their will follows without trouble the guidance of their intellect, and their lives are little haunted by regret. Others are oppositely constituted; and are so in degrees which may vary from something so slight as to result in a merely odd or whimsical inconsistency, to a discordancy of which the consequences may be inconvenient in the extreme.' *Varieties* [*of Religious Experience*] p. 141."

314A = *IJ* 548.

314B–D = *IJ* 550–53. A duplicate of MS 251A–C; this one is clean; the earlier one has minor revisions.

315–21 = *IJ* 553–62 (excluding Hal's interlude on 560). In the MS., instead of looking "like Warhol with a tan" (*IJ* 553), Lenz resembles "Cesar Romero after a hideous mishap" (cf. *IJ* 276, 894). The MS's footnote to "hydrolysis" (*IJ* 557 and n. 232) reveals one of Wallace's drug sources: Anthony B. Radcliffe's *Pharmer's Almanac: A Layman's Guide to the Pharmacology of Psychoactive Drugs* (1985; rpt. Ballantine, 1991). The stories Lenz and Green exchange (*IJ* 557–59) are weirder and more exotic in the MS., regarding, e.g., Elvis's twin brother *in utero* Enos, mirror-cults, and a "pocket of persons in Rhode Island and Delaware who believe the Biblical Antichrist appeared and walked among the earth for a seven-year period between 1972 and 1979 in the guys [*sic*] of televised *Dating Game* game show host Jim Lang." (Handwritten at the beginning of this episode is the note "All typos intentional.")

321A = *IJ* 227. In the MS it's "Helen L. Slansker, 33," working out of Tucson rather than "Erythema AZ" (*IJ* 227); there's no such town, of course, but every Gaddis fan will recognize *erythema* as the skin disease from which Wyatt Gwyon suffers in *The Recognitions* (p. 43).

322–27 = *IJ* 563–65. The MS version is much longer because Wallace took some snippets and dispersed them elsewhere in the finished novel.

327–29 = *IJ* n.90, 1000–1002. Day is not quite as verbose in the MS version (which, e.g., lacks his final paragraphs on the un-American, illogical nature of AA [*IJ* 1002]).

330–42 = *IJ* 575–89. The MS contains about 400 words at the beginning that Wallace cut (mostly Lenz boasting that many of the Ennet House females "want him to X them from all possible angles of attack in the worse possible way" and telling Green about the screenplay he's writing) or moved around (e.g., to n.239). At the equivalent to the end of the paragraph at the top of *IJ* 578, Wallace cut this amusing bit: "A Euro-punk now crosses the frame, abundantly leathered, with prolix hair, pale, spikes radiating from skull and wrists, jackboots, pale and with a long jaw, taking forever to cross the alley's mouth. Lenz tells Green there've historically been Euro-punks for decades: he says the definition of a Euro-punk's: two haircuts, one head" (MS 333). The MS underlines Green's familiarity with Hawaiian music (i.e., it's his consciousness that identifies the Don Ho album): "A slack-steel guitar. Influences on West Coast jazz circa the 1940s and 1950s. Green had read up on all things Hawaiian, in grade school, sitting silently in the library corner's beanbag chair under a poster of Chuck Norris holding up a book and saying reading is *fundamental*" (MS 340).

343–44 = *IJ* 589–93. This brief sequence shows more revision than any other episode in the manuscript. "Hugh" was another early name for Orin. The MS lacks the two paragraphs from "He keeps trying to imagine Madame Psychosis" through "because Mario never changes" (*IJ* 590). To Mario, the Ennet House originally "smells like God" before Wallace changed that to "smells like an ashtray" and reworked the God reference (*IJ* 591). (It was about this time that Wallace, the son of atheists, got religion.) In the MS Mario hears a recording of a Madame Psychosis show, but "it's not a live broadcast, because tonight on WYYY Miss Diagnosis is doing a Pig-Latin reading of John's Revelation that Mario could only take five minutes of" (MS 344). After the line (added by hand) "It is increasingly hard to find valid art that is about stuff that is real in this way" (*IJ* 592), Wallace cut this paragraph, from a letter Mme. Psychosis once read aloud on her show:

> "So but I'd always feel strange, then, when we fucked [amended to "did it"]. It was like an all-body hallucination — that, beginning at opposite ends of the world, we hurtle toward each other, each bound for the opposite point that had launched the other, and that in the best of worlds we'd pass each other in opposite flight, impossibly close, sliding past each other like two planes of glass, too smooth to touch. But that here we snag somehow. I get caught on you. Something catches, keeps us from hurtling on past each other to the place we need to get to, each other's place. We're caught on each other in mid-hurtle. We struggle and thrash, trying to disengage. It's no use." (MS 344)

344–46 = *IJ* 593–96. Another heavily revised interlude.

347–53 = *IJ* 200–211. This is the chapter I suggested to open the novel, and while Wallace obviously didn't agree, he did move it closer to the front. He originally wrote "severe cyctic acne" before substituting the all-purpose Boston adjective "wicked" (*IJ* 200). After the sentence ending "techniques and public relations, etc." (*IJ* 203), the MS has a 2500-word footnote (pp. 348A–D) concerning a "professional stem-artist" named Gordon W. Eagan, "a three-decade heroin addict who claimed without bravado to have raised and fed into his right arm sums equal to the yearly GNP of most small Caribbean nations." Set in November YDAU, it details his various scamming techniques; one of his cons was fellow-Ennet resident Ken Erdedy, who now reacts "with a kind of celebrity-recognition-type fervor." In the MS the cummings tatt is spelled correctly (cf. *IJ* 208).

353–66 = *IJ* 601–19. The MS version of the climactic fight scene is very close to the final version, footnotes included. Lenz seems to be wired on cocaine, not "Bing" (*IJ* 605; in fact, many of the amusing slang terms, like "eating cheese" for ratting, were added later). The Nuck's .44 was originally a mere .22. At this point in the MS there's a handwritten page, 360A, describing the shooter's stance: *IJ* 609.

366A–E = *IJ* 596–601. Orin is age 26 in the MS version of this interlude, which is about half the length of the book version.

367–76 = *IJ* 620–26. Instead of "Hal and Mario have both been to a few" (*IJ* 622), the MS reads: "I've been to a few" (MS 370), one of many indications that Hal is in some sense the narrator of the novel. (On the other hand, see 433–43 below.) The MS has Luria P — instead of Hugh Steeply in Tine's office (*IJ* 622); the WYYY engineer has a spine-split copy of *The Tao of Physics* instead of *Metallurgy of Annular Isotopes* (*IJ* 624).

377–88 = *IJ* 627–38. The Syrian Satelliter and *Moment* profiler were added later to the chapter's first paragraph. The descriptions of the students' eating habits were greatly expanded for the novel. The Darkness gives an extended account of one of his parents' "connubial battles" (MS 378–79). Mrs. Incandenza originally used green pens rather than blue (*IJ* 631; MS 381 has the note: "change all pens she chews on to green pens"; contemplate for a moment going through the entire novel looking for such instances). After Stice cites his old man's dictum (*IJ* 633) someone in the MS adds: "A Bedouin contortionist" (MS 382). In the MS Struck taunts the others by relating "how he was on the phone to this girl in 16s down at the Bradenton School he was going to X before 1 Jan. or die in the effort, says he was on the line to this girl and how she relates that her doubles partner had an attack of the moists for one of Struck's intimate circle up at ETA, very casually," then goes on to describe her with as much attention to her tennis style and equipment as her physical attributes (MS 383–84). Struck: "But so Fern says she knows the guy by sight but isn't sure of the name. . . . She says the one with the long arms and the hands like a strangler." "That's half the guys at this school," someone objects (MS 385). (Turns out Troeltsch is the lucky guy, which is greeted with incredulity all around.)

388–97 = *IJ* 651–62. The MS's opening paragraph is more perfunctory than the novel's (which still economically sets the scene with short sentences). Stice's service motion is in only the McEnroe tradition; expanded to McEnroe-Esconja for the novel. The MS description of Gately in the hospital is much more crowded; instead of asleep alone (*IJ* 654), he is "thrashing" in bed from pain: "Calvin Thrust is at Gately's bedside, arms crossed, gasper unlit, watching Gately thrash and flush fever-bright. Pat Montesian, Joelle ver N., Bruce G., and Gately's sponsor Bobby H are down the corridor in the CC reception area, listening to the vending machines hum and gurgle and want coins, waiting to go in and be there for Don Gately. The US Marshal stationed at Gately's room's door has received notice of one visitor at a time, he said" (MS 390–91). After the reference to "Queer" Tony, the MS pictures Randy Lenz on the north side of the Mass Pike trying to thumb a ride westward. Orin embraces not the "Swiss" hand-model but "the Italianate wife of the Italianate mayor of a Phoenix suburb" (MS 391).

397–413 = *IJ* 666–82. The MS has only one footnote (n.272) to the novel's seven for this chapter, a typical ratio. Traub is called Farb in the MS. The MS notes "a concentration of adolescent-high graffiti on the wall," e.g., "'All Hail Alberta. O.I. 'N E.I.' in a heart, with arrows" [Orin Incandenza + Elaine (as

Avril is called a few pages earlier) Incandenza?], "Spore-factor Six — 13 Million Triobonds Can't Be Wrong," "Gone fission," and higher than the rest, "Happiness Need No Longer Be Pursued" (MS 401–2; cf. 233–51 above).

Thierry's last name is Ontan in the MS. Pat Cash is "in asylums by the mid twenties" rather than simply "vanished by the twenties of age" (*IJ* 676). (There are many similar handwritten changes to imitate French syntax in this chapter.) Thierry's interpolations on *IJ* 679 were added later. In the MS DeLint notes that "The founder's Academy motto was 'I CARRY MY MASK IN FRONT OF ME AT ALL TIMES'" (see 32–38 above) but that Schtitt changed it to "'CONTRARIA SUNT COMPLEMENTA,' which is from the man Niels Bohr, who meant substances and events are of necessity the same things, the players and the games are the opposites that are just the two sides of of [redundancy *sic*] the one thing they must transcend, to achieve it'" (MS 412; see *IJ* 81 for the final motto, but and also see *IJ* 713 and n. 298 for an extremely loose translation). Wallace cut some interesting tennis comparisons that DeLint makes: "Hal to me is reminiscent of a girl named Goolagong, Australian, the 1970s, same touch and control, a sentient stick, the best pure female player in the era of late King and the young Evert, but she'd have these Incandenza-like lapses where she'd go into what her coach Tony Roche called going 'Walkabout,' an Australian mumbojumbo term, a kind of trance where she'd kind of zone out, puncture her gestalt, seem not to care. Also this girl Mandlikova in the 80s era of Navratilova and Austin. Face like Jimmy Connors but the best little hiney in the history of tennis. Incredible strokes, natural player, but would leave herself and hover" (MS 412–13).

414–17 = *IJ* 682–86. Matty is 26 in the MS instead of 23. Note 278 (*IJ* 1052) was originally the episode's last paragraph.

417–19 = *IJ* 548–49. With a few exceptions (pp. 448–60, 474–76), the MS is very clean from here to the end, with justified margins, and sequentially paginated (by hand) without alphabetical inserts.

419–22 = *IJ* 686–89. In the MS DeLint isn't described in detail as he is in the novel, and Hal watches a different set of cartridges: "He watches the Alberto V05 parody [*Cage*; see 469 below] and 'Pre-Nuptual [*sic*] Agreement Between Heaven and Hell' and 'Dark Logics' and then 'Adultery In a Narrow Bunk,' . . . He watches 'Death in Scarsdale' and 'Transparent Tigers' and 'Homo Duplex' and 'Kinds of Pain'" (MS 419–20), followed by *Medusa v. Odalisque* and *Wave Bye-Bye to the Bureaucrat.*

422–24 = *IJ* 689–91. Not dated in the MS.

424 = *IJ* 692. Note how the spacing is off in the published version: there should be a 3-line section break at the top of 692.

424–30 = *IJ* 692–98. The MS lacks the introductory sentence. A first-person "I" appears a few times in this chapter of the MS. Ernest Feaster was originally surnamed Harris.

430–32 = *IJ* 698–700. Again, not dated in the MS. At the end there's a note "section not finished"; the episode is resumed at *IJ* 714.

432–33 = *IJ* 700–701. The MS has only the Troeltsch and Schtitt/Mario interludes; the other three were added later. Again, there should be a 3-line section break at the top of *IJ* 701.

433–43 = *IJ* 701–11. In the MS, Bridget watches *Blood Sister* alone with Hal at first (and indulges in Haagen-Dazs instead of yogurt). Fran is "pie-faced" in the MS rather than "hanuman-faced" (*IJ* 703, an Indian monkey). The novel's "It remains to be determined . . ." (*IJ* 707) was originally "It's unclear to me whether Joelle ver Nooy, whom Hal doesn't personally know . . ." (MS 438), which complicates the question of who exactly narrates this novel. In the MS, Joelle thinks of Gately with "unabashed" rather than "fearful sentiment" (*IJ* 707). The MS has "jig" for the novel's "colored" during the Mattapan man's story (*IJ* 707–11; i.e., Wallace decided to filter it through the Southerner Joelle's sensibility rather than the black Bostonian's).

443–47 = *IJ* 711–14. The MS continues beyond the point where the novel ends this sequence as Bridget offers to tell Hal the funny thing Pemulis did earlier that day (*IJ* 702–3). Pemulis gave her a lift in the truck, and at a stoplight noticed a blind man with cane and sunglasses. As the man crossed in front of him, Pemulis put the truck in neutral and gunned the engine, scaring the blind man half to death. "Section not finished" scribbled at bottom.

448–60 = *IJ* 755–69. At the top of the first page Wallace has written "Found Drama II." In the opening paragraph Bernadette Longley and Fran Unwin were on the courts, but Wallace replaced them because this episode apparently occurs while they're watching *Blood Sister* with Hal. The MS, like the novel, has a "second tenor" mysteriously turn into a "baritone" within a few sentences (*IJ* 756). The Gilbert Treffert poster (*IJ* 757) was originally Gilbert LaTouche. The 49-star U.S.A. flag (*IJ* 761) originally had 46 stars. Both MS and novel end with one of Wallace's prettiest paragraphs (*IJ* 769).

461–68 = *IJ* 769–74, 782–85. The Moms' dog was originally called Roger rather than S[amuel?]. Johnson. After Hal says he doesn't know whether he misses Orin or not (*IJ* 771), Mario asks: "Remember when you were really little and Himself would always call you his Little Button, like Come To Papa My Little Button, and one day in the driveway in Weston you disagreed, you made your hands like fists down at your sides and put one foot down hard and went to Himself you went I Am *Not* A Little Button. And Orin was there and he went That's What All The Little Buttons Say, Kid" (MS 463). There is no break or interruption in the MS version.

469–73: cut. Six short sections; if one analog to *IJ*'s "anticonfluential" structure is channel-surfing, one can think of these as mildly interesting snippets until the main program resumes. The first is entitled "JAMES INCANDENZA'S FIRST ATTEMPT EVER AT SOMETHING FILMED, 'CAGE I,' NEVER PUBLICLY SEEN BECAUSE IT'S DULL AND HEAVY, A 28-SECOND PARODY OF AN ALBERTO V05 COMMERCIAL, FEATURING AN OLD PRE-DIGITAL TELEVISION SET, A CLEAN WALL MIRROR, AND TWO IMAGES IN BOTH, ONLY ONE OF WHICH IS ATTRACTIVE." A brief script follows, with the model saying things like: "*Don't hate me because I'm beautiful. Hate yourself because you're not.*"

The second is "HAL INCANDENZA'S FIRST 2 WRITTEN COMMENTS ON ANYTHING EVEN REMOTELY ECONOMIC . . . ," in which young Hal praises the penny, concluding: "Pennies seem more like a synecdoche of fear and aggression — have pennies at the ready, ready to direct them outward, lest the pennies come back your way, for you to have to lug around, or keep in a jar."

The third section lacks a title and reads in its entirety: "Assuming you're not bedridden or institutionalized for detoxification or something, ie. assuming you're just like an average US person, can you remember the last time a whole day went by without your buying something? No matter how small. *Something*. Is this a bit weird?" (MS 470).

The fourth section has like a 150-word title about what Geoffrey Day thinks about after waking up in the middle of the night, feeling like "A SMALL PALE SOUL PREY TO THE WHIMS OF A GREAT ROARING NATURE, LIKE PASCAL UNDER REMOTE SKIES, AT NIGHT": "We are romantics, Americans, today," it begins. "Romantics believe that nature is the spirit's repository and projector"; unlike "the farmers of yore," who treated nature with respect, modern-day Americans like Lenz say "the great thing about nature is it's one big toilet." (It's a subtle passage that resists abridgement.)

The fifth section explains "WHERE THE TRADEMARK OPENING

LINES OF MADAME PSYCHOSIS'S 'SIXTY MINUTES MORE OR LESS WITH MADAME PSYCHOSIS' ON WYYY CAME FROM: DR. JAMES INCANDENZA'S THIRD SHORT FILM, 'DARK LOGICS,' ALSO UNSEEN PUBLICLY BECAUSE IT'S TERRIBLY OBLIQUE AND DRY, CONSISTING MOSTLY OF STILL SHOTS OF ILLUMINATED MANUSCRIPTS HAVING THEIR PAGES TURNED BY A SKELETAL HAND: FRAUDULENT MATHEMATICAL DERIVATIONS OF GHASTLY THEOREMS FROM BENIGN AXIOMS, THE ADOLESCENT DIARIES OF FAMOUS DICTATORS, EXCERPTS FROM POST-GENESISTIC CHAPTERS OF A KIND OF PSEUDO-CONTEMPORARY BIBLICAL-TYPE THING, VIZ:" This is followed by quotations from the *Book of Perry and Clive*, *Book of Otto*, and the *Book of Betsi and Brad*, all in a parody of Genesis.

The final section is "HAL INCANDENZA'S ONE EXTANT WRITTEN THING ON DUCKS, SUBMITTED 21 NOVEMBER YR./WHOPPER FOR THEN-PRORECTOR JANICE SNEE'S OPTIONAL AND PRETTY EASY 'NEW ENGLAND ECOLOGY WORKSHOP,' A KIDS' CLASS, HAL BEING ONLY TEN AT THE TIME, WHICH ACCOUNTS FOR A CERTAIN STRAINED, TIP-TOE-LIKE QUALITY TO THE PROSE OF HIS MEDITATION ON THE DUCKS IN BOSTON'S PUBLIC GARDEN." Hal notes that "ducks' trade secret" for flourishing in their cold, wet environment is their "oily exudationary layer," which if compromised by "a mom using a spray bottle with a weak boric acid solution to scrub the duck clean and oil-free before a son picks it up" will cause the duck to "fall prey to the full fury of the wet, cold environment in which it makes its natural home."

474–75 = *IJ* 785–87. In the MS Hal's conversation is described as "upscale Boston speech."

475–86 = *IJ* 795–808. MS is almost identical to the book version.

487–520 = *IJ* 809–45, 846–51. The MS has fewer paragraph breaks in this long sequence. MS reads "your display of reluctant virtue" instead of "reluctant *se offendendo*" and its accompanying note (*IJ* 814). Wallace expanded the paragraph now spanning *IJ* 817–18 to include the details about Pat's (and Joelle's) red hair and physical appearance. Mrs. Lopate (*IJ* 818) is called "the Thing, the catatonic lady from the Shed" in the MS. There's no section break in the MS as on *IJ* 827. *Cheers!*'s Norm is spelled correctly in the MS. The poseur "Schwulst" (*IJ* 835) replaces the MS's "Bochco." (Steven Bochco is a writer/producer best known for his work on *Hill Street Blues*; *Schwulst* is a German word for "swelling, tumor," or figuratively, "bombast, turgidity.") Wallace shortened the MS's "the car-switching hour" to "the switching hour"

(*IJ* 837), probably to bring out the pun on "witching hour" (and maybe even to allude to *Hamlet's* "the very witching time of night" [3.2.413].) No section break in MS between *IJ* 845–46.

520–23 = *IJ* 851–54. The MS lacks a date and the details about the Boards and A.P.s being three weeks away (*IJ* 851). In the MS "the opponents were to be the Ukrainian Jr. Davis and Jr. Wightman Cup teams," and throughout the rest of the MS it's the Ukrainians rather than the Quebecois who are expected.

523–32 = *IJ* 854–64. In the MS, Orin's "only aesthetic interest in Joelle had been in a face he could make into anything anybody watching might wish" rather than "first aesthetic and then anti-aesthetic" (*IJ* 855). At the point where the novel states, "What's unendurable is what his own head could make of it all" (*IJ* 860), the MS has Gately remember Ferocious Francis describing at length what *his* head made of his problems (MS 528–29). Joelle's family bull was originally called "Big Nig"; her Uncle Lum was originally Uncle Punk. At the point where the novel's episode ends, the MS continues with Gately's "memory of the summer at 13 he worked in Beverly for old Gus Carty the lobsterman. . . . The thing Gately remembers best, besides the odor, is the way all the trapped lobsters' eye-stalks were always stuck out protruding between the reticular bars of the trap, every single eye-stalk of every single one, so the eyes always looked out at open space. The advantage of eyes that projected way forward: the eyes never had themselves behind bars. A lobster's ommatophoric Denial" (MS 532, a variant on *ommatophorous*, "bearing an eye, as an eye-stalk" [*OED*]; cf. *IJ* 891).

532–42 = *IJ* 864–76. In both MS and book the digital display reads "11-18-EST0456" (*IJ* 865), even though this scene is presumably a continuation of *IJ* 851–54, dated 11-20. "The window was unobserved above The Darkness's breath-line" (*IJ* 865) originally read "above the Wraith's breath-line." And in fact, there are several places in this episode where "The Darkness" originally read "the Wraith." Hal even calls him "Wraithster" at one point (MS 539). (Q.v. *IJ* 943, where Stice "thinks he's been somehow selected or chosen to get haunted or possessed by some kind of benefactor or guardian ghost.") In addition to imagining his father's ghost and black spiders (*IJ* 870), Himself "claimed to be tormented by an apparition of Ethel Merman that wouldn't shut up and let him sleep" (MS 538; Wallace probably remembered he already used Merman earlier w/r/t the DMZ'd soldier [*IJ* 214]). After Stice shrieks "Jesus God put it back!" the MS continues: "The little second face's blue eyes protruded like ommataophorous [*sic* — that word again!] eyes" instead of "like cartoon eyes" (*IJ* 871).

543–53 = *IJ* 883–96. Wallace added to the MS the foreshadowing to "Fackelmann's eliminated map after the insane scam on Sorkin" (*IJ* 886). Gately's girlfriend's name is abbreviated in the MS Pamela H.-J.

553–61 = *IJ* 896–902, 906–11. The MS begins with reference to "Stice's detachment," not "defenestration" (which would be correct only if you decide "fenestration" can mean getting stuck to a window, which it usually doesn't). In the MS Hal experiences not a panic attack but "an attack of jeda-vu" (another interesting word choice). The oft-mentioned film cartridges are described as "the size of old 45-rpm records but had the glassy shine and diffractory reflective qualities of the first-generation compact disks Disney Leith had brought in to class" (MS 554). All of the material from "Her smile in the wedding photo is homodontic" to "the Moms and C.T. have never represented themselves as anything other than unrelated but extremely close" (*IJ* 901) isn't in the MS. There is no section break in the MS.

Wallace added the first paragraph after the section break on 906 to the resumption of this episode. In the MS, the Moms had Himself interred in her family cemetery in Ste. Thérèse des Monts, Quebec, rather than in L'Islet Province (*IJ* 907); similarly, Hal flew to "Ste. Thérèse des Monts, a small town built around spud-storage facilities fewer than twenty clicks south of the Baie des Chaleurs" rather than St. Adalbert (*IJ* 910). Kieran McKenna was first described as having a "little retroussé nose" before it got downgraded to a "little porcine snout" (*IJ* 909). "Peterson's *The Cage*" (*IJ* 911) isn't in the MS (which suggests Wallace learned of this "1947 classic" [*IJ* 986, n.b] after he already gave the title to three Incandenza films). The MS identifies the quotation "For while *clinamen* and *tessera* . . ." (*IJ* 911) as coming from Harold Bloom's *The Anxiety of Influence*, pp. 122–29 (which Wallace coyly acknowledges in n.366).

561–85 = *IJ* 902–6, 911–38 (excepting the interlude on 916). A long, uninterrupted sequence in the MS, very close to the book version. Gately's "cognomen" (*IJ* 902) was originally a "moniker." In the MS, the wienie recites *Howl* more plausibly in Pig Latin instead of Chaucerian English (*IJ* 906). In the MS, Otis P. Lord for a while is in the bed next to Gately's, there to get the Hitachi monitor over his head removed, but Wallace later deleted all these references except for the bed-frame assembly-work on *IJ* 918–22. The Dworkinite protest group was originally called Womyn's Exploitation-Preventionand-Protest Phalanx: WEPPP rather than FOPPP (*IJ* 929). The crucial paragraph on *IJ* 934 beginning "His fever is way worse" is only partly present in the MS (and the brief interlude not at all), which then continues "And so but the next morning found Gately and Fackelmann still there in the corner. . . ."

585–98 = *IJ* 941–58. Again Hal refers occasionally to The Darkness as the Wraith or Wraithster in the MS. Originally there was no reference to the "print of Lang directing *Metropolis*" (*IJ* 951). The "another attack" mentioned at the bottom of *IJ* 951 reads "another attack of jamais-vu," which is maybe what he meant earlier by "jeda-vu." (*Jamais* is French for "never.") The MS lacks the reference to *Consummation of the Levirates* (*IJ* 952; Levirates follow the Jewish practice where the brother of a deceased man marries his widow; Hal's illustrated rug presumably depicts an orgy of such weddings. The biblical Onan refused to consummate his Levirate duty and had his map eliminated by his god as a result, but lives on in the various O.N.A.N. puns in *IJ*). Wallace added the three paragraphs on *IJ* 954–55 from "Then it occurred to me" through "to cripple myself to avoid (or forgo)."

598–99: cut. Two pages of brief AA testimonials, e.g.:
"If you're having trouble with spirituality, welcome to the club." — Charlie M., Brookline Young People's Group, Monday, 11/16/YDAU
"I came in to save my ass and found my soul was attached." — Cheryl U., BYP, Monday, 11/16/YDAU
"They say it's good for the soul, but I don't feel nothing inside you could call a soul." — Nell G., The Allston Group, Friday, 11/13/YDAU

599–601 = *IJ* 958–60.

601–2: cut. Orin leaves distracted phone messages on Hal's answering machine. He notes how moths and insects are attracted at night by his lighted window, trying to get in, then wonders if "this is what we are to God, little night-things whapping at a lit window, trying to get in" (MS 602).

602–9 = *IJ* 972–81. The main narrative of the MS concludes just as the novel does; Wallace knew early on how he wanted it to end. But after the final sentence's "and the tide was way out," there are these enigmatic lines:

18 — Hal and Helen, Hal and Exhibition, Pemulis and DMZ
19 — Gately and Joelle. 'They sewed his eyes open and Superglued the back of his head to the wall and propped the TP viewer in front of him and put something in the viewer. The chinks had propped up mirrors all around him so he couldn't look away'

Then there's a handwritten note "SECTION UNFINISHED," followed by

"Resume sec. after filmography." No clue.

610–16 = *IJ* 985–93. The MS version of Incandenza's film bibliography, added as an appendix, is close to the novel's, with a few exceptions: in the MS, the authors of "The Laughing Pathologists" (*IJ* 985, n.24a) were limited to Comstock and Posner, and they treated Michael Snow (instead of E. and K. Snow) as well as John Waters. Following *Union of Theoretical Grammarians in Cambridge*, the MS adds:

> *Union of Publicly Hidden in Lynn.* B.S. Meniscus Films, Ltd. Documentary cast w/ narrator P.A. Heaven; 78 mm.; 60 minutes; color; sound. Filmed proceedings in a Boston, MA suburb of "anonymous" meeting of the Union of the Hideously and Improbably Deformed, a support group for aesthetically challenged persons struggling with issues around light and sight. MAGNETIC VIDEO, PRIVATELY RELEASED BY MENISCUS FILMS, LTD.

Cage III and *No Troy* appear in different positions than in the novel.

□ □ □ □ □ □ □

And so but it should be obvious by now that not only did Wallace make very few cuts — about 40 pages, and almost none of the ones I suggested, as it happens — he wound up adding a considerable amount of new material. In 1994 and 1995 Wallace wrote the opening sequence (*IJ* 3–17, set a year later than the main narrative rather than several years in the past, as he originally had it), the mold-eating incident (10–11), several scenes featuring Orin (65–66, 565–67, 574–75, 971–72, 1038–44), Pemulis's drug lecture (66–67), *all* of the Marathe/Steeply dialogues outside Tucson and most of the Wheelchair Assassins material, Mario's first and only romantic encounter (121–26), the hilarious e-mail about the bricklayer's accident (138–40), the explanation for why videophony didn't work (144–51), the workout (198–200), the helpful calendar of subsidized time (223), the discussion of the "billowing shape" (648–51), the Bain/Steeply correspondence (663–65, 1047–52), all of the material on pp. 714–55, the funny scene with Marathe and Kate Gompert in a bar (775–82), several Rod Tine scenes and related interrogations, Pemulis hiding then losing the old sneaker containing the DMZ (700, 916), Joelle's apprehension and release (934, 938–41, 958), the Assistant District Attorney's talk with Pat Montesian (960–64), the forthcoming exhibition fête (964–71), and maybe half of the endnotes. That is, Wallace added at least 200 typeset pages of new material to the manuscript, plus expanded many of the previously written episodes, before it was subjected to his editor's shears. In a testy letter to David Markson dated 28 November 1995, Wallace complained:

"the fucker's cut by 600 pages from the first version, and though many of the cuts (editor-inspired) made the thing better, it fucked up a certain watertightness that the mastodon-size first version had, I think." That page-count seems mighty high: I suppose it's possible that, after revising and expanding the original manuscript, then adding some 200 pages of new material, Wallace wrote an additional 400 pages, all while teaching at ISU, but that seems a bit much even for a prodigy like him. (Perhaps he was speaking of manuscript pages versus typeset pages.) At any rate, it's to his editor's credit that, instead of insisting on further reductions, Pietsch decided to market the novel's gargantuan size as part of its appeal. Despite the cuts, Wallace was grateful; in the same letter to Markson he goes to on to say: "But still, the house is being so essentially brave publishing something so long and hard — they're out so much money just printing the thing you wouldn't believe it. . . ."

The finished novel was delivered mid-1995 to Little, Brown, which issued a first state of galleys in two paperback volumes, offset and reduced from Wallace's final typescript. (Larry McCaffery's set is the only one I've ever seen.) A second state of galleys, the "Signed Advance Reader's Edition" (whose print run has been variously estimated at 200, 500, and 1000 copies), was produced in the fall of 1995, and the handsome book appeared in January of 1996.

As a coda, I'd like to reprint the review I wrote of the published novel for the *Review of Contemporary Fiction* [see pp. 359–60 above]. (That Spring 1996 issue was not uncoincidentally the "Future of Fiction" issue Wallace guest-edited.) Friends aren't supposed to review the books of friends, but we were pretty lax about that sort of thing at *RCF.* Dave later told me his editor liked my review enough to enlarge and post it on his office wall, and that I was the only reviewer to note that, while set in the future, the novel was a response to "the need to excel in the Reagan eighties."

I now regard *Infinite Jest* as perhaps the most important novel published in the 1990s and am grateful I had the opportunity to follow its gestation. Dave paid me a fine if undeserved compliment by inscribing my copy of the first edition "For Steve — Thank you. Your suggestions in 93/94 made this better."

In Memoriam
David Foster Wallace

I knew him, Horatio. Not exactly a fellow of infinite jest — more Hamlet than Yorick, mild-mannered and self-deprecating rather than loud and merry — but an extremely decent human being, which made the shocking news of his suicide in September 2008 all the more painful. The greatest writer of his generation, yes, but I remember the gent who went easy on me the one time we played tennis together, gave much-needed advice on my orangutanic serve, and who politely asked to play full out before proceeding to blow me off the court.

His loss to contemporary fiction is devastating, because more successfully than anyone he demonstrated what the next stage after postmodernism might look like. Born in 1962, he came of age in the Seventies, the most ludicrous decade in the 20th century except for the appearance in America of totemic postmodern masterpieces like Pynchon's *Gravity's Rainbow*, Gaddis's *J R*, Delany's *Dhalgren*, Coover's *Public Burning*, Barthelme's *Dead Father*, Barth's *LETTERS*, and Sorrentino's *Mulligan Stew*. How does an ambitious young author follow *that* parade? Certainly not by reviving Hemingwayesque understatement, as some writers in the Eighties did, and certainly not by merely imitating Pynchon, Gaddis, et al. They had taken irony about as far as it could go — it was being co-opted by the culture at large anyway and was losing its bite — and these postmodernists pretty much exhausted the mine of classical literature, myth, and fables their modernist forebears had used to structure their work. Besides, they appealed mainly to highly educated readers and were representative of high culture, which in the Eighties was becoming as obsolete as spats and top hats. So for an aspiring writer like Wallace, *Quo vadis?* (as he asked in a special issue of the *Review of Contemporary Fiction* I asked him to edit).

He could have written precious, experimental works published by small presses and enjoyed by a chosen few. For example, Janice Galloway's *The Trick Is to Keep Breathing* (1989) is a brilliant dramatization of one of Wallace's signature themes (depression), but its experimental format limited its audience. With his background in mathematics he would have excelled at the rule-based fictions generated by the OuLiPo group, and in all likelihood could have produced something like Georges Perec's *Life A User's Manual* (1978). Wallace's brilliant solution was to craft shiny new fiction that would attract the big New York publishers, appeal to a wide range of readers, yet display the kind of intellectual rigor and formal innovation that should make the cognoscenti think.

Post-postmodernism could be as brainy as postmodernism but draw its materials from pop culture rather than (or in addition to) high culture. It could leave irony to older writers who still found it a potent weapon (Gaddis, Sorrentino) and revive the compassion readers once felt for characters in novels. It could explore a wider variety of formal approaches — short fictions made up of one half of an interview, a therapy session, a dictionary entry — in a wider variety of narrative voices. Wallace's two novels were literally forward-looking, both ostensibly set a dozen or so years in the future but dramatizing what we were likely to become if we continue living the way we do now. His superb nonfiction pieces built on the New Journalism of Wolfe and Thompson and added features from fiction and academic criticism. As Pound urged, he made it new.

His innovations and novelties were not mere showpieces but techniques applied to the somewhat old-fashion purpose of making the reader *feel*. After postmodernists and their critics demolished the grand narratives that had sustained Western culture for thousands of years, Wallace perfectly captured the disorientation, ennui, and bone-deep sadness of a generation not so much "incredulous toward metanarratives" (as Lyotard put it) as unaware there had ever been such a thing. He did it in meticulously crafted language that echoed and parodied the new lexicon of post-postmodernism, a kind of slacker mandarin (as I put it in my review of *Infinite Jest*) made up of slang, fractured syntax, corporate-speak, advertising lingo, political blather, self-help bromides, and post-industrial tech-talk, as well as the barely literate mumblings of junkies, drunks, and the poor. The maniacal detail, the lexicographer's precision, the footnotes, the willingness to unfurl sentences to Proustian lengths — all this made him a lord of language who not only captured the way modern America *sounds* in all its cacophony better than any of his contemporaries, but whose stylistic versatility is the equal of anyone in literature: Joyce, Rabelais, whoever.

Unfortunately, this mastery of art and language was not enough to keep his personal demons at bay. Wallace wrote his suicide note a decade ago in the opening lines of one of his stories: "The depressed person was in terrible and unceasing pain, and the impossibility of sharing or articulating this pain was itself a component of the pain and a contributing factor in its essential horror."

Like Hamlet, he had a fatal tendency to overthink everything. Now cracks a noble heart. Good night, sweet prince.

Of Cause and Consequence

I'm always surprised how little advantage writers take of the expressive possibilities of punctuation. Most of them, even the flamboyantly creative ones, limit themselves to the meat-and-potatoes basics of the comma and period, ignoring the colon, the dash, the ellipsis, the parenthesis, emphatic italics, and especially the semicolon. The British call a period a "full stop," but sometimes you don't want to come to a halt at the end of an independent clause; you want to link it to the next independent clause by something more than sequentiality, and that's where the semicolon comes in. It is a signal that the thought expressed in the first independent clause is not yet complete, not truly independent; it indicates the next clause is not a new thought but a continuation and conclusion, like the second line in a couplet. *Then* you can use that full stop.

Flipping through most novels, you rarely see a semicolon, even though creative works like novels are precisely where you would expect to see creative use of punctuation. I grabbed two at random from a stack of bound galleys I am preparing to sell, Bret Easton Ellis's *Lunar Park* (2005) and John Updike's *Widows of Eastwick* (2008). I see a few colons in Ellis's novel, some expressive use of dashes and ellipses, but not a single semicolon, even where his sentences cry out for them. Wouldn't "Please, I thought. Please let someone save him" (178) read better as "Please, I thought; please let someone save him"? Wouldn't a semicolon work better than a full stop in the middle of these two sentences: "I kept my gaze fixed on the horizon. The sky was turning black, and the clouds roiling in it kept changing shapes" (213). You could argue that those are two separate actions — the narrator fixes his eyes on the horizon, and *then* notices the sky is turning black — but since the second clause is the consequence of the first, a semicolon would be better. (I haven't checked this galley against the published version, but I hope someone changed the final clause to "and the roiling clouds kept changing shapes.")

"Consequence" is the word Strunk and White use in their famous *Elements of Style*. (I have the illustrated edition of 2005, which sports a big semicolon by itself on the back cover.) When there is a "cause and consequence" relationship between two independent clauses, they suggest it is better to use a semicolon than a period. The two examples they give are short sentences: "Mary Shelley's works are entertaining; they are full of engaging ideas," and

"It is nearly half past five; we cannot reach town before dark." Yet many writers, especially minimalists under the influence of Hemingway and Carver, prefer to use full-stopped sentences rather than link them via semicolons. Here's Ellis again: "I could hear the soft, snapping sounds of something approaching. And it was moving eagerly. It wanted to be noticed. It wanted to be seen and felt. It wanted to whisper my name. It wanted to deceive me. But it wasn't making itself visible yet" (95). Ellis was probably trying to create dramatic tension, but it's more like being stuck in stop-and-go traffic. And while it's not necessarily wrong to start a sentence with "And or "But," it should be avoided, unless you use them creatively like Pynchon ("A-and . . .") or Wallace ("And so but . . .").

Flipping through *The Widows of Eastwick*, I see one semicolon at the beginning of chapter two: "Satan's mark is upon our pleasures; else we would not be driven to repeat them, even when sated, until they devour us" (98). Most writers would have used a comma there — indeed, this is a misuse of the semicolon per Strunk and White, for the second half is not an independent clause — but the semicolon creates more of a pause than a comma would: not as much as a full stop, but just enough to let us feel Satan's mark upon our pleasure of reading well-wrought prose. Flipping through his pages, I don't see any further semicolons, nor do I see any instances where they are called for; Updike knows what he's doing.

Other novelists known for their elaborate style use semicolons sparingly, it seems. I see only a few in Gass's *Tunnel*, even fewer in Theroux's *Darconville's Cat*. (There are more in his *Laura Warholic*, but only because I put them there while copyediting the manuscript. He left them in, but we shouldn't discount the work of copyeditors; perhaps *Lunar Park* was festooned with semicolons that were deleted by a semicolon-hating editor.) Wallace seems to go out of his way to avoid them in *Infinite Jest*, even when he knows full well they're called for, as here: "A big one being this pretense that overt eccentricity was the same as openness. I.e., that they were all 'exactly as crazy as they seem' — the punter's phrase" (751). Every copyeditor in the world would instinctively change that to ". . . same as openness; i.e., that they . . . ," but, like Updike, grammar maven Wallace knew what he's doing and deliberately flaunted the rule for semicolons in an act of "overt eccentricity."

While one doesn't expect writers to be as creative with punctuation as the late German novelist Arno Schmidt — a typical sentence in *The School for Atheists* reads: "TIM : »Keeps all Your senses fully occupyd. — *HEARING* ? : one door sighs; the next griggles; the third farts" (109), which illustrates an additional use of semicolons in lists — one hopes that writers will realize there are more punctuation marks than the comma and period; semicolons and other wallflowers deserve an occasional spin on the dancefloor of prose.

Beowulf and Postmodernism

Not having studied Anglo-Saxon since grad school, nor having kept up with *Beowulf* criticism in particular, I'll take Ted Morrissey's word for it in *The* Beowulf *Poet and His Real Monsters* that most recent criticism on the Anglo-Saxon poem remains fixated on old-fashioned philological study. While these textual issues are important — especially when one's interpretation hinges upon a proposed emendation or the accurate identification of the dialect of a certain word — Morrissey's illuminating monograph demonstrates the advantages of bringing newer critical strategies to bear on the poem, especially "postmodern" ones that might seen incompatible with this premodern work. Looking at *Beowulf* through postmodern eyes fosters a greater appreciation of the craftsmanship and subtlety of this masterpiece.

For example, one the earliest theorists of postmodernism, architecture critic Charles Jencks, argued that po-mo works are characterized by "double-coding," whereby the artist appeals to both popular and elite audiences by encoding for the latter group subtle allusions, references, and ironies that will probably go unnoticed by the larger popular audience who focus on the more obvious and appealing aspects of a work. In his essay "What Was Postmodernism?" (*electronic book review*, 2007), Brian McHale gives as an example animated movies like *Aladdin*, which "appeal to children through slapstick and cuteness, and to their parents through pop-culture allusions and double entendres that go right over youngsters' heads." *Beowulf* strikes me as a deliberately "double-coded" work, with exciting fights scenes that would delight the *scop*'s mead-muddled audience, but at the same time are encoded with theological and political issues, intertextual references to other works, and some dazzling wordplay for the benefit of the connoisseurs and intellectuals of his time. Double-coding is also in effect as the poet ostensibly tells a tale set in Denmark and Sweden in the sixth century but that is also (if not *really*) about England in a traumatized period several centuries later, a trans-historical strategy that would probably go over the heads of the tipsy masses but would not be lost on the more sober thanes in the hall. The popular aspects of a double-coded work will always appeal to a larger audience; Howell D. Chickering Jr. speculates that "Beowulf's tragic third fight with the dragon was more frequently read than his earlier adventures, since folio 182, where this adventure begins, is quite worn out" (*Beowulf: A Dual-Language Edition*

[Anchor Books, 1977], 246). In contrast, Hrothgar's serious sermon on pride (lines 1700 ff.) shows little sign of wear.

Postmodern works also flaunt a heightened self-consciousness about their status as artificial literary creations, metafictionally drawing attention to the artist behind the work. No one would mistake *Beowulf* for a chapter in the *Anglo-Saxon Chronicle*, partly because the poet frequently draws attention to himself and to his artistry. On a half-dozen occasions, the first-person "*ic*" pops up to remind the reader that the tale isn't telling itself, but is rather a dramatized reconstruction of what the *scop* has only heard. The *scop* is self-consciously aware that he is *performing* his story, not merely reporting it, and highlights this process at line 871, the morning after our hero's first encounter with the monster Grendel. The anonymous author self-consciously introduces his stand-in into the proceedings, whereupon this wordsmith

> found new words, bound them up truly,
> began to recite Beowulf's praise,
> a well-made lay of his glorious deed,
> skillfully varied his matter and style. (trans. Chickering)

Suddenly the reader realizes the previous 870 lines have not been a historical account of Beowulf's actions but a fanciful re-creation — a literary *performance*; the poet, having "unlocked his word-hoard" (l. 259), has armored himself with words to perform a glorious linguistic deed to rival if not outdo Beowulf's wrestling match of the night before. For the *story* of Beowulf's deeds, you can read the Cliffs Notes; the poem is a *performance* of the story, a showy display of the poet's wrestling match with words in which he emerges triumphant. (Beowulf only tears off an arm.) Look at me, at *my* prowess, the word-warrior proclaims, not at Beowulf, whose own later account of his fight with Grendel (lines 2069 ff.) is deliberately bland in comparison. One of the few interesting things about Robert Zemeckis's comically crude film version of *Beowulf* (2007) — aside from the golden splendor of Angelina Jolie — was Beowulf's postmodern awareness that he was the protagonist in a work-in-progress to be called *The Song of Beowulf*.

The poet's innovative, unconventional use of words is another feature associated with postmodernism, as Morrissey argues in his second chapter, and which he goes on to align with the obsession with diction that trauma victims display. I was previously unaware of trauma theory, but Morrissey argues convincingly that this branch of postmodern theory shines new light on several murky aspects of the poem, on what some readers call its disjointedness and downright weirdness. *Beowulf* enacts on both a formal and verbal level the effects of trauma on a people (and on a gifted poet) subjected to centuries of warfare, sickness, and disorder, resulting in a poem closer to nightmare than elegy. Morrissey shows how other postmodern strategies illuminate the poem, and respectfully suggests these new approaches can supplement, not supplant, the more traditional philological approaches. Those earlier approaches have for too long treated *Beowulf* as a period piece, but these new approaches give the lay a startling relevance in the 21st century: I am writing this at the end of 2012, after the quick succession of Hurricane Sandy, the slaughter of children in Newtown, Connecticut, and fears of going off a fiscal cliff have somewhat traumatized Americans — who are not as bad off as the Anglo-Saxons of the Dark Ages, to be sure, but are now in the appropriate mood to appreciate the traumatized world of *Beowulf*.

Mōdraniht 2012

Maximalism Down Argentine Way: *Adam Buenosayres*

English-only lovers of maximalist novels have been deprived of one of the finest examples of the genre for 66 years. But in the spring of 2014, McGill-Queen's University Press published the first English translation of Leopoldo Marechal's 1948 novel *Adam Buenosayres*, admirably rendered and annotated by Norman Cheadle of Laurentian University in Ontario. In retrospect, this outlandish meganovel can be seen as the first explosion in what came to be called the Boom, yet the absence of an English translation (and its relative obscurity in Latin America) kept Marechal from taking his rightful place at the forefront of Señores Cortázar, García Márquez, Fuentes, and others.

It's a big novel, 618 pages in the new English translation. Maximalist novels don't necessarily have to be big: they need only display maximal use of the full resources of language, its complete lexicon, its wide array of rhetorical devices. Maximalists laugh at Strunk & White's strictures, and regard minimalists as pussies. Their novels can come in small sizes, such as Djuna Barnes's compact *Nightwood*, Arno Schmidt's dense novellas, and Mark Leyner's clown-car-packed books, along with even shorter ones by Ronald Firbank and W. M. Spackman. But most maximalists need room, need space to spread their linguistic wings, as in the best-known examples of the genre: François Rabelais's *Gargantua and Pantagruel*, Laurence Sterne's *Tristram Shandy*, Hermann Melville's *Moby-Dick*, James Joyce's *Ulysses*, and any number of novels published later in the 20th century and into the 21st. (David Mitchell's *Bone Clocks* appeared as I was writing this [August 2014].)

Minimalist Anton Chekhov once complained to maximalist Maxim Gorki that his style "wore him out," the aforementioned Spackman reports (in an essay on maximalist Leo Tolstoy): "The sheer Russian downpour of modifiers exhausted his attention — a simple statement that a man sat down on the grass became, helplessly, 'a dignified, pigeon-breasted, middle-sized personage with a short reddish beard seated himself on the green but now stroller-trampled grass, seated himself without a word, and began staring timorously and twitchily about.'"[1] Maximalists place the emphasis not so much on

1 "Being Fair about Lyof Nikolayevich," *Canto* 1.4 (Winter1977), 76.

a character's actions (as minimalists do) as on the language describing those actions, sharing (if not hogging) the stage with their creations. This can be mishandled, resulting in prose denigrated as "overwritten," and indeed Spackman goes on to complain that often in Tolstoy there is "a kind of insanity of functionless, crammed in, lumbering, and exasperatingly superfluous detail." But when done with wit, virtuosity, and a giddy love of language, such prose can be more exhilarating than exhausting.

Many big, maximalist novels are set, appropriately and even symbiotically, in big cities such as Alexandria (Lawrence Durrell's quartet), Beijing (Cao Xueqin's *Story of the Stone*), Berlin (Alfred Döblin's *Berlin Alexanderplatz*), Boston (David Foster Wallace's *Infinite Jest*, Alexander Theroux's *Laura Warholic*), Chicago (Mark Smith's *Death of the Detective*, Leon Forrest's *Divine Days*), Dublin (Joyce), Glasgow (Alasdair Gray's *Lanark*), Havana (Guillermo Cabrera Infante's *Three Trapped Tigers*, José Lezama Lima's *Paradiso*), London (George W. M. Reynolds's *Mysteries of London*, Charles Dickens's *Bleak House*, Wyndham Lewis's *Apes of God*, Julián Ríos's *Larva*, Martin Amis's *London Fields*, Zadie Smith's *White Teeth*), Los Angeles (James Frey's *Bright Shiny Morning*), Mexico City (Carlos Fuentes's novels, Fernando del Paso's *Palinuro of Mexico*), Montreal (Norm Sibum's *Traymore Rooms*), Mumbai (Salman Rushdie's *Midnight's Children*, Vikram Chandra's *Sacred Games*), New York City (William Gaddis's *Recognitions* and *J R*, Paul Goodman's *Empire City*, Joseph McElroy's *Women and Men*, Sergio de la Pava's *Naked Singularity*), Paris (Victor Hugo's *Les Misérables*, Marcel Proust's *In Search of Lost Time*, Georges Perec's *Life A User's Manual*), San Francisco (Karen Tei Yamashita's *I Hotel*), St. Petersburg (Dostoevsky's *Crime and Punishment*, Andrei Bely's *Petersburg*), Tokyo (Hiraga Gennai's *Rootless Weeds*, Haruki Murakami's *1Q84*), Vienna (Robert Musil's *Man without Qualities*, Heimat von Doderer's *Demons*), Istanbul (Buket Uzuner's *I Am Istanbul*), and points in between. *Großstadtromane*, the Germans call them.

Buenos Aires in the 1920s is the setting of Marechal's novel, a time of avant-gardism and anarchy. The title character and his brainy friends discuss everything from aesthetics to theology to politics to sociology with the reckless enthusiasm and unearned confidence of readers in their twenties, drunk on books and high on theory. Adam Buenosayres — his surname was Marechal's childhood nickname, the way one might call a flashy dresser in shades "Hollywood" — is a poet in crisis: he is having doubts about both his poetic vocation and the young woman he's in love with, and the novel records his inability to surmount those doubts. Opening with his funeral six months later, it dramatizes his last three days on earth, from Maundy Thursday to Holy Saturday of the Catholic Holy Week.

While Adam's personality and fate recall Goethe's Werther, the novel itself ostentatiously recalls Joyce's *Ulysses*, both in size and linguistic extravagance. After reading a Spanish translation of *A Portrait of the Artist as a Young Man*, Marechal read Valéry Larbaud's French translation of *Ulysses* in 1929 and began writing his novel shortly after; he then abandoned it for many years, but resumed work in 1945 after reading the first Spanish translation of Joyce's novel. Adam has much in common with Stephen Dedalus, his friend Samuel Tester resembles Buck Mulligan, and their conversations with others about Argentine identity recall those about Irish identity in *Ulysses*. There's a terrific scene in a brothel that recalls Joyce's Nighttown, and even a classroom episode reminiscent of the second chapter of *Ulysses*.

But it's the linguistic extravagance of *Ulysses* that most inspired Marechal, though he also seems to have been under the influence of Lautréamont and Rabelais. *Adam Buenosayres* is "lousy with metaphors" (151), as the narrator mocks. Self-doubting Adam chastises himself for "reading into the signs of things much more than they literally say" (341); watching children play a game called Angel and Devil, he begins brooding on "the soul's responsibility" and soon imagines angels and demons fighting over his soul. Adam's metaphoric tendencies generate the freewheeling imagery throughout the novel, dramatizing not the growth of an artist honing his gifts (as with Stephen in *A Portrait*) but the death of an artist at the hands of "his imagination's monstrous offspring" (349).

Sometimes the linguistic extravagance is played for laughs: Marechal takes as much delight in loud, tasteless clothing as Pynchon would decades later. Here's Adam's principal:

> He wears — and swears by — a greenish-skyblue-grey suit, with spongy tones and rare glints of indigo, astonishing colours which, according to the scholar Di Fiore, could be produced only in the workshop of the great outdoors, or in one governed by the most niggardly economy. Nonetheless, his outfit is brightened by three vehement notes: a shirt the colour of magpie vomit (Adam Buenosayres's definition), a frenetically green bow tie, and boots of hallucinatory yellow. (325)

When the narrator apostrophizes an alluringly disreputable teenager nicknamed La Bebe, his gives us a textbook example of maximalist prose:

> Your story was fit for the lyrics of a tango,[2] it blossomed in the intricate arpeggios of the bandoneón, became legendary in the plangent voices of *malevos* howling their melancholy to the fiery sunsets in the barrio Villa Ortúzar! Yesterday, your fifteen springtimes were a floral bouquet, your short little skirt and your sunlit braids set off wild conflagrations in the neighbourhood's sensibility; coach drivers sighed for you as

2 For an idea of what that might sound like, seek out Astor Piazzolla's gorgeous, surrealistic *María de Buenos Aires* (1968).

> they headed evening-ward, a carnation in their ear and a brawl in their heart. Yesterday, at dances on the patio, at the hour when night seems to spring directly from the body of a guitar, the twinkle in your eye and the swing of your hips slowly unsheathed passion, lust ferocity — daggers quick to jump at a challenge. Yesterday, your image lightened the dead hours of lumberyards, and haunted the silence of phantasmal general stores, when a hand of *truco* would suddenly die on the table, impaled by a listless ace of spades. (227)

If that doesn't make you swoon, this novel is not for you.

While Joyce inspired the form of the first two-thirds of *Adam Buenosayres*, Dante inspired the last third, which consists of two documents from Adam's hand. "The Blue-Bound Notebook" is, like Dante's *Vita Nuova*, a mystic account of how he met his dream-girl Solveig (named after the romantic lead in Ibsen's *Peer Gynt*) and his crushing realization that his idealization of her bears no resemblance to the vapid girl who falls for one of his friends instead. (I found this the least interesting portion of the novel, but perhaps I'm too old for such stuff.) The final section is a 223-page infernal descent modeled on Dante's *Inferno*, itself a literary topos based (as Adam notes) on the briefer infernal descents in Homer and Virgil. In the vengeful spirit of Dante, Marechal roasts Argentine society in the hellish fires of his imagination, peppered with further doubts by Adam of his poetic vocation, and especially of literary topoi like this one: after leaving the fifth circle of hell, he develops

> a boundless anger against all those wits who, displaying an arrogance both absurd and malicious, had ever dared to cobble together a literary Inferno. Poking their noses into other people's lives, washing their dirty laundry in public, conducting a moral autopsy on their neighbours and making them sweat in violent infernal sports: all these seemed to me exercises which, contravening the sweet laws of mercy, betrayed a limitless wickedness. (527)

Almost every level of Argentine society is castigated here in various vignettes and hallucinatory skits, ending with the metamorphosis of a man into an insect à la Kafka. Adam self-consciously apologizes for following Dante's schema so closely, but his Virgil (a friend named Schultz) brushes away such objections when he is accused of unoriginality after his lecture on the origin of social classes; no doubt speaking for Marechal, he bristles: "If I used someone else's schema, and nothing more than a schema, I have on the other hand fleshed it out in quite an original fashion" (477).

This is Marechal's claim to fame. *Adam Buenosayres* may be too closely modeled on Joyce and Dante to qualify as a truly original work, but it is fleshed out with bravura displays of linguistic virtuosity. There are not only parodies of various genres of popular Argentine fiction, but also of the efforts of Marechal's fellow avant-gardists of the 1920s, including a young Jorge Luis

Borges, who appears here as Luis Pereda. (Cheadle's copious annotations unlock this *roman à clef*.) There is a street-fight rendered in epic Homeric style, a dialogue modeled on Plato's *Symposium*, and a phantasmagoric midnight scene on the edge of town out of a gothic horror novel. And throughout this novel "lousy with metaphors" are reams of imaginative imagery, and in fact the novel ends with Adam spinning out one simile after another as he describes the monster at the bottom of hell:

> Nastier than a fright at midnight. Got more gills than a dorado. Serious as a monk's codpiece. More ingratiating than a rich man's dog. Sharp-pointed, like an old man's knife. More puckered than an immigrant's tobacco pouch. Shit-smeared, like the boot of a Basque dairyman. More ornery than a draw-wheel nag. Uglier than a pig's somersault. Tougher than a vizcacha's paw. Skittish as a washerwoman's pony. Solemn as the fart of an Englishman. (618)

Adam may be unable to control his image-making habit, and may resent it for encouraging him to symbolize Solveig into a poetic abstraction, but Marechal's better controlled linguistic abilities are stupendous. For other readers, his dramatization of the avant-garde milieu of 1920s Buenos Aires might be the novel's main attraction — their romantization of lowlifes (presaging the Beats' interest in criminals and writers like Genet), their nationalistic obsession with *martinfierrista* ideology, their disgust with invasive British capitalism (recalling the Irish-English conflicts in *Ulysses*) — but for aficionados of maximalist prose, the endless inventiveness of the language, and Marechal's willingness to push it to extremes, is the novel's chief delight.

Adam Buenosayres is not the only 20th-century maximalist novel that waited an ungodly amount of time for an English translation. Within the next year, we've been promised English translations of Miklós Szentkuthy's encyclopedic *Prae* (1934) and Arno Schmidt's gigantic *Bottom's Dream* (1970). It's interesting to speculate how our fiction might have been impacted had these three novels been translated into English within a few years of their publication. Our roster of maximalist novels may be longer now. Or maybe not: few novelists of any era are capable of such works, so we should be grateful for the ones we have, and grateful to Norman Cheadle and McGill-Queen's University Press for providing this superb example.

The Avant-Pop Novels of J. P. McEvoy

The 1920s saw a surge in experimentation with the form of the novel. In *Ulysses* (1922), James Joyce used a different style for each chapter, including the play format for the notorious Nighttown episode. Jean Toomer's "composite novel" *Cane* (1923) consists of numerous vignettes alternating between prose, poetry, and drama. John Dos Passos in *Manhattan Transfer* (1925) abandoned traditional narrative for a collage of individual stories, newspaper clippings, song lyrics, and prose poems. Taking his cue from European Surrealists, Robert M. Coates likewise deployed newspaper clippings, along with footnotes, diagrams, and unusual typography, in *The Eater of Darkness* (1926). Djuna Barnes's novel *Ryder* (1929) includes a variety of genres — poems, plays, parables — and is written in a pastiche of antique prose styles. William Faulkner scrambled chronology and used four distinct narrative voices in *The Sound and the Fury* (1929), and later even added a narrative appendix. These were all serious novelists who disrupted nineteenth-century narrative form to reflect the discontinuities, upheavals, and fragmentation of the early twentieth century, a time when many new media emerged that would rival and in some quarters supplant the novel in cultural importance and popularity.

But literary historians have overlooked a novelist from the same decade who deployed these same formal innovations largely for comic rather than serious effect, adapting avant-garde techniques for mainstream readers instead of the literati. Between 1928 and 1932, J. P. McEvoy published six ingenious novels that unfold solely by way of letters, telegrams, newspaper articles, ads, telephone transcriptions, scripts, playbills, greeting card verses, interoffice memos, legal documents, monologues, song lyrics, and radio broadcasts. Ted Gioia described *Manhattan Transfer* as a scrapbook, which could describe McEvoy's novels as well, and in fact a reviewer of his first novel used that very term.[1] Given their concern with a variety of media (vaudeville, musicals, movies, newspapers, greeting cards, comic strips, radio) and their replication of

1 "*Manhattan Transfer*: The American Novel as Scrapbook," http://www.fractiousfiction.com/manhattan_transfer.html. T. S. Matthews, *New Republic*, 25 July 1928, 259. The most famous predecessor for the "scrapbook" novel is Bram Stoker's *Dracula* (1897); for a literal example, see *The Scrapbook of Frankie Pratt* by Caroline Preston (2011).

the print forms of those media, they might better be described as multimedia novels. But perhaps the best, if anachronistic, category for McEvoy's novels is avant-pop, that postmodern movement of the late 1980s/early 1990s which (per Brian McHale, quoting Larry McCaffery) "appropriates, recycles and repurposes the materials of popular mass-media culture, 'combin[ing] Pop Art's focus on consumer goods and mass media with the avant-garde's spirit of subversion and emphasis on radical formal innovation.'"[2]

Since McEvoy is all but unknown, a brief biographical sketch follows.

An orphan, Joseph Patrick McEvoy told the *Rockford Morning Star* later in life that he didn't "remember where he was born — but he has been told that it was New York City and that the year was 1894." Newspaper comic historian Alex Jay, who records that remark in a well-researched profile,[3] gives a number of possible birthdates ranging from 1894 to 1897; the consensus today is 1895. Possibly born Joseph Hilliek or Hillick, the boy was adopted by Patrick and Mary Anne McEvoy of New Burnside, Illinois. The same *Rockford Morning Star* piece reports him as saying "he didn't go to school — he was dragged. This went on for a number of years, during which time McEvoy grew stronger and stronger — until finally he couldn't be dragged any more. This was officially called the end of his education." In the contributors' notes to a 1937 periodical, he wrote (in third person): "While he was still a guest in his mother's house, J. P. McEvoy started his writing career at the age of fifteen as Sporting editor of the *South Bend Sporting-Times*."[4] He later admitted (in first person), "I remember my first assignment as sports editor for the *News-Times* [*sic*] was to cover a baseball game. I was a descriptive writer. I became so interested in what was going on that I omitted the detail of scoring the game. I had to call *The Tribune* (a rival newspaper) to get the score."[5] In 1910 he enrolled at the University of Notre Dame, which he attended until 1912.

In 1920, a stationery industry journal called *Geyer's Stationer* gave this account of his early career (again from Jay):

> It is interesting to take a peep into Mr. McEvoy's past. He early acquired the art of hustling — perhaps that is why he is able now to do the work of two or three men. At Christian Brothers' College in St. Louis he was the star bed maker. One hundred and fifty a day was his regular chore. Later, at Notre Dame University, he was a "waiter"

2 *The Cambridge Introduction to Postmodernism* (New York: Cambridge University Press, 2015), 83.

3 "Ink-Slinger Profiles: J. P. McEvoy," <http://strippersguide.blogspot.de/2015/06/ink-slinger-profiles-by-alex-jay-jp.html>, posted 8 June 2015. This treasure trove of research is the source for many of the biographical details that follow.

4 *North American Review* 244.1 (Autumn 1937): 206.

5 Quoted in Ray Banta, *Indiana's Laughmakers: The Story of over 400 Hoosiers* (Indianapolis: PennUltimate Press, 1990), 115.

> at meal times and a newspaper man in the evenings. He worked on the *South Bend News* from six in the evening until two in the morning. When pay day came he required no guard to protect him — $4.00 constituted his salary!
>
> When he came to Chicago, after graduating, he obtained a position as cub reporter in the sporting department of the old *Record-Herald*.

He created several comic strips there beginning in 1914, and moved on to the *Chicago Tribune* in 1916 for further strips before joining the P. F. Volland Company, which published books, postcards, and greeting cards. McEvoy published two illustrated books of sarcastic verse with Volland, both in 1919: *Slams of Life: With Malice for All, and Charity Toward None, Assembled in Rhyme* — with a postmodernish introduction in which McEvoy refers to himself in the third person as "his favorite author" — and *The Sweet Dry and Dry; or, See America Thirst!*, a mélange of poems and strips protesting the passing of the Eighteenth Amendment prohibiting the sale of alcohol. *Slams of Life* in particular trumpets the linguistic ingenuity that enlivens his later writings. The mostly comic poems are bursting with wordplay, slang, raffish rhymes, typographical tricks, and flamboyant diction: the first sesquipedalian word in one poem is "Absquatulating," and the opening stanza of "The Song of the Movie Vamp" reads:

> I am the Moving Picture Vamp, insidious and tropical,
> The Lorelei of celluloid, the lure kaleidoscopical,
> Calorific and sinuous, voluptuous and canicular,
> And when it comes to picking pals, I ain't a bit particular.

Many are quite literate, even erudite: "That's a Gift" namedrops the historians Taine, Gibbon, and Grote, while another ranges from "the Ghibelline and Guelph" to "Eddie Poe." The latter's "The Raven" is parodied in "A Chicago Night's Entertainment," and "Lines to a Cafeteria or Glom-Shop" is a takeoff on a canto from "Kid" Byron's *Don Juan*.[6] A poem with the baby-talk title "Bawp-Bawp-Bawp-Bawp-Pa!" acknowledges the ancient Greek orators "Who slung a mean syllable over the floor / Isaeus, Aeschines, Demosthenes, too," and McEvoy seems to have been au courant with the latest poetry and art as well, for another one is entitled "An Imagist Would Call This 'Pale Purple Question Descending a Staircase.'" He introduced Sinclair Lewis at a talk before the Booksellers' League in Chicago in 1921; reporting the event, *Publishers Weekly* identified McEvoy as the author of *Psalms of Life*, a sanctification of his *Slams* that probably amused him.[7]

6 *The Sweet Dry and Dry* includes a parody entitled "The Boobyiat of O Howdri Iam."
7 "Lewis Talks to Chicago League," *Publishers Weekly*, 19 March 1921, 914.

McEvoy wasn't happy at Volland, despite his lavish salary ($10,000 a year, equivalent to around $130K today) and the prestige of being "the first writer of greeting-card sentiments to be admitted to the Author's League."[8] In the author's note at the end of his *Denny and the Dumb Cluck* — a 1930 novel satirizing the greeting-card business — he writes:

> For many years I was editor and poet laureate of P. F. Volland and Co. and the Buzza Co., leaders in the manufacture and distribution of greeting cards, and among other minor atrocities I have compiled 47,888 variations of Merry Christmas. Also I have sat in on art conferences without number, where we met such important crises as "Shall we face the three camels east, or would it be better to put one of those Elizabethan singers out on the doorstep, holding a roll of wall paper?"

Until he resigned from Volland in 1922, McEvoy continued to write for the *Chicago Tribune*. It ran a serial called *The Potters* in 1921, illustrated by a friend he had made at Notre Dame named John H. Striebel (1891–1962), with whom he would later collaborate. *The Potters* was described as "a new weekly humorous satire in verse on married life in a big city" and was later turned into a successful play and published in book form in 1924.

By then McEvoy had left Chicago and was living in New York City, leaving behind both greeting cards and comic strips to write for the stage. First he wrote a revue called *The Comic Supplement* (1924), which was produced by Florenz Ziegfeld and starred W. C. Fields.[9] McEvoy wrote the original "Drug Store" sketch, one of Field's favorites and reprised in some of his later films. Ziegfeld forced unwanted changes on McEvoy's script, but later repented and invited him to begin writing for the Ziegfeld Follies. McEvoy cowrote the 1925 production (with Fields, Will Rogers, Gus Weinberg, and Gene Buck), and continued to contribute skits and songs until 1926.

In 1926 he wrote a two-act revue entitled *Americana*,[10] a smart but zany show that Gershwin biographer Howard Pollack describes in terms that anticipate McEvoy's novels: "*Americana* . . . satirized American life, including an after-dinner speech at a Rotary Club and an awkward attempt by a father to talk to his son about sex; it also took aim at opera ('Cavalier Americana') as well as Shakespeare by way of [composer Sigmund] Romberg ('The Student

8 James Curtis, *W. C. Fields: A Biography* (New York: Knopf, 2003), 157.

9 For details, see Curtis (157–64) and especially chapter 23 of Simon Louvish's *Man on the Flying Trapeze: The Life and Times of W. C. Fields* (London: Faber and Faber, 1997). Louvish says they had a lot in common, physically and temperamentally, and concludes, "McEvoy's influence on Bill Fields was profound and long-lasting" (254). They appear together in a photograph on p. 255.

10 It was registered with the Library of Congress as *Americana: A Novel Revue* — an inadvertent (or not) pun setting the stage for the revue-like novels McEvoy would soon write.

Prince of Denmark'). Critics welcomed the show as refreshingly clever — a 'revue of ideas,' as the *Times* headline stated. . . ."[11] His other revues — *No Foolin'* (1926), *Allez Oop* (1927), and *New Americana* (1932) — were less successful but provided plenty of backstage material for his novels.

It was at the Ziegfeld Follies that McEvoy met the inspiration for his first novel. Louise Brooks (1906–1985) was a featured dancer in the 1925 edition, and caught the eye of Paramount Pictures producer Walter Wanger, who signed her to a five-year contract later that year. McEvoy thought the wild-living Brooks would make an attractive heroine for a comic novel, and after naming her "Dixie Dugan" began writing a fictional account of her madcap adventures in show biz. *Show Girl* — made up of letters, telegrams, newspaper clippings, and so forth — was serialized in *Liberty Magazine* from 14 January to 14 July 1928, illustrated by his Notre Dame classmate John Striebel, who modeled Dixie on Brooks. It was published in book form by Simon & Schuster in July of the same year, and was an immediate success, going through five printings in two months for a total of 31,000 copies in print — not to mention reprints by two other publishers, two British editions, and a German translation (*Revue-Girl*, adapted by Arthur Rundt). *Show Girl* deals with Dixie's zigzagging path to success on Broadway; in its sequel, *Hollywood Girl*, Dixie (like Louise Brooks) travels out to Hollywood for further risqué adventures. Like its predecessor, *Hollywood Girl* was first serialized in *Liberty* (22 June–28 September 1929), then published by Simon & Schuster in book form later in 1929. Both were quickly made into movies, *Show Girl* (1928) and *Show Girl in Hollywood* (1930); it was initially reported that Brooks would play Dixie, but she didn't get the part, possibly because she was under contract to another studio (though she had been loaned out before). Both films starred Alice White instead, who resembled It girl Clara Bow rather than the vampy Brooks. Stills from the films were tipped into later printings of both novels, an early example of media synergy.

In 1929, McEvoy's former employer Florenz Ziegfeld, who appears as a character in *Show Girl*, produced a musical entitled *Glorifying the American Girl* with a script cowritten by McEvoy, and then staged a musical version of the novel, on which Gershwin again collaborated.[12] The lamest but longest-

11 *George Gershwin: His Life and Work* (Berkeley: University of California Press, 2006), 377. Gershwin wrote a song for the show ("That Lost Barber Shop Chord"). McEvoy was assisted by Morrie Ryskind and Phil Charig, and worked with composers Con Conrad and Henry Souvaine on the score. Conrad (1891–1938) writes the music for the musical in McEvoy's first novel, *Show Girl*.

12 See Pollack 451–61 for a detailed account of the musical, who notes that the script "lost much of the charm of the original novel" (453). Ethan Mordden agrees: "Very little of McEvoy's satirical view of how scandal and crime sell fame came through" (*Ziegfeld: The*

lasting spin-off of *Show Girl* is the comic strip *Dixie Dugan*, which McEvoy and Striebel began in October 1929 and which ran until October 1966, long after both had died.[13] The show-biz premise was soon dropped for a series of light romantic adventures, and today the strip is held in low esteem by most comic book historians. As Jay notes, McEvoy appeared in the 17 October 1939 edition of the strip, metafictionally depicted arguing with Dixie over money made from the franchise. A forgotten movie version, also called *Dixie Dugan* and starring Lois Andrews, was released in 1943.

McEvoy followed *Hollywood Girl* with four more novels in the same multimedia format. *Denny and the Dumb Cluck* (Simon & Schuster, 1930) is about a greeting-card salesman named Denny Kerrigan, who was first introduced in *Show Girl* as a long-distance love interest of Dixie's. (The "dumb cluck" of the title is Denny's new girlfriend, Doris Miller.) In the same author's note quoted earlier, McEvoy admits

> The truth is *Denny and The Dumb Cluck* is a grudge book. It was I who originated the most famous Christmas Greeting of all — Wishing you and yours a Merry Christmas and a Happy New Year. You have probably used it yourself, not knowing — nor caring, which is worse — that it was stolen from me, that I have not received one cent of royalties for it.
>
> I was robbed of that beautiful sediment [*sic*: a pun often used in his novels] and I swore that I would bide my time and some day I would get even. *Denny and The Dumb Cluck* is my answer.

McEvoy's fourth novel, a satire of the comic-strip business entitled *Mr. Noodle: An Extravaganza*, was serialized in the *Saturday Evening Post* from 15 November to 20 December 1930 (a little too elegantly illustrated by Arthur William Brown) and published in book form by Simon & Schuster in April 1931. In the fall of that year they also published *Society* — serialized as "Show Girl in Society" in *Liberty* between 30 May and 8 August, again illustrated by Striebel — which picks up the Dixie Dugan story where it left off at the end of *Hollywood Girl* and, after a satiric view of high society in both Europe and the U.S., brings her zany story to an end. McEvoy's final novel, *Are You Listening?*, was serialized in *Collier's Weekly* between 17 October and 12 December 1931 (illustrated by Harry L. Timmins) and quickly made into a movie with the same title before it was published in book form by Houghton Mifflin in August of 1932. McEvoy's last two novels apparently didn't sell well, for they

Man Who Invented Show Business [New York: St. Martin's Press, 2008], 268).

13 Jay records McEvoy's remark that he stopped writing the strip around 1936 and turned it over to his son Denny and Striebel. See the feature story on the origins of the strip in *Modern Mechanix*, April 1934, 57, 143–44 <http://blog.modernmechanix.com/dixie-dugans-fathers/#mmGal>.

are nearly impossible to find today.

In 1930, at the height of McEvoy's success, Broadway columnist Sidney Skolsky ticked off some amusing if questionable trivia about him:

> His first piece of writing appeared in the South Bend *News*. He inserted a job-wanted advertisement.
>
> For some unknown reason he is afraid to enter a laundry.[14]
>
> Lives at Woodstock, N. Y. Is the proud possessor of two blessed events and a St. Bernard dog. The two children are now attending school in California. The dog, dying of loneliness, is to be shipped there next week.
>
> The only jewelry he wears is a black opal ring. Wears this because everyone says it is unlucky.
>
> Is very fond of people who resemble him.
>
> He saves unused return postal cards.
>
> Never actually writes a play or story. He dictates everything. Always has two secretaries working. Never revises any of his manuscripts. *Show Girl* has fourteen chapters. It was dictated at fourteen settings.
>
> He is unable to part his hair.
>
> Believes there should be a law against bed makers who never tuck in the sheets at the foot of the bed.
>
> As far as comedians go he starts laughing if he's in the same city as Jimmy Durante.
>
> Always buys two copies of a book. One to read and one to lend.
>
> His full name is Joseph Patrick McEvoy. His mother name him Joseph. His father named him Patrick. Not caring for either, he became J. P. McEvoy.
>
> He has a picture of his wife in every room.
>
> Still receives royalties on some of the greeting cards he wrote. His favorite is the following:
>
> *Eve had no Xmas*
> *Neither did Adam.*
> *Never had socks,*
> *Nobody had 'em.*
> *Never got cards,*
> *Nobody did.*
> *Take this and have it*
> *On Adam, old kid.*
>
> He was once an amateur wrestler. Gave it up because he didn't like being on the floor.
>
> He hates to see people in wet bathing suits.
>
> His first book to be published was a volume of poetry titled *Slams of Life*. He has the names of those who bought it. Two more sales and he could have formed a club.
>
> Smokes a cigar from the moment he turns off the shower in the morning until he puts on his pajamas at night.
>
> His pet aversions are women's elbows, chocolate candy all melted together, fishing stories, fishermen, fish, Laugh, Clown, Laugh; radio talks on how to make hens

14 For the reason, see McEvoy's "A Jeremiad on Laundries" in *Slams of Life* (58–59).

lay, buying new shoes, mixed quartets, Laugh, Clown, Laugh; runs in silk stockings, three-piece orchestras, waiters who breathe down his neck and Laugh, Clown, Laugh.

When in New York he puts up at the Algonquin. If working on a story or play he and his wife occupy separate rooms.

His first writing for the stage was a vaudeville sketch. *Out of the Dark,* written with John V. A. Weaver. It played only two performances in a four-a-day vaudeville house.

His favorite composers are Tschaikovsky, and George Gershwin. His favorite conductors are Toscanini and Frank Kennedy of the Fifth Avenue bus line.

Has two mottoes. One for the home and one for the office. The motto hanging in his house is: "Let No Guilty Dollar Escape." The motto hanging in his office is: "Watch Your Hat and Coat."

Dislikes all the Hungarian Rhapsodies from number one to twelve.

His idea of a grand time is hearing Paul Robeson sing anything, going to Havana, being petted by any brunette not over five feet five, depositing royalty checks from Simon & Schuster, throwing pebbles into a lake, reading anything by James Stephens, eating kalteraufschnitt mit kartoffelsalat and attending a Chinese theater with a Chinaman.

He once got sick eating a sandwich that was named after him.

After he quit running a column in the Chicago *Tribune* the circulation of the *Tribune* dropped from forty thousand to a million.[15]

McEvoy continued to work in movies and publishing throughout the 1930s and 1940s. He appears in the opening credits of the 1933 film *The Woman Accused* as one of the ten authors who wrote a chapter each of the serialized novella (in *Liberty*) from which the screenplay was adapted; he collaborated again with W. C. Fields on the latter's 1934 films *You're Telling Me!* and *It's a Gift*; wrote nonfiction accounts of his life in upper New York State; published a children's book called *The Bam Bam Clock* (Algonquin Publishing Co., illustrated by Johnny Gruelle); and he wrote a humorous advice column called "Father Meets Son" for the *Saturday Evening Post* (published in book form by Lippincott in 1937). He coauthored the screenplay for Shirley Temple's musical *Just around the Corner* (1938), along with an article on her ("Little Miss Miracle") in the 9 July 1938 issue of the *Saturday Evening Post*, which reproduces a photograph of the author sitting next to the ten-year-old actress. He wrote the book for *Stars in Your Eyes*, a 1939 Broadway revue starring Ethel Merman and Jimmy Durante (the latter had a cameo in McEvoy's first novel). Other notable magazine contributions include an interview with Clark Gable about *Gone with the Wind* in the 4 May 1940 issue of the *Saturday Evening Post* (there's a photo available of a tuxedoed McEvoy dancing with Gable's co-star Vivien Leigh), and a profile of Walter Howey, editor of William Randolph Hearst's *Boston American*, in the June 1948 issue of *Cos-*

15 *Times Square Tintypes* (New York: Ives Washburn, 1930), 245–48.

mopolitan. He was famous enough to be featured in magazine ads for White Owl cigars, "just off the plane from Havana" (reproduced by Jay).

McEvoy spent the rest of his life contributing to *Reader's Digest* as a roving editor, travelling with his third wife, and entertaining a veritable who's who in America. Visitors to his large estate near Woodstock included members of the Algonquin Round Table, Frank Lloyd Wright, Clarence Darrow, Rube Goldberg, and avant-garde composer George Antheil. "One hectic weekend," a local newspaper reported (per Jay), "almost the entire membership of the American Society of Artists and Illustrators attended a fabulous weekend party." In 1956, McEvoy published his last book, *Charlie Would Have Loved This* (Duell, Sloan and Pearce), a collection of humorous articles. He died on 8 August 1958.

"GET HOT!": THE DIXIE DUGAN TRILOGY

For most readers in 1928, *Show Girl* looked utterly unlike any novel they had ever seen. Preceding the title page is a teaser with some hype from the publisher's Inner Sanctum imprint,[16] and the title page itself is an elaborate cast list "In the order of their appearance," as in a theater program or the opening credits of a silent film. Each "performer" is followed by a saucy descriptive line, beginning with "Dixie Dugan: The hottest little wench that ever shook a scanty at a tired businessman." The novel proper begins with a dozen pages of letters — familiar enough from epistolary fiction — which are quickly followed by a cavalcade of telegrams, Western Union cablegrams, newspaper articles (in two columns and a different font) and letters to the editor, playlets in script form, police reports (IN SMALL CAPS), poems and greeting card verses, a detective agency log, various theater materials (ads, reviews, notices, house receipts), one-sided telephone conversations, a dramatization of a business convention, radiograms, even a House of Representatives session reprinted from the *Congressional Record*.

All of this narrative razzmatazz supports a screwball-comic Broadway success story that occurs over a six-month period in 1927. (Nearly every document is dated, from May 1st to October 22nd.) The first half of the novel tracks Dixie's hectic rise to notoriety. As this 18-year-old Brooklynite explains in a letter to her long-distance boyfriend Denny Kerrigan, she's hell-bent on

16 "*Show Girl* was what *The Inner Sanctum* calls a Life Saver. Part of it showed up on a gray afternoon and promptly ran away with the working day of our staff. It was read and accepted in twenty-four hours. Laughter is an irresistible salesman. [¶] A number of other customers fell in line. *Liberty* laughed and bought *Show Girl* for serial publication. *First National* is filming it and a musical comedy is in the offing."

joining the chorus line of the Ziegfeld Follies.[17] He, on the other hand, writes that he wants to "get married and get a little apartment in Chicago, and I'll come home to you every Saturday night after my week on the road selling mottoes and greeting cards in Indiana" (98).[18] Failing her Ziegfeld audition, Dixie instead becomes a specialty dancer at the Jollity Night Club, where she attracts the smoldering glances of "a tall, dark-haired, black-eyed tango dancer" named Alvarez Romano, who turns out to be the son of a South American president. (She enjoys making out with him: "And when he kisses — well the kid goes sorta faint and dreamy and don't care-ish and can barely get through the front door and slam it shut" [19].) She also attracts the attention of a 45-year-old Wall Street broker named Jack Milton,[19] who one night after the show invites Dixie and other dancers to a party with his Wall Street buddies. He gropes and mauls her, only to be interrupted by Romano, who stabs him.

The *New York Evening Tab* (i.e., the *New York Morning Telegraph*) turns it into a salacious scandal, and as a result Dixie is deluged with job offers, endorsement deals, and marriage proposals. The *Evening Tab* begins running Dixie's first-person life story, ghostwritten and completely fabricated by reporter Jimmy Doyle, whom Dixie describes as "cute as a little red wagon and writes beautiful and I think he's hot dog" (98). Fairly literate (though he confuses Swinburne with Browning), he describes his "bogus autobiography" to a Hollywood friend as follows, in a representative example of McEvoy's jazzy style and his contempt for tabloid readers:

> Well, I'm still Dixie Dugan and my contribution to the Fine Arts is monastically entitled "Ten Thousand Sweet Legs." Boy, it's hot. With one hand I offer them sex and with the other I rap them smartly over the knuckles with a brass ruler and say "Mustn't touch. Burn-y, burn-y." Then I sling them a paragraph of old time religion and single standard and what will become of this young generation. (I hope nothing ever becomes of it. I like it just the way it is.) And then another paragraph like the

17 Her age is not given in the novel, but in the sequel set a year later, Dixie writes: "As for me I am nineteen years old and what is technically known as a virgin although I have been most thoroughly and thrillingly mauled on many occasions . . ." (*Hollywood Girl* 37). She also states "I am now five feet two inches tall and weigh 110 pounds" (36) — Louise Brooks's stats.

18 Barry Shank offers some informed observations on Denny and his profession in *A Token of My Affections: Greeting Cards and American Business Culture* (New York: Columbia University Press, 2004), 148–51, one of the only treatments of McEvoy in recent criticism (though he gets some plot details wrong). Of McEvoy's *Slams of Life*, Shank writes, "As an attempt at satire, the book fails to sustain a critical viewpoint. But it functions quite well as a document of the cheap cynicism that seemed to haunt those who produced culture on demand for commercial purposes in the first half of the twentieth century" (147).

19 His formal name John Milton is given a few times; apparently McEvoy liked the idea of naming a horny Wall Street broker after the Puritan poet.

> proverbial flannel undershirt that is supposed to make you hot and drive you crazy, and presto! the uplifted forefinger, "But this is not what you should be interested in, children." And then a little Weltschmerz and then the old Sturm und Drang — a Sturm to the nose followed up with a Drang to the chin — the old one-two. So, as you may gather, this opus is the kind of love child that might result from an Atlantic City week-end party with the American Mercury and True Stories[20] occupying adjoining rooms. So much for literature! (77–78)

Spying on Dixie one night outside the theatre of her new show, Jimmy sees Romano abduct Dixie (to take her back to "Costaragua" to marry her), abducts Dixie himself when their limousine crashes, and then convinces her to lay low while his newspaper milks her disappearance for weeks. The recovering Jack Milton hires detectives to find her, offers to underwrite a musical for Dixie, and enlists Jimmy to write the book and lyrics for it.

The second half of the novel documents the progress of the musical from its contentious beginning — Milton hires show-biz producers who rewrite Jimmy's script and bring in outside contributors[21] — to its disastrous out-of-town opening, to its eventual success after Jimmy takes charge and restores his original conception. Retitled *Get Your Girl*, the musical makes Dixie a star, and Jimmy realizes he loves Dixie as much as she does him: "Besides being cute and all that she's got a quick mind, a keen sense of humor and says just what she thinks," he writes to his Hollywood friend. "And she really thinks" (195). Meanwhile, Dixie's three suitors come to different ends: she rejects the marriage proposal of her sugar daddy, Jack Milton. Denny Kerrigan, still pining for Dixie, makes a big splash at a greeting-card convention in Atlantic City (where he catches Dixie's show), and heads home with a promotion if not with the girl. On a darker note, Alvarez Romano returns to Costaragua to help his father lead a counter-revolution, is captured, and sentenced to death. He escapes, but all his fellow prisoners are slaughtered, as a two-page article from the *Evening Tab* reports in gruesome detail. McEvoy places that tragedy near but not at the conclusion of the novel in order not to spoil the happy ending: Dixie finds success and love, conveyed by some clever parodies of notable theater critics of the day (Percy Hammond, Alexander Woollcott, Alan Dale, Walter Winchell) and a flurry of giddy radiograms.

Aside from the novelty of its format, the most appealing aspect of *Show Girl* is its language. Often sounding like a risqué and snarky P. G. Wodehouse,

20 *American Mercury* was the leading literary journal in the 1920s; *True Story* [*sic*] featured sleazy "sin-suffer-repent" confessions by women (often male ghostwriters).

21 Real-life Broadway veterans Con Conrad (music), Sammy Lee (choreography), Herman Rosse (scenic design), and Walter Donaldson and Gus Kahn (additional songs). Several celebrities make cameos in the novel, including Florenz Ziegfeld, Jimmy Durante, and evangelist Aimee Semple McPherson, and many others are namedropped.

McEvoy offers a fruity cocktail of slang and flapperspeak, most of it from Dixie herself. She slings words and phrases such as "into the merry-merry" (show biz), "a good skate" vs. "a wet smack" (a fun vs. dull person), "gazelles" and "gorillas" (young women and nightclub predators), "butter and eggers" (theater audiences), "ginny" (tipsy), "static" (unwanted advice), "goopher dust" (a legal loophole), "blue baby" (a dud play), "clucks" (dumb people), "crazy as a brass drummer," and exclamations like "Tie that one," "skillabootch," and "Get hot!" (encouragement shouted at a good dancer). Glib Jimmy Doyle has already been quoted, and throughout McEvoy inserts some clever song lyrics, parodies, and greeting-card verse; he even has Denny quote and praise a song from his own musical *Allez Oop*. There are times when the insider theater lingo becomes hermetic ("the old comedy mule stunt . . . an easy hit in the deuce spot . . . an unsubtle comedy team in 'one' with Yid humor and soprano straight . . . novelty perch turn in four . . . the choice groove next to shut" [52]), but all the slang and shoptalk is a constant delight. One reviewer said "Five years from now *Show Girl* and *Hollywood Girl* will need a glossary."[22] Dixie agrees: she starts a diary in the latter for the benefit of her future biographers:

> I can refer them to you Diary and they can see for themselves I'm not handing them a lot of horsefeathers. I suppose too Diary we should keep posterity in mind because when they came across a word like horsefeathers and didn't know what it meant we should have it defined somewhere, so for the sake of posterity horsefeathers means a lot of cha-cha and cha-cha means what diaries are usually full of. (*Hollywood Girl* 35)

Dixie is the first of many independent, untraditional young women in McEvoy's novels. She is a self-proclaimed representative of "flaming youth" (a 1923 novel and silent movie), and at times sounds surprisingly 21st-century: "The real ambition of our young generation . . . is to be cool but look hot" (7). At a time when most young woman wanted to get married as soon as possible, Dixie tells Denny, "I don't want to marry you or anybody else. . . . I'm young and full of the devil and want to stay that way for a while" (94) — a sentiment that will be voiced by many of McEvoy's young heroines.

In *Show Girl* McEvoy introduces other themes that will run through all of his novels, dark undercurrents beneath their playful surfaces. His contempt for the general public has already been noted in Jimmy's condescending remarks on his newspaper readers, an attitude that McEvoy will later extend to theater audiences, greeting-card customers, comic-strip fans, and radio listeners. When Jimmy meets with the Broadway producers who want to dumb down his play, we get this exchange:

22 *Saturday Review of Literature*, 30 November 1929, 491.

DOYLE (*bitterly*): I suppose if you got "Romeo and Juliet" you wouldn't produce it unless you could buy a balcony cheap.

EPPUS: "Romeo and Juliet"? Pfui! I seen that once. There wasn't a hundred dollars in the house.

KIBBITZER: That kind of play don't make money. You got to stick to things people understand. (112–13)

Kibbitzer later makes a pass at Dixie, and sexual predation in show business is another recurring theme. Dixie breezily dismisses that incident — "Well, that's what a female gets for having Deese, Dem and Doze" (118) — but along with her earlier sexual assault at Jack Milton's party and the lascivious advances of club "gorillas," McEvoy dramatizes how dangerous show biz is for "gazelles" like her.

The mendacity of the media is mostly played for laughs here, with the joke on the dumb clucks who take celebrity gossip as gospel and actually believe the "sediments" expressed in greeting cards, but corruption is handled more seriously. When the police arrive at Milton's wild party and arrest Alvarez, Dixie notes that one of the guests, "Wilkins his name was, a big politician I found out later — got the cops off to one corner and gave them some sort of song and dance" that keeps their names out of the papers the next day (30, 32). Near the end, Alvarez's father travels to New York and promises Milton the oil concession in Costaragua in exchange for financing his revolt; Milton gets a few of his Wall Street pals together and decide "that would be the patriotic American thing to do. Our country may she always be right," Dixie remembers him saying, "but right or wrong we've got to have oil." Milton enlists an Alabama congressman named Fibbledibber to convince his fellow representatives via patriotic rhetoric that America's honor depends upon &c &c &c, and sure enough Congress authorizes the Marines to intervene in the South American country. These darker elements add depths to what would otherwise be a light entertainment — depths that were drained by the producers of the 1928 movie version (no doubt of the same mindset as Kibbitzer & Eppus), according to those who have seen it. The novel is dark and daring, like Louise Brooks; the movie is blonde and harmless, like Alice White.

Show Girl's reviews were as boffo as those for Dixie's performance in *Get Your Girl*. Marian Storm quite rightly praised it as "a show-case of language. Whirling, whizzing, dizzying — a bombardment upon eye and ear of monotonous, accurate, faithful ugliness, of snappy similes." Proposing a new criteria for literature, the *Springfield Republican* said, "If making 'whoopee' is one of the aims of literary art, Mr. McEvoy has scored a literary success." Ziegfeld himself reviewed it for the *Saturday Review of Literature* — despite appearing in *Show Girl* as a character! — and described it as "show business 'hoked up' to the saturation point. . . . The action races by and every typographical ingenuity is used to emphasize and amplify the 'punch stuff'" — slinging slang as deftly as Dixie, but perhaps not entirely comfortable with seeing his profession mocked.[23]

Published a little over a year later, *Hollywood Girl* is one of the first and still best satires of Hollywood — a clichéd subject today but a novelty in 1929, when the industry was still young and making the transition from silent films to talkies. It begins seven months after the conclusion of *Show Girl*, and ends a year later (i.e., May 1928–April 1929), and features a similar story arc. *Get Your Girl* having run its course, Dixie is back in Brooklyn looking for work while Jimmy tries to write a new star vehicle for her, vowing to marry Dixie as soon as it is staged. When Dixie learns that flamboyant movie director Fritz Buelow[24] is in New York casting his next epic — *Sinning Lovers*, based on "The Charge of the Light Brigade"[25] — and is "hot for a jazz-mad baby that could make yip yip and faw down in a new squeakie," as Dixie puts it (14), she finagles an interview and passes a screen test, on the basis of which she's given a tentative contract and sent to Hollywood. She gets only bit parts at first, and then none at all, and learns the studio will not be renewing her contract.

At this low point, nearly halfway through the novel, Dixie delivers an emotional, 18-page interior monologue modeled on Molly Bloom's at the end of *Ulysses*, at the end of which Jimmy calls her and vows to help. (He too is now in Hollywood as a screenwriter.) He feels a publicity party is what she needs to attract work, which results in a remarkable chapter entitled "Hollywood Party: *A Talking, Singing, Dancing Picture with Sound Effects*," another 18-page tour de force that ends with the suicide of an "aging" actress. ("I'm thirty two," she tells Dixie, "and in this business if you're [a woman] over thirty you're older than God" [124].) While the party rages, Dixie goes off with Buelow to another party and is nearly raped. All this Sturm und Drang is heightened by troubling rumors that a Wall Street syndicate of bankers, including Dixie's old admirer Jack Milton, will be merging the major studios, eliminating jobs, and moving the whole business back east.

At about the same structural point in *Show Girl* where Jack regains control of his musical, Dixie learns she has been given the lead in *Sinning Lovers*, once again thanks to Jack Milton. (Ironically, the studio had decided to give

23 All quoted from the 1928 edition of *Book Review Digest*.

24 He is called Fritz von Buelow only on the cast list in the front of the book, and is apparently based on McEvoy's friend Erich Von Stroheim, who also makes a few cameos in his novel under his real name.

25 In 1929, the idea of making a romantic movie out of Tennyson's 55-line poem was absurd, but in 1936 there appeared *The Charge of the Light Brigade*, starring Errol Flynn and Olivia de Havilland.

the role to the aging actress the same night she committed suicide.) Dixie is tempted to accept Milton's marriage proposal after she and Jimmy have the last in a series of fights, but after the preview version of the movie flops, she drops him because he wants to give up on the film (and on her career). She is shocked at his philistine views: "Jack says so far as the bankers are concerned if it doesn't make money it's not a good picture and I says what about Caligari[26] and he says I never saw it and from all I've heard of it I never want to see it . . ." (205). Fortunately, another producer and director step in, save the film (retitled *Loving Sinners* under pressure from the censorious Hays office), and the movie makes Dixie a star, as attested by another raft of rave notices (more real-life reviewers, this time representing Los Angeles).

But this is where the novel takes a surprising turn. Unexpectedly, Jimmy Doyle is *not* called in to save the screenplay, make up with Dixie, and marry her at the end. Instead McEvoy lets fame and riches go to her head: Dixie starts hanging out with silly rich people, indulges in trivial pursuits, and only two weeks after meeting Teddy Page, a "New York millionaire sportsman and young society aviation enthusiast" (227), she elopes with him in Las Vegas. She's aware he's a binge-drinking, hell-raising skirt-chaser, but she's convinced she can change him. "It's only because he hasn't met the right kind of girl" (235). (Cue reader's rolling eyes.) The penultimate page of the novel features a tipped-in wedding photo of the couple (with a dead ringer for Louise Brooks as Dixie), followed by an announcement in the *New York Times* that Page's wealthy family has cut ties with him.[27] This unexpected ending is a daring subversion of the wedding bells convention typical of most romantic books and movies, but *Hollywood Girl* is not a typical novel.

In addition to all the narrative bells and whistles of *Show Girl*, the sequel sports a publicity release, cast lists and shooting schedules, the morality clause from an actor's contract, interoffice memos, six drafts of the opening sentences of a letter, screenplays (complete with camera directions), a full-page ad in *Variety*, and some unpunctuated, modernist-looking dialogue. Plus there's a parody of Edgar Guest (reminiscent of the poems in *The Sweet Dry and Dry*) and that Joycean monologue. Dixie starts and abandons a diary, which feels like a narrative crutch on McEvoy's part, but Dixie is so entertaining that it would be churlish to complain. There's another slew of slang: "maddizell," "laying down a few flat arches" (dancing), "belchers" (talking pictures), "dog

26 *The Cabinet of Dr. Caligari*, the 1919 German Expressionist masterpiece.

27 The final page of the *Liberty* serialization (28 September 1929, 73) is much more elaborate: the *Times* announcement mimics the paper's actual display and text fonts, and the extended photo includes several wedding guests and a caption, not just the wedded couple as in the published book.

house" (a bass violin), "sitzplatz" (sitting place=ass), and "Hot cat!" (expressing excitement). Jimmy is as glib as ever, as when he is asked by a reporter for his first impression of Hollywood: "Offhand, it looks a little bit like Keokuk [in Iowa] on a Sunday afternoon, except that the houses and vegetation seem to have been retouched by one of those disappointed virgins who go in for painting china" (67). But he can't top Dixie on the difference between the Big Apple and the Windy City: "New York is a jazz-band playing diga-diga-doo but Chicago is just a big megaphone with an overgrown boy hollering through it: Look at me, ain't I big for my age" (40).

Like the first novel, there are a few celebrity cameos, including Dixie's counterparts Louise Brooks and Alice White, aptly enough, and Aimee Semple McPherson via the radio airwaves. Von Stroheim is seen working with Gloria Swanson on *Queen Kelly*, a production as costly and strife-ridden as *Sinning Lovers*, and fans of old Hollywood will revel in all the namedropping, tech talk (UFA angles, lap dissolves), and insider dope.

Sexual predation is even more prominent here than in McEvoy's first novel, and creepier: *Show Girl* is PG-13, *Hollywood Girl* R-rated. Director Buelow is a letch who indulges in Trump/Bush "locker room banter" and seduces the *Evening Tab* reporter who interviews him near the beginning of the novel (and who begins dating Jimmy at the end, when he returns to his job there), and plans to do the same with Dixie. (First, she has to fend off his manager with a joke about pedophilia.) Warned by Jimmy that Buelow "was on the make for me," Dixie tells her diary "of course he's on the make and what of it, all men are, only some are sneaky and don't admit it . . ." (42). Jimmy tells her she will have to put out to be put in Buelow's movie, which causes their first spat, but Dixie sees plenty of that after she's been in Hollywood a few months. She keeps saying no to all the men who hit on her, including Jimmy's Hollywood correspondent, unlike those who say yes: "that's how you get along say yes talk about yes-men you never hear of the yes-girls but they're the ones with the Minerva cars and three kinds of fur coats I guess I could get there too if I said yes . . ." (81).[28] The novel is frank about the sex appeal of movies. The aging star says of the latest starlets,

> they've got one thing I haven't got — youth. They've got young necks and young legs and young eyes. And nice slim, soft young bodies. And you can't fool the camera when it comes to those things. And that's what they want out here in this business. Youth. Young flesh. And they feed it into the machine and out comes thousands of feet of young eyes and young legs and young bodies. Reels and reels of it. And that's

28 This occurs in Dixie's monologue, echoing the closing line of Molly Bloom's monologue in *Ulysses*: ". . . and yes I said yes I will Yes." Like alcohol, *Ulysses* was prohibited in America at this time, but McEvoy managed to obtain both.

> what people want to see. Men go there and watch them hungrily all evening and then go home and close their eyes when they kiss their wives. (124)

McEvoy would have used a different verb than "kiss" if he thought he could get away with it. A month later Dixie is almost raped by Buelow, and after her success she speaks of budding actresses in terms of prostitution:

> Hardfaced mothers from all over the country dragging their little girls around to studios ready to sell them out to anyone from an assistant director to a property man just to make a little money off them. Agents with young girls tied up under long term contracts at a hundred a week leasing them to studios for ten times that and pocketing the difference. Hundreds of pretty kids from small towns, nice family girls, church girls, even society pets going broke and desperate, waiting tables, selling notions, peddling box lunches on the street corners — I could tell you stories that would curl your hair. (223–24)

Passages like this are what make *Hollywood Girl* closer in tone and intent to *Caligari* than *Singin' in the Rain.*

These intimations on immorality in show biz perhaps account for the curious number of biblical allusions in the novel, beginning on the first page, when Dixie blithely answers an imaginary interlocutor: "Where've you been? On Broadway, sez I. Where on Broadway, sez you. Up and down, sez I — up and down, between Forty-eighth and Forty-second, looking for a job" — the final word punning on the source of Dixie's diction, Job 1:7: "And the Lord said unto Satan, Whence comest thou? Then Satan answered the Lord, and said, From going to and fro in the earth, and from walking up and down in it." Over the next few pages there are allusions to the twelve apostles, Jonah and the whale, the book of Genesis, Noah's ark, and the Four Horsemen of the Apocalypse. Though based on Tennyson's poem, *Sinning Lovers* inexplicably begins with the Garden of Eden (with Dixie in Eve's role), and when Dixie resignedly decides to marry Milton, she says, "sometimes I feel like that bimbo in the Bible who sold out for a mess of pottage" (cf. Gen. 25:29–34; "bimbo" is used of men and women in the novel). The most sustained biblical allusion is the radio broadcast Dixie and Jimmy endure while in a restaurant: from L.A.'s Angelus Temple Aimee Semple McPherson delivers a hokey sermon on Daniel in the lion's den, spread over four pages in small caps (174–77), exhorting her listeners to tune out "all the jazz bands and the frivolous things of this world" and to sing along with her (to the tune of "Yes Sir, She's My Baby"):

> *Yes sir here's salvation*
> *No sir don't mean maybe*
> *Yes sir here's salvation now*

Goodbye sin and sorrow
Welcome bright tomorrow
For we've got salvation now (177)

This is too ludicrous to take seriously, and though Dixie occasionally refers to herself in terms such as "a devil on wheels" (231), she is hardly Satan, much less Eve, Esau, or Daniel, and her thoughtless elopement at the end makes a mockery of finding salvation. Nor is McEvoy calling for readers to renounce "the frivolous things of this world" like Broadway musicals and Hollywood epics; for his purposes, the Bible is no longer a moral guidebook but a source of wisecracks, but the recurring biblical references add one more unexpected level to the novel.

As with *Show Girl*, the reviewers ignored the dark depths and stayed at the bright surface of the novel, which they found a little dimmer than its predecessor. "The book is amusing, filled with Hollywood madness and Hollywood slang," said the *New York Times*, "but it lacks the easy, hilarious fun of 'Show Girl,'"[29] not considering the possibility that McEvoy was aiming at something more than "easy, hilarious fun."

Two years later, McEvoy concluded Dixie's sassy saga with *Society*, which picks up the same day *Hollywood Girl* left off.[30] The first half of the novel documents the first few months of Dixie and Teddy's impulsive marriage: honeymooning down in Mexico and then up in Monterey, Teddy continues drinking and chasing after women, which soon drives Dixie to Hollywood to resume her career. But they make up, and Dixie begins learning more of Teddy's rich family: his 18-year-old sister Serena, whom he calls "a wet smack and dumb as a duck" (6), who is preparing to make her debutante debut that fall; his 16-year-old sister Patricia, a hellion already wearing heels who has seen Dixie's film and runs away from private school to pursue a similar career in Hollywood; and Teddy's predictably stuffy mother and father; in order to trace his daughter, the latter hires the same Open Eye Detective Agency that searched for Dixie in *Show Girl*. Mr. and Mrs. Teddy Page, as they are called — Dixie loses much of her independent identity after she marries: "Teddy is my career now" (42) — then sail to France to continue their honeymoon, but during the crossing Teddy lusts after an Apache dancer called Le Megot — "cigarette butt or a snipe," as Dixie translates, and described as "one of the sexist little devils I ever saw with a wild shock of hair, a slim lazy

29 Quoted in *Book Review Digest* for 1929.

30 However, there is an inexplicable dating discrepancy: *Hollywood Girl* ends in April 1929, but *Society* begins in April 1930. A few references in the past tense to the Crash of '29 indicate the novel is indeed set in 1930, the bulk of it from April to December, and concluding around the time of the book's publication in the fall of 1931. Cf. note 33 below.

body, big black eyes and a red mouth that must drive men crazy" (70). Upon arrival in France, Dixie sends a telegram wittily announcing "LAFAYETTE I AM HERE" (74), but no sooner is the honeymooning couple settled in Paris than Teddy sneaks off to London "on business" to catch Le Megot's act at the Kit Kat Club. Meanwhile, Dixie is escorted around Paris by an Italian gigolo who had tried to seduce her during the ocean crossing. After another big fight — Dixie throws "a complete set of Victor Hugo at [Teddy], all of which he managed to dodge with the exception of Volume II of 'Les Miserables'" (109) — they make up and head down to the Riviera.

At that point, halfway through novel, the plot takes a metafictional turn: we learn that Jimmy Doyle is in Paris, working for Colossal Pictures again and "gathering material for a high society movie" (105–6). Excited to learn that Dixie is also in France, he telegraphs his producer with a revised idea: "COULD COMBINE EUROPEAN ANGLE SOCIETY AND DIXIES POPULARITY" (108, *sic*) — which sounds like a note McEvoy made to himself after finishing *Hollywood Girl*. Dixie continues to party with the idle rich and tells Jimmy she's having fun, or "fun in a way. But it's no pleasure — if you know what I mean. We're all so bored — Teddy's friends and their friends — and they work so hard to be amused — and nothing really makes 'em really laugh — only when they're full of champagne and are their real selves but don't know it" (123). Dixie is excited to learn she's pregnant, but just then Teddy gets involved in a sex scandal and both have to sneak back to New York. As the Page family prepares for Serena's obscenely expensive coming out ball at the Ritz-Carleton on Thanksgiving Eve ($50K, around $750K today), Patricia reconnects with the young communist radical she had met while en route to Hollywood, and attends a rally in Bryant Park at which he speaks the night of Serena's ball. Learning the cost of the ball, her Red beloved leads a protest march to the Ritz, which is broken up by the police — or as the headline in the communist *Daily Worker* puts it (177):

> TAMMANY COSSACKS DEFEND SACRED RITZ
> FROM CONTAMINATION BY STARVING WORKERS
> THOUSANDS OF DOLLARS FOR ORCHIDS
> WHILE MILLIONS CRY FOR BREAD.

Early the next year, Jimmy returns from France, manuscript completed, and tracks Dixie down in Palm Beach, where she is drinking to excess, experiencing cramps, and having doubts about becoming a mother: "I'm so tired of this silly empty life and realize the baby is going to tie me down tighter than ever" (188). On the next page we read a news account of an explosion on a yacht, in which Dixie was seriously injured. When she learns she has lost the fetus, she declares herself through with it all. Her decent father-in-law arranges a quickie Mexican divorce (and a generous stipend for life), and Dixie agrees to star in Jimmy's movie *Society Girl*, "A Sensational Expose of the Haut Monde At Play" as a full-page ad on the penultimate page describes it. The movie is a "smashing hit" (with more fake quotes from real reviewers of the time), and Dixie and Jimmy decide to rest by sailing together for France. Meanwhile, Teddy is already on to his next showgirl, who Walter Winchell informs us (in a tidbit from his column) is "the third gel from the left in Earl Carroll's Fannyties" (205).[31]

Though *Society* lacks the hellzapoppin' energy and jazzy lingo of its predecessors — which in fact would be inappropriate for the leisurely pursuits of the rich and fatuous — the novel is more ingenious than the average satire of high society due, once again, to the novelty of its materials. The title page resembles a formal invitation, *set in a copperplate font* and even blind-stamped. In addition to the usual letters, telegrams, playlets, and news clippings, we're treated to Dixie's ocean crossing diary, shipboard schedules and announcements, formal invitations and cards of introduction, menus, invoices, legal documents, a Junior League report by Serena on "A Trip through a Biscuit Factory," and best of all, several chapters from *The Memoirs of Patricia Page (To Be Opened Fifty Years After Her Decease)*, an amusingly self-dramatizing, misspelt account of the 16-year-old's runaway adventure. There are self-conscious narrative winks from McEvoy, as when the stage direction in one playlet describes the head of the Open Eye Detective Agency as "one of those fiction detectives who can only be found in real life" (33), and when Jimmy remarks on the coincidence of booking a hotel room next to Dixie's: "If a fellow wrote that in a book they'd say he certainly had to reach for that one" (118). As Jimmy adapts his film plans to fit Dixie's life, and even asks her to supply background material on debutantes (which she does in snarky fashion), it becomes obvious that his *Society Girl* is a metafictional mirror image of McEvoy's *Society*, a film of the novel/novel of the film.

The darker themes in the first two novels are lighter here: sexual predation takes the forms of handsy gigolos and rampant adultery. As early as page 3 Dixie reports that one of Teddy's rich friends "went right on the make for me — didn't seem to mind I was on my honeymoon. Teddy didn't either. Seemed flattered if anything." A dozen pages later he shacks up with his ex-fiancée, and his tomcatting ways result in the suicide of one betrayed husband. Prostitution imagery is used for both debutantes — their coming out balls are

31 A Joycean pun on Carroll's stage revue *Vanities*. "Known as 'the troubadour of the nude,' Carroll was famous for his productions featuring the most lightly clad showgirls on Broadway" (Wikipedia).

sales displays for the marriage market — and for "society girls who are poor as church mice and yet have to keep up a swank front and be seen everywhere in the swellest clothes and what they won't do to get by would put a Follies girl's gold digging into the 'come into the drug store with me while I get some powder' class" (18). Patricia's communist friend reprises Alvarez Romano's role in *Show Girl* to introduce political elements in the novel, railing against the decadence of capitalist society in America and aristocratic privilege abroad, which McEvoy records in garish detail.

He also slips homosexuality into the novel. In a brilliantly rendered playlet set in a Paris nightclub called Le Fétiche, two Harvard boys "doing postgraduate field work in abnormal psychology" marvel at the lesbians. "A rosy-cheeked, bright-eyed contralto in tweeds" sings three new stanzas of Cole Porter's "Let's Do It, Let's Fall in Love" (1928), another opportunity for McEvoy to show off his gift for parody:

> Bugs do it —
> Slugs do it —
> Evil-looking thugs in jugs do it —
> Let's do it —
> Let's fall in love.
>
> In holes the nice little mice do it —
> Tho they are pariahs — lice do it —
> Let's do it —
> Let's fall in love.
>
> . . . .
> The Infusoria in Peoria do it —
> And the better classes in Emporia do it —
> Let's do it —
> Let's fall in love. (93, 98)

This scene is followed by a letter from a *Variety* reporter describing the sights to be seen on the way south to the Riviera, including "a little hideaway tucked between [San Rafael and Toulon], entirely populated by the most delightful pixies, male and female, but you'll never find it unless you meet one of three people, names enclosed here in sealed envelope. They'll take you there if they like you" (103). In a trilogy about show business, it's about time McEvoy mentioned the gay element, though it was a daring move for a commercial novelist in 1931.

Though Dixie takes up with high society, she's never taken in by it. She mocks as she learns "society patter" and affected enunciation, yet can still deliver snappy similes such as "he closed up like Trenton on a Sunday night" (89; i.e., stopped talking). As she occasionally reminds people, she's still just an Irish "punk" from Brooklyn, and despite a number of poor choices throughout the novel, she retains her best qualities. Teddy's father praises her "spirit and independence in refusing alimony or settlement" (202), and the news item that concludes the novel indicates she's single: she has reunited with the love of her life from *Show Girl*, but she hasn't married him. Perhaps McEvoy merely wanted to leave the door open for another sequel, but it's more likely that he intended Dixie to follow in the dance steps of his original model, Louise Brooks, who except for two very brief marriages spent most of her life single. (We can only hope that Dixie doesn't wind up like our Miss Brooks did.)

Society is blander than its predecessors, but together the Dixie Dugan trilogy is an endlessly inventive portrayal of female independence as well as a damning indictment of show business, politics, sexual attitudes, and society at large. "To those who have followed him since 'Show Girl,' Mr. McEvoy has always meant humor and bite," wrote the *Saturday Review of Literature* of *Society*. "The ridiculous and the sharply ironical were always blended," and though the reviewer felt "the irony has wilted and the humor become worn" in the third novel, it's that blend of humor and bite, of ridicule and irony — shaken and stirred with linguistic and formal ingenuity — that makes the trilogy as a whole a mordant, madcap masterpiece.

FADE TO BLACK: THE FINAL NOVELS

McEvoy's 1930 novel *Denny and the Dumb Cluck* is a spin-off from *Show Girl*, which documented the failure of greeting-card salesman Denny Kerrigan to convince Dixie to abandon show biz and move to Chicago to marry him. Denny gets top billing in this novel, which begins two years later with a letter dated 11 May 1929 and ends about a year later, and which marks McEvoy's turn toward darker, more bitter satires of American culture.[32] The novel is festooned with greeting-card verse, whose saccharine sentiments are undercut throughout by the vulgar businessmen who peddle the stuff and the "dumb clucks" who fall for it. Although marketed as a humorous novel,[33] the novel contains attempted suicides, mental breakdowns, divorce proceedings,

32 Thus the novel occurs during the inexplicable 1929–1930 gap between *Hollywood Girl* and *Society*, which is perhaps what McEvoy intended by re-dating the latter, hoping nobody would notice.

33 The novel was published by Simon & Schuster's Inner Sanctum line, an experiment at pricing new novels at $1.00 (instead of the usual $2.00) and using stiff paper rather than cloth covers. They were color-coded: blue for "books in a more or less serious vein," green for detective and mystery novels, and red for "books of a lighter nature" (ii). *Denny* was classified as red.

Chicago mob slayings, and concludes with the murder of the president of Denny's card company. Even the Hollywood happy ending, in which Denny regales his bride (the "dumb cluck" of the title) with the story of that murder during their honeymoon near Niagara Falls, is undercut by signs of what a terrible husband he will be. The novel is dedicated to Santa Claus.

Like McEvoy's earlier novels, *Denny* is an assemblage: letters, press bulletins and newspaper clippings, company memos (some shouting in ALL CAPS), telegrams, divorce papers and trial transcriptions, a hotel bill, two lengthy monologues, and selections from a lonely hearts newspaper column penned by "Carolyn Comfort" — actually a "white-haired [male] tobacco-chewing reprobate" (148).[34] It differs from his earlier novels in its structure: they proceeded chronologically, with their multiple story-lines interlaced, but *Denny* is divided into eight semi-independent sections that focus on specific story arcs. Part 1, dated from 11 May to 12 June 1929, concerns Denny's modus operandi to selling the Gleason Greeting Card Company's wares to the female owners of card shops (all with twee names like "Ye Arte Moderne Snuggery"); as he writes to his supervisor Al Evans, this entails "taking out the lady buyers and getting them all warm and confused so they'll overstock themselves and have to work like hell making profits for you and me eh Al?" (22).[35] At loose ends one Sunday in Chicago, he meets "the dumb cluck": a young woman named Doris Miller, estranged from her rich family in Indiana because she moved to Chicago "to make her own way" as a singer — another of McEvoy's admirably independent young women. But when Denny recites one of his company's lovey-dovey greeting cards and passes it off as his own spontaneous creation, Doris falls for him. "Poetry always gets dames," he smirks to Al (15). But after she spots the poem in a greeting-card shop window, she attempts to drown herself. She is rescued, then explains her reason for the attempted suicide to a reporter who gussies it up for a human interest story for the *Chicago Herald Examiner* (reproduced on pp. 23–25), which leads to a spike in sales for the "Heart Throb" card Denny quoted. Denny hears about the sales but is unaware of his role in the spike.

The next section, however, begins with a letter by Al dated more than two months earlier (3 March) instructing his salesmen to make a big push for the new idea of a Father's Day card, and concludes with a newspaper report dated 17 June 1929 noting Al's admittance to a sanatorium for a nervous breakdown, the result of his stress-inducing sales efforts. This section features heart-rending letters from his wife to her mother on the disastrous effects of his work on their marriage, and also introduces the Gleason Company's "staff Poet Laure-

34 Nathanael West's *Miss Lonelyhearts* was published three years later in 1933.

35 Al and a few other characters from the greeting-card subplot in *Show Girl* reappear here.

ate" (3), Terence McNamara, a hard-drinking party animal (obviously a stand-in for McEvoy himself) whose marriage is likewise troubled. Section three is undated but apparently takes place in April, for it deals with sales plans for Mother's Day cards. Denny gets nowhere with the proprietor of Ye What Ho Gifte Shoppe, "One of those long legged short-haired Greenwich village gals that wear batik bloomers and talk about their complexes" (60). She has eyes only for a milquetoast customer who shops frequently for cards to send home to mother. (In an ironic twist typical of McEvoy's novels, he turns out to be a hired assassin.) Denny reports to Al about a crime wave in Chicago, and passes along his (and apparently his creator's) doubts about his profession and his country: "Boy, you and I picked a piker's game when we decided to spread cheer throughout the land. It's nothing to cheer about if you ask me" (69).

Section four documents McNamara's divorce proceedings, dated between 14 September and 5 October 1929.[36] His wife testifies to his numerous drinking binges on greeting-card related holidays and irresponsible behavior, including the time when McNamara flipped out when his kids recited a Valentine's Day greeting-card poem to him. But when the poet takes the stand, he wins over judge and jury by answering entirely in greeting-card "sediments" (as it is often spelled in this and other McEvoy novels).

The final four sections are undated. Section five apparently takes place later in October 1929, for greeting-card president George Gleason is in New York City looking for a replacement poet after firing McNamara for bad publicity. This startling section is a 23-page monologue delivered by Gleason to a Ziegfeld showgirl in his hotel room — she is currently dancing in *Whoopee!*, which closed 23 November 1929 — whom he plies with liquor and tries to seduce until she panics and attempts to jump out the window. In section six, which seems to take place in late October or early November (though there's no mention of the Wall Street crash during the last week of October), Denny searches for Doris, while the dumb cluck pours her heart out to Carolyn Comfort's lonely hearts column. Section seven must be set in late January of 1930, for football season has just ended and Denny is peddling Valentine's Day cards. He's having a difficult time making a sale to the owner of Ye Merrie Lyttle Nooke in South Bend, Indiana, "a little pug-nosed Mick" who is distracted by unrequited love for a theology student at Notre Dame, and is secretly contemptuous of her wares: "There is a card lying here on the table be-

36 McEvoy drew upon his own 1922 divorce trial for this section. Jay quotes from a news story in the Portland *Oregonian* (27 August 1922), in which McEvoy accused his estranged wife of failing to take proper care of their children despite a generous alimony and "of gay 'carryings on' in her home at late hours after the children had been put to bed." She countercharged "that McEvoy was too friendly with other women."

fore me as I write, a sample Valentine given me by that fool salesman, Denny Kerrigan, who sells the Gleason line. It says 'Love is bright as sunshine, love is sweet as dew' and a lot more. But it isn't anything like that at all, darling. Love is bitter and dark and cruel beyond all the cruel dark and bitter things of this world" (177). Her heartbroken letters to the student express true emotions in stark contrast to the false ones offered on greeting cards. After reading a newspaper announcement of her beloved's ordination into the priesthood, clueless Denny writes to the woman about his new idea for a line of cards: "CONGRATULATIONS ON YOUR ORDINATION."

The final section jumps ahead a few months to Denny and Doris's honeymoon, and is mostly taken up by Denny's account of George Gleason's murder the previous February by a disgruntled customer. There's no explanation for how Denny found and made up with Doris, for since Denny is talking to her (another one-sided monologue to a silent woman), there wouldn't need to be. Doris obviously knows how it happened, but the reader doesn't, who might be excused for thinking McEvoy grew impatient and didn't want to write a penultimate section on their reunion and courtship. Denny had suffered some sort of accident in section six that entailed a hospital stay with his face in bandages, and unbeknownst to him Doris nursed him and took dictation for his letters to Al about his search for "that dumb cluck" (156). They obviously reconnected, so McEvoy apparently felt he could cut to the honeymoon and wrap it up.

Despite the ostensibly happy ending, this is a harsh novel, which is to be expected from an author who set out to write a "grudge book" to "get even" with the greeting-card industry, as he admits in the author's note at the end. It was *too* harsh for some reviewers: "The book is American in the same way that chewing gun, comic supplements and loud speakers are American," complained Edwin Seaver in the *New York Evening Post*. "It is a violent, noisy book." Contemptuous of the publisher's attempt to market the novel as light humor, V. P. Ross wrote, "It is too ugly to be delectable, too grotesque to be tragic, and too longwinded to deserve the laurels of humor."[37] But it is precisely those qualities that give *Denny and the Dumb Cluck* its edge, its Voltairic clash between ideals and reality, its anticipation of the irony-clad black humor of 1960s novels. A standard boy meets-loses-marries girl novel taking jabs at greeting cards would be too simple. McEvoy used that sideline to stand for American business practices in general, many aimed at persuading "dumb clucks" to purchase their goods and services. He even hints that the New Testament's promises of immortality are as false and hollow as greeting cards

37 *Outlook* 155 (27 August 1930): 667. Seaver's review appeared in the 9 August issue of the *Evening Post*, p. 5.

when Denny flips through a Gideon's Bible in a hotel room.

The language isn't as slangy as that in the Dixie Dugan novels, though there are some amusing euphemisms ("you illegitimate sons of Rin-tin-tin's mother") and synonyms for drinking binges ("out on a bat"). There is also what appears to be McEvoy's self-conscious defense of his "humorous" approach to writing versus that of "serious" writers, many of whom flocked to Paris in the 1920s. Denny writes to Al about the old drunk who writes the lonely hearts column:

> For years he has done everything in the newspaper racket and found that nobody cared, so now he runs the Lonely Hearts Corner and hopes to save enough money to retire and go to Paris to write a novel. He says he needs a couple of years off from the job so he can gather material. I says, what about all these letters you get from the Lonely Hearts? I should think that would be swell stuff for a writer. A lot of hooey! says he. Now, take that story you were telling me about that girl you tried to find — you know, the one you picked up in a restaurant and took for a lake ride. She jumps off a boat because she thinks you wrote those bum sediments you're always quoting! Well, I don't blame her. I'd jump off myself to escape you. Now, I suppose you think there's a story in that? Sure, says I. Crazy, says he. That just proves you'd better stick to peddling cheer. You'd starve to death if you tried to write. Now me, for instance, I know how, but I've nothing to write about and I can never save up enough to get ahead and settle down for a couple of years to do serious work. You know my dream, says he. I want to get a little studio in Paris near Montparnasse, and just sip wine, nibble cheese, and observe life and write about it. (150–51)

You can imagine what that novel would be like, if the old sot ever got around to writing it. But McEvoy *did* find "a story in that" attempted suicide, a polyvalent one that expands to indict all of American society at the bitter end of the Roaring Twenties when it all came crashing down, and didn't need to take a few years off in Paris to write it.

Having settled his score with the greeting-card business, McEvoy turned next to the comic-strip industry. The first half of *Mister Noodle* takes place in Chicago, where McEvoy got his start in strips, and I can't improve on the plot summary provided by James A. Kazer in *The Chicago of Fiction*:

> The story of Charlie "Chic" Kiley from Gum Springs, Illinois, is told through letters to his mother, news clippings, telegrams, and transcripts of conversations. Kiley takes drawing classes at the Art Institute and works in the art department of the *Chicago Star*. Overnight he becomes a nationally known comic strip artist when he introduces *Mister Noodle*, a strip composed only of profiles (since that is all Kiley can draw). He also effortlessly achieves social status, receiving memberships in the Chicago Athletic, Forty, and Midday Lunch clubs. With his newfound security he is able to marry his girlfriend and he soon has a one hundred thousand dollar per year contract for his syndicated strip. However, when he relocates to the syndicate's offices in New York City he succumbs to the temptations of beautiful women, nightclub entertainments,

> and drink. When an actress falls from the balcony of his penthouse the scandal fills the Midwest with moral indignation and his comic book gets cancelled. Only when he returns to Chicago and reconnects with his small town does he get the inspiration for a new comic strip and rediscover success. This satire of the syndicated comic book industry makes pointed comparisons between Chicago and New York to the detriment of the latter.[38]

It's important to note that the novel satirizes only certain aspects of the comic industry, specifically the undeserved success of certain hacks and low-brow taste of many readers. The first time Kiley submits his poorly drawn strips to the editor of the *Chicago Star*, his boss tells him, "This paper has printed hundreds of questionnaires and prize contests for the correct answers on the simplest subjects, and we have found by experience that the average person knows only three things. . . . He knows his name; he knows his parents; and he knows where he lives. And that's all he does know. Remember that if you're going to be a comic-strip artist. . . . Always tell 'em something they already know. The better they know it the better they like it" (41). Talentless hacks pandering to the lowest common denominator is what irked McEvoy, not the genre itself; later in the novel, when a Russian director named Ivan Stalinsky sails to America to make a movie of Kiley's strip,[39] the director expresses what might be McEvoy's own views during a gangplank interview with the *New York Evening Tab* (the same rag that figures so prominently in *Show Girl*):

> "The comic artist is the real modern artist. Comic artists were the first expressionists, and the colored supplements in your Sunday papers, with their vivid reds and greens and blues, are brutal and frank as the life they underscore, and it is only because I have always made pictures with real people rather than actors that I welcome this opportunity to come to your America and make a new comédie humaine, using the real Noodles of American life to reënact and interpret the salty humors of everyday existence. . . . You can say for me," he added, "that the Supreme Author is a Humorist, and Life is a mad comic supplement He created to amuse the angels." (125)

McEvoy placed the final sentence up front as the epigraph to the novel, but then again, the entire statement may only be a swipe at the lofty claims sometimes made for the genre. The author definitely has his tongue in cheek when Kiley's editor tells him, "Don't forget the last frontier of old-fashioned virtue

38 *The Chicago of Fiction: A Resource Guide* (Lanham, MD: Scarecrow Press, 2011), 236–37.

39 When Stalinsky finally visits a Hollywood movie lot, a scene rendered in play form, the stage directions state he is shown around by a studio exec "overawing him with the lavish opulence of American technical resources and at the same time secretly frightening and depressing him with the remorseless rhythm of this great machine, spawning and spewing in callous complacence an endless flood of elegant marshmallows" (136–37), which can be read as McEvoy's final verdict on the movie industry.

is the comic strip" (47).

Unlike the previous novels, the documents that make up *Mister Noodle* are not dated, except for a clip from *Vanity Fair* on the last page dated 1932, a year *after* the novel was published. Apparently the events occur between 1929 and 1930 — a character on page 71 recites lyrics from "Just You, Just Me," a hit song introduced in the 1929 musical *Marianne*, though again there's no mention of the Crash of '29 — and everything happens at a more rapid pace than in the previous novels, effectively conveying the "overnight-success" aspect of Kiley's career. This is a deliberately unfunny novel about the funny papers, featuring one of McEvoy's most despicable protagonists. Not only is he talentless, but he owes his success to others: his girlfriend Dorothy — whom he meets at the Art Institute and later elopes with — gave him the idea for the strip in the first place, which Kiley then adjusts to his boss's low view of comics (which Kiley later parrots as his own). After he becomes successful, he has a team produce the strip for him while he gallivants around New York City, and even when he returns to Illinois in disgrace at the end, he has learned nothing. Kazer's description of the conclusion is misleading: Kiley returns to Gum Springs to recuperate, but is subjected to a brilliantly rendered monologue by his ignorant Irish Catholic mother about murders, mayhem, and madness out in the sticks: hardly the stuff of inspiration. When Kiley then meets with his former *Chicago Star* editor and claims he has ideas for a new strip, he junks them as soon as his boss feeds him an idea for a new strip called *Mister Whoosis*, which Kiley claims for his own creation when he boasts to his New York syndicate boss of his imminent return to the big leagues. The novel ends with another hick comic artist arriving in New York and getting carried away at the idea of living the high life, obviously on course to repeat Kiley's fall. Or not: the last page of the novel reproduces a clip from a future issue of *Vanity Fair* stating, "We nominate for the Hall of Fame, Willie Timmerman, because — " (186).

The *Chicago Star* editor's final lecture to Kiley is a cynical but informed overview of the comic-strip business, especially its lack of originality, and undoubtedly represents McEvoy's conclusions after fifteen years in the business. When Kiley tells him that he has an idea for a strip that has never been done before, the editor (named James P. Mason) cuts him off:

> Worse. Doomed to failure. The most successful strips running today were always successful, long before they were strips. Mutt and Jeff was a big hit when it was called Weber and Fields, and it's a bigger hit now when it's called Amos 'n' Andy. Same idea. Big dumb guy picking on a little smart guy. German dialect, colored dialect, Brooklyn dialect — same thing. Little Orphan Annie is Cinderella. Bringing Up Father — Abe Kabibble — every burlesque show for the last fifty years has had a Jiggs and an Abe. The Gumps? Mr. and Mrs.? Any family comic? Has anything ever

happened in any of 'em that hasn't happened a million times in a million homes?

CHIC: I know, but they aren't funny.

MASON: They don't have to be funny. Did you ever watch anyone read a comic page? Did you ever see him laugh? Was there ever a laugh in Little Orphan Annie? One of the most successful comic strips running. People don't want to laugh so much as they want to feel superior to somebody else. (179–80)

There are discussions like this throughout, with references to many strips and comic artists, which should make *Mister Noodle* valuable for comic historians, written by someone who was there at the beginning. For literary historians, *Mister Noodle* is valuable as a demonstration of how to take an unoriginal story-line (rube seduced by the big city) and make it new by way of formal and linguistic innovations. In addition to McEvoy's usual documents, which as always provide a you-are-there immediacy to the proceedings, there are some amusing parodies of the gossip columnists of the time. Kiley's arrival in New York is announced by a word-drunk columnist reaching for the literary stars:

AVE! MISTER NOODLE!
An Inquiry into the Irrefragable Tenuities
(From the Editorial Page of the New York World)

Swims into our ken a new planet — the algebraic mystification of orbital aberrations, the torturing ellipse of tortured ellipses, the Theseus before the throne of the Minotaur, half bull, half man, quaint Cretan symbol of American ideology — Mister Noodle — planet X — crying in the wilderness, eating the wild locusts of ephemeral fame, preparing the way for a greater-than-he, forsooth, or peradventure, if you will quibble — but I shout "Gold! Gold!" as did wild-eyed Sutter long ago — and mayhap I will grant you, a Fool's Gold, but your Au may be my FeS_2, and who will bid me nay, for fool's gold is the guerdon of fools — always the king on the throne has paid the fool on the stool stones for bread, darkness for light, the louring brow for the laughing lip — and so, in like manner — Measure for Measure, said the Mortal Poacher with immortal finality, or vice versa — we too long and too smugly, I fear, have been paying Mister Noodle of the earth earthy — Punchinello Redivivus! — with Jovian frowns from our high, crystal parapets, remembering not that Jove walked with the sons of men by day and talked with the daughters of men by night — Danaë? Shower of gold? FeS_2? Why not? — and from the little despairs of men, brewed by an alchemy lost to us the great courage of the gods against the cosmic crepuscle of the Götterdämmerung. (Ya sagers, all, shouting in the terrible twilight that finally swallowed warm, shining Olympus and cold, dread Erebus alike.) Vale, Great God Pan! Ave, Mister Noodle! (97–98)[40]

Columnist Walter Winchell is parodied twice, once upon Kiley's arrival and once after his disgrace: "A certain cocky alien from Chicago, who was King Fish in the ookie-ookie racket a few months ago, and then faw down on his

40 This sounds like Percy Hamilton, who is parodied near the end of *Show Girl* (212).

you-know-what with a big phfft is out of the camphor again and trying to merge a meal ticket on a local rag . . . no soap" (163). On the train from Illinois to New York, Kiley makes the acquaintance of "The Boop-a-Doop Sisters," two nightclub chippies who provide a sassy stream of slang throughout the rest of the novel, even some pig Latin.

As in his previous novels, McEvoy takes the faults of a minor — some in the 1920s would have said trivial, even disreputable — medium of pop culture as a metonym for the faults of America at large. He presumably wrote *Mister Noodle* in the gloomy months following the Wall Street crash, which perhaps justifies the *New York World* columnist's despairing evocation of Wagner's *Twilight of the Gods*. Reviewers used to the fizzy fun of the Dixie Dugan novels were shocked at the novel: one complained "Its humor is cruel," another that "There is a great deal that is coarse and unnecessarily realistic," and a third that it "is hard, brittle, cruel almost to literary sadism"[41] — which sound like the reviews Faulkner's *Sanctuary* received the same year. Neither *Mister Noodle* nor *Society* (also published in 1931) sold well, and perhaps for that reason McEvoy changed publishers for his final novel.

In contrast, reviewers were very impressed by *Are You Listening?*, and quite rightly so. It is his most compelling performance, his most technically ingenious "stunt" (as one reviewer called it), his grittiest and most realistic novel, and his most powerful dramatization of the impact of new media on the public. The media in question is commercial radio: only a decade old by 1932, "The invasion by this sort of *blah* is now history," one of the novel reviewers lamented (William Rose Benét, he who labeled it a stunt):

> One hears it not only in every apartment but on every street corner. It has turned any imaginative life that exists for the man in the street into a mixture of ballyhoo slogans, thickly syrupy sentiment — usually about all the wrong things — and sensational thought images. . . . [T]he industry in its infancy has so far managed to spread more blatant vulgarity on the air than one would even have suspected. This is probably what a democracy loves. It is certainly what it continues to listen to without noticeable protest.[42]

McEvoy's "noticeable protest" puts it even more dramatically: a broadcaster describes radio as going "into every home, every factory, every story, every place where men and women meet to eat, sleep, drink, work or play; this tremendous voice from which there is no escape; this modern jungle drum beating from coast to coast . . ." (236). For some lonely souls in the novel radio provides companionship — "Turn it on in the morning and let it run. Keeps

41 All quoted from the 1931 edition of *Book Review Digest*.
42 "The Ghost in the Radio," *Saturday Review of Literature*, 20 August 1932, 52.

them company" (143) — but one character who can't escape it lambastes radio for "babbling all day like a half-witted relative" (129).[43]

The main story-line concerns the three O'Neal sisters, who have left Middletown, Connecticut, to try to make it in New York City. The eldest, Laura, went there to become a concert singer, but now performs for Radio WBLA (pronounced *blah*, as Benét notes). She shares an apartment with her younger sister Sally, who works as a receptionist at WBLA all day and parties all night. Their airhead kid sister Honey, nearly 18 when she moves in a little later, is "trying to crash Broadway" (40) but has to settle for bit parts on the radio, and eventually for a gig as a celebrity gossip reporter for the *New York Morning Tab*. All three have trouble with men, none more so than Laura, who is romantically involved with Bill Grimes, a continuity writer for WBLA. He's stuck in a hellish marriage with a shrew who won't grant him a divorce until he can afford to pay a huge alimony; near the end, he accidentally strangles her to death, then flees with Laura as WBLA, in cahoots with the police department and the *Morning Tab*, livecasts the manhunt for them. Because of the radio reports' reach, the couple is ID'd and arrested in Florida, Bill is convicted of manslaughter, and is sent to Sing Sing (which was recently wired for radio). The novel ends with all three sisters listening, from different locations in different moods, to a live radio broadcast of Cab Calloway and his Joy Boys singing "Life Is Just a Bowl of Cherries" from the Cotton Club.[44]

The novel elapses over about a year's time — undated, but apparently from May 1931 to spring 1932 — and is partly conveyed by way of radio broadcasts, set in ***boldface italics***: announcer palaver, jingles, speeches (including one from the Vatican by the pope), skits plugging ludicrous products, musical interludes, and live shows from various locations, including the notorious Nut Club in Greenwich Village. (There are also some short-wave police bulletins near the end.) The broadcasts alternate with the main mode of the novel: unpunctuated dialogue, one-sided telephone calls (with unspaced Célinesque ellipses …), monologues, and *italicized shouting* in a larger point size. The earthy dialogues are often interrupted and undercut by the airy nonsense of the broadcasts, usually for darkly ironic purposes. (Saccharine love songs provide musical background for spats between couples; a noted judge delivers a speech praising Prohibition hours after his all-night, booze-filled yacht party; peaceful Christmas hymns are interrupted by the barked police

43 This recycles a stage direction in a restaurant scene in *Hollywood Girl*: "*Above the clatter of dishes and the bumble bumble of voices a radio loud-speaker, pleasantly ignored, drools and cackles with the idiotic insistence of a half-witted relative at a family dinner*" (168).

44 There are footnoted permission acknowledgments for this and some other songs quoted in the book. McEvoy hadn't done so in previous novels and may have run into legal problems.

reports on the manhunt.) And as in all of McEvoy's novels, there is extensive behind-the-scenes dramatizations of putting a show together, especially the frustrating attempts of creative people to meet the needs of their commercial sponsors. WBLA's producer regards radio as "a theater of the air. The advertising is incidental, but so far as the public is concerned, a necessary evil" (90). The sponsors, of course, feel precisely the opposite: one client, after hearing a Shakespearean skit created for the Eureka Exterminator Quarter Hour, wonders "if some of it won't be hard to understand. Of course I understand it, but then you know how the average person is — especially when it comes to words like — like — like well, some of those words the girl used. . . . Seems we use a lot of time on the air without saying something about our product. Couldn't we mention that it comes both in liquid and powder form, or something like that?" (184). The frequent time-of-day announcements are called *M-O-R-I-S-O-N WATCH TIME* after its sponsor, which anticipates the subsidized years in David Foster Wallace's *Infinite Jest.*

McEvoy's reliance on dialogue to carry the narrative is reminiscent of other novelists of the time such as Ronald Firbank, Ivy Compton-Burnett, Evelyn Waugh (*Vile Bodies*), and Virginia Woolf (*The Waves*). In the radio bits, he demonstrates his gift for satire and pastiche, but the dialogue is impressive for its unvarnished realism from a wide variety of characters, from radio personnel and sponsors to Wall Street investors to speakeasy owners and gangsters. (Just before he strangles his wife, Grimes tells her that her psychologist "just wanted to lay you" [219], perhaps the first appearance in fiction of the vulgar verb.[45]) By way of dialogue McEvoy ingeniously conveys everything that a third-person narrator in a conventional novel would — appearances, actions, settings — putting the reader in the same position as a radio listener creating visual images from dramatized scripts.

The best lines are delivered by McEvoy's female characters, most of whom reveal how difficult it is to be a woman, especially in what Sally O'Neal calls "this man's town" of New York. When station announcer Buddy Law tells her he can't see how girls stand it, she answers, "Buddy, when you're a girl you learn to stand almost everything. That's what being a girl means" (15). Both Sally and Honey party hearty in defiance of their conventional, religiose mother, who visits and lectures them on a woman's place in the world (safely married at home in an apron), while older sister Laura is so exasperated by her failed career and troubled relationship with Grimes that she attempts suicide. She complains of her neighbor Mrs. Peters, who turns on her radio "in the morning and never lets up until two o'clock the next morning," but her mother tells her she does so because "She's lonesome and sad. How would

45 The earliest example recorded by the *OED* is John O'Hara *Appointment in Samarra* (1934).

you feel if you used to be a famous actress, and now because you're not young any more you can't get a job and have to sit home and listen to the radio." Laura replies, "Well, that's just tough if she grows old and gets out of step. Who can help that?" (129). Later, Mrs. Peters offers some sound advice to Honey, who can't decide whether to accept a rich man's invitation to attend a football game in Chicago: "Remember, it's always the woman who holds the key to any situation like this. It can be any kind of situation she chooses, and the man must abide by her decision. If I haven't learned anything else in my fifty years, I've learned that men accept a girl on her own valuation of herself. If she wants respect for herself, she must have it for herself first" (167). As in his other novels, McEvoy portrays independent women in a positive light, but in *Are You Listening?* he poignantly captures the despair of women trapped in hopeless situations. The psychologist who treats, "lays," and then abandons 50-year-old Mrs. Grimes doubts his smart secretary's diagnosis that she's dangerous: "Why? Just because she's emotionally starved, repressed, and somewhat inclined to hysteria? What of it? Most married women of that age are." "True," his secretary responds, "but she's a potential manic-depressive, starved, thwarted, on the edge of her menopause and fixed on you. You know that's a bad spot" (195; like "lay," this may be one of the earliest appearances of the word "menopause" in fiction). Both Laura and Alice Grimes suffer psychotic meltdowns, Sally and Honey fend off near-rapes, and in another scene a gangster Sally is dating knocks a woman unconscious. The plight of women alternates with the ubiquity of radio both formally and thematically in this gender-sensitive novel.

Despite its grim theme, there are some amusing bits. Answering the phone while the station's broadcast blares overhead, Sally wisecracks, "If there's anything that's good for a hangover, it's German on a loudspeaker" (45). There are clever Gilbert and Sullivan parodies that recall the McEvoy of *Slams of Life*, and the listening audience is treated to musical performances by such groups as the New Art Plumbing Symphony Orchestra (under the direction of Arturo Garfinkel) and the Beau Brummell Dandruff Dandies' Jews' Harp Trio playing the overture to Wagner's *Tannhäuser*. (His *Tristan and Isolde* is incorporated into an ad for bathroom fixtures.) But as in McEvoy's other late novels, the humor is black.

Even though the aforementioned William Rose Benét called *Are You Listening?* a "'stunt' novel" and stated "There is nothing a bit 'literary' about the book," he praised it to the skies, pompously concluding his review: "Mr. McEvoy has been ere this a champion of the comic spirit. He has also, however, seen the cruel significance behind all the moronic chatter now burdening the ether, and has praiseworthily evoked it in this novel for us to see. Underneath all the japery, it mutters in our ears like the ghost of Hamlet's father!" Hollister

Noble, in a rave review for the *New York Times Book Review*, praised the "consistent balance between the serious delineation of character and the mocking irony of [the radio station] environment," and complimented McEvoy "for two distinct achievements. He has re-created with amazing fidelity, through the rapid-fire conversation of his characters, the very breath and life of the studio. And at the same time he has skillfully handled a great variety of characters, each of them early delineated and definitely individual. All of them have the full flavor of reality, and Mr. McEvoy is most adept in depicting their collisions with the fantastic complexities and whirling enigmas surrounding them."[46] Perhaps heeding the show-biz advice of always leaving them wanting more, McEvoy ended his performance as a novelist on that high note.

The final line of McEvoy's final novel is "Are you listening?," which would be echoed 43 years later in the final line of William Gaddis's multimedia novel *J R*, spoken into a telephone: "Hey? You listening . . . ?"[47] McEvoy resembles Gaddis in many ways: both have a caustic sense of humor and dim view of America; a high fidelity ear for dialogue and the vernacular; and a penchant for the comic-ironic juxtaposition of public statements vs. private sentiments, high art vs. low entertainment (in *J R* Gaddis uses Wagner much the same way McEvoy does). Both use documents in fiction — *J R* has several, and his novel *A Frolic of His Own* is filled with legal documents, a play script, letters, newspaper clippings, brochures, even recipes — and both satirize the frivolous uses of technology in the arts: like the Russian director in *Mister Noodle*, Gaddis in his final, posthumous novel *Agapē Agape* stares agape at "the lavish opulence of American technical resources and at the same time secretly frighten[ed] and depress[ed by] the remorseless rhythm of this great machine, spawning and spewing in callous complacence an endless flood of elegant marshmallows" (*Noodle* 136–37). Three other innovative fictions of the 1970s that come to mind are the vaudevillian skits, speeches, and news reports that make up Philip Roth's *Our Gang* (1971), Jerome Charyn's novel in the form of a literary quarterly, *The Tar Baby* (1973), and Robert Coover's use of show-biz tropes to indict American culture in *The Public Burning* (1977), another novel comprised of documents, monologues, poems, and parodies. Whether regarded as a covert avant-gardist of the 1920s, as a harbinger of the Black Humor of the 1960s and certain multimedia novels of the 1970s, or as an avant-popster *avant la lettre*, J. P. McEvoy deserves to be rediscovered and reprinted.

46 "Tuning for the Moonstruck Static of Radio Land," *New York Times Book Review*, 28 August 1932, 4.

47 *J R* (New York: Knopf, 1975), 726. There's no evidence Gaddis knew McEvoy's work.

PART 3: PERSONAL MATTERS

Nympholepsy

I have heard the mermaids singing, each to each.
I do not think that they will sing to me.
—T. S. Eliot, "The Love Song of J. Alfred Prufrock"

In early December 2000, at the age of 49, I suffered an attack of nympholepsy. Since that is not something your average HMO would diagnose, it took me a few days to identify the malady. Three factors, I realized, had led to the attack: (1) the return into my life of a 17-year-old, rose-lipt girl named Morgan Bertolucci,[1] who had been released from a treatment center for anorexia; (2) the reading of David Markson's then-forthcoming novel *This Is Not a Novel*, which, among other things, quotes Housman's lines "The rose-lipt girls are sleeping / In fields where roses fade"; (3) and the realization that soon I would turn 50, and that I was still alone — never married, no long-term relationships — and in all likelihood I would die alone without ever knowing what it is like to love and to be loved. The attack struck just as I finished reading Markson's novel, and I wept uncontrollably for the next five minutes.

At first I thought the weeping was merely the result of the masterful orchestrated pattern of death and loss in Markson's novel, which (among other things) catalogues the deaths of dozens of artists in terse one-liners:

A. E. Housman died of a heart condition.

Shostakovich died of a heart condition. . . .

Henry Adams died of a stroke.

Addison died of dropsy.[2]

The relentless accumulation of these death notices in Markson's novel, along with several references (like the Housman) to the transience of youth and ambition, creates a tide of emotion that should overwhelm any reader.[3] Markson was of course astounded and pleased when I told him how his novel had reduced me to tears, but when I conveyed this in an e-mail to another writer,

1 Not her real name (changed at her request), which is a similar Welsh-Italian combination.
2 David Markson, *This Is Not a Novel* (Washington, DC: Counterpoint, 2001), 172–73.
3 Since my friend Markson was 73 and in poor health, I also knew "David Markson died of ______" would be the eventual coda to the novel. [He died ten years later in 2010 of unknown but apparently natural causes. — 2016 note.]

Thomas McGonigle — who also read the novel in galleys and had a more sober reaction — he e-mailed back to say Markson's novel didn't warrant that reaction and I should look further for the cause of those tears. At first I dismissed this, ascribing it to Tom's rather cynical attitude toward things in general, but a week later I realized he was right. Markson's novel may have opened the floodgates for those tears, but they originated elsewhere.

For without realizing it, or wanting to, I had fallen hopelessly in love with Morgan. The previous May she had come to work at the same Borders book store where I was an assistant manager. She seemed to be a typical high school girl, a little prettier perhaps and much better read (I soon discovered), certainly very mature for her age, but she was little more than one of my more pleasant colleagues for the first two months. I noticed she was quite thin, but didn't think much of it. Then one day she almost had a fainting fit and had to call for her parents to drive her home; it turns out she was anorexic, and was put in a local hospital for immediate treatment. This took me completely by surprise, and my heart went out to her: I had heard of anorexia, of course, but had never known a victim, and it seemed especially unfair that someone as wonderful as Morgan should be so afflicted. After some hesitation — I knew what some people would think of a 49-year-old man taking such an interest in a teenage girl, despite my knightly motives — I arranged to visit her in the Denver children's hospital to which she had been taken. My heart collapsed at the sight of her: pale, broken, depressed. We stumbled through a conversation, and I left her with some reading material. She said she appreciated the gesture, so the following week I called and asked if she would like another visit, and she said she would "love" one, but the day before the scheduled time she called to say she was being transferred to a treatment center in Arizona and had to cancel my proposed visit. After a month or two, I found myself continuing to think of her and so, again with some hesitation, I called her parents to get the address and wrote her a get-well letter. We exchanged a few letters that fall and I looked forward to her return to the store in late November.

She walked into the store the day after Thanksgiving for the evening shift and looked great: no longer the pale, broken girl I had seen last July but a winsome beauty with her natural charm restored, and completely cured, she said. I took her to the deli next door during her dinner break that night and told her that I was going to devote myself to keeping her happy thereafter. (Her anorexia had been due in large part to depression, and she claimed to have few friends.) Talking to her during that dinner, and during a few lunches that followed, not only gave me a greater appreciation of her many endearing qualities, but reminded me of a simple joy I had missed out on most my life: the company of a pretty girl who seemed to like me. But she was more than just a pretty face (there were other teenage girls working at Borders, as attractive as

Morgan): she was quiet, a bit shy, introverted, bookish, artistically inclined — qualities I shared and that led me to regard her as a soul mate, despite our age difference, qualities I had always looked for in a girlfriend but had never found. And of course she possessed numerous lovable qualities I lacked; I could fill the page with them. I had been waiting all my life for someone like this on whom I could lavish all my dammed-up care and affection, and thus Morgan became the unwitting victim of this flood of emotion. (Morgan, it must be said, never regarded me as more than an older friend; she never took me up on my open-ended invitation to take her anywhere, any time, to do anything she liked. In fact, she began using homework as an excuse to turn down my lunch invitations.) It was at that point I finished reading Markson's novel and suffered my attack.

A week or so later, Tom's e-mail still rattling me, I saw Morgan bantering flirtatiously with another Borders employee closer to her own age and I realized I was jealous — not happy to see her readjusting and making new friends, but jealous — and I had to admit to myself that I was in love with her, that I really wanted to be her boyfriend, not her big brother or mentor. I wanted to play Angel to her Buffy, not Giles. The impossibility of that devastated me even as I told myself how inappropriate, unprofessional, even foolish, my infatuation was. But we don't choose who we love; love chooses us — which is why the ancient Greeks considered Cupid more a pest than a friend. (I didn't even consider confessing my love to Morgan: I knew she didn't feel likewise and that such a confession would only embarrass her, or worse; I may have been foolish but I wasn't stupid.) I wasn't the first older man to fall for a younger girl, but something else was at work here, and after a few days' thought, I identified it: nympholepsy.

I had come across the word a few times in my reading, and remembered that it appears in Nabokov's *Lolita,* that peerless monument to unrequited love. Taking down my hardcover copy of Alfred Appel's annotated edition, I fumbled beneath *Lolita*'s tight white jacket for a few minutes until I found what I was looking for. On page 19 Humbert Humbert identifies himself as a "nympholept," and in his notes Appel quotes *The Penguin English Dictionary*'s definition of "nympholepsy," viz., "a species of demonic enthusiasm supposed to seize one bewitched by a nymph; a frenzy of emotion, as for some unattainable ideal," and then adds: "more specifically, in *Blakiston's New Gould Medical Dictionary*, it is defined as 'ecstasy of an erotic type.'"[4]

4 Vladimir Nabokov, *The Annotated "Lolita,"* ed. Alfred Appel, Jr. (New York: McGraw-Hill, 1970), 339–40. On p. 131 Humbert states: "The science of nympholepsy is a precise science. Actual contact would do it in one second flat." Here and elsewhere (as in his 1967 interview with Appel in *Wisconsin Studies in Contemporary Literature*), Nabokov seems to

Although the erotic element was overstated — my feelings for Morgan were not overtly sexual; I had fantasized about what it would be like to kiss those rosy lips, but not much beyond that[5] — the notion of frenzy at the sight of an unobtainable ideal sounded right. I had recently watched the movie *American Beauty*, where the Kevin Spacey character's vision of the cheerleading temptress Mena Suvari[6] results in a similar frenzy and triggers a midlife crisis. Morgan was my nymph, and was as unattainable as any nymph spied in the distance in Arcadia. As I languished in lovesickness during those final weeks of December — I thought about Morgan constantly, even dreamed of her at night, something I thought only happened in silly love songs — I tried to find out more about this word, this malady.

The Oxford English Dictionary, which like most people my age I own in the two-volume compact edition (it was always on offer in the back of magazines at a reduced price in the 1970s and everyone I know seems to have sent away for it), gives a brief record of the word's usage. The *OED* offers this sniffy definition of nympholepsy: "A state of rapture supposed to be inspired in men by nymphs; hence, an ecstasy or frenzy of emotion, esp. that inspired by something unattainable." It cited Richard Chandler's *Travels in Greece* (1776), from which its definition derived; a melodious couplet from Byron's *Childe Harold's Pilgrimage* ("A young Aurora of the air, / The nympholepsy of some fond despair"); and three other instances in which "nympholepsy" was similarly used in the sense of regret for an unattainable ideal. Each writer moved further away from the original sense of being blasted by the sight of an actual nymph. Later editions of the *OED* cited writers who, like Nabokov, used "nympholepsy" to describe an attraction to younger girls: a few grades above pedophilia, perhaps, but with no mythological or psychological overtones.

I leafed through my tattered copy of *The Anatomy of Melancholy*, and while nymphs abound in the forests of Burton's erudition, I was surprised not to find anything on nympholepsy. Nothing in *The Golden Bough* or *The White Goddess*, those treasure chests of myth and magic that enthralled me when younger. Nor did searching the Internet yield much. I learned a poet named Rodger Kamenetz had published a volume entitled *Nympholepsy* (Dryad Press, 1985) — which proved disappointing — and that a Canadian singer named Elle recorded a CD of the same name (Fearless Records, 1998). The

have regarded "nympholepsy" merely as an attraction to young girls.

5 Fortunately, Morgan never acted or dressed remotely sexy, else I would have burst into flames.

6 In real life, the 21-year-old Suvari married 37-year-old cinematographer Robert Brinkmann, an interesting instance of life imitating art.

distinguished Greek translator Richmond Lattimore had published a poem as an undergraduate at Dartmouth called "Nympholepsy." A few online sex dictionaries defined the word as "a trance state induced by erotic fantasies or daydreams," without giving a source. I discovered William Faulkner had written a little-known short story called "Nympholepsy," an early effort posthumously published, about a lonely workman's unexpected twilight encounter with a skinny-dipping Southern gal, who flees into the woods like an unattainable nymph out of Greek mythology. One search engine even took me to some sort of goth/sex site, with a digitized photo of a vixen who looked anything but unattainable.

Despite their mixed signals, all of these definitions and examples more or less confirmed my self-diagnosis of nympholepsy. My nymph Morgan was unattainable, and I realized that, pushing 50, I would in all likelihood never attain a beautiful young woman like her.[7] Most middle-aged men are vain enough to imagine they are still capable of attracting a younger woman — and a lucky few actually can — but those with any sense reach a point where they abandon that illusion. And it's a difficult illusion to give up. Nympholepsy is not just the attraction to young girls, but *despair* at the attraction to young girls; nymphs may symbolize some unattainable ideal, but they are also real girls with oodles of charm, and for older men such creatures are usually untouchable and unattainable. *Hinc illae lacrimae.*

It wasn't until I began writing this essay in April 2001 — in February I had left the bookstore in Colorado where Morgan and I had worked together, largely for professional reasons (I had become a buyer at Borders' main office in Ann Arbor, Michigan) but partly to escape the nymph's bewitching spell, which had made an emotional wreck of me — that I learned of a new book that promised to provide more background: Jennifer Larson's *Greek Nymphs: Myth, Cult, Lore.* Unfortunately it wasn't due out for a while, so I beguiled the time by trying to recover from the attack of nympholepsy.

Like some convalescents who masochistically don't really want to get over their illness, however, I unwisely nursed my love for Morgan. We had parted sweetly with promises to keep in touch, perhaps getting together that summer — Morgan had wildly suggested a trip to England to see her favorite band, Radiohead, to which I had enthusiastically agreed — so I began writing long, flamboyant letters to her, but I soon learned she obviously didn't miss

7 The desire of an older man for a younger girl is considered perverse by some people, mostly those ignorant of biology, history, and evolution. Men's "brains are hard-wired to find nubile teenagers highly desirable and particularly beautiful," as Nancy Etcoff notes in her *Survival of the Prettiest: The Science of Beauty* (New York: Doubleday, 1999), 24. The heterosexual man who *isn't* attracted to nubile teenagers would be the true pervert. How we act on that attraction is another matter.

me as much as I missed her. My letters went unanswered for weeks, and eventually elicited only perfunctory responses, and then none at all. I sent her gifts, which she didn't acknowledge. She rarely answered her e-mail. As painful as her unexplained withdrawal was, I realized it was for the best. I had enlarged some photos of her taken before I left and posted them on my wall and at my office at work, but decided I had better remove them if I wished to recover. But I couldn't stop thinking of her, and still dreamed of her at night.

My choices of reading matter didn't help. I picked up a copy of the new Everyman's omnibus of Updike's Bech stories, and remembered a passage in *Bech: A Book* that had humiliated me when I read it 25 years earlier: when Bech expresses his surprise that a charming Bulgarian poetess is unmarried, a countryman of hers asks Bech:

> "In America, only the uncharming fail to marry?"
> "Yes, you must be very uncharming not to marry."[8]

I made the mistake of reading *Echo*, the latest novel by Francesca Lia Block[9] — a writer I had turned Morgan on to — about a gifted but troubled teenage girl suffering from anorexia, a painful reminder of why I had taken an interest in Morgan in the first place. The miserable Michigan weather didn't help my mood; it reminded me of New Jersey, where I had spent the worst four years of my life earning a PhD at Rutgers. Quite often I had to suppress the urge to cry. As I've always done in times of sorrow, I turned to music, my first and truest love, for consolation. I was tempted to burn a mix CD to match my mood, one song for each of Morgan's 17 years:

1. "Alone Again Or" by Love
2. "Wild World" by Cat Stevens[10]
3. "You've Got to Hide Your Love Away" by the Beatles
4. "Younger Girl" by the Lovin' Spoonful
5. "Days" by the Kinks[11]
6. "To Love Somebody" by the Bee Gees
7. "Cherish" by the Association

8 John Updike, *The Complete Henry Bech* (New York: Everyman's Library, 2001), 49.

9 If unfamiliar with her enchanting work, see my "Fairies and Nymphs: The Fiction of Francesca Lia Block," *Rain Taxi* 5.4 (Winter 2000/2001): 32–33. [See pp. 79–82 in this volume.]

10 I sang these first two classic break-up songs at a Borders employee talent night two weeks before I left Colorado. Morgan was in the audience, but afterward didn't comment on the songs.

11 Not the 1968 original but the live, more expansive version on *To the Bone* (1996). The late Kirsty MacColl recorded a gorgeous version of this bittersweet song, one of Ray Davies' finest. God save the Kinks.

8. "What Becomes of the Broken-Hearted?" by Jimmy Ruffin[12]
9. "Nowadays Clancy Can't Even Sing" by Buffalo Springfield
10. "All This and More" by Procol Harum
11. "Don't Give Up" by Peter Gabriel (with Kate Bush)[13]
12. "Cry Baby" by Lisa Germano[14]
13. "The Walking (and Constantly)" by Jane Siberry
14. "Has He Got a Friend for Me?" by Maria McKee[15]
15. "Loneliest Person" by the Pretty Things
16. "I Shall Not Care" by Pearls before Swine (words by Sara Teasdale)[16]
17. the Largo from Bach's Concerto in F Minor for keyboard and strings (BWV 1056), Glenn Gould, piano

But I decided against it, knowing I'd be tempted to slit my wrists by the time the CD ended.[17] I re-read an old favorite of mine, Sherwood Anderson's *Winesburg, Ohio*, and lingered on the story "Tandy," about a man who declares: "'I am a lover and have not found my thing to love. That is a big point if you know enough to realize what I mean. It makes my destruction inevitable, you see.'" Turning to address Tom Hard's seven-year-old daughter, he goes on:

> "There is a woman coming," he said, and his voice was now sharp and earnest. "I have missed her, you see. She did not come in my time. You may be the woman. It would be like fate to let me stand in her presence once, on such an evening as this, when I have destroyed myself with drink and she is as yet only a child."[18]

In one of my letters to Morgan I recommended *Winesburg, Ohio*, and told her to pay special attention to "Tandy"; I never learned whether she read it or not.

April was the cruelest month, the liquid l's of Eliot's line logrolling into

12 Dave Stewart (not the ex-Eurythmic but the ex-Hatfield and the North keyboardist) released an innovative version of this song in 1980 with ex-Zombie Colin Blunstone handling the vocals, but in times of sorrow pathos beats innovation.

13 This song caused uncontrollable weeping during a similar breakdown when I was 34.

14 I could fill this entire CD with the songs of this self-styled "emotional wench," the saddest woman on record. It wasn't until I wrote this essay that I realized Morgan is what Lisa probably looked like as a teenager.

15 McKee reverses the pronouns of Richard Thompson's original, but I want her desolate version here, gender confusion be damned. Besides, McKee's brother Bryan MacLean wrote "Alone Again Or," above. MacLean, who died in 1998 at the age of 52, never married. (Have I mentioned I'm a music geek? And you know how popular they are with the ladies.)

16 A fine but little-known poet who committed suicide in 1933. Pearls before Swine was a fine but little-known folk-rock group of the '60s.

17 Indeed, the perfect music video for the Bach piece would depict a suicide submerging himself in a bathtub, sipping from a flute of Champagne, slitting his wrists, and watching the blood slowly (*largo*) stain the water red. His eyes close during the final two measures.

18 Sherwood Anderson, *Winesburg, Ohio*, ed. Charles E. Modlin and Ray Lewis White (New York: Norton, 1996), 79.

others: lovesick, lackluster, lethargic, listless, lonely, loveless, lugubrious, ludicrous, lost. Loser.

Nympholepsy is discussed only briefly in Larson's *Greek Nymphs*, which finally arrived in June, a month after my fiftieth birthday (alone again, naturally). And more disappointing, the notion of nympholepsy as a rapture inspired by something unattainable is apparently a late, unhistorical invention. In her excellent, erudite book Professor Larson identifies three major forms of nympholepsy, a concept that degenerated from positive to negative over the centuries:

1. Originally it meant "a heightening of awareness and elevated verbal skills believed to result from the nymphs' influence on a susceptible individual,"[19] not unlike being inspired by the Muses (who, as Larson shows, were related to nymphs). In Plato's *Phaedrus*, for example, Socrates ascribes his heightened eloquence to the nearby presence of nymphs. Oracle-mongers conned their marks by claiming their prophecies were inspired by nymphs. A nympholept was usually a man who lived apart from society and produced poems or oracles inspired by a particular nymph, whose shrine he maintained. The shrine was usually in a hillside cave, dark as a strip club; in return for his devotion he would be "possessed" by the nymph in "sexual terms," as Larson says (18), though what physical form this took she doesn't say. But picture a middle-aged man devoting a website to his favorite teenage star, and "worshiping" her accordingly; it's appropriate that many such websites are called "shrines."[20] (When I moved to Ann Arbor, where I knew no one, I felt I was going into exile; my nymph inspired this fanciful essay, though I stopped short of erecting a shrine to Morgan.)

2. "In the postclassical period, however, possession by the nymphs began to be seen as an abnormal and dangerous state hardly distinguishable from illness" (13). This could take the form of a mental seizure; it was believed anyone who saw a nymph went mad. But tales were also told of physical seizure, in which a nymph or group of nymphs would become enamored of a beautiful man and drag him into their cave for sex. (We don't need archaeological evidence or antique inscriptions to know a man came up with *that* fantasy.) Nymphs are closely identified with rivers and lakes, and often this seizure led to drowning the unlucky swain, as in the Echo and Narcissus story or that of the sailor boy Hylas. The late-Victorian painter J. W. Waterhouse prettily

19 Jennifer Larson, *Greek Nymphs: Myth, Cult, Lore* (New York: Oxford University Press, 2001), 13; hereafter cited parenthetically.

20 See, for example, "Tigger's Jennifer Love Hewitt Shrine," where the correct use of punctuation and orthography suggests an older webmaster.

illustrated both subjects; for years I used to have a reproduction of his *Hylas and the Nymphs* (1896), which portrays an adorable gaggle of girls enticing the young lad to join them in the river. Water nymphs are of course kissing cousins of mermaids and sirens, who similarly lured men to destruction.

3. Finally, under sex-negative Catholicism, nympholepsy became a form of demonic possession: "the classical nymphs were syncretized with malignant demons, both the fallen angels of Christian orthodoxy and older Greek demons like the *lamiai* and *gelloudes*" (Larson 63). Nymphs were thrown in with the large class of supernatural beings known as *exôtika* ("things outside or beyond"), an unholy lot that included demons, vampires, succubae, and other fantasy figures of the perverted Christian imagination. In the Church's poisoned view, alluring girls were the Devil's handmaidens, the divine daughters of Greek myth turned out like whores. The demonization of sex appeal is one of the blackest of the Church's many sins.

In healthy contrast, the ancient Greeks celebrated the sexuality of their nymphs. "Nymphs were the earliest equivalent of sex symbols," another scholar writes. "They were usually depicted nude or attired in flimsy garments. As part of the pervasive fecundity of nature, they suggested sexual freedom unencumbered with institutionalized life."[21] Back to Larson: "The nymph is also an idealized mythopoetic version of the village girl at the peak of her sexual desirability, so that her interactions with mortal men can hardly avoid connotations of sexual attraction. Just as gods are attracted to nubile maidens, men are attracted to nymphs" (65). It is worth pointing out the word *nymph* is from the Greek *numphê*, meaning "bride," or more broadly, a girl of marriageable age. In ancient Greece, as in most of the world until a century ago, that meant a girl between the ages of 12 and 18. (Puberty indicates the readiness for sexual activity; it goes without saying the artificially prolonged childhood imposed upon contemporary teenagers causes untold psychological and physiological damage.)

The nubility of young girls skipped hand in hand with the fecundity of nature, which is why nymphs were always associated with water, trees, and hills. (There were no urban nymphs.) The promiscuity of these country lasses was merely a manifestation of profligate nature. It wasn't until our own era that this degenerated into hoary old jokes about the farmer's daughter and leering tales of the half-nekkid gals of Tobacco Road and Dogpatch. (Although, speaking of *Li'l Abner,* the definitive representation of nympholepsy as an erotic seizure can be seen in the 1959 movie version in the person of Stupefyin' Jones, perfectly portrayed by Julie Newmar in a black leotard and

21 Robert E. Bell, *Women of Classical Mythology: A Biographical Dictionary* (New York: Oxford University Press, 1993), 327.

fishnet stockings, whose toxic sexuality paralyzes any male onlooker.) The ancients expected that teenage sexual energy to be harnessed eventually in marriage — "Unmarried girls were associated with the wild and compared to spirited horses who needed to be 'tamed' or fields to be 'cultivated'" (Larson 89)[22] — but until then it was a thing of beauty and a joy forever.

So it is easy to see how nymphs came to represent an ideal, especially later when men in cities were cut off from nature and girls were bundled up in yards of clothing. It's easy to wax nostalgic over the fantasy of beautiful maidens haunting the countryside, swimming naked in rivers, or indulging in their favorite pastime of dancing.[23] And it's easy to see why some men would prefer to see girls remain in that idealized state. Nymphs are emblems of innocence, but innocence on the verge of experience. The nymphs of Ovid's *Metamorphoses* are always imperiled by a god or mortal eager to change those innocent girls into experienced women, and even though this is a necessary, even positive transition for human females, the more sentimental among us regret that innocence can't be preserved forever. One reason Keats so admires his Grecian urn is that it freezes and immortalizes that final flowering of innocence before it is deflowered:

> Forever warm and still to be enjoy'd,
> Forever panting and forever young.

Keats's nymph "cannot fade," he consoles the Bold Lover, and "though thou hast not thy bliss, / Forever wilt thou love and she be fair." But of course real women "fade," and eventually die, a tragedy all the more poignant when one remembers not the accomplished, experienced adults they became, but the innocent girls they once were. This is why leafing through your high-school yearbook can be heartbreaking.

Those lines of Housman quoted near the end of Markson's *This Is Not a Novel* are from his poem "With Rue My Heart Is Laden," short enough to be quoted in full:

> With rue my heart is laden
> For golden friends I had,
> For many a rose-lipt maiden
> And many a lightfoot lad.

22 Morgan strongly identified with the heroine of the book she gave me as a going-away present, Paul Goble's children's classic *The Girl Who Loved Wild Horses* (1978).

23 Like Herod in Oscar Wilde's *Salomé*, I would have given unto half of my kingdom to see Morgan dance, but it's probably just as well I never did — for surely I would have lost my head.

By brooks too broad for leaping
 The lightfoot boys are laid.
The rose-lipt girls are sleeping
 In fields where roses fade.[24]

When I came across that final couplet on page 166 of Markson's novel I immediately thought of Morgan, and the realization that her beauty would someday fade, that she would soon leave the dollhouse of innocence for the motel room of experience, played a major role in my tearful breakdown. Like Lewis Carroll, who lost interest in girls after they grew up, I wanted to freeze Morgan in the perfection of 17, to keep my Alice in Wonderland.[25] With rue *my* heart was laden.

But innocence can also be alluring, a disturbing paradox driven home by the novel I had read during my move from Colorado to Ann Arbor. Tom Robbins' rollicking *Fierce Invalids Home from Hot Climates* stars an iconoclastic CIA agent named Switters, a swashbuckler in his mid-thirties who is attracted to teenage girls, specifically to his 16-year-old stepsister Suzy. Like Morgan, Suzy is "at a juncture where innocence and sophistication converged," still "vacillating between poise and awkwardness."[26] Switters rationalizes his illegal attraction with several well-reasoned arguments (see pp. 134–37, 159–61), but admits to himself that, as much as he wants to ravish her, he also wants "to shield her, with every means at his disposal, from the slings and eros of adult rage and fortune, to deflect the poison bullets of the 'real world,' which is to say, the marketplace, so that not one would ever blast a hole in the magic tutu of her childhood" (163). I felt exactly the same way about Morgan, but I knew I was powerless to shield her, to deflect those bullets. I wanted to be Morgan's catcher in the rye, but my Phoebe was ready to leap off the cliff into adulthood. She had already taken up smoking and was planning to get a tattoo, and if still a virgin, she wouldn't be for long. She would soon leave for college, where she'd no doubt get drunk, get high, get laid, get in trouble, eventually graduate and get a good job, get married to a great guy, and, if not live happily ever after, would certainly lead a more fulfilling life than I had.

Morgan will fall in love, and be loved, as most people are. My attack of nympholepsy was partly due to my bitter regret at missing out on all that, on

24 A. E. Housman, *A Shropshire Lad* (1896), #54.

25 *Alice* was much on my mind that winter of discontent with Morgan. I read Martin Gardner's new edition of *The Annotated Alice*, watched again Dennis Potter's splendid film *Dreamchild* (1985), and taped a charming new version of *Through the Looking Glass* starring a 25-year-old(!) Kate Beckinsale as Alice.

26 Tom Robbins, *Fierce Invalids Home from Hot Climates* (New York: Bantam, 2000), 65, 67. This too I recommended in a letter to Morgan, though again I don't know if she ever read it.

the most basic need of humankind: to find a mate, to have and to hold, in sickness and in health. To love somebody. And now it was too late. Not only am I a half-century old, but a lifetime of rejection and disappointment, of being stood up, turned down, and passed over, has convinced me that whatever it is women look for in a man, they don't see it in me.

I was reminded again of *Winesburg, Ohio*, not "Tandy" this time but "Adventure," the tale of a premature spinster so agitated by "her desire to have something beautiful come into her rather narrow life" that one night she runs naked out into the rain; upon returning, she reprimands herself: "'What is the matter with me? I will do something dreadful if I am not careful,' she thought, and turning her face to the wall, began trying to force herself to face bravely the fact that many people must live and die alone, even in Winesburg."

Even in Ann Arbor.[27]

27 Update from the Life Imitates Art Dept.: in October 2001, awaiting publication of this essay, I drove an hour to sit in a nearly deserted theater to watch *My First Mister*, a touching film about a troubled 17-year-old girl who befriends a lonely 49-year-old man. Still she haunts me.

Postscript. I can now view Morgan with the equanimity of Edith Wharton's Newland Archer: "When he thought of Ellen Olenska it was abstractly, serenely, as one might think of some imaginary beloved in a book or a picture: she had become the composite vision of all that he had missed" (*The Age of Innocence* [NY: Norton, 2003], 208).

Rethinking the History of the Novel

When I was a kid, I was taught that Columbus discovered America in 1492, and I had no reason to doubt my teachers on this point; after all, there was a holiday to commemorate the event. But then in 7th grade, while perusing the shelf of new releases in my school library — I was already a book nerd at that age — I picked up a book by Charles Boland entitled *They All Discovered America*, an account of the large number of explorers who apparently landed in America well before Columbus. This book rocked my worldview, and my distrust of authority figures and conventional wisdom began at that point.

Something similar happened a decade later. As an undergraduate in the early 1970s, I was led to believe the novel originated in England in the 18th century, and no professor told me otherwise as I pursued my PhD in the 1980s. Sometimes *Don Quixote* or *The Pilgrim's Progress* was mentioned as a prototype, but according to conventional literary wisdom the novel experienced a kind of virgin birth with *Pamela*, Samuel Richardson's epistolary novel of 1740. But outside the walls of academe, in those alternative classrooms called used-book stores where I spent so much time in the 1970s, I kept coming across books that certainly *looked* like novels but obviously predated *Pamela*. There was not only Lady Murasaki's *Tale of Genji*, a huge novel written around 1010, but also the shorter *Tale of the Lady Ochikubo*, written a few decades earlier in Japan. I picked up the Everyman's edition of *The Story of Burnt Njal*, a 13th-century Icelandic fiction that was labeled a "saga" but looked and read very much like a realistic novel. I came across multivolume Chinese novels from the Ming Dynasty like *The Plum in the Golden Vase*, a sordidly realistic novel from Shakespeare's time. I read Robert Graves's *White Goddess* and was puzzled by his reference to "a novel called *The Recognitions*" that dated from the 4th century. What? There were novels in the 4th century?

I also came across older works of fiction that didn't resemble conventional novels but reminded me of the unconventional, experimental ones I was reading at the time. Apuleius's *Golden Ass* (written in the 2nd century AD) read like something John Barth might have written, while Petronius's *Satyricon* (written a century earlier) looked and read very much like a Thomas Pynchon novel. Rabelais's 16th-century *Gargantua and Pantagruel* resembled any number of gargantuan, Rabelaisian 20th-century novels from James Joyce's *Ulysses* to Gilbert Sorrentino's *Mulligan Stew*.

It dawned on me that most academics had a too-narrow definition of the novel genre, which they limit to realistic fictions set in identifiable sociocultural contexts, especially ones that make psychological probes into human nature. While that definition might exclude a few of the titles I've mentioned, it describes most of the others to a T. (For example, *The Tale of Genji* is a realistic novel that displays more psychological insight than almost any European novel before the 20th century.) I also suspected most professors were unaware of the diversity of experimental novels that bloomed in the 20th century, and thus unaware of how heterogeneous the genre is. Before I began writing my history of the novel, I surveyed the various definitions of the genre offered by critics, and they all seemed to be based on a narrow selection of canonized classics, from Jane Austen to Henry James. Each definition I read excluded any number of experimental novels on my shelf — that is, books that had been labeled "novels" by their authors and publishers — but which were either unknown to these critics or ignored as part of a lunatic fringe. Granted, I have a lot of weird novels on my shelf, for innovative experimental fiction was my specialty at that time. But still, any definition that excludes that many examples is obviously flawed and useless. Once you add unconventional novels into the mix — things like Burroughs's *Naked Lunch*, Johnson's *The Unfortunates*, and Barthelme's *Snow White* — the only elements that all these fictions have in common are that they are written in prose and are longer than a short story, so I used those basic criteria for my definition of a novel — that is, a book-length work of fiction — which is basically the one novelist E. M. Forster uses in his classic *Aspects of the Novel*. (Parenthetically, even stating that novels are written in prose is problematic, for there are such things as novels in verse and hybrids like Nabokov's *Pale Fire* and Danielewski's *Only Revolutions*, but let's not complicate matters.)

I also realized there was a problem with nomenclature. When critics in the 19th century began discovering and writing about some premodern novels, they labeled them "romances," or "sagas," or satires, folk epics, tales, pastorals, legends, picaresques, or such-like terms. Since they didn't closely resemble the conventional, realistic novels of their own time, these myopic, ethnocentric academics felt they needed to be called something else, which allowed later historians of the novel to ignore them. Or I should say, those who were even aware of them: I suspect most professors have never even heard of *The Tale of Lady Ochikubo* or the 4th-century *Recognitions*, so their status as novels was a nonissue for them.

I'm sure you've all read T. S. Eliot's classic essay "Tradition and the Individual Talent." He argues that "what happens when a new work of art is created is something that happens simultaneously to all the works of art which preceded it." Then he goes on to say: "after the supervention of novelty, the *whole* existing order must be, if ever so slightly, altered; and so the relations, proportions, [and] values of each work of art toward the whole are readjusted; and this is conformity between the old and the new." I interpret that to mean that when an unconventional novel like *Pale Fire* or *Gravity's Rainbow* appears, it alters our conception of the novel genre in general. That is, it should not be regarded as a radical departure from the genre, or some experiment that can be banished to the lunatic fringe; rather it is an expansion of elements that have always belonged to the genre. And if you are a literary historian, it prompts a reconsideration of any number of premodern book-length prose fictions that were not previously considered part of the novel tradition — ones like Petronius's *Satyricon* that don't resemble an Anthony Trollope novel but that do resemble Pynchon's. As Eliot says, we must "readjust" our view of the genre to accommodate the new work, and that in turn allows us to readjust our view of earlier prose fiction works that were not previously considered novels.

This point is illustrated in the preface to an eccentric Brazilian novel of 1880, *The Posthumous Memoirs of Brás Cubas*, by Machado de Assis. Admitting he was influenced by Sterne's *Tristram Shandy*, the narrator states upfront "that serious people will find some semblance of a normal novel, while frivolous people won't find their usual one here." In other words, a serious reader (like T. S. Eliot) will see past the unconventional structure and technical eccentricities to see how an experimental novel like this one does indeed belong to the history of "normal" novels — as Eliot likewise did with Joyce's *Ulysses* — whereas "frivolous" people will not make the connection and dismiss it as "not really a novel" — a phrase I often see in Amazon reviews of postmodern novels.

Adding to the confusion is the fact that the novel is the most volatile and unfixed genre there is, resisting all critics' efforts to confine it. About halfway into Venedict Erofeyev's experimental Russian novel *Moscow to the End of the Line* (1969), which is subtitled "An Epic Poem" for Gogolian reasons, the narrator says, "God knows what genre I'll be in by the time we reach Petushki. Since Moscow it's been all philosophical essays and memoirs, poetry and prose, Turgenev-style. . . . Now, it's a whodunit!" Novelists laugh at critics' attempts to define and confine their workspace.

Anyway, I was still mulling all this over when things suddenly got personal. In the early years of the conservative Bush administration of evil memory, there was a corresponding reactionary backlash against the innovative, unconventional novels I love, as though their liberal-minded creators were trying to sabotage the great tradition of the novel that began with *Pamela*. These conservative critics identified Joyce as the architect of this anarchy, and attacked later saboteurs like Barth, Pynchon, Gaddis, Barthelme, and DeLillo. This struck me as a view that could only be held by someone woefully ignorant of literary history. Joyce was hardly the first to depart from the great tradition of the novel — I've already mentioned *Tristam Shandy* and *Brás Cubas*, and I could add dozens more — and his followers were simply doing what the most interesting novelists have always done: keeping the novel "novel." The narrow definition preferred by some critics applies only to the most recent segment of fiction's long arc, so I set out to identify that long arc and, more importantly, to establish a continuum between ancient novels and postmodern ones — which is why I continuously namedrop modern novels in the course of my survey. It's as much a history of avant-gardism in fiction as it is a history of the novel. And a defense: I was sick and tired of hearing conservative critics talk trash about the novelists I love and had written about, hence the rather truculent tone of the introduction to volume 1.

As I began, I wondered why no one had previously written a comprehensive, international history of the novel. There are any number of histories of painting, of opera, of dance, of puppetry, of almost every other art, but as I gathered the materials I needed I noticed that the only histories of the novel were specialized studies of particular periods and nationalities. Even ambitious books like Margaret Anne Doody's *True Story of the Novel*, as capacious as it is, mostly confines itself to tracing the influence of ancient Greek and Roman novels on later European ones. Not a word about the *hundreds* of novels written in the East during the same period — and I mean novels by any definition you care to use. But I soon discovered why no one else had taken on this task. First, once you define the novel as any book-length fiction, as I did, thousands of examples written before the Renaissance qualify for inclusion, from all across the world. There's a reason why most academics specialize in a particular period: no one has the time to read all novels and to familiarize him/herself with all the critical literature that has accrued around them. And no one knows that many languages: serious critics need to read a work in the original, but no one commands the dozens of languages needed for a universal history of the novel. (In my two volumes, I deal with over 600 novels written in over 30 languages.) That means one has to rely on translations, when they exist, and often it means dealing with inferior or abridged ones. And in cases where a noteworthy novel has not been translated, one has to rely on summaries, which is worse yet.

And then there's the need to familiarize oneself with a culture well enough not to make tourist-like blunders. In order to write about medieval Byzantine novels, for example, one has to first acquaint oneself with the culture in which those novels were written, the reader expectations at the time, the political and theological climate, and so on. For each period I gleaned enough from secondary sources to get a general idea of each period, but I quickly learned why specialists devote a lifetime to one subject area.

If I had thought about all this before I began, or spent a year or so researching and writing an outline of the work as more conscientious writers do, I doubt I would have undertaken the project. But illustrating Alexander Pope's warning that "fools rush in where angels fear to tread," I foolishly threw myself into the project and began rushing through nearly 4,000 years of fiction.

At first I planned to focus solely on innovative, experimental fiction, starting with Petronius's *Satyricon*, and then moving on to Achilles Tatius's wacky 2nd-century Greek novel *Leucippe and Clitophon*. But I quickly realized that in order to explain how these novels departed from the norm, I had to first explain what the norm was in the Classical world, which sent me back several centuries earlier to Xenophon's *Education of Cyrus*, which was written in the 4th century BC, so that I could fill in the development of the Greek novel. Then I realized that prose fiction began even earlier than that, which sent me back to ancient Egypt in the 20th century BC. Another challenge had to do with plot summaries: when writing a paper on *Moby-Dick*, say, a critic can assume the reader knows the work and can proceed with the argument. But who reads Achilles Tatius, or Xenophon, or even Petronius these days? Potted plot summaries can be boring, but it's difficult to discuss a novel's technical innovations without first giving a sense of what the book is about, or without using its characters' names, so I tried to devise a way of summarizing a novel while alternating with critical commentary, and not always successfully according to some of my harsher critics. That's one more reason why specialists write only for other specialists.

But since I was writing not for specialists but for a general audience, I also adopted a different style. Before beginning the actual writing, I just assumed I'd be writing in the standard academic manner, but over the years I had grown tired of that bloodless, wooden mode. I prefer colorful, lively writing, prose that is witty and actually fun to read rather than a chore. My first publications appeared in scholarly journals and by university presses, but beginning in the 1990s I started writing book reviews for places like the *Washington Post*, the *Nation*, and the *Chicago Tribune*, and I enjoyed the more relaxed, urbane tone they encouraged. (Book reviewing, by the way, was great training, for my two-volume history is essentially hundreds and hundreds of book reviews strung together.) A year or two before starting, I remember thinking that it would be fun someday to write a big, deliberately eccentric book filled with quaint and forgotten lore, along the lines of Burton's *Anatomy*, Frazer's *Golden Bough*, or Graves's *White Goddess*. Some of my favorite novels have the same qualities, and the creative writer in me was looking for an opportunity to scratch that particular itch.

But I'd sort of forgotten that ambition when I finally decided to begin the actual writing of my novel-history, and I dragged my feet for a few months because I didn't want to write in the standard academic mode. But one day, for reasons I no longer remember, I started reading David Grinspoon's *Lonely Planets*, a then-current overview of the state of knowledge about the possibility of life on other planets. Although it is a rock-solid, well-researched book, the tone is pop-science casual: Grinspoon occasionally goes off on personal digressions and anecdotes, throws in quips and jokes, and uses rock lyrics for epigraphs, but without compromising the informational value of the work. I was about halfway through it when the proverbial lightbulb popped up over my head and I said to myself "*This* is how I should write my book." Since I planned to write an *alternative* history of the novel, why not use an alternative to the standard academic style, one that resembles the type of prose I like to read and that I use myself whenever possible. I gave myself permission to have fun with the project, hoping that the reader would likewise have fun with it, and figured that a lively tone would offset the massive amounts of material readers would have to wade through, mostly about novels they had never heard of, much less read. At that point I also recalled my earlier ambition to write a big, eccentric book someday, so I decided to indulge that sweet tooth as well. And having made those liberating if reckless decisions, the floodgates of creativity opened up: I dashed off the 36-page introduction during a week's vacation in the spring of 2004, and was off and running.

That sense of fun sustained me for the next eight years, but it stopped being fun as I neared the end the second volume. The first volume was written in three and a half years' time while working full-time at another job, but in January 2010 I was laid off. At that point, I was about a quarter of the way into writing the second volume, and since I fortunately had enough money in the bank to coast for a few years, I decided to devote myself full-time to finishing it. At first, it was wonderful to focus solely on reading and writing, but after a while it became more like a chore, which was exactly what I had hoped to avoid when I began. It became like working in a factory: I'd read a novel, then write about it, read the next one and write about it, and so on and so on, broken up only by occasional trips to the library for background reading. During the last seven or eight months of writing the second volume, I realized it had stopped being fun, and while I tried not to let it show in my prose, by the time I wrote the last page of the second volume, I had no desire to go on to the third volume that I had been planning on from the very beginning.

But even if I had maintained my enthusiasm, I doubt I would have persisted. I literally did not know what I was letting myself in for when I began the first volume, and the second volume proved to be much, much longer than I anticipated. So when I viewed the prospect of a third volume, I had a much clearer notion of what that would entail, and that's when I converted from Pope's fool to an angel who fears to tread. My second volume ends in 1800, and after that date the number of novels published is enormous and unwieldy. Even though I had planned to narrow my focus at that point and concentrate only on innovative, experimental novels, I realized it would take me another five years *at least* working full-time and another thousand pages to cover 1800 to the present, and I finally had to admit that I had bitten off more than I could chew. Now I understood why no one had written a comprehensive, universal history of the novel before, and also understood why such things are only attempted in multi-volume university press series overseen by general editors with troops of contributors at their command.

I had other more mundane reasons for tapping out when I did, and I could offer the lame excuse that there are plenty of histories of the novel from 1800 onwards; it's that early period before Jane Austen that needed coverage. As I say, if I knew at the beginning what I know now, I wouldn't have undertaken the project, but I would have thereby deprived myself of a great scholarly adventure that forced me to read hundreds of fascinating novels that I otherwise never would have read, so it was all worthwhile *for me*, and it's been gratifying to hear that it was worthwhile for at least some readers.

Publishing Rikki Ducornet

I had the honor of being Rikki Ducornet's publisher during the first half of the 1990s, when she went from a cult author published mostly by small presses to a nationally recognized one published by the major New York publishers.

In 1991 she sent a packet to us at Dalkey Archive Press seeking a U.S. publisher for her second novel *The Fountains of Neptune*, which had been published two years earlier in Canada. Along with a copy of it, she enclosed the manuscript of *The Jade Cabinet*, along with the latest *Ontario Review* containing a selection from it. I was impressed by *The Fountains of Neptune*, but I really loved *The Jade Cabinet*. After getting the boss's OK, I told Rikki that we would like to publish both right away, so she extricated herself from Ontario Review Press (whose Joyce Carol Oates wanted to publish the new novel) and we brought out *Fountains* in 1992, and *The Jade Cabinet* in the spring of 1993. By then we were already talking about publishing her other works: first an expanded edition of her 1980 short-story collection *The Butcher's Tales*, which we brought out in spring of 1994, and then a corrected reprint of her 1984 novel *The Stain* in the fall of 1995.

Earlier in 1995 we also published her new novel *Phosphor in Dreamland*. That summer, Rikki told us she would be out west and the idea of doing a mini reading tour to promote it came up. By that point I really hated being around Dalkey's publisher and, eager for any excuse to get away from the office, I volunteered to fly from Illinois out to California. Once there, I rented a car and met Rikki for the first time at her son Jean-Yves's place in Oxnard, outside of L.A. I drove her to a daytime reading at Chapman University in Orange (at Mark Axelrod's invitation), and maybe one at Dutton's in Brentwood, another L.A. suburb. I accompanied her to a recording studio where Michael Silverblatt interviewed her for his wonderful *Bookworm* program. Then we drove north to San Francisco. I believe Rikki gave a reading at Black Oak Books in Berkeley, and also at some performance space in San Francisco, where she shared the bill with Dale Peck. (He read from his novel *Martin and John*, which we both found whiny and annoying.)

During the early 1990s she occasionally contributed to our journal, the *Review of Contemporary Fiction*, and at my request she did the cover art for our translation of René Crevel's 1933 surrealist novel *Putting My Foot in It*. By 1996 she had caught the eye of the New York publishing world, and the last project I worked on with Rikki was typing up the manuscript of *The Word "Desire,"* which Henry Holt published in the fall of 1997. (Rikki showed her appreciation by dedicating one of its stories to me.) By then I had quit Dalkey and moved back to Denver, where she then lived, and we saw each other occasionally over the next few years. I once invited her to do a reading at the Borders bookstore where I worked, and also interviewed her for a local arts magazine called the *Bloomsbury Review* (January/February 1998). In 2001 I moved to Michigan, but we've kept in touch ever since, and I've read each new work of hers upon publication with deepening admiration.

Like many editors, I need only read the first few pages of a work to tell if it's something I want to publish, and *The Fountains of Neptune* quickly seduced me. The sensibility was cultured but unorthodox, the form achronological but cohesive, and the content an intriguing mix of science, psychoanalysis, myth, and fairy tale. But it was the author's quicksilver way with words that did it: after a few more pages I was intoxicated by the colorful, imagistic diction, the Rabelaisian raunch, and the rum-fueled fancy displayed by the denizens of the Ghost Port Bar as they swap increasingly phantasmagoric sea tales. She had me (at page 15) at her description of the sea as "a green-eyed witch; she speaks in tongues," which seemed to describe la Ducornet as well.

For all the whimsy and wordplay, there was also a toughness of mind on display, a blazing intellect stoked by wide reading, a deep contempt for conservative thinking and their repressive institutions, a pro-sex swagger, and an uncompromising allegiance to the unconventional, the heterodox, the subversive. My kind of book, my kind of author.

There was even more whimsy and wordplay in *The Jade Cabinet*, appropriately so in a novel featuring Lewis Carroll. This may be my favorite novel of hers. It is a paean to English eccentricity, but also a parable about substantiality vs. ethereality, of commerce vs. aesthetics. Above all, it is an investigation into the mysteries of language, everything from hieroglyphics to muteness. The villain of the piece is a cartoonishly vulgar Victorian industrialist, and the whole thing reads like Dickens's *Hard Times* reimagined by Jorge Luis Borges.

This is the first book of Rikki's that I edited, though "copyedited" would be more accurate, for I did little more than correct a few typos, maybe suggest a few word changes. Unlike some editors who feel a manuscript is unpublishable until they work their magic on it, I take a hands-off attitude toward writers who know exactly what they're doing, as Rikki clearly did. It was fun to work with the graphic elements — handwritten sentences and hand-drawn sketches and diagrams — and Ducornet enlisted the help of her friend Rosamond Purcell to supply the artwork for the cover and endsheets.

I can't remember whether it was my idea or Rikki's suggestion to bring out next an expanded edition of her early short-story collection, *The Butcher's Tales*, which Toronto's Aya Press had published back in 1980 and which Rikki had sent me. Here in miniature were all the qualities I appreciated in her novels, along with excursions into surrealism and science fiction. I deliberately placed at the end an early story that concluded with the lines, "Sleepers awaking, our grey flesh tingling beneath the warm tongues of sister suns, the old dreams stirred; our blood flowed fast now, darkening, already inventing a new language for Desire." That struck me as an appropriately sensuous description of Rikki's whole fictional project: inventing a new language for desire. Most of Rikki's novels have historical settings, set in times and places when "desire" — not "love" but capital-D *Desire* — was regarded as disruptive and irreligious, a threat to decent society. Rikki respects it for the life-affirming force of nature it is, and in her work finds new, more positive ways to speak of it. We called our edition *The Complete Butcher's Tales* because it also included all the stories she had written since 1980, and once again Rosamond Purcell supplied the outré cover art and endsheet illustrations. I remember that, years later, the conventional-housewife publicity coordinator at Borders wouldn't allow me to display it for Rikki's reading because she found the cover obscene.

Shortly after *The Complete Butcher's Tales* came out in the spring of 1994, Rikki sent me the manuscript of her next novel, *Phosphor in Dreamland*, handwritten on legal-sized paper. Previously she had hired typists to prepare her works for publishers, but I volunteered to type this one myself on my newish Apple word-processor, figuring I could copyedit it as I went along. Perhaps because of this hands-on involvement, *Phosphor* remains one of my favorite Ducornet novels. I'm not a quick typist, so the procedure allowed me to savor every word as I went along, to attune myself to her cadences, to trace the twists and turns of her syntax. (Cadence was especially important to her; Rikki rejected a few of my diction suggestions because of rhythm). There were even more graphic elements than in *The Jade Cabinet*, including a portfolio of drawings we decided to include as an appendix (not something every publisher would allow). I designed the book's interior, and it was my idea to use a tiny seashell for section dividers.

My snail's pace also allowed me to marvel at her manipulation of tone: though the novel is as airy and sunny as its Caribbean setting, it deals with oppression, environmental degradation, religious fanaticism, and madness. The balance between light and dark elements resembles *The Jade Cabinet* in this regard — Ducornet's subsequent novels tip much more to the dark — as does its antiquarianism and natural history excursions. I noted the seamless shifts between the 17th century and the present, and how she used the modern natural history museum as both setting and form — the novel imitates a tour of an exotic museum — and I followed the slowly developing love story between the docent narrator and the artist Polly. (The *Wunderkammer*, or cabinet of wonders, is another model for the novel's form.) I watched how she cleverly worked her interest in Swift into the novel, and I recognized in her puritanical "Clean Sweepers" an allusion to the Promise Keepers, a boys-only evangelical Christian group making fools of themselves at that time in Colorado, where Rikki was living. I would have appreciated these things had I simply read the novel, but typing it was like looking over Rikki's shoulder as she composed the work, a Pierre Menard feeling of participating in its creation.

My years at Dalkey Archive were depressing and frustrating, but Rikki and a few other writers kept me sane and entertained. For that reason, I am as grateful to her as she is to me (as she has graciously said) for publishing her works during that crucial period in her brilliant career.

Index